TWILIGHT

—— *of* ——

MARXISM

TWILIGHT

— *of* —

MARXISM

Medjugorje,
the
Downfall of Systematic Evil,
and the
Fulfillment
of the
Secret *of* Fatima

Thomas W. Petrisko

St. Andrew's Productions

Pittsburgh, Pennsylvania   Ave Maria, Florida

First Edition: August 2022

Hardback ISBN: 978-1-891903-59-5
Paperback ISBN: 978-1-891903-60-1
eBook ISBN: 978-1-891903-61-8

Distributed by:
St. Andrew's Productions
5168 Campbells Run Rd., Ste 104
Pittsburgh, PA 15205

Telephone: 412-787-9735
Web: saintandrew.com
Email: standrewsproductions@yahoo.com

Books are available at special discounts for bulk purchases in the United States for individuals, organizations, institutions and corporations.

Special thanks to all the publishers that granted permission to quote their works. The author and publisher are grateful to all whose materials have been used in one form or another in this book. If any materials have been inadvertently used in this work without proper credit being given in one form or another, please notify the pub-lisher in writing so that future printings of this work may be corrected accordingly.

To read additional *"Praise for Twilight of Marxism,"* go to
standrewsproductions@yahoo.com

CONTENTS

IN MEMORY

In memory of Father René Laurentin and John Haffert, spiritual
titans of their day,
and the pillars of God's dawning triumph in the world.

ALSO BY THOMAS PETRISKO

The Miracle of the Illumination of All Consciences
The Fatima Prophecies
Call of the Ages
The Last Crusade
The Prophecy of Daniel
St. Joseph and the Triumph of the Saints
The Sorrow, Sacrifice and Triumph: Visions & Prophecies of Christina Gallagher
Glory to the Father
In God's Hands: The Miraculous Story of Little Audrey Santo
The Kingdom of Our Father
Inside Heaven and Hell
Mother of the Secret
The Ideal You
Inside Purgatory
Fatima's Third Secret Explained
False Prophets of Today
The Face of the Father
For the Soul of the Family: The Apparitions of the Virgin Mary to Estela Ruiz
Living in the Heart of the Father
P.S. Your Sandwich May Be Killing You
St. Philip and the Apostles of the Father
Original Separation
The Mystery of the Divine Paternal Heart of God Our Father

Thomas Petrisko writes a freelance subscriber email (digital) newsletter for **SUBSTACK** (see ***substack.com***), under the title ***Consider the Fig Tree***. It deals with Catholic themed issues including prophecy, mystics, apparitions, saints, miracles, contemporary news, related Church and secular events, and excerpts from his books that are relevant to the times at hand.

To Theo Adam Meyers,
our first grandchild.

Praise for
Twilight of Marxism

"*Twilight of Marxism* is a remarkable book, a work of erudition and breadth, brave and encyclopedic in its story telling of a tragic century gone by, one whose shadow the world still lives under.

The twentieth century, wrote Pope John Paul II, was a "theater in which particular historical and ideological processes were played out, leading toward a great eruption of evil, but also providing the setting for their defeat."

Petrisko's magisterial work captures this historical "theater"—both the human and the spiritual sides of it—in a gripping, engaging narrative that not only spans the twentieth and twenty-first centuries but brings the reader face to face with the ungodly times at hand.

A superb compendium of research, full of intimate detail, meticulously compiled from a great number of well and little known sources, by any measure this book is a triumphant accomplishment, a valuable chronicle that historians will someday treasure.

Most importantly, *Twilight of Marxism* demonstrates in an inspiring way why Jesus Christ is and always will be the Lord of history."

—Roy Abraham Varghese,
Author/editor of over twenty books,
including *Cosmos, Bios, Theos,*
which **Time Magazine** called
"The year's most intriguing book about God."

Praise for

Twilight of Marxism

"*Twilight of Marxism* is inspiring, marvelous, a masterpiece. It is an opus magnum work on the coming fulfillment of the prophecies of Fatima.

Mark Twain said, "If I'd had more time I'd have written less." It is hard to say in a sentence or two how significant I believe *Twilight of Marxism* is for the times in which we live.

Hopefully, it will be an actual grace that moves its readers to pray and fast more fervently to lessen the birthing pains of the coming Era of Peace promised by Our Lady at Fatima.

In 1917, Our Lady of Fatima predicted that the "errors of Russia" would spread throughout the world if her message was not heeded. Petrisko notes that the "errors of Russia," militant Marxist atheism, in its variant form of "practical atheism," has metastasized in the cultural organs of the West and manifest in the deadly symptoms of legalized abortion, euthanasia, same sex marriage, and transgender ideology. The war on marriage and the family signals what Fatima visionary Sister Lucia predicted would be "The Final Battle" between Christ and AntiChrist.

In a divine counter stroke, Our Lady came again at Medjugorje to dispel the miasma of practical atheism. Her appearances of forty years and the countless conversions and miracles attributed to her intercession provide solid evidence that "God exists," His mercy abounds, but a day of reckoning is coming as the prophet Zecheriah foretold: "Awake O Sword."

Twilight of Marxism brilliantly weaves together threads of cosmic and human history in a spellbinding apocalyptic narrative. Read this at your peril for you may end up fasting on bread and water as Our Lady, the "Gospa," asks us to do."

—D. Brian Scarnecchia, M. Div., J.D.
Professor of Law, Ave Maria School of Law

Scarnecchia is the main NGO Representative to the United Nations for the Society of Catholic Social Scientists and author of *Bioethics, Law and Human Life Issues: A Catholic Perspective on Marriage, Family, Contraception, Abortion, Reproductive Technology, and Death and Dying*.

Praise for

Twilight of Marxism

"First and foremost, let me say this book is a masterpiece, an extraordinary work of storytelling on a subject few, if any, have ever tackled in this fashion.

Twilight of Marxism is an intelligent, comprehensive and enthralling look at the fraught times at hand, of the horrific past century, and of a hopeful future that envisions a coming triumph of good over evil.

But Petrisko makes it clear. That promising future could come at a steep price, one that has been looking back in the mirror at us since August 6, 1945, the day the first atomic bomb was dropped on Hiroshima.

As a Command and Control expert in the field of nuclear weapons for over 43 years with the U.S. Air Force, it is that price I would like to address. One doesn't need any apocalyptic prophecies to understand the dangers the world finds itself in today. Despite the end of the Cold War, there are still thousands of nuclear weapons spanning the globe with the terrifying potential to radically change life on Earth as we know it. The staggering threat of a world holocaust is as alive today as it ever was and did not go away with the collapse of the Soviet hegemony.

With this in mind, one can't help assume then, after reading *Twilight of Marxism*, that it is this nightmare that the Virgin Mary was warning of at Fatima and is perhaps a part of the mysterious contents of the Secrets of Medjugorje.

Petrisko's invitation to the reader to take a good, hard look at this critical issue, especially in light of the Virgin's many warnings, can only be seen as another call to awaken us to a deadly reality staring up at us from the abyss. As the author makes abundantly clear, God is generously, lovingly sending Mary to ask us one last time to turn away from sin, to pray, and come back to Him, before it is too late.

Yes, a new era of life on Earth is promised to be coming. But, at what price might we pay to finally see it. Read this profound book and decide for yourself."

—Gerard Beer,
Former Cyber-Security, Bio-Terrorism,
Chemical and Nuclear Triad Senior Command and
Control Officer / Contractor for the U.S. Air Force.

66 It is a characteristic of any decaying civilization that the great masses of the people are unaware of the tragedy.

Humanity in a crisis is generally insensitive to the gravity of the times in which it lives.

Men do not want to believe their own times are wicked, partly because they have no standards outside of themselves by which to measure their times. If there is no fixed concept of justice, how shall men know it is violated?

Only those who live by faith really know what is happening in the world; the great masses without faith are unconscious of the destructive processes going on, because they have lost the vision of the heights from which they have fallen."

—Archbishop Fulton Sheen,
Communism and the Conscience of the West, 1948

AUTHOR'S FOREWORD

"How awesome are you, Elijah!...You are destined, it is written, in time to come to put an end to wrath before the day of the Lord, to turn the hearts of fathers toward their sons...Blessed is he who has seen you before he dies."
—Sir 48:4,10,11

TRUTH TRANSCENDS TIME AND TIME CRYSTALIZES TRUTH, SO IT IS said. Perhaps these realities led me to want to finish this book, which I began twenty years ago.

Twenty years is a long time. When I started back then, I was well aware that the visions of the Virgin Mary to three children at Fátima in 1917 and to six young people at Medjugorje in 1981—sixty-four years apart—were viewed by theologians to be divine bookends that coddled a heavenly strategy, one that anticipated a radical change to life on earth.

While the primary theme of the message emerging from the two Marian apparitions was resounding and unequivocal—a call to the world from the ethereal Mother of Jesus Christ to abandon its evil ways and return to God—the eschatological overtones of both were unprecedented.

A new era was gearing up just below the horizon, both revelations hinted, and would manifest itself after some galvanizing upheavals jarred the status quo. The nature of these future trials, however, remained unknown, concealed in prophecies officially labeled Secrets, a cryptic sounding term that piqued curiosity even with non-Catholics.

But for those of us who do more than browse these affairs, this was old news.

For me, there was certainly no sense of a call to revisit the history of all of this in another book, especially since it was common knowledge in Marian circles. I had covered much of this story in two earlier works of mine, *Call of the Ages* and *The Fatima Prophecies*.

There were, however, some provocative issues surrounding the two heavenly visions that begged to be better understood and I, like other empiricists of Catholic mysticism, couldn't resist their lure.

Winston Churchill once described Russia as a riddle, wrapped in a mystery, inside an enigma, and that same perception seemed a worthy assessment of the prophetic mysteries surrounding Fátima and Medjugorje. Needless to say, the sibling apparitions posed some compelling questions:

- Why had Fátima's promise of a coming victory of good over evil in the world and a subsequent "era of peace" not materialized after the fall of the Soviet Union?
- Why did the Virgin Mary state at Medjugorje that humanity needed to come back to God—while there was still time?
- How can the "Triumph of the Immaculate Heart" follow the consecration of Russia if Russia was never consecrated?
- What exactly did Mary mean when she stated that Medjugorje would realize the secret prophecies she foretold at Fátima?

And there was one last question which especially roused my curiosity:

- Are the Virgin Mary's secret revelations at Fatima and Medjugorje connected to unfulfilled prophecies in the Old Testament, the Gospels and the Book of Revelation?

These were just some of the questions I wanted to probe in what I suspected would be a little book that preached to the choir. At the time, I hoped to do so after a brief dusting up on the more intricate history of Fátima and by tunneling a little deeper into the core of Medjugorje.

But I was wrong.

Fátima, I discovered, held more than just some hidden enigmatic subtleties waiting to be unearthed. It was, rather, a hedgerow maze, a labyrinth of old and new trails that led to and away from the answers I hoped to find.

To this day, what transpired there in 1917 cannot be fully understood; it's as mystifying as anything in the history of the Judeo-Christian experience, highly reminiscent of the more implausible events written of in the Old Testament that defy reason.

Two of the child visionaries at Fátima were told by the Virgin Mary they would soon die—and did! The sun, swollen and unhinged, plunged from the sky before the terrified eyes of 100,000—then abruptly receded back into the heavens. And all of Mary's riveting prophecies landed dead on the mark: the Second World War arrived on schedule, out of Russia flowed the bloody red scourge of Communism, and a future Pope—seen in a vision to get shot—got shot.

All as foretold.

Furthermore, a taunting tale of intrigue followed the Fátima story for the next eight decades that added to its eccentricity. This ongoing conundrum would eventually come to involve international political leaders, a foiled nuclear war, and a half a dozen popes that couldn't free themselves of Fátima's demanding attention no matter how hard they tried.

Just digging below the surface with Medjugorje didn't suffice either.

Perhaps more than Fátima, this was a puzzle with too many pieces. And the harder I tried, the more difficult it was to put the pieces together: millions of pilgrims, thousands of apparitions, hundreds of healings, dozens of miracles, ten secrets, six visionaries and four decades in the making. A smorgasbord of enmeshed facts and factors all stewing in a deep, dark pot of Catholic mysticism—with no end in sight.

Medjugorje is the largest Marian apparition in history in multiple ways, with the potential, come the realization of its ten secret prophecies, to be perhaps the biggest event in the history of the Church... maybe the world.

And *that*, in a way, says it all.

It soon became obvious to me. To explore beneath the surface of Fátima and Medjugorje—in the manner that was necessary to make sense of it all—was starting to look as if I had bitten off more than I could chew.

I pushed forward, but accomplished little.

I was like a vehicle without enough fuel to finish the trip. To assemble and dissect these two colossal events was going to take a substantial amount of research—which meant a considerable amount of time.

I wrote nearly a hundred pages—twelve chapters—and slowly ground to a halt, finally setting it aside. My suspicions were correct. I would need to immerse myself in a sea of materials to get to the level of knowledge necessary to grasp the complexity of the story I was hoping to understand, yet alone write about.

For the next fifteen years, the manuscript sat in a little cardboard box that started to fall apart from being moved around so much. I kept Fátima and Medjugorje on my read list, but shied away from even thinking about trying to write again.

In 2014, I finished *The Mystery of the Divine Paternal Heart of God Our Father*— a book that argues why the Catholic Church needs a feast day in the Father's honor—and haphazardly started to more notice the box containing the manuscript, now parked in a corner of my bedroom closet.

I also found myself thinking more about those unanswered questions I still had surrounding the mysteries of Fátima and Medjugorje.

I recalled how the lone surviving visionary of Fátima, Lúcia dos Santos—who passed away at the age of 97 in 2005—said that "the Fátima week" wasn't over, that there was much more to unfold and come to light, much more to happen.

And how *could* Fátima be over?

No "triumph" of God has descended upon the world.

Humanity isn't bathing in an "era of peace."

And while Medjugorje—with its haunting Ten Secrets—remained perhaps the best source for some resolution to these mysteries, none of the Virgin Mary's inauspicious foretellings there had yet to see the light of day.

Gradually, in lieu of all this, I began to ponder looking for some answers to my questions again.

One day, I experienced somewhat of an epiphany.

I believed I saw that maybe the Spirit was out ahead of me on this. Although writing the book would still take a lot of research, I suddenly realized that I might have in my possession a generous amount of the material needed to do so, perhaps more than I knew.

Beginning in 1988, and methodically over the next twenty-five years, I had acquired a treasure chest of information on Fátima and Medjugorje.

Stashed away in my basement and garage, I literally had accumulated boxes and crates of letters, articles, reports, periodicals, newspapers, newsletters, and audio and video cassettes.

And, after checking around our office building, I emerged with a "cat that ate the canary" look on my face. As I foraged through several large storage rooms, I found that I owned well over a hundred books on Fátima and Medjugorje. I had gradually acquired them one by one at the many conferences that I was invited to speak at over several decades.

Seen as a whole—to go with what was available on the Internet—I realized a vast historical record of both apparitions was in my possession, perhaps as comprehensive as I could ever hope for outside of pillaging a Catholic college library.

Besides possessing the reservoir of resources, I also began to wonder about the many strong, personal relationships I had developed over the years with individuals that were intimately involved with Fátima and Medjugorje.

Some of these chosen souls had stayed at our home, or sat on the board of directors of our organizations, and I had gotten to know them quite well.

Consequently, over the years, a number of these blessed men and women had shared with me their extraordinary experiences, whether with political leaders, visionaries, Vatican officials, or even the Pope. I also had conducted interviews with some of them that held anecdotal, yet captivating revelations that were never published.

Had all of this been for a reason?

In May of 1989, I crossed paths with the world renowned French Scholar Father René Laurentin at the *National Conference on Medjugorje* at the University of Notre Dame. Struck with almost childish awe at just being in the same room with him, I remember thinking on the first day there that I hoped to get near enough to him, before the weekend was over, to shake his hand.

Little did I know then that by the mid-90s, the great theologian would be spending several days or more every year at my home in Pittsburgh before moving on to conduct his annual lecture at the University of Dayton, where he taught a seminar on Mary most summers.

That year at Notre Dame, I had been the guest of Ed and Jan Connell. They were a husband and wife attorney tandem who I met at a prayer group in Pittsburgh. We soon became best of friends, with Jan going on to write two of the most enlightening books ever written on the apparitions at Medjugorje, based on her multiple interviews with the six visionaries.

My relationship with Jan Connell permitted me to get a truly intimate understanding of Medjugorje and the visionaries, as she would often enlighten me about them in unique and insightful ways, even privileging me with prepublication drafts of her books for my review and edification.

Over the next several years, I kept meeting more individuals who were involved with Medjugorje in a special way. Theologians Michael O'Carroll of Ireland and Richard Foley of England, who both penned books on Medjugorje, became advisors on the board of one of our organizations. Father Edward O'Conner, another author and the former head of theology at Notre Dame—and also the spiritual director of the *National Conference on Medjugorje*—became a close confidant and edited my first book.

I also got to know Medjugorje author and expert Denis Nolan and his dear friend, Sister Emmanuel Maillard, who lived in Medjugorje and whose excellent book, *Medjugorje: the 90's*, was published by our company, Saint Andrew's Productions.

My family and I were also very blessed with personal visits to our home and our offices from some of the Franciscans of Medjugorje, including Father Phillip Pavich, Father Jozo Zovko and Father Petar Ljubicic—the priest chosen by the visionary Mirjana Dragićević Soldo to announce to the world the Ten Secrets of Medjugorje. In fact, it had been after Father Petar and his translator spent a couple days at our home that I became more convinced that I should write a book on Medjugorje.

But it wasn't until shortly after that—when I surprisingly received a large crate shipped to my office out of nowhere—that I became certain of that decision.

One of Medjugorje's earliest and greatest advocates in the United States—a close friend of mine named Stan Karminski—had passed some years before. Unbeknownst to me, his wife, Marge—acting on behalf of Stan's wishes—sent to me all of his records and files on Medjugorje. This unexpected cache of documents, which totaled in the thousands of pages and was historically priceless in my eyes, became a final sign to me to write about Medjugorje.

It had also been Stan—perhaps not by accident—that introduced me to the Fátima people that came into my life during this same period.

One summer, during the mid-90s, when I was visiting my in-laws in the Philadelphia area where Stan also resided, he and I got together and traveled north to the *101 Foundation* in Washington, New Jersey.

There, I met the inimitable servant of God, Dr. Rosalie Turton, who introduced me to John Haffert, the co-founder of the multi-million-member Blue Army and the author of over twenty books on the apparitions at Fátima.

Like Laurentin, Haffert was a living saint who consulted with several Popes concerning Fátima and even interviewed John F. Kennedy—who was a member of the Blue Army—on his television show in 1959, the year before he was elected President of the United States.

After this, Haffert and I began to communicate on a regular basis, sometimes several times a week by fax or phone. Providentially, it would be through him that I was taken into a more personal and profound understanding of Fátima and the visionaries, especially the lone surviving Sister Lúcia.

Haffert met with Lúcia a handful of times, starting right after World War II in 1946, and he interviewed over 200 individuals who witnessed the Miracle of the Sun at Fátima on October 13, 1917.

No one, in my opinion, knew and understood the apocalyptic and eschatological constitution of Fátima better than him. Until the day he died, Haffert believed the threat of nuclear annihilation was one of the looming prophecies of Fátima.

During this period, I also met a man named James Hardiman, who wrote a book on Fátima in 1993, *The Song of the Three Shepherds*. Hardiman authored twelve novels and was a leading executive in Hollywood, where he worked for Walt Disney Productions, Columbia Pictures and CBS

Television. In 1968, Hardiman was named the Hollywood Showman of the Year by the Screen Publicists Guild, an award given to only one person annually, two of whom were the renown film director, Stephen Spielberg, and the celebrated actor, Paul Newman.

Hardiman wanted to make a major motion picture on Fátima. It was something he believed God was calling him to do, especially after he visited Fátima and snapped— directly in front of the Basilica of Our Lady of the Rosary of Fátima—one of the most miraculous of photographs.

At the time, Hardiman wrote to me and asked if I would be the executive producer of his movie on Fátima. This was something, obviously, I hadn't a clue as to what was involved and respectfully declined. We did, however, remain in touch and he authorized his exclusive permission for me to publish his extraordinary photograph, an indication to me that perhaps I was to write about not just Medjugorje, but Fátima too.

Around this same time, I also got to know Bishop Pavel Hnilica of Czechoslovakia and the famous Soviet dissident, Josyp Terelya. Hnilica, once the youngest bishop in the world, lived and worked in Fátima for years. Like Haffert, he interviewed Sister Lúcia multiple times and was an advisor to Pope Paul VI and the close friend of Pope John Paul II.

Terelya, a well-known Catholic conference speaker in the 90s, who was a Ukranian political prisoner freed by Soviet Premier Mikhail Gorbachev, was not so much connected to Fátima as he was about Fátima.

Like Alexandre Solzhenitsyn, Terelya's brutal life in the Gulag drew the attention of the world, and he was later welcomed by Pope John Paul II at the Vatican and President Reagan at the White House. Terelya was a living testament to the nightmare Mary foretold would descend upon Russia and I had the honor of traveling with him back to Ukraine right after the Iron Curtain fell. For over ten years, I got to interact with both these living saints, as they brought the message of Fátima to reality in my life.

Almost all of these heroic individuals are gone now. But they believed in the promise of the "Triumph of the Immaculate Heart" and that Medjugorje was where the world would secure this destiny—where the Secret of Fátima would be brought to fulfillment.

Over time, I came to realize their influence on my life was something I needed to not take for granted, and this helped me decide to finish this book.

In 1917, the Virgin Mary appeared at Fátima for a reason.

Mary hoped "to prevent"—she explained on July 13th—the "errors of Russia," an approaching atheistic scourge foretold by her to come out of that country and "spread throughout the world."

In Russia, this "error" would come to life in the form of Communism, as a militant, Masonic funded Marxist revolution explodes in Petrograd on October 25, 1917—just two weeks after the closing apparition at Fátima.

This menace finds traction in the coming decades with Soviet Communism methodically advancing far and wide as predicted, extending its godless tyranny to over a third of the world's population by the 1980s.

But by that time, it also becomes obvious that the Virgin Mary said "errors of Russia"—not error—at Fátima for a reason, as an array of theories gleaned from Marxist thought proliferate in Western culture, bringing a host of new evils upon the world by the end of the century.*

These ideologies—a virtual new religion of reality —thrive today in secularism, and as Pope Emeritus Benedict XVI warned, are collectively instilling in societies a universal dictatorship of humanism.

Known as "Cultural Marxism," it is another form of authoritarianism that is intolerant, atheistic, and because of technology, as great a threat to civilization as Communism, if not more.**

At Medjugorje, it becomes evident that the apparitional woman who came to Fátima—on the eve of the October Revolution more than a hundred years ago—has remained in the world to see to an end to *all* of the "errors of Russia." And to set the stage for the fulfillment of the

---

*   On June 26, 2000, the Vatican released *The Message of Fátima*, a theological commentary on the Secret of Fátima by Cardinal Joseph Ratzinger, the Prefect for the Congregation of the Doctrine of the Faith. It acknowledged the spread of the "errors of Russia' in the 20th century, describing them as atheistic systems that waged war against Christianity, marked by a "a tragic human lust for power and evil."

**   Italian Marxixt Antonio Gramsci (1891-1937)—known as the "Godfather of Cultural Marxism"—is credited with first theorizing that Western states could only be toppled by first infiltrating and subverting the "pillars of their culture"—i.e., religion, family, education, media, corporations, councils, police, law (high culture), along with race, sex, arts, entertainemnt, etc. (low culture). In short , Gramsci believed there needed to be a cultural revolution before a political revolution could firmly take hold, which is what the West is experiencing today. He, in essence, saw Marxist thought as a counter religion. Wrote Gromsci, "Socialism is precisely the religion that must overwhelm Christianity." [Over the last fifty years, a considerable number of academics have written that not only is Cultural Marxism a religion, but Marxism itself is, in its essence, a religion. See chapter eleven of this book, "The Errors of Russia," for more on this subject]

last prophecy of Fátima: the promise of a "triumph" over systematic evil and a "period of peace" on earth.

This prophesied time slowly ascends the horizon. But first must come an upending and turbulent transition between the world of today and the world of tomorrow, a transition that some say will fulfill ancient prophecies in the Bible.

And that is what this book is all about.

In approaching this work, I want the reader to know that there was a reason that I revisited in this writing many of the horrific details of the suffering and carnage that make up the violent history of the twentieth century.

The Virgin Mary appeared at Fátima in an attempt to head off the inexplicable misery that unfolded throughout that unprecedented period. Unfortunately, her hopes were not to be realized.

Now, at Medjugorje, her pressing appeal to mankind strives to do the same, only the "errors" (of Russia) that were to be prevented must now be defeated.

No one more than Mary can see what the future holds for humanity as it is to progress from one age to another. By recalling and coming to grips with the anguish of the past, perhaps we can better respond to the exigency of the present.

Life, as we know it, is to experience a radical metamorphosis.

The last throes of the Age of Reason are underway.

Historic moments and epic events are moving into place. A dramatic shift in human consciousness is to unfold as a "divine reset" of the world and the Church takes hold.

Tomorrow—I believe—will be nothing like today.

As God did with John the Baptist, through the Virgin Mary's appearances at Fátima and Medjugorje, a mother's voice is heard crying in the wilderness of a fading era, pleading with her children to come home as night falls.

All who can hear her voice are invited to answer her loving but urgent call.

Thomas W. Petrisko
February 11, 2022,
Feast of Our Lady of Lourdes

66 She (Russia) will spread her errors throughout the world, causing wars and persecution of the Church. The good will be martyred, the Holy Father will have much to suffer, various nations will be annihilated."

—The Virgin Mary,
Portugal,1917

66 If you live in a graveyard, you can't weep for everyone."

—Aleksandr Solzhenitsyn,
Russia,1968

PREFACE

*"A great sign appeared in the sky, a woman clothed
with the sun, with the moon under her feet, and
on her head a crown of twelve stars."*

—Rv 12:1

O N MAY 13, 1917, THREE SHEPHERD CHILDREN OUTSIDE THE VIL-
lage of Fátima in west central Portugal, eighty-eight miles north
of Lisbon, reported an apparition of the Virgin Mary. Over the next six
months, they would experience five more encounters with the vision.

The apparition appeared to launch an appeal to humanity to turn
away from evil and sin and come back to God, the visionaries were
told, before a series of harsh events contained in a three-part "secret"
prophecy came to fulfillment.

To prevent the coming perils—which included World War II and
Communism— the Virgin Mary said she would return to request the
consecration of Russia by the Pope and the bishops of the Catholic
Church, along with a worldwide prayer initiative known as the
Communion of Reparation.* This vision took place in 1929 at Tui,

---

*   For those outside the Catholic Church, it is necessary to understand that the request
for the "consecration of Russia" by the Virgin Mary is a matter of the Catholic religion
that lies entirely in the realm of faith. To the secular world, this ritual will have little
meaning and may appear strange and even cultish. But inside the Church, such ceremonies are a well-established tradition and are believed to be sanctifying, powerful and
in keeping with how God worked with his chosen people in ancient Israel.

     In the Old Testament, the patriarchs and prophets of old were often seen to be told
by God to perform what would appear to be unrelated or inconsequential acts that
produce miraculous outcomes, such as what followed after Solomon prayed to God
to accept the consecration of the Temple of Jerusalem (2 Chr 7:1-22). At Fátima, the
requested consecration of Russia by the Pope and all of the bishops of the Catholic
Church in order to prevent approaching trials is to be viewed in this same light of faith.
It is seen to be in keeping with Scripture: "For nothing is impossible for God." (Gn 18:14,
2 Kgs 3:18, Jer 2:17, Mt 19:26, Lk 1:36)

Spain, to the lone surviving visionary, but failed to bring about the desired response.

The Catholic Church began a canonical process of investigation to study Fátima on May 3, 1922. The apparitions were declared supernatural by the Church on October 13, 1930.

On June 24, 1981, an apparition of the Virgin Mary was reported in the rustic hamlet of Bijakovići, located ninety-six miles southwest of Sarajevo in what was the nation of Yugoslavia at the time.

By the end of the following day, six youths emerged as the visionaries in what has become known throughout the world as the apparitions at Medjugorje. Some fifty million people have traveled to the village in Hercegovina over the past forty years.

As at Fátima, an appeal to renounce evil and sin and return to God was reported to be the message of the vision. Once again, confidential prophecies—known as the Ten Secrets of Medjugorje—are being received by the six visionaries from Mary.** The mysterious foretellings are said to involve world transforming events of considerable magnitude—believed greater than Fátima—that are to unfold within the lifetimes of the visionaries.

On March 17, 2010, Pope Benedict XVI empaneled a seventeen-member board, known as the Ruini Commission, to study the events at Medjugorje. It completed its work on January 17, 2014. Though not officially approved by the Church, a pre-released copy of the commission's report in 2020 disclosed the panel concluded the first seven apparitions at Medjugorje were *"constat de supernaturalitate"*—determined to be supernatural.***

In May of 2019, the Holy See sanctioned official Church pilgrimages to the shrine. On August 2, 2020, Archbishop Luigi Pezzuto, the Vatican's apostolic nuncio to Bosnia-Hercegovina, addressed the annual gathering of youth in Medjugorje on behalf of the Pope.

** As of early 2022, three of the visionaries at Medjugorje had received all ten secrets from the Virgin Mary. The other three received nine.

*** Andrea Tornielli, "The Conclusions of the Ruini Report on Medjugorje," *The National Catholic Register, nc.register.com*. Posted by Andrea Tornielli / CNA/EWTN News on Wednesday, May 17, 2017, at 9:02 p.m.

No judgement as to the veracity of the succeeding visions at Medjugorje has been rendered primarily due to their volume and to the fact that the events there have not concluded.

The Ten Secrets of Medjugorje remain secret.

PART I

TO PREVENT THIS

"You understand, venerable brethren, that we speak of that sect of men who, under various and almost barbarous names, are called socialists, communists, or nihilists, and who, spread over all the world, and bound together by the closest ties in a wicked confederacy, no longer seek the shelter of secret meetings, but openly and boldly marching forth in the light of day, strive to bring to a head what they have long been planning—the overthrow of all civil society whatsoever."

—Pope Leo XIII,
Quod Apostolici Muneris,
December 28, 1878

CHAPTER ONE

THE FIRE THAT WASN'T

"So, Moses decided, 'I must go over to look at this
remarkable sight, and see why the bush is not burned.'"
—Ex 3:3

THE BLAZE ON MT. CRNICA IGNITED SPONTANEOUSLY.
Seconds later, the flames sprung so high the fire could be seen from a considerable distance. Below, the habitants scattered within the five little villages realized this could spell trouble—especially for Bijakovici which sat at the base of the little hill. [1]

Responding with urgency, a caravan of police, firefighters, and militia arrived, piled out of their vehicles, and sealed off the area. [2]

But suddenly, it was gone.

For fifteen minutes, a raging inferno.

Now, nothing. [3]

An even stranger discovery was unearthed by investigators as they ascended to the top of the hill. Upon inspection, no evidence of the conflagration could be found—not a trace of smoldering bushes or burnt trees, no charred weeds, or blackened grass. Not a gasping spark or a floating ash.

Dismissed by skeptics as absurdity, the fire was no mirage for the locals living around Crnica. And not only was the blaze witnessed by over five hundred people, the incident was certified by government authorities assigned here to oversee this stealthy slice of Herzegovina. [4]

Ironically, the security had been ratcheted up for just this purpose—to impede the cascade of bizarre disturbances spilling out almost every day from the previously tranquil region.

By now, the embarrassing affairs—religious provocations as they were classified—were seen as dangerous and seditious, [5] drawing international attention, and giving Communist Party officials in Sarajevo and Belgrade the jitters.[6]

For bemused journalists already familiar with the unfolding spectacle peeking through the cracks of the Iron Curtain in the fall of 1981, the steady flow of reports coming from the handful of quasi-medieval hamlets nestled together were already coalescing in their files under a single name:

Medjugorje.

CHAPTER TWO

JUDGEMENT DAY

"Then God's temple in heaven was opened, and the
ark of his covenant could be seen in the temple.
There were flashes of lightning, rumblings, and
peals of thunder, and a violent hailstorm."

—Rv 11:19

NOT MANY KNOW OF THE HORRIFIC TEMPEST THAT DESCENDED upon Medjugorje shortly after midnight on June 24, 1981. But it manifested eerily like Scripture's violent squall that Christ tamed on Galilee.

One account memorialized it in almost novelesque language:

"The night before had been sticky—hot and oppressive, heavy with menace. At one in the morning, a storm of Homeric force split the sky." [1]

The raging blast of nature not only rattled the heavens, it heaped a good share of havoc on earth, too. Within minutes, the entire hamlet was shaken awake, scrambling through the streets to help fight a dozen fires and limit the damage from blowing debris.

"It's like the Day of Judgment out there," hollered a frenzied Iva Vasilj to her still bedded down husband after a brief reconnaissance of the smoking village. [2]

Hail, sheets of rain, barrages of lightning that streaked in all directions, and crashing—almost deafening—thunder drove Iva to her panicked assessment. Reluctantly, husband Pero, a peasant tobacco farmer, threw off the covers to venture out. Startled, he found that the storm had incited so many blazes, the undermanned local fire department couldn't cope with them all.

The utilities building was destroyed, as was a makeshift discothèque in the old meeting hall. Fire trucks from the municipal capital of Čitluk arrived and saved half the post office, but both the power and the phones were knocked out.[3]

Smoke belched out of the pine trees directly below the Vasilj's home, where burning trees looked like large candles. Drained by it all, it would be dawn before the couple's fears lifted.

Like the other villagers, the Vasiljs were no strangers to the wild storms that frequently blow in over the Adriatic and onto the plains of western Herzegovina. In 1933, the residents even erected a towering concrete cross on the local mountaintop that seemed to help repel the dark side of nature.

But this unharnessed gale punished the area so brutally, recalled Iva, she wasn't certain nature was all that was behind it. "I grabbed a crucifix and a bottle of holy water," she confessed, "and went around sprinkling half the village." [4]

Trying moments produce unpredictable responses, even from the steadiest of souls. But Iva Vasilj's exorcism tactics unveil her suspicion: perhaps the devil was in the details of the violent midnight storm that slammed into Medjugorje on that night, before the first day of the apparitions.

Of course, if something evil played a role, no one will ever know. Throughout the world over the previous twenty-four months, however, the devil seemed to be not just in the details, but the architect of the blue prints.

For hundreds of years, the people of Herzegovina have felt the pain and fear that comes with storms—all kinds of storms—especially those brought on by anger and hatred, leading to chronic war and endless death in their land.

Now, the entire planet, like this tortured land of the Southern Slavs, was looking at an approaching storm on the radar of life—a thermonuclear storm.

Over the twenty-four months prior to the summer of 1981, a parade of international events and crises escalated tension levels between the East and the West to perhaps an all-time high.

In June of 1979, the President of the United States, Jimmy Carter, approved a new guided missile system called the MX, furthering the arms race. Although Carter and Soviet Union President Leonid Brezhnev would later that month sign the Salt II agreement in Vienna—a treaty that if ratified would limit long-range nuclear missiles and bombers to 2,250 apiece per nation—the world felt no safer.

And it wasn't.

The Soviet invasion of Afghanistan in December 1979 quickly doused any optimism that the Cold War was thawing. Fears of a second Soviet invasion into Poland were in the air, too.

Then, things got worse.

The United States boycotted the Olympics in Moscow the summer of 1980 in response to the Soviet's plunge into Afghanistan, while the nation's Congress moved to allow the draft registration of all 19 and 20-year-old men for the first time since 1972 and the Vietnam War.

It was an ominous sign.

During this same period, an Islamic fundamentalist revolution in Iran exploded, giving birth to a hostage standoff involving fifty-two Americans. This new Middle East crisis, along with escalating violence in Israel, Lebanon, and Afghanistan, threatened to spark a conflict so vast it was bound to involve a confrontation between the United States and the Soviet Union—a potential nuclear confrontation.

The Iranian hostage crisis ended in January 1981, after 444 days. But, just three months later, the President of the United States, Ronald Reagan, was shot by John Hinckley Jr. as he stepped into his limo in downtown Washington, D.C.

And again, six weeks later, bullets flew in St. Peter's Square, after a reported agent of an Eastern Bloc Communist country, Bulgaria, hired Mehmet Ali Ağca to assassinate Pope John Paul II.

The attempted assassination took place sixty-four years to the day—May 13, 1917—of the first apparition of the Virgin Mary at Fátima.

By the spring of 1981, many believed the world stood at its most dangerous moment in history, conjuring up flashbacks of the air raid drills and fallout shelters that were part of everyday life during the first two decades after World War II. Too many confrontations across the globe had the East and the West postured in a showdown, threatening to pull their thousands of nuclear missiles out of their subterranean holsters.

Needless to say, the entire world was on edge, with people everywhere holding their breath. As with the Cuban Missile Crisis of October 1962, no one dared imagine the unimaginable.

In 1917, a new era in hostility arrived.

A world war was in full bloom, and for the first time ever, literally millions were dying across the globe. In Portugal, beginning on May 13 of that year, the Virgin Mary's apparitions at Fátima to three shepherd children—ten-year-old Lúcia dos Santos, nine-year-old Francisco Marto, and his little sister, Jacinta, who was seven—defined the moment and urgency of the times.

The horrible carnage of World War I would soon end, Mary informed the children in the second portion of a confidential three-part prophecy given to them on July 13, 1917. Destined to become universally known as the Secret of Fátima, the good news about the First World War was immediately tempered by a word of caution from the apparition: a still ghastlier world war lurked in the future if humanity did not alter its course—if it did not cease, insisted the Virgin Mary, "offending God."

And there was more.

Out of Russia, Mary explained to the children, would emerge a coming scourge—soon to be understood as atheistic Communism—that would "spread its errors" throughout the world. Unless the Catholic Church and the faithful responded in the ways that Mary was to return to request—one being the "consecration of Russia" by the Pope and all the bishops—wars, suffering, martyrdom, and persecutions would befall the Church and the world.

Even worse, the Virgin told the three little visionaries, if her pleas were not heeded, "various nations will be annihilated"—a dire and haunting prognostication that incited talk of a coming doomsday and the "end of the world" for decades to come.

And then there came the third and last part of the prophetic Fátima message.

Written down twenty-seven years later on January 3, 1944, wax sealed inside an envelope by the lone surviving visionary—now a nun known as Sister Lúcia—and then kept in the custody of the Bishop of Leiria for thirteen years, the third part of the Secret of Fátima was transferred to the Vatican in 1957 so it would "not fall into the wrong hands." [5]

Expected to be revealed in 1960, the Vatican let it be leaked to a Portuguese news outlet on February 8 of that year that the third part of the Secret would not be released. It then remained concealed under lock and key for decades by a series of Popes.[6]

Rumored to harbor even greater prophetic angst than the first two parts of the Secret, insiders at the time grew to understand it would probably never see the light of day—or at least as long as there continued to be a Cold War.[7]

As occurred with the Virgin Mary's terrifying revelation from her apparition at La Salette, France, in 1846, unnerving bootleg renditions of the mysterious foretelling began to circulate.[8] And, not surprisingly, the bogus prophecies sounded true to the third part of the Secret's reputed content; gargantuan natural disasters, nuclear warfare, deadly plagues, civil wars and even cosmic disturbances causing millions to perish from one moment to the next were described [9]—sensational claims that kept alive the Secret's reputation for possessing shock and awe.[10]

What was finally disclosed by the Vatican on June 26, 2000, however, was nothing of the sort, leaving the long-awaited, allegedly catastrophic foretelling to fizzle out a dud almost overnight.

To the amazement of millions worldwide—after decades of anticipation—the contents of the so called "Third Secret of Fátima" contained none of the expected apocalyptic rhetoric.[11]

But what did come forth was provocative.

Discarding words, the revelation turned out to be not a message from the Virgin Mary at all, but Sister Lúcia's description of a baffling vision the three children witnessed.[12]

It was a vision that would not be immediately understood to hold the esoteric mysteries and climactic overtones that it did, since no corroborating text—although rumored to exist—was released with it.

But when examined closely, the third part of the Secret was found to possess—in perplexing symbolism—what seemed again to be another serious forewarning from Mary of a momentous time in the future. A time that many Fátima followers felt had not yet seen the light of day, despite an effort by Cardinal Angelo Sodano and others that attempted to assign its meaning to the past.[13]

The vision had two scenes.

Crying, "Penance, Penance, Penance," while holding a flashing sword that gave off flames that "looked as though they would set the world on fire," there appears an angel who towers over the Earth and to the left of a lofty, radiant Virgin Mary. The angel is seen to be casting divine wrath upon a sinful world, only to find the effort mitigated by Mary's interceding right hand.

A second scene of a war-torn city, with many religious depicted as victims—including a martyred pope—trails the first scene congruently. More or less, it conveys the understanding that the Church will be at the center of a painful and sorrowful calamity in the future and is to greatly suffer for the glory of God.

The nuclear imagery was unmistakable and worthy of St. John's *Apocalypse,* wrote the Prefect of the Congregation for the Doctrine of the Faith, Cardinal Joseph Ratzinger (the future Pope Benedict XVI), in *The Message of Fatima,* an official commentary on the Secret of Fátima provided by the Vatican on the day the mysterious prophecy was released.

"The angel with the flaming sword on the left of the Mother of God," said Ratzinger, "recalls similar images in *The Book of Revelation.* This represents the threat of judgement which looms over the world. Today the prospect that the world might be reduced to ashes by a sea of fire no longer seems pure fantasy: man himself, with his inventions, has forged the flaming sword." [14]

Sister Lúcia—93 years old by then—offered no new insights at the time of the disclosure or any helpful words to confirm Ratzinger's attempted interpretation, other than to say it was the role of the Church to best discern the vision's meaning.

But, in an earlier May 12, 1982, letter to Pope John Paul II that was released by the Vatican on the same day as the third part of the Secret, Lúcia *did* present an interpretation of the vision, revealing that the prophetic imagery in it was intended to convey a more profound realization of the serious implications of the second part of the Secret— the spread of the "errors of Russia" throughout the world that Mary warned about in 1917 at Fátima.[15]

In essence, Lúcia's letter wanted to make it perfectly clear to the Pope that the third part of the Secret was intended to magnify the incessant dangers associated with the spread of systematic atheism, especially in the form of the unconstrained march of militant Communism—the rapacious red revolution germinated in Russia, now over six decades in the making.

Lúcia's letter also implied that dreadful consequences—perhaps the fulfillment of Mary's prophecy that "various nations will be annihilated"—were inevitable unless the consecration of Russia was finally enacted by the Pope.

On March 25, 1984, two years after receiving Sister Lúcia's letter, Pope John Paul II—along with those bishops who chose to accompany him—finally performed the long awaited consecration, though not of Russia, but of the world.

Asked after if the Pope's act was accepted by God, Lúcia said it was done, but it was "already too late!" [16]

Too late?

What did Lúcia mean that it was "too late?"

Without question, her words were again in reference to the spread of the errors of Russia, the now global tsunami of atheistic Marxist ideology that had flooded every corner of the planet in ways seen—and unseen.

What was *seen* was alarming.

By the mid-80s, twenty-three countries and one third of the world's population were under Communist rule, with news of Soviet inspired insurgencies, revolutions, and guerrilla wars continuing to pop up on a steady basis.[17] Simply put: the world had become very "Red"—and very dangerous.

Less than a year prior to Sister Lúcia's letter to the Pope, the growing concern of a nuclear confrontation between the East and the West again proved itself to be viable in an undeniable and alarming way.

The New York Times, in an article published on September 27, 1981, divulged a new U.S. Defense Department report on the Soviet Union's present military might. The analysis painted a picture of a huge and dynamic military machine that gave the impression of "relentless and almost overwhelming Soviet military power."

The numbers in the report said it all.

Eighty Soviet divisions—over two million troops—were now deployed supposedly for the defense of Eastern Europe, with another twenty-five divisions stationed in reserve. This did not include the hundreds of thousands of Warsaw Pact soldiers on standby.[18]

In addition to the man power, 51,000 tanks and 7,260 combat aircraft, along with 250 SS-20 medium range missiles, were in place up and down the Iron Curtain. The missiles were loaded with over 750 nuclear warheads. And, for the first time, the report found that the Soviets had taken the lead in the development of high-powered lasers, as well as direct energy weapons. [19]

The massive visible presence of the Soviet military along its border with Eastern Europe, as well as in other strategic locations around the globe, was disturbing though not surprising.

But what was *unseen* was surprising.

By the mid-80s, there was an unsettling reality fermenting that was becoming undeniable: a metamorphosis of life in the West was underway, with socialists sharing power or ruling in some European nations and leftist, Marxist thought running amok in the cultures and institutions that lined both sides of the Atlantic.*

Simply put: the great Judeo-Christian foundation that held up Europe and America for centuries seemed to be crumbling. And this pervasive disintegration of traditional values was becoming as much a worry to some as the prowling Soviet bear.

In essence, to go with the Cold War, a spiritual and ideological ice age was descending on Western civilization—bringing with it the fear that there lurked a growing enemy within, to go with the enemy at the gate.

While the Virgin Mary prophesied at Fátima that a great return to God was to come into the world, there still remained the gnawing suspicion that Sister Lúcia's concerns of the "complete fulfillment" of the Secret of Fátima carried within it one more dreadful and final chapter. One more possibility—as Cardinal Ratzinger sublimely put it in his interpretation of the Secret—that the world might be "reduced to ashes by a sea of fire."

---

*   The social changes in America were becoming so great that the eminent Jesuit theologian, professor and papal advisor, Fr. John Hardon S.T.D., stated in 1998: "The United States of America is the most powerful Marxist country in the world." [From a lecture delivered by Father John Harden on April 4, 1998, at the CMF Regional Conference held at the Cardinal Mindszenty Foundation in Chicago. Published by the Cardinal Mindszenty Foundation, August 1998.]

Needless to say, by the summer of 1981, one didn't need any new prophecies to make this case.

And so comes again—to a fragile and even more dangerous world—reports of the apparitional woman from Heaven.

And as Abraham was saved at the last second from sacrificing his beloved Isaac, who on earth could argue with the timing at Medjugorje.

But why Medjugorje?

Why in Communist Yugoslavia behind the Iron Curtain of all places?

Why in a blood-soaked country—a place that has never known peace—would the Virgin Mary appear declaring she was coming as the *Queen of Peace*?

On the surface, it seemed puzzling, undeniably laced with mystery, and certainly a bit ominous.

But underneath, there were clues that something profound was at hand—that a unique moment in history was settling into place—and that this broken land of sorrows was being chosen to bring to fulfillment the last prophecies of the Secret of Fátima.

CHAPTER THREE

LAND OF THE DEMONS

"But the Lord's eyes are upon the reverent, upon those who hope for his gracious help, delivering them from death, keeping them alive in times of famine."

—Ps 33:18

O NE DOESN'T NEED TO SOLICIT OPINIONS FROM HISTORIANS TO begin to understand a place that a 1993 ABC News documentary deemed worthy of such an ignominious title as *The Land of the Demons*—a region where more hatred has flourished at times than perhaps anywhere on earth, and where after centuries of endless human carnage, chronic fear and anxiety have become embedded within the people's DNA. [1]

Yes, the former Yugoslavia—the historic epicenter of cultural clashes, with a graveyard of empires and emperors vaster than Afghanistan— could not be a more deserving candidate for celestial assistance. And perhaps not a better target-specific place for the Virgin Mary to come with the hope of preventing the Third World War.

While the news media often focuses on the chronic hostilities in the Middle East, Korea, Africa, and other intermittent global hot spots, the land of the Southern Slavs holds no rivals for quantity of violence spanning eons.

Over the centuries, this region has sponsored bloody brawls between popes and kings, cultures and civilizations, governments and churches. Throw in a generous number of endemic clashes between bickering peoples, tribes, villages, towns, cities, and neighboring nations, and you have the incarnation of Dante's Inferno.

The reality of the land is this: whether Croatian, Serbian, Bosnian—Christian, Orthodox, or Muslim—these people have never known peace in their lifetime, or in the lifetimes of their forefathers.

In *Black Lamb, Grey Falcon*, author Rebecca West wrote in 1941 about what sizes up to be ground zero for domestic warfare:

> Were I to go down to the market place, armed with the powers of witchcraft, and take a peasant by the shoulders, and whisper to him, "In your lifetime, have you known peace?" wait for his answer, shake his shoulders and transform him into his father, and ask him the same question, and transform him in turn into his father, I would never hear the word "Yes", if I carried my questioning of the dead back for a thousand years. I would always hear, "No, there was fear, there were our enemies without, our rulers within, there was prison, there was a violent death." [2]

Barbarous details aside, the region has failed miserably as a melting pot for individuals and nations, cultures and faiths. In the competitive spirit of Cain and Able, fratricidal clashes win the gold medal here, as the land is the antithesis of brotherly love.

The Roman Empire fractured in this place, as would the emerging Christian faith, accomplishments found on the résumé of no other region in the world.

Historians say, however, there is a major reason for all this malevolence.

The country that Medjugorje and its surrounding villages occupy is known as Bosnia-Herzegovina, one of six republics coalesced into post-war Communist Yugoslavia.

The vast magnitude of the population is descendant of the original Slavic group—the Slaveni.[3] The names Serb and Croat were drawn from a second group of migrants, thought to be Iranian tribes, which in the seventh century occupied the northern part of the region.[4]

Over time, the two groups assimilated, but even in the Middle Ages they did not call themselves Serbs or Croats. They referred to themselves as Bosnians—a geographical term more than cultural or ethnic.[5]

The specific region where Medjugorje sits is what is called the Brotnji Plateau, which was a province of the Roman Empire called Illyrian.[6] Its history can be traced back to the first century—and that's exactly how far one needs to travel back in time to understand the hostilities in this part of the world.

Beginning with their location east and west of the old Imperial Dividing Line, and then later in their form of Christianity, the issues that have caused groups to consistently spill each other's blood have included language, fanatical doctrines, state religion, and misguided allegiances to foreign occupiers.

But more than anything else, scholars believe that all this hatred stems from the original line of division established between the East and the West almost two thousand years ago.

Historians say this is where one must start to understand the profoundness of the divisions between the peoples, as well as the reasons for the longevity of the fratricidal disputes.

In A.D. 284, the Roman Emperor, Diocletian, came to power. He proceeded to divide the empire into two self-governing regions, a western half still administrated by Rome and an eastern half controlled by Constantinople.[7]

The Emperor Constantine instituted a reunion of the two empires, but on the passing away of Theodosius the Great in A.D. 395, a second division was made.[8] This line of division ran north-south from the Sava near Sirmium (Sremska Mitrovica) to Lake Scutari (Skadar) in the present Montenegrin-Albanian border. [9]

Over the centuries, this line remained a permanent feature on the cultural map of Europe. Thus, it separated Byzantium from Rome,[10] or in reality, the Greek from the Roman cultural heritage.[11] Eventually, it also separated the Eastern Orthodox from the Roman Catholic Church and users of the Cyrillic script from those of the Latin.[12]

From the fifth through the eighth centuries, invading hordes descended upon the region, and it changed hands quite frequently. In the seventh century, the Slovenes and Croats were introduced to the Christianity of Rome, which had been progressively establishing itself in Europe and Africa.

Then, in the ninth century, the Serbs were converted by the Eastern Church.[13] Charlemagne's empire controlled enclaves throughout the territory in the eighth century,[14] but by the ninth century, a war had emerged for the souls of the Slavic people between the two Christian confessions—the Eastern Church of Byzantium and the Western Church of Rome.[15]

With this, the region was infused with more distrust, animosity, and division, as everyone from the Bogomils to the Crusaders to the Turks bloodied the soil over the next five centuries.

After some brief respites during the reign of the Ottoman Empire, fire and sword laid waste again to the land for several more centuries until replaced by bullets and bombs—courtesy of warring Austrians, Hungarians, Slovenes, Russians, Germans, Croatians, Serbians, and Muslims.

Throw in the assassination of Austrian Archduke Franz Ferdinand in Sarajevo on June 28, 1914, which set off World War I, forty years of communism under the tyrant Marshal Tito, the fact that this region would bear witness in the 1990s to the only war fought on European soil since World War II, and one can see the land's bloody birthmark proudly withstands the sands of time.

Geopolitically speaking, the line of demarcation in the former Yugoslavia between the East and the West appears humanly indelible, still forever the crossroad between conflicting faiths and political ideologies.

Consequently, it remains a tinderbox for tensions and hostilities, a region always capable of tripping a war overnight that could rapidly escalate into a global confrontation between dozens of nations.

Feelings of rancor, suspicion, hatred, and division have ruled hearts here for almost two thousand years, but so did they rule in the heart of the region's Roman forefather—the despotic Emperor, Diocletian.

Known as the last of the Roman tyrants, the last of the Roman antichrists, Diocletian undertook the final great persecution of the early Christians.

The Christian faith multiplied considerably in the years before Diocletian's reign, and thus, in A.D. 303, the Emperor issued a series of edicts beginning the greatest period of martyrdom and suffering for Christians throughout the history of the Roman Empire.

Known as the *Diocletianic*, or "Great Persecution", assemblies were prohibited, churches destroyed, and the Scriptures were burned. In the end, the failure to eradicate Christianity totally was said to be one of the great disappointments of Diocletian's life.

Diocletian was a native son of Dalmatia, now Croatia, where he built the last great Roman palace in Split and returned there to retire in A.D. 305. He died on December 3, 311, not far from—what would be a short drive down the highway today—a sequestered huddle of five rural villages that sit in the shadow of a mountain capped with a huge, towering concrete cross.

The cross overlooks a Catholic shrine the world has come to know as Medjugorje.

Some will read into the stormy morning at Medjugorje a foreshadowing sign of the supernatural events that emerged later that day.

This may or may not be true.

But a stronger, more worthy application of such faith is noted in something else that came with the clock striking midnight on the 24th of June: it was the feast day of Saint John the Baptist, the legendary precursor of Christ.

Indeed, if history now stood at a confluence of time as never before, the Baptist's day of honor—which celebrates the life and mission of a prophet who besought temporal repentance to prevent eternal sorrow—is a date more than worthy to be understood as providential.

In retrospect, it could be coincidental the Virgin Mary suddenly appeared on a little hill in a Communist nation on such an important day on the Church calendar, at perhaps the most perilous moment in human history.

But highly unlikely.

As at Fátima, where the crowing rooster is not just a part of the town's fabric but Portugal's symbolic bird of truth and justice, Mary's arrival in another bucolic village—whose streets are also patrolled by St. Peter's eternal friend—seemed to signal the dawning fulfillment of a moment birthed in the fullness of God's time, accompanied again by no shortage of divine markers. Scripture counts sixty-four generations between Adam and Christ, and sixty-four years stretched between Fátima and Medjugorje.

"The chaff will burn in unquenchable fire," the Baptist roared, and such could be argued was the case for the world that humid, muggy, June day in 1981.

It was a day that started off before dawn with a baptismal soaking from the heavens above, followed by the surprise appearance from an illuminating lady floating on a hillside, whose later words at Medjugorje would come to sound like the desert preacher himself—words that forewarned that some kind of judgement was near.

At Fátima, Mary prophesied the ending of one world war and the coming of another. She predicted persecutions of the Church and the Holy Father. She warned of the "annihilation of nations." [16]

But she also foretold a coming change in epochs of history, a great triumph of good over evil, and an era of peace that would settle the earth.

Now on the feast day of the greatest prophet of them all, the Virgin Mary was in Medjugorje appearing to twice as many visionaries as at Fátima—and returning to a world a thousand times more dangerous than in 1917—to attempt to fulfill her words. [17]

CHAPTER FOUR

MAKE WAY FOR MARXISM

*"Thus says the Lord: Cursed is the man who
trusts in human beings, who seeks his strength in
flesh, whose heart turns away from the Lord."*

—Jer 17:5

FÁTIMA.
   To understand Medjugorje, one must understand Fátima. And
to understand Fátima, one must understand prophecy.

Prophecy is the testimony and legacy of Fátima, beginning with
Mary's first foretelling words there:

"The war is going to end." [1]

The "Great War for Civilization"—World War I—was nearing its
end. Mary confided this preknowledge to the three shepherd children
on July 13 [2] and again on October 13, 1917.[3]*

It was a pivotal disclosure.

In Portugal, far from the blood-filled muddy trenches of the Western
Front in France, the Virgin's words envisaging the war's approaching
conclusion would have been welcome news—if only widely circulated
at the time.

The conflict had been costly to Portugal.

While not a major combatant, and not officially entered into World
War I until 1916, by its termination in 1918, 12,000 Portuguese troops
laid dead. Another 82,000 civilians perished from food shortages

---

* Mary also spoke about World War I in May and September of 1917, asking the children
  both months to pray the Rosary "to obtain" the end of the war.

related to the misery at hand. And by 1920, 138,000 more succumbed to the Spanish Flu, a horrific two-year pandemic that affected 500 million worldwide and killed an estimated 50 million or more.[4]

All in all, it was for Portugal, as for most of Europe, an apocalyptic time. Five long years of anguish, suffering, and death—a godforsaken, devastating fraction of history—one perhaps unseen before in such a brief portal of human existence.

But, though not seen, the trying age had been imagined.

And while probably unpreventable, the ghastly era had been prophesied well in advance of the Virgin Mary's apparitions at Fátima.

For more than a hundred years before Mary appeared in Fátima, novelists were dallying in the literary frontier of future shock, prognosticating worldwide calamities and technological-driven doomsdays.

Attentive and sensitive to the morose changes consuming the post-Enlightenment age, writers brandished short stories and fictitious narratives of a perilous world to come, a time that would flirt with mankind's very existence.

Centered on future trials brought on by the modern age, many of the novels approached "end of the world" scenarios not just as stories of survival, but as living in an unavoidable epoch to come.

Seen as already previewed in *The Book of Revelation*, some writers assumed that mankind's destiny was already carved out in stone. What remained, though, were the details—something the novelists enjoyed bringing to life based on Saint John's account of the final days of planet Earth.

Quite a few lofty names in writing threw their pens into this arena. But it was one man whose novels became the rage. Mastering the apocalyptical theme, H.G. Wells saw a future in upheaval and chaos, as massive conflicts driven by advanced technology in weapons bring death and destruction everywhere.

By the mid-eighteenth century, though, one didn't need to search the imagination or read novels to encounter this storyline. The future had landed, as upheaval abounded and a metamorphosis of life on earth started to unfold in every sphere of endeavor—from religion to culture, politics to science, philosophy to art, transformation defined the age.

It would be, however, the terrifying advances in technology that spelled the most trouble. As in the novels, the future appeared to be moving towards a precipice, thanks to the rapidly-accelerating field of the art and science of killing.

The progress mankind made in conducting warfare from the end of the eighteenth century through the early twentieth century was stunning in breadth and sweeping in results.

By the mid-nineteenth century, the dawning age of modern warfare had arrived.

Field guns undid castles and fortresses. Artillery capabilities altered land and sea battles. Improved roads and canals allowed armies to become more mobile. And the innovation of conscription, which requisitioned men by law into the armed forces, brought into existence armies reminiscent of the barbarian hordes of the ancient world.[5]

By then, some governments were mobilizing the youth of both sexes. This brought whole nations in step with the military, and mega-sized battles were waged.

At Leipzig, 539,000 fought in 1813. At Solferino in 1859, 300,000 men fought in a battle that stretched over 60 miles. Before 1861, the United States Army was 16,000; however, by the end of the American Civil War in 1865, the Confederacy had called up ninety percent of its male population (1,400,000) and the union forty-five percent of its men (2,900,000).[6]

The technological innovations in munitions, hand guns, and rifles progressed steadily throughout the nineteenth century, too. Bullets became cylindrical in shape. Pistols and revolvers became mass produced, and rifle accuracy grew dramatically. By the 1860s, some companies produced 1,000 rifles a week. Soon, rapid-firing guns were developed, and by 1900, machine guns could massacre charging infantrymen. In South Africa, automatic firing guns that shot 2,000 rounds in three minutes were used for the first time.[7]

Artillery had its own critical development. Large shells could now rip apart wooden boats. This forced the development of ironclad ships, such as the Monitor and the Merrimac in the American Civil War. Armored wagons and trains were soon developed and rushed into service. Submarines, torpedoes, land and sea mines, and steam-driven battleships added to the avalanche of military toys. [8]

The maturing science of killing knew no end, validating the dreams of the novelists while forcing their imaginations to try and stay ahead.

The vast technological and organizational preparations for modern warfare seemed to be hinting at what some politicians feared to be approaching by the mid-nineteenth century—a "great war."

This would be one that industry and government together could advance beyond anything ever before seen. One in which a nation, because of its industrial/military capabilities, could wage to grab "world power," and maybe even more, "world control."

But, if not careful, as American Civil War statesman Henry Adams observed, the rapid advance in military capabilities also previewed a direr possibility—the danger of "world destruction." [9]

And it was this theme that seemed to dominate the message of a flurry of reported miracles that intensified right after the French Revolution and continued right up to the Virgin Mary's historic 1917 appearance in Fátima.[10]

Issuing alarming forecasts of approaching trouble beginning in the mid to late 18th century, by the early nineteenth century, the prophecies appeared to be everywhere—and, in retrospect, World War I seemed to be their common premonition.

These revelations would later be seen collectively by Marian theologians as an opening act of prophetic thunder, delivered in preparation for the lightning-charged historical/political prophecies of Fátima in 1917.

By the mid-nineteenth century, the prophets hinted, if not asserted, that a future series of events would carry with them worldwide implications. Unparalleled evil and sin, and their consequences, were descending upon the earth, the revelations echoed, with inevitable sorrow to follow.

According to Professor David Blackbourn of Harvard University, the total number of alleged nineteenth century apparitions ran into "the many hundreds." [11] Blackbourn says that, for the most part, historians have divided the reported miraculous events of the past 225 years into what he calls "waves," with the first wave beginning in the aftermath of the French Revolution.[12]

This wave was emphasized by a handful of renown female mystics of the age, such as Catherine Emmerich, and an outpouring of reports of weeping statues and images of the Virgin Mary, most notably the "Weeping Madonnas" of Rome—twenty-six different pictures across the city that exhibited supernatural characteristics in which the Church was moved to investigate.

This period was followed by—right before the political upheaval of the 1830s in France—a second great wave.

The beginning of this second wave was highlighted by a well-known 1836 Church-approved apparition in Paris to Catherine Laboure, who would be declared a saint by the Catholic Church. Here, the warnings of approaching calamities intensified, as the Virgin Mary prophesied to the holy nun:

"The entire world will be overcome by evil of all kinds." [13]

Such dire words were increasingly noted with the second wave, culminating with a vision of Mary high up on a mountainside at La Salette, France, in 1846 to two youngsters, 11-year-old Maximin Girard and 15-year-old Melanie Calvat.

Troubling and controversial for decades, the Catholic Church approved the vision in September, 1851, but would not release a secret message given by Mary to Melanie that reportedly contained unparalleled apocalyptic content.[14]

Over the next ten years, such frenzied prophetic alarm continued to spread across Europe.

At Lichen, Poland in 1850, a Church-approved apparition predicted that a worldwide calamity approached, in which millions would die in epidemics and bloodshed. It was a revelation that previewed the first quarter of the twentieth century as clear as any.

The vision also foretold that out of Poland would come "the hope for all tormented mankind," a prophecy seen to herald the coming of Poland's future son, Pope John Paul II.[15]

Around the same time, in Australia, a mystic named Theresa Steindel reported that Mary told her a "great affliction" neared, one that eerily sounded like a reference to the coming nuclear age:

"There will be terrible disease. Radiation will come from above and cover buildings with flames." [16]

Finally, in 1860, somewhat of a climax to this second wave is noted.

The Secret of La Salette, given to Pope Pius IX on July 18, 1851, was finally revealed.[17] Handwritten text copies of the Secret had circulated in religious communities for years, but not publicly. Now, the bally-hooed Secret emerged, and it was—as rumored—terrifying.

Unimaginable and profound immorality was coming, with Hell itself to be opened, unleashing a great struggle between the Devil and the Church on earth. Wars, natural disasters, plagues and an apostasy of faith also lay ahead.

In unprecedented detail, the La Salette message warned that there approached an age of great trouble and suffering, ignited visibly and invisibly by despotic evil and atheism, culminating with Rome (the Catholic Church) deserting the true faith, subsequently inducing the rise of the Antichrist:

> God will strike in an unprecedented way. Woe to inhabitants of the Earth. God will exhaust His wrath upon them, and no one will be able to escape so many afflictions together... God will allow the old Serpent to cause divisions among those who reign in every society and in every family... Justice will be trampled underfoot and only homicides, hate, jealousy, lies and dissension will be seen without love for country or family... Physical and moral agonies will be suffered. God will abandon mankind to itself... Churches will be locked up or desecrated... A great number of priests and members of religious orders will break away from the true religion... There will be bloody wars and famines, plagues and infectious diseases... Lucifer, together with a large number of demons, will be unloosed from Hell...They will put an end to faith little by little...Nature is asking for vengeance... The Earth will be struck by calamities of all kinds... The seasons will be altered... A general war will follow which will be appalling...All civil governments will have one and the same plan, which will be to abolish and do away with every religious principle, to make way for materialism, atheism, occultism, and vice of all kinds... Rome will lose the faith and become the seat of the Antichrist.[18]

The time to make way for "materialism, atheism, occultism, and other vices" was, indeed, at hand—especially the time for Marxist atheism.

While various conceptions of atheism were no stranger to civilization, it was considered prior to the nineteenth century a somewhat rare and eccentric view. Although some theoretical systems are believed to go back as far as the 6th century B.C., the actual term "atheism" itself did not clearly emerge until the 16th century.

But as is well established, long before the rise of the great monotheistic religions of Judaism, Christianity and Islam—before the Greeks and Romans and their pantheon of gods—there is abundant evidence that most ancient peoples believed in the existence of deities. Atheism and atheists appear to have never been in vogue.

Now, as the Virgin of La Salette foretells, the golden age of "philosophical" and "political" atheism was descending upon the world, as the tendentious theories of Feuerbach, Marx, Engels, Freud, Darwin, Nietzsche and a trail of scholastic nihilists start to surface and bring inspiration to the budding revolutionaries of the coming age.

Consequently, this brings to fruition through the advent of atheistic Communism a new political–sociological phenomenon of atheism as never before witnessed in history. It is a worldwide emergence of systematic atheism—albeit the masses are forced to participate as it is deemed vital to their promised economic good fortune—that radically changes life on earth forever.

By the 1980s, more than a third of the world comes to live under some form of Marxist regime, as the prophecies of the 19th century—especially Mary's haunting words at La Salette—become indisputable reality.

Notre Dame historian Thomas Kselman, in his book *Miracles and Prophecies in Nineteenth Century France*, noted that the function of the many revelations during this period should not be viewed as God being punitive, but rather as corrective.

The prophecies, wrote Kselman, insisted the world's political order align itself with the supernatural order, and strive for the creation of a "Godly kingdom on earth."[19]

Blackbourn emphasized a similar view: he saw that the classic Marian vision of the 19th century contained an intense vision of a better world, of peace, hope, or plenty.[20]

This perspective is well taken, as more and more prophecies in the second half of the nineteenth century began to insist that a coming victory of good over evil through Mary would emerge after a "great trial." The plethora of Marian apparitions and cults in nineteenth century France was evidence that the "Age of Mary" had dawned, wrote Kselman.[21]

At a village named Lourdes in France, this understanding was especially conveyed. In 1858, 14-year-old Bernadette Soubirous reported eighteen apparitions the Church would validate. Aided by an outpouring of miraculous healings, a new, more elevated understanding of the Virgin Mary emerges at Lourdes that stretches into the twentieth century. Now, far from a role player, Mary is becoming better understood as Heaven and Earth's Queen, chosen by God to forward a divine rescue plan to all humanity.[22]

Shortly after Lourdes, two more apparitions would come to be approved by the Church, both pointing to a coming triumph of good over evil on earth through the powerful intercession of Mary.

At Pontmain, France, on the evening of January 17, 1871, four children described a beautiful lady in the sky—covered with stars on her dress—who foretold the village would be saved from the invading Prussian army.[23] Within eleven days, the Prussians withdrew from France, and an armistice was signed.

Six years later, on August 21, 1879, at Knock, Ireland, twenty-two people witnessed a vision of the Virgin Mary, Saint Joseph, and Saint John the Evangelist, hovering beside the village church. Upon studying, the Church approved the miracle.

And—to add to the silent, mysterious vision— theologians concluded that a book Saint John was seen holding at Knock was most likely *The Book of Revelation*, an esoteric sign, they offered, of Mary's coming defeat of the Red Dragon as disclosed in the book's twelfth chapter. [24]

The harsher prophecies intensified.

Something unfathomable and unparalleled was said to be drawing near.

Studying an 1883 apparition at Hartervald, Germany, Blackbourn noted that there was an apocalyptic tone here that exceeded "anything to be found in 1876–77." [25] Kselman observed that Europe was submerged in prophetic madness from 1870 to 1879. Quoting a priest from the period, he writes,

"Everywhere there is talk only of miracles and prophecies..." [26]

Then, on October 13, 1884—the future anniversary date of Fátima's great Miracle of the Sun—Pope Leo XIII is reported to have had, although there is no official Vatican documentation of the event, a profound mystical experience.

As with the Secret of La Salette, the Pope is said to have been led to understand in a vision that there neared the unleashing of all of Hell on earth, as a great spiritual war, both in this world and beyond, would soon explode. It would, for many, validate and substantiate the truth of the prophetic times at hand.

Joseph Trembly of the Edmund Burke Institute, and a columnist for the *Catholic News Agency* (CNA), describes one of many versions of Leo's reported experience:

> On October 13, 1884, Pope Leo XIII, just after celebrating Mass, turned pale and collapsed as though dead. Those standing nearby rushed to his side. They found him alive but the Pontiff looked frightened. He then recounted having a vision of Satan approaching the throne of God, boasting that he could destroy the Church. According to Pope Leo XIII, the Lord reminded him that His Church was imperishable. Satan then replied, "Grant me one century and more power over those who will serve me, and I will destroy it." Our Lord granted him 100 years. The Lord then revealed the events of the 20th century to Leo XIII. He saw wars, immorality, genocide, and apostasy on a large scale. Immediately following this disturbing vision, he sat down and wrote the *Prayer to St. Michael*. For decades it was prayed after Mass, until the 1960s. [27]

Taken as a whole, the mystical events of the nineteenth century reveal an undeniable conclusion. A cataclysmic rendezvous with tragedy, suffering, and death—an epoch time of great distress—was soon to come.

This period would be, according to some mystics, the beginning of "*The Great Tribulation*" foretold in the Gospels, whose roots go back to the Old Testament prophecies of Isaiah, Daniel, Ezekiel, and Zechariah. [28]

At Pontmain on that evening in 1871, the Church recognized a terrible war ended abruptly through Our Lady of Hope's intercession. Forty-three stars were counted around Mary that night at Pontmain, and forty-three years of peace followed—bringing France to 1914 and the First World War. [29]

World War I was called "The Great War" not simply because of the unprecedented scale of the conflict, but because of perceived moral implications.

From its onset, the Allies believed the struggle was against a great evil in Germany. Then, as the unprecedented horror of the massive conflagration unfolded, the war conjured up thoughts of the epic battle of Armageddon. Ironically, a battle at Megiddo in Israel—the site of the foretold, final clash in Saint John's *Revelation*—took place there in late September, 1918.

By the time Mary appeared at Fátima on May 13, 1917, the apocalypse of a world at war could not end soon enough. An estimated 16 million deaths, along with 29 million wounded, would mark the final casualty toll, justifiably earning the conflict another name — "The Great Slaughter."

But just as noteworthy was *how* so many died.

As the novelists and prophets foresaw, the advancements in technology proved to be inhumane. Countless dead were severed, decapitated, or shredded to pieces by the power of the new ordinances. Thousands were killed by lethal, torturous disabling agents such as chlorine and mustard gas. Millions were psychologically impaired by the emotional brutality of the war's unprecedented horror.

It was a war, perhaps even more than World War II, that still lives in us today through so many sayings and euphemisms that it created, such as, no man's land, the trenches, sniper, dogfight, tailspin, nosedive, booby trap, shell-shocked, and others, including—for those joking about their own looming demise— "pushing up daisies."

In retrospect, it's not hard to understand how the long withstanding words of Lieutenant-Colonel John McCrea's poem, *In Flanders Fields*, seemed to best define a struggle that not only killed the body but brought torment forever to the living soul.

Indeed, the Great War had been a dreadful misadventure, and by 1917, the abysmal reality of the conflict was well known by all the parties.

No one could dissent, the immense suffering needed to end.

In Rome, one man felt he would try again to do just that.

World War I was 29 months old when Giacomo Paolo Giovanni Battista della Chiesa—Pope Benedict XV—decided to reach out once more in a special way for divine assistance to end the nightmare.

After years of fruitless appeals, beginning with his November 1, 1914, encyclical *Ad beatissimi Apostolorum* (Appealing for Peace)—which called on the belligerents to end the conflict—Benedict determined it was time to turn again to the Virgin Mary.

The war, by then, tormented him.

"Who could realize," observed the Pope, "they are the children of the same Father in Heaven?"

On May 5, 1917, Pope Benedict commenced a novena and added a new invocation to the *Litany of Loreto*. The litany, a prayer to Mary seeking her maternal help, invokes the recitation of her many titles. First composed in 1587 for public use by Pope Sixtus V, it is credited by believers with often securing divine favors in desperate times of need. Now, Benedict would add a new Marian title to its conclusion:

"Queen of Peace, Pray for Us."

In a letter to the Vatican Secretary of State, Cardinal Pietro Gasparri, the Pontiff—who called World War I "the suicide of civilized Europe"—poured out his heart for Mary to come to mankind's aid and end the war:

> There is raised, therefore, toward Mary, Mother of Mercy and omnipotent grace, this loving and devoted appeal from every corner of the earth. From the noblest temples to the last chapel, from the royal palace and from the mansions of the rich...from the humblest dwelling, from every place in which the souls of the faithful find refuge from the plains and seas red with blood...bring to her anguished cries of mothers and spouses, the weeping innocent little children, the longing of every generous heart. That her most tender and benevolent solicitude be touched and that the peace we seek for this devastated world be granted.[30]

Eight days later, the Virgin Mary appeared to the three peasant children at Fátima, Portugal. Known since ancient times as "The Land of Holy Mary," [31] the Virgin assured them that World War I was going to end. As welcome a revelation as anyone could ever hope for; Pope Benedict's plea to Mary would come to be understood as having been well received.

The good news, however, would be quickly tempered.

The apparitional woman added a note of caution—and a dreadful sounding prophecy. A great scourge was coming out of Russia, and another war, if the world did not change its course and return to God.**

It would be a war, stressed the Virgin of Fátima, "worse" than the first one. [32]

**   Some Fatima writers have argued that although Nazi Germany is viewed as the primary catalyst for bringing about World War II, Mary's words in the second part of the Secret, as relayed by Sr. Lucia, are understood to imply that the Second World War wouldn't have materialized if not for "the errors of Russia, " i.e., the 1917 Bolshevik, Marxist revolution in Russia. Writes one author: "It cannot be said that Russia was the only country responsible for "Hitler's War." The (Fatima) Secret does not say that. However, without excluding the other nations responsible, it is true that it (the Secret) still places Bolshevik Russsia, and not Nazi Germany, on the first rank of nations responsible for the war... Bolshevik Russia was not only the great beneficiary of this atrocious war, but it was also the most effective active accomplice of the Nazis, and even instigated the war. This historical truth gives the Fatima Secret an unexpected profundity...." (*The Whole Truth About Fatima*, Volume II [English edition, 1989], pp. 689–690)

CHAPTER FIVE

THE MUSEUM OF THE WORLD

"If you belonged to the world, the world would love its own; but because you do not belong to the world, and I have chosen you out of the world, the world hates you."
—Jn 15:19

TEN-YEAR-OLD LÚCIA DOS SANTOS HAD PLENTY OF WORRIES. By September, the fifth month of the apparitions at Fátima, not a day went by that wasn't filled with difficulties and unease.

"Heroic suffering", wrote one writer in describing her plight.

Blamed by her mother for foolish, childish imaginings, and even trickery, Lúcia struggled to cope with the family crisis now at hand. [1] It was a predicament her mother blamed totally on her, even going so far as to tell a man that Lúcia was "nothing but a fake, who is leading half the world astray." [2]

Continually mocked and threatened as a criminal, much of the abuse centered on her refusal to reveal the Virgin's Secret. But, while her enemies were many, her friends were more, evidenced by the growing number of pilgrims that kept coming to Fátima.

In June, at the second apparition, about fifty people gathered to observe the heavenly encounter. In July, the number had swollen to around 4,000, and by September, 25,000.

This, unfortunately, caused the Santos family to be knee deep in problems. They could no longer grow food due to the damage on their farm from the crowds. [3] Their flock of sheep also needed to be sold since they were unable to graze, and the family desperately needed income. [4]

And then, as the time neared for the October apparition, a rumor spread that the authorities intended to explode a bomb close to the children—at the very moment of Mary's appearance.[5]

But even that was not Lúcia's greatest worry.

The Virgin promised a miracle in October. So now, tens of thousands would be converging on Fátima, with great expectations. So distressing was this situation that Lúcia's mother felt it could cost the girl—the youngest of her seven children—her life, telling her that they needed to go to confession "because if there is no miracle, we will be killed." [6]

It also didn't help the anguished Lúcia that the local parish priest—Father Manuel Marques Ferreira, a zealous, prudent pastor—felt it could all be "a deceit of the Devil." [7]

Fortunately, the great Miracle of the Sun at Fátima on October 13th (see Chapters 19 & 20) did not disappoint, though the anxiety felt by her family on that day was palpable until the very last minute. [8]

A year after the last apparition in October of 1917, both of Lúcia's cousins and fellow visionaries fell ill at the same time with the Spanish Flu.[9] The two, as the Virgin Mary foretold, eventually succumbed—Francisco on April 4, 1919,[10] and Jacinta on February 20, 1920.[11] Lúcia's father also passed away from a sudden attack of double pneumonia on July 31, 1919.[12]

Alone and deeply saddened by the loss of three loved ones in less than a year, Lúcia sought peace in Lisbon and then Santarém, if only for a while from her home in Aljustrel, the tiny hamlet in the rainy, rocky hill country called Aire where she lived a half a mile south of Fátima.

At the time, despite the great miracle that occurred during the last apparition, many of the residents in Aljustrel remained leery of her and continued their mistreatment. Consequently, instead of peace, she found nothing but torment wherever she went.

In the eyes of the world, Lúcia wrote in her *First Memoir*, she was either "a saint or a hypocrite ... a visionary or a sorceress." [13] Unlike her deceased cousins who were "taken to Heaven"—as Mary promised on the second apparition—she was forced to remain in what she called the "museum of the world." [14]

Encouraged by others, Lúcia entered a boarding school run by the Dorothean Sisters on June 17, 1921. It was a move that lifted her "oppressive sadness", one that allowed her to continue with fulfilling Mary's request that she learn to read. [15]

After submitting herself to the first canonical interrogation on the apparitions in 1924, Lúcia subsequently joined the Dorothean Community in October of 1925.[16] Tucked away now by Church authorities at convents in Pontevedra and Tui in Spain, Lúcia would begin a new round of struggles, this time with her confessors and superiors in her efforts to bring to light Mary's requests and promises.

Fulfilling her words at Fátima, the Virgin Mary—and Jesus—appeared to Lúcia in the second half of the 1920s, requesting that the Church begin to spread a special devotion amongst the faithful to offset the sin of the world—*The Communion of Reparation on the First Saturdays.*[17]

Then, on June 13, 1929, Mary appeared to her for a second request.

This time she returned, as she had told Lúcia she would in 1917, to ask for the Pope—in conjunction with all the bishops in the world—to consecrate Russia to her Immaculate Heart.

If both appeals were properly and timely enacted by the Church, Lúcia said the Virgin promised that the Second World War would not come to fruition, and Russia would not spread its deadly errors throughout the world.[18]

Nothing, however, transpired.

By the 1930s, Lúcia dos Santos—now Sister Lúcia of Mary [19]—felt guided by the past and troubled by the future. Still living in Tui, her chronic worries—some old, some new—were ever present.

Most of all, as time marched on and nothing happened, Lúcia couldn't help but ponder the contents of the foreboding Secret, carrying it within her, as she would write, "inviolate." [20]

As had been the case with Jacinta, the gnawing foreknowledge that the Second World War approached especially ate at her though she did not address this in her first two memoirs in 1935 and 1937 since it was not a request of her superiors.

Lúcia also knew that before World War II would commence, Mary had promised a great celestial sign that would cue the war's onset.

This divine harbinger, the visionary understood, unfortunately meant one other thing: a significant outpouring of misery and death would soon roll again over Europe and across the world, as with World War I.

By 1938, however, the die was cast.

All of Lúcia's pleas, on behalf of Mary's requests, fell upon deaf ears, and so came to fulfillment the Virgin's first prophecy concerning World War II:

"When you see a night illuminated by an *unknown light*, know that this is the Great Sign given to you by God that He is about to punish the world for its crimes, by means of war, famine, and persecutions of the Church and of the Holy Father." [21]

World War I was fought in the trenches with great misery. The trenches protected against poison gas, giving soldiers more time to put on gas masks. Dysentery, cholera, typhoid, and "trench foot" were common diseases. Gigantic rats were common too. At Fatima, Mary spoke of World War I four times.

Top Photo Credit: U.S Army Military

Left Photo Credit: Das Bundesarchiv-German Federal Archive

Pope Benedict XV appears to have heard of the apparitions at Fátima. On April 29, 1918, he replied to the Portuguese Bishops and alluded to Fátima, saying that their country, because of its devotion to the Immaculate Conception, "Truly merited some very extraordinary aid from the Mother of God."

Photo Credit: Vatican Archives

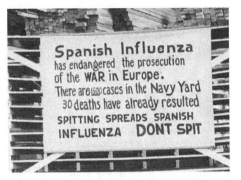

All districts of Portugal were affected by the Spanish Flu. The pandemic first hit the southeastern districts and the main cities, such as Lisbon. Excess mortality, however, was highest in the northeast, where Fátima was located. Jacinta and Francisco Marta, the two youngest Fátima visionaries, died during the pandemic.

Left Photo Credit: Library of Congress

Right Photo Credit: U.S. National Archives

In her *Second Memoir*, Lúcia describes how the Spanish Flu affected Francisco and Jacinta. Both children, Lúcia notes, offered up to God all their sufferings from the flu, including severe chest pains. Lúcia writes that during Francisco's illness, he suffered "heroic patience", never allowing the "slightest moan or the least complaint escape his lips."

Photo Credit: St. Andrews Productions

CHAPTER SIX

AN UNKNOWN LIGHT

"There will be powerful earthquakes, famines
and plagues from place to place;
and awesome sights and mighty signs will come from the sky."
—Lk 21:11

OR MORE THAN FIVE HOURS, ON THE EVENING OF JANUARY 25, 1938—the Feast of Saint Paul's conversion on the road to Damascus, where a "light from the sky suddenly flashed around him" (Acts 9:3)—a remarkable illumination of the evening skies occurred over all of Europe and much of Asia and North America.[1]

The almost magical-looking, red glow of the heavens extended from the grasslands of Siberia to the Pacific coast of California, visible as far south as San Diego. Scientists reported that it was an aurora borealis. [2]

But in Tui, Spain, Sister Lúcia asserted otherwise.

The extraordinary celestial display, the nun insisted, was the "Great Sign" promised by the Virgin Mary at Fátima in 1917 to mark the advent of World War II. [3]

To say the least, the sky that night was special, as the wondrous event— vast and far-reaching—was witnessed by millions.

Curiously, almost immediately, scientists seemed to understand that it was more than just a unique aurora borealis. Observed from one side of the world to the other, the sweeping panorama was so breath-taking in scope that its overwhelming presence seemed uncanny, even ominous, to many.[4]

Transcending descriptions of aurora borealis events dating back centuries, the solar spectacle quickly sent researchers scouring the records to find a comparable phenomenon.

The heavenly mural, they said, was distinguished by three characteristics:

- It was noted to have plunged well below the latitude of 50 degrees, something rarely seen before. [5]
- It did not limit itself to the North Pole region as was usual, but stretched over half the globe in its breadth. [6]
- It was predominantly blood red in color—with two giant three-mile-high "red spots" at its center [7]—creating an alluring, somewhat frightening appearance of the heavens being angrily ablaze.

It was this third extraordinary, uncharacteristic quality that caused experts to wonder how it could even be an aurora borealis. The vast, towering red sky, scientists wrote, seemed to totally contradict the customary multicolored, predominantly greenish manifestations of the past.[8]

On January 26, 1938, an article in *Le Petit Dauphinois* captured the uniqueness of the previous evening:

> The breadth of the spectacle observed was such that the blazing sky resembled the brilliance of dawn. The people were astonished at first, then admired this celestial manifestation, which is rarely seen in these latitudes; then as the phenomenon prolonged itself they grew disturbed. Some curious scenes—especially in our countryside—were witnessed as the horizon remained purple. A thousand controversies swirled around this strange vision, which was believed to be a vast fire in the mountains, or gigantic military maneuvers with searchlights; it was even believed—and this was the almost unanimous and not the least interesting observation—that the sun was going to rise... At eight o'clock, the animation which was continually increasing, changed on certain points into a real terror. [9]

Exceptional, rare, gigantic, and beautiful—these were all words used by writers to describe the scene. Panic, confusion, terror, and fright were the words they applied to its onlookers.

This paradoxical language exposes the quandary that viewers of the phenomenon found themselves in that night. Even heady scientific journals described the event in uncharacteristically mangled and unscientific prose.

The Bulletin of the Astronomical Society of France and Monthly Review of Astronomy, Meteorology and Globular Physics wrote:

> The sun had been invisible all day. But now, more than two hours after sunset, the clouds are dispelled. The northeast, northern, and northwest horizons light up as though dawn were going to break all over again. For practical purposes it is dawn…But a nocturnal dawn, with a strange light… Gradually, up above, the sky turns fiery red and an irregular red arch appears… In the streets there is panic, "Paris is on fire!" In several villages of the province, firemen are mobilized… An immense blood-red glow was extending over the sky.[10]

Quite a few astronomers, scientists, and meteorologists documented the heavenly pageant of January 25, 1938. Their words add further life to the event's preternatural identity.

Professor Pers of the Faculty of Sciences at the University of Grenoble wrote, "The sky was ablaze like an immense moving furnace, provoking a very strong blood-red glow." [11] Said an official from the Observatory of Pic du Midi de Bigorre in the French Pyrenees Mountains: "It constitutes a rare phenomenon for this latitude… The first impression was of a gigantic conflagration." [12] Stated a scientist in Italy, "Almost all the spectators believed that the sky was being lighted up by an enormous fire; and I myself believed the same thing at first. The apparition lasted almost two hours, from ten o'clock until midnight. Its color was intense red." [13]

In France, many everyday people also monitored the unforgettable evening, reporting some unique and curious observations. "Yesterday evening there was a great red cloud; it was like a sheet of blood," wrote a ten-year-old student at La Chapelle-Saint- Laud in Maine-et-Loire.[14] "The whole sky seemed to be on fire…it was announcing the end of the world! The cocks, undoubtedly fooled by this aurora, began crowing as if it were sunrise," said a man in Picardy. [15] "I observed that during the whole duration of the phenomenon that the dogs in the village and surrounding area began barking and howling," noted another man in the region of Vaucluse.[16]

Throughout the world, there came a number of odd stories related to the strange-looking sky.

According to the *Associated Press*, thousands of telephone calls to government authorities in France and Switzerland inquired whether the sky was ablaze "from fire or war," or if it was "the end of the world." [17] Off the coast of North Africa, an admiral suddenly ordered a destroyer cruising near the shore to turn off course towards the northwest, believing that a great fire lay ahead of the warship in the distance.[18] Nearby, in Tunisia, the red sky was so starkly visible over almost all of the country that the frightened natives were convinced it was "a warning of the divine wrath." [19]

Audio mysteries were also reported in association with the celestial event.

Carl Stromer, a Swedish astrophysicist, said a deputy of his stationed on Njuke Mountain heard "strange noises" when the solar event reached its height.[20] From the mountain top, the sky reportedly appeared to be an "ocean of flames" emitting "curious sounds from above that lasted about ten minutes, rose in volume, and then vanished." The sounds resembled, the assistant thought, "the crackle of burning grass." [21]

That evening, radio and telegram communications were affected in many countries, as was the earth's magnetic field. Even the Trans-Atlantic Cable was interrupted from 8:00 p.m. that night until 11:00 a.m. the following morning.[22]

It was for this reason that *The New York Times* and other U.S. newspapers reported the story a day later. The headline of the paper the following day, however, would perfectly capture the magnitude of the event:

"Aurora Borealis Startles Europe; People Flee in Fear, Call Firemen."

Under this read the subhead:

"Britons Thought Windsor Castle Ablaze—Scots See Ill Omen-Snow Clad Alps Glow—Short Wave Radio Halts."

Communication between Sister Lúcia and her immediate superiors suffered no delays. After witnessing the sky aglow from her convent bedroom window, the cloistered nun notified them that the Great Sign—promised by Mary at Fátima in 1917—had been served.

A Portuguese author, G. Freire, would discover that Sister Lúcia did not wait until she penned her next memoir to tell others, but did so immediately, alerting her bishop, Dom Jose Alves Correia da Silva, her provincial superior, Canon Galamba de Oliveira, and her confessors. [23]

It appears that some suspected rather early what the illumined sky was really all about. Father Robert O'Leary, a seminarian living in Vienna at the time, was gathered with his classmates in the seminary chapel for nightly prayers that fateful evening.

Suddenly, a great red glow poured through the chapel windows. It quickly became so bright that their superior, Father Aloysius von Gross-Kappenburg, cancelled the session.

The priest then immediately ordered everyone to put on some work clothes and go into the town, suspecting the city was on fire. "I went to my room on the fourth floor and opened the window," recalled O'Leary. "The sky was red with billowing clouds of flames. But to my amazement, there was no fire in the town. We all went outside, as the Superior had told us, to help the burning town. But no place could we find the fire. It was as though there were rolling flames over the world."

The next day, the seminarians wondered aloud what had caused the extraordinary "night of fire." Father O'Leary remembers that the professor of Dogmatic Philosophy simply refused to comment,

"I had the impression that he knew something," says O'Leary, "because he was nervous about it." The professor of Moral Theology also declined to answer. Finally, though, their professor of Scripture, Father Vollmacher, revealed what he thought may have occurred:

"That was Fátima, the warning...the warning of Fátima."

As with other news reports, the Nazi-influenced Austrian newspapers reported the following day that the mysterious red sky had been an aurora borealis, although stronger than usual. Father Vollmacher, however, immediately demurred, again telling the seminarians what he felt were the implications of it all:

"We are going to have a war..." [24]

Completing her *Third Memoir* on August 31, 1941, two years into World War II, the lone surviving visionary of Fátima recalled the fateful night of the Great Sign:

> Your excellency is not unaware that, a few years ago, God manifested that sign. which astronomers chose to call an aurora borealis. I don't know for certain, but I think if they investigated the matter, they would discover that, in the form in which it appeared, it could not possibly have been an aurora borealis. Be that as it may, God made use of this to make me understand that His justice was about to strike the guilty nations. [25]

Confronted by examiners over the decades, Lúcia never veered from her position. The illumined sky that evening was unmistakably the foretold Great Sign, designating the beginning of World War II.

Father Joaquin Alonso, appointed by the Bishop of Leiria to prepare the definitive study of Fátima, noted Lúcia's unswerving position in his final report of 1975:

"She has never thought that this was a merely natural phenomenon." [26]

Though confident it was the Great Sign, Lúcia offered no evidence—human or divine—to support her assertion. An early investigator, Father Hubert Jongen, questioned Lúcia in 1946 as to why she believed it was not an aurora borealis; she simply replied, "Because I don't think it was." [27]

History would prove Lúcia right—it *was* the Great Sign.

Because with the Sign…came the war.

World War II is considered to have formally commenced on September 1, 1939, with Germany's invasion of Poland, followed by France and Britain's declaration of war on Germany two days later.

Many, however, contend that the annexation of Austria on March 12, 1938, six weeks after the appearance of the Great Sign, is the true beginning point of the war. For the record, some place the start of the war even earlier, with Japan's invasion of Manchuria in 1937 or Russia in 1938.

But there is possibly an even greater alignment between the Great Sign and the onset of World War II—one more exact in relationship to the date of the solar event.

On January 30, 1939, Hitler revealed in a speech that he had decided on the invasion of Austria a year before in January 1938—the same month and year the Great Sign amazed and disturbed the Western world. [28]

Regardless of the war's precise onset date, once Lúcia knew the Great Sign had been given, she immediately pressed forward with her attempts to get the Church to respond to the Virgin's two desires. [29]

Writing in a letter on March 19, 1939, to Father Jose Aparicio, a former spiritual director, she asserted that "world peace or world war depends" now on the fulfillment of the Virgin Mary's requests. [30]

In a second letter, dated June 20, 1939, her language borders on desperate. Seen in the context of Germany's approaching invasion of Poland in September, her words reveal an awareness that any opportunity to prevent the war had all but slipped away:

"Our Lady promised to delay the scourge of war if this devotion was propagated and practiced. We see her avert the chastisement to the extent that efforts are made to propagate it. But I am afraid that we cannot do more than we are doing and God in His anger will lift the arms of His mercy and let the world be ravaged by this chastisement. It will be a chastisement such as never before, horrible, horrible." [31]

Two months later, on August 10, 1939—now just weeks before the official start of World War II—Father Aparicio noted in his discernment that Sister Lúcia's words indicated to him that she knows exactly what is coming:

"She speaks categorically, like someone who has seen future events. I even think that Our Lady has revealed them to her." [32]

Pope Pius XI did not exactly know the future.

But by the late 1930s, he had a good sense of what was coming—and he certainly knew of Fátima.

Although Lúcia's *First Memoir* was not written until December, 1935, Pius XI had already been informed of Lúcia's efforts in 1930, and again in 1937. [33]

A year later, by a collective petition of the Portuguese bishops in June of 1938, the Pope was once more made aware of the urgency of Fátima's requests.[34] Lúcia was even comforted in this knowledge by her confessor, Father Bernardo Goncalves.

"I remember well that my confessor," wrote Lucia, "told me that the Holy Father (Pius XI) had heard the message graciously and had promised to consider it." [35]

The Pope decided, however, to take no action, even at the hour, wrote one author, "of imminent peril." [36]

Pondered for decades by Fátima researchers, the Great Sign, first and foremost, fulfilled in January of 1938 what Mary said on July 13, 1917, that it would. It announced in a timely fashion that God was about to punish the world for its crimes. War, famine, and persecution of the Church and the Holy Father soon followed, as foretold.

When examined more closely, however, the Great Sign was found to resonate a deeper message, one rich in symbolic language that some believe make it even more significant than the Miracle of the Sun at Fátima in 1917. This is because its symbolism seemed to be associated not only with the past, but the future.

According to some Fátima writers, the cherry-painted sky on the ominous night of the Great Sign signified that God—in His wisdom—was speaking to His people with just one word: red.

It can be inferred, they postulate, that the vivid, red torrents that flowed across the sky meant that rivers of blood were about to flow with World War II.[37] That blood—as demonstrated in the breadth of the phenomenon—would flow from one end of the earth to the other.[38] And, the two giant red spots that were seen in the center of the phenomenon represented, like their bright red flags, the two evils of German Nazism and Soviet Communism, primary participants of the coming bloody carnage.

One other symbolism in the Great Sign has been noted, though meant for what was to come after the war. The sprawling red glow that hung so low over much of the world that evening was seen to be prefiguring the universal conflagration of Communism that descended after World War II. [39]

Indeed, like a monstrous tsunami, the coming red wave of atheistic totalitarianism would submerge all nations and every hemisphere, transcending oceans and borders, thus symbolically turning Earth as red as Mars.

Before she died in 1920, little Jacinta Marta seemed to understand exactly what was approaching with World War II. She spoke of how the war would be "worse" than the last one—how so many would suffer, how unrepentant sinners would be lost.

Like Lúcia, who lived for decades with angst over all of the looming consequences contained in the Secret, Jacinta felt haunted in her waning months by how dreadful the times would be. [40]

"Jacinta, what are you thinking about?" Lúcia inquired one day of the very sick little girl. "About the war that is coming," she replied, "so many people are going to die and almost all of them are going to go to Hell. Many homes will be destroyed, and many priests will be killed.

" Look, I am going to Heaven, and as for you, when you see the light which the Lady told us would come one night before the war, you run up there too." [41]

CHAPTER SEVEN

A GRUESOME WAR

*"You will hear of wars and reports of wars; see
that you are not alarmed, for these things must
happen, but it will not yet be the end."*

—Mt 24:6

DESPITE THE LEAGUE OF NATIONS.
Despite the vivid memories of the filthy trenches, the muddy
bomb craters, and the barbed wire of no-man's land.

Despite Łódź, Mons, Ypres, the Somme, Tannenberg, Gallipoli,
Passchendaele, the Armenian Genocide, and the mass slaughter of a
generation, seismic rumblings within the nations were being felt across
Europe by the time the Treaty of Versailles was signed on June 28, 1919—
five years to the day of the assassination of Archduke Franz Ferdinand.

The Spartacist Uprising in Germany, hot on the heels of the
Bolshevik Revolution in Russia, meant one thing to those with a finger
on Europe's pulse—the "Guns of August" could roar again. Less than
a year removed from the Armistice, the smell of another war lingered
heavily in the air.

The newspapers got wind of it early.

Long before Germany, Japan, and Italy set out on their course to
subdue the planet, long before words like "blitzkrieg" and "kamikaze"
defined World War II—the so-called "Good War"—the press began to
speculate that World War I—The "War to end all Wars"—would see
another chapter.

In February, 1919, a British daily newspaper, *The Manchester
Guardian*, published an article that even went as far as to use the term

"World War II," imagining hypothetically the coming of the Second World War much the way people today speak of World War III. [1]

The article would have sounded like old news to the visionaries at Fátima.

The three little prophets had been served notice by the Virgin Mary on July 13, 1917, that a second world war— "worse" than the first— would inch its way above the horizon, soon to appear if humanity did not alter its path.

Needless to say, no course correction was coming.

World War II—the largest single event in human history—arrived on the divine schedule. And as foretold, it would be worse—incomprehensibly worse.

World War II, distinctly characterized, was gruesome—too gruesome to recall, too gruesome to recount. Like all wars, death would be its principle legacy, as the number of fallen best bemoans the tragedy of war.

But gruesome would be this war's identity.

More than The Great War, World War II's buried shame, its lurid dishonor, and its unparalled violence would never out run the light of day—not then, and not now.

After suffering 92,000 casualties and killing more than 200,000 Chinese in the battle for Shanghai, the Japanese seized the capital city of Nanking. There, they methodically slaughtered and defiled 300,000 citizens.

Taking revenge for Shanghai, in full defiance of the Geneva Conventions, the Japanese stabbed, set afire, lynched by the tongues, machine gunned, beheaded, and buried citizens alive—holding sadistic killing contests to determine who could decapitate the most people. [2]

More than 80,000 women were systematically raped at Nanking, then often bayonetted to death.[3] The Japanese forced fathers to rape their daughters, brothers their sisters, and sons their mothers.[4] Those females who survived were shipped off to become "comfort women" for the Japanese soldiers who would occupy China through 1945.

Altogether, the Japanese methodically defiled and murdered half of Nanking's six hundred thousand citizens.[5]

News of the atrocities was celebrated in Japan. Criminal soldiers of the Imperial Japanese Army were even praised as glorified heroes in the newspapers for their wicked acts.[6]

By the war's end, it is estimated that the Japanese had murdered 10 to 15 million Chinese.

From the Beer Hall Putsch of 1923 to the Battle of the Bulge in 1945, Hitler showed that he had no appetite for bluff and preached a war without rules.

And so it came to be.

From Russia to France, from Poland to Italy, everywhere the Swastika marched, indiscriminate killing of anyone and everyone became a way to divine and realize the Fuhrer's will.[7] Killing became—for many of the soldiers of the Third Reich—mundane. It occurred not only in the killing fields of war, where time-honored rules of war are often abandoned, where the stress of the moment causes one to lose control. No, it was more, much more.

It was killing in the streets and in the doorways, in the alleyways and the sideways. It was killing for revenge. It was killing for sport. It was killing as if killing were not killing. As one German soldier described it, "I shot everything."

Throughout Europe and across Asia, in Northern Africa and the Middle East, German soldiers—who would have never hurt an animal before the war or laid a hand to their child—became like barbarians. They seemed to possess no human decency. Survivors remember the Nazi's degrading and murdering people in every form and manner conceivable.

To kill one, to kill a few, to kill thirty, to kill fifty innocent civilians became commonplace. Round them up and kill them. Plain, everyday, ordinary men now did such with ease, whispering to their conscience that it did not matter. Telling themselves no one will ever know. Happy, willing executioners in the Fuhrer's name—in oath to Adolph Hitler—suppressed all responsibility, all concern, and any shame.

And there came other atrocities.

Forced prostitution, the razing of towns and villages, human shields and human experimentation, biological warfare, group rape, countless open air massacres, and of course, the Holocaust—the systematic genocide of millions—all to satisfy a demonic obsession to inflict pain and shed blood.

The Holocaust, in fact, overshadows Germany's greater plan for even more killing and for celebrating it.[8] Indeed, Hitler—nominated for the Nobel Peace Prize in 1939—wanted not only to completely eradicate the Jews, but reportedly planned to create the "Museum of the Extinct Races" to forever show the world the degeneracy of Jewish life—and to honor himself for ridding it. [9]

Hitler also planned to erase Poland and the Soviet Union as states, to exterminate their ruling classes, and to kill tens of millions of Slavs— Russians, Poles, Belarussians, Ukrainians, and others.[10]

According to newly discovered documents, if the German invasion of the U.S.S.R. had gone as planned, 30 million civilians would have been starved to death that first winter,[11] and tens of millions more would have been killed, expelled, assimilated, and enslaved.[12]

This was the Nazis' final plan in the East.[13]

Unpredictable, unprecedented, and unethical.

All came to define the aerial bombing that transpired throughout World War II.

But, in the history of warfare, none of these terms capture the complete picture of what the massive bombing brought to bear on its victims and their surroundings.

Seen objectively and understood subjectively, aerial warfare dictated and defined the conflict. It decided the outcome—one of obliteration and desolation never before seen on earth.

As the son of General Dwight D. Eisenhower, Second Lieutenant John Eisenhower told his father as they surveyed the Normandy beaches following the D-Day invasion of France on June 6, 1944, "You'd never get away with this if you didn't have air supremacy." To which General Eisenhower replied, "Without air supremacy, I wouldn't be here." [14] *

---

*   Dwight Eisenhower saw a spiritual war unfolding in the world. Jack M. Holl, in his book, *The Religious Journey of Dwight D. Eisenhower* (Eerdmans Publishing, Grand Rapids, MI, 2021), writes, "Eisenhower continued to see the world in terms of a dialectical struggle between divine and demonic forces throughout his life…"

Indeed, the bombings of cities, harbors, industries, railways—every conceivable target—created unimaginable terror and total ruination, and left vast, gory scenes of maimed and dead.

Strategic bombing in World War II killed as many as 60,000 civilians in Britain, 67,000 in France, 100,000 in Italy, 351,000 in China, 500,000 in the U.S.S.R., and 653,000 in Germany. Tens of thousands more disappeared across the globe from an angry sky that once showered only soft drops of rain and pearly white flakes of snow.

As so shockingly preserved on film, the indiscriminate bombing virtually erased much of the urban landscape in Germany. It reduced beautiful structures of antiquity to massive piles of rubble.

The tragic destruction of so many historic cities seemed almost sacrilegious in a way, yet ironically fitting with the accompanying desecration of so much human life; in Germany, 33 percent of Berlin suffered irreparable destruction, 61 percent of Cologne, 64 percent of Düsseldorf, 75 percent of Hamburg, 83 percent of Bochum.

Europe, one writer thought, looked to be a barren moonscape.

And then there was Dresden.

In just three days, from February 13 through 15 of 1945, 772 heavy bombers of the British Royal Air Force and 527 bombers of the United States Army Air Force dropped over 3,900 tons of bombs and high incendiary explosives on Dresden.[15]

This ignited a firestorm that torched most of the city.

Afterwards, seen from the air, Dresden looked like a large, disarticulated skeleton—stripped of its skin, virtually eviscerated.

On the ground in Dresden, the survivors described the horror of the bombing as being under attack by both man and nature. People were not only burnt and injured, but melted. Some were so disfigured that no words adequately described what they had morphed into.

In the streets, uncontrollable panic and chaos reigned as thousands of blazing buildings collapsed, with burning shards slowly drizzling on the scurrying masses below. Later, cremated people, adults shrunk to the size of children, and scattered pieces of arms and legs were discovered within the humbled structures.

When the bombing finally ceased, the firestorm adopted a life of its own. Everywhere one looked, people could be seen running aimlessly while ablaze. Over time, as the conflagration swelled, the wind whipped up such that many were literally blown back into the fires they had just emerged from—seemingly vacuumed up into the fiery hell on earth.

After the attack, scorched couches on the streets were seen to have dead civilians sitting on them, appearing to be still alive [16]—as if the ordeal had been a dramatic play, now closing with a more serene and calming final act.

Dresden, ghoulish in its hellish unfoldment, lifted the savagery of aerial bombardment to the next level. Out of 28,410 houses in the inner city, 24,866 were gone. As many as 100,000 died.[17]

Ironically, the annihilation of Dresden—a mostly civilian city with no extraordinary military significance—was not necessarily ordered to defeat Germany and the Nazi regime, or to strategically expedite the war in a major way.

Rather, the savage bombing by the Allies was primarily undertaken to warn the Russians of what a superior force could do to them if they failed to honor the agreements made at the conferences.[18]

It would be Hiroshima and Nagasaki, though, that would unveil the ultimate end game in aerial warfare.

And, the epitome of the gruesomeness of World War II.

In Japan, two atomic drops previewed the consummate future of owning the airspace above your enemy. Complete annihilation—the fate that Mary said at Fátima awaited various nations—would now be the status quo.

So complete was the devastation of the two cities that the visible, unsettling remains of war were left barely visible at all. After 8:15 a.m. in Hiroshima on August 6, 1945, and 11:01 a.m. in Nagasaki, three days later, what remained were only memories.

For ethicists, the atomic bomb previewed new parameters of the inhumanity of humanity. Complete cessation of mankind and the incineration of the planet, perhaps the end of the world, were no longer inconceivable. This challenged the cognitive development of morality theory that separates us from other animals.

For the spiritually minded, the mystery and eeriness of Saint John's *Apocalypse* was no longer restricted to the imaginations of novelists and the visions of Old Testament prophets. In just three days, Hiroshima and Nagasaki brought the world face-to-face with the Apostle's frightening account of the "end times."

The most famous book of prophecy, written so far in the past and meant for some day in the future, was now alive in the present—where it remains forever frozen in time. Indeed, depending on an array of variables, any day could now be the Earth's last day.

Marthe Robin, a 1940s French mystic and stigmatist, noted not long after the war:

"This atom bomb—when one thinks that small nations will also have it—and only two fools will be needed to ravage everything." [19]

Yes, World War II *was* significantly worse than World War I, as Mary foretold at Fátima. And while the number of casualties can never reveal the depth of this tragedy, they cannot be ignored. Instead, they must be grasped and pondered, as they validate the gruesomeness of it all.

And the numbers, more than anything, reveal what the Virgin Mary's use of the word "worse" fully meant.

World War II was fought by more soldiers over more of the planet, with the greatest destruction of human life and property, than any previous war.

Seventy million soldiers participated; 16 million were killed, nearly one out of every four. Twenty-five million were wounded in battle. There came over 50 million civilian deaths to go with the military losses. This figure rises to over 80 million when war-related disease and famine are included.

In truth, the exact total of killed, wounded, and missing—soldiers and civilians—will never be known, can't be known. People vanished, families were scattered. Cities, towns, and villages were leveled or burned to the ground with their inhabitants in them. Nothing, for many, can prove they existed.

In all, over ten million "disappeared."

But what *is* known of the number who died is incomprehensible.

The fatality figures per nation crystalize this reality.

China suffered 4 million military and 20 million civilian deaths. One organization—*Research Starters of the National World War II Museum*—reports that as many as 50 million Chinese may have perished.

The Soviet Union lost 8 to 10 million soldiers, and 24 million civilians. Japan suffered over 2.1 million military and 2.6 million civilian deaths. Germany lost 5.5 million soldiers and 6.6 million civilians. France lost 217,000 soldiers and 567,000 civilians. The United Kingdom lost 383,000 soldiers and 451,000 civilians. And the United States saw 407,300 military losses along with 12,100 civilian deaths.

One would expect the major combatants to suffer great losses. But across the map, the figures remain numbing.

Austria saw 268,000 military and 384,700 civilian deaths. Czechoslovakia suffered 25,000 military and 345,000 civilian losses. Finland lost 95,000 soldiers and 97,000 civilians. And the former Yugoslavia had 446,000 military losses, and over one million civilian deaths.

In Europe alone, forty million men, women, and children died. The continent was, for the most part, turned into a huge cemetery, soaked in blood.

Moreover, the statistics prove the whole world truly was at war.

India saw 87,000 soldiers perish along with 1.5 million civilians. The Philippines lost 57,000 soldiers and over 500,000 civilians. And the Dutch East Indies, now Indonesia, experienced 3 to 4 million deaths, mostly civilian.

Staggering casualty figures for the great battles of the war round out the morbid picture.

At Guadalcanal, there were 38, 000 casualties, at Iwo Jima 48, 000, and at Okinawa 150,000. The Battle of the Bulge saw 181,000 casualties in six weeks.

But it was in Russia that the figures spiraled off the chart. At the siege of Leningrad, there were a total of 1.5 million military and civilian losses. At Stalingrad, an unfathomable 1,971,000 total casualties are recorded.

The war's most ignoble statistics? From the two atomic bombs, 146,000 died at Hiroshima, and 80,000 at Nagasaki.

Five million died in prisoner-of-war camps over the course of the war.

And, using the broadest definition of the infamous World War II atrocity, 15-20 million people were lost in the Holocaust—the Final

Solution—the Nazi-sponsored, systematic annihilation of the Jews and many other groups designated as undesirable. [20]

According to Sister Lúcia, the motivation behind this incomprehensible genocide was the primary reason Mary specifically stated in the Secret of Fátima that World War II was to be "worse" than its predecessor. Wrote Lúcia in 1955 concerning this matter at the request of the Father General of the Carmelite Order:

"In what sense would it (World War II) be worse? In the sense that it would be an atheistic war that attempted to exterminate Judaism, which gave the world Jesus Christ, Our Lady, the Apostles—who transmitted the Word of God—and the gift of faith, hope and charity. The Jews are God's elect people, whom He chose from the beginning: 'Salvation is from the Jews.'" [21]

By November 1942, Germany and Italy controlled Europe and much of North Africa, and *Operation Barbarossa* was underway in Russia. Not content, the Middle East and beyond were in the Third Reich's sights.

Japan, after 200 years of strict seclusion, was more than just awakened—it was aggressively on the move. Casting completely aside ancient isolation policies, Japan showed after Pearl Harbor that it was on a reckless quest for power and dominion—every bit as ambitious as its Axis partners. Leapfrogging into China and then south, the Empire of the Rising Sun soon held territory in twelve nations, with no plans to call it quits.

In the spirit of Alexander and Caesar, Attila and Napoleon, the twentieth century was getting a taste of the latest round of megalomaniacs out to conquer the world. This time, though, the tyrants dreamed bigger and operated smarter, conquering by not just the point of a gun but by the rhetoric of their ideas—ideas that revealed a desire to not only control the flesh, but the mind and soul. Needless to say, they were philosophies not compatible with religion, especially Christianity.

Foretelling more than just war, the Virgin Mary predicted at Fátima that with World War II there would come religious persecution. And so it was, as the Axis powers sought to erase the need for any "power" from above.

In Japan, the government forced every subject to practice State Shinto and recognize the Emperor as divine. Those who opposed the imperial cult, including the Oomoto and Soka Gakkai rites of Shinto, were persecuted, as, of course, were Christians.

Christianity and Japan go back a long way, and much of it is not very pleasant.

Long before the twentieth century, the government banned the religion and drove it underground, brutally oppressing its practitioners for centuries. World War II added to this legacy, although the government did not outlaw the Catholic Church or totally prohibit worshiping in Japan.

But as the Japanese juggernaut rolled across the Pacific, Christians—especially Catholics—became swept up in their maniacal methods. As they did in Nanking, the Japanese troops raped and killed nuns in the Philippines, most notably at the Manilla Massacre. There, they also murdered priests and many Catholic parishioners at a church called Our Lady of Remedies.

In Guam, churches were converted to prisons and the religious beheaded. In China, the Japanese followed a killing policy against religious communities (especially Hui Muslims) who saw 220 mosques razed and countless people slain, with many girls turned into sex slaves. Hui cemeteries were destroyed and survivors went jobless and homeless by decree.

Throughout South East Asia, it was much of the same: The Japanese looted and burned churches, temples, and shrines wherever they went.

In Europe, Adolf Hitler launched an all-out assault on the Catholic Church.

Far from divine and excommunicated by the Church in 1937, Hitler was an adroit politician, using religion in his speeches to aid him in his rise to power. Once in office, however, he targeted religion, especially Catholics, who made up a third of the German population.

First liquidating the *Catholic Centre Party*—influential during the Kaiserreich and the Weimar Republics—he then set about to shut down religious organizations, businesses, and newspapers.

After that, the gloves came off.

Angered by the Pope, the Fuhrer moved decisively to break the Church's back. In Germany, he interned thousands of priests, especially at the Dachau Concentration Camp, a death bin known as the "priests camp." Over the course of the war, 1,034 priests would succumb at Dachau.

Across Europe, it was no different.

The Nazis persecuted Jews, Catholics, and other religious everywhere. In Poland, as in Germany, an estimated 3,000 Catholic priests were executed. Eighteen hundred died in concentration camps.

Years before—on July 20, 1933—the Vatican signed an agreement with Germany, the *Reichskonkordat*. Intended to prevent Nazi persecution of Catholic institutions, it unfortunately was only as good as the paper it was written on.

Once perfectly clear as to Hitler's true intentions, Pope Pius XI, who succeeded Benedict XV on February 6, 1922, confronted the dictator in his 1937 encyclical, *Mit brennender Sorge*. Denouncing the regime for its racial and nationalistic idolatry—the basis of Nazi ideology—Pius accused the Nazis of "sowing fundamental hostility to Christ and His Church." And, sensing a greater evil was brewing, the Pope decried the "threatening storm clouds of religious extermination" gathering over Germany.

Aware of the two-headed monster vying to devour Europe, a following encyclical, *Divini Redemptoris*, took aim at the evil of Communism, too, warning it was "intrinsically perverse." Personally, Pius XI viewed both ideologies as Satanic.

Then, after the 1938 Kristallnacht attack on the Jews, Pius joined Western leaders in their protest of the Nazis' antisemitism. This angered Hitler more, further deteriorating the Church's relationship with the Third Reich.

History reflects well on Pius XI's reign. He was a holy man who did much good in the service of the Church. His writings confronted the evils of the day, and he canonized many great Catholic men and women—Theresa of Lisieux, Bernadette of Lourdes, Thomas More, John Fisher, Robert Bellarmine, John Bosco.

But if there was any hope in preventing World War II, any chance of impeding Communism in its infancy by heeding Fátima's requests, it would have had to have occurred during the reign of Pius XI.

While Popes Pius XII and John Paul II are both known as "Fátima" Popes, it was only Pope Pius XI that was cited by name in the Secret of Fatima by the Virgin Mary on July 13, 1917. [22]

Unfortunately, the good Pope did not take action, although it is said his advisors did not serve him well on the matter of Fátima and, as time has gone on, it is clear that a deeper look at what he truly understood about Fátima needs to be undertaken.

Pius XI died on February 10, 1939, six months before Adolf Hitler began his "Lebensraum" into Poland, the invasion to secure living space for the German people,[23] and not long after Joseph Stalin ended his "Great Terror" in Russia—the fait accompli purge of millions of Russian people. [24]

His successor, Pope Pius XII, rebooted the Church's efforts to counter the rising threat in Germany. A virulent pre-war critic of Nazism, Pius XII issued on October 20, 1939, his first encyclical—*Summi Pontificatus*—denouncing the invasion of Poland.

Although enraged, he was not surprised by Hitler. As apostolic nuncio to Germany from 1917 to 1930, the former Cardinal Eugenio Pacelli dispatched a confidential memo to American officials a year before ascending to the Chair of Peter. Any compromise with the Nazis, Pacelli made clear, should be "out of the question." To the American consul general, a year later, Pacelli labeled Hitler "a fundamentally wicked person" and an "untrustworthy scoundrel."

Upon his election as Pope on March 2, 1939, the Nazis immediately accused him of being anti-German. The Soviets pitched in, expressing their displeasure in a mutual condemnation that, ironically, would someday help show that Pius XII was not soft on the two atheistic tyrannies that threatened to erase all Christianity.

And this—the obliteration of Christianity—was exactly what *was* at stake.

With Britain standing virtually alone in the early days of the conflict, newly appointed British Prime Minister Winston Churchill identified what the free world was fighting for:

"Upon this battle depends the survival of Christian civilization…if we fail, then the whole world…will sink into the abyss of a new Dark Ages." [25]

Sister Lúcia, like Churchill, did not hesitate to communicate her thoughts as to how to preserve Christian civilization.

On February 6, 1939, just four days before the death of Pius XI, Lúcia informed her bishop that "the war predicted by Our Lady is imminent," petitioning again through her superiors that the Vatican perform the consecration of Russia and institute the Communion of Reparation devotion. [26]

Dispatching a letter from Tui to Pius XII on December 2, 1940, the diminutive nun requested that the Holy Father, in union with the bishops, consecrate the world—with "a special mention of Russia"—to the Immaculate Heart of Mary. [27] Assuring the Pope that the Lord promised to shorten the days of tribulation, Lúcia's plea seemed to argue that it was better late than never. [28] But the hierarchy of the Church remained firm, refusing her appeal. [29]

Finally, on October 31, 1942, the Silver Jubilee of the apparitions at Fátima (1917-1942)—convinced through the efforts of Sister Lúcia and the bishops of Portugal, and by the miserable plight of the war—Pius XII performed the consecration. [30]

Six weeks later, he repeated it at St. Peter's Basilica in Rome before 40,000 onlookers. [31] But though done, it was not in the manner Mary requested. [32]

Pius XII's effort would shorten the war, Lúcia revealed she was told, but would not resolve the full problem at hand—the ominous march of the first of the "errors of Russia"—Communism. [33]

On August 15, 1945, the Feast of the Assumption of Mary—the same day that St. Francis Xavier came to Japan in 1549—the surrender of Imperial Japan was announced. Germany, Japan, and Italy stood defeated, and World War II was relegated to the past.

Another prophecy of the Virgin of Fátima had come and gone.

But the Secret of Fátima still contained unfulfilled portions, prophecies believed to be no less the magnitude than the two world wars. And, as occurred at the end of World War I, the new peace appeared fragile and incomplete, destined to be short lived.

One didn't need to know of Fátima to see what was coming.

The Soviet Union was fomenting trouble everywhere, transcending borders and oceans, and working to poison every nation around the globe with its toxic, Marxist ideology. The Red Revolution, the Red Terror, the Red Menace—the Red Dragon (Rv 12:3)—surged on. **

Two years later, another war was declared—a Cold War.[34]

In a speech describing relations between the Soviet Union and the United States, given before the South Carolina House of Representatives on April 16, 1947, a longtime advisor to several Presidents defined the moment:

"Let us not be deceived," declared Bernard Baruch, "we are today in the midst of a Cold War. Our enemies are to be found abroad and at home. Let us never forget this: our unrest is the heart of their success. The peace of the world is the hope and the goal of our political system. It is the despair and defeat of those who stand against us." [35]

An "era of peace" was coming, the Virgin Mary promised in the second part of the Secret of Fátima of July 13, 1917.

But not quite yet, it appeared safe to say in 1947.

Nor did it look promising in 1949, when China, the most populated nation in the world, turned Communist.

Nor did it in the early 1950s after a major conflict exploded in Korea.

But if not an era of peace now, when?

Evil, defeated on such a grand scale in World War II, seemed on the march again, more threatening than ever in the form of godless

---

** Fr. Stefano Gobbi, an Italian priest, locutionist, and founder of the Marian Movement of Priests, reported the Virgin Mary told him the "Red Dragon" (Rv 12:3) was " atheistic Communism" and "Marxist atheism." and that the "Beast" (Rv 13:1-4) was FreeMasonry. (See Messages 267, 404 and 405 in the book, *To the Priests, Our Lady's Beloved Sons*). To date, no official investigation has been performed by the Congregation for the Doctrine of the Faith (CDF) to discern the supernatural character of Gobbi's locutions. A letter from a member of the CDF asked Gobbi to state explicitly messages are his own meditations, but this was later clarified by the CDF as not an official act on their part.

Communism. And, by August 1949, yoked with nuclear weapons, how could it ever be defeated?

How could Mary's era of peace ever dawn in a world so dark, so sinful and so dangerous?

Perhaps only Sister Lúcia knew.

Ordered by Bishop da Silva to write the third part of the Secret of Fátima on January 3, 1944, Lúcia jotted down the mysterious revelation and folded the piece of paper.[36] She then placed it in an envelope, waxed it shut, wrote the year "1960" on it, and hand delivered it to the Titular Bishop of Gurza, Dom Manuel Ferreira, who delivered it to Bishop da Silva.

Lúcia reportedly advised that he (Silva or a successor), the Archbishop of Lisbon, and the Holy Father in Rome could read it before—or some say by the latest—1960.[37]

Only after then was it to be revealed to the public.

Eventually, on April 16, 1957,[38] thirteen years later, the third part of the Secret of Fátima would find its way to The Vatican Secret Archive [39] in Rome, and finally into a small wooden safe in the papal apartments of Pope Pius XII, which bore the inscription, *Secretum Sancti Offici* (Secret of the Holy Office).[40]

There, Lúcia's letter would sit for years, its dreaded words remaining undisclosed even to Bishop da Silva and Pius XII, both of whom refused to read it—although the bishop permitted a photograph of him and the legendary envelope, which appeared in *Life Magazine* on January 3, 1949.[41]

In 1958, all the world would again come to know its whereabouts, as a photograph of Pius XII's safe—citing its excitatory contents—appeared in the French weekly, *Paris Match*, on October 18.[42]

And so, all eyes looked towards 1960 and the moment the Church would disclose the Secret's contents, feared by most to hold little news about peace, but instead news foretelling of a coming, even worse nightmare than the two world wars.

News, perhaps, of an event involving "incalculable self-destruction" that a future Pope would beseech God to keep away.[43]

News, perhaps, that would require Mary return—this time to a little mountainous plateau in the Alps of Herzegovina—where a rustic hamlet named Medjugorje had unknowingly been preparing for her arrival years before the outbreak of World War II.

The German army totaled 13.6 million soldiers in World War II. In 1935, the army reached its projected goal of 36 divisions, just 17 months after Hitler announced German rearmament. The Italian army saw nearly 4 million serve in World War II. Many Italian POWS were later permitted to join the Allies.

Photo Credit: Das Bundesarchiv-German Federal Archive

Mussolini and Hitler

**Photo Credit:
Ladislav Lupa**

Pope Pius XI

Photo Credit: Vatican Archives

Pope Pius XI repudiated "Nazi Racial Theory" as a so called "myth of race and blood." He urged Mussolini to ask Hitler to restrain his anti-Semitic actions in Germany. According to recently released documents that reveal Pope Pius XII's efforts behind the scene, the much maligned pope saved nearly two million Jews.

**Photo Credit:
Vatican Archives**

Pope Pius XII

CHAPTER EIGHT

A DIVINE COLLISION

*"First, I give thanks to my God through Jesus Christ for all of
you, because your faith is heralded throughout the world."*
—Rom 1:8

The Feast of Saint John the Baptist is a holy day of obligation in this part of Christendom.

Besides the spiritual graces, the celebration traditionally showers some corporal benefits on the Catholic inhabitants of Medjugorje; after morning Mass, work and school are finished for the day for many.

In a region once regarded as the poorest and most undeveloped in the former Yugoslavia—where people had to grow their own food, raise farm animals, and preserve water—where there was no plumbing and electricity until 1962—some may argue against the wisdom of such tradition.

But Catholic traditions supersede economic concerns here.

The people place God above mammon.

And not just mammon.

By the looks of the massive cross they constructed on the local mountain in 1933, God stands above everything the eye can see. [1]

Now known as Mt. Krizevac or Cross Mountain, its former aliases over the centuries could make it into a mountain range of its own: Sipovac, Titovac, and finally Grmliavinac [2]—the Mountain of Thunder and home of Gromovnik, the dreaded Spirit of Thunder. [3]

Once the site of various unholy rituals and sacrifices by a bevy of pagan invaders, legend has it that the evil and angry Gromovnik summoned annual storms to pulverize the inhabitants below.

Mammoth hail stones, hurricane force winds, and unbidden fires collectively spelled doom for the villagers and their burgeoning yearly harvests. [4] Terror and fear of this vicious cycle held the people hostage until rescued by what the locals saw as divine intervention.[5]

In 1932, Pope Pius XI is said to have had a dream that issued a heavenly mandate for a towering cross to be erected on the "highest Golgotha in Hercegovina" in honor of the nineteen-hundred-year anniversary of the crucifixion of Jesus.[6]

Obedient to the nocturnal command, Pius sent for Medjugorje pastor Father Bernardine Smoljan to come to Rome and aid the Pope with bringing his dream to life.[7]

Father Smoljan proved to be the man for the moment. Excavating and hauling by hand over twenty tons of rocks, sand, and other essentials to the summit of the mountain, the good priest directed the weary, yet devout Catholics of the region to complete the onerous undertaking in less than three months.

With thousands gathering on the mountain to celebrate, the 30-foot high cross was dedicated on March 16, 1934. Adding to its glory, a hefty number of sacred relics were embedded in its inner structure, including a relic of the True Cross of Jesus Christ—courtesy of a pleased Pius XI.[8]

Once erect, the colossal cross boldly stood guard over the Brotnjo plateau, immediately credited with ceasing the perennial debilitating storms and fires, as well as sending the cruel and now-impotent Gromovnik into exile.

The vast Brotnjo plateau region, where Medjugorje sits in western Herzegovina, contains little industry and was mostly known in 1981 for its sparse agriculture of tobacco, grapes, pomegranates, and wheat.

Most of Brotnjo is stony, and fertile crop-growing land is scarce with scant vegetation. Large trees are rare, and the ground is flat but carefully utilized. Workable fields are bordered by stones, used as makeshift fences. Since rain was limited, few wells and springs existed. Instead, water tanks and stone cisterns collected the precipitation which was then marshaled by hand to the cattle and tobacco plants.

For centuries, the men of the region loaned themselves out as migrant workers in Sweden, West Germany, Belgium, France, and Switzerland, leaving their families to work the rocky farmland.

The women and children did not miss a beat, as the wine and tobacco remained excellent. The tobacco, known as Herzegovina Gold, remained plentiful. The wines, especially the white Žilavka and the red Blatina, won awards in Europe for their superior quality.

The Church of St. James in Medjugorje was surrounded by both crops at the time, as it took center stage amidst the five hamlets that blended into each other yet maintained their sovereignty, detectable only when outbursts of bygone animosities resurfaced between them from time to time.

The other villages are Miletina, Vionica, Surnanci, and Bijakovići, holding about 500 families in all back then. Today, they have become virtually one town.

The parish emerges in historical documents for the first time in the sixteenth century.[9] It then vanishes and reappears in various recorded accounts of the village, almost always associated in some regard to the Franciscans.

As throughout the lands of the Southern Slavs, the Franciscans—who arrived in the fourteenth century as missionaries to help eradicate a heresy called Bogomilism that began in Bulgaria and spread throughout the Balkans [10]—have labored to maintain the Catholic faith in Herzegovina, erecting and maintaining monasteries throughout the area. During the Ottoman reign (1478-1878), the region experienced great hardships, with many Franciscan martyrs recorded.[11]

The struggles of the past centuries did nothing to eradicate the violence that stalks the people of western Herzegovina, including more slain men of the cloth. Some sixty-six Franciscans (five from the parish of Medjugorje) were murdered by the Partisans—the Communists of post-World War II Yugoslavia—during and after the war in the region, and almost a thousand overall were killed in the Yugoslav Republics of Croatia and Bosnia-Herzegovina.[12]

Seven of the murdered priests were shot in the head in Mostar on February 7, 1945, and dumped in the Neretva River. Among them? — Father Bernardin Smoljan, the builder of the lofty mountain cross in Medjugorje. [13]

Throughout Hercegovina, the mostly Croatian people remain strong and loyal to the Catholic faith to this day. This is found to be especially true in parishes like St. James, which is still under the auspices of the Franciscans—commonly referred to as friars by the locals—and from which at least nineteen priests and twenty nuns have over recent decades come to serve across the globe.[14]

The construction of the present St. James was started in 1934 and completed in 1969, replacing an old church built in 1897, five years after its founding.[15] The church is consecrated to Saint James, the Elder—the Saint of Pilgrims—and sits in the diocese of Mostar.

Brandishing two medieval-style towers on both sides of its front entrance, and described upon its opening as extremely oversized for the small population it served, the concrete-slabbed building dominated the surrounding fields and miniscule houses of the plateau in 1981.

The previous church was originally situated at the very edge of the village in neighboring Bijakovići, about 200 yards away from the present St. James. Bijakovići is a slightly elevated, hamlet of boxy, white calcite houses, strung like pearls on both sides of old cart-worn streets of clay and stone, lying at the base of Podbrdo.

Like the other four villages, it was undeveloped and rustic in the early 1980s, with farm animals scurrying across the roads or peeking out of backyard pens. As everywhere else across the plateau at the time, fields of tobacco plants sprang up all around the two street town, sharing the open terrain with rows of grapevines and various dwarf-sized trees that dot the dark, red soil.[16]

It was in Bijakovići where two teenage girls, Ivanka and Mirjana, both still in high school and on summer vacation, got together that first late afternoon commemorating the Baptist's glory.

They planned on wasting some time along the bottom paths in the shadow of the stony Podbrdo. It was to be a casual excursion of relaxation, hopefully holding a few laughs, and just the innocent joy attached to such youthful leisure.

And so it would be here that the two young girls collided—like the Titanic's fateful rendezvous with the invisible iceberg—with their own unforeseen destiny.

It would be a fateful collision—dramatic, shocking, and, like the Titanic, destined to attract the eyes of the world.

CHAPTER NINE

"IS IT A SNAKE?"

"But who am I that the Mother of my
Lord should come to me?"

—Lk 1:43

IT WAS A LITTLE AFTER FIVE O'CLOCK ON THAT HOT, MUGGY Wednesday of June 24, 1981, when Ivanka Ivanković and Mirjana Dragićević strolled down the streets of one world and landed—one could say—in another. [1]

And for these two girls, it is fair to say, there would be no going back.

Tall, dark-haired, strikingly pretty, and undeniably innocent-looking, Ivanka Ivanković was born in the miniscule hamlet of Bijakovići on August 21, 1966. By the age of fifteen, though, she had moved with her family to Mostar, seventeen miles down the road from Medjugorje.

As the vivacious young girl did every year, Ivanka returned to Bijakovići in the spring of 1981, assisting her grandparents in the tobacco fields and vineyards that the family owned and cultivated for decades.

While her immediate family dwelled in Mostar, they owned an inherited home and some property in Bijakovići that Ivanka helped look after. This kept the teenager occupied from sunrise to sunset during the summer months.

Her father, Ivan, was doing seasonal work in West Germany that summer, while her beautiful—said to be saintly mother—Jagoda, had just passed away after a long illness, only little more than a month before the apparitions commenced. [2]

Ivanka had one older brother, Martin, and one sister, Daria, who both, like her, attended school in Mostar. Her grandmother, Iva, was up in years, and Ivanka's role in Bijakovići was to personally assist her, something she also did on weekends during the school year.

Those who knew the young girl the best at the time described her as a typical teen, well balanced and happy, and surprisingly somewhat religious, as had been Jagoda. Ivanka did, people agree, always have her sights set on marriage and a family.

But that summer, the shocking death of her mother hit her very hard. At the cemetery, it is said she collapsed upon the coffin in heart-broken grief, struggling to accept the inevitable burial.

Mirjana Dragićević did not permanently reside in Bijakovići either.

Born on March 18, 1965, the soft-spoken young girl was a year older than Ivanka and seemed even more mature than her age.

Described by the locals as an attractive, blonde-haired "modern girl" who was bright, sophisticated, and well-educated, the 16-year-old Mirjana lived most of the year with her parents in the busy, diverse Sarajevo, a city known as the "Jerusalem of Europe" because of its multi-cultural blend of peoples, religions and ethnicities.

Seeking better employment opportunities, Mirjana's parents had moved to the bustling city from Bijakovići before she was born. At the time, her father, Izzo, took a job in a radiology lab in Sarajevo, while her mother, Milena, had recently found new work in a local boutique.

Mirjana's younger brother, Miroslav, who is almost nine years younger, was said to be a very intelligent little boy, who simply adored his big sister—except, perhaps, on the day Mirjana announced she was going to be a nun, causing him to joke that he would have to call his sister, Sister Mirjana. [3]

As had become an annual custom for her, Mirjana vacationed every summer at her aunt Slava and uncle Simon's home in Bijakovići. There, she toiled in the tobacco fields, picking and stringing the leaves during the day while spending her down time with her closest friends, Ivanka and Vicka Ivanković.

Like Ivanka, Mirjana was known to be somewhat strong in her faith for a teenager, a faith that was a cherished tradition in her family. Going back as far she could remember, the Rosary was prayed every day in her home. Indeed, the Gospa—Croatian for Madonna—was said to be a member of the family in the Dragićević household.

Preparing the night before to take advantage of the perks of the Baptist's annual day, the teenage girls decided they would use their extra time off to mosey along the back roads and trails of Podbrdo and Crnica, the camel humped hills that pretend to tower over Bijakovice.

Rendezvousing at Ivanka's house in the late afternoon, the two finally gave up waiting on their other close friend, Vicka, and headed down the street and up a rock-gorged path.

There, walking on a trail that winds its way around and ultimately intersects with the larger hill, Crnica, the girls sang some of their favorite songs being piped out of Zagreb's hottest radio station and talked about the latest fashions in Sarajevo, along with the previous night's horrific storm.[4]

Having ventured as far as they wanted to go, they then casually reversed their way back towards Bijakovići, eventually settling on a place to sit in the shade at the base of the smaller hill.

Suddenly, as they began to relax, Ivanka glanced up and to her left.

In the hazy distance, two to three hundred yards up Podbrdo, the teenager spotted a shiny, luminous silhouette of a person, hovering above the boulders and brush. It appeared virtually motionless in the air, holding still as could be.

The figure seemed to possess the outline of young woman.

"Mirjana, look, Our Lady!" a nervous and somewhat frightened Ivanka stammered out loud without thinking as she pointed towards the glowing girl—not sure exactly what she was seeing, or even if she was hallucinating.

Mirjana, adrift in her own thoughts, shrugged her shoulders and continued to stare ahead, not wanting to be bothered with such nonsense. "Come on. Why on earth would Our Lady appear to us?"

But then, noticing an alarmed expression beginning to evolve on Ivanka's face, a now slightly concerned Mirjana suggested the two hasten along the trail and down the hill to the safe confines of Bijakovići.

Descending to the bottom of the path, the still spooked pair walked a bit until they ran into a little thirteen-year-old shepherd girl, Milka Pavlović, just departing her home. Milka disclosed she was on her way to retrieve her small flock of grazing sheep on Podbrdo, not far from where the two girls had just fled.

For a few moments, the three held court and briefly chatted, whereupon Milka gently foisted Ivanka and Mirjana to assist her with her chore. Unable to say no, the gang trudged back up the stony hill.

Reaching the hillside pasture, Milka let the sheep into the pen, and the girls headed once again back towards home. The time was now about 6:15 p.m. Minutes later—as they meandered down Podbrdo—they passed by the spot where Ivanka first eyed the illuminating lady.

And there—as before—Ivanka spied the shining figure of a woman floating motionless on the slope of the hill.

"Look, there she is again!"

Now more intrigued, Mirjana decided this time to focus her eyes on the exact area Ivanka was pointing at. As did Milka. And—within seconds—the three agreed. There, on the side of the hill hovered a radiant young girl in a lustrous silver-grey dress with a long white veil. This time, she seemed to be holding something in her arms very protectively.[5]

Shocked, the trio froze, completely speechless and aghast, but concentrating hard to remain focused on the shimmering lady. While time now seemed to be standing still, the longer the girls stared, the more they began to realize who it was they were casting their eyes upon.

Like an oil painting springing to life, what had to be the Blessed Virgin Mary slowly became more and more visible before their incredulous eyes.

It was the Madonna, they all felt, bathed in a magnificent white light that revealed and illuminated all her celestial glory. Spellbinding and incomprehensibly beautiful—as they would later struggle to explain—Mary's appearance simply transcended human words. [6]

"We couldn't see her face," Mirjana recalled, "and anyway, we didn't know what the Madonna would really look like. But something inside us really insisted that it was the Madonna. We knew it was her, but we felt confused, and just stood there looking at her."

Ivanka concurred—it had to be the Madonna.[7] But though excited, she felt paralyzed by the surge of conflicting emotions: "We didn't know what to do, where to put ourselves. We felt a mixture of joy and fear. So much joy, yet so much fear. It's impossible to describe it."

Mentally processing that the radiant vision was the Most Holy Virgin was challenging, but it was even more difficult to contemplate what—or who—Mary was holding wrapped in a blanket.

Again, though, there could be only one conclusion.

"I saw the Madonna holding Jesus in her hands," insisted Ivanka.[8] It had to be Jesus, Mirjana agreed, arguing that no earthly mother would take a baby up that hillside. [9] The glowing lady repeatedly covered and uncovered the infant.

Then, the three seemed to innately sense the woman was summoning them in a nonverbal way to approach and see her child.

Still frightened and now somewhat befuddled, Ivanka, Mirjana, and Milka became even more at a loss for words, not sure what to do next. Mirjana remembers asking herself if she was dead or alive, wanting to pinch herself to see if she was dreaming.[10]

Suddenly, the carefree rustlings of a surprise visitor could be heard stumbling upon the scene, hurdling the three teenage girls out of their bliss and back to reality.

There, a short distance from them down the hill, stood Ivanka's and Mirjana's effervescent, forsaken pal—a smiling, curious Vicka—staring up at her dumbfounded friends.

Puzzled at first, Vicka took a guess at what was going on.

"What is it?

"Is it a snake?" [11]

CHAPTER TEN

THE MOTHER OF GOD IS VISITING EARTH

"The woman herself fled into the desert, where a special place had been prepared for her by God."

—Rv 12:6

"Vicka exudes joy ... Her spirit is truly ebullient," wrote renowned international author, Janice Connell, in her bestseller, *Visions of the Children.* [1]

"Vicka is the most talkative... the most controversial of the seers. She does not tremble before the truth as she sees it," concluded Father Janko Bubalo in his award-winning, *A Thousand Encounters with the Virgin Mary at Medjugorje*—the first book that centered totally on just one of the Medjugorje visionaries—Vicka.[2]

"Face to face, Vicka would prove perhaps the most radiant human being I had ever encountered," penned three time Pulitzer Prize nominee Randall Sullivan in his masterpiece account of Medjugorje, *The Miracle Detective.* [3]

"Vicka is the charmer of the group... She simply radiates delight... There is nothing artificial about her," discerned theologian Joseph Pelletier, in *The Queen of Peace Visits Medjugorje.* [4]

The third member of the inseparable summer gang—and oldest of the visionaries—Vicka Ivanković shares the same last name with Ivanka, but is no relation to her fellow villager.

Like Ivanka, she was born in Bijakovići on July 3, 1963, and has Croatian blood flowing in her veins. While she goes by Vicka, her real name is Vida, which in Croatian means—of all things— "vision."

Her parents, Pero and Zlata, raised eight children, forcing her father to work in West Germany for fifteen years to provide for his large family. Like her two friends, this meant she had to work the farm at an early age, tending to the grapes, tobacco, and other chores while living at home with her mother and five younger siblings. Two older sisters married young and had already moved out.

Vicka went to grammar school in Čitluk and was enrolled in a Mostar middle school for textiles in the summer of 1981. Of medium height, with curly brown hair and dark eyes, the 17-year-old Vicka was described as being very strong willed and bold, yet compassionate and sincere. Honest to a fault, those who knew her well said she was incapable of telling a lie.[5]

Foremost about her, though, was Vicka's unremitting, radiant smile and her endless conviviality—something no one who meets her forgets. It is a gift that empowers her with a lovable charm and contagious joy that is described as infectious and extremely disarming.

Usually dressed remarkably simple, the Franciscans who first interrogated Vicka about the visions noted she had no great thought for her appearance, a trait they believed confirmed her natural humility. Years later, of all the visionaries, none seemed to attract the pilgrims like Vicka, perhaps because of her so down-to-earth manner.

At least as much—if not more—than Ivanka and Mirjana, Vicka's family was also well known for their faith long before the apparitions began. Indeed, her father Pero was touted by many for his holiness, and her 88-year-old grandmother (also named Vicka) was sure to be heard nightly throughout the village cackling the family bedtime prayers.[6]

To no one's surprise, it would be grandmother Vicka who discerned post haste on the first day of the apparitions that Mt. Podbrdo's lady of light might need a splash of holy water to test what side she was coming from.[7]

Having failed mathematics during the previous year at the textile school—thereby sentencing herself to summer-school classes—Vicka missed the feast day Mass of the Baptist at St. James that morning because of a final exam in Mostar.

Returning home around noon on a sweltering hot bus, the exhausted girl grabbed lunch and fell into a long nap. Awakened rather late in the afternoon by her sister Zdenka, Vicka spotted a message from Ivanka and Mirjana that said to meet at Mirjana's aunt's house.

Completely refreshed, the rambunctious teenager set off—in her bedroom slippers—to do just that. But when she got to Jakisa's house, her friends had already departed for Podbrdo without her.

Nevertheless, suspecting their whereabouts, Vicka immediately headed down the asphalt road and towards the backyard hill.

As she hastened her way up Podbrdo, Vicka noticed her three friends were apparently focused on something that had grabbed their attention. Still uncertain what it was, she scampered the rest of the way up the hill to join them.

Once on the scene with the other three girls, though, a surprise was at hand. Ivanka and Mirjana wasted no time inviting Vicka to cast her eyes upon a visitor stationed about a thousand feet up near the top of Podbrdo.

"Look! Up there—the Madonna!"

"What do you mean, the Madonna? What is wrong with you?"

Stunned, confused, and scared, as soon as Vicka issued her feisty rebuke to her three friends, the vivacious young girl took off. And—like Mirjana—she didn't bother to steal a curious gander of the vision either. Rather, in a blink of the eye, she fled—slippers in hand—straight down Podbrdo barefoot, finally coming to rest at a stone wall in front of some houses in Bijakovići.

There, she let loose a good cry.

"I only wanted to cry. How can they play with the Virgin Mary?" she recalled afterwards, speaking as if what the others had done was almost blasphemous.

Up on Podbrdo, however, the scene had come full circle for the once-disheveled Mirjana.

Although she had wanted nothing to do with the apparitional woman the first time around, she now found herself hypnotically fixed on the mesmerizing sight—unable to let go, unable to grasp the full implications of what she was really seeing.

She kept thinking that it was not possible that this was the Virgin Mary, though her heart was totally convinced. Years later, Mirjana recalls thinking at the time that the Blessed Mother would never be willing to come to Medjugorje...to Herzegovina.

But, she remembers, after finally deciding to take a stronger look, she knew it was her:

"I was 16. I thought that Blessed Mother was in Heaven. I never thought of her as willing to come here. I didn't think I was worthy to be near the Blessed Mother. When Ivanka had told me to look at the mountain, I looked at Ivanka. I thought something was wrong with her. I wondered what was happening. But, I did look and see her." [8]

Ivanka, like Mirjana, became more confidant it was Mary, too.

Soon, both girls' conviction grew into certainty, as the longer they stared at the shimmering woman, the more assured they became that it truly, truly was the Madonna.

"Oh, I was certain. I knew exactly who it was...my whole being knew without a doubt that this lady of unexplainable beauty was the Mother of God," remembers Mirjana. [9]

Likewise, Ivanka was certain, too. Together, her mind and heart told her it had to be the Virgin Mary:

"The first time I saw her outline; it was the same as I'd seen in holy pictures. That's all I can say. I can't say it any better...But when I saw the Madonna again, this time holding the baby Jesus in her hands... I was sure." [10]

Back in Bijakovići, still barefooted, a tearful Vicka staggered upon two boys, 21-year-old Ivan Ivanković—not a relative to her or Ivanka—and 16-year-old Ivan Dragićević, who was carrying a plastic bag full of freshly-picked apples.

Declining an apple, a nervous Vicka beseeched the two young men to return with her to Podbrdo to see the Virgin, adding they could opt out on actually looking at the vision if they were not quite comfortable with that part. [11]

The two Ivans, both from Bijakovići, agreed to the mission, serendipitously making Vicka the first to spread the news of the apparitions.

Now in the secure company of the brave young lads, a calmer Vicka felt reassured of her safety and led the way back to where the others still lingered on Podbrdo.

Once together again with the other three girls, Mirjana, Ivanka and Milka wasted no time helping point Vicka and the boys in the direction of the glowing figure.

And this second time around—like Mirjana—Vicka let herself look.

Casting her full attention on the upper portion of the hillside, within moments the young girl's eyes caught hold of a dazzling sight. There before her, about a yard off the ground up on the side of the hill, floated a beautiful lady bathed in white, her face aglow.

Vicka also noticed that the woman was holding a baby. Overwhelmed and stunned by the magnitude of the uncanny experience, she immediately turned to ask Ivan Dragićević if he saw her, too.

A reply, however, was not to be heard.

Beyond shock, Vicka discovered the younger of the two Ivans was no longer at her side, having fled down the hill—much like she herself had just done minutes before—in alarm, surrendering his bag of apples at the scene.

Back now on the streets of Bijakovići, the shaken boy went so far as to scale the stone fence in the village to further insure his successful escape.

Ivan Dragićević had just turned 16 when the apparitions began.

Born in the hamlet on May 25, 1965, by 1981 his life had become very mechanical, as he needed to go to school and complete family chores almost every day.

Like most of his neighbors, his father and mother—Stanko and Zlata—were farmers. The family did, however, live in a fairly large house, together with Ivan's two younger brothers.

As with the others, the Dragićević family was of strong faith, often attending Mass every day. The Rosary was also a daily family fixture, although Ivan confesses it was more of just a habit to him then.[12]

At the time of the apparitions, Ivan was a tall, timid, and retiring boy, who looked rather serious to those who didn't know him. Possessing thick, dark, curly hair, which he wore over his ears and combed down on his forehead, it can be inferred that his image indirectly contributed to his stoic persona.

He was, however, known in the village as a good-hearted, steady boy, who though serious and pensive, was always pleasant. While he says he knew the other visionaries, they were only casual friends and neighbors at the time, with nothing else in common besides their youth.

While Ivan was not overtly prayerful by nature, he did have a reputation for being forthright and trustworthy. He was instantly seen by many in the community as incapable of partaking in any form of deception—especially with such serious matters as the apparitions.[13]

The opening day was perhaps a bit too overwhelming for him, though, catching the teenage boy completely off guard. Unlike Mirjana and Vicka, who both returned to Podbrdo after their initial encounter with the apparition, once Ivan departed the hill he felt no gnawing inspiration to return—not even for his apples.

He also later admitted that he was not sure from the brief first encounter that day with the apparition that it *was* the Blessed Mother.[14]

As occurred with Mirjana, however, Vicka's second time around proved a different story.

Now staring like the others at the shimmering light glistening on the hillside, the ever-beaming, joy filled young girl quickly became spellbound by the beautiful, shining lady it enveloped. And the more Vicka looked, the more her curiosity begged for understanding.

"Can you see anything?" Vicka inquired of Ivan Ivanković and Milka.

"I can see something completely white, turning," Ivan answered Vicka.[15]

"I see Our Lady," said Milka.[16]

With such affirmative replies, Ivan Ivanković and Milka Pavlović officially become visionaries, yet after this first evening, neither would ever see an apparition of Mary again in Medjugorje.

Milka's sister, Marija, would arrive the next day and forever remain one of the permanent group of visionaries at Medjugorje. But Milka could not return. Her mother didn't take to the news too well, and prohibited her to go back the following evening,[17] exiling her to a distant field to ensure her obedience.

When Milka did return on the third evening, she saw nothing. To this day, Milka possesses a calm, quiet nostalgia about it all, harboring no envy, regrets, or bitterness.[18]

Milka has, however, contributed to a better understanding of the events on the first day. In some accounts, she has filled in some superfluous yet necessary details, such as the fact that during the "second apparition" on the first day (which she witnessed), the precise location is simply not verifiable because the girls continually moved around for 20 to 30 minutes while discussing their observations.

Ivan Ivanković was unimpressed by it all that first evening. Retrieving his buddy's abandoned apples, he departed the hill to look for his shaken friend.

The following day, Ivan declined at first to go back, thinking he was too old for matters that to him seemed childish. Vicka would later defend his decision: "Why would he want to hang around with kids like us?"

By the evening of the second day, though, Ivan Ivanković suffered a change of heart and returned to Podbrdo, but witnessed nothing.

Ironically, the young man, a lathe factory worker, would later be arrested and jailed for two months for violating a strictly-enforced police order that forbade the visionaries and their followers from returning to the hill.

During that time, some of the visionaries received a vision from Mary of Ivan Ivanković in a prison cell, in which the Virgin told them that he was being "a witness to the truth."

As with her two close friends, once more calm and settled, Vicka quickly became engrossed by the beautiful lady in light.

Seemingly frozen in time and space, she remembers focusing her eyes hard on the vision to pull it in more distinctly. She would later describe in detail the experience to a BBC film crew in 1986:

> I saw it—and what I saw was very white. I saw a gown, dark hair. All the time, she was covering and uncovering something she held in her left hand. I was not able to see what else she was doing, but it looked like she was showing something.

Then, she called to us to come closer—but who was going to get any closer? We were saying to each other: "She is calling us, but who is going to go?"

None of the visionaries on the first day remember for certain how long the apparition lasted. Some accounts say up to forty-five minutes, others recall it lasted merely until the Madonna vanished, with no true sense of the amount of time that passed. But, more or less, it appears the children finally departed as darkness descended, and they could no longer see the vision. It also had started to rain, as Vicka recalled.

Soon enough, though, the six were in their homes trying to relay to their families what exactly had happened. But their explanations proved inadequate and unconvincing. Although they tried to be as sincere and forthright as they could, few in their households could buy into their mystical madness.

In a couple of homes, hysterics actually filled the air—especially at Milka's, where the little girl was told it was a figment of her imagination, or worse. "You should have caught her," one opined.[19] "Did she send greetings to your mothers and fathers? " another further jested.

At Vicka's, the reactions to the alleged heavenly encounter were mixed, with most preferring to downplay any reality to the matter. Vicka remembers sitting on her couch crying while being teased by her sister, "Maybe they saw a flying saucer." [20] But suddenly, casting the humor aside, her uncle took aim at the vacationing girl from Sarajevo, Mirjana, warning that she seemed like a "clever city girl", perhaps capable of conceiving such a bizarre ruse. [21]

Vicka's parents, unlike her playful siblings, recommended she keep quiet about it all, if she didn't want people to think she was mad.[22] Only her grandmother casually let slip that she wasn't that ready to dismiss the children's flight-of-fancy, warning everyone that it could be the Devil disguised as an angel of light to fool people.[23] Recalled Vicka, "There was real commotion. Some perhaps believed, some wondered… everything conceivable was said." [24]

Ivanka's home proved no different. Skepticism held the front row. When told about everything that happened, her grandmother moved to solve the mystery, "Come now, it was somebody watching sheep who had put a flashlight on his head." [25]

At Mirjana's, her uncle cared little about what actually happened on the hill and immediately became more concerned that such nonsense could get everybody in a lot of trouble with the Communist authorities.[26]

Down the road, Ivan's family wasn't buying in either and seemed unconcerned about his brief, but frightening episode with the ghostly sight. "They just laughed," recalled Ivan. "They thought we must have seen the glow from a shepherd's torch or a wil-o'-wisp." [27]

All in all, the visionaries claim they were not too troubled by their family's reactions. Vicka said she just smiled and told herself it didn't matter, as long as she knew the truth, "They couldn't influence me no matter what they said or did." [28] Recalled Mirjana, "I took it as though they believed me. If they didn't believe me that was their personal affair. I wasn't annoyed in any way." [29] Ivan held a similar attitude, "I would have preferred that they believed, but if they didn't want to, that was their personal affair." [30]

One intriguing anecdote associated with the first day is worth noting, though.

Later challenged over Ivanka's immediate certainty that it was the Virgin Mary she was seeing, Vicka cleverly retorted that it would have been even *more* foolish for Ivanka to have claimed otherwise,

"I don't know, who is she going to think about? A beautiful young mother with a child? A crown on her head? A lady just like Our Lady?" [31]

Besides Vicka's insight in exposing the obvious, there also emerges through her—for the first time—some of what would come to be very distinct elements of the Medjugorje apparitions.

Vicka noticed on day one that the Virgin Mary's dress appeared a silvery-gray color, with a white veil, an eventual defining characteristic of the Madonna of Medjugorje, versus the all-white, or white-blue attire the Virgin famously wore at earlier apparition sites such as Fátima and Lourdes.

She also established that Mary wore a crown of stars, had dark hair, and appeared about 19 or 20 years old.

And, the bubbly girl emphasized, the Virgin Mary floated in the air—on a cloud—not touching the ground. [32]

The vision's feet, she insisted, were never in sight.[33]

Like the apparitional Madonna herself, the shocking news of Mary's surprise visitation on Podbrdo traveled unseen throughout the five villages that evening.

But, almost everywhere, talk persisted well into the night, with many curious souls shuffling by the homes of friends and neighbors to ask questions. It seemed, not surprisingly, that everyone had an opinion. [34]

Notwithstanding their shock from it all, the children recalled experiencing a deep peace that first night, wallowing in a unique feeling of happiness, though none of them slept very well. Only Mirjana reports that she stayed up all night, praying and shivering in fear. [35]

And while their parents and elders were concerned the neighbors might call them liars or worse, such a worry did not develop for the most part.

Moreover, it could be argued that the opposite began to unfold in the villages.

The locals, while not completely convinced, were generally kind and sympathetic—revealing the deeper faith and solidarity of the Croatian people. This was something that could be expected in a region so used to serious trials and tribulations, followed often by the need for compassion, friendship, loyalty, and support.

And so, it would be just another storm in Herzegovina which the people would again ride out together.

A little down the trail in the village of Medjugorje, Iva and Pero Vasilj—still shaken by the earlier storm the night before—took in the curious news without losing any sleep this time.

When a local boy dropped by and told them about the apparitions, the biblical-like tempest of the previous twenty-four hours now seemed to make more sense to the couple.

"Oh," pondered Iva aloud, "so that's why there was all that thunder and lightning last night. The Mother of God is visiting earth." [36]

Yes, the Virgin Mary was visiting again.

But not just any part of the earth. Since the 1940s, Yugoslavia was a place where the Mother of God was not very welcome.

All because of—as Mary predicted at Fátima—the "errors of Russia."[37] *

---

*   The use of the word "errors" (of Russia) by Mary at Fatima on July 13, 1917, may have been for a reason. Mary can be seen to be echoing Pope Pius IX's words in his November 9, 1846, encyclical, *Qui Pluribus* (On Faith and Reason). Communism, wrote Pius in what was his first encyclical, was dark, deceitful, cunning, and depraved— "a filthy medley of errors." The encyclical was released two years before Karl Marx's and Friedrich Engels's *Manifesto of the Communist Party* in 1848, known today as *The Communist Manifesto.*

The six Medjugorje visionaries seen in ecstasy during an apparition at St. James Church.

Photo Credit: St. Andrews Productions

Jacov lived with his mother, Jaka, until she passed away when he was twelve.

Photo Credit: St. Andrews Productions

This photograph of the visionaries was taken on Mt. Podbrdo during the first week of the apparitions in June of 1981

Photo Credit: St. Andrews Productions

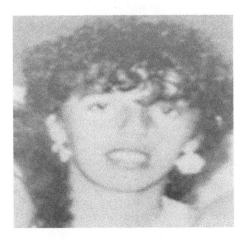

Milka Pavlović experienced only one apparition of the Madonna on June 24, 1981.

Photo Credit: St. Andrews Productions

Mt. Podbrdo and Mt. Crnica. The two hills in Bijakovići have been described as camel humps. They were the home of wild boars and wolves for many years before the apparitions.

Photo Credit: St. Andrews Productions

The village of Bijakovići has been described as a two-street town. All of the visionaries were born there, except Mirjana.

Photo Credit: St. Andrews Productions

Built in 1933, the towering cross on Mt. Krizevac can be seen from a great distance. Father Bernardin Smoljan, the pastor at St. James in Medjugorje at the time, was murdered in Mostar on February 7,1945, by Tito's Communist Partisans.

Left Photo Credit: St. Andrews Productions

Right Photo Credit: St. Andrews Productions

PART II

THE ERRORS OF RUSSIA

66 Not a single problem of the class struggle has ever been solved in history except by violence. When violence is exercised by the working people, by the mass of exploited against the exploiters— then we are for it."

—Vladimir Lenin,
Report on the Activities of the Council of People's Commissars,
January 24, 1918

CHAPTER ELEVEN

THE ERRORS OF RUSSIA

"Now the Spirit explicitly says that in the last times
some will turn away from the faith by paying attention
to deceitful spirits and demonic instructions through
the hypocrisy of liars and branded consciences."

—1 Tim 4:1-2

H E WOULD BE DEAD IN LITTLE MORE THAN A YEAR.
But for the moment, he bathed in glory.

On February 23, 1981—almost four months to the day before the Virgin Mary's first apparition at Medjugorje—the 26th Congress of the Communist Party of the Soviet Union opened.

It was kicked off with a five-hour address by the General Secretary and the Chairman of the Presidium of the Supreme Soviet. A marathon of a speech, Soviet television carried only the beginning and the end of his talk that day, giving it ten minutes of total airtime.

But the beginning and end were all that mattered.

If you were looking to gauge the direction of the U.S.S.R., that was all you needed to hear. As had occurred every five years, the Congress commenced by vehemently reaffirming the party's mission through its most prophetic voice—comrade Leonid Brezhnev.

At the time, the Soviet Union was not doing well. While supersized and super-powered, it suffered from a growing decline in economic growth, a frightful decline in food production—consequences of the disastrous Afghanistan invasion—and a perennial decline in cooperation with its yoked neighbors.

This time, the problem in the Soviet fold was a series of unsettling events in Poland that were becoming embarrassing. As with Hungary in 1956 and Czechoslovakia in 1968, trouble with its satellite members did not reflect well on communism as the ideal alternative to capitalism. But these were backroom issues the Kremlin always found ways to manage, usually with the help of some tanks.

Most worrisome, though, was the Soviet Union's growing estrangement from the United States and the West. The continued alienation between the superpowers was causing talk of war—nuclear war.

By 1981, this dilemma preoccupied the mind of Brezhnev.

Twice before, with Cuba in October 1962 and seven years later with China in October 1969, the threat of nuclear confrontation for the Soviet Union had come perilously close to reality. Now, more than ever, Brezhnev's words to the Congress seemed poised to show he would act if justified.

Concluding his 110-page address, Brezhnev—who would succumb to a heart attack on November 10, 1982—made a stirring pledge. Never would the Soviet Union allow itself to be deterred from its goal of a worldwide Communist revolution:

> Our aim is Communism and it is a majestic aim. Every labour achievement, every year of heroic accomplishment, and every five-year plan brings us nearer to that aim. This is the standpoint from which the party assesses the coming five-year period. Much will have to be done.
>
> The tasks that will have to be fulfilled are big and complex. But we will most definitely carry them out...
>
> Honor and glory to the Communist Party of the Soviet Union, a party of builders of Communism!
>
> May our great country, the Union of the Soviet Socialist Republics, continue to grow stronger and flourish!
>
> Long live peace! Long live Communism! [1]

Received with assiduous attention, punctuated with prolonged applause, and welcomed by mandatory approval, Brezhnev's vision of the road ahead for his party revealed one thing for certain: nothing in the present was considered a detriment to the future.

Cut from the godless mold of his villainous predecessors—Lenin, Stalin, Khrushchev—Brezhnev's leadership embraced Karl Marx's guiding principle: the ends justify the means.

Physically, he appeared chiseled from the same mold, too.

With aplomb, the Soviet General-Secretary reflected the image of the classic Russian oligarch. As if handed down to him in some malevolent fashion, Brezhnev was gifted with a menacing demeanor that left the impression that not only did he never smile, but was physically incapable of doing so.

Day in and day out, his face permanently wore the frozen expression of a death mask. Revealing some say—as with his autocratic forefathers—the blackened soul of a ruthless Communist.

His nasty comportment was no act.

Brezhnev ascendancy to the General Secretariat post meant, if anything, that he had enough cruelty in his past to justify his anointing. And, as his address was written to convey between the lines, the party's future would not be comprised by a reluctance to wield the Soviet nuclear sword.

This was an intention he would affirm again later that same year.

On October 27, at a Kremlin dinner in honor of Ali Abdullah Saleh, the President of North Yemen, Brezhnev warned,

"The stakes in this dangerous game are the threat of a world nuclear war, the prospect of the death of hundreds of millions of people." [2]

Brezhnev was a Communist—inside and out. And if the Lady of Fátima warned of persecution coming from Russia, here was a man who was comfortable in the role of the persecutor.

His speech that cold February day in Moscow left the party with what it wanted to hear: the onward march of Communism would not be deterred by such petty issues as food shortages and unemployment.

As with the Nazis in the closing days of World War II—who marshalled vast resources to maintain their extermination camps versus utilizing them to defend Germany from the advancing Allies—the ultimate goal of the Soviet Union remained on schedule in the winter of 1981: world domination through world revolution, at any price.

The same way it all began on that godforsaken October day in 1917.

Less than two weeks after the last apparition at Fátima, the revolution in Russia was off and running—officially sprung by way of an armed insurgency in Petrograd on October 25, 1917.

The October uprising—Red October—was an insurrection led by "the Reds," better known as the Bolsheviks, a name that means "one of the majority."

The Bolsheviks were a renegade Marxist faction of the Russian Social Democrats Worker's Party, founded in 1903 by Freemasons Vladimir Lenin and Leon Trotsky, along with Dr. Alexander Bogdanov, a philosopher and science fiction writer.

They changed their name to the Russian Communist Party (of Bolsheviks) in March 1918; to the All-Union Communist Party (of Bolsheviks) in 1925, and to the Communist Party of the Soviet Union in October, 1952.

The Bolshevik Communists hoped to get it right from the start. Claiming to be pure in their objectives, they aimed to create a political-economic system that operated on the principle that a society's problems arise from the unequal distribution of wealth—just as the Communist Manifesto of Marx and Engels reasoned.

To resolve this perceived injustice, the distinctions between classes—especially between the rich and the poor—needed be addressed. And that meant one thing: there would probably have be a dispute. This was because the wealthy, said Marx, never voluntarily surrender their goods, property, and status.

Most of all, Marx stressed that it must be a revolution of the poor—of the workers—to be successful. Translated, this meant that class anger, stimulated by agitating envy in the working class, would be the best way to bring a successful overthrow of powers.

This type of change involves one other ingredient: force.

Theoretically, Marxists are guarded in their advocating of force, deferring to casually note its "probable necessity." In truth, though, force is not only the key to bringing a successful Communist revolution, but essential to maintaining one.

Indeed, so-called "social equality" appears only sustainable—as Communist nations would embarrassingly demonstrate time and again—by calling upon military muscle to insure the proletariat never demurs too much from the cause. This, not surprisingly, would come to be seen as Communism's modus operandi, the very heart of its success.

But while history would show force at the heart of Communism's success, time would reveal that atheism was what party apparatchiks believed to be the soul of its survival.

Marx, Lenin, Stalin, Mao, and countless other Communist despots over the decades, all held firmly to this single premise. More than anything, the absence of a deity—freedom from the tyranny of believing in a God that didn't exist—was what a nation needed most to move out from the chains of class struggle.

This is what every true Communist maintained—no pun intended—to be gospel. In thesis, this was small print in the Communist Manifesto. But in practicality, it would be written in all capital letters in the Bolshevik Party's playbook right from the very beginning.

And so, wherever Russia's "errors" came pushing in, the presence of God and religion needed to be escorted out—quite often before the smoke from the barrels of the guns had time to vanish.

In Portugal, seven years before the Bolshevik's seized power in Russia, this reality struck hard and fast.

With the violent overthrow of the monarchy and the expulsion of the Braganca dynasty by the Portuguese Republican Party on October 5, 1910, a new Masonic government—openly dedicated to atheism—was installed.

Lisbon, its leaders heralded, would become the atheist capital of the world.[3]

The Portuguese insurgents possessed a rabid hatred for religion. This led to immediate action following the coup. Within five days of seizing power on October 10, the new government—whose symbol was the Red Star [4]—declared all Catholic convents, monasteries, and religious orders were to be closed, with their assets confiscated. To insure cooperation, bishops were exiled and priests imprisoned. [5] All members of religious orders that resisted were considered as "enemies of the state."

The new provisional government of Portugal was just getting started.

They then expelled the Society of Jesus from Portugal, halted all religious teaching in schools, and abolished wearing religious garb in public.[6] To smear salt on the wound, they forbade the ringing of church bells.

On October 18, the government issued a decree abolishing the religious oath in courts of justice. Then, on October 25, they terminated a two-centuries old traditional oath for professors and students by which they had sworn to defend the Dogma of the Immaculate Conception.

And they still weren't done.

Next, the revolutionary authorities ordered a complete secularization of the state. Divorce was institutionalized, as was the legality of civil marriages. Cemeteries were secularized, and any religious dress at all was prohibited on "pain of imprisonment"— even by those who received permission to remain in Portugal to teach. Finally, public religious holidays were not to be celebrated.[7]

All of this culminated with a new "Law of Separation of Church and State,"[8] enacted on April 20, 1911, causing Masonic Grand Master Magalhaes Lima to publicly state that within a few years, no person in Portugal would wish to become a priest.

Minister for Justice and future Prime Minister of Portugal, Alfonso da Costa, went further, declaring,

"Thanks to this law of separation, in two generations, Catholicism will be completely eliminated in Portugal." [9]

While Portugal's government was not Communist, its new leadership was extremely antireligious, satiated with the teachings of a familiar name: Karl Marx.[10]

This begs the question—exactly what *did* Karl Marx think about God?

Marx's ideas on capitalism, class separation, and politics are well expounded by way of his two books, *The Communist Manifesto*, which called for a forcible overthrow of all existing social conditions, and *Das Kapital*, a foundational, theoretical text in materialist philosophy, economics, and politics, and the most cited book in the social sciences before 1950.

But what is less scrutinized is Marx's emotional bond with atheism. Which, when magnified, appears to be the driving force behind his passion to bring down the status quo.

Devoted to the atheistic philosophers Kant and Voltaire and later Hegel, Marx despised the role of religion in society—and he desired to change it. He was heavily influenced by a professor named Bruno Bauer, who taught that the Christian Gospels were fantasies and that an atheistic movement greater than Christianity was coming. Bauer's book, *Criticism of the Synoptic Gospels,* denied the historicity of Christ and portrayed His life as a mythical invention.

Inspired by his mentor and close friend, Marx set out to bring about Bauer's dream of a godless society. In his doctoral thesis at the University of Berlin, Marx proclaimed that, in the country of reason, the existence of God cannot have any meaning. He believed this was especially true for Christianity.

"The social principles of Christianity preach cowardice, self-contempt, abasement, submission, humility," sneered Marx. "The social principles of Christianity are hypocritical...So much for the social principles of Christianity." [11]

A young lawyer named Georg Jung, a contemporary, said Marx called Christianity one of the most "immoral religions." [12] But to be clear, Marx wanted all religions done away with. "In truth, all gods I hate," became his admission, Marx's motto against religion.

It was a maxim that went hand in hand, Bishop Fulton Sheen believed, with another axiom of Marx:

"Communism begins where atheism begins." [13]

In essence, Marx hated God, period: "The more of himself that man gives to God," he espoused, "the less he has left for himself." [14]

But Marx's opposition to religion went well beyond the intellectual level. His life reveals it was personal. He not only had a profound hatred for God, but a visible affinity for the dark side, one that those closest to him couldn't help but sense, either consciously or subconsciously.

Historian Paul Kengor, in his book, *The Devil and Karl Marx*, writes that Marx's father said his son was "governed by a demon," and that Marx's own son referred to him as "my dear devil."

Likewise, Marx's wife called him a "wicked knave" and his partner, Friedrich Engels, said he was a "monster of ten thousand devils." [15] Others who knew him didn't hesitate to say or write that he was "possessed," or "under a spell," and that he often acted and looked so; one friend of his said he had "eyes like a wet goblin." [16]

Death seemed to stalk Marx as four of his seven children died in infancy, and two of his surviving children, daughters Eleanor and Laura—along with Laura's husband, Paul Lafargue—committed suicide.

The respected scholar and academic, Robert Payne, in his celebrated 1968 book, *Marx: A Biography*, had a chapter titled, "The Demons." [17] Wrote Payne about the evil that shadowed Marx, "He had the Devil's view of the world, and the Devil's malignity. Sometimes he seemed to know that he was accomplishing works of evil." [18]

Marx would nurture his hatred for God and religion his entire life. His book, *Contribution to a Critique of Hegel's Philosophy of Right: Introduction*, perhaps best reveals—since so many choose to quote from it—his passionate disdain for any human need to worship a creator and his belief that one needed to eschew all religion:

> Religious misery is at once the expression of real misery and a protest against it. Religion is the groan of the oppressed, the sentiment of a heartless world, and at the same time the spirit of a condition deprived of spirituality. It is the opium of the people.[19]

To many scholars today, Marx's overt disdain for religion confirms their thinking: Marxism—though viewed primarily as a philosophical system, or as an economic/political action theory—is in reality a secular religion.

This is a premise that has grown over time. "It could be argued," wrote Trevor Ling in *Karl Marx and Religion*, "that the bulk of the literature today supporting the view that Marxism is a religion is so great that it cannot easily be set aside."

There is a reason for this growing consensus of opinion: Marxism can now be clearly seen to contain an anti-Judeo-Christian philosophy/theology at its core, one that, ironically, tries to parallel the communal belief structure of the two religions while rejecting their supernatural tenets.

Boston College professor Peter Kreeft noted the similarities between Marxism and Judaism, "Marx, like Moses, is the prophet who leads the new 'Chosen People'—the proletariat—out of the slavery of capitalism, into the 'Promised Land' of communism, across the Red Sea of bloody worldwide revolution."

Bruce Ashford, Provost of Southeastern Baptist Theological Seminary, believes Marxism literally apes Christianity, "Marx constructed his ideology as the antithesis to Christianity and is best understood theologically…Marx identifies the great "evil" of the world as material inequality and subsequently urges society to turn to the "holy scriptures" of Marxist ideology in order to to find "salvation."

Joseph Schumpeyer, in his book, *Capitalism, Socialism, and Democracy*, sees Marxism as a religious guide on how to theologically save the world from evil: "...Marxism is a religion. To the believer it presents...a plan of salvation, and the indication of the evil from which mankind, or a section of mankind, is to be saved."

As with the other religions, the Devil is found in Marxism, and, writes Kengor, it is by way of Marx himself.

Perhaps not surprisingly, Marx is found to have been aware of his demonic leanings. "Thus Heaven I've forfeited, I know it full well," he penned in a poem in 1837, "My soul, once true to God, is chosen for Hell." [20]

In another poem, Marx wrote, "See the sword—the Prince of Darkness sold it to me. For he beats the time and gives the signs. Ever more boldly I play the dance of death." [21]

Kengor sums up succinctly Marx's demonic leanings:

"Karl Marx wrote not only about the Hell that was Communism, but about Hell itself." [22]

Awarded the Karl Marx Medal and smacked on the lips by East Germany leader Erich Honecker with the socialist fraternal kiss in 1979, Brezhnev is not fondly recalled as a pious man.

Besides his bushy eyebrows, the Secretary General was known for his penchant for medals, the length of his leadership of the U.S.S.R., and, most of all, the *Brezhnev Doctrine*—the Soviet Union's right to use military force to maintain the strict rule of the Communist Party in nearby socialist countries.

Force.

Once again, it was a word Marx and Engels deflected somewhat as taboo, but not one his Russian protégées were afraid to use. Lenin, Stalin, Khrushchev, and Brezhnev all mastered the application of force. Which—translated—meant inflicting any and all violence, terror, and military might necessary to ingrain the Communist agenda on its subjects.

Of the four Soviet tyrants, Brezhnev was perhaps known the least for unbridled force. But though his legacy for being ruthless did not rival his predecessors, he is known for perhaps one of the most notorious acts of bloodshed in history.

Leonid Brezhnev is accused of ordering the murder of Pope John Paul II. [23]

Following years of investigation, a 2006 report released by Italy's Mitrokhin—a governmental parliamentary commission—found that Soviet Premier Leonid Brezhnev asked the main intelligence directorate, or GRU, to eliminate the Polish-born pontiff. [24]

Brezhnev did so because of Pope John Paul II's passionate opposition to communism in Eastern Europe—a persistence of the Pope that annoyed Brezhnev to no end.

Upon release of their findings, Mitrokhin's head, Paola Guzzanti stated:

"This commission believes, beyond any reasonable doubt, that the heads of the Soviet Union took the initiative of eliminating Pope Karol Wojtyla, and they conveyed this decision to the GRU." [25]

With this discovery, Brezhnev enters into the greatest conundrum of the twentieth century: the ongoing fulfillment of the prophetic contents of the Secret of Fátima. [26]

The June 26, 2000, Vatican release of the third part of the Secret of Fátima strongly carried the interpretation—though not officially—that the children's vision of the bishop dressed in white, who is shot and killed by gunfire, represented the attempted assassination of John Paul II.

In lieu of this expounded opinion—given by both Cardinal Angelo Sodano,[27] the Secretary of State at Fátima on May 13, 2000, and by Cardinal Ratzinger [28] in the Vatican commentary, *The Message of Fatima*, on June 26—Brezhnev's place in the unfolding mystery of the Secret is, to a great degree, indirectly acknowledged by their words.

While Brezhnev's dark role in the fulfillment of the Secret of Fátima took time to arrive and then uncover, the same cannot be said in identifying the roles of his predecessors, beginning with Vladimir Lenin.

Unlike Brezhnev, the part of the main character in Russia's atheistic revolution has never been shrouded in mystery.

Quite the contrary.

In fact, without Lenin, the Virgin Mary may never had mentioned the "errors of Russia" at Fátima in the first place.

Perhaps, she might not have needed to come to Fátima at all.

CHAPTER TWELVE

VISAGES OF LUCIFER

*"Be not emulous of evil men, and desire not to be with them;
For their hearts plot violence, and their lips speak of foul play."*
— Prv 24:1-2

THE ARCHITECT.
No words better define Lenin.

Seen as the principle mastermind of the Bolshevik Revolution, the evil that the Virgin Mary foretold would begin in Russia—and spread throughout the world—appears to only have been able to come from a man evil enough to bring it forward.

The third of six children of a wealthy middle-class family, Vladimir Lenin was born Vladimir Volodya Ilyich Ulyanov on April 10, 1870, but would change his name in 1901 to Lenin—one of 160 aliases and countless pen names he used for the ten million words he would write in his lifetime.[1]

Baptized at Saint Nicholas Cathedral in Simbirsk a few days after he was born, Lenin grew up in a Christian home but was remembered as an extremely destructive child—one who openly confessed to misbehavior. He was, however, an outstanding student, extremely zealous in his studies, especially in one subject: religion.

But at the age of sixteen, his life suddenly took a downward turn away from God with the passing of his father. Becoming erratic and confrontational, Lenin shortly thereafter renounced his faith, a decision he would come to boast of:

"I broke sharply with all questions of religion. I took off my cross and threw it in the rubbish bin." [2]

Not long after, Lenin was hit with another tragedy.

A year past his father's death, his anarchist brother, Alexander—known as Sasha—was implicated in a plot to kill Tsar Alexander III. Tipped off, the police arrested Sasha, who was hung on May 8, 1887.

Traumatized by his brother's execution and wanting retribution—then further incensed after his university expelled him—Lenin slowly grew attracted to the ideas of his deceased sibling. Soon, he began meeting with a revolutionary cell organized by a militant socialist named Lazar Bogoraz.

Bogoraz desired to resurrect the People's Freedom Party—which Lenin fit the bill to help bring about. With this, social activism became his life. Leftist political organizations, demonstrations, arrests, and exiles characterized his efforts in the 1890s, as he inundated himself with the teachings of Karl Marx.

Over the next twenty years, Lenin relentlessly pursued his agenda.

He traveled throughout Russia and Europe, wrote and spoke on capitalism and imperialism, and called for an international civil war between the classes. To say the least, the maturing revolutionary became indefatigable in purpose.

Later, it became evident why. Lenin strived to change the future, motivated by his own contemptuous past and by occult and Gnostic ideas.

Peter Struve, a colleague of Lenin during the 1890s, identified the single most dominant element of the blossoming revolutionary's personality: incessant, unabated hatred. Others would add chronic anger, racism, and class envy, as well as a burning desire for revenge.

Vladimir Lenin, close associates concur, was capable of drawing on inexhaustible reserves of such emotional fuel in the pursuit of his mission. And his mission was abundantly clear to those around him: he hungered to bring down the government, the Tsar, and the Church in Russia.

Over time, his writings would show his contempt for the Church and religion was in total agreement with Karl Marx's own thinking:

"Religion is the opium of the people—this dictum by Marx is the cornerstone of the whole Marxist outlook on religion." [3]

Piggybacking on the tribulations of World War I, Lenin and his inner circle—with financial help from Freemasons in Europe and America and from the German Kaiser—seized control of Russia on October 25, 1917.

The following day, Lenin appeared undisguised in public for the first time in months to a thundering wave of cheers.

The moment the Masonic Marxist dreamed of had finally arrived.

Indeed, the evil foretold at Fátima was now identifiable, perfectly characterized in one menacing, villainous-looking man with a demonic disposition.

Lenin—whose chiseled goatee highlighted a countenance that seemed to harbor visages of Lucifer himself—would rightly forever become the ideal poster face of Soviet Communism. Without question, his sinister expression showcased a coldness inside that was the perfect home for the evil he would shower upon Russia—and eventually the world.

John Reed, an American journalist, wrote of Lenin's cold, dark, but unflappable appearance that historic October day in Petrograd:

> A short, stocky figure with a big head set down on his shoulders, bald and bulging. He had little eyes, a snobbish nose, a wide generous mouth, and a heavy chin; clean shaven now, but already beginning to bristle with the well-known beard of his past and future.
>
> Dressed in shabby clothes, his trousers much too long for him. Unimpressive to be the idol of the mob, yet loved and revered as perhaps few leaders in history have been.
>
> A strange popular leader—a leader purely by virtue of intellect; colorless, humorless, uncompromising, and detached, with picturesque idiosyncrasies—but with the power of explaining profound ideas in simple terms, of analyzing a concrete situation. And combined with shrewdness, the greatest intellectual audacity.[4]

That morning, waiting for the applause to die down, Lenin coolly commenced with the task at hand,

"We shall now proceed to construct the socialist order." [5]

And so it came to be.

The dawning despot immediately proceeded to call for private property to be transferred to the state's ownership. Then, on January 20, 1918, a decree proclaimed the separation of Church and state and suppression of all the Church's legal rights. And, to consolidate his authority, Lenin ordered the execution of anyone with ties to the former monarchy, including the entire family of Tsar Nicholas II.

This would be mere baby steps towards the regime's love affair with blood.

Over the next five years, to go with the Bolshevik's murderous tyranny of the Russian people, an ensuing civil war would bring perdition to hundreds of thousands across the country, serving as the formal introduction to Communism's one and only indisputable record of accomplishment: massive death.

And with all the death would come premeditated, systematic terror, eventually termed "Red Terror." Perhaps recalling Marx's 1849 vow, "When our turn comes, we shall not make excuses for the terror," [6] Lenin said at the time: "The way of terror is the only one open to us and we cannot avoid it. Do you imagine that without the brutal, uninhibited revolutionary terror, it would be possible for us to prevail?" [7]

Bolshevik terror took many forms, especially with the construction of concentration camps—a model system of imprisonment that caught the eye of Hitler—where enemies of the new regime perished by the tens of thousands.

Peasants, wealthy, soldiers, people of former influence—anyone who appeared capable of any opposition to the Bolsheviks—were erased without pity.[8]

Insufferably cold and calculating, Lenin insisted that terror was the only way "to give a lesson to the whole breed so that for several years, they do not even think anymore of any sort of resistance." [9]

Not long after the October Revolution, leftist organizations desiring to imitate the Russian revolt began popping up all over the map.

But this was no accident.

Marxist conjecture contained a strategic plan that was at work.

The errors of Russia were now on the move.

Many of these societies had been around for years. Fomented across Europe in the 1880s, a proliferation of Communist parties had been founded, all adhering in principle to the ideals of a classless society and collective ownership of property.

Once the Bolsheviks solidified power in Russia and assembled the Soviet Union, Lenin's dream of ushering in a worldwide Communist revolution took center stage. Anxious to revisit nations that failed to bring Marxist change, Lenin formulated a program to aid them. He also did so because he believed that the revolution in Russia would not survive the power of what he saw as Western imperialism.

"Anglo-French and American imperialism will inevitably strangle the independence and freedom of Russia," wrote Lenin, "unless world-wide socialist revolution, unless world–wide Bolshevism, conquers." [10]

Russia, in fact, did not exactly hold a soft spot in Lenin's heart. Worldwide revolution was for him the goal all along.

"I spit on Russia!" Lenin declared. "That's only one stage we have to pass through on our way to world revolution. We are going to tear the whole thing down. We shall destroy and smash everything…nothing will remain standing." [11]

Through the work of the Communist International—a party organ founded in 1919 and better known as the Commintern—financial aid and assistance for Communist parties throughout Europe was put in place.[12]

The Commintern identified those nations and peoples who were ripest for political uprisings, targeting underdeveloped societies or those especially stricken with ongoing poverty and noticeable internal instability. Consequently, either through political transition or by force of arms, the Bolsheviks were ready to assist these states.

By the early 1920s, the seeds were planted for the ascension of Marxist parties in Asia, Africa, and the Americas.

And while some would embrace adapted forms of Communism, they together shared in one undeniable truth: they were all the diseased fruit from the same poisonous tree: Vladimir Lenin.

CHAPTER THIRTEEN

THE SPREAD OF RED

*"Then the dragon became angry with the woman and went
off to wage war against the rest of her offspring, those who
keep God's commandments and bear witness to Jesus."*
—Rv 12:17

D EMENTED, DETERIORATED, AND A SHELL OF HIS FORMER SELF, BY
the beginning of 1924, Vladimir Lenin was all but finished.

The wily rebel had survived an assassination attempt and several
strokes. But by now, trapped in a body ravaged by syphilis, the failing leader could only stammer and mutter as he spent his fading days
grounded in a wheelchair, virtually motionless.[1]

In weeks, Lenin would be dead.

And so the stage was set.

The genocidal reign of Joseph Stalin was pulling out of the gate. And
if the Virgin of Fátima knew one compelling truth about the spread of
the errors of Russia, it was what lay ahead once this pariah ascended to
the pinnacle of totalitarian power.

Following in Lenin's footsteps—in more ways than the eye can see—
Stalin also felt a change in his name could do him some good.

A native of Gori, Georgia, Joseph Stalin was born Josif Vissarionovich
Dzhugashvili. To create a public persona as a true revolutionary, however, he changed his name to Stalin, which in Russian indicated to
others the image he wanted to convey: I am the man of steel. [2]

In less than a century, he would be the man of murder.

Lacking Lenin's demonic glare, or Brezhnev's gangster physiognomy, the diminutive Stalin—who stood barely 5'4"—possessed his own menacing air, accentuated by clusters of smallpox scars and a mustache that looked like a manicured paint brush.

Due to a deformed left arm and webbed left foot that together altered his gait, Stalin's presence did not always trigger immediate intimidation. Nevertheless, the savvy leader cunningly cultivated his innocuous image to his advantage, cleverly assuaging others to often underestimate him or his macabre intentions.

Abused as a youngster by children in his village, Stalin harbored a lifelong cruel streak for anyone who bothered him or failed to give him respect. As with Lenin— somewhat ironically—an interest in theology motivated him to study at the Georgian Orthodox Seminary in Tbilisi.[3]

But the allure faded as he grew more enamored with the philosophers and radicals of the age. His favorites? The subversives who preached social revolution, three fellows named Karl Marx, Friedrich Engels, and Vladimir Lenin.

Nurtured on their tendentious theories of social transformation, the short-in-stature Stalin would show that he was not short in will. Soon turning his philosophic interests into action, the blossoming anarchist began to devote all his energy to leftist movements, becoming battle-tested in the street warfare of a rebel rouser.

And, as time went by, he perfected his craft.

Returning from exile in Siberia in 1905, as a result of the first of many arrests, Stalin—though never an orator like Lenin or an intellectual like Trotsky—grew into an engaging activist and a ruthless organizer.

Forever holding meetings, publishing pamphlets, and coordinating protests, strikes, and demonstrations, Stalin, like Lenin, assimilated unassumingly into his emerging destiny.

As he grew in confidence and became increasingly brazen, nothing for the cause was too much for Stalin to take on. A man of many talents—and few inhibitions—he went so far as to provide a helping hand with robberies, kidnappings, extortion, and bank heists to aid in easing the Bolshevik's struggling finances.

The now-blossoming anarchist even earned a moment of fame after being identified in the notorious June 26, 1907, Tiflis Bank Robbery—a much-publicized day of disrepute for Stalin and his cronies. The prominent heist resulted in several deaths and a cache of 250,000 rubles (three million dollars today).[4]

In 1917, Stalin was released once more from exile and returned to Petrograd. There, he became involved in the first phase of the October Revolution, helping to establish the new order and implement provisional rule.

With Lenin's endorsement, the self-proclaimed man of steel—with the heart of stone—was selected by the Bolshevik Central Committee to be part of a four-man "Chetverka", along with Lenin, Trotsky, and Sverdlov. Together, the council was to lead the infant government forward. This post was soon followed by his appointment as the People's Commissar for Nationalities' Affairs.

By the early 1920s, after serving in a military capacity in the post-revolution Russian Civil War and the Polish-Soviet War, the veteran activist undertook the steps necessary to position himself within the Communist Party to become the undisputed heir to Lenin.

He was now, history would show, at the crossroad of his infamy.

Moving to consolidate his dictatorial power after Lenin died on January 21, 1924, Stalin separated, then eradicated all opposition.

Over the next two decades, the mendacious leader saw to the exile, execution, or murder of all the big names of the October Revolution: Trotsky, Kamenev, Bukharin, and Zinoviev. He was even suspected to have had poisoned Lenin's widow, Nadezhda Krupskaya.

Now, ever more methodically, the cunning First Secretary of the Communist Party began to lay down the lines of a résumé that would one day establish him as the most dreaded tyrant in the history of the world.

So dreaded was Stalin that the renowned Russian author and Soviet dissident, Aleksandr Solzhenitsyn, tells of a speech made by Stalin at which all the listeners were afraid to be the first person to stop clapping:

"All looked around despairingly and clapped on, sweat standing out on their foreheads, exhaustion stealing over them," wrote Sozhenitsyn.

It's also a résumé that reads that Stalin—like Marx and Lenin—was involved with the occult. He is said to have entered into trances and communicated with spirits and demons, and liked to dabble in magic and the astral world. [5]

While working under Stalin often meant death for party comrades, living under his rule would come to mean the same for everyday folk.

Seeking to turn Communist rhetoric into viable action, Stalin moved to institute a policy that transferred citizens from the countryside into the city. This would allow—experimental Bolshevik theory held—the Soviet Union to better industrialize its economy and to collectivize its agriculture. Tragically, and deliberately, it also incubated a deadly famine; five million perished, mostly by starvation.

Growing obsessively paranoid by the 1930s, Stalin unleashed next what came to be known as the "Great Terror." Consumed by a mounting fear of betrayal, the tyrant conducted a vast cleansing of the enemies of the working class. This purge saw an estimated 750,000 Communist Party members and military personnel executed.

It also caused the exile of 3 million to the Gulags—forced labor camps—eventually adding many more to the death tolls. As a result of Stalin's maniacal policies, estimates range from 10 to 14 million people died in the Soviet Union during this period.

The "errors of Russia"—spread ever so profusely under Stalin—were now becoming quite visible and undeniable. Little by little, word was leaking out that something ungodly was unfolding in the country.

And the end was nowhere in sight.

Over the next decade, countless numbers would succumb in the Soviet Union under Stalin. Just as alarming, though, would be the unfurling of communism throughout the world under his stewardship by way of the Soviet Communist Party's Commintern.

This began with Russia's neighbors.

To aid an uprising against the Chinese, who ruled Mongolia, the Soviets invaded the country in 1921. By 1924, a new Marxist government was in place: The Mongolian People's Republic.

During this same period, due to the demand generated by the Russian revolution, the Commintern began to support fledging Communist groups across Europe.

In theory, the Commintern was designed to strike while the iron was hot—and this is exactly what it did. The Bolsheviks were especially keen on a struggling Germany, where World War I sanctions and reparations invited insurgencies across the nation.

In the region of Bavaria, a Communist uprising grabbed control and created the Bavarian Soviet Republic. The revolt, however, didn't succeed, as it was put down by a right-wing paramilitary organization called the Freikorps.

In Hungary, a similar rebellion took place in 1919. This time, the Communists—led by the infamous Bela Kun—became part of a coalition government. Neighboring Romania experienced its own problems, too. Again, however, the changes were short lived, as the rebel leaders ended up executed or on the run.

Two years later, in northern Italy, another ambitious communist effort would be successfully put down by the government, as would one in Bulgaria in 1923. By then, though, it was becoming undeniable: Communist ambition was brewing everywhere.

Across Europe, attempted Communist insurrections became a steady part of life during the economically troubled 1930s. Most of these dalliances were products of a crafty Russian agitator—the Kremlin's Grigory Zinoviev, who had been one of only two members of the Bolshevik Central Committee to vote against armed revolt in 1917, based on his entirely orthodox Marxist views.[6]

Through shadow organizations such as the *Profintern* (trade unions), *Krestintern* (peasants), *Sportintern* (organized sports), and the *International Red Aid* (humanitarian aid), Zinoviev engineered a sizeable amount of strife in many countries.

Over time, under his tutelage, umbrella groups would penetrate every sector of a vulnerable nation's society. He was especially active through *The Young Communist International*—the youth branch of the Commintern—for in the young, Communism preached, "lay the future."

Zinoviev's efforts weren't restricted to Europe.

In Asia, the *Profintern* established the Pan-Pacific Trade Union Secretariat (PPTUS). This was one of many Asian front groups that successfully organized communist trade unions in Japan, China, Philippines, Korea, New Zealand, Vietnam, and Australia.

By the late 1930s, the Commintern invested in another approach. It now began to aggressively operate through what was called *The Popular Front Policy*. This was an attempt to bring greater Socialist-Communist collaboration with other activist groups in Europe, the United Kingdom, and the United States.

In essence, the Popular Front strategy was viewed as a more politically expedient tactic. It aimed to appear compatible with capitalism in order to gain easier participation through coalitions in governments.

In truth, however, the overthrow of capitalism remained unchanged. Marxism—as it would continue to show—was proving to be a beast with many heads.

And that it remained.

Through whatever means it could muster, the Red Storm pressed on. Communism, as its leadership never denied, was rapidly moving towards building a new world—an unprecedented atheistic, tyrannical civilization—far beyond anything the outside world imagined that first, cold October day in Petrograd in 1917.

By 1945, dozens of countries were experiencing Communist uprisings or succumbing to insurrections, leading many to believe there would be no end to "the spread of Red."

In the convent of the Dorothean Sisters at Vilar, near Porto in Spain, the humble voice of the prophet who first announced the coming of this scourge went on record to agree: there would be no end coming to the deadly march of Communism that was underway.

Interviewed on July 15, 1946, by one of the most illustrious of contemporary historians, William Thomas Walsh, Sister Lúcia spoke for the first time directly to the world through an outside voice that carried immense respect and credibility.

Born in Waterbury, Connecticut, and educated down the road at Yale, Walsh was known as one of the most gifted writers and intellectuals of the era. In rapid succession, the noted man of letters had generated novels, plays, biographies, and poetry that repeatedly generated prestigious awards for literary excellence.

Upon hearing the story of Fátima, the renowned author set aside all his other works to visit Portugal to investigate the 1917 visions. His book, *Our Lady of Fatima*, was published in 1947 and soon became recognized as the single most factor in drawing the attention of millions almost overnight to the story of the apparitions.[7]

As he witnessed Eastern Europe being taken over after World War II by Stalin and saw Communism—the errors of Russia—progressing everywhere, Walsh decided during his private audience to pose a pressing question to Fátima's cloistered surviving voice concerning the unceasing spread of the cancerous ideology. [8]

"Does this mean, in your opinion," Professor Walsh inquired of Lúcia, "that every country, without exception, will be overcome by Communism?"

"Yes," Lúcia answered without hesitation.

"Did Our Lady ever say anything to you about the United States of America?"

"No," replied Lúcia, but with an amused smile that caused Walsh to believe that perhaps the United States was not so important in the general scheme of things as he imagined.

Lúcia then made it clear to Walsh that a remedy was still available:

"What Our Lady wants is that the Pope and all the bishops in the world shall consecrate Russia to her Immaculate Heart on one special day. If this is done, she will convert Russia and there will be peace. If this is not done, the errors of Russia will spread through every country in the world." [9]

The errors of Russia continued to spread.

Prior to 1945, Communism existed primarily in the countries that came to form the Soviet Union. They were, in 1922, the original four republics within the Tsar's former empire: The Russian and Transcaucasian Soviet Federated Socialist Republics and the Ukrainian and Belorussian Soviet Socialist Republics.

Over the years, additional Soviet republics were established: The Turkmen and Uzbek Soviet Socialist Republics in 1924; the Tadzhik Soviet Socialist Republic in 1929; and the Kazakh and Kirgiz Soviet Socialist Republics in 1936.

In that same year, the Transcaucasian Republic dissolved, and its territory separated into three new republics: Armenia, Azerbaijan, and the Georgia Soviet Socialist Republic.

In 1940, the Karelo-Finnish, Moldavian, Estonian, Latvian, and Lithuanian Soviet Socialist Republics were formed. And finally, in 1956, the Karelo-Finnish Soviet Socialist Republic became autonomous. In all, a total of fifteen republics made up the early Soviet Union.

After World War II, Stalin engineered possession of Eastern Europe, subsequently adding Poland in 1945, as well as Bulgaria, Yugoslavia, and Albania in 1946, Czechoslovakia and Romania in 1948, and Hungary and East Germany in 1949 to the Soviet sphere.

These nations became known as the Eastern Bloc. Thus, by 1950, an impressive collection of puppet allies and comrade states were in Stalin's stable.

But Stalin's greatest success would be his role in securing the world's most populated nation into the Communist fold: China.

Some argue that Stalin did not help Mao Tse-Tung substantially with encouraging Communism to take hold in China.

Nothing could be further from the truth.

During a presentation to the Stalin Society on October 18, 2009—in commemoration of the 60th anniversary of the People's Republic of China and the 130th anniversary of Stalin's birth—the Chairman of the Marxist-Leninist Communist Party of Great Britain, Harpal Brar, quoted Mao himself in lifting the veil on Stalin's involvement:

> As you all know, Marx is dead and so are Engels and Lenin. Had there been no Stalin, who would there be to give directions? But having him—this is really a blessing. Now there exist in the world a Soviet Union, a Communist party and also a Stalin. Thus, the affairs of the world can go well. We must hail him, we must support him, and we must learn from him… We must learn from him in two respects: his theory and his works.[10]

Barr then cited words from Mao's own *Selected Works*, to ensure there could be no doubt:

> The Soviet Union alone has helped China with its aviation and supplies…Stalin is the true friend of the cause of liberation of the Chinese people. No attempt to sow dissention, no lies and calumnies, can affect the Chinese people's whole hearted love and respect for Stalin and our genuine friendship for the Soviet Union.[11]

In retrospect, Mao's words concerning Stalin were no small compliment.

Coming from the only person believed to have exceeded Stalin in total human carnage in all of history, the founder of Red China certainly knew who deserved credit for his own unholy success.

Mao Tse-Tung, according to multiple published sources, is credited with overseeing the death of as many as 90 million people, a deed that stands alone in all of human history.

And while this feat leapfrogged him over his mentor, it also generously lends more merit to the ignoble legacy of his beloved ally and "true friend," Joseph Stalin.

China did not succumb to Communism until 1949.

By then, Communism had already moved into Thailand in1942, Vietnam in 1945, and Korea in 1948. Cambodia and Laos would fall in 1976, after South Vietnam collapsed, while Communist insurgencies arose in Burma, Malaysia, and Indochina.

The Southern and Western hemispheres were next to see the spread of Red.

The Cold War saw Communism move into South Yemen and pockets of the Middle East in 1967 and then throughout Africa, with governments set up in the Republic of the Congo in 1970, Ethiopia in 1974, and Somalia in 1976. Likewise, Communists came to power in the former Portuguese colonies of Angola and Mozambique after civil wars in 1975. In Africa, over the years, some twenty-six movements are recorded.

In the West, Fidel Castro's Cuban revolution arrived in 1959, while a litany of other Central American nations found themselves in sometimes decade long confrontations with Communism. Nicaragua, El Salvador, Guatemala, and Honduras all witnessed guerrilla movements spearheaded by Marxist revolutionary groups, as would Grenada and Venezuela.

By the 1970s, the steady march of Communism—now known in the West as *Soviet Expansionism*—was understood to be a worldwide juggernaut, as over one third of the world's people were living under some form of Marxism.

This became a statistic some Christians saw pointing to Chapter 12 of *The Book of Revelation*: "Its [The Red Dragon] tail swept away a third of the stars in the sky and hurled them down on earth." [12]

Communism's bloody methods were no secret by then, either.

Consequently, this reality aroused strong resistances and all-out wars in many nations that were determined to fight to escape its grasp.

"Better Dead than Red" became more than just a slogan—especially for the persecuted Catholic Church and millions of its faithful.

CHAPTER FOURTEEN

KILLING GOD

"Who will separate us from the love of Christ?
Will anguish, or distress, or persecution, or
famine, or nakedness, or peril or the sword?"
—Rom 8: 35

PERSECUTION.

The Virgin Mary's prophecies at Fátima foretold not just the spread of the errors of Russia, but of the "persecutions" destined to come with it.

Mary even used the word twice in the second part of the Secret.

And—to no surprise—it would be the nefarious Stalin who would most ensure that this prophecy would come to pass.

Nurtured well in Marxist thought, if there was one thing Stalin understood, it was the need to bury religion. Moreover, the maniacal autocrat believed this effort was paramount if the so-called "Peoples' Revolution" was to succeed.

To Stalin, it was clear: Communism would not triumph in this world if the masses continued to take their lead from a deity in another. For him, therefore, the goal was set: total eradication of religion, especially Christianity.

And to bring this transformation, as with the revolution itself, there would be a need for force—massive, ruthless, and brutal force—just as Lenin initiated against all religion when the Bolsheviks first seized control of Russia in 1917.

Like Karl Marx, Vladimir Lenin voiced his profound hatred of God and religion.

"Any religious ideas, any idea of any God at all, any flirtation even with a God," Lenin wrote in a November 13, 1913, letter to Maxim Gorky, "is the most inexpressible foulness…the most dangerous infection." [1]

As occurred in Portugal in 1910, Lenin moved quickly in 1918 to implement a policy of separation of Church and state. In essence, it was a declaration of war by the Bolsheviks on religion—one that would see the most unparalleled persecution of religion in history.

The new government immediately demanded all Church property—convents, churches, monasteries, and any possessions of value—be nationalized. Next, all priests, nuns, brothers, monks, and pious laity were to be shuffled off to prisons, psychiatric wards, or corrective labor camps. And for many, if deemed an enemy of the state, the Gulag camps became their permanent home.

Anatoly Lunacharsky, Lenin's first minister of education, concurred with Lenin's thinking and went a step further. If the revolution was to truly succeed, it would be necessary to "kill God." [2]

In 1922, The eminent Cardinal Joseph Mercier published the first report on the vast persecution taking place in Russia, especially noting the eradication of the religious:

> Statistics for the victims of the persecution are frightening. Since November 1917, 260,000 simple soldier prisoners and 54,000 officers; 18,000 land proprietors; 35,500 'intellectuals'; 192,000 workers; 815,000 peasants; 28 bishops; and 1,215 priests were put to death.
>
> To these last figures, we must add an as yet unknown number of priests of both Orthodox and Catholic who were condemned and executed these last months for refusing to cooperate with the decree ordering the confiscation of holy objects. [3]

This was only the beginning.

Stalin, now becoming known as the "colossus of terror," quickly reinforced both Lenin's and Lunacharsky's thinking with even bolder action.

"A fight to the death must be declared on religion," declared Nikolai Bukharin, the founding editor of *Pravda* and one of Stalin's chief henchmen. The government, he preached, "needed to take on religion at the tip of the bayonet." [4]

By 1928, a new wave of persecution was underway, prohibiting any religious activity. This meant no trace of religion was permitted in public. No secret, underground worship either, as those caught suffered even more dire consequences.

Then, in April of 1929, the Sixteenth Soviet Party Congress decided on a second general purge, passing a law that led to another outbreak of persecutions. The new law brought with it the creation and distribution of propaganda films and museums to spread antireligious fervor, along with the further destruction of religious monuments and places of worship.

Several months later, on August 27, 1929, the "Continuous Week" was introduced, suppressing Sunday as the day of worship. There would also be more killing. From 1929 to 1933, and estimated 15 million perished by persecution, especially a class of citizens known as the Kulaks.[5]

Stalin especially turned up the heat on the Russian Orthodox Church, which held the greatest number of the faithful. Members of the community had long suspected what was coming. As far back as January 1918, only months into the revolution, the Church's head—Patriarch Tikhon of Moscow—had labeled the Bolsheviks "the monsters of the human race," [6] and he excommunicated all who supported the revolution.[7]*

Ten months later, in November 1919, Tikhon delivered an appeal to Europe:

---

*   Russian Orthodox Patriarch Tikhon took his monastic vows at the Pskov Seminary and Theological Academy in St. Petersburg in 1891. At that time he adopted the name Tikhon in honor of St. Tikhon of Zadonsk. His real name was Vasily Ivanovich Bellavin.

Bishops, priests, monks and nuns, are shot down en masse under the vague pretext of "counter-revolution." Through a refinement of cruelty, the supreme consolation of the Sacraments is refused them, while their relatives cannot obtain a Christian burial for their bodies.[8]

By 1932, Stalin's fresh assault on the Orthodox had more than validated Tikhon's opening alarm. But even more was to come. The Communist Party's "Society of the Godless" [9]—an organization dedicated to purging any religion remaining in Russia—detailed on May 15 its five-year plan:

"Not a single house of prayer shall remain in the territory of the U.S.S.R., and the very concept of God must be banished from the Soviet Union as a survival of the Middle Ages and an instrument for the oppression of the working masses." [10]

The five-year plan was aggressively implemented. In 1937 alone, thousands of Orthodox priests were shot.[11] Those who survived were sent off to prison. With the clerical carnage also came the destruction of more houses of worship. To erase God in the Soviet Union meant to erase all of Him, especially any physical presence.

Between 1927 and 1940, the number of Orthodox churches in Russia fell from 29,584 to less than 500.[12] All Orthodox schools were also closed. By the 1930s, any churches and schools that were not wrecked or burned to the ground were converted to museums. Religious publications were expressly prohibited.

Catholicism—no longer even considered a religion by the state but redefined as a "religious association" —felt the same torch. By 1926, no Catholic bishops remained in the country.[13]

By the end of the 1930s, there were only two functioning Catholic churches left in Russia out of the 1,200 that had existed in 1918— The Church of Saint Louis in Moscow and Our Lady of Lourdes in St. Petersburg.[14]

But all of this was still not enough for the Bolsheviks.

Stalin's agenda was about more than just murdering the religious and closing churches. Rather, it was a two-pronged attack—the abolition of religion and the propagation of atheism.

The Bolsheviks desired to sanitize the nation of any faith, something never undertaken before in such a methodical manner. They aimed not to just kill believers and their spiritual houses—but to kill "belief" itself.

It was not just atheism, wrote Aleksandr Solzhenitsyn, but "a ferocious atheism." [15] Thus, conversion to atheism became a national movement.

All religious teaching to minors was outlawed. In the public schools, children were even encouraged to report their parents to the authorities if they witnessed the practice of religion at home.

By 1932, the Society of the Godless—also known as the League of Militant Atheists—was now 5.6 million strong. It began recruiting "atheistic missionaries" to canvas the Soviet Union. Their motto: "Struggle against Religion is a Struggle for Socialism." Its journal, *The Bezbojnik* (The Godless) organized conferences and blasphemous demonstrations.[16]

Stalin's successor, Nikita Khrushchev, would go so far as to revoke the legal rights of parents to teach religion to their children. A decade later, university students were required to take a special course: "Fundamentals of Scientific Atheism."

Perhaps the epitome of all of this came in 1961 when Khrushchev promised that in ten years he would "present the last Christian in the U.S.S.R. on television for all to see." [17]

World War II somewhat slowed the push to eradicate Christianity in the Soviet Union. But the effort immediately restarted with the surrender of Germany. This time, it was with a different focus.

Having virtually eliminated the Orthodox and Catholic Churches in Russia, the Soviets turned their full attention to the Catholic Church in Ukraine. In 1946, the Eastern Rite was formally disbanded, with its property confiscated or destroyed. Eighteen bishops were then executed, with the remaining whisked away to Siberian forced-labor camps.

One man witnessed it all—and lived to write about it.

Josyp Terelya, a Catholic underground activist who survived twenty years in the Gulag, detailed in his and Michael Brown's book, *Witness*, how millions bore the brunt of the Soviet war on God in Ukraine after World War II.[18]

Terelya's father, a staunch Communist, kept the party's statistics in the Carpathian region. At the end of World War II, there were an estimated 700,000 Eastern Rite Catholics, 459 churches and chapels, 281 parishes, and 359 priests in the region.[19]

Overall, before 1945, the Ukrainian Church held 4 million faithful and 2,772 parishes nationwide.[20] By the 1960s, the Church was completely decimated. No churches remained open, and all religious services were held in secret, usually in the woods.[21]

Altogether in Ukraine, wrote Terelya, more than 1,000 churches were destroyed, with millions incarcerated or killed for the faith—usually disappearing without a trace.[22] Perhaps as well as anyone, Terelya captured in his book the brutality of the Communist assault on religion in the U.S.S.R.:

> The arrests and trials did not stop. By night, they would haul off the priests, and the priests would never be seen again. I ran into some of them later, in the bottomless pit of the Soviet prison system. The most visible manifestation of their extermination was the closure or outright destruction of Church buildings. Perhaps never before in history has destruction or transferal of Christian edifices occurred on such a massive scale…
>
> Church steeples were toppled, artwork pillaged, icons ruined, and bells were smashed—not just in Ukraine but throughout the Soviet Union. Picture in your mind a wrecking crane knocking the cross off the top of a church. Picture a baroque building collapsing into a heap of dust. Picture the authorities clamping chains and padlocks across the front doors…
>
> Catholicism was torn down all around me. Worshippers had to hide their prayer like a criminal hides his smuggling… The struggle between the Church and the Communists was a never ending one. [23]

After World War II, the purging of God in Eastern Europe mirrored the tactics of the Soviet Union, and often went further.

It was a period of great persecution for the Church in the East, one in which Pope Pius XII was led in his 1951 Christmas address to coin the term, the "Church of Silence", which reflected how the Christian communities there saw "their hands bound and their lips closed."

In Romania and Bulgaria, the Orthodox Church suffered bloody persecutions of the clergy and the faithful. In Bulgaria, many Catholics were considered spies and arrested. Cardinal József Mindszenty was tortured so badly in Hungary, he became unintelligible.

In Czechoslovakia, the authorities proceeded somewhat differently. The Communists took over the Church, discharging priests to work camps and imprisoning most of the bishops. Over a six-year period, they held trials for public view—with execution usually the sentence.

The Communists attempted to run the Church in Poland, too, arresting Cardinal Stefan Wyszyński and his secretary, Father Antoni Baraniak. The Cardinal's secretary was interrogated 145 times over two years. Although not murdered, Father Baraniak had his fingernails pulled out, his flesh burned, and his kidneys battered—all in a failed effort to have him testify against Wyszyński. [24]

In Albania, all religious practice was suspended. God, the Communists declared, "did not exist." In 1967, the government went so far as to impose a ban on every religion in the nation, making Albania the first and only constitutionally atheist state. Every church and mosque in the country was closed—a total of 2,500 altogether—while 500,000 people were imprisoned, of which 100,000 died.[25] People still prayed, some later revealed, "under the covers."

Around the world, in every nation where the Communists seized control, it was the same. Persecution reigned, just as the Virgin of Fátima foretold—and not just with Christians. Communism was merciless on all faiths, persecuting followers of Islam, Buddhism, Judaism, and any religion that recognized a higher power.

The first Premier of the People's Republic of China, Chou En-Lai, promulgated the Communist Party's feelings in his country not long after the 1949 revolution. "We Communists are atheists," declared Mao's well-known right-hand man,[26] who spent decades keeping his word on this matter.

In China, as in the Soviet Union, temples, churches, and monasteries were converted into archives of the state, used then for museums, hospitals, schools, and insane asylums.

Buddhism, Islam, and Christianity were all ruthlessly oppressed, seen as vehicles for foreign ideas and misguided loyalties attempting to permeate Chinese society. Priests, monks, and practitioners of every faith were arrested, exiled, killed, or forced to renounce their beliefs. Succeeding generations were then taught to reject religion and learn, as in the Soviet Union, "scientific atheism." [27]

After Mikhail Gorbachev became the last head of the Soviet Union, a special commission was assembled to investigate the crimes committed under the Communist regime, including those against religion.

Headed by Alexander Yakovlev, the investigative body found about 200,000 religious of various denominations had been murdered, and an additional 300,000 arrested. The commission documented the destruction of 40,000 churches.[28]

The Marxist-Leninist doctrine of militant persecution was an historical assault on religion of all creeds. But it desired, most of all, to obliterate Christianity.

In retrospect, the Virgin Mary's prophecy at Fátima concerning Russia was worded in the gentlest of ways. Mary, it can be seen, was warning not exactly of the spread of communism but the consequences: massive death, persecution, destruction, and the worst consequence of all—mandated or acquired atheism.

Jesus taught to fear those who can kill the body and the soul.[29] Communism—unlike anything before in the history of the world— was clearly out to destroy both, exactly as Christ's words forewarned.

Thus, by 1981, not a country under its grip escaped this effort.

One Communist nation was different, though.

In Yugoslavia, there emerged a seemingly more open and independent system. Unlike the other Eastern European nations that walked carefully in line with Moscow under fear of its power, Yugoslavia seemed almost defiant to the Kremlin.

Its brand of totalitarianism, under an autocrat named Tito, permitted a looser economic society and other cultural oddities that, for a Communist state, were unheard of in the age of Joseph Stalin.

Historians agree, Yugoslavia experienced a different style of Communism.[30]

Perhaps, though, it was just the right place—the perfect climate—for a heavenly visitor.

Karl Marx

Vladimir Lenin

Joseph Stalin

Photo Credit: John Jabez Mayal, International Institute of Social History

Photo Credit: Pavel Semyonovich Zhukov

Photo Credit: Public Domain of Russia

Atheism fueled the efforts of Marx, Lenin and Stalin. All had occult ties and expressed extreme anger and hatred towards religion.

Russian Tsar Nicholas II and the Romanov family were executed by the Communists on July 17, 1918. On July 17, 1998, the 80th anniversary of their murder, the family's remains were reburied in an official ceremony in St. Petersburg.

Photo Credit: Boasson and Eggler, St. Petersburg. (U.S. Public Domain)

Mao Tse Tung

Photo Credit: China Public Domain

Josip Broz (Marshall Tito)

Photo Credit : Slavic Wiki.com

Aleksandr Solzhenitsyn

Photo Credit: Mikhail Eustafiev

Dr. Thomas Petrisko with former Soviet dissident Josyp Terelya in 1994 at the chapel in Hrushiv in Ukraine. Josyp Terelya spent twenty years in the Soviet Gulag. Over one half million people are reported to have seen Mary above this chapel in Hrushiv.

Photo Credit: Thomas W. Petrisko

CHAPTER FIFTEEN

ENEMY OF THE STATE

*"Blessed are you when they insult you and persecute you and
utter every kind of evil against you falsely because of me."*
— Mt 5:11

JUNE 25, 1981, BEGAN NO DIFFERENT THAN ANY OTHER DAY IN
Medjugorje.

The six visionaries—unaware of their new status—retained their
morning schedules; they fed the animals, tackled the tobacco fields,
and squeezed in any errands requested by their folks.[1]

After their chores, Vicka and Milka's sister, Marija, got a ride into
Čitluk with a neighbor, Marinko Ivanković. There, the girls caught a
bus into Mostar to attend summer school.[2] Nothing new. Nothing out
of the ordinary. It was a typical summer day in Herzegovina.

But as the late morning and early afternoon unfolded, the ongoing
reactions from family members, friends, and neighbors mounted on
their collective psyche.

Soon, the kids began to sense that it was not a typical day. People
were staring; they overheard teasing and gossiping; and the worry on
their families' faces was evident.[3]

No, it was not a normal day.

And, unbeknownst at the time, most of them would never experience a normal day in their lives again.

But that was a reality not yet fathomed, any more than they could
have imagined what had unfolded over the previous twenty-four hours.

Gradually, as the day moved on, the children's thoughts trended away from their problems and towards a mutual vanishing point: the inviting allure of Podbrdo that evening and the possibility of a second encounter with the radiant lady.

"We dreamt about it and talked about it. Ivanka, Mirjana and I agreed that we would again go to the site at about the same time of day. If it really is Our Lady, perhaps she will come again," recalled Vicka.[4]

Vicka remembered Ivanka suggested they test their courage and see what fate may hold. The resilient teenager argued that if they saw the vision again it would be "good." If not, the whole affair would be over, "quieting the ridicule." [5] The three agreed. But something more, something strange was at work, recalled Mirjana.[6]

The youngsters confessed to sensing an "inner urge" to return to the rocky hillside, as if something was mysteriously pulling them there beyond their control. To each, it was like a divine calling that, paired with their reasoning, began to mount throughout the day.

Whatever it was, it was contagious, for they all reported to experience it.

"I was terrified! But the next day around the same time we felt the desire to go to the same place. I felt in my heart that I must go back. The others felt the same way too. We just all…felt an immense desire to go back to that place," explained Mirjana. It was something within, she would write years later, that was too strong for her to ignore.[7]

Ivan Dragićević spoke of it too. Although the teenage boy scampered off Podbrdo the first day, he was back on board by the next afternoon. Rattled for sure, Ivan reassumed his quiet, reserved nature, admitting only to experiencing a great shock the day before.[8] But something inside of him beckoned a return to the hill—something he couldn't fight.

Even little Milka, already prohibited to return by her mother, felt the urge to go back. She later confessed to feeling almost drawn to the hill, as if being innately summoned in her soul to once again gaze upon the beautiful lady in light. [9]

Of all the visionaries, however, it seems Mirjana Dragićević struggled the most with the decision to go back.

The teenage girl wanted to return and wasn't fretting over what people thought, though, much like Lúcia at Fátima,* she had been teased unmercifully all day long by some boys who threatened to "climb Podbrdo and catch the Virgin."[10]

Without any doubt, Mirjana said she knew to follow her heart. But she was unable to sleep at all that first night and still trembled with fear the next day. It was a feeling of dread that wouldn't lift.

Her uncle and aunt offered no resistance to her returning on the second day, and said they would come too.[11] Her grandmother was also supportive, advising Mirjana to step up her prayers if she hoped to find peace—and if she hoped to once again be in the presence of the Madonna.

And so the day progressed, with the stage for the coming evening beginning to take shape. And although Ivan Ivanković and Milka Pavlović would not return to Mt. Podbrdo that evening, two other youngsters would providentially replace them: Marija Pavlović, fifteen, the older sister of Milka, and a little ten-year-old boy named Jacov Čolo, who learned about the celestial visitation from Mirjana, his cousin.

Tall and quite thin at the time, Marija Pavlović's soft brown eyes and childlike expression caused her to radiate a joyful, honest, and trusting simplicity. When she smiled, dimples extended more visibly her warmth in a calm, captivating way.

Marija seemed to possess, some would come to write, a spotless heart.

Born on April 1, 1965, Marija entered a family that was very poor. Her father, Philip, a farmer, and her mother, Iva, raised six children and struggled to make ends meet.

Marija's three brothers, Pero, Andrew, and Ante, were working in Germany at the onset of the apparitions. Her older sister, Ruzica, was already married, while Milka attended the local grade school.

---

*   "Look Lúcia, there's Our Lady on the roof." This was how a group of boys taunted Lúcia after the second apparition at Fátima on June 13, 1917.

Before the visions, Marija aspired to become a florist,[12] although she was at the time finishing her apprenticeship as a hairdresser in Mostar.[13] Of all the visionaries, she was considered the most religious, possessing a pious personality that reflected her deep spirituality, prayerfulness, and humility.[14]

A friend who knew Marija well at the time described her as "just beautiful."[15] Not surprisingly, after the apparitions began, she was the first to say she wanted to become a nun.[16]

Upon hearing about her sister Milka's experience, Marija almost immediately confessed to secretly festering a strong desire to also see the Madonna.[17]

Her teasing of Milka on the first night was meant to be playful, she would insist afterwards, confiding how she certainly meant no harm.[18]

Jacov Čolo—whose first name in Croatian means "James"—was only ten years old when the visions began.

Born on May 6, 1971, Jacov was said to be a typical little boy of his age, enjoying pop music and football.[19] Those who knew Jacov best say he was always very private, shy, and gracious, and not a bad student.

Through the early days of the apparitions, Jacov quickly revealed his high intelligence, a clever wit during stressful times, and his firmness of faith—although his spiritual side sometimes collided with his energetic, restless youthfulness. Often, it was hard for him to stay still for great lengths of time, especially during the often three-hour prayer sessions.

Jacov was the only child of Ante, a migrant worker in Austria who parted the family when his son was eight years old.[20] The young boy was said to live in great poverty with his mother, Jaka, who was afflicted with illnesses. [21]

When he was twelve, two years after the apparitions began, his mother passed away, [22] and Jacov went to live with his uncle Philip and Aunt Iva, Marija and Milka's parents.

Once informed by his cousin Mirjana of the heavenly vision, Jacov begged to come along on the second day. Mirjana remembers that when Jacov first heard that she had seen the Blessed Mother, he said that he, too, would desire to see her more than anything else in the world.[23]

The fact that Jacov emerged as a visionary through Mirjana begins to reveal the critical role she—perhaps in a different way than any of the five others—plays in the events at Medjugorje.

From the beginning of the apparitions through the decades that followed—to what is foretold to come in the future—none of the six is revealed to be a more centralized character than Mirjana Dragićević. [24]

The second of the children to see the Virgin, she would become the first to receive all the hidden prophecies—known as the "Ten Secrets"—and the first to no longer experience daily apparitions. Her final daily apparition, which lasted forty-five minutes, occurred on December 25, 1982. [25]

It is also to be through Mirjana—and a priest of her choice—that the Ten Secrets will someday be announced one by one to the world. [26]

Like Lúcia at Fátima—who she shares many similarities with including the same month of birth, March—she will remain the hub of the wheel at Medjugorje, central to the story in countless ways as time moves forward.

Mirjana will also, like Lúcia, reveal a terrifying experience with Satan.

The only of the six visionaries to release a book on her personal experiences surrounding the visions, Mirjana's 2016 memoir details the many early sufferings of the visionaries, along with the nightmarish ordeals she and her family experienced living in the topsy-turvy world of Yugoslavia in the early 1980s.

It was a time when—and a place where—the ghosts of World War II still lingered in countless ways. [27]

After heavy bombing by the Axis powers in the early years of World War II, Yugoslavia surrendered to Germany and Italy in April of 1941.

The country was then divided amongst its member states, with the largest area becoming the newly created "Independent State of Croatia." This entity included Croatia, Slovenia, parts of Dalmatia, and all of Bosnia and Herzegovina. It was also subdivided by a southeast to northwest line that created German and Italian zones of occupation.

For the most part, the Germans and Italians ran the show, supported by a Croatian nationalist paramilitary group called the Ustasi. This group was led by a man named Ante Pavelić, an extremist who master-minded the October 9, 1934, assassination of the King of Yugoslavia, Alexander Karadordevic, during a state visit to France.

Secure behind the Axis powers' authority, Pavelić undertook a brutal campaign against the Muslim and Serbian population. In 1943, as the Allies took control of the war, the Germans fully replaced the Italians in the greater Croatian state, but did nothing to reign in Pavelić.

Meanwhile, hiding in the mountains and forests as the war engulfed the Balkans, the Partisans—a Serbian resistance underground militia led by a man named Josip Broz—grew in size, strength, and support. They effectively responded to the Ustasi, reversing many of the gains made by Pavelić and his Nazi collaborators.

Their success swelled even more after the Catholic Church, under Archbishop Aloysius Stepinac, withdrew its support of Pavelić, openly denouncing him and his supporters. [28]

Broz's Partisans, however, were not just Serbian.

They included the military wing of the Communist Party in Yugoslavia, previously outlawed in 1921.[29] Illegal and decimated by Stalin's purges over time, the Communist Party was all but extinct in Yugoslavia until Moscow revived it by choosing Broz to mastermind its resurrection.[30]

Broz, who had witnessed the Bolshevik Revolution in Russia when visiting Petrograd in 1917, [31] proved to be the right man for the moment. Over the years, after some prison time, he joined the Russian Red Army before gradually emerging in Yugoslavia in 1934 under his code name of "Tito." [32]

Designated as First Secretary of the Communist Party of Yugoslavia in September 1937, [33] by 1941, Tito had built up a force of more than 12,000 bodies. By 1943, his Partisans—with the help of the western Allies—had effectively undertaken a Marxist civil war in Yugoslavia, one the Allies fully supported with a public declaration: "We have pro-claimed ourselves the strong supporters of Marshall Tito because of his heroic and massive struggle against the German armies." [34]

During this time, Colonel Draža Mihailović's Serbian Chetniks were also waging an effective struggle against the Germans. The Chetniks—who took their name from the armed band of Serbs who had opposed the Ottomans years before—wore peasant clothes, grew their hair and beards long, and espoused a Greater Serbia ideology, one committed to the restoring the Serbian Royal Family as rulers of Yugoslavia.[35]

In the early months of World War II, the Partisans and the Chetniks cooperated in various operations, however, this gradually evaporated as more and more Chetnik units came to fight on the side of the Germans and Italians against the Communist Partisans.[36]

Ultimately, by the war's end, Tito's Partisans emerged in complete control of the country. By then, Tito had secured a promise from the Soviets to leave Yugoslavia once the Germans were defeated and Belgrade was liberated.

Triumphantly, the victorious Partisans entered Sarajevo on April 6, 1945, and liberated Zagreb a month later.[37] Soon after, the remnants of the Ustasi and the Chetniks were eliminated, and Communist Yugoslavia was born.

Three important consequences emerged from Tito's triumph.

First, Serbia ascended into the dominant post-war structure of Herzegovina, especially with its military. Secondly, Bosnia became the center point of Yugoslavian defense theory. And finally, the royal Yugoslavian era was officially over as the Communist regime set about to immediately construct a new society of "brotherhood and unity." [38]

That would not come about, however, until a reign of counter terror was conducted at the end of the war.

The sins of the Pavelić regime and the Ustasi were many; thus, the Serbian Communists butchered the Croats—as many as 16,000 in one day. [39]

The era of Tito was now at hand.

Beginning in 1945, it would extend into 1980, a year before the apparitions began in Medjugorje. And, of all the Soviet-backed Communist regimes to emerge after World War II, the government in Yugoslavia would be the strangest, seen by the West to hold a glimmer of hope—although few knew exactly what that hope could be.

Unlike the other Eastern European nations that treaded carefully in line with Moscow for fear of its military power, Tito constantly defied the Kremlin in economics, military, and foreign policy.[40]

But it was more than Tito's clashes with the Kremlin that made him an anomaly; his brand of Communism was seen to be different.

First and foremost, it appeared to condone a more tolerable society, promoting a concept known as "National Communism." This openness earned Tito a reputation as being "the only good Communist," a Marxist dictator who was actually loved by some in the West, yet was still respected as a worthy adversary. [41] In fact, in the eyes of many, Tito was second only to Stalin in the world of Communism. [42]

But although ultimately estranged from Moscow, no illusions should be made as to Tito's flavor of Communism. The Soviet system was his envy, and he sought to imitate it in many ways.

The Yugoslavian Constitution of 1946 was modeled after the U.S.S.R.'s of Stalin in 1936. [43] This primarily meant that no individual state had any right to self-determination, as in the Soviet Union. It also meant the possibility to secede from Yugoslavia was politically unthinkable. [44] To guarantee this, Tito's Partisans of World War II became the People's Army. [45]

Indeed, there was an intimate interlocking of all party and state functions in the nation, symbolized at the summit by Tito's role as head of the government, the party, and the army. [46] This was a classic case of the dictatorship of the proletariat, as defined by Lenin and practiced by Stalin in the Soviet Union. [47]

In Yugoslavia, Tito's human rights record was every bit the equivalent of his more despised Eastern Bloc peers. Behind the scenes, the bespectacled leader ruled with polished charisma, calculated cunning, and an iron fist, much the same as Romania's Nicolae Ceausescu, Albania's Enver Hoxha, and Poland's Wojciech Jaruzelski.

Defined in no uncertain terms, Tito governed as an all-powerful, Communist dictator, determined to ape the Soviet Union in most every way, especially in solidifying and maintaining his own power.

It was a challenge he acknowledged was demanding for a lot of obvious reasons.

"I am the leader," said Tito, "of one country, which has two alphabets, three languages, four religions, five nationalities, six republics, surrounded by seven neighbors; a country in which live eight ethnic minorities."

In January 1953, Tito became President of Yugoslavia and President of its Federal Executive Council. Ten years later, he arranged to be named president for life.

Openly clashing with Stalin, Tito did get along somewhat better with Khrushchev and Brezhnev.[48] But he still moved to build his own bloc of nonaligned nations, earning him the title "Father of the Non Aligned Movement." [49]

But while not aligned with Moscow, day-to-day life in Yugoslavia was not much different for most citizens. As in all Communist nations, arrests, liquidations, seizures of property, and church closings were part of his order.

While religion was permitted, faith-based education was gradually replaced with the teaching of Marxist philosophy. And, as in the Soviet Union, the persecutions were constant, especially of nationalists and religious.

Priests, bishops, and practicing laity were often arrested and charged with undermining the state, with over 200 executed in the very first months after World War II.[50] Even Archbishop Stepinac, who stood up to the Ustasi, as well as the Communists, was sentenced to sixteen years of hard labor.[51] Likewise, relations with the Vatican were severed, with the state putting on trial some citizens for "Nationalist Catholicism." [52]

Vatican II led to a thaw in the relations of all the Communist nations with Rome, as well as a renewal of dialogue with the Orthodox Churches. Tito even visited Pope Paul VI in 1971.[53] But because of the scars that World War II left in Yugoslavia, there was still much left to be desired. The atheistic government especially feared religion in Croatia and kept a watchful eye over every move the Vatican made there.

Still, the people continued to push back.

Over the decades, resurgent nationalism appeared over and over again in the Yugoslav Republic of Tito. Tension especially mounted in Croatia and Kosovo, as underground movements emerged after Communist repudiations.

All in all, Tito's economics were what separated Yugoslavia the most from the rest of the Eastern Communist bloc nations. Starting in 1963, he moved the government from the rigid centralized Soviet system of economics towards a new, more industrialized program that became known as Market Socialism.[54] That changed the nation significantly; however, despite the improved economics, the threat of Croatian independence reemerged.

In 1971, an uprising in Zagreb had to be put down by the military, with Tito muttering how Russian tanks could roll in the streets as they had in Prague in 1968.

Tito died on May 4, 1980, one year before the Virgin Mary's apparitions in Medjugorje began. By then, the Yugoslavia Republic was again extremely restive, witnessing various protests and arrests. No matter how hard it tried, Yugoslavian Communism could not contain the increasing threats of resurgent nationalism within its republics.[55]

And Tito kept brawling with the Soviets until the very end.

One of his final acts of policy was to condemn, as he had denounced the invasion of Prague in 1968, [56] Leonid Brezhnev's decision to order the Soviet Union military's invasion of Afghanistan.[57]

Needless to say, right up to the last days of his life, Tito maintained his feisty clashes with the big brother next door, who he feared but continued to stand up to.

Tito annoyed Stalin, perhaps, more than most realize. In 2012, a Slovenian scholar added a new dimension to this story.

Claiming that it was not a stroke that killed the 74-year-old Stalin on March 5, 1953, historian Jože Pirjevec writes that after the Soviet tyrant unsuccessfully tried to have Tito assassinated twenty-two times, Tito had Stalin murdered.

In his book, *Tito in Tovarisi* (Tito and His Comrades), Pirjevec outlines—through circumstantial evidence—that Tito knew that his bitter enemy would never stop attempting to kill him. So, he finally did something about it.

Tito, he claims, had Stalin poisoned with potassium cyanide. In a letter to Stalin, discovered on Stalin's desk after his death, Tito wrote:

"Stop sending people to kill me. We've already captured five of them, one of them with a bomb and another with a rifle...if you don't stop sending killers, I'll send one to Moscow, and I won't have to send a second." [58]

This ended up, Pirjevec argues, to be exactly what Tito finally did.

Tito's Yugoslavia was more frightening than fascinating for Mirjana Dragićević.

Like craters in the moon that expose the scars of a violent bygone age, Mirjana's memoir no sooner begins than she addresses her own anguished past; the sorrowful and agonizing impressions pummeled deep into her soul by Tito's totalitarianism.

Recalling life in the former Yugoslavia before the apparitions, Mirjana's book painfully revisits the daily rigors of the Communist state, especially what it was like to live in constant fear, and how the need for secrecy preoccupied day-to-day living.

Mirjana dwelled, one concludes from her writing, in a prison of constant paranoia—a gloomy world of distrust that required quick thinking upon every decision, before and after each word said aloud or whispered in secret.

In essence, Mirjana makes one thing clear: functioning day to day in Communist Yugoslavia was forever about remembering that one's every step and word would be looked upon by the authorities with suspicion.[59]

Education in Tito's Yugoslavia, she reveals, was no different than in Stalin's Soviet Union. Atheistic principles were the cornerstone of all learning. Mirjana tells how her classroom history books idealized the heroic designs of Marx, Engels, and Lenin.[60]

God and religion, on the other hand, were fables.[61]

She was mandated to pledge allegiance to the Socialist Federal Republic of Yugoslavia that promised unity and brotherhood.[62] And— as in the Soviet Union, China, and Cuba, where images and statues of Lenin, Mao, and Castro were strategically positioned for citizens to have to endlessly encounter—countless likenesses of comrade Tito's vainglorious grimace were everywhere the eye could see in Yugoslavia.

This cult of adulation peaked annually on Tito's birthday, when government-sponsored rallies nationwide celebrated his life.[63] These sanctimonious affairs, Mirjana writes, were especially crafted to involve the youth, as they were to be shining examples of love and devotion for the leader. [64]

Through sporting events and musical presentations in Tito's honor, school children were foisted upon to spearhead the nation in celebrating his life and heroic achievements.[65] Mirjana recalls how teachers would require students to submit poems and songs that praised Tito and Communism, with the state media extolling publically the finest submissions.

Ironically, in May of 1981, just a month before the apparitions began in Medjugorje, Mirjana was chosen to appear on television to recite a poem honoring President Tito. [66]

And then there flowed Mirjana's recollections of the extremely dark side of living under Tito's brand of Communism.

First and foremost, this involved the duplicity of the government-sponsored spies found in every town and village, forever reporting innocent people to the authorities for innocuous and bogus crimes.[67] Many of these victims, she states, were clandestinely taken away and murdered, subsequently dumped in unmarked graves.[68]

One of these tragic victims was her own grandfather, Mate, who was accused of being an enemy of the state. Forcibly removed from his wife and five children in the middle of the night without warning, justification, or evidence, Mate was never to be seen again, buried somewhere that only God knows.[69]

Soon to be labeled a Croat fascist [70] and a subversive enemy of the state herself, [71] Mirjana says she became for the Communist authorities a prime target of the regime because of the apparitions at Medjugorje.[72]

Over the next eight years, this would become a harrowing ordeal for her—mentally, physically, and emotionally. But, Mirjana persevered, often recalling how her mother said that if you died for God, you would live forever, but if you said no to God, you could die forever.[73]

Like the hundreds of millions of others who lived through the consequences of the spread of Marxist errors, Mirjana came to understand that on any given day—at any given time—she could disappear like her grandfather Mate, perhaps never to be seen or heard from again.

CHAPTER SIXTEEN

"THEY'LL SAY WE'RE MAD"

"The Kingdom of God is at hand. Repent,
and believe in the Gospel."

— Mk 1:15

JUST A SHORT STRETCH DOWN THE ADRIATIC SEA FROM THE PROVince of Herzegovina and across a small leg of the Mediterranean sits the nation of Israel.

Surrounded by enemies on all sides, with survival at all cost its unnegotiable position, the nation unofficially revealed on June 25, 1981—less than twenty-four hours after the Virgin Mary's groundbreaking appearance in Medjugorje—what was already the world's worst-kept secret.

Confessing by way of an interview with Moshe Dayan, its celebrated eye-patched army general and former Defense and Foreign Minister, Israel admitted it had developed the ability to produce and manufacture nuclear weapons. And, Dayan warned in *The New York Times* story, it could do so rather swiftly if Arab countries produced them.[1]

The *Times* also reported that same day how United States Undersecretary of State, James L. Buckley, had been assured by Pakistan's highest leaders that their country wasn't developing or planning to develop a nuclear bomb. But Pakistan also made no promise not to seek such in the face of India's already successful effort.[2]

Five years later, Pakistan confessed it did have the ability to make a nuclear bomb. And, a little more than a decade after that, it admitted having successfully conducted five nuclear tests.

Seismic data had long before revealed Pakistan's secret.

The nuclear storm clouds were becoming more visible.

At Medjugorje on June 25, the four visionaries, Ivanka, Mirjana, Vicka, and Ivan—who decided to return to the hill on the second evening—gathered together after their day concluded and began to stroll towards Mt. Podbrdo, this time by way of the asphalt road through the middle of Bijakovići.[3]

As they walked and interacted, the four carried with them a "whatever will be, will be" attitude. As Ivanka reasoned, they all believed it was the right decision, even if the Virgin didn't appear again.

"We decided to go," said Vicka, "if we see her, that is okay. If we do not see her, what can we do?" [4]

As it gradually became known that the children were planning on returning to the hill, a growing number of curious villagers decided to tag along too.

Marinko Ivanković, the next-door neighbor to both Milka and Vicka, wanted to be present.[5] He decided to come after learning about what had taken place from Vicka and Marija on their morning ride into Čitluk—especially upon hearing of Ivan Dragićević's involvement, a youngster he esteemed to be "a sensible boy." [6]

Similarly, there came to Bijakovići that evening the sometimes down, but never out, Iva Vasilj of Medjugorje. She held no second thoughts on trailing along.

"I didn't even stop to lock up," Iva recalled, "if any thieves came along, they could have cleaned us out." [7]

In all, the number of stragglers following the children up the hill ranged from fifteen to twenty.[8]

As occurred at Fátima upon the second apparition, the cornerstone at Medjugorje was about to be set.

Somewhere around 6:00 p.m., the four children arrived at the base of Podbrdo. Led by Ivanka again, with Mirjana at her side, they gradually started to scale the hill with their supporters marching close behind.

Suddenly, everyone halted.

The four—almost afraid to breathe—collectively thought they had just witnessed something remarkable span the sky above. Something they said that looked like "lightning." [9]

A moment later, it happened again. And then again. And with the third bolt of light, everyone realized something extraordinary was starting to unfold.

Unlike the previous day, when Ivanka simply spotted Mary already positioned on the hillside, this time the Virgin's arrival was spectacular: three flashes of brilliant light that illuminated the hillside and dazzled the eyes of the children.

It was a heralding intervention of divine wonder, undoubtedly worthy of the arrival of Heaven's Queen.[10] Witnessed not only by the visionaries and others on the hill, but by many in the villages below;[11] the regal celestial signal was followed almost instantly by a euphoric cry from an excited Ivanka:

"Look the Madonna!"[12]

Abruptly lifting and then turning their heads upward, Vicka and Mirjana seemed to instinctively lock onto Ivanka's discovery. And, as if rehearsed, their perfectly harmonious stare at the same place on the hill all but confirmed what onlookers suspected: the Virgin Mary had returned to Podbrdo.

"Suddenly a light shone," explained Vicka, "and Our Lady appeared."[13]

Wasting not a moment, the animated Vicka immediately raced down the hill to try and find Marija and Jacov,[14] both of whom she had promised to retrieve if Mary appeared again. Upon hearing Vicka call her, Marija departed her home so fast she put on a pair of her father's oversized shoes, losing both by the time she got to the hill.[15]

Returning with the two at her side, the now six children huddled together and gazed upward at the light-bathed Lady, who was hovering a good distance higher up the hill than the previous day.

Although the two newest members of the group could not distinctly make out the vision, the other four reveled in the sight.

"We saw the Blessed Mother alone. This time she did not have the infant Jesus in her arms. I saw her very clearly as if she was right next to me...It was daylight, she was quite visible," recalled Vicka.

The considerable distance should have reduced the visibility of the apparition to a mere speck. But such was not the case. Instead, the visionaries reported that they saw Mary as if magnified in some way.[16]

Whether supernaturally aided or not is unknown, but the next thing that occurred was also unexplainable. Responding to the Madonna, who beckoned the children to come nearer by extending her arms, the six youngsters suddenly raced effortlessly up the side of the mountain—as if "propelled" or had "wings"—despite countless piles of rocks and scores of jagged bushes.[17]

According to the onlookers, what should have taken at least ten to twelve minutes, somehow occurred in less than two, even with some more lost shoes along the way. Mirjana would later say it felt as if they coasted up the hill.[18]

Once up the treacherous slope, another oddity occurred.

Witnesses say all the children suddenly came to a complete halt, about six feet in front of where the bright light had settled. Again, their abrupt, simultaneous stoppage was hard to comprehend. Later, the children attributed the entire experience to an "interior force"[19] that simultaneously guided them up the hill and ultimately dropped them to their knees before the Virgin Mary, somewhat like a rapidly descending jet that lands and frantically brakes to a complete stop.

Mirjana's uncle, who witnessed the strange episode, said the entire escapade terrified him.[20] Others concurred—what unfolded was, all agreed, not natural.

Vicka was not sure what exactly happened:

"We just ran towards the Madonna, as if something was pulling us through the air. I was terrified. I was also barefoot, but the thorns didn't scratch me. When we were a few feet away from her, we felt as though we were thrown to our knees. Jacov was kneeling right in the middle of a thorn bush and I was sure he'd been hurt. But he came out of it without a scratch." [21]

Racing up the hill after the children, the twenty or so villagers found the six settled on a bed of rocks, praying while trying to whisper with each other.

When asked by Vicka, Marija reported initially that she couldn't see the Madonna. She did, however, notice something in white that was gradually becoming clearer.[22] Then, after making the sign of the cross and joining the others in prayer, the blurred contours of a woman evolved into a clear image before her straining eyes.

First her face, then her hands took shape, Marija recalled, like "a mist clearing." Finally, in all her mesmerizing splendor, there floated above her the incomprehensible-looking Madonna, in a long grey dress and white veil.[23] It was, Marija instantly realized, the inexplicable vision her sister Milka had so desperately tried to describe the night before.

Almost the same occurred with Jacov.

The ten-year-old could not see the apparition when standing lower on the hill. Then, he ascended Podbrdo and began to pray. Like Marija, the vision first appeared to him somewhat misty, nebulous, and indistinct. But slowly it cleared and came into focus, becoming definitive, intense and breathtaking. So much so, that it caused him to comically tumble backwards, landing in another clump of jagged bushes. [24]

Although the six arrived almost simultaneously, the mysterious force drew Ivanka and Vicka to crumple to their knees first. Together, the two girls slowly feasted their eyes on the Madonna.

Unlike the evening before, Mary appeared extremely young up close, "nineteen or twenty" years old, and even more strikingly beautiful than on the first day.[25] And as the apparitional woman extended a divinely, penetrating gaze upon them, they reported feeling emotions that were beyond words.

The Virgin's magnetic eyes, the girls tried to explain, were so vivid and so expressive, so kind and tender, they somehow radiated her love and ethereal presence upon them. [26]

"She was beautiful, smiling and happy," recalled Vicka. "Why, one can't begin to describe it." [27] After freeing himself from the brambles, Jacov, too, rejoiced in his first glimpse of Mary. "I can die now that I've seen the Virgin," he later mused.[28]

For Mirjana, who now had seen the Madonna two days in a row, it was too much. She fainted, as did Ivanka. "We were so afraid," said Mirjana, "when we saw her the second day, we fainted." Asked why she fainted, she could only say it was because she didn't understand anything, and because she was seeing the Mother of God.[29]

As had Vicka the day before, Mirjana began to register every little detail she could remember about Mary's stunning appearance.

Foremost was a beautiful blueness that surrounded the Virgin, bathing and illuminating her. Mary's skin was an olive tone, Mirjana recalled, with eyes so deeply blue they reminded her of the Adriatic Sea.[30] And, like Vicka noted after the first day, she agreed that the Virgin's hair was curly black with locks hanging out from under the veil, and that she wore a blue-gray iridescent dress.[31]

Most of all, the heavenly vision radiated a peaceful, maternal love that was vibrant, breathtaking, and intense.[32] And, Mirjana marveled, the Madonna spoke perfect Croatian in a voice that sounded almost musical in quality.[33]

The ragtag gang of onlookers became spellbound, too, just watching the children with their faces aglow, locked into their mystical, almost romantic looking ecstasy. Afterwards, some reported that the visionaries seemed to be staring upward at a focal point just a few feet in front of them, while actively engaging their celestial guest.

They repeatedly noticed that the youngsters were moving their eyes and nodding their heads in apparent responses to Mary. But, no conversational sound was heard by anyone.[34]

Consistent with a pattern leading up to that point, Ivanka became the first to speak to the Madonna.[35]

Without hesitation, she immediately asked Mary a question about her recently deceased mother, Jagoda, who had died alone in the hospital.[36]

Her mother was doing well the Virgin replied in a melodic voice, revealing that she was in Heaven and that Ivanka needn't worry.[37] Mary then advised her to continue to obey her grandmother, and to strive to be especially good and helpful since she was elderly and no longer able to work.[38] Except for Jacov and Marija,[39] all the visionaries heard the Virgin address Ivanka.

Mirjana spoke up next.[40]

Rattled somewhat by all the harassment she endured that day, she strongly urged the Virgin for a sign for the onlookers,

"Dear Madonna, they won't believe, when we go home."

It was an argument known to have been made by visionaries in the past who endured the doubting ridicule of the masses.[41] "They'll say we're mad," added the young girl to bolster her case.[42]

The Virgin just smiled.

And with this brief exchange, the mystical encounter for day two was essentially over. But before Mary departed, the children asked her one last question.

Would she return for a third day?

"Yes," the Virgin assured them as she started to hover higher in the air, bidding them a final adieu as she went, "Go in God's peace."

Evaporating into the foggy mist, the apparitional figure then vanished into the sky, as all six visionaries could be seen rotating their straining necks in the same direction as her fading light.

The apparition was over.

But suddenly, the aftermath of the spectacle brought with it some unexpected drama. Overwhelmed by the news of her mother, upon descending the hill, Ivanka immediately broke down and wept uncontrollably in the arms of her grandmother.[43]

But as she explained what the Virgin had said, another fuss erupted on the way home. Although Ivanka's mother had been a good and pious woman, some in the crowd could not believe it was possible she had already entered through the pearly gates.

Eternal bliss, a few felt, was a formidable challenge, not something that could occur so fast after one's earthly departure. Or at least it appears, not something anyone expected to hear about with someone they actually knew.

It is worth noting that the Virgin would later elaborate on this spiritual reality in another appearance at Medjugorje:

"You must realize that the humble performance of your human and Christian duties is enough to make you worthy of Heaven." [44]

For various reasons, almost everyone wept after the apparition on the second day, which lasted ten to fifteen minutes.[45] Excitement and bewilderment, caused by colliding emotions, filled the air and was best released through the shedding of some joyful tears.

But there were the usual thorns to go with the roses.

As the visionaries descended the hill, several people demanded to inspect the bodies of the six, especially the bottoms of their feet. Some were baffled and intrigued, even suspicious, at the lack of any cuts, scrapes, or scratches.[46]

And, as occurred on the first evening—despite witnessing for themselves some truly extraordinary moments—most of the visionaries' family members continued their benignly, rancorous opposition to their claim that the Virgin Mary was appearing to them.[47]

Ivanka's brother called her insane,[48] while her grandmother asked her to come to her senses.[49] Ivan's folks became angry, mostly because he claimed to see what others couldn't. [50]

But a shift was beginning.

Some began to believe in the children, especially after contemplating and later discussing more of what they had witnessed. Even a few family members came on board.

Although Mirjana's aunt and uncle would phone her parents in Sarajevo, cautioning them that she might be suffering a nervous breakdown, they said they believed her. As did her grandmother, Jela.

Vicka's mom said she believed her, too, counseling her daughter to speak the truth without fear.[51] And, after day two, grandma Vicka appeared to have no doubt the children were experiencing an unearthly encounter, preparing them to test the spirits come Friday evening.

Overall, the visionaries began to experience within a sense of redemption, as day two confirmed for them the reality of their experience, both individually and collectively.

This was especially true for Ivan.

After fleeing the first day, the second day had just as powerful an effect in the opposite way for him, for he had now met the Madonna and would never again be the same:

"The first moment I saw Our Lady a change took place in me—in my soul and in my heart. Something like a current streamed through me from head to toe. Somehow, everything in me became entirely different and new. It was especially true on the second day of the apparitions, when we became close to Our Lady and talked to her."[52]

One onlooker was especially affected by the events that transpired on day two at Medjugorje.

Marinko Ivanković—who mistakenly believed the apparition that evening was at 7:15, not 6:15—couldn't get over the sobbing Ivanka and all that he heard had occurred with her. Together with what Vicka and Marija had told him in the morning, he became that day a firm believer in the unfolding events.[53]

This would become critical to the early story of Medjugorje, for from that day on, the 39-year-old Marinko befriended the six, who he felt badly needed help, especially since some of them at the time had little support from their families.

Henceforth, he would assume the role of the children's dominant supporter, organizer, and adult leader—their forever advisor and trusted friend.

Indeed, Marinko became the confidant of the children and because of his dedication and sincerity, they would come to lean on him heavily, even trusting him to advise on what questions they should present to the Virgin.[54]

He also faithfully began to keep a record of the early events at Medjugorje. His value in this capacity is heightened by the fact that official documentation of the early days was confiscated by the police on August 17, 1981, and never recovered.[55]

Several more events from the second day of the apparitions would also come to be very significant in the history of Medjugorje.

When asked what they were praying while kneeling in front of the Virgin, Vicka said they recited seven Our Fathers and seven Hail Marys. Contrary to later reports that the Virgin Mary herself implemented this prayer regime, it was Mirjana's grandmother who first suggested the prayers, a Croatian tradition in the region in honor of the Seven Sorrows of Mary.[56] Afterwards, the Madonna said it pleased her and recommended they add the Creed.[57] The Virgin would later join in praying with them, but without reciting the Hail Marys.[58]

A phenomenon surrounding a watch that Mirjana was wearing also occurred on this day, with the numbers changing on the face and the arms moving backwards. Although greater mysteries occurred that second day—such as the celestial flashes of light, the children's rapid ascent of the hill, and their apparent immunity from injury—the changes to Mirjana's watch were truly considered miraculous by the visionaries themselves. Mirjana reportedly still keeps the watch in her possession and detailed the incident in her book. [59]

There are some events that were said to have occurred on the second day of the apparitions that did not.

It was not until the third day that the Madonna announced exactly who she was.[60] And it was also on the third day that Vicka Ivanković boldly confronted the apparitional woman as to her origins. [61]

The three most critical elements of the second day, however, were not what happened before, during, or after the apparition, but what the second day itself would later come to represent at Medjugorje.

First, it would be this date, June 25, not the day before, that the visionaries said Mary requested be celebrated as the official anniversary day of the apparitions at Medjugorje.[62]

The permanent body of six visionaries also came together for the first time on this second day.[63]

Two other youngsters in the village would later reportedly receive interior visions and locutions: nine-year-old Jelena Vasilj in December 1982, and Marijana Vasilj in March 1983, also nine but of no relation to Jelena. However, as with Ivan Ivanković and Milka Pavlović, the two were never to be considered part of the core group.

Finally, from this second day of the apparitions, July 25, 1981, until December 25, 1982, all six children claimed to receive an apparition of Mary every day between approximately 6:30 and 6:45 p.m.

Mirjana Dragićević reported that the full group's last daily apparition was December 25, 1982, [64] although they were not altogether that day.

While much unfolded on the second day that is significant in Medjugorje's overall history, the second apparition, more than anything, set the stage for what was about to come.

Peace and joy had resounded that evening, but a strange, foreboding sense of concern lingered in the air after everything was over.

Times were changing. Lives were changing.

And, though it all seemed for the good, an unsettling future would soon be at hand in many ways for the people of Medjugorje—and well beyond.

CHAPTER SEVENTEEN

"GOD EXISTS"

"Behold, I know your thoughts, and the
arguments you rehearse against me."

—Job 21:27

C ARS, TRUCKS, WAGONS, DONKEY CARTS—YOU NAME IT, IT ARRIVED. By late Friday morning, a steady caravan of everything and anything with wheels came meandering into Medjugorje.

Outside the only entrance to the town, the vehicles of the earliest lined both sides of the roads long before noon, sparing only enough space for a farm tractor here and there to muscle in.

In town, clusters of bodies traveling on foot could be seen drifting through the streets, roaming about the five villages in unguided and random directions. The invading horde—whether divinely summoned, merely curious, or coerced by friends and family—had one thing in common: questions.

Where is the hill of apparitions?

Who are these visionaries?

What time will the Madonna appear?

On top of the congestion, the legendary Herzegovina summer heat baked the air on this third day of the apparitions, forcing one and all to seek fluids, shade, and some respite as they navigated their way through the back roads and dirt paths towards Podbrdo.

As for the locals, it was becoming obvious: the cat was out of the bag. Thousands were flooding into Medjugorje, and the air was thick with a restless tension as much as the suffocating heat.

In less than 48 hours, without the help of newspapers, radio, or television—in a Communist nation no less—countless numbers had become aware of the mystical malaise occurring here, putting their lives on hold to come and investigate for themselves. Some would confess traveling from as far away as Krajina, 300 miles northeast of the Brotnji plateau.[1]

Medjugorje, it can be said, was under siege... and would never be the same again.

Early that evening, taking an alternative path beyond the houses, the six children and Marinko strolled along the bottom of Podbrdo, slightly below the place of the first apparition.[2]

As they approached the hill, the group began to recite the Rosary along with the prayer regimen of seven Our Fathers and Hail Marys. Needing no invitation, the burgeoning crowd eagerly joined in. It was about 6:30 p.m.

Suddenly, moments into the Apostles Creed, three brilliant peels of white light,[3] like a storm of silver meteors, raced across the open sky, bathing not only the hill, but the region for miles around.[4]

Witnessed by many, the eyes of the six visionaries instinctively reacted to the three flashes, grabbing and following the nucleus of one primary beam of light as it narrowed, condensed itself, and finally settled up the hillside near an old wooden cross that sat next to a large boulder. [5]

The Madonna was back.

First informing the faithful Marinko as to where to go, the six were off and running, effortlessly navigating with uncanny speed once again the huge rocks and barbwire bushes that impeded their way to the resting place of the light.[6]

There, they found the Virgin Mary, suspended off the ground and dwelling in the center of the luminescence. Collapsing to their knees before her and facing northeast, Mary warmly greeted her anxious darlings:

"Praise Jesus."

This time, as prearranged, before any of the six responded to the Virgin's salutation, the vivacious Vicka sprung a surprise on the apparitional lady.

Armed by her wily grandmother to combat the diabolical, the young girl—assisted by Marinko—quickly moved to sprinkle a jar of holy water laced with blessed salt on the hovering Virgin, ensuring she utilized every last drop.[7]

"If you are the Madonna stay with us. If you are not, depart from us!"[8]

The apparition remained.

Noticeably pleased with the children's spiritual moxie, the heavenly-looking Lady smiled and then quickly set about to commence with the work at hand.[9] But before another word was spoken, there came a second surprise of sorts.

As had occurred the day before, Ivanka and Mirjana suddenly passed out. They were a bit "woozy," as Vicka termed it.[10] This incited panic, confusion, and even the departure of the Madonna.[11]

Pulverized by the intense heat and the pressure of the crowd, an estimated 3,000,[12] the two parched girls needed to be moved into some shade—but not for long. Revived and fortified, they quickly returned to the group, joining in the prayers and songs that had not ceased. And soon, the apparitional Lady reappeared, looking "happier than yesterday," noted Vicka.[13]

Now, with thousands of eyes focused on the ecstatic children,[14] an indescribable spectacle unfolded before the massive hillside audience—the world of the here and now started to be seen mysteriously interacting with the world of the ever after. And, unlike the day before, the massive crowd gradually pressed closer and closer to take in every moment.

They were, thought one man, hoping it was real— though wondering if it wasn't—wondering if they were fools—while hoping they were blessed.

Calmly settling the children, the Madonna proceeded to address their readied questions.

As she had the day before, Ivanka inquired again of her mother's status,[15] wondering this time if she needed prayers or Masses.

Safe and secure in the bliss of Heaven, Mary assured the heartbroken girl that her mother required no additional spiritual intervention.

Taking her turn next, Mirjana's question followed in the same vein, inquiring if her recently deceased grandfather, Ilija, was okay.[16]

"He is well," the Virgin informed her, though not making it clear of his heavenly arrival.[17]

While both replies to Ivanka and Mirjana were relatively brief, and not profound or prophetic, they were significant. For with them came the beginning of the next chapter in the extraordinary story that was just starting to take hold.

After two days of anxiety, fear, confusion, and elation, Mary's patient, loving response on this third evening was just what Ivanka and Mirjana needed to hear, for the Virgin's tender, calming words quieted the restlessness of the two girls, as well as the entire group.

This gentle moment, in essence, was perfect, for it permitted the tension of the previous days to rapidly dissipate, like air suddenly freed from a rocketing balloon.

Now at ease and no longer terrified by the unworldly encounter or the massive crowds that surrounded them, the children's conversations with Mary henceforth will be seen to take on an almost earthly character, seemingly oblivious to its true nature.

Moreover, from this day forward, the six visionaries would come to understand that Mary is truly with them, first and foremost, as a mother. And, like a good earthly mother, she is one they can trust and turn to, one who they know in their hearts will never let them down. One who is on their side and will ferociously protect them.

Day three also brought with it another important reality.

Although crowds have attended public apparitions of the Virgin Mary for centuries, they never before came armed with the perks and prowess of the modern world, something that began to be witnessed on the third day of the apparitions at Medjugorje.

Loaded with clicking cameras and recording devices,[18] not only did those in the gallery snap pictures and record to their heart's content, but this would eventually lead to much more. Soon, attending news media would come to even broadcast or film live the mystical encounters, as if covering a sporting event or reporting breaking news. [19]

Consequently, unbeknownst at the time, a whole new and unprecedented realm in the treatment of miracles was dawning with the apparitions at Medjugorje, as the eyes and ears of not just the assembled masses could witness the unfolding scene, but millions the world over.

This reality especially affected the Catholic Church and its responsibility to discern reported miracles. In just a short period of time, the effects of such intrusive media coverage raised the bar on the assessment of all such sacred mysteries, as Church examiners entrusted with investigating such events confessed to suffering difficulties from so much attention.[20]

By the mid-1990s, discerning a reported miracle would become a matter that few bishops in the Catholic Church would welcome much, if at all. Even the Vatican would come to bemoan what some in the Magisterium termed, "The Medjugorje Virus," [21] a two-decade avalanche of alleged miracles that some thought was because of all the media attention on Medjugorje, the so called "Marian Corridor." [22]

Wrote one Rome based journalist,

"The Vatican was particularly concerned that modern means of global communication were making the Church's cautious, considered approach obsolete. By the time local bishops or the Vatican could even begin to investigate, they had already become news." [23]

The onslaught of news reporting may appear to be negative one if perceived from only one perspective. But there also came, in some people's eyes, many positive developments from the increase in press coverage. Because of the sheer quantity of reports throughout the 80s and 90s, millions who had never heard of such events were casually introduced to them.

Sometimes framed by reporters as attempts to "unlock mysteries" or "solve the unknown," interest in Medjugorje and similar spiritual-based stories soared, spiking the curiosity of countless viewers who often by accident would see the broadcasts.

In America, major television networks, such as CBS, ABC, and NBC, as well as many of their local affiliates, sent investigative crews to Yugoslavia to film first-hand accounts of the events in Medjugorje. The print media did no less, as newspapers, magazines, and wire services worked hard to unearth new, extraordinary stories of the miraculous there.

Because these reports emanated out of a place called Medjugorje—an alien-sounding destination that was lodged behind the Iron Curtain where atheism was promoted by the state—such stories couldn't help but almost automatically attract somewhat incredulous viewers.

Over time, many of the TV programs and print articles often led to related experiences of individuals who would "discover God" or "return to their faith."

The so called "Medjugorje Virus," one could argue, was not a bad virus to catch.

As the apparition continued to unfold on the third day, and the children now calmly interacted with the Madonna, there arose out of the circle of onlookers a bevy of requests for the sick or for departed loved ones. Some of these were relayed to the Madonna by the visionaries, who sympathetically took in and conveyed to Mary what they could.[24]

Then, the most important exchange up to this point between the children and the Virgin Mary took place. While sounding rather insignificant on the surface, it would begin to define the apparitions at Medjugorje and their singular connection to Fátima in a major way:

Who are you?

"I am the Blessed Virgin Mary".

Why have you come?

"I have come to tell you that God exists." [25]

Why Medjugorje?

"The faith is strong here. There are many true believers."

What do you desire?

"I wish to be with you and to call the world to conversion." [26]

After these cryptic but illuminating replies to the children's questions, the Virgin suddenly asked the youngsters to arise from their knees, perhaps for them to better cope with the still exhausting heat.

Now, standing upright and aligned before Mary, the children proceeded with more questions, especially determining that the time was right to ask of her what they desired the most—and what the crowd was starting to clamor for on the third day: a sign to demonstrate that she was truly present.

But like the day before, this request proved to be to no avail.

Turning to Scripture this time, the Virgin Mary explained to the youngsters the intrinsic value of having faith without proof. And, while they were able to see her, said Mary, they should not feel unworthy of such a privilege. It was not for them to understand how, why, and who

God picks for such graces. Lastly, she reminded them that God doesn't necessarily select the cream of the crop.[27]

Completing her mission for the day with these words of wisdom, her third visitation to Podbrdo was finished. But, as she had the day before, Mary promised again to return, alerting them in advance that she would appear the following day down the hill closer to the place of her initial apparition.

"Go in God's peace," the Virgin encouraged the children, departing in her cocoon of light.

The third day was over.

But suddenly, it wasn't.

While those nearest to the apparition began to excitedly share with each other what they had just witnessed, the six children slowly and discreetly disbanded, passing unassumingly through the throng and down the hill, virtually unrecognized by the crowd.

First to depart, a reticent Marija decided to exit the main descending path through a tiny valley on the hillside called Lokvetina.[28]

But once on the backward trail, she suddenly circled off the path to her left, stood, looked up, and then collapsed to her knees. To Marija's overwhelming surprise, a tearful, distressed Madonna was now hovering in the air above her, positioned before a multicolored cross.

Out of nowhere, the Virgin had unexpectedly returned. [29]

And for a reason.

To the young girl's amazement, Mary immediately began to deliver a poignant and passionate plea that would reveal, in essence, that the purpose of her apparitions would transcend the needs of Medjugorje and even Yugoslavia.

As the Virgin had briefly alluded just minutes before to all six visionaries, a worldwide appeal for peace was to be at the center of her mission:

"Peace, peace, only peace. Reconcile yourselves. Peace must reign between God and men, and between men," [30] Mary told the startled Marija, engaging her in a conversation that lasted ten minutes. [31]

Then, after completing their extraordinary encounter together with a prayer, the Virgin once again ascended, slowly fading into the blueness of the surrounding light.

Overwhelmed with tears herself as she recovered from the encounter, Marija struggled to rise and walk, feeling faint, unable to even speak. Fortunately, though, a small group that witnessed the second apparition was able to assist her home.

Afterwards, from this singular, jolting episode, a young Marija Pavlović declared that she would never be the same again.[32]

Day three was now truly over.

But the drama of Medjugorje was only beginning.

To no one's surprise, the beautiful lady in light revealed herself to be who the children suspected all along: the humble, Mother of Christ, who disclosed she had come to Medjugorje on a mission of mercy.

Mary was coming again to help the world find peace. Only this time, there would soon come a significant addendum to her plea:

"Before it is too late!"

Mary's message to the children on the third day especially confronted the greatest impediment to that peace in the world: the pervasive winds of atheism sweeping across the planet.

No, not just the theoretical atheism of Communism, so visibly entrenched in Yugoslavia and the governments of the East and throughout the world, but also the more insidious, practical atheism taking hold in the culture of the West.

And so, the Madonna opened her mission at Medjugorje with the most rudimentary of statements, one she would repeat there over the next four decades:

"GOD EXISTS!"

On the surface, it's an understated-sounding disclosure if ever there was one. But, Mary's words are far from elementary in their intent. They deliver a concise, profound summation of the problem at hand, exposing the root of the danger she first sought "to prevent," as she declared at Fátima.

Simply put: where little or no belief in God prevails, there often follows little or no love between people. And, where love is lost, the void is invariably replaced by division, anger, and hatred—all of which are seeds of violence and stepping stones to hostility and war.

In the world of the early 1980s, and to this day, this dilemma portends to not just the danger of war, but *nuclear* war—the ultimate

Sword of Damocles hanging over humanity for decades now and the not-so-hidden motivation behind the Virgin Mary's intervention at Fátima, and everywhere throughout the world since.

It's a paramount revelation regarding the importance and significance of Mary's coming to Medjugorje, specifically noted by Mirjana in her 2016 memoir, who writes how the Cold War of that time brought the world to the brink of nuclear catastrophe.[33]

First and foremost, then, is this profound declaration by Mary on the third day at Medjugorje of the undeniable existence of a divine Creator, implying the world needed to come back to the safety of this reality, to retreat from the stranglehold of atheism that was beginning to grip not just the governments of the people, but their hearts.

Contained in the Virgin's words is a second implication: mankind needs to accept this truth because it is flirting with annihilation if it doesn't, as so clearly defined in the Secret of Fátima.

As a weeping Madonna conveyed to Marija Pavlović on this day at Medjugorje, peace needed to come soon.

And only God could bring this peace.

Peace.

If peace on earth is to be achieved, the Virgin of Medjugorje reveals that a process must begin and unfold. It is to start with those who already have faith in God, those who live by the Creator's laws and teachings—especially His call to love and forgiveness, to renunciation of evil and especially its root, sin.

Sin—both the prophets of yesterday and the visionaries of today stress—holds consequences. It destroys peace and produces societal ills, it leads to moral plagues that grow into cultural cancer.

Most of all, sin separates mankind from God.

It was their own behavior, the prophets of the Old Testament often told God's chosen people, that led to their undermining, that created their difficulties and suffering. As with Adam and Eve, sin precedes a fall.

But it is more than just the suffering that sin brings.

Sin, Christ explained, erases the freedom that God grants men and women. It makes them slaves of their own selfish interests instead of collaborators in the Creator's work and His world. Worst of all, sin destroys any chance for peace. Both world wars came from sin, the Virgin made clear at Fátima.

And now, an ocean of sin threatens the very survival of the planet.

Thus, Mary comes to the strife-torn land of Herzegovina to begin a desperate effort before the clock strikes midnight.

It's a place she acknowledges on this third visit that has many strong believers—those of enduring faith—who will be drawn to cooperate with her plan, as they are battle tested in their pain and suffering, in their own failing to love and forgive.

It is this plan, the Virgin will come to explain, that seeks commitment to prayer, fasting, and conversion, a plan that involves endless attempts at reconciliation, and one that will take dogged work to succeed.

In essence, in saying "yes" to Mary's plan, these simple, yet trustworthy Croatian partisans become her loyal, first disciples. Those, she knows, who can advance her plan to others through their humble, yet unmistakable example.

In the final analysis, it is clear: the Madonna is in Medjugorje to begin her work with souls who have great faith, in order to save the world from the danger posed by those with little or no faith—the atheists, the unbelievers, or as Mary would come to say, those who simply don't know the love of God.

Henceforth, from this remote, peasant village, located on a historic crossroad of civilization, a divinely-guided peace movement begins, takes hold, and spreads. Mary's ultimate desire is that it will travel from one soul to another, one nation to another, one era to a new era—the era of peace she envisioned at Fátima.

With the end of the third day at Medjugorje, another reality emerges.

It is clear that this effort is to be carefully guided by the Virgin through the words, actions, and lives of the six children—her chosen instruments of peace—who will be rather quickly reinforced by a seemingly endless-growing army of collaborators from throughout the world.

The first recruits to this army emerge on this third evening, as the suffering, needy, and lost children of Yugoslavia respond in the thousands to a grace clearly already at work in their hearts, just days into the Virgin's hillside arrival.

From these courageous ones—after this day—will follow millions.

The third day of the apparitions at Medjugorje reverberated with pro-fundity, and this truth did not escape those looking to find exactly that. Wrote reporter Gitta Sereny of *The London Sunday Times*:

> Tapes made on the third day vividly record the tumult as the children described to the crowd what the Madonna looked like and valiantly tried to transmit questions to her and report her replies. Many wanted news of departed relatives; others begged for help for their loved ones, often pushing severely handicapped infants into the children's arms. [34]

Father Svetozar Kraljević, who would pen a groundbreaking expose on the early days at Medjugorje, *The Apparitions of Our Lady at Medjugorje*, illuminated the importance of the third day in his semi-nal work:

> On the third day, and ever since, pilgrims—from the region and all over the world—have experienced the love and hospitality of the local people, who have become the most outspoken witnesses to the truthfulness of the visions. [35]

Theologian and distinguished professor, Father Joseph A. Pelletier, also did not ignore the profound significance of the third day of Mary's apparitions at Medjugorje. In his book, *The Queen of Peace Visits Medjugorje*, he noted that Medjugorje was, like Fátima, a call to all:

> On the third day, when Our Lady was asked by Ivanka what she wanted, she gave a summary of the message that would be expanded upon in the days ahead. Her message was peace, the peace that can only come from conversion or reconcilia-tion with God and with one's neighbor. [36]

Indeed, Mary's call for peace would be the reverberating message of the third day. It is a message destined to be repeated over and over the next four decades at Medjugorje.

True peace can only come from faith in God, the Madonna stressed in an overtly visual and verbal way on this day. But she also emphasized that people would still need to act to bring this peace, because the paramount danger to civilization wasn't going to just go away.

Moreover, time remained of the essence, and this too was what the sorrowful exuding Virgin hoped to impress upon Marija in a most unforgettable way that evening on the pathway near her home.

Filled with unspeakable anguish after her solo encounter with the Madonna, Marija said she came to innately understand the gravity of what was beginning to unfold through the apparitions.

"It was an overwhelming experience," recalled Marija of Mary's surprise visitation to her, "I saw the Madonna weeping, and the sight drove me to commit myself totally to her request. She had come to inspire all of us to search for peace—peace in our own hearts, peace within our families, peace in the world." [37]

The importance of this critical day at Medjugorje can be weighed only in relation to the haunting danger of nuclear annihilation that hung over the world that summer.[38]

Succinctly crafting the moment at hand in her masterful 1988 account of the visions, *Spark from Heaven*, British journalist and author Mary Craig— an objective driven investigator of the apparitions—did not let this truth escape her in framing the significance of the third day.

It was a day Craig felt profoundly revealed Mary's mission at Medjugorje was to save the world from fiery destruction:

> Thus, was the essence of the Medjugorje message revealed. The Madonna's desperate plea for peace would go echoing round a world which, in the summer of 1981, seemed to hover on the brink of self-destruction. Relations between the superpowers were at their lowest ebb; and there were real fears of a Soviet invasion of Poland—they had invaded Afghanistan the previous year—that might engulf the world in nuclear war.
>
> In those dark days, few people would have rated the chances for peace as being very high. Though the very idea chilled the blood, the time for building fall-out shelters seemed to be at hand. [39]

CHAPTER EIGHTEEN

A CRUEL BOMB

"Lo, the Lord empties the land and lays
it to waste; He turns it upside
down scattering its inhabitants."

—Is 24:1

F ALLOUT SHELTERS, BUILT TO ISOLATE OCCUPANTS FROM AN atomic bomb's radioactive debris, did not exist in Japan—or anywhere else—in August of 1945.

The need, though, would only be days away.

The 13th U.S. Marines, one of the regiments of the 5th Marine Division, was redeployed in Hawaii after being removed from Iwo Jima in March 1945.[1]

The regiment was getting ready for its next assignment: the assault landing on Kyushu, the southernmost of the Japanese islands. Planners estimated initial casualties of 100,000 or more.[2]

It was a conservative estimate.

Around the clock outside Tokyo, a crew of Japanese professional radiomen monitored all signals emanating from United States transmitters. Early on August 6, 1945, they picked up a call signal from the island of Tinian, first heard three weeks earlier.

Throughout that August day, the Japanese radiomen continued to hear the signal, which they called New Task Company.[3] What they didn't realize was that it was coming from the highly-secretive 509th Composite Group, that indeed, had a new task. [4]

Its mission: drop the atom bomb on Japan.

After months of soul searching, the decision was made to drop atomic bombs on Japan. Ethically, the experts concluded there was nothing new in the bomb that was not already available in TNT or fire bombs. All that remained was determining where they would be dropped.

That decision was shaped by a consensus of where it could make the deepest impression, preferably a city hitherto untouched by bombing. Four names came up—Kyoto, Kokura, Niigata, and Hiroshima. [5] A fifth was considered at the last minute— Nagasaki.[6]

Around midnight on August 6, 1945, the chaplain of the 509th said a brief prayer. Seven B-29 crewmembers ate breakfast, and an hour or so later, they were airborne and headed toward the beautiful city of Hiroshima. The city, which was known for its spectacular willow trees and its picturesque views of the Chugoku Mountain Range, had received only twelve bombs throughout the war.

At 8:15 a.m., the Enola Gay arched upwards and to the right on a 60-degree angle. Now, it was 8,900 pounds lighter. Below it, an atomic bomb named *Little Boy* was hurtling towards Hiroshima.

In 45 seconds, it would hit.

First Lieutenant Morris R. Jeppson, who oversaw the console monitoring the bomb circuits, started his own count: "40…41…42…" He stopped. A thought raced through his mind: "It's a dud!" [7]

But an instant later, Jeppson thought he had gone blind.

The world turned purple as an immense flash of bright light stunned his brain. Below, a ballooning ball of angry fire stretched across 1,800 feet, with a temperature at its core of 100 million degrees!

Seconds before, people on the ground had observed falling parachutes that carried radiation instruments. The Japanese cheered because they thought the enemy planes overhead were in trouble. Suddenly, without a sound, the parachutes vanished, as there no longer appeared a sky over Hiroshima.

Those who survived said the first instant of the atomic explosion was pure light—blinding and intense, yet beautiful and awesome. One witness said the flash turned from white to pink and then to blue as it rose and a bulbous cloud blossomed.

Others said they saw fire in six colors. It reminded them, they thought, of a huge photographic flashbulb popping over the entire city.

But most saw nothing at all.

They were completely incinerated exactly where they stood, literally melted by radiant heat. Others were shredded by blast waves that carried glass, bricks, beams, and solid debris.

The drop had been perfect, only 200 yards from the designated aiming point.[8] Seventy thousand casualties, instantly. At two-and-a-half miles from ground zero, the heat still burned the skin. At one-and-a half miles from the point of detonation, a printed newspaper page, exposed to the heat, had the black letters burned completely out of the white paper.

In the sky, the Enola Gay arched upward.

A minute after the explosion, tail gunner Bob Caron saw a shimmering light rushing toward the plane and braced to be hit by the shock waves. It resembled, he thought, a heat wave rising from an asphalt road surface.

After two shock waves, it was over. The crew looked back to scan what they wrought. By now, a perfect mushroom cloud had risen four miles into the sky.

Below, Hiroshima was gone.

"My God!" said Captain Robert A. Lewis, who was Colonel Paul W. Tibbets Jr.'s copilot, "What have we done?" [9]

All that remained of the city was an atomic desert.

Within the innermost one-mile radius, everything was leveled.[10]

Almost everything.

Eight blocks from the epicenter of the blast sat the Church of Our Lady of the Assumption. Inside were four Jesuit priests and four others.

Even though flaming death surrounded them, they were not killed, not even affected by the radiation.[11] Although they were wounded, and the church was in ruins; they had survived.

"In that house, the Rosary was prayed every day," Father Hubert Shifner, one of the survivors, would later say on American television. "In that house, we were living the message of Fátima." [12]

Over the years, some 200 scientists examined the unlikely survivors to try and discover what saved them from incineration.[13] No conclusions, no objective leads.

What did the other survivors say?

They agreed with Father Shifner. Like the eight that stowed safely away in Noah's Ark, they had secured refuge in what is often described as the Ark of Mary, a mystical source of refuge which many Catholic writers have stated is mankind's safest sanctuary for the times at hand.

It took two atomic bombs to end World War II.

On August 9, three days after Hiroshima, a second bomb named *Fat Man* was dropped, flattening Nagasaki.

Realizing that Japan could be wiped off the face of the earth, and dreading the reality of succumbing to the advancing Soviet Red Army—an intolerable idea after witnessing communism emerging in China—Japan's Emperor Michinomiya Hirohito chose to surrender to the United States.[14]

On August 15, 1945—the Feast of the Assumption of Mary—the war was over.

That same day, Hirohito addressed his nation in defeat. He told his people during his famous "Jewel Voice Broadcast"—the first time that a Japanese emperor spoke directly to the common people—that Japan's enemy had begun to employ a "cruel bomb", the power which to "do damage is, indeed, *incalculable*, taking the toll of many innocent lives."[15]

This was a bomb, Hirohito told his people, that if the war continued, would result in the "ultimate collapse and obliteration of the Japanese nation and would lead to the total extinction of human civilization." [16]

Then, closely echoing the Virgin Mary's most optimistic words at Fátima, Hirohito concluded:

"We have resolved to pave the way for a *grand peace* for all the generations to come." [17]

Two weeks later, General Douglas MacArthur seemed to reflect the possibly darker implications of Mary's admonition at Fátima.

Aboard the U.S. battleship Missouri in Tokyo Bay on September 2, 1945, the pompous MacArthur signed the final papers and declared in his radio address that if the world ever went to war again, it would be, "Armageddon." [18]

The problem, MacArthur summarized, "is theological." [19]

The Second World War had consumed the nations as Mary predicted at Fátima.

For those who had survived its wretchedness, it felt like Armageddon had already come and gone. The conflict was, as the Virgin said it would be, a "worse war," much more terrible than World War I.

It took two atomic bombs over four days to end the Second World War. But it took less than a moment for the world to realize that nothing would ever be the same.

The Earth was now a nuclear planet on the eve of destruction—every day.

A few years later, the Soviets began to test nuclear weapons. With this capability, the West now faced a heightened, more dangerous threat in Communism. Every nation, as one writer put it, "was now as vulnerable as an island."

All of this presented an extraordinary reality.

Were these two ghastly twentieth-century horrors— Communism and nuclear weaponry—destined to bring to fulfillment the more apocalyptical prophecies in the Old Testament and *The Book of Revelation*?

Could the heavens rain fire, as Saint Peter foretold in Scripture, and as so many visionaries have warned since the middle of the nineteenth century?

Had prophecy and history finally intersected in such a visibly undeniable way?

Perhaps General MacArthur's words of a coming "Armageddon" possessed a striking truth beyond their sensational value.

World War II was over.

Eighty to one hundred million people laid dead. But somehow, the planet was an even more dangerous place.

Now, with the Soviet Union's development of nuclear weapons, the post-war nations of the West quickly discovered they could not slip into complacency.

The agreements reached at Potsdam and Yalta with the Soviets were precariously flawed and held the potential for renewed hostilities. From Eastern Europe to South Korea, the planet was looking like a powder keg.

The United States and the Soviet Union—one could say—had split the atom and divided the world.

Stalin realized the deck was stacked in his favor, and he was not the kind of leader to discard opportunity. By 1946, the despot wasted no time tightening his hold on Eastern Europe. And with fall of China to Communism in 1949, no one needed an in-depth analysis of the state of world affairs. As in the early years following World War I, the writing was on the wall. Another world conflict was beginning to look like an inescapable conclusion.

Only this time, the stakes were going to be much higher.

Containing the spread of communism was now only half of the problem for the West.

With the nuclear genie out of the bottle, many nations throughout the world felt they also would need to possess such weapons to feel safe, secure, and respected. But unlike transitioning from the bronze to the iron age, the trajectory in the evolution of nuclear warfare would unfold rather quickly.

Consequently, the containment of nuclear proliferation was instantly no less a crisis than the containment of communism.

In the final analysis, both dilemmas showed themselves to be of similar nature. They were both conduits to massive suffering and death.

One—slow and methodical like a lethal poison—begins to kill once in the system of a people or nation. Communism, by the 1950s, held no misgivings. Its dirty little secret was known: it was another form of totalitarianism, complete with pompous dictators and disingenuous promises.

The other—apocalyptic by its very nature—was now the ultimate tool to accomplish worldwide control, or worldwide suicide. Nuclear weapons were what evil men with evil intentions could only have dreamed of throughout history.

Their containment, though, proved to be a two-edged sword.

Not only was the number of nations possessing doomsday weapons a problem, but there was the need to limit the stockpiling of such weapons with the nations who developed them.

And then there was a third concern: bigger, more powerful, nuclear weapons could be just around the corner.

On November 1, 1952, this last concern became reality.

Racing forward with its program, the United States tested its first fusion device—a thermonuclear hydrogen bomb—on the island of Elugelab in the Eniwetok Atoll of the Marshall Islands.[20]

An awesome sight, it was the birthday of an awesome nightmare.

As noted, fusion—not fission—was the primary difference between this bomb and those dropped in Japan in 1945. The two words to the average person sound quite similar. But in the world of nuclear science, there was a gaping difference.

A fusion bomb is 1,000 times more powerful than a fission bomb.[21] Long advocated by Dr. Edward Teller—an original member of the Manhattan Project—the physicist referred to it as a "super bomb."

Upon remote detonation that day, the H-bomb's bulbous cloud mushroomed out over 100 miles [22] and contained as much force as the combined weight of all the bombs dropped on Germany and Japan in World War II,[23] vaporizing the island completely.[24]

"The island of Elugelab is missing," President Dwight D. Eisenhower was informed by Atomic Energy Commission Chairman Gordon Dean after the test.[25]

Nine years later to the day, the Soviets set off a fifty-megaton hydrogen bomb,[26] code named the Tsar Bomba, the king of bombs.[27] It was, nefariously, the most powerful explosion in history—and remains so to this day.[28]

In December 1987, the United States and the U.S.S.R. made major strides at a summit held in Washington. Agreements were reached on arms control; nuclear weapons; nuclear testing ; chemical weapons; conventional forces; exchange of citizens, students, and scientists; trade; the environment; energy; space; and more.[29]

The highlight of the summit, however, occurred on December 8—the Feast of the Immaculate Conception—with the signing of the IMF Treaty (The Intermediate Range Nuclear Forces Treaty).[30] It would eliminate almost 2,700 missiles.[31]

Nine nations, according to the Stockholm International Peace Research Institute, today possess nuclear weapons: The United States, Russia, the United Kingdom, France, China, India, Pakistan, Israel and North Korea, with the United States and Russia holding vast numbers.

One nation, South Africa, once possessed nuclear weapons, but dismantled them in 1989.

The United States, the Federation of American Scientists (FAS) estimates, has over 5,428 nuclear weapons with 1,650 active warheads. Russia is believed to have 5,977 nuclear weapons with 1,588 active warheads. China is the third largest nuclear power with approximately 350 warheads, followed by France (290) and the United Kingdom (225).

As of early 2022, the FAS estimates there were a total of 12,700 nuclear warheads on the planet.

All of this means, despite the treaties, one ignoble thing.

On any given day, the planet could be incinerated with little or no notice.

At Fátima, the apparitional woman's words touched upon the anguish of the twentieth century.

After announcing the coming end of World War I, Mary predicted the Second World War would erupt during the Pontificate of Pope Pius XI.

She saw how Russia and the atheistic errors of Marxism, once forged together, would sweep the earth.

She correctly anticipated that more wars, more pain, more famine, and more persecution would come if men did not change their sinful ways, if her requests were not granted.

But in unveiling all of the trials and tribulations that were to come during the twentieth century—in sharing all of this prescient knowledge with her children on earth to prevent their fulfillment—how did the Queen of Peace fail to speak of the approaching perils brought about by nuclear devastation?

Why did the Virgin not reveal that fire could rain from the sky upon all the world?

How did she not foretell that the power of the sun—the power to dissolve the elements—would soon overshadow all civilization?

According to one man, Mary warned of all of this at Fátima and more on a rainy day back in 1917.

Just not in the way people expected.

CHAPTER NINETEEN

SO ALL MAY BELIEVE

"I am the Lord, the God of all mankind!
Is anything impossible to me?"

—Jer 32:27

THE DARK CLOUDS SWIFTLY PARTED.

Like curtains drawn open to commence the show, the heavenly assistance from above permitted the voice of a child to introduce the day's main performer.

Rising before an audience of 100,000, ten-year-old Lúcia dos Santos—under the guidance of an interior impulse [1]—lifted her head and pointed to the sky:

"Look, the sun!" [2]

The multitude assembled at Fátima on October 13, 1917, had not come on short notice.

For three months, word circulated that a "miracle" would occur there in October. It was a miracle whose day, hour, and place were foretold. Lúcia repeated this to whoever came to question her. [3]

And so they came—the poor and the wealthy, the humble and the mighty, those who believed and the ones who scoffed.

From the farthest corners of Portugal—a nation known for its deep devotion to the Holy Spirit—the invitation had been received and accepted by the thousands, numbers swollen by hundreds of packed coaches from Germany, Italy, France, and neighboring Spain. Together, they blended with the many who had flown in from the British Isles, North and South America, Asia, and even Australia.[4]

Although World War I still gripped the world—especially in Europe, where Germany prepared for its coming 1918 "peace through victory drive"—tens of thousands arrived in Fátima.

Marching like a great unruly army, they converged on the land of the *Terra Santa Maria*—a nation so old that no one knows for sure who founded the capital city of Lisbon.

All in all, it was an avalanche of response from almost everywhere, despite the efforts of the government and the newspapers to dissuade attendance, and regardless of the police and the military's efforts to intimidate the people along the way. Even a ferocious storm off the Atlantic that hammered the region for days failed to stymie the onslaught.

To say the least, the call to Fátima had been answered, as hordes of barefooted pilgrims, carrying wicker baskets of food and water jugs filled to the brim, clogged the roads and muddy byways of the tiny Iberian Peninsula nation that day.

William Thomas Walsh, in his 1947 classic, *Our Lady of Fatima*, captured the uncanny sight:

> Fathers and mothers carried sick or lame children in their arms for incredible long distances. Fishermen left their nets and boats on the beaches of the Vieira and took to the oozy roads. Farmhands from Monte Real, sailors from ships in the harbors of Porto or Algarve, factory workers from Lisboa, *serranas* from Minde or Soublio, ladies and gentlemen, scrubwomen, waiters, young and old, rich and poor, all sorts of people were plodding through the mud and pelting rain that night.[5]

Past the miles of pine trees and the endless rows of olive groves, to the Cova da Iria they were headed—a vast, natural hollow situated on the top of a hill in the deserted, almost inaccessible, Serra de Aire Mountains, the geographical center of Portugal, eighty-eight miles from Lisbon.

And just hours from its destiny.

Seventeen-year-old Dominic Reis was living near Porto that day, over 100 miles from Fátima. Two days before, his father had told his mother, "We're going to Fátima. We're going to see what happens…" Departing a day early, the train was full by 6 a.m. that morning, with not a seat to be found.[6]

Everywhere along the way, Dominic remembers how people, laden with their heavy burros, were on the move. Dressed in every possible fashion—some without shoes—the caravans of saturated bodies and beasts sloshed steadily forward through the maze of puddles in the cold and cutting rain, impeded only by weekend soldiers hired by the government to discourage the people from going to the Cova.[7]

Home from the war in France, Augusto Mendes rose at 4 a.m. to leave for Fátima from Torres Novas, a small town in Santarém that sent a bus full of people. His brother, Carlos, had gone to the apparition in September and at first decided against returning. But, that morning, Carlos suddenly changed his mind. Eight hours later, the two found themselves—along with a third brother, Candido—standing right next to the visionaries.[8]

Dona Maria Teresa Charters was in the crowd that day, too. A member of a prominent family from Leiria, she was 26 years old at the time and traveled to Fátima with several relatives. She remembers finally arriving after a long six-hour trek from Leiria. Maria came, she said, because "if something was going to happen, I wanted to see it with my own eyes."[9]

The same, however, could not be said for Avelino de Almeida. It was not his burning faith that brought Almeida to Fátima, but his responsibility as managing editor of *O Seculo*, the largest newspaper in Lisbon.

A Freemason who cared little for priests, sacraments, doctrines, or creeds, Almeida had to cover the story because it had become too big to ignore. Acknowledged as one of the best newspaper reporters in Portugal, his writing was known for his cynicism for the apparitions, but in a way that was respectful of others and their beliefs:

> Thousands of persons are heading to a wild expanse of country near Qurem to see and hear the Virgin Mary. Let pious souls be not offended and pure believing hearts be not afraid,

we have no intention of being a scandal for those who sincerely hold their faith and whom the miraculous still attract, seduces, bewitches, consoles and fortifies, as has been the case for thousands of years.[10]

Likewise, Mario Godinho had no desire to spend his day at Fátima. Mario was an engineer who was a member of another important and distinguished Portuguese family from Vila do Paco. Though he would later be credited with being the first to take a photograph of the three visionaries, that day he was at Fátima as a skeptic. A man of science, Godinho was convinced that nothing would happen.

But, he had to go.

Why?

His mother made him.

In need of a way to get Fátima, Mrs. Godinho knew her successful son could haul her and several other family members in his oversized convertible Peugeot.[11] Godinho recalls that while driving on a "poor and miserable road" eighteen miles from the village, he saw "hundreds and hundreds of people and many kinds of vehicles." Once at Fátima, he preferred the comfort and dryness of his car to any pending miracle looking to be found somewhere in the pouring down rain.[12]

At least, until he noticed the hordes of people looking up at the sky.

The sky.

No one who came to Fátima that day suspected the miracle would be connected to the sky. In July, a miracle was promised to occur in October. But not a clue was revealed to the children as to its nature.[13]

At the apparition at Valinhos on August 19, after the time in which the children were imprisoned,[14] Mary again promised:

"In the last month, I will perform a miracle."[15]

Then, at the apparition on September 13, the Virgin for the third time confirmed to the three children that the miracle was still on schedule:

"In October, I will perform a miracle so that all may believe."[16] But again, Mary said not a word to the visionaries as to what would take place.

By October 12, tens of thousands had converged on Fátima, with thousands more arriving by the hour. [17] For days now, there had been no visible sky, only a thick blanket of low, dark clouds dropping endless reserves of rain.

The sky, it's safe to say, was the last place anyone expected to find what they came looking for that day.[18]

All of Portugal was galvanized by the morning of October 13.[19]

Despite the threats, mockery, and actions of the authorities, the eyes of the entire nation were focused on the shepherd children and their bold prognostication.

The Masonic government, though condescending, saw an opportunity being handed to them. A "colossal fiasco" was expected, as one writer put it.[20] Once the miracle flopped, it would hopefully further serve as a death blow to "the myth, the superstition, and the fanaticism of religion in the country."

It was, political leaders felt, "an opportunity to bury once and for all the already moribund religion of Christianity in Portugal." [21] In Santarém, a neighboring town, a hundred or so local Masonic members even held a contemptuous parade to lampoon the Fátima visions.

The faithful, filled with hope after years of persecution, believed the visionaries were instruments of the Almighty; no measures of intimidation or ridicule would persuade them otherwise.[22]

With the miracle, there would come a resurrection of the faith, so downtrodden since the 1910 Marxist-inspired Masonic revolution in Portugal. In a country known for centuries for its Christian heritage, many saw the hand of providence coming to the rescue.

Looked at objectively, the presence of reporters from Portugal's major newspapers signaled the magnitude of that decisive, rainy day for the country.[23]

And rain it did that day.

By mid-morning, the adversarial weather climaxed its misery on Fátima's stoic visitors. It was cold. It was wet. It was muddy. And a new round of hostile, biting winds, throwing sheets of water into the faces of the shivering pilgrims, made some think the nasty weather might even chase away the miracle.

The Cova da Iria— "The Cove of Peace," named after the 7th century 20- year-old Portuguese virgin and martyr Saint Iria or Saint Irene [24]— was by then a miserable swamp.

Once at the Cova, though, the crowd bonded.

Joining in song while reciting the Rosary over and over in a rhythmic chant, a feeling of excitement and anticipation prevailed.

By noon, vantage points in the large field were at a premium, with people squeezed into every last foot of space. Photographs of the day reveal that perhaps more than a hundred thousand were there, hiding under a phalanx of black umbrellas beneath the gray, morbid sky.

Nevertheless, an army of latecomers continued to force their way through the deep, muddy marsh, causing the massive crowd to congeal and sway uncontrollably.

Towards the epicenter of the horde, the crush of bodies at one point became too great, causing the path of the three approaching visionaries to disappear from sight. This ignited a split second of panic, as the youngest visionary—seven-year-old Jacinta—was separated from her father and began to cry.[25]

But order was quickly restored.

Coming to the children's rescue, a group of men hoisted them to their shoulders, high stepped through the deep water and mud, and safely delivered them to the designated area of the Cova, where the apparition would take place.

There, a lone grassy piece of pasture with a small holm oak tree—adorned with colorful ribbons and flowers thanks to a local woman named Maria Carreira—waited, ready to hold once more on its crest the Queen of Heaven.[26]

Three months before, the Virgin promised the children a sign in October "so that all may believe."

Finally, that day, that hour, was here.

The greatest foretold miracle in the history of the world was about to unfold.[27]

Ten-year-old Lúcia dos Santos took charge of the moment.

Though mocked unmercifully by neighbors and relatives right up until the very end, she firmly instructed the massive crowd to shut their umbrellas [28] and begin the Rosary,[29] and for Jacinta and Francisco to kneel next to her.

With the three little children now humbly kneeling on the ground, Lúcia slowly began to lead the prayer.

Suddenly, the young girl alerted her two little cousins that a distant light was starting to approach:

"Be quiet, be quiet."

"Our Lady is coming. I have seen the flash."

"Look carefully, Lúcia," cried out her terrified mother, "make no mistake!"

There would be no mistake.

Within seconds, those closest to the visionaries saw a fifteen-foot high white-looking mist slowly descend and engulf the children, as if to safely encase them within the Virgin's presence.

Instantly enraptured by the vision, all that could be discerned by the nearest onlookers after that was the soft voice of the servant child: [30]

"What do you want of me?"

Now hovering directly over the holm oak tree and in front of the three little shepherds, the Virgin immediately set about to accomplish her mission.

Fulfilling a promise concerning her identity that she had made to them in July, Mary revealed what by then was well understood: "I am the Lady of the Rosary," immediately adding, "I would like a chapel built here in my honor. Continue to pray the Rosary every day."

Next, as she had foretold in June, the Virgin confirmed the approaching end of World War I: "The soldiers will be coming home." [31]

Finally, after receiving petitions for the sick and needy from Lúcia, Mary closed out her appearance with words the visionary would come to repeatedly emphasize to all who would listen for the next eight decades:

"Do not offend God anymore, He is already too greatly offended." [32]

With this, the Lady of the Rosary concluded what she came to say.

But not with what she had come to do.

Rising slowly above the three visionaries, beams of bright light suddenly emitted from both her hands towards the sky. Then, as the apparitional woman ascended ever higher, a reflection of the Virgin's own radiant light projected upwards and onto the blazing sun.

And with this—Lúcia knew in her heart—the moment for "all to believe" had truly arrived.

CHAPTER TWENTY

THE DANCE OF THE SUN

"Ask now of the days of old, before your time, ever
since God created man upon the earth; ask from
one end of the sky to the other: Did anything so
great ever happen before? Was it ever heard of?"
—1 Dt 4:32-34

IF THE MIRACLE PROMISED AT FÁTIMA WAS TO COME, THE BURGEON-
ing throng at the Cova da Iria sensed the time had arrived. For
something in the heavens seemed astir.

Positioned perfectly above the crowd—as if keeping in harmony
with Lucia's directives—a now overtly, radiant looking sun sat high in
the noon sky behind a few remnant clouds.

But, all of a sudden, it looked as if to be moving—as if on the loose.

"I saw the sun as if it were a ball of fire," remembered attorney Carlos
Mendes, "begin to move in the clouds." [1]

Move, it did, and it was just beginning.

Now all alone in the open sky, with the remaining clouds fleeing,
the brilliant golden orb appeared to not only move, but spin and glow
as if it were coming to life—as if it were breathing. It appeared, the
startled onlookers could see, to be turning brighter and brighter, more
brilliant, more golden than ever.

And, along with this baffling activity, there came another mystery.

As the crowd continued to stare directly into the slowly emerging solar phenomena, they came to realize that no harm was being
incurred upon their eyes; the power of the sun was not to be feared.
It was, the astonished witnesses described, like gazing at a benevolent,
shiny moon that was uncannily bright yet welcoming and harmless. [2]*

---

* In another Fatima oddity, Adolf Hitler writes in *Mein Kampf* that he was blinded in
WW I on October 13, 1918, one year after the Miracle of the Sun.

And yet, even greater surprises were about to unfold.

Not content to be simply moving, spinning, and magnificently aglow, the now enhanced and radiant-looking sun suddenly took off across the vast, open sky, as if on parade before the spellbound crowd. Shining even more intensely, it then began to swing forward and backward, again and again, all the while throwing off an array of brilliant colors.

Described by spectators as a colossal wheel of fire, the multiple beams of colored light began to not only stream across the sky but also flood the countryside below, striking and reflecting off the ground, the trees, and even the people's clothes.

"I looked at the sun and saw it spinning like a disc, rolling on itself," recalled Antonio Antunes de Oliveira, who was 32 years old at the time. "I saw people changing color. They were stained with the colors of the rainbow." [3]

This mesmerizing "dance of the sun"—as it would come to be forever known through an *O'Seculo* newspaper story published two days later—went on for several minutes, enthralling the captive masses below.

Then suddenly, the rhythmic, prancing orb drew itself to an abrupt halt, as if commanded to stop.

But not for long.

Pausing for several moments—as if to welcome applause—the twirling, pulsating sun then started dancing around the heavens all over again in an encore performance, and then again in a third waltz across the clear blue sky that now held not a cloud in sight. [4]

As the mighty sphere wavered by the third time, people noticed it was intensifying even more, projecting greater power and more strength. Some remarked that it now appeared to be growing, as if expanding exponentially in diameter. Again, a fascinating, hypnotic whirlwind of light and color continued to exude from it in all directions, completely bathing the Cova and its guests.

The best, however, was still to come.

Appearing now to be losing its balance in the heavens completely, the engorged globe wobbled for a second or two, stabilized itself, and then began to fall towards the Earth like a renegade comet on course to incinerate the planet.

While many couldn't help but just stare in disbelief, a panorama of hysterical reactions soon exploded on the ground. Throughout the Cova, said one witness, there arose "indescribable confusion and terror." [5]

Some people fled, panicked beyond their wildest imagination. Others fell to their knees in prayer, pleading with God for mercy. A few—concerned with their eternal salvation—started to confess their sins aloud. Most, however, remained froze in their tracks, stoically awaiting their fate.

"The world is going to end," muttered a 32-year-old man from Ameixoeira. [6]

"We are going to die," thought a 26-year-old woman from Leiria.[7]

In some areas of the Cova, a relatively quiet, yet fatalistic dread set in.

Even unbelievers— mostly there that day out of mere curiosity— would later confess to be stricken with a morbid despair.

"These were seconds, moments, that seemed like hours," a reporter from the *Dario de Noticias* would write. [8]

Unabated by the horrified and panicking crowd, the now monster-sized sun continued to drop steadily towards the Earth, drawing closer and closer to the horizon. It appeared to desire, said one man, to crush the Earth with its fiery weight. [9]

As it neared, an eerie darkness began to descend with it.

First appearing somewhat shaded and then almost purple in color, the entire Cova da Iria slowly succumbed under what could only be described as a foreboding, eclipse-like effect that was now being cast by the tumbling, massive ball of fire.

At the same time, the nearer the sun crept, the more the people throughout the hollow started to appear yellow, almost jaundiced in skin color.

Finally, as if to cap the growing list of mounting terrors, there suddenly swept over the crowd an intense feeling of radiating, suffocating heat. [10] It was, it seemed, as if the sun was now so close it was actually beginning to bake the air.

In mere seconds, the cool autumn day had somehow morphed into a hot summer afternoon.

The remaining moments of the prodigious miracle sound like excerpts peeled from the more wondrous pages of the Old Testament.

Now, like beams shot from a laser, the sun's deep red rays began bleeding through the trees, as one might observe in a magnificent sunset viewed from high upon a mountain top. But this scene did not look like just any sunset, as the fallen sun had swollen so large that it literally filled the sky behind the trees with its huge, red, pulsating presence.

On the ground, in harmony with the apocalyptic-looking sky, there unfolded a scene for the ages, as the once passive and pious horde now scrambled and scattered in every direction, desperately attempting to outrun what was perceived as the imminent justice of an angry God.

To go with the massive pandemonium, there arose a cacophony of screaming, crying voices that meshed together, reverberating in an unharmonious chorus of anguish that could be heard throughout the Cova.

While some remained on their knees, humbled before the power of God, many believed all hope to be gone. The world, they thought, had but moments until it would be consumed in fire.

"I had the impression," said Higino Faria, as he recalled the terrified faces that surrounded him, "that it was the day of final judgement." [11]

It was, countless voices throughout the Cova da Iria could be heard echoing over and over, "the end of the world." [12]

Then—as quickly as it began—it was over.

The cascading ball of horror, ever so real—bent on destroying the planet—suddenly and unexpectedly drew itself to an abrupt and screeching halt.

Its terrible, renegade descent stopped cold in its tracks.

Quivering in place for a second, the once recalcitrant sun then slowly, methodically started to roll itself back towards its firmament in the heavens.

It also, at the same time, began to mystically shed its volume and girth, no longer appearing excessively massive and bright.

Within a sheer matter of moments, a completely normal-looking sun could be seen resting in its mooring in the sky, as if nothing that day had ever taken place.

On the ground, though, something extraordinary was taking place.

Discovered gradually and somewhat incidentally by the crowd as they struggled to process what they had just gone through; the people began to become aware of the fact that everything in the Cova da Iria was now completely dry.

No water. No puddles. No mud.

Not a drop of the rain that had pummeled Fátima for days could be found.

It was as if it had never rained at all.

"As soon as the sun went back in the right place, the wind started to blow hard," recalled Dominic Reis over forty years later in a 1960 television interview, "...and in a few minutes, the ground was dry as this floor here. Even our clothes were dry and looked as though they had just come from the laundry. I believe, I thought. Either I'm out of my mind or this was a miracle, a real miracle!" [13]

Newspapers from throughout Portugal ran articles with photographs of the October 13, 1917, Miracle of the Sun at Fátima. The above article came from an October 1917 Portuguese magazine. The journalist states at the conclusion, "I affirm what I saw. The rest is with science and the Church."

Photo Credit: St. Andrews Productions

CHAPTER TWENTY-ONE

MORE THAN A SIGN?

*"For who has known the mind of the Lord
or who has been his counselor?"*
—Rom 11:34

THE MIRACLE OF THE SUN WAS OVER IN MINUTES.

The prodigious experience, however, left its memory indelibly imprinted in the minds and hearts of the thousands there that day. And, it would live on forever in the accounts that quickly became part of the public record in Portugal.

Having sent reporters and photographers to ensure an accurate summation of Portugal's date with destiny, two of Lisbon's newspapers printed front page stories of the extraordinary event.

To the dismay of the atheistic government, the papers covered the events in a relatively objective manner, forever validating Fátima and its Miracle of the Sun. Wrote *Diário de Notícias* on October 15, 1917:

> According to the testimony of thousands and thousands present there, the sun appeared like a dull silver plate spinning around in a circular movement as if it were moved by electricity... there were people who seemed to see the sun leave its supposed orbit, break through the clouds and descend to the horizon... in a common effort to explain the phenomenon, many crying out in fear that the giant orb would precipitate itself to the earth on top of them, and imploring the protection of the Holy Virgin.[1]

O Seculo, Lisbon's largest daily newspaper, was even more descriptive of the momentous day:

> One could see the immense throng turn towards the sun, which appeared free from the clouds and in its zenith. It looked like a plaque of dull silver, and it was possible to look at it without the least discomfort. It neither burned nor blinded the eyes… At that moment, a great shout went up and one could hear the spectators nearest at hand shouting: "A miracle! A miracle!"

> Before the astonished eyes of the crowd, whose aspect was biblical as they stood bareheaded, pale with fright, eagerly searching the sky, the sun trembled, made sudden incredible movements outside of all cosmic laws—the sun danced according to the typical expression of the people. Few there that day were reluctant to give their testimony. Many of notable status spoke freely and without reservation. [2]

John Haffert, co-founder of the worldwide Fátima apostolate known as the Blue Army, returned to Portugal over four decades later to interview the surviving witnesses that he could locate from that day.

In his book, *Meet the Witnesses*, their memories of the miracle are found to have remained strong and vivid. Perhaps more than anything, these individual's words preserve the best, most truthful record of that singular event in history.

Present at the Cova that afternoon was Dr. Manuel Nunes Formigão, a priest who previously questioned the children after an earlier apparition in September. He recalled the extraordinary "dance of the sun" in detail:

"The sun in its zenith appeared in all its splendor. It began to revolve vertiginously on its axis, like the most magnificent fire wheel that could be imagined, taking on all the colors of the rainbow and sending forth multicolored flashes of light, producing the most astounding effect. This sublime and incomparable spectacle, which was repeated three distinct times, lasted for about ten minutes. The immense multitude, overwhelmed by such evidence of such a tremendous prodigy, threw themselves on their knees." [3]

Another prominent witness was a man named John Carreir. He recalled the panic that set in as the sun descended upon the Cova:

"I saw the sun spinning around and it seemed to come down on us. It revolved like a bicycle wheel. Afterwards, it returned to its place. I wasn't afraid, but I heard people cry out. 'Oh, we are going to die! We are going to die!'" [4]

A farmer, Antonio de Oliveiro, also remembered the fear that rang out as the sun hurled towards the Earth:

"I looked at the sun and saw it spinning like a disc, rolling on itself. I saw people changing color. They were stained with colors of the rainbow. The sun seemed to fall down from the sky...They were afraid and screaming." [5]

A priest named Father Joao Menitra believed his life was over:

"I looked and saw that people were in various colors-yellow, white, blue. At the same time, I beheld the sun spinning at great speed and very near me. I at once thought: I am going to die." [6]

A widow named Maria dos Prazeres recalled the peak hysteria of the crowd during the last moments of the solar miracle:

"I saw the sun turn upon itself; it seemed to fall from the sky... The people around me were crying..." [7]

This sense of the apocalyptic—the feeling of a cosmic annihilation descending from the heavens as the miracle climaxed—appears to have never escaped the witnesses of that surreal day. Over time, though, some preferred to focus on the event as a heavenly intervention, a gift from God to His people.

Interviewed many years later, Carlos Mendes testified that he came to feel a true sense of the divine that day:

"Wan faces, standing here. From every side, great ejaculations, acts of contrition, of the love of God. An indescribable moment! We feel it. We remain dominated by it... What I saw at Fátima could not help but affect my interior life. And I am sure that all who saw the miracle... cannot fail to be impressed by its greatness." [8]

Though the Miracle of the Sun is associated with Fátima, researchers determined the solar event was visible over a vast area, approximately 600 square miles.[9]

In some regions, however, it would have been more difficult to see, due to the village's location in the midst of the Serra de Aire Mountains. The small town of Pombal, thirty-two miles north of Fátima, was the most distant location found to have had witnesses.[10]

The fact that so many on the outskirts of Fátima experienced the miracle quickly dismissed critics who attempted to argue it was a product of collective hallucination or mass hypnosis at the Cova. Moreover, their testimonies—some uncovered decades later—further substantiate the immensity of what took place that afternoon.

In Leiria, eighteen miles away from Fátima, a bright red flash in the sky was reported by a woman who wanted to go to the Cova that day but was forbidden by her husband.[11] In the town of Alburitel, nine miles out, a spinning, revolving sun, that suddenly came down in a zig zag towards Earth, was reported by a young school boy along with his classmates. Together, the children fled the school and hid amongst a group of terrified adults in the streets." [12]

In Minde, eight miles from Fátima, an American building contractor named Albano Barros witnessed the sun "fall from the sky."[13] Likewise, in San Pedro der Moel, an oceanside village thirty miles from Fátima, a Portuguese poet named António Vieira observed the miracle.[14] Years later, in 1935, Vieira recalled the experience:

"On that day, October 13, 1917, I had forgotten the prediction of the three shepherds. I was surprised and charmed by a spectacle in the sky. It was truly astonishing, which I witnessed from this balcony." [15]

The total circumference of the miracle was no small piece of real estate. Yet, after the event was studied, no scientific evidence could register the breadth of the phenomenon—or, that it even happened at all. Professor Frederico Oom, director of the Lisbon Observatory, told a reporter from *O Século*:

"If it were a cosmic phenomenon, astronomical and meteorological observatories would not have failed to record it. And this is precisely what is missing, the inevitable recording of all the disturbances in the world systems, no matter how small they may be." [16]

And that's just it. It wasn't a cosmic phenomenon of any sort. It wasn't something that could be physically measured and documented.

It was a miracle.

And it *did* take place.

"Of the historic reality of this event," said Dr. Pio Sciatizzi, an Italian professor of mathematics and astronomy, "there can be no doubt whatsoever." [17]

Ironically, the failure of any scientific evidence was a blessing in disguise for another reason: it helped to solidify the Catholic Church's approval of Fátima.

Wrote Bishop Dom José Correia da Silva on October 13, 1930:

"This phenomenon—which no astronomical observatory registered and which therefore was not natural—was witnessed by persons of all categories and of all social classes, believers and unbelievers, journalists of the principal Portuguese newspapers, and even by people miles away. Facts which annul any explanation of collective illusion." [18]

The plunging sun at Fátima on October 13, 1917, was no illusion. The experience was real, as the thousands would testify.

Perhaps, for many witnesses, it was *too* real.

Lasting minutes before their eyes, it would be branded forever in their souls.

It signaled, wrote Fátima author Antonio Socci, "something different about the epoch in which we are living—perhaps an apocalyptic turning point in the history of humanity." [19]

However, as the decades following the miracle went by, questions concerning its constitution arose.

What was God's intent in serving up such a frightful event that left such an emotional impact?

Why did the miracle involve the sun?

Was the miracle related to the prophecies contained in the Secret of Fátima?

Over the years, many came to believe the miracle was more than a sign the Virgin Mary gave to prove her presence at Fátima, to confirm that "God exists."

It appeared, rather, to have a greater purpose, a symbolic significance that perhaps only time would reveal.

And in 1945, that time arrived.

CHAPTER TWENTY-TWO

A TURNING POINT IN HISTORY

"For lo, the day is coming, blazing like an oven, when all the proud and all evildoers will be stubble. And the day that is coming will set them on fire, leaving them neither root nor branch, says the Lord of hosts."

—Mal 3:19

BY 1950, BISHOP FULTON SHEEN WAS CONVINCED OF SOMETHING. Internationally renowned for his radio and television ministries, the saintly bishop believed the Virgin Mary delivered perhaps her most profound prophecy at Fátima on the afternoon of October 13, 1917, the day of the great Miracle of the Sun.[1]

Only Mary did it without words.

Overwhelming the audience's senses and emotions, the extraordinary solar miracle that day left the 100,000 [2] in attendance stupefied. In no uncertain terms, almost all who departed after the sun's grand finale were bewildered by its magnitude, its ferocity—the divine wonder it extracted from deep within their psyche.

But the miraculous phenomenon aroused not only shock and awe, but anxiety and fear.

Years later, many would best remember the relief experienced as the sun retreated back into the firmament. The miracle—which lasted about 12 minutes—caused many to feel more thankful for its ending than its coming. [3]

And for good reason.

The seconds of terror seemed like hours, leaving them happy just to be alive.[4]

Why?

Why did God seemingly hurl the sun upon the crowd at Fátima?

Three times in the months leading up to October 13, the Virgin Mary promised a miracle "so that all may believe." But the beautiful yet alarming, ricocheting sun that day went well beyond what anyone could see as a benevolent sign from a loving God.

The roaring globe of fire, instead, seemed to echo some of God's earlier works. Those found on the sterner pages of the Old Testament, where rivers turned bloody red and plagues of insects blackened the sky.

Therefore, one thing had to be true.

The Miracle of the Sun contained something more within it than was foretold.[5]

As time went by, many suspected the miracle's extraordinary constitution held a deeper message—one that God wanted to give to the world for a reason.

Then, after two historic days in August 1945, the answer to this mystery became plain as day. The power of the sun—released in the atomic bombs dropped over Hiroshima and Nagasaki—revealed the esoteric implications and the hidden symbolism of the great miracle.

Fiery horror rained from the sky on those two days in Japan—just as it did when the sun plunged from the heavens at Fátima.

Even U.S. President Harry Truman, in his statement after the bombing of Hiroshima, did not fail to note the association between the atomic bomb and the sun. "The force from which the sun draws its power has been loosed," stated Truman in his official announcement of the atomic bombing of Japan. [6]

Soon after, Bishop Fulton Sheen—ever perceptive in the ways of the Almighty—came to realize that the dramatic resolution of World War II was related to the Miracle of the Sun. For him, it was another prophecy of the Virgin of Fátima fulfilled.

Reflecting on it all, the astute Sheen saw how the two singular events were intimately linked. He understood how the nuclear age—symbolically foretold through the Miracle of the Sun at Fátima—had been realized in Hiroshima and Nagasaki.

Describing the two atomic bombings as "the birthday of the modern world," Sheen realized also that turning to Mary would be the only answer in containing this nightmare:

"At Fátima, the fact that Mary could take this great center and seat of atomic power and make it her plaything, the fact that she could swing the sun like a trinket at her wrist, is a proof that God has given her power over it." [7]

Many came to quickly see not just the ferocity of the atomic bomb but what it meant to the faceoff between the East and the West that was intensifying.

Throughout the West, noted names grasped how the horror of the atomic bomb and the ambitious designs of Communism yielded a compounding crisis of unimaginable danger.

"Each one of the inhabitants of our planet should think now, on this day," President John F. Kennedy told the United Nations on September 25, 1961, "when this world of ours will no longer be inhabitable." [8]

Bernhard Philberth, the renowned physicist, concurred with Kennedy: "With nuclear energy, a possible end to our immediate surroundings looms up in an alarming manner." [9]

Even Eugène Ionesco, one of the foremost figures in the world of theater at the time, famously entered the discussion in a most awaited speech that drew international attention at the opening of the Salzburg Festival in 1972:

"Hell is predominating today. Everything has become problematic. Any catastrophe is possible tomorrow. We live under the threat of cosmic destruction." [10]

Church figures chimed in too, citing the great danger of nuclear weapons to the survival of the planet.

"How grievous and enormous then must be the sins of our God-defying century for the warning of nuclear war and world Communism to be wrung from a God of love and mercy. How unspeakable must be the crimes and abominations of our age for the Omnipotent to hurl the sun terrifyingly towards Earth… Is this not the story of Sodom and Gomorrah all over again?" wrote Catholic author Francis Johnston. [11]

"We are racing against a deadline," noted Fátima spokesman Monsignor William C. McGrath, "… when Russia's superiority in atomic weapons will usher in a D-Day of universal death. We sincerely hope and pray that a faithful response to the message of Fátima will result in the conversion of Russia and the crumbling of world Communism into chaotic ruin." [12]

But Cardinal Yu Pin, the exiled Archbishop of Nanking, voiced the gravity of the situation perhaps best. Nuclear weapons in the hands of Communists, he noted in 1978, could lead to the end of the West:

"The world is at the turning point of history and the fate of mankind hangs in the balance. A perspective of the world today does not exempt the United States from future control by Communism...for eventual world Communist enslavement. We are in the last period of time sufficient to change the course of history... We must encourage the faithful to pray fervently and promote the message of Fátima..." [13]

Even an Italian priest from San Giovanni Rotondo—known to the world as Padre Pio— rued the times at hand not long before his death:

"Pray, get others to pray, for the world is at the threshold of perdition." [14]

While she would often comment on the errors of Russia as realized in Communism, Sister Lúcia made no direct effort to confirm or deny the nuclear symbolism of the Miracle of the Sun.

Nor did Fátima's hierarchal trustees. Father Joaquin Alonso, Fátima's official documentarian, went so far as to stress in his findings that any reported "cosmic-theological interpretations" of the Miracle of the Sun were wholly devoid of historical foundation, and what occurred at Fátima "does not admit of fantastic interpretations." [15]

These were undoubtedly efforts to ensure that no such understandings were part of the official record of the events at Fátima. But Pope John XXIII clearly alluded to Fátima's implicit nuclear message. While Pope Paul VI believed the fall of the sun was not only a warning of nuclear war, but an "eschatological sign of the end times."*

Paul VI's apostolic exhortation, *Signum Magnum* (The Great Sign)— understood to be the Virgin Mary in *The Book of Revelation* (Rv 12:1)—was released on May 13, 1967, the fiftieth anniversary of the

---

*   In a notable irony, Pope Paul VI died on August 6, 1978, the 33rd anniversary of the dropping of the first atom bomb on Hiroshima. His immediate successor, Pope John Paul I, would then die on his 33rd day in office. [It is also worthy to note that it was 33 years from Pope Leo XIII's vsion/experience with Satan in 1884 to Fátima in 1917.]

first Fátima apparition. This was seen as a move that especially signaled Paul's desire for the apocalyptic message of Fátima to remain alive and significant to the Church, [16] a Church he warned was filling with "the smoke of Satan" after his encyclical on contraception, *Humanae Vitae*, met with strong resistance. [17]

And then there comes Pope John Paul II.

In his March 1984 "Act of Entrustment of the World" prayer—viewed as the most successful attempt at the consecration of Russia prior to the 2022 consecration by Pope Francis—the Pope bemoaned not only the danger of nuclear war but of "incalculable self-destruction," going so far as to echo Emperor Hirohito's words in his address to the Japanese people on August 15, 1945.[18]

With the Miracle of the Sun, the prophetic Virgin previewed at Fátima—as she had foretold World War II and Communism—the coming of an historic 20th century event that would change the world in a dramatic and irreversible way. But, some have warned, the great miracle that October day was only half of the Virgin's nuclear alarm at Fátima.

Over time, the Great Sign of January 25-26, 1938—the strange and unique aurora borealis that overshadowed a great swatch of the planet that evening—also came to be seen as being rich in symbolism of the approaching nuclear age—and perhaps more.[19] (See Chapter 6)

According to a highly respected American nuclear physicist, the Great Sign prefigured not only the advent of the nuclear age but potentially an unprecedented danger hidden within it —one holding such extraordinary consequences that his warnings even drew the attention of Hollywood.

CHAPTER TWENTY-THREE

THE SONG OF THE SWORD

*"Then the angel took the censer and filled
it with burning coals from the altar,
and hurled it down on the earth. There were peals of thunder,
rumblings, flashes of lightening, and an earthquake."*

—Rv 8:5

DIAGNOSED BY SCIENTISTS AS AN AURORA BOREALIS, THE SOLAR phenomenon of January 25, 1938, was the Great Sign that the Virgin Mary preannounced at Fátima on July 13, 1917.

The sign would, Mary foretold, signal the onset of the Second World War.

That it did, as many historians opine that the war began six weeks later with Hitler's annexation of Austria on March 12, 1938.

As with the Miracle of the Sun, however, the Great Sign came to be seen as ominous, with Fátima experts discerning it also held the prophetic symbolism of the coming age of nuclear weapons.

And, perhaps, even more.

According to some, the symbolic makeup of the Great Sign hints at the truly unimaginable. It appears, they argue, that the sign was intended to take the approaching menace of nuclear weapons—already prophetically symbolized in the Miracle of the Sun in 1917—to the next step, to an even more horrifying degree of potential danger, perhaps to the level of Pope John Paul II's concern of "incalculable self-destruction."

Father Edward O'Conner, a former head of theology at Notre Dame University, writes:

It has been prophesied that there will not be a Third
World War, yet many of the prophecies seem to be alluding to something worse to befall the world from the hands
of man.[1]

Does the Great Sign symbolically hint of "something worse"?
But what could be more terrible than a nuclear war?

The exact constitution of the Great Sign of January 1938 remains
an enigma.

Was the Great Sign an aurora borealis that God, in his foreknowledge, used to signal the start of World War II?

Was the Great Sign an aurora borealis that God enhanced to such
a degree that its unique characteristics were intended to reveal His
divine hand at work, thus confirming it truly was a sign?

Or, was the Great Sign a completely miraculous intervention like
the Miracle of the Sun at Fátima in 1917—a global "Burning Bush"
manifestation—intended to not only mark the coming of the Second
World War, but to symbolically convey the unknown and frightful
consequences associated with nuclear weapons—perhaps beyond
Hiroshima and Nagasaki?

One nuclear scientist thinks the Great Sign was exactly that—a warning of a greater danger from such weapons than just their application.

At an April 1986 meeting of *The American Physical Society* in
Washington, D.C., Dr. Rand McNally—a prominent nuclear physicist
at the Fusion Energy Division of Oak Ridge National Laboratory in
Tennessee—presented his theory of what actually occurred on the evening of January 25, 1938. [2]

Besides appearing to confirm Sister Lúcia's opinion in her *Third
Memoir*—that a "closer scientific investigation" of the phenomenon would reveal "it could not have been an aurora borealis"—Dr.
McNally's work opened up a new, more profound contemplation of
the solar prodigy.

After decades of investigation, the scientist came to a conclusion. The fiery red, angry-looking sky on the evening of January 25—an unprecedented celestial event according to many scientists—was "not a natural aurora."[3]

It was, McNally wrote, "similar in nature to the false aurora created by an atomic explosion."[4]

Relying on years of research, McNally contends there is a theoretical possibility that a large enough nuclear detonation (50 megatons or more) can set off a deadly chain reaction in the atmosphere.[5] This could then evolve into what he termed a "nuclear tornado."[6] A nuclear tornado, McNally explained, would be a ferocious, massive conflagration that would use the atmosphere as fuel to sweep out of control across the planet.

The esteemed nuclear physicist based his findings on a mathematical understanding of the genesis of a thermonuclear reaction and its potential, hidden consequences. Moreover, McNally pointed out, this *was not* simply a new discovery. The scientists who worked on the *Manhattan Project* were very aware of this possibility in 1945.[7]

Most significantly—in light of today's nuclear arsenals—McNally stressed that only "one" high yield-to-weight nuclear explosion would be necessary to ignite the atmosphere and trigger this crisis.[8]

In other words, an all-out nuclear war, or any war for that matter, is not needed. One large nuclear weapon—deliberately or accidently detonated in a conflict or through a test—could generate the reaction. In fact, McNally says, an error by just one person could trigger the catastrophe.

This dangerous scenario was demonstrated by the height and breadth of the Great Sign of 1938, according to McNally.[9] He discovered this after comparing the alleged aurora borealis that year to a nuclear test that took place on an island in 1958.[10] That test created a magnetic dynamo in the upper atmosphere, six minutes after the detonation.[11] Using the findings of that test, he demonstrated that the phenomenon of 1938 could not have been a natural aurora.[12]

In 1961, McNally wrote to a Soviet scientist about the dangers of high megaton testing. This was after Soviet military leadership boasted of planning to detonate a 100-megaton device.[13]

Over the years, in repeated letters to scientific organizations, McNally mathematically outlined the consequences of such testing and the risks of igniting a nuclear tornado. He urged nations to ban all nuclear weapons.

McNally, a Catholic who visited Fátima, upholds Lúcia's contention that the phenomenon of 1938 was, without question, the Great Sign foretold by Mary on July 13, 1917. But, he suspects, besides the Sign marking the onset of World War II, it was also intended by God to symbolically convey the approach of something more ominous than the war—the hidden potential of nuclear weapons for an unimaginable catastrophe!

They say a picture is worth a thousand words.

If so, then it appears that Mary may have prophetically warned at Fátima of the coming nuclear age not once, but twice, in the strongest language possible: two miraculous panoramic, celestial murals of unprecedented magnitude, filled with divine symbolism.

The first, witnessed by tens of thousands at Fátima in 1917.

The second, witnessed by millions the world over in 1938.

John Haffert, perhaps Fátima's greatest lay advocate, devoted much of his work to the significance of these two "visual prophecies." In, *Her Words to the Nuclear Age*, Haffert writes:

> A fireball, which the crowd thought was actually the sun, plunged towards the Earth over the mountain at Fátima. It was objectively real. It was not something created in the imagination of those tens of thousands of witnesses... Everyone who saw it, at least within a six-mile radius, thought it was the end of the world...and they felt the heat.
>
> But then came the second miracle, even more significant to our nuclear age: the Great Sign that Our Lady said would indicate that all the prophecies she had made were about to unfold upon the world...leading to the annihilation of several entire nations. When the Great Sign appeared in 1938, there were not merely tens of thousands who thought the world was going to end but millions...the world seemed to be on fire on the night of January 25 – 26, 1938.[14]

Haffert—who wrote twenty books on Fátima and first interviewed Sister Lúcia less than twelve months after the first atomic bomb was dropped—held great regard for Dr. McNally's theory.[15] He also did not believe the Great Sign of 1938 was meant to only signal the onset of World War II. Rather, he suspected the makeup of the Great Sign symbolically warned of Mary's unfulfilled words at Fátima of "the annihilation of nations," a prophecy he saw hovering over the world for decades as if in a holding pattern waiting to land.

In the mid-80s, Haffert produced a five million dollar major Hollywood movie starring Martin Sheen titled *State of Emergency*.* The title came from the words President John F. Kennedy used to describe what day-to-day life would be like for a child born into a nuclear world.

The film fictionally presented the dangers of a nuclear tornado and how the Great Sign of 1938 was warning of such a calamity. It was a warning, Haffert always insisted, designed not for the world of the mid-twentieth century, but for the future:

> A warning is given that something may be avoided. But World War II began only two months after the Great Sign. This left no time for it to have any possible opportunity to prevent the war. We must presume the Sign was intended for today...when it is known. The remaining chastisement foretold at Fátima is far more terrible than the Second World War. Our Lady said several nations will be annihilated...this is what the Great Sign refers to. The purpose of the Great Sign is to warn us.[16]

A weeping Madonna—near the conclusion of *State of Emergency*—parenthetically sums up this great soul's six-decade long plea for civilization to save itself from a fiery holocaust before it was too late.

Appropriately, *"Too Late?"* was the title of one of John Haffert's last books.

There is another significant nuclear connection with Fátima.

---

*   Martin Sheen starred in a movie about Fátima, *A State of Emergency*, in 1986, and in a movie about Medjugorje, *Gospa*, in 1995.

In 1973, a series of reported supernatural events—approved by the Catholic Church in 1984—occurred at a convent occupied by the Community of the Sisters of Junshen in the city that experienced the second atomic bombing in World War II—Nagasaki, Japan.

A wood-carved statue of the Virgin Mary in the convent wept blood there one hundred and one times. The statue, along with a nun named Sister Agnes Sasagawa, both miraculously manifested the bloody stigmata in the right hand.[17]

The supernatural events at Akita climaxed on October 13—the anniversary date of Fátima's Miracle of the Sun—when Mary delivered a dreadful warning to Sister Agnes of a cataclysmic future:

"As I told you," the Virgin Mary said to Sister Agnes, "if men do not repent and better themselves, the Father will inflict a terrible punishment upon all humanity. It will be a punishment *worse* than the Deluge, such as one will never have seen before. Fire will fall from the sky and will wipe out a great part of humanity, the good as well as the bad, sparing neither priests nor faithful. The survivors will find themselves so desolate that they will envy the dead." [18]

A fiery punishment worse than the Deluge? Coming from a prophecy out of Nagasaki?

Considering the circumstantial evidence, one can only conclude that this divine warning of fire falling from the sky—delivered from such a remarkable location—must be related to a potential nuclear scenario. No other explanation bears even the slightest consideration.

Besides the link to Nagasaki, the direct connection of Akita with Fátima immediately presents itself as undeniable in meaning in another way: the October 13 date of the Akita message is inescapably connected to the October 13, 1917, Miracle of the Sun at Fátima, and, therefore, the nuclear symbolism of the solar miracle that day.

At Fátima, Mary warned of a worse war than World War I.

At Akita, the Virgin warned of a worse punishment than the Deluge.

Both the Second World War and the Deluge were of global significance. Mary's words, however, are even more ominous at Akita. This is because the Deluge left no survivors except for the eight stowed away in the Ark. It was, *Genesis* implies, a chastising event for the sin of the world, historically incomparable in magnitude and devastation.

On April 22, 1984, Bishop John Ito declared the events at Akita to be supernatural and granted the approval of the Church.[19]

Asked by a journalist, "What is the message of Akita?"

Ito replied, "It is the message of Fátima." [20]

But Akita is more than just the message of Fatima. It's a revelation that appears uncannily similar to some of the more grave prophecies in Scripture, too.

Indeed, both the Old and New Testaments are replete with warnings—thunderous clamorings from the prophets and even Christ—of a future age that is to be consumed by so much evil, sin, and apostasy that God will move to radically shake up the status quo in an even more calamitous way than in the times of Noah.

In Matthew, in Mark, Christ foretells a period of great tribulation before His Parousia, one "such as has not been since the beginning of the world until now, nor will ever be" (Mt 24:21). He even cites the prophet Daniel's foretellings of this coming unimaginable woe.

Isaiah, Ezekiel, Malachi and a number of other Old Testament prophets also speak of a time of unparalleled divine justice stationed on the distant horizon. Known in Scripture as the "Day of the Lord," it is said to be followed by an age of harmony between God and His people.

No words more succinctly expound this coming time than Zechariah's "The Song of the Sword," which seems to anticipate Mary's prophecies at Akita and Fatima of great upheaval in the hierarchy of the Church, of tremendous human carnage throughout the world, and a subsequent era of tranquility that basks in the love and peace of God.

The fact that this well known passage in Scripture is from Zechariah 13—a number that undeniably recalls both Fatima and Akita—causes one to certainly wonder if this is no accident.

THE SONG OF THE SWORD

> Awake, O sword, against my shepherd,
>   against the man who is my associate,
>   says the Lord of hosts.
> Strike the Shepherd
>   that the sheep may be dispersed'
> and I will turn my hand against the
>   little ones.

In all the land,
>two-thirds of them will be cut
off and perish,
>and one-third shall be left.
I will bring the one-third through fire,
>and I will refine them as silver is refined,
>and I will test them as gold is tested.
>They shall call upon my name, and I will hear them.
I will say, "They are my people,"
>and they shall say,"The Lord is my God."

Zech 13:7–9**

** According to *The New American Bible,* in Mt 26: 31, the Evangelist quotes from this verse, in somewhat different form: " I will strike the shepherd, and the sheep of the flock will be dispersed." This verse is also understood to refer to a future time of great unrest in the Church and the world, according to various Catholic private revelations.

CHAPTER TWENTY-FOUR

THE LANGUAGE OF TEARS

*"No one can lay hold on anything unless
it is given him from on high."*

—Jn: 3:27

O NLY ONE PERSON WOULD BE NOW NEEDED TO LAUNCH A NUCLEAR nightmare on all of civilization. And by 1960, not just U.S. President John F. Kennedy, but much of the world worried that man had arrived.

Assuming leadership of the Soviet Union in 1953 with the death of Joseph Stalin, Nikita Khrushchev commenced on a reckless path that put more chill in the already icy Cold War.

Telling Western ambassadors at a reception for Poland's Władysław Gomułka at the Polish Embassy in Moscow on November 18, 1956, "We will bury you," [1] followed by a bizarre shoe-pounding rant during a Plenary Meeting of the UN General Assembly on October 12, 1960, in New York,[2] the short, bald leader of the nuclear ladened Soviet Union was not exactly the man people wanted to see holding the keys to a war chest full of doomsday weapons.

The surreal moments by the Soviet leader were shown to be not without merit for such trepidation. Two years later, the erratic Khrushchev managed to engineer the world's first nuclear showdown between the United States and the Soviet Union—a *thirteen-day* heart-pounding debacle that had people looking for mushroom clouds to spring up at any moment.

Known as the Cuban Missile Crisis of October 1962, the two-week confrontation over the Soviet's placement of offensive nuclear missiles in Cuba would be the moment the two superpowers came closest to an apocalyptic slugfest, so close there were unsubstantiated reports that Pope John XXIII tried to mediate between Kennedy and Khrushchev by giving them a peek of the Third Secret of Fátima.[3]

The missile scare wound down with a settlement. But the eyes of the world would forevermore remain on the two grappling nations. A decades-long match of nuclear chess was underway, with few doubting there wouldn't be another nail biting confrontation.

It was—as one prominent Vatican journalist described it—a "planetary rivalry," with Fátima's Third Secret seeming to now have "planetary importance." [4]

The eyes of the Virgin Mary appeared to notice the mounting danger, too.

The same year Khrushchev assumed the helm of the Soviet empire, a weeping statue of the Virgin in Syracuse, Sicily, drew the attention of the world.

Overwhelming in symbolism for the fragile post-war nation of Italy, Mary's teardrops won unanimous approval from an episcopal conference and by the local bishop in little over three months.[5]

"Will men understand," remarked Pope Pius XII in reference to the weeping Madonna of Syracuse, "the mysterious language of those tears?"

The days following World War II were mysterious for sure.

As if in harmony with General MacArthur's apocalyptic rhetoric, the air seemed filled with more and more "signs of the times"—curious events that people the world over began to see as pointing to biblical prophecies. This thinking seemed justified with the birth of Israel in 1948, an end times-caliber prophecy bar none.

By now, Pius XII certainly understood the times and the tears—and the good Pope continuously tried to do something about them.

On October 31, 1942, Pius consecrated the world to Mary's Immaculate Heart, with a veiled reference to Russia.[6] The long desired papal act, however, was not accompanied in union with the bishops of the world, as requested at Fátima. By 1943, Sister Lúcia already noted that the attempt was incomplete. [7]

In 1944, Pius XII took further action.

Pointing again to Mary as the answer to the world's bloody brawl that was now in its fifth year, the Holy Father imposed the Feast of the Immaculate Heart upon the Universal Church, declaring it to be annually celebrated on August 22.[8]

Though World War II would end soon after, the weary pontiff needed to stay on the offensive, as he could see that Marxism's errors were about to swallow half of Europe. With the nuclear genie now out of the bottle, however, Pius couldn't help but state the obvious in a Christmas message to his cardinals in 1945:

"The world is on the verge of a frightful abyss…men must prepare themselves for suffering as mankind has never seen." [9]

Two years later, Pius instructed Cardinal Benedetto Masella to go to Fátima in his name to crown a statue of Our Lady of Fátima, Queen of the World. [10] The crown itself came as a gift from the women of Portugal who contributed their wedding rings and jewelry for its construction. It weighed an incredible 44 pounds and held in it 950 diamonds, 313 pearls, 17 rubies, 14 emeralds, 269 turquoises, and 2,650 precious stones. [11]

Then, on November 1, 1950—in his boldest move to date—Pius XII declared the Dogma of the Virgin Mary's Assumption into Heaven.[12] It would be the fourth Marian dogma, and the second to be proclaimed in little less than a century.

Fátima would stay at the forefront of Pius XII's reign in the new decade. He would even come to refer to himself as the "Pope of Our Lady of Fátima," declaring, "Fátima is a summation of my thinking." [13]

Breaking precedent, in 1951, Pius had the holy year conclude at Fátima rather than in Rome.[14] The following year, the pontiff formulated again what some say was the only explicit consecration of Russia to the Immaculate Heart of Mary up to that point.

But, once more, Sister Lúcia said it was not valid.[15]

Finally, in 1954, Pius issued an encyclical on the Queenship of Mary,[16] directly referring to Mary's miraculous appearance at Fátima. This was shortly followed by his raising the Church of Our Lady of the Rosary at Fátima to the rank of a minor basilica on November 12. [17]

The work of this great servant must have been on the right tract.

This is because Pope Pius XII reported that he personally experienced in Rome in 1950 on four occasions (Oct. 30, 31; Nov. 1, 8) what some believe was a solar event very similar to Fátima's Miracle of the Sun: [18]

> At a certain moment, having lifted my eyes above the papers I had in my hand, I was struck by a phenomenon that I had never seen before. The sun, which was fairly high, looked like a pale, yellow opaque globe completely surrounded by a luminous halo, which nevertheless did not prevent me at all from staring attentively at the sun without the slightest discomfort. A very light cloud was before it. The opaque globe began moving outward, slowly turning upon itself, and going from left to right and vice versa. But within the globe, very strong movements could be seen in all clarity and without interruption.[19]

All of this occurred while a statue of the Pilgrim Virgin of Fátima was present in the Vatican at the time. [20] This was a fact that the Holy Father did not fail to note.

Pius XII's entire reign can be viewed as one in which God directly and visibly worked to combat the errors of Russia through him. A collection of odd coincidences seems to bear witness to this truth.

At the hour of Mary's first appearance at Fátima—noon on May 13, 1917—Pope Pius XII was consecrated a bishop. At that same hour, blood was shed in a Moscow church.[21]

In May 1946, when Stalin held his greatest May Day parade with over a million lock-stepped uniformed marchers processing through the heart of Red Square, Pope Pius XII sent *a legate a latere* to Fátima to honor Our Lady of Fátima in the presence of a million white handkerchief-waiving pilgrims. [22]

Finally, the infamous Joseph Stalin was fatally struck down on the anniversary of the election of Pope Pius XII to the Chair of Peter, March 5, 1953—which also happened to be Pope Pius's birthday. [23]

By the late 1950s, the lone surviving visionary of Fátima well understood the seriousness of the Madonna's tears, too. And, like Pope Pius, Sister Lúcia continued to take action.

On December 26, 1957, Father Augustin Fuentes Anguiano, a Mexican priest who had been appointed vice postulator of the causes for the beatification of Francisco and Jacinta Marto, interviewed Lúcia.[24] Upon releasing some of his findings, a crisis of sorts erupted. [25]

Throughout the West, the conversation generated a new level of interest in Fátima, elevating its urgency, as Lúcia's reported words sounded more apocalyptic than ever—something the Vatican was not pleased about.

The meeting set off a stir for other reasons, the most prevalent being the publishing of distorted versions of the interview. But a review of the authentic dialogue, as published by Father Alonso, revealed a clear, mystical picture of the times at hand.

A "terrible chastisement" was about to befall a sinful world, Alonso reported Lúcia had, indeed, told Father Fuentes.[26] Alonso quoted Fuentes as speaking of a message he received from "the lips of Lúcia" herself:

Fuentas: *I would like to tell you only of the last conversation I had with her, which took place on the twenty-sixth of December last. When I visited Sister Lúcia in her convent, I found her very concerned, pale, far from well. The first thing she said to me was this:*

Lúcia: Father, the Blessed Virgin is very sad because no one heeds her message, neither the good nor the bad. The good continue in their life of virtue, but without paying any attention to the message of Fátima. Sinners keep following the road of evil, because they fail to see the horrible chastisement that is about to befall them.

Believe me Father, God is going to punish the world, and very soon. The chastisement of Heaven is imminent. In less than two years, 1960 will be here, and what will happen then? If we do not pray and do penance, it will be very grievous for all of us. Our Lady has said repeatedly, 'Many nations will disappear from the face of the Earth, and Russia will be the instrument of Heaven's chastisement for the entire world, unless we obtain the conversion of that poor nation.' Father, the Devil is carrying on a decisive battle with the Virgin

Mary. He sees that his time is getting short, and he is making every effort to gain as many souls as possible. He wants to get hold of consecrated souls.

Our Lady did not tell me that we are living in the last epoch of the world, but she did give me to understand that, firstly, we are going through a decisive battle at the end of which we will either be of God or of the Evil One ; there will be no middle way; secondly, that the last means God will give to the world for its salvation are the Holy Rosary and the devotion to the Immaculate Heart of Mary; and thirdly, when God in His Providence, is about to chastise the world, He first uses every means to save us, and when He sees we have not made use of them, then He gives the last anchor of salvation, His Mother. [27]

Throughout the world, Lúcia's alarming words triggered concern.
Horrible chastisement?
No middle way?
Decisive battle?
As with her conversation with Professor Walsh on July 15, 1946— when he asked her if she "had any revelation about the end of the world," and Lúcia stated, "I cannot answer that question" [28]—Fátima's apocalyptic reputation was once again in the news on both sides of the Atlantic.

In subsequent remarks over the next three decades, Lúcia continued to hold one reason for such serious and alarming talk: the unrelenting march of Marxist atheism.

It was a march that tried to show it wasn't afraid of the Virgin of Fátima, either.

In Budapest Hungary, on March 2, 1953, the Communists put on a play mocking Our Lady of Fátima. Reported by *Newsweek Magazine*, the journalist noted that "it didn't draw a laugh or a sound of applause from the audience." [29]

Nothing in the news, though, seemed to contradict Lúcia's view.

In Germany, as an encore to its blockade of Berlin in 1948-49—called a prelude to World War III—a wall was erected in 1961 to separate the eastern side of the city from the western. Or, rather, to keep the people living in the Communist sector of Berlin from departing to the free sectors of the West.

Throughout Eastern Europe, it was no different.

All along the Iron Curtain, hostilities continued to flare as people sought to resist the Communist stranglehold on life. Around the world—from Africa to South and Central America, from Southeast Asia to the Middle East—Communism stayed on the prowl. Violence, anarchy, and restlessness pervaded.

No nation, as Lúcia insisted, was safe from Marxism's toxic tentacles.

Even in the United States, the effects of atheistic thinking were spreading as American society by the late 1960s became strained, decadent, and leftward leaning.

But how could this be in a nation that proclaimed to be blessed with a gift of freedom that came from God?

How could this happen in a country fervently opposed to Communism since Lenin first set up shop in Russia?

Ironically, America's incredible freedom was beginning to reveal itself as a double-edged sword.

After World War II, the nation set out to turn its war-time production into the manufacturing of goods for peace-time use. Business flourished. Labor prospered. A scientific revolution followed, brought about largely by the atomic research. There was a baby boom. It was an exciting time to live.

A new medium of communication—television—brought entertainment into millions of homes. With the development of super highways, international airports, and mass transportation, factories churned out new lines of products that could be shipped from one end of the world to another. Soon, modern appliances and plastic devices of every kind turned life in the country into an unending quest for convenience and pleasure.

Twenty years later, something occurred that was not foreseen.

The post-war generation—who had everything—had been transformed into a new breed of malcontents. They were disgruntled souls. Large on talk, they propounded radical philosophies and opinions on everything from sex to politics. Everyone had an opinion, but they were generally unenlightened opinions.

Over the next two decades, television brought the philosophies of the Sixties into every home in America, and the erroneous ways of this generation were made to seem normal. What had once been socially taboo was now portrayed as morally acceptable, even beneficial.

Out went religion, the traditional family, decency, and God. In came a variety of lifestyles, beliefs, and movements that sought to deconstruct and redefine society. From pro-choice to political correctness, from radical feminism to New Age beliefs, from homosexuality to white collar crime, the economic and intellectual fruits of the post-World War II era had backfired.

By the late 1980s, the West had become more like the old Wild West—dangerous and lawless, shameless and guiltless. Like with Communism, the people had become slaves to a tyranny—not so much of the body, but of the mind and soul, just as Mary foretold. In retrospect, some wrote the fruits of the *Enlightenment* were reaching a climax. [30]

Mary warned at Fátima of the spread of Russia's errors. But she didn't elaborate on how or where this would happen. Now, as godless behavior swept through the West, both questions could be answered.

The vast and deadly philosophical, atheistic driven tenets of Marxism knew no rules, as it took aim on all of civilization. Every nation was its goal through any means possible. Consequently, preventing government coups and defending border invasions were only part of the solution.

At its heart, this new danger was a way of thinking. Marxist atheism could infect a culture, it was apparent, without a revolution or a military invasion, without a vote cast or a bullet fired. [31]

Years after General Douglas MacArthur's closing remarks to end World War II on the U.S.S. Missouri, the tireless Bishop Fulton Sheen continued to warn of what was coming in the West, especially in America.

Sheen spoke of an approaching time of confusion, of an apostasy of the faith that together could lead to immense trouble. Especially clear to him was how dire the situation was becoming as he watched America become a moral abyss and a paradise for freethinkers. Fertile ground, he thought, for rejecting the teachings of Christ and for nurturing the rise of a godless reality of life:

"We live in the days of the Apocalypse," observed Sheen, who wrote a series of books confronting atheism and its role in a coming climax of our era. "Great forces—the Mystical Body of Christ and the mystical

Body of the Anti-Christ—are beginning to draw battle lines for a cataclysmic contest." [32]

On the evening of October 16, 1917, just three days after the Miracle
of the Sun at Fátima, seven Franciscans met at the Seraphic College in
Rome to form the Militia of the Immaculata.

Maximilian Maria Kolbe, who Pope John Paul II canonized on
October 10, 1982, founded the organization to convert sinners, here-
tics, and schismatics, primarily Masons.

Kolbe took the action after witnessing a Masonic parade in Rome
that wound its way through the streets of the Eternal City brandishing
banners that stated "Lucifer will rule in the Vatican" in the century to
come. [33]

Theologians emphasize that Mary did not come to Fátima to only
prophesize the approaching hazards of Communism and the Nuclear
Age. Rather, her warnings came with solutions.

The Church needed to do its part, especially the Pope and the bishops. And the people needed to do their part. Prayer, sacrifice, and
living in peace with one another were necessary in order for love and
hope to triumph over anger and hatred.

Most of all, what was needed was what Lúcia pleaded at Fátima:
"Men must cease offending God who is already so much offended." [34]

By 1981, however, it was strikingly clear. The response had not been
nearly enough. The pervasive confrontation with the "errors of Russia"
raged on, in ways seen and unseen. And, there were now also enough
nuclear weapons to scorch every inch of the Earth.

Thus, in Yugoslavia, Mary was busy at work.

And, as her words would start to reveal at Medjugorje, she seemed
to be saying that a closing chapter in this drama was falling into place.

The Soviet Union's Tsar Bomba. The largest atomic bomb ever detonated.

Photo Credit: Croquant-CC BY SA 3.0

Dr. Rand McNally. He warned of the danger of a "nuclear tornado."

Photo Credit: St. Andrews Productions

John Haffert wrote 25 books on Fátima. The co-founder of the Blue Army, Haffert agreed with Bishop Fulton Sheen on the nuclear symbolism contained in Fátima's Miracle of the Sun in 1917.

Photo Credit: St. Andrews Productions

Bishop Fulton Sheen was the first to recognize that the Miracle of the Sun was terrifying for a reason: it was meant to divinely preview the coming nuclear age.

Photo Credit: St. Andrews Productions

Soviet President Nikita Khrushchev
and President John F. Kennedy.
The Cuban Missile Crisis in October
1962 lasted 13 days, a number that
once again pointed to Fatima.

Photo Credit: U.S. Department
of State

On June 25, 1981—the
day after the first appearance of the Virgin Mary
at Medjugorje—Israeli
leader Moshe Dayan let the
world know that Israel had
nuclear weapons.

Photo Credit: Israel Defense
Forces (IDF). Designated
Public Domain by
Israel government.

The bombing of Hiroshima,
August 6, 1945.

Left Photo Credit: Peace Memorial
Museum / AP

Edward Teller was
known as the "Father of
the Hydrogen Bomb."

Right Photo Credit:
Open Media Ltd.

PART III

HEROES AND VILLAINS

66 When I first met Pope John Paul II a year ago in Alaska, I thanked him for his life and his apostolate. And, I dared to suggest to him that in the example of men like himself and in the prayers of simple people everywhere, simple people like the children of Fátima, there resides more power than in all the great armies and statesmen of the world."

—President Ronald Reagan,
Address to the Assembly of the Republic of Portugal, Lisbon,
May 9,1985

CHAPTER TWENTY-FIVE

THE DAWN OF SOMETHING GOOD

"And you brought them in and planted them on the mountain of your inheritance—the place where you made your seat, O Lord, the Sanctuary, O Lord, which your hands established."

—Ex 15:17

FOR EIGHT DAYS, FATHER JOZO ZOVKO PRAYED.

Shut off from the outside world, Jozo was instructing a Catholic retreat for nuns at a secluded convent in Kloštar Ivanić, a remote village of 6,000 tucked away in northern Croatia near Zagreb, and 250 miles from his new assignment at the Franciscan parish of St. James in the village of Medjugorje. [1] The priest welcomed the time away to devote to some intense, personal intercession on behalf of his new parishioners. [2]

The undeniably handsome, youthful-looking 40-year-old Franciscan, whose olive complexion and warm smile fit well with his easy going yet intense nature, had been transferred to Medjugorje from Posušje, a town north of Imotski in northwestern Herzegovina.[3] There, he had been happy at his parish.

But now, he was homesick for those days. In the little more than eight months at St. James, the idealistic Jozo discovered his new flock somewhat less passionate in the practice of their faith than hoped for. [4] This was especially disheartening since he had arrived filled with a fresh enthusiasm bolstered by his efforts to improve his own spiritual life.[5]

Indeed, the parish at Medjugorje proved to be a challenging assignment, so much so that Jozo confessed that he sometimes felt like those Israelites who were sorry to leave Egypt.[6] Upon settling in at St. James, Jozo found it needed a bottom-up fix, as the people had lapsed into spiritual doldrums.

There was little family prayer, no sacramental priorities, and few had any clue about any need for fasting and penance. Catholic devotions and practices were missing everywhere. And most now ate meat on Friday because it was, "okay with the Church." [7]

The old teachings were "hard," the members of St. James laid on Jozo.[8] The youth, the parents, and even the Third Order Franciscans balked at his suggested changes to bring more religious structure into their parish.[9]

Gradually, the persistent Jozo initiated prayer meetings and catechism classes to incorporate his approach. But the response to these efforts was lukewarm.[10] On Sundays, his sometimes marathon sermons were said to be inspirational, but only for those who remained awake.

Over time, the priest came to sense his stunted, uninspired parish, like so many of the day, needed a source to reignite their spiritual energy.

And so Jozo committed himself to the only source he could think of to hasten such a change—prayer. He even asked the nuns at the retreat to beseech Heaven with him to help cajole his "anemic" sheep into the light.[11] It was a light he believed his parishioners could find, because they did exhibit great personal faith.

Unbeknownst to Jozo, their strong faith was not just an observation of his; it was real in ways beyond his knowledge. And because of it, his flock's search for the light would not be arduous or long.

Some may say it only took eight prayer-filled days to ignite.

Or rather…to appear.

On June 24, the last day of the retreat, Father Jozo Zovko went into Zagreb for a Christian Renewal Group meeting.[12] There, the first traces of the divine assistance he sought surfaced.

"Father Jozo," one of the Renewal members enthusiastically greeted him, "have you heard that Medjugorje was struck by lightning during the night? They say the Post Office has been burned down, and a lot of other damage has been done." [13]

Jozo hadn't heard. But he did try several times to reach Father Zrinko Cuvalo, his assistant pastor and fellow Franciscan at St. James, only to no avail.[14] Now, he knew why. The telephone lines were still out in Medjugorje.

From Zagreb, Jozo hastened to his former parish in Posušje, then to Split. There, he discovered more about the monstrous storm, but nothing else.

On Saturday, June 27, Jozo headed back to St. James. But first, he and Father Viktor Kosir drove an extra twenty miles north of Medjugorje to a hospital in Mostar, where Jozo's mother had been admitted for a broken leg the night before he departed for the retreat in Croatia.[15]

Exiting the hospital, the two Franciscans crossed paths with an ambulance from the *Health Home* in Čitluk. It was delivering a woman Jozo vaguely recognized from his parish named Dragica Ivanković.

Dragica, a fiery personality from the village of Bijakovići, had been injured at work. Like Jozo's mother, she now owned a broken leg and a bandaged-up hand—courtesy of a chunk of metal that landed on her that morning.[16]

"Where is Fr. Zrinko? What's happened to him?" Dragica barked at Jozo as the two came eye to eye.

Puzzled by the inquiry, Jozo sought whether Father Zrinko Cuvalo had encountered some misfortune while he was away.

"No, no, nothing of the sort," Dragica replied. "Nothing's happened to him, but you need get over to Medjugorje as fast as you can. Our Lady has been appearing to some children! [17] Go to Zrinko, the Madonna has appeared." [18]

An extraordinary utterance to say the least, Jozo remained speechless for a moment.[19] He then dismissed any seriousness to Dragica's puzzling remark, attributing it to her being in a state of shock and possibly incoherent from her injuries.[20]

Still, the two friars picked up the pace back to Medjugorje with a more heightened curiosity of what in the world *was* going on there.

What was going on there, the good priest would soon discover, was something *not* of this world. And, within minutes of his arrival in Medjugorje, Father Jozo Zovko's life would change forever. [21]

Pulling into the parking lot of St. James that lazy Saturday afternoon, the two Franciscans discovered mayhem. Thousands were descending upon the little town, scattering every which way, making Dragica's assessment now seem like an understatement.

Vehicles were parked all around the church, as the commotion surrounded not just the center of Medjugorje but spread up and down the streets throughout the five villages, especially in the direction of Bijakovići.

Two nuns, Sister Marcelina Susac and Sister Vladimira Vucic, both scheduled to be reassigned, wasted no time detailing to Father Jozo the provocation behind the sprawling confusion: [22]

"Six children are saying that Our Lady is appearing to them. People are gathering at the apparitions up on the hill. They are coming from all of Brotnjo, Ljubuska and Krajina. The parish yard, the space around the church and the roads are full of cars and a great crowd of people." [23]

"Has Father Zrinko spoken to the visionaries?" a shocked Jozo wanted to know.

"Yes, and he's recorded the conversations." [24]

Jozo quickly spotted the recorder laying on a table in a gathering room and listened to the tapes. Zrinko, who sounded like a police detective in his cross examination of the children, [25] conducted interviews of Ivan and Vicka that morning.[26] And from what Jozo could draw from the conversations, something incredulous was unfolding on the side of the hill named Podbrdo, just a short drive down the road from the back of St. James.

While far from getting the whole story, Jozo learned from the recording that early in the evening of Wednesday, June 24, a group of children from Bijakovići saw what they believed to be a bright, glowing figure holding a child and floating on the hillside of Podbrdo. Intrigued and puzzled, they believed it was the Virgin Mary and reported the experience to their families.

Then, around the exact same time the following day, it happened again—this time to as many as six children, while witnessed by a crowd of twenty or so friends, neighbors, and relatives who climbed the hill with them.

The six, Jozo drew from the tape, had names: Ivanka Ivanković, Mirjana Dragićević, Vicka Ivanković, Ivan Dragićević, Marija Pavlović, and a little boy named Jacov Čolo.

Jozo further learned that by Friday, the rumor mill had somehow exploded the news across Bosnia and Herzegovina, Croatia and well beyond, as thousands journeyed to the village, coming from as far as seven hours away.

One other aspect of the burgeoning crisis became apparent to him: the tension surrounding the drama sounded like it was already wearing heavily on Father Zrinko. And, based on the sound of his voice during his interrogation of the two children that Saturday morning, the priest wasn't exactly hiding it very well. [27]

Not exactly possessing the charm of Bing Crosby in the *Bells of St. Mary*, Father Zrinko Cuvalo exhibited a gruff, terse style that incited adults, let alone kids, to reverse paths when spied ahead. [28] Children, though, had always trembled before his stern countenance—all children, not just the ones Jozo heard Zrinko grill to the bone on the tape. [29]

Described as hard-headed and skeptical, though compassionate and selfless, Zrinko repelled people and knew why. It was his face, the friar admitted, a face he said he couldn't help he was stuck with:

"My expression puts them off. They don't like my face. Well, that's too bad. I am what I am, and I can't help my face." [30]

Zrinko had dodged the bullet the first day after the visions, as news of the commotion on Podbrdo and around Bijakovići stayed away from St. James—probably because no one knew for sure what to believe, who to believe, or what to expect after that evening. Nor did it probably matter, since most, even the children, felt that the playful, youthful drama might be over.

But day two launched the spectacle into the stratosphere, as family and neighbors witnessed brilliant lights flashing across the sky, the children leapfrogging up the hill as if under control of a puppet master, and then an array of human emotions erupting once the Madonna softly faded into the waiting heavens.

Something bizarre, perhaps supernatural, had materialized for sure on Podbrdo and by the end of the second day, fear, anxiety, wonder, and awe shared the moment, like gasping patches of smoke slowly belching from a doused fire.

That evening, the onset of Zrinko's problems knocked on his door—literally.

The batty woman from Bijakovići, Dragica, ordered her husband Marinko to St. James to beg the priest to come and console the troubled children, and to inquire of him some pastoral wisdom to help deal with the ongoing madness fomenting outside the couple's front door. [31]

With Jozo out of town, the elderly Franciscan had been doing well holding down the fort up to that point. But now Marinko's surprise visitation would change all that quickly, bringing him the news of the roiling mysticism that was brewing on the slopes of Podbrdo.

Permitting Marinko a brief opening statement, Zrinko feigned listening for a minute to pacify his anxious guest, then abruptly shooed him back out the door, more perturbed that the automobile mechanic entered the rectory shirtless, dirty, and soaked in sweat than about any scuttlebutt of a hillside Madonna.

To Zrinko, it was a joke. [32]

"Marinko, forget the childish games, and we can both go and get some rest," he advised as he bid him good night. [33]

Dismayed and speechless, Marinko reported back to his already agitated wife that the priest couldn't care less if the Virgin Mary was appearing on the hill, or anywhere else for that matter. [34]

In his mind, Zrinko truly did dismiss the news outright that evening, almost immediately chalking up the Podbrdo visions to fantasy, motivated by typical adolescent, psychological eccentricities. [35]

But the priest's dawning dilemma did become gnawingly palpable to him, he would later admit, and he fell asleep that night feeling guilty over his poor behavior,[36] innately dreading that some aftershocks approached from the pesky apparitions come the break of day. [37]

Early Friday morning, Zrinko drove down the highway to a monastery in Široki Brijeg for a Franciscan meeting and retreat.[38] There, Father Kosir reported his fellow brother looked a little troubled, unusually quiet and withdrawn, but said Zrinko revealed to no one what was bothering him.[39]

The out-of-town spiritual excursion filled up most of the priest's day, but upon returning to Medjugorje that evening, Father Jozo's frazzled right-hand man was blindsided; four priests from neighboring towns, one being the Bishop of Mostar's secretary, were waiting for him at St. James, all quite inebriated with excitement upon hearing about the visions earlier that day at a gathering of priests in Studencima.[40] Now, the animated priests were in Medjugorje demanding to meet the visionaries.[41]

Even worse for Zrinko, on Podbrdo remained the remnants of the thousands who had come that day, slowly gravitating homeward while basking in the highly-charged atmosphere that lingered on from the apparition.

Jumping into a car, Zrinko and his four guests snaked their way down and around a short dirt road to Bijakovići, eventually pulling up to a lingering crowd spattered around Marinko and Dragica's house.[42]

There, several of the visionaries could be seen still fending off questions being hurled by the stragglers, while tears and prayers flowed and echoed everywhere in the background.

Spotted the moment they exited their vehicle, the five priests soon found themselves inundated with confession requests and a deluge of questions about the apparitions. [43]

Finally, after being unable to corner or even identify for sure the children amidst the ruckus, a tired, bewildered Zrinko asked some of the visionaries' parents to bring their kids to the church the next morning before Mass, so he could talk to them.[44]

With this, the weary friar decided to retreat to St. James to unwind and try to decipher it all.

A considerable number lingered in Bijakovići late that evening, trading opinions and swapping stories, all the while hoping to hear a little extra from the visionaries. It was an eventful day that nobody wanted to see end.

And in a way, it wouldn't.

The sun had set on the evening, but it was the dawn of something no one ever expected to experience in their lifetime in this imprisoned land—a piece of the world so bereft of the joy and hope that all people hunger for in life.

Now, suddenly, both joy and hope filled the air like the discovery of a couple of new stars in the sky, and while tears flowed, they were coming from faces with smiles, not frowns.

Indeed, sleep could wait, as there was a sense that something good was about to happen to people who had been waiting their turn for exactly that.

That evening, the Virgin Mary had dropped some key words reflective of her mission in Medjugorje—words such as peace, prayer, reconcile.

Words that began to reveal the seriousness of her intervention.

Words that would soon begin to work their way over, under, and around the Iron Curtain.

CHAPTER TWENTY-SIX

NO BETTER THAN
AN ATHEIST

*"See I am laying a cornerstone in Zion, an approved stone
and precious. He who puts faith in it shall not be shaken."*
—1 Pt 2:6

WITH THE SUN STRETCHING UP OVER THE HORIZON ON A LAZY Saturday morning, an unscheduled visitor arrived at Father Zrinko's door.

Cackling through the morning air louder than the roosters strutting the streets of the rustic village, in galloped Dragica. And, unlike her docile husband, she swiftly beheaded the priest with a verbal guillotine, taking no pity on his sleepy state or respect for his revered collar.

Everybody she knew was converging on that hill, Dragica bellowed. The mayor, the police, priests from out of town, friars, even the bishop's secretary, and "Heaven knows who else." [1]

And what was Father Zrinko doing about it?

Dragica didn't wait for his reply:

"Who do you think you are, behaving as though this has nothing to do with you? Are you a human? Are you a priest? You're no better than an atheist, you should be run out of the village." [2]

Browbeaten badly by Dragica, Zrinko sensed where all this was headed.

And it wasn't good.

Having acres of illegally-assembled masses, congested nightly on a hillside in anticipation of a celestial visitation—in Communist Yugoslavia no less—wasn't exactly a healthy situation for a Catholic priest to find himself in 1981.[3] No one needed to warn him. He was well aware it posed a guaranteed one-way ticket to prison—or worse.

Years later, these thoughts of his were proven not to be symptoms of paranoia. The Communists at the time had their own list of suspected provocateurs, and it came to be discovered the name of Father Zrinko Cuvalo ranked near or at the top. Thus, with the handwriting on the wall, and no Jozo to dump the mess on, Zrinko knew time was of the essence.

Nervously, the humbled priest apologetically dismissed Dragica and waited for the parents of the six visionaries to bring them to St. James for a closed-door meeting. The hardly-bothered pastor of the night before was admittedly now a worried wreck:

"It wasn't that I actually believed the children's stories. What worried me was trying to decide what I was dealing with: was it a dangerous conspiracy, mere rumor, a piece of childish mischief—irrational states of mind?" [4]

Four of the children, Ivanka, Vicka, Ivan, and Marija, arrived that morning and attended Mass at St. James, with two of the visionaries going to confession. [5]

Then, in a small back room, with his tape recorder running, the frazzled Zrinko proceeded to rake them over the coals, all but putting a gun to their heads to force them to confess their plot. [6]

Zrinko felt he had good cause for his acerbic methods.

If the problem started with the children, the fastest way to end it would be with them, too. And the sooner, the better.

Interrogating them all morning in the parish house, Zrinko listened closely for inconsistencies, gaffes, and anything that smelled fishy—but with no success. No matter what he asked, the children calmly responded, confidant not only in their answers but in their brazen truthfulness.

"Did you lie?" a bristling Zrinko all but accused Ivan, after spinning his wheels for too long and making no progress. [7]

"I don't lie," the 16-year-old boy fired back. [8]

The tape was rolling, but it might as well have remained blank.

Zrinko heard nothing that sounded like a note of deception in them. But even though the children radiated honesty and sincerity, Zrinko couldn't get himself to trust their explanations.

Determined to press on, the agitated priest mentally scrolled through his list of plausible scenarios: a deliberate government conspiracy intended to hurt the Church; childhood mischief on a grand level; or, the children were taking drugs that self-induced an irrational, imaginary state, igniting within them the heavenly raptures.[9]

Though an air of truthfulness continued to win the day, Zrinko would not allow himself to be convinced their experiences were real and that there was even a remote chance that the Blessed Virgin Mary was truly appearing in Medjugorje. Someone or some group—some kind of conspiracy, he kept thinking—must be putting them up to this.[10]

Winding up his quasi court proceeding, Zrinko's testy, closing remarks unveiled his deeper, more foreboding concerns:

"One of these days, we'll find ourselves standing in the criminal dock together," the anxious friar predicted, taking a last, desperate stab that possibly some fear of the Communist authorities might spring loose a confession.[11]

But no luck.

The youngest of the group—ten-year-old Jacov—even let out a laugh, inciting Zrinko to become apoplectic with anger,

"And that means you too little boy. It's no laughing matter!" [12]

Despite Zrinko's gestapo tactics, the children gave no ground.

It was all true, the four maintained; they had seen the Madonna—the *Gospa* as they repeatedly referred to her in Croatian—and that was all there was to it.

By noon, the friar dismissed the kids and drove off annoyed to Čapljina for a short meeting.

Unlike Jacov, there wasn't much Zrinko felt like laughing about.

But he certainly must have smiled with some relief the moment he returned from Čapljina and saw that Father Jozo had finally pulled into Medjugorje.

Discarding any pleasantries, the exhausted assistant pastor at once let loose on Jozo a summation of his living nightmare.

Drugs, a Communist plot, and a ring leader named Mirjana Dragićević headlined his theory concerning the visions, with an emphasis on the drugs and the clever young city girl who attended school in Sarajevo.[13]

"People are saying she brought drugs with her, maybe in cigarettes. She started giving drugs to the children, and now they're claiming to see visions." [14]

By now, Zrinko could only envision the worst.

It was day four and—if he was sure about one thing—the six children were not going to easily admit to anything. And, there was a greater concern mounting: more and more people were now flooding into the Medjugorje region from farther and farther away. People were even hitch-hiking. Zrinko warned the growingly attentive Jozo: "We've got a big problem on our hands." [15]

Voicing no disagreement with Zrinko's appraisal of the situation, the somewhat outwardly amused Jozo garnered what he could from his assistant pastor and concluded what was now obvious to him; he needed to size up the children himself. He would do this, Jozo determined, by recording his own interviews with them and then comparing their responses to Zrinko's. Then, he would see where this led him.

With their plan in hand, the two rattled priests headed out the door and up the road to Bijakovići, only to pass a slow moving truck that was carrying the six kids on their way to St. James.

Although Jozo had been pastor at St. James since November 11, 1980, the dynamic priest discovered as he met with the visionaries that he had no memory at all of them or their families. [16]

It did come out that Vicka had attended one of his catechism classes, but that was the only personal contact he had with any of them beyond their attendance at Mass.

Dispensing with all of the introductory pleasantries as fast as he could, Jozo chose to begin his interviews with Mirjana, since she'd been labeled the bad girl from the cosmopolitan metropolis who was allegedly the mastermind of the scam.

But Mirjana's replies convincingly disarmed the priest, and he quickly concluded the young girl didn't do drugs. She was, Jozo felt, quite a normal teenager who was interested in boys, and not religion. [17]

His probing endeavor with the other five followed in the same suit; no cracks were discovered in the children's accounts—or in their heads, for that matter. Unfortunately, the six appeared to be a group of quite earthy youngsters.[18] This was not exactly what he was hoping for. Still, regardless of what was emerging, he decided to press on.

Hours passed, with Jozo finding himself as baffled as his assistant. Finally, like Zrinko, he vented his frustration on one of them—little Jacov.

Staring the boy in the face, Jozo point blank told the ten-year old he had never seen the Blessed Virgin Mary. To which the diminutive Jacov unhesitatingly responded,

"I saw her like I see you." [19]

Helplessly won over by their youthful innocence and completely stumped by their admirable candor, Jozo decided next to peruse the children's taped responses until he could come across something that could help him solve this mystery.

But what he discovered was not what he was looking for.

Ironically, Jozo slowly began to realize that his interrogation was revealing consistencies in everything from how Mary looked to why she was appearing in Medjugorje. And although the children's wording varied, it became more and more clear to the priest that all six were describing a mutual experience.

One thing, most of all, became especially certain to him, the children all strongly agreed that no human words could fully describe the beauty of the apparitional Madonna, or adequately convey the feeling that was experienced when in her heavenly presence.

Still—no matter how believable the children sounded and appeared—Jozo continued to ponder the possibility of outside corruption from the larger towns down the road where they attended school. He couldn't help but wonder, as did Zrinko, if they were being manipulated. [20]

"Most of them go to school in Mostar or Čitluk. Anybody could have got at them and put them up to this nonsense. There has to be someone stage managing them," thought the befuddled Jozo. [21]

As for the six young visionaries—still extremely overwhelmed by what they had gone through over the past three days on Podbrdo—it seemed almost inconceivable why the two priests—of all people—seemed the most doubtful. [22] For them, it was becoming a compounding crisis, something their youthful states left them unprepared for in any way.

Wrapping up the meeting, Jozo softened his demeanor. As he prepared to dismiss them, he advised the children to pray and study the

Bible, and to read about Lourdes and Fátima, two places of historic Marian apparitions. Two places also, not surprisingly, that the children had never heard of.

Jozo then handed out some prayer books and rosaries, along with a book titled, *The Apparitions of the Blessed Virgin Mary*.[23] With that, the interviews were over, as the six happily fled through the door and back to Marija's house to talk amongst themselves before departing for that evening's apparition.

But their planned respite wasn't to be.

Though the Franciscans were done with them, others weren't.

Salivating to cross-examine them too, the government's SUP, or Secret Police, suddenly arrived on the scene in Bijakovići and demanded the six immediately go with them to see a doctor. [24]

"When I need a medical check-up, I'll arrange one for myself," Vicka muttered to the police as she was escorted out the door. [25]

Warned by Marija's parents as they were taken away to resist any pills or injections, the children were hastily squeezed into government vehicles and carted off five miles to Čitluk, the municipal capital, for some lengthy questioning at the police station. [26]

Once there, the SUP immediately began to curse and badger the kids, accusing them of being liars and worse.

Then—just two hours before that day's apparition—they were swept over to the offices of a general practitioner, Dr. Ante Vujicic, who was to see if he could diagnose what ailed them. It was another goading experience, and a much greater level of intimidation. [27]

"They at SUP took us to some doctors as though for a checkup. As though we were sick, or drug addicts, or...who knows what they thought," remembered Vicka about the ordeal. [28]

As with Jozo and Zrinko, the Communists also smelled a sinister ploy, only from the opposite side of the playing field—some religious shenanigans by the Catholic Church to spark an uprising within the people's regime. [29] Consequently, the government officials, with a little assistance from medical and psychological tests, hoped to release to the public some unfortunate news about the beguiled children.

But no such luck.

To the chagrin of the Communists and Father Zrinko—who later admitted he had hoped that medical test results would reveal mental instability or drug use and bring an end to this mess—Dr. Vujicic discovered nothing but healthy, well balanced, and normal children. Even worse for the authorities, their sound mental states were now formally documented. [30]

Decades later, Mirjana Dragićević would jest in her book that she possessed official government papers that validated her sanity—proof, she noted—that few can offer in defense of their own mental status. [31]

CHAPTER TWENTY-SEVEN

EYES TO THE SKY

"He is your glory, he, your God, who has done for you those great and terrible things which your own eyes have seen."
—Dt 10:21

FORETELLING THEIR NEED FOR A MORE EXTENSIVE PSYCHIATRIC examination in the near future in Mostar, and subtly intimating that it would be no more pleasurable than their visit today, the authorities released five of the six visionaries a little before 6:00 p.m.[1]

Only Ivan, for some unknown reason, was detained for further questioning. [2]

Cramming into the small car of a local man, whom the children ran into at a nearby hotel, the five youth wasted no time departing Čitluk for Bijakovići. [3]

But as they approached Medjugorje, another problem in their problem-filled day surfaced. The police had blocked the main street leading into the town, and dozens of abandoned vehicles now lined both sides of the road. This brought traffic from every direction to a dead halt. [4]

As the authorities busied themselves writing out tickets and taking registration numbers, [5] and with precious little time left before the Madonna's arrival, the five rambunctious children quickly took matters into their hands: they exited the stranded car and began to race as fast as they could towards the hill. [6]

The Madonna would come, they felt confidant, and nothing was going to prevent them from being there—especially after all they had been through that day. Even if they were going to be shot, Vicka later quipped, they were headed to Podbrdo for their fourth rendezvous with the Queen of Heaven. [7]

Unbeknownst to them at the time, other interested parties were adhering that evening to similar vows concerning the rocky little mount. The Communists recruited Dr. Darinka Glamuzina, an atheist physician, to be there and investigate the celestial encounter. [8] While, in a similar move, a still very distraught Jozo decided to dispatch to the hill in his steed Fathers Zrinko and Kosir. [9]

Not wishing to appear in any way supportive of the rumpus on Podbrdo, Jozo decided he would observe the spectacle from a distance under the shadow of a sprawling cypress tree. [10]

Jozo's growing dismay was now twofold.

Besides the mystical mayhem unfolding in his parish, the anguished friar bemoaned the fact it so illustrated his failures as an inspirational pastor:

"The crowds were swarming up the hill like bees. Thousands of gullible idiots, waiting for something spectacular to happen," he bemoaned. "Why couldn't the truths of the Gospel move them like that? What was wrong with them?" [11]

And of course—in a way—he was right.

There would total an estimated five thousand that evening on Podbrdo.[12] Animated and excited, with their eyes fixed to the sky or upon the faces of the children, the people were like migrating birds, looking for a new place to feed. Needless to say, in Jozo's eyes, Bijakovići wasn't the right place.

At the time, Jozo believed he was watching thousands of fools.

Little could he imagine the millions who would follow in their footsteps.

That evening, Marinko and Mate Pavlović—another neighbor of the visionaries—suggested a test to probe the mystical proceedings at hand. [13]

The two men predetermined that the five children (Ivan did not attend) would ascend the hill in two separate parties along different trails, wanting to see if one group noticed the apparition before the other. Whichever group sighted the Madonna first would then have to alert the other.

Ivanka, Mirjana, and Vicka formed one party on a path somewhat higher up the hill. Marija, Jacov, Mate, and a civilian-attired Father

Zrinko, [14] who asked to stay close to better observe the apparition, formed the second group near the bottom of Podbrdo.

As both groups gradually began to shuffle along the two trails, there suddenly came a burst of blinding light that panned over the upper slopes of Podbrdo.[15] Now familiar with her ways, the six knew well that the cascading flashes could only mean one thing: the Madonna's arrival was imminent.

Having just reached an area slightly below where the apparition was seen on the first day, the group on the lower part of Podbrdo immediately launched themselves up the hillside.

As occurred on the previous two evenings, the visionaries hurdled rocks and bushes at an impossible speed, ascending so rapidly to where the light had settled that they left the stunned Zrinko frozen in his footsteps.[16]

That night, Father Kosir would inform Jozo that what took place at that moment was not humanly possible, a physical action he would describe as beyond comprehension to him: "No person on Earth was capable of such a feat, and certainly no child." [17]

Hundreds of witnesses observed this phenomenon during the first week of the apparitions. But, over time, skeptics began to belittle as exaggerated folly the reported episodes of the children being almost "carried by the wind" up the hill.

Mariologists would later come to note, however, that such an oddity was reported by witnesses at other apparitions, most notably the visions at Lourdes.

There, the lone visionary—Bernadette Soubirous—was also described as "soaring up the slope" of the Massabielle Grotto and "going down the zigzags of the slope at an extraordinary speed." It was documented that Bernadette seemed "nimble as a young mountain goat, going bounding towards the bank of the cave." [18]

Coming to a halt about sixty-five feet farther up Podbrdo,[19] and more to the left than on the second day, the two groups became separated from each other at first by the massive crowd, but eventually managed to reunite beneath the floating Madonna—whose eyes that evening seemed to be spanning the countryside near and far as she awaited their arrival. [20]

"She gazed over the people…she smiled…she gazed over Krizevac and over the fields," said Vicka, who noticed that Mary appeared pleased with all that she was taking in. [21]

Like the visionaries, the huge crowd was soon on the run, too. Within moments of seeing the children begin to race up the hill, the many thousands reacted, rolling up Podbrdo en masse until they gradually came to form a concentric circle around the six kids.

As everyone seemed to be finally settling into place, there suddenly arose a new problem: the Virgin Mary, the children revealed, had vanished.[22]

The aggressive restlessness of the onlookers as they ascended the hill, the children would later speculate, had accidently violated an undefined perimeter around Mary, causing her departure. Some, they ventured to guess, had gotten too near. [23] This perplexing dilemma would happen three times.[24]

Eventually, after the third episode, a group of local men shoved their way through the multitude and secured a zone around the visionaries, thereby preventing the anxious crowd from intruding on the space closest to the epicenter of the vision. [25]

Finally, as this remedy took hold, a rather pleased Madonna reappeared and began to speak to the children—her "angels," as she would address them for the first time. [26]

"Praise be Jesus," Mary began, exuding a joyful smile that the visionaries said never departed her face that evening, even during the inadvertent interruptions.

But unlike the previous two nights, when both apparitions approximated at least thirty minutes in length, today would be different. Only four questions were to be entertained by Mary, of which two were almost the same as the previous day.

The first question, forwarded through little Jacov this time, originated from Fr. Jozo, who inquired whether the Gospa had anything to say to the priests? [27]

"Let them believe strongly and guard the faith," Mary replied to Jacov. [28]

Then, as they had requested on the preceding evenings, the children again beseeched a sign from Mary to prove her presence.

This time, Vicka pleaded their case. [29] But once more, it was to no avail: "Let those who do not see me believe as if they see," came Mary's response, intimating once more that the people would have to rely on their faith to accept her presence. [30]

While all of the visionaries believed a miraculous sign would be the best way to silence their persecutors, it was perhaps Mirjana who hoped for such a grace the most.

More than the other visionaries combined, by the fourth apparition, Mirjana's critics had grown, as the stressed out young girl continued to hear mounting accusations that she was hallucinating from drugs— or as was heard at Fátima[31]—had epilepsy.[32]

Not alone in such misery, a troubled little Jacov also let the Virgin know that some people "treat us as liars." [33]

Together, all six saw a sign as the best way to quiet their adversaries, whether they be the local tormenters, the doubting priests, or the hostile authorities. But, Mary had only words of wisdom for them—and some practical advice:

"My angels, there is always injustice among people. Pay no attention to what people say." [34]

Finally, Ivanka asked the apparition her name once again.

"I am the Blessed Virgin Mary." [35]

With her reply, and affirmation of another visit the next day, Mary gradually dematerialized, fading up and away into her surrounding light and the warm summer night's air.

While the apparition was rather short, it was enough, as the brief encounter with the Virgin could be seen as revealing a mother who knew exactly what her children needed the most on this day—some well-deserved rest.

Much less drama occurred with the fourth apparition than with the first three.

But in certain ways, the day was a watershed moment for the visions, starting with the great number of onlookers who were present—especially those in attendance who came with ulterior motives.

After the vision ended, Dr. Darinka Glamuzina is said to have departed in shock. While some accounts have her returning several days later, it is certain that she would refuse to ever play a role again on behalf of the Communist authorities in Yugoslavia with regards to Medjugorje.

Dr. Glamuzina reportedly asked that day if she could touch the apparition, causing Mary to reply, "Let her come forward; there will always be Judases who do not believe." [36]

According to Vicka, the doctor did indeed appear to come in contact with the Virgin's left shoulder, and reported later that she had "felt some sort of tingling in her hand" at that moment. Some accounts report that she later converted from the experience.

Likewise, Fathers Zrinko and Kosir were deeply affected by what transpired that evening and would later admit to leaving dumbfounded, bewildered, and more worried than ever. They realized, the friars explained, that the situation was out of hand and coming to a head. [37] Their candid accounts of the day, however, would later serve well to help chronicle the unfolding of the fourth apparition.

Finally, as he sat, observed, and pondered it all from a distance, Father Jozo Zovko also reportedly became more deeply disturbed by the evening's end, passing beyond skepticism and exasperation into outright hostility. [38]

Indeed, as the next day would reveal, an anguished Jozo was now more determined than ever to try and solve what was truly unfolding in Bijakovići. Little could he imagine that all the madness he had just witnessed… would soon center totally around him and the parish of St. James.

The fourth day of the apparitions started to reveal the beginnings of some of the downside of what was occurring in Medjugorje.

As with what could be expected with such a large crowd, a few of the disillusioned could be heard muttering and cursing as they exited the hill, upset that they didn't see any visions themselves. [39]

But one man, who was certain it was all a deception in the first place, left instead forever convinced of the vision's validity. And his opinion carried considerable weight in the local villages.

Jozo Vasilj, often called Postar because he worked as the village postmaster for many years, was immensely respected in these parts. Accepted by many as a godfather type figure, Postar was a stubborn old curmudgeon who got out of the gate slow with it all.

A firm nonbeliever in the apparitions when he initially heard about them, Postar grew into perhaps the village's number one "doubting Thomas" after the first three days, asserting that he knew a hoax when he saw one.[40]

But although Postar stubbornly refused to tag along with his wife and mother on the previous evenings, his gnawing curiosity finally got the better of him that Saturday. [41]

Arriving early with his family, Postar soon found himself enlisted in crowd control and with providing ad hoc security for the six children.[42] So absorbed with these duties, he wasn't even aware when the apparition began, confessing that he saw and felt nothing the whole time it took place. [43]

However, as the crowd descended Podbrdo after the vision was over, Postar accidentally—or perhaps providentially—came upon Mirjana, who could be seen experiencing a second apparition with the Virgin on a remote, descending trail off the hill. [44]

As had occurred with Marija the evening before, the Virgin Mary suddenly reappeared to Mirjana as she was making her way down Podbrdo to go home. Postar just so happened to notice her a short distance ahead of Vicka and Jacov, who decided to stop and discreetly observe the fascinating encounter.[45]

Camouflaged by a massive bush that concealed a large rock that he was huddled behind,[46] an amazed Postar watched Mirjana captured in ecstasy, while he simultaneously eavesdropped in on Vicka and Jacov, who he could hear quietly conversing.[47]

Then, as he secretly followed Vicka and Jacov a little more down the path, Postar distinctly heard Vicka remark to Jacov, "Ode!"—a Croatian term meaning, "She's going." [48]

At that very same moment, Postar caught sight of the more forward Mirjana slowly lifting her eyes to the sky as if to trace Mary's departing ascension into the heavens above.[49]

Shocked and overwhelmed by what he witnessed, a sweating, sobbing Postar melted into the bushes to collect himself. To this day, the retired postmaster has never gone to another apparition, as he desires no more proof. The incredible feelings from those moments have never left him and he says it's all he will ever need.[50]

With the close of the fourth day, the most unique phenomenon that *is* Medjugorje also began to show itself.

No, not the voracity of the six children in staunchly defending their experience. No, not the fact that thousands were descending upon the village, a prelude to its future. But a greater phenomenon: the mystery of how one by one, a host of individuals can be seen to be being plucked out of their safe, comfortable lives, and called to assist in God's plan at Medjugorje.

Indeed, from the very earliest days of the apparitions, it becomes apparent that the grace pouring into Medjugorje was to be not just for the village and the visionaries, but for many others in a variety of unique ways.

Over time, Postar came to understand that God had designed the moment on the hillside just for him. And with this reality, he soon came to also realize that the miracle unfolding in Medjugorje was designed all along to include him, in order for him to share it with those that would come to cross his path.

Like Postar, there are others that can be seen very early on to be similarly predestined to play a part in God's plan at Medjugorje. Most notable are both Dragica and Marinko Ivanković, who were clearly chosen in their providential roles, with the husband and wife tandem called to be the first to inform the two parish priests of the apparitions, at separate times and places.

This simply cannot be dismissed as coincidence.

Pivotal people at pivotal places at pivotal moments shadow the day to day unfolding of the story of Medjugorje in an uncanny and unending way. Many of these individuals have written about their somewhat miraculous experiences.

Moreover, throughout the history of Medjugorje, a tapestry of divine threads masquerading as coincidences takes the stage over and over again, leaving countless souls with tears in their eyes that God has chosen to use them in a special way to bring his plan of peace to the world.

Alone and separated from his fellow visionaries that evening, Ivan felt left out. But, like Postar, it appears Mary would find a way to have him involved.

In their concern for their son after returning from the frightening ordeal with the police in Čitluk, Ivan's parents asked him not to go to the hill that night, fearing the authorities might seize him again.[51]

Already depressed from the secret police's interrogation and now experiencing severe stomach pain, the young boy obeyed his parents and stayed home, yet couldn't escape feeling treasonous that he wasn't with the others on Podbrdo. [52]

But, another surprise was forthcoming.

As Ivan stood on a roadside below the hill, Mary suddenly appeared to him, smiled, and told him to take courage and be at peace. [53] It was a most appropriate ending to a day that saw little peace for Ivan or any of the children.*

Like at Fátima, the problems for the visionaries were just beginning.

---

* The history of Medjugorje is filled with accounts of apparitions that suddenly occur to the visionaries, such as the ones experienced by Marija on day three and Mirjana and Ivan on day four. These apparitions, as well as the fact that Mary appeared to the visionaries on their trips outside of the village, have been used by critics as evidence against the veracity of Medjugorje. However, such transient experiences have been reported by mystics for centuries, and while they depart the parameters of what the critics see as acceptable for a classic Marian apparition, they are not unique to Medjugorje. Fátima's Lucia also reported being surprised by "spontaneous" apparitions that she had no idea were coming at that moment or that day. (See *A Pathway Under the Gaze of Mary* by the World Apostolate of Fatima.)

CHAPTER TWENTY-EIGHT

HEROES AND VILLIANS

*"He who walks honestly walks securely, but he
whose ways are crooked will fare badly."*
—Prv 10 10:9

FOR FATHER JOZO ZOVKO, SUNDAY COULDN'T COME SOON ENOUGH. With only a day of calamity under his belt, he was already more than eager to use his homily to slow down the runaway madness streaming from Podbrdo—or at least take his best shot at doing so. But in cautioning his listeners that true revelation would always be recognizable by its "fruits," he somehow failed to see his overflowing church as a rich harvest itself—one that had already fallen from the tree and rolled into the pews. [1]

Jozo's blindness to this reality, nevertheless, was not without good cause.

The circumstances surrounding the situation were more than troublesome as the nervous friar and the not so indomitable Zrinko were running out of time to find the answer to what was behind the visions.

This was 1981 Communist Yugoslavia, where atheism was the official state religion. As such, the two priests knew the government would soon make quite clear that it had no intent on sharing the spotlight.

After morning Mass, Jozo continued his passionate plea to those who attended his weekly Sunday catechism class. [2] He even warned them that Satan might be behind the strange events.[3] Then, pushing the pedal to the metal, Jozo took aim at Vicka's sister, Ana, who was in attendance:

"I'm afraid your sister and the others are trying to make fools of us. How long are they going to keep up this hoax?" [4]

With tears flowing down her face, an angry Ana fired back: "I know my sister," she told Jozo sternly, "she doesn't tell lies." [5]

The sky was filled with golden sunlight that day, but Jozo's world was dark and cloudy. As he watched some 15,000 people whisking past St. James around 5:00 p.m., he was happy to find a group of youngsters who had showed up to pray with him in the church, instead of galloping up Podbrdo for the evening apparition.[6]

But his optimism was short lived.

"When I finished the prayer, I turned around and they had all gone, every one of them to the hill." [7] Abandoned like Christ in Gethsemane, Jozo's spirit sank to a new low. "I wanted to cry out: 'God, what do you want of me? All these people are convinced you're up there on that hill. What am I supposed to do about it?'" [8]

The danger now was growing by the minute, and while Jozo remained at St. James, Father Zrinko flowed with the crowd to try and minimize the crisis, dressed once again in civilian clothes to blend in.

Afraid that the police were infiltrating the hill, Zrinko urged every brown-robed Franciscan priest and any nuns he crossed to exchange their religious garb for whatever he could find for them back at St. James. [9]

In Zrinko's mind, every little thing that could downplay the pious makeup of the scene on Podbrdo mattered. By then, his fear was mounting that the Communists would pull up one evening in force and haul off all the priests and nuns.[10]

"It's as though you see something coming at you," said Zrinko about his thinking by then, "but you're not sure what it is, what you should do about it, or how you can protect yourself. But you know that whatever it is, it has the power to destroy you." [11]

Like the previous two afternoons, the hot Herzegovina sun baked the air this fifth day of the apparitions.[12] But Mary arrived again on schedule, accompanied by a blast of white light that sprayed the hill like an oversized spotlight shining on a solo stage performer.

Making their way through the massive crowd, Marija, Jacov, and Vicka were trudging up Podbrdo when they immediately spotted the towering light.

"Look! Look! Look!" [13] Marija cried out.

Seconds later, as on the previous evenings, all six were racing up the hill at what Father Victor Kosir would describe this time as "superhuman speed." [14]

Though just as extraordinary, the conversation with the Virgin this evening was, for the most part, unremarkable from the previous two evenings in content. Mary chose to focus her message again on advising those in attendance, especially the priests, to believe and have faith.

But the apparition *was* remarkable in one unique way.

A man named Grgo Kozina, who knelt right next to the visionaries, recorded the entire celestial encounter on tape. Grgo also served as sort of a play-by-play announcer to the crowd, with the children relaying to him every question submitted to the Virgin along with her answer. He then, in turn, relayed both the question and the reply to the crowd. [15]

"Did she come?" Girgo can be heard asking on the tape recording.

"Yes. Yes. Yes. She came," the visionaries tell him.

Then, Girgo's voice can be heard rattling off each question, one by one, and Mary's subsequent answer:

Dear Madonna, what do you wish of us?

"Faith and respect for me."

Dear Madonna, what do you wish from our priests?

"That they believe firmly."

Dear Madonna, why don't you appear in the church so that everybody can see you?

"Blessed are those who have not seen and believe."

Dear Madonna, which do you like better: that we pray to you or sing to you?

"Do both: sing and pray."

Dear Madonna, what do you wish from these people who have gathered here?

"Let these people, who do not see me, believe the same as the six of you, who see me."

Dear Madonna, will you leave some sign here on Earth, so that we can convince people that we are not liars, that we do not lie, that we do not play games with you?

"Go in God's peace."[16]

Mary's final words are not what the six, once again, were hoping to hear.

Nor would the visionaries' subsequent words to Father Zrinko after the apparition be what he was hoping to hear.[17] Though Zrinko stood next to the children throughout the apparition—which, according to Grgo Kozina's tape recording lasted almost an hour— the priest decided to subject the children to a brutal interrogation immediately after the Virgin Mary departed, right on the hill.[18]

Zrinko: *Tell me. Did you see anything this evening?*

Vicka: I did.

Zrinko: *Tell me! Why didn't you say, "There she is!" as you cried out the other night, when you say you saw her the first time?*

Vicka: I did say that!

Zrinko: *You did not.*

Vicka: I did!

Zrinko: *I did not hear it—and I was right in front of you!*

Vicka: What are you saying? I told them that! [19]

Confessing later to being purposefully loud and antagonistic—saying that he was playing the devil's advocate with Vicka and the other visionaries that evening [20]—the closing moments of the fifth day of the apparitions reveal the looming sense of danger all parties felt was closing in on them. [21]

The children, in desperate need of their sign from the Madonna, sensed that the large crowds were not necessarily going to remain friendly forever without some kind of confirmation that all of this was real.

While the priests, knowing the ugly history of the Church and the Communist authorities in Yugoslavia—going back to World War II and the Partisans—could see that there was no way that this situation could go on much longer without someone being held accountable.

Despite a softening demeanor at the conclusion of his interview with the children the day before, by Sunday morning Jozo's thinking had taken a 180-degree turn. The priest again determined that he needed to crush their charade. No longer was he just exasperated, but now outright antagonistic towards the apparitions and, therefore, the six children.

Jozo and Zrinko knew the situation was beyond out of hand [22] and, if fraud wasn't the cause, then it had to be the girl from Sarajevo who must have brought some hallucinogenic drugs with her from the city. [23]

"She looks too pale to me," Zrinko told Jozo, recommending that they focus on Mirjana once more.[24] The friar had told Mirjana on Sunday morning that if these were real apparitions, the Virgin would have delivered some kind of important message. Mirjana responded by assuring him that she would again ask the Madonna for a sign.[25]

Being compliant and submissive to the priests' demands were the only ways Mirjana knew how to respond.

But such was not the case with Vicka.

Asked by the priests if Mary became vexed when the crowd pressed on her and perhaps touched her veil during Saturday's apparition, Vicka told them,

"Look, Our Lady cannot be vexed. She is not like us. She had no problem." [26]

Asked why the Virgin's veil was so long in the first place, Vicka replied, "How should I know?" [27]

And, when Jozo wanted to know why the Virgin disappeared so many times, Vicka told him he should "ask her yourself." [28]

For Jozo, by Sunday evening, the moment at hand was now quite clear. The children were playing with God. Playing with religion. Playing with people's lives.

Consequently, come the next day, he made up his mind that he was going to bring it all to an end.

Heroes and villains.

Every good story needs them. And if the first week introduced the heroes of Medjugorje, the coming weeks and months would unveil a parade of villains to add plenty of menace to a thickening plot.

Come Monday morning, June 29, Father Jozo Zovko—a villain at present—began once again to interrogate four of the children, with Vicka and Jacov absent.

Now hardened and seemingly powered by an overdose of adrenalin, Jozo hammered away at those visionaries in attendance at St. James that morning. Mirjana, his primary suspect, found herself especially facing a barrage of threats intended to crack her defiant will.

But again, it would be to no avail.

Fortified by an evening with her parents, who arrived the day before from Sarajevo and concluded that their daughter was well enough for them to return without worry,[29] Mirjana responded to Jozo's threats by telling him the Madonna would appear to them even if we were placed in jail.[30] Vicka upped Mirjana, "Even in America." [31]

"Stop deceiving people!" [32] Jozo commanded Ivanka next.

Denying that she was deceiving anyone, Jozo exploded, "We are here in front of God and the Cross! It is terrible to play with religion! God cannot leave it unpunished!" [33]

Ivanka, though, wouldn't give an inch, "But I've seen. I see her as I'm seeing you." [34]

"Do you realize the crowd is terribly disturbed?" Jozo pressed on. "They see no sign! You don't change! The people feel deceived by you, taken advantage of! How can you do it?" [35]

"I believe I see her. What can I do?" [36]

At the daily Mass that Monday—filled to the rafters for the Feast of Saint Peter and Saint Paul—Jozo issued a public statement concerning the apparitions. He pledged his fidelity to the Church and his love of the Virgin Mary, leaving open slightly the possibility that the happenings in this parish might be possible, but for the children's benefit alone. [37]

With those words, the friar departed for Mostar to again visit his hospitalized mother. [38]

But the day was just getting started for the children.

Fearing a Croatian nationalist uprising emerging through the Catholic Church,[39] government orders from Sarajevo were issued to Mostar and Čitluk.[40] The scandalous affair in Medjugorje needed to be immediately contained before a crisis erupted.[41]

Thus, off again to the police station in Čitluk, and then to the neuropsychiatric department of the Safet Mujic Hospital in Mostar,[42] went the six, as a diagnosis of mental illness or hallucination was needed by the authorities to fulfill their plan.[43]

Unfortunately, the pediatric specialists there found no mental illness or evidence of drug-induced behavior. Passing every test, Dr. Mulija Dzuzda declared them sound and healthy.[44]

This caused the Communists to resort to Plan B—intimidation of the children through a nefarious scheme of fear and terror.

First, they were taken to the hospital's morgue and forced to eye corpses undergoing different stages of autopsy. Then, the visionaries were brought to the hospital's psychiatric patient wing and left to mingle with the severely mentally ill patients.

While there, a "lady doctor"—as the children described her—haphazardly examined them as a group.[45] She then insinuated, a deeply disturbed Mirjana recounted, that they could be found mentally ill and forcibly "shut up with mad people." [46]

A Franciscan priest who was visiting Medjugorje that same day and would be assigned there in the future, said that he found Mirjana so shaken from this ordeal that when he asked her if she would go to the hill of apparitions again, she said she "very much doubted it." [47] Overwhelmed by the cumulative experiences of the day, Mirjana told the visiting friar, "If they question me once more, I'll have a nervous breakdown." [48]

All the children agreed the goings that day were dreadful, except for Vicka.

Asked a series of questions about it all a few years later by Father Janko Bubalo in an interview session for his book on Medjugorje, the ever animated Vicka claimed to have seen right through the Communist's scheme that day and panned it for what it was: [49]

Bubalo: *Did they inform you where you were headed?*

Vicka: They said to see the doctors in Mostar.

Bubalo: *And you were off?*

Vicka: We were off. What else could we do?

Bubalo: *And, ultimately?*

Vicka: They brought us to some psychiatric place. Why, until then, I barely heard of such a thing. When we arrived, they told us to get out and the examination began.

Bubalo: *And the referral cards for the exam?*

Vicka: What referral cards?

Bubalo: *And, who was called first for the exam?*

Vicka: They took all of us in a room at one time.

Bubalo: *And who examined you?*

Vicka: Some lady.

Bubalo: *Did she examine each of you individually?*

Vicka: No, no! All at the same time. Why, there wasn't any sort of exam to speak of. She kept making inquiries and aggravating us.

Bubalo: *And how did she appear?*

Vicka: She attempted to make of us some kind of sickies… that we were imagining things; that we are some kind of addicts; that we are fooling the people, and the like… She attacked me for being dressed in the latest style—like the Virgin's girl that I am. Lord! Who can recall it? We could hardly wait to get out of there as fast as possible and to go home to look after our own business.

Bubalo: *Someone said they took you into a mortuary?*

Vicka: Yes, that too. I suppose they wanted to scare us with whatever.

Bubalo: *And, for example, did they frighten you with anything?*

Vicka: Not at all, not with anything!

Bubalo: *Really, with nothing?*

Vicka: Lord! I told you. They didn't frighten me at all. What can they do to me? Someone is dying all the time. So, let them die! I only wanted to get into the vehicle and get back home as quickly as possible.

Bubalo: *You didn't say anything to me as to what the lady doctor had to say to you?*

Vicka: She said whoever brought us there was nuts, and that we were completely normal children. What else could she say? [50]

On the sixth night on apparition hill, the crowd was again massive, exceeding the estimated 15,000 the day before.[51]

"Overflowing—one on top of another. You couldn't stand upright anywhere," remembered Vicka, not knowing that this large crowd would also be the last for a while. [52]

But a noteworthy evening it was, as the Virgin Mary began to further elaborate on her mission in Medjugorje, telling the visionaries, "There is but one God, one faith," [53] and that the people were to believe "firmly, with no fear," [54] echoing the memorable first words of Pope John Paul II from just a few years before in Saint Peter's Square in Rome.

Most of all, though, was what would occur that evening with a little boy named Daniel Setka, who had turned stiff and blue four days after his birth and was never healthy.[55] Daniel was eventually diagnosed as suffering from *spastic hemiparesis* and *epilepsy*.[56] By age two and a half, he was still unable to speak or walk, and could barely hold his head up.[57] His parents searched far and wide for a medical solution, but without success.

Being religious, they made pilgrimages to holy shrines, again to no avail.[58] Upon hearing about the visions, they journeyed from Podgorje to Medjugorje in hoping that they could somehow present Daniel to the Virgin during an apparition. The boy's father beseeched the visionaries several days before that evening to intercede with the Virgin for a cure for his son.[59]

Vicka says she will never forget the moment she first saw Daniel at her parents' home on the afternoon of June 28, 1981, "The father held him in his arms. The little boy looked half dead. He hung his head on his father's left shoulder. Really, he looked terrible." [60]

After telling the visionaries repeatedly on this evening to not be afraid, and that they would persevere the persecutions as long as they continued to believe and have recourse to her, Vicka asked the Virgin to help the little boy.

Mary then slowly gazed upon Daniel, "Tenderly, tenderly…" recalled Vicka.[61] "She looked at the child for two or three minutes," said Mirjana, who remembers the Virgin's look was full of mercy. [62]

Finally, the Madonna told the visionaries, "If his parents believe firmly, then he will be healed." [63]

That evening on their way home, the family stopped at a café near St. James Church in Medjugorje to get something to eat. There, out of nowhere, the little boy spoke his first words. [64]

"Daniel could neither speak nor walk," said his mother in recalling the moment. "But somehow he'd become stronger since we visited the site where the Madonna appeared. Suddenly, as we sat at the restaurant table, Daniel raised his hand, banged the table, and said, 'I want a drink.' I immediately shouted, 'He's been cured!'" [65]

The next day, the parents took him back to Podbrdo. While weak, Daniel managed several steps after his parents put him down.[66] Then, the boy started to climb upon some rocks.

Standing atop one of them, he abruptly proclaimed loud and clear, "Mama, look, I'm walking." [67]

But as the day begun, so would it end.

Like an angry bear awakened from hibernation, the Communist authorities worked late into the evening that Monday to move to shut down the apparitions. *The Socialist Alliance*, a party organization that operated a branch in every city and mandated all citizens enroll, called to order an emergency meeting of the Bijakovići Cooperative Commune, which received its orders from the Čitluk Commune.[68]

The purpose of the assembly that day?

The gatherings on Podbrdo must be "obstructed" at all costs. [69]

By now, alarmist voices in the party from Sarajevo to Belgrade were decrying that a subversive nationalistic movement was at hand. Croatian terrorists were accused of being behind the Medjugorje children.

In addition, reported cries of "Rise Croatia," [70] along with the singing of Croatian songs and a Croatian flag raising, were rumored to have occurred on the hill during the past week.[71] The entire affair, it was said, was being instigated by the deceptive "Ustasi Franciscan priests," under the guise of the "so-called Marian apparitions in Bijakovići." [72]

For Father Jozo Zovko, all of this meant one thing: another face-to-face visit with the visionaries come morning.

The noose was tightening—and he and Zrinko could feel it.

CHAPTER TWENTY-NINE

"PROTECT THE CHILDREN"

*"Have mercy on me, God, have mercy on
me. In you I seek shelter. In the shadow of your
wings I seek shelter till harm pass by."*

—Ps 57:1

EXORCISM.

This could be the solution to the problem with the children, proposed Father Tomislav Pervan when he and Franciscan Provincial Novice Master, Father Ivan Dugandzic, arrived at St. James early on Tuesday, the seventh day of the visions.[1]

Asked to remain outside the parish office by Father Jozo while he and Zrinko conducted another round of interviews with the visionaries, the two visiting priests quickly made things worse.

As they discussed their view of the situation, the mothers of Vicka and Jacov—who were sitting in the waiting area—couldn't help but hear their opinions of what was behind the onset of the apparitions. [2] By the time Jozo reemerged from his office, both of the women were in tears, as Pervan continued to ramble on that the visionaries were under the influence of the Devil.

"You can't blame the mothers for what the children are supposed to be seeing," [3] Jozo murmured to Pervan, a Scripture scholar, as he ushered the visiting friar into his office.

After speaking with the children about their terrifying visit to the morgue and the psychiatric hospital the previous day, Jozo knew the two women were already upset; the timing of Pervan's arrival couldn't have been worse, he thought.

For Jozo, things had already gotten off to a bad start that morning. Confronting Ivanka first, who was still a wreck from the day before, the desperate priest again insinuated that the Devil *was* involved in the events on Podbrdo—though not in the way Pervan hypothesized.[4]

"Can't you see Satan is here, and not the Madonna?" Jozo told a restless and weary Ivanka.

"It is her," replied Ivanka. "I know it." [5]

Attempting a different angle, Jozo then asked the girl a trick question, "How long did it take Marinko to write up those questions, the answers, and what you should say?"

"He did not write the answers, only the questions."

Didn't she think that it would be better if a priest wrote the answers?

"What answers?" retorted a now-bothered Ivanka. "The Madonna answers, not us." [6]

Next, it was Mirjana's turn.

Aware that the girl was deeply affected by Monday's experiences at the mental ward, Jozo decided to prey on her fragile state in attempt to elicit a confession:

"God terribly punishes anyone who misleads people. Do you know that?"

Mirjana answered affirmatively.

Jozo pressed on: "Those who are misleading people, those who are transmitting the wrong messages, they are severely punished. How is it that you are going to get out of this?"

"What can I do," said Mirjana, "when I see her and other people can't?" [7]

"It may be tomorrow that God terribly punishes you six."

"I don't think He will." [8]

"Why won't He?" interjected Zrinko.

"Because we are not lying." [9]

After making no progress with Vicka and Jacov either, Jozo asked the visionaries one last thing: can the apparitions be moved from the hill to the church?

The children told him they will speak with the Madonna.[10]

As they departed St. James, Jozo handed them a list of questions he wanted them to ask Mary that evening. Another round was over—and at the bell, the six were still standing.

As the children and their parents left, the phone rang at St. James.

Immediately, Father Jozo and Father Zrinko were to travel to Čitluk and explain to the Communist authorities what was going on in Medjugorje.[11]

Arriving shortly thereafter, the local Chairman of the Communist Party didn't mix words with the two friars; the priests needed to immediately "extinguish the charade" in Bijakovići.[12]

No explanations were accepted by the party chief.

The demonstrations on Podbrdo were "religious" in character, he assured them, and the Catholic Church was being held responsible.[13]

There were consequences—even for himself, he let be known—as high-level officials in Sarajevo and Belgrade were prepared to take strong action if it all didn't cease fast.[14]

The best they could try to do, Jozo responded, was to move the apparitions into St. James. That would work, the chairman nodded, just so long as they "don't do it on the hill." [15]

While Jozo and Zrinko huddled in Čitluk with the Communist hierarchy, a pair of social workers, one from the Council of the Republic in Sarajevo, had meanwhile arrived in Bijakovići and arranged for a meeting with the children at Vicka's house.[16]

Ljubica Vasilj and Milica Ivankovic,[17] both local women, explained they had been instructed to spend some time with the visionaries to review their experiences of the past week.[18]

They then suggested undertaking somewhat of a leisurely outing around the region to conduct and fulfill this assignment. Failure to cooperate meant that the SUP would replace them in the task, warned the ladies.[19]

Minutes later, except for Ivan, the visionaries were down the road and off into the countryside with the social workers. Their outing included stopping by an historic waterfall in Kravica, then a popular restaurant in Čapljina, and finally at an ice cream stand in Cerno.[20]

Entertained and completely distracted the entire day, as the merry crew drove back from the Dalmatian coast late in the afternoon, the children suddenly became aware that it was almost 6 p.m. This caused them to realize something else; the entire excursion had been nothing but a ruse to prevent their attending that evening's apparition.

As they neared Cerno—a distance of about six miles from Medjugorje—they demanded to be let out of the car in order to pray. [21] At first reluctant, the women ultimately decided to pull over. [22] Once out, the five children immediately kneeled in a nearby field, staring in the direction of Mt. Krizevac.

With the towering white cross visible in the distance—there suddenly appeared in the sky a brilliant, glowing ball of light moving in their direction. As the pearly white orb neared, the astonished visionaries could make out in its center the figure of the Virgin Mary, her long veil flowing in the air behind her like the cape of a superhero. [23]

"We were praying our usual prayers. Then I looked up the hill and saw the light coming down towards us," explained Ivanka of the extraordinary apparition. "Those two women saw it too! I asked them and they said they had seen it. I kept on looking at the light, and then… out of it came the Madonna." [24]

Moments later, Mirjana found herself trying to explain to the Virgin what had happened to them and what the police in Medjugorje were now ordering:

"They've forbidden us to go to the hill anymore," Mirjana informed Mary. "Will it upset you if we wait for you in the church?" [25]

Nodding in agreement to Mirjana's proposal—and once more promising to return the next day—the Madonna then departed as quickly as she came, back in the direction of Medjugorje. There, over 20,000 disappointed souls still massed, debating about the visionaries' whereabouts. [26]

Moving out of the field and onto the road, the children commenced their way back to Medjugorje, too. Only now they had to walk, as their two hosts for the day were long gone, having fled in fear upon witnessing Mary's luminescent arrival. [27]

In Medjugorje that seventh night, after everyone departed, a sigh of relief temporarily filled the air in the rectory at St. James and in the homes of the visionaries.

No, they weren't out of trouble.

But the priests and the children were pleased that the apparitions would now be held in the church. Perhaps—at least for a while—there would be less drama, less controversy.

The calm, however, was short lived.

The authorities were still at work.

The police had grabbed Marinko, and he was being held in Čitluk for questioning. [28]

While it wasn't going very well for the children and the priests, things weren't going any better for the government.

By the afternoon of July 1, 1981, television and newspaper reporters were arriving in Medjugorje from all over Yugoslavia [29]—with inquiries coming in from as far away as Italy—concerning the reported miraculous healing of little Daniel Setka.[30]

Communist officials were enraged.

Now, a massive amount of media attention suddenly focused on Medjugorje.

And that wasn't all.

That morning, they had been blindsided by the resignations of the two social workers. The women, dumbfounded and frightened by the phenomena in the field, stated they could not continue after what they witnessed.[31] Not long after, they both left the vicinity—one moved to Sarajevo, and the other to Germany. [32]

Meanwhile, the SUP arrived in town again, calling for a public meeting at the school house of all the villagers. They wanted to make sure that everyone understood that the visionaries were officially banned from the hill.[33]

The secret police then took the opportunity to criticize some of the parents of the children, starting with Vicka's father who, though working in Germany, was accused of not financially supporting his family.[34] This negligence, the authorities said, caused his wife to lose control of her eight children.

Marija's father was singled out, too, with officials calling him an alcoholic who was mentally disturbed.[35] Finally, the police felt it wouldn't hurt to point out that Jacov's parents were divorced.

The ploy, though, seemed to backfire.

After hearing the litany of insults, many of the villagers became even more supportive of the children, with their parents starting to be viewed as martyrs.[36]

Later that day, two more government SUP agents arrived in Medjugorje and went straight to the visionaries' houses. While Ivan and Mirjana were not home, [37] the agents did manage to round up the rest of the children and force them into their van, with Jacov's mother managing to somehow snatch him back through a rear door as it pulled away.[38]

But the SUP didn't get far.

Like the evening before, as they headed down the road from Bijakovići, another extraordinary incident unfolded out of nowhere.

With the children pounding hard on the windows of the van as it neared Medjugorje, the agents felt they had no choice but to stop and scold them. Suddenly, the Virgin's presence was perceptible to the children, only in a way that Vicka would later describe to Father Bubalo as a kind of internal vision. [39]

Though not aware of this development, as the SUP gazed into the back of the van and looked upon the children's somewhat distant looking faces, they immediately panicked and ordered everyone to get out of the vehicle. [40]

Then, with the officers in a state of bewilderment, the three girls spontaneously took off, racing as fast as they could into a nearby tobacco field. [41] This forced the police to abandon the van and chase them on foot.[42]

Around the same time, just down the road a stretch, there sat alone in St. James Church a shell-shocked Father Jozo, more bewildered and overwhelmed than ever. [43]

And not without cause.

He had just received another threatening communication from the authorities in Čitluk. If he were unable to control the demonstrators flocking into Medjugorje by the thousands that day, the priest would now face criminal charges. [44]

Feeling helpless on what was now the eighth evening of the apparitions, Jozo was also becoming more uncertain about what to do with the children. That morning, a local woman who had been a fierce opponent of religion—even going so far as to scream on Podbrdo during one of the apparitions, "God exists, but only in your imaginations, idiots!"—reported experiencing a radical conversion.[45] She even demanded that Father Zrinko hear her confession. It was, the shaken friar claimed, the most powerful confession he heard in his thirty-year priesthood. [46]

Thus, with a heavy heart, a troubled mind, and a Bible in hand, Jozo went into the church to pray alone, not knowing what to do next.

"I felt like Moses before the Red Sea and I knew that I could speak only to God," Jozo would later explain. "No man could have answered my need. I prayed, 'God, I know you talked to Abraham, to Moses and to others. Now there are thousands of people here these days. Tell me where the river is going. I do not know where the mouth of that river is, nor what its source is.'" [47]

Just then, deeply engrossed in his conversation with the Lord, Jozo says he heard a voice say to him:

"*Come out and protect the children.*" [48]

Setting his Bible aside and genuflecting, Jozo instinctively hurried over to the main door of the church, [49] opened it, and in fled the three children who escaped the SUP. [50]

"The police are chasing us. Hide us," the children pleaded with the stunned priest.[51]

Moving swiftly, Jozo took them to the rectory and locked them in an unoccupied room. Moments later, as the dazed priest stood outside the front doors of the church, an agent came hurrying by and asked Jozo if he saw the children.

"I did," he admitted, as the officer rambled past him and hurried down the street. [52]

That evening, the Madonna would appear to all six visionaries in the rectory of St. James for the first time. [53]

And, Father Jozo celebrated Mass before what was most likely the largest attendance at a worship service since the church opened in 1969.[54]

Once considered oversized for the five villages, St. James suddenly seemed too small for the many thousands there who believed in the Madonna of Medjugorje.

It was a throng of believers that now included—for the first time that evening—a priest named Jozo Zovko.

CHAPTER THIRTY

THE TWO MADONNAS

"When Jesus saw his mother and the disciple there whom
he loved, he said to his mother, 'Woman, behold your
son,' Then he said to the disciple, 'Behold your mother.'"
—Jn 19:26-27

A SMALL PIN WITH THE IMAGE OF A FACE.
It wasn't much—but it said everything.

The Black Madonna of Czestochowa—worn boldly and proudly by Lech Wałęsa on the lapel of his suit coat—meant one thing to the man, as well as the Polish people who saw it glued to his chest.[1] The Virgin Mary was with him.

And if Mary was with him, then nothing would prevail against him.

By July of 1981, the face of Walesa, like that of the Black Madonna, *also* meant one thing to the Polish people: *Solidarity*—the first independent non-governmental trade union in a Soviet-bloc country.

Founded by Walesa at the Lenin Shipyards on August 14,1980, *Solidarity* quickly became a glimmer of light, peeking through a hole in the Iron Curtain. [2] And, along with the current Polish Pope, Karol Wojtyła, the union seemed to represent the fact that something profoundly spiritual was at work in Poland.

While Father Jozo Zovko now believed it was the fire of the Holy Spirit blazing the path in Yugoslavia those early days of July 1981, farther north in Eastern Europe, the Communists were determined that very month to douse the same fire in Poland.

Confronting an economic crisis from the year before, First Secretary Edward Gierek's Polish government decided to raise meat prices, while slowing the growth of wages.[3] This instigated a series of strikes and factory occupations.

Beginning in Warsaw on July 2, 1980, the unrest soon spread to major industrial centers. Then, at the Lenin Shipyards in Gdansk, a popular crane operator named Anna Walentynowicz, who was an activist, was fired.[4] This outraged the workers there even more and caused them to organize.

Over the next year, *Solidarity* went from a trade union to a national movement, with eighty percent of the total Polish work force eventually joining the organization.

"History has taught us there is no bread without freedom," the *Solidarity* program proclaimed, suddenly forcing the Communist government in Poland to change its labor policies.[5]

But by early 1981, the Soviet Union had seen enough.

Installing its favorite son, General Wojciech Jaruzelski, as premier on February 11, 1981, the Communist government adopted a strong arm position on *Solidarity* and began to prepare a crackdown.[6]

Particularly well-liked by Premier Leonid Brezhnev, Jaruzelski had a proven track record for Soviet loyalty—at any price. Eleven years before, he had personally approved a top-secret Soviet plan to invade Western Europe.[7] The strategy included turning Poland, his homeland, into a nuclear wasteland for use as an invasion corridor for a two-million-man strike. [8]

Jaruzelski, a Pole, was certainly no son of Poland—and the Soviets knew it. This meant *Solidarity* and Lech Wałęsa's days were numbered.

In Yugoslavia, Father Jozo Zovko's fate moved along the same path.

Like Wałęsa and his Black Madonna, the Virgin of Medjugorje would soon be his closest friend.

While the Communist Party in Poland was not too happy that summer of 1981, it's safe to say that neither were their comrades in Yugoslavia, where they kept making things worse for themselves.

On July 4, the fortieth anniversary of Fighters Day in Yugoslavia—so named for the 1941 anniversary of the Partisan or Communist uprising in the nation during the early days of World War II—Brando Mikulic, a high-ranking party official, proclaimed to several hundred thousand in historic Tjentište that Croatian nationalists were spreading a ridiculous story about the Virgin Mary appearing in Medjugorje. [9]

Mikulic took care to note how the alleged visions were occurring in the very area where the most atrocious crimes in Yugoslavia during World War II had been committed by the Ustasi.[10]

The aim of the bogus ruse, he assured the massive crowd, was to intimidate uneducated people and try to fool them, and to manipulate them politically in order to make them serve those who work against the interests of nations and nationalities.[11] Mikulic's objective was to ridicule the apparitions and use them as political fodder.

His strategy, however, backfired badly.

In Tjentište that day, there just happened to be a large number of national television and radio reporters, as well as foreign journalists and correspondents.[12] The significant media presence had been initially sent to cover the anniversary celebration. However, once they heard Mikulic mention the reported visions, they pounced.[13]

The story was soon picked up by European television-based news agencies, and it was rebroadcasted from one end of the continent to the other.[14]

The cat was now out of the bag.

To the dismay of the angry Communist authorities in Yugoslavia, a horde of journalists from throughout the West immediately began arriving in the country, trying to locate the stealthy little hamlet with the cryptic-sounding name.[15]

Ironically—or perhaps, providentially—thanks to the Yugoslavian government, the annoying visions in Herzegovina went from an internal conundrum to an international sensation in little more than a blink of the eye.

Medjugorje, as one writer put it, "quickly became a household word." [16]

"Did not Christ come to liberate you and me and all of us who have been in slavery for forty years, so that this evening or tomorrow we may kneel before him and say: 'Break these chains, break these shackles, break the fetters which bind my life with the evil of sin. You alone have the key?'" [17]

Jozo's sermons now packed a punch.

Awakened in their spirit, his flock no longer slept through them. And his enemies, mostly government attendees, now hung on every word too, hoping that he would hang himself—and the visionaries—with proof of sedition.

With Jozo on board with the apparitions, though, things could be expected to go a little smoother for the six visionaries, at least in the short run. But, unfortunately, they still didn't have what they desired most—a sign from the Virgin.

However—while it wasn't easily discernable—the quiet, hidden hand of God *was* at work all around the children.

Over and over, through *little signs*, it appeared Mary was leaving her fingerprints on a number of mystifying events in Medjugorje, but as with the case of little Daniel Setka, faith would be the powder needed to dust the evidence.

The most telling proof of the divine at work was in the long confessions lines.[18]

Every day in Medjugorje, hundreds were lining up to let go of their sinful pasts, like joy-filled children waiting their turn to talk to Santa Claus. Jozo especially delighted in this, as in his eyes there could be no greater a sign of the apparitions' authenticity than people turning to the Church.

For him, the blindness of sin being healed was better than the blindness of sight being restored. The Sacrament of Confession, Jozo told his listeners, destroys one's own idols and leads to freedom, putting Jesus back in first place.[19]

But as Christ said, "Which is easier, to say, 'Your sins are forgiven'; or to say, 'Rise up and walk?'" (Mt 9:5), so it would be in Medjugorje. Promising to prove whether or not Mary was really appearing in Medjugorje, a blind man named Jozo Vasilj decided to mimic one of Christ's most memorable miracles in the Gospels.

Vasilj took dirt from apparition hill, mixed it with thyme and water, and then rubbed it into his eyes in order to attempt to restore his sight. After doing this, he prayed the Creed with deep conviction. He then opened his eyes and immediately told his wife he could now see her.

Thinking he was kidding, the woman gave it no thought until—to her shocking amazement—he confronted her regarding the short length of her dress. Not content, he then repeated the mud pasting process on his infected left arm, wrapped a towel around it, and went to sleep. The next morning, Jozo Vasilj found his arm had completely healed. [20]

Another man, Matija Skuban, from Germany, reported that he had felt a powerful current flow through him while praying in St. James on July 20, 1981. He wasn't sure what had happened or why it occurred. But minutes later, when he rose for Communion, he discovered his paralyzed left leg had been healed. [21]

Similarly came the story of Damir Coric. Damir was in his third year of high school in 1979 when he lost all feeling in his legs, and eventually was left unable to walk. Diagnosed with a brain disorder called *Hydrocephalus Internus*, Damir proceeded to undergo five surgeries that left him worse. Now unable to stand, or even sit up in bed, he soon developed difficulty eating and had to drink through a straw. His mother, Mara, thought God was "going to take him." [22]

Asking some girls who were going to Medjugorje to please bring her some flowers or earth from Podbrdo, Mara and her husband started to bathe their son in the soil and flowers from apparition hill. Although nothing happened, his mother continued to believe.

Finally, she took Damir himself to Medjugorje in the late summer of 1981. There, on the second trip, after being prayed over by Vicka, the teenage boy said he could feel the heaviness of his body lifting. Within a short time, Damir was completely healed. [23]

Likewise, there came the healing of Marica Kvesic, who was 17 years old when she suffered a sudden paralysis of her arms and legs. As with Damir, she lost all function and reportedly didn't have, according to her mother, Andja, "the strength of a kitten in her body."

All hospital treatments rendered her condition worse, and Marica spent the following year in a wheelchair. Diagnosed with *Polyradiculoneuritis* with *Quadriparesis*, doctors went so far as to say in 1980 that she would never walk again.

In desperation, Andja took her daughter to Medjugorje, where she started to improve immediately. Within a short period, Marica was completely able to walk and eventually hiked the 32 miles from her home in Posusje to Medjugorje in gratitude. [24]

By mid-July, less than 30 days after the onset of the apparitions in Medjugorje, physical healings were being reported to St. James on a constant basis. Minor ailments were especially vanishing left and right.

From backaches to eczema, rashes to neurological conditions, people kept reporting their *little miracles.* [25]

But the vast number of healings was just the beginning of the signs.

During this time, the entire five-village community surrounding St. James underwent a transformation.

Old disputes between enemies were now cast aside and forgotten. Neighbors began to help each other in the fields. And, Father Jozo especially noted, some parishioners reported that using foul language, as well as drinking and being boisterous, were behaviors that were no longer necessary—they were, people now told him, "not of God."

Most significantly, there emerged an attitude of work can wait, as evening Mass became a must for many of the villagers.[26]

With the many miracles and changes in Medjugorje came more prevalent news accounts. One article, which appeared in the Communist weekly magazine, *Arena,* written by a reporter named Peter Pavlović, especially set off another round of growing interest in the village because of its favorable slant.

The story, which detailed the many miraculous healings, received broad attention and, to the chagrin of the Communists, caused another surge of pilgrims and reporters to descend on Medjugorje.[27]

The second wave of journalists now began to even linger in the village in hopes of breaking the next big story. [28]

Then, there were the growing number of reports of strange and otherworldly happenings that were becoming commonplace in Medjugorje.

On July 14, the visionaries and about fifty followers from the local villages climbed Podbrdo around 11:00 p.m., at the request of the Virgin. Suddenly, seven or eight people began to point out a ball of light that was shooting directly towards them as if it came out of a hole in the sky.

"It was like a shining balloon that came down quickly," explained Vicka of the phenomena. The strange light then seemed to stop directly over a sunken area of the hill that had been somewhat excavated. In its center was staked a wooden cross. [29] Once the ball of light halted, it literally burst, recalled the witnesses, scattering thousands of tiny looking stars everywhere.

With the hillside now awash in light from above, the entire group fell to their knees in awe, with some children and adults crying. Below, throughout the villages, countless numbers of people witnessed the phenomenon and immediately began to rush the hill. Recalled Marinko, "We started praying aloud. We prayed for about 45 minutes altogether. We were all crying. I shall never forget that night." [30]

The evening ended with two Madonna-like shapes—one glowing and the other like a silhouette—appearing by the cross on top of Mt. Krizevac. The radiating Madonna looked like "white fire," thought Marinko. But after he got his camera and took a photograph, only the non-glowing Madonna was ultimately visible.[31]

In early August, another celestial mystery unfolded.

This time, a massive cloud formation appeared in the sky over Mount Krizevac. It spelled out the word *Mir*, which means "peace" in Croatian. According to accounts, even Father Jozo saw it, using it that evening in his homily to recall Scripture's foretelling of the coming of signs in the sky. [32]

As summer rolled into fall, reports of little miracles throughout Medjugorje were being registered at St. James on a regular basis.

One fascinating account had the sun especially behaving oddly, as it was seen turned on its axis, pushing forward towards the Earth, and giving off long rays of light, only to then retreat a few moments later. Around 150 statements originated from this phenomenon alone. Wrote one witness,

"I noticed the sun doing strange things…it began to swing to and fro. Finally, a ray of light separated itself from the sun and travelled like the rays of a rainbow towards the place where the Virgin had first appeared. It then rested on the church tower, on which a clear image of the Virgin appeared."

Other oddities were reported.

One person saw figures around the sun. Others reported seeing the shape of a cross on the sun. Some said they saw six small hearts appear in the sky—centered around a large heart and a white cloud—cover the hill at the site of the first apparition. Such phenomena caused many to cry, pray, or even run away. [33]

Miles away from Medjugorje, in a nearby village, almost the entire population—which had gathered for a funeral procession—reported seeing the sun one afternoon perform similar wonders. Immediately after it was over, the crowd felt compelled to pray together for about ten minutes. [34]

A priest visiting Medjugorje at the time, Father Umberto Loncar, who scoffed for days at such reports of signs in the sky, was forced to eat his words. He witnessed the phenomena too, and felt compelled to tell about it:

"At six-twenty exactly, I saw a huge red and violet cloud over Cerno... After the cloud disappeared from sight, I descended to the terrace between the rectory and the church. Precisely at 6:40 p.m., the red and violet figure of a magnificent lady arose from the hill of Crnica. The red and violet faded in intensity as she ascended in the sky; then she disappeared. The last thing I saw was a brilliant white scarf that dangled from her feet and swung in the air." [35]

Even the invincible Iva Vasilj, the maternal grandmother of Ivanka, reported a remarkable sight in the heavens above Medjugorje:

"I had gone to our tobacco fields at sunset to pick the leaves," explained Iva. "Suddenly a real cold wind got up, and as we looked up, the sun was dancing, and the head and shoulders of a woman came out of it and went towards Krizevac. There were balloons coming out of the sun—red, purple and blue. I was paralyzed with fright. The neighbor's fifteen sheep were so frightened that they huddled stiffly together." [36]

While more such reports abounded as the seasons changed—perhaps granting the visionaries some relief—none of this made the authorities any happier. To the contrary, the Communists became more determined to find a way to shut down Medjugorje.

Banned from the hill, over the following weeks the visions took place anywhere the children could find that escaped the eyes of the SUP: in the Church, at their homes, in the fields, even in cow sheds.[37] Constantly followed, the six sometimes drove miles to break free of police surveillance.[38]

None of this erratic activity surrounding the apparitions, however, discouraged the massive crowds. In fact, quite the opposite occurred; the people continued to come to Medjugorje, where confession lines were now seemingly endless and the church filled beyond capacity every evening for Mass.

Demands for St. James to be closed were now being repeatedly refused by Jozo, who by the beginning of August, sensed his days—like Lech Walesa in Poland—were numbered.

This reality became more evident to him after another band of young people singing Croatian hymns and chanting anti-government rhetoric scaled Podbrdo noisily one evening.

"I shall be going away soon," Jozo predicted shortly thereafter to a visiting friar who was assigned to serve at Medjugorje in the near future, "be ready to take my place." [39]

CHAPTER THIRTY-ONE

THE JUST WILL PREVAIL

*"You belong to God, children, and you have
conquered them, for the one who is
in you is greater than the one who is in the world."*

—1 Jn 4:4

THE KNOCK ON THE RECTORY DOOR CAME AT 7 A.M.[1]
It was followed by a second knock on Jozo's door by Zrinko, who wanted to let him know that two representatives of the Mostar Ministry of the Interior had arrived. [2]

"Let them wait," replied Jozo, as he finished his morning preparations.

Minutes later, as the weary priest stepped out, the purpose of the early morning visitation was established.

"You're to come with us," said one of the agents.

Sparing goodbyes to save everyone from getting upset, as Jozo was led outside to a tiny Volkswagen, a waiting police officer wanted to know if he was to be handcuffed.

"No," came the reply from his superior, surprising Jozo, as he thought it was a preplanned certainty once he spotted the TV cameras rolling.[3]

Driving off at what Jozo remembered to be at a dizzying speed, the besieged friar was later transferred into the back of a black police van, which hurried him to Mostar. There, in a building he didn't recognize, Jozo was placed in cell number eighty-three.[4]

Back at St. James, the remaining agents thoroughly searched the parish offices. They also bodily frisked five local Franciscan nuns, who were accused of operating a secret electronic device that projected the apparitions into the eyes of the children.[5] All of this, the authorities claimed, was conjured up by Jozo.[6]

Before departing, the agents confiscated boxes of documents, books, letters, and audio cassettes of the first interviews of the visionaries.

And, not to be overlooked, approximately $4,000 in cash from the collection boxes. [7]

For weeks, this day—August 17, 1981—had been foreseen, over and over. But a series of events in the early days of the month finally pushed it to fruition.

By then, government harassment of the priests, the villagers, and the visionaries had increasingly stepped up. The priests were constantly being interrogated "for hatching the entire plot." The scheme was designed, the Communists now claimed, to raise money for an extension to the church.[8]

At the same time, the authorities alleged the children were part of an insidious plot of nationalistic sedition. Frustrated and vexed by it all, the Yugoslavian government finally declared a state of emergency in Medjugorje. [9]

The key players, according to the government, were not only the priests and the children, but also their parents, as well as certain pilgrims who were "regulars" in Medjugorje. Soon, government informers were planted everywhere to observe all the main characters in order to pin charges on them.

Then, on August 11, the authorities in Čitluk had moved again to close down the apparitions. They began by calling Jozo to their headquarters, ordering him to abolish evening Mass and to stop the people from going up the hill. This time, they had produced so-called incriminating documents obtained from their informants that allegedly proved Jozo started everything.

"We know you're the man behind all this," the Communist officials told him. "We have witnesses. We can put you behind bars." [10]

"You've absolutely no justification for doing so," countered Jozo. "How can there be witnesses to something that didn't happen? A witness is not someone who's ready to swear to whatever you tell him, even when it's a lie." [11]

Seeking to placate the authorities, Jozo said he would attempt to stop the activity on the hill. But he refused to end the evening Mass.

The following day, the police arrived and arrested two people on the hill, one of them being first-day-only visionary, Ivan Ivanković.

They also established constant guards on Podbrdo at every point of entry.

Two days later, on August 13, a couple more squads of special police arrived in Medjugorje from Sarajevo. This time, they blocked access to the church and arrested Father Ferdo Vlašić. Indicted soon after for being a cleric-nationalist, both he and Ivan wound up incarcerated in Mostar for the next two months.[12]

Finally, on August 16, Bishop Pavao Zanic of Mostar released a statement on the apparitions.[13] Zanic, who wept for joy upon first hearing of the visions and visited Medjugorje five times during the first weeks,[14] was an avid supporter of the children's honesty and publicly proclaimed, "These children are not telling lies."[15]

His statement, which was subsequently published in a major Croatian publication, was immediately regarded as "deliberately provocative" by the government.[16]

It also served to be the straw that broke the camel's back for Father Jozo Zovko.

By then, though, his arrest was a fait acompli.

With the arrest of Jozo, the entire parish of Medjugorje fell into a deep and dark depression, one that is revealed in the parish ledger:

> When the bell rang for Mass, the church filled up in dead silence. The people were looking at the set faces of the priests and nuns, the scattered altar cloths, overturned vases, wide-open cupboards all around. When Father Zrinko came to the altar to address the people, he could hardly speak: "This is the hardest day of my life," he said, and everyone began crying. During Mass they tried to sing, but they gagged on the words. The sisters said they couldn't bring themselves to say the Glorious Mysteries of the Rosary, and said the Sorrowful ones instead.

> At the end of Mass, in the middle of the seven Our Fathers, the visionaries stopped dead, and hurried to the side room opposite the sacristy. There was a hush, prayerful and expectant, and all eyes were fixed on the door where the children were. Then, Jacov came to the microphone, "Our

Lady called us into that room. Where she was waiting for us. She told us to tell you: '*Don't be afraid. I want you to be happy and to let joy show on your faces. I shall look after Father Jozo.*'" [17]

Television news that evening out of Sarajevo reported the arrest.[18] The newscaster announced that Jozo, Bishop Zanic, and others were extremists and that they gravely abused religious freedom under the guise of advancing and restoring the Ustasi.[19]

Once Jozo was in custody, the authorities proceeded to torture him.

A resident of Medjugorje, Mladen Bulic, crossed paths with Jozo in a hospital somewhere around the end of August. He later presented a written testimony of what he learned concerning the friar's confinement in jail:

> In the middle of August, 1981, I had been hospitalized for throat problems for five days. On August 25, I was at my bedroom window. I saw a militia car. Two policemen came out, holding my parish priest, Father Jozo, dressed in civilian clothes. I hurried down the stairs to greet him because a week before he had been incarcerated. On the stairs, I met Father Jozo with two policemen.
>
> I moved towards him to shake his hand, but the two policemen pushed me away nervously. I noticed that the small group had stopped in the hallway, while waiting for a patient to leave the doctor's office. Father Jozo's ears were bleeding. Seeing how he was walking, I thought he would stay in a wheelchair for the rest of his life.
>
> I got closer and asked him, "How are you doing?"
>
> He turned towards me with a smile and said "You see."
>
> Looking at his smile, I saw that teeth were missing. The right cheek was swollen. They had beaten him savagely.
>
> One of the policemen came to me and said, "If you keep on talking, we will beat you too."

I did not let them intimidate me. I answered, "You cannot do anything. I am a patient, and I have a right to be here!"

Father Jozo went into the doctor's office with the policemen. When he came out, he asked me, "How are things going in Medjugorje?"

I answered, "All is well. Do not worry."

A policeman said, "There is nothing to worry about because tonight we will cut his head off."

I answered, "You cannot do anything to him; you were able to beat him up; you cannot kill him."

At that point, Father Jozo turned his head and told me to be silent because it was dangerous to talk.

Afterwards, I learned about ten days later, the policeman who had beaten him up died of a heart attack. The main policeman was telling Father Jozo that he was an enemy of the state and the government, and that he would be worn thin, and they would get him a little bit at a time. The policeman had chained him and put weights on his arms and legs to hurt him. But when in the morning, they came back to take Father Jozo, they found him freed of his chains; and his cell, which did not have a lamp, was illuminated. [20]

When finally brought to trial in October, Jozo charges were threefold.

Through his sermons, the Franciscan priest was said to be repeatedly referring to the Israelites' forty years in the desert as a symbolic reference to Communism's forty-year rule in Yugoslavia.

He also, in declaring it sometimes necessary to shed one's blood for the faith, was accused of using doublespeak to incite violence against the regime.

Lastly, Jozo was charged with promulgating the rise of religion in Croatia and Herzegovina as a path to power, once again, in opposition to the state and the people.

All of these charges, eighteen witnesses for the prosecution testified, proved Jozo was the mastermind behind the apparition hoax in Medjugorje.

Three hundred and thirty people volunteered to speak on behalf of Jozo, all were denied. No theological experts were permitted to explain Jozo's reference to the "forty years in the desert" cited in his homilies. And, a request for the taped sermons to be played in court was not permitted. [21]

Not surprisingly, the trumped-up charges prevailed in the court proceedings against Jozo. Alarmed by the restlessness in Poland brought about by the Catholic Lech Wałęsa and his *Solidarity* movement, the Communist government in Yugoslavia wanted to ensure it showed no weakness in dealing with its own Catholic revolutionaries.

On October 22, 1981, Father Jozo Zovko was sentenced to three-and-a-half- years' imprisonment. [22]

The court—in order to show its rationale side—ordered the money taken from St. James's coffers to be returned. [23]

Through Jozo's arrest and conviction, the Communist authorities in Yugoslavia intended to bring an end to Medjugorje.

But it proved to be only the beginning.

Like the suffering of so many martyrs in Church history that have mystically seeded a greater cause at hand, Jozo's plight was the spiritual fuel used to take Medjugorje to the next level.

In fact, by the fall of 1981, no longer would Medjugorje be just a pilgrimage for the homespun of Yugoslavia. As word spread about the sanctuary of miracles in Herzegovina, nothing seemed to dissuade travelers from all over Europe—regardless of so many obvious impediments.

The one who would come the most to Medjugorje at this time, however, would be the Virgin Mary herself, for by the time Jozo was arrested, she had already nurtured an extraordinary relationship with each of the six visionaries and was starting to harvest the fruits.

Although apparitions have been reported for centuries, with many a visionary becoming the vehicle of a divine message, something unprecedented began to unfold with the six in Medjugorje.

Mary, the Church-proclaimed spiritual mother of all God's people on Earth, appeared to be in Medjugorje in a way designed to prove she truly was a "personal" mother to all.

And, through the visionaries there, she began to demonstrate this reality in a very special way.

By mid-July, the communication unfolding between Mary and the children was becoming quite profound and intimate. The visionaries were starting to be taken into the world of the Virgin; a world where the importance of strong faith, persistent prayer, and the power of the Sacraments was what embodied the practice of living a good and holy life.

In their answers to questions regarding Mary's words, a profound understanding of God was starting to be seen—a wisdom that revealed how far they had come under her spiritual tutelage in just two months.

Asked by a priest if she experienced Mary as one who gives graces or one who prays to God, Vicka answered, "As one who prays to God." Asked by the same priest if prayer was more powerful in one place than another, Vicka said it all comes down to one's faith, not the location where the prayer was said. [24]

Vicka wasn't the only one that now appeared to be revealing spiritual growth. Regardless of the question, all six seemed to understand the ways of God in a new, more enlightened way that revealed the presence of the Madonna in their lives.

One evening, Mary asked that the visionaries—who were accompanied by about forty others—to go to the prairie at Gumno (Gumno means threshing floor in Croatian), a farmer's field about 200 yards from Vicka's home.[25]

There, the Madonna appeared and even permitted the people to come near enough to her to be in contact with her dress. [26] A few who participated claimed to feel a sensation from the apparition, similar to what the atheist pediatrician, Dr. Glamuzina, reported on Podbrdo that she experienced. Others became overcome with emotion.[27] All in all, the evening was used by Mary as a teaching moment to emphasize prayer, fasting, the seriousness of sin and the need for the Sacrament of Reconciliation. [28]

Mary also continued to teach the children about the times at hand.

On the same day, August 2, Marija reported an apparition at her home in which the Virgin told her that a "great battle is about to take place. A battle between my Son and Satan. Human souls are at stake." [29]

Four days later, on August 6, the *Feast of the Transfiguration*, Mary said to the children for the first time, "I am the Queen of Peace." [30] It was a pivotal moment in the apparitions, for Fátima and Medjugorje were being directly linked by Mary in a special way that appeared intentional.

Mary first appeared at Fátima on May 13, 1917, eight days after Pope Benedict XV had added a new invocation to the *Litany of Loreto*: "Mary, Queen of Peace, pray for us." Now, Mary was referring to herself in Medjugorje as the Queen of Peace.

Twice more before the end of 1981—once at the end of August and again in October [31]—Mary would emphasize to the children that she was in Medjugorje as the Queen of Peace. [32]

On August 17—the day Jozo was arrested—the visionaries expressed to Mary the heavy sadness canvassing Medjugorje.

"Be not afraid," the Virgin told the children to tell the people. Instead, the faithful needed to "be filled with joy, a joy that needs to be seen on your face." [33] Christian suffering, Mary told the villagers, was a great gift of faith, and Jozo would be rewarded by God for his present distress, as would they all.

Yes, Jozo was gone, but the Virgin Mary's plan at Medjugorje was pushing forward.

The visionaries were learning the ways of God, as were the priests and the people.

It was becoming clear; the future was being laid out before them. It was a future that connected the work begun at Fátima to Medjugorje, a work which Mary was hinting, through the secret messages being given to the visionaries, that was not complete, that remained unfulfilled.

The work in Medjugorje—as at Fátima—would involve some coming changes in the world. Undeniably, they were changes the Madonna could see.

And those in Medjugorje were given a glimpse.

Responding to a question concerning the recent upheaval in nearby Poland given to Marija by a young local Franciscan, the Virgin replied,

"In a little while there will be great conflicts there, but in the end, the just will prevail." [34]

CHAPTER THIRTY-TWO

SOLIDARITY

*"I will drive them out little by little before
you, until you have grown numerous
enough to take possession of the land."*

—Ex 23:30

U PHEAVAL.

If one had a crystal ball in 1981 to see the upheaval ahead in Eastern Europe for the remainder of the decade, to call it shocking would be an understatement.

And yes, it would be events in Poland that would marshal in the coming unrest.

A bellwether nation in the emerging resistance to Communism that was picking up steam in Eastern Europe, Poland—a country so religious it was said by critics to have "not experienced the Enlightenment"— would become the catalyst for the unthinkable: a coming challenge to the Marxist hegemony that first premiered in Russia in 1917. [1]

The movement arising in Poland was political in nature.

But what was emerging there seemed to be driven by more than just a human longing for freedom.

Something spiritual seemed at work.

This view starts with the obvious: the Catholic Church was now headed by a native son of Poland.

But soon after, it also became clear that *Solidarity*'s leader, Lech Wałęsa, shared the Holy Father's *Totus Tuus* allegiance to the Blessed Virgin Mary.

The two Polish leaders shared one other thing, too: both were the target of the same assassin—Mehmet Alì Ağca.

Just months before he would attempt to kill the Pope, Ağca stalked Wałęsa in Rome. Planning to knock off the Polish union leader with a suitcase bomb, the Bulgarians called off the hit at the last moment because the Italian police had been tipped off. [2]

But there would soon appear another dominant figure in this story.

And, like Poland's Wojtyła and Wałęsa, he too would be spiritually motivated to envision the end of Communism. All it would take for him to emerge was the right time and the right opportunity.

And that didn't take long to happen.

At 6 a.m. on December 13, 1981, Poland exploded. [3]

From Warsaw to Gdańsk to Kraków, tanks rumbled through the streets and bullets whizzed through the air. Scores of police vehicles sped around everywhere, looking for leaders of *Solidarity*.

The Communist government's crackdown on the union had finally come. Over 80,000 soldiers and 30,000 policemen were mobilized in a massive show of force. [4]

The flexing of so much government muscle was not surprising. *Solidarity* now had over 9 million members, almost a third of the population. [5] It had undeniably become a monolithic force that the Polish authorities were not sure how to deal with.

Within days of the action, it looked like the problem had been put to rest for good. With Wałęsa in prison, the union's funds confiscated, and hundreds of deaths reported, the end of *Solidarity* seemed at hand.

In Rome, Pope John Paul II was reported to be surprised and anguished.[6] It was a profound humiliation for Poland, Father Stanislaw Dziwisz publicly professed on behalf of the Holy Father.[7]

Appearing before the nation on television, Poland's Prime Minister Wojciech Jaruzelski announced that the country would be governed in the short run by the Military Council of National Salvation,[8] a committee of 15 generals and five colonels. Marshall Law would now be in force.

Poland, Jaruzelski declared, was in a "State of Emergency." [9]

It would soon be argued by political analysts in the West that Jaruzelski had had no choice. The Polish Prime Minister was said to have known a Soviet invasion was coming, one that would bring massive bloodshed. He believed, therefore, there would be less danger, suffering, and instability if the Polish military did the dirty work instead of Soviet soldiers. [10]

Jaruzelski, some think, was hinting at such when he spoke to the nation:

"I am speaking to all Poles. Our country is threatened by mortal danger. The danger is coming from forces hostile to socialism. The new Military Council will stop the fall of the state." [11]

Solidarity issued its own statement to the people of Poland and the world:

"We appeal to you: help us in our struggle by mass protests and moral support. Do not watch passively the attempts to strangle the beginnings of democracy in the heart of Europe. Be with us in these difficult moment... Solidarity with *Solidarity*, Poland is not yet lost." [12]

One man was immediately with *Solidarity*.

"We need to hit them hard, and save *Solidarity*," President Ronald Reagan told a National Security Council meeting not long after the imposition of martial law in Poland.

Reagan was mad. But he also sensed the time was at hand when the United States could perhaps fulfill Pope Pius XII's words—favorites of Reagan: "God had placed a wounded world into the hands of America." [13]

Meeting with liaisons from the Holy See first, Reagan immediately initiated a series of communications with the Pope, telling him on December 29 that the United States would not let the Soviet Union dictate Poland's future with impunity. [14]

For Reagan, the uniqueness of the moment at hand was not lost on him.

As his former advisor Richard Clark would note, Reagan thought of Poland as a means to the disintegration and collapse of the main danger, the real adversary, the Soviet Union. [15]

Long disappointed over the West's abandonment of Eastern Europe after World War II, the President made it known to his advisers that the United States refused to abandon Poland again. [16]

In prison and alone with only their Madonna—one in Poland and the other in Yugoslavia—Lech Wałęsa and Jozo Zovko were hundreds of miles apart on January 1, 1982.

But they were bonded in a way that was special, in a way that two other separated men suffered together in prisons at the hands of another tyrannical empire—Saints Peter and Paul. Unlike the two Apostles, however, Wałęsa and Zovko would live to fight another day.

But not for now.

As the Communist authorities in both countries moved to tighten their stranglehold on events, it was slowly becoming apparent to them that the situations were different than before.

The times at hand were not the same as Hungary in 1956 or Czechoslovakia in 1968. The world had changed, and so had the people living behind the Iron Curtain. Consequently, brute force would be unable to dictate the outcome of the Communist's dilemmas in Poland and Yugoslavia.

In Medjugorje, no matter how bad the authorities wanted it, the apparition of the Virgin Mary was not going away.

With Father Jozo melting into the labyrinth of the Communist prison system in Yugoslavia, Father Zrinko Cuvalo had to take the wheel at St. James.[17] He was now backed up by Father Tomislav Vlašić, the former pastor at Saint Francis of Assisi in Capljina.

Vlašić was an acclaimed scholar,[18] who first visited Medjugorje on the fifth day of the apparitions in June and quickly became involved in helping his fellow friars with the visions.[19] Upon finishing his tenure in Capljina, he was transferred to Medjugorje and arrived on August 18, the day after Jozo was arrested. [20]

Though officially designated as Zrinko's assistant pastor, by October he found himself inundated with many of Jozo's other responsibilities, which included the pastoral needs of the pilgrims coming for the apparitions. [21]

Indeed, while bedlam and chaos filled the air in Medjugorje, so did visions of the Virgin Mary. By the end of 1981, people were coming to Medjugorje from all over Europe and beyond.

Moreover, not only were the apparitions still occurring daily, so also was the mystical madness that surrounded them. And while the good friars kept reminding people that miraculous oddities weren't import-ant— "not what Medjugorje is all about," they repeated—no one could help but ponder why so many signs and wonders were now occurring on a non-stop basis.

In October alone there came a plethora of odd sightings, especially towards the end of the month.

On October 21, 22, and 26—and once more on December 19—the massive concrete cross on Mt. Krizevac turned into a column of light, taking the shape of a 'T.' [22] The cross then turned into a luminous figure of the Virgin Mary, though not clearly defined.[23] This phenomenon lasted about a half an hour the first two times, and 15 to 20 minutes the next two occurrences. [24]

On October 28 came the mysterious fire on the hill, which suddenly appeared and then completely vanished. The authenticity of this phe-nomenon was sworn by over 500 witnesses.[25]

And there came more extraordinary, personal stories.

A local woman named Anka Pehar reported that as the sky was getting dark one evening, and she gazed in the direction of the two smaller hills, she noticed on Crnica a funnel-shaped light that slowly rose from the ground. As it did, the light then got wider.

Suddenly, she saw the Madonna in it, with her arms spread open wide. The huge illumined image of Mary then floated across the sky, moving in the direction of St. James. Anka was soon joined by four others who also saw the same thing. The phenomenon lasted for over an hour. [26]

In late October, a priest who came to Medjugorje to celebrate Mass, Father Janko Bubalo, reported that he was in the rectory of St. James when he heard a disturbance outside. Looking out the window, he saw a crowd of about seventy, including four or five priests, with their eyes all focused on Mt. Krizevac. The mass of people all reported seeing the same uncanny sight: a massive, glowing silhouette of the Virgin Mary on the top of the mountain. [27]

These types of unexplainable sightings would continue throughout the remainder of the year, with such reports from pilgrims and the res-identsof the five villages starting to seem almost normal at Medjugorje.

But to one man, all the supernatural signs meant nothing.

Although Father Zrinko Cuvalo was now in charge at St. James—and by default the entire dilemma surrounding the apparitions at Medjugorje—none of this implied he now believed in what was going on there.

And, by late 1981, the stubborn friar still held onto his doubts.[28]

With Zrinko now pastor, the Communists hoped their dilemma had a sympathetic ally on the inside.[29] The villagers, on the other hand, were less than thrilled.

Zrinko was *Zrinko*, and now with more authority, the worst was feared.

The parishioners were right.

The cantankerous priest maintained his bullying demeanor, [30] especially with the many pilgrims that he perceived to be mindless:

"People simply couldn't be allowed to do what they pleased. That's why I bullied and shouted at them. I knew it was unpleasant behavior, especially from a priest, but it was the best I could manage. I was rude to them all: male, female, young, old, cleric, lay. I even snapped at the elderly friars." [31]

Zrinko lambasted the Communists, too, questioning the presence of the plain clothed police he often identified at Mass, "What are you here for? Have you taken up mysticism and superstition?" [32]

Just looking suspicious would draw his wrath. Although he confessed afterwards, he sometimes attacked innocent pilgrims that he suspected were informants. [33]

As for the visions, by the time the cold weather hit, Zrinko permitted them to be permanently held inside of St. James.[34] Now, every evening, a set routine was followed: after beginning the Rosary, a small group of people—including visiting priests, scientists, nuns, and foreigners—were all escorted to a small chapel for the apparition.

There, they would begin a separate prayer regime. This consisted of the Creed, the seven Our Fathers, Hail Marys, and Glorias. Usually, around the second or third Our Father, the visionaries would simultaneously fall to their knees.

Instantly, their eyes could be seen focused above and forward on a spot that was assumed to hold the Virgin Mary. As on the hill, the Madonna was described as being three dimensional and in the flesh.

On most evenings, Mary would converse with them all together or individually for about fifteen minutes. Then, when the vision was over, the children would go back into the church and join in the prayer.[35]

On the second day of Jozo's trial, Zrinko witnessed a brilliant illuminating white aura around the cross on Mt. Krizevac. [36] Still, he refused to allow himself to be influenced, a mindset that continued over the next several months. [37]

But then one day, Zrinko heard the confession of a barren woman who was angry at God and suddenly experienced a radical conversion. Her story, the priest found, brought him to accept that "the finger of God" was in the events taking place in Medjugorje.[38]

"It was this woman's breakdown that brought light into my own darkness," admitted Zrinko, "she made me realize that God must have some hand in the situation, regardless of any doubts I might have. It was a moral sign, far clearer for me than the light around the cross or the fire on the hill." [39]

By January of 1982, the darkness in Poland was something no one had any doubts about.

Solidarity's leaders throughout the nation were in jail.

Marshall Law was in force and would remain so for the next year and a half. And, by the end of the year, with the death of Soviet President Leonid Brezhnev, a new Communist tyrant was in charge.

Yuri Andropov—known as the "Butcher of Budapest," who crushed the 1956 Hungarian uprising—was now the head of the Soviet Union. Andropov, a Marxist hardliner, opposed any political reform. For Poland and the rest of Eastern Europe, this meant the darkness would remain.

But, as with Father Zrinko, Mary revealed in Medjugorje that God had a hand in the situation. Change was coming in the Soviet Union, she revealed, especially in its heart—Russia. [40]

The revelation appeared to be another subtle link to Fátima, where after revealing her foreboding Secret to the three little shepherds on July 13, 1917, Mary promised,

"In the end…Russia…shall be converted." [41]

Apparition sites and miraculous signs and wonders have always gone hand in hand. But nothing, it is said, can compare with what has unfolded at Medjugorje.

Left Photo Credit: St. Andrews Productions

Right Photo Credit: St. Andrews Productions

Father Zrinko Cuvalo became the pastor at St. James after Father Jozo Zovko was imprisoned in August of 1981.

Photo Credit: St. Andrews Productions

After his release from prison, Father Jozo Zovko traveled the world speaking about Medjugorje. His story was eventually made into a movie that was released in 1995 called *"Gospa."* He is seen here visiting the author and his family in Pittsburgh in 1993.

Photo Credit: Thomas W. Petrisko

Dragica and Marinko Ivanković were the first to tell the priests about the apparitions at separate times and places, including Fr. Jozo who is seen here with them.

Photo Credit: St. Andrews Productions

Solidarity peaked at 10 million in September, 1981, representing one third of the country's work-age population. It received underground financial support of an estimated 50 million dollars from outside the country, including the Vatican and the United States.

Photo Credit: Tadeusza Kurka

Lech Walesa led the Gdansk Shipyard strike which gave rise to Solidarity in 1980. By 1983, Walesa had won the Nobel Peace Prize. By December 1990, he was elected President of the Republic of Poland.

Photo Credit: Gledymin Jablonski

The December 1981 crackdown on Solidarity in Poland saw the use of 1,750 tanks, 1,908 combat vehicles, 9,000 cars, and 110,000 soldiers and police.

Photo Credit:
J. Zolnierkewicz

General Wojciech Jaruzelski imposed martial law in Poland on December 13, 1983, sending in the military to make mass arrests. In 2008, he went under trial for war crimes related to that decision. He died in 2014.

Photo Credit: Poland Government / Public Domain Photograph

CHAPTER THIRTY-THREE

THE WORLD IS IN GRAVE DANGER

*"And if those days had not been shortened, no
one would be saved; but for the sake
of the elect they will be shortened."*

—Mt 24:22

THE SOVIETS DIDN'T TAKE KINDLY TO THE NEWS THAT A POLE WAS Pope.

They knew of Karol Wojtyla.

He was a leading architect at Vatican II of *Dignitatis Humanae,* the Declaration on Human Freedom.[1] Likewise, stuck behind the Iron Curtain for most of his life, they were well aware he was no fan of Communism. His well-known opposition to the experimental city Nowa Huta—the City without God built near Krakow between 1949 and 1951—was not appreciated.[2]

Outraged and fearful the new Polish Pope would stoke anticommunist sentiments in Eastern Europe, the Soviet leadership issued orders to the KGB to infiltrate Pope John Paul II within hours of his election.[3]

The Italian Secret Service, *Sisde,* based on information from Czechoslovakia, revealed that Soviet KGB operations—codenamed *Pagoda* and *Infection*—immediately instructed intelligence agencies in the Warsaw Pact to "discredit the Church and the Pope with disinformation and provocations that *do not* exclude his physical elimination." They would strategize this through their other intelligence arm—the GRU.[4]

To stay on top of John Paul II's every move, the KGB further plotted additional steps to engineer his demise. Through a Benedictine monk who worked inside the Vatican as a mole, they managed to plant a bug inside a statue of the Virgin Mary that stood on a table in the private study of the Vatican Secretary of State, Cardinal Agostino Casaroli. [5]

The man in charge of the KGB at the time?

Yuri Andropov.

To many Kremlin experts, the rise of Andropov to the pinnacle of power in the KGB was more than just the ascension of a party hardliner. He was a legitimate strongman who was also a trusted, diehard Marxist.

"Andropov," wrote David Remnick in *Lenin's Tomb: The Last Days of the Soviet Empire*, "was a throwback to a tradition of Lenin's asceticism [6]... he was profoundly corrupt." [7]

Andropov's résumé as Chairman of the Committee for State Security (KGB) confirms this view. As head of the highly feared spy agency since 1967, he had designed the brutal suppression of all political dissidence in the Soviet Union over the previous two decades.

In the 1970s, Andropov spearheaded an aggressive, renewed campaign to eliminate religion in the U.S.S.R. This was, he said, in order to create the ideal atheist society that Marxist-Leninism had originally envisioned. [8]

Andropov also supervised the planning of the 1968 invasion of Czechoslovakia. At the time, even leaders of the Warsaw Pact viewed him with trepidation and paranoia. To them, Andropov was a monster, known as the leader who substituted the KGB for the Communist Party.

He especially held keen interest in the Vatican. [9]

In 1969, Andropov directed an intensification of espionage against Rome, with a specific interest on the activities of Pope Paul VI. Every department of the Vatican was eventually infiltrated by spies.[10] Upon the election of Karol Wojtyla, Andropov was ordered by the Kremlin to research how and why Wojtyla somehow became leader of the Roman Catholic Church.[11]

His analysis concluded what one would expect; it was a plot hatched by Washington to dismantle the Warsaw Pact.[12] And, his KGB report noted, it included another Polish connection central to it all: Zbigniew Brzezinski, U.S. President Jimmy Carter's National Security Advisor. [13]

With the founding of *Solidarity*, Pope John Paul II almost immediately became involved with behind-the-scene efforts to discourage Brezhnev from intervening militarily into Poland.[14]

By the summer of 1982, though, with the Soviet economy struggling and Moscow concerned with a new American missile—the Pershing II—no one was sure what Moscow might do next. [15] This uncertainty worsened with the death of Brezhnev in November and the rise of the dangerous Andropov to the ultimate seat of power in the U.S.S.R.

Remnick reveals that when Andropov assumed power, several members of Brezhnev's inner circle were so frightened of him that they "shot, gassed or otherwise" did away with themselves.

One man in the West must have known who he was dealing with at the time.

It was during Andropov's reign that Ronald Reagan labeled the Soviet Union, "The Evil Empire."

On July 21, 1982, just four months before Yuri Andropov assumed power, the Madonna gave the six visionaries at Medjugorje a powerful, thought provoking revelation:

"Through fasting and prayer, one can stop war, one can suspend the laws of nature."[16]

Mary's message was significant: prayer could do the impossible.

Her words, it seemed, were reminiscent of what she said at Fátima on July 13, 1917. On that day, she promised to return to ask for the consecration of Russia to her Immaculate Heart and for a special prayer devotion called the Communion of Reparation:

"To prevent this (God's punishment of the world for its crimes through war, famine, and persecution), I shall come to ask for the consecration of Russia to my Immaculate Heart, and the Communion of Reparation on the first Saturdays. If my requests are heeded, Russia will be converted, and there will be peace..."[17]

By early 1982, this reality was being made clear again.

Like at Fátima, Mary was in Medjugorje to ask for prayer to bring peace and prevent war. It was also clear as to why.

The "Triumph" foretold at Fátima had not been realized, and only more prayer could bring it to fulfillment.

Prayer could bring peace. Prayer could stop wars. Prayer could stop even a thermo- nuclear war. Mary seemed to be alluding to this over and over at Medjugorje.

The Virgin had no advice on any peace conferences, treaties, or negotiations. Not that they weren't important. But what would bring peace for sure—what could prevent war for certain—was prayer.

And, from the looks of things by the summer of 1982, Mary needed lots of prayer.

And so it would begin: a spiritual movement to prevent war and bring peace to the world like never seen before, centered on prayer.

And, the Virgin promised at Medjugorje, God would answer this prayer:

"The world is on the point of receiving great favors from me and my Son. May the world keep a strong confidence." [18]

At Medjugorje that first year, what began to emerge after every apparition was something special.

The faithful were truly coming to pray—and the prayers were from the heart.

Loud and strong, the people sounded like a choir, as if they wanted their prayers to be heard in Heaven just by the sheer volume of their voices. It was impressive, wrote one theologian:

> The prayer…is pure and hard like the rocks of the mountain where the apparitions began. The voices are rough without any intonation. They recite the prayer in strong, well carved syllables, almost hammered out. It is really from the soil, as though from a rock that this prayer goes up to Heaven. It goes up like a flame, not smoke. It is not complicated, exaggerated or affected. It is impressive. It seizes you not at an emotional level but in a much deeper area of your being…that place where man discovers himself to be indwelt by God, the Creator. [19]

Yes, something impressive was emerging in St. James.

On many evenings, half the people in the church would stand for a good two hours. This, in itself, was difficult, especially in the winter, when it was cold in the unheated building. [20]

Likewise, when summer came, the church would be excessively hot and draining. [21] Despite the austere conditions, though, the people came, every day, every night, week after week, month after month. To outsiders who started to visit from all over, it appeared that the parishioners were not drawn to pray. Rather, they *longed* to pray.[22]

In the spring of 1982, a prayer group, one of what would soon be many in Medjugorje, spontaneously began among a group of young boys. Despite the length of the daily services, which began at 5:20 p.m. and concluded around 9:00 p.m., the boys would meet afterwards and continue with more prayer, at least once a week.

The reason for this was clear: the Virgin asked for more prayer.

There was an urgency to her mission in Medjugorje, Mary revealed, one that transcended human understanding. It involved the world, and Satan's destructive plans for humanity. And, of course, prayer:

"It is necessary for the world to be saved, for it to pray strongly, while there is time." [23]

"Satan exists! He seeks only to destroy...pray, and persevere in prayer." [24]

"I have come to call the world for conversion for the last time." [25]

Over the coming months, Mary would establish in Medjugorje a virtual school of prayer for these intentions. It appeared that she was leading her followers to a new level of understanding about the power of prayer, in one's life and in the world:

"I wish to urge you once more to pray, dear children." [26]

"Pray without ceasing." [27]

"It is necessary for the world to be saved, for it to pray strongly and to have the spirit of faith." [28]

"Kneel down my children and pray. Persevere in prayer." [29]

"Through prayer, one obtains everything. Pray so the world will welcome my love." [30]

By the summer of 1982, a second dominant theme emerged more clearly in the apparitions at Medjugorje: strong faith needed to accompany prayer.

When one profoundly believed, prayer was extremely effective.

This understanding was given not just for the visionaries and the people, but also the priests. When one priest requested the children to ask Mary a question about the frequency of the apparitions, she reminded him to have faith in God and pray:

"Be patient. Everything is developing according to God's plan, His promises will be realized. May one continue to pray. To do penance and to be converted." [31]

When the children asked what one must do in order to have more cures, Mary said it all came down to faith and prayer:

"Pray, Pray and believe firmly. Say the prayers which have already been requested. Do more penance." [32]

Responding to a question one visionary asked about the sick, the Virgin replied:

"Have them believe and pray; I cannot help him who does not sacrifice and pray. The sick, just like those who are in good health, must pray and fast for the sick. The more you believe firmly, the more you pray and fast for the same intention; the greater is the grace and mercy of God." [33]

Intense prayer and strong faith bring results.

This was the Virgin's mantra.

To obtain what was necessary in life, to provide for one's family, to heal the division in the world and unite it in peace—this all came down to these two spiritual realities. Even she, the Madonna revealed to the visionaries, had to pray to God for her mission to succeed in Medjugorje:

"I cannot do anything without the help of God. I, too, must pray like you. It is because of that I can only say to you; pray, fast, do penance and help the weak." [34]

The Queen of Peace was appearing in Medjugorje to bring peace. And, as at Fátima, her plan was unfolding.

This plan, however, was to be different from her plan in Portugal.

While strong similarities are noted with Fátima—the call to prayer, penance, and conversion—Mary would also plead more at Medjugorje for fasting. She wanted for people to deny themselves, so the power of their personal sacrifice could be used by God.

The world of the 1980s had considerably changed from the time of Fátima in 1917. Bountiful amounts of food, clothing, and what were considered necessities in the past, were more available.

In the West, the average citizen was now awash in what would be considered luxuries: automobiles, televisions, appliances, and other modern conveniences. There now existed indoor heating and air-conditioning, bathrooms, and hot water.

Overall, the quality of life was undeniably better almost everywhere than a half century before. Thus, fasting and abstinence, or sacrificing in some way, was what Mary asked her faithful to embrace.

At Fátima, propagation of the Communion of Reparation of the First Saturdays devotion was at the center of her plan. But this does not emerge at Medjugorje. Mary did mention on August 6, 1982, the importance of the First Saturdays: *"One must invite people to go to confession each month, especially the First Saturday."* But none of her messages attempt to conclusively anchor her success at Medjugorje to this devotion, as at Fátima.[35]

Likewise, Mary's revelations at Medjugorje carry no requests from the Pope and the Church hierarchy, or the need for any specific act by the Church to be fulfilled.

On September 16, 1983, Mary did call upon the Holy Father to join in her quest for peace: "I recommend to everyone, and to the Holy Father in particular, to spread the message which I have received from my Son here at Medjugorje. I wish to entrust to the Pope, the word with which I came: MIR (Peace), which he must spread everywhere." [36]

Overall, the heart of Mary's message at Medjugorje is the same as at Fátima. The world was in grave danger of crossing over a precipice. The Virgin Mary is here, therefore, to prevent that from happening.

But at Medjugorje, Mary's call is more focused on the person—for people to respond individually and then collectively. This is what she asks to bring change.

In essence, anyone who hears the Madonna's call needs to do what she requests: to pray, to fast, to convert—to give their life to God—with all their heart.

The message of Medjugorje, according to some, is best understood in relation to the dangers of the 1980s and today, as compared to the early twentieth century.

The errors of Russia had moved beyond the state and into the people—especially in the West. [37] Changing the people, therefore, not just the state, was now what was needed to save the world.

Indeed, Mary's messages at Medjugorje concerning the future in Poland and Russia seemed to already be hinting that a political change in these nations—and beyond—was coming. Moreover, her words also seemed to preview the battle lines of the future were in the West, where atheism in the individual and in the culture was gathering steam:

"The West has made civilization progress, but without God, as if they were their own Creators.[38] Monthly confessions will be a remedy for the Church in the West. One must relay this message to the West." [39]

At Medjugorje, the visionaries may not have fully understood the historical and global ramifications of the Virgin's visitation. But, by the summer of 1982—one year after the apparitions had begun—the children did understand very well what Mary was trying to teach and show them.

Love—love for God, love for one another—a new world where love won out over hate—was what the Madonna of Medjugorje was all about.

The world was going to change, the visionaries were coming to understand, but it would take a lot of work to bring this change. [40]

CHAPTER THIRTY-FOUR

GOD HAS A PLAN

*"No disciple is superior to the teacher; but when fully
trained, every disciple will be like his teacher."*
—Lk 6:40

I F THE VIRGIN MARY OPENED A SCHOOL FOR HOLINESS IN
Medjugorje, it is clear that her six front row students were paying attention.

While some criticize the simplicity of Mary's messages in Medjugorje,
describing them as banal, it is a simplicity of brevity, not of wisdom.

No shortage of divine inspiration is found when contemplated:

"Do not pray now, be silent and let me pass through your hearts." [1]

"Love is the only power which saves." [2]

"Faith is learned by opening oneself in humility." [3]

"As soon as you see sin confess it, so that it does not remain hidden
in your soul." [4]

At Medjugorje, Mary comes as a preeminent teacher of the faith at
the conclusion of a faithless century, writes author and correspondent
Gabriel Meyer in his book, *A Portrait of Medjugorje*.[5]

While the Virgin's words are somewhat of a paper mountain, con-
trasting greatly with her relatively few words at her other famous
apparitions, this does not discredit her presence. Rather, one theologian writes, it makes Medjugorje a giant among Marian events.[6]

Father René Laurentin calls the many revelations at Medjugorje "a
Marian Pedagogy." [7] It proves, he says, the inexhaustible patience of a
Mother. [8] Having studied them, Laurentin notes the messages intend,
as their primary function, to help the substance of the Gospel enter
into daily life. [9]

The messages state nothing new or startling, agrees Meyer, who was based in Medjugorje for *The National Catholic Register*.[10] Meyer says that Mary's words are about essential piety: "They largely restate basic Christian truths: the necessity of prayer, the importance of personal faith, the need for repentance and conversion, the efficacy of fasting." [11]

But a number of the Madonna's teachings can be clearly defined as unique to Medjugorje. For example, where the Virgin asked for the Rosary at Fátima, she now requests all fifteen decades of the prayer. [12] And, the Madonna of Medjugorje adds, not in a mechanical way: "I do not need 100-200 Our Fathers." [13]

She also asks that prayer be sincere, inviting people to prayer from the heart and not to pray in a routine fashion.[14] Fasting, Mary tells the visionaries, is to be intense and purpose-filled. For those able, "two days a week on only bread and water." [15]

The most compelling message of Medjugorje, says Meyer, has to do with reconciliation: "Peace, peace, peace," says the Virgin at Medjugorje, over and over again. "Make peace with God and with each other." [16] In a region historically known for discord, Meyer points out, it is a message that reaches deep into the ethnic and religious division in the society. [17]

But it's not just *what* Mary says, but *how* she says it.

Like any good teacher, the Virgin knows success comes not by intimidation, not by demand, not through fear; rather, it comes through invitation and love.

Mary invites at Medjugorje. She asks for a free response: "I do not want to force anyone," "I wish to call you to grow," "I invite you to," "Today, I would like to give you," and "I am calling you."

The Madonna also uses phrases like, "I desire," "I appeal," "I am asking you," and "I beg." Then, at the conclusion of each message, Mary shows her appreciation: "I thank you for having responded to my call." [18]

Overall, at Medjugorje, Mary inspires and supports. She understands, she comforts, and she especially rejoices. When she witnesses a positive response to her messages, it is said that she smiles.

The visionaries say that the Virgin is always courteous and patient, caring, and full of concern. To them, her kindness, affection, and motherly interest are apparent. Mary simply wants all to reflect her

Son, Jesus, sometimes shedding tears to move the six to grasp the gravity and seriousness of her coming.[19]

At Medjugorje, it is clear. The Madonna is a protectress of her children and the faith. She seeks only to help and support: "I wish to console you in all your temptations. I wish to fulfill you with the peace, joy and love of God." [20]

That she does. To anyone who studies her words, it's apparent that the Virgin has come to give pastoral care to her children: "I want to shepherd you..."; "I want to wrap my mantle around you." [21]

Examined individually, each visionary reveals a very personal assimilation of the heavenly messages and human truths stemming from his or her experience with Mary.

Mirjana Dragićević's role in the visions is unique.

Perhaps more than the others, she will play a critical part in the unfolding of the prophetic events to come. Her personal relationship with the Virgin, in lieu of this role, has been somewhat shaped with this reality in mind.

Mirjana has great compassion for the unbelievers who face terrible consequences down the road because of their estrangement from God.[22] They are choosing, she says, things that are passing away [23] and, consequently, wasting their lives.[24]

Mirjana tells people that the Blessed Mother has come to the world in love and mercy. She comes to help people realize there is a life after death.[25] Heaven, therefore, is worth any price.[26]

God, Mirjana informs, knew each person before He made the world, breathing His love into them in their mother's womb.[27] She says that prayers to God have special meaning and are all that really matter, because they strengthen a person's faith. Not surprisingly, Mirjana believes the whole world needs to experience God's love through their faith. One does this, she adds, by preparing their heart so that it longs for God.

And, while Mirjana stresses that prayers for unbelievers are vital, she also emphasizes that each person, even those with faith, have parts of them that do not believe. This is why we all sin and why some people go to church only out of custom or tradition. [28] Every day, therefore, we all need to pray for faith, for hope, for love—so we can be better believers.

The Virgin has taught Mirjana that nothing matters in this life but faithfulness to God's will. [29] Today, many people, she says, have "goals" that sadly do not include the things that will bring them Heaven. [30] Life on Earth, Mary has told Mirjana, can be compared to the life of a flower. It is beautiful while it lasts; but it is very short.[31]

The apparition at Medjugorje is the most important of its kind in the history of the world, Mirjana says Mary has also told her.[32] Thus, it makes the Virgin sad that people are not receiving all that she is bringing to the world. Each of Mary's children is special to her, and she loves each the same—no less than the visionaries. Therefore, she wants all her children to know she is here on Earth for *them.*

As she emphasizes in her book, Mirjana understands that people should not force others to believe, or tell others how to live. Instead, their lives should be an example to those people—an example of God's existence and God's love.[33]

In interviews, Mirjana has stressed the following: [34]

- Those who know Mary should try to pray fervently, intensely, and frequently for those who do not believe.

- Mary will never forsake anyone who calls to her. She will pray *with,* and *for,* any child who invites her.

- The Virgin said that Jesus, her Son, redeemed every person by His passion and death on the Cross. And, He gave all people on Earth to His mother before He died on Calvary.

- The way to God is laid out in the sacred Scriptures. The truth is in the Scriptures and in the Church's teaching. Mary is always desiring her faithful to read the Bible.

- Mary said that if Catholics lived their faith, the whole world would be Catholic.

- God makes all things well for those who trust in Him.

- Mary said that many people today choose things that are of no eternal value. Many are unaware of divine truth, drunk on the pleasures of the world, blinded by intellect, and crippled by selfishness.

- Mary is in Medjugorje to call the entire world back to God.

- The Virgin says that we should never judge one another. She herself judges no one. She loves. She teaches and guides. God alone judges.

- Mirjana says that Mary told her that people go to Heaven in full conscience; that which we have now. At the moment of death, we are conscious of the separation of body and soul. It is false, therefore, to teach people that we are reborn many times and that we pass to different bodies. One is born only once. The body, drawn from the earth, decomposes after death. It never comes back to life again. Man receives a transfigured body. Whoever has done very much evil during his life can go to Heaven if he confesses, is truly sorry for what he has done, and receives Communion at the end of his life.

Being the first chosen to appear to by the Virgin Mary, it would seem logical that Ivanka has been especially led by her since that moment.

Perhaps more apparent than the others in some ways, Ivanka seems to conduct herself in imitation of Mary; always somewhat silent and serene, humble and thoughtful.

Amongst the six, she is almost hidden at times, preferring to stay in the background, away from attention. Like Mirjana, though, her words reveal that she knows Mary well. And, she has taken to heart what she has learned from the Queen of Peace.

God has a plan for each soul, says Ivanka, and it begins with assigning a soul a Guardian Angel who has a name you can discover through prayer. [35] Most importantly, since our Guardian Angel always sees God, he, therefore, always sees God's plan for us. It is a plan, Ivanka explains, each person must follow to get to Heaven and it involves much prodding from our Guardian Angel, especially to repent. [36]

Once again, Ivanka emphasizes, it all comes down to prayer. Prayer brings grace and, ultimately, grace leads to repentance. The Our Father, she notes, is an especially important prayer, for it can guide our days in helping us to find God's will. [37]

All those who turn to Mary for help in seeking God's will receive her love, her power, her tenderness, Ivanka advises. No one is refused.

Mary cares for all her children, whether they know her or not. She is, Ivanka reminds, their *Mother*. [38]

Ivanka has been told that the Virgin Mary loves her children with "the Father's love"—a Father who wills pain and discomfort for none of His children. But, God does want His children to sacrifice. Those who sacrifice by fasting, Ivanka stresses, build a closer relationship with God because it greatly pleases Him. Fasting, she stresses, cures people of the sickness of sin.

Most importantly, according to Ivanka, Mary is all about humility. The Virgin once said to her, "Ivanka, I am humble because I know God." Humility, Ivanka learned, is a *fiber* of the soul, [39] a condition of it. It is not an external characteristic, but rather, a sign of one's relationship with God.[40] Therefore, it cannot be ascertained with the senses.

In interviews, Ivanka has emphasized the following: [41]

- Peace and simplicity are the fruits of prayer and fasting. They are gifts from God.
- The Virgin Mary wants her children to avoid places of temptation. They can easily take our mind and heart off of God.
- People should fast with love because the reward is very great.
- Mothers who work should never feel guilty. Prayer will help to experience the peace they need in their busy lives.
- One can recognize the presence of Satan where there is hate, anger, rage, violence, and disorder. When someone's actions are agitated and harsh, this is an obvious indicator of the Evil one's presence. Prayer stops the Devil's power.
- Allow God to be a Father. Accept His loving plan for your life.
- Angels communicate with us when we offend God. This is because it troubles them and they let us know. The angel will give us no peace until the action that offends God is halted.
- Mary knows what's in every person's heart. She has been given immense powers in Heaven and on Earth to come to the aid of her children. Her power comes from Jesus's love for her.
- Mary has come to Medjugorje to call all the people on Earth to her Son, Jesus—to His ways.
- Jesus is the way home to God the Father.
- The Mass is for all people on Earth. It is offered for non-Catholics, even if they don't realize it. The Mass is the power of Jesus's sacrifice on the Cross that gives people the strength to walk

their path on Earth towards the Eternal Father's waiting arms. The Mass helps all of God's children to find His will for them.

The Virgin Mary has been dictating the story of her life to Vicka.[42] Thus, to say the visionary knows Mary and her message is probably an understatement.

Like Mirjana and Ivanka, it's clear: it all comes down to doing God's will—and according to Vicka— that comes down to the Commandments, the Bible, and prayer.[43]

Mary has been teaching Vicka especially about God's love—a love that is stronger than all the evil in the world, all the temptation in the world. [44] God's love, she says, is what will lead the world to peace and joy, even in the midst of great suffering and temptation. And the Virgin Mary, adds Vicka, is the perfect example of *living* this love. Mary is the perfect mother, sister, and servant of God, she is able to teach us about Him.[45]

Vicka says Mary wants all people on Earth to have faith in God. She wants them to know that He is with His children day and night, cares for them, longs for them. God calls to us in the wind, says Vicka, and in the words of Jesus. Like Mirjana and Ivanka have stated, He is calling the world now in a special way at Medjugorje.

Vicka has told many that to experience God's gifts is to experience God.[46] Through prayer, she has learned that every person on Earth lives their whole life right before the face of God Our Father, surrounded by His angels and Saints. Everything that comes upon her path every day, Vicka now knows, comes from the Father. He wills it. He allows it. Her only choice is to accept it. She must trust, she says, that God is her Father and that He loves her no matter what.[47]

Vicka wants everyone to know that at Medjugorje, Mary is especially asking for the family Rosary. It will renew the family; the Virgin has told her. Moreover, parents must pray the Rosary for their children, she says, and children must pray it for their parents. This because the Rosary is the chain that binds generations to eternal life.[48] When families pray the Rosary, Satan is helpless.[49]

Most significantly, Mary told Vicka that people who are serious about their prayer will change *through* prayer. This is because prayer and fasting is the one sure way to God, who can bring the desired change no matter what.

In interviews, Vicka has revealed the following: [50]

- Prayer and fasting open our eyes to truth. Suffering also opens our eyes to truth, but often by the time the suffering comes, it is too late to eliminate the cause.
- Some people's lives and choices expose them to more sin. They need to go to confession often and, for them, the way is harder.
- Prayer is the key to the Heart of God.
- When God permits a great suffering, we need to accept it with love. The Virgin says God has a reason He has given a person a suffering and knows when He will take it away. He only asks patience. That is why we should never say, "Why me?" The suffering is a gift, and out of love, we should ask God if there is something more we can do for Him.
- The Virgin told Vicka that priests must protect the faith. They need to pray the Rosary with their people.
- Faith is a precious gift but it takes work to protect this gift.
- Prayer, fasting, and penances, like suffering, are like a mantle that covers those with no faith. It is what the Blessed Mother wants from her followers. It is a total surrender to God's will. The Virgin seeks those who will pray and fast and do penance for those who can't or won't.
- If we voluntarily break the Commandments through ignorance or weakness, it gives Satan power over our lives. It then takes God's grace, and our cooperation, to rescue us.
- The Virgin Mary says the Mass needs to take first place in a person's life. At Mass, Jesus comes to us in physical way. It's a the most sacred, holy moment.
- The Blessed Mother has said to Vicka that these are her last apparitions.

Ivan, like Ivanka, is quiet and enjoys solitude.

By the second year of the visions, Ivan entered a seminary, but found it was not God's will for him.[51] Right from the beginning, though, he says he realized the seriousness of the apparitions and tried to use them to truly better himself on a consistent basis.

He quickly developed a devoted prayer life and his words, in a certain way, give any listener a keen insight into Mary's mission at Medjugorje in ways that are different from the others. There was a rumor that the Virgin Mary had shown Ivan his future right up until his death, but he has repeatedly explained that this was not true and just a misunderstanding.

The Virgin, says Ivan, brings a message that focuses on the fallacies of this world. Materialism is destroying the beauty of God's great gift of life, and people are living lives that lack order and proper direction.[52] Strong prayers are the remedy, he emphasizes, and that is why Mary has come to Medjugorje—to tell and teach the world about the power of strong, faithful prayer.

Through prayer, the Virgin Mary has greatly helped Ivan when he is experiencing temptation. He now knows his weakness and God's strength. Prayer has taught him to rely on Gods strength to change, especially old habits. One, however, must decide to pray and then concentrate on the prayer, he reminds his listeners.[53]

Ivan especially understands how sin deprives one of eternal love. If we knew how much God loves us, we would never sin. Sin, he stresses, wounds us so much that we become unaware of God—we refuse His love.[54] It's in the Eucharist, therefore, that we receive the armor to resist sin. We should try to make the Mass the center of our lives and receive the Eucharist daily, he suggests, if we can.[55]

It is Satan, Ivan reminds his listeners, that tells us that we are not good enough, or that our prayer is not good enough. Because of Satan's influence today, Mary is very concerned about the youth of the world and family life in general.

The world, Ivan repeats often to listeners, offers the youth only drugs, alcohol, and immorality.[56] This causes great suffering for the youth; it ruins their lives and destroys families. It also causes a high divorce rate. Divorce, Ivan says, is a product of sin.[57] Wherever there is divorce, there is sin. And, he reminds, wherever there is sin, there is Satan.[58]

In interviews, Ivan has spoken of the following:[59]

- There is an "awareness" blindness that people develop. People often attach great importance to other people, certain material objects or status in life, such as homes, automobiles, or social and professional positions. As they go through life, these things become proportionally greater and greater until they devour a person's awareness of them. If that happens, they are no longer able to experience peace and joy. Many people are suffering from this illness. They die of hunger from these things.

- Sin is often the result of strong temptation and weakness.
- God expects parents to help and guide their young. The parent's first job is to create a loving environment of respect for one another, one that children can see. If there is little love or respect between parents, a child's spirit is sickened. It creates a perfect atmosphere for Satan to work in.
- Prayer groups should pray for world peace. They should pray for the sick and the abandoned, the born and the unborn, the hungry and the homeless, the poor and the lonely. They should also try to do corporeal works of mercy.
- Mary desires all people to be in prayer groups and to fast. Prayer without fasting, he says, is like a soldier with one leg in battle. One is more easily defeated by Satan.
- The call of the Blessed Mother in Medjugorje is to change hearts. If you change hearts, you change society. The Virgin Mary promises that where families pray together, there will be harmony and unity. It is a process that must start when children are babies. When children are grown, it can often be too late.
- The authority of parents must rest on love. Parents must restrict the freedom of their children out of love and an awareness of Satan. Children must obey their parents out of love. Sacrificial love brings extraordinary blessings from God for parents and children.
- The Virgin Mary says that three generations in one household is very pleasing to God.
- Mary is the Mother of all people. She is calling from Medjugorje all her children on Earth.
- The family is greatly threatened by the disease of materialism. Families blame work for having no time to pray together. This is often the excuse. But it's really a lie, one that many people are living.

There are six visionaries in Medjugorje. But only one was chosen on March 1, 1984, by the Madonna to receive and deliver her monthly message to the world: Marija.[60]

Surprised by Mary on the third day of the apparitions as she departed Podbrdo by a side trail, her life was forever changed even more from that moment on. It was a type of conversion experience that immediately took her to a whole new level of spiritual reality.

Since then, her primary message to the pilgrims at Medjugorje surrounds the necessity of conversion. People need to convert, as does the world. Marija hammers away day after day this singular message: God is the only source of everlasting peace and joy. So, convert, she tells everyone, and discover His peace and joy. [61]

People, says Marija, will find in Medjugorje the way to what they are looking for in life. But first, they need to understand what the great gift that their life really is.[62] This can happen through the blessings that are distributed by Mary in Medjugorje. Once again, as the others have emphasized, it is through prayer and fasting that one can tap into these blessings. The Madonna, Marija emphasizes, wants her children to turn to her for every need, little or big. She wants to be their *true* mother.

As with the other visionaries, Marija wants her listeners to realize how serious sin is, and its effects. She says that sin wounds us gravely and separates us from God, who is our source of abundance and joy, of love and goodness. A cloud of darkness, the Virgin Mary told Marija, has enveloped the entire planet because of sin.[63] Thus, the call to conversion at Medjugorje is to *all* the people on Earth—people of all faiths and races and nationalities.[64]

The Eternal Father, Marija tells everyone, is the deepest longing of every human in their heart.[65] And, through Medjugorje, they can find a way to express that longing. Most of all, it is prayer from the heart, she stresses, that opens hearts to find their heavenly Father.

Marija says that through prayer, we can taste the Father's love.[66] And, once we do, we are never satisfied, for the Father has a scorching love for each child of His.[67] It's a love that ignites a flame in our hearts that is so intense that it extinguishes all fatigue, all fear, and all self-love.[68]

In interviews, Marija has spoken of the following: [69]

- The gift of the *bread of sorrow for sin* restores a person's heart to the presence of God's love.

- Marija says she has offered her life completely, without limitation, without exception, totally to the Virgin Mary in order that God's plan being manifested at Medjugorje can be realized in the world.

- The blessings of the Virgin Mary at Medjugorje are not for us alone. We are intended to be a conduit of God's love for others. As His blessings flow upon us, we receive them and pass them on. In that way, God's love and blessings flow through us to others.

- People need to make the commitment to faithfully give time to God every day as a gift to Him.

- Sin darkens a person's capacity to think wisely.

- This is a time of great grace and mercy. Now is the time to listen to Mary's messages at Medjugorje and change our lives. Those who do will never be able to thank God enough.

- The will of the Virgin Mary is a clear mirror of God's will.

- Prayer and fasting give us discernment to distinguish between good and evil.

- Satan is permitted to test every soul. Not even Jesus was spared.

- Grace is like a drop of water on a flower that makes it open and bloom. Grace can open a sinful soul and make it beautiful and new again. That grace especially comes through repentance and sacramental confession.

Jacov was the only child amongst the six visionaries when the visions began in 1981.

Consequently, like Jacinta and Francisco at Fátima, his experiences and perspectives are fascinating. He was, to say the least, truly enraptured by what was happening at the time. And, therefore, his sincerity in desiring people to believe him was undeniable during the first months of the apparitions, when there was so much ridicule. His comprehension of the Virgin's message, however, in lieu of his age at the time, was no different than the others in content, and held a uniqueness that resonated with listeners.

According to the Franciscans, Jacov took to the Virgin's message quickly and never hesitated from the beginning to share what he was learning from Mary. It was information and advice that added up to a smorgasbord of spiritual treasures, making his listeners smile and feel confident that his experiences validated the authenticity of the visions in a special way. The Virgin, says Jacov, from the very beginning has filled his heart with the desires of Heaven. [70] Because of this, he always counts the minutes and moments of her arrival on the days of her apparitions, which is now only once a year. Nothing on Earth, he empathizes often, can satisfy his heart like the joy and happiness he experiences in the presence of the Madonna.[71] Mary has taught Jacov to trust that God's love makes all things well, if we totally surrender to it.[72] Consequently, in his life, he understands he has been chosen as a messenger of Mary's apparition at Medjugorje, and that is his role. No matter the hardships, God will make all things well for him. He embraces both the joys and the sufferings that come with his role, as he understands that those who receive great spiritual blessings also receive heavy crosses. Mary, Jacov says, is in Medjugorje to help the world understand that her Son wants all people to turn to Him. She wants the world to know Jesus more intimately as our brother, our Savior, our Lord. The means to this, he tells people, is deep interior prayer—and the greatest interior prayer is the Mass.[73]

All creation, says Jacov, has a relationship with the Eternal Father. Therefore, the more intimate our relationship with Jesus in the Mass, the more intimate our relationship with the Eternal Father.

This begins, Jacov explains, with a person's heart. The Blessed Mother wants our hearts to be attracted to the things of God and not to people and materialism. People and possessions, he says, cause us to lose control of our lives, to lose our true freedom. This is something we don't even realize is happening to us. [74]

When our hearts are all ours, Jacov asserts, we put God in first place and then have *interior freedom*. God can then enter our hearts and drive out illusions and attachments. [75] His love can then flow through us to others, and we become filled with this love. In essence, Jacov says we become like Mary, as our love flows out to the world. [76]

In interviews, Jacov has spoken of the following: [77]

- The Virgin Mary has asked people to be careful of the problem of the tyranny of the memories—past pains, sorrows and even sinful memories that brought pleasure, that need to be surrendered to God.

- If we attach our hearts to people and things, we lose our hearts for God. We must put God in first place in our lives.

- People have the laws of God—which is the path to Heaven—written in their hearts. But they reject them. This causes Mary great sadness.

- The human heart is often most untrustworthy. It can refuse God's mercy. Prayer and fasting helps the human heart hear and see God. We then can choose God and accept His love.

- The Virgin has told Jacov that people must forgive. Not to forgive hurts us more than it hurts them. When we pray and fast and truly forgive, we have peace. This is the path the whole world needs to take.

- The Virgin Mary says that those who know God, love God. They are a sign of His love, His peace, His generosity.

- There is not a single creature that is unloved by God.

- When fasting is for love of self instead of love of God, it has a reverse affect. It has no lasting value.

- Our motives are important. We need to pray that all of our motives are pure.

- The human heart is very weak. It is fasting, prayer, forgiveness, and reconciliation that frees the human heart.

- Those who have little suffering are as dear to God as are those who suffer greatly. One's attitude toward suffering is what matters, not the degree. People should never compare sufferings. Any comparison is our own human judgement. Only God can see the human heart.

- Everyone should have a "prayer corner" somewhere in their home. This is a special place where they can be alone and feel near to the Lord.

<hr/>

Being near to the Lord is what every heart desires. It is a soul's deepest longing, the greatest good it can find in life. At Medjugorje, the Virgin Mary made the visionaries aware of this truth.

But she did not shy away from the opposite of this truth: the worst experience a soul can have is separation from God, in this life and for all eternity.

Hell is that permanent separation from God.

And at both Fátima and Medjugorje, the Virgin has made sure the visionaries grasped this reality.

CHAPTER THIRTY-FIVE

"I HAVE SHOWN YOU HELL"

*"Then he will say to those on his left, 'Depart
from me, you accursed, into the eternal
fire prepared for the devil and his angels."*

—Mt 25:41

APOCALYPTIC.
The term is used often by many writers to describe the message of Fátima. And it's not difficult to understand why:

- There is the foretelling of World War II and Communism, along with the mysterious warning of the "annihilation of nations" in the second part of the Secret.
- There is the haunting symbolism of the coming nuclear age, contained in both the Miracle of the Sun on October 13, 1917, and in the Great Sign of January 25-26, 1938.
- There are the ominous, silent mysteries of the third part of the Secret, represented in the vision of the angel with the flaming sword, the ruined city littered with martyrs, and a slain pope at the top of a mountain.

"Fátima is unfolding," wrote theologian Eduardo Sigüenza, "and it contains Biblical and apocalyptic repercussions for all humanity, even in the Third Millennium." [1]

Sigüenza's understanding is twofold.

Many of the contentious and frightening elements of Fátima have found fulfillment. And those that haven't are poised on the horizon, awaiting perhaps a final dawning through some future manifestations.

Over the years, however, a concentrated effort has been made to shift the message of Fátima away from such uncomfortable themes, perhaps rightfully so for many reasons. The message of the Gospel is always one of hope, conversion, and mercy. No miraculous intervention, therefore, should be different.

Yet, Christ didn't shy away from the reality of God's justice in this world—and in the next.

And, at Fátima, neither did the Virgin Mary.

This brings us to an undeniable fact: the most contentious and frightening part of the Secret of Fátima has not been extensively examined to this very day: the vision of Hell.

So, what was the Virgin Mary desiring to tell the world in the first part of the Secret when she showed the three little shepherd children a terrifying glimpse of Hell? In her *Fourth Memoir*, Lúcia described in detail the vision:

> As Our Lady spoke these last words, she opened her hands once more, as she had done during the two previous months. The rays of light seemed to penetrate the earth, and we saw as it were a sea of fire.
>
> Plunged in this fire were demons and souls in human form, like transparent burning embers, all blackened or burnished bronze, floating about in the conflagration, now raised into the air by the flames that issued from within themselves together with great clouds of smoke, now falling back on every side like sparks in huge fires, without weight or equilibrium, amid shrieks and groans of pain and despair, which horrified us and made us tremble with fear.
>
> The demons could be distinguished by their terrifying and repellant likeness to frightful and unknown animals, black and transparent like burning coals. Terrified and as if to plead for succor, we looked up at Our Lady, who said to us, so kindly and so sadly:
>
> *"You have seen Hell where the souls of poor sinners go. To save them, God wishes to establish in the world devotion to my Immaculate Heart. If what I say to you is done, many souls will be saved and there will be peace."* [2]

Mary's words concerning Hell stuck to the children's hearts, especially little Jacinta who asked questions of Lúcia about Hell.

"That Lady also said that many souls go to Hell! What is Hell, then?" Jacinta asked Lúcia. [3]

"It's like a big deep pit of wild beasts, with an enormous fire in it—that's how my mother used to explain it to me—and that's where people go who commit sins and don't confess them. They stay there and burn forever!"

"And they never get out again?"

"No!"

"Not even after many, many years?"

"No! Hell never ends!"

"And Heaven never ends either?"

"Whoever goes to Heaven, never leaves it again!"

"And whoever goes to Hell, never leaves it either?"

"They're eternal, don't you see! They never end!" [4]

"That was how, for the first time, we made a meditation on Hell and eternity," Lúcia wrote in 1935. [5] After the vision of Hell on July 13, 1917, Jacinta would never lessen her concern over souls going to Hell and would constantly sacrifice for the conversion of sinners. [6]

Over the years, Fátima writers have offered commentaries on the divine intentions behind the vision of Hell. These opinions most often explore its value in shaping the visionaries into more perfect instruments to God's will. Many believe, however, the vision especially set the stage for the next two parts of the Secret of Fátima.

Lúcia's memoirs establish how the vision of Hell deeply affected the three visionaries. In her *Third Memoir*, she wrote: "The vision lasted but an instant...Otherwise, I think we would have died of fear and terror." [7]

Lúcia also noted the vision's permanent effect on Jacinta, greatly influencing her until the day she passed away.[8] According to Lúcia, Jacinta looked upon Hell and forever saw the ruin of souls who fall therein. [9]

"The vision of Hell filled her with horror to such a degree," wrote Lúcia, "that every penance and mortification was as nothing in her eyes, if it could only prevent souls from going there." [10]

Indeed, the vision led Jacinta to become a living witness to Hell's reality in a way that was more than to just testify to its existence. Jacinta truly wanted to help prevent people from going to Hell: "Oh, Hell! Hell! How sorry I am for the souls who go to Hell. And the people down there, burning alive, like wood in the fire." [11]

Lúcia wrote that a shuddering Jacinta would often kneel down for long periods of time, reciting the prayer over and over that Mary taught them:

"O my Jesus! Forgive us, save us from the fire of Hell. Lead all souls to Heaven, especially those who are most in need."[12] *

Jacinta would also ask Lúcia and Francisco to join her in saving souls from Hell:

"Francisco! Francisco! Are you praying with me? We must pray very much to save souls from Hell! So many go there! So, many... Why doesn't Our Lady show Hell to sinners? If they saw it, they would not sin, so as to avoid going there. You must tell Our Lady to show Hell to all people." [13]

With the foreknowledge of the coming of World War II, and how many people would die, how many souls would be lost, Jacinta became even more concerned about eternal punishment.

Asked by Lúcia what she was thinking one day, Jacinta remarked, "About the war that is coming. So many people are going to die, and almost all of them are going to Hell." [14]

Unlike his sister, Francisco worked hard at not thinking about the vision of Hell in order to minimize his fears.[15] When Jacinta became overwhelmed by fear, he would tell her, "Do not think of Hell so much. Think about our Lord and Our Lady instead. I never think about Hell so that I won't be afraid." [16]

---

* Original version of prayer as appeared in Lucia's memoir.

One day, however, Francisco disappeared for a long while in a maze of large rocks, located at the bottom of a great ravine. When Lúcia and Jacinta finally found him, he was trembling on the ground, unable to get up.[17]

"What's the matter with you? What happened," they asked. In a voice suffocated with fear, he told them, "One of big beasts from Hell was just here." [18]

Considering their age at the time, Lúcia also saw the vision of Hell as the embodiment of an important message: it is never too soon to teach children about the reality of Hell.

"Some people, even the most devout, refuse to speak to children about Hell, in case it would frighten them," said Lúcia. "Yet God did not hesitate to show Hell to three children, one of whom was only six years old, knowing well they would be mortified to the point of, I would almost dare to say, withering away in fear." [19]

Over the years, after Lúcia's memoirs were released, she was often confronted about the vision of Hell. Father Ricardo Lombardi, the founder of *The Movement for a Better World*, asked her on October 13, 1953: [20]

"Do you really believe that many people go to Hell? I myself hope that God will save the greatest number."

"Many are those who are lost," replied Lúcia.

"Certainly the world is a cesspool of vices…But there is always the hope of salvation," replied Lombardi.

"No, Father, many are lost." [21]

William Thomas Walsh also attempted to minimize the number who went to Hell in his famous interview of Lúcia on July 15, 1946. [22]

"Our Lady showed you many souls going to Hell. Did you get the impression from her that more souls are damned than saved?"

"I saw those that were going down," Walsh recalled a somewhat "amused" Lúcia answered, "I didn't see those that were going up." [23]

The vision of Hell powerfully shaped the three visionaries at Fátima regarding their mission. Theologians, however, have pointed out other merits.

First, and foremost, the vision directly confronted an important teaching of the faith—one that has become either ignored, downplayed, or dismissed outright. Most people live as if Hell doesn't exist, a fact that has been repeatedly confirmed by modern surveys. While many people say they believe in Heaven, they often deny the existence of Hell.

At Fátima, the Virgin Mary had already told the children in an earlier apparition they were going to Heaven, so the vision of Hell, theologians point out, couldn't have been for their sake.

Instead, it was given for the benefit of others. [24] It was given, they emphasize, for people to understand one's eternal destination is based on how a person lives his or her life. It was given, then, to awaken the reality of sin.

The Church has always taught that a healthy awareness of Hell is what people need to move away from sin and back towards God. Needless to say, Christ's words in Scripture are meant to be taken literally:

"For what does it profit a man, to gain the whole world and forfeit his life? For what can a man give in return for his life?" (Mk 8:36-37)

The journey of every soul born into the world is perilous. This is why the risk of eternal damnation at one's personal judgement is an established tenet of the Christian faith. The vision of Hell at Fátima added nothing new to this spiritual reality. But it did reinforce this truth in an age rapidly hurling away from such a belief.

It is important that the vision of Hell be seen in relationship to the rest of the Secret of Fátima.

The vision of Hell was the first part of the Secret of Fátima for a reason.

It was what Mary had come to warn of more than everything else—more than World War II, more than Communism. Even more than nuclear annihilation, the Virgin Mary came to Fátima to warn of Hell.

This is because no human suffering, regardless of its nature, is worse than eternal suffering. Consequently, the salvation of souls is the primary message Mary delivered at Fátima.

While the Virgin would say in the Secret of Fátima that she came to prevent the many serious earthly calamities that were gathering on the horizon—especially universal atheism—she came first and foremost to prevent people from going to Hell.

Appointed by the Bishop of Leiria to assemble the definitive study of Fátima and perhaps the world's foremost expert on the apparitions of Fátima, Father Joaquin Maria Alonso noted this fact:

> The mystery of Hell is connected with the establishment of devotion to the Immaculate Heart of Mary. Our Lady's intercession can obtain from God the salvation of souls who would otherwise be condemned. Note well this idea already dominates the whole text (of the Secret of Fátima). And we should not be misled by the ideas which follow. Powerful as they may be, they are all subordinated to the salvation of souls...[25]

Sister Lúcia understood that the salvation of souls from Hell was the primary message of the Secret of Fátima, too. Over the years, she continually reminded listeners of this truth. In an interview on December 26, 1957, Lúcia told Father Augustin Fuentes:

> My mission is *not* to announce to the world the material chastisements which will surely come if the world does not pray and do penance. No. My mission is to indicate to everyone the imminent danger we are in of losing our souls forever if we remain obstinate in sin.[26]

Lúcia remained true to her mission, regardless with whom she spoke. After his highly publicized meeting with Lúcia in the Carmel of Coimbra on July 11, 1977, the future Pope John Paul I—Cardinal Albino Luciani—was said to have told his brother that the conversation with Lúcia "deeply troubled him." No one knows if this is true, but he did speak publicly of one thing after the visit: Fátima's message of the reality of Hell:

> Hell exists and we could go there. At Fátima, Our Lady taught us this prayer, "Jesus, forgive us our sins, save us from the fires of Hell" ...There are important things in this world, but there is nothing more important than to merit Heaven by living well. It is not only Fátima that says so, but the Gospel. [27]

CHAPTER THIRTY-SIX

THE CENTURY OF SATAN

"Now is the time of judgement on this world; now
the ruler of this world will be driven out."

—Jn 12:31

"Do not be afraid. I have shown you Hell so that you may know the state of those who are there." [1]

Sixty-four years after Fátima, the same alarm is sounded at Medjugorje. Hell exists, and the souls of people are going there.

Like at Fátima, Mary showed the visionaries the eternal dwelling of the damned. Their words again leave no doubts.

Hell is hell, and it is real.

In the center of Hell was a great inferno, recalled Vicka of her encounter with the frightful abyss, there was an ocean of flames, [2] a vast sea of fire. [3]

Almost identical to Lúcia, Vicka remembers how souls looked like normal people before they went into the fire, but when they reappeared, they were filled with rage and didn't have a human shape anymore.[4] They became grotesque animals, unlike anything on Earth, as if they were never human beings. She described them as horrible appearing, angry, and ugly.[5]

The more someone was against God's will, Vicka came to understand, the deeper they went into the fire, and the more rage they exhibited. [6] Their anger, she understood, was against God. She remembers them raging and smashing around, all the while hissing, gnashing and screeching.[7] Their goodness and beauty was destroyed by their own hands.[8]

Vicka learned that people in Hell didn't believe in God when they were in this life. They denied him, she says, even at their death. [9] Consequently, they become one with Hell in this life—in their bodies—and at death, go on to be the same.[10] In Hell, they continue to deny God.[11] Thus, it was their will to go to Hell, something they wanted and chose.[12]

Vicka doesn't recall feeling any heat or experiencing any fear in Hell. She believes a special grace protected her, as she was with the Virgin Mary.[13] But, like Jacinta at Fátima, the visionary acknowledges the experience changed her forever. Now, the conversion of sinners is what she prays for. This is because she knows now what awaits them if they refuse to convert.[14]

Jacov saw Hell with Vicka, although he seldom talks about it.

The self-chosen suffering there, he has said, is beyond one's ability to comprehend. Thus, it causes him pain to just think about it because he realizes that no one needs to go there. Hell is, Jacov believes, the ultimate waste.[15]

Marija remembers seeing Hell as a large space with a great sea of fire in the middle of it.[16] She says she witnessed many people there, especially noticing a particular beautiful young girl who approached the fire. As the girl drew near the fire, she became animal-like and lost all her beauty, appearing no longer human.[17]

Marija was also led to understand that all those in Hell *choose* to be there. The Virgin told her that at the moment of death, one sees all their choices—what they have done with their life. Consequently, if it was a life of sin, they choose Hell.

People, asserts Marija, condemn themselves.[18]

Ivan, though he witnessed it, prefers not discuss Hell at all,[19] while Ivanka says that she did not want to see it.[20]

But Mirjana, who also chose not to visit or to see Hell—although she writes in her book that Mary showed her a glimpse of what awaits those who reject the love of God—unexpectedly had Hell come to her. [21]

Out of nowhere, on April 14,1982, Mirjana had a personal encounter with Satan that God permitted as a test. Describing the experience as terrifying, it is to this day something Mirjana says she doesn't like to think about.[22]

On January 10, 1983, she explained in an interview what took place:

It was approximately six months ago, though I don't know exactly and cannot say for sure. As usual, I had locked myself into my room, alone, and waited for the Madonna. I knelt down, and had not yet made the Sign of the Cross, when suddenly a bright light flashed and the Devil appeared. It was as if something told me it was the Devil. I looked at him and was very surprised, for I was expecting the Madonna to appear. He was horrible—he was all black all over and had a...He was terrifying, dreadful, and I did not know what he wanted.

I realized I was growing weak, and then I fainted. When I revived, he was still standing there, laughing. It seemed that he gave me a strange kind of strength, so that I could almost accept him. He told me that I would be very beautiful and very happy, and so on. However, I would have no need of the Madonna, he said, and no need for faith. "She has brought you nothing but suffering and difficulties," he said; but he would give me everything beautiful—whatever I want.

Then something in me—I don't know what, if it was something conscious or something in my soul—told me: No! No! No! Then, I began to shake and feel just awful. Then he disappeared, and the Madonna appeared, and when she appeared my strength returned—as if she restored it to me. I felt normal again. Then the Madonna told me: "*That was a trial, but it will not happen to you again.*"

The Virgin then told her:

Excuse me for this, but you must realize that Satan exists. One day he appeared before the throne of God and asked permission to submit the Church to a period of trial. God gave him permission to try the Church for one century. This century is under the power of the Devil, but when the secrets confided to you come to pass, his power will be destroyed. Even now he is beginning to lose power and has become aggressive. He is destroying marriages, creating divisions amongst priests and is responsible for obsessions and murder. You must protect yourselves against these things through fasting and prayer. Carry blessed objects with you. Put them in your house and restore the use of holy water. [23]

Mirjana's experience is reminiscent of a similar encounter with Satan that occurred at Fátima with Lúcia, although it took place in a dream.

In the weeks leading up to the Virgin Mary's revelation of the Secret on July 13, 1917, Lúcia's mother took her to see Father Manuel Ferreira, the parish priest.[24] After questioning Lúcia, Father Ferreira muttered that it all could be "a deceit of the Devil." [25]

Soon after this—now buried in doubts and temptations—Lúcia reported a dream in which Satan came to mock her:

> I saw the Devil laughing at having deceived me, as he tried to drag me down to Hell. On finding myself in his clutches, I began to scream so loudly, and cry out to Our Lady for help, that I awakened my mother.[26]

The Book of Revelation speaks of a great war between "a woman clothed with the sun" and a "huge red dragon." [27] Catholic Tradition holds these two combatants to be the Blessed Virgin Mary and the Devil.

In her famous interview with Father Fuentes in 1957, Sister Lúcia said that a "decisive battle" was underway, and that Satan was making every effort to gain as many souls as possible. [28]

Similarly, at Medjugorje, Mirjana reported that Mary told her that the Devil was granted one century to wage war with extended power over the world. [29]

In a December 1983 report to Pope John Paul II concerning the urgency of the message of Medjugorje, the similarity of Mirjana's revelation of this "century of Satan" to what Pope Leo XIII reportedly described after the vision he is said to have experienced on October 13, 1884, is specifically noted.

A number of Mary's messages at Medjugorje seem to allude to this confrontation unfolding between her and her Biblical adversary.

In fact, so many of Mary's revelations speak of Satan by name that it appears to be by design, perhaps in order to leave a clear record that substantiates the great spiritual battle that unfolded during this period of time on Earth.

At Medjugorje, Mary goes to great length to establish not only the reality of Hell, but the reality of Satan. She has stated: "The Devil tries to reign over the people;"[30] "Satan exists; He seeks only to destroy;" [31] "Satan says only what He wants. He interferes with everything;" [32] "Every disorder comes from Satan;" [33] "God gives you the grace to defeat Satan." [34]

The Virgin especially notes her personal war with him regarding her work in Medjugorje: "Satan wants to destroy all my plans;" [35] "Satan continues to hinder my plans;" [36] "Satan is continually trying to thwart my plans;" [37] "Satan is strong. He wishes, with all his strength, to destroy my plans." [38]

Each of the visionaries at Medjugorje gives a different perspective of the reality of Satan and his tactics. When looked at as a whole, they lift the veil and shed light on the mechanics of demonic evil in the world today.

Ivan speaks quite forcefully about the Devil's influence. The enemy wants us to sin, he says, this then makes us blind and deaf to God. Sin occurs, he tells people, because of strong temptation, personal weaknesses, individual shortcomings, and what the Devil knows about each of us. Consequently, whenever there's sin, there is Satan. Ivan says that sin wounds us and makes us less aware of God. Then, the Devil can trick a person into getting involved with alcohol, drugs, and immorality. [39]

In our world today, Ivan points out, all of these things cause much suffering and are especially responsible for the moral decline of the young. But, he says, sin also occurs when parents are tempted by the Devil to attach too much significance to people, objects, and status symbols such as automobiles, houses, or professional and social positions.

Over time, this materialism becomes exponentially greater, until it affects a person or a family's awareness of what matters in life, robbing them of peace, love, and joy, and permitting Satan to use his power to divide and conquer. [40]

Grace—especially available in the Sacrament of Reconciliation—is a remedy for materialism, stresses Ivan. Prayer and fasting will also restore our direction, especially if we can pray the Rosary every day. All of this, he says, will change people and society one family at a time. [41]

Ivan also says that Mary has promised that for families who pray together there will be harmony and unity, and less demonic interference. It must begin, he emphasizes, when children are babies. It is also a process that children must obey, however, out of love of their parents.

Sacrificial love, says Ivan, brings great blessings for parents and children.[42]

As with Hell, Jacov almost always prefers not to talk about Satan.

Surprisingly, he did respond to a question in one interview, "Our Lady has said that Satan wants to turn us away from her plan and from prayer. I believe Satan wants to dissuade us from all this. But we must fight against this." [43]

Fear, emphasizes Vicka, is a great problem and often comes from Satan. He then uses fear to disturb and rob us of our peace. This causes us to close ourselves to God, so we don't pray like we should. Like Ivan, Vicka sees Satan devouring the youth of today, with the modern world offering so many transitory temptations.

The Devil, emphasizes Vicka, is using every single moment—every opportunity—to attack the young people of the world. This is because he has immense power now and is very deceptive. Satan, she says, tries to make us confused, wanting us to see evil as good. He also tries to give us kindness, and to distract us by getting us upset and agitated over things. [44]

We can recognize the Devil by a gut instinct and when we lose our peace, she says. And, every day, we must ask God to keep Satan away and protect us. We also need to pray hard, have blessed objects, and to wear a Scapular, as these really work.

Vicka assures people that when they do these things, Satan can do nothing to us. [45]

The Blessed Mother, says Ivanka, wants us to avoid sources and places of temptation, for Satan uses them. Ivanka says we can detect the presence of Satan wherever there is hatred, rage, violence, and disorder. Where people's actions are harsh and agitated, his presence is obvious.[46] Peace in our hearts is what we should have, says Ivanka. This will tell us that we are doing the right things to keep Satan away. [47]

Marija concerns herself with the damage to the young people caused by Satan today. She says that Mary asks us to pray with great intensity and with a great spirit of sacrifice for the youth. Rock music, Mary has told her, can have diabolical messages.[48] This is because evil comes in many different forms, and it's up to people to see this through prayer.

Like Vicka, Marija knows that fear comes from Satan. Trusting in God the Father, therefore, is what she says is needed to conquer demonic fear, to defeat Satan.[49] She recommends that each person use their innate ability to distinguish between evil and good. They need to see their incorrect choices, and in this way, block Satan's opportunities and stop the sin in their life. Sin, she likes to tell her listeners, separates a heart from God's love. [50]

In 1994, Marija reported that the Virgin had spoken to her about "consecrations" that some people make to Satan. Mary spoke of it, she said, not to frighten us, but to encourage us to pray. The Virgin affirmed that these persons could still repent, annul such contracts, and turn towards God during their time on Earth. [51]

Because of her personal experience with the Evil One in 1982, Mirjana has strong insights into the ways of Satan. Today, she explains, you can see the Devil's power everywhere—no one is satisfied, people cannot get along with each other, there is divorce, broken marriages, abandoned children—born and unborn. There are grudges and bitterness within families—between brother and sister, parents and children, husband and wife. All this, Mary told Mirjana, is the handiwork of the Devil.[52]

Mirjana points out that wherever there's lack of love, Satan is influencing that person. She says the Devil always allures people, and is always trying to turn a true believer away from the road to Heaven. Satan, she has learned, is evil itself, and often comes disguised.[53] One can sense his presence where there's conflict, confusion, and disorder. [54]

He particularly enjoys destroying family relationships, cautions the visionary.[55] Mirjana especially wants people to know that he is deceptively powerful; he can distort memories and even distort what "people think is reality." [56]

Mirjana also emphasizes that anger is a favorite tool of the Devil. She says he likes to make family members argue with each other, where sin then becomes exponential in its effects. [57] Prayer, fasting, blessed objects, and holy water break his power. As for her own efforts, she says she tries to pray three Rosaries a day to allow her to forgive and help her to love. [58]

Warn your friends and loved ones about Satan's power, Mirjana urges listeners, because the Devil is out to "steal Heaven from us." [59]

The towering cross on Mt. Krizavec was erected in 1932.

Photo Credit: St. Andrews Productions

Medical studies of the visionaries were conducted while they were in states of ecstasy.

Photo Credit: St. Andrews Productions

By 1990, there were on average 10,000 confessions a day in Medjugorje.

Photo Credit: St. Andrews Productions

The visionaries on Mt. Podbrdo during the first week in 1981.

Photo Credit: St. Andrews Productions

CHAPTER THIRTY-SEVEN

ON THE BRINK

"It shall be a time unsurpassed in distress
since nations began until that time."
—Dn 12:1

IT'S WEDNESDAY, AND IN ROME THAT MEANS ONE THING: POPE JOHN Paul II is being driven around Saint Peter's Square in his famous popemobile.

His driver, Sebastiano Baglioni, knows to roll around the plaza slowly enough for the Holy Father to reach out and bless people and pick up a child here and there to kiss. Two aides are with him: his butler, Angelo Gugel, and his personal secretary, Father Stanisław Dziwisz, who carries with him the text of the Pope's remarks that day.

John Paul II will announce two important initiatives on this occasion: the establishment of the *Pontifical Council for the Family* and *The International Institute of Studies on Marriage and the Family*.[1] Both of these, the Pope will tell an audience of 20,000, are meant to be a "new sign of the Church's care and esteem for the institution of marriage and family."[2]

The timing of the announcement is relevant.

A referendum on abortion will be coming in just four days, in which two thirds of Italians will vote in favor. In addition, Sister Lúcia will respond to a letter from the Institute's founding president, Cardinal Carlo Caffarra, with some memorable words:[3]

"The final battle between the Lord and Satan will be about marriage and the family...because this is the decisive issue."[4]

This will come to be seen as a prophetic statement.

But on this day, something else that holds even greater prophetic overtone is about to unfold.

5:13 p.m.

As the Pope hands back 18-month-old Sara Bartoli to a parish priest, a young, black-haired, intense-looking man taking photographs, suddenly draws out a gun.

The man's passport says he is a 23-year-old Turkish citizen named Farum Ogzum. But he is actually 25-year-old Mehmet Alì Ağca, an escaped, convicted Turkish murderer, hired by the Bulgarian Secret Service, with a wink from the Soviet GRU and a nod from the KGB.

Ağca's weapon of choice is a Belgian Browning 9 mm handgun—the pride of the Nazi Waffen-SS in World War II. It holds *thirteen* cartridges, a fitting number considering the day.[5]

It is May 13, 1981, the sixty-fourth anniversary of the first apparition at Fátima.

As John Paul II's tiny vehicle nears, Ağca reminds himself of his plan. He believes the Pope is wearing a bulletproof vest and will shoot him in the abdomen—multiple times if possible.

Holding the gun with two hands as his target approaches, Ağca lifts his head, stretches out his arms, and fires two shots. [6] Though not perfect, the Turkish assassin fulfills his mission. One bullet glazes the now-standing Pope's left elbow while the other crashes into his abdomen, beginning the loss of a massive amount of blood.

Now collapsed into the arms of Father Dziwisz, and shielded by the body of a Swiss guard, the popemobile rushes to the Arco delle Campane. There, John Paul II is transferred to a new Vatican ambulance that he blessed just the day before.[7] He also gave his blessing, the Holy Father said at the time, "to the ambulance's first patient." [8]

From Saint Peter's, the Pope is rushed in a mere eight minutes to the Gemelli Clinic—a trip that usually takes thirty. By 5:55 p.m., Pope John Paul II, who has lost 75 percent of his blood at this point, is in surgery. It does not conclude until 11:25 p.m.

Around midnight, the hospital makes the announcement the world is anxious to hear: the Pope will live.

Sympathetic communiques pour into the Vatican from everywhere. One is quite notable.

"I am very indignant at the criminal assassination attempt on you," reads a telegram from Soviet President Leonid Brezhnev, "I wish you a quick and complete return to health." [9]

As he regained consciousness, John Paul II realized who saved his life.

Sensing the Virgin Mary's protection throughout the ordeal, he would later say that one hand fired the gun while another guided the bullet's path.[10]

This unconscionable deed, committed upon the man viewed symbolically as heaven on earth—was a testimony to man's defiance of God in the clearest of terms.

"An act of unspeakable evil," said President Ronald Reagan, "an assault on man and God." [11]

Yet, before the world, it has the opposite effect.

With Pope John Paul II's insistence that the Virgin Mary interceded to save his life—an assertion not impugned by his surgeon, Dr. Francesco Crucitti, who spoke of the zigzag route of the bullet that dodges the Pope's major organs [12]—the horrifying act became an extraordinary sign of God's presence.[13]

And of the Virgin Mary's visions at Fátima.

For John Paul II, his shooting becomes a sign—one calling him to action. The Pope immediately thinks of consecrating the world to the Immaculate Heart of Mary.[14] A prayer he wrote, which he called an Act of Entrustment, is prerecorded and broadcasted from the Basilica of Saint Mary Major in Rome on June 7, 1981.[15]

But because John Paul II knew Brezhnev might invade Poland if provoked, the prayer does not mention Russia by name, and is not done in union with the world's bishops.[16] It was, in essence, a replication of Pius XII's actions.

And, once more, not what Mary seeks.

On July 17, 1981, as the Holy Father recovered from a second hospitalization due to infection, he was visited by a man named Dr. Gabriel Turowski, an immunology professor and an old friend of the Pope from Poland. The Pope's encounter with Turowski makes him even more aware of the relationship between the date of the assassination attempt and Fátima.[17] As a result, the Pope calls for the original text of the third part of the Secret of Fátima.

The next day, Cardinal Franjo Seper, the Prefect of the Congregation for the Doctrine of the Faith, removes two envelopes containing the Secret from the Archives of the Holy Office. One envelope— a white one—contained the original Portuguese text of Sister Lúcia. The other—an orange one—held an Italian translation. He then gives both to Archbishop Eduardo Martínez Somalo, who delivered them to the Pope on the 9th floor of the Gemelli Clinic.[18]

After studying Lúcia's words, which make reference to a pope ten times, John Paul II becomes convinced of its relevance to the shooting—and of the urgent need to fulfill the consecration.

"In these three months, I have come to understand," the Pope tells Bishop Pavel Hnilica who visited him in the hospital, "that the only solution to all the problems in the world, the deliverance from atheism and rebellion against God, is the conversion of Russia. The conversion of Russia is the content and meaning of the message of Fátima." [19]

Thus, John Paul plans to try to fulfill the request for the consecration again.

On the morning of May 13, 1982—the first anniversary of the attempted assassination—the Holy Father journeys to Fátima and meets with Sister Lúcia for twenty minutes. There, before one million people, he celebrates Mass at the Basilica and consecrates the world to the Immaculate Heart of Mary.[20]

Once more, though, the act is incomplete.

This time, the Pope had intended to make it in union with all the bishops of the Church. But the invitations to join him arrived too late for them to participate in the ceremony.[21] There is also no mention of Russia. Sister Lúcia would inform the apostolic nuncio to Portugal of this deficiency herself on March 19, 1983.[22]

Afterwards, however, she suggests in a letter that there would be some benefit from the attempt: "It is late, and Communism has spread throughout the world. It will have its effect, but each of us must respond to the consecration." [23]

If the consecration was the one thing needed to stop the pervasive Communist agenda, it needed to come soon. This is because the world was truly getting more perilous. And Lúcia, some posture, knew more than she ever completely revealed. [24]

A letter dated May 12, 1982, from Sister Lúcia to Pope John Paull II offers a window into her thinking at the time: [25]

Since we did not heed this appeal of the Message [the enactment of the Consecration of Russia and the propagation of the Communion of Reparation devotion throughout the Church], we see that it has been fulfilled, Russia has invaded the world with her errors. And if we have not yet seen the complete fulfillment of the final part of this prophecy, we are going towards it little by little with great strides... And let us not say that it is God who is punishing us in this way; on the contrary it is people themselves who are preparing their own punishment...[26]

"Little by little, with great strides," was a phrase that perfectly described the relentless march of Marxism throughout the world, as well as the nuclear showdown that was inching closer between the East and the West in early 1983.

And it *was* getting worse by the day.

With Andropov now in charge, both the internal affairs of the U.S.S.R. and Soviet foreign policy were on the offensive. [27] Brezhnev had suffered from poor health over the previous few years, now things were on an upswing again.[28]

But the Soviets found themselves on the defensive too, which added to the tension. Suspicions were mounting that the Soviets directed the Bulgarian Secret Service plot to assassinate Pope John Paul II.

The issue almost skyrocketed into a global crisis between the East and the West, but Pope John Paul II reportedly asked Washington to keep quiet and not publicize the issue. He did not want the matter, it is rumored the Pope said, to "start World War III." [29]

By 1983, though, plenty of other dangers loomed to jumpstart such a nightmare. And they all stemmed from the same source: The Soviet Union, and the sphere of nations now under its influence.

How dangerous was it?

The word "brink," used in a number of book titles to describe the fraught times at hand, seems to say it all:

- 1983: REAGAN, ANDROPOV, AND A WORLD ON THE BRINK
- THE BRINK: PRESIDENT REAGAN AND THE NUCLEAR WAR SCARE OF 1983

- **War Scare: Russia and America on the Nuclear Brink**
- **1983: The World at the Brink**
- **Standing On the Brink: The Secret War Scare of 1983**

The year 1983 would be "a hot one in the Cold War," wrote historian Paul Kengor.[30]

An authority on Reagan, Kengor saw the ultimate confrontation shaping up—one that came down to human freedom or world enslavement. It was, he wrote, "no mere battle of bombs and bullets; but a battle of moral will and faith, of right versus wrong, of good versus evil." It was, up to the West to "save the world from this godless force." [31]

Kengor was right.

By 1983, Communism looked like it would conquer the planet.

It was a fungus, seeping into every nook and cranny of the nations. It was a tidal wave, unable to recede because an ocean of evil was pushing it forward. It seemed like every week, the press would report yet another coup, another revolution.

But the West—behind a determined Ronald Reagan—started to push back.

As the year began, Reagan took his opposition to Communism to the American public and the world.[32] After a decade of détente, he had seen enough. He believed the Soviets were not to be trusted with their lies.

Reagan shared the belief of many others that the Cold War was not some giant misunderstanding that could be worked out. To him, it was a true war—a *just* war—with moral consequences. [33]

In January 1983, *Voice of America* broadcasted for the first time a religious service worldwide—including in the Soviet Union and Eastern Europe—thanks to Reagan.[34]

The Christmas Eve Service from the National Presbyterian Church in Washington was just the beginning.[35] Liking what he saw, Reagan promptly declared the United States had a duty to assist in getting broadcasts of religious services into totalitarian countries.[36] Consequently, he pushed forward with more such programming through *Voice of America* and *Radio Free Europe*.[37]

Then, on February 3, 1983, Reagan declared Proclamation 5018—*The Year of the Bible, 1983*.[38] The President urged Americans to use religion as a means to carry the United States forward through the great challenges that lied ahead. [39] Although the action was nothing major, it did begin to shed light on Reagan's deeply religious roots.[40]

Over the years, Reagan's political opposition to Communism became well-established. But what is not fully understood is that it was greatly motivated by his spiritual compass—an internal scope that held no reservations in attributing the avalanche of evil in the world to one cause: sin. [41]

On March 8, 1983, Ronald Reagan took to the podium at the Citrus Crown Ballroom of the Sheraton Twin Towers Hotel in Orlando, Florida, to speak to an assembly of Christian faithful. He began by recognizing the power of prayer and its crucial role in the office of the presidency. He then confronted a series of important social and cultural issues: drugs, abortion on demand, adultery, school prayer, pornography, teen sex, birth control, and the Hyde Amendment, which prohibited the taxpayer funding of abortion.[42]

Finally, Reagan got to his point:

"We know that living in this world means dealing with what philosophers would call the phenomenology of evil or, as theologians would put it, the doctrine of sin...There is sin and evil in the world and we're enjoined by Scripture and the Lord Jesus to oppose it with all our might." [43]

It was an opposition, Reagan stated, that meant confronting the greatest evil and sin of all: Marxist-Leninism as embraced by the Soviets.[44] To Reagan, the heart of this matter was that Soviet Communism denied the soul.[45] He believed this surpassed the most important element in a person's life: freedom to know, love, honor, and worship your Creator.

To deprive one of this, Reagan thought, outweighed all the other ways Communist states deprived their citizens. The Soviets' repression of speech, the press, and even one's livelihood were insignificant compared to the immorality of choking their people's souls.[46] This, to him, was the ultimate sin.

Reagan told his audience:

> Let us pray for the salvation of all of those who live in that totalitarian darkness—pray they will discover the joy of knowing God. But until they do, let us be aware that while they preach the supremacy of the state, declare its omnipotence over individual man, and predict its domination of

all the peoples on the Earth, they are the focus of evil in the modern world.[47]

The atheist U.S.S.R., Reagan proclaimed that day in Florida, was "an evil empire." [48] Along with his Polish counterparts—Wojtyła and Wałęsa—he was now more determined than ever to resist their efforts every step of the way. And, he believed that God was on his side.

"Think of it," Reagan told the National Religious Broadcasters. "The most awesome military machine in history [the U.S.S.R.], but it's no match for that one, single man, hero, strong yet tender, Prince of Peace." [49]

Two weeks later, Reagan took that next step.

On March 23, 1983, the United States revealed it was working on something new militarily. Reagan called it the Strategic Defense Initiative.

The media labeled it *Star Wars*.

The program called for building a sophisticated ground and spaced-based defense apparatus that would intercept Soviet missiles. While the system was far from operational, it struck a deep fear in the Soviets. This was because it created a way for the United States to be no longer tied to the theory of MAD (Mutual Assured Destruction).

MAD was a doctrine of military strategy and national security. It held that the full scale use of nuclear weapons by both sides in a war would cause complete destruction of both the attacker and the defender—thereby assuring their "mutual destruction."

Reagan called MAD the "suicide pact." [50]

The Soviet response to *Star Wars* was swift. If the process went on, responded Marshall Sergei Akhromeyev, "We will have nothing to do but to take up retaliatory measures in the field of both offensive and defensive weapons." [51]

While the U.S. and the U.S.S.R. anted up the nuclear stakes in the spring of 1983, along came another surprise: a second attempted assassination on Pope John Paul II.

This one occurred on almost exactly the same date as in 1981, only this time *at* Fátima.

On May 12, 1983, a man named Juan María Fernández Krohn yelled "down with the Pope," and tried to stab John Paul II with a bayonet as he ascended to the main altar at the basilica at Fátima. [52] The Pope, wounded slightly, blessed Krohn and continued on as security dragged him away.

A month later, the world took another hard swallow.

The unpredictable Yuri Andropov moved to tighten his grip on the Soviet Union. Already General Secretary of the Communist Party, he consolidated his power on June 16, 1983, by becoming Chairman of the Presidium of the Supreme Soviet, or President of the Soviet Union.

For the West, it was again time to pause and assess who this Soviet leader was.

Andropov seemed irrational and unpredictable; he was the closest in thinking to Lenin and Stalin that had arisen in the U.S.S.R.[53] He had even changed his name like they did, from Grigory to Yuri and had lied about his past on different occasions as he worked his way up in the party. [54] Like his founding predecessors, upon assuming the highest office, he began ridding those he didn't like or trust.

In just fifteen months, Andropov would dismiss eighteen ministers and thirty-seven first secretaries.[55] Like Stalin, he initiated criminal cases against some of the highest party and state officials.[56]

Was he capable of the eccentric decision making of Lenin and Stalin?

Could he bring mass chaos and death upon the world through a nuclear war?

In August, worldwide attention fell again on Andropov. *Reader's Digest* published "The Plot to Murder the Pope," an investigative article on the attempted assassination of Pope John Paul II.

Written by Claire Sterling after a four-month investigation, the article showed how all the tracks led back to Moscow. Mehmet Ali Ağca had not acted alone, and he was part of a Turkish group under the direction of the Bulgarian Secret Service. He even spent fifty days in Bulgaria. Sterling revealed how the Bulgarian Communists were some of Moscow's principal surrogates for terrorism and subversion and "do what the Russians want them to do." [57]

At the time, *Reader's Digest* was published in sixteen languages, with 100 million readers. [58] The Russians, up to then, had defenders in the West. These supporters argued that the Soviets weren't crazy enough to kill the Pope—even with the scary Andropov at the helm of the KGB.

Wrote the Italian newspaper, *Il Giornale Nuovo*: "The news reaching London is that the Reagan Administration's Sovietologists continue to be skeptical about the whole thing, maintaining that it is virtually unthinkable that the Soviet Union could have acted with such reckless imprudence." [59]

Now, Sterling's article virtually proved the Russians ordered the hit. And the reckless face behind it was Yuri Andropov.[60]

What came next did nothing to lessen concerns over Andropov.

On September 1, 1983, a Korean Boeing 747 passenger airline—KAL 007—on route from New York City to Seoul via Anchorage, was blown out of the sky by a Soviet Su-15 jet fighter as it flew over the Sea of Japan near Moneron Island, west of Sakhalin. All 269 passengers and crew on board were killed, including a U.S. Congressman from Georgia.

The Korean airliner, which had strayed into Soviet-prohibited airspace, was downed with air-to-air missiles. At first, the Soviets denied knowledge of the incident. Later, they admitted to shooting down the plane, claiming it was on a U.S. spy mission.

Finally, Andropov and the Soviet Politburo postulated that KAL 007 was a deliberate provocation of the United States to probe the Soviet Union's military preparedness, possibly to "provoke a war." [61]

Reagan mixed no words:

"It was a massacre…an act of barbarism, born of a society which wantonly disregards individual rights and the value of human life and seeks constantly to expand and dominate other nations." [62]

The unconscionable attack was one of the tensest moments of the Cold War.[63]

Until what came next—just weeks later.

CHAPTER THIRTY-EIGHT

A REHEARSAL FOR ARMAGEDDON

"Thus the word of the Lord came to me: Son of man, speak this prophecy: Thus says the Lord, God: Cry, Oh, the day! for near is the day, near is the day of the Lord; a day of clouds, doomsday for the nations shall it be."

— Ez 30:1-3

TODAY HE IS KNOWN AS THE MAN WHO SAVED THE WORLD.[1] In 1983, however, his actions got him a reprimand... and then demoted.[2]

On September 26, the Soviet early warning command center reported the launch of multiple USAF Minuteman intercontinental ballistic missiles from bases in the United States. If such an attack were to come, the Soviet Union's strategy was simple: automatically launch an all-out immediate nuclear counterattack.

Stanislav Petrov, a lieutenant colonel of the Soviet Air Defense Forces, was the duty officer on an overnight shift that day. He was situated in Sepukhov Bunker 15 near Moscow. This was the command center responsible for the early warning satellite network that watched for an impending nuclear missile attack.

Looking closely at the data, while ignoring a computer alarm and a lit-up screen that displayed the word "LAUNCH" in large red letters, Petrov noticed a single missile approaching, then four more—but ultimately, not hundreds.

Due to the low number of missiles, he determined that it must be a false alarm. His decision, history would write, prevented not only retaliatory Soviet strike, but a full scale nuclear war. At the time, the Soviets possessed 35,804 nuclear warheads.[3] The U.S. had 23,305.[4]

The Earth—for all practical purposes—would have been no more.

Four years before, a classified 1979 report by Congress's *Office of Technological Assessment* estimated that a full-scale Soviet assault on the United States would kill 35 to 77 percent of the U.S. population—or, between 82 and 180 million people. A U.S. counterstrike would kill 20 to 40 percent of the Soviet Union's population, or between 54 and 108 million people. The combined death toll would be between 136 and 288 million.[5]

And that's just from the nuclear missile exchange.

Because of disturbed global temperatures and extremely disrupted agriculture that would follow, *The International Physicians for the Prevention of Nuclear War* estimated the potential death toll from starvation would be another two billion.[6]

Indeed, Petrov did the world a pretty big favor.

An investigation into the Soviet false missile debacle later determined a satellite warning system had malfunctioned that day. Petrov, though, was relentlessly interrogated afterward and never rewarded for his decision.

Three more false incidents were reported over the following months.

A day before the false nuclear attack incident, President Reagan gave a speech in New Yok City at the annual Pulaski Day Banquet. There, before an audience of Polish Americans, Reagan called the KAL 707 passenger plane downing a crime. He then linked it to a Soviet World War II slaughter of Polish military officers in the Katyn Forest:

"You know that downing a passenger airliner is totally consistent with a government that murdered fifteen thousand Polish officers in the Katyn Forest. We cannot let the world forget that crime, and we will not."[7]

Reagan then, for the first time, announced his commitment to a free and democratic Poland. [8] His incendiary words immediately exacerbated the already-inflamed state of affairs.

Several days later, a bellicose Andropov fired back.

Reagan, the Soviet leader's statement read, was on a crusade against socialism.[9] "Attempts are being made to persuade people," warned Andropov, "that in general there is no room for socialism in the world." [10]

The public rhetoric between the U.S.S.R. and America was by now becoming high-stakes poker, being played out before the eyes of the world. And it would not let up. In October came another round.

Just two days after a couple of terrorist truck bombs detonated at the U.S. Embassy in Beirut, Lebanon, killed 240 U.S. troops, the United States mounted a military invasion of the tiny Caribbean island of Grenada.

One week before, on October 19, Grenada had been seized by a hard line Marxist group led by Bernard Coard, a revolutionary who was backed by Cuba and the Soviet Union. Fearing the military use by the Soviets of a new airport under construction, Reagan took decisive action.

On the morning of October 25—citing the need to protect U.S citizens and to restore order and democracy—American soldiers invaded the island and removed Coard. [11] Thirty Soviets and 600 Cubans were taken in the process.[12]

The Soviets immediately denounced the attack.[13]

Equating the Grenada invasion with their downing of the Korean jetliner, the Soviet mouthpiece *Pravda* said the invasion showed the United States at its "foulest." [14] *Tass,* their press agency, called the action a "brazen occupation." [15] It was, the Kremlin bemoaned, "hypocritical." [16]

Over the next few weeks, Moscow relentlessly painted Reagan as a "trigger happy cowboy." [17] Some in the Western press agreed. Reagan, wrote a critic, behaved "like the Russians",[18] an allusion to the Soviets' interventions in Afghanistan and Central America.[19]

The Kremlin then took it a step further.

If they felt their new Central America Communist ally, Nicaragua, was threatened, they would intervene.[20] In Andropov's mind, the Grenada invasion confirmed what he feared most about Reagan: he was an American President willing to use force.[21]

But as extraordinary as the year had been up to then, the alarming madness was not over. The apocalyptic roller coaster that was 1983 held one more surprise, one that would prove to be the most serious crisis of the year.

Some say of all time.

Able Archer 83 was a code name for NATO military exercises that began on November 7, 1983.

The purpose of the war games was to simulate a period of conflict escalation between NATO and The Warsaw Pact. The maneuvers would culminate with the U.S. military attaining a simulated DEFCON 1 coordinated nuclear attack.

Though done almost yearly, the five-day exercise involving all of NATO's forces in 1983 was tactically different. This time, there were changes added to the regime, among them a new, distinctive format of coded communication, a host of new radio silences, and changes involving high-level leaders of the governments.

All of this worried the Soviets for a reason.

They had just observed another large annual NATO exercise two months before called *Autumn Forge* (a prelude to *Able Archer*) that stretched from Norway to Turkey.[22] Those maneuvers saw 40,000 U.S. and NATO troops moved across Europe, [23] including over 19,000 troops airlifted from overseas in one hundred and seventy missions, conducted under radio silence.[24]

Along with the war games that year came the new Pershing II mid-range nuclear missiles, which were beginning to arrive in Western Europe that fall. The Pershing II, because of its mobility and trajectory, could reach Moscow in eight to ten minutes. This left the Soviets with a lot less time to respond if attacked.[25]

Herb Meyer, the Vice Chairman of the National Intelligence Council, even jested that the time it would it take the Pershing II missiles to hit their targets was roughly how long it takes some of the Kremlin's leaders to "get out of their chairs, let alone to their shelters." [26] Mikhail Gorbachev would later describe the Pershing II missiles as "a gun pressed to our temple." [27]

To Moscow, all of this smelled of trouble and *Able Archer 83* became the straw that broke the camel's back. The Soviets postured that if the exercises were a ruse for a nuclear first strike, they needed to take action before it was too late.

On November 9, the seventh day of *Able Archer*, Western Intelligence reported that Soviet pilots had been placed on alert at their air bases in East Germany and Poland.[28]

Moscow, indeed, was taking action.

It readied all forces, preparing to be attacked.[29] Air units were put on standby. Planes were loaded with bombs. Seventy SS-20 intermediate-range ballistic missiles were put on high alert.[30] Conventional forces were prepared for combat. Even nuclear submarines—docked at different ports or at sea—were sent under the Arctic ice to escape radar and sonar detection.[31]

On top of that, there was a dangerous problem arising from an intelligence-gathering program that had been installed by Andropov two years earlier. [32] It was initiated out of his fear that Reagan was preparing a nuclear first strike.[33]

Code named RYAN, the program was designed to determine from agents abroad if a U.S. strike was coming. Its slogan, according to KGB General Oleg Kalugin, was: "Do not miss the moment when the West is about to launch war." [34]

RYAN soon became a red herring.

Russian agents abroad began to feel obliged to file intelligence-gathering evaluations, [35] so not to lose face with Andropov.[36] But this ultimately created a vicious spiral. Many agents began to report alarming information that they did not believe in. If there were lights on in buildings at night, if there was an increase in the call for blood at donor centers, if there was any out-of-ordinary behavior, it all got reported to Andropov. [37]

This, in turn, fed his paranoia.[38]

Andropov often viewed these reports as credible indications of a potential nuclear attack.[39] This apparently led to foreign Soviet agents receiving nonsensical instructions. There were times when Operation RYAN, remembers Russian defector Oleg Gordievsky, "more closely resembled the Marx Brothers and Dr. Strangelove." [40]

Able Archer 83 exacerbated all this madness.

Historians would later write that due to suspicion, belligerent posturing, and blind miscalculation on the part of both sides, there almost came war. The West was especially naïve about the situation and deliberately escalated it in many ways. At the time, the White House wanted to "stare down the Soviet bear," said Nate Jones a Cold War historian.[41] All this, it was said, became "a rehearsal for Armageddon." [42]

Years later, Thomas Blanton, Director of the National Security Archive and Thomas Nichols, a professor at the Naval War College, concluded that *Able Archer 83* may have brought the world the closest to nuclear war since the 1962 Cuban Missile Crisis.

Historian Richard Rhodes believes it was perhaps even more dangerous.[43] This is because during the Cuban Missile Crisis, both sides were at least aware of the great danger and working to resolve the dispute.[44]

Israeli historian Dmitry Adamsky called *Able Archer 83* the "moment of maximum danger" of the Cold War.[45]

One factor especially made it so: Yuri Andropov.

Andropov's mentality reportedly made him unpredictable, according to Oleg Kalugin, a former KGB chief of counterintelligence. The Soviet helmsman, Kalugin believes, was apparently so distrustful of American leaders that he was very capable of ordering a first strike nuclear attack.[46]

Others agree.

While previous Soviet leaders rattled the nuclear sabre, Andropov was all for using it.

Alexander Yakovlev, a Kremlin advisor to Mikhail Gorbachev, feared Andropov could blow up the world. "In a way," said Yakovlev, "I always thought Andropov was the most dangerous of all of them." [47] The West, wrote journalist David Remnick, should have been much more frightened when he ascended to power because he was "a beast." [48]

Andropov believed the only way to defeat anticommunists was with extreme, overt force and held a hardline nuclear war doctrine.[49] And, to exacerbate his obsessive thinking, he believed the number one anticommunist was Ronald Reagan.

He was probably right.

Reagan once said that Communism "is neither an economic or a political system—it's a form of insanity." [50] He even wondered if it was an evil traceable back to the fall of Adam and Eve in Paradise. Said Reagan in one of his anticommunism speeches:

> Whitaker Chambers said that Marxist-Leninism is actually the second oldest faith, first proclaimed in the Garden of Eden with the words of temptation, "Ye shall be as gods." The Western World can answer this challenge, he wrote, "but only provided that its faith in God and the freedom He enjoins is as great as Communism's faith in Man."

I believe we will rise to the challenge. I believe that Communism is another sad, bizarre chapter in human history whose last pages even now are being written. I believe this because the source of our strength in the quest for human freedom is not material, but spiritual. And because it knows no limitation, it must terrify and ultimately triumph over those who would enslave their fellow man.[51]

After Reagan's Evil Empire speech, Andropov said Reagan was a liar and insane and compared him to Hitler.[52] He even claimed Reagan had ties to the Mafia.[53]

By the summer of 1983, Andropov's mindset became even scarier. On June 16, 1983, the Soviet leader addressed the Central Committee, telling them, "The prospect of nuclear war is overhanging mankind."

Then, on September 29, Andropov issued a blunt, worrisome statement through *Pravda* that affirmed no hope of improving Soviet-U.S. relationships while Reagan remained president.[54]

Two months later, on November 27, Andropov claimed through *Pravda* and *Izvestia* that Reagan was bent on world domination.[55] The Soviet leader, it appeared, was becoming more obsessed with what Reagan might do. Likewise, the West was becoming more obsessed with what Andropov might do.

The uneasy feeling about Andropov didn't just circulate in high circles. Years later, soldiers stationed in Germany remember being on various levels of alert all the time.[56] No one was ever sure what was a drill or not.

The rumor was that Andropov knew the Soviet Union was collapsing, [57] and decided that the only way it could survive was militarily.[58] He reportedly ordered the Warsaw Pact to invade Western Europe three times, only to be stopped by the KGB each time.[59] Whether or not this really occurred is unknown.

Able Archer 83 took its toll on an already extremely bleak situation. Ironically, on November 20, 1983, just days after *Able Archer 83* concluded (with the American public clueless about the latest crisis), one hundred million people tuned in to a two-hour ABC television doomsday docudrama called *The Day After*.

The movie depicted a hypothetical nuclear war between NATO forces and the Warsaw Pact, and what life would be like for survivors. It was followed by a town hall discussion on the reality of the movie's storyline. To this day, the show remains TV's highest-rated movie for number of viewers.[60]

On November 24, 1983, Soviet and U.S. talks on intermediate range nuclear weapons in Europe were suspended.[61]

On December 9, 1983, the Soviets broke off all arms control negotiations.[62]

At Medjugorje, a significant development is found to have occurred at this very moment during this precarious year. After the apparition of November 30, 1983, Marija Pavlović told the Franciscans that the Virgin Mary wanted a letter or report to be written and immediately sent to the Pope:

"The Supreme Pontiff and the Bishop must be advised immediately of the urgency and great importance of the message of Medjugorje." [63]

The communique to Pope John Paul II was written on December 2, 1983. It did, indeed, inform the Holy Father of the urgency of the message of Medjugorje, which seemed to fit like a glove with the urgency of the moment in the world.

Mary, the report stated, was in Medjugorje for the conversion of the world. But, it noted, "one cannot expect the whole world to be converted." Thus, the future would be decided, the letter explained to the Pope, through prophetic events that were coming—events now locked away in what the visionaries said were ten secrets.[64]

1983 brought the world the closest to "the annihilation of nations," Mary's haunting prophetic utterance at Fátima. By the year's end, the future appeared shrouded in peril. Another twelve months like the past, and the planet could become a heap of smoldering ashes—either deliberately or by accident.

The year did end, however, with a visual message to humanity—one with instructions on how to prevent such a global nightmare.

On December 27, 1983, Pope John Paul II showed that reconciliation and forgiveness were the paths to peace. In an extraordinary moment before the eyes of the world, the Holy Father came face-to-face with Mehmet Ali Ağca, his would-be assassin of May 13, 1981, during a three-hour visit to Rome's Rebibbia Prison.[65] Ağca was serving a life sentence at the high-security facility.

The Pope, dressed in white robes and a scarlet cape, and Ağca, wearing a light blue flight jacket and slacks, met for twenty-one minutes.[66] "This will remain for me a historic day in my life as a man, as a Christian, as Bishop of Rome," said the Pope after huddling with Ağca in a corner of his cell. "Today, after more than two years, I was able to meet my attacker and repeat the pardon I immediately granted him after being shot. Ağca is my brother," John Paul II explained, "whom I have sincerely forgiven." [67]

The Pope requested prayers for his assailant. Ağca, who, as John Paul departed, knelt and kissed his ring.

It was later revealed that the fascinating meeting between the two held a secret.

Ağca wanted to know two things: Why the Pope wasn't dead? And who was the mystery woman of Fátima who saved him?

"He wanted to know about the Secret of Fátima, and what the Secret actually was," John Paul II would later write. "This was his principal concern. More than anything else, he wanted to know this." [68]

The Pope's secretary, Father Stanislaw Dziwisz, later added to the John Paul's disclosure:

"All Ağca cared about were the revelations of Fátima," wrote Dziwisz in a book he released several years after John Paul II died. "The only thing that interested him was figuring out *who* had prevented him from killing the Pope…Who was this Virgin Mary, this 'goddess of Fátima?'" [69]

Fátima haunted Ağca—and perhaps, its mysteries surrounded him in more ways than one. It would later come to light that a very special nun had blocked and tackled Agca right after the shooting in Saint Peter's Square.

Her name? Sister Lúcia.[70]

On December 27, 2014—the thirty-first anniversary of John Paul II's visitation to the prison—Mehmet Ali Ağca visited Saint John Paul II's tomb in Saint Peter's Basilica and laid white roses.[71]

A Vatican spokesman, Father Ciro Benedettni, said it was a surprise visit and lasted only a few minutes. Italian TV ran a brief video of the visit to the Basilica.[72] In it, Ağca, who reportedly converted to Christianity in 2010, is heard to remark as he departed,

"A thousand thanks, Holiness. This is a miracle that goes on. The mystery of Fátima goes on. Long live Jesus Christ!" [73]

CHAPTER THIRTY-NINE

BIG BROTHER

"But the earth shall be filled with the knowledge of the Lord's glory as water covers the sea."

—Hb 2:14

BY DECEMBER 1983, THE WORLD FEARED AN EXPLOSION WAS COMING.

And it was—in Medjugorje.

Three days before Pope John Paul II met at Rebibbia Prison with Mehmet Ali Agcar, the village of Medjugorje received a notable visitor.

Father René Laurentin, an eminent French scholar and world-renowned Mariologist—the recipient of innumerable awards and ultimately the author of over 150 books—arrived in the remote village on the afternoon of December 24, 1983.

Laurentin was greeted with zero fanfare and nowhere to stay. His luggage had been subject to a two-hour search, and the nature of his business in Yugoslavia had been subsequently investigated at the airport police station.[1]

This was just the beginning of his woes.

Returning a year later, the French theologian was humiliatingly stripped searched, dragged before a judge, heavily fined, and kicked out of the country. He would be forbidden to return for one year. [2]

The chilly greetings would not deter Laurentin's interest in Medjugorje.

He would go on to pen over fifteen books on the apparitions. But it would be the product of this first visit that would introduce Medjugorje to the world.

And introduce the world to Medjugorje.

Laurentin was born in Tours on October 19, 1917, just four days after the last apparition at Fátima.

Called to serve in the French Army during World War II, he was decorated with the Military Cross, two citations, and the Legion of Honor before being taken a prisoner of war in Belgium in May, 1940. He subsequently spent five years at Oflag IV-D Elsterhorst, a prisoner-of-war camp near Hoyerswerda, Germany. [3]

After the war, Laurentin was ordained a priest on December 8, 1946. He then was trained in classical theology, receiving a Doctor of Letters from Sorbonne in 1952 and a Doctorate of Theology from Institute Catholique in 1953. [4]

Because of his background, he was not inclined toward apparitions: "I did not search them out, they came and looked for me," he wrote.[5]

That same year, Monsignor Pierre-Marie Theas, the Bishop of Tarbes and Lourdes, asked Laurentin for a theology of Lourdes.[6] Thirty volumes later, the work revealed almost as much about him as Lourdes.

Laurentin exhibited, his peers noted, not only the gifts of a brilliant theologian but also that of a masterful historian and a journalist, "par excellence." [7] He would go on to be praised for the exactitude of his chronicles on Vatican II and many other scholarly endeavors.

René Laurentin possessed, wrote Cardinal Albert Decourtray, "scientific rigor, spiritual contemplation, and the zeal of a pastor." Soon, the humble French theologian became an advisor to popes.[8]

He is, a reporter for *The National Catholic Register* noted, "the eminent Marian scholar in our time." [9]

All of these skills would be needed in his writings on Medjugorje, where Laurentin knew a challenging investigation awaited him.

Besides the Communists and the local bishop, who was at first favorable to the visions and then became obdurate, the Church was not exactly going through a period of welcoming new miracles.[10]

"Real discernment," wrote Laurentin, "such as that made by Bishop Laurence at Lourdes, in a manner exemplary for his day, does not seem possible any longer…I have shocked people every once in a while in these recent years by saying that if Lourdes were to take place in our own day the apparitions would not be recognized." [11]

Laurentin wasn't in Medjugorje to help advocate for its approval by the Church. But what he found happening there kept him coming back—and kept him writing.

When confronted on why he felt so positive about Medjugorje, why he kept writing books on the apparitions, Laurentin said he had nothing to do with it. It was, he insisted, all "Our Lady." [12]

His detractors questioned his sustained presence there, but as one writer on Medjugorje pointed out, "Laurentin is just the sort of man you'd have to bring in on something like Medjugorje anyway." [13]

The distinguished Irish Theologian Father Michael O'Carroll, went a step further; he believed Laurentin to be unparalleled in the Church's history in such matters:

"In no previous apparition or series of apparitions has a theological expert of the quality of Father René Laurentin been present from an early stage. He is scarcely rivaled in knowledge and critical judgement in the entire history of apparitions." [14]

Of his eighty books on the Catholic faith written by the time of his arrival in Medjugorje that cold December day in 1983, only one subject of his works generated conversion: Medjugorje.[15]

Not long after Laurentin's initial trip to Medjugorje, he published *Is the Virgin Mary Appearing in Medjugorje?* In France, over 75,000 copies were quickly sold, and the book generated a flood of French pilgrims to Yugoslavia. It was then translated into other languages. And, before you knew it, people from all over Europe started to head to Medjugorje.

Laurentin was to Medjugorje what yeast is to bread.

The fuse was lit.

And the explosion was about to occur.

Laurentin's first book on Medjugorje was no pep rally on visions or hysterical treatise on child visionaries. It was loaded with facts, with insightful information.

It questioned everything and walked a reader to his or her own conclusions, based on the evidence. It examined every reported element of the apparitions from both sides with no reservations.

From the history of the events, to even a long-running dispute between the Franciscans and the local diocese, it tackled all the hard questions. Professionally chronicled and well written, it pandered to nothing and no one.

The author, it was clear, brought no agenda to the work.

Laurentin wrote that his book attempted to discern Medjugorje according to the principles he applied "in my previous studies at La Rue du Bac (1830), La Salette (1846), Lourdes (1858), Pontmain (1871)." [16] He labeled it a work of research,[17] one he chose not to have graced with an imprimatur as to not upstage the local bishop.[18]

From his own words, it is clear that Laurentin sought to probe Medjugorje's mysteries guided by his heart and conscience, and especially the charisms of the visionaries:

"I felt myself outdone, challenged, in my investigator's mind set. I cursed this task which obliges me to interrogate, analyze, photograph, pursue, into their interior castles these people whose life is so full so that I could obtain precise details that my historian's conscience demanded." [19]

Written in January of 1984, Laurentin's book revealed three significant facts about the apparitions at Medjugorje:

1. By then, an estimated two million had gone on pilgrimage to Medjugorje. [20]
2. A generous number of Church hierarchy and other heady theologians had already visited Medjugorje and left impressed with what they witnessed. [21]
3. The six visionaries had been examined by a number of doctors and scientists, who all conducted tests, studies and evaluations. These included:

- Dr. Ludovic Stopar, a specialist in hypnotherapy and parapsychology, who found the children to be absolutely normal with no pathological indications.[22]
- Dr. Maria Magatti, a neurologist who studied the children's reaction to stimuli and concluded the ecstasy was genuine.[23]
- Dr. Lucia Capello, a neurophysiologist who examined the children's synchronized movements: falling to their knees, moving their lips, turning their eyes upward, and more. She concluded

there was "no natural explanation" and that it "indicates that there is something that is seen only by the visionaries and not by observers." [24]

- Dr. Mario Botta, a heart specialist who stated that the ecstasy did not alter the children's normal physiology "but elevates it to a higher plane." [25]
- Dr. Enzo Gabrici, a neuropsychiatrist who found no sign of hallucination, epileptic syndrome, or any disorder that could affect consciousness. [26]
- Dr. Anna Maria Francini, a professor of medicine, who stated that during ecstasy, she had never seen attention and interest manifested to such a degree of intensity. [27]
- Dr. Henri Joyeux, a French professor of medicine at the prestigious University of Montpellier. He concluded the phenomena of the apparitions at Medjugorje cannot be explained scientifically: "According to the experiments carefully conducted, we can affirm that there has been no pathological modification in the parameters which have been investigated... During the ecstasy there is a perfect convergence of their eyes and there is a strong feeling of a face to face encounter between the visionaries and a person we cannot see." [28] (Joyeux published a book with Laurentin and various medical colleagues that further investigated the phenomena at Medjugorje.)

All of this medical testing showed, Laurentin wrote, that while in their ecstatic states, the visionaries exhibited "traits consistent in authenticity" with the traditional criteria and experience of the Church in such matters. [29]

One member of the International Committee of Lourdes, Dr. Ivan Tole, ventured another noteworthy opinion: "Three or four of the healings (at Medjugorje) are certainly miraculous." Another doctor, Dr. Mangiapan of the Lourdes Medical Bureau, thought as many as nine were worthy of further study. [30]

Laurentin's book, indeed, sought the facts and truth—and his readers could see this. Soon, because of his work, Medjugorje became known throughout the world.

This, in turn, led to more.

In France, by the summer of 1984, organized pilgrimages to Medjugorje were springing up across the country. [31] Returning home, many were touched deeply by their experience there. This, in turn, spawned a massive prayer movement in the country, as prayer groups began to organize everywhere.

Consequently, the Rosary alone was now being prayed every day by countless numbers of people who perhaps weren't praying at all just a short time before. If the Virgin Mary's plan to save the world from self-annihilation was to come through the power of prayer, her effort was gathering momentum.

Laurentin wasn't just busy in France with Medjugorje, he was also making sure things were going well in Rome, where meetings with the Pope and others helped stave off criticism from those who were skeptical about apparitions.

Rumored to have been told by Church hierarchy to be more prudent in his activism for the Herzegovina visions, Laurentin was forced to set the record straight:

"Three times, briefly and in private, I spoke with the Pope," Laurentin revealed in his fifth book on Medjugorje, "he read the books which I sent to him on these occasions. He did not ask me to practice prudence, nor did he give me any other restrictive warning. I am ready to verify it under oath. My works, known in Rome, had been able to help Rome clarify things, and as a result of such works, the judgement of Monsignor Zanic against Medjugorje was not accepted. If such displeases those who wished a condemnation, and who were looking consequently to discredit me, that is their concern." [32]

As seen from the massive daily crowds in Medjugorje by early 1984—with people constantly fingering beads and waiting in long lines to have their souls repaired—the spiritual explosion taking place in Medjugorje was an objective reality.

But it still must have not been enough; through her messages to the six visionaries, Mary continued to press for more prayer.

In January and February of 1984 alone, of the known messages published during this period, the word "pray" or "prayer" is found ninety-seven times.[33] While the messages at first glance appear repetitious, closer scrutiny reveals that each holds its own unique appeal to prayer.

The revelations clearly seemed to be pressing for more prayer for a reason.

It was as if by the sheer quantity, something was soon to come.

A message given on January 27, 1984, personifies the Virgin's relentless push for prayer, especially from those willing to profoundly take her words to heart:

> Pray and fast. I wish that you deepen and continue your life in prayer. Every morning, say the prayer of consecration to the Heart of Mary. Do this in the family. Recite each morning the Angelus, five Our Father's, Hail Mary's, and Glory Be's in honor of the Holy Passion and a sixth one for our Holy Father, the Pope. Then say the Creed and the prayer to the Holy Spirit. And, if it is possible, it would be well to pray a Rosary.[34]

The references to the Pope, Mary's Heart, and the Rosary are telling.

They were integral elements to her appeal at Fátima. Curiously, the following day, Mary mentioned that her call to prayer is so her "heart" can reach out to the world:

"I wish that all of you pray, and that my heart extends to the whole world. I wish to be with you." [35]

In lieu of the escalating tension between the two nuclear superpowers by end of 1983, one can safely surmise that the Virgin Mary's anguished appeal for prayer at Medjugorje involved some race against time that only Heaven knew existed.

A message given by the Virgin on February 17, 1984, does nothing to dispel this notion:

"My children, pray! The world has been drawn into a great whirlpool. It does not *know* what it is doing. It does not realize in what sense it is sinking. It needs your prayers so I can pull it out of this danger." [36]

The world, Mary seemed to be saying, was totally ignorant and completely blind to the spiritual forces behind the eminent danger. What it needed most, therefore, was something only she could bring: peace, true peace. The peace she had spoken of from her very first days at

Medjugorje. The peace that she said was the reason she had come as the Queen of Peace.

It was the peace that even the sky over Medjugorje boldly proclaimed in huge letters one day in August, 1981. That day—August 6—was a day those who saw the word "MIR" span the sky say they will never forget. It was also memorable for another reason.

It was the day the first atomic bomb was dropped on Hiroshima.[37]

On January 16, 1984, President Ronald Reagan delivered a speech on Soviet-American relations. Although the previous year repeatedly brought the two nations to the brink of conflict, Reagan chose to dwell on a more positive future, one aimed at securing peace:

> During the first days of 1984, I would like to share with you and the people of the world my thoughts on a subject of great importance to the cause of peace—relations between the United States and the Soviet Union…We're witnessing tragic conflicts in many parts of the world. Nuclear arsenals are far too high, and our working relationship with the Soviet Union is not what it must be…
>
> We must and will engage the Soviets in a dialogue as serious and constructive as possible, a dialogue that will serve to promote peace in the troubled regions of the world, reduce the level of arms and build a constructive working relationship…That is why 1984 is a year of opportunities for peace. [38]

Peace.

Talk of peace. It was what everyone needed to hear.

But it was "1984"—the year memorialized in the title of George Orwell's famous novel of the same name—and the Communist nations were now emblematic of the horrifying world his classic envisioned.

"The more the Party is powerful, the less it will be tolerant; the weaker the opposition, the tighter the despotism," imagined Orwell. [39]

The renowned author's words looked clairvoyant when considering Yuri Andropov's Soviet Union of February, 1984. The U.S.S.R. and the nations of Eastern Europe eerily resembled Orwell's society of official deception, secret surveillance, and manipulation by an omnipresent "Big Brother."

A visible despotism could also be seen in Andropov, who was not only alarming the West, but also his Communist cronies in the Kremlin.

Then came a new mystery in the turbulent world that was the Soviet Union; the principle figure in the real-life dystopia was missing. Since August of 1983, the enigmatic Yuri Andropov had not been seen in public.

But, on February 11, 1984, the mystery was solved.

Yuri Andropov was dead.

The Soviet leadership announced that he died in Moscow at the age of 69, reportedly from renal failure. [40] It was later learned that he had been running the country from his hospital bed for quite a while. [41] Now, his disconcerting fifteen-month reign of the Soviet Union was over.

"It will be a world of terror as much as a world of triumph," wrote Orwell. [42]

With Andropov gone, hope prevailed that maybe some of the terror in the world went with him.

That would remain to be seen.

But if there was ever a time for Fátima's foretold "Triumph" to arrive, that time was now.

CHAPTER FORTY

DELIVER US

"Even to the death fight for the truth, and the
Lord your God will battle for you."

—Sir 4:28

SISTER LÚCIA WAS 76 YEARS OLD IN 1984.

The lone surviving visionary of Fátima was only ten when the Virgin Mary appeared to her in 1917 and first spoke about the need for the consecration of Russia by the Holy Father.

On that day, the Virgin promised that she would return to her to formally request the action be undertaken. Twelve years later, on June 13, 1929, that day came.

Lúcia, now 22, was living in Tui, Spain, when Mary made the official request for the Pope and all the bishops to consecrate Russia:

> The moment has come in which God asks the Holy Father, in union with all the bishops of the world, to make the consecration of Russia to my Immaculate Heart, promising to save it by this means. [1]

From 1929 to 1984, Popes Pius XI, Pius XII, John XXIII, Paul VI, John Paul I, and John Paul II failed to successfully make the consecration—or, never attempted at all. This added up to 55 years of disappointment and frustration for Lúcia.*

---

*   Wrote Father Rene Laurentin, "Never have the popes been pushed so far to obey, at the level of the universal Church, the request of a visionary." Aura Miguel, *Totus Tuus,* p.98.

For the world, it was much worse.

It permitted the coming of wars, famine, persecutions, and death—massive death. It led to millions living under the yoke of Communism.

All the wars that have taken place, Lúcia told Cardinal Ricardo Tito Jamin Vidal of the Philippines in a later interview, "could have been avoided..."[2]

What *could* have been. What *should* have been. None of it mattered now. The present and the future were all that counted. And things weren't looking up.

Though Andropov was dead, the man chosen to replace him—Konstantin Chernenko—was not a radical departure from the status quo. Lúcia's letter to John Paul II of May 12, 1982, could not have spelled it out any clearer as to why the consecration needed to be done.

The complete fulfillment of the prophecy that Lúcia warned of in the letter—the onward march of Marxist atheism, militant Communism and the risk of nuclear war—*were* getting nearer. [3]

Now, less than two years later, they were visible.

The Soviet downing of KAL 007 brought with it immediate consequences. The brazen act affected the balance of power in Europe.[4] Prior to the attack on the jet, Great Britain, Italy, West Germany, Belgium, and Holland all had governments that refused upgraded missile installations in their countries. After the Soviet attack on the airliner, they changed their minds. All agreed now to accept the new medium-range missiles, with some receiving them just two months later in November of 1983. [5]

Realizing its military advantage was slipping in Europe, the Soviets began to contemplate their options. Having developed in 1979 a plan to invade Western Europe—known as *Seven Days to the Rhine* [6]—some in the Kremlin argued that it would be wise to revisit that roadmap.

Writes Antonio Socci, in *The Fourth Secret of Fatima*:

> Facing the prospect of collapse and military vulnerability, for the first time the Kremlin took under consideration the military option, that is, the possibility of a "preventive" attack on Europe. All indications are that this would have involved an atomic conflict, a road with no return. [7]

It was exactly then, notes Grzegorz Górny and Janusz Rosikon in *Fatima Mysteries*, "when a global nuclear war was imminent," that Pope John Paul II would make his next attempt to perform the consecration.[8]

After the 1982 consecration came up short, John Paul II knew he would need to do it again.

Guided by his own spiritual compass, the Holy Father chose the date of March 25, 1984, *The Solemnity of the Annunciation.* The consecration would take place during the closing ceremony for The Holy Year of the Redemption.

Taking action three months in advance—with the letters dated December 8, 1983, *The Feast of the Immaculate Conception*—all the bishops of the world were invited to join him in the Act of Consecration.[9] The Pope even invited the Orthodox bishops to accompany him, and five patriarchs participated.[10]

To make sure it was enacted properly this time, John Paul II studied all the previous consecrations and consulted Lúcia on at least two occasions. In the history of the Church, never had a pope done so much to fulfill the request of a visionary of private revelation, wrote one Fátima authority.[11]

As John Paul II knelt in front of the original hand-carved statue of Our Lady of Fátima, the Capelinha—flown in from Fátima by the Bishop of Leiria himself to Rome for the special day—he slowly began to read the consecration prayer in front of an estimated 200,000 that had gathered in Saint Peter's Square.[12]

The tone of his words reflect how serious the moment was for him personally:

> The power of this consecration lasts for all time and embraces all individuals, peoples, and nations. It overcomes every evil that the spirit of darkness is able to awaken, and has in fact awakened in our times, in the heart of man and in his history. How deeply we feel the need for the consecration of humanity and the world—our modern world—in union with Christ himself. [13]

The words of the consecration that day, wrote Cardinal Tarcisio Bertone, were designed by the Pope to be commenting on the message of Fátima in its sorrowful fulfillment.[14] They pleaded with Mary, the Mother of the Church, to help a world overwhelmed by the spirit of darkness.[15]

In its essence, the consecration besieged the Virgin to deliver the world from a litany of trials and troubles, many of which were warned of through Fátima: [16]

- From famine and war, deliver us.
- From nuclear war, from incalculable destruction, deliver us.
- From every kind of war, deliver us.
- From sins against the life of man from its very beginning, deliver us.
- From hatred and from the demeaning of the dignity of the children of God, deliver us.
- From every kind of injustice in the life of society, both national and international, deliver us.
- From readiness to trample on the Commandments of God, deliver us.
- From attempts to stifle in human hearts the very truth of God, deliver us.
- From the loss of awareness of good and evil, deliver us.
- From sins against the Holy Spirit deliver us, deliver us.[17]

In its fullness, the consecration seemed to be an expanded *Our Father*, asking God, through the intercession of the Immaculate Heart of Mary, to deliver us from evil. The Pope repeated the word "evil" four times and the words "deliver us" ten times in the relatively short prayer.

What laid hidden beneath each word, however, was the true aim of the prayer: for God to deliver the world from the evil scourge of Marxist atheism, from the tyranny of Communism, from the endless spread of the "errors of Russia."

In the March 27, 1984, edition of the *L'Osservatore Romano*, it was reported that at a certain point in the prayer, Pope John Paul II departed from his prepared text and said:

"Enlighten especially the people whose consecration and entrusting you are waiting from us." [18]

This was a veiled reference, it was believed, to Russia.[19]

Witnesses close to John Paul II that day saw him make lengthy pauses during the prayer, adding more to the suspicion that he was mentioning Russia by name, perhaps repeatedly. [20]

One man wanted to drive a stake into the heart of the beast through the consecration.

His thinking?

If the Pope and the bishops were to finally ask that the world be delivered by God from such evil—the evil foretold at Fátima to begin in Russia—then it wouldn't hurt to have the consecration prayer recited in a target-specific way. That is, in Russia itself.

Better yet, in the Kremlin.

Bishop Pavel Hnilica of Czechoslovakia arrived at this determination. And he set out to make it happen.

Hnilica's story is one for the ages. Studying at a seminary in Trnava, a city in today's western Slovakia, the 29-year-old was arrested by the Communist government's secret police on April 13, 1950.[21] He was sent to various labor camps and forced to join the military that summer.

Somehow, though, he still managed to become a priest, eventually ordained clandestinely in a hospital by his imprisoned bishop, who entered the facility to undertake medical tests.[22]

Then, on February 2, 1951, at barely 30 years of age, Hnilica was again consecrated in secret, this time as a bishop—in the same hospital.[23] This was done to allow seminarians to be secretly ordained into the priesthood by him in Czechoslovakia, since all the existing bishops in the country were imprisoned. Hnilica's ordination made him the youngest bishop in the world at the time. [24]

The Czechoslovakian bishop came to Rome during the Second Vatican Council, having fled his native country to seek aid for the Church in the East. During the Council, he met and became close friends with many in the hierarchy of the Vatican. He would go on to accompany Pope Paul VI to Fátima as a papal legate.

There, he got to know the Bishop of Leiria, João Venâncio, and became intimately involved with the message of Fátima. Upon meeting privately with Sister Lúcia, she told him that over the course of the apparitions, both private and public, Mary had mentioned Russia many times. It was a disclosure that perhaps further motivated his clandestine visit to the Kremlin.

With the Pope's blessing, Bishop Hnilica and Monsignor Leo Maasburg—an Austrian priest ordained at Fátima—traveled to

Moscow on March 22, 1984, landing at Sheremetyevo International Airport late in the afternoon. [25]

After several close calls with security in the Kremlin, the two self-described "tourists" performed the consecration on March 24th, first at the Church of Saint Michael the Archangel and then at the Church of the Dormition.

They topped off the madcap adventure by celebrating Mass in the Kremlin, too, discreetly concealed behind an opened copy of the Soviet newspaper *Pravda* that they pretended to be reading. [26]

The two arrived back at Saint Peter's the next day, just as John Paul II commenced the ceremony. The Pope, upon hearing of their success, took it as a confirmation from the Virgin that this consecration effort finally fulfilled her request at Fátima. [27]

At first, there were rumors that Sister Lúcia said it wasn't acceptable.[28]

But, she would eventually repeatedly confirm that the consecration was performed to Heaven's satisfaction.[29]

Over the next two decades, multiple letters from her validated John Paul II's Act of Entrustment—most notable her correspondences of August 29 and November 8, 1989, July 30, 1990, and November 21, 1999. Along with a number of published interviews that she gave on the validity of the consecration— the question got to the point that it seemed like overkill. [30]

Her August 29 letter can be viewed as her strongest attempt to make it painstakingly clear that the consecration was accepted:

> On October 31, 1942, in a letter from his Holiness Pius XII, they asked me then if it was done as Our Lady had asked; I said no, because it lacked the union with all the bishops of the world. After this, Pope Paul VI made it on May 13, 1967. They asked me if it was done as Our Lady requested. I answered no, for the same reason, it lacked the union with all the bishops of the world. It was made again by Pope John Paul II on May 13, 1982. They asked me then if it was done. I said no. It lacked all the bishops of the world.

Then, this same supreme Pontiff, John Paul II, wrote to all the bishops of the world asking them to unite with him and he gave orders for the image of Our Lady of Fátima to be taken from Capelinha and brought to Rome, and on March 25, 1984—publicly and in union with all the bishops of the world who wished to unite—made the consecration as Our Lady requested. They asked me then if it was made as Our Lady had asked for it, and I said yes. Since then it is done. [31]

Lúcia apparently felt these efforts of hers were necessary, as a small but insistent faction still held that the consecration was not completely fulfilled in the way Mary requested at Fátima.

They believed, therefore, the result was incomplete.

The objections this time primarily centered around the fact that the "world," not "Russia," had been the object of the consecration, and that the act was called an "entrustment", not a consecration.[32]

Something must have been done right, though.

At Medjugorje, on the same evening of Pope John Paul II's consecration, a message from the Virgin Mary alluded directly to a major breakthrough in her efforts to bring peace to the world. On what would be that day her one-thousandth apparition in Medjugorje,[33] the Madonna told the children:

"Rejoice with me and my angels. Because a part of my plan has already been realized!" [34]

The Virgin Mary's message at Medjugorje is perhaps too panoptic and nonlinear for some to conclusively connect to Pope John Paul II's effort that same day in Rome.

But a series of strange and extraordinary events—several that undeniable point to Fátima—followed not too long after that memorable day. Even Mirjana Soldo noted this in her book, citing how after the consecration of March 25, 1984, the U.S.S.R. experienced a host of military disasters, of which the worst was on the very anniversary date of Fatima, May 13, 1984. [35]

Indeed, the Soviets did.

As Mirjana observed, a series of major setbacks suddenly struck the U.S.S.R. as if in a chain reaction to the consecration.

On May 13, 1984—the anniversary date of Fátima and just seven weeks after the consecration—a fire began near the Severomorsk Naval Base, which was the headquarters of the revered Northern Fleet of the Soviet Navy. Severomorsk is a town of 55,000 in Murmansk Oblast, on the Kola Peninsula in Russia. Because of its military secrets, the town was considered a closed city.

The fire lasted four days and caused a massive chain reaction of explosions, killing between two to three hundred people.[36] Most significantly, it destroyed at least nine hundred of the Northern Fleet's torpedoes and missiles. The blaze also destroyed five hundred and eighty of the Fleet's S-125 Neva/Pechora surface to air missiles, and three hundred and twenty of the Fleet's SS-N-3 Shaddock cruise missiles, capable of carrying nuclear warheads.

Jane's Defense Weekly—an authoritative British Military publication—said the explosion crippled the fighting capacity of the Northern Fleet. In fact, the eruption was so powerful it was at first thought to be a nuclear detonation. Western intelligence sources classified it as the "greatest military disaster to the Soviets since World War II," saying the facility would not be fully operational for a couple of years.[37]

Two years later, yet another nuclear related accident occurred in the Soviet Union.

This time the eyes of the world would come to be focused on it.

On April 26, 1986, a sudden surge of power during a reactor systems test destroyed Unit 4 of the nuclear power station at Chernobyl near the town of Pripyat in northern Ukraine, about 65 miles from Kiev. The accident and fire that followed sent enormous amounts of radioactive material into the environment.

In response, the government had to close off the area within eighteen miles of the plant and evacuate 115,000 people within the most heavily-contaminated areas. In subsequent years, another 220,000 needed to be moved out of the region.[38] The Chernobyl accident contaminated wide areas of Belarus and Ukraine and affected millions of people.** To this day, it is considered the most disastrous nuclear power plant accident in history. [39]

Then, on the night of May 12, 1988 —the eve of the anniversary date of the first apparition at Fátima—the Soviet Union suffered another

---

**   Though ambiguous, some have argued that Chernobyl means "wormwood" in the Ukrainian language, the name of the fallen star in *Revelation's* "Third Trumpet" prophecy.

massive military blow. As thousands prayed at an all-night vigil at Fátima, another explosion shut down the Soviet Union's sole missile motor plant. *The Associated Press* reported:

"A major explosion has shut down the only plant in the Soviet Union that makes the main rocket motors of that country's newest long range nuclear missile, according to U.S. officials." A Pentagon statement further added that the accident destroyed several buildings at a Soviet propellant plant in Paulogriad. [40]

Curiously, just a week before on May 3, 1988, a similar series of blasts ripped apart a Nevada facility owned by PEPCON, a company that produced the ammonium perchlorate used in the fuel of almost every missile and rocket system. [41]

To this day, NASA calls the Nevada accident the "largest domestic non-nuclear explosion in history." [42] The explosions were felt ten miles away, and experts compared them to a 1-kiloton nuclear detonation. The blasts even caused minor earthquakes measuring 3.0 and 3.5 on the Richter scale at observatories in Colorado and California. [43]

During this period, the Soviets also lost two nuclear submarines due to mechanical malfunctions, as well as suffering what amounted to defeat in Afghanistan after ten years of war. They withdrew from the country in February of 1989. [44]

But what was to happen by the end of 1989 would leave even the most stringent doubter of the 1984 consecration's mystical efficacy on rubber legs. Before the eyes of the world, there would come what many claimed to be an unfathomable miracle— one that even to this day seems impossible to fully comprehend. [45]

CHAPTER FORTY-ONE

THE END OF THE EVIL EMPIRE

*"Be not provoked with evildoers, nor envious
of the wicked; for the evil man has
no future, the lamp of the wicked will be put out."*
—Prv 24:19-20

BY MID-JANUARY 1871, A GENERAL CLIMATE OF FEAR HAD OVER-taken the French village of Pontmain.

Located two hundred miles west of Paris, the community of five hundred was in line to be gobbled up by the advancing Prussian army of Prince Otto von Bismarck. With Paris under siege, it looked like all of France would soon fall and become part of a greater German empire. Thirty-eight young men from Pontmain had been conscripted to serve in the French army, adding to the worries of the townspeople.

Then, on the morning of January 17, Pontmain received some more bad news: the Prussian army was closing in on Laval, only thirty-three miles away. Abbe Guerin, the saintly village priest, addressed the faithful at Mass that morning:

"Let us add penance to our prayers, and then we may take courage. God will have pity on us; His mercy will surely come to us through Mary." [1]

Eleven hours later, Father Guerin's words were fulfilled—not only for Pontmain but for all of France.

At about 5 p.m. that day, as the sun was setting, the Virgin Mary appeared in the sky above a small house to two boys, 12-year-old

Eugene Bernadette and his 10-year-old brother, Joseph. Two young girls, Francoise Richer, age 11, and Jeanne Marie Lebosse, 9 years of age, would happen by and also see the apparition.[2] But no adults witnessed the vision.

Mary's stay was brief—about three hours—but transforming.

She had come to bring the panicking villagers some good news; their prayers were to be answered:

"**Pray My Little Children. God Will Hear You in a Short Time**," read a slowly unfolding scroll of words that appeared below the floating Virgin, "**My Son Permits Himself to Be Moved**." [3]

That evening, a group of Prussian soldiers encountered a vision outside of Laval. "A Madonna is guarding the country and forbidding us to advance," the men are said to have reported to their superiors.[4]

The next morning, Pontmain and its neighbors received a surprise: the Prussian army had withdrawn. Eleven days later, an armistice was signed.

Suddenly, the war was over.

Prayer, and the Virgin Mary's intercession, helped bring it to an abrupt end.

The Church saw it that way, too.

The single apparition at Pontmain was approved by Bishop Joseph-Hippolyte Guibert on January 18, 1872, a little more than a year later. [5]

There is a significance to what happened at Pontmain.

It set the way for what was coming: a series of intercessions by the Virgin Mary that would follow over the coming years on behalf of those threatened or overwhelmed by war.

Mary knows about war.

She lived on Earth at a time that saw her own native land seized and occupied by an invading army. And—long before the Romans—her Jewish Scriptures taught her about the many wars Israel fought with its neighbors and conquering empires from afar.

Her besought intercession in such affairs is legendry.

From Cologne in 1474, to Lepanto in 1571, to Peterwardein in 1716, the accounts of how praying to Mary helped end conflicts and bring victories are compelling.[6]

Just as compelling, though, are her intercessions of the last two centuries.

Like at Pontmain.

And, for that matter, throughout the twentieth century.

Responding to the urgent pleas of Pope Benedict XV—who was beside himself over so much ruin and carnage from World War I—and to the millions who doggedly beseeched Heaven for an end to the war, the Virgin Mary came to Fátima in 1917.

There, as at Pontmain, she announced that the war was going to end. Within a year, it was over.

Leaving a spiritual formula at Fátima to prevent a second world war—which Church leaders and the faithful failed to apply—Mary comes again to the rescue of humanity in World War II.

On October 31, 1942, Pope Pius XII consecrated the world to the Immaculate Heart of Mary in Rome, submitting finally to more than a decade of pleadings from Sister Lúcia and others in the Church.[7]

The consecration, however, was flawed, as its object was not Russia and was not done in union with all the Church's bishops, as requested by Mary at Tui in 1929. [8] The Virgin Mary, however, secured the blessings of the Almighty from Pius XII's attempt. As at Pontmain and with World War I, she had come to the rescue of a distressed world.

On February 28, 1943, Sister Lúcia revealed this welcome news to Archbishop Ferreira, the Bishop of Gurza:

"The good God already showed me His satisfaction with the act, although it was incomplete according to His wishes, achieved by the Holy Father and several bishops. He promises, in return, to soon put an end to the war. The conversion of Russia is not for now." [9]

The promise to end the war can be seen to begin to materialize within days of Pope Pius XII's act of consecration. Fátima author Frére Michel de la Sainte Trinité writes:

> The six months which followed this blessing…marked a veritable turning point in the war. Indeed, after this date, the war slowly moved to its end.[10]

In *The Fourth Secret of Fatima*, Antonio Socci noted how the war suddenly took a decisive turn for the better:

> God immediately kept his promise: November 3, 1942: defeat of the Germans at Al Alamein, after ten days of terrible combat; November 8: the landing of the Anglo-Americans in North Africa; February 2, 1943: the capitulation of Stalingrad by the German Sixth Army; Churchill delivers the famous speech: "The wheel of destiny has turned." [11]

But, Socci noted, not only did the conversion of Russia *not* occur, the spread of Communism was very evidently progressing:

> The war soon ended, although one could not call "peace" that which began in 1945, with half of Europe ending up in Soviet hands, and the Communist nightmare, and the beginning of the "Cold War" that so many historians have described as "the Third World War." [12]

Without a doubt, the fall of Eastern Europe into the Soviet sphere does serve as evidence of Lúcia's revelation: "the conversion of Russia is not for now." A second letter, written by Lúcia on May 4, 1943, to Father Bernardo Goncalves, reiterated that the consecration was deficient and would not deter the spread of Communism:

> Our Lord promises the end of the war to be soon, with regard to the act which his holiness has deigned to perform. But as it was incomplete, the conversion of Russia will be later.[13]

The Second World War, though, is seen to have been in the Virgin Mary's hands all along. World War II officially became a "world war" when the United States entered the day after Japan's surprise attack on Pearl Harbor, December 8, 1941—the Feast of the Immaculate Conception of the Virgin Mary.

It came to its miserable, but thankful, conclusion with the announcement of Japan's surrender on August 15, 1945, the Feast of Mary's Assumption into Heaven.

In February 1946, as Eastern Europe was being dragged into the Soviet stranglehold, Father Hubert Jongen—a Dutch Montfort Father—inquired of Sister Lúcia if she thought the world was going through a period of Russian domination because Russia has not been specifically consecrated?

Replied Lúcia, "I think Our Lady's words are being fulfilled: 'If not, she (Russia) will spread her errors throughout the world.'" [14]

Needless to say, after World War II, the great danger Mary had spoken of at Fátima was becoming increasingly visible. Marxism was on the move, spreading its "errors." Besides the loss of Eastern Europe, there came the fall of China in 1949, with Communism now entrenched throughout Southeast Asia.

On October 14, 1951, Lúcia reminded Pope Pius XII again—through a priest named Father Gustav Wetter, the rector of the Collegium Russicum in Rome, who visited her at the Carmel at Coimbra—that what Our Lady of Fátima requested had not been done. [15]

Then, in May of 1952, the Virgin pressed Lúcia to try harder:

"Make known to the Holy Father," Mary instructed Lúcia, "that I am still waiting the consecration of Russia to my Immaculate Heart. Without this consecration, Russia will not be able to convert, nor will the world have peace." [16]

A month later, Sister Lúcia successfully navigated this appeal to Rome.

Finally, Pius XII, inundated by personal signs—especially the four Fátima-like solar miracles at the Vatican in November of 1950 during the days of his proclamation of the dogma of Mary's Assumption into Heaven—yielded and decided to once again perform another consecration. [17]

Indeed, the sun phenomena that Pius witnessed at the Vatican, some held, was as if God Himself was asking the Holy Father for the consecration, for him to respond to Fátima. "The prodigies," wrote Fátima author Mark Fellows, "may have also been intended as a directional arrow urging Pius on to consecrate Russia to the Immaculate Heart. That Papa Pacelli witnessed—repeatedly—the signature miracle of the Fátima apparitions could hardly have been a coincidence." [18]

On July 7, 1952, ten years after his first attempt, Pius XII explicitly consecrated the people of Russia to the Immaculate Heart of Mary. This time, he did it through an Apostolic Letter, *Sacro Vergente anno*.[19] In the letter, the Pope openly cites Russia by name. The date is also important: it is the Feast of Saints Cyril and Methodius, the apostles of the Slav peoples.

But, the effort was deficient in multiple ways, according to Father Alonso in his Fátima study of 1973.[20] Most glaringly, Alonso pointed out that it lacked all the bishops throughout the world enacting the consecration in union with the Holy Father.

Astonishingly, however, Sister Lúcia *again* reports positive news from Pius's effort. Although the attempt is still flawed, great graces are to be accorded to the world, reports Lúcia. These benefits would not be recognizable immediately, but again are sizable. Europe is apparently saved from a Soviet invasion that was in the making. And, the murderous Stalin is gone for good. [21] Writes Antonio Socci about this amazing turn of events:

> Notice the dates. Everything happened within the turn of eight months from the consecration of Russia to the Immaculate Heart of Mary. Who saved Europe from that projected and proclaimed Soviet invasion and "pulled the tyrant (Stalin) from the throne?"
>
> The anonymous hand of history...or the powerful hand of the *Woman of the Magnificat,* thanks to the solemn act of the Holy Father...the Pope finds a hearing in Heaven, obtaining great graces, but which—being partial—does not obtain the realization of the extraordinary promises of Fátima.
>
> In fact, it is true that the bloodiest of the anti-Christian tyrants of the universe disappeared and that Western Europe was saved from Communism, but Russia is far from converting, the Cold War continues and will become dramatic, and with ascent of Khrushchev to power, the persecution of the Church of the East will continue. [22]

Socci's observation is precise. Deterred slightly by Stalin's death, Communism methodically marches on. The Virgin Mary is successful, however, in saving the world once again from a major crisis, although no one at the time realized that a war was so close to taking place in Europe.

Pius XII would not attempt the consecration again.

Nor would his successor, Pope John XXIII, who would be the first to read the third part of the Secret of Fátima in August 1959. John read it at the papal summer residence at Castel Gandolfo, but decided it should remain confidential to only him and a handful of close advisors. [23]

Instead, John XXIII's focus would be on calling a Church Council— Vatican II. The new Pope was also viewed by some to be perhaps a little at odds with Fátima, although he had visited the shrine as the Patriarch of Venice in 1956. He opened Vatican II with remarks regarding "prophets of doom." [24] This followed his silencing of Sister Lúcia in 1959, a move which prohibited her to meet or speak with people about the message of Fátima. [25]

At the time, concerns were running high that Lúcia could become a renegade voice with regards to the third part of the Secret of Fátima. Its anticipated 1960 deadline for release was drawing near, and some were unsure what she might do.[26] It was even speculated—for no legitimate reason—that Lúcia might give a radio message to the world. [27]

John XXIII's successor, Pope Paul VI, did not attempt a *new* consecration. He is also frowned upon by some for dismissing Lucia's request to meet with him privately at Fátima in 1967. The Rome monthly, *Inside the Vatican,* seemed to view both Popes as not wanting to overdo it with Fátima:

> John XXIII (1958 to 1963) and Paul VI (1963-1978) gave rather lukewarm support to the spread of the Fátima devotions ... and opposed carrying out the consecration of Russia by name, which Lúcia continued to insist Our Lady had requested. Both Popes could have used the occasion of the gathering of all the world's bishops in Rome for the Second Vatican Council to make such a consecration; neither chose to do so. [28]

Pope Paul VI did, though, on November 21, 1964, proclaim Mary, the "Mother of the Church." [29] He also recalled Pope Pius XII's consecration of October 31, 1942, by personally renewing it that day in the presence of the Fathers of Vatican Council II. [30]*

Pope John Paul I, Albino Luciani—who reigned only thirty-three days—was permitted no time to address the need for the consecration of Russia. As previously noted, Luciani met with Lúcia a year before becoming Pope. One Vatican periodical even claimed she addressed him repeatedly that day as "Holy Father." Lúcia, however, denies the rumor that she foretold to him his election to the papacy, yet alone its brevity. [31]

And so comes Pope John Paul II's date with destiny.

The Pope's June 7, 1981, Act of Entrustment on the Solemnity of Pentecost that was broadcasted from the Basilica of St. Mary Major in Rome—weeks after his attempted assassination—was recognized immediately as deficient.[32] Nevertheless, it must be pointed out that just a few weeks later, on June 24, Mary arrived in Medjugorje. Perhaps this failed attempt contributed to bringing into the world another significant, but unrecognized grace.

The following year—on the anniversary date of his shooting, May 13, 1982—Pope John Paul II tried again. This attempt was at first declared by some as finally fulfilling Mary's request at Fátima.[33] Lúcia, however, soon dismissed it as inadequate, claiming that the consecration as requested by the Virgin was still not done correctlly and not accepted by Heaven. [34]

But—once more—Lucia revealed that God would in some way, as in 1942 and 1952, respond favorably: "It is late, and Communism has spread throughout the world. It (the attempt) will have its effect, but each of us must respond to the consecration." [35]

That the incomplete consecrations of 1942, 1952, and 1982 still led to the shortening of World War II, the salvation of Western Europe from a Soviet invasion in 1953, and other unknown but special graces in 1982, is nothing short of extraordinary.

It also causes one to wonder.

---

*   For some reason, Sister Lúcia mistakenly mentions in her letter of August 29, 1989, that Pope Paul VI's renewal of May 13, 1967, was a formal attempt at the consecration, but insufficient.

If such divine favors were secured from three incomplete and unaccepted consecrations, what could hope to be seen if—once and for all—the consecration was finally accepted? [36]

Perhaps the world—it's fair to say—would see something quite phenomenal happen.

Perhaps it would witness the impossible.[37]

Perhaps the inconceivable.

And that it did.

It all is seen to have begun right after the Pope's Act of Entrustment of March 25, 1984.

To go with the bizarre military and nuclear setbacks in the Soviet Union and beyond, cracks started to appear almost immediately in the Soviet stranglehold of Eastern Europe.

In Poland, Hungary, and East Germany, strikes and labor disputes began to become constant.[38] In Romania, thousands demonstrated against Nicolae Ceausescu's personal dictatorship.[39]

In Czechoslovakia, hundreds of thousands signed petitions demanding more freedoms.[40] And in Yugoslavia—a country nonaligned with the Warsaw Pact—signs of nationalism and economic turmoil were again on the rise.[41]

Then, in the summer of 1989, partially-free elections were held in Poland and Hungary. [42]

Not long after this, one of history's most immortal series of political events unfolded in rapid succession. Like the Great Wall of Jericho, the Communist nations of Eastern Europe came tumbling down—one after another—with the pièce de résistance being the fall of the Berlin Wall in Germany.

On November 9, 1989, raw emotion, euphoria, and chaos erupted in Berlin. Before the eyes of the world, the greatest party Europe has ever seen took place.

And boy, it was some celebration.

Germany—sawed in two for decades—was suddenly one again. The end of World War II had finally come for the country. And Berliners, not sure of it all, could only smile and laugh, even the border guards, who were now—you could say—unemployed.

While President Ronald Reagan's 1987 speech in Berlin called on Soviet General Secretary Mikhail Gorbachev to "tear down this wall"—a 15-foot-high set of parallel barricade walls that physically and ideologically divided the city—not even the most optimistic soul could imagine this would happen. But now, just two years later, the 27-mile-long partition, which ran through the heart of the city for 28 years, was suddenly a relic of a bygone era.

Over time, Berlin had come to represent how the West viewed Communism. Never mind the stories of terror and imprisonment, of atheism and death that was life in every Communist nation. By the 1980s, the struggle against the Red Menace was very black and white. It was good against evil, life versus death. And Berlin, more than anywhere, showcased this reality.

In Berlin, the Cold War became theater—an espionage thriller—where a great drama played out daily. And to live with or without freedom was the plot.

Looking back, it's easy to understand why.

Berlin, the city of shadows—its storied Wall, its Checkpoint Charley, its Nazi remnants—perfectly captured the stalemate going on between the East and the West. And the notorious concrete partition became the ideal stage prop to contrast the two worlds.

Mile after mile, on both sides of the gray, graffiti-covered barrier, one could always picture pale faces lurking in the darkness, secret agents who were daring spies, and midnight deals involving microfilm and fake passports. From hot air balloons to hidden tunnels and secret compartments in the trunk of a car, the challenge of making it over, under, or through the Wall was what Berlin was all about.

The Cold War, and its dark side of Communism, was perpetually on display in Berlin. The emotional temperature of the city never rose above freezing.

Hope was alive. Hope was dead. In Berlin, it depended on the day of the week. The Wall gave off both messages. John F. Kennedy stood in front of the Wall and reminded the world that "we are all Berliners." Moscow parked some tanks behind it, warning of the folly of trying to become an ex-Berliner. Hope—springing eternal—was in a stare down with twenty-seven miles of despair in the moribund city.

For decades, though, there remained a kernel of faith—often on life support—that lived in the hearts of Berliners on both sides of the Wall. There was coming, these foolhardy souls liked to believe, an agreement, an invasion, an earthquake—*something* that was going to end that Wall.

Then, one day, the Wall was no more.

Overnight, it went from a concrete barbed wire barrier— formidable as the Alps were to Hannibal—to stacks of souvenir rocks piled up in stores across the globe. Hope had leaped from hundreds of candles melting at the base of the Wall to hundreds of feet dancing on it.

But that wasn't all.

The Iron Curtain—symbolized so perfectly by the Berlin Wall—suddenly came crashing down with it. [43] In what seemed like just moments, decades of totalitarianism were over.

Communist Eastern Europe, and then the heart of the Evil Empire itself—the Soviet Union—were relegated to what Reagan foretold: the dust bin of history.

The mighty power of Rome—forever threatened by betrayal within and barbarians at the door—took hundreds of years to waste away. The Soviet kingdom, at the peak of its military prowess and with a third of the world under its influence, collapsed overnight.

And for those who witnessed it all through the eyes of faith, its fate was sealed the moment Pope John Paul II consecrated the world to the Immaculate Heart of Mary.

Prayers—supplications lifted to Heaven from the heart—not weapons, brought down the Berlin Wall…then the Iron Curtain…and finally the Evil Empire itself.

In human terms, the end of the Cold War seems to have come about like a strategy concocted while playing a board game. It had no single author and fell into place through a chain of coincidences, extraordinary timing, and that invisible element called luck.

Brezhnev dies, Andropov dies, Chernenko dies—all men who had plotted the death of the Pope. In a reversal of fates, they, not the Pope, somehow meet their Maker in a span of less than three years.

Mikhail Gorbachev, a man with a massive, ominous-looking birthmark on his forehead, who is secretly baptized a Christian, assumes the reins of power in the Soviet Union. He introduces *"perestroika,"* which ends central planning and commences a policy of greater economic awareness and restructured labor efficiency. He implements "*glasnost*," a policy of more openness and transparency with political and social issues.

Reagan—the fox in the henhouse—watches and waits.

He launches Star Wars.

He collaborates with dissidents in Poland.

He becomes best friends with a Pope in the Vatican.

Patiently and cleverly, the ex-Hollywood movie star deliberately rattles and rattles the Soviet house of cards. Soon, a not-so-happy proletariat rises up and seals the deal. All of sudden, overnight, Lenin's utopian dream—morphed into a juggernaut of 140 million dead in less than a century—comes to a brake-screeching halt.[44]

It all officially ended, not surprisingly, on a string of very notable days.

On October 13, 1990, the anniversary date of Fátima's Miracle of the Sun, the first public Mass since the Communist Revolution of 1917 was celebrated in the iconic Cathedral of the Intercession of the Most Holy Virgin in Moscow's Red Square.

On December 8, 1991, the Feast of the Immaculate Conception, Soviet President Mikhail Gorbachev—the eighth and final leader—announced the dissolution of the Soviet Union.

On Christmas Day, December 25, 1991, Gorbachev relinquished power, and the hammer and sickle red flag of the Soviet Union is lowered for the last time.

On January 1, 1992—the Solemnity of Mary, Mother of God—the Soviet Union officially ceases to exist, replaced by fifteen new sovereign states, including Russia, which raises the prerevolutionary tricolor flag over the Kremlin.

The bloodless collapse of the Soviet empire was the will of God.

It came to reality though the intercession of the Virgin Mary—and through the response of people.

It came through mighty and powerful people like the popes and the presidents who knowingly or unknowingly cooperated with God's grace.

It came through little and humble people like the children in Fátima and Medjugorje who trusted the Virgin Mary's words.

And it came through the prayers and fasting of millions of faceless souls that kept hope alive—who proved the impossible was possible when one had faith.

Faith. Prayer. Fasting.

Christ said faith could move mountains.

The Virgin Mary said prayer and fasting could end wars.

The peaceful collapse of Communism in Eastern Europe and the Soviet Union was nothing short of a mountain that was moved.

And with it, the Cold War came to an end. [45]

CHAPTER FORTY-TWO

DEMOCIDE

*"For our struggle is not with flesh and blood but with
principalities, with the powers, with the world rulers of
this present darkness, with the evil spirits in the heavens."*
—Eph 6:12

"The world is at the turning point of history and the fate of
mankind hangs in the balance. Compromise with Marxist
countries and providing help and moral support serves
only one basic reality: greater strength for eventual communist enslavement.

We are in the last period of time sufficient to change the
course of history and inspire a cry to *"wake up!"*

Marxism finds in religion today invaluable allies in its quest
for global domination. The fantastic plan to turn the Church
into an instrument of Communist conquest would be unbe-
lievable if we did not see it happening before our eyes.

To have Catholics favorable to Marxism lends support
to the Marxist cause on religious grounds. Some even
present Jesus as the 'subversive man from Nazareth' and
are involved in organizations to help bring Marxism to
power...We must encourage the faithful to pray fervently
and promote the message of Fatima...Catholics must be
prepared to suffer martyrdom."

Cardinal Yu Pin,
Exiled Archbishop of Nanking

POWER *KILLS*, THE TITLE OF ONE OF PROFESSOR RUDOLF J. RUMMEL'S two dozen books, not only describes the substance of the book but Rummel's life's work.

Frequently nominated for the Nobel Peace Prize for his lifelong study of war, violence, and mass killing, Rummel is probably best known for exposing Communism's bloody trail through statistical evidence. He coined the term "Democide," meaning the synthesis of mass murder and genocide. Democide, he demonstrated, will often be found much more in non-democratic governments.

Rummel's work doesn't lie. He confirmed what the world witnessed and cannot deny. Marxist-Leninism, in its Soviet incarnation, brought hell on earth—before, during and after the Cold War. The researcher devoted fifty years of his life analyzing the morbid numbers to prove it.

In January 2002, *Inside the Vatican* published a letter-to-the-editor that Rummel wrote under the heading, "**MASS MURDER UNDER COMMUNISM**." The following is an excerpt:

> With the passing of Communism into history as an ideological alternative to democracy, it is time to do some accounting of its human costs.
>
> Few would deny any longer that Communism—Marxism-Leninism and its variants—meant in practice bloody terrorism, deadly purges, lethal gulags and forced labor, fatal deportations, manmade famines, extrajudicial executions and show trials, and genocide. It is also widely known that as a result millions of innocent people have been murdered in cold blood.
>
> Yet, there has been virtually no concentrated statistical work on what this total might be. For about eight years, I have been sifting through thousands of sources trying to determine the extent of democide (genocide and mass murder) in this century. As a result of that effort, I am able to give some conservative figures on what is an unrivaled Communist hecatomb, and to compare this to overall world totals.
>
> ...Of course, even though systematically determined and calculated, all these figures are only rough approximations. Even were we to have total access to all Communist archives,

we still would not be able to calculate precisely how many the Communists murdered.

Consider that even in spite of the archival statistics and detailer reports of survivors, the best experts still disagree by over 40 percent on the total number of Jews killed by the Nazis. We cannot even near thus accuracy for the victims of Communism. We can, however, get a probable order of magnitude and a relative approximation of these deaths within a most likely range.

With this understood, the Soviet Union appears the greatest megamurderer of all apparently killing nearly 61,000,000 people. Stalin himself is responsible for almost 43,000,000 of these. Most of the deaths, perhaps around 39,000,000, are due to lethal forced labor in gulag and transit thereto.

Communist China up to 1987, but mainly from 1949 through the Cultural Revolution—which alone may have seen 1,000,000 murdered—is the second worst megamurderer. [Rummel's total for the People's Republic of China, which includes his inclusion of those that perished in Mao's famine (1958-1962), is 76,702,000.]

Then there are the lesser megamurderers, such as North Korea and Tito's Yugoslavia...Pol Pot and his crew killed some 2,000,000 Cambodians from April 1975 through December 1978...In sum, the Communists probably have murdered something like 110,000,000. [Rummel notes this does include the estimated 30,000,000 of the Communist countries subjects that died in aggressive wars and rebellions that these nations provoked.]

How can we understand all this killing by the Communists? It is the marriage of an absolute ideology with the absolute power. Communists believed that they knew the truth, absolutely. They believed that they knew through Marxism what would bring about the greatest human welfare and happiness.

And they believed that power, the dictatorship of the proletariat, must be used to tear down the old feudal or capitalist order and rebuild society and culture to realize this utopia. Nothing must stand in the way of its achievement. Government—the Communist Party—was thus above the law. All institutions, cultural norms, traditions, and sentiments were expendable. And the people were as lumber and bricks, to be used in building the new world.

Constructing this utopia was seen as though a war on poverty, exploitation, imperialism, and inequality. And for the greater good, as in a real war, people are killed. And thus, this war for the Communist utopia had its necessary enemy casualties; the clergy, bourgeoisie, capitalists, wreckers, counterrevolutionaries, rightists, tyrants, rich, landlords, and noncombatants that unfortunately got caught in the battle...

The irony is that Communism in practice, even after decades of control, did not improve the lot of the average person, but usually made living conditions worse than before the revolution...

But there is a larger lesson to be learned from this horrendous sacrifice to one ideology. That is that no human beings can be trusted with absolute power.[1]

Professor Rudy J. Rummel,
University of Hawaii,
Kaneohe, Hawaii, U.S.A.

Dr. Rummel died in 2014, but his work lives on and can still be found on the University of Hawaii's website.

His name and his work will also live on in another way; Rummel is the man who put a face on "the errors of Russia."

CHAPTER FORTY-THREE

THE DIVINE PLAN

*"In all wisdom and insight, he has made
known to us the mystery of his will
in accord with his favor that he set forth in him
as a plan for the fullness of times, to sum up
allthings in Christ, in heaven and on earth."*

—Eph 1:9

A MIRACLE.
No word better described the mystery of Communism's overnight collapse in Eastern Europe and the Soviet Union.[1] Many voiced this causally, with no intention of implying the divine was at work.

But others meant it.

Not surprisingly, some delved into the personal lives and faith formation of the three principle participants involved in the drama: John Paul II, Ronald Reagan, and Mikhail Gorbachev.

Did God choose these three men?

Are there clues He was preparing them all along to bring down Communism?

Did the Virgin Mary play a discernable role in the extraordinary events surrounding them—a Pope, a President, and a Premier?

Raised a Protestant, Ronald Reagan's father was Catholic.

In November of 1904, his parents were married at Immaculate Conception Catholic Church in Fulton, Illinois. [2] Along with his older brother, Neil, Reagan was baptized on July 21, 1922, at 11 years of age. That day, the 40th President of the United States would say that when he emerged from the water he felt "called by God." [3]

It was a call Reagan immediately answered.

The future Hollywood star began attending the Disciples of Christ Church in Dixon weekly with his mother, Nellie. There, at age fifteen, he started teaching a Sunday school class and wouldn't miss a worship service in two years.[4]

Nellie—who is remembered as a living saint—imbued in her son her love of Christianity.[5] She especially taught him what guided her: a trusting sense that all things were part of God's plan—even the most disheartening setbacks. In the end, everything always works out for the best, Nellie told her son.[6] For Reagan biographers, this would come to be seen as the cornerstone of the man. From Nellie's Protestant influence would also come Reagan's love of Scripture, his spiritual confidence, his courage to speak the truth, and an indomitable trust in the providence of God.[7]

Reagan's sense of the mystery of God, however, came from his Catholic roots.

In a speech at University of Notre Dame in May of 1981, he talked about this side of himself. Recalling his 1940 movie, *Knute Rockne, All American*, Reagan said he felt almost mystical playing the role of George Gipp.[8] It was, he thought, the role that led him to understand what it took to attain the unattainable, to achieve the impossible.[9]

What it took, Reagan said he learned, was an indefatigable faith, one that calls on a person to persevere, to never quit—to go in there, as the Gipper put it, "with all one's got." [10]

It was this kind of faith that Reagan found in Mother Teresa of Calcutta.

The diminutive religious visited him at the White House on June 4, 1981, not long after his attempted assassination.[11] The visitation, it's believed, left an indelible mark on him and his faith.[12]

Mother Teresa told Reagan that day how she and her fellow sisters turned to God in a powerful way right after he was shot. The nuns, she informed him, stayed up for two straight nights praying for him to live.[13] The attempt on his life held a deeper purpose, she further enlightened him. "Because of your suffering and pain, you will now understand the suffering and pain of the world." [14]

The meeting humbled Reagan to the point of being speechless.[15] His Catholic roots were stoked. But the living saint wasn't done. Mother

Teresa touched on his Protestant, providential side, too: "This has happened to you at this time because your country and the world need you." [16] According to one biographer, the words proved transformative, leaving Reagan with an affirmation of a higher duty [17]—a confirmation of a divine calling—one he began to sense following the shooting.[18]

Not long after, Reagan discovered that Pope John Paul II experienced the same mystical intuition after he was shot.[19] On June 7,1982, the two kindred spirits met for the first time in Rome. They discussed their miraculous survival from the assassination attempts and agreed they survived for a reason.

Consequently, from that point on, the President and the Pope would share in this divine reality.[20] They believed in it. They talked about it. They stayed faithful to it.

It was known to them as the DP—the Divine Plan. [21]

The two leaders would come to share one other thing: the Virgin of Fátima and Medjugorje.

Ronald Reagan practiced no devotion to the Virgin Mary.

He was not acquainted with her apparitions.

But he is suspected to have crossed paths with Fátima during his Hollywood days.[22] Reagan was president of the Screen Actors Guild in 1952 when Warner Brothers released the movie, *The Miracle of Our Lady of Fatima,* [23] which according to one biographer, Reagan surely knew about.[24]

After he was elected President of the United States, Reagan surrounded himself with a number of Catholic aides: Al Haig, Bill Casey, Dick Allen, and Bill Clark; speechwriters such as Tony Dolan, Peggy Noonan, and Peter Robinson were also Catholic.[25] Some of them began to speak of Fátima with him.

Historian Tomasz Pompowski documented that one senior staffer, Bill Clark, a very devout Catholic, further expanded Reagan's understanding of the Fátima apparitions in two long talks and in some shorter conversations. [26]

Then, in 1982, Pope John Paul II presented Reagan with a book of interviews on Fátima from the Vatican Library.[27] Consequently, from all accounts, Reagan not only appears to have become favorable to the visions, but was motivated and inspired by them.

Ultimately, this was demonstrated to be true.

Speaking before *The Assembly of the Republic of Portugal* on May 5, 1985, the President addressed the subject of the apparitions and the world-renowned basilica at Fátima.[28] It would be the only time in Reagan's presidency he would publicly speak of Fátima.[29]

Recalling a conversation with Pope John Paul II, Reagan told the Portuguese legislators:

> I dared to suggest to him [that in] the example of men like himself and in the prayers of simple people everywhere, simple people like the children of Fátima, there resides more power than in all the great armies and statesmen of the world.[30]

Now, the mystical side of Reagan was taking hold.[31]

A few months later—right before his first meeting with Gorbachev in Geneva, Switzerland, on November 19, 1985—the President was handed some additional information on Fátima by speechwriter Tony Dolan, the architect of the 1983 *Evil Empire* speech.[32] Dolan presented Reagan with two rosaries that day—one for him and one for Gorbachev [33], and a memo explaining Fátima.[34] By then, said Dolan, Reagan knew all about Fátima because it was long a "part of the anticommunist movement." [35]

Then in June 1987, prior to a G-7 economic conference in Venice, Italy, Reagan met with his Ambassador to the Vatican, Frank Shakespeare. The ambassador remembers that Pope John Paul II wanted the President to better understand how the influence of Mary's message at Fátima shaped the Pope's perspective on the Cold War and Russia.[36] Through this understanding, Reagan and John Paul II shared, Shakespeare believed, an almost "mystical bond." [37]

Approximately six months after, on December 8, 1987, the Feast of the Immaculate Conception, Ronald Reagan and Mikhail Gorbachev signed the INF Treaty during a three-day summit held in Washington, D.C. The arms control agreement eliminated all of the two nation's land-based ballistic missiles, cruise missiles, and missile launchers within specified ranges.

At the time, the Pilgrim Statue of Our Lady of Fátima had been sent to President Reagan by Father Juan Villanova, chaplain of the Sanctuary of Fátima in Portugal.

"It was upstairs in Nancy's and my bedroom at the White House," Reagan later mentioned in thanking the priest, while he and Gorbachev "were meeting downstairs." [38]

One other point about Fátima and Reagan is worth noting.

Reagan, according to *Inside the Vatican*, will come to "suggest he has knowledge of the (Third) Secret" of Fátima, although the specific details of who he said this to—and when—were not cited by the periodical. [39]

Then, there's Medjugorje.

During the same 1987 summit with Gorbachev, President Reagan received a letter from Medjugorje visionary Marija Pavlović. The communique was sent to him through Ambassador Alfred Kingon, who visited the tiny village in Yugoslavia. Kingon was Reagan's Representative of the United States of America to the European Communities, an appointment known today as the Ambassador to the European Union. [40]

Born in Brooklyn in May 1931, Kingon was a businessman, investor, and editor before coming on board with the Reagan administration in 1982. [41] He was not a Catholic. In fact, he had no formal religious affiliation. [42] But he did harbor one strong spiritual interest: a sincere belief in the apparitions of the Virgin Mary. [43]

Over time, Kingon and his wife visited Marian apparition sites in Spain, Belgium, and Egypt. [44] His interest in Medjugorje—which Kingon thought was real and important [45]—came, once again, through Reagan's speechwriter, Tony Dolan. Dolan had traveled to the village in 1986 to pray for someone close to him that was ill. [46]

On Kingon's third day in Medjugorje, the ambassador met visionary Marija Pavlović and a young American girl named Kathleen Parisod. [47] Marija was speaking to a group of American pilgrims, with Parisod serving as her translator.

Shortly after, over lunch, a conversation developed between Kingon, Marija, and Father Svetozar Kraljević, among several others, concerning Soviet-U.S. relations and the upcoming talks on nuclear disarmament that December. [48] This led to Marija excusing herself and then returning with a letter that she handed to Kingon and asked him to give to President Reagan. [49]

Upon returning to Brussels on November 13, 1987, Kingon sent a package to the White House containing Marija's letter, as well as a written explanation of his own.[50]

Then, on December 6—the day before the nuclear disarmament summit was to start—Kingon received a call from the White House. Reagan had received the package and read Marija's letter.[51]

Several months later, in February 1988, the Croatian Catholic newspaper, *Sveta Bastina,* published the reported contents of the letter sent to President Ronald Reagan from Marija: [52]

> Dear President Reagan, The Blessed Mother appears every day in this small village of Medjugorje in Yugoslavia. She sends us a message of peace. We know that you do your best to improve the peace in the world and we remember you every day in our prayers. We want you to know that you can rely on our prayers and sacrifices. In this way we want to help you in your difficult task. Our Holy Mother said that with prayer and fasting even wars can be averted. May this message help you, and Mary's daily appearances be a sign to you also that God loves His people. United in prayer, in the Hearts of Jesus and Mary, we express to you our *Love,* and greet you with the peace of the Queen of Peace. [53]

After reading the letter, Reagan is reported to have remarked, "Now, with a new spirit, I am going to meet with Mikhail Gorbachev." [54] The President also asked Kingon for Marija's address in order to personally write back to her.

On Christmas Day, Marija received an autographed picture of Reagan, which said, "To M. Pavlović—With heartfelt thanks and every good wish. God Bless you. Ronald Reagan." [55]

While some accounts allege Reagan actually called Marija, and that Reagan made comments about Medjugorje at the summit ceremony, these events did not occur.[56] Kingon later said that it was *he* who called Marija.[57] Ambassador Kingon confirmed to historian Paul Kengor, however, that he later met with Reagan concerning Marija's letter and that the President told him he was "very moved." [58]

All of these events that involved the Virgin Mary while Reagan was in office must have moved him. At his funeral at the Washington National Cathedral in June of 2005, the famous Irish tenor Ronan

Tynan sang perhaps the most moving song in all of Catholicism, Franz Schubert's 1825 classic, *Ave Maria.*[59] It was a hymn Reagan personally chosen for his funeral a decade earlier, long before being afflicted with Alzheimer's disease.[60]

Mikhail Gorbachev's life came under the microscope with the fall of the Soviet Union.

Who was this man that oversaw the collapse of the Soviet empire?

Was it just his policies of *glasnost* and *perestroika* that led to the fall of Communism?

Or did it help that Gorbachev had a gentler side—a spiritual core—that allowed God to work in him and bring "the miracle?"

A proclaimed atheist, Gorbachev was not raised one. He was known, in fact, to have been secretly baptized into the Russian Orthodox faith by his mother and both grandmothers during the Stalin era.[61]

And, despite the government's strict frowning upon religion at that time, he grew up in a home surrounded by practicing Christians. Almost all of his family, he admitted, were "believers," [62] and he came to realize that their faith was important to them. [63]

Surprisingly, the Soviet Premier did not hide this spiritual history. Gorbachev liked to share that his grandmother read him the Bible as a child, [64] and that she displayed her Orthodox icons on an iconostasis across from a table that held his grandfather's portrait of Lenin.[65]

Curiously, he once noted, the home had on the wall—hidden behind the mandatory picture of Joseph Stalin—one very special icon: The Blessed Virgin Mary.[66]

Little is known about Gorbachev during the years he rose through the ranks of the Communist hierarchy. But somewhat of a curtain was lifted on his personal side once he secured the highest office. And, it's not unfair to say that his Christian roots started to show.

Gorbachev, as far as anyone could tell, didn't "sound" like much of an atheist. During their first summit in Geneva on November 19 and 20, 1985, Ronald Reagan noted right away that Gorbachev liked to utter remarks such as, "Only God knows" and "God help us." [67]

At one point, Reagan recalled the Soviet Premier told him that their two countries have never been at war and let us "pray God that it never happens." [68] That same evening, Gorbachev quoted Scripture in an impromptu toast at a formal state dinner.[69]

On December 8, 1987, Gorbachev was at it again: "I am convinced," he asserted at the signing of the INF treaty, "It is God's will that we should cooperate." [70]

Michael Reagan, the President's adopted son, wrote that Gorbachev talked about God's will all the time. "At each of their summits, my father would open with a prayer for guidance, and Gorbachev would close with the words, 'If it's God's will.'" [71] It is important to note, Gorbachev never tried to hide from these remarks, repeating them even in his 1996 book, *Memoirs*.[72]

As their Cold War negotiations developed over the years, Reagan repeatedly said that he felt Gorbachev was a "closet Christian." [73] Once, after an invigorating session, Reagan told aide Michael Deaver, "He believes!" [74] On another occasion, during a lively dinner conversation involving Reagan, Gorbachev, and their wives (Nancy and Raisa), the Soviet leader pointed to Raisa and said. "Ask *her*, she's the atheist." [75]

Almost immediately after assuming office, Gorbachev brought vast changes in the practice of religion in the U.S.S.R. He openly criticized the Soviet policy of atheism, saying it had taken a rather "savage form," that it had "waged war" on religion.[76] And he began to permit what was inconceivable just a few years before.

Christmas celebrations were now seen on television, priests were invited to participate in televised debates, clergymen were allowed on government committees, and the Bible began to be printed by the state.[77] Even American televangelist Robert Schuller broadcasted a sermon on Russia's lone television station.

In December 1989, Gorbachev traveled to Rome. There, he met privately with Pope John Paul II. In his brief remarks after, he again noted that all believers have a right to practice freely their religious life and satisfy their spiritual needs.[78] Some allege that during his conversation with the Pope, Gorbachev asked for forgiveness for the sins of Communism. [79] While that's probably a stretch, one Catholic historian, George Weigel, saw the meeting with the Pope as the "symbolic moment of surrender of Communism to God." [80]

Years later, during his *Hour of Power* show on October 22, 2000, Schuller interviewed Gorbachev. The Soviet Premier cautioned that people should not categorize nations into first rate and second rate because all nations are "God's creation." And, he added, "God knows what He's creating."

In another curious revelation from the show, Gorbachev told Schuller of a meeting between George H. Bush, Francois Mitterrand, Margaret Thatcher, and Brian Mulroney, in which they analyzed the end of the Cold War era. At the end of the meeting, Gorbachev recalled it was he that added a final word: "And, we must remember Jesus Christ."

Explained Gorbachev with regards to his permissive attitude towards religion,

"There can be no freedom without spiritual freedom, without human beings being able to choose." [81]

Questions surrounding Gorbachev's spirituality continued long after he left office.

Because so much has been written that contradicts his atheistic claims, some still suspected what Reagan argued: Gorbachev was a closet believer. Gorbachev has publically maintained his atheism, however, regardless of the skepticism.

But on March 18, 2008, another red herring arose with regards to this matter.

Gorbachev and his daughter, Irina, paid a surprise visit to Assisi, the home town of Saint Francis in Italy. There, the self-described atheist was seen on his knees in silent prayer for thirty minutes at the tomb of Saint Francis.[82] Witnesses that day were moved by his piety.

Father Miroslavo Anuskevic, a Lithuanian priest at the Basilica of Saint Francis, said he watched Gorbachev, eyes closed, praying anonymously alongside his daughter in silent meditation with very oriental intensity.[83]

"Francis is, for me, the *alter Christus*, the other Christ," Gorbachev said afterwards as he departed Assisi, "His story fascinates me and has played a fundamental role in my life. It was through Saint Francis that I came to the Church, so it was important that I came to visit his tomb... I feel very emotional to be here at such an important place not only for Catholics but for all humanity." [84]

Once more, Gorbachev's words created a stir.

News organizations the world over ran the story the next day: **"Mikhail Gorbachev Admits He Is a Christian,"** proclaimed a *London Telegraph* headline.[85] *La Stampa,* an Italian newspaper, labeled Gorbachev's behavior a "spiritual perestroika." [86] Some declared Gorbachev was "now a Catholic."

Within days, though, Gorbachev drifted back to his "I am an atheist" mantra. "To sum up and avoid any misunderstandings," an official statement released by him read, "let me say that I have been and remain an atheist." [87]

As one writer noted, however, after the Assisi incident, a man who talks like this and spends a half hour on his knees at the tomb of a saint "doesn't sound much like an atheist."

Mikhail Gorbachev assumed the leadership of the Soviet Union in March of 1985, exactly one year after Pope John Paul II's act of consecration of the world. From that moment, according to Sister Lúcia in a 1992 interview, Gorbachev "unknowingly was an instrument of God." [88]

As with President Reagan, sometime in the early winter months of 1988, Premier Gorbachev received a letter from Medjugorje visionary Marija Pavlović. The document was delivered to him at the Kremlin by Soviet Ambassador Anatoly Dobrynin, through the joint efforts of U.S. Ambassadors John Matlock and Alfred Kingon.[89] The letter, like Reagan's, sought to convey to Gorbachev the Virgin Mary's message of peace at Medjugorje.[90]

Was Sister Lúcia right in saying Gorbachev was an instrument of God?

Was the Virgin Mary influential with him in helping bring an end to Communism?

Perhaps the hidden icon of the Virgin behind the portrait of Stalin in his childhood home says it all.

For Karol Jozef Wojtyła, God was everything.

From his youth, the question of faith drove him. To Wojtyla, it became the first and ultimate reality. He believed man cannot exist without God, and that this truth is transcendent. Absolute truth and absolute moral values, therefore, led him to want to be a priest— and a strong fidelity to the Virgin Mary would be at the heart of his calling.[91]

Wojtyła devotion to Mary began as a child.[92] The future saint then drew closer to the Virgin after he lost his mother, Emilia, at the age of nine.[93] From that time on, he would seek the comfort of Our Lady of Perpetual Help at his local church in Wadowice.[94]

He and his father would also begin to make pilgrimages to the nearby Shrine of Kalwaria Zebrzydowska, particularly on the Feast of the Assumption. There, they would walk *The Way of the Cross* and ask Mary to help them cope with their loss.[95] At the age of ten, Wojtyla began to wear the *Brown Scapular of Our Lady of Mt. Carmel,* which he received at the shrine.[96] This, he said, taught him to rely on Mary's maternal protection.

Around age 20, he was introduced next to Saint Louis de Montfort's treatise on *True Devotion to Mary,* which teaches one to totally consecrate their life to the Mother of Christ. "I was already convinced that Mary leads us to Christ," he would say, "but at that time I began to realize that Christ leads us to His Mother." [97] Saint Louis de Montfort's book, he would later write, "was the decisive turning point in my life." [98]

Karol Wojtyła was ordained a priest on November 1, 1946.[99] Two weeks later, he began his studies at the Pontifical University of Saint Thomas Aquinas in Rome.[100] By then, he and the Virgin had become inseparable.

Now, he was pouring his heart out to the Black Madonna of Poland, who he carried with him in his heart wherever he went. The famous Black Madonna—or, the Icon of Our Lady of Częstochowa, which goes back to the 1300s—had become his source of strength during World War II and after the Soviets occupied Poland.[101]

Tragically, by now, the Virgin Mary was the only one he had left.

His parents were both dead, as was his brother. He also had witnessed many of his Jewish friends and their families taken away and murdered in the Holocaust.[102] All before turning 25 years of age. [103] Thus, it would be through Mary that he would overcome the many difficulties of living under Communism and ascend through the Church to the Chair of Peter in 1978, becoming the first non-Italian Pope in over 400 years.

On his first trip back to Poland, Pope John Paul II returned to the Shrine at Częstochowa. There, he made it clear the Black Madonna was and would remain his trusted guide.

"The call of a son of Poland to the Cathedral of Saint Peter," he said on June 4, 1979, "contains an evident and strong link with this holy place, with this Shrine of great hope. 'Totus Tuus', I had whispered in prayer so many times before this image." [104]

Totus Tuus— "*I am Totally Yours.*" This was John Paul II's maxim. He said it. He wore it. Now, he was turning to Mary to guide and define his papacy—both literally and symbolically.[105]

On December 7, 1981, a small but significant step to immortalize this reality took place. A mosaic of the image of Mary—*Mater Ecclesiae* (Mother of the Church)—was mounted on the façade of the Apostolic Palace overlooking Saint Peter's Square.[106] Carved at the base of the mosaic were Pope John Paul II's own coat of arms and his now famous motto.[107]

The Madonna would now keep a perpetual vigil over the Square, said John Paul II, because she "has always been united to the Church, and has always been felt as being particularly close during the most difficult moments in history." [108]

Of course, the Pope was thinking of his own difficult moment just six months before on May 13, 1981—the day he was shot in Saint Peter's Square. That day, the Madonna held him in her arms, as she is seen doing with Jesus in the radiant blue mosaic.

That day, the prophetic mission that was his destiny—Fátima— would become ingrained into his papacy by the shedding of his blood.

As Pope John Paul II recovered in the hospital in May of 1981, he requested to see the Bishop who had twice been secretly ordained in Czechoslovakia—first as a priest and then as a Bishop— Pavel Hnilica.[109]

Hnilica, who had been living in Rome for years, first met the young Wojtyła during Vatican II, and the two remained close.[110] The Slovak Bishop told John Paul II several days after his election to the Chair of Peter that God had chosen him for a great mission. Now, after the attempted assassination and his review of the mysterious third part of the Secret while recovering in the hospital, Fátima would become central to his thinking.[111]

The apparitions at Medjugorje would become part of John Paul II's thinking, too. And he saw the connection to Fátima: "Medjugorje is the fulfillment of Fátima," the Pope told Hnilica in a private conversation before the fall of the Iron Curtain.[112] On another occasion, Hnilica said John Paul II told him, "Medjugorje is a continuation of Fátima.

The world has lost its sense of the supernatural. It will find it again in Medjugorje."[113]

Medjugorje, the Pope seemed to be saying, was what was needed to push Fátima across the finish line. The worldwide movement of prayer and fasting emanating out of the little village in Yugoslavia—that John Paul II was rumored over and over again to be unofficially in support of [114]—was perhaps something he understood to be the spiritual straw necessary to break the camel's back, to bring to an end the Soviet empire.[115]

It is interesting to note that Lúcia once said that God would permit the collegial consecration of Fátima to be done when "a sufficient number comply with Our Lady's requests." [116] Great changes in the world, she told John Haffert of the Blue Army in 1946, "would definitely follow." [117]

Was it Medjugorje that finally helped secure that "sufficient number" to permit the collegial consecration of the world in 1984?

Did the international prayer movement that emerged from Medjugorje secure the downfall of the Soviet empire?

After the collapse of Communism was underway in Eastern Europe, Monsignor Angelo Kim—President of the Korean Episcopal Conference—seemed to reveal this had been Pope John Paul II's mindset in regards to the unfolding events. During his visitation with the Holy Father in Rome in the fall of 1990, Kim thanked the Pope for helping free Poland from Communism.

"No, not by me," John Paul II replied to Monsignor Kim, "but by the works of the Blessed Mother, according to her affirmations at Fátima and Medjugorje." [118]

At a conference at Notre Dame University in May of 1992, Ambassador Alfred Kingon spoke on whether or not he believed the Madonna of Medjugorje played a role in helping to end the Cold War, in helping to bring to fulfillment—through Ronald Reagan, Mikhail Gorbachev, and John Paul II—the Divine Plan:

> The Cold War ended. Communism began to manifest its inevitable decline. The Berlin Wall came down. What role did all of this play? Is it true that Mary defeated Communism? If

I've learned anything in life, I've learned this; the only will of God is love; all the rest are the choices of men... Our job is to surrender to God. And I think that's what happened.

All of us who pray. All who prayed responding to Mary's call, and all who proved in general allowed the inner calls, and the conditions changed, and men responded to the changed conditions. That was precisely the Marian message of Medjugorje.[119]

Kingon, the non-Catholic, maintained his belief in Medjugorje.

Interviewed years later by a journalist about Medjugorje, the ambassador asserted: "The whole world is going to change." [120]

Asked in Medjugorje if he knew anything about the changes taking place behind the Iron Curtain, visionary Ivan Dragićević replied at the time that we must conclude that people's prayers and fasting were successful. [121]

Ivan, like Kingon, then added, "The changes there are not finished." [122]

Leonid Brezhnev

Photo Credit: Ulrich Kohs (Commons:

Konstantin Chernenko

Photo Credit: Kommyhnctnyeckar

Yuri Andropov

Photo Credit: Tass (Designated

Mikhail Gorbachev

Photo Credit: Ronald Reagan Library

Pope John Paul II was shot by Mehmet Ali Ağca on May 13, 1981. They met in Rebibbia Prison on December 27, 1983.

Left Photo Credit: Vatican News, VA

Right Photo Credit: Keystone France / Getty Images

◄ Stanislav Petrov: the man who saved the
world in September of 1983.

Photo Credit: Queery-54

Pope John Paul II's consecration of the world on March 25, 1984.

Photo Credit: Vatican News

The Berlin Wall fell on November 9, 1989. Germany was reunited the following year.

Photo Credit: Lear 21 CCSA/ COM: CERT/ German Freedom of Panorama

Reagan spearheaded the effort that led to the end of the Cold War. Here he is with British Prime Minister Margaret Thatcher, a staunch ally. He claimed to know the 3rd Secret of Fátima.

Photo Credit: U.S. Federal Government

Bishop Pavel Hnilica consecrated Russia in the bowels of the Kremlin. He is seen here with the author and his family ten years later.

Photo Credit: Thomas W. Petrisko

PART IV

ONE SOUL AT A TIME

" Gradually it was disclosed to me that the line separating good and evil passes not through states, nor between classes, nor between political parties either—but right through every human heart— and through all human hearts."

Aleksandr Solzhenitsyn,
The Gulag Archipelago,
1973

CHAPTER FORTY-FOUR

"LET THE PEOPLE GO TO MEDJUGORJE"

"I will give you a new heart and place a new
spirit within you, taking from your
bodies your stony hearts and giving you natural hearts."
—Ez 36:26

I T WAS A FRIGHTENING DISCLOSURE.
   "The consecration of the world by Pope John Paul II and the bishops," said Sister Lúcia in an interview in Coimbra, Portugal, "prevented an atomic war that would have occurred in 1985." [1]

It would not be until 1993 that Lúcia made this shocking statement concerning the significance of the consecration in history.[2] Lúcia also explained that in no way was the consecration a cure all for the many woes of humanity, visible and invisible.

In short, though the immediate threat of nuclear confrontation between the East and the West was averted, the great struggle at hand was alive as ever, especially the spiritual war raging behind the scenes.

"Begin to work for God," Lúcia urged in the same interview with Cardinal Ricardo Vidal of the Philippines, "because now, the Devil is arising and working against God and all of His works." [3]

Lúcia's opinion appeared in harmony with the visionaries at Medjugorje.
This was precisely the situation.

By now, anyone aware of Fátima's prophecies could see that there was much ahead before humanity would see the foretold "era of peace." Both the unrevealed third part of the Secret of Fatima and the Ten Secrets of Medjugorje testified to that reality.

One thing, though, was becoming evident; it appeared that before anymore secrets were revealed, Mary would forge ahead at Medjugorje with her mission to bring the world to conversion—to bring to God whoever responded to her call. And more and more were responding.

Wrote Antonio Gaspari in the November 1996 issue of *Inside the Vatican:*

> When we speak of the fruits Medjugorje bears for the Church, even critics are silent. Today pilgrims—both Christian and non-Christian—arrive in Medjugorje from every corner of the world.
>
> With more than 16 million visitors, the site has become the scene of an exceptional spiritual revival. More confessions are heard in Medjugorje than in any other parish of the entire world; more than 150 confessors work without interruption here every day.
>
> In the year 1990, 1,900,000 people took Communion (more than at Fátima); 30,000 priests and bishops have visited the site. Many conversions are reported, even among those who come out of curiosity, or simply to accompany friends or relatives. In the USA, 600 Medjugorje prayer groups have been formed; in Austria 500; several hundred in Italy.[4]

By the spring of 1990, there were 10,000 confessions a day, 30,000 Communions at Medjugorje.[5] But the many conversions were not limited to the pilgrims coming to the village.

Throughout the world, there came countless stories of people being introduced to Medjugorje and experiencing a sweeping transformation. The apparition, wrote Laurentin, "reawakened faith on a global scale."[6]

"Conversion, then, is the basic message from Medjugorje," opined Father Svetozar Kraljević, in explaining the phenomena of Medjugorje throughout the world. "We can well conclude that the accumulation of sin is so intense that it has brought mankind to the brink of self-destruction. It is not within the means of man to fashion a system of protection that would save him from the fate that man is preparing for himself. God, nonetheless, offers the only option: conversion." [7]

These encounters with God—these life changing conversions through the Virgin of Medjugorje—were often extraordinary in nature.

Suddenly, without foreknowledge, everyday people would report "flash conversions." Swept, one could say, out of their old lives and into new ones, almost overnight. Many of these individuals, from every walk of life—often quite successful in their careers, businesses and professions—would then immediately want to help spread the message of Medjugorje.

This chain-effect evangelization through the newly converted would cause Medjugorje in the early 1990s to explode, taking it beyond what any renowned miracle in modern Church history had seen in so brief a period of time.

Was there a reason?

At Medjugorje, the Virgin is calling people without waiting for tomorrow, Laurentin felt, because "tomorrow will be too late." [8]

One of these flash conversions was a remarried Lutheran newspaper columnist and publisher from Myrtle Beach, South Carolina, named Wayne Weible.

After hearing about Medjugorje from a fellow Sunday school teacher, Weible's journalist curiosity took over. Within a day, he borrowed a videotape and a book on Medjugorje. He quickly consumed the book. Then he and his wife, Terri, curled up on the couch to watch the video. There, it happened:

> As I watched in fascination, I suddenly felt a strange sensation: someone—was speaking to me! It was not an audible voice but one that seemed to be within me. Incredibly, I somehow knew it was the Virgin Mary. I felt a numbing sensation throughout my being. Everything in the room seemed to fade away, until there was just me and what was happening on the television screen. And the voice within, with its

message: "*You are my son, and I am asking you to do my Son's will*" ...Unable to breathe, I managed to glance at Terri: had she heard it too? She was watching the screen, interested, but relaxed. I realized it was only happening to me...[9]

The Virgin, Weible revealed, told him that night to write about Medjugorje. This he says he was told would become his life's mission.[10] In just months, Weible assembled a series of columns he wrote on the visons into a small tabloid-sized newspaper and began to distribute it.

Before he knew it, millions of the papers were flowing out of Myrtle Beach to all four corners of the globe.[11] The soon to be ex-Lutheran found himself following them into hundreds of churches from America to Europe to Russia. Millions would hear his personal testimony about Medjugorje.[12]

Weible was not a one-man crusade.

From 1985 to 1995, there would emerge many like him. Each would bring a different calling, a different skill to the cause. The now-worldwide dissemination of Medjugorje was picking up steam. The cumulative effect of these chosen souls—who came from everywhere—is immeasurable.

One of the first visitors to Medjugorje from the United States was a man named John Hill.

Quite successful in life, Hill became convinced of the events in Medjugorje. Consequently, he opened up what he called the "*Center for Peace*" near Boston, which then distributed information on Medjugorje throughout the nation.

Around that time, there came Stan and Marge Karminski of Philadelphia. They had filmed the village and its ongoing miracles during their 1983 and 1984 visits. [13] After sharing a video with some friends, the Karminskis soon found themselves distributing tens of thousands of copies of the video throughout the country and beyond. Demand always exceeded supply, they discovered. The Karminskis' are called Medjugorje's "First Family of the United States" with Stan known as "the Father of Medjugorje in America." [14]

Across the state in Pittsburgh, came another husband and wife duo. Jan and Ed Connell, both lawyers, kept crossing paths with people telling them about Medjugorje. Convinced they needed to go, they returned determined to tell the world about Mary's urgent plea to all mankind. Using their many skills, a series of newsletters and books containing enthralling interviews with the visionaries were published, bringing the most intimate picture of the six children and their experiences to date. [15]

In Westmont, Illinois, another husband and wife team joined the cause. Larry and Mary Sue Eck decided after visiting the Marian shrine that an official magazine on Medjugorje needed published. Filled with photographs and stories depicting the many healings, conversions, and miracles pouring out of the village, *Medjugorje Magazine* added another dimension to the growing effort to evangelize the message of the apparitions.[16]

Down south, an Alabama organization known as Caritas of Birmingham began an effort that would span the globe. Founded by a man who preferred anonaminity, the organization would play a vital role in assisting visionary Marija Pavlović to donate a kidney to her brother, and with generating millions of dollars of relief aid during the war in the Balkans in the mid-1990s.

Overall, across the United States, the "Medjugorje Movement" took off. More than 200 Marian centers, often called Centers of Peace after John Hill's original center, sprung up across the country. [17]

There would follow annual Medjugorje or Marian conferences in cities like Chicago, San Diego, Pittsburgh, and South Bend. The organizers of these efforts arranged for group pilgrimages to Yugoslavia too, which soon saw millions more visiting Medjugorje—often repeatedly.

Released from prison in February of 1983, Father Jozo Zovko went from one-time opponent of the visions to perhaps its greatest advocate.

Most significantly, Jozo came to a profound understanding of the uniqueness of what was happening in the village. [18] Medjugorje, Jozo explained, was about Mary's call to *"real"* conversion.

"Medjugorje comes from Heaven. It is the pure gift of God," said Jozo. "This is why it was hard for me to accept it in the beginning. Unless a person wants to change, the message of Medjugorje is calling your soul a liar. Medjugorje calls you to give up all the presuppositions you brought with you and begin to approach things in a radically new way: the way of prayer. Medjugorje does not produce Pharisees…Medjugorje is about confrontation of the soul with God." [19]

This pure gift of God was not only for the laity. Church hierarchy were hearing the call and answering it—and not just by traveling to Medjugorje. Deeply touched by what they personally experienced, they lent their voice to Mary's effort in Medjugorje.

- "When I go to any shrine, I do not go to admire the churches or monuments; I sit in the confessional and from the confessions I hear, I can evaluate just how good the shrine is. I have been to Medjugorje; I did not seek out the visionaries or the priests. I just heard confessions for two whole days and this was enough to convince me that Our Lord is present in Medjugorje, and so is Our Lady." —*Bishop J. Carboni, Italy.* [20]
- "We have more conversions from Medjugorje than any place in the world! I don't recall in history anything comparable to the Medjugorje events."— *Bishop Nicholas D. Antonio, United States.* [21]
- "'By their fruits you shall know them.' Here, the fruits are so manifest, so clear and impressive, both in Medjugorje itself and among those who return home after a pilgrimage, that they simply cannot be ignored."—*Bishop Seamus Hegarty, Ireland.* [22]
- "I have noticed that the people who return from Medjugorje become apostles. They renew parishes. They form groups in which they get together and prayer groups. They pray before the Blessed Sacrament. They hold lectures, lead discussions and bring others to Medjugorje; and these circles, these prayer groups, spread out more and more. They renew the Church." — *Cardinal Giuseppe Siri, Italy.* [23]
- "The theology of Medjugorje rings true. I am convinced of its truth. Everything concerning Medjugorje is authentic from the Catholic point of view. All that happens there is so evident, so convincing… There is only one danger alone for Medjugorje— that people will pass it by."—*Cardinal Hans Urs von Balthasar, Switzerland.* [24]

Considered one of the greatest theologians of his age, Hans Urs von Balthasar never became a cardinal. He passed away two days before his investiture.[25] Nevertheless, he is often referred to as such in respect. He was the director of Pope Benedict XVI's doctoral thesis and his mentor,[26] and reportedly Pope John Paul II's favorite theologian.[27]

No official remarks are on record concerning Medjugorje by Pope John Paul II.

But how could there be? It would have been improper for obvious reasons. However, from personal statements attributed to him, the Polish Pope appears to have been not just favorable, but highly supportive of the appparitions there.[28]

As noted, this is a contentious subject since John Paul II never formally endorsed Medjugorje. But it is impossible to deny such an accumulated body of statements by him on Medjugorje from so many highly-placed Church figures and reputable news sources.

According to Irish theologian Michael O'Carroll, "Everyone in Rome knew how Pope John Paul II felt about Medjugorje,"[29] This was a fact Rome's many publications confirmed. Wrote *Inside the Vatican*: "It is common knowledge the Pope is sympathetic to the Marian site."[30] Said Vatican correspondent John Thavis, "John Paul II has a soft spot for Medjugorje."[31]

There was a reason for this.

Apparently, during audiences with the Pope, many bishops reported either going to or coming from the village. John Paul II would then quite often make a favorable comment to them about Medjugorje. Investigative author Randall Sullivan wrote that while he was in the Holy City, he met with top Vatican officials on the study of miracles. There, he found many curiously muted on the subject of Medjugorje. He eventually understood, said Sullivan, that this was due to the Pope's "undisguised sympathy for the devotions in Bosnia." A number of bishops, confirms Sullivan, privately reported the Pope to be "deeply moved by what was taking place in Medjugorje."[32]

In June 1986, twelve Italian bishops at a papal visitation addressed a question to the Pope: "Holy Father, what should we advise about pilgrimages to Medjugorje?" John Paul II replied, "I'm astonished at this question. Aren't you aware of the marvelous fruits it is producing? Let the people go to Medjugorje, if they convert, pray, confess, do penance and fast."[33]

The Archbishop of San Antonio, Patrick J. Flores, reported a simi-lar question and response given to him: "Let the people go there," the Pope told Flores, adding, "Go, and when you get there, pray for me." [34] Bishop Murilo Krieger of Brazil told the Pope of his three pilgrimages to Medjugorje. "Medjugorje is a great center of spirituality," the Pope replied. [35]

"Only good things are happening in Medjugorje," Archbishop Harry Flynn said John Paul II told him during his *ad limina* visit in 1988.[36] Bishop Michael D. Pfeifer of San Angelo wrote in his pastoral letter that the Pope spoke very highly about the village—how Medjugorje has changed lives, and that the messages are not contrary to the Gospel. [37]

It is a fact that Pope John Paul II expressed a personal desire to go to Medjugorje. "I want to go to Split, to Maria Bistrica, and to Medjugorje," he told a Croatian delegation in 1995 that included Croatia's Vice President, Cardinal Kuharic and a journalist named Ante Gugo. This story was published in the Croatian daily newspaper, *Slobodna Dalmacija* on April 3, 1995. [38]

Likewise, the President of Croatia— Franjo Tudjman—said John Paul II told him twice, "I also wish to come to Medjugorje." [39] This sen-timent was confirmed by Bishop Pavel Hnilica, who met with the Pope once a week and revealed John Paul told him, "If I weren't the Pope, I'd have been in Medjugorje already." [40]

In October 2005, six months after the death of Pope John Paul II, Marek Skwarnicki published a book in Polish of the letters he and his wife, Sophia, received from the Holy Father.

The book is titled, *John Paul II: I Send You Greetings and Bless You, the Pope's Private Letters*. In some of the correspondences, Pope John Paul II spoke of Medjugorje.

In a letter, dated December 8, 1992, the Holy Father wrote, "... I thank Sophia for everything concerning Medjugorje. I, too, go there every day as a pilgrim in my prayers: I unite in my prayers with all those who pray there or receive a calling for prayer from there. Today we have understood this call better." [41]

John Paul II writes on May 28, 1992, "...and now we every day return to Medjugorje in prayer." [42] On December 6, 1993, the Pope wrote of the war in the Balkans and of Medjugorje: "...I know that Sophia looks very much to Medjugorje and, of late, towards Ostra Brama, for the reason of her entire past. I, actually, was in Ostra Brama, I even quoted from Mickiewicz, there. I was not in Medjugorje but I also look in that direction. Please tell your wife about it. I look in that direction and it seems to me that one cannot understand today's terrible events in the Balkans without Medjugorje." [43]

Again, referring to the ongoing war in the Balkans, John Paul II writes on February 25, 1994, of Medjugorje's uniqueness: "...Sophia is writing me about the Balkans. I guess Medjugorje is better understood these days. The kind of "insisting" of our Mother is better understood today when we see with our very eyes the enormousness of the danger... I thank you because I myself am very much attached to that place. It can be there is only one such sanctuary in the world." [44]

Pope John Paul II was the "Pope of Fátima," wrote Giuseppe De Carli in the 'Introduction' to *The Last Secret of Fátima* by Cardinal Tarcisio Bertone. [45]

But was John Paul II also the "Pope of Medjugorje?"

Many believe so. He often expressed his faith in Medjugorje, according to Denis Nolan, an expert on the history of Medjugorje. [46]

Wrote Nolan:

> The late Cardinal Tomášek had made public the Holy Father's remark in his presence, "If he were not the Pope he would like to go to Medjugorje to help at the work with the pilgrims." [47] The Holy Father invited numerous priests and bishops to go there.[48] He received several of the Medjugorje visionaries, among them Mirjana Dragićević.[49] Upon visiting Rome in 1987 he spoke for 20 minutes with her in private [50]...He recognized the visionary Vicka, when she presented him with a rosary that had been blessed by Our Lady specifically for him. The Pope said to her, "Pray for me and I will pray for you," [51]

Nolan especially notes Pope John Paul II's message to the village during the war in 1992: "Tell Medjugorje that I am with you." [52] Around this same time, *Inside the Vatican* reported that during a meeting with the Superior General of the Franciscan Order, the Holy Father said to him,

"All around Medjugorje, bombs have been falling, and yet, Medjugorje itself was never damaged. Is this perhaps not a miracle of God?" [53]

Father René Laurentin, who repeatedly met with the Pope on Medjugorje, says John Paul II never showed "any doubt on the supernatural character surrounding the event." Laurentin recalled the Pope's words to a medical commission that determined the phenomenon of the visionaries' experiences were unexplainable. "The world is losing its sense of the supernatural," Laurentin writes the Holy Father said to the commision, "people rediscover it in Medjugorje through prayer, fasting and the Sacraments." The French theologian also emphasizes how the Pope's remarks that day were "recorded by the commission's secretaries." [54]

After March 1984—the month the Pope consecrated the world—the Virgin Mary's messages at Medjugorje appear to become more crystalized.

It would be that same month that Mary chose one of the visionaries, Marija Pavlović, to give a weekly message to the world.[55] Prior to then, the messages were either personal or confined to the parish and locale populace.[56]

She had come to Medjugorje, the Virgin explained in these "official" messages, to invite, to correct, to help humanity overcome the difficulties and temptations of its fragile existence—to help people "realize the divine light" they carry within.[57] The focus of many of the messages was now on getting to Heaven and the importance of understanding life in terms of one's infinite existence. Medjugorje, the messages showed, was just as much at home with eternity as it was with time: [58]

"I am your Mother and therefore I want to lead all of you to perfect holiness. I want every one of you to be happy on Earth and every one of you to be with me in Heaven. This, dear children, is the reason of my coming here and my desire." [59]

At Medjugorje, like at Fátima, the primary purpose of her intervention now became even clearer. Mary has come for the salvation of souls, to build holiness in the individual, and to nurture a passionate love for knowing God. [60]

Medjugorje, the Virgin's words showed, teaches us to live with an awareness that we exist on Earth temporarily; that one must always be prepared for the "end time" in this life. [61]

At Fátima, Mary showed the visionaries a scene from Hell. She spoke to them about going to Heaven. At Medjugorje, she goes a step further. She takes them to visit the celestial abodes.[62]

Moreover, she brings to life the full world of the eternal. She says "all will choose" their destination by how they live, and that this life is the only life given by God:

"It is false to teach people that we are re-born many times and that we pass to different bodies. One is born only once. The body, drawn from this earth, decomposes after death. It never comes back to life again. Man receives a transfigured body." [63]

While speaking of this world being the complete basis for life in the next, the Virgin brings to our attention the full drama of salvation. She speaks of angels and evil spirits who ceaselessly interact with us, either leading us to or away from God:

"I call on every one of you to consciously decide yourselves for God and against Satan.[64] You are ready to commit sins and to put yourselves in the hands of Satan without reflecting." [65]

Father Gabriel Amorth, an exorcist for the Diocese of Rome and the Vatican,[66] appreciated Mary's words concerning this uncomfortable but real spiritual dimension of human reality. Founder and President of *The Association of Exorcists*, Amorth performed more than 30,000 exorcisms in his sixty plus years before he died in 2016.

"Generally, it is the casting out of devils that is given first place among the Messianic signs when they are referred to in the Gospel," said Amorth. "At Medjugorje, too, among the other extraordinary favors granted by the Virgin, there are many reported cases of people freed from demonic possession." [67]

Added Amorth, "Satan hates Medjugorje because it is a place of conversion, of prayer, of transformation of life." [68]

Yes, Medjugorje, is a place of conversion—real conversion—of complete conversion. As Mary said, "Dear children, I am calling you to a complete surrender to God." [69]

So then, what is real conversion? What is complete surrender to God? Once called, how does one maintain such a change to their life?

Mary's words supply the answers:

- Complete Conversion: "Today I am again calling you to complete conversion, which is difficult for those who have not chosen God. I am inviting you, dear children, to convert fully to God. God can give you everything you seek from Him." [70]
- Peace and Reconciliation: "Live peace in your heart and in your surroundings, so that all may recognize the peace, which does not come from you, but from God." [71]
- Pray from the Heart: "Today I call you to prayer from the heart, and not just from habit." [72]
- Confession once a Month: "Make your peace with God and among yourselves. For that, it is necessary to believe, to pray and fast, and go to confession." [73] "One must invite people to go to confession each month, especially the First Saturday. I have invited people to frequent confession. Do what I have told you," [74] and "Monthly confession will be a remedy for the Church in the West. Whole sections of the Church could be cured, if the believers would go to confession once a month." [75]
- Frequent Mass: "Let holy Mass be your life," [76] "Jesus gives His graces in the Mass. Therefore, consciously live the holy Mass and let your coming to it be a joyful one. Come to it with love and make the Mass your own," [77] and "Come to Mass, the time is being provided to you." [78]
- Adoration of the Blessed Sacrament: "Unceasingly adore the Most Blessed Sacrament of the Altar. I am always present when the faithful are adoring. Special graces are then being received." [79]
- Fasting: "Fast strictly on Wednesdays and Fridays," [80] and "The best fast is on bread and water. Charity cannot replace fasting... everyone but the sick must fast." [81]
- Pray the Rosary: "Every day, pray at least one Rosary: the Joyful, Sorrowful and Glorious mysteries," [82] and "Let the Rosary always be in your hands as a sign to Satan that you belong to me." [83]

- Avoid Sin: "I want each of you to be happy, but in sin, nobody can be happy," [84] "I call each of you to begin to live as of today that life which God wishes of you and to begin to perform good works of love and mercy. I do not want you, dear children, to live the message and be committing sin which is displeasing to me," [85] and "Dear children, you are ready to commit sin, and to put yourselves in the hands of Satan without reflecting. I call on each one of you to consciously decide for God and against Satan." [86]

- Read Scripture: "I'm going to reveal a spiritual secret to you: If you want to be stronger than evil, make yourself a plan of personal prayer. Take a certain time in the morning, read a text from holy Scripture, anchor the divine Word to your heart, and strive to live it during the day, particularly during the moment of trials. In this way, you will be stronger than evil." [87]

- Read and live the Virgin Mary's Messages at Medjugorje: "I want you, dear children, to listen to me and live my messages," [88] "If you live the messages, you are living the seed of holiness," [89] and "I ask you to accept and live the messages with seriousness... Little children, each day, read the messages which I have given you and transform them into life." [90]

- Family Prayer: "These days, I am calling you to family prayer," [91] and "Today, I am asking you to pray, pray, pray. In prayer you will experience great joy and the solution to every hopeless situation. Thank you for making progress in prayer. I am grateful to all of you who have begun praying in your families." [92]

Mary's prescription for "complete surrender to God" encompasses all of these points being practiced on a regular basis. In the end, though, a deep conversion is founded on faith and prayer, especially prayer. Prayer, it was clear, was the hub of the wheel. Prayer was what was needed to change the individual—and ultimately, mankind.

The world—Mary's words were saying at Medjugorje—needed to see it was missing something—something lost that needed to be found, something it had to rediscover before it could hope to find peace.

The world needed, the Mother was making clear, to return its Father—God the Father.

"I am your Mother," Mary says at Medjugorje, "and I always want you to be closer to the Father," [93]—to know the Father, [94] to hear the call of the Father, [95] to be one heart in one Heart with the Father. [96] This was a call, the Virgin explained, that needed to go out to a world that did everything "without the Father," [97] causing it to "wander in darkness" [98] because it has "forgotten Him." [99]

But now, through faith and prayer—through real conversion—Mary was inviting humanity to find the peace it was searching for in its Father, to experience a new beginning in Him, a taste of Heaven on Earth. "The Father is not far away from you," the Virgin told Mirjana in 2011, "and He is not unknown to you." [100]

Medjugorje, Mary declared, was to be a path for this new beginning with Him:

> I desire for God's will to be fulfilled completely here; and that through reconciliation with the Father, through fasting and prayer, apostles of God's love may be born—apostles who will freely, and with love, spread the love of God to all my children—apostles who will spread the love of the trust in the Heavenly Father and who will keep opening the gates of Heaven.[101]

Heaven, the Virgin stresses at Medjugorje, is the goal.

Like at Fátima, it is the primary purpose of her intervention. Consequently, as Mary often emphasizes that God exists, so she emphasizes how Heaven exists—so much so that the visionaries were given a peek of the "Promised Land."

CHAPTER FORTY-FIVE

THE PROMISED LAND

"Let the children come to me, and do not prevent them,
for the kingdom of heaven belongs to such as these."
—Mt 19:14

THE PROMISED LAND.
This was the Hebrew desire and pursuit in the Old Testament that God ordained to be a foreshadowing of what should be every Christian's ultimate goal—Heaven.

Although early Christians embraced the basic tenets of a Jewish heaven, Christ provided a full revelation through His life and words. Jesus explained that not only was Heaven a place where God lived, but a special sanctuary prepared for His children:

"Come ye blessed of my Father, inherit the kingdom prepared for you from the creation of the world (Mt 25:34)."

Today, Catholics are taught to regard Heaven as a condition *and* a place of supreme beatitude. It is a condition because souls see the divine essence of God. They enjoy the "possession of God" in pure light.

It is a place because after the Resurrection, according to theologians, all bodies will need a place to exist. Jesus and Mary had earthly bodies that are now, the Church teaches, in Heaven.

Consequently, our faith implores us that the pursuit of Heaven needs to be our greatest longing in life, and while Heaven's location is not established, that does not permit us to ignore its existence.

Over the past two centuries, the Virgin Mary has made sure the faithful do not ignore Heaven's existence.

At Rue du Bac in Paris in 1830—the apparition considered by theologians to be the beginning of *The Age of Mary*—the Virgin Mary appeared to St. Catherine Laboure and spoke of "Heaven and Earth" and how "the Saints in Heaven" were interceding before the throne of God for her. [1]

In 1846, at La Salette, France, Mary told the two visionaries, Melanie Calvat and Maximin Girard, that Heaven closely "directed all things on Earth" and responded to the "cries of the oppressed." Mary cautioned at La Salette that there were mounting efforts to "deny the existence" of Heaven.

At Lourdes in 1858, Mary told the youthful Bernadette Soubirous, "I do not promise to make you happy in this world, but in the next." On her death bed, Bernadette muttered, "Heaven, Heaven," as she explained to those around her that she would not be denied Heaven because of "not longing for it enough."

At Fátima, the powerful vision of Hell given to the children illustrated the consequences of not attaining eternal life in Heaven. During the second apparition, Mary promised Jacinta and Francisco that they would soon "go to Heaven." This caused Jacinta to later remark, "I would enter a convent with great joy, but my joy is greater because I am going to Heaven."

Now, at Medjugorje, there is again no shortage of talk of Heaven. But this time, Mary has done more than just speak of the celestial abode.

She took two of the visionaries for a visit.

On November 1, 1981—All Saints' Day—Vicka and Jacov literally disappeared from Earth. They were taken, the two would come to reveal, to Heaven. [2]

Jacov's mother, Jaka, confirmed what happened.

The two kids, she says, mysteriously vanished into thin air right out of her house.[3] Immediately worried that the police had snatched her son again, the poor woman says she frantically searched her home and yard for twenty minutes. [4] Then, as suddenly as it began, it was over. Vicka and Jacov were found by her standing in the kitchen, back at home. [5]

Surprisingly, the moment he returned, Jacov explained to his mother that he hadn't wanted to go Heaven. He even tearfully begged Mary to leave him behind, to just take Vicka. [6] "She has seven brothers and sisters. I am an only son," little Jacov argued with the Madonna. [7] Unfazed, Mary told him not to be afraid, and off they went. [8]

To this day, Jacov does not say much about what happened. Heaven, he tells people, is a region of great light and happiness. [9] He remembers seeing many people praying, conversing with each other and appearing to be filled with joy. Words, he says, rob Heaven of its true splendor. [10]

Over the years, Jacov has been reluctant to reveal more, as the memory of Heaven remains bittersweet for him. At times, he associates his visit to Heaven with sadness, because he is still deprived of its permanent reality. Thus, he says he tries not to think about it. [11]

If he dwelled on Heaven too much, Jacov jests, he would die of loneliness. [12]

Vicka, on the other hand, holds no reservations. She joyfully relives her unique experience with others, eagerly recalling the inexpressible beauty as well as the multitude of angels and souls she beheld there. [13]

In his extensive interview with Vicka, Father Janko Bubalo asked the young girl to describe everything she could remember of the day she visited Heaven.

It all began that morning, Vicka told Bubalo. She and Jacov first traveled to Čitluk and returned to Bijakovići around 3 p.m. [14] After stopping at her house, they then went to Jacov's— where the Virgin suddenly appeared without notice.

"Praise be Jesus!" Mary greeted them and abruptly said she would like to take them to Heaven. [15] Both of them, she says, immediately became frightened, and Jacov started to cry. But before they knew it, Mary took Vicka by the right hand, Jacov by the left, and they slowly lifted upward toward the ceiling, together. [16] Suddenly, Vicka recalls, the house disappeared; they were off to Heaven. [17]

Once there, Mary began to point at different areas for them to gaze at together. Heaven, explained Vicka, was a very vast space [18] with no buildings or boundaries anywhere [19], filled with beautiful light, people, flowers, and angels—all radiating an indescribable joy. [20]

"Your heart," recalled Vicka, "stands still when you look at it." [21] She remembered a narrow tunnel that awaited people who enter Heaven, but was told nothing about it.[22] She did recall, though, that everyone would respond to the Virgin Mary as they would pass by. [23]

"Heaven is a big wide space, limitless," explained Vicka. "There is a glowing light that doesn't exist on Earth. I saw many people, and they are all very, very, happy. They sing, they dance…they communicate in a way unknown on Earth. They know each other from the *inside*. They wear long robes; I noticed three different colors, but these colors are not like the ones on Earth, they looked yellow, gray and red. There were about thirty people. They were all very, very beautiful. No one was too short or too tall. There was no one skinny, fat or suffering. They were all very good looking." [24]

Vicka says they saw these people walking, talking, and praying, with small angels flying above them. [25] Though the people spoke, she could not understand them.[26] Overall, she stressed, it's impossible to describe with words the great happiness in Heaven.[27]

But suddenly, as Jacov relayed, the trip to Heaven was over. In a split second, she and Jacov found themselves back in Jaka's kitchen. Feeling confused at first, she remembers that they were immediately discovered by his distressed mother. [28]

Ivan didn't go to Heaven, but he has seen it, and says it is worth any cost.

People there, he recalls, are happy and live in the fullness of God. It is better than anything you can imagine, [29] Ivan stresses, adding that life here is not the end.[30]

Ivanka reports that she saw Heaven, as in a picture. All she can say is it was beautiful— very, very, beautiful. She says she saw no homes, no trees—only people, who looked as though they had bodies and were wearing, as Vicka noted, robes. Everyone there was filled with a happiness that she cannot explain or forget. [31] Ivanka especially relishes the memories of the angels she saw there, who fascinated her with their radiating presence. [32]

Mirjana says she witnessed Heaven like a video or a movie that unfolded before her, although it didn't last very long.[33] In Heaven, recalled Mirjana, she saw happy, healthy looking people, both men and women.[34] The faces of the people radiated a type of inner light that revealed their joy.[35] Everyone in Heaven, she thinks, looked to be about thirty years of age.

Mirjana also remembers seeing people walking around a beautiful park. The trees, meadows, and the sky looked totally different than anything on Earth.[36] The grass and flowers were so beautiful, she emphasized, that it is impossible to adequately describe them. [37] While she could see the souls in Heaven, they couldn't see her.[38] But, she realized, they had everything they needed and wanted nothing. [39]

The visionaries at Medjugorje report being shown Heaven for a reason: to be a witness to its reality.[40] This was because many people on Earth, Mary emphasized to them, do not believe it exists.

"Heaven is a reward," Mirjana says the Virgin made clear to her, "for those who remain faithful to God to the end." [41]

CHAPTER FORTY-SIX

UNFULFILLED?

"See to it that no one captivates you with an empty seductive philosophy according to human tradition, according to the elemental powers of the world and not according to Christ."
—Col 2:8

ACROSS EASTERN EUROPE AND ASIA, NEW FLAGS—LIKE THE RED, white, and blue Russian banner now flapping over the Kremlin—heralded that freedom and independence were alive. But, like Cain and Able, the once sibling nations of the now estranged Soviet family did not exactly see eye-to-eye.

Nowhere was this more evident than in the former Yugoslavia, where by 1992, the Cold War would seem like the good old days. As with the Israelites circling in the desert, longing to return to the bountiful confines of their slave masters in Egypt, new sufferings made the yoke of Communism seem infinitely preferable.

Yugoslavia, with its historic cauldron of brewing hostilities, was a microcosm of an often angry Old World. Its ethnic groups—Serbs, Croats, Muslims, Albanians, Slovenes—possessed a legendary hatred for each other. The Virgin Mary's 1981 arrival in Medjugorje brought hope the fratricidal atmosphere would dissipate.

But it was not to be.

In 1991, declarations of independence in Croatia and Slovenia stirred a violent backlash from Serbia. Almost instantly, the former Yugoslavian army, under Serbian authority, set out to impose its will. For the umpteenth time, war broke out in the land of the Southern Slavs.[1]

Millions were driven from their homes. Towns and villages got shelled into rubble. Incidents of ethnic cleansing and rape, as well as the presence of mass graves, were reported by the hordes of refugees clogging the roads. Even the ancient fortress walls of the medieval city of Dubrovnik became pockmarked with over 2000 shell holes.

By 1995, 100,000 lay dead with two million displaced before a U.S.-brokered peace settlement finally took hold in November that year. [2]

The former Yugoslavia was just one of a lengthy list of new clashes during the 1990s. The many struggles arising in Eastern Europe, the former Soviet Union, and across the globe threw cold water on any ideas that Fatima's prophesied era of peace was imminent.

A partial register of the conflicts over the decade sets the scene:

- 1991-Gulf War, 55,000 dead.
- 1991-92-South Ossetia War, 1,000 dead, 125,000 refugees.
- 1991-93-Georgian Civil War, 20,000 dead, 260,000 refugees.
- 1991-97-Algerian Civil War, 150,000 dead.
- 1991-02- Sierra Leone Civil War, 50,000 dead.
- 1991-19 Somali Civil War, 300,000-500,000 casualties.
- 1992-Transnistria War, 1,000 dead, 3,000 wounded.
- 1992-East Prigorodny Conflict, 650 dead, 99,000 refugees.
- 1992-93-Abkhazia War, 35,000 dead, 250,000 refugees.
- 1993-05-Burundian Civil War, 300,000 dead.
- 1994-96-First Chechian War, 90,000 dead, 500,000 displaced.
- 1994-Yemeni Civil War, 7,500 dead.
- 1994-97-Iraqi-Kurdish Civil War, 5000-8000 dead.
- 1997-Albanian Civil War, 2,000 dead.
- 1998-00-Eritrean Ethiopian War, 300,000 dead.
- 1998-99-Kosovo War, 13,500 dead, 1,500,000 displaced or refugees.
- 1999-09-Second Chechen War, 150,000 to 250,000 dead. [3]

One conflict deserves special attention since it bears undeniable similarities with Medjugorje: the ghoulish genocide hatched in Rwanda; an ungodly nightmare that even visionary Mirjana Dragićević Soldo writes about in her book. [4]

Rwanda lies in the center of Africa, 750 miles from the nearest sea. The original natives were pygmies. They were followed by the Bahatu tribe, who sought to escape the advancing Sahara Desert. By the sixteenth century, the Nicotes arrived with great herds of cattle. Eventually, the territory became settled by Europeans, and by the twentieth century, Rwanda passed from German to Belgium hands and finally garnered independence on July 1, 1962. Today, it is home to about nine million.[5]

Rwanda is coined the Switzerland of Africa because of its emerald green hills and white-tipped mountains.[6] But after the 1990s, it became more known for its bloody red rivers that swept along the bodies of the many who perished in the mother of all massacres.

In the spring of 1994, during the same period the war in the Balkans erupted in Eastern Europe, the worst genocide since World War II took place in Rwanda.

One ethnic group, the Hutus, sought to eradicate another, the Tutsis. And they almost did.

By the time the conflict ceased—in less than 100 days—800,000 to 1 million Tutsis had been gored to death,[7] mostly by machete.[8] Hundreds of thousands were left maimed. Countless succumbed to disease. Throughout central Africa, millions paraded in refugee columns that grew to be miles in length.[9]

At the time, the media could make no sense out of it. To better express the evil that the tragedy evoked, secular journalists incorporated spiritual language.

"Hell On Earth," declared the cover of *Newsweek Magazine*.[10] Proclaimed *Time Magazine,* **"There Are No Devils Left in Hell…They Are All in Rwanda."** [11] Wrote *Time:* "Rwanda serves as a modern laboratory for anyone trying to figure out which factors will matter and which will not in the pursuit of peace." [12]

One factor in the pursuit of peace was not mentioned: The Queen of Peace.

Apparitions of the Virgin Mary began in Rwanda in 1981, the same year, once again, as Medjugorje.[13] Mary came to a region known as Kibeho, where she warned six young boarding school girls and a pagan boy, by word and vision, of an approaching holocaust.

One graphic vision lasted eight hours. It revealed a nightmarish future: rivers and lakes of blood, people murdering one another, abandoned corpses without heads, dead babies everywhere.[14]

"I am talking to the world," Mary pleaded to Anathalie Mukamazimpaka, one of Kibeho's visionaries, "but you do not understand." [15]

Rwanda's Bishop Gehany granted an initial sanction of the visions on August 15, 1988.[16] Thirteen years later, on June 29, 2001, the Catholic Church fully approved the apparitions.[17]

"Now we can say," reflected Bishop Augustin Misago of Gikongoro on the twenty-fifth anniversary of the Kibeho visions, "that this (the apparitions) was a prediction of the tragedy of Rwanda." [18]

As Mary remarked to Anathalie, it was a message Misago stressed was "for the whole of humanity." [19]

Why such an avalanche of wars starting in the early 1990s? If Pope John Paul II's 1984 consecration of the world was accepted by God, wasn't an "era of peace" to follow?

The question was put to Sister Lúcia:

"Tell them that the wars that are occurring now in Russia and in the world are civil wars and not world wars. It is a normal pattern. And the Virgin did not refer to these wars…the Virgin only referred to the wars that were being promoted by the errors of Russia…spread all over the world." [20]

Regardless of the consecration, Lúcia explained, wars were still part of the landscape. But, the recent bloodshed was no longer related to the spread of communism. Likewise, Pope John Paul II's Act of Entrustment was not to be taken as a harbinger that the era of peace had arrived. "The Triumph," the 86-year-old nun firmly established, is an "ongoing" process. [21]

At the time, the Fátima visionary's words were intended to smooth over some percolating doubts about the consecration's efficacy, as well as any improper expectations in its aftermath.

But instead, Lúcia's remarks sparked more controversy.

The interview—given in Coimbra, Portugal on October 11, 1993, to his Eminence Ricardo Cardinal Vidal of the Philippines and ten others [22]—brought almost an immediate backlash of negative comments and inflammatory accusations that gathered traction in the secular and Catholic media. [23]

Some insisted the 1984 consecration, since it failed to mention Russia, was incomplete, regardless of what Lúcia said.[24] Others said that the much-publicized meeting of Vidal with Lúcia did not actually take place.

One dissent went so far as to suggest that a "fake Lúcia" held the interview. [25] Even Carlos Evaristo, the Portuguese translator that day—who later published a book about the lively controversy—was accused of fraud.[26]

For better or worse, the entire affair ended up almost an historical event on the Fátima timeline. [27]

Lúcia's explanation, however, was without acrimony.

The Entrustment was accepted. Regardless of all the ruckus, despite it not being exactly what the Virgin requested, it was valid. History, she patiently pointed out, proved it. Lúcia told Vidal:

> It's true. God uses every stone, even the atheist Communists that were fighting the most against everyone. They changed from one moment to another, without conditions, or protests, and without contestation. This is an act of God! A great miracle! It is a conversion. It proves the mercy of God and the love of God for mankind...

> We were at the beginning of a nuclear war and all of a sudden these projects that the nations had—the United States against Russia—that were on the verge of exploding the whole world—from one moment to another.

> At the moment the Holy Father made the consecration, these projects of war changed. And these projects of war changed into projects of peace. This is not natural! These projects to terminate everything have now changed into projects to liberate! [28]

Sister Lúcia never veered from this position. Everything that happened surrounding the collapse of Communism after the 1984 consecration was miraculous. In her opinion, one had to be blind to the power of God to *not* see the evidence. In a book published years later, Lúcia polished her account of how the consecration ended the Cold War:

> It is well known to all that this was one of the most critical moments in the history of humanity, when the great powers, hostile to each other, were projecting and preparing for a nuclear atomic war that would destroy the world, if not all, for the most part, with what chances of survival? And who would be able to dissuade these men to change all this to the contrary? Asking for a meeting in order that an embrace of peace may happen? Changing their plans from war into plans of peace?
>
> Who but God was able to act on these intellectuals, these wills, these consciences in order to lead them to such an exchange, without fear, without fear of opposing revolts? Of yours or foreigners? Only the power of God, who acted in all, caused them to accept in peace, without riots, or opposition, and without conditions. [29]

The fall of the Soviet empire brought liberation.

Besides basic human rights, individuals now had political and economic freedom. Most of all, with the cessation of government promulgated atheism, there came religious liberty. The right to convert, to worship, to choose a religion—was now a choice.

With regards to Fátima, however, clarification of another issue arose.

Many believed the "conversion of Russia"—spoken of by Mary in the second part of the Secret—meant "a conversion to Catholicism." [30] Even Father Joaquin Alonso, Fátima's official documentarian, wrote so. [31]

Now, to the surprise of many, Lúcia said this was *not* what the Virgin Mary intended her words to mean. The visionary addressed this issue in an interview with another prince of the Church, his Eminence Anthony Cardinal Padiyara of India, on October 11, 1992:

"Has the conversion of Russia then taken place?" Lúcia was asked by the official translator.

"Yes, the news speaks for itself."

"Is the conversion of Russia not interpreted as the conversion of the Russian people to Catholicism?"

"Our Lady never said that. There are many misinterpretations around. The fact is that Russia, the Communist, atheistic power, prevented people from carrying out their faith. People now have an individual choice to remain as they are or to convert. This they are now free to do, and many conversions, in fact, are taking place..." [32]

These volatile issues surrounding Fátima—an outbreak of new wars; the missing "era of peace;" the consecration of the world, not Russia; the true meaning of the conversion of Russia—along with the still veiled contents of the Third Secret of Fátima—kept a contentious storm swirling around Lúcia throughout the early 90s.

And it is easy to see why.

The issues all seemed to be signs of contradiction that the Pope's "Entrustment" had been completely fulfilled. [33] And, much of this also seemed to be hinting that Marxist-Leninism had not gasped its last breath.

Was there an explanation to help make sense of it all?

The Entrustment of the World by Pope John Paul II on March 25, 1984, was a watershed moment. It finally fulfilled—to the best of the Church's ability—the request Mary made at Tui in 1929 and her original words at Fátima in 1917. [34] But it was understood as far back as October 1940—when the consecration of the world, not Russia, was first discussed—that this might bring less of the promised response by Heaven. [35]

The consecration of Russia by the Pope and the bishops was designed, according to Mary's words at Fátima, "to prevent this." This meant "to prevent" the Marxist-Leninist revolution from "spreading"—to stop what Mary warned Russia's "errors" would bring throughout the world: wars, martyrdom, and the persecution of the Church and the Holy Father. [36]

Anything less undertaken could be expected to obtain less. [37]

And, in the end, less *was* undertaken.

Without a doubt, the consecration was not executed in the manner requested. This fact weighed on Pope John Paul II's mind.

In a 1990 interview with Cardinal Paul Josef Cordes, the Vice President of the Pontifical Council of the Laity and a close friend of the Pope, Cordes tells how John Paul spoke of this to him:

> It was 1984, and during a private lunch with the Pope, I spoke of the consecration he had done, I recall that he thought, sometime before, of mentioning Russia in the prayer of benediction. But at the suggestion of his collaborators he had abandoned the idea. He could not risk such a direct provocation of Soviet leaders. I also recall how this renunciation of the public benediction of Russia weighed heavily on him.[38]

Fátima author Antonio Socci concurred. He emphasized in his 2006 book, *The Fourth Secret of Fatima*, that the consecration of 1984 *was* definitely valid, but indeed, John Paul knew it could not be expected to deliver all it was once intended to bring:

> This does not mean that the Consecration of 1984 was not accepted by Heaven and has not obtained its beneficial effects, but the Pope knew from the first—and said so—that it was not the consecration requested at Fátima, and that it would *not* be able to have the effects promised there by the Madonna.[39]

Furthermore, the vast amount of time it took for the consecration to be finally performed—to whatever level of acceptance—could in no way be perceived as anything but also detrimental to the outcome.[40]

This reality is indisputable.

By 1984—some six decades after the fact—much had transpired, most of which being the pernicious spread of Marxism. And, not just in the form of Communism. Time had, indeed, taken its toll.

Fátima expert Father Andrew Apostoli reflected on this reality:

Unfortunately, various factors contributed to delaying the consecration of Russia to Mary's Immaculate Heart. This delay allowed Russia to spread her "errors" around the world, causing the great evils Our Lady warned us about. [41]

Shortly after the 1984 consecration, Sister Lúcia was asked by Father Luis Kondor, the Postulator of the Cause of the Beatification of Francisco and Jacinta, if the consecration was done as requested.[42]

It was done, Lúcia confirmed, but added it was "*too late.*" [43]

Kondor then asked Lúcia what would signal God's acceptance of the consecration and the fulfillment of the promises it carried.

"Look to the East," Lúcia replied.[44]

Lúcia appears to reveal two understandings in this response.

The first is that she has a certain degree of awareness that a geopolitical change was coming shortly in the *East*, as fulfilled with the fall of Communism in Eastern Europe and the Soviet Union.

Secondly, by affirming the consecration was done in an acceptable manner, but was *too late*, Lúcia reveals that she is aware that Marxist atheism—the errors of Russia—will carry on in ways beyond the collapse of the Soviet empire.

Lúcia also spoke of this in her 1993 interview with Cardinal Vidal: "Atheism…Atheism still exists…Everything referring to materialism spreads from atheism, from Marxism." [45]

When examined, Lúcia's history surrounding this issue perhaps reveals a latent awareness of this coming scenario. In her 1946 meeting with historian William Thomas Walsh, Lúcia acknowledged the world would eventually be intoxicated with the plague of Marxism if the consecration of Russia wasn't performed in an expeditious and proper manner.

Did this mean that "every country, without exception," would be overcome, Walsh asked her that day in 1946.

"Yes," Lúcia replied.[46]

Released on May 1, 1991, Pope John Paul II's encyclical, *Centesimus annus*, examined the collapse of Communism.

The Pope saw that fundamental anthropological errors were at its core. Communism, he writes, held a false vision of human nature and society. These errors gave rise to misleading economic and political solutions.

But Marxist atheism, the Pope noted, was at the root of the problem and remained a danger. [47]

Two weeks later, John Paul II visited Fátima again.

There, he warned that the heart and soul of Communism—atheism—was still alive and busy at work in the post-Soviet world. If not vigilant, a challenge from another form of this same intrinsic evil would befall humanity.

The Pope called that day on the Virgin Mary once more:

"The danger to substitute Marxism with another form of atheism exists, which by flattering the liberty tends to destroy roots of human and Christian morality. Nations who have recently acquired their liberty and now are engaged in constructing their future, need you." [48]

CHAPTER FORTY-SEVEN

A PANDEMIC OF ATHEISM

"Fools say in their heart, 'There is no God.' Their deeds are loathsome and corrupt; not one does what is right."
—Ps 14:1

"GOD IS DEAD," HERALDED GERMAN PHILOSOPHER FRIEDRICH Nietzsche in 1882. [1]

Nearly a century later, *Time* magazine revisited the subject.

"Is God Dead?" the weekly publication inquired in its famous April 8, 1966, issue, plastering in oversized red letters the provocative question across its cover. [2]

Nietzsche incorporated the phrase in a figurative way to convey his conviction that the Enlightenment killed any real possibility of the existence of God. Over time, however, his proponents altered his words to mean that the Christian God who once existed has ceased to exist.[3]

Time's iconic piece was intended to deliver a different message.

The evils of earth were so many and terrible that if God wasn't literally dead, He was—by His inaction to stop the atrocities of the 20th century—irrelevant.[4]

"As always," argued *Time*, "faith is something of an irrational leap in the dark, a gift of God. And, unlike in earlier centuries, there is no way today for churches to threaten or compel men to face that leap; after Dachau's mass sadism and Hiroshima's instant death, there are all too many real possibilities of Hell on earth." [5]*

---

* On April 15, 2022—Good Friday—*The New York Times* published an Op-Ed in favor of atheism titled, "In This Time Of War, I Propose We Give Up God." Author Shalom Auslander argued that God is responsible for "war and violence," and for "oppression and suffering," suggesting that people stop teaching children about Him. "If He were mortal, the God of the Jews, Christians, and Muslims would be dragged to the Hague. And yet we praise Him." Perhaps now, wrote Auslander, "is a good time to stop emulating this hateful God."

Hell on earth—some have written—is what you get when those who declare God deceased conjure up plans to manage the planet in His steed, such as the Freemasons commenced centuries ago.

With the Protestant Reformation of the sixteenth century came the hope of fraternal organizations for an even greater reformation, a reformation of the world— "a new world order." [6]

It would be an order centered on the power of the state, where the importance of family, property, and religion would be minimalized. [7] No more divine laws, no pesky virtues. Morality, patriotism, and freedom were also found missing in their vision of tomorrow. But, they boasted, paradise on earth would arise.

"There is one main dogma of Freemasonry, there is one religion, only one true, only one natural; the religion of humanity," wrote Henri Delassus, a French theologian from the late 19th and early 20th century who worked tirelessly to expose and condemn the goals of the Freemasons.[8]

This hope of the wicked—birthed in secret societies dedicated to social change through financial control and war—would be denounced for centuries by the Church. By the time Mary appeared at Fátima in 1917, eleven Popes—Clement XII, Benedict XIV, Pius VI, Pius VII, Leo XII, Pius VIII, Gregory XVI, Pius IX, Leo XIII, Pius X and Benedict XV—condemned efforts of Masonic societies to bring an anti-Christian, atheistic civilization.[9]

"Tear away the mask of Freemasonry," wrote Pope Leo XIII in *Humanum genus* in 1884 in response to Marxism, the industrial age, and the radical changes taking place in Italy and Europe, "make plain to all what it is. It aims at the utter overthrow of the religious order of the world which Christian teaching has produced, and the substitution of a new state of things—based on the principles of naturalism." [10]

Communism, the child of the secret societies and condemned by so many popes, fulfilled this dream when it seized hold of Russia in 1917.[11] By the 1930s, Pope Pius XI declared its roots were undeniably spiritual, labeling it "intrinsically evil." [12]

In *Divini Redemptoris*, he confronted the true origin of the atheistic cancer metastasizing everywhere: "There is another explanation for the rapid diffusion of the Communist ideas now seeping into every nation great and small, advanced and backward, so that no corner of the earth is free from them... It's directed from one common center... It is Satan's army on earth. It is in a certain sense Satan himself, the adversary of God and the children of God." [13]

"Atheistic Communism," stated Bishop Pavel Hnilica, referring to Pius XI's words in an address delivered almost fifty years later on July 24, 1988, at Marienfried, Germany, "surpasses all previous persecutions in the Church—even that of Nero or Diocletian—not only in its extent, but also in its violence. The whole world is threatened with falling back into a barbaric state, a state worse than before Christ came...

"The hour of the battle against God is the hour of Mary." [14]

At Fátima on May 13, 1917, the hour of Mary officially commenced.

Mary came to Fátima to confront atheism, systematic, Marxist atheism.

Even before her apparitions that year, the first appearance of the angel at Fátima in the spring of 1916 to the three children revealed the focus of her coming mission.

The prayer the children are taught by the angel, "My God, I believe, I adore, I hope and I love you. I beg pardon for those who do not believe, do not adore and do not love you," is understood by theologians to be an "anti-atheism" prayer.[15] It is recognized as the opening overture in the great counter attack of Mary to come at Fátima against an implacable atheism about to be let loose on the world.

Mary knew that a systematic godlessness—after centuries of formulation—was on the verge of becoming operational in Russia. The Virgin's plan, as revealed to the three shepherd children, was to head the danger off at the pass, to contain the plague before it spread.

But such was not to be.

Militant Communism, the *first* of the "errors" Mary foresees emerging in Russia, breaks out and spreads rampant for decades. Finally, in 1984, Pope John Paul II brings the runaway train of Soviet totalitarianism to a halt. In essence, the Church, through the consecration of the world, administers a punishing, supernatural blow to the antichurch.

But the contagion of Communism had already slipped away from the scene of the crime by then. Like a virus that reproduces by injecting its genetic material into a host cell and then dividing, causing a new virus in a new form, the lifeblood of Communism— atheism—survives, having long before split itself and burrowed into the cultures of the world.

There, concealed in a new host, it secures a place in the hearts of the people as opposed to the halls of the government.

Father David Bellusci, Ph.D., a professor of Theology and Philosophy at Catholic Pacific College, succinctly captured in an article what is now well understood as being "Cultural Marxism," a tentacle of the "errors of Russia":

"The Virgin Mary warned (at Fátima) of 'Russia spreading its errors throughout the world," noted Bellusci, "'causing wars and persecution' of the Church... Was Mary's warning only in reference to the "hard" Communism of military intervention? Or did it also relate to "soft" Communism, now referred to as "Cultural Marxism?"

"(Cultural Marxism) goes much further than barricades, army tanks and barbed wire fences characterizing Communist regimes... Cultural Marxism paves the way to social reconstruction through imposed change; the state imposes on its people how to think, and if one disagrees there are consequences...it brings to completion what began with the "Enlightenment." **

Cultural Marxism (Known also as Neo-Marxism, Post Modernism, New Faith, and more.)—the "errors of Russia" that inflame societal engineering today—is the application of Marxist theory to culture. It is, in principle, akin to its dogmatic predecessor; it views western culture as the key source of human oppression, as Marx viewed western capitalism.

Cultural Marxism, however, is at the same time different.[16]

It is harder to identify, more difficult to read. It has no single gospel or master blueprint. It has no supreme plan of action, no lineage of iconic sages. But its ultimate objective is the same as Communism—to make the mind, body and soul a slave to atheistic ideology in order to build an atheistic reality.

Repackaged by 20th century philosophers grasping to creatively expound on Marx and Nietzsche, Cultural Marxism espouses the tenets of naturalism, humanism, and materialism and is the nucleus of many contemporary social/political doctrines and a host of ascendant, atheistic fermented ideologies, such as critical race theory, wokism, cancel culture, group think, sexual and gender ideologies, and countless more.

** Father David Bellusci, OP, "Mary Is the Answer to the Question of Cultural Marxism," December 2, 2017, https://bccatholic.ca/voices/fr-david-bellusci-op/mary-is-the-answer-to-the-question-of-cultural-marxism.

As a whole, these movements possess one unspoken, collective truth. They endeavor, following in the longstanding footsteps of Freemasonry, to supplant Judeo-Christian culture—the nuclear family, marriage, faith, nobility, patriotism, law and order, sexual morality, and other pillars of historically Western society—with an intellectual/theological-modeled form of secularism.

Though not condemning of religion as Communism, Cultural Marxism exalts man and the planet, and whisks aside any deity who comes with earthly commandments or heavenly beatitudes. Its minions disdain tradition and seem blind to common sense. They challenge laws and boundaries, disrupting order as needed. They defame—no, mock—Judeo-Christian values.

Most significantly, Cultural Marxism functions by stealth in education, the media, the courts, the government.[17] Once in authority, however, like Communism, it reveals itself to be totalitarian, seeking to regulate not only the way people act, but how one thinks.

In 2010, Pope Benedict XVI identified these "ideological currents" —these "winds of doctrine"—to be the crisis of our age. As John Paul II exposed the "culture of death" that arose from the Marxist mindset, Benedict denounced "aggressive forms of secularism," especially in the West, where people live "as though there were no God." [18] Such ideologies, Benedict said, were intolerant, and seek to create in society a culture within which religious belief is hard to find, to hold and to proclaim.[19] St. Paul, he reminded, warned of such human deception and trickery that entices people into "error," [20] which gives rise, Benedict concluded, to "a false reality based on false truth," on toxic rationalism. [21]

This "modern atheism"—satiated today by science as much as philosophy—now permeates civilization and is creating a "new faith in man"—a budding "theology of humanism"—based on the premise it can engineer intellectually, morally superior people (Social Darwinism), who, in turn, will build a temporal "heaven on earth."

No war, revolution, or election will eradicate this thinking. No proclamation of a spiritual leader or decree by a civil authority is going to end it. The philosophers and secret societies of the past—in the wake of Communism's collapse— could not have imagined such a perfect reincarnation of their disordered hope for humanity.

But as omnipresent as this great deception is (See Rv 12:9: "The huge dragon, the ancient serpent, who is called the Devil and Satan, who *deceived the whole world*"), it remains powerless before one truth—the Virgin Mary, the omnipotent Mother of God.

Mary's words at Fátima defined her mission. They previewed the future.

It was a revelation that allowed mankind to share in the foreknowledge of God. The outcome of her visitation, revealed in the Secret of Fátima, is the one thing for certain that is really *no* secret at all.

History's verdict on Fátima is sealed and delivered.

"In the end," assured the Queen of Heaven and Earth, "My Immaculate Heart will Triumph." The key, or the secret to this Triumph, is contained in those same words: My Immaculate Heart.

Three times Mary refers to her Immaculate Heart in the second part of the Secret of Fátima, almost as if her victory will be threefold in the final outcome.

And, perhaps, it will be.

The fascist scourge of World War II, though not prevented as desired by Mary, was brought to an accelerated conclusion with the consecration of the world by Pope Pius XII in 1942, according to Lúcia.

The second head of the three-headed atheist monster, Communism, was severed in 1984, with Pope John Paul II's Entrustment of the World which secured an end to the Cold War.

Both these victories, brought about through the Church's obedience to God's request at Fátima, are already visible, definitive "triumphs" of Mary's Immaculate Heart. And—in no uncertain terms—begin to fulfill Jesus's insistence to Lúcia that the Triumph be recognized in this way—that it is to come though the Immaculate Heart.

But the full Triumph did not come after the 1942 or 1984 consecrations. Why?

The Church, while it took time, fulfilled its role.

Flawed as the efforts were over the years, Lúcia upheld both consecrations—to a lesser degree—were accepted by God. Moreover, both brought tangible and visible results in confirmation, as witnessed in the swift outcome of WWII and the collapse of the Soviet imperium. [22]

But since what Mary asked of Lúcia was not done precisely as requested in 1929, it must be presumed that herein lies the problem—that somewhere in the language used by the Popes, or with the object of the consecration, or with the level of participation of the bishops, there is to be found the reason the world is still plagued with atheism, dominated by Marxist and Masonic forces, and still in danger of nuclear annihilation.

Although Pope Pius XII used the word "consecrate" in his prayer and alluded to Russia in his text of 1942, and Pope John Paul II discreetly mentioned Russia in his Entrustment Prayer of 1984,[23] it is a fact that neither openly cited Russia, and that many believe John Paul II's "entrustment" was not the same as the "consecration" Mary asked for.

On July 7, 1952, ten years after he consecrated the world with an implied reference to Russia, Pope Pius XII, in a second attempt—this time by a special Apostolic Letter, *Sacro Vergente anno*—explicitly consecrated the people of Russia. Unfortunately, the world's bishops did not participate, a gross omission that again derailed the outcome.

On October 8, 2000, sixteen years after the 1984 act, Pope John Paul II repeated his Entrustment of the World prayer. But he left out, once more, the same two words— "consecrate and Russia." [24]

Inside the Vatican editor-in-chief Robert Moynihan noted the significance of this omission:

> Two words. Two small words. Many on October 8—as Pope John Paul II together with some 1500 of his bishops in St. Peter's Square "entrusted" to the Virgin Mary the entire world—were waiting to hear those two words. But they were disappointed.
>
> The words not spoken were "*consecrate*", rather than "entrust", and "*Russia*", rather than the "entire world" ... The fact that the words "consecrate" and "Russia" were not used saddened some of the many millions worldwide who are devotees of the "Message of Fátima" ...for these simple believers, the precise words requested by the "Lady", and no others, should have been used. [25]

Church officials confirmed to *Inside the Vatican* that the Pope preferred in 2000 to use the same language that he did in 1984— "entrustment" not "consecration." [26] And, though the Cold War was over, the Pope again avoided citing "Russia" as the object of the act for a reason.

"Rome fears the Russian Orthodox might regard it as an offense," explained Moynihan. "If Rome were to make specific mention of "Russia" in a prayer, it's as if Russia especially is in need of help when the whole world, including the post-Christian West, faces profound problems." [27]

As noted, Pope John Paul II had remained concerned by the fact the 1984 consecration omitted a specific reference to Russia. [28] "He talked in a small circle," recalled Cardinal Cordes of his conversation with the Pope, "about how he felt this urge inside also to mention Russia at that consecration." [29]

Lúcia reported concerns too.

Three days prior to the 1984 Entrustment ceremony, at a pre-celebration of her coming seventy-seventh birthday on March 28, Lúcia is said to have responded to a Mrs. Pestana—who was in attendance and mentioned to her the upcoming consecration that Sunday, March 25—by replying, "That consecration *cannot* have a decisive character." [30]

It is no secret that in the immediate period after the Entrustment, Lúcia would not confirm its validity. She even sounded irresolute: "There was not a participation of all the bishops and there was no mention of Russia. Many bishops gave no importance to this act." [31]

In his book, *Fátima: Intimate Joy, World Event*, author Frere Francois de Marie des Anges captured the "post-Entrustment" take on the Pope's latest effort: "In the months which followed the act of offering of March 25, 1984—which was only a renewal of the act of 1982—the principal scholars of Fátima agreed in saying that the consecration of Russia had not yet been done as Heaven wished it." [32]

Time would see Lúcia's uncertainty transition to conviction. This was because, she would say, a large number of the bishops participated in the consecration for the first time, as requested by Mary. On February 17, 2005, however, there came a better understanding as to why Lucia had a change of heart.

Cardinal Tarcisio Bertone, in an interview with *La Repubblica*, revealed Lúcia reported to him that she received an apparition of the Virgin after the first Entrustment of the World by Pope John Paul II.

"Lúcia had a vision in 1984, the last public one, of which she has never spoken, during which the Madonna thanked Lúcia for the consecration in her name, which she had requested from the mystic." [33]

The 1984 Entrustment did not bring the Triumph promised at Fátima.

But it brought a sea of change.

The Soviet Union dissolved, Eastern Europe became liberated from Communism, and without a doubt, the entire world began to breathe a lot easier.

Lúcia not only came to state the act was accepted,[34] but would emphasize how the results speak for themselves.[35] Indeed, though the Entrustment failed to bring all that was hoped for, a prodigy was witnessed before the eyes of believers and unbelievers alike with the sudden end of the Cold War. [36]

But because what transpired was so undeniably miraculous—so clearly related to the Pope's act for those looking at it through the eyes of faith—did this mandate that the consecration should not be repeated again?

Or, would one last consecration—this time naming "Russia" as requested by Mary—bring the complete transformation of the world, the final blow to the Marxist, atheistic juggernaut that has ravaged humanity for over a century?

Considering John Paul II's intuitive "urge" to name Russia—and his lingering concerns years later— some began to believe this was reason enough to consider that it should be done again.

But there was more to weigh as to considering why another consecration needed to be contemplated, especially in looking at the history of the language used by the Virgin Mary and Lucia with regards to this matter—and at another more pertinent factor that has been, perhaps, not realized.

There are two realities with regards to the issue of the language that was used concerning the consecration: what the Virgin Mary said to Lúcia, and what Lúcia said to others about the consecration.

The following is what Mary told Lúcia on three occasions:

> **At Fátima, July 13, 1917,** Mary said to the three visionaries: "I shall come to ask for the consecration of Russia to my Immaculate Heart and the Communion of Reparation on the First Saturdays. If my requests are heeded, Russia will be converted, and there will be peace." Mary also said: "In the end, my Immaculate Heart will Triumph. The Holy Father will consecrate Russia to me, and she will be converted, and a period of peace will be granted to the world." [37]

> **At Tui, June 13, 1929,** Mary said to Lúcia: "The moment has come in which God asks the Holy Father, in union with all the bishops of the world, to make the consecration of Russia to my Immaculate Heart, promising to save it by this means." [38]

> **At Coimbra, May, 1952,** Mary said to Lúcia: "Make it known to the Holy Father that I am always awaiting the consecration of Russia to my Immaculate Heart. Without the consecration, Russia will not be able to convert, nor will the world have peace."

As can be seen, Russia is the object of the consecration in every communication of Mary with Lúcia that is known verbatim. It is certain there are others, but they are not documented, or have not been released.

The second reality is related to this first one. History reveals that every known communication of Lúcia's never failed to name Russia as the object of the consecration. The following is a partial look at the record:

> **May 29, 1930:** Letter to Father Goncalves from Lúcia: "The good Lord promises to end the persecution in Russia, if the Holy Father will himself make a solemn act of reparation and consecration of Russia..." [39]

> **May 18, 1936:** Letter to Father Goncalves from Lúcia: "Intimately I have spoken to the Lord about the subject, and not too long ago, I asked him why He would not convert Russia without the Holy Father making the consecration?" [40]

October 24, 1940: Letter to Pope Pius XII from Lúcia: "In 1917 in Fátima, in the portion of revelations designated by us as secret, the Blessed Virgin announced the end of the war that was afflicting Europe and predicted a future one that would begin in the reign of Pius XI. To prevent this war, she said, 'I will come to ask for the consecration of Russia to my Immaculate Heart and the Communion of Reparation on the first Saturdays.'" [This letter was not sent.] [41]

December 2, 1940: Letter to Pope Pius XII from Lúcia: "In 1917, in the portion of the apparitions that we have designated 'secret', the Blessed Virgin revealed the end of the war that was then afflicting Europe and predicted another forthcoming saying that to prevent it, she would come to ask for the consecration of Russia to her Immaculate Heart as well as the Communion of Reparation on the First Saturday." [42]

August 31, 1941: Reply of Lúcia to Bishop da Silva in the form of Lúcia's *Third Memoir*: "Be that as it may, God made use of this to make me understand that His justice was about to strike the guilty nations. For this reason, I began to plead insistently for the Communion of Reparation on the First Saturdays and the consecration of Russia." [43]

February, 1946: Reply of Lúcia to Father Huber Jongen in an interview:

Jongen: *What did Our Lady ask?*

Lúcia: The consecration of Russia to the Immaculate Heart of Mary by the Pope, in union with all the bishops of the world.

Jongen: *Did she ask for the consecration of the world?*

Lúcia: No. [44]

July 15, 1946: Reply of Lúcia to Professor William Thomas Walsh in an interview:

Walsh: *Lúcia made it plain that Our Lady did not ask for the consecration of the world to her Immaculate heart. What she demanded specifically was the consecration of Russia. She did not comment, of course, on the fact that Pope Pius XII had consecrated the world, not Russia, to the Immaculate*

Heart in 1942. But she said more than once, and with deliberate emphasis...

Lúcia: What Our Lady wants is that the Pope and all the bishops in the world shall consecrate Russia to her Immaculate Heart on one special day. If this done, she will convert Russia and there will be peace. If it is not done, the errors of Russia will spread through every country in the world. [45]

May, 1952: The Virgin Mary at Coimbra to Lúcia (Lúcia then communicated this message to Pius XII in June, 1952.): "Make it known to the Holy Father that I am always awaiting the consecration of Russia to my Immaculate Heart. Without the consecration, Russia will not be able to convert, nor will the world have peace.[46]

December 26, 1957: Reply of Lúcia to Father Augustin Fuentes in an interview: "Many nations will disappear from the face of the Earth, and Russia will be the instrument unless we obtain (through the consecration) the conversion of that poor nation." [47]

July 2, 1959: In a message that Lúcia received on this date from the Curia of Coimbra, she was informed that she could no longer speak about, or meet with anyone concerning, the message of Fátima, without permission from the Holy See. In a May 9, 1973, letter to her Salesian nephew, Father Valinho, Lúcia writes, *"I may accept only visits from members of my family, and I may no longer answer questions without explicit permission from the Holy See." This decision erects a more than twenty-year gap in the published communications of Sister Lúcia and the message of Fátima, including any comments on the consecration.* [48]

May 12, 1982: Reply of Lúcia to Father Umberto Maria Pasquale, S.D.B. in an interview published in *L'Osservatore Romano* on this date:

Pasquale: *Has Our Lady ever spoken to you about the consecration of the world to her Immaculate Heart?*

Lúcia: No! Father Umberto! Never! At the Cova da Iria in 1917, Our Lady had promised: I shall come to ask for the

consecration of Russia...In 1929, at Tuy, as she had promised, Our Lady came back to tell me that the moment had
come to ask the Holy Father for the consecration of that
country (Russia). [49]

[Father Umberto reports receiving a small note from Lúcia
two years prior to the interview in answer to a question he
had concerning the consecration. The note read: "Reverend
Father Umberto, in replying to your question, I will clarify:
Our Lady of Fátima, in her request, referred only to the consecration of Russia." Coimbra 13-V-1980, Sister Lúcia]. [50]

March 19, 1983: Reply of Lúcia to papal nuncio, Archbishop
Portalupi, Dr. Lacerda, and Father Messias Coelho acting on
behalf of the Holy Father with regards to the standing of
Pope John Paul II's consecration of 1982.

Lúcia: "In the act offering of May 13, 1982, Russia did not
appear as being the object of the consecration. And each
bishop did not organize a public and solemn ceremony of
reparation and consecration of Russia. Pope John Paul II
simply renewed the consecration of the world executed by
Pius XII on October 31, 1942. From this consecration we can
expect some benefits, but not the conversion of Russia." [51]

October-December, 1983: Quote of Sister Lúcia in article
by Father Pierre Caillon of Centre Saint Jean, Sees, (Orne)
France. (Published in the monthly periodical *Fidelite
Catholique*, reprinted in *Fátima Crusader*, Issue 13-14, p.3):
"The consecration of Russia has not been done as Our Lady
had demanded it. I was not able to say it because I did not
have the permission of the Holy See." [52]

Lúcia's unwavering conviction that Russia must be the object of the
consecration was still front and forward not long before the Pope's
1984 "Entrustment" of the world. This is quite evident in her May 13,
1982, letter to Pope John Paul II. It refers to Russia five times, three
times by name.[53]

Mary's words—as well as the excerpts from Lúcia's letters, public statements, and memoirs—all name Russia specifically as the object of the consecration. They also reveal the absolute necessity for the consecration of Russia by the Pope to be done in collegiality with the bishops.

But whether the object of the consecration is Russia or the world, it has always been assumed that the purpose of the consecration was for one reason: to address the "errors" of Russia, to mystically refute and dismantle the worldwide effusion of Marxist generated atheism through this singular act, consummated on a singular day.

But was there another reason why Mary asked for the consecration of Russia?

And could it have something to do with why Mary referred to Russia five times in the Secret of Fátima on July 13, 1917?

CHAPTER FORTY-EIGHT

THE LIGHT COMES FROM THE EAST

*So if they say to you, 'He is in the desert,' do not go out
there; if they say, 'He is in the inner rooms,' do not believe
it. For just as lightning comes from the east and is seen as
far as the west, so will the coming of the Son of Man be.*

—Mt 24:26

I T WAS THE MOST TREACHEROUS CROSSROAD IN HISTORY.
While some believe the 1984 consecration—regardless of the
fragile political climate at the time—should have cited Russia by name,
it is hard to argue with Pope John Paul II's reasoning.

In his eyes, the state of the world was at stake.

The Vatican's diplomatic policy of *Ostpolitik*—a controversial strategy involving the cessation of public Church criticism of Communist
regimes and a constant openness to negotiation with Communist officials—long held the need to minimize the consequences of Church
actions. This was because it was known they could trigger reprisals on
the faithful behind the Iron Curtain by Communist authorities.*

---

* The policy of *Ostpolitik* is believed by some to have been behind the reason why in 1962
the Vatican and the Russian Othodox Church came to a reported agreement (known
as the Pact of Metz or the Vatican-Moscow Agreement) that the Russian Orthodox
Church would send observers to Vatican II under the condition that no condemnation
of Communism would be made at the Council. (See Alexis Ulysses Floridi, *Moscow
and the Vatican*, Paris: France-Empire, Paris, 1979, pp.147-48. See also, "Fatima: The
Vatican Moscow Agreement" by Atila Sinke Guimaraes, November 2, 2013, catholictra-
dition.org.)

But now, the risk of an international crisis by citing Russia in the consecration appeared genuine and exponentially greater than anything before.[1] This concern is upheld with Lúcia's 1993 revelation to Cardinal Vidal that a nuclear war was avoided in 1985. [2]

There was also apprehension in the Vatican at the time—as one author put it—of causing an "apocalyptic rupture" with the Russian Orthodox Church.[3]

Vatican experts say these two issues decided the final wording of the 1984 consecration.

But there may have been another variable that eased that decision.

It appears Sister Lúcia—based on her pre and post-consecration statements—had more than an inkling Pope John Paul II would again consecrate the world, not Russia.[4] This matter is said to have been discussed between them beforehand, as it is a fact that the Pope asked for her input,[5] the same as he had prior to the 1982 consecration attempt. He also would consult her prior to his announcing of the third part of the Secret of Fátima in 2000.[6]

One author writes that Lúcia "already received and read the text of the Pope's consecration formula three days in advance" of the 1984 consecration. [7] If so, this could explain why Lúcia—whose cumulative writings over the years never failed to include Russia by name as the object of the consecration [8]—seemed to somewhat humbly acquiesce her long held position on this critical matter.[9]

This related issue—the history of Lúcia's documented insistence that it is "Russia" that must be consecrated—cannot be viewed as of inconsequential significance. The record shows that Lúcia not only sought the consecration of Russia in all her efforts as outlined in the previous chapter, but had been led through Mary to nurture in her heart a deep, unwavering love for Russia.[10]

This was an affection for the Russian people further intensified by her growing understanding of their sufferings under communism. In fact, her writings seem to reflect that she believed their misery would only find amelioration through the consecration.

A 2015 biography of Sister Lúcia by the Sisters of Coimbra, *A Pathway Under the Gaze of Mary*, reveals her affection for the Russian people. It also hints of how Lucia viewed the assuaging prospects of the consecration:

> Ever since the apparition of July 13, 1917, Lúcia had carried Russia in her heart, and her love for this country grew exponentially. Her tenderness for this land (Russia) and its people, was present until her death. Just hearing the name Russia was enough to get her notice and attention on what this land meant, and she cherished the dream of going to Russia someday... She very much wanted to visit this land that was in her heart since she was ten years old, and live her final days there.[11]

In July of 1950, Lúcia wrote a letter to a Russian woman named Irene who lived in France. It reveals her devotion to the Russian people was truly just as the Sisters of Coimbra described in their biography:

> I know that the Russian people are great, noble and cultured, capable of walking the path of truth, justice, and goodness. Since I saw this fondness of Our Lady for them, I cherish them as a people and desire nothing more than their salvation.[12]

A second letter of Lúcia's to a Russian man named Liktor Vladdimir in 1978, almost thirty years later, shows how Lúcia's sentiments for Russia remained unabated for decades:

> I know that the dear Mother of Heaven and Our Mother loves the dear Russian people and wants to help them find a better way. I asked her, therefore, that the Immaculate Mother keep them in her heart, and lead them to Jesus Christ our Savior.[13]

Bishop Pavel Hnilica, who knew the Fátima visionary well, also revealed an intriguing event surrounding Lúcia and her profound concern and love for Russia.

> One day, returning from Fátima, where I had met Sister Lúcia, I recounted to Mother Teresa what the visionary had

told me. It was that the Madonna of Fátima, in various apparitions, both the official ones in 1917 and private apparitions to Sister Lucia in the following years, expressed an interest in Russia at least twenty-two times. "This insistence," I said to Mother Teresa, "is proof of the Madonna's extraordinary solicitude for the Russian people." [14]

These documents demonstrate even more that those who wondered how Lúcia could ever accept the consecration of the "world"—instead of Russia—had legitimate reasons to express their incredulity.

Nevertheless, in lieu of Lúcia's confirmation of the acceptance of that consecration—along with her impeccable character and John Paul II's indisputable sanctity—it is reasonable to conclude that the 1984 Entrustment of the World *was* God's will for that moment in time.

This is realistic, logical and highly likely in lieu of the paramount Soviet nuclear threat of the day. Heaven could certainly see why an amended consecration needed to suffice considering the apocalyptic atmosphere swirling around this arduous decision.

This conclusion permits another assumption.

It also causes one to suspect that if Mary knew there would someday come a true "consecration of Russia," it may have been something the Virgin felt she need not make Lúcia aware of at the time. God is known for withholding mysteries to even His most chosen, as seen in Scripture and with the saints. This would account for Lúcia's view that because the 1984 Entrustment of the World was accepted, "there was no need" for another consecration. [15]

After the release of the third part of the Secret of Fatima in 2000, a growing debate over the next two decades surfaced again surrounding this very tenable issue. This debate was no longer a matter of whether or not the 1984 consecration was valid and accepted.

It was.

Rather, it was a matter of whether or not a "consecration of Russia" was perhaps still needed, even wanted by Heaven, to secure the full triumph foretold at Fatima.

Inside the Vatican editor Robert Moynihan took an objective, penetrating look at this question: [16]

Over the years, there has been considerable controversy in Catholic circles over this question: Has Russia ever been consecrated to the Immaculate Heart of Mary in precisely the way Mary asked for that consecration at Fátima?

Some Catholics argue that John Paul II's consecration in1984 was sufficient, and they point to the fact that Sister Lúcia seems to agree with them. [Moynihan refers here to, and published in full, Lúcia's August 29, 1989, letter to Sister Mary of Bethlehem which acknowledged the acceptance of the consecration.]

Others continue to maintain that even the 1984 consecration was in some way "flawed" and so, ineffectual. This group proposes that the Pope "re-do" the consecration, or, as they would put it, "do it for the first time in the right way."

In the context of the "Fátima Secret," the answer to this controversy is important: if the consecration of Russia has been performed, then the "conversion of Russia" should follow, and with it a "period of peace" for the world; if the consecration has not been performed, then it should be performed as soon as possible.[17]

According to some Fatima experts, there was another reason why Mary specifically requested the "consecration of Russia," and it appears to be a credible reason.

It is essential, some contend, to bringing the reunification of Rome with the Orthodox, to reversing the thousand-year-old schism with the Eastern Church—what some call "Russia's greatest error." This, they opine, was a major reason why Mary asked for the consecration of Russia in the first place.

There is much to examine concerning this conjecture. But before looking at this matter, it is necessary to ask a couple of simple questions.

What exactly is a schism?

And what were the reasons the Eastern and Western branches of the Church became divided so long ago?

A schism is a formal separation or division of a body, organization or institution, caused by differences of opinion or belief, often in doctrine. It usually involves an official secession of one group from the other, of which the most famous in history is the renowned "Great Schism of 1054" in the Catholic Church.

That year, Pope Leo IX sent an emissary—Cardinal Humbert of Silva Candida—a former French Benedictine abbot, from Rome to Constantinople. The cardinal's meeting with Patriarch Michael I. Cerularios was intended to be a mission of conciliation, but shortly unraveled.

Humbert, a reportedly tactless and narrow-minded man, launched into a contemptuous criticism of Cerularius that severely soured the negotiation. This threw it into a downward spiral.[18] On Saturday, July 16, 1054, in the Cathedral of Hagia Sophia, Humbert ended up excommunicating Cerularios, who in turn excommunicated him a week later. [19]

At that time, it is believed the primary point of dispute was the use of unleavened bread during the celebration of the Mass.[20] But the Great Schism actually was the end result of centuries of tensions involving political, cultural and theological disagreements between the Eastern and Western sides of the Church.[21]

The other points of dispute—along with issues that arose after the schism—were the liturgy, the Trinitarian doctrine, the primacy and authority of the papacy, and the language of the Nicene Creed, especially the question of whether the Holy Spirit proceeds from the Father or from the Father and the Son, a disagreement known as the *Filioque Controversy.* [22]

The mounting threat of Islam, rival missionary expansion in the Slavic territories, and the Fourth Crusade in 1204 would also come to exacerbate the division.[23] The Fourth Crusade, diverted from the Holy Land, attacked and captured Constantinople. The attack caused the deaths of thousands of Orthodox Christians along with the desecration of their churches and icons.[24] To this day, the fallout from this tragedy lingers.

The Orthodox Church continued to share a common heritage and doctrine with Rome after the schism, as set forth in the first seven councils, but were no longer aligned with the Pope and the Roman Catholic Church. [25]

In defining the concept of schism within a religious context, it must be noted that schism is not heresy. [26]

Although schismatics may come to believe heretical doctrines—and their partiality for these doctrines may originate in the circumstances of the schism—to be a schismatic is not to be a heretic. [27] And, conversely, heresy is not schism. [28]

But schism matters very much indeed if we are to regard the unity of the Church as a central feature of God's design for the world, and therefore vital to Mary's plan at Fátima.

This is in fact how *Lumen Gentium*, the dogmatic constitution *de Ecclesia* of the Second Vatican Council, sees the need for unity within the Church: [29]

> **By her relationship with Christ, the Church is a kind of sacrament or sign of intimate union with God and of the unity of all mankind. She is also an instrument for the achievement of such union and unity.** [30]

In this declaration, we see a principal goal of the economy of salvation is the undoing of human divisions—divisions within the human family, and division between the human family and its Creator. [31]

These two types of division are seen as mutually implicated, one leading to the other. This affirmation of the Second Vatican Council was not a fleeting gesture, but an attempt to articulate a deeply held conviction of Scripture and Tradition. [32]

In the pre-history of *Genesis*, disunity is described in the story of the Tower of Babel, which leaves humanity estranged from God and divided among itself, especially fragmented by an inability to communicate, which symbolizes the division.[33]

Immediately after this comes the beginning of the history of salvation, summoned in the call of Abraham. From there, our entire biblical path unfolds. It is the path to the remaking of the original unity of the human family with itself and with God, but remains continuously impeded and marred by sin. [34]

By the time we get to the New Testament, we see the unity of the disciples is a major preoccupation of Christ, even on the night before

His Passion. This unity of the Apostles is also viewed as not just a good in itself, but indefinitely extended in the fellowship of the Church throughout the ages.[35] Christ's prayer emphasizes this fact:

> **I pray not only for these, but for those also who through their words will believe in me. May they all be one, Father, may they be one in us. As you are in me and I am in you, so that the world may believe that it was you who sent me.** [36]

In St. Paul's *Letter to the Ephesians*, a clear indication that Jesus's prayer was not simply a pious wish is confirmed, as the unity of the Church is spoken of as an ongoing and living reality given by the Father in and through Christ:

> **God has made known to us his hidden purpose...To be put into effect when the time was ripe; namely, that the universe, all in heaven and on earth, might be brought into a unity in Christ.** [37]

Paul's letter sees the Church as a family where all nations can be at home. It is the privileged means of bringing about unity in Christ:

> **You are no longer aliens in a foreign land, but fellow citizens with God's people, members of God's household...** [38]

Consequently, as a result, it is not simply that the Church ought to be one; it is one, and cannot but be one. Paul also then warns of any division in the future, and employs the term "schism" with the Church in Corinth: [39]

> **I appeal to you, brothers, for the sake of our Lord Jesus Christ, to make up the differences between you and instead of having schisms among yourselves, to be united again in your belief and practice.** [40]

Beginning with Ignatius of Antioch, through Basil, Cyprian and a number of esteemed early writers, the "mystery of unity" in the Church is developed over the centuries, especially around the authority of the bishops and the Pope.[41]

It was well foreseen that misunderstandings and disagreements at the levels of faith and theological formation could likely become causes of a break in the unity of the Church. And, it is understood this could be exacerbated through *communio imperfecta*—imperfect communication. [42]

But, despite such foreknowledge, the great East-West Schism of 1054 arrives, due to a culmination of theological and political differences between Rome and Constantinople which, as noted, developed over time.

A more exhaustive look of this history is not for this undertaking. Rather, the question at hand is the age old one. What can be done to overcome this separation?

In 1979, Pope John Paul II framed the crux of the issue:

"It seems to me, in fact, that the question we must ask ourselves is whether we still have the right to remain separated." [43]

Of course, the answer to the Pope's question is self-evident; the Church does not have the right to remain separated. Unification, both sides are quite aware, is indisputably God's will. Without any doubt, the Church must become whole to fulfill its mission.

It especially needs to become one in order to share in each other's gifts, which is the only way to fulfill the perfection God calls the Church to seek.

This mystery of unity in diversity was prefigured in the creation of Adam and Eve. The Church Fathers taught that Adam and Eve were created equal in dignity but with complementary and distinct roles. This reflects the unified relationships of the Divine Persons in the Trinity. [44]

This same unity in diversification existed in the Church from the beginning and is exemplified in the complimentary roles of St. Andrew and St. Peter. [45] It was Andrew who discovered Jesus and then told Peter, who recognized Jesus as the Messiah.

So it is with the Church today.

The East can help the West to rediscover what has been lost or deemphasized over the centuries. And the West can help the East recognize Jesus in the Petrine ministry. Each must give to the other what it lacks to create the better whole, a unified Church of Christ on earth. [46]

Moreover, the practice of the faith has much to benefit with the assimilation of the unique attributes of both Churches.

The Eastern Church tradition calls Christians to holiness by contemplating Christ more in His divinity than His humanity. It inspires adoration and wonder, one that holds a balanced attitude of reverential fear and awe before God's majesty, combined with a humble and child-like love of Him.[47]

The Western Church tends to emphasize the humanity of Christ. Because of the rationalistic culture of the West, the Roman Church tends to identify with the mind, or reasoning powers, in its attempt to understand divine truth and to use information and knowledge to grow in sanctity.[48]

The differences between the Eastern and the Western Church is perhaps well summarized in the iconography of the two traditions. In the Latin, or Western tradition, images of the Saints often appear with haloes around their heads. In Eastern iconography, an aureole completely envelopes the bodies of the Saints. [49]

In recent decades, the successors of St. Peter have recognized the significance of rediscovering the "light from the East" as a means of reestablishing the unity that existed in the beginning. [50]

On May 2, 1995—the Feast of St. Athanasius—Pope John Paul II released an Apostolic Letter, *Orientale Lumen*, in which he expressed his hope for the Church to end the division. In the letter, the Pope stated that he had a passionate longing "that the full manifestation of the Church's catholicity be restored to the world...which is preserved and grows in the life of the Churches of both the East and the West." [51]

His successor, Pope Benedict XVI, also strove to make progress in the direction of unification. On his very first visit outside of Rome, he attended a Eucharistic Congress and promised to make "reconciliation with the Orthodox Church a fundamental commitment" of his papacy. [52]

Curiously, Benedict made this pledge in Bari, Italy.

Bari is just a short distance from the port city of Trani, which had been a point of contact between Rome and Constantinople at the time that the excommunications between the Pope of Rome and the Patriarch of Constantinople were exchanged in 1054. [53]

CHAPTER FORTY-NINE

A DIVINE FORMULA?

"I will make of you a great nation, and I will bless you; I will make your name great, so that you will be a blessing."
—Gn 12:2

THE OVERTURES BY JOHN PAUL II AND BENEDICT XVI TO SEEK unity are vital.

But the question at hand is not what the Pope can do to bring about a reconciliation of the Churches, but what Mary asked the Pope to do with regards to this matter, as many suspect was intrinsically woven into her request at Fátima.

In other words, did Mary's appeal for the consecration of Russia hold within it a divine formula to open the door to the reunification of the Orthodox Church with Rome?

It appears, when one closely looks at Fátima, that this may very well have been the case.

This is first and most thought to be present through the pivotal presence of the Virgin Mary herself at Fátima, who is treasured by both churches.

Remarked Cardinal Ratzinger, the future Benedict XVI, in 2002, "The Catholic Church and the Orthodox Church have done well keeping her a central figure." [1]

At Fátima—two years before the opening appearance of Mary on May 13, 1917—the groundwork is believed to have been laid for a call to the Church to mend its division. This is demonstrated, it is argued, in the mysterious visitations to the children from an angel in 1916, who comes three times.

The scenes—described by Sister Lúcia in her memoirs—sound very reminiscent of the divine transcendence of God as emphasized in the Eastern Church.

"We knelt down, with our foreheads touching the ground," recalled Lúcia, "and began to repeat the prayer... an extraordinary light shined on us...the angel left the chalice suspended in the air... he (the angel) prostrated on the ground and repeated with us, three times, the same prayer...'My God, I believe, I adore, I hope and I love you...'" [2]

In addition to these profound Eastern forms of imagery, it has been pointed out that the Angel at Fátima gave Holy Communion to three children, who were nine, seven, and six years of age respectively. Two of which, Francisco and Jacinta, had received no formal catechesis at the time, yet alone their First Holy Communion.

Such a unique unfolding appears to once again subscribe to the customs and practices of the Eastern Church, which permits babies and children to participate in the Sacraments of Initiation—Baptism, Confirmation and the Holy Eucharist. [3]

There are other correlative elements of the Fátima story that point to the Orthodox faith. But, none more relevant than the appeal by Mary for the consecration of Russia.

With this action, Mary is seen to be delivering a divine request that this country (Russia) be consecrated, to be made holier and dedicated to a "higher purpose," and therefore, such a supplication must be seen as of the highest order in the realm of a call to the sacred.

This is something the Orthodox have traditionally treasured. [4] In the Orthodox Christian faith, the call to consecration is understood to be very special, viewed as a solemn dedication, filled with profound symbolisms, many of which are biblical elements taken from the Old Testament that recall the consecration of the Tabernacle and of the Temple of Solomon.

Orthodox consecrations usually involve relics and the reciting of petitions, prayers, and hymns. They are often complex services involving processions led by bishops who represent Christ the King, who enters the consecrated object and defeats the power of the Devil.

The Roman Catholic Church sees a consecration as being special too. It sets apart a blessing, a benediction, or a prayer on behalf of a person or thing, from that of a consecration, in that the object of a consecration passes from the common order to a new state, and therefore becomes more directly a vehicle of the will of God. [5]

Consequently, as in the case of ancient Israel, Mary's appeal at Fátima for the explicit consecration of the nation of Russia at God's request, signifies that it is His divine will to set this nation apart for Himself, so that it may be a "light to the nations."

Thus, Russia, while foretold by Mary at Fátima to be a terrible scourge of the world because of her errors, is also singled out at Fátima to become—once consecrated—an extraordinary blessing to all mankind.

The belief that Russia will someday be a bellwether Christian nation is not just a supposition arising from a theological dissection of the message of Fátima.

The Russian people themselves are said to have instinctively felt their terrible sufferings were meant to someday be used by God to further His Kingdom on Earth. [6]

"A universal mission of Holy Russia in the service of the reign of God remains the grandiose idea shared by quite a good number," wrote Catholic philosopher, theologian, Father Andre Richard.

Richard writes that the very heart of the message of Fátima—the call to consecration and reparation—must be understood in relation to the word "Russia." The word "Russia" in the message of Fátima, he explains, refers both to the "state" and to the "people." Thus, in lieu of this perspective, the conversion of Russia, Richard insists, must mean two things: its conversion from Marxist atheism *and* its destined reunification with the Catholic Church. [7]

Though separated in the eleventh century from the Western Church, the ancient oriental and Russian Orthodox are descendants of Apostolic Christianity, maintaining true Apostolic succession and in agreement substantially with the Latin Church and its fundamental teachings on everything from the seven Sacraments to the final Resurrection. Even those oriental and orthodox churches not originally in communion with Rome can trace their origins as local churches to the Apostles themselves. [8]

Thus, while the western world, for the most part, remains ignorant of Russia and its legacy of faith, the Russian people see themselves as possessing an historic culture and an historic faith. It is a faith that has remained very much alive despite its travails during the days of tsarist Russia and its Marxist and post-Communist successors. [9]

Vladamir Sergeyevich Solovyov, a nineteenth century Russian philosopher, theologian, and poet, played a significant role in the spiritual renaissance of early twentieth century Russia. In 1889, he wrote *Russia and the Universal Church*. Although baptized into Eastern Orthodoxy, he favored the healing of the schism with Rome and believed in papal supremacy. [10]

For Solovyov, the idea of a nation is not what she thinks of herself, but what God thinks of her in eternity. According to him, God's plan for Russia is, once reunited with the Catholic Church, to help bring new Christian life to Europe and the world. [11]

This future, Father Gustav Wetter—author of the monumental work *Dialectical Materialism*—ventures will come only through and because of Russia's horrific experience with Marxism. Through the cross of Communism, he writes, it becomes more plain to see God's plan for Russia. Wetter believes that " the theory of Lenin on the contradiction in the essence of things, leads inevitably to the alternative—the mystery which can only be that of the living God, Jesus Christ." [12]

Father John Mowatt, a former director of the Byzantine Centre of the Blue Army in Fátima, concurs with Wetter's understanding. He too believes the Communist revolution was a transitory step to the reunification of the Orthodox Church with Rome, in line with Russia's divine calling to lead the nations after the Triumph:

> The Church in Russia itself had to be reborn in the fire of revolution so that, freed of its role as a tool of the state, it might more fruitfully work for the eventual transformation and transfiguration of Russia's soul. The spiritual potentialities of Russia have yet to be realized in history and the religious vocation of the Russian people has yet to come to the fore. [13]

Mowatt adds that this hopeful future is because of the great love the Russian people have had for the Virgin Mary for centuries. He sees their devotion to her as unparalleled and the reason why Russia is at the center of the message of Fátima. Russia is needed, he says, to help lead the world to the truth possessed in Christianity. [14]

Many prophecies over the centuries in both the East and the West are found to herald this hope too. Not the least are Mary's words at Fátima and Medjugorje. [15]

On June 13, 1929, the Virgin Mary appeared to Sister Lúcia in Tui, Spain, and told her "the moment has come for the Pope, in union with the bishops, to consecrate Russia."

The question, therefore, arises: what determined "the moment has come?"

Of course, one can say it was now so because God's will, in and of itself, determined this moment. But in terms of a human rationale, it can be conjectured "the moment" had come for another reason.

Fátima was now only months away from being fully approved by the local bishop, thereby positioning the Pope to be able to act with no reservations with regards to the status of the apparition in the eyes of the Church.[16]

Furthermore, while the errors of Russia were spreading, as Mary foretold at Fátima in 1917, they had yet to formally proliferate beyond what was now simply a greater Russia; Bolshevik Communism had extended by 1929 only into the annexed neighboring Soviet states of Ukraine, Uzbekistan, Belarus, Tajikistan, Moldova, Kyrgyzstan, and Turkmenistan.[17]

Thus, from a human perspective, the moment appeared ripe for the consecration to accomplish all that God desired to bring about through Mary's prophetic words at Fátima.

So what exactly was intended with the timely execution of the consecration of Russia?

From all that was to follow throughout the remainder of the 20th century, we can assume in retrospect—with Lúcia's words in confirmation—that the many wars, persecutions and sufferings that occurred during this period because of Communism would not have come to realization; they would have been, as Lucia stated, "avoided." [18]

The all-embracing efficacy of the consecration would have seen to their prevention, as Mary's words guaranteed at Fátima. [19] Moreover,

Marxism, in all its malignant deviations, would also have been stymied before ever seeing much of the light of day.

In essence, the benefits of the consecration are easily applied to envisioning the full "defensive" nature it was intended to provide against the dark clouds of atheistic morass gathering below the horizon.

But have we contemplated the *full* measure of what the consecration was intended to achieve in the world?

Can we, for a moment, imagine the "offensive" graces that were divinely envisioned to come with its timely enactment?

It is impossible to grasp in its providential design the great treasure of good that God intended to shower upon the world if Russia had been properly and timely consecrated, but we can get somewhat of an authentic peek into this question from what occurred in Portugal before, during, and after World II.

In that tiny nation—after it was consecrated to the Immaculate Heart of Mary by its bishops in 1931, 1938 and 1940—a volcanic eruption in faith occurred that changed life there for the better in countless ways.

What was witnessed in a short period was unprecedented in perhaps the history of Christianity, and with it came a political and societal renewal unlike ever seen before. [20] The complete metamorphosis of the nation was so great it left Church leaders speechless, literally dumbfounded by what they observed unfolding throughout the *Land of Holy Mary.* [21]

"To express what has been going on here for twenty-five years, the Portuguese vocabulary has but one word, "miracle," gushed Cardinal Emanuel Cerejeira on May 13, 1942, during the Jubilee celebration of the Fátima apparitions. "Yes, we are firmly convinced that we owe the wonderful transformation of Portugal to the protection of the most holy Virgin." [22]

We will cover the history of this in an upcoming chapter.[23] But, it seems safe to say that if what occurred in Portugal because of the consecration had been extended at large at the time, not only would the great suffering of the 20th century been avoided, but mankind would now be living in an idyllic spiritual age.

Moreover, not only would a renaissance in the faith throughout the world be at hand, but some like to think that such a universal awakening would have been greatly forwarded by the reunification of the Catholic and Orthodox Churches.

CHAPTER FIFTY

"I WANT MY 'WHOLE CHURCH' TO KNOW"

"Do you not know? Have you not heard? Was it not foretold to you from the beginning? Have you not understood?"
—Is 40:21

OBEDIENCE.

No single virtue of Sister Lúcia stands out more.

To God, to the Virgin, to her superiors, Lúcia incessantly strived to be obedient to their requests. But that doesn't mean she didn't ponder things. And if there was one issue she couldn't completely understand, it was why "Russia" had to be consecrated.

Wasn't there an easier way to address the situation?

Couldn't the consecration be replaced with something else?

Was there some way Russia could be converted without it?

In a May 18, 1936, letter to her spiritual director Father Bernardo Goncalves, Lúcia reveals that she asked the Lord to tell her why He would not convert Russia without the Holy Father making the consecration? [1]

"Because I want my *whole* Church," Christ answered Lúcia, "to acknowledge that consecration as a triumph of the Immaculate Heart of Mary, in order to later extend its cult and to place devotion to this Immaculate Heart alongside the devotion to my Sacred Heart."

"But my God, the Holy Father probably won't believe me, unless you yourself move him with a special inspiration," replied Lúcia.

"The Holy Father. Pray very much for the Holy Father. He will do it, but it will be *too late*. Nevertheless, the Immaculate Heart of Mary will save Russia.

"It has been entrusted to her." [2]

From this dialogue, we see Christ's words speak of His "whole Church" and of the critical role of the "Holy Father."

Such words are insightful.

This is because they seemingly point to the consecration being not only the remedy for the errors of Marxism, but also the vehicle for the Church becoming "whole" again, for a reunification that will emerge through the galvanizing and medicinal graces divinely embedded in the act. Statements by Lúcia reinforce this suspicion, especially comments made in 1946 that allude to the "Eastern Church" and the conversion of Russia. [3]

Father Robert Fox, in his book *Rediscovering Fátima*, noted this surreptitious reality: "Lúcia has always thought of the conversion of Russia as not limited to the return of the Russian people to Orthodox faith or the rejection of Marxist atheism, but rather a total, perfect conversion to the Roman Catholic Church." [4]

Father Joaquin Alonso, Fátima's documentarian, was of the same mindset. He believed Lúcia clearly understood the consecration was designed to bring about the reunification of the Churches.

"We must affirm," writes Alonzo, "that Lúcia has always thought that "conversion" is not limited to the return of the Russian people to the Christian-Orthodox religion, rejecting the Marxist-atheism of the Soviets, but rather refers purely, simply and fully to the total, integral conversion of Russia to the one true Church of Christ, that being the Catholic Church." [5]

In his book, *The Light Comes from the East*, Hugh Owen identified why the consecration of Russia was—and remains—intended to serve as the means for the reunification of the divided Church:

Just as the "conversion of Russia" depends on the consecration of Russia by the Pope and the bishops in union with him—a sign of their recognition of Russia's sacred mission to the nations, as the first among Eastern Christian Churches of the world—so the "reorientation" of the Church will not succeed without a simultaneous recognition of the paternal authority of the successor of St. Peter, our "Holy Father." [6]

It appears no accident that Pope Pius XI—the only Pope mentioned by name in the Secret of Fátima—is the Pope that Christ asks Lúcia to appeal to for the consecration of Russia.

Pius XI—Ambrogio Damiano Achille Ratti—was the former papal nuncio to Poland (1919-1921) and had a great love for the Slavic people. It was said that he desired to be the "Pope of the Reunion." [7] Pius developed this ambition from his contacts with the Orthodox while serving as the Vatican's ecclesiastical diplomat in Warsaw. [8] Later, as Pope, he received intelligence reports that suggested the revolution in Russia might prove providential in mending the separation between the Orthodox and Rome. [9]

His destiny appeared marked out for him.

Fátima authority Fre Michel de la Sainte Trinite, author of the prodigious *The Whole Truth About Fatima*, concurs with this view. He bemoaned the tragedy of the lost opportunity that presented itself to Pius when "the moment" had come in 1929:

Poor Russia, dominated by Bolshevism, and still a victim of its centuries-old schism, would have been saved by both evils at the same time. Moreover, deliverance would have come at the request and on the decision of all the Catholic bishops obeying their head—this Bishop of Rome (Pope Pius XI), whose universal primacy of jurisdiction as successor of Peter—the Russian Church had refused to recognize. [10]

Fátima, Fre Michel opines, was a masterpiece of divine strategy. If Mary's words are obeyed, he insists, the consecration would have knocked out both Communism and the albatross of the schism:

Yes, let us admire the astonishing, divine, stratagem through which God willed to bring back to His flock, by the millions, the multitude of his sheep led astray in the schism, and at the same time assure world peace. What fullness of wisdom in this great design of mercy! This already would suffice to show that this was not of man, but of God.

The more we examine it, the more we understand its divine coherence. We understand that this design is irrevocable, and that God does not will to change any part of it. When Sister Lucy asked him why He would not convert Russia without the Pope making the consecration, Our Lord responded, "Because I want my 'whole Church' to recognize *that* consecration..."[11]

The observation that God's "design is irreversible" and that "He does not will to change any part of it" deserves reflection. Fre Michel's words, in essence, again reveals why the earlier consecrations failed to bring the full Triumph—and why the world struggles today with Marxism in its many malignant variations. It is clear; the "design" was altered, and consequently, the "result" was altered.

Some say the situation is no different today. God's "plan" at Fátima is "explicit" with regard to the outcome. It remains, therefore, immutable that only Russia can serve as the object of the consecration in order to bring the complete prophesied outcome.

The critical role of the "consecration of Russia" in bringing unity within the Church was never spoken of by Mary at Fátima. Nor did Lúcia speak of it in her writings.

But it was perceived by one very significant player in the Fátima timeline.

Pope Pius XII—the self described "Pope of Fátima" —grasped the reality of this singular threshold.

Though it was the "world" that Pius consecrated, we see in the words of his petition to Mary—transmitted over the radio on October 31, 1942, and then repeated on December 8 in St. Peter's Basilica—that he directly alluded to the consecration not only remedying the errors of Marxism, but the schism too:

> Give peace to the peoples (referring to Russia) separated by *error and schism*, particularly those who have a special devotion to you and among whom there was no home where your venerable icon was not honored, and where, at present, it may be hidden in the hope for better days. Bring them back to the One fold of Christ, under the One true shepherd.[12]

More than twenty years later, at the close of the third session of the Second Vatican Council on November 21,1964, Pope Paul VI renewed Pius XII's consecration. He again connected the consecration to unity with the Orthodox Church.

"Look with benign eyes on our separated brothers," Paul beseeched the Virgin Mary. "Condescend to unite us. You who brought forth Christ as a bridge of unity between God and men." [13]

CHAPTER FIFTY-ONE

THE CONSECRATION OF RUSSIA

*"They shall call upon my name, and I will hear them. I will say,
"They are my people," and they shall say, "The Lord is my God."*
—Zec 13:9

AT FÁTIMA, GOD PRESENTED A PLAN.

Its goal was to save the world from a great suffering and to guide it towards a time of peace. The plan requested the assisitance of the Pope and the bishops, as well as the prayers of the faithful.

Failure to follow the plan would result in consequences, which were spelled out at Fátima through extraordinary socio-political prophecies that came to fulfillment over the course of the 20th century. The end of World War I, World War II, Communism, nuclear destruction, persecution, famine, and the threat of "annihilation" were predicted in word or vision and then became reality before the eyes of all.

At Medjugorje, this same process is at hand.

The Virgin has unveiled a plan.

It again involves the world and she asks that this plan be understood as a continuation of Fátima. The plan involves prophecies and Secrets; it warns of consequences: "You cannot imagine what is going to happen nor what the Eternal Father will send to earth." [1]

The plan at Medjugorje touches on all the major themes found at Fátima. Mary emphasizes the reality of sin and Hell, about the need for conversion and the significant role of the Church. She speaks about people, about nations, about God. As at Fátima, she has discussed the coming of her "Triumph."

And—once more—she foretells the "Triumph" will involve Russia.

No request for the consecration of Russia is heard at Medjugorje.

Nor is it found at any Church sanctioned apparition before or after Fátima.

This is not surprising.

It seems highly unlikely that such an appeal from the Virgin Mary would be heard anywhere else. The request for the consecration of Russia was the center piece of Fátima's revelation. Consequently, such a call from another apparition site would detract from this singular, unprecedented moment in the life of the Church.

But Mary's words at Medjugorje regarding the future of Russia— given in October of 1981 to the visionary Marija Pavlović, who, at the time, submitted a question to the Virgin from a Franciscan priest from Mostar—cannot be dismissed as just a casual response to an inquirey during that evening's apparition. [2]

Rather, when contemplated, it is no less a pivotal, strategic disclosure by Mary, one designed to show that Medjugorje was in step with Fátima. It was, quite simply, a glimpse of what is to come with the Triumph of the Immaculate Heart.

Forty years have gone by since those early days at Medjugorje. Over time, a mountain of words has been recorded from the many apparitions that the six visionaries have experienced, either individually or collectively.

Some of the Virgin's most poignant, compelling disclosures at Medjugorje, however, are found in the first six to twelve months. And they were—seen now in retrospect—to have been for a reason.

Like with Fátima, the revelations appear to set the stage for the substantial amount of prophetic fulfillment that is to come, one that will leave Medjugorje with indisputable evidence of the Virgin Mary's "time of visitation" in the land of the Southern Slavs.

The Virgin's words concerning Russia are one of those prophetic revelations. The message was brief, but to the point. Author Mary Craig gives this account in *Spark from Heaven*:

> At some time in October (1981), Father Ivica Vego, a young
> Franciscan from Mostar, asked Marija to put three questions

to the Madonna: about Poland; about the Hercegovina problem; and about the East-West struggle. She replied that in Poland great conflicts would soon take place, but that "*right*" would prevail in the end. (Indeed, the imposition of Marshall Law, or, as the Poles preferred to call it, General Jaruzelski's war against the Polish nation, was a mere two months away. But few people would claim that now, since the crushing of *Solidarity,* "*right*" has been seen to prevail in the unhappy land.) In the "Hercegovina Issue", much prayer and patience were needed, the Lady advised. But it was her reply to the third question that was the strangest. The Russians, she prophesied, would come to glorify (literally, make "manifest") God to the world; while the West, though it had attained undeniable technological mastery, had lost God in the process. [3]

Several verbatim variations of Mary's exact message that day are found. But Father René Laurentin's version, recorded in his book, *Is the Virgin Mary Appearing at Medjugorje?* is the most circulated:

> Russia is the people where God will be most glorified. The West has advanced civilization, but without God, as though it were its own creator. [4]

Laurentin footnotes one of his sources for this message as Father Svetozar Kraljevic's book, *The Apparitions of Our Lady at Medjugorje.* [5] But Kraljevic's book (English edition) does not quote Mary's words verbatim as Laurentin's does and other versions do.

This leads one to suspect that there was a precise, original quote of what Mary said to Marija as exactly relayed to Father Ivica Vega that day, of which Laurentin accessed in addition to Kraljevic's work. [6] (This is perhaps confirmed, as Laurentin reports a different version of the same message in his book, *Messages and Teachings of Mary at Medjugorje.*)

Kraljevic's book, however, does disclose a significant addendum concerning this entire matter. He reports that Father Vega "tried to learn more about the future of the West," which caused, Father Kraljevic writes, Marija Pavlović to become "flushed" because "the question impinged upon the Secrets." [7]

Several points concerning this prophecy deserve attention.

Regardless of Mary's exact words, it is clear the message appears to "divinely" validate a coming "conversion" of Russia.[8] Indeed, we can see that Mary is making it clear; God's plan for Russia is a great one. Russia is, as Craig wrote, to "manifest God to the world," and this plan will be actualized and the results evident.

It is also noteworthy that Mary was speaking of "Russia" at a time before Russia was independent, as the Soviet Union was still in existence when the message was given at Medjugorje in October of 1981.

Needless to say, all of this points to Fátima.

Consequently, some questions must be asked.

Is Russia's conversion to occur without Russia ever being consecrated as Mary requested at Fátima?

Or, by revealing what she did at Medjugorje, was the Virgin indicating that her precise words at Fátima will someday be fulfilled, that Russia will be consecrated?

At Fátima, Mary said:

> In the end, my Immaculate Heart will triumph. The Holy Father will consecrate Russia to me, and she shall be converted, and a period of peace will be granted to the world.[9]*

It is significant that Mary's words at Medjugorje assert the Russian "people" will glorify God the most. This language appears to confirm what French Theologian Father Andre Richard insisted was intended by the Virgin Mary at Fátima.

Wrote Father Richard:

> The word Russia, in the message of Fátima, refers to the *state* and to the *people*. In lieu of this perspective, the conversion of Russia must mean two things; its conversion from Marxist atheism and its destined reunification with the Catholic Church.[10]

---

*   It must be noted that while Pope John Paul II consecrated the world, not Russia, in 1984, it would have been impossible for him to consecrate Russia at that time as an independent nation anyway, since it was still part of the Soviet Union.

Clearly, Mary's words at Medjugorje—which speak of the "Russian people"—do exactly that; they seperate the "people" from the "state." One suspects, therefore, this was for a reason.

Through the eyes of faith, it is believed that Pope John Paul II's 1984 consecration of the world led to the liberation of the Soviet Union— which included the "nation" of Russia at the time—from the grips of Marxist/ Communist rule.

Since then, the Russian government has over time come to politically and economically support Christianity—primarily the Orthodox Church. As of 2017, twenty-five thousand churches have been constructed or rebuilt in Russia with the aid of the state since the fall of Communism.[11] In addition, the government is seen to be openly advocating the fundamental princilples of Christianity through legislative and bureaucratic reforms. In a series of constitutional amendments proposed in 2020, there included a proclamation of "Russia's faith in God" and that marriage is to be defined in law as "the union of a man and a woman."[12]

But for the most part, the "people of Russia" are still living a very secular existence, caught up in the lures of the same materialistic and sensual trappings as the West. In reality, experts write, most Russians are "atheists" at heart, as when under Communism.[13]

Gene Zubovich, in a 2018 article published in *Religion and Politics*, defined the state of religion in Russia, despite the government's faith based measures:

> Governments sometimes promote belief systems that explain life's meaning, and rituals that remind us of it, because it lends them legitimacy. But these quests seem to always remain incomplete. This is certainly true of Soviet atheism, and it is also true of Russian Orthodoxy... Most Russians identify as Orthodox but only 6 percent of them attend church weekly and only 17 percent pray daily. Russians are largely unchurched and often don't conform to the doctrines of the Orthodox Church. The Soviet Union had been the first country to legalize abortion in 1920, and the rate of abortions is more than double compared

to the U.S. and enjoys widespread support despite strong objections from the Orthodox Church. And contrary to Orthodox teaching, attitudes toward divorce and pre-marital sex remain lax...Many Soviet rituals invented by atheists remain widely popular. Stamps and medals, many of them instituted to counter religious influence, are still in wide use. One can hardly visit a statue or monument in Russia without encountering a wedding party, and the civil registration office—ZAGS—is still the preferred choice for weddings. [14]

Critics of the Russian government's public position and action in favor of God and religion are suspicious and cynical, calling them politically motivated. [15]

This view is not without merit, especially considering Russia's 20th century history.

While the Russian Orthodox Church experienced intense persecution and was forced to make a public declaration of total submission to the Bolshevik regime in the early Soviet period (the Church had only 200-300 active parishes in the Soviet Union by 1939 while there were roughly 50,000 before the revolution), the exigencies of World War II caused Stalin to soften his stance on the Church and allow it more freedom. But the Russian Orhodox Church was in subservience to the state for the remainder of the Soviet period.

Towards the end of Mikhail Gorbachev's reign, his policies of glasnost and perestroika sparked hope that the Russian Orhodox Church was about to experience a great revival. In 1988, there were major celebrations throughout Russia as churches and monasteries were reopened and the people seemed eager to restore their religious traditions.

However, that did not last. Soon after the collapse of the Soviet Union, Russian Orthodoxy split again and a new relationship between the Russian Othodox Church and the state slowly took hold.

Today's Russian Orhodox Church has moved from institutional survival by means of decades of total cooperation with an atheistic state (the Soviet Union) to one that has again aligned itself with the state (Russia) in creating what some call a "militant religious nationalism." [16]

It is a worrisome and dangerous development that many believe once again called for the consecration of Russia.

"Consecrate Russia Now," read the headline of an article reporting the appeal of an American cardinal at a conference in Rome on May 20, 2020. Cardinal Raymond Burke, former head of the Vatican's highest court, stated that Russia—more than ever—should be consecrated exactly as requested by Mary at Fátima.

In his talk, *Fatima: Heaven's Answer to a World in Crisis,* Burke extolled the dangerous times humanity had entered and said the answer lies in the consecration of Russia:

> The consecration of Russia to the Immaculate Heart of Mary is more needed today than ever. When we witness how the evil of atheistic materialism, which has its roots in Russia, directs in a radical way the government of the People's Republic of China, we must recognize that the great evil of Communism must be healed at its roots through the consecration of Russia, as Our Lady directed.[17]

Just a month before, Italian Archbishop Carlo Maria Vigano called for the consecration of Russia too, "Let us not forget Our Lady's unheeded appeal for the Pope and all the Bishops to consecrate Russia to her Immaculate Heart, as a condition for the defeat of Communism and atheistic materialism." [18]

The public clamor to consecrate Russia has added a growing number of voices in recent years. In April of 2017, prominent European Catholic historian Dr. Robert de Mattei also called for the consecration of Russia, declaring all the previous consecrations "partial" and incomplete." [19]

A month later, German Cardinal Paul Cordes echoed this plea, "Today, once again, we hear the call of Our Lady of Fátima to consecrate Russia to her Immaculate Heart, in accord with her explicit instructions." [20]

In 2016, Bishop Athanasius Schneider of Kazakhstan stated the same, "Pray that the Pope may soon consecrate explicitly Russia to the Immaculate Heart of Mary, then she will win." The consecration will," said Schneider, "fulfill more completely and perfectly the desire of Our Lady of Fátima." [21]

Even world renowned Vatican exorcist, Father Gabrielle Amorth—not long before he passed way—publicly appealed in 2015 for another consecration attempt, "A specific consecration of Russia has not yet been made. You can always do it. Indeed, it will certainly be done." [22]

A petition asking for the consecration of Russia to the Immaculate Heart of Mary was initiated in 2017 by the Rome-Life Forum in response to the widespread appeal. It drew the signatures of many illustrious Catholics from throughout the world. [23]

Not surprising, the argument on behalf of those in the Church who assert that the time for such consecrations is over is still heard.

While acknowledging the shortcomings of the 1984 act, Father Andrew Apostoli pointed out in his 2010 book, *Fatima for Today*, that Pope John Paul II's "Entrustment of the World" brought about what it was primarily intended to do. [24] The Soviet empire collapsed, noted the Franciscan theologian, and the nation of Russia is "continuing to experience *somewhat* of a conversion from atheism to Christianity." [25]

The world, however, does not appear to be experiencing a conversion.

Marxist atheism is eating away at its soul. And with each day that goes by there is the growing feeling that something needs to be done to confront this mounting danger, a danger that could radically change the world overnight. [26]

On February 22, 2022, that danger struck.

Russia invaded Ukraine and in response to an appeal by the Bishops of Ukraine, Pope Francis, in union with those bishops throughout the world who responded to his invitation to join with him, consecrated Russia and Ukraine to the Immaculate Heart of Mary. The consecration took place on March 25th, the same date that Pope John Paul II consecrated the world in 1984. **

** On Ash Wednesday, March 2, 2022, in response to Russia's military invasion of Ukraine, Ukraine's Latin Rite Bishops sent a letter to Pope Francis to request that he publicly perform the act of consecration to the Immaculate Heart of Mary. "We humbly ask your holiness to publicly perform the act of consecration to the Immaculate Heart of Mary of Ukraine and Russia, as requested by the Virgin of Fátima," said the letter, published on the Ukrainian Bishops' website that same day.

While some critics still questioned the validity of the consecration, most agreed that the language of the prayer, along with the Pope's call for collegiality from the world's bishops, appeared to properly satisfy Mary's words at Fátima in 1917, as well as her official request for the consecration at Tui, Spain, on June 13, 1929. ***

Based on the history of previous consecration attempts, extraordinary and visible events in time can be expected from this act.

But still, questions arise.

Will the consecration of Russia bring the sweeping changes to the world that many are hoping and praying for? Or did it, some wondered, simply fulfill Jesus's words to Lucia that she wrote of in her May 18, 1936, letter to her spiritual director, Father Jose Bernardo Goncalves:

> "The Holy Father. Pray very much for the Holy Father. He will do it, but it will be too late." [27]

One thing, however, is for certain regarding the March 25, 2022, consecration.

While the need for the proper consecration of Russia seems to have been finally fulfilled, the second part of Mary's original twofold request at Fátima has not.

At Fátima in 1917, and again at Tui in 1929, Mary asked not only for the consecration of Russia but also for "the Communion of Reparation on the first Saturdays."

This second request—in the opinion of Fátima scholars—was also never properly satisfied.

United to the consecration of Russia by Mary, the Communion of Reparation was, in essence, an appeal to the hierarchy of the Catholic

---

*** In lieu of the March 25, 1984, "Consecration of the World" and its mystical, catalystic effect on the fall of theoretical, Soviet Marxism (Communism), it is not unlikely that the March 25, 2022, "Consecration of Russia" will divinely target the ideological, cultural errors of Marxism in much the same way. This means that although this last consecration was undertaken in response to Russia's military invasion of Ukraine, its greatest effect will be on the Marxist-atheistic culture of the West. The U.S. Supreme Court's overturning of Roe v Wade—the 1973 abortion ruling that led to the death of millions—on June 24, 2022, was perhaps the first visible sign of this upshot of the consecration, i.e., the beginning of the downfall of all of "the errors of Russia." (For a similar perspective, see "The Consecration of Russia Overturned Roe v Wade," by Kennedy Hall, https://onepeterfive.com/consecration-russia-overturned-roe-v-wade/.

Church, and to its faithful, for a special worldwide movement of sacrifice and prayer.

This was necessary, according to Lucia, because the need for reparation of sin carried as much importance as the consecration of Russia.

Once more, Lucia's letters allow us to grasp the enormous gravity attached to this matter. In a March, 1939, letter (the exact date is not verifiable) to Father Goncalves, Lucia writes that Christ said to her:

> "Ask, ask again insistently, for the promulgation of the Communion of Reparation in honor of the Immaculate Heart of Mary on the First Saturdays. The time is coming when the rigor of My justice will punish the crimes of diverse nations. Some of them will be annihilated." [28]

Likewise, in a letter to her former Jesuit confessor, Father Jose da Silva Aparicio, dated March 19, 1939, Lucia states:

> "On the practice of this devotion (the Communion of Reparation), together with the consecration to the Immaculate Heart of Mary, world peace or world war depends." [29]

And again, on June 20, 1939, Lucia informed Father Aparicio:

> "War or peace of the world depends upon the practice of this devotion joined with consecration to the Immaculate Heart of Mary. Hence, I would want it spread…" [30]

Lucia's letters show that the consecration of Russia was never intended to be the sole means of fulfilling Heaven's requests to help bring peace to the world. Divine justice demands reparation for sin. Therefore, Mary strategically yoked the consecration of Russia to the Communion of Reparation.

Moreover, since so much time has passed since then, it is logical to assume that the need for reparation today—in consideration of the billions of abortions over the last fifty years alone—is now exponentially greater than one can ever fathom.

All of this points to a glaring reality.

The Virgin Mary has come again—this time to Medjugorje—for an undeniable reason: to secure the prayer and reparation needed to pull the world back from a precipice...and to bring to fulfillment the Secrets she began at Fatima. [31] ****

****   Vatican journalist, Antonio Socci, writes that the fulfillment of the remaining prophecies at Fátima and Medjugorje will be verifiable; they will be public and uncontestable as the coming of Communism and World War II fulfilled earlier prophecies of Fátima: Socci writes: "This Our Lady announces after making a series of historico-political prophecies (all of which, as we have seen, came to pass: revolutions, persecutions and wars); therefore the "Triumph" prophesied by Mary will have a resounding historical, and even cultural and political, obviousness. Like the victory at Lepanto, but much greater." Antonio Socci, *The Fourth Secret of Fatima*, p.217.

CHAPTER FIFTY-TWO

"THE SECRETS I BEGAN AT FATIMA"

"At the time when you hear the seventh angel blow his trumpet, the mysterious plan of God shall be fulfilled, as he promised to his servants the prophets."

—Rv 10:7

TWO REQUESTS WERE MADE BY THE VIRGIN MARY AT FÁTIMA IN order to prevent the errors of Russia from spreading. "I shall come to ask for the consecration of Russia to my Immaculate Heart," she told the three shepherd children on July 13, 1917, "*and* the Communion of Reparation on the First Saturdays."

As noted, the second request—the Communion of Reparation to Mary's Immaculate Heart—is a devotion; for five consecutive Saturdays of the month, Catholics are to go to confession, receive Holy Communion, pray five decades of the Rosary, and meditate on their mysteries to make reparation for the sins committed against the Immaculate Heart of Mary.

Not surprisingly, Fátima writers recognize the practice of this devotion has been woefully lacking since the beginning. Some believe so much so that, perhaps as much as the flawed consecrations, it is a primary reason the world has not seen the promise of Fátima.

In 1993, Sister Lúcia hinted as much,

"The Communion of Reparation is the means to combat atheism, because atheism is what condemns the most to Hell...the Virgin is interested particularly in the Communion of Reparation." [1]

In essence, God's people *individually* need to do more.

To many, this is what it appears Mary set out to accomplish through Medjugorje. She comes to arouse Catholics, and all people, from their spiritual doldrums—spurring them to want to bring the fullness of her prophetic words.

"At Fatima," wrote theologian Joseph Pelletier, "Our Lady asked for the consecration of Russia to her Immaculate Heart, promising the conversion of that country and a period of peace for the world through the consecration…

"It would seem , though, that there has not been enough prayer and penance to bring this about and to obtain these prayers and penance is one of the reasons she has come to Medjugorje." [2]

As at Fátima, Mary seeks prayer at Medjugorje—especially the Rosary.

She asks for penance, sacrifice, and renunciation. She leads souls to reconciliation. But contrary to Fátima, her strategy appears to be more simple and accommodating to today's modern world. [3]

Thus, rather than ask for a renewed effort to spread the *First Saturdays* devotion, Mary instead asked for much of what the devotion contained, but in a singular fashion.[4] In this way, due to perhaps less structure, the Virgin's requests are still inviting and appear more likely in today's world to precipitate a sustained response.[5]

Indeed, the Virgin's call at Medjugorje is similar to Fátima; however, it's taking place in a new world at a different time. But, as urgent as Fátima's call was in 1917, Mary's call is much more so today.

"Fátima's plea was to the Church; Medjugorje's call is to all humanity." wrote Jesuit Professor Father Edward Carter. [6]

Others agree.

"The message of Medjugorje is aimed at the whole world," notes British author and journalist Mary Craig.[7] "It is a planetary call for conversion," observed Father Tomislav Pervan, a former head pastor at Saint James in Medjugorje. [8]

But it's even *more* critical than that, argues Carter, a theologian who taught at Xavier University in Cincinnati. Carter, who compared

Fátima and Medjugorje in his book, *The Spirituality of Fatima and Medjugorje*, sees the two apparitions as inseparable and designed by Heaven to rescue humanity from destroying itself:

"Fátima initially outlined what is needed to save mankind. The messages of Medjugorje, while confirming the need, tells us in great detail how to accomplish it." [9]

In essence, Fátima sought to prevent the world from a great suffering. Medjugorje seeks to save the world…period.

With the Soviet Union only months away from its last gasps, the Virgin Mary confirmed at Medjugorje what reportedly Pope John Paul II and others observed: "Medjugorje is the fulfillment of Fátima." [10]

Only now, Mary's own words would validate this understanding.

Medjugorje, the Virgin revealed, is not just the continuation of Fátima in its essence, spirituality, and sharing of mutual goals. Rather, the Virgin's mission in Medjugorje is to literally finish what she foretold at Fátima in her three-part Secret.

She had come to secure the Triumph of the Immaculate Heart.

In two messages given at Medjugorje in late 1991 and one on Christmas Day in1992—Mary's words, in light of her revelations at Fátima, define her precise mission in Medjugorje:

> **I invite you to self-renunciation for nine days so that, with your help, everything that I desire to realize *through the Secrets I began at Fátima, may be fulfilled*. I call you, dear children, to now grasp the importance of my coming and the seriousness of the situation. I want to save all souls and present them to God. Therefore, let us pray that everything I have begun be fully realized.** (August 25, 1991) [11]

Father René Laurentin, upon learning of the Virgin Mary's message that day at Medjugorje, acknowledged its significance: "The connection with Fátima was confirmed by the message of the Virgin on August 25, 1991." [12]

One month later, the Virgin Mary reestablished that the climax of her work at Medjugorje would bring to fulfillment what she prophesied at Fátima on July 13, 1917:

Therefore, dear children, help my *Immaculate Heart to triumph* in the sinful world. I beseech all of you to offer prayers and sacrifices for my intentions so I can present them to God for what is most necessary. (September 25, 1991) [13]

Then, on Christmas Day, 1992—one year to the day that the Soviet Hammer and Cycle flag was lowered over the Kremlin for the last time—Mary recalled her promise of an era of peace:

Today is a day of peace, but in the whole world there is a great lack of peace. That is why I call you all to build *a new world of peace* with me... (December 25, 1992) [14]

Through these three messages, the Virgin's final push at Medjugorje to bring fulfillment to Fátima is confirmed.* The Soviet Union and its militant form of Marxism were history. Thus, it was now time for Mary to turn her attention to the remaining errors of Russia, the surviving bastions of Communism and the residual toxins of Marxism that had seeped into minds and hearts the world over.

It was also time, Mary counseled at Medjugorje, to look at people separated from God in a different way. This was because it wasn't so

---

* The Virgin's three messages at Medjugorje in 1991 and 1992 point to Fátima's promise of "the Triumph of the Immaculate Heart." They also reveal much more when closely examined. First and foremost, they confirm the Triumph is still to take place. Mirjana's often repeated statement that Mary said to her, *"What I started in Fátima, I will finish in Medjugorje. My heart will triumph,"* further contributes to this truth. With this understanding, it is important, therefore, to revisit Mary's exact words at Fátima on July 13, 1917: *"In the end my Immaculate Heart will triumph. The Holy Father will consecrate Russia to me, and she will be converted, and a period of peace will be granted to the world."* Perhaps, ironically, in light of the fact that some Fátima supporters do not support Medjugorje, it is in these three messages at Medjugorje that they find redemption for some of their own convictions. This is because 1) the messages concur that the Triumph was not attained with the 1984 consecration and 2) based on Mary's words at Fátima, there very well could be the need for another consecration of Russia. This is because the Virgin's words specifically indicated at Fátima that the Triumph will follow the consecration of Russia, which did not occur until March 25, 2022.

much the fact that unbelievers didn't believe, as they just didn't *know* God, or His love.

Unbelievers, Mirjana would say Mary told her, do not "feel God as their Father." [15] These struggling souls, the Virgin recommended, needed to be seen in a new light.

"All of the horrible things happening in our world today come from those who do not know the love of God," said Mirjana, "but she (Mary) is not necessarily speaking of atheists. Unfortunately, many people who think of themselves as religious do not know His love yet either." [16]

Mirjana revealed the Virgin Mary told her to pray each day for "those most in need of prayer, because bad things—wars, divorces, drugs, suicides, abortions—are happening in the world because of the *unbelievers*. So, in praying for them, you pray for a better world for yourself." [17]

During her annual apparition on March 18, 1989, Mirjana reported that Mary shared with her that day her deep concern for unbelievers:

> Yet, one more time she beseeched all of us to pray, to help her by our prayer for unbelievers, for those—as she says— who do not have those delights of experiencing God in their heart with a living faith.
>
> She said that she does not wish again to threaten. Her wish, as the Mother, is to warn us all, to beseech us because they do not know about the Secrets. She spoke about how she suffers in this regard because she is the Mother of all. The rest of the time passed in conversation about the Secrets. [18]

Eight years later, on July 2, 1997, Mirjana spoke to a group of youth in Medjugorje and shared more about this spiritual reality:

> On the second of each month, I pray with Gospa for unbelievers. We cannot save them without our prayers and our example. She asks us to give these prayers our priority, and to witness especially with our lives so that through us, unbelievers might see God and God's love. If only you could see the tears on Our Lady's face for unbelievers, you would certainly dedicate all your devotion and love to their conversion. [19]

Mirjana would come to further explain that even calling those who lack faith "unbelievers" was not exactly the way to look at them through the Virgin's eyes. She says that when she asked Mary who these unbelievers were, the Virgin told her again that they were all those who do not see the Church as their home and God as their Father. Mary then told her not to even call them unbelievers, because even by saying that, one judges them.[20]

Father Slavko Barbarić well understood the implications of this truth.

He taught that an unbeliever is not just someone who calls himself godless or says that he does not know whether God exists, but someone who says that he "believes" and "knows the Word of God" but does not live according to it and does not do what is good. [21]

Some have written of a deeper concern for unbelievers—or people who do not know God—goes hand-in-hand with a fundamental reality: many of these individuals are in positions of great power today and, therefore, the security and future of the world lies with their decisions.

This, it has been noted, poses considerable danger because of nuclear weapons, and because of an ever expanding pandora's box of scientific and cultural evils that threaten humanity like never before.

Mirjana has hinted in some of her statements of the serious need to pray for unbelievers.[22] She wrote in her book that Mary told her that when you pray for them, you pray for yourselves and for *your own future*. [23]

Father Barbarić's words reveal that he understood this reality early on at Medjugorje. Whether viewed as unbelievers, people who don't know God, or just simply atheists, the magnitude of this truth was apparent to him.

In the mid-80s, Father Barbarić spoke perhaps prophetic words:

"We live in a world full of atheism. There is a personal, practical atheism and an organized atheism. The practical atheism of the Christians is more dangerous to the faith than the organized type. We must start to pray, to start with Our Lady, who is asking us for faith. Practical atheism means that I have everything and do not need Our Lord; I know Our Lord exists but I have everything. It is the most dangerous atheism for the faith, for peace, for love. A poor person…is open to Our Lady, to mankind. Practical atheism means: I don't need you." [24]

Barbarić's words make it clear that he also understood the deeper implications of Fátima and why Mary needed to come to Medjugorje. He saw how Medjugorje fulfilled Mary's mission at Fátima to bring the defeat of systemic atheism through personal conversion:

"One could say that at Fátima, Our Lady announced 'Atheism' and said: Fight against atheism [Communism]. Our Lady invites us now at Medjugorje to pray and fast for those who do not believe!" [25]

Perhaps visionary Ivan Dragićević put it best, "Today we always ask when Russia will be converted, but no one asks, "When are *we* going to be converted?" [26]

Millions lost their lives because of World War II and through the savagery of Communism.

No one knows how many lost their souls.

Now, an inestimable number of people throughout the world are under the influence of a tsunami of atheism that stems from the "errors of Russia," from Marxism.

But the plan of the Virgin Mary is a divine plan. It is deliberate, patient, and most of all, perfect. And, it thrives on one very special element: the love of a perfect Mother who wants to lead every one of her children to God.

"If it is necessary," the Virgin once said at Medjugorje, "I will appear in each home." [27]

The connotation was clear.

The Mother of all has come for all—even if it means pursuing one soul at a time.

CHAPTER FIFTY-THREE

ONE SOUL AT A TIME

*"For the Son of Man has come to seek
and to save what was lost."*

—Lk 19:10

A NEUROPHYSIOLOGIST, Dr. Marco Margnelli journeyed to Medjugorje in the summer of 1988.

He would go there on a mission: to expose the fraud.[1]

By 1984, medical tests done on the six visionaries by doctors from various European nations came to a collective, decisive conclusion: the state of ecstasy the children entered during the apparitions was not the result of a diagnosable medical condition.[2] They were found by every examining physician to be physically and mentally healthy.

But this didn't end the testing. It simply passed the buck into the hands of some other doctors who wanted to look for "religious hysteria."[3]

Two Italian physicians, including one specializing in the field of "Religious Delirium" who worked at the Institute of Criminology at Milan University, were permitted to study the visionaries not only during their ecstasies, but also throughout the course of their normal lives.[4] The physicians looked for patterns observed repeatedly in "delirious people with a mystical bent."[5]

Their findings, however, suggested nothing different. The visionaries showed no sign of any pathological state.[6] On the contrary, they were found to be peaceful, calm, and gentle in all circumstances.[7] Their lives reflected only good will and kindness,[8] and they were discovered to be happy. [9] All the visionaries wanted to do, the psychiatrists stated, was "report what was happening to them." [10]

For Dr. Margnelli, a "convinced Marxist" as *Inside the Vatican* described him,[11] this suggested that possibly the original medical findings were in error.[12] Margnelli was a specialist in ecstasy and altered states of consciousness.[13] He was the author of a study titled *La Droga Perfetta*, which sought to establish a parallel between changes in consciousness induced by chemical means and religious experience. [14]

Upon arriving in Medjugorje, Margnelli conducted his own medical tests.[15] He looked for any evidence that would contradict or expose it (Medjugorje) as a fake.[16]

His findings?

"As a scientist, I can only declare that the children really pass into another state of consciousness."[17] For him, it was a mystery. "We are certainly in the presence of an extraordinary phenomenon." [18]

But by the time Margnelli was finished with his research, he was somewhat uninterested in the results.[19] He had moved personally into non-scientific thinking about Medjugorje. [20] Margnelli remained puzzled by what else he had observed: the absolutely synchronous movements of the visionaries during the apparitions; the miraculous healing of a woman from Milan that he personally met, and some pictures taken by his friends that showed the forty-foot cross on Mt. Krizevac vanishing.[21]

One mystery especially gnawed at him—the birds outside of St. James.

Every evening before the apparition was to occur in the rectory, birds would gather in the trees around the church before sunset. By the hundreds, they would chirp and coo, at times deafening loud.[22] Then, suddenly and simultaneously, the birds would all go silent the moment the apparitions began.[23] This "absolute silence of the birds," Margnelli confessed, troubled him to no end. [24]

Perhaps this was an understatement.

Returning to Milan, the atheist Margnelli became a practicing Catholic just a few months later.[25]

Randall Sullivan came to Medjugorje with the same professional skepticism.

Describing himself as the "miracle detective," [26] Sullivan set out to investigate the apparitions in order to write a book on what he labeled a "spooky subject." [27]

By then, Sullivan was not arriving in a sleepy little rural village that couldn't be located on a map. Medjugorje was now a bustling, internationally known destination where millions had visited. The visionaries were no longer called children. In fact, five of the six by the end of 1994 were married with children of their own. [28]

Sullivan was no run-of-the-mill writer. Like the respected Margnelli, he was a prestigious author and award-winning journalist, penning acclaimed pieces for *Rolling Stone*, *Esquire*, *The Guardian*, *Men's Journal*, and other popular periodicals. [29]

Over his career, he would be nominated three times for the Pulitzer Prize in writing. [30] His book, *LAbyrinth*, would go on to be made into a Hollywood movie. [31]

One more thing about Sullivan: he was for the most part, like Margnelli, an atheist.

Sullivan confessed that he wondered what was out there. [32] But, that's about it. He had been raised by atheistic parents who saw religion as a crutch for the weak minded. [33] Both his siblings were also avowed atheists. [34]

Brash and confident, Sullivan's detective foray seemed to set off an alarm immediately upon his arrival in Medjugorje, where he planned to stay for a month but remained for almost two. [35]

He first began his investigative mission in Rome, however, in order to find out how the Roman Catholic Church goes about the discernment of miracles. While there, he interviewed a number of Church experts in the Vatican; ultimately, he departed with a Pandora's box of questions, rather than the conclusive answers he was looking for.

Two realities, though, surfaced.

There was an ongoing struggle in the Catholic Church as to its direction. This, he discovered, affected everything the Church did, even with the investigation of miracles. [36]

The second reality was the reason he was in Rome in the first place: Medjugorje.

"In Rome," wrote Sullivan, "my own interest in that tiny Bosnian parish would increase each time I spoke its name aloud. There was no single word, I discovered, that so instantly could produce a rapturous smile, derisive snort, or an uncomfortable silence in the Holy See as 'Medjugorje'. What fascinated me was that those who extolled Medjugorje as a sacred place of unparalleled power all had made pilgrimages across the Adriatic to experience the village firsthand, while those who scoffed knew only what they had read or heard." [37]

The timing of Sullivan's visit to Medjugorje blended perfectly with his detective agenda.

He arrived there during the war in the Balkans, immediately establishing a background for his story that couldn't fit better. Hostility, suspicion, mistrust, and danger shadows his account as he ventures through the back roads and quaint towns of rustic Croatia, Bosnia and Hercegovina.

Then, once in the village, his perceived persona as an American journalist seeking to harm Medjugorje was planted front and center. To almost everyone, Sullivan was a red flag, a bad guy, the enemy.

In the minds of those he encountered there, including some of the visionaries, his *Rolling Stone* magazine legacy marked him as someone who was the exact opposite of what Medjugorje was all about.

Sullivan reveals how he perceived that Jacov gave him an uneasy glare on his first day there,[38] while Ivan later openly challenged him as to the purpose of his mission: "You are not here for truth. You are here to make a joke of us." [39]

But it's Mirjana—whose home he stays at for a while—that decides to test whether or not the reporter can withstand the hidden, subduing graces of Medjugorje.

Sensing the Madonna was at work, she pushes Sullivan in a direction that determines the major theme that emerges in his book: his burgeoning conversion. Pressing her to reveal God's secret plan in Medjugorje, Mirjana confronts the prestigious author: "I know why you first come to me—you are an unbeliever." [40]

Then, informing him that their interview would be suspended until he took a better look at who he was and what he believed, [41] Mirjana tells Sullivan point blank that he must climb Mt. Krizevac.[42] Somewhat surprisingly, the self-proclaimed miracle sleuth caves in to her request. He not only decides to embark on Mirjana's challenge, but does so that very same day.[43]

Plodding to the summit of the mountain, as he listened to his inner self ponder the foolishness of every step, Randall Sullivan's destiny rapidly unfolds.

First, an isolated bundle of storm clouds, complete with lightning bolts and thunder, explodes directly above Mt. Krizevac—or as Sullivan perceives it—above *him*.

Immediately he senses there is a reason: it has to do with his past. [44]

Then, a mysterious group of French nuns, along with a compassionate young woman, cross his path and come to his aid after the storm, only to unexplainably vanish from the mountain minutes later. [45]

Together, the two uncanny experiences, along with the hour-long trek up the mountain past the stations of the Cross— during which he hauls his sins—causes something inside of him to give.

Randall Sullivan—the unbeliever—undergoes what he calls his *first* religious experience.[46]

Physically, he laughs uncontrollably. Emotionally, he sheds a river of tears. He admits feeling, he writes, a liberation in his soul.[47] Consequently, from that moment, the modus operandi of his work in Medjugorje shifts.

But the transformation is a process. It seems to grab hold of his life. The book that Sullivan is in Medjugorje to write will not be published for almost nine years. Apparently, this is the time Sullivan needed to come to terms with himself—and with Medjugorje.

Sullivan, like Margnelli, grasped what was really taking place in Medjugorje.

The Virgin Mary, it can be said, was reclaiming her children.

One soul at a time.

Dr. Marco Margnelli and Randall Sullivan, as Mirjana says, were "unbelievers"—two souls never forcibly indoctrinated by a Communist regime, yet far from any belief in God.

Margnelli, an Italian, and Sullivan, an American, chose their ways in Western cultures that permitted them every freedom, including religion. But although the West was free, its vision of life over the previous several decades had become increasingly blind to God and religion.

Man was in. God— if not dead—was definitely out.

Moreover, by the late 80s and early 90s, the media and entertainment industries had begun to power up this anti-religion message, especially with regards to morality and traditional values. Margnelli and Sullivan were just two of millions swept up in the "unbeliever" crusade conquering the planet.

News of the Virgin Mary's apparitions in Medjugorje, however, would fly somewhat under the anti-religion radar. Considered by the secular press to be novel, harmless, amusing, and mostly bizarre, the story of Medjugorje made for good reading and intriguing television.

While the media didn't necessarily believe what was taking place, they didn't have to. People, they understood, love information about strange and unexplainable events.

And in Medjugorje, they found plenty of both.

Stories and shows about Medjugorje popped up everywhere:

- The Keston Magazine (UK) – July 29, 1982
- The Keston Magazine – December 1, 1983
- Libre Belgique – January 9, 1984
- The Spectator (UK) – June 2 – 9 – 16, 1984
- The Guardian – September 17, 1984
- Religion in Communist Lands, Vol. 12, N.3 – December,1984
- The (London) Sunday Times – October 6, 1985
- The (Dublin) Sunday Press – January 20, 1985
- La Stampa – June 20, 1985
- Paris Match Magazine – July, 1985
- Il Tempo – October 9, 1985
- The New York Times – November 18, 1985
- The Reader's Digest Magazine – February, 1986
- Time Magazine – July 7, 1986
- The Philadelphia Inquirer – May 24, 1987
- The Washington Post – July 17, 1987
- Newsweek Magazine – July 20, 1987
- BBC News – February 8, 1987
- The International Herald Tribune – July 21, 1987
- The Times of London – July 27, 1987
- ABC News 20/20 Show – June 17, 1988
- The Miami Herald – September 6, 1988
- The Oprah Winfrey Show – November 23, 1988
- Birmingham News – December 2, 1988
- The Arizona Republic – August 16, 1989
- NBC Unsolved Mysteries Show – September 27, 1989

- U.S. News and World Report Magazine – March 12, 1990
- NBC Inside Edition Show – September, 1990
- Life Magazine – July, 1991
- Phoenix New Times – July 5, 1992
- The Wall Street Journal – November 9, 1992
- The Joan Rivers Show – December 8, 1992
- The Atlanta Journal / The Atlanta Constitution – June 12, 1994
- The Arizona Republic – November 13, 1994

"I have come to tell you God exists!" [48]

This assertion—deliberate and provocative—Mary voiced on the third day of the apparitions at Medjugorje. Many in the media who had done much to distract the world from this truth now seemed to be making amends through the vast attention focused upon the little Slavic village.

And, the story of Medjugorje was getting through.

By the mid-90s, tens of millions had heard about the apparitions. This spawned another wave of individuals to take action on behalf of the Virgin Mary's pleas to help spread her messages.

By then, a worldwide Marian movement had emerged and began networking across continents. It was a movement that included renowned figures in religion, politics, entertainment, sports, and the arts.

With the prominent names, another reality became clear.

Mary had not just come for unbelievers, but for anyone and everyone:

- **Mother Teresa of Calcutta**, founder of the *Missionaries of Charity* and winner of the 1979 Nobel Peace Prize: "I know that many people go there and are converted. I thank God for leading us during these times in this way. I like the picture of Medjugorje that Our Lady blessed during the apparitions. I would go willingly to Medjugorje, but many people would go because of me and this would not be right." [49]
- **Milona Von Hapsburg**, direct descendant of the Hapsburg Austrian Royal Monarchy: "I started to come back to Medjugorje regularly and during one year I came back every month. My whole life was peeled off me; like an onion, I was peeled. My ideas about life, the plans I had for life, the life I was living,

my work, everything just went away from me, and slowly but surely the values that were being underlined and stressed in Medjugorje were taking over." [50]

- **Mother Angelica**, founder of EWTN: "I'm convinced Medjugorje was given to us by God. Our Lady was sent by Him to renew the entire Church. This is most obvious to me by the very fact that Our Lady is telling us, asking us, begging us to change our lives for the better. She asks us to pray, pray, pray, to practice fasting, to mortify ourselves." [51]

- **Reverend David Du Plessis**, world-renowned leader of the Pentecostal Church: "There is no question whatever in mind. This series of apparitions is definitely from the Lord. All the people in the area have been converted to Jesus. They're all reading the Bible. Mary is encouraging this. The message cannot be questioned." [52]

- **Lola Falana**, the top female entertainer in the world in the 1970s: "When the television showed the crowd of pilgrims which ascend the Hill of Apparitions, I experienced a great desire to go there, to walk with them, but my legs were inert, dead. Then, with tears in my eyes, I prayed to the Blessed Mother to heal me, promising her that if one day I would be able to walk again, I would go there." Falana was healed of MS within a month and went to Medjugorje. [53]

- **Jim Caviezel**, Hollywood actor who played Christ in *The Passion of the Christ*: "Through Medjugorje, I experienced how the Rosary is a powerful prayer and what a gift we have when we attend Holy Mass every day." [54]

- **Cardinal František Tomášek**, a staunch and widely known anti-communist during the years of the Cold War in Czechoslovakia: "I am deeply convinced of the apparitions in Medjugorje, and am deeply grateful. Step by step the Immaculate Heart of Mary will Triumph. And I am also deeply convinced that Medjugorje is a sign for this." [55]

- **Archbishop Phillip Hannan**, the Bishop who delivered the eulogy at the funeral Mass for President John F. Kennedy and the graveside eulogy for Senator Robert Kennedy: "The whole parish has been revitalized. Almost every parishioner has become very devout—attending daily Mass, fasting, praying, standing in line to go to Confession. Their devotion is Christ centered...can there be anything but good in it?" [56]

- **Alberto Salazar**, an Olympic Marathon runner: "Medjugorje for me was just a time of returning to the Catholic Church and returning to my commitment to Christ." [57]
- **Alfred Williams**, Austrian lay evangelist who distributed 15 million Fátima brochures through the Blue Army: "The millions of Rosaries that have been prayed and offered up, the fasting on bread and water by the multitude, the millions of confessions, the change of lives by uncounted people from all over the world who have visited there—my God, what else do you *want* to prove the validity of this phenomenon." [58]
- **Andrea Bocelli**, world-renowned tenor: "I am going to Medjugorje to receive a message, not to give a message." Bocelli gave a concert in Medjugorje on August 7, 2008.[59]

Bernard Ellis, a businessman who sold steel to Third World countries, lived in the suburbs of London with his wife, Suzanne, in the early 1980s.

Extremely successful for over twenty-five years, Ellis was raised an Orthodox Jew and once thought of becoming a rabbi. By then, he had pretty much seen the world, though he never heard of Medjugorje.

But Sue, a Catholic, was well aware of the rustic little village of miracles. And, the more she discovered, the more she became convinced that it was the one place she hoped to go.

So, Sue hatched a plan.

For her birthday in 1983, she would ask her husband to take her on a vacation to Dubrovnik in Croatia. Then, once there, she would see if they could take a stroll over to Medjugorje, some two-and-a-half hours up the Adriatic coast by car.

Executed to perfection, Bernard and Sue Ellis landed in Medjugorje in August of that year, although not so much to Bernard's liking as Sue's. Still, it was her birthday, and Bernard figured being the only Jew in a Catholic town would go pretty much unnoticed.

It didn't.

The locals and religious took to them both so warmly, that the couple began to repeatedly return. Sue, for the spiritual graces. Bernard, for the peace and relaxation he found in the village.

In 1985, during what Bernard referred to as a "regular visit" to Medjugorje, they overheard that visionary Marija Pavlović was going to witness a late night apparition at the site of the massive cross on Mt. Krizevac. For Sue, it was an easy decision—they were attending.

Arriving at the top of the mountain early that evening, the couple decided to sit at the base of the concrete cross to wait for the apparition to begin. Soon, they found themselves in pitch black darkness surrounded by several thousand people, all singing and praying in pious anticipation of the vision.

Suddenly, there emerged a small group carrying a lantern that cut its way through the crowd, with Marija Pavlović at its center. As the people parted to let them through, Bernard could see that Marija was headed directly towards him and Sue, with the visionary eventually stopping right at his shoulder.

Moments later, Maria fell to her knees and started to pray.

As she did, a man accompanying Marija asked Bernard, in a badly-mangled English syntax, a question,

"*Are you English?*"

"Yes," Bernard answered.

"*Tell the crowd in English that the Mother of God is appearing to Marija Pavlović; everybody kneels, no photographs and pray.*"

So, Bernard turned and shouted through the darkness to the throng:

"Everybody kneel, the Mother of God is appearing to 'Maria Pablobic', no photographs, everyone pray."

Upon hearing him, the people dropped to their knees.

Except for Bernard. His religious tradition forbade him to do so.

But, that didn't last long.

Seeing how he had told everyone to kneel, it dawned on him that remaining upright wasn't going to work. So, on his knees he went— right next to Marija.

For Bernard, the moment of truth had arrived.

Not only was he stuck late at night on a cold mountaintop somewhere in the middle of Bosnia and Hercegovina—with several thousand fanatical Catholics waiting for an invisible lady from Heaven to drop in—he was doing so on his knees.

"There were stones on the ground and they were cutting into my knees. I felt very uncomfortable. I wondered whether Catholics had special kneecaps that allow them to kneel. These were the thoughts going through my head when the apparition was taking place."

Then, minutes later, another looming disaster.

On the top of his very prominently bald head, Bernard suddenly felt a tiny splash. As if to crown the evening off with one last insult, it was starting to rain.

"I felt a drop of rain fall on my head and I thought it was going to pour…We were going to get soaked…And I wondered what any Jewish man was doing in such a situation."

Finally, the apparition was over. But not for everyone.

Around Marija, members of her entourage quickly jumped to their feet. They then shoved little handheld tape recorders in front of her face so she could repeat the message given to her by the Virgin.

Almost simultaneously, others then began to swiftly translate her words into different languages. As before, Bernard was drafted to aid the cause for the English-speaking members of the crowd.

"I can't remember the exact words," recalled Bernard, "it was something to do with returning to living in the light of the Gospel, otherwise, the world would inflict a great tragedy upon itself."

But, as Bernard slowly worked his way to the end of the message, his eyes suddenly gazed upon something startling.

"A tear rolled down the cheek of Our Blessed Mother," he told the crowd, "and landed on the cloud she was standing."

Instantly, Bernard realized what this meant.

The good Jewish husband had just been christened by the good Jewish Mother—the Mother of God herself.

"I thought to myself, I must have been right under that cloud. That night it did not rain."

On Holy Thursday, April 13, 1987, Bernard Ellis was baptized and confirmed into the Catholic Church. Coincidently, it was also the first night of the Jewish Passover that year.

Bernard recognized the significance:

"The first night of the Jewish Passover and Holy Thursday do not always fall on the same day, but on this year it did. For Jewish people, the Messiah will come on the first night of the Passover. It's a tradition and they wait for the Messiah to come on that night. For me, the Messiah did come on that night when I was Baptized, Confirmed and received my First Holy Communion."

There was one more so-called coincidence.

Bernard says it was a present for him from the Blessed Mother on that day.

"April 13th also happened to be my birthday! Born again on my birthday! What a wonderful grace for a Jewish man!" [60]

CHAPTER FIFTY-FOUR

"PROTECT MEDJUGORJE"

*"But the Lord is faithful; he will strengthen
you and guard you from the evil one."*
—2 Thes 3:3

ASK MARY IF CROATIA WILL EVER BE FREE?
This was what Father Petar Ljubicic requested Mirjana Dragićević to inquire of the Madonna long before the war broke out in the Balkans.

"Yes," Mirjana was told, but only after considerable suffering and pain.[1]

Mary's lone tear drop on the head of Bernard Ellis would pale in number to what she would shed for her children when war hit the former Yugoslavia in 1991.

The conflict affected Medjugorje greatly, but the village somehow remained an oasis of peace in the middle of it all. Pilgrims from as far away as America continued to come, despite the danger.

Extraordinary accounts of what appears to have been divine protection surfaced repeatedly throughout and after the war. The April 28, 1993, edition of the French newspaper, *Le Monde*, went so far as to call Medjugorje "the protected zone of the Virgin Mary." [2] Indeed, the neighboring town of Čitluk was severely bombarded, and attempts to bomb Medjugorje were reported to have been ordered.[3]

But none succeeded.

A captured Serbian pilot who was shot down on May 8, 1992, spoke about this mystery, "I could not bomb the Church of Medjugorje. If I got close to it, I could not see it anymore; some kind of fog hid it from my eyes." [4]

The pilot's story even prompted a front page article in the November 9, 1992, *Wall Street Journal*. Read the headline: **"Forward into Battle? Not Here Where the Virgin Reigns."** [5]

Another pilot, U.S. Air Force Captain Scott O'Grady—who was shot down over Bosnia in an F-16 fighter jet on June 2, 1995, while on a mission to enforce a no-fly zone—also reported an extraordinary experience related to Medjugorje.

Forced to hide for six days, twenty-miles south of Bihac behind Serbian lines, O'Grady said he began to pray to Our Lady of Medjugorje. He had heard about Medjugorje from his mother's friend, who once spoke about the village.

Suddenly, on his third day in hiding, O'Grady said he beheld Mary in a vision:

"I turned to Our Lady in prayer. Before long, I felt a definite presence. It grew more and more vivid, until I could see it, shimmering in my mind's eye! I knew I would not die. It's hard to put into words, but I saw the vision, but yet, also felt it. The feeling was powerful, very warm, and comforting...[6] Our Lady of Medjugorje saved me." [7]

Other reports appear to support that Mary was keeping a protective eye over the shrine.

Six missiles, fired into the village on May 8, 1992, all fell on waste ground less than a quarter of a mile from the church. The attack killed a dog, a cow, and a chicken, and it caused damage to an empty house.[8]

Three unexploded bombs were also discovered in the muddy fields surrounding Medjugorje, [9] and another two landed near a gas station at Tromedja's crossroads near Medjugorje. But no one was ever injured or killed in the villages from the fighting.

In addition, St. James Church was not damaged in any way throughout the war, unlike the great number of churches in Croatia, Bosnia, and Herzegovina that were totally destroyed. In the diocese that holds the city of Sarajevo alone, out of 144 parishes, only 54 survived.[10] In Mostar, the historic cathedral was destroyed, including its library of over 30,000 books.[11]

During the horrific conflict, Father Jozo Zovko served as the guardian of the Franciscan Monastery in Široki Brijeg.[12] There, he spent most of his time aiding victims of the war.

On June 17, 1992, however, Jozo traveled to Rome and met with Pope John Paul II. In an open letter, he wrote about his audience with the Holy Father:

> My unforgettable meeting with our Pope took place on June 17, 1992. So many friends of Medjugorje had prepared this meeting! I had to accomplish my mission of peace with the General of my order and with the Pope. The Pope had been informed of my mission and the General of my order also. I had already made a brief report to them on my mission of peace and my meetings with different politicians. Since I had the papers in my hands, I also decided to give the Pope the image of the Blessed Virgin (of Tihaljina) with the messages.
>
> He was surrounded by some cardinals and priests. I took his hand and kissed it. He told me "Good morning", and with love, he listened to me introduce myself: "Holy Father, I am Father Jozo from Medjugorje. At the end of my mission, I want to leave you this report with the image of the Blessed Virgin and her message."
>
> The Pope answered me: "Medjugorje, I know, I know, Medjugorje... Protect Medjugorje. I am with you. I bless you. Courage. Courage, I am with you. Support Medjugorje. Greet them all for me. I bless all of them. I know you are suffering in this war." He held my hands more tightly. I continued telling the Pope about the political situation and the sufferings of our people. Full of sadness, he blessed me again while he held my hands tightly. I thanked him for everything that he had done for us, for the Croats and for the independence of our country. [13]

Six months later, on January 10, 1993, Jozo would meet again with Pope John Paul II. This time it would be in Assisi, where he would present a talk on Saint Francis and participate with religious from all over the world in praying for peace.[14]

Not just the Pope would become visibly involved with Medjugorje and the war.

Once again, as with the Cold War and President Ronald Reagan, it appears Medjugorje found a way into the White House and the Oval Office.

James Flickinger, an attorney from Grand Rapids, Michigan, experienced a conversion through Medjugorje in November of 1990. Not long after, he became involved with relief efforts for the refugees of the war in Bosnia and Herzegovina. Flickinger, along with two friends, made ten trips there during the war, bringing in over 5 million dollars in direct medical aid.

The program was so successful, news of it reached the White House, prompting an invitation to meet with President Bill Clinton in December of 1996.[15] At first reluctant to attend for personal reasons involving the President's policies, Flickinger noticed the invitation was for December 8, the Feast of the Immaculate Conception, and changed his mind.

The meeting couldn't have gone better, he would later report, as the three men met with the President and members of his staff. While everything from military solutions to the attitude of the people in Bosnia were discussed, the three also told Clinton about Medjugorje and the need for prayer to bring an end to the war. [16]

"I had expected reserved reactions from the President," wrote Flickinger in a letter published by Wayne Weible describing the meeting. "The response could not have been warmer. There were broad smiles and vigorous nods of approval to the call for prayer. Also interesting was President Clinton's reaction to our gift to him of a rosary, blessed in Medjugorje. I expected he would thank us and perhaps set it on his desk. That didn't happen. He held it in his hands until the time we left the meeting. Later, we had the opportunity to talk further with the other people who had been invited to the meeting. Two of them were very involved with Medjugorje. They also felt compelled to come to the White House meeting to emphasize the need for our nation to pray for true peace." [17]

That same day, President Clinton met with television evangelist, Reverend Robert Schuller, who had a weekly worldwide show called,

The Hour of Power. Schuller, on his very next show, spoke of his meeting with Clinton, and told his audience that the first words out of the President's mouth to him were, "Ask our world to pray for peace in Bosnia-Hercegovina!" which Schuller did. [18]

For the most part, as Mirjana would note in her book, Medjugorje was insulated from the worst of the war. It appeared as if the village was in a safeguarding bubble, the visionary commented.[19] The ex-mayor of Medjugorje, Dragan Kozina, agreed, "You have to believe that either we were very lucky, or that someone was protecting us." [20]

But many tears were still shed.

Over 100,000 died in the region.[21] And, a number of friends and family members from Medjugorje were injured or killed because of the brutal conflict, including Stjepan Soldo, the 22-year-old brother of Mirjana's husband, Marco, who was killed in a car accident while delivering aid. [22]

On November 21, 1995, the Dayton Peace Agreement, known as *The Dayton Accords*, was signed in Dayton, Ohio—home of the prestigious internationally-recognized Marian Library at the University of Dayton—and the war in the Balkans was over. [23]

The time for shedding tears was finally nearing an end in the village.

But not for the Madonna of Medjugorje.

As the war was winding down, just across the Adriatic Sea in Italy, a sixteen-inch-tall, white plaster statue of Our Lady of Medjugorje began to weep tears of blood in Civitavecchia, a city a little more than fifty miles northwest of Rome.[24] The reported miracle began on Friday, February 2, 1995, and quickly became the talk of Italy.[25]

The statue was purchased as a souvenir by Father Pablo Martin, the parish priest of St. Agostino's Church in the Pantano district of Civitavecchia, during a pilgrimage to Medjugorje in September of 1994.[26]

Scientific investigations by laboratories confirmed the drops of blood pouring out of the *La Madonnina's* eyes were of human origin, setting off an even greater stir.

Because of the drama that would swirl around the little statue for the next several years, the story eventually became an international news event.[27] Soon, like at Medjugorje, thousands were coming from all over to see for themselves the weeping Madonna of Civitavecchia.[28]

As with Bernard Ellis, through the power of her teardrops, the Virgin Mary was continuing to call the world back to God. But it was a call that needed to be answered, the Madonna would continue to say in Medjugorje, "while there is still time." [29]

Jim Caviezel

Photo Credit:
En Wikipedia.org

Bernard Ellis

Photo Credit: St.
Andrews Productions

Rita Klaus

Photo Credit: St.
Andrews Productions

The Risen Saviour statue in Medjugorje has seen a constant flow of water from its right knee.

Photo Credit: St. Andrews Productions

At her June 25, 1988, annual apparition, Ivanka was photographed in ecstasy. The eyes of her baby daughter, Christina, appear to also be locked in on the vision.

Photo Credit: Renee Laurentin

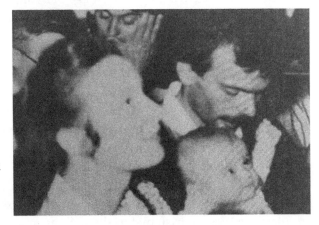

CHAPTER FIFTY-FIVE

OPENING SECRETS

*"I became preoccupied with her, never
weary of extolling her. My hand
opened her gate and I came to know her secrets."*
—Sir 51:19

IT WASN'T THE BEST OF TIMES—OR THE WORST, CONSIDERING ALL that unfolded in the twentieth century.

But it may have come close.

The late 1990s seemed to flirt with Dickens' prose. The world was anxious, without a compass, and schizophrenic in many ways; yet at the same time, it was riding a post-Cold War sigh that mixed well with a scientific renaissance.

Personal computers, hand-held cell phones, emails and websites—all ushered in a sea of change, a new age of living on earth. Spearheaded by the Internet, a technology boom swept across the planet. The pace of life was transformed, even in rural areas once known for tranquility and easy living.

In the West, it was all about the individual.

The pursuit of more personal wealth, pleasure, and convenience defined the closing years of the second millennium, especially in America. There, people caught luxury fever, spending money on anything that called itself "bigger and better."

The East pushed to keep up.

Nations with massive populations like India and China began to modernize, bringing societal changes that witnessed citizens trying to emulate the West's garish materialism. Sunglasses and trendy hairstyles were dead giveaways that something was happening in countries where oxcarts and chickens had paraded the streets not long before. For the most part, life was relatively good, and getting better.

Behind the scenes, though, the dark, godless side of humanity was getting darker, almost black. The cascade of regional wars continued, with rogue nations, drug cartels, and Islamic terrorists taking turns grabbing headlines.

While, out of sight, there was underway the greatest holocaust in history.

The slaughter of the unborn, occurring in the tens of millions a year worldwide, almost single-handedly caused one to wonder if God's justice could not be far off.

The backdrop to all this—though thought about and discussed much less—was the ever-present danger of nuclear annihilation. While not carrying the palpable fear that stalked the planet for decades, hundreds of nuclear weapons were still plugging silos and hiding in oceans, ready to launch at a moment's notice.

Y2K—a worldwide computer glitch predicted to occur the moment the clock struck midnight at the turn of the millennium—ensured the calamitous century ended with a somewhat-fitting apocalyptic scare.

All of this demonstrated one thing: the era of peace foretold at Fátima was not only unfulfilled, but looked more and more to be humanely unattainable—that is, unless some extraordinary help arrived from above.

That help was on the way.

At Medjugorje, unlike at Fátima, the message from almost the very beginning was clear: the future would not be determined by mankind's choices alone.

Through what little was known of the Ten Secrets to be revealed there, a divine schedule was seen to be part of the plan.

Its appointment card had even been written out and handed to Mirjana.

On Christmas Day, 1982, Mirjana Dragićević reported that she received the Virgin Mary's tenth and final Secret. Mary then presented her with something that seemed like a rolled up scroll that had the ten secrets written on it.[1] Upon handing it to her, the Madonna advised the teenage girl to show it to a priest of her choosing at the appropriate time. [2]

At first, Mirjana didn't ponder what she held in her hands. But then it hit her: how, she wondered, was she holding an object not of this world? [3]

Though it was surreal, the scroll looked very earthy. Mirjana described it as a beige-colored material akin to parchment—not quite paper and not quite fabric, but something in between.[4] She said that when she unrolled and read it, she saw the Secrets written in a simple, elegant cursive handwriting with no decorations or illustrations. The Secrets were unnumbered but appeared in the same order that Mary had given them to her.[5]

The first Secret was at the top, and the tenth at the bottom of the scroll.[6] Each Secret brought with it the date of the event foretold.[7] And, Mirjana discovered, only she was able to read it. She had a cousin in Switzerland, an engineer, examine the material in order to identify its composition, but he could not say what it was.[8]

Years later, Mirjana revealed a bemusing event concerning the scroll.

During the war in the early 90s, her family was forced to flee after Sarajevo came under bombardment. At the time, Mirjana kept the mysterious parchment there instead of Medjugorje. Ultimately, it was left behind in her parent's apartment.

Discovering that a Spanish battalion of over two hundred United Nations peacekeepers stationed in Medjugorje was scheduled to be transferred to Sarajevo, Mirjana decided to take a chance. She inquired if some of them could attempt to retrieve the heavenly message, along with other personal documents.[9] This, the soldiers successfully did.[10]

Not long after, one of them knocked on Mirjana's door in Medjugorje and simply handed her a bundle of papers, along with the scroll. The man was, Mirjana described somewhat amusingly, oblivious to his role in what had just transpired.[11]

Two more points concerning the scroll and its contents are worth mentioning.

Some early accounts report that Ivanka also received a celestial piece of parchment with the Ten Secrets written on it. This misinformation, however, was clarified when Ivanka denied it to Father Laurentin, explaining to him that Mary simply taught her a code to use for transcribing the Secrets safely.[12]

Secondly, after Mary entrusted Mirjana with the Tenth Secret, she instructed the visionary to choose a priest for a special role. Ten days prior to the event described in the First Secret, Mirjana is to tell this priest what is predicted to happen, and when it will occur. Mirjana and he are then to *both* pray and fast for seven days before the priest is to reveal it to the world, three days prior to its occurrence. All ten secrets are to be revealed in this manner.[13]

In an interview conducted with Mirjana on October 7, 1988, the visionary hypothetically explained how the public revelation of the Ten Secrets to the world will unfold someday:

> About the Secrets. I have got the Ten Secrets. I received a date for each Secret; when and where it is going to happen. I was instructed to choose a priest in whom I would have confidence. That priest would be approved by Our Lady as suitable for that particular purpose. For example, ten days before the Secrets will occur, I need to reveal that to him, and he is supposed to fast on bread and water for seven days. And three days before the event, he is to reveal to the people what is going to happen.[14]

On June 27, 1985, Mirjana chose for this role a 39-year-old priest named Father Petar Ljubicic.* A tall Franciscan who wore thick, oversized glasses, Ljubicic was known for his warm smile and his compassion for orphans and the very poor.[15]

Born in 1946 in the village of Prisoje, sixty-five miles from Medjugorje, Father Ljubicic became a Franciscan in 1967 and was ordained in 1972. He would become Vicar at Vitina from 1972 through 1978, at Tihaljina from 1978 to 1982, and then at Seonica from 1982 to 1986.[16]

---

*   In her 2016 book, *My Heart Will Triumph*, Mirjana indicated it may not be Fr. Petar Ljubicic who reveals the Secrets, writing that it "doesn't necessarily have to be that way." It depends, she said, on "God's will." A June 2021 Italian video posted online of a Q&A session with Mirjana appeared to confirm this possibility. Being so young at the time of her first choosing Fr. Petar, one can't help but wonder if his present age is now a concerning factor with regards to the time of the announcement of the Secrets. Mirjana's growing reality of this over time may be much more of a consideration behind this situation than any accusations of her "changing her mind."

Stationed almost an hour and a half away, Mirjana was questioned about the wisdom of her selection at the time. Shortly after, though, Father Ljubicic was mysteriously transferred to Medjugorje.[17]

Quiet and extremely reserved, Ljubicic almost immediately opined after talking to Mirjana about the Secrets that it looked as though the First Secret might "be very disturbing." [18]

It was also around this time that another Franciscan arrived in Medjugorje, one who would become quite instrumental in helping Mirjana with the burden of the Secrets.

Father Slavko Barbarić was assigned to the parish in September of 1985. Born in Dragićina in 1945, just a few miles down the road from Medjugorje, Barbarić was ordained in 1971 and served in a parish in Graz, Austria, for a year. He then served in Čapljina for five years.[19] From 1978 to 1981, he worked on doctorates in sociology and psychotherapy at Freiburg University in Germany before being assigned to Medjugorje.

Barbarić's intuition before he arrived, he confessed, was that Medjugorje was a case of "fantasy and collusion." [20] Formally indoctrinated so well on the workings of the mind, he would, ironically, become most known at Medjugorje for his teachings on the spiritual workings of the heart.

With so much trepidation smoldering during the last days of the twentieth century, mostly because the end of the second millennium brought with it an air of doomsday that seemed to hover over the planet, curiosity in the contents of Mirjana's heavenly scroll mounted.

The signs of the times in the late 90s many believed, pointed to the budding fulfillment of the Ten Secrets of Medjugorje. [21]

But it would be the contents of another mysterious piece of paper—one holding the most celebrated of all the Virgin Mary's secrets—that suddenly popped up in the news again in the spring of 2000.

The so called Third Secret of Fátima was back in the headlines.

Beginning in November of 1999, after the Portuguese Bishops' ad limina visit [once every five years] with the Pope, there arose rumors that the third part of the Secret of Fátima would be revealed.[22]

This had occurred not too long before.

In 1996, Cardinal Ratzinger, the Prefect of the Congregation for the Doctrine of the Faith, curiously traveled to Fátima on October

13 to deliver the homily. Which was all he did. Two hundred thousand from across Europe and beyond gathered that day, but went home disappointed.

This time there would be no disappointment.

On January 13, 2000, Rome's popular daily, *Il Massaggero*, flashed the headline: **"Pope to Reveal Third Secret in May."**

And, indeed, that is what John Paul II would do.

On May 13, 2000, Cardinal Angelo Sodano officially announced at Fátima, after the beatification ceremonies that day of the two other visionaries, Francisco and Jacinta Marto, that the Holy Father was going to publicly open the third part of the Secret and let the world in on its mysterious contents.

The Secret concerned, noted Sodano in his prepared statement that day, "the war waged by atheistic systems against the Church and Christians" in the last century of the second millennium.

"On this solemn occasion of his (John Paul II's) visit to Fátima," Sodano stated in his prepared statement, "his Holiness has directed me to make an announcement to you. ...In order that the faithful may better receive the message of Our Lady of Fátima, the Pope has charged the Congregation for the Doctrine of the Faith with making public the third part of the Secret of Fátima, after the preparation of an appropriate commentary." [23]

"No great mystery is revealed; nor is the future unveiled," wrote Cardinal Joseph Ratzinger in his theological commentary: *The Message of Fátima*.

Released by the Vatican on June 26, 2000, the forty-three-page booklet addressed not only the third part of the Secret, but the entire Secret of Fátima.[24]

However, the long awaited text of the third part of the Secret—written originally by Sister Lúcia on January 3, 1944, in Tui, Spain, under obedience to her bishop—turned out *not* to be a message at all from the Virgin Mary to the children at Fátima.

Instead, the document contained only Lúcia's description of a vision that the three young visionaries experienced in the summer of 1917, one saturated in theological and historical symbolism:

THE THIRD PART OF THE SECRET REVEALED AT THE COVA DA IRIA—Fátima, on 13 July 1917.

I write in obedience to you, my God, who commands me to do so through his Excellency the Bishop of Leiria and through your Most Holy Mother and mine.

After the two parts which I have already explained, at the left of Our Lady and a little above, we saw an Angel with a flaming sword in his left hand; flashing, it gave out flames that looked as though they would set the world on fire; but they died out in contact with the splendor that Our Lady radiated towards him from her right hand; the Angel cried out in a loud voice: '*Penance, Penance, Penance!*'. And we saw in an immense light that is God: 'something similar to how people appear in a mirror when they pass in front of it' a Bishop dressed in White 'we had the impression that it was the Holy Father.'

Other Bishops, Priests, men and women Religious going up a steep mountain, at the top of which there was a big Cross of rough-hewn trunks as of a cork-tree with the bark; before reaching there the Holy Father passed through a big city half in ruins and half trembling with halting step, afflicted with pain and sorrow; he prayed for the souls of the corpses he met on his way; having reached the top of the mountain, on his knees at the foot of the big Cross he was killed by a group of soldiers who fired bullets and arrows at him, and in the same way there died one after another the other Bishops, Priests, men and women Religious, and various lay people of different ranks and positions. Beneath the two arms of the Cross there were two Angels each with a crystal asper-sorium in his hand, in which they gathered up the blood of the Martyrs and with it sprinkled the souls that were making their way to God. [25]

—Tui, 3–1–1944.

Expected to set off fireworks, the disclosure—as well as the Vatican's commentary—left many feeling like a child who is told there is no Santa Claus. The contents of the third part of the Secret revealed nothing near what was expected.

Soon, a chorus of accusations rippled through the media. Wrote one Rome based reporter years later about it all:

> The Third Secret of Fátima was the Vatican equivalent of *Area 51*; any attempt at an official explanation was bound to ignite new conspiracy theories… Where were the end-of-the-world scenarios?… Where was the divine punishments for a world gone wrong? … And if the Third Secret did not warn of the apocalypse or a global catastrophe like nuclear holocaust, why had the Vatican kept it secret for so long? [26]

The Vatican's commentary, pointed out critics, had a primary—some thought perhaps somewhat disingenuous—objective; it was to establish the attempted assassination of Pope John Paul II on May 13, 1981, as the single event of significance foretold in the third part of the Secret.

The slain Pope seen in the vison, the commentary postured, was the culminating climax of a century of totalitarian evils.[27] All of which had been prophesied at Fátima to descend upon the world and the Church. All of which also—including the attempted assassination of the Pope and the fall of Communism—were now fulfilled prophecy.

This brings up, some say, the second objective of the Vatican's document: it was intended to permanently assign the third part of the Secret to the past,[28] as well as, in essence, the prophetic content of the second part of the Secret of Fátima, too.[29]

In this regard, the three principal voices of the disclosure concurred. Said Cardinal Tarcisio Bertone, "The period of history marked by tragic human lust for power and evil has been brought to an end." Declared Cardinal Sodano, "The events to which the third part of the Secret of Fátima refers now seem part of the past." Wrote Ratzinger, "First of all, we must affirm with Cardinal Sodano…the events to which the third part of the 'secret' of Fátima refers now seem part of the past. Insofar as individual events are described, they belong to the past." [30]

Bertone maintained this mindset in his 2008 book: "The media have doggedly refused to resign themselves to the fact that the prophecy is no longer open to the future, but refers to something that now belongs to the past." [31]

Unintendedly, the Vatican's interpretation of the third part of the Secret perhaps started to take shape right after the attempted murder of the Pope. In reviewing the contents of the Secret of Fátima on July 18, 1981—as he convalesced in the Gemelli Clinic from an infection caused by a tainted blood transfusion on the day he was shot that May—John Paul II became convinced that the Pope slain in the vision of the third part of the Secret was a mystical foreshadowing of his failed assassination attempt.

Mary, he believed, intervened to save him.[32]

While not in keeping with what the vision foretold, the Holy Father's conclusion was theologically acceptable. This is because no true prophecy of a concerning future is etched in stone. As Cardinal Ratzinger explained, "even a catastrophic or apocalyptic one (prophesy), cannot be inevitable." [33]

By its very nature, prophecy is a call to alter a foretold troublesome path ahead by taking action that attempts to disarm the looming danger. This is best depicted in the Old Testament's account of Jonah and the pending chastisement of Nineveh that is averted.[34]

John Paul II's survival—versus the fatal plight of the Pope in the third part of the Secret vision—can be viewed in this way, too. Perhaps, through years of prayer and penance, the prophesied outcome was foiled. [35]

No dispute was heard from Lúcia concerning this position. The Fátima visionary stated that it was up to the Church to discern the third part of the Secret and had no official statement on its commentary.

Lúcia was, however, informed ahead of time. Dr. Joaquin Navarro-Valls, the head of the Vatican's Press Office and Pope John Paul II's official spokesperson, told journalists that several weeks before the beatification of Jacinta and Francisco on May 13, Sister Lúcia was made aware of the Pope's decision to reveal the third part of the Secret and had been asked to review the Vatican's interpretation. [36]

Critics, however, insisted the interpretation was wrong.

Besides the fact that Pope John Paul II survived—which some claimed contradicted the whole intent of the third part of the Secret of Fátima [37]—other parts of the vision were seen to suggest more than just the attack on the Pope. Some went so far as to say the third part of the Secret foretold a future crisis in the Church that will involve another Pope who has yet to arrive. [38]

But there arose even greater objections.

Statements concerning the third part of the Secret made by Church officials in the mid-80s and early 90s—all *after* the attempted assassination of John Paul II—did not line up well with the commentary's emphasis on the assassination attempt. Simply put, their remarks at that time appeared to be speaking of something more that was still to come.

This was especially noted with regard to Vittorio Messsori's 1985 book, *The Ratzinger Report*. Cardinal Ratzinger told Messori that "to publish the 'third part of the Secret' would mean exposing the Church to the danger of sensationalism, exploitation of the content." [39]

Ratzinger also did a 1996 radio interview with Portugal's main Catholic radio station, *Radio Renascenca*, in which he denied any "apocalyptic visions," something the now released Secret was found to hold in the eyes of many. [40]

There also came into question comments made by those who read the third part of the Secret during the reigns of Popes John XXIII and Paul VI. To many, their remarks seemed at odds with the Church's commentary on the vision. Most of these opinions centered on the belief, wrote *Inside the Vatican,* that either "a great chastisement or a great apostasy—one that would involve the highest levels of the Church"— were predicted to come in the Secret. [41]

This suspicion—that of a great apostasy—had been fueled for years by Lúcia's own words from her *Fourth Memoir,* which stated at the end of the second part of the Secret, "In Portugal, the dogma of the faith will always be preserved; etc..." It was a statement that seemed to imply that such would not be the case for the Church or the faith throughout the rest of the world.

Many leaders of the Church appeared to still hold this opinion of the contents of the third part of the Secret. "In the Third Secret, it is foretold," Cardinal Maria Luigi Ciappi, Pope John Paul II's own personal papal theologian, once said, "the great apostasy in the Church will begin at the top." [42]

Asked by the editor of *Ill Giornale* if he was satisfied with release of the third part of the Secret and the Vatican's commentary, the great Mariologist Father René Laurentin replied,

"Not at all. There are some things that don't convince me." [43]

CHAPTER FIFTY-SIX

A FOURTH SECRET
OF FATIMA?

*"Both what is still hidden and what has already been
revealed concern us and our descendants forever,
that we may carry out all the words of this law."*
— Dt 29:29

FOR MANY MARIAN FOLLOWERS, ALL OF THE CONTROVERSY SUR-
rounding the announcement of the third part of the Secret of
Fátima meant one thing: there was a missing piece to the revelation
that was not released by the Vatican—a suspected narrative given
by the Virgin Mary which not only interpreted the vision but was
believed to hold a warning to the Church, especially with regards to a
future council.

This part of the original text, some hailed, remained deliberately concealed.

"Mystery Half Revealed," read the headline of the Italian daily
newspaper, *La Repubblica*. "The celebrated 'Third Secret,'" said the
paper, "cannot be reconciled with the dramatic events of May 13, 1981.
There is no Pope who is struck down 'as if dead.' The scene is another. A
Pope killed by 'soldiers who shoot him with bullets and arrows.' It does
no good to invoke the language of symbols and metaphors. No one will
be able to put it into the heads of people that the prophecy is mistaken.
It is not an illusion; it points elsewhere." [1]

That the third part of the Secret was not fully released is a charge
that will not go away.

This so-called missing text is even believed by some to have been the source of inspiration behind Pope John Paul II's reported words at Fulda, Germany, in November, 1980.

At Fulda, in response to the question, "What about the Third Secret of Fátima. Should it not have been published in 1960?" the Pope gave a surprising reply to a small, semi-private gathering, that was presumably believed to be "off the record." His comments, however, were published in the German magazine, *Stimme des Glaubens*, who obtained a tape of the question and answer session.

The Vatican did not issue a denial of this controversial story that soon spread around the world.[2] John Paul II reportedly said that day:

> Because of the seriousness of its contents (The third part of the Secret of Fátima), in order not to encourage the world power of Communism to carry certain coups, my predecessors in the Chair of Peter have diplomatically preferred to withhold its publication. On the other hand, it should be sufficient for all Christians to know this much: if there is such a message in which it is said that oceans will flood entire sections of the Earth; that, from one moment to the other, millions of people will perish...there is no longer any point in really wanting to publish this Secret. Many want to know merely out of curiosity, or because of their taste for sensationalism, but they forget that to know implies for them a responsibility. It is dangerous to want to satisfy one's curiosity only, if one is convinced that we can do nothing against a catastrophe that has been predicted. [3]

What is going to happen to the Church? the Pope was then asked.

> We must prepare ourselves to suffer great trials before long, such as will demand of us a disposition to give up even life, and a total dedication to Christ and for Christ. With your and my prayer, it is possible to mitigate this tribulation, but it is no longer possible to avert it, because only thus can the Church be effectively renewed. How many times has the renewal of the Church sprung from blood! This time, too, it will not be otherwise. We must be strong and prepared, and trust in Christ and His Mother, and be very, very assiduous in praying the Rosary. [4]

The existence of a withheld document—referred to as the "Fourth Secret of Fátima" [5]—has been denied by all the principal figures involved—most prominently, Cardinal Tarcisio Bertone.

In 2008, the cardinal, with the help of an Italian journalist, Giuseppe De Carli, released a book on the whole affair, *The Last Secret of Fátima*. In it, Bertone—who spent many hours face-to-face with Sister Lúcia on multiple occasions—says that the part of the text (of the third part of the Secret) where the Virgin speaks in the first person wasn't censored for the simple reason that it never happened: "The text these people talk about just doesn't exist." [6] Such talk, Bertone added, is "absolutely crazy." [7]

Others agreed. If the Church was trying to hide some perilous prophecies—or a harsh message from Mary about Vatican II—Fátima scholars argue that Popes Paul VI (who read the Secret on March 27, 1965 [8]) and John Paul II would never have "espoused the whole philosophy of Fátima and visited the shrine in Portugal." [9]

Sister Lúcia, the one who would know for sure, was adamant until she died in 2005 that there was no such text. Confronted by Bertone, who handed her a photo static copy of her original letter and asked if it was the one and only third part of the Secret, Lúcia replied:

"This is my letter. This my writing. Yes, this is the Third Secret, and I never wrote any other." [10]

Doubters of Lúcia cited her age and other hypothetical reasons for her statement, such as her vows of obedience or a furtive quid pro quo agreement with the Vatican that permitted her to publish her books.

Over time, this issue became a thorn in her side that was repeatedly revisited. [11]

On October 26, 2001, another fly in the ointment appeared surrounding this issue.

The Rome periodical, *Inside the Vatican*, published an article titled, "The Secret of Fátima: Is there Something Else?" The story claimed Sister Lúcia had recently sent Pope John Paul II a letter warning him that his life was in danger. [12]

"News has arrived," wrote the journal, "that Sister Lúcia dos Santos, the last surviving visionary of Fátima, sent to the Pope a few weeks ago a letter in which she warns him clearly that his life is in danger. According to Vatican sources, the letter affirms that the events described in the Third Secret of Fátima have yet to occur, and it (the letter) was delivered shortly after September 11 to John Paul II by the Bishop Emeritus of Fátima-Leiria, Alberto Cosme do Amaral." [13]

The article reported that the letter from Sister Lúcia encouraged the Pope to reveal the "entire" Third Secret, stating, "It has been said that it (the letter) contains the warning: 'Soon there will be great upheavals and chastisements.'"

Not surprisingly, the story quickly mushroomed.

When asked, the Titular Bishop of the Diocese of Fatima-Leiria— Serafim de Sousa Ferreira de Silva—did not deny Lúcia sent the Pope a letter. But the letter, the bishop explained, did not express danger to the Pope. [14]

Adding to the drama, twenty-one days after the article was published, Archbishop Tarcisio Bertone was seen returning to Coimbra to meet with Sister Lúcia. It was rumored the visit was to have Lúcia deny everything and to demonstrate to the world that the Third Secret and the Consecration of Russia were closed matters—which is exactly what happened.

Bertone, in a January 2002 interview with *Inside the Vatican*, once again calmed the seas around the third part of the Secret:

"Sister Lúcia reconfirmed that the Third Secret has been revealed in full and that there is no more to the Secret. The rest are inventions of journalists and also some priests. Unfortunately, there are pseudo-prophets who use the prophecies of Sister Lúcia to advance their apocalyptic ideas."

Likewise, Bertone stressed again, "Sister Lúcia said that the consecration was completed as the Virgin Mary desired...It is absurd to continue to deny certain facts." [15]

All of this ongoing controversy took its toll.

In Rome, even steady Vatican press observers were taken back by the latest Fátima affair. *La Stampa*'s Marco Tosatti went so far as to label it "an unusual, not to say, unprecedented event in the bimillenial history of the Church." [16]

With the different storms surrounding the release of the third part of the Secret of Fátima in 2000 not going away, there suddenly appeared another event that some saw as related to it all: the terrorist attack on the United States on September 11, 2001.

For those who doubted the Vatican's explanation of the third part of the Secret, this shocking event added fuel to their suspicions that the Secret contained controversial prophesies.

Not surprisingly, a few months after the 9/11 terrorist attack, Cardinal Bertone was forced to respond again. This time he was asked as to whether or not the events of September 11 were referenced in the third part of the Secret but not released. "It is not true that she (Lucia) predicted the events of September 11th. She told me this clearly," explained Bertone. [17]

By now, though, it was becoming obvious. The third part of the Secret wasn't going away. The world had too many big problems to let it.

"The cracks which were opening in the official interpretation of the Fátima affair after 2000 were becoming nosier and more numerous…," wrote Antonio Socci in *The Fourth Secret of Fátima*. "The Triumph of the Immaculate Heart of Mary is not seen in the world—far from it— much less the promised peace and 'conversion of Russia.' Above all, after September 11, 2001, it appeared clear that the maternal warnings of the Madonna concerning imminent chastisements were not consigned to the past." [18]

Socci's book and a couple of others—*The Secret Still Hidden*, by an American lawyer named Christopher Ferrara, and *The Secret Not Revealed* by Marco Tosatti—were sound exposes on the history of the third part of the Secret. All construct strong arguments on the existence of a missing text based on a trove of circumstantial evidence that includes some very germane documents and personal testimonies.

One testimony in particular—that of an Archbishop Loris Capovilla given to a journalist named Solideo Paolini, who published it in his book, *Do Not Despise the Prophecy: Reconstruction of the Unpublished Part of the Third Secret*—stated there were indeed two different texts of the Third Secret.[19]

On September 21, 2007, however, Capovilla is seen in a filmed interview, released by Cardinal Bertone, issuing an apparent retraction of his statement.[20]

There *was* one person who appeared very pleased by the releasing of the third part of the Secret: Mehmet Ali Ağca, the Turkish attempted assassin of Pope John Paul II.

Going back to December 27, 1983, when the Pope met with Ağca in his cell at Rome's Rebibbia Prison—at which time Ağca inquired about the shooting and its connection to the prophecies of Fátima—the Turkish assailant had personally woven himself into the mystery of the Secret of Fátima.

John Paul II's 2005 book, *Memory and Identity*—as well as his secretary Father Stanislaw Dziwisz's 2008 memoir, *Life with Karol*—makes no secret of the fact that Fátima was the primary interest of Ağca that day in prison.

Then, over the years, as Ağca learned more about Fátima, he claimed that the shooting was part of the unreleased third part of the Secret of Fátima. At his second trial in1986, Ağca spoke mysteriously about it, turning the courtroom proceedings into a spectacle. [21]

After Cardinal Sodano stated on May 13, 2000, that the third part of the Secret of Fátima foretold the 1981 assassination attempt on Pope John Paul II, Ağca—speaking through his lawyer, Marina Magistrelli, on May 14, 2000—said he felt relieved from the weight of responsibility by the disclosure of the Secret: "I was an unwilling instrument in a mysterious design; now I know this with certainty." [22]

To this day, the controversy lingers.

In 2016, the third part of the Secret sprang to life a couple of times again.

A German theologian named Ingo Dollinger claimed Cardinal Ratzinger personally told him that there is a part of the Third Secret that is not yet released.

"There is more than we have published," Dollinger quotes Ratzinger as saying to him not long after the June 2000 release of the third part of the Secret. Pope Emeritus Benedict XVI issued on May 21, 2016, an immediate denial through the Vatican Press Office.[23]

Then, a few months later, Robert Moynihan, the Editor-in-Chief of *Inside the Vatican*, revealed that many years before (2007), he too—as Solideo Paolini—met with the late Archbishop Loris Capovilla concerning the third part of the Secret.

In his July 29, 2016, Moynihan *Letter #49*, Moynihan tells how he had in mind to write about his second meeting with Capovilla, how they spoke of the third part of the Secret of Fátima, and how they had discussed that the envelope containing the Secret—shown on Italian TV by Cardinal Bertone—did not reveal the writing Capovilla said he made on its exterior at the request of Pope John XXIII in August of 1959.

"Perhaps there was a second envelope," Moynihan reports Capovilla— elevated to a cardinal in 2014—remarked to him. [24] Moynihan recalled the meeting:

> I stopped there. For Capovilla on that day had not clarified for me the matter of the Third Secret. He had left it open, mysterious. And he had clearly intended to leave it so. He had intentionally led me to believe that there was something not clear about the publication of the Secret or Secrets—that there might even have been two different letters, with two different envelopes, with two distinct texts.
>
> But, at the same time, he had left me in the dark about what that something might be. He had clearly had some hesitation about speaking definitively on the subject of the letter, as if he had been asked not to do so by some higher authority. As I understood him, he was hinting to me that there did exist some other version of the Third Secret, a version different from the one that was revealed and published [in 2000], but he would not say so clearly and categorically. [25]

The following year, a compelling contribution to this affair is noted. It perhaps even ends the controversy, barring the surfacing of the alleged document.

In 2017, an American author, Kevin Symonds, released an impressive 600-page work on the subject: *On the Third Part of the Secret of Fatima*.

After researching all of the sources that contribute to the ongoing polemics surrounding the third part of the Secret—especially those surrounding Sr. Lúcia and the Vatican—and after obtaining permission to research the archives of the Sanctuary of Fátima, Symonds revealed that Lúcia had been given a prophetic insight into the third part of the Secret, which she was not allowed to communicate to others. [26]

This fact, Symonds noted, could account for why the text of the third part of the Secret seemed incomplete to some people. Referring to the biography of Sr. Lúcia, *A Pathway Under the Gaze of Mary*, Symonds writes,

> The Carmelite biography revealed that there was indeed more to the third part of the Secret than was released in the year 2000. The Sisters, however, were careful to note that this was not because of an alleged Vatican conspiracy. The matter was over a hitherto unknown command given to Sr. Lúcia on or around January 3, 1944, not to reveal "what is given to you (Sr. Lúcia) to understand of its significance." [27]

Symonds further adds that a little known but significant development in the history of the Third Secret controversy came about in 2016.

The French writer Yves Chiron—respected for his works on Pope St. Pius X and his writings on apparitions—revealed that he wrote a letter to Benedict XVI on the subject of Fátima and received a response. Chiron says Benedict wrote back and stated, "A fourth secret of Fátima does not exist. The published text is entire and there exists nothing else." [28]

Symonds's book confronts head on the various conspiracy theories, arguing with documented references—through relevant sources in their original languages—that what the Vatican published in 2000 *was* the whole text as written in1944.

He concludes that the vision that makes up the third part of the Secret—the martyrdom of the Church— flows out of the second part of the Secret that warns of the errors of Russia, just as Lúcia's May 1982 letter sought to explain to Pope John Paul II.

Therefore, Symonds argues, there is no other text—no Fourth Secret—that narrated the vision, just as Sr. Lúcia, Pope Benedict XVI, Cardinal Bertone and others contend. [29]

One man will never be convinced.

Fátima author Father Paul Kramer said he is still certain there is a missing text. And, he says, he was told years ago at Fátima that this Fourth Secret would someday see the light of day:

> Without claiming any kind of prophetic accuracy, I can say that that when I was in Fátima in 1991, I was informed that the Carmelites of Fátima had received news from Sister Lucy and her fellow sisters at the convent in Coimbra that Our Lady had appeared to Sister Lucy not long before May of 1991, and told her that the Third Secret is going to be revealed during the course of a major war.
>
> So, the war will break out, it will be a sudden war, it will be a blitzkrieg, and the true Church will be driven underground. But at the beginning of this war, when the Pope realizes that keeping the Third Secret hidden no longer makes any sense —because the Russians have now made their move—he will reveal the missing text of the Third Secret. [30]

Kramer's foretelling is just one more piece to add to a puzzle begun over a hundred years ago. More pieces can be expected. But unless a missing text is revealed, there appears to be no way of proving a "Fourth Secret of Fátima."

There is no known direct connection between the third part of the Secret of Fátima and Medjugorje.

It is curious, however, to note that it was released by the Vatican on June 26, 2000, one day after the anniversary of Our Lady of Medjugorje.

One can't help but also notice that Mirjana Soldo, in her 2016 book, *My Heart Will Triumph*, not only wrote about the Third Secret, but published the entire text in her book. [31]

Mirjana writes that some speculated that the Third Secret predicted the assassination attempt on John Paul II, while others—citing the fact that the Pope survived—thought it represented something that had *not yet* happened. [32]

Was there a reason, some wondered, why Mirjana included the Third Secret in her memoir? As usual, there is always more mystery to add to a mystery.

CHAPTER FIFTY-SEVEN

ABORTION: THE GREATEST "ERROR OF RUSSIA"

"Before I formed you in the womb I knew you,
and before you were born I consecrated you."

—Jer 1:1, 5

THE CHURCH'S INTERPRETATION OF THE THIRD SECRET WAS JUST that, an interpretation.

And it quickly moved to establish that fact.

Perhaps sensing the disagreement its commentary could invite, Cardinal Ratzinger emphasized this understanding, declaring there was no official definition, or understanding.[1] "It is not the intention of the Church to impose an interpretation," explained Ratzinger at a press conference in Rome on the same day that the third part of the Secret was released.

The vision in the third part of the Secret, Ratzinger thought, appeared to be a synthesis of history that involved the world, the Church and its hierarchy over at least a half century, with the attack on Pope John Paul II appearing to be "the central point."[2]

Everything, though, was now in the past. Cardinals Bertone and Sodano concurred with this view, while agreeing the interpretation was not definitive. But ten years later, at Fátima on May 13, 2010, Ratzinger, now Pope Benedict XVI, appeared to suddenly leave open the question of the Secret's unfulfilled prophetic implications:

"We would be mistaken to think that Fátima's prophetic message is complete. May the seven years which separate us from the centenary of the apparitions hasten the fulfillment of the prophecy of the Triumph of the Immaculate Heart." [3]

Benedict, many immediately postured, seemed to be implying that there remained more to come with Fátima. The Pope, however, quickly moved to distance himself from this misinterpretation of his thinking. Those who sought to see his words that day as implying he had reopened the door to his understanding of Fátima's prophetic message were mistaken.

In an interview with author Peter Seewald, Benedict said he was referring at Fátima to "the whole power of evil that came to a head in the major dictatorships of the twentieth century—and that in another way is still at work today." The Triumph will draw closer, the Pope told Seewald, but implied such an understanding in a much broader sense to the further "coming of God's Kingdom" on earth. Such "triumphs of God, triumphs of Mary," Benedict explained, "are quiet but they are *real* nonetheless." [4]

While clearing the air on his remarks at Fátima, Benedict's perspective was somewhat eye opening. It revealed his overall view of Fátima was not the same as thought, or was that of his predecessors.

"From his answer, one can see that Benedict has a *spiritual* interpretation of the "triumph" of the Immaculate Heart of Mary", wrote Fátima author Kevin Symonds. "This interpretation conflicts with another, more literal one that holds a literal world-wide era of peace will be given once the Holy Father consecrates Russia." [5]

Regardless of Benedict's understanding, exculpatory evidence that the Secret of Fátima is *not* fulfilled is well established. The problems arising from the errors of Russia, from Marxism in one form or another, were undeniable and visible everywhere.

In the accompanying documents released the same day as the third part of the Secret, a letter from Sister Lúcia to Pope John Paul II—dated May 12, 1982—was also released. In it, Lúcia states that the third part of the Secret was a symbolic revelation of the second part of the Secret, specifically referring to the spread of the errors of Russia.

"The third part of the Secret," wrote Lúcia, "refers to Our Lady's words, 'if not [Russia] will spread her errors throughout the world, causing wars and persecutions of the Church...' The Third part of the secret is a *symbolic revelation*, referring to this (the second) part of the message." [6]

In this letter, Lúcia clearly establishes that the third part of the Secret refers to something other than the assassination attempt, which was already a year in the past. Rather, she points to the fact that atheistic Marxism, principally seen as Communism at the time, was alive and on the move.

At the time (1982), Lúcia's letter is seen to be appealing for Pope John Paul II to attempt once more the consecration of Russia in order to stymie the steady march of Soviet expansionism. This the Pope would do in 1984. But we now clearly understand that Marxist driven atheism, with its intrinsic errors and mutated forms, had already eclipsed Soviet Communism.

Lúcia's words in 1993, after the fall of the Soviet Union, indicate she also understood well in advance the nature of this beast. She was aware that the war with atheism was far from over. Fátima, said Lúcia at the time, was in its "third day" of a "long week" and that the other "errors" of Marxism were formidable concerns:

> Atheism is still the greatest instrument used by the Devil in these days. Because it is a grave sin against God which denies His very existence giving way to all sorts of evil doings like abortion. Everything... spreads from atheism, from Marxism. People expect things to happen on their own time limit... Fátima is still in its third day. The Triumph is an ongoing process. [7]

To this day, the errors of Russia live on.

The Fatima week has not ended. The "Triumph" remains an ongoing process. And, as Lucia mentioned, the greatest error of Russia now canvasses the globe—the murder of the unborn, fueled by the greatest lie in history: "Abortion is a woman's right to choose."

In a January 2000 editorial, *Inside the Vatican* editor Robert Moynihan confronted this reality concerning the broader prophetic makeup of Fatima and how abortion needed to be recognized as one of the "errors of Russia." Abortion, Moynihan noted, was the ultimate error, transcending Communism in its destruction of human life.

> Many think that Russia "spread its errors" throughout the world in its support for Marxist-Leninism, and that those "errors" are now receding. But many forget that another "error" remains.
>
> Under Lenin in the 1920's, Russia became the first modern state to legalize abortion. Is that not the "error" that has spread throughout the world, and remains, and provides the basis for the "culture of death" which has grown so strong and all-embracing even as Communist ideology has collapsed?
>
> If this is so, if the conversion of Russia is still to come and if it will usher in a period of peace for the world, will it not be marked by a conversion of people to life, away from abortion? [8]

Moynihan's words define the true profoundness of Fátima's warning.

Abortion, the now incomprehensible, worldwide, legal holocaust, stalks the human stage. It has permeated all civilization and is the greatest visible consequence of the "errors of Russia."

According to the World Health Organization (WHO), there are 40-50 million abortions a year worldwide, or a 125,000 abortions a day. The Guttmacher Institute—the statistical arm of Planned Parenthood which both the United Nations and the World Health Organization consider reliable and authoritative—estimated approximately 56 million abortions occurred each year between 2010-2014.

In the year 2020, 43% of all deaths worldwide came from abortion, according to the American Center for Law and Justice, including 40 million surgical abortions.

An estimated 64% of all abortions occur in Asia and the abortion rate (the number of abortions per 1,000 women aged 15-44) is the highest in Russia at 53.7 abortions a year. Some women in Russia report having over 20 abortions.

While the United Nations lists China's official abortion rate at 19.2, it's actual abortion rate is much higher. According to China's 2010 census, there were approximately 310 million women of reproductive age in the country. An estimated 13-23 million abortions happen annually in China, resulting in an adjusted abortion rate that may be as high as 74.2. The United States abortion rate (2008) was 19.6.

The following abortion data is from '*Abort 73*,' which draws from the UN's World Abortion Policies Report: [9]

ESTIMATED ABORTIONS PER YEAR [millions]

Region	2010-2014
AFRICA	8.3
ASIA	31.5
LATIN AMERICA	4.4
NORTHERN AMERICA	1.2
EUROPE	8.2

The American Life League estimates from 1973 through 2018, there were 61.8 million abortions performed in the United States.

But these are only surgical and medical abortions.

In addition, the organization estimates that 14 million chemical abortions occur in the United States each year, resulting in a projected total well in excess of 610 million chemical abortions between 1965 and 2009. [10]

The conclusions from all of this are mortifying.

When the estimated number of abortions as a whole across the globe over the last fifty years are looked at—statistics that take into account surgical, medical(IUD) and chemical abortions—it becomes clear that the total number of deaths of innocent children is in the "billions."

What this means for our purposes is this: the second part of the Secret of Fátima, as well as the third part—its "symbolic face" according to Sister Lúcia—are both unfulfilled to a great degree, and, consequently, the primary reason the world cannot expect to see the fulfillment of Fátima.

The "Triumph" will not come until the errors of Russia—the pervasive blight of atheistic thought that guides humanity, that guides abortion, that guides the *Culture of Death*—is eradicated completely.

As Mother Teresa—St. Teresa of Calcutta today—alluded many times, there can be no peace in the world until there is peace in the womb. Only then, Catholic writers emphasize, will a triumph of God—the Triumph of Fátima—be seen.

But there are deeper implications.

The promise at Fátima of the Triumph of the Immaculate Heart was a serious proposition. It confronted the world with the reality that it cannot maintain its sinful path, not only because it leads to misery and death, but because it's not God's will for His creation.

Now, Mary returns at Medjugorje to not just sound the same alarm, but to confirm the work begun at Fátima will be successfully completed. Like in the times of Noah, a great transformation is to take place. And, it promises to be unlike anything ever seen before.

God's plan—shared with mankind through prophecy—is to be prophecy fulfilled.

Fátima launched this turning point in history.

Medjugorje will see it to its inescapable conclusion.

"We find ourselves before a prophecy that announces a radical and extraordinary change in the world," wrote Antonio Socci in *The Fourth Secret of Fatima*, "an overthrow of the mentality dominating the modern world." [11]

It's an overthrow that Socci states will flow out of the "events contained in the Third Secret of Fátima"[12] and into events, he writes, "belonging to the Ten Secrets of Medjugorje." [13]

Indeed, the Ten Secrets of Medjugorje, asserts Catholic author Ted Flynn, will bring biblical scale changes to the world unlike anything ever seen before.

"What will happen at Medjugorje," said Flynn, "will be a complete paradigm shift in world affairs. It will make the parting of the Red Sea seem insignificant as a miracle and will be the equivalent of a polar shift for the world. It will be that significant." [14]

"All the Secrets force me to pray." [15]

It was a disclosure by Marija Pavlović that Father Laurentin struggled to understand while pondering the clarity of the gaze in her eyes.

Marija had been transformed, Laurentin noted, by something he had not seen in any young girl before. She was deeply affected, he thought, by the knowledge of what was contained in the Secrets.[16]

The Secrets.

The visionaries—who never discuss the Secrets among themselves—say the Ten Secrets of Medjugorje involve warnings, signs, and chastisements that will bring all of mankind to a renewed awareness that God exists. [17]

Most significantly, their unfolding centers on the Third Secret—a revelation by its number alone—that immediately recalls the daunting history of Fátima's Third Secret in a way that appears to be no accident.

Like the uncanny parchment they are recorded on, the Ten Secrets are said to arrive in a way more mysterious than the scroll that was handed over to Mirjana by the Virgin Mary.

Each Secret is to be preannounced to all mankind—one by one.[18]

But if mysterious describes the coming arrival of the Ten Secrets, apocalyptic defines their nature, even more so than the Secret of Fátima, according to theologians.

"There is a marked apocalyptic significance in the Ten Medjugorje Secrets, even stronger than was the case at Fátima," wrote British Theologian Father Richard Foley. [19]

"The Marian apparitions at Medjugorje have strong apocalyptic elements, perhaps even more so than the apparitions at Fátima in 1917," asserted Father Robert Faricy, a professor of Mystical Theology Emeritus at the Pontifical Gregorian University in Rome. [20]

"At Fátima, Our Lady prophesied World War II as a punishment for the sins of that era. At Medjugorje, she tells the world that its lack of faith and consequent sinfulness are about to extract a costly toll," said theologian Father Joseph Pelletier. [21]

"She, who is still Our Lady of Fátima, has explained Fátima and its apocalyptic message at Medjugorje," opined mysticism expert and prolific author Father Albert Hebert. [22]

Father Luigi Bianchi—an Italian author and an acknowledged expert on Fátima—noted an undeniable, symbolic lesson unfolding through the Virgin Mary's major apparitions.

"The hours of the apparitions follow a progression," explains Bianchi, "At Lourdes, they took place in the morning. At Fátima, at noon. At Medjugorje, in the evening. Is it the end of a long day, and the announcement of the Eighth Day?" [23]

Father Bianchi poses a rhetorical question, but its answer is "yes."

It is "yes" because it appears that God is indicating at Medjugorje that our trouble-filled world has reached a critical point. Unlike at Fátima, where the future could still be determined by a proper and substantial response to the Virgin's requests, no such precise conditions are associated with the Ten Secrets of Medjugorje.

The Pope and the bishops are not known to play requested roles in a prophetic drama. The faithful, while asked to pray and do penance, can only mitigate the intensity, not prevent, the unfolding of the Secrets.

God's plan, say the visionaries in regards to the Secrets, will be realized by a series of future events. [24] A climax, therefore, to what Mary began at Fátima and is concluding in Medjugorje, is a fait accompli.

Why?

Because the Virgin has announced that God desires to bring to an end the era of atheism and for the world to enter an era of peace. Therefore, through Mary's intervention, through her words at Fátima and Medjugorje, she has announced that He Himself will guide its arrival.

It will come through God's mercy and justice.

But it will come

All of this means one thing: the world cannot out run the future that is posed to descend through the unfolding of the mysterious Ten Secrets of Medjugorje.

Down through the years, the visionaries have been consistent with this message. The following statements range from 1983 to 2015:

- "First, some of the Secrets will be revealed—just a few," said Mirjana in Medjugorje on January 10, 1983, "then, the people will be convinced the Madonna was here. Then, they will understand the Sign." [25]
- "The Secrets and their revelation—the happenings that are tied with the secret messages—are going to happen for sure," Ivan told Father Zoran Ostojich on November 19, 1989, in Chicago. "Our Lady said that the beginnings of these happenings and the revelation of each Secret *will* be proclaimed." [26]
- "Our Lady talked to me about the Fifth Secret," revealed Ivanka on June 25, 1997, after her annual apparition at her home in Medjugorje, "and then spoke the following message, 'Dear children, pray with the heart to know how to forgive and how to be forgiven.'" [27]
- "Our Lady spoke to me about the Secrets," stated Jacov after his annual apparition of the Virgin Mary on December 25, 2010, "and, at the end said, 'Pray, pray, pray.'" [28]
- "I have nine Secrets. I was only talking about the Third Secret earlier," Vicka disclosed in a 2015 interview. "The only thing I can say is the Seventh Secret was half reduced, because of our prayers and sacrifices." [29]

"The Secrets are their destiny," observed Irish Theologian Father Michael O'Carroll, about the six visionaries at Medjugorje. [30]

Yes, they are.

But the Secrets are also mankind's destiny.

It is a destiny—if we take the visionaries at their word—that will have a dramatic bearing on history in a way never seen before. [31]

"They say that with the realization of the Secrets entrusted to them by Our Lady," offered one of the friars at Medjugorje, "life in the world will change. Afterwards, men will believe like in the ancient times. What will change and how it will change, we don't know given that the seers don't want to say anything about the Secrets." [32]

Unlike the Secret of Fátima—which foretold the Second World War and that a universal evil would emerge out of Russia—no significant clues are found as to what to expect. Rather, their content is shrouded in mystery.

Mary's own words concerning the Ten Secrets, however, are delivered in a tone that reflects their rather pressing and grave nature:

> The Sign will come; you must not worry about it. The only thing that I would want to tell you is to be converted. Make that known to all my children as quickly as possible. No pain, no suffering is too great to me in order to save you. I will pray to my Son not to punish the world; but I beseech you, be converted.
>
> You cannot imagine what is going to happen nor what the Eternal Father will send to Earth. That is why you must be converted. Renounce everything. Do penance. Express my acknowledgement to all my children who have prayed and fasted.
>
> I carry all this to my Divine Son in order to obtain an alleviation of His justice against the sins of mankind. I thank the people who have prayed and fasted. Persevere and help me to convert the world. [33]

CHAPTER FIFTY-EIGHT

THE WINTER OF TOMORROW

*"He answered them, 'It is not for you to
know the times or seasons that the
Father has established by His own authority.'"*
—Acts 1: 7

"YOU COULD WRITE DOWN THE SECRETS, PUT THEM IN AN ENVE-
lope, seal them, and leave them with me," a Church official told
ten-year-old Jacov Colo in the early days of the Medjugorje apparitions. "I could write down the Secrets, put them in an envelope and
leave them at home," Jacov replied. [1]

Adroit in countering any attempt to dislodge their contents, Jacov—
as did all the young visionaries at Medjugorje—knew from the very
beginning that the Secrets were *secret*. [2] And, their determination to
protect them has been well noted by many.

Historically, this has been true with the Secrets the Virgin Mary has
revealed to her chosen ones, especially children.

In 1932, at the Church approved-apparitions in Beauraing, Belgium,
three of the five visionaries claimed they received Secrets that not even
the Pope could be told. One of the visionaries—an 11-year-old boy
named Albert Voisin—upon examination, did say his Secret was sad,
which was in itself enough to spark concern.[3]

During another Church-approved apparition in Belgium the following year, this time in the town of Banneux, Mary gave 12-year-old
Mariette Beco two Secrets that she would not reveal during interrogations. Again, curiosity filled the air. Mariette is alleged to have even
told her father, while pointing to her chest,

"Papa, even if you would place your gun here, I would not tell!" [4]

The same kind of thinking with young visionaries is found at Fátima, as Lúcia's *First Memoir* reveals how little Jacinta said to her shortly before she died,

"Never tell the Secret to anyone, even if they kill you." [5]

Anyone aware of the Ten Secrets of Medjugorje and their mysterious contents can't help but be curious a little, wondering what the fate of the world is to be. But this has always been part of awaiting the fulfillment of prophecy, especially when *secrets* are involved.

In Scripture, the idea of divine secrets is prefigured in Saint Paul's *Letter to the Ephesians* when he speaks of God's secret plans.[6] Theologians say that Mary's secrets exist in this same context because they involve what Saint Paul declared to be the "mystery of Christ."

But when did the Virgin Mary start giving Secrets?

Mary has been reportedly appearing since the first century. In A.D. 40, she is believed to have manifested before her death to the Apostle James the Greater in Zaragoza, Spain. However, many consider this event a bilocation, not an apparition.

Her appearance to St. Gregory the Wonderworker (A.D. 213-270), according to St. Gregory of Nyssa, is said to be the earliest recorded vision of Mary, while her first "classic" apparition is believed to have occurred in Syro-Malabar, India, to three young boys at a spring in A.D. 335.

While the Virgin may have given secrets to other visionaries over the centuries, it was during the nineteenth century apparitions at Rue de Bac, Paris, that the mystery of her secret messages begins to clearly unfold. It all started here, say Mariologists, when a nun named Catherine Laboure revealed that she had been given, "Several things I must not tell." [7]

Saint Catherine's words are the starting point for this mystery. But it was with the Church-approved apparitions in 1846 at La Salette, France, in the diocese of Grenoble, that this element of the Virgin's revelations piques significant interest, not just to the faithful, but also to Church hierarchy.

And it's not surprising why.

Once the presence of secrets at La Salette was known, public speculation about their content and nature became rampant. Everyone wanted to know if the "special knowledge" in the secrets concerned them in any way, and if so, what could be done to escape harm.

At La Salette, public figures, institutions, different interest groups, members of religious orders, clerics, bishops, cardinals, and even the Pope became involved in a drama surrounding the secrets—one that stretched all the way into the twentieth century.

It all began when two children, 14-year-old Francoise-Melanie Calvat-Mathieu and 11-year-old Pierre-Maximin Giraud, reported that when the Virgin Mary appeared to them on a mountain in the French Alps near the village of La Salette on September 19, 1846, she gave each of them a secret message.[8]

At first, the children apparently made no reference to the secrets in their accounts of the apparition. But upon repeated interrogations during the first week, Maximin and then Mélanie revealed that personal secrets were confided to them.

On October 12, 1846, Father Melin, a priest from the village of Corps, composed a letter to Victor Rabillou, a librarian in Bourgoin, that briefly noted the secrets' existence. This was the first document to cite their presence; but at this point, the secrets were considered to be of a personal, not public, nature. [9]

The earliest written account of the apparition in mid-October 1846 again disclosed the secrets. This came from the notes of Father Louis Perrin, the newly-appointed pastor of La Salette who interviewed the children.[10]

According to available documentation, the visionaries initially refrained from even speaking of the secrets for fear of revealing them. But once they were known to exist, an almost ceaseless investigative effort was begun to dislodge them.

Over time, the children repeatedly out-maneuvered their interrogators, but this did nothing to inhibit the efforts. Threats of punishment and death, bribes, tricks, and pretense all failed to get the children to reveal the secrets. [11] On the positive side, their determination was seen as evidence of their integrity—and thus, increased the probability that the apparition was authentic.

As the months went by, the pressure on the children continued.

When asked if the secrets concerned Heaven, Hell, the world, religion, or other matters, Mélanie replied, "It concerns that which it concerns; if I tell you this you will know it, and I don't want to tell it." [12]

In the spring of 1847, a report written by Dr. Armand Dumanoir, a Grenoble lawyer, suggested for the first time the possibility of the children's secrets being of public relevance.

"After these words," wrote Dumanoir, "the Lady gave each of them a secret which appears to consist in the announcement of a great event, fortunate for some, unfortunate for others." [13]

With this document, a new stage in the mystery of Marian apparitions was upon the world. Church officials now began to intensify the investigative process. The public also began to voice its interest, especially given the great social and political turmoil in France in 1848. [14] Many began to speculate that the children's secrets were vital for understanding the unfolding contemporary events.

At this time, Church officials also began to write letters of inquiry to the priests involved with the children. By 1849, rumors were running amok, with the contents of the secrets at the center. Various scenarios were being outlined, with even the Second Coming of Christ foretold to be at the culmination. [15]

Reported efforts involving two future Saints, Catherine Laboure, the visionary at Rue du Bac, and then an actual visit to little Maximin by the Cure of Ars, Jean Vianney, all contributed to efforts to encourage the children to reveal the secrets.

But they would not budge.

Finally, in June of 1851, Pope Pius IX was informed that the children were willing to transmit their secrets to him. The Pope agreed to the arrangement.

On July 2, Maximin sat down and recorded his secret, after which he reportedly said, "I am unburdened. I no longer have a secret. I am as others. One no longer has any need to ask me anything. One can ask the Pope and he will speak if he wants." [16]

The next day, Mélanie wrote down her secret. Claiming she forgot something, she repeated the action on July 6th. The children said that they finally agreed to tell the secrets because they now understood the Pope's position within the Church. But, further information disclosed that both children believed they were graced with special signs from Heaven that permitted the disclosures. [17]

The Secrets of La Salette were then given to Pope Pius IX on July 18, 1851.

The Pope opened and read them in the presence of the Grenoble officials. Ironically, this series of events—which finally brought the secrets to the Pope—also exacerbated speculation that they were apocalyptical in content.[18] Reports and rumors about the audience with the Pope further fueled this speculation. Other reports from a handful of clerics who read the secrets also emerged. Together, the public began to piece together a picture that fit in with their apocalyptic suspicions.

Some of the rumors, nevertheless, were true.

Witnesses who observed the children write their secrets reported their facial expressions and other behavioral aspects. One witness noted that Mélanie asked how to spell "Antichrist." The length of the texts was also noted as to which of the two secrets was longer.

In addition, Pope Pius IX's reaction upon reading the secrets seemed to convey more information.[19] According to the representatives present, the Pope stated after reading Maximin's message, "Here is all the candor and simplicity of a child." [20]

However, while reading Mélanie's secret, the witnesses said that the Pope's face changed and reflected strong emotion. Upon finishing, he reportedly stated, "It is necessary that I reread these at more leisure. There are scourges here that menace France, but Germany, Italy, all Europe is culpable and merits chastisement. I have less to fear from open piety, than from indifference and from human respect. It is not without reason that the Church is called militant and you see here the captain." [21]

Afterwards, further comments were attributed to the Pope by respected sources. Cardinal Lambruschini, First Minister to Pius IX and Prefect of the Congregation of Rites, reportedly said, "I have known the fact of La Salette for a long time and, as a bishop, I believe it. I have preached it in my diocese and I have observed that my discourse made a great impression. Moreover, I know the Secret of La Salette."

Cardinal Fornaric, Nuncio to Paris, remarked, "I am terrified of these prodigies; we have everything that is needed in our religion for the conversion of sinners, and when Heaven employs such means, the evil must be very great." [22]

Upon returning home from Rome, Father Perrin told Mélanie that he was unsure of what she had written, but judging by the Pope's reaction, it wasn't flattering. He then asked the girl if she knew what the word "flattering" meant. She replied, "To give pleasure," and then Mélanie added, "but this (the secret) ought to give pleasure to the Pope—a Pope should love to suffer." [23]

And that is what the Secrets of La Salette apparently brought to Pius IX—considerable suffering. Asked years later about the contents of the

Secrets, Pius said, "You want to know the Secrets of La Salette? Ah, well, here are the Secrets of La Salette: If you do not do penance, you will perish." [24]

As the years went by, the Secrets of La Salette became irrevocably present in the public realm. This knowledge convinced many Catholics that to know the contents of a secret revelation was crucial to understand the critical times in which they lived.

The Church also found itself in a most uncomfortable situation after La Salette. While wanting to reap the fruits of authentic events, the presence of secrets placed its very trustworthiness on the line. Church officials were torn between understanding the public's desire to know, and its mission to protect sound doctrine from contamination and confusion.

This problem has not gone away.

According to one investigative writer, thirty-one alleged apparition sites in two dozen countries in the course of the twentieth century alone have been discovered to have secrets given to visionaries. [25]

In short, there is no limit to the ramifications of what the Secrets of La Salette have meant to the drama of many later Marian apparitions—especially to those that have also revealed secret messages, such as at Lourdes, where the Virgin gave Bernadette Soubirous three secrets she never revealed, [26] and especially at Fátima.

Like with Pius IX and La Salette, the anguish brought upon the popes of the twentieth century due to the Secret of Fátima is evident and well documented. From Pope Pius XI through Benedict XVI, every pope for almost a century labored under the controversies surrounding the Secret of Fátima.

These are controversies—in many minds—that remain unresolved.

At La Salette, two Secrets were given by Mary, one to each of the visionaries.

At Fátima, there were three parts to what Sister Lúcia termed to be one Secret.

But now, at Medjugorje, there are Ten Secrets being given to each of the six visionaries.

What is Mary doing at Medjugorje with so many Secrets?

"The word 'secret' has a magical effect on people," said Mariologist Father Joseph Pelletier, "it arouses curiosity and stimulates interest.

God makes use of this to draw attention to the message He wishes to transmit through His heavenly messenger." [27]

"It is certain that the Secrets of Medjugorje contain impetus for us," advised Father Slavko Barbarić. "The messages tell us what we have to know for now. The fact of secrets is found again and again in Marian apparitions; obviously they belong to the educational method of the Blessed Mother, which trains one to patience and an ability to wait. We must wait for much until the time for it has come." [28]

Father René Laurentin says it's apparent that Mary is giving so many Secrets to her visionaries at Medjugorje because the times are urgent and the future is threatened:

"The world is destroying itself. It is vehemently preparing its own destruction for having struggled, forgotten, or relegated the essential: God and His law of love, which the messages of Medjugorje recall. The Secrets announce to a large extent, the imminent destructions which are not extrinsic punishments, but imminent justice, the self-destruction of a world which entrusts itself to evil through deviation and frenzy." [29]

Laurentin, once again, can be seen to be addressing the fact that the apparitions at Medjugorje have strong apocalyptic elements, as seen at Fátima, and are reminiscent of passages found in Scripture.

Examples of the apocalyptic in the Bible are many, but predominantly recalled in the Old Testament books of *Daniel, Ezekiel*, and *Zechariah,* along with certain chapters in the New Testament, most notably *The Book of Revelation.* [30]

Theologians say that Jesus's most apocalyptic statements in the Gospels are found in *Mark*, Chapter 13; and especially in *Matthew*, Chapters 24-25:

"Nation will rise against nation, and kingdom against kingdom; there will be famines and earthquakes from place to place." [31]

Apocalyptic, though, is not only about content, but also style, and the two cannot be separated.

Apocalyptic style embraces symbols, images, and visions to express religious concepts. In *Daniel*, Chapter 7, the mysterious Son of Man figure is used by Jesus in His teaching on the end of the world.[32] In *Matthew*, Chapter 25, Jesus speaks of the separation of the sheep from the goats to symbolize the Last Judgment.[33] *The Book of Revelation* abounds in symbolism and allegorical language that is comparable to that of the Old Testament.

Apocalyptic is also different from prophecy.

Prophecy calls us to change, to convert our lives to God.[34] It condemns sin and infidelity to the Lord. Most of all, prophecy calls us to faith and leads us to prayer, to confession. It calls us to reconciliation with God and with one another. This will bring the peace, Mary's chosen ones tell us, that God wants His children to experience in their lives and in the world.

At Medjugorje, what is occurring is both "apocalyptic and prophetic," says mystical theologian Father Robert Faricy.[35] Faricy states that this is found at Medjugorje in a variety of ways: the Ten Secrets and their implied content; the many references to the Devil; the promised Sign that is to appear on Podbrdo and the mysterious wonders witnessed in the village—strange lights, solar miracles, visions experienced by visitors, and the many miraculous healings. [36]

Most of all, the apparitions announce that the future belongs to the Lord, which is a strong confirmation of the prophetic makeup of the revelations. Writes Faricy:

> The messages are prophetic, but many elements that make up the content of those messages are apocalyptic. Prophecy tells us what to do. Apocalyptic tells us what God intends to do. It sees history as completely under the Lordship of Jesus Christ. The future belongs to God. He is the Lord of history, in charge of the world and everything in it. The future lies hidden in the Lord's hands because it belongs to Him. He holds the future, and He makes it present to us now in a mysterious and hidden way, through signs and symbols.
>
> Furthermore, apocalyptic confronts evil squarely. Its strong vision of God's power and lordship makes possible a clear vision of evil in this world. Belief in the reality of Satan, in fact, comes from the Old Testament apocalyptic tradition. In the New Testament, the apocalyptic victory is already present in Jesus, He defeats sin, death and Satan, triumphing by His Cross and Resurrection.[37]

We especially find much of this in the Ten Secrets of Medjugorje, says Faricy.

The Secrets, from what is known about them, are to confront the evil of today with the power of God, who completely tells us what He is going to do, that He is the Lord of history and that He will defeat sin, death and demonic influence.

As the Virgin has said at both Fátima and Medjugorje, we see God's intent to change the world through the apparitions of Mary *will* come. [38]

"The Ten Secrets tell us we can have hope in the future," assures Faricy. "They console us because they say to us that we do not know what the future holds but we do know who holds the future—the Lord...True, the future holds some terrible things. But it belongs to the Lord. The *terrible things* coming do not dim His Lordship or His victory. We can trust in Him." [39]

"I have chosen you; I have confided in you everything that is essential. I have also shown you many *terrible things*," said the Virgin Mary to a stunned Mirjana on December 25, 1982, the day she received her Tenth and last Secret. "You must now bear it all with courage. Think of me and think of the tears I must shed for that. You must remain brave." [40]

Mary's words of encouragement in discharging the final Secret to Mirjana are revealing. Something very challenging awaits her, and—for that matter—the whole world.

So, the obvious question stands before us: what kind of *terrible things* was Mary speaking of, in giving such consoling yet serious advice to her official mouthpiece, the one chosen to reveal the Ten Secrets to the world?

In an age when no one has to be told that nuclear missiles can flash through the air like Zeus throwing lightning bolts, there's no need to strain the imagination as to what could come upon mankind. The potential divine justice of tomorrow's world certainly has already been crafted by the hands of today's man.

"We didn't need an apparition to convince us that nuclear war is a possibility," observed Father Slavko Barbarić at Medjugorje. "If a house is on fire, it doesn't burn down because the mother shouts fire." [41]

Indeed, as when Mary came to Fátima during the throes of World War I, today's dangers are before us, firmly in place, poised to strike. Mary has not come to bemoan the obvious.

In 1917, the world was very aware of its man-made misery. The Secret of Fátima simply foretold that another round of even *worse* misery—a second world war and more—was in the cards if her words were not heeded.

The *terrible things* contained in the Ten Secrets of Medjugorje that Mary speaks of are presented in this same light. We need only to look around and see how we have already constructed a world flirting with destruction. Mary comes again to try to wake us up to this reality, before it's too late.

"Regarding the question of the apocalyptic dimension," explained Father Barbarić, in a July 14, 1987, interview in Medjugorje, "Our Lady has pointed the way to peace. Certainly we understand the possibility for catastrophe to occur... It depends on us to avoid catastrophe." [42]

Yes, it does.

But, Mary's call at Medjugorje to the world at this time goes beyond a plea to save it from catastrophe.

The Ten Secrets—unlike the Secret of Fátima—do not hold a plan within them to prevent their coming, only to mitigate them. This is because Mary has come this time not to stop the errors of our age but to *end* them, and to prepare the world for a new era that *needs* some trying times to help it get here.

Times that will come with the Secrets.

Medjugorje's call, therefore, is first and foremost an awakening; it's a call to every person on earth to be aware of their eternal plight—and to their temporal one—in light of what the Secrets hold. Indeed, the message contains a resounding urgency to respond to the graces being given at this time in history.

"Hasten your conversion," the Virgin told the six visionaries in a message shared with the world in the spring of 1983, "do not await the Sign which has been announced, for people who do not believe, it will be too late." [43]

Two years later, this urgency is heard again:

"Now is the time for conversion. I have been exhorting you for the last four years. Be converted before it will be too late." [44]

Twenty years later, this plea continued to resound at Medjugorje:

"Today, the Lord permitted me to tell you *again* that you live in a time of grace. You are not conscious, little children, that God is giving you a great opportunity to convert..." [45]

These messages—as with her message to Mirjana on the day she received the Tenth Secret—seems to indicate that what is to come will not come easily, but will come swiftly. Some difficult—what the Virgin Mary called "*terrible*"—days lie ahead, with eternal consequences at stake for those who continue to choose to ignore the presence of God in their life. This is why Mary told Mirjana "to think of the tears I must shed."

While Pope John Paul II wrote of the "springtime" that is to come in the Church and the world in the new millennium,[46] the message at Medjugorje is clear: whether one is a believer or not, the autumn of today is leading to the winter of tomorrow.

"I have prayed," the Virgin Mary told Mirjana on November 6, 1982, "the punishment has been softened. Repeated prayers and fasting reduce punishments from God, but it is not possible to avoid entirely the chastisement. Go on the streets of the city, count those who glorify God and those who offend Him.

"God can no longer endure that." [47]

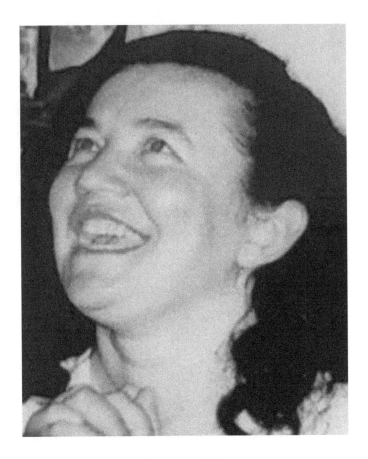

Vicka Ivanković Mijatovic

"I'll just say this: whoever does not believe without a sign will not believe with a sign. And, I'll tell you this too: woe to him who delays his conversion waiting for a sign."

Photo Credit: Renee Laurentin

PART V

TIME OF DECISION

" I ask you to pray for the conversion of everyone. For that, I need your prayers."

—The Virgin Mary
Medjugorje,
April 8,1984

CHAPTER FIFTY-NINE

THERE WILL BE THREE WARNINGS

*"Indeed, the Lord does nothing without revealing
his plan to his servants, the prophets."*

—Am 3: 7

H E WILL GO BEFORE THE LORD IN THE SPIRIT AND POWER OF THE prophet Elijah, wrote Saint Luke of the coming of John the Baptist.[1] Needless to say, the Virgin Mary's arrival in Medjugorje on June 24, 1981—the feast day of the Baptist—was meant to be strategic with regards to her mission.

It was, in essence, a theological exclamation point on the start of her mission.

Like Elijah and the Baptist, Mary was in the world to make straight the path of the Lord. She had come to lay the axe to the root, to call down the fire, and no better day on the Church calendar signaled this spiritual D-Day than the Baptist's feast.

The Virgin's early words at Medjugorje, however, were measured.

God's allotted period of her visitation was somewhat set.

A certain time for conversion, she repeated, was underway. Divine mercy, though incomprehensibly infinite, was on a finite schedule.

We are living in a time of grace, wrote Mirjana in her 2016 book, echoing the Virgin's words. After this, she made clear, will come "the time of the Ten Secrets, and then the time of Mary's triumph." [2]

While those who follow Medjugorje ponder the length of these periods, one thing is known for sure; with each minute, each hour, each day, the time of the Secrets draws nearer as the time of grace slips away, gone forever.

Mirjana, in 2007, perhaps best defined the moment, "Our Lady said that this time in which we live is a time of decision." [3] It should be a decision to change, to convert one's life to God, she writes in her book, to prepare for the future by "preparing your soul."

This is *not* done, Mirjana made abundantly clear, by "erecting bunkers and stockpiling supplies." [4]

Time.

It's the friend of the young and the foe of the old.

It can be on your side; it can be against you. It waits for no one. Time, like life, has a past, a present, and a future. Jesus, cautioned against the future: "Do not worry about tomorrow; tomorrow will take care of itself."

But the Lord was speaking about the concerns of the temporal world, not the eternal. The Secrets of Medjugorje—whatever they may hold—sound more like "the day of the Lord coming like a thief in the night," and one needs to be prepared. [5]

It is a day that we can assume is undeniably closer, just by contemplating a few of the words Mirjana used in speaking about the Secrets in her book.

Referring back to an incident in 1985 that involved Ivanka receiving the Tenth Secret, Mirjana called it a time when the Secrets were still "many years away," a remark that leads one to logically conclude that she is inferring that such can no longer be said to be the case. [6]

So, just what is known about these Ten Secrets that point to the more serious warnings in Scripture regarding one's eternity?

Why will it be too late for some by the time the Third Secret arrives?

Some of Mary's early messages at Medjugorje speak directly of the contents of the Secrets, but most of what we know comes from the visionaries. Essentially, they have said only what they are able to say since the Secrets are, well, secret.

This conundrum involving "the secrecy of the Secrets" has been noted before.

In Lourdes, two parish priests asked Bernadette, "Would you disclose your Secret to the Pope?" Bernadette replied, "The Blessed Virgin forbids me to disclose it to any person. The Pope is a person."

At Fátima, the parish priest commended the three children, "You are doing well, my children— what for yourself, and or God—to keep the Secret of your souls." [7]

The same is found at Medjugorje.

But some of the visionaries' words do provide a salient look into this mystery.

The six visionaries—polite and patient over the years—cannot escape the shadow of their Secrets. Day in and day out, for decades now, people have bombarded them with questions about them.

What is in them?

When are they coming?

Will the Secrets be good or bad?

At Fátima, the three children would retire into absolute silence— "to the point of rudeness"—when having to answer the everyday people who tortured them with questions about their Secret. [8] Quite perturbed by it all, their delicate consciences eventually only surrendered to the requests of priests, who they felt had, as one writer put it, "somewhat of a legal right to ask such questions." [9]

Over time, the six visionaries at Medjugorje have adopted a twofold response to public questions surrounding the Secrets: 1) the Secrets are off limits; 2) their contents—while disconcerting—are of no paramount concern if one's soul is right with God.

Though it has been almost forty years since the Ten Secrets were first revealed to be part of the Madonna's revelations at Medjugorje, most of what is known about them came about in the first ten years.

During this time, we find almost all of the known messages in which Mary herself actually speaks of the Secrets. It's also during this period that the visionaries appear to be somewhat more forthcoming during personal interviews regarding them.

Perhaps because of their desire to prove the apparitions were true, or because of the trust built up between them and some of their early inquisitors—or because of youthful indiscretions—these early dialogues give us the best insight into the overall nature and content of the Ten Secrets.

It's known that the visionaries at Fátima received their three-part Secret from the Virgin Mary on July 13, 1917. But no such precise starting date is established as the official beginning of the revelation of Ten Secrets of Medjugorje.

Father Svetozar Kraljević, in his seminal work, *The Apparitions of Our Lady of Medjugorje, 1981-1983: An Historical Account with Interviews,* provided what appears to be the first substantive look at the Secrets.

At the time, Father Kraljević was a true insider at Medjugorje. Sent to the United States in 1975 to finish his theology training, he was ordained in 1977 and then served in New York City.

Returning home in 1982 to visit his relatives, less than a year after the apparitions began, he was suddenly told his passport was no longer valid and could not return to the United States. Consequently, Father Svet—as he is best known—immediately set his sights on going to Medjugorje, which he had already heard about in America. This led to the penning of his book. [10]

Around this same time, Father René Laurentin began to write, *Is the Virgin Mary Appearing at Medjugorje?* The book included within it a small, reconstituted Croatian book on Medjugorje written by Father Ljudevit Rupčić.

Rupčić, imprisoned by the Communists three times,[11] was a New Testament exegesis professor at Franjevacka Teologija [12] (Franciscan School of Theology) and had also taught at the University of Zagreb.[13] His original book, *The Apparitions of Our Lady at Medjugorje*—the first of five books on Medjugorje, with the last coming in 1991—was published in Croatia in 1983.[14] It contained what appears to be the first formal contact with the visionaries, which included several of his questions to them regarding the Secrets.

At the time, Rupčić confessed, he wasn't too convinced about the visions, perceiving Medjugorje as a "joke." [15]

Because both Kraljević's and Laurentin's books were scheduled to be published around the same time, Laurentin was permitted a pre-publication look at Father Svetozar's manuscript. In this way, said Laurentin, he would try not to harmonize the books but to maintain their differences. [16]

The bibliography of Laurentin's first book reveals he reviewed, to his knowledge, all the reports, articles, and short pamphlet-type writings available on Medjugorje at the time, including any dialogues with the visionaries that addressed the Secrets. Likewise, Kraljević's book, though not profoundly informative about the Secrets, also contained interviews with the visionaries that shed light on them.

Together, the two books start to reveal the seriousness of their content.

It must be noted that none of these early works attempted to establish an official timeline on the revelation of the Secrets. This would later begin to take shape, although haphazardly and unintendedly, through the publication of Laurentin's second book on Medjugorje, *Messages and Teachings of Mary at Medjugorje, Chronological Corpus of the Messages.* Laurentin coauthored this effort with Father René Lejeune, a professor who had worked at Alger, Strasbourg, São Paulo, and Geneva.[17]

By 1985, Laurentin felt that it was necessary—even in compliance with Mary's request to "study and live" her messages—that a complete corpus of all available messages since the beginning of the apparitions be assembled in chronological order.

This effort by Laurentin and Lejeune would come from a variety of sources: the visionaries, the priests, the diaries and journals kept (especially Vicka Ivankovic's diary of the apparitions and Ivan's diary that he kept while in the seminary), and especially the official records of the Franciscans, who maintained a logue of the events and messages at Medjugorje in what was termed "the parish chronicle," or better known as "The Chronicle of the Apparitions," as referenced by Dr. Ljudevit Rupčić and Dr. Viktor Nuić.[18] Laurentin and Lejeune especially referred to a 1986 book by Father Y. M. Blais titled, *Five Hundred Messages to Live.*[19]

It appears that all contemporary compilation books and website histories of the Virgin Mary's early revelations at Medjugorje were drawn out of this effort by the two men.

While the history of the Virgin's messages at Medjugorje primarily emerges from this book of Laurentin and Lejeune, there is a question of the preciseness of the Virgin's words in the early messages. Rupčić and Nuić addressed this issue in their 2002 book, *Once Again, the Truth About Medjugorje*:

"The visionaries themselves cannot guarantee letter by letter what Our Lady said. If the four Evangelists differ amongst themselves in their reports about the same event, then there is no wonder that perhps the visionaries differ in their reports. Fr. Tomislav Vlašić himself on page 40 of the *"Chronicle of the Apparitions"* writes that it is evident that the visionaries do not relay word for word the replies that they received, but in their own words which can give the response a different tone and as such it is necessary to take account of that when referring to the inadequacy of the children's memories, their manner of expression and their behavior." [20]

This documented assertion forces us to conclude that almost all of the early messages at Medjugorje— prior to the beginning of the weekly "parish messages" on March 1,1984—must be understood as not being "verbatim accounts" of what the Virgin Mary said to the visionaries on any given date. Of course, it can be assumed that some are precise, but there is no way of knowing for sure.

From Laurentin and Lejeune's work, we discover that the words *Secret* and *Secrets* do not appear at all in Mary's messages given during the first year, which runs from June 24 to December 31, 1981. Some points of interest with regard to the Secrets, however, do manifest during this initial period.

The more serious nature of the Virgin's message at Medjugorje, which Father Robert Faricy defines as "apocalyptic" in theme, starts to develop early.

First, on June 26, Mary tells the visionaries, "I wish to convert and reconcile the whole world—to convert all of you." Then, on August 2, she discloses the reason why: "A great battle is about to take place. A battle between my Son and Satan. Human souls are at stake."

With this declaration, Mary's words echo for the most part what Sister Lúcia of Fátima reportedly stated the Virgin told her about a great spiritual battle unfolding in the 20th century, most notably revealed in her December 26, 1957, interview with Father Augustine Fuentes Anguiano, the vice-postulator for the beatification of Francisco and Jacinta.[21]

By September, the Virgin is seen to be stressing the seriousness of her coming.

She now consistently asks for conversion, something that will be forever a staple of her message in Medjugorje. And, during this period, there emerges a running exchange between Mary and the children concerning their requests for a sign. These conversations gradually evolve from talk of a sign in general, to the coming of the Great Sign that will become the cornerstone of the Third Secret.

The most revealing message that the "sign" Mary is speaking of *is* actually one of the Ten Secrets comes on September 4, when the Madonna says to the children, "The sign will be given at the end of the apparitions." From this point on, dialogue regarding the sign can be seen to grow more specific, as the promised sign is slowly revealed as the Great Sign contained in the Ten Secrets.

Then, on October 12 and 17, and again on October 22, the first substantive indication of the Secrets is found. It occurs in a discussion the visionaries have with Mary concerning ongoing reports of supernatural phenomenon erupting in the village, including claims that many people saw the cross on Mt. Krizevac transform itself into a light, and then into a silhouette of the Virgin.

"Is the whiteness of the cross a supernatural phenomenon?" the children asked of the Virgin. "All of these signs are designed to strengthen your faith," Mary responds, "until I leave you the visible and permanent Sign."

With this response, Mary's answer directly points to the presence of the Secrets, which are to reveal the Great (permanent) Sign. But, it's unknown whether or not at this time she is still referring to the Sign outside of the broader context of it being one of the Ten Secrets.

The dialogue between Mary and the visionaries that occurs six days later, on October 28, again points to the Third Secret—the "permanent Sign." Several hundred people see a mysterious fire burning on Podbrdo that suddenly vanished. Mary subsequently confirms to the visionaries its mysterious nature, and in doing so, alludes to the Secrets: "The fire seen by the faithful was of a supernatural character. It is *one* of the signs; a forerunner of the Great Sign."

As can be seen, her words directly speak of the contents of the Secrets. However, it is still not confirmable from the Laurentin and Lejeune corpus of messages that the visionaries at this time understood the Great Sign as one of the Ten Secrets.

In November, two more messages speak of the urgency surrounding the Virgin's visitation at Medjugorje. On Sunday, November 22, Mary stated "The world must find salvation while there is time." One week later, on November 29, she virtually repeats herself: "It is necessary for the world to be saved while there is time."

These become the last messages in 1981 that can be understood to be indirectly associated in some way to the Secrets.

There is no specific mention of the Ten Secrets in the first seven months of the apparitions in 1982, according to Laurentin and Lejeune's corpus.

There are, however, two revelations that are relative to the Secrets and are of significant importance because of the amount of discussion surrounding them over the years.

On Sunday, May 2, 1982, the Virgin told the visionaries, "I have come to call the world to conversion for the last time. Later, I will not appear any more on this Earth."

Then, on June 23— just prior to the first anniversary of the visions— Vicka asked Mary a set of questions that were posed by priests. Within her answers (recorded in the parish chronicle), Mary confirms her previous statement, "These apparitions are the last in the world."

To this day, there is no consensus on the exact meaning of the Virgin's words.

It is worthy to note that Mary has made similar statements before, as during her Church-approved apparitions at Beauraing in 1932 and 1933. On December 23, 1932, Mary told the five children in Beauraing, "Soon, I shall appear for the last time." [22]

One other message at Medjugorje stands out during this time frame, which could be seen by some to be related to the Secrets' apocalyptic overtones. On July 12,1982, Mary was asked if there would be another world war. She replied, "The Third World War will not take place."

On August 15, 1982, the subject of the Ten Secrets is first acknowledged in the Laurentin and Lejeune message timeline. Its entry again originates from the St. James parish chronicle:

"The vision lasted about seven minutes. The Gospa entrusted *a new Secret* to Vicka and Ivanka—only to them. The others saw that it was about a Secret, but they did not understand anything."

The historical relevance here is twofold.

Not only is the presence of the Ten Secrets documented for the first time in the Laurentin and Lejeune book, but from what *is* written, it is clear that an *undocumented reality* of the Ten Secrets has been ongoing for quite some time—possibly, according to other sources, as early as July, maybe even June, of 1981.

Fathers Barbarić and Vlašić allude to this in their 1985 book, *Open Your Hearts to Mary Queen of Peace*: "These visionaries say that, from the very beginning, Our Lady told them she would confide ten secrets to them for the whole of humanity." [23] Likewise, Mirjana is also on record as telling one interviewer that the Virgin began to speak about the Secrets in the first week of the apparitions. [24]

On August 31, 1982, the Virgin Mary spoke again of the Great Sign. This revelation alludes to the fact—which the visionaries have asserted concerning all Ten Secrets—that each Secret will come to pass, at least to some degree, regardless of the world's response:

"The Great Sign has been granted. It will appear *independently* of the conversion of the people."

Over the remaining months of 1982 and throughout 1983, Mary's messages to the six visionaries— as documented by Laurentin and Lejeune— reveal little more of importance involving the Ten Secrets as a whole. But a significant development does come into play before the end of 1983 concerning the reality of the Ten Secrets.

As cited previously, Marija told the Franciscans that the Virgin Mary wanted a letter sent to the Pope concerning the exigency of the message at Medjugorje:

"You must warn the Bishop very soon, and the Pope, with respect to the urgent and the great importance of the message for all humanity." [25]

By virtue of this letter—for the first time—somewhat of an official, written summary from the Church is compiled concerning the nature and history of the apparitions at Medjugorje. A significant portion of the factual information for it is attained from a meeting with Mirjana on November 5, 1983. [26]

Most noteworthy, within the letter's contents, there is found a brief summary of the existence and makeup of the Ten Secrets.

December 2, 1983

After the apparition of the Blessed Virgin on November 30, 1983, Marija Pavlović came to see me and said, "The Madonna says that the Supreme Pontiff and the Bishop must be advised immediately of the urgency and great importance of the message of Medjugorje."

This letter seeks to fulfill that duty.

1. Five young people (Vicka Ivanković, Marija Pavlović, Ivanka Ivanković, Ivan Dragićević, and Jacov Čolo) see an apparition of the Blessed Virgin every day. The experience in which they see her is a fact that can be checked by direct observation. It has been filmed. During the apparitions the youngsters do not react to light, they do not hear sounds, they do not react if someone touches them, they feel that they are beyond time and space.

All of the youngsters basically agree that:

- "We see the Blessed Virgin just as we see anyone else. We pray with her, we speak to her, and we can touch her."
- "The Blessed Virgin says that world peace is at a critical stage. She repeatedly calls for reconciliation and conversion."
- "She has promised to leave a visible sign for all humanity at the sight of the apparitions at Medjugorje."
- "The period preceding this visible sign is a time of grace for conversion and deepening of faith."
- "The Blessed Virgin has promised to disclose ten secrets to us. So far, Vicka Ivanković has received eight. Marija Pavlović received the ninth one on Dec 8, 1983. Jacov Čolo, Ivan Dragićević and Ivanka Ivanković have each received nine. Only Mirjana Dragićević has received all ten."
- "These apparitions are the last apparitions of the Blessed Virgin on Earth. That is why they are lasting so long and occurring so frequently."

1. The Blessed Virgin no longer appears to Mirjana Dragićević. The last time she saw one of the daily apparitions was Christmas, 1982. Since then, the apparitions have ceased for her, except on

her birthday (March 18,1983). Mirjana knew that this latter would occur.

2. According to Mirjana, the Madonna confided the tenth and last secret to her during the apparition of December 25, 1982. She also disclosed the dates on when the different secrets will come to pass. The Blessed Virgin has revealed to Mirjana many things about the future, more than to any of the other youngsters so far. For that reason, I am reporting below what Mirjana told me during our conversation on Nov 5, 1983. I am summarizing the substance of her account, without word for word quotations.

Mirjana said,

Before the visible sign is given to humanity, there will be three warnings to the world. The warnings will be in the form of events on the Earth. Mirjana will be a witness to them. Three days before one of the admonitions, Mirjana will notify a priest of her choice. The witness of Mirjana will be a confirmation of the apparitions and stimulus for the conversion of the world.

After the admonitions, the visible sign will appear on the site of the apparitions of Medjugorje for all the world to see. The sign will be given as a testimony to the apparitions and in order to call people back to the faith.

The Ninth and Tenth Secrets are serious. They concern chastisement for the sins of the world. Punishment is inevitable, for we cannot expect the whole world to be converted. The punishment can be diminished by prayer and penance. But it cannot be eliminated. Mirjana says that one of the evils that threatened the world, the one contained in the Seventh Secret, has been averted thanks to prayer and fasting. That is why the Blessed Virgin continues to encourage prayer and fasting: "*You have forgotten that through prayer and fasting you can avert war and suspend the laws of nature.*"

After the first admonition, the others will follow in a rather short time. Thus, people will have some time for conversion.

That interval will be a period of grace and conversion. After the visible sign appears those who are still alive will have little time for conversion. For that reason, the Blessed Virgin invites us to urgent conversion and reconciliation.

The invitation to prayer and penance is meant to avert evil and war, but most of all to save souls.

According to Mirjana, the events predicted by the Blessed Virgin are near. By virtue of this experience. Mirjana proclaims to the world: "Hurry, be converted; open your hearts to God."

...Holy Father, I do not want to be responsible for the ruin of anyone. I am doing my best. The world is being called to conversion and reconciliation. In writing to you, Holy Father, I am only doing my duty. After drafting this letter, I showed it to the youngsters so that they might ask the Blessed Virgin whether its contents are accurate. Ivan Dragićević relayed the following answer: 'Yes, the contents of the letter are the truth. You must notify first of all the Supreme Pontiff and then the Bishop.'

This letter is accompanied by fasting and prayers that the Holy Spirit will guide your mind and your heart during this important moment in history. [27]

Yours in the Sacred Hearts of Jesus and Mary,
Father Tomislav Vlašić,
December 2, 1983

CHAPTER SIXTY

WHILE THERE IS TIME

*"At that time there shall arise Michael, the
great prince, guardian of your people…"*

—Dn 12:1

S HE NEEDED TO BE SECRET ABOUT THE SECRET.

This was what the Virgin Mary asked of Sister Lúcia concerning
the second part of the Secret of Fátima, which involved fortold chastisements of all humanity.

While Lúcia would begin to reveal some of the first part of the Secret
in 1925—the vision of Hell—it was not until 1941 that she deliberately
set about to make the powerful, prophetic second part of the Secret of
Fátima known in writing. [1]

Prior to then, not only had Lúcia not written of it, but she had not
truly spoken of it publicly.

In fact, though Lúcia was interviewed at her convent by a number
of notable visitors in 1946 alone; Father Hubert Jongen on February 3
and 4; Professor William Thomas Walsh, with Fathers Galamba, Roca
and Furtado on July 15; Father Louis de Gonzague, accompanied by
John Haffert (who also met with Lúcia in1952 and 1955) on August 12;
and Canon Casmir Barthas on October 17 and 18, nothing was publicly forthcoming about the Secret of Fátima.

Lúcia's multiple visits with Father Thomas McGlynn—the sculptor
who Lúcia helped perfect the famed statue of Our Lady of Fátima—
beginning in February of 1947; Father Gustav Wetter on August 14,
1951—who delivered a message to Pius XII for her; Father Joseph
Schweigl on September 2,1952—an Austrian Jesuit who was sent to

Fátima by Pius XII to interrogate Lúcia about the Third Secret, and others less notable were also kept confidential at the time.

Aside from the books that would emerge from these audiences with Lúcia, only Father Ricardo Lombardi, the well known Jesuit and founder of *The Better World Movement*—who was a friend of Pius XII—wrote and published a circumstantial account of his meeting with Lúcia. It appeared in the Vatican newspaper, *L'Osservatore della Domenica*, on February 7, 1954, and within it Lúcia reveals the seriousness of the Virgin's message at Fátima.

The story reported how Lombardi interviewed Lúcia in October 1953— "behind the grill at Coimbra"—and in answer to a question said to the priest, "If humanity does not seek to perfect itself, given the way in which it behaves now, only a limited part of the human race will be saved." [2]

In essence, it would not be until 1957—with the controversial disclosure of Father Fuentas—that a substantive interview with Lucia concerning Fátima's grave message is revealed.

This would come almost forty years after the apparitions at Fátima.

At Medjugorje, the opposite is found to occur.

The mysterious existence of the Ten Secrets is brought to life relatively early on in the history of the visions. But, unlike at Fátima, this is especially a result of the probing interviews with the visionaries that were conducted there at the time.

Four of the most significant interviews ever done with the visionaries at Medjugorje took place in 1982 and 1983. They were published in books by Father René Laurentin, Father Svetozar Kraljević and Father Janko Bubalo.

The first of these dialogues involves all six visionaries and Father Ljudevit Rupčić. A highly edited version of the interview was published in Laurentin's 1984 book, *Is the Virgin Mary Appearing at Medjugorje?*

The Croatian professor presented to the children sixty-two questions, some of which involved the Secrets. At the time, Rupčić met with each of them separately and gathered their independent and converging answers.

He would repeat this same sixty-two question interview in1987.

It is with this seminal interview of Rupčić that the curtain on the Ten Secrets of Medjugorje begins to be drawn back.

The following is a portion of the original, *unedited* transcript of Rupčić's interview conducted in December of 1982, the same month the report on Medjugorje was sent to the Pope. It involves only those questions that concern the Secrets. It is not known if this version of the interview has been ever published before.

Rupčić: *Has the Lady entrusted some Secrets to you?*

Marija Pavlović: Yes, I know six secrets. The rest of us; some have seven, some eight. They pertain to us, the Church, people in general.

Jacov Čolo: Yes, they pertain to our lives, and people.

Vicka Ivanković: Yes, I have seven of them. The first pertain to our church in Medjugorje, to the Sign, the whole humanity and everybody, the Church in general and there are some for us.

Ivanka Ivanković: Yes, I have eight. They pertain to us, personally, the Church and the world.

Mirjana Dragićević: Yes, I have nine entrusted to me. They pertain to us, the Sign…the whole world, and Medjugorje.

Ivan Dragićević: Yes.

Rupčić: *Did the Lady have a message for the world?*

Marija Pavlović: All the messages relate to the world. There are messages for peace, for faith, conversions, prayers, fast and penance.

Jacov Čolo: You have to pray, fast, return to faith, so that there will be peace.

Vicka Ivanković: She tells us to pray, do penance, return to faith, peace; the most important is the message for peace. She announced this!

Ivanka Ivanković: The "Lady" said that it is most important to have strong faith, that we should pray every day at least seven Our Fathers', seven Hail Marys', seven Glory Bes' and the one "I Believe." And to fast on bread and water on Fridays.

Mirjana Dragićević: She emphasized that prayers are important. Faith, fast; that with this, wars and catastrophes can be averted. Today we have very much of this.

Ivan Dragićević: That you must return to your faith, and that it become more secure and deep, and that way be transferred from knee to knee.

Rupčić: *Are you allowed to tell the Secrets to others?*

Marija Pavlović: We cannot. The Lady told us whom we will tell.

Jacov Čolo: We cannot until she tells us.

Vicka Ivanković: No. We cannot until she tells us.

Ivanka Ivanković: No, to no one.

Mirjana Dragićević: No.

Ivan Dragićević: No.

Rupčić: *Are the Secrets good or bad about the world?*

Marija Pavlović: Well now, that is a secret.

Jacov Čolo: There is good and there is bad.

Vicka Ivanković: There is good and bad.

Ivanka Ivanković: There is good and there is bad.

Mirjana Dragićević: There is good and there is bad.

Ivan Dragićević: (Rupčić: *Same as above.*)

Rupčić: *When will the Lady allow you to reveal these Secrets?*

Marija Pavlović: I don't know. She will tell us when, and to whom.

Jacov Čolo: Don't know.

Vicka Ivanković: When she tells us.

Ivanka Ivanković: Don't know.

Mirjana Dragićević: She didn't tell us yet.

Ivan Dragićević: When she allows it.

Rupčić: *Did the Lady promise to do anything special by which the remaining will know that she is the Lady?*

Marija Pavlović: The Lady said she will leave a sign for those who do not believe.

Jacov Čolo: Yes, she will leave a Great Sign.

Vicka Ivanković: She said she will leave a Great Sign.

Ivanka Ivanković: Yes, the Lady said that she will leave a Great Sign on the mountain of the apparition.

Mirjana Dragićević: Yes.

Ivan Dragićević: Yes.

Rupčić: *When will that Sign be given?*

Marija Pavlović: And that is a secret.

Jacov Čolo: We know this but can't reveal it.

Vicka Ivanković: We know but cannot say.

Ivanka Ivanković: It's not important.

Mirjana Dragićević: That is one of the Secrets.

Ivan Dragićević: That is a secret.

Rupčić: *Will this special sign, which is announced by the Lady, be seen by everyone?*

Marija Pavlović: It will be.

Jacov Čolo: It will be.

Vicka Ivanković: It will be.

Ivanka Ivanković: Certainly

Mirjana Dragićević: Yes.

Ivan Dragićević: Yes.

Rupčić: *When will the Sign be?*

Marija Pavlović: And that is a secret.

Jacov Čolo: We know this, but cannot reveal it.

Vicka Ivanković: I know. I am not allowed to tell. Otherwise, I would.

Ivanka Ivanković: I know.

Mirjana Dragićević: This I cannot tell you.

Ivan Dragićević: This a secret.

Rupčić: *Would you swear that that which you have said is the truth?*

Marija Pavlović: I would.

Jacov Čolo: I would.

Vicka Ivanković: I would a hundred times, not once!

Ivanka Ivanković: Why naturally, yes.!

Mirjana Dragićević: Naturally I would!

Ivan Dragićević: I would! [3]

The second of these dialogues involves Mirjana Dragićević and Father Tomislav Vlašić. It was conducted on January 10, 1983, just a month after Father Rupčić's interview.

Identical extracts of this interview were published in both Kraljević's book, *The Apparitions of Our Lady at Medjugorje* and Laurentin's *Is the Virgin Mary Appearing at Medjugorje?*

Through these two books, the Ten Secrets of Medjugorje start to attract significant attention by the mid-80s. This is enhanced by the fact that they hold the first known published interview to take place with Mirjana after she received the tenth and final Secret.

> Question: *You said that the 20th century has been given over to Devil?*
>
> **Mirjana**: Yes.
>
> Question: *You mean the century until the year 2000, or generally speaking?*
>
> **Mirjana**: Generally, part of which is in the 20th century, until the First Secret is revealed. The Devil will rule till then. She told me several Secrets and explained them to me; and I have them written down in code letters, with dates, so I won't forget them. If, say, tomorrow a Secret is to be revealed, I have a right, two or three days before, to pick whatever priest I want and tell him about it. For example: "The day after tomorrow, such and such will happen." The priest, then, is free to do as he thinks best with that information. He can write it out before it happens, then read it to others after it happens. He can also tell it to the people; "Tomorrow, such-and-such will happen." It's up to him to decide what to do with the information.
>
> Question: *Were these Secrets ever revealed before, to anybody in previous generations?*
>
> **Mirjana**: I can't answer that. Anyway, you know all the Secrets that have been told before. You know some of them, but not all.
>
> Question: *So then, I don't know all of them; but since you've been told not to talk about them, I won't ask you to. That's all right—as it should be. But I'll ask you if you know when the Secrets will be revealed.*

Mirjana: I know. I know every date of every Secret.

Question: *But you can't say anything about this?*

Mirjana: I can't.

Question: *Can we suppose, then, that one might say that three Secrets would be revealed before the Great Sign appears; then the rest of the Secrets will be revealed, one by one? Is there anything to that?*

Mirjana: Nothing like that, but something like this. First, some Secrets will be revealed—just a few. Then—then, the people will be convinced that the Madonna was here. They will understand the Sign. When Jacov said that the Mayor will be the first one to run to the hill, he meant that generally, people of the highest social class. They will understand the Sign as a place or occasion to convert. They will run to the hill and pray, and they will be forgiven. When I asked the Madonna about unbelievers, she said: "*They should be prayed for, and they should pray.*" But when I asked again, recently, she said, "*Let them convert while there is time.*" She did not say they should be prayed for.

Question: *You can say nothing specifically until the moment the Madonna says you can?*

Mirjana: Yes.

Question: *Can we say that some of the Secrets belong only to you, personally?*

Mirjana: No. None of the Secrets is personally for me.

Question: *Not you, then, but Ivan has some personal Secrets.*

Mirjana: My Secrets are all for mankind generally, for the world, Medjugorje, for some other areas, and about the Sign.

Question: *The Sign will pertain to the parish?*

Mirjana: Yes, to Medjugorje. But there is something else.

Question: *Something else?*

Mirjana: Nothing for me personally.

Question: *After these Ten Secrets, after these eighteen months of apparitions, what do you tell the people they should do? What do you say to priests? To the pope? To bishops, without revealing the Secrets? What does the Madonna want us to do?*

Mirjana: First, I would like to tell you how it was for me at the end, and the…

Question: *All right.*

Mirjana: Two days before Christmas, the Madonna told me Christmas Day would be the last time she would appear to me. (I didn't quite believe this.) On Christmas Day, she stayed with me forty-five minutes and we talked about many things. We summarized everything that had been said between us. On behalf of many people, I asked what they should do. Then she gave me a very precious gift: she said she would appear to me on my birthday every year for the rest of my life. Also, independently of the Sign—and anything else—she said she will appear to me when something very difficult happens—not some everyday difficulty, but something quite grievous. Then she will come to help me. But now, I have to live without her physical presence, without her daily, personal visits. I say to all people: Convert! - the same as she said: "*Convert while there is time!*" Do not abandon God and your faith. Abandon everything else, but not that! I ask priests to help their people, because priests can cause them to reject their faith. After a man has been ordained, he must really be a priest, bring people to the Church. The most important point is that the people convert and pray.

Question: *What is the greatest danger to mankind? What does it come from?*

Mirjana: From Godlessness. Nobody believes—hardly anybody.

Question: *Why did the Madonna introduce herself as the Queen of Peace?*

Mirjana: You know very well the situation in the world. The situation is very tense. Peace is needed—a just and simple peace. [4]

In 1987, Mirjana met privately with Pope John Paul II in Rome. She reported that the Holy Father "knew" she had received all ten secrets, but could reveal no more of their conversation other than that John Paul said to her, "If I were not the Pope, I would be in Medjugorje." [5]

On February 27, 1983, Father Svetozar Kraljević interviewed Ivanka Ivankovic for his same book, *The Apparitions of Our Lady at Medjugorje.* Through this interview, a little more is learned about the purpose behind the Secrets.

> Kraljević: *The Queen of Peace. Does she mean to imply something by that name?*
>
> **Ivanka**: I think that, in calling herself Queen of Peace, she shows that she means to reconcile the world.
>
> Kraljević: *How does she reconcile the world?*
>
> **Ivanka**: Merely by coming to the world, she reconciles it—at least a little. People have converted, and begun to believe, and pray a little more. The Madonna said that with prayer and fasting, wars could be stopped.
>
> Kraljević: *Bearing in mind what you know about the future, tell me if the Madonna of Medjugorje will reconcile the world even more.*
>
> **Ivanka**: I think she will. Because she is the Queen of Peace, I think she will reconcile the whole world.
>
> Kraljević: *Will the Great Sign help in achieving this?*
>
> **Ivanka**: Yes, when the time comes.
>
> Kraljević: *Will the Sign appear very soon, or later.*
>
> **Ivanka**: It will appear at the proper time. [6]

Over two years later, on May 7, 1985, Ivanka received her last daily apparition and was given the Tenth Secret. Mary told Ivanka that day, "Whatever I have told you during these years, and the Secrets I have revealed to you, for now, do not speak of them to anyone until I tell you." [7]

The fourth and last of these early, pivotal interviews occurred between Vicka Ivanković and Father Janko Bubalo, a local Franciscan. It was published in Bubalo's award-winning book, *A Thousand Encounters with the Blessed Virgin in Medjugorje.*

Bubalo, a renowned Croatian poet who was imprisoned by the Communists a few years before the apparitions began, said he heard about the visions by the third or fourth day. [8]

Vicka, who will reportedly release a book some day on the life of the Virgin Mary based on Mary's dictations to her, [9] gave the interview with Father Bubalo through a series of meetings with him that concluded at the end of 1983, with some additions, the author notes, in 1984.[10] (It should be noted that Bubalo also conducted extensive interviews at the time with Ivanka and Marija.)

> **Bubalo:** *Usually Vicka, when one speaks of the Virgin's apparitions, Secrets are associated with them. This is the case here in Medjugorje, also.*
>
> **Vicka:** I don't know anything about that. Would you believe that I knew almost nothing about the apparitions of the Virgin in Lourdes, and I've been meeting with the Virgin at Podbrdo and Medjugorje, more than a year. I even knew, somehow, to sing the song, *From That Grotto* without having any notion of what it is about. And to be honest, I don't want to speak of any other Secrets except those of Medjugorje, if any of that interests you.
>
> **Bubalo:** *It interests me. Naturally, it interests me. I have attempted to broach the subject before, but, nonetheless, it continues to be a secret to me.*
>
> **Vicka:** What can I do! A secret is a secret.
>
> **Bubalo:** *I think you are entirely too closed on the subject.*
>
> **Vicka:** You can think what you will, but I know what I may and may not.

Bubalo: *Good. To the extent I was able to enter the subject, you, the Seers, don't talk about the Sign nor about the Secrets amongst yourselves.*

Vicka: Little or not at all.

Bubalo: *And why is that? Whenever I ask something about the subject, as, for example, did the Virgin truly forbid any discussion on the subject, you simply pretend as though you don't hear the question.*

Vicka: And we don't. We don't wish to speak of the subject and that is it.

Bubalo: *Good. Then tell me first off, how many Secrets did the Virgin say she would impart to you?*

Vicka: You certainly know that much. But here: she told us that she would impart Ten Secrets.

Bubalo: *To each of you?*

Vicka: To each of us, as far as I know.

Bubalo: *And are the Secrets the same for each of you?*

Vicka: They are and they aren't.

Bubalo: *And how is that?*

Vicka: Just so. The main Secrets are the same, but perhaps some of us have a secret which applies to us alone.

Bubalo: *Do you have such a Secret?*

Vicka: I have one. It is for me alone, since it concerns me only.

Bubalo: *Do the others have any such Secrets?*

Vicka: That I don't know. It seems to me that Ivan does.

Bubalo: *I know that Mirjana, Ivanka, and Marija don't have any since they told me. I don't know, however, for little Jacov. He didn't want to answer me on that point, while Ivan said that he had three which concern him only.*

Vicka: So, alright. I told you what I know.

Bubalo: *But tell me, in their order, which Secret is only for you?*

Vicka: Let's let that be. That is important only to me.

Bubalo: *But, can't you at least tell me that much without revealing your Secret?*

Vicka: Well, it's the Fourth. And, now be satisfied.

Bubalo: *Good, then, Vicka. Can you tell me how many Secrets you have received thus far?*

Vicka: So far, eight.

Bubalo: *In order, then. Generally speaking, it is known that in the Secrets the Virgin has foretold of something ghastly for mankind. Is that so?*

Vicka: Well, you can say it is known. So, what then?

Bubalo: *And you can't, then, say any more on the subject?*

Vicka: Nothing. That is sufficient.

Bubalo: Mirjana suggested something even more dreadful in her Ninth and Tenth Secrets.

Vicka: So, we heard! It is good for us to reflect on it.

Bubalo: *And you can say nothing more?*

Vicka: What can I? I know nothing more about it than you do.

Bubalo: *Can you at least say this much: do you know what will take place based on each of the Secrets?*

Vicka: I know for those I have already received.

Bubalo: *And do you know when it will take place?*

Vicka: I won't know until the Virgin tells me.

Bubalo: *Mirjana says that she knows exactly what and when things will happen.*

Vicka: She knows. The Virgin told her because she no longer has apparitions.

Bubalo: *According to that, you can't say, nor do you know, if any of the Secrets will be made evident to the world before the evidencing of the Virgin's Sign?*

Vicka: There, I told you I don't know. What I don't know, I don't know! [11]

As in the times of the Old Testament, an intense period of transformation is expected to come through the unfolding of the Ten Secrets of Medjugorje. Consequently, the Ten Secrets have become in some eyes almost legendary in stature—destined, it is believed, to bring divinely ordained change.

In lieu of the potential magnitude of such prophecies, therefore, could the events foretold in the Secrets of Medjugorje be alluded to in the Bible? Do they concern prophesied times spoken about in the *Gospels* or *The Book of Revelation*?

No, the visionaries say, Mary never said that.[12]

Some, however, are not sure.

Theologians Foley, Faricy, Laurentin, and some of the Franciscans at Medjugorje, are on record as having said that Medjugorje's message is "apocalyptic." Still, none have gone so far as to claim the events contained in the Secrets are specifically alluded to in Scripture.

But others think such a possibility should not be ruled out.

Something extraordinary is unfolding in Medjugorje, and it's their opinion that it might be part of a bigger picture. One of Mary's messages—some have postulated—perhaps hints of this reality:

"If you pray; God will help you to discover the *true* reason for my coming. Therefore, little children, pray and read the Sacred Scriptures so that through my coming you discover the message in Sacred Scripture for yourselves." [13]

Asked if he thought the times foretold in *The Book of Revelation* had arrived, Father Tomislav Vlašić answered, "Yes, certainly." He then expanded on his answer: "We must really be aware that we are now in the time of great events when God wants to work a change for us, and thus the visionaries say these apparitions are the last for humanity and that with these events the time of Satan is finished. It is true: a new page has turned, something will come." [14]

Attorney Jan Connell, who interviewed the visionaries' multiple times over decades for her newsletters and books, also seemed to speculate about the significance of Medjugorje with regards to Scripture.[15]

Connell saw the Virgin of Medjugorje as traceable to *The Book of Revelation*, pointing out that the visionaries said that Mary has a crown of twelve stars and that she stands on a cloud, as described in *Revelation* 12:1. [16]

Father Albert Herbert, another prodigious author and an expert on Catholic private revelation involving prophecy, went so far as to write that Medjugorje *is truly* the fulfillment of Scripture:

"We must grasp the transcendental presence of Mary, the presence of the Woman clothed with the Sun, the Woman of the *Apocalypse*... Right now, we claim and affirm Mary of Medjugorje to be the splendid figure of the Twelfth Chapter of *Revelation*, with the moon under feet and on her head a crown of twelve stars." [17]

After the prophetic implications of Fátima were better understood, many writers said they thought they saw in Fátima the times fortold in *The Book of Revelation*.[18]

Pope Paul VI's apostolic exhortation, *Signum Magnum*, released on May 13, 1967—which coincided with his visit to Fátima that day—was viewed to be in this light especially because of its title, *The Great Sign*, which again recalled *Revelation* 12:1. [19]

Now, at Medjugorje, where the Virgin Mary announces she will bring the Secrets of Fatima to fulfillment, a closing chapter to this mystery is descending upon the world.

Indeed, the Ten Secrets of Medjugorje are said to carry within them not only the mercy and justice of God, but a definitive conclusion to the spiritual war that has been unfolding over the last several centuries, a climactic final phase that Fatima's Sister Lucia saw approaching and often spoke of in a cryptic, almost biblical sounding way.*

In her controversial, 1957 interview with Father Fuentes Anguiano (See Chapter Twenty-Four), Lucia said she was told a "decisive battle" was about to be played out between "God and the Evil One," a battle in which there would be "no middle way." [20]

---

*   On Sunday, August 2, 1981, the Virgin Mary gave the visionary Marija Pavlovic a message at Medjugorje that appeared to confirm Sister Lucia's words: "A a great battle is about to take place. A battle between my Son and Satan."

This was a revelation Lucia would later expand upon in 1983 with her well known letter to Cardinal Carlo Caffarra, the founding President of *The John Paul II Institute for Studies on Marriage and the Family.*

Once more, her language in the letter sounded again as if foretelling events prophesied in Scripture.

"The final battle between the Lord and Satan will be about marriage and the family," Lucia revealed to Caffarra, "because it is the decisive issue." [21]

This "final battle" over "marriage and the family," said Cardinal Caffarra, is "being fulfilled today."

In an interview published in *Aleteia* on May 19, 2017, Caffarra described how he has come to believe that Satan is attempting to destroy the two "sacred pillars of creation"—man and woman—through abortion and homosexuality, in order to fashion his own "anti-creation." [22]

As with Lucia, Cardinal Caffarra's insights strike a biblical chord.

"I began thinking a few years ago that Sr. Lucia's words are taking place," the Cardinal told Diane Montagna of *Aleteia*, "If we read the second chapter of *Genesis*, we see that the edifice of creation is founded on two pillars."

"First, man is not *something*; he is *someone,* and therefore, he deserves absolute respect. The second pillar is the relationship between man and woman, which is sacred. Between the man and *'the woman.'* Because creation finds its completion when God creates *'the woman.'* So much so, that after He created woman, the Bible says God rested.

"Today, what do we observe? Two terrible events. First, the legitimization of abortion. That is, abortion has become a 'subjective right' of woman…we say that abortion is a good; it is a right. The second thing we see is homosexual relationships, with marriage. You see that Satan is attempting to threaten and destroy the two pillars so that he can fashion another creation." [23]

This assault on "the two pillars of creation" has been successfully underway in the world for some time now, but has not breached the sanctity of the Catholic Church. The Church, under the recent guidance of Popes Paul VI, John Paul I and II, and Benedict XVI, has resisted efforts to undermine its positions, boldly upholding its moral teachings on contraception, IVF, abortion, euthanasia, and homosexuality.

The encyclical letters of Pope Paul VI and Pope John Paul II, *Humanae vitae* (Of Human Life) and *Evangelium vitae* (The Gospel of Life), significantly reinforced these moral pillars.

However, as we enter into the climax of this great spiritual war, it is clear that these teachings are now primary targets of Satan, essential to fulfilling his goal of stripping away the Church's moral authority in the world, in constructing, as Cardinal Caffarri stated, an "anti-creation." [24]

Needless to say, it should come as no surprise that the toppling of the Church's moral foundation is near the summit of Satan's plan, second only to destroying its Sacramental mysteries (Mt 24, Dn 12). Pope Paul VI's ominous statement in 1972, "The smoke of Satan has entered the Temple of God," has always been most associated with *Humanae Vitae*, which has endured relentless criticism since its release on July 25, 1968.

The term "anti-Creation" that Caffarri adopts to summarize Satan's objectives in this war is also quite astute and relevant, since the Evil One's aim in dismantling the moral pillars of the Church is essentially motivated by his great hatred of the "Creator of creation"—God the Father.

At their core, both abortion and homosexuality strike directly at the First Person of the Holy Trinity, at His Fatherhood—at His Divine Paternal Heart— the womb of the Father's "everlasting love," where each and every soul is "created" in the Creator's image. ("Before I formed you in the womb I knew you, and before you were born I consecrated you "(Jer 1:1, 5).

Thus, in essence , all attempts to impede, disfigure, or destroy the life the "Author of Life" wills to create—whether through contraception, abortion, same sex relations—is an attempt to undermine the Eternal Father's Divine Paternity, to vanquish His Fatherhood from the hearts of His children, which has been the Evil One's goal since the Garden.**

Satan, however, has been given only so much time to win this spiritual war—a century or one hundred years—according to Pope Leo XIII's reported 1884 prophetic vision (See Chapter Four).

And that allotted period, according to Mirjana Dragecevic Soldo, will officially come to its conclusion with the unfolding of the First Secret of Medjugorje.

**   The attack on life through abortion, contraception, and homosexuality—directly aimed at the divine paternity of the Father—has led some to argue that the Triumph of the Immaculate Heart will not be completely fulfilled until the Church declares a feast day for God the Father, which will honor in perpetuity His Divine Paternity. For more on this subject see my books, *Original Separation and The Mystery of the Divine Paternal Heart of God Our Father*. Also see Fr. Jean Galot's book, *Abba, Father, We Long to See Your Face*.

An Italian priest reportedly took this picture of Mary during an apparition at St. James Church in Medjugorje in the early 1980s.

Photo Credit: Pittsburgh Center for Peace

Mirjana's "second of the month apparition" drew huge crowds for many years. The monthly apparition ended in March of 2020.

Photo credit: Pittsburgh Center for Peace

A 1974 painting by Vlado Falak, which hung in St. James Church in Medjugorje, appears to have previewed the coming apparitions of the Virgin Mary in 1981.

Photo Credit: Pittsburgh Center for Peace

CHAPTER SIXTY-ONE

THE POWER OF SATAN
WILL BE DESTROYED

"For the accuser of our brothers is cast out."

—Rv 12:10

66 **I** SPOKE WITH MIRJANA AND SHE SAID THAT THE FIRST SECRET IS one catastrophe in one place in the world," said Draga Ivanković, who lived in Bijakovići at the time of the first apparition and is a cousin to three of the visionaries. "She knows where. She will tell it, ten days before to Father Petar (Ljubicic); and three days before it will happen, he will tell it to the people. All the people will know this for three days before it happens. There will be three such warnings before the Sign on apparition mountain.

"The three warnings are for the people to convert. The Sign is going to be something very convincing, and it will last forever. They say it will be very beautiful. If I remember correctly, one time Our Lady said that they should take a picture of the mountain because afterward it will be changed. I do not know when the First Secret will take place, but she says 'soon.' If you believe, do not be worried." [1]

Worry.

No one should worry about what is coming with the Ten Secrets of Medjugorje—all six visionaries concur—as long as one has taken the time to have their slate wiped clean with God.

But if not, by the time the Third Secret rolls around, it certainly sounds like it could become a concern. [2]

Like a line drawn in the sand, the appearance of the Great Sign on Podbrdo, where the first apparitions took place, is understood by some to be a metaphorical "crossing of the Red Sea" with regards to the world's future.

With this miraculous event, something incomprehensible is in the works. And from the sound of the visionaries, few will be able to deny its divine origin.

But before then—the First Secret must come.

The First Secret is considered a warning.

It will be proof, the visionaries tell us, of the Madonna's presence in Medjugorje. [3] And, following its fulfillment, there is to come an intense period of grace in which many people will convert. [4]

But, there is something more that is foretold to take place.

As with the appearance of the Great Sign, the First Secret is to be understood in a way that transcends its physical manifestation, for its unfolding is to affect the spiritual world, too.

The First Secret, according to Mirjana Dragićević Soldo in interviews over a period of more than ten years, will *break* the power of Satan.[5] It will end, she says Mary explained to her, a designated length of time—one century—that God granted Satan to extend his influence over humanity in a more effective, some would say powerful way. [6]

This mysterious and prophetic revelation—often written of but never officially documented—is said to have originated with Pope Leo XIII from a brief vision he experienced after celebrating Mass in the Vatican. As previously discussed, that mystical experience reportedly may have led to his composing of the well-known *Prayer to Saint Michael*.[7]

In the letter to Pope John Paul II of December 2, 1983, it was noted how the Virgin Mary spoke to Mirjana about this so-called "Century of Satan" and revealed to her that it would end with the unfolding of the Ten Secrets of Medjugorje.[8]

The report to the Pope, however, did not make it clear that the Devil's long-awaited demise would actually occur with the fulfillment of the very "First Secret," which Mirjana later explains during a January 10, 1983, interview published in Father Kraljević's book, *The Apparitions* of *Our Lady at Medjugorje*, and in subsequent other interviews over the years.[9]

In essence, the First Secret is to administer a decisive blow in the spiritual war that both Lúcia of Fátima and the visionaries of Medjugorje have spoken about in interviews.

So, what will this First Secret be?

Mirjana appears to be the best source to shed a little light on this question.

Mirjana's final daily apparition occurred on December 25, 1982, which lasted forty-five minutes.[10] On that day, the Virgin Mary promised her that she would appear from then on only on her birthday each year, March 18, [11] or at times when she was experiencing "difficulties or had special needs."[12] Time would show that some of this divine assistance would be in the form of interior locutions, not just apparitions.[13]*

On March 18, 1983, the Virgin kept her word and appeared to Mirjana on her birthday, and again on the same date in 1984.[14] That day, Mary told the young girl before her departure, "This year, probably, we will see each other again on account of the Secrets." [15]

On August 25, 1984, according to Father Slavko Barbarić, Mirjana received a special apparition in which Mary said to her, "Wait for me on September 13; I will speak to you about the future." [16] The Virgin appeared to her that day as promised, and once more that year on Christmas Day, in an apparition that lasted a half an hour.[17]

After the September apparition—which saw a weeping Madonna appear because of all the unbelief in the world [18]—Father Barbarić asked her a question:

"Are you happy to know the future?"

"One word suffices to make me cry all day long," answered Mirjana, "the Virgin is very sad with all the unfaithful people."

"Which unfaithful people," Barbarić wanted to know, "those who go to church but do not practice their faith, or those who do not know God?"

---

*   In August of 1987, this format changed. At that time, the Virgin Mary told Mirjana that she would also start to appear to her on "the second of every month" in order to pray with her for non-believers. These monthly apparitions took place from September 2, 1987, through March 2, 2020. On March 18, 2020, Mary announced to Mirjana that she would no longer appear to her on the second of every month.

"They are both the same," explained the visionary, "all adults have the capacity to know that God exists. The sin of the world consists in the fact that they are not interested in God."[19]

In 1985, Mirjana reported —according to the parish chronicle—receiving either locutions or apparitions on twelve occasions,[20] including one highly publicized "special apparition" on Friday, October 25, 1985, in which she received a more insightful look at the First Secret.

On that day, Mirjana experienced an intense vision during the apparition that allowed her to somewhat witness an event contained in the First Secret. Since she knew of this apparition a month in advance, she asked Father Petar Ljubicic (the priest chosen by her that June to reveal the Ten Secrets to the world) to be in attendance. Petar's personal experience that day proved to be very moving, as he reported witnessing the visionary's eyes filled with tears at one point.[21]

The official parish chronicle account, published in *Medjugorje Gebetsaktion* (1986, No.2), and reprinted in Father René Laurentin's 1988 book, *The Apparitions at Medjugorje Prolonged*, reads:

> We began to pray at 1:50 p.m. When she appeared, the Blessed Virgin greeted me: *Praised be Jesus.* Then, she spoke of unbelievers: *They are my children; I suffer because of them. They do not know what awaits them. You, must pray more for them.* We prayed with her for the weak, the unfortunate, and the forsaken. After the prayer, she blessed us.
>
> Then she showed me, as in a film, the realization of the First Secret. The Earth was desolate. *It is the upheaval of a region of the world.* She was precise. I cried. Why so soon? I asked. *In the world, there are so many sins. What can I do if you do not help me? Remember that I love you.* How can God have such a hard heart? *God does not have a hard heart. Look around you, and see what men do; then you will no longer say that God has a hard heart. How many people come to church, to the house of God with respect, strong faith, a love of God? Very few! Here you have a time of grace and conversion. It is necessary to use it well. Pray very much for Fr. Petar, to whom*

I send a special blessing. I am a mother; that is why I come.
You must not fear for I am there. [22]

Afterwards, Mirjana reported that Mary prayed over Father Ljubicic two times in Latin during the apparition. "I was happy because Our Lady was happy with my choice." said Mirjana. "The heart of Father Petar is completely opened to the Savior. A reward is waiting for him. We prayed an Our Father and a Glory Be for the success of Father Petar in the task which is confided to him."

The Virgin stayed for eight minutes that afternoon before departing.[23]

During the fall and winter of 1985 to 1986, Father Robert Faricy lived in Medjugorje for several months. On what would be his fifth visit, the eminent mystical theologian from Rome decided to keep a daily journal of the activities unfolding in the village, which he commenced writing on Friday, October 11, 1985.[24] His logue was later made into a 1987 book titled, *Medjugorje Journal, Mary Speaks to the World.*

On the day after the apparition / vision experience of Mirjana, Father Faricy documented the following account of what occurred in his journal:

> ***October 26, Saturday Night:*** Yesterday Mirjana had a visit from Our Lady. It lasted eight minutes. A month ago Mirjana heard Our Lady's voice tell her she would come on October 25. So, Mirjana knew ahead of time. She told Father Petar, and he was there during this vision. He says that, at one point, Mirjana's eyes filled with tears. Afterwards, she told him that Our Lady had showed her, as in a film, the coming of the first of the Ten Secrets. It will be a severe warning to the world. She already knows the date. She'll tell Father Petar ten days before it happens, and he'll make some kind of public announcement three days before it happens… Our Lady is showing Vicka and Jacov the future of the world. Apparently, things look bad.[25]

The following month, Mirjana received another special apparition which once again involved a vision of the First Secret. Father Laurentin chronicled the official account of the event in his book, *The Apparitions at Medjugorje Prolonged*:

> ***November 30, 1985***: Mirjana had another apparition, a little shorter than the one of October 25. The Italian priest, Father Boniface, was present. Again, Mirjana saw, as in a film, the unfolding of the first message. "It will be unhappy; it will be a sorrowful sign," she confirmed. "It will come in a short time." She (Mary) prayed for unbelievers and for Father Petar, so that Father Petar will be able to prepare himself for this task. After the apparition, Father Bonifacio said to Father Petar, "Certain people say that you will not reveal the contents of the Secret." "If I have the right to reveal it, then ten days beforehand, I will know it and three days before, I will say it," he answers. [26]

Father Faricy, still living in Medjugorje at the time, recorded again his thoughts concerning Mirjana's second vision of the First Secret on November 30,1985, in his daily journal:

> ***December 2, Monday***: Sister Janja told me tonight that she hopes I can be here when Petar gets from Mirjana the Secret to be revealed to the world, the prediction of some kind of imminent catastrophe that apparently will take many lives. Mirjana had another vision of it last Friday, seeing the disaster as one might see it in a film. She is badly shaken. Both Petar and Janja seem to think the fulfillment of the revelation given to Mirjana will come quite soon, at most in a few months. Petar looks nervous about his role in the matter: to know about it ten days before it happens and to announce it three days before.[27]

Several weeks after, on Christmas Day 1985, Mirjana received a third apparition/vision involving the First Secret. Wrote Father Tomislav Vlašić on January 23, 1986, in his and Father Barbarić's book, *I Beseech You, Listen to my Messages and Live Them*:

> ***December 25, 1985***: Mirjana now has more frequent apparitions; her last one was on 25th December 1985. Mirjana

again witnessed an event referring to the First Secret, the first warning to the world. She was sad. [28]

Almost two months later, Mirjana experienced yet another special apparition, and once more reported a vision of the First Secret. Wrote Father Faricy in his daily logue:

> **February 16, Sunday:** The chief news was that yesterday, Saturday, February 15, Mirjana had a vision of Our Lady at her house here in Bijakovići. It lasted five or six minutes; and during it she saw again the First Secret, as though in a film.[29]

The accounts of the four separate "like a film" glimpses into the First Secret by Mirjana appear to be the most telling reports of any of the Ten Secrets, except for the coming of the Great Sign with the Third Secret. Mary spoke to Mirjana one more time about the First Secret on June 4, 1986. [30]

While nothing highly specific is revealed in all of these accounts, they do reinforce the sublime significance of the First Secret, perhaps because it is directly aligned with the end of Satan's period of enhanced influence.

The phrase "as in a film," which Mirjana uses to describe both the October and November 1985 visions of the First Secret—as well as the vision in February 1986—are the exact same words she would come to use to describe how she was given to understand some of the Ten Secrets in her 2016 book, *My Heart Will Triumph.*

In her book, Mirjana writes that Our Lady relayed most of the events of the Secrets to her through words, but also showed her some of them *"like scenes of a film."* When she saw these glimpses of the future during apparitions, people near her, she wrote, often noted the intense expressions on her face and asked her about it after. [31]

In his 2007 book, *Tower of Light,* investigative journalist Michael Brown published an extensive interview that Mirjana gave to Father Petar Ljubicic on October 26, 1985, one day after her initial vision of the First Secret. Ljubicic released a transcript of it later that year. [32]

In the interview, Mirjana discusses the state of the world in context with the coming of the Ten Secrets, especially the First Secret:

Ljubicic: *How would you assess the current situation around the world?*

Mirjana: There never was an age such as this one, never before was God honored and respected less than now, never before have so few prayed to Him; everything seems to be more important than God. This is the reason why she cries so much. The number of unbelievers is becoming greater and greater. As they endeavor for a better life, to such people, God Himself is superfluous and dispensable. This is why I feel deeply sorry for them and for the world. They have no idea what awaits them. If they could only take a tiny peek at these Secrets, they would convert in time. Certainly, God always forgives all those who genuinely convert.

Ljubicic: *Did she (Mary) perhaps alert us to other things we must do, in addition to praying and preparing for that time? Perhaps something concrete?*

Mirjana: Father, I wish you only knew how I feel on some days! There are times when I feel that I could go mad. If Mary wasn't here, if she didn't fill me with strength, by now I would have surely gone mad. When I see how people believe, especially in Sarajevo, how they use God and His name in swearing, how thoughtless they are, how they curse God… These wretched ones have no idea what awaits them in the near future. It is then, as I observe them, that I take pity on them. I feel so sorry for them and pray and cry and pray, pray so much for them. I pray to Mary to enlighten their minds because, as Jesus said: they truly do not know what they do. And yet, the first two Secrets are not at all that severe and harsh. What I mean is yes, they are severe, but not as much as the remaining ones.

Ljubicic: *Are the Secrets perhaps of a notable, distinct character, or more of a spiritual nature?*

Mirjana: Distinct. Distinct.

Ljubicic: *Distinct?*

Mirjana: Yes, distinct. It will be visible. It is necessary in order to shake up the world a little. It will make the world pause and think.

Ljubicic: *Something like a catastrophe?*

Mirjana: No, it will not be anything as huge as that. That will come later. It will be something that will give the world something to think about seriously, allow it to see that she was indeed here, and to realize that there is God, that He exists.

Ljubicic: *After that, will there be anyone who will say, "This is some sort of a natural phenomenon," or along those lines?*

Mirjana: Perhaps some staunch unbelievers might say something like that after the First and Second Secrets.

Ljubicic: *I am just curious whether anyone will be able to say, "I feel something, that something will happen soon", or along those lines.*

Mirjana: Well, you can see there are some rather peculiar things going on in the world. People are unhappy, dissatisfied, avarice reigns everywhere, hardly anyone admits that they ever have enough of anything. Yet, none of this gives any clues about the Secret. The Secret stands on its own. The Secret will abundantly speak for itself and requires no prior clues or signals.

Ljubicic: *Once again, concerning the First Secret, who will experience, see, and be convinced and then be able to say: "Truly that which has occurred or is occurring is the manifestation of the Secret?" Who will be able to see all that?*

Mirjana: All those who will be here or in the places where the Secret will unfold.

Ljubicic: *Let me assume that this involves a specific place. All those who will wish to see and experience this sign or whatever the Secret is, will they have to come to that particular place to see and experience this?*

Mirjana: Well, Father, surely no one wishes to watch disasters, distress, and misfortune. I don't think that this kind of thing attracts people at all. Why, would people go to see something of that sort? It is one thing to see a sign, quite another to go and see suffering or disaster. Who would, for example, go to Italy to see a dam collapse? Who has that kind of desire? I don't think that anyone does—and that is how it will be with this Secret. Whatever is in the Secret, it will, of course, be something that everyone, everywhere, will immediately hear about.

Ljubicic: *Tell me, if the Secret involves a location rather than a condition or a situation, wouldn't it be desirable to have as many people as possible see—to have as many eyewitnesses as possible—even though it may not be a joyful thing or something pleasant to look at?*

Mirjana: Father, it will be obvious. It will be something that people will hear about very far.

Ljubicic: *The manifestation of that Secret, will it only be a momentary thing or will it be something that will last for an extended period?*

Mirjana: It will last for a little while.

Ljubicic: *Little while?*

Mirjana: Little.

Ljubicic: *Will its effect be lasting or permanent or will its effect be momentary and passing?*

Mirjana: How can I explain that without encroaching on the Secret? Let me just say that it won't be good at all, it won't be pleasant.

Ljubicic: *After that, if any one were to come here knowing that such and such had occurred, will that person be able to see anything—any evidence that something, indeed, did happen here?*

Mirjana: Yes, yes, yes.

Ljubicic: *It will be visible?*

Mirjana: Yes.

Ljubicic: *This whole situation: it seems that she (Mary) is trying to prepare us and to "dress" us with saintliness, God's love and perfection, so that we greet Our Lord when He comes. Is there anything that signals something of that? Of that nature?*

Mirjana: Just as any mother, she cares for her children. She wants us to come and meet God the Father well-prepared. She doesn't want us to weep and wail when it's too late. God said that He forgives at any time- providing the soul repents sincerely. All she asks for, the one thing she waits for, is for all of us to repent so that we may be forgiven. What follows are the Secrets that are really unpleasant. I would be happy if everyone would finally understand that. I cannot tell the Secrets, but once they begin to be fulfilled, then it will be too late.

Ljubicic: *Will the interval between the First and Second Secret be lengthy?*

Mirjana: That varies according to the Secrets. What I mean is that, for example, the time between the First and the Second Secrets is of a certain period, between the Second and the Third is of a different length. For example, and I stress, for example, the First Secret may take place today and the Second one already tomorrow.[33]

In another of his books, *The Day Will Come*, Michael Brown writes about a second interview with Mirjana by Father Petar Ljubicic in which the First Secret is again discussed:

In a later interview with the same priest, Mirjana expanded upon the other Secrets, urging especially conversion of the young. They were especially the ones Mary wept over, she explained, "I now know about things that are not particularly pleasant," said the visionary, whose daily apparitions halted in 1982, when she received the Tenth Secret—the first of the six to do so. "I believe that if everyone knew about these same things, each one of these people would be shocked to their senses and would view our world in a completely different light.

Of course, my greatest advice to all is to pray for all the unbelievers. You see, Mary expends the greatest amount of time talking about that very thing. We must also not forget the elderly and the infirm. They are ours too. They sacrificed their whole lives. Many of them lived their entire lives for God in prayer. Their senior years shouldn't have to be sad and miserable."

I cannot elaborate much more, it's hard for me to do that. You see, so much is tied to the Secrets. If the people saw the First Secret, as it was shown to me, all of them would most certainly be shaken enough to take a new and different look at themselves and everything around them. [34]

In interviews with Father Ljubicic on the subject of the Secrets, the humble friar always emphasizes that much prayer and fasting will precede the announcement of the First Secret, as well as the fact that Mirjana will definitely be in Medjugorje for the announcement of the Secret.[35]

None of the other five visionaries have said anything more that is substantial to add to what is known about the First Secret. They have all, more or less, primarily referred to it as a warning that will validate the Virgin Mary's presence in Medjugorje.

Will life on earth be more pleasant after the "First Secret"?

"We shall see," offered Marija Pavlović. [36]

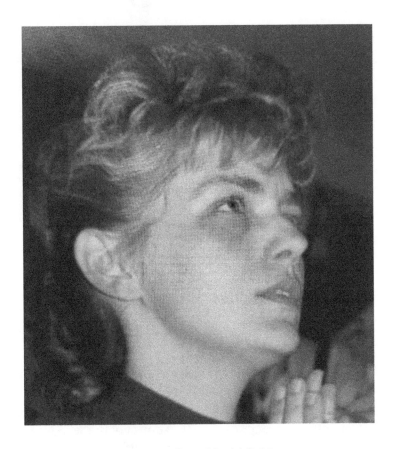

Mirjana Dragićević Soldo

"Each individual on earth will play a role as the Secrets unfold."

Photo Credit: Pittsburgh Center for Peace

CHAPTER SIXTY-TWO

AN APOCALYPTIC MOOD

*"Many false prophets will arise and deceive
many; and because of the increase in evil
doing, the love of many will grow cold."*
—Mt 24:11-12

T HERE IS SOMETHING MORE THAT IS RELEVANT TO THE FIRST
Secret—and all of the Ten Secrets for that matter—that came
about around this time and changed forever how the mystery of the
Secrets was to be publicly approached at Medjugorje.

As books and articles with interviews of the visionaries started to circulate—revealing conversations with them that disclosed more of the
substance and nature of the Secrets—there is found emerging a coordinated response by the Franciscans on the subject of the Secrets in general.

In essence, it is agreed that an increased effort is needed by all the
parties in Medjugorje—principally the visionaries and the priests—to
refrain from speaking too much about the Secrets. "The present not
the future," it is agreed, should be the concern.

Father Tomislav Pervan, the head pastor of St. James in
1985, explained:

> Today in the world an apocalyptic mood is spreading, So I
> want to keep a distance from it. For it is not a question of
> tomorrow, the day after tomorrow, or what will happen in
> ten years, but today. It is not a question of the end of time,
> but of the present time, what I and everyone else need and
> must do today and now.

We are called to do what we must do; convert, pray, turn to God. This our task today, not something that will perhaps happen or can happen. This is the meaning of the Secrets of the apparitions of Mary in general, and this is also the case with Medjugorje. [1]

Father Philip Pavich, an American friar working in Medjugorje, thought the same as Pervan. He believed that those who zero in on the reported nature of some of the Secrets cause an "unhealthy distortion" of the message.

Such a view causes unfounded apprehension and inflicts fear in Pavich's view, which he says is not the reason Mary is appearing in Medjugorje: "We don't see it as the end of the world," said Pavich, preferring to recognize a higher purpose to Medjugorje. [2]

This approach to the Secrets becomes something that Father Slavko Barbarić especially begins to emphasize both privately and publicly. Both he and all the Franciscans understood that the mounting curiosity surrounding the Ten Secrets had the potential to derail the real message of Medjugorje.

The Virgin Mary, they begin to stress, has come to show the path to peace, not the road to perdition.

Investigative writer Randall Sullivan says that Barbarić told him that he had "advised the visionaries to say nothing further on the subject (the Secrets)." This was because it encouraged a "kind of fatalism" in people, causing them "to live in the future, rather than in the present." [3]

On November 15, 1985, Father Barbarić confronted this reality in a talk he presented in Medjugorje. The friar invited his listeners to understand that Mary brings only love, hope, and peace, even with regards to the Secrets:

> Mirjana said she saw the First Secret as if in a film and said, "My God, does this really have to happen?" Our Lady is supposed to have answered that it is, "*Not God but sin that does it*" … Owing to this bit of news, I feel many have been overcome with fear, with anguish…Our Lady is talking a lot about the Secrets and invites us to prayer… especially for the unbelievers…All these messages will have no meaning for us if we respond with fear. We must respond with confidence, with love and say, 'Everything is in God's hands and today I need

to carry out all my duties with love and hope. This I have understood and this I tell everyone—the apparitions never bear a new revelation; they are always an impulse, to pray, to fast, to love, to be reconciled, to make peace. And so, not even these secret messages can bring anything new. [4]

On December 30, 1985, after Mirjana received from the Virgin Mary her second look at the First Secret, Father Barbarić again states that both revelations of the First Secret are to bring hope and nothing else:

During the two locutions of 25 October and 30 November, Our Lady showed her, she says, the first admonishment, the First Secret, as in a film. The admonishments, all Mirjana is telling us, must be understood in the context of the apparitions… By coming to us, Our Lady wants to tell us that it is possible to find a path to peace once again. For this reason, the apparitions are always a fact giving us renewed hope, they never want to give us anguish and fear, but always hope. [5]

By July of 1987, Father Barbarić's position on the issue is well defined. He told author Jan Connell that the friars do not speak about the apocalyptic events in connection with Medjugorje— that it was really not their primary orientation. Medjugorje, he stressed to her, had become a place of hope. He felt this was in keeping with what the Blessed Mother said: "I come to lead you to peace and to bring you peace."

Mary, emphasized Barbarić, invites us to fast and pray, in order to receive and achieve this very peace. [6]

As with Father Barbarić, Father Tomislav Vlašić also started to carefully craft his talks and sermons at Medjugorje to more emphasize the proper way to understand Mary's messages, especially the Secrets.

Referring one day to an article on his desk in which the headline read: "**Medjugorje Secrets Predict Dire Events**," Vlašić remarked to a journalist that "reports like this do a disservice to readers." [7]

On the same day of the initial vision of the First Secret given to Mirjana—the priest told a group of pilgrims:

Today, Mirjana had an apparition of Our Lady lasting eight minutes…Father Petar, who was present, merely told me, "I saw tears in Mirjana's eyes" …When we talk of these events, there are people who get frightened…we must not get frightened, but we must be converted. Conversion is an act of hope. Fear is an act of desperation, and we must have an act of hope. If you live an act of hope, if you live conversion, ahead of you can only be joy…[8]

The following day, the friar again sought to put this issue into a proper perspective to a group of pilgrims from Italy:

Yesterday, Mirjana had an apparition …the visionary saw, as in a film, the taking place of the first Secret, of the first warning to mankind…I spoke to the visionary today. She told me this, "You can tell everybody—we are in a time of graces, at a time of Our Lady's call, who wants to lead us to salvation" …When one usually talks of these things, that is, the announcements made by the visionaries, people become afraid. But why are you afraid? This means we have not discovered faith…what the visionary emphasizes is conversion, a purification of the heart, a total opening to God in order to live in God. [9]

A week later, on November 2, 1985, the Feast of All Souls, he explained during a talk given in Medjugorje that what is coming in the future, is exactly what the world needs to move out of this dark moment in time:

The last apparion to Mirjana took place on 25 October, a week ago. After the apparition, Fr. Petar asked her what happened? Why were you so sad? "Our Lady showed me for the first time, as in a film, the events of her first warning. It is very severe. That is why I am sad." I then spoke to the visionary who once again repeated that this is the period of grace when many graces are granted, it is the period of conversion… The visionary stresses this aspect of joy and hope we must possess when looking at the future… This moment of crisis in mankind as a whole is very favorable for us Christians to discover God. It is indeed a grace to discover God. Truly I say to you—blessed are you if you have some sufferings. Not, however, are you blessed in your sorrows, but blessed are you, if in your sorrows, discover God and eternal life.[10]

Over the years, some writers have distorted the six visionaries' words concerning the Secrets, or have tried to insinuate the Secrets reopen old Catholic prophecies that emphasize cataclysmic events.[11]

These corrupted interpretations are found in books and newsletters as well as on some websites. Several books released over the years contain the Medjugorje visionaries' strong objections to these deliberate distortions or exaggerated predictions.

In the same interview with attorney Jan Connell in 1991, Mirjana was asked if she ever said "areas of the planet would be destroyed" and that "no life" would grow there. The visionary denied such statements, making it clear that she never said any such thing nor has ever spoken about such calamities.[12]

Bogus versions of the Secret of La Salette—along with the Third Secret of Fátima—became legendary for their grossly exaggerated direr predictions. While unfortunate, such distorted accounts are inevitable with prophecy. Connell asked Mirjana about similar rumors associated with Medjugorje, such as the coming of "three days of darkness," deadly earthquakes and tidal waves, and other frightful catastrophes. Mary had "not spoken" about any of those predictions, Mirjana stressed to Connell, making it clear that such rhetoric only hurts the true message of Medjugorje.[13]

Vicka echoed Mirjana's assertion concerning such inflammatory talk. Author Michael Brown writes: "Vicka Ivanković told me talk of the end of the world, the Second Coming, and the Antichrist were not in my Secrets." [14]

Marija emphasized much the same, "I do not speak of the Second Coming of Christ, of catastrophes, destruction, or evil. With prayer and fasting, even war can be eliminated. The Blessed Mother says prayer and fasting can change even the natural law." [15]

Ivan has especially denounced those who peddle the sensational in association with the Secrets of Medjugorje, who paint Mary as a prophetess of "doom and gloom." [16] At a talk in 2008, he emphasized that "Mary has not come to criticize us, or tell us about the end of the world." [17]

The record shows that dispelling alarm with regards to the Secrets is something that Ivan has emphasized for years at his talks. As far back as 1996, before a large gathering in Windsor, Ohio, Ivan told the crowd: "Today, people are talking about terrible things that will happen in the world, the 'three days of darkness.' I would like to have you understand one thing that I'm going to tell you. Our Lady did not come to bring us terror. She is not coming to bring us darkness. She is coming to us as a mother of light and a mother of hope." [18]

Asked again a year later at another of his talks about catastrophic predictions, Ivan responded, "That is not coming from Our Lady to us and so I don't know where it is coming from." Confronted moments later with another such question, this time about Word War III, the frustrated visionary simply answered, "No." [19]

The specific events to unfold with the First Secret are unknown.

But there may be an interesting side story involving the First Secret at Medjugorje and the powerful vision Mirjana received in October 1985.

In retrospect, it's clear, Mirjana's experience that day was not just another apparition of the Virgin Mary. And, it was not just another revelation involving the Secrets. Rather, when looked at as a whole, it appears God could have possibly guided some of what occurred surrounding that day for a reason.

It was in October of 1917 that Satan finally succeeded in bringing to fruition in Russia his attempt to bring a 'triumph of atheism' in the world, the very same month and year that Mary came to Fátima to prevent such an ignominious effort from succeeding.

And, it was *exactly* on October 25, 1917, that Vladimir Lenin and the Bolsheviks announced they had seized power in Petrograd, Russia, and began to commence with their godless revolution—the same date that Mirjana received the extraordinary vision of the First Secret—the Secret that, when it comes to pass, will bring an end to Satan's extended influence over mankind on Earth.[20]

Was God, by giving the powerful vision of the First Secret on this specific date, trying to irrefutably mark that He is the Lord of history—that, as He was in control of the *beginning* of the hellish, Marxist nightmare that fell upon the world on that very date, so too is He is in control of its *end*?

Will this date be seen perhaps again someday as the Secrets unfold?

The Second Secret of Medjugorje is also described as a warning by the visionaries.

It will witness, they say, many more people convert after it is fulfilled.

However, a great number of people— "particularly in the West"— will still try to argue "a natural explanation" for the events contained in both of the first two Secrets, according to the visionaries. [21]

Medjugorje author, and perhaps its greatest evangelist, Wayne Weible, wrote in his final book that he believed the Second Secret involves the widespread prophecy of a coming extraordinary event known as the *Miracle of the Illumination of all Consciences*. [22]

Known also as *The Warning*, this is to be a prophesied moment in time when every human being in the world is to see the state of their soul in God's eyes. Many conversions are foretold to come because of it. [23] Nevertheless, there is no evidence at all—or any words to this effect stated by the visionaries— that this miracle makes up or is part of the Second Secret, or any of the Ten Secrets of Medjugorje.

Father Petar Ljubicic spoke about the First and Second Secrets during a panel discussion at Notre Dame University on May 27, 2007:

"We must say that the first two Secrets are involved with Medjugorje. They will be a warning of that which is to take place, because Our Lady did appear first in Medjugorje. And the parishioners of that parish of St. James are called to live those messages and to spread them as well. Many will be surprised, because they weren't really taking into account what will take place." [24]

After the Second Secret, there will come the appearance of the Great Sign—the fulfillment of the Third Secret on Mt. Podbrdo. And, like the First Secret, it promises to be a watershed event in the history of the world.

Indeed, when what is foretold comes to pass, perhaps future generations will come to see Mt. Podbrdo in the same way as Mt. Sinai, Mt. Tabor, and Mt. Carmel are viewed today: as a holy place that witnessed God—as Scripture says—*stoop down* to mark His presence among His people in an everlasting way.

Fr. René Laurentin

**Photo Credit:
Pittsburgh Center
for Peace**

Fr. Robert Faricy

**Photo Credit:
Pittsburgh Center
for Peace**

Fr. Ljudevit Rupčić

**Photo Credit:
Ljudĕvĭt Rupcic**

**Fr. Petar Ljubicic was chosen by
Mirjana to reveal the Ten Secrets
of Medjugorje. He stayed with the
author at his home for a couple of
days in 2000.**

Photo Credit: Thomas W. Petrisko

**Janko Bubalo interviewed Vicka
multiple times for his book, *A
Thousand Encounters with
the Blessed Virgin Mary
in Medjugorje*.**

Picture Credit: Janko Bubalo

CHAPTER SIXTY-THREE

THIS WILL CHANGE EVERYTHING

*"This shall be the Lord's renown, an
everlasting imperishable sign."*

—Is 55:13

D READ, SUSPICION AND OUTRIGHT FEAR ACCOMPANIED THE alleged contents of the Third Secret of Fátima for decades. From runaway oceans submerging regions of the planet—to cascading missiles setting cities ablaze—to new and deadly plagues turning the Earth into a massive graveyard—doom and gloom is a phrase that fit the infamous Third Secret of Fátima like a glove.

This time, though, the narrative could not be more reversed.

The Third Secret of Medjugorje—similarly to that of Fátima—has weathered decades of discussion. This "third secret," however, has been more associated with wondrous anticipation, not nail biting unease.

Its fulfillment is to be a sign of hope, a harbinger of a future that is to hold joy and help to bring peace. [1]

Extensively spoken of by all six of the visionaries at Medjugorje, the Third Secret will fulfill Mary's promise to leave a sign. And, like at Fátima on October 13, 1917—when her promise to leave a sign was fulfilled by the sun supernaturally appearing to drop from the sky like a ball of fire—at Medjugorje a pre-sign of the Third Secret involved a supernatural fire that appeared on Mt. Podbrdo on October 27, 1981. [2]

While no one except the visionaries has any facts regarding the Sign's true makeup, speculation has ranged from the sudden appearance of a chapel on apparition hill, [3] to an underground spring emerging there (as at Lourdes), [4] to an earthquake somehow creating an inland waterway that links the Adriatic Sea to Mt. Podbrdo in Bijakovići. [5] One author even suggested perhaps a column of fire similar to what the Israelites experienced is coming. [6]

In 1984, a Catholic priest who was a "water diviner" thought that he detected two powerful streams of water underground on the hill. If they continue to converge, he theorized, the streams will eventually unite and burst out and up to the surface, perhaps creating the 'Great Sign.' Seeking to study the area more, the government heard of his activities and had him arrested along with one of the friars. They ended up being held for questioning at the police station for two hours. [7]

Marija said in a May 2008 interview that the Virgin Mary told her that one day a chapel should be built not at the site of the first apparitions, but further down on Podbrdo. [8] However, this request, Marija made clear, is not associated with the Sign. [9]

Known also as the Great Sign, many of its characteristics have been revealed by the visionaries: [10]

- It will be visible. [11]
- It will appear on Mt. Podbrdo at the sight of the first apparitions. [12]
- It is for all humanity, not just Catholics and Christians. [13]
- It will be permanent. [14]
- It will be on the Earth and not in the sky. [15]
- It will be beautiful. [16]
- It will appear spontaneously. [17]
- It will be visible to everyone that comes to Medjugorje. [18]
- It will be indestructible. [19]
- It will be near but not before the end of the apparitions. [20]
- It will be accompanied by miraculous healings. [21]
- The visionaries know exactly what it is. [22]
- The visionaries know exactly when it will appear. [23]

- It will confirm the Virgin Mary's apparitional presence in Medjugorje.[24]
- It will be preceded by two warnings.[25]
- It is given in order to call people back to the faith.[26]
- It is something that has never been seen on Earth before.[27]
- It will be rejected by some who will not believe it is a sign from God.[28]
- Some people will remain unbelievers even after the Sign comes.[29]
- Those who are alive will witness many conversions because of the Sign.[30]
- Those who wait until the Sign comes to believe will have little time for conversion—for some, it will be too late.[31]
- It will happen in the lifetime of the visionaries. [32]
- It will be seen that human hands could not have made it.[33]
- It will be able to be photographed and filmed.[34]
- It is the one Secret the visionaries know they share in common. [35]
- It will be much more beautiful when seen by one's own eyes in Medjugorje. [36]
- To experience the Sign with the heart, one must come to Medjugorje.[37]
- There will be conversions during the Sign's manifestation. [38]
- The Sign will be for the Church so there can be no doubt of Mary's presence in Medjugorje. [39]

During his interview with Vicka Ivanković for his book, *A Thousand Encounters with the Blessed Virgin Mary in Medjugorje*, Father Janko Bubalo asked the visionary what she could tell him about the Great Sign:

> Bubalo: *I see that this is really tedious to you, but nonetheless, at least tell me where the Virgin will give that Sign.*
>
> **Vicka:** On Podbrdo. At the sight of the first apparitions.
>
> Bubalo: *Will the Sign be in the heavens or on Earth?*
>
> **Vicka:** On Earth.
>
> Bubalo: *Will it appear spontaneously, or will it gradually appear?*
>
> **Vicka:** Spontaneously.

Bubalo: *Will everyone be able to see it?*

Vicka: Whoever comes here will.

Bubalo: *Will the Sign be temporary or permanent?*

Vicka: Permanent.

Bubalo: *And will the Sign be able to be destroyed by anyone?*

Vicka: By no one.

Bubalo: *You think that, or...*

Vicka: The Virgin said so.

Bubalo: *Do you know exactly what the Sign will be?*

Vicka: Exactly!

Bubalo: *Do you know when the Virgin will make it evident to the rest of us?*

Vicka: I know that also.

Bubalo: *Do each of you know that?*

Vicka: I don't know, but I think that not everyone knows it up to now.

Bubalo: *I failed to ask, is the Sign a special Secret, or...*

Vicka: It is a particular Secret, but it is also one of the Ten Secrets.

Bubalo: *For certain?*

Vicka: What else, but for certain.

Bubalo: *And why is the Virgin leaving the Sign here?*

Vicka: Why to show the people that she is here among us.

Bubalo: *And what do you think, what would happen to any one of you that might somehow reveal the Secret of that Sign?*

Vicka: I don't think about the possibility for I don't think that could happen.

Bubalo: *Well, at one point, the Bishop's Commission asked that you describe what the Sign would be like, and when it would occur, and that the notation be sealed in your presence and be kept safely until the Sign occurs.*

Vicka: That is true.

Bubalo: *But you did not want to agree with that. Why?...*

Vicka...I don't want to say any more about the subject. But, I'll just say this: whoever does not believe without a sign will not believe with a sign. And, I'll tell you this too: woe to him who delays his conversion waiting for the Sign. I once told you that many would come, and perhaps, even bow to the Sign, but will, nonetheless, not believe. Be happy you are not among them! [40]

Over twenty-five years later, on January 2, 2008, Father Livio Fanzaga, a priest of the Scolopian Fathers, interviewed Vicka on *Radio Maria Italia* in a live broadcast from Medjugorje. In this discussion, Vicka—who has had several visions of the Great Sign [41]—revealed a little more of what she knew about this coming prodigy:

Fanzaga: *I was really struck by what the Madonna said about the Third Secret, which concerns the Great Sign on the mountain. You visionaries said that it will be a visible Sign, an indestructible Sign that comes from God. However, she also added, "Hurry and convert yourselves. When the promised Sign on the hill will be given, it will be too late" (September 2, 1982). Another time, she also said, "And even after I've left this Sign on the hill which I have promised you, many will not believe. They will come to the hill. They will kneel, but they won't believe (July 19, 1981). Why is it, in your opinion, that people will see the Sign but they won't convert?*

Vicka: The Third Secret is about a Sign that she will leave here [Medjugorje] on the mountain of the apparitions. This Sign will remain forever. It is given above all for those people who are still far away from God. The Madonna wishes to give these people who will see the Sign a chance to believe in God. I was able to see this Sign.

Fanzaga: *You have already seen the Sign?*

Vicka: Yes, I saw it in a vision.

Fanzaga: *Jacov once said in an interview with Radio Maria that in order to see the Sign it will be necessary to come here to Medjugorje. Is that true?*

Vicka: Yes, it's true. The Sign will remain on Podbrdo and one will have to come here to see it. This Sign will be indestructible and will remain in that place forever. I want to say about those people who will see it and not believe. The Madonna leaves everyone free to believe or not, but those are ones whose hearts are too closed. It's the same thing as the Madonna said to us, "If one wants to go to Heaven, he will go to Heaven, if one wants to go to Hell, he will go to Hell." Those people who are far away from God and do not want to believe, these will not believe in the Sign. For those who do not know God but have good intentions and a desire to love, these will be benefitted by the Sign. But I think that those who do everything against God, they will run away from the Sign. They will not believe.

Fanzaga: *So, this is a time of grace. This is the time of conversion, "Do not wait for the Sign in order to convert yourselves," the Madonna said. Well, so why leave a Sign like some last extreme help? Is it in order to move the Church to recognize the apparitions as authentic?*

Vicka: Yes, certainly it will be for the Church, so that they will have no doubt that the Madonna had been among us. And it is also for those who are still far away from God. So, the Madonna is thinking about both groups of people. And then it is up to us—how to be ready to respond to the Sign—to respond to her call through the Sign. Everyone who comes, who will see, you know, you can say, "I don't believe it" and this is your personal idea—that's what you believe. But that the Madonna is here, that she is present, that she leaves this Sign— a Sign no man can make; it is something only God can make. And so nobody will be able to say that it is a small thing or something else. This arrives in such a way, that they won't have words to say what it is. [42]

In 1993, Vicka told another interviewer how she had seen the Great Sign. It was, she again confirmed, a final and wondrous warning for unbelievers: "It will be beautiful, very beautiful, I have already seen it three times," Vicka emphasized. [43]

Two years later, in August of 1995, it was reported that Vicka had said that the Great Sign would appear "when only one of them (the visionaries) will still have the daily apparitions." She added, at the time, that the Virgin did not explain what she means when she said, "Do not wait for the Sign, when the Sign comes, it will be too late." [44]

Sister Emmanuel Maillard, from the Community of the Beatitudes living in Medjugorje, quotes Jacov Čolo saying the same at that time: "The very first Secrets will be revealed and they will prove that the apparitions are real." [45] As for the Great Sign, Jacov added, "I saw it. It is very beautiful." [46]

In her October 26, 1985, interview with Father Petar Ljubicic, Mirjana Dragićević also discussed the coming of the Great Sign:

> Ljubicic: *Out of the Ten Secrets that each of you will receive—and you and Ivanka [Ivankovic] already did—do you know which of them will be exactly the same? I mean, which Secrets will be exactly the same for you, for Ivanka, and the others?*
>
> **Mirjana:** No, I don't know.
>
> Ljubicic: *Someone said that only three of the Secrets that each of you received are identical, while all the others are different.*
>
> **Mirjana:** The one about the Sign is identical. I am positive about that because there will not be six different Signs.
>
> Ljubicic: *Not on the same spot.*
>
> **Mirjana:** The Sign is the same Sign. Personally, I never spoke about the Secrets with any of the others. After all, in the same way that the Secrets were entrusted to me, that is how they were entrusted to the others as well.

Ljubicic: *Thus far, I never spoke with you about the permanency of the Sign. Each of you maintain persistently that it will be indestructible, permanent, and very large. Accordingly, one will be able to understand it as something tangible.*

Mirjana: Yes, the Sign will be indestructible and permanent. Naturally, it will be clear to everyone that it is not something constructed and erected. Nobody will be able to say that it was brought and placed in that particular spot by, let us say, someone from Medjugorje.

Ljubicic: *The Sign's manifestation—will it be during the day or night? By asking that, am I encroaching on the Secret?*

Mirjana: Oh, that is a secret. I cannot answer that because that touches upon…the Secret already has a specific date and time.

Ljubicic: *Does the Secret have a specified minute and second?*

Mirjana: I know the exact day and hour.

Ljubicic: *Do you anticipate that there may be some people, some souls, who will perhaps "feel" something, without anyone else's knowledge or anticipation, that something is about to happen and will, therefore, come in large numbers?*

Mirjana: I do not know. But I did have the opportunity to ask Our Lady something to that effect. I do know that, during the Secret's manifestation, there will be spiritual conversions.

Ljubicic: *There will be conversions?*

Mirjana: Yes, there will be conversions.

Ljubicic: *Do you think that of those who will convert, a majority of them will be those who were suspicious, who doubted, who didn't believe?*

Mirjana: There will be all kinds: those who were just suspicious, those who didn't believe at all, and others.

Ljubicic: *Do you think that there will be those who will remain hardened—despite the explicit, tangible, visible signs and warnings?*

Mirjana: Yes.

Ljubicic: *There will be?*

Mirjana: Yes, there will be.

Ljubicic: *Yes, of course, just as there always were. Even today, so many see the obvious works of God, yet simply reject Him because they are so hardened, just as the Pharisees did.*

Mirjana: Those are the ones who have shut their souls to God.

Ljubicic: *It seems that Our Lady is drawing attention to our greatest enemy, Satan. It seems that he is increasing his attacks, that he is attempting to create confusion and entangle the entire situation.*

Mirjana: He is responsible for the unbelievers, Satan. This is why she said to bless the home with Holy Water on Saturdays. He is the one who makes people into unbelievers. Who else?

Ljubicic: *Do you think that Godlessness is growing or decreasing today?*

Mirjana: Father, it is increasing. A miracle is *necessary* for Godlessness to decrease.[47]

Fr. Petar Ljubicic has been interviewed many times about the Secrets. He has also spoken specifically of the Great Sign in his talks at Medjugorje and throughout the world. At Medjugorje, on April 22, 1989, Ljubicic talked about the Third Secret:

> Our Lady says *all* of the Secrets *have* to come to pass. Some can be lessened, but they all have to be accomplished. I can only say the first two Secrets are warnings, and after they are revealed, it will be clear to everyone that Our Lady is here on the hill of apparitions, Our Lady promised to leave a Sign, and we can only guess what it will be. It will be approximately where a cross marks the apparitions of Our Lady.
>
> The Secrets will be revealed one by one. Ten days before, they are to be revealed, I will be told and I will then pray and fast

for seven days, and three days after that I will reveal it. The Seventh Secret has been lessened through prayer. The Third Secret is the only one that is good and that will be the Sign that Our Lady will leave on the mountain.

The word Secret does not have the same meaning in English as it does in Croatian. In Croatian, it means "a message that has not been revealed." The message of Medjugorje is peace, the promise that Jesus brought when he walked the Earth. But the messages that will be revealed are warnings in a sense of what sin will bring. [48]

Mirjana's confidence in the Great Sign is noteworthy.

The visionary told Father René Laurentin in January, 1986, "After the Sign will be shown, one will be obliged to believe." [49] In Mirjana's January 10, 1983, interview published in Father Svetozar Kraljević's book, she also seemed to imply that the Virgin Mary's presence will be associated with the appearance of the Great Sign in a special way.

In a footnote that is found on the bottom of the first page of the original transcript of the interview, we read: "This statement (of Mirjana) seems to imply that Our Lady will be present at Medjugorje on the day the permanent Sign appears." [50]

In another small, uncirculated booklet published in 1983, *Our Lady Queen of Peace, Queen of the Apostles*, there is found a message from Mary to the visionaries that also speaks of the Great Sign and atheists.

This revelation can be seen to confirm Marija Pavlović's response to Father Rupčić in his interview of the visionaries in December of 1982. At the time, Marija said that the Sign would be "for those who do not believe." The author of the booklet writes:

> They say that Our Lady has promised to leave a visible Sign on the mountain where the first apparitions occurred. Mary told them: *The sign will be given for the atheists. You faithful already have signs and you have to become the sign for the atheists.*
>
> Following this visible Sign, there will be many miracles and healings. All the visionaries say that they have seen this Sign

in the apparitions, they know the date when the sign will come; but they say that before the Sign comes there will be a warning or admonishment to the world. Our Lady says this: *You faithful must not wait for the Sign before you convert; convert soon, this time is a time of grace for you. You can never thank God enough for His grace which He has given, this time for deepening your faith and for your conversion. When the Sign comes it will be too late for many.* [51]

As noted, one of the very first interviews with the visionaries at Medjugorje was conducted by Father Ljudevit Rupčić at the beginning of December 1982. It consisted of sixty-two questions, some of which involved the Secrets.[52]

In 1987, Rupčić repeated his initial inquiry.[53] In this second interview, Father Rupčić asked the visionaries two new questions with regards to the Great Sign.

1. Are you sure that the Great Sign is going to appear on the hill of apparitions?
2. Are you disturbed that it is late in arriving? [54]

The visionaries' responses were as follows:

Marija: I am sure that it will arrive like Our Lady told us. Everything is under the control of Our Lady, both the Sign and the apparitions. It is Our Lady who knows the best time when this Sign will appear? All that is her plan.

Ivan: It is certain that this Great Sign will appear as Our Lady has said. I am not at all disturbed.

Vicka: I only know that there will be, on the site of the apparition, a visible Sign and I am not disturbed as to whether the time is long before its manifestation.

Jacov: I am sure that the Sign will be manifested. I am not troubled that it has not taken place up to the present.

Mirjana: Of course, I am convinced. There is nothing to be troubled about since I know the exact date. Everything must follow its course.

Ivanka: Yes, absolutely. Everything will develop according to God's plan.[55]

Clearly, the Great Sign is very much at the center of what the future holds with Medjugorje.

This is because all of the visionaries concur that its appearance will reinvigorate faith throughout the world. The Sign will be, as a correspondent from Rome saw it, "An emblem of gratitude" for believers—and "a last call" for nonbelievers. [56]

Is it the miracle that Mirjana told Father Ljubicic was necessary to wake up the world?

Over the years, the visionaries have maintained a unified conviction of the Great Sign's strategic purpose: it is to prove the Virgin Mary appeared at Medjugorje.

Their words reflect this confidence:

- "The most powerful armaments and explosives in the world could not destroy it," Ivanka declared. "Nothing," she asserts, "will harm the Madonna's plans." [57]
- "The people will be convinced the Madonna was here," insists Mirjana concerning the Great Sign, "they will understand the Sign." [58]
- "When the Permanent Sign comes," said Jacov, "people will come here from all over the world in even larger numbers. Many more will believe!" [59]

Father Slavko Barbarić, who often spoke privately with the visionaries concerning the Sign, appeared to hold the same confidence that it is to be an extraordinary manifestation of the truth of God's presence in Medjugorje:

"Yes, people will come from everywhere. And, there will be a reason why. I am no prophet. But, if anything should happen at all...it will only happen in and through Medjugorje, through the Mother of God. The world will be shown clearly where lies authentic power. I am thinking here, among other things, in the Sign that was promised in the Secrets." [60]

Barbarić was awed by a possible theological mystery surrounding the Great Sign foretold to come at Medjugorje.

In an interview he conducted with Archbishop Frane Franic of Split on December 16-17, 1984—just five days after Franic had met with Pope John Paul II in Rome to discuss the case of Medjugorje—he asked the Archbishop if the Great Sign at Medjugorje could be associated with the *Great Sign* foretold in Chapter Twelve of *The Book of Revelation*. [61]

> Barbarić: *Every week, I speak with the visionaries in the name of the parish. I have asked them a number of times about the Sign. They always say, "Our Lady instructed us. We have seen it. We know. There is no need to worry. As for us, we must pray and fast." They say that there would have been other signs if we had accepted the messages better and if Our Lady had not found so much resistance. Ought we to understand the talk about the Great Sign in terms of the Apocalypse?*

> **Archbishop Franic**: The *Apocalypse* does talk about the Great Sign: "*A woman, clothed in the sun appears in the skies with a dragon opposing her.*" Maybe the Sign is beginning to be realized in this way. When the prophets spoke, they did not know what they were saying in their prophecies. For example, prophets in the *Old Testament*, spoke about Christ as King of Kings. They did not comprehend properly what God was saying throughout time… They did not know how all of this would end. The talk about the Great Sign is prophetic language. When the children speak, they do not understand many of the things they say since they did not study theology. Therefore, we are here to explain all their expressions about the words, messages, signs, and so on. [62]

> Barbarić: *It seems to me it is the "Great Sign" which is perplexing to our Bishop. The children say it will come soon. That is Biblical talk.*

> **Archbishop Franic**: Exactly. And to try to catch the children in a contradiction like this is unnecessary. What do they know? They do not know exegesis or hermeneutics. [63]

While the Great Sign may have profound and ancient biblical implications, it also appears to be a line of demarcation for our present times.

Asked by Jan Connell if many people would die between the time of the first chastisement and the promised Great Sign at Medjugorje, Mirjana again reminded people that after the visible Sign appears, "those who are still alive will have little time for conversion." [64]

Is the future of the human race to be a *utopia* or a *dystopia*?

This question was put to over 130 of the most inventive minds in every field of endeavor in 2009. Their answers were then published in a book titled, *This Will Change Everything*. [65]

These brilliant, gifted men and women were asked to envision what world-transforming discoveries or events lie ahead. They were asked to foresee the developments of tomorrow that could change the world forever overnight.

Confronting whatever ideas that they could imagine, the great thinkers pondered whether universities and churches would become relics, what doomsday scenarios were inescapable, and what could possibly bring ecological renewal to the planet.

Revolutions, they foretold, in science and politics, in religion or philosophy, could force a new way of life upon humanity.

Will inventions unfurled from the hands of man save the planet?

Are there discoveries coming that will transform life as we know it?

Is civilization on the brink of a great new day?

What will change everything?

In a cluster of little hamlets snuggled together between the mountains in a remote region of Herzegovina, the ultimate answer to this question may soon be revealed.

The "Great Sign" at Medjugorje—without a doubt—will change everything.

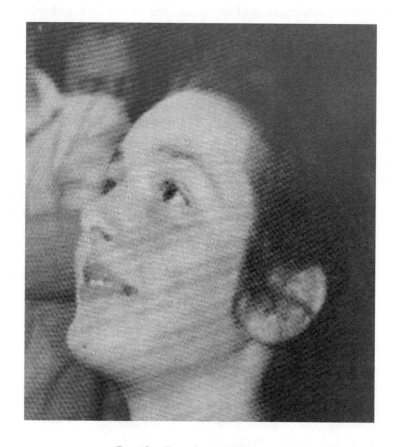

Ivanka Ivanković Elez

"The Madonna has come to Medjugorje to call all people on earth to her Son, Jesus, for the final time."

Photo Credit: Pittsburgh Center
for Peace

CHAPTER SIXTY-FOUR

"I KNOW THE FUTURE OF THE WORLD"

"For I know well the plans I have in mind for
you, says the Lord, plans for your welfare
not your woe! Plans to give you a future full of hope."
—Jer 29 :11

"Do not fool yourself thinking I am good, and my brother who lives next to me is not good! You will not be right. I, as your Mother, love you and therefore I warn you.

The Secrets are here, my children. It is not known what they are, but when you do learn, it will be too late.

Return to prayer! Nothing is more needed than prayer. I wish that God would allow me to explain to you at least a little about the Secrets, but even this is too many graces He is giving." [1]

—The Virgin Mary at Medjugorje,
January 28, 1987

WHILE THERE IS LITTLE THAT MARY IS PERMITTED BY GOD TO reveal about the Secrets of Medjugorje, one not so little thing is certain about them: their number.

There are Ten Secrets of Medjugorje—more than any other well documented Marian apparition in history, either approved or not by the Church. [2]

But why Ten Secrets?

Is there a mystical significance to this number?

According to Biblical scholars, ten is considered a perfect number. It consists of the number four—the number of physical creation—and the number six—the number of man. Ten is also considered the number of man's perfection, which is believed to be confirmed by the presence of ten fingers and ten toes.

It is said that the number ten represents the authority of God and His governance on Earth. Some have written that it is a symbol of obedience, responsibility and completeness of order with regards to God's laws.

In the Bible, the number ten is found two hundred and forty-two times, and the word *tenth* is found another seventy-nine times. Not surprisingly, we begin to find the number ten right away in the Old Testament.

In the first chapter of *The Book of Genesis*, the phrase "God said" is written ten times, which is said to testify to God's creative power. God is then found telling Abraham that He would not destroy Sodom if ten righteous men could be found there.

Further on in *Genesis*, Abraham's servant takes ten camels with him on the way to procure Rebekah to be the wife of his son, Isaac. After he meets her, two gold bracelets weighing ten shekels are placed on Rebekah's wrists, and there is an effort made to restrain her for ten days before she is to depart to Isaac.

The next book in the Old Testament picks up where *Genesis* leaves off.

In *Exodus*, we read of the ten plagues that fall on Pharaoh and Egypt, a pivotal story in the Jewish timeline. This is followed shortly by the "Ten Commandments" being given to Moses by God on Mt. Sinai, perhaps Scripture's most recognizable moment with regards to the number.

The number ten, or multiples of ten, continue throughout the Old Testament.

In the Temple of Solomon, ten pillars line the west side of the Court. Inside, where ten linen curtains hang, there are ten lavers, ten lamp-stands and ten tables and it is on the tenth day of the first month that a lamb is to be chosen to sacrifice in the temple for Passover.

Most memorably, God is seen in *Isaiah* to cause the shadow on a sundial to go back ten degrees and the Jewish faithful are encouraged to tithe—meaning "give a tenth"—of their income to the Lord.

In the New Testament, Jesus is found to cure ten lepers and there were ten days between His ascension to Heaven and Pentecost. Jesus also uses the number ten in many parables: *The Parable of the Ten Virgins*, where five virgins are found to lack the necessary oil to be ready for the bridegroom; *The Parable of the Ten Gold Coins*, where ten disciples are given ten gold coins in a test of their stewardship; and *The Parable of the Lost Coin*, where a woman with ten coins misplaces one but rejoices greatly upon discovering it.

If there is a reason why there are Ten Secrets of Medjugorje, it will probably be never known. But the history of the use of the number in the Bible offers considerable insight and much to ponder with regards to this question.

Two other Scriptural uses of the number ten appear relevant and significant to the times at hand, and perhaps the apocalyptic nature of the Ten Secrets of Medjugorje.

There were ten generations from Adam to Noah that lived on Earth before the world was purified of its evil by the Great Flood. And, it was after the Tenth Plague stuck Egypt and Moses received the Ten Commandments on Sinai that the Jewish people departed to begin a new life in the "Land of Milk and Honey."

Did these three events in the timeline of ancient Israel foreshadow the role the Ten Secrets of Medjugorje are to play in God's plan to redirect the path of humanity?

Does the foretold era of peace represent "the Land of Milk and Honey?"

In her book, Mirjana Dragićević Soldo stresses that the Ten Secrets are not all negative.

It will be time of great joy, Mirjana reportedly alluded concerning the Fourth, Fifth and Sixth of the Secrets, for those who choose to convert. [3] But, offsets Vicka, terrible things await those who do not turn back to God. [4]

Ivanka said following her June 25, 1988, apparition, that she and the Virgin discussed the Fourth Secret, after which she stated that it was very important for people to do God's will. [5]

Vicka, in her extensive interview with Father Janko Bubalo, also remarked that her Fourth Secret applied to her alone, causing many to wonder if the visionaries were receiving different Secrets.

In one of their books, Fathers Barbarić and Vlašić did note the existence of other secrets:

"These visionaries say that the Ten Secrets refer to the whole world and are linked together in a chain. There are also *other* secrets, personal secrets for the children or for certain people who are connected with these future world events." [6]

On June 25, 1989—during her annual apparition—Ivanka revealed that she and the Virgin discussed the Fifth Secret. [7] Father René Laurentin, who was present at the apparition that day, recalled that he watched the young woman's "transparent joy" at the beginning of the vision become "somber," and then "serious and grave." [8] It was an indication to him that the content of Ivanka's Fifth Secret may be somewhat concerning. [9]

When asked by Jan Connell about what occurred during the apparition, Ivanka said that Mary discussed with her both the Fifth and Sixth Secrets that day, and that the Madonna was asking everyone in the world to pray and fast.[10]

Ivanka further commented on her practice of fasting on bread and water for forty days every year at Lent, as her family has for generations.[11] She said she started doing this because the Blessed Mother told her that fasting will stop wars, adding somewhat curiously, "I know the future of the world—not just my own history—but the future of the world." [12]

What did the Blessed Mother tell you? Was it a good future? Connell inquired.

"The Blessed Mother has told me everything. There are good things and bad things. The important thing to know is God loves each of us. We are His children." [13]

Is it a long future? persists Connell.

"For some it is long. For some it is short," replied Ivanka.[14]

After a number of her annual June 25 apparitions, Ivanka revealed how Mary continued to speak to her about the first six Secrets. (For the record, the Virgin discussed with Ivanka the First Secret in 1987 [15] and in 2011;[16] the Second Secret in 1987;[17] the Third Secret in 1988;[18] the Fourth Secret also in 1988;[19] the Fifth Secret in 1989; [20] 1997; [21] 2010 [22] and 2012; [23] and the Sixth Secret in 2000 [24] and 2005.[25])

These conversations concerning the first six Secrets have not been shared with the public. But in the early days of her yearly visitations from the Virgin Mary, Ivanka, like Mirjana, said her "primary suffering" involved the Secrets, though not specifying one Secret more than another. [26]

After the emotionally-draining June 25, 1989, apparition, Ivanka did share with Father Laurentin a little of what was said:

"The Blessed Virgin spoke of the Fifth Secret, she asked us urgently to pray, for we are in great temptation and danger; the world and material goods make us slaves. Satan is at work according to his plan. Even those who have already begun their conversions allow themselves to be taken in by the material. That is why the Blessed Mother wishes we would support one another in prayer. She intercedes for us close to her Son." [27]

In December of 1982, Father Ljudevit Rupčić asked all the visionaries a specific question: Did Our Lady confide any Secrets to you? [28]

Several of the visionaries, in their answer to this question, mentioned that some of the Secrets involved the Church:

> **Marija Pavlović**: Yes, I know six Secrets. The others know seven or eight. They have to do with us, the Church, people in general. [29]
>
> **Vicka Ivanković**: Yes, I have seven. The First Secret has to do with our church at Medjugorje. It has to do as well with the Sign, humanity in general, and each person. The Secrets speak of the Church in general. There are some which concern us. [30]
>
> **Ivanka Ivanković**: Yes, I have seven. Some concern us personally, others the Church and the world.[31] (Ivanka, according to Father Janko Bubalo, received from Mary a narration of the past, present and future life of the Church that she has recorded, but is not permitted by her to release at the present [32])

It is known that the last four of the Ten Secrets are considered grave, that the first three are described as warnings, and that these three visionaries—Marija, Vicka, and Ivanka—all told Father Rupčić that they had received, up until then, no more than seven Secrets.[33]

Consequently, it appears that these three visionaries' responses to Father Rupčić's question—which all speak of the Church—may involve Secrets Four through Six.

Author and investigative reporter, Michael Brown, believes so, too:

"Little was said about the Fourth, Fifth, and Sixth Secrets, leading to speculation that these were the ones having to do with the Church." [34]

Wayne Weible also wrote in his last book that these three Secrets— four through six— "may refer to the Church." [35] Once again, though, such speculation that these Secrets involve the Church, also presumes the six visionaries are receiving the same Secrets, which Laurentin says, "is not evident." [36]

Father Rupčić's 1982 interview unearthed one other specific note of interest concerning the Secrets and the Church. When asked, Vicka gave a most candid answer to the Croatian priest's question, "Did Our Lady have a message for the Pope?"

"He (the Pope)," said Vicka, "should consider himself as the father of all people and not only Christians. That he tirelessly and courageously promotes the message of peace and love for all men. This is *found among the Secrets* that she gave us, but we shouldn't speak about it now, only when she permits us to say it. There is a little of everything." [37]

Several years later, during a January 24, 1985, interview with Archbishop Frane Franic of Split, Vicka added to her disclosures concerning the Church, "A new era begins for the Church, one in which the Church *cannot trust* any human power or human strength but rely on the power of the Cross, on the love of Christ, and the Holy Spirit." [38]

Vicka's words here sound a bit ominous, causing one to ponder all the prophecies of apostasy, betrayal and schism that have been foretold to come upon the Church some day, a day many believe has begun to unfold.

Mirjana, in her book, also spoke of the Church and the Secrets being related.

She said that between the time we are living in now—the time of grace—and the time of the Triumph, will be the time of the Secrets. It will be during this time, she noted, that the priesthood of the Catholic

Church will serve as a bridge to get *through* the Secrets and into the time of the Triumph.[39]

Similarly, in a question and answer session at a talk he gave in Seattle, Washington, on October 29, 1997, Ivan made it clear that some of the Secrets involve the Church.

> Question: *Is there any "reason" given for the Secrets and is mention made of any timetable?*
>
> **Ivan:** I believe so; that there *is* a reason why she gave them to us. The Secrets Our Lady gave are tied with the world, with the Church, and one day will be revealed. It's also other things that are involved in the Secrets.[40]

Exponentially wiser today from doing countless interviews, as well as from simply maturing, Vicka's slip of the tongue concerning the Secrets and the Pope is one of many found in the early archives of Medjugorje during such question-and-answer sessions with the visionaries.

From appearing to allude that the Secrets are part of the *Apocalypse* and the Second Coming of Christ,[41] to refusing to deny that many could perish between the time of the First Secret and the Third Secret (the Great Sign), [42] to admitting the Ten Secrets will be painful to the whole world, [43] misspeaks, gaffes, misunderstandings, translation errors, and perhaps some true accidental disclosures are found when one looks closely at the various discussions the children conducted with their inquisitors in the first years of the apparitions. Perhaps one of those "accidental" disclosures occurred in the 1980s. At the time, the youthful visionaries were in the process of receiving the Secrets and also had subsequent apparitions with Mary that discussed or previewed the Secrets in visions. Quite often, these experiences left them in tears.* After one such event, one of the visionaries was asked why they were so distressed and reportedly replied, "How can't I cry when I see blood and little children."**

---

* Marija, Vicka, Ivanka, Mirjana and Jacov have all been reported to have cried at an apparition.

** This account comes from two highly reputable sources that were both at the apparition.

It was made clear by the visionary that the vision did not involve dead children, but only blood on the ground around them. Perhaps similarly to Sister Lucia's description of the Third Part of the Secret of Fatima, in which she was shown a slain Pope, along with bishops, priests, religious, and various lay people who were "martyrs" and whose "blood was being gathered up," this reported vision may well have been symbolic imagery rather than a literal event.

On another occasion (March 25, 2022)—when asked during an interview on *Radio Maria* by Father Livio Fanzaga, "Do you think there is a danger of nuclear war?" or "Is this just the Devil's way of intimidation?,"—one of the Medjugorje visionaries, Marija Lunetti, answered, "Aaah…I don't want to go into the Secrets, but…."

One disclosure of the contents of the Secrets, however, was not an accident.

Dr. Ludvik Stopar, a theistic parapsychologist and psychiatrist, trained in hypnotherapy, reported that he hypnotized Marija Pavlović.

And, Stopar admitted, he got Marija to reveal the Secrets to him.

Stopar studied general medicine at the Medical University of Graz in Styria, Austria, and psychiatry, hypnotherapy and parapsychology at the University of Freiburg im Breisgau, Germany.[44] He then became director of the Amber Polyclinic of Maribor in Yugoslavia.

Stopar visited Medjugorje on four occasions to examine the visionaries.[45] With regard to Medjugorje, his report found the children to be absolutely normal, but it also revealed that one of the subjects, Marija Pavlović, had been subjected to hypnosis by him.

Dr. Stopar was interviewed by Father René Laurentin concerning this matter sometime in 1982-83, as reported by Dr. Henri Joyeux and Laurentin in their book on the scientific and medical studies on the apparitions at Medjugorje.

Laurentin: *Why did you go to Medjugorje?*

Stopar: Parapsychological phenomena are my line of work. I could not be uninterested in these events which have taken place in my own country.

Laurentin: *When did you go to Medjugorje?*

Stopar: Four times: in May, 1982, November, 1982, June, 1983, and November, 1983. Each visit lasted five to ten days.

Laurentin: *Your memorandum, written in German, was made known to me about a year ago. It was given to me under the seal of secrecy, but it is well known today and you yourself have published a summary of it in a Brazilian periodical. In this you claim to have separated the 90% subconscious from the 10% conscious level of the visionaries and in this way you have been able to establish their sincerity. What then was your method and on whom did you carry it out?*

Stopar: Hypnosis, administered to Marija Pavlović, who appeared to me to be the most intelligent and the most mature of the visionaries and who was therefore the most suitable for the test.

Laurentin: *Did you use touch eye contact?*

Stopar: Neither. She closed her eyes. Once asleep, she breathes as if asleep. During the two previous days I had her give me an account of the visions without hypnosis. I asked her to repeat the account under hypnosis and she did this for one hour. While hypnotized only the subconscious level operated. The 10% conscious level was asleep. There was no difference between the two accounts; both were the same.

Laurentin: *You do not want to say that she gave exactly the same account, in exactly the same words?*

Stopar: No, certainly not. She used different words but the meaning was the same.

Laurentin: *Were there other differences?*

Stopar: In the early account, not under hypnosis, Maria kept the Secrets confided to her by the apparition, very strictly. Under hypnosis she told them to me.

Laurentin: *But surely, a violation of conscience! Now, the Secrets are no longer a secret?*

Stopar: You can trust my professionalism. The Secrets remain as secret for me as for Marija. I would not confide them, even to you. It is as serious as the seal of the confessional.

Laurentin: *When I questioned Marija about this hypnosis, I was surprised that she does not seem to remember what she said to you.*

Stopar: This is quite normal. Marija excused herself at the end of the hypnosis: "Excuse me, Doctor, I cannot understand what happened to me; I went to sleep while talking to you."

Laurentin: *One thing did surprise me. When I asked, "Did the Doctor ask your permission?" She replied, "No."*

Stopar: If I had asked, I am sure she would have refused. In therapy, one does not ask permission. [46]

No further information on this intriguing episode has ever surfaced. It appears, since there is no evidence to the contrary, Dr. Stopar remained true to his word concerning the Secrets.

However, the question arises as to whether or not Marija's involvement with Dr. Stopar at the time was considered personal therapy, or merely her cooperating with a researcher of the apparitions.

Unpleasant. Serious. Grave.

The last four of the Ten Secrets of Medjugorje have found no shortage of colorful words to best capture the drama of their reputed content. The early interviews conducted with Mirjana, Ivanka, and Vicka in 1982 and 1983 opened the window wide for people's imaginations concerning these Secrets—and nothing since has done much to close it.

As a whole— strictly from a curiosity standpoint—the early interviews with Mirjana are especially priceless. This is because they deliver more than just information. They are a captivating, human look into the life of a visionary, of Medjugorje, and the universal problems at hand that the sin of the world has created once again at this moment in history.

They also reveal the challenges of being a prophet, whether thousands of years ago or today.

As with the prophet Jeremiah in the Old Testament—who loved his people but needed to present them with the cold, hard facts—Mirjana tells it like it is: God is intent on bringing change in the world, whether welcomed or not, and trying choices will soon be coming for everyone.

But her human side shines through.

The Seventh Secret—perceived by the young visionary as a troubling disclosure—becomes a personal quest for Mirjana to have lifted from her people.

Thus, it is clear. Although she is a prophet working for the Lord, the divine justice rising on the horizon is coming for her, too, for *her* world—and the world of her family, which she soon understands is all of humanity.

So, like Abraham, like Moses, like so many of the prophets, she attempts to argue on behalf of her fallen brothers and sisters. She tries to reason with the Almighty, to get Him to sheath His sword (1Chr 21:27), to turn away from His wrath (Prv 24:18).

But, though successful in *softening* the fury of the Seventh Secret,[47] Mirjana's heart is again broken, her mind overwhelmed once more, by what she learns must still come:

"Then she (Mary) told me the Ninth Secret and it was even worse. The Tenth Secret is totally bad and cannot be lessened whatsoever. I cannot say anything about it, because even a word would disclose the Secret before it is time to do so." [48]

Ivan Dragicévic´

"The Madonna has been permitted by God to come here. She knows what is coming in the future. She is calling God's children back on the path to Heaven."

Photo Credit: St. Andrews Productions

CHAPTER SIXTY-FIVE

THE DESTINY OF HUMANITY

*"It shall be a time unsurpassed in distress
since nations began until that time."*

—Dn 12:1

DECADES HAVE GONE BY WITHOUT ANYTHING OF TRUE SIGNIFI-
cance coming to light regarding the Secrets of Medjugorje,
especially the last four of the Ten Secrets.

And nothing more should be expected.

After years of interviews, the visionaries are weary of such questions
and have no new answers. But the fraught content of the last of the
Secrets is indirectly alluded to now and then by them and this helps to
keep their momentous nature front and center:

- Ivanka— when asked if every person on Earth will soon become
  aware of God's presence—replied that this would occur *sooner*
  than many suspect.[1]
- Jacov—in hinting that there are some mighty changes ahead—
  confirmed that Mary is in Medjugorje to reconcile the whole
  world—and *will* do so.[2]
- Ivan—in trying to explain what Mary hopes to accomplish
  through the apparitions—stated that people will understand
  one day why Mary has been in Medjugorje so long.[3]

On the Feast of the Assumption in 1982, three of the visionaries
received the Eighth Secret and they all said it was "very grave." [4]

On November 19 of that same year, some of them were given the Ninth Secret and described it as "extremely grave, and wept because of it." [5] Vicka—it was said—grieved uncontrollably after receiving her Ninth Secret on April 22, 1986.[6] Asked by Father Bubalo if the Virgin's Secrets foretold something "ghastly awaited mankind," she replied, "Well, you can say it is known." [7]

All of this confirmed what Mirjana—unfairly criticized by some at the time—had reported years before.

Although Mirjana received her Tenth Secret in 1982, the Virgin Mary continued to speak to her on occasion about the Secrets during her annual apparitions and during so-called "special apparitions."

Years have gone by since Mirjana revealed the substance of such conversations, though slight references to her confidential discussions with Mary about the Secrets are noted throughout the 80s and 90s.[8] She did, however, refer again in 1992 to the Tenth Secret as "especially" grave. [9]

Mirjana also revealed in her book that on June 14, 1986, Mary appeared to her and told her this would be the last of her special apparitions involving the Secrets because she had explained everything that was necessary.[10] Mirjana further wrote about a special prayer to Jesus—for those who do not know the love of God—that Mary taught her which is connected to the Secrets. She says she will reveal it some day when permitted along with a book on the story of the Virgin's life as revealed to her through visions.[11]

It remains, however, with Mirjana's January 10, 1983, interview—published in Father Svetozar Kraljevic 's book—that we learn the most about the last four of the Ten Secrets:

Question: *You have been given the last of the Secrets?*

Mirjana: Yes, the Tenth.

Question: *Can you tell me what it relates to?*

Mirjana: I cannot; but I can tell you that the Eighth Secret is worse than the other seven. I prayed for a long time that (the Seventh Secret) might be less severe. Every day, when the Madonna came, I pestered her, asking that it be mitigated.

Then she said that everyone should pray that it might be lessened. So, in Sarajevo, I got many people to join me in this prayer. Later, the Madonna told me that she'd been able to have the Secret lessened. But then, she told me the Ninth Secret and it was even worse. The Tenth Secret is *totally bad* and cannot be lessened whatsoever. I cannot say anything about it, because even a word would disclose the Secret before it's time to do so.

Question: *I won't press you. Anyway, though, the Tenth Secret has to do with what will definitely happen?*

Mirjana: Yes.

Question: *Unconditionally?*

Mirjana: Yes. It will happen.

Question: *What does the Madonna say? Can we prepare ourselves for what will happen?*

Mirjana: Yes, prepare! The Madonna said people should prepare themselves spiritually, be ready, and not panic; be reconciled in their souls. They should be ready for the worst, to die tomorrow. They should accept God now so that they will not be afraid. They should accept God, and everything else. No one accepts death easily, but they can be at peace in their souls if they are believers. If they are committed to God, He will accept them.

Question: *This means total conversion and surrender to God?*

Mirjana: Yes. [12]

"The plans of the seers, the tears of some of them after having had the Eighth, the Ninth, and the Tenth Secrets," observed Father Laurentin, "assures us that these last Secrets announce the wages of sin." [13] These Secrets, the French theologian said he was told by the visionaries, were quite intense.

But in what form will the events contained in these last of the Secrets be served?

As with the Third Secret of Fátima, many writers have scoured for small indiscretions on the part of the visionaries. They hope to find something said by accident, a word or two muttered in haste or frustration. Something that leaks some specific detail about the Secrets.

In his book, *Medjugorje: Facts, Documents and Theology*, Irish theologian Michael O'Carroll, reports that in an interview with the Canadian newspaper *L'Informateur*, one of the visionaries was asked if there would be a nuclear situation in the future and reportedly responded by saying that this was "part" of the Secrets. "Something unconsciously given away?" writes O'Carroll.[14]

O'Carroll also dwelled on a stirring message one of the visionaries received from the Virgin Mary on August 15, 1985:

"My angel, pray for the unbelievers. They will tear their hair, brother will plead with brother, and they will curse their past godless lives, and repent, but it will be too late. Now is the time for conversion. Now is the time to do what I have been calling for these four years. Pray for them." [15]

Is this message hinting of fear or pandemonium, perhaps because of some serious chastisements to be permitted by God, whether from war, disease or an unknown calamity that disrupts human life on Earth?

Or is it hinting of one's personal anguish at the consequences of not repenting and standing before, perhaps unexpectedly, the judgement seat of God?

During the early years at Medjugorje, the word "chastisement" was often used with regards to God's coming justice upon the world for its sins, especially as suspected to be forthcoming in the last four of the Ten Secrets. It's a term that many used to define the nature of these more serious sounding Secrets, one in which the visionaries heard countless times.

Asked in an interview by attorney Jan Connell if the messages at Medjugorje involve chastisements for the sins of the world, Vicka simply responded, "Yes." She then added that such events must surely come if people did not return to God.[16] Vicka also said that leading people to conversion now prepares them for such moments,[17] and that with prayers, fasting and penance, the punishments can be lessened.[18]

On the other hand, when Ivanka was asked about chastisements in a 1996 interview, she responded, "Our Lady never said anything about chastisements in Medjugorje." [19] But previously when questioned by Father Janko Bubalo as to whether or not it was true that the Virgin showed her a glimpse of the terrible contents that make up the Ninth Secret, Ivanka—almost in tears from just thinking about it—replied, "Why, I would have died had she shown it to me." [20]

These responses by Vicka and Ivanka invite the question as to what exactly *is* a chastisement, as it seems to be a confusing term, not just for visionaries, but for many.

To many people, the word "chastisement" implies a harsh event, such as a plague, a war, an earthquake—some life disrupting act—that originates in the divine will of God and is then consummated by Him.

This understanding appears to primarily emanate from the divine punitive events described in the Old Testament. In essence, God conceives a punishment and deliberately sends it upon His people.

Many spiritual leaders, books and articles further this singular understanding in a reckless fashion—insinuating through the haphazard, magnified and over use of the word chastisement—that major calamities should be viewed as the vengeance of God. But the truth of the matter is, theologians say, God is not a Machiavellian plotter hiding behind the clouds, prearranging a shower of retributions to rain upon the world.

In fact, it is quite the opposite.

While both the Old and New Testament make it resoundingly clear that God certainly does intervene to correct and redirect His children, the how, when and why behind such divine activity is a mystery in itself. This is because no one knows the will of God. But we can use faith and reason to get a little better understanding of it all.

Undoubtedly, it sounds as if the chastisements the Virgin warns of in her apparitions spring from the cumulative, inescapable consequences of humanity's sinful behavior. This would leave, as Fátima author John Haffert writes, no need for divine wrath:

"It seems logical man would bring about his own chastisement. There is the theological principle that God does not multiply miracles. Since a holocaust is right at hand, waiting to happen, why would God send some miraculous fire to wipe out entire nations especially in light of His promise after the Deluge? No evil comes from God, only from sin." [21]

Again, Haffert's understanding is not to rule out God's freedom to intervene in His creation as He deems necessary. But as his words imply, theology makes it clear that most prophecies of approaching chastisements should be seen in relation to God's permissive will, not his ordained.

Moreover—as can be seen at Fátima and Medjugorje—it is God's desire to help in such calamitous times. He wants, Mary's words reveal at both apparitions, to prevent or mitigate a coming chastisement, promising to do so in response to people's prayers, sacrifices, and renunciation of sin.

At Fátima, Mary's words in the second part of the Secret called for the prevention of the foretold chastisement. On July 13, 1917, she told the visionaries: "He (God) is about to punish the world for its crimes by means of war, famine, and persecutions of the Church and the Holy Father. To prevent this…"

At Medjugorje, Mary invited the mitigation of the severe Seventh Secret. Said Mirjana on January 19, 1983: "She (Mary) said that everyone should pray that it (the 7th Secret) might be lessened…I got many people to join me in this prayer. Later, the Madonna told me that she'd been able to have the Seventh (Secret) lessened."

God's intent—both apparitions make evident—is to attempt to use the warning of the approaching chastisement to draw His people back to Him. He demonstrates His infinite mercy in this way, and by coming to the rescue of His people after a chastisement befalls them.

During the 1930s, Sister Lúcia's letters reveal that she often worried that God could no longer withhold from the world the justice it so deserved for its sins. The Virgin Mary's requests to prevent the chastisements had gone unheeded, and Lúcia sensed the approach of World War II was at hand. But, like Haffert, Lúcia makes it clear that the approaching war was not the will of God, or that it was God that was sending it:

> It does not mean that God wanted a war, as He is the Lord of peace, goodness and love: "Love one another as I have loved you." That is the Lord's law. His First Commandment. Yet He allows wars, just as He allows sin, on account of the gift of

freedom that He endowed us with, so that we might serve Him, be obedient to Him, and love Him freely. If we use this gift to wrong people, then we are responsible before God, before our consciences, before humanity, which suffers the consequences of our errors. [22]

The Franciscans at Medjugorje convey a similar understanding of chastisement when addressing the pilgrims there. They are well aware of Mary's warnings of God's justice being served. Yet, the friars explain that this justice originates from the hands of man.

"Our Lady says it is not God, but sin that does it," Father Slavko Barbarić said about the Ten Secrets and the foretold "justice" in them. [23]

The priests and visionaries at Medjugorje frown on references to the Ten Secrets that focus on chastisements. This kind of talk, they emphasize, separates the Secrets from the true message of Medjugorje.

Attempts to sensationalize the Secrets, the friars understand, provoke fear and siphon off hope. Consequently, such efforts work against helping people understand the positive outcome the Secrets are intended to achieve in the end.

With that reality noted, however, there appears to be an inescapable "Day of the Lord" descending upon humanity—a time in which the world will have to answer for mankind's ocean of crimes —especially the billions of abortions that undeniably cry out to God for justice.

Not surprisingly, some believe this epoch of history, as in the age of Noah, may involve a purification that is to emanate from God's ordained will—a divinely sent correction of the human race that is part of His anointed plan, long anticipated in what St. Paul called in his *Letter to the Galatians*, "the fullness of time." [24]

Such a transformation—it is hard to deny—would seem to go hand in hand with what some of the Secrets at Medjugorje reportedly are to bring upon the earth. Moreover, with regards to Medjugorje, it has been ventured that the events contained in the Secrets may be not just world changing, but truly eschatological—events related to the final destiny of humanity—as suspected by theologians of Fátima.

"The significance of the (Medjugorje) Secrets can be understood with reference to Fátima," wrote Denis Nolan in *Medjugorje: A Time for*

Truth a Time for Action, "the Secrets of Medjugorje are believed to be eschatological in nature and will be revealed slowly before the events they predict unfold." [25]

Others agree.

Fátima author Father Luigi Bianchi writes: "Medjugorje is the Fátima of our day… an eschatological dawning…to rise with the Third Millenium." [26]

Father René Laurentin ehoes this opinion: "Medjugorje has an apocalyptic, even eschatological flavor. Mary has come for the 'last times.'" [27]

Father Janko Bubalo goes so far as to say that this was detectible right from the beginning at Medjugorje: "The very first words of the Virgin in her encounter with the seers was of an eschatological nature." [28]

Most significantly, to speak of an escatological time means to be talking of the Lord coming back in glory, the final days leading to the Parousia. "The Last Judgement will come when Christ returns in glory," reads the *Catechism of the Catholic Church*, "only the Father knows the day and the hour; only He determines the moment of its coming. Then through His Son Jesus Christ He will pronounce the final word on all history." [29]

There are no public messages from Mary at Medjugorje that specifically speak of such an "end times" scenario. Nor have any of the visionaries spoken of such a happening.

But while Marija has said she does "not speak of Christ's Second Coming" and Vicka says that this is "not part of her Secrets," the visionaries have made comments that seem to reveal Mary has spoken to them in some way about the inevitable return of the Lord in the end times, perhaps in a broader sense with regards to the purpose of the Secrets, in a way to prepare for this eventual reality.

"I cannot say anything about that because Our Lady has said nothing specific," said Vicka when asked about "the last events mentioned in the Apocalypse" by *Informateur De Montreal* on October 7, 1992. [30]

"An evangelization has begun toward the Second Coming, I cannot say anything," replied Ivan when asked in November, 1990, by *The National Catholic Register* if the Virgin Mary told him anything about the Second Coming in relation to *Evangelization 2000*. [31]

"Many people ask whether the Blessed Mother has said anything about the Apocalypse and the Second Coming of Christ," inquired Jan Connell of Mirjana in her 1990 book, *Queen of the Cosmos*. "I would not like to talk about that," replied Mirjana.[32] In the *Afterword* of the 2009 revised edition of her book, Connell writes of Ivanka: "Ivanka knows ten secrets that she says involve the final chapters of the earth's history." [33]

Most interesting comes several statements by Father Slavko Barbarić and Father Tomislav Vlašić in late 1985 that were published in their book, *Pray with Your Heart*. The remarks by the friars also seem to reflect that an eschatological element is associated in some preparatory way with the Secrets of Medjugorje:

> — "I wish to tell you how I have interpreted these apocalyptic messages. In the *New Testament* we have a book bearing the name of *The Apocalypse*. In this book you can read of many dreadful things St. John saw in his visions, and how he described many disasters...But you see, all this cannot be explained just in terms of physical catastrophe; this must always be interpreted in terms of conversion...In other words, they help our faith. Our faith must always have this quality of waiting...In the *New Testament*, mostly in *The Apocalypse*, there is a word which the Church has been repeating many times, Marantha! In other words, come Lord Jesus!" (Father Slavko Barbarić, November 15, 1985.) [34]

> — "When Mirjana announced the content of the last locution, many telephoned to ask... when? how? These messages are apocalyptic, and in order to understand them, one needs perhaps to read once again *The Apocalypse* of St. John... These apocalyptic messages have a purpose—our faith must be awake and not asleep...one element of faith is the element of waiting, of keeping vigilant. The apocalyptic messages require us to be awake, not to sleep as regards our faith, our peace with God, with others, and as regards our conversion." (Father Slavko Barbarić, December 7, 1985) [35]

> — "I spoke to the visionary today. She told me this. 'You can tell everyone we are at a time of graces, at a time of Our Lady's call, who wants to lead us to salvation. Mankind is going through some very tough moments, through which a harsh purification will take place. After the sign it will be too late.' The visionary is saying that mankind will reach a point where there will be a meeting with God, when there will be a manifestation of God, and this, she says, will be a period

of faith, of conversion, and that is why Mary is inviting us to conversion." (Father Tomislav Vlašić, October 26,1985) [36]

At the time, this entire matter generated a substantial amount of interest at Medjugorje. Father Laurentin, in his June 1987 book, *Latest News of Medjugorje*, reports that on February 28, 1987, Father Alberto Bonifacio posed the question of the return of Christ with the friars at St. James in Medjugorje, seeking to understand what exactly the visionaries may have been told about this issue. [37]

Likewise, on February 12, 1987, Father Angelo Mutti asked Father Vlašić a couple of questions concerning what he and Father Barbarić were speaking of in their 1985 book. Mutti published the friar's response in the June 7, 1987, issue of *Echo from Medjugorje*, a monthly publication from Mantova, Italy, that was one of the earliest and most widely distributed sources of news on Medjugorje in the mid-80s. [38]

> Mutti: *In a message given by Mirjana, she says that Our Lady has come to prepare us for the Second Coming of Christ. What does she mean by this?*
>
> **Vlašić**: Mirjana has stressed this several times. I have asked her: "*Do you mean the meeting with Christ that comes after death, or do you mean the coming of Christ, here on Earth?*" She replied that she means the coming of Christ on Earth and that Our Lady has come "to prepare" the way for this second coming. Each one of us realizes, in our hearts, that this is Our Lady's purpose and that she has wrought in us a great awareness of God. Mirjana reminds us of Our Lady's words, "*These apparitions of mine are the last for humanity.*" [39]
>
> Mutti: *This coming of Christ; is it to be an intermediary coming, before the end of the world; will He be visible to us or only appear in our hearts?*
>
> **Vlašić**: The visionary (Mirjana) gives no such details—when it will happen or what will happen—she just says that this is "the preparation" for this event. It seems that Our Lady is preparing us for a new quality of life; what will happen next is contained in the Secrets; the effect they will have on humanity; we do not know. All we can do at this point is adore the Lord and await Him, just like the "prudent virgins." [40]

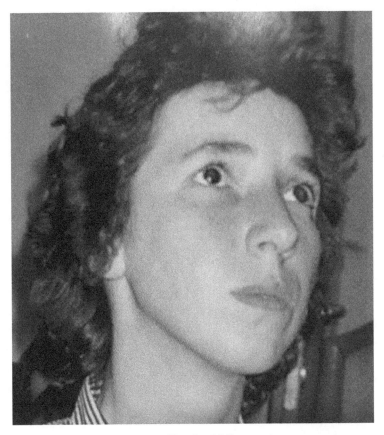

Marija Pavlović Lunetti

"The punishments mentioned by Our Lady do not come from God, they are the fruit of man's moral perversions. It is only men who prepare the punishments forecast in the Secrets that Our Lady has entrusted us with."

Photo Credit: Pittsburgh Center for Peace

CHAPTER SIXTY-SIX

THE WOMAN CLOTHED IN THE SUN

"Jesus said: I saw Satan fall like lightening from the sky."
—Lk: 10:18

THERE IS A MYSTERY SURROUNDING THE SECRETS OF MEDJUGORJE—one that has received little to no attention. It involves a revelation that Mirjana made with regards to the date of March 18, which is her birthday and the day she receives her annual apparition—but also, she says—a date connected to the Secrets.

"Only when the events contained in the Secrets start to unfold," Mirjana writes in her book, "will the world understand why she (the Virgin Mary) chose the 18th of March." [1]

The hidden significance of this date is a mystery that asks to be pondered.

But it is not a new kind of mystery in Judeo-Christian history.

Down through the centuries, there has often been found a linkage of events that have occurred on the same date—a chosen calender number—for some divine reason.

In recent history, a series of events associated with the number thirteen—or the 13th day of a given month—have been observed. And, they appear to be pointing to, or connected with, Fátima.

Mary appeared at Fátima on the 13th of May, June, July, September and October of 1917. It is believed she first appeared on the 13th because of the role this date played with Queen Esther and her heroic rescue of the Jewish people, who were scheduled for annihilation on the 13th of the month as described in *The Book of Esther.**

Mary's appearance at Fátima has been also related to *Revelation* 12:1— "a woman clothed with the sun" —which, as can be seen, are two numbers (12 and 1) that add up to "13."

Pope John Paul II's attempted assassination of May 13, 1981, and the Church approved miracle at Akita, Japan, on October 13, 1984— as well as events surrounding the collapse of Communism and the Soviet Union—are just some examples of this mystery already cited in this writing.

But there are many more, some fairly recent and others that go back centuries.

The older ones are especially of interest.

Pope Leo XIII's reported overhearing of a conversation between God and the Devil, which foretold a century of evil and may have spawned the *Prayer to St. Michael*, is alleged to have occurred on October 13, 1884. Likewise, quite mysteriously, a ten-year old St. Theresa of Lisieux was cured of an illness through a miraculous smile from an image of the Virgin Mary on May 13, 1883, the year before Pope Leo's vision.

Were these events connected to Fátima in some way?

Over the centuries, the 13th is a date found again and again in Church history. Two events are noteworthy because they occurred in Portugal.

In 1385, an army on the way to battle led by a general named Nuno Alvares Pereira—later beatified by Benedict XV in 1918 and canonized by Pope Benedict XVI in 2009—stopped at a church in a village named Ceica, in the country of Querem. This would be in the diocese of Leira-Fátima today.

There, Nuno—a mystic—prayed to the Virgin Mary to bring his army victory. The following day, Nuno's army passed through what is today the village of Fátima. On this site, the entire army experienced a miracle. The soldiers claimed to hear angels singing and then witnessed a vision of St. Michael raising his sword in a sign of victory.

---

* In Judaism, 13 also signifies the age at which a boy matures and celebrates his bar mitzvah—becoming a full member of the Jewish faith. And, according to the Rabbinic commentary on the *Torah*, God is understood to possess 13 attributes of mercy.

Nuno himself is said to have ridden through what became known as the Cova da Iria, the future field where the Virgin Mary would appear in 1917 to the three children. In this meadow, the general is said to have been divinely told that the ground he knelt on was holy. And— one-day—God would bring a great victory over evil on this very spot.

This miracle occurred on August 13, 1385.

Two hundred years before, there is found another link to Fátima and the 13th.

On October 13, 1147, historian A. Fernando Castilho writes that a "miracle of the sun" was reported during a battle near Lisbon in Portugal. This event led to the country's liberation from the Moors on October 25 of that year.

For some reason, the mystery of the number "13" is found even further back in Catholic history and lore. One tradition even holds that Sts. Peter and Paul were both killed by the Romans on October 13th—one in 64 and the other in 67A.D.

As with the number "13" and Fátima, Medjugorje, Mirjana and the number "18" are found intertwined in ways beyond just Mirjana's birthdate on the 18th of March, and the fact it is the day she receives her annual apparition of the Virgin Mary.

The first yearly apparition that Mirjana received on March 18, 1983, was on her "18th birthday" (1965-1983). She notes in her book that it was exactly one month before—February 18, 1983—that Father Jozo was released early from prison. This was because, she writes, the government reduced his 3-year sentence to "18-months." [2]

Mirjana also writes that on her last daily apparition of December 25, 1982, she and Mary "summarized our entire 18 months together."[3] This period, it must be noted, ran *exactly* 18 months to the day. It extended from June 25, 1981, until December 25,1982. [Note: Mary did not speak at all to the visionaries on the first day of the apparitions, June 24, 1981.]

The "significance of the date will be clear," Mirjana has said many times about the real reason for the March 18 annual apparition date.[4] This leads one to wonder if there are some clues to be found concerning this number in Judeo-Christian history.

In Judaism, the number 18 is a special number, it emphasizes the importance of life and is often found in celebrations.

At weddings, bar mitzvahs, and when making donations, Jews often give gifts of money in multiples of eighteen. This symbolically gives the recipient the gift of life or luck—a blessing from God as meant to be understood in the number.

Likewise, Jewish prayers especially center around the number 18. The Amidah, which is the central prayer of every service, was originally composed of 18 blessings, and is still referred to as the Shemoneh Esrei—the Hebrew words for the number 18.

The Talmud records a number of reasons for the number 18, including the 18 times that the forefathers Abraham, Isaac and Jacob are mentioned together in the Torah and the 18 times God's name is cited in the Shema Yisrael.

But most of all, it is noted that the number 18 is understood in the Jewish faith to be a symbol of their slavery and bondage. In the Old Testament, the word bondage is mentioned 18 times and two of the ancient enemies of Israel—Eglon the Moabite King and the Phillistines, with the help of the people of Ammon—held them in bondage for 18 years.

Needless to say, it is feasible that the present mystery may in some way be related to this fact, only with regard to the world's present bondage to sin.

In Catholic history, March 18 is most known for the death of St. Cyril of Jerusalem, who died on March 18, 386. St. Cyril is recognized for advocating the veneration of relics and arguing on behalf of the doctrine of Transubstantiation, the belief that the bread and wine of Communion become the actual body and blood of Christ.

Other events of Catholic significance are noted on this date.

On March 18, 1123, the First Lateran Council opened in Rome. It was the first ecumenical council held in the West, convened by Pope Callixtus II. Two centuries later, on March 18, 1314, thirty-nine Knights Templar were burned at the stake in Paris. [Note: It was on October 13, 1307, that scores of the Knights Templar were first arrested in France.]

It is likely, however, the mystery behind this date and the Secrets of Medjugorje has little to do with mainstream Catholic history. Rather, it would seem to be more inclined to be associated with the history and message of Fátima.

Mary appeared at Fátima to confront atheism.

But it was not just atheism she came to address, but a specific onslaught that neared—the atheism effusing from Marxism. It would be Marxism that fueled the Bolshevik Revolution in Russia and it is Marxism that still thrives in our atheistic world of today.

Thus, the Virgin's promised victory—her "Triumph"—will be a triumph over not just atheism, but Marxist driven atheism. This is the reason Mary warned at Fátima of the "errors of Russia"—the multitude of errors derived from Marxism that she knew would manifest beyond just Communism.

With that said, it would not be surprising if the mysterious reason for the date—March 18—refers directly to this issue, to something that will shine a light on the defeat of "Marxist" atheism.

It is noteworthy to mention that Karl Marx's life was no stranger to the number "18" or to the "month of March."

Marx was born on May 5, 1818.

He died on March 14, 1883.

But most significantly, the date of "March 18" is found to have played a pivotal role in the rise of Marxism. It is a date that Marx himself saw as singular and historic.

In Paris, France, on March 18, 1871, radicalized socialist workers seized control of the city in an uprising known as "The Paris Commune." Afterwards, in his reflection on the insurrection, Marx declared that the emancipatory truth held in his writings was now evident for the world to see through this groundbreaking event in France.[5]

The revolt made Marx famous[6] and he penned a book on it, which Lenin read in 1917.[7] Marx declared the Paris Commune, "the glorious harbinger of a new society"[8] and "a historic experience of enormous importance."[9]

During their 71-day control of the city, the anti-Catholic leaders of the Commune proceeded to execute the Archbishop of Paris, Georges Darby, and a significant number of priests—the despised "black crows," as the revolutionaries termed them.[10]

To many, even Vladimir Lenin, the Parisian insurgency is considered to be the official birth of the practical implementation of Marxism, an historic precursor to the coming of Communism in Russia and the numerous Marxist movements that followed.

The coming triumph of the Virgin Mary is understood to have officially commenced with the Virgin Mary's 1531 apparition in Mexico, where "Our Lady of Guadalupe" [a total of 18 letters in 4 words] is recognized by Marian theologians—due to the apocalyptic message conveyed through the miraculous image on St. Juan Diego's tilma— as the "Woman Clothed with the Sun" who comes to wage war with Satan as foretold in St. John's closing narrative (Rv 12:1-18) to the New Testament.

This understanding becomes evident at Lourdes, where the Virgin Mary's declaration, "I am the Immaculate Conception," opens the way for the fulfillment of an array of prophecies that tie Mary directly to "she" who is to "crush the head" of the Serpent in *Genesis* 3:15, which also, as can be seen, totals 18.

At Lourdes, the mystery of the number 18 is found front and center, as Mary appeared there 18 times in 1858 to Bernadette Soubirous and spoke to her for the first time on February 18th. Lourdes was later approved by the Church on January 18, 1862, with no reason given for this date by Bishop Bertrand-Severe Laurence of the Diocese of Tarbes.

Most significantly, the 18th and last apparition at Lourdes took place on July 16th—the Feast of Our Lady of Mt. Carmel—a feast that directly recalls God's triumph over the false prophets of Baal through the wondrous Elijah. It is a triumph seen again as a foreshadowing sign of God's coming victory through the Virgin of Revelation. (See Epilogue for this full story.)

At Fátima, the understanding of the significance of Elijah's victory to Mary's coming Triumph is confirmed when Mary appears as Our Lady of Mt. Carmel during the last apparition in October of 1917, and where her first apparition on May 13th —a date in which the month (5) and the day (13) add up again to 18—is clearly meant to call to mind Queen Esther's role in the salvation of the Jewish nation.

Now, theologians tell us, what the Virgin Mary began at Guadalupe, laid the foundation for at Lourdes, and confirmed at Fátima, will be fulfilled at Medjugorje—her glorius and long awaited victory over an age of unprecedented evil and systemic atheism.

It is to be, as Mirjana has stated, a victory that will see—with the unfolding of the First Secret at Medjugorje—the defeat not just of the evil of this world, but of the world of darkness, of Satan.

A victory, quite fittingly, that points to the Lord's words in *The Gospel of Luke*—and once more—to the number 18: "I saw Satan fall like lightening from the sky" (Lk 10:18).

CHAPTER SIXTY-SEVEN

TIME IS SHORT

*"But woe to you, earth and sea, for the Devil has come down
to you in great fury, for he knows he has but a short time."*
—Rv: 12:12

Mirjana Dragićević Soldo receives most of the attention with regards to the Ten Secrets of Medugorje. This is primarily because she will someday reveal them by way of her chosen spokesperson, Father Petar Ljubicic.

But the other five visionaries have spoken considerably about the Secrets too, and it is often in their casual remarks—sometimes in response to questions unrelated to the Secrets—that something thought provoking is forthcoming.

Ivan Dragićević, who rarely mentions the Secrets—perhaps because of an early controversy he got innocently ensnared in while in the seminary [1]—often carefully alludes to them in his talks.

At one event, Ivan stated, "The Secrets refer to both good and bad" and the "difference depends on us." On another occasion, he told an interviewer that God permitted Mary to come to Medjugorje because "the Blessed Mother knows *what* is coming in the future." Both of these subtle remarks hint not only of the transforming nature of the Secrets, but of humanity's ability to affect—through prayer and conversion—their outcome. [2]

In 1989, Ivan was asked, "Based on what you know now, having had nine Secrets, how do you understand Our Lady's presence here in Medjugorje?"

"The Blessed Mother," he thoughtfully replied, "is here urgently calling us—everyone in the world—to change our lives, to come back to God now." [3]

A few years later, at a talk at the Franciscan monastery in Vienna on January 18, 1993, Ivan told his listeners that knowledge of the Secrets is intended to invite change. First emphasizing that Mary has not come to frighten anybody, he then pointed out a glaring reality: "People cannot deny the state of the world." It was an allusion to the fact that a time may be coming for God to intervene in a necessary way—the way of the Secrets.

"One thing is for sure," Ivan told the crowd that day, "since the beginning, the Mother of God said the greatest threat to humanity was that it could annihilate itself. And this happens in many ways: by means of wars, drugs, alcohol, by means of an immoral life...I cannot speak of the Secrets...these will be known when the time comes, but anybody can recognize certain things by the time we are living. I do not want to say anymore. Each person has been given the capacity to draw conclusions." [4]

Twenty years later, at a talk in Medjugorje on June 24, 2011, Ivan continued to stress that knowledge of the Secrets carries responsibility. His testimony that day, in some way, was reminiscent of John Paul II at Fulda. There, the Pope warned in 1980 of the inherent danger of knowing the Third Secret of Fátima and doing nothing about it.

Ivan's words hit the same chord:

"But one day when the time comes—when some things get revealed—you will understand *why* the apparitions are such a long time and *why* every day. Later on, we will understand some things. Later on, our eyes will be opened when we see *physical changes* that are going to happen in the world. This is so important to understand. I'm not going to tell you the Secrets. The time in front of us is the time of great responsibility." [5]

It is an important responsibility, Ivan knows, because he says he has seen the Virgin "cry over abortion," over "divorce, priests and war." [6] The world has a future, he stresses, "only if it turns back to God." [7]

Ivanka Ivanković-Elez has not spoken much about the Secrets.

Ivanka did, however, tell interviewer Jan Connell to please tell people to take the Secrets "seriously." [8] It was a noteworthy response, perhaps emanating from the fact that Ivanka takes the Secrets quite seriously herself.

The visionary has revealed that she and Mary discussed the Seventh Secret in 2006, [9] the Ninth in 2008, [10] and the Tenth in 2009, [11] although nothing was specifically disclosed. In some of those years, Ivanka says, Mary talked to her about the "future." [12]

All in all, though, it's apparent; the Secrets are something that never leave Ivanka.

Asked on August 6, 2001, "Are we getting closer to the time when the Secrets will be revealed?" Ivanka's response revealed her on-going awareness of them, "Every day," she replied, "We are getting closer and closer." [13]

Curiously, one of the most difficult apparitions Ivanka experienced was on the morning of June 25, 1993, but it did *not* involve the Secrets.

Before a group of about 60 people squeezed into her home—including an Italian TV crew—Ivanka received her annual apparition, which was seven minutes long that day. At its conclusion, she burst into tears and rushed out of the house.[14] The next day, she revealed to Sister Emmanuel Maillard what happened:

"The Virgin showed me some terrible and indescribable events. What I saw had nothing to do with the Secrets. It's like a new warning, because these terrible things can still be averted by prayer and fasting. Conversion and giving one's self to Jesus are necessary more than ever. Do not be blind, become converted." [15]

Father René Laurentin, who was present that day, said Ivanka told him what she saw was horrible and that the event was near.[16] When Father Slavko Barbarić heard what occurred, he visited Ivanka himself to find out what exactly unfolded.

Upon returning to the rectory, Barbarić told everyone, "These terrible things will happen soon. They concern the world in general." Barbarić added that Ivanka told him, "This was the most painful apparition of all." [17]

Of the six visionaries at Medjugorje, it is Marija Pavlović-Lunetti who appears to handle the touchy subject of the Secrets the best.

While Marija has done as many interviews as the others, she seems to know best how to artfully evade answering questions concerning the Secrets. But, she does so, without refusing to talk about them, or appearing annoyed with persistent curiosity.

Indeed, in examining Marija's words in such conversations, the visionary does not refrain from the substance and nature of the Secrets. She is also very sensitive to their volatile content. In an in-depth 1986 article by Notre Dame theologian Edward O'Conner, she is reported to have admitted to have burst into tears when one of the Secrets was revealed to her.[18]

Almost always, though, Marija simply speaks of what she knows without using the words *Secret* or *Secrets* too much.

Do not wait for the sign to be converted, she exhorts pilgrims, telling them the Virgin wants people to respond now.[19] Asked if all people on Earth will believe in God by the time the Great Sign comes, she paraphrases one of Mary's more serious messages. The Blessed Mother has said, she replies, that "those still alive when the Sign comes will witness many conversions."[20] Asked if it will be too late for those who wait for the Great Sign, she answers that "this is the time of great grace and mercy, the time to change our lives."[21]

But her sixth sense to be careful with what she says is always present when she hears the word "secret."

Asked if the Ten Secrets speak of God's will that people love each other—upon hearing the question mentions the "Secrets"—she gently replies, "We cannot say anything about the Secrets."[22] Asked if one should worry about the Secrets? "No, about the Secrets, we can say nothing." Said Marija in a 1988 interview, "Because they are secrets—when they are to be revealed—we will know what they concern. But for now, there is nothing to worry about."[23]

For Marija, and perhaps all the visionaries, "now" can be a very relative term.

This reality is illustrated in a message from the Virgin Mary to Marija during a late night prayer meeting on Podbrdo on October 5, 1987:

"Pray! Pray! Pray!", Marija says the Madonna told the gathering on the hill that evening, "You must be converted…Time is short." [24]

Renzo Allegro, an Italian journalist and author, republished an interview he did with Marija Pavlović in 2001 that he originally conducted in 1989.

It is a special account, Allegro wrote, because Father Slavko Barbarić—after putting him through what he described as a real interrogation—phoned Marija and got her to agree to do a more probing interview with him.

Allegro describes his conversation with Marija that day as a long, detailed, serene, and pondered account, conducted with no feeling of haste and with enough time for clarifications to confirm details.

The interview was taped and ran from noon into the evening at Marija's home in Medjugorje. The reporter says he considers it a "document" and believes it should be brought to the attention of all those who wish to know the intimate details of the events at Medjugorje through Marija Pavlović's *exact* words.

In it, Marija opens up significantly about the Secrets.

The following is an excerpt in which Allegro discusses the Secrets with Marija:

> Allegro: *You told me that you have seen Our Lady every day since 1981. Have you got accustomed to these encounters?*
>
> **Marija**: No, it is not possible to get used to these things. Every time feels like the first. As well as *seeing* Our Lady, myself and the other seers *feel* her presence, her love, her protection and her worries. It is a wonderful miracle that is repeated each day.
>
> Allegro: *What does "feel" the worries of Our Lady mean?*
>
> **Marija:** Our Lady is not always happy. Her face sometimes wears a shadow of sadness. When she talks to us about some subjects, you can see that she is suffering. On two occasions, I have even seen her weep.
>
> Allegro: *On which occasions?*

Marija: When she told me some Secrets about the future of the world. I cannot speak about these things for the moment.

Allegro: *What are the most important things that Our Lady has said to you over the course of the years?*

Marija: Her messages, her requests, and her suggestions are all important. Throughout these years, she has been our teacher and our mother. She has helped us to grow. She is very gentle when she speaks to us. She never gives orders. She expresses her desires and leaves us completely free to carry them out. The things she tells us are not the same for all of us. She has entrusted special tasks to each of us and with her teachings. She has shown us how to do them. Right from the beginning, she told us that she would tell us Ten Secrets. They are Secrets that are destined to be revealed, but only when she says so. The first one of us to receive all the Secrets was Mirjana. In fact, she received her last apparition on December 25, 1982. Our Lady has entrusted Mirjana with the task of informing mankind when the "Great Sign" is about to arrive. It will be a glorious Sign that should appear on Podbrdo as a proof of the authenticity of the apparitions. This "Great Sign" will be visible to everyone and will come in order to persuade the world to be converted once and for all. If this does not happen then there will be a punishment. The "Great Sign" will be preceded by three celestial admonitions. Ten days before their coming, Mirjana will inform a priest so that he may warn the world. Mirjana is an effusive, cheerful girl. On meeting her, someone said, "The Secrets Our Lady has confided to you must be beautiful because you are always happy." She replied, as soon as I think of them I begin to cry." Our Lady recounted the story of her life to Jacov, Ivanka, Vicka and me, just as it really happened during her stay on earth at Nazareth. It was wonderful. One day, this account will also be made public. In fact, Our Lady has told Vicka to write down what she recounted. Vicka has done so and is waiting for Our Lady to tell her to publish it.

Allegro: *The Secrets that have been entrusted to you, are they beautiful or horrid?*

Marija: Beautiful and horrid at the same time. In general, 'Secrets' of this type concern sad events. However, they are not inescapable events. They are always conditioned by something. Our Lady says "this will happen if…" For example, the Seventh Secret entrusted to me has already been made redundant. It was about painful events but, thanks to the prayers and repentance of people at Medjugorje, things have changed. Our Lady always said, "With prayer and repentance, anything can be obtained."

Allegro: *You say that Our Lady is so gentle, good and thoughtful. So how do you explain that she threatens humanity with punishments and catastrophes?*

Marija: Our Lady never threatens punishments. Nor does she say that God punishes mankind. It is mankind that, straying from the truth by doing evil, prepares serious catastrophes. The punishments mentioned by Our Lady do not come from God, they are the fruit of man's moral perversions. It is only men who prepare the punishments forecast in the Secrets that Our Lady has entrusted us with. With her apparitions, her messages, and her advice, she tries to make mankind reflect, until they realize what kind of abyss they are heading for. Our Lady often says, "I adore the freedom that God has given you." Yet, she weeps when she sees how often men use this freedom to do evil to their neighbors.[25]

Like Mirjana, Marija says that Medjugorje will bring the fulfillment of Fatima. In a June 25, 2016, interview with Father Livio Fanzaga for *Radio Maria*, Marija commented on this dawning reality. In response to Father Fanzaga asking if Mary was realizing her plans through the faithful at Medjugorje, Marija replied:

"We don't know what the plans of God and of Our Lady are, but this evening Our Lady told us, 'I call you to persevere in prayer so that with you I can realize my plans (message of June 25, 2016).' "I think Our Lady is realizing the Triumph of the Immaculate Heart, as she said in Fatima, even through us, because we have said yes to holiness, yes to living the Commandments of God, yes to life, and to rejoice in the Law of God…We are poor instruments, but when the Lord takes us, He transforms us…"

Of the six visionaries, perhaps none of them stresses two critical points about Mary and the Secrets as much as Vicka Ivanković-Mijatovic.

The Secrets, she repeats in interviews, can be "substantially lessened" by prayer and penance. Through Mary's intercession, because of God's love, Vicka says this can happen. Needless to say, she wants people to remember this reality and emphasizes often how the Seventh Secret has already been mitigated.

Vicka's second concern is that people realize the Madonna has come to call "all of her children." Mary wants, emphasizes Vicka, everybody in the world to be saved. The Madonna is the Mother of every person on Earth, she has a "mother's love" for them all and her messages are for everyone, she tells people. [26] This emphasis is well noted as countless numbers of various religions, races and ethnicities have been drawn to Medjugorje over the past four decades.

Vicka, like the others, has uttered some thought provoking responses about the Secrets during interviews. Father Laurentin reported one involving a question asked by a cousin of hers as reported in *The Echo from Medjugorje* (1993):

> Question: *Do you remember that you cried when you received the 7th, 8th, and 9th Secrets, and so did Marija? You say that the Secrets do not speak of the war at hand. So what is awaiting us?*
>
> **Vicka**: You just gave the answer to the question yourself. [27]

When her interviews are examined, Vicka, though warm, vivacious and colorful, is extremely honest and blunt, even more than Mirjana. In *Queen of the Cosmos*, her exchange with Jan Connell concerning the future reveals she had no interest in soft pedaling the reality of what she knows is coming in the Secrets:

> Question: *Will the people who listen to the Blessed Mother and change their lives and convert have it easier during the chastisement?*

Vicka: Of course. That is why we are trying to lead people to conversion. We have to help people convert. We have to prepare them for the chastisement. We help them with our prayers and the things we are doing. Everything we are doing at Medjugorje is to show people the right way to live the messages.

Question: *Will God's mercy stop at some point?*

Vicka: If we are open to the Lord's mercy, it never stops. If you don't want God's mercy, it stops for you.

Question: *When the permanent sign comes in Medjugorje, will it be too late for many to convert?*

Vicka: Yes.

Question: *Will the permanent sign happen in your lifetime?*

Vicka: Yes.

Question: *What happens to those people who don't really believe enough right now to convert and want to wait until the permanent sign comes?*

Vicka: For those people, it will be too late. [28]

In another interview, conducted by *Informateur De Montreal* on October 7, 1992, Vicka was asked about *The Book of Revelation*:

Question: *The Apocalypse says that the Devil will be in chains one day. Is that only symbolic?*

Vicka: I believe Satan will be defeated only if we accept the Madonna's messages. If we convert and live like the Madonna teaches us, then we will have a period of peace. It depends on us. If we do not change, it will not happen.

Question: *Do you believe that the last events mentioned in the Apocalypse have started to happen?*

Vicka: I cannot say anything about that, because the Madonna has said nothing specific. Thus, I do not know.

Question: *Many people believe that it is the beginning of the end.*

Vicka: It could be, but the Holy Virgin has said nothing on that subject. [29]

Vicka did not have an answer to the last question. But, at face value, it was a curious inquiry.

The question forwarded, if pondered, is very serious at its core. When one asks a visionary if it's the beginning of the end, the *end* means the "end of the world."

So, is it even possible the world might be approaching its conclusion?

Mary's known words at Fátima, according to Lúcia's revelations, never mentioned such a dire possibility.

But recently, that understanding may have changed.

Something lost has been found.

CHAPTER SIXTY-EIGHT

THE LOST PROPHECY
OF FATIMA

"Arise, Lord, let no mortal prevail; let the nations
be judged in your presence. Strike them with terror,
Lord. Show the nations they are mere mortals."
—Ps(s) 9-10:20-21

MUCH OF WHAT IS KNOWN ABOUT FÁTIMA COMES FROM SISTER Lúcia's memoirs, letters and interviews. This trove of information was accumulated over a period of approximately eighty years, up until her death in 2005.

While the other two visionaries, Francisco and Jacinta, are on record for statements regarding the Virgin Mary and the apparitions, most of this also came through Lúcia.

There is one primary source besides Lúcia, however, that is considered factual and trustworthy. These are the partially released interviews, books, and relevant notes of Dr. Padre Manuel Nunes Formigão—known as the "fourth seer of Fátima." [1]

Father John De Marchi, who lived in Fátima for years, and got to know the environment, customs, and characteristics of the people firsthand there, wrote in 1950 a highly acclaimed account of the apparitions, *Fatima; The Facts*. It was republished in 1980 as *Fatima: From the Beginning.* [2]

Because of De Marchi's concern for detail, it is considered an authentic historical document. [3] In the book's *Introduction*, he writes that the information in his book comes from six primary sources, of which he ranks second the findings of Dr. Formigão.[4]

De Marchi credits Formigão with the first reliable publication on the subject of Fátima in 1921.[5] His book, *Os Episodios Maravilhosos de Fatima* (The Marvelous Events of Fátima), was based on his interrogations of the children, together with his personal impressions of the apparitions. Over the years, Formigão published other articles and books on Fátima, often under the pen names Visconde Montelo and Mira Ceti. [6]

At the time of the apparitions in 1917, Formigão was 34 years old. He was the canon of the Patriarchal See in Lisbon and a professor at the Seminary and Lyceum at Santarem.[7] He held two doctorates, one in theology and the other in canon law from the Gregorian University in Rome. [8]

Needless to say, this gifted man's time was at a premium. He had no keen interest in apparitions, but Formigão kept hearing about Fátima and decided to attend the September 13 apparition.

Described by De Marchi as a man of tact and prudence, Formigão was not awed with what he observed that day. He stood over 600 feet away from the visionaries, and dismissed any alleged light phenomena to an optical effect caused by the height of the Serra de Aire Mountains. [9]

Reserved yet benevolent, he was, however, impressed by the three children.[10]

Two weeks later, on Thursday September 27, Formigão returned to Fátima to question and study the visionaries. He interviewed all of them, starting with Francisco. And, he forcefully confronted Lúcia about a rumor. It was said she revealed a bogus version of the Secret of Fátima to the authorities who imprisoned the children in August.

Formigão: *In order to free yourself from the mayor on the day he imprisoned you, did you tell him something as if it were the Secret, thus deceiving him and boasting of it afterwards?*

Lúcia: That is not true. Senhor Santos really did want me to reveal the Secret, but I could not and did not do so, although he tried in every way to make me do what he wanted. I told the Mayor everything that the Lady had said to me except the Secret. Perhaps it was because he thought I had told him the Secret too. I never wanted to deceive him.[11]

Convinced of the children's sincerity, on October 11, 1917, two days before the last public apparition, Formigão returned again to Fátima.[12] This time he interviewed Manuel Goncalves, who knew the families of the Fátima visionaries, as well as the visionaries once more. [13]

Remaining near Fátima, he attended the October 13 apparition and that same evening undertook a third investigation of the children. It is noted that he considered it important to not delay in getting their separate accounts of that day, especially before they were left alone together and conversed.[14]

Consequently, through asserting his authority as a priest, Formigão managed to rid the children of the crowd that assembled at the house by 7 o'clock that evening, and subsequently interrogated each them individually about the day's events. [15]

By then, the children were extremely fatigued. They had "not had a single moment of peace since daybreak and the strain intensified after the miracle," according to De Marchi's account.[16]

Still, Formigão proceeded to ask Lúcia forty-eight questions, Jacinta twenty-six, and Francisco twenty-seven. Some of their answers concerned him.

But Lúcia's answer to one question looked extremely troublesome:

> Formigão: *Did the Lady tell you who she was?*
>
> Lúcia: She said she was the Lady of the Rosary.
>
> Formigao: *Did you ask her what she wanted?*
>
> Lúcia: Yes, I did.
>
> Formigão: *What did she say?*
>
> Lúcia: She told us to repent; not to offend our Lord who was greatly offended; to say the Rosary and to ask pardon for our sins; that the war (World War I) would end *today* and we would expect our soldiers (back) in a short while. [17]

World War I did not end that day, that week, that month.

This meant to Formigão that there now hung over Fátima—despite the great Miracle of the Sun—a huge impediment in getting the apparitions approved by the Church. Lúcia's statement created, noted De Marchi, "serious objections to the veracity of the apparitions." [18]

It was for this reason that Formigão headed back to Fátima to subject the visionaries to another severe inquest.

On October 19, Formigão again questioned Lúcia:

> Formigão: *On the 13th of this month Our Lady said that the war would finish on that same day? What were the words that she used?*
>
> Lúcia: She said *"The war will end today. You can expect the soldiers very shortly."*
>
> Formigão: *But listen, Lúcia, the war is still going on. The papers give news of battles after the 13th. How can you explain that if Our Lady said the war will end on that day?*
>
> Lúcia: I don't know; I only know what I heard her say, that the war would end on that day.
>
> Formigão: *Some people declare that they heard you say that Our Lady had said that the war would end shortly. Is that true?*
>
> Lúcia: I said exactly what Our Lady had said.[19]

On November 2, a final interview was conducted. [20] But it too failed to illicit any change in Lúcia's answers. For the most part, Jacinta was in agreement with Lúcia in her responses to Formigão's questions. But it would come to be seen that the children had already spoken that day of the apparition, and that Jacinta thought she might have heard something different than Lúcia concerning what Mary said about the war, and told her so.[21]

Formigão, despite his findings, continued to believe the children. He concluded they were exhausted, especially Lúcia. This fatigue, he wrote, affected their recall:

> Lúcia especially, on account of the severe ordeal by interrogation which she had undergone, was utterly worn out and excessive fatigue prevented her replying with the care and attention which we desired. Her answers were at times almost mechanical and she was frequently unable to recall certain circumstances of the apparitions which was not the case before October 13. [22]

At the official inquiry of the apparitions held on July 8, 1924, at the Asile de Vilar at Oporto, this matter still hung over Fátima like a storm cloud threatening to spoil an important day. [23]

But incredibly, Jacinta—passed away some five years by then— would come to the rescue of her beleaguered cousin, Lúcia. On this day, Lúcia came under strong questioning as to this very troubling and possibly irreconcilable issue arising out of Formigão's multiple interviews.

By then, though, she had come to accept that her memory had failed her during his questioning. But not because of exhaustion.

Lúcia told the commission:

> I think Our Lady added this: "*People must be converted. The war will end today and the soldiers can be expected soon.*" My cousin Jacinta, however, told me afterwards at home that Our Lady had said this: "*People must be converted. The war will end within a year.*" I was so preoccupied with all the petitions which people wanted me to lay before Our Lady that I could not give all my attention to her words. [24]

In lieu of everything considered, the commission accepted Lúcia's explanation.

As Formigão contended, it was concluded that the children were exhausted in body and mind on the evening of October 13. Thus, they were in no condition to reply with exactitude to the questions put to them by him.[25] It should be noted that Dr. Formigão was himself a member of the commission.

Although Jacinta maintained similar answers to Dr. Formigão in the follow up interviews of October 19 and November 2, it appears that she might have done so only because she did not want to be in conflict with Lúcia's version of what Mary said on October 13.

It was Lúcia who the Virgin Mary directly conversed with, not her or Francisco. And this— from the very beginning in Jacinta's eyes— made Lúcia more certain of what was said by Mary.[26]

During Formigão's final interview of November 2, Jacinta is on record as saying: "Lúcia heard better than I did what the Lady said." [27]

In the end, however, it was Jacinta who heard better what the Lady said.

Likewise, it would be Jacinta's memory, not Lúcia's, that would be the decisive factor in helping to resolve this critical issue with Fátima's investigatory panel.

And so, this brings us to something else that Jacinta reported that Mary said that day—a mysterious revelation only recently brought to the forefront with regards to the prophetic message of Fátima.

And once again, Jacinta and Lúcia do not share the same memory.

Perhaps because it was buried at the end of his book on Pope Benedict XVI, it went relatively unnoticed. But Vatican journalist and international author Antonio Socci divulged a somewhat startling disclosure in 2018 that casts a new light on the prophetic message of Fátima.

Virtually hidden in the closing chapters of his book, *The Secret of Benedict XVI: Is He Still the Pope?* (English edition), Socci unveils a heretofore unheralded, remarkably overlooked phrase from a message that the Virgin Mary delivered to the three little shepherds. The message is not found anywhere in the released writings of Lúcia—or for that matter in mainstream Fátima literature—but is present in the official documents.

Given by Mary on October 13,1917, the final apparition which climaxed that day with the Miracle of the Sun, this lost prophecy of Fátima —perhaps as much as any other Fátima message in word or vision—perfectly illustrates why Fátima is regarded as apocalyptic.[28]

Socci reveals that this issue came to his attention after a friend of his from Padua visited Fátima. While there in 2017, this person came upon a course being conducted at the shrine on the messages of Fátima. It was titled, "A Course on the Message of Fátima: The Triumph of Love in the Dramas of History." [29]

According to its sponsors, the seminar—offered also by the Diocese of Leira-Fátima [30]—was being given "for those that have not had the opportunity to encounter the message that, in the Cova da Iria, God gave to the people of our time through the Blessed Mother." [31]

It, in essence, was designed to present the fundamental elements of the apparitions at Fátima.

Subsequently, for those who enroll in the class, there also came a booklet that contained historical documentation on all of the apparitions at Fátima.

And it was in this booklet, that Socci discovered a surprising annotation.

Within the small manual, there is found in the final section a chapter on the apparition of October 13, 1917. This chapter detailed that day's events at Fátima.

On page 40, the text reads: [32]

And taking on a sadder appearance, the Blessed Mother said: "May they not offend any more Our Lord, who is so greatly offended! If the people will amend, the war will end, but if they do not amend, **the world will end.**" [33]

CHAPTER SIXTY-NINE

"IT'S THE END OF THE WORLD"

*"The end of all things is at hand. Therefore, be
serious and sober for prayers."*
—1 Peter 4:7

"A BRIEF BUT TERRIBLE PHRASE," WRITES ANTONIO SOCCI CON-cerning his initial impressions of the obscure Fátima message.[1] Indeed, the gravity of the disclosure is both surprising and significant. Socci expanded on his amazement of such a lost prophecy:

> I have never read this expression, which is so disturbing, in the official texts found in the bookstore. In fact, in the *Memorie di Suor Lúcia, Volume I* (Memoirs of Sister Lúcia) …the apparition of October 13,1917, is recounted twice, but this phrase is not there. It is the same in the other books and interviews of Sister Lúcia. Who therefore reported those words of the Blessed Mother? And when? Where is the source? Are they reliable words? [2]

The disarming words, Socci soon discovers, do not come from Sister Lúcia, but Jacinta. And they too were spoken by the Virgin Mary on October 13.

One more fact becomes known; their source is solid, virtually impeccable: the inimitable and resolute Dr. Manuel Formigão. [3][*]

The reliability of the disclosure is also resolved satisfactorily.

Socci finds that multiple, official Fátima documents validate Jacinta's words to Dr. Formigão, confirming what must be said is the obvious; the shrine would have not been using Jacinta's revelation in the course's manual if this matter had not been verified. Socci opines that this situation alone "guarantees its authenticity and reliability." [4]

Besides Formigão, two other sources concur with this revelation.

One is a letter of a Father Manuel Pereira da Silva, who was present at the October 13 apparition. Father da Silva writes of a friend named Father Antonio Pereira de Almeida, who reportedly both saw and heard the children speak about "the end of the world" if people "do not do penance and change their lives." [5]

The second source is a document that reports another interview with the children that same evening by a Father Jose Ferreira de Lacerda. In answer to Lacerda's 22nd question, Jacinta again states Mary said, "*If the people do not amend, the world will end.*" [6] Lucia answers the same question of Father Lacerda but without including this phrase. [7]

Furthermore, Socci is correct about Lúcia's writings, especially her memoirs, which directly recount these words of Mary on October 13. In two of Lúcia's memoirs, she echoes what Jacinta recalls, but gives different versions, neither of which mention the words "the world will end."

Writes Lúcia in her *Second Memoir* of 1937,

> Now, your excellency, here we are at the 13th of October. You already know all that happened on that day. Of all of the words spoken at this apparition, the ones most deeply engraved upon my heart were those of the request made by our heavenly mother: "*Do not offend God anymore, because He is already so much offended.*" [8]

---

[*]   In looking closely at the histories of Fátima and Medjugorje, an interesting observation can be ventured. Formigão appears to be to Fátima as what Laurentin is to Medjugorje. His role in providing the early documentation on the children and the apparition, his books and writings, his invaluable assistance in protecting the visionaries and Fátima from missteps by Church authorities, are all paralleled to a degree by the indispensable role of René Laurentin at Medjugorje.

Four years later, in her 1941 *Fourth Memoir*, Lúcia writes,

> They must amend their lives and ask forgiveness for their sins. Looking very sad, Our Lady said, *"Do not offend God anymore, because He is already so much offended."* [9]

In this second account, we find Lúcia mentions, like Jacinta, the need for people to amend their lives. She also recalls the sadness of Mary that is found in Jacinta's version, and repeats her claim that the Virgin said the Lord is offended and should not be further offended.

One person aware of Jacinta's words that Socci does not mention is Father John De Marchi.

In his book, *Fatima from the Beginning*, De Marchi also unveils Jacinta's shocking disclosure, however, he throws another twist into this story. Contrary to what Socci reports—that Formigão unearthed Jacinta's startling remark when he interviewed her at home on the evening of October 19th—De Marchi claims that this specific disclosure came during a talk between Jacinta and Dr. Formigão that took place while they were walking on a road together.

Writes De Marchi of Jacinta's prophetic statement:

> Can we then discover among the different affirmations of the children the nearest approach to the exact truth? We think that it lies in the declaration of Jacinta on the 19th of October when she and Dr. Formigão were quietly walking along the road from Aljustrel to Fátima. When asked what Our Lady had said on the last occasion she replied: *"I have come here to say that men must not offend Our Lord anymore because he is already very much offended, and if they amend their lives the war will end, and if not, **the world will end**."* [10]

In lieu of this extraordinary revelation, several questions are pertinent.

Did Mary actually say what Jacinta claims she heard on October 13 at Fátima?

If so, did the Virgin mean it literally?

And, did Lúcia—as occurred with her misunderstanding of Mary's words concerning the end of World War I—not hear Mary correctly or heard the alarming phrase but decided out of fear not to ever mention it?

There are conflicting realities to discern in forming an opinion on these questions. But the dust begins to clear when the matter is looked at as a whole.

First of all, if Jacinta's words were considered worthy enough to be contained in an official text of a course offered at the shrine of Fátima, then certainly their merit cannot be easily dismissed. In essence, to be included in such an official Fátima publication, her words would have had to have been considered not just factual in their occurrence, but truthful in their content.

This means there was a mindset arrived at by the administrators at Fátima that Jacinta had not misheard the Virgin. It also means the officials felt this message deserved to be made public, not censored or dismissed as a mistake.

It is interesting to note that when in Lisbon not long before she died, according to the letters of her caretaker, Madre Godinho, Jacinta said: "If men do not amend their lives, Our Lady will send the world a punishment worse than anything it has known before and it will come first to Spain."

Jacinta's words appear to be in reference to Communism's role in the Spanish Civil War. Godinho's letters also reveal that Jacinta spoke of "great events" which would be realized "about 1940." These revelations indicate that Mary disclosed much to Jacinta in their private meetings towards the end of her life and lend support to the credibility of her "end of the world" assertion.[11]

But, perhaps the message is meant to be interpreted in a different way.

Some may argue that if Mary said this, perhaps she meant "the end of the world" as we presently know it—the end of this age, this era— not the final Christian eschatological Parousia. If such is the case, it would certainly ease the entire matter, as this revelation would comfortably flow with Mary's unfulfilled prophecy at Fátima of a coming "era of peace."

This then brings us to Lúcia.

The decision at Fátima to include Jacinta's message in the text of the course's manual would have had to been undertaken with the reality that Jacinta's version of Mary's words that day differ from Lúcia's accounts in her two memoirs.

But considering all that Lúcia presented to the world over her lifetime in bringing to reality the message of Fátima, her account had to have been also seen as sincere and credible. She undoubtedly wrote what she believed she heard. Moreover, in looking at the history of her courageous life, it is clear she would not have shied away from the gravity of Jacinta's revelation if she believed it was what Mary truly said.

There is also the fact that Lúcia wrote her memoirs as a mature adult—schooled in the faith—versus the child that Jacinta was at the time that she spoke to Dr. Formigão and others. This further reinforces the trustworthiness of Lúcia's account.

All of this, however, is placed somewhat under question by the fact of Lúcia's admitted mistaken recall of Mary's words concerning the end of the war.

It is a mistake that occurred during the October 13 apparition that involved the same portion of Mary's message that day. Consequently, it cannot be completely out of the question that Lúcia perhaps did not hear correctly this part of the message too.

Lúcia testified before the investigative commission that Jacinta heard correctly that day with regards to Mary's words about the war, and that she had not. She also stated she was preoccupied with other concerns during the apparition and did not concentrate on what was being said by the Virgin: "I could not give all my attention to her words." [12] Moreover, Lúcia herself establishes this was the primary reason for hearing the message incorrectly, not exhaustion. [13]

Thus, one cannot help but wonder if this same inattention to Mary's words caused Lúcia to not clearly hear the Virgin's message concerning "the end of the world," the same as Jacinta did.

Two final observations are worthy of this entire matter.

There is the curious reply that Lúcia made to Professor William Thomas Walsh in 1946 when she said, "I cannot answer that question," in response to his asking if she had "any revelation about the end of the world."

And, there is also the now more relevant remark that she made to Father Fuentas in 1957 when she told him, "Father, the Most Holy Virgin did not say explicitly that we are coming to 'the end of the world,' but there are three reasons that I am led to believe it." [14]

These intriguing answers of Lúcia to Professor Walsh and Father Fuentas seem to flirt with Jacinta's claim that Mary warned about "the end of the world." Was there an unknown reason? Something subconscious?

Not many fretted much about "the end of the world" in1917.

Most likely because nuclear weapons did not exist to arouse such talk.

But Jacinta stated she heard these words come from the Virgin Mary. And Mary's words were delivered on the same day, at the same time, that the long awaited "sign" was given at Fátima—the day the crashing sun upon the crowd symbolically forewarned of an approaching future that held real "end of the world" concerns.[15]

This sign—the Miracle of the Sun—was the sign Mary had promised for months that she would give in order to prove she was appearing to the children at Fátima.Countless numbers had heard about the foretold harbinger. Tens of thousands came to see it. But, when the sign finally took place, it ended up causing untold numbers to anxiously cry out loud almost exactly what Jacinta claims Mary said just moments before: "It's the end of the world!"

One man's book chronicles this extraordinary fact.

In, *Meet the Witnesses*, John Haffert tried to recapture Fátima of October 13, 1917. Haffert interviewed in 1960 over 200 witnesses of the Miracle of the Sun. He documented what the people saw, felt, thought and said about it all.

Ironically—perhaps providentially—the testimonials sound as if coordinated to substantiate Jacinta's claim that Mary warned of "the end of the world."

"Even my mother grabbed me to her," explained Dominic Reis to Haffert, who was seventeen at the time and later moved to America. "She started to cry: "It's the end of the world." "What did you think of all of this?" Haffert asks Reis on his 1960 television show, "The people around me were saying that they thought it was the end of the world. They were very much afraid."[16]

Mrs. Guilhermina Lopez da Silva told Haffert no different: "My former neighbor, Dona Nazare Pinheiro, when she came back from Fátima that day, told me that she had seen the sun coming down like a spinning wheel, she was so frightened that she fell to her knees reciting the *Act of Contrition*, believing it to be indeed the end of the world."[17]

Antonio Antunes de Oliveira said the much the same: "I looked at the sun and saw it spinning like a disc, rolling on itself. I saw the people changing color. They were stained with colors of the rainbow. The sun seemed to fall down from the sky." Were you afraid, Haffert asks? "I was afraid the sun would fall down because the people said the world would end." [18]

Maria das Prazeres, a thirty-one-year-old widow, lived about an hour's walk from Fátima. She overheard the same talk throughout the crowd, "The people around me were crying: 'the world is going to end.'" [19]

Jose Joaquim da Silva was close enough to hear the visionaries talking before the apparition. During the Miracle of the Sun, Jose remembered clearly, one cry in the crowd stood out: "The persons around me were seeing something extraordinary. They cried out with fear. They were saying that the world was going to end." [20]

Manuel da Silva, who lived in Fátima, could not forget what he saw that day in the Cova da Irea during and after the Miracle of the Sun. The people, he recalled, were throwing themselves to their knees as the sun got closer and closer to the Earth. They were crying and praying aloud, and pleading with God. "Did you think it was it was the end of the world," asked Haffert. "Yes", Manuel answered.[21]

The significance of such a threatening reality is better understood today. This is because since the mid-1940s the planet has been living day to day under the shadow of nuclear annihilation. [22]

Antonio Socci, quoting Pope Paul VI's words to the French philosopher Jean Guitton, captured perfectly how an "end of the world" mindset took hold everywhere by the 1960s, even in the Vatican. [23]

"At times I reread the Gospel about the end times," Paul VI told Guitton as he weighed the nuclear tense days that were now at hand, "and I note that, at the moment, some signs of this end are emerging. Are we near to the end? This we will never know." [24]

Pope Paul VI would himself become one of the signs of the nuclear nightmare that descended upon the world. He died on August 6, 1978, the anniversary of the first atomic bomb dropped on Hiroshima.

Prophecy is not the future etched in stone.

Fulfilled prophecy depends on response—or a lack of it.

This is a critical point that deserves emphasis.

"To return to the 'prophecy' relayed by Jacinta", writes Socci, "we must consider that we are dealing with private revelations and that is a conditional prophecy, that is, it indicates what may happen if humanity does not repent and does not change its ways." [25]

In 2000, the Vatican illustrated this point in its theological commentary, *The Message of Fatima*. Pope John Paul II's survived assassination attempt—believed to be foreshown in the vision of a slain Pope in the third part of the Secret of Fátima—was seen as a terrible prophecy prevented through the intercession of the Virgin Mary. [26]

At Fátima, Mary announced her coming Triumph. But her prophetic words will only find fulfillment through the choices and actions of humanity. Lúcia always spoke of the future with this in mind.

At Medjugorje, the visionaries carefully instruct their listeners that tomorrow is conditional, both the bad and the good. It is as if to remind us that if a threatening prophesy can avoid fulfillment, there remains the possibility a welcomed prophesy might not find fulfillment.

In faith, the visionaries at Medjugorje maintain that what Mary has foretold to them will take place. But over the years, they often speak of the urgent need to repent, for mankind to reverse its ways, in order to insure a positive outcome.

"I believe Satan will be defeated," said Vicka, "only if we accept the Gospa's messages. If we convert and live like the Gospa teaches, then we will have a period of peace. It depends on us. If we do not change, it will not happen." [27]

Such "change" has yet to happen.

Some forty years after Mary arrived in Medjugorje—and more than a hundred years since Fátima—the world has still not heard the plea of its Mother.

Socci noted this reality:

"It would be difficult to affirm that such repentance has happened. It seems rather that the exact opposite has happened. Mankind has taken the opposite rout." [28]

During a talk given in Medjugorje in1986, a visiting priest told his listeners of Mary's call for conversion. "Our Lady once said," he remarked to a small audience, "you must understand; I have come to save you, to save your families, and to save the world." [29]

In 1997, ten years after this priest's exhortation, it did not sound like the Virgin Mary believed this effort was making much progress: "You are creating a world without God," she warned at the time. [30]

Ten years later, in 2008, things sounded no better. "This world," the Madonna of Medjugorje bemoaned, "is further from God every day..." [31]

Five years farther down the road, it looked as if the Virgin felt the situation was getting worse: "This world...is without joy in the heart, and is without a future." [32]

By the fall of 2020, her call sounded almost the same as when she began.

"God loves you and is sending me to save you, and the Earth on which you live." [33]

Will the world continue to ignore the prolonged appeal of the Queen of the Prophets?

Are the Ten Secrets the only remedy left to awaken people?

Will *even* they succeed?

Or could, as little Jacinta believed Mary said, "the end of the world" be approaching?

Author Jan Connell asked Mirjana this very question in the early 90s:

"Mirjana, many evangelists these days talk about the end of the world. Will the world survive the Secrets you know?"

"God's world is unchanging," replied Mirjana, "All passes away but God's will. Those who pray understand." [34]

Years ago, I sat down with Father Petar Ljubicic, the quiet, stoic friar that Mirjana chose to announce the Ten Secrets, and asked him some probing questions about the world's fragile future, the nuclear dangers that haunt mankind, and the seriousness of the message of Medjugorje.

What he said was hopeful, but Father Petar believed it all came down to using the time still being granted by God in a propitious way.

"We can't put it off," Ljubicic emphasized to me, "now is the most important time and we must use it. That's the main point. We can't put it off...for it will be too late!" [35]

CHAPTER SEVENTY

A CONVERSATION WITH FATHER PETAR LJUBICIC

"For there is nothing hidden that will not
become visible, and nothing
secret that will not be known and come to light."

—Lk 8:17

SURPRISINGLY TALL, INNATELY PLEASANT, AND FILLED WITH ZEAL for the Lord and his mission; if the Ten Secrets of Medjugorje are said to have some harshness in them, their chosen presenter certainly doesn't have any in him.

Swinging through the northeastern United States in early February of 2000, Father Petar Ljubicic presented a talk on a cold winter afternoon at Franciscan University in Steubenville, Ohio, and spent a couple of days, along with his translator, defrosting at our home in the suburbs of nearby Pittsburgh.

Ljubicic was a delight to be around; one found his humility came as natural as his smile and unpretentious graciousness. His prominent glasses made up as much of his persona as his brown Franciscan robe, and one can't imagine what he would be like without them.

Our children were blessed to meet him, and my wife and I were left with no doubts that he was the perfect ambassador for the message of Medjugorje. Love, peace—and that Croatian warmth one finds when in Medjugorje—all radiated from him in his short stay with us.

At the time, I was thinking about writing a small book on Medjugorje and publishing another edition of our internationally distributed

Marian newspaper—one featuring Medjugorje— that would be released the following year.

Of course, if one wanted to address the Ten Secrets in these endeavors, Father Ljubicic was as good a source as it gets, perhaps even better than the visionaries, since they were long known by then to be carefully policing their every word.

Ljubicic's openness and enthusiasm in discussing Medjugorje and the Secrets with me was a little surprising, for I thought by then that he would be fatigued by it all. But he wasn't. Moreover, his candor left me feeling that what he said would be edifying to the reader, for the interview did not come off as another repetitious dialogue on Medjugorje.

The following is the entire interview, published here for the first time. Ljubicic's translator, in my opinion, was excellent; he was unhesitating and clear in presenting my questions to Father Petar and confident in the delivery of Father's exact answers in return to me.

The interview was tape recorded and took place on the campus of Franciscan University in Steubenville, Ohio. It was conducted after Father Ljubicic had given a talk to the students that morning, which was followed by a lively question and answer session with them. [1]

Question: *Father, I thought we would begin with a prayer.*

Ljubicic: Good! Lord, we believe you are present with us here. You are always with us, if we know that or not. You are our Creator. You lead this world. Give us that gift-that grace-that we recognize You. That we come to know You. That we open ourselves to your Spirit. And that everything we do, we do for your greatness, and for our salvation. Bless all of our work in this time. Bless all of those we will be meeting tonight. Bless all of those who are opening themselves to you and want to come to know You. We pray too, Lord Jesus: save all people. You came to be our Saviour, to be the Saviour of everyone. Mary, Queen of Peace, pray for us. Pray for all those who look for your Son that they may find Him. Thank you for coming as our Mother and that you want to bring us Jesus, so that in Him we can have everything that we need. [Father Petar then led us in praying a Hail Mary and a Glory Be.]

Question: *Father, can you tell us a little bit about where you grew up in Croatia, you know, your early days, your childhood?*

Ljubicic: I was born in a little village about a hundred kilometers from Medjugorje.

Question: *What's the name of that village?*

Ljubicic: Prisoje. I am the first child of parents who waited a long time. My mother didn't have children for five years. She was in fear that she wouldn't have children at all. And she prayed to God and said to the Lord, "Lord if you give me children, I'll consecrate all of them to you. And that's how I was born. The first child of ten.

Question: *In what year?*

Ljubicic: 1946. I finished grade school there (Prisoje) and then went to the minor seminary. Then to Split and onto Dubrovnik. Then I began studying theology in Sarajevo and went onto finish in Germany. I became a priest in 1972. I'm a Franciscan priest 28 years now. What I know of myself is that I knew I wanted to be a priest. I had a strong desire to preach the "Good News."

Question: *Good! Father, I have a lot of documentation on the early days of Medjugorje. So, I'm not going to really ask much. We'll talk a little bit about that, but I just kind of would like to know what your thinking is today, of the memories of those first days. Our Lady continues to speak to us at Medjugorje. She said this is "a time of grace." Father, what is your opinion of the apparitions today after almost twenty years? And why are they continuing? Why are they still continuing? Why do you think these apparitions are still going on?*

Ljubicic: The world—and we—are in a great danger. There are horrible things around us. There is poverty and sickness. There's a great crisis in the world. And, its right for help to come from Heaven- to help get us out of this crisis. God wants all people to be saved. That is why I think these apparitions are a great help, for God to show us how much He loves us. That's why I see, that's the reason, that the apparitions have been lasting so long. Our Lady wants all people to realize they are God's children, that God loves them, and that He waits to see all of them in Heaven.

Question: *When did you first hear about the apparitions? They began on July 24,1981. How much longer after that did you first hear of these apparitions?*

Ljubicic: The first couple of days I heard of it. But I wasn't able to go right away.

Question: *When did you go?*

Ljubicic: I was helping the people for their Confirmation at my location. I went on the 27th of June. From the beginning. I believed that God is at work there especially when she (Mary) spoke to Vicka and Ivanka. My feeling was these children can't be lying. I went with a priest then. And then, in the first months, we heard confessions in the Church. Through these confessions, I truly came to see how open people were and how much confession meant to them.

Question: *When did you first meet Mirjana?*

Ljubicic: I saw her just like the other visionaries. I didn't know any of them before the apparitions started. I saw her after a couple of times there, and had a couple of words with her. But I wasn't especially tied to her. But she saw something in me, and I don't know what it was, but others told me she saw something in me and she wanted…she was going to pick me as the one to give the Secrets to. I thought that those people were joking with me. But, then she came to me and told me for me to get ready because I'll be the one to tell the world the Secrets when it comes to that time. The Secrets are about certain happenings that will happen, certain things that will happen at a certain time and certain places. She received something from Our Lady like a "sheet" —kind of like paper or cloth—but it's not something that looks…it looks sort of like…

Question: *Have you seen this?*

Ljubicic: No. I haven't. A few people have seen it. All of the Secrets are written on that sheet. Everything is written on it-what will happen and when. Ten days before the first Secret happens, the Secret will be able to be read. It will appear on that sheet. Now it's invisible. And then the Secrets…Every time another Secret comes-ten days before-it will show up on that sheet. The first two Secrets are warnings. The third Secret is of a Sign that will appear on Apparition Hill.

Question: *How did you feel when you first heard the news for sure that Mirjana said, "Yes—it's you." How did you feel personally inside? Did you feel worthy? Did you go into prayer?*

Ljubicic: On one side, I felt joy. On the other side, I felt a great responsibility. Why was it me? By what reason did she have? What does this mean?

Question: *Did you have any fear?*

Ljubicic: Maybe I'm not even conscious of the responsibility that is upon me. No. I don't fear it. It's something on the outside. It's almost like it doesn't *really* concern me. I won't *let it* affect me.

Question: *Now, to announce these Secrets—because you are the one that Mirjana chose—did you need to have your "Superior"—and this is just an example, because this would affect all the Franciscans throughout the world, since this a Franciscan parish—did you need to tell the Bishop or your superior about this, so that they weren't afraid of any embarrassment?*

Ljubicic: This is a private thing. I don't have to clear it with anyone.

Question: *Why must you fast to announce these Secrets?*

Ljubicic: That's what Our Lady asks for to Mirjana. Seven days of prayer and fasting.

Question: *So how will you fast? Just on bread and water those seven days?*

Ljubicic: Yes. Bread and water and then the three days before making public the Secrets, also.

Question: So there will be ten days that you'll fast?

Ljubicic; The three days before the Secrets, I don't have to fast. It's just the seven days before revealing. [2]

Question: *Ok.*

Ljubicic: Three days before the Secret, I tell the world.

Question: *Where will you reveal it at? In Medjugorje?*

Ljubicic: Yes, I'll tell it in Medjugorje.

Question: *And then, will you be available to answer questions when people ask? You know, there's going to be worldwide media there. Are you prepared? Do you understand the media is going to be coming?*

Ljubicic: I'll give Croatian television the monopoly of my interviews if the Communists aren't back in power at that time. [3]

Question: *I figure the media in the United States, the Western media, is going to converge on this.*

Ljubicic: I don't have to [do interviews].

Question; *Has Mirjana talked to you about what you are to do as far as announcing it?*

Ljubicic: Nothing special when it comes to this. Then, she'll tell me what I have to do.

Question: *Have you been closer to Mirjana since you began your involvement with the apparitions?*

Ljubicic: I was in Medjugorje for ten years. So, I saw her very often and often talked to her. What we are waiting for now is the time for the Secrets to be revealed, to come.

Question: *Father, do you remember the time that they saw the fire on the hill, not where the cross is on Mt. Krizevac, and when they went up there the fire was gone. Reportedly, Our Lady said that's a sign of the Great Sign. Do you remember anything about that? What can you tell me about that?*

Ljubicic: There was a great fire on "Apparition Hill", and at the time that the fire appeared on Apparition Hill, the Communists wouldn't allow people to go up there. But the fire appeared. This was at the beginning of the apparitions. There was also a sign in the sky written— "MIR", which means "peace"—between Apparition Hill and Mt. Krizevac. About five hundred people saw that.

Question: *Did you see that also?*

Ljubicic: I didn't see that.

Question: *There was reportedly another sign, or fire, on the hill where the Cross is too. Do you know about this?*

Ljubicic: I don't know of a fire but often times the cross on Mt. Krizevac used to disappear and there was a silhouette that appeared of the Blessed Mother, in place of the cross. Many people saw the silhouette of Our Lady.

Question: *The priest who sent the letter to the Pope, Father Tomislav Vlašić, do you know if he had ever gotten a response from the Pope, because that letter dealt with Mirjana and the Secrets?* [4]

Ljubicic: I don't know.

Question: *You don't know?*

Ljubicic: No.

Question: *Has Mirjana shared anything about these Secrets with you at all, other than what she has shared publicly?*

Ljubicic: [Author's note: I have at this time decided to not publish Fr. Ljubicic's response to this question, and to two follow-up questions related to his reply. My decision was based on the fact that his answer was both surprising and remarkable, and on the fact that I have been—and remain—unable to find anywhere else what he revealed to me. Consequently, I did not want this singular issue to distract and possibly overwhelm the paramount essence and greater purpose of this book.]

Question: *Fr. Rene Laurentin, Fr. Michael O'Carroll, Fr. Ljudevit Rupčić. They have all talked about some of the Secrets possibly containing a nuclear element. Do you think that's possible? Have you heard anything like that?*

Ljubicic: No. I don't know of anything of that.

Question: *Our Lady said that when she came to Medjugorje, that she came—and she said this on August 25, 1991— "I have come to fulfill the Secrets I began at Fátima." What is your feeling on what this means?*

Ljubicic: They say that Medjugorje is the fulfillment or a continuation of Fátima. Maybe this means the finishing off of what has started at Fátima. The realization of everything that Out Lady started there.

Question: *Well, she (Mary) promised an "Era of Peace" there. So, do you think that she's come to Medjugorje to bring people to the level of prayer that will finally cause this to happen?*

Ljubicic: What was the end of the question?

Question: *I think Our Lady at Fátima gave a plan of peace which was really a plan of prayer. In Medjugorje, is she trying to get more prayer to finally bring the "Era of Peace?"*

Ljubicic: It's conversion. The call to prayer and the Rosary. A call to a strong faith and for penance. Because in Fátima, she said, "Penance, penance, penance!"

Question: *Mirjana has said that the 9th and 10th Secrets are very serious. You talked today about the first thee Secrets. What can you tell us about the remaining Secrets?*

Ljubicic: I have asked [Mirjana] about the first three, and the others I haven't been too concerned with. When the time comes, I'll get more information about them.

Question: *Our Lady spoke about "a century of peace" in her message of December 25,1999. What do you think she means by "a century of peace"? That was the last message of the last year of the millennium.*

Ljubicic: In the future... this next century... a century of peace. I don't know how to explain it, except that all us are hoping, and want that peace to come.

Question: *Our Lady said, "The world must convert while there is still time." What do you think she means by that? Is it the time before the Secrets? The time before the end of the "period of grace"?*

Ljubicic: What that means is this. What man puts off for more and more-he then has less time to convert. Because we must always think about that. That if I don't use the graces that our Lord gives me now, then I am even less ready to accept the grace that God gives me tomorrow. Because I'm just putting it off more and more. That's what we see when they asked Jesus for a sign for the Jews to convert. Jesus told them that another sign won't be given to them. The prophet Jonah, he was in the stomach of a fish for three days and the Son of Man will be in a tomb for three days. This means he will die and rise again. And when Jesus rose, those who wanted to convert, converted. And those who didn't want to believe, paid the guards to say that the Apostles stole him while they were sleeping. They don't want to convert. Who doesn't convert now, there's little hope will convert tomorrow. Now is the most important time and we must use it. That's the main point. We can't put if off…for it will be too late.

Question: *One last question. Mirjana's has ten Secrets. The other five visionaries have nine or ten Secrets. Are they all the same Secrets? Or, are the other visionaries going to announce their own Secrets too?*

Ljubicic: None of the others have said anything. None of them have said anything but it has come to the conclusion that everyone has the Secret of the Sign that will appear on Apparition Hill. They don't talk about the Secrets amongst themselves so they don't know whether they are the same ones or not.

Question: *Ok. So, Mirjana is the only one who's going to announce her Secrets?*

Ljubicic: I don't know anything, except for Mirjana.

Question: *Thank you Father.*

Jacov Colo

"Many wonder what Our Lady is saying in these Secrets. What will happen? I think the most important thing is that we accept her messages. If we have accepted them and have God in our hearts and in our lives, we need worry about nothing."

Photo Credit: Pittsburgh Center for Peace

CHAPTER SEVENTY-ONE

"PRAY, PRAY, PRAY"

"Not as man sees does God see, because man sees the
appearance, but the Lord looks into the heart."
—1 Sm 16:7

Jacov Čolo is extremely reserved about the Secrets.
When asked if the world should convert now, however, he doesn't hesitate.

"That is why Mary is here." [1]

She has come, he then offers without prompting, to convert and reconcile the whole world.

Will such an unfathomable transformation of humanity happen?

"Yes." [2]

Since June 25, 1981, Jacov Čolo—who turned ten years old just three weeks before—has been receiving apparitions of the Virgin Mary.

The youngest of the six visionaries, the early photographs of him in ecstasy were fascinating. The sight of a child, totally consumed in mystical wonder, was not something one sees every day.

But in contrast to such a blessing at that young age, comes the fact his mother died just two years later and his father was nowhere to be found to raise him.

From the beginning, Jacov has gone out of his way to avoid publicity.

He does not desire attention and never will. To his credit, he shunned the role of the quasi-celebrity that the visions tried to cast upon him in the early years. And, he didn't relish speaking much back then. While he was the youngest of the six by far, he clearly identified his calling:

"My role is not as a prophet. I am a witness to the messages the Blessed Mother is bringing to the whole world here at Medjugorje." [3]

Consequently, there is little of substance on record from him during the early years of the apparitions, especially with regards to the Secrets, which he almost totally refused to speak about.

Father Milan Mikulich of Portland, Oregon—born just 25 miles from Medjugorje—was one of the first priests from America to visit Medjugorje. He headed there in November, 1981, just five months after the apparitions began.

By 1983, Mikulich had publish articles on the visions in the journal, *Orthodoxy of the Catholic Doctrine*. On February 6, 1984, the Franciscan interviewed little Jacov and asked him a couple of questions about the Secrets—which proved an exercise in futility.

> Mikulich: *Are the nature of these Secrets more positive or negative for us?*
>
> **Jacov:** There are some that are good, and some are not so good, but there are more that are good.
>
> Mikulich: *What number are good and bad?*
>
> **Jacov**: That I may not say. [4]

Almost ten years later, Jacov remained silent as ever concerning the Ten Secrets.

In the early 90s—around the time of the start of the war in the former Yugoslavia—I presented Jacov with a list of questions in an interview that took place in Medjugorje.

The following is an excerpt of that dialogue. It has not been published before:

> Question: *Our Lady said this is the last time she will ever appear. What does this mean?*
>
> **Jacov:** Our Lady didn't say this to me.

Question: *What does Mary ask of the world today that is different from the beginning of the apparitions?*

Jacov: During these twelve years, she is always calling us to pray. But she especially calls us to pray for peace.

Question: *It has been written that when the first Secret of Medjugorje is revealed, Satan's powers will be broken. Is this true? What is going to happen?*

Jacov: I don't want to talk about the Secrets.

Question: *Will all the Secrets take place before the end of this decade?*

Jacov: I don't want to talk about that.

Question: *Has Our Lady spoken to you about the Pope lately?*

Jacov: Not to me personally.

Question: *Is the world making progress in its conversion?*

Jacov: Our Lady never said anything about that. But she is very happy if people come here to pray.

Question: *Has Our Lady ever wept tears? Has she ever wept tears of blood?"*

Jacov: I have seen Our Lady weeping. But never tears of blood.

Question: *Is the Second Coming of Jesus part of the Secrets?*

Jacov: I don't know that.

Question: *Tell us about the Great Sign?*

Jacov: Our Lady promised us that she will leave a Great Sign on the Hill of Apparitions and we know when it will be.

Question; *It has been twelve years since the apparitions began. Has the Gospa indicated the apparitions may end soon?*

Jacov: I don't know anything about that.

Question: *Tell us about God's peace?*

Jacov: Our Lady invites us all the time to peace. This is the reason for her coming here. That is why she came here—for peace. First, she calls us to peace in our hearts. And, if we have peace in our hearts, we can start to pray and to love everybody. We can do anything!

Question: *Has Mary spoken to you of the Fátima message, the consecration of Russia and the era of peace that is promised the world?*

Jacov: Never.

Question: *Many say the Church and the Pope must suffer much. Has Mary spoken of this to you?*

Jacov: There is no message to me especially for this. One time, she gave a message for priests.

Question: *Has Mary spoken about abortion to you?*

Jacov: Not to me personally.

Question: *Did Our Lady and the prayers of her children bring about the fall of Communism?*

Jacov: She hasn't said anything special about this.

Question: *Jacov, the whole world has sunken into a deep darkness, and Mary is said to be concerned about the whole world as much as much as the war that is taking place here. What does all this mean to us? What should we do?*

Jacov: When Our Lady came twelve years ago, right at the beginning of the apparitions, she said we should pray for peace, and that her messages are not only messages for Medjugorje, they are messages for the whole world.

Question: *Is there anything special you would like to tell Americans?*

Jacov: I would just like to call all people to pray. Our Lady calls us for these twelve years to pray, especially now, for peace in our country. And, of course, for all the world. [5]

In reading between the lines, one begins to notice how the visionaries at Medjugorje often speak of the Ten Secrets as much as from what they know, as they do not know.

They understand what the Secrets contain. But they don't know the total breadth or outcome of the events. They don't know because it is unlikely it has been revealed to them.

At Fátima, the Virgin Mary did not tell the three shepherds all the details of the nightmare that World War II and Communism would launch upon the world. Mary did not tell them seventy million would die from the war. She did not explain how Communism would come to cover a third of the planet. She refrained from explaining the errors of Marxism, how nuclear weapons would come to haunt life on earth.

Similarly, the visionaries at Medjugorje are given only so much.

As a result, it appears they have adopted a careful, resigned approach. This helps them maintain a positive outlook and the optimism needed to speak about the Secrets.

Most of all, they understand it is senseless to worry.

At a Marian conference in the United States in November of 1997, Jacov revealed his steady approach with regards to the contents of the Secrets.

> I know many of you are wondering, "What are the Secrets?" I can't tell you what they are. Many wonder what Our Lady is saying in these Secrets. What will happen? I think the most important thing is that we accept her messages. If we have accepted them and have God in our hearts and in our lives, we need worry about nothing. We should not think or worry about the Secrets. [6]

Less than a year later, while visiting a friend, Marija Paulic, in Sunrise, Florida, Jacov Čolo received the surprise of his life. [7] As he waited in prayer for his daily apparition that afternoon in Marija's home, the Virgin suddenly appeared. She carried with her a major announcement for him.

Author and filmmaker Sean Bloomfield wrote about this significant day:

> The Virgin finally appeared—a blissful moment which, according to the six seers, is impossible to describe in earthly terms no matter how many times it happens. To Jacov's shock, however, the Blessed Mother announced that this would be her last regular apparition to him. No reason was given. She concluded their meeting by requesting that Jacov prepare to receive the Tenth and final Secret during a *special* apparition the following morning. [8]

The startling apparition that day proved pivotal in Jacov's life. As was the date it took place—September 11, 1998—the same date the terrorist attack on the United States would come three years later.

The following morning at 11:15 a.m., the Virgin returned to Jacov:

> When she came she greeted me as always with *'Praise be Jesus.'* While she was confiding the Tenth Secret to me, she was sad. Then with a gentle smile, she said to me: [9] *"...From today, I will not be appearing to you every day, but only on Christmas, the birthday of my Son. Do not be sad...Let people always see in you an example of how God acts on people and how God acts through them. I bless you with my motherly blessing and I thank you for having responded to my call."* [10]

The apparition ended at 11:45 a.m. According to a witness, Jacov was overwhelmed with grief, not just because of the Tenth Secret, [11] but because it meant the end to his daily apparitions. [12] A long and hard struggle for him would now begin. Not surprisingly, the news spread swiftly across the globe.

Bloomfield picks up the story:

> The parishioners and priests of Medjugorje, including the late Fr. Slavko, were taken aback when they received word of Jacov's last daily apparition occurring in the USA. They had always thought it would take place in Medjugorje, where Mirjana and Ivanka had each received the Tenth Secret.

No one, however, was more affected than Jacov. He became depressed and withdrawn for many months, struggling with the absence of seeing Our Lady every day. Eventually, through ardent prayer, he came to understand that he had to be like everyone else who did not see the Virgin every day. Anyone, he allotted, could be close to her praying with their hearts.

Three years later, the symbolic reason for the date and location of Jacov's last daily apparition became apparent on September 11, 2001. Al Qaeda terrorists crashed hijacked planes into the World Trade Center buildings and the Pentagon. The attacks killed thousands and ushered in a new era of war, fear and uncertainty. It would later be revealed that many of the terrorists who piloted the planes had spent a substantial amount of time in Florida, preparing for the attacks and attending flight schools. Their plans, in fact, were being hatched at the same time that Jacov received the Tenth Secret.

A beautiful statue of Our Lady sits in Marija Paulic's living room where Jacov received his Tenth Secret. The statue often weeps inexplicably leaving the believer to decipher what it could mean.

When asked in 2003 if the Secrets he has received have anything to do with 9/11 attacks and the problem of Islamic terrorism, Jacov paused and then reluctantly said, "I should not answer that." [13]

Jacov's last daily apparitions in the United States—and potential association with the coming 9/11 terrorist attacks in 2001—leaves much to ponder and more questions.

Are the Secrets associated with terrorism?

Does the United States play a role in some way?

Is the weeping statue in Florida a sign of something to come?

Most of all, one can't help but read between the lines of Jacov's reply concerning the Secrets and terrorism: "I should not answer that."

From his response, it seems as if there was a desire in his heart to affirm that the question was perhaps on the right track.

Jacov last reported he and the Virgin talked about the Secrets in 2010. After which, Mary said to him, "Pray, pray, pray." [14]

CHAPTER SEVENTY-TWO

"EVERYTHING WILL BE FINISHED IN MEDJUGORJE"

"Then the kingship and dominion and majesty
of all the kingdoms under the heavens
shall be given to the holy people of the Most High."
—Dn 7:27

A GROUP VISITING MEDJUGORJE ONE DAY WAS TOLD THE STORY OF the Secrets by a tour guide while visiting Podbrdo. The man explained the role of the Secrets, the celestial parchment with its cryptic writing, that the Secrets will be revealed three days in advance, and how each one will be announced by a priest.[1]

One pilgrim inquired whether the Secrets held benign or dangerous events, and whether or not it would be a good idea to be in Medjugorje at that time.

The guide just shrugged.

"Let's put it this way," he replied, "you'll get three days to get to Medjugorje—or three days to get out!"[2]

"Totally bad."

In stark imagery, Mirjana's choice of words to describe the Tenth Secret is disconcerting.

But when the source of her words—the complete, original interview from 1983 is examined—another picture emerges. In fact, this document reveals a profoundly clearer understanding. The Secrets of Medjugorje are not so much about physical chastisements—as at Fátima—as they are about God's intent to use the events in the Secrets to alter the direction of life on earth.

The Secrets, it becomes clear, are going to move the world and the Church into a new time. It is to be an era, wrote Wayne Weible, that has been foretold by saints and mystics for centuries.

"The Blessed Mother," wrote Weible, "has said at various times in her messages that once all the Secrets occur, the Earth will be purified. The Tenth Secret will bring this purification. The Ten Secrets are in reality a great merciful grace. They are not about punishments, but about love— holy, divine love." [3]

Of course—when seen in this light—this then changes the Secrets from something "totally bad" to totally good.

The Ten Secrets, the visionaries tell people, must be understood this way.

They are to transform the world for the better, while their harsher side can still be significantly lessened. [4] They will bring—as not just Weible, but others point out—a climax to the Virgin's intervention on Earth.

And, say both Mirjana and Ivanka, every human being will play a part in the unfolding of the Secrets.[5] The assertion that every person on Earth will play a role is significant. This is because it shows the proper approach to the great mystery of the Secrets.

Viewed by many as a string of intense events that God will permit to purify the world, the Secrets, as the visionaries came to realize, are actually a gift to mankind through the mercy of God. This is why every person will be involved.

In some manner, people will be confronted individually, as the Secrets come to pass, with a better understanding of the meaning of life on earth, of the presence of sin and evil in the world, and of their own reality of God. They then will see the need to respond appropriately.

Mirjana, perhaps differently than the other visionaries, came to a deeper understanding of this truth about the Secrets in an ironic way— through her prayerful quest to have the Seventh Secret mitigated by God.

She received the Seventh Secret in her parent's apartment in Sarajevo and its contents troubled her greatly. So, she asked Mary if it was possible for the Secret to be lessened. After the Virgin replied "Pray," she rallied family and friends to pray with sincere conviction and intensity for this intention over a period of eight months. [6]

Told the Secret was softened, the Virgin Mary then said to her, "But you must never ask such things again." [7] Mirjana explained to the friars that the Virgin said this to her because "God has His plan" for the conversion of the world—a plan that strongly "necessitates the unfolding of the Secrets." [8]

In these words, we discover that only in the unfolding of the Secrets— God's plan—will there come peace, the *era of peace* prophesied at Fátima. In essence, as Scripture holds, justice and peace will kiss. [9]

After this time comes to pass, will the Virgin Mary ever appear on Earth again?

This question stems from two of the messages Mary gave in the early days of the apparitions that stated these would be her "last apparitions." [10]

Over the years, five of the six visionaries are on record confirming that Mary did say this to them. As noted, some of them have emphasized that they are not certain what this means. Perhaps Vicka helps put this curious issue in the proper perspective:

> For me, the message that the Madonna has given is very clear: this is the last time that she will be present here on Earth *in the way* she has been present at Medjugorje for such a long period of time. I heard her speak those words, because I was the one who received them personally.[11]

> But that does not mean we should be troubled or frightened. After all, God rules the world. He is present in this world and we must always be ready for His will. If these then must be the last apparitions of Mary, it means that God wants it so… and we must recognize this will, this love of God, as always, with joy and serenity.[12]

Marija, in a revealing interview with *Caritas of Birmingham* on February 24, 2004, shed more light on this mystery:

Question: *Marija, several of the visionaries on various occasions said that these are the last apparitions on Earth. What did Our Lady say to you about this?*

Marija: Our Lady said from the beginning that these are the last apparitions on Earth in which we can hear Our Lady, touch Our Lady, speak with Our Lady; where we can pray with Our Lady; apparitions where it is possible that we 'have' Our Lady. In other apparitions—people have spiritual experiences—but not like us, the six visionaries in Medjugorje; where Our Lady speaks to us. This is really the last and special grace. Normally, one person may see Our Lady [like Bernadette or St. Catherine of the Miraculous Medal, who also touched Our Lady.] But here, six visionaries are a number which is very credible. But this is the last where we can touch Our Lady, speak to her, etc., in this way. [13]

Question: *Also, is it after the Secrets are revealed, will there not be any need for the apparitions?*

Marija: Our Lady is with us so she can give us knowledge of the Secrets and to help us through the Secrets. After the Secrets are realized, Our Lady will not need to come anymore. [14]

Mirjana is found to be in agreement with this assertion. She told author Jan Connell that she received the same understanding, "She (Mary) said after the Secrets are realized she won't need to come again." [15]

On January 2, 2008, Father Livio Fanzaga interviewed Vicka on *Radio Maria Italia*. The two talked about the Ten Secrets, the end of the Virgin Mary's apparitions, and how people need to use the remaining time of grace for conversion.

Fanzaga: *When the time of the Secrets comes, the Fourth through the Tenth Secrets—Secrets which are evidently very difficult, it means that in any event, in the time of the*

Secrets—we will always have the Sign of Our Lady which will comfort us. But you also said the last time, last year, that during the time of the Ten Secrets, one of the visionaries will still have the daily apparitions of the Madonna.

Vicka: Yes, it is certain, it is something I repeat now. We will see who it is. There is still me, Marija, and Ivan. Afterwards, we will see who the Madonna has chosen, who of us three remains with the apparitions. Or, maybe it will be someone else that the Madonna has chosen.

Fanzaga: *So you, Ivan, and Marija, one of you three. Someone said something to Mirjana like, "Vicka said that during the time of the Ten Secrets there will be one visionary who will continue to have the daily apparitions" but Mirjana said that she didn't know anything about this. What does that mean? That this was told personally to you by the Madonna?*

Vicka: Yes, the Madonna told me personally. Afterwards, we shall see. The Madonna didn't say, "Vicka, it will be you." Now, we just wait to see who it will be. She said that when the time comes, to the person who will continue to have the apparitions, she will explain every 'how and what' to that person.

Fanzaga: *The Madonna also spoke of false prophets, "Those who make catastrophic predictions are false prophets. They say: in that particular year, on that particular day, there will be a catastrophe. I have always said that the chastisements will come if the world does not convert. Therefore, I invite everyone to conversion. Everything depends on your conversion." So, now I ask you, if we convert, will there still be the Ten Secrets, or no?*

Vicka: No, no. The Ten Secrets will take place for sure. The Madonna has already given them. She has described nine of them to me and now I am waiting for the last one. I can only tell you about the Secret which is the Sign on the mountain which I already spoke about and now I only want to say this about the Seventh Secret: The Madonna said that half of the Seventh Secret has been cancelled because of our prayers. She recommends that we continue praying because with our prayers we can lessen other Secrets.

Fanzaga: *So, in essence, the discourse is this: the Madonna urges us to convert, she tells us not to wait for the Sign on the mountain, and in any event, "All the Secrets I have confided will be realized and also the visible Sign will be made manifest. When the visible Sign comes, for many it will already be too late (December 23, 1982)." What does that mean?*

Vicka: The Madonna did not explain why it will be "too late" and I did not ask. She only said that we are now living "in a time of grace."

Fanzaga: *So it is important to convert before the Sign is manifest?*

Vicka: Every day the Madonna calls us to conversion, to the conversion of hearts, you understand? And twenty-seven and a half years later the Madonna is still among us and our hearts are still too closed, too distant. I don't know. I don't know what it could be, but "too late" could be right.

Fanzaga: *You have always said, and also the Madonna of Medjugorje, that when we talk about the Ten Secrets, we must do so always inviting everyone to hope. In fact, in one of the Madonna's messages, she said, "We must never take away hope." The Madonna didn't come to frighten us but to call us back to responsibility and to conversion in a context which always inspires hope. The Madonna even once said, in the first year of the apparitions: "For the Christian, there is only one attitude with regard to the future: hope of salvation." (June 10, 1982)*

Vicka: Well, you see, the Madonna is here among us to save our souls, truly; she did not come in order to boss us, 'do this, do that or else'—she is here to occupy herself with our souls, she says she is the Mother of everyone and loves everyone. "You do not know how much I love you; If you knew you would cry for joy." We are still a long way away from her joy—you understand? All those things, simple things—she always gives us hope. And then you read her face which she shows you—it is so sad! But she gives you so much joy! She lifts you up, she gives you strength! And this is so encouraging.

Fanzaga: *In all my radio broadcasts, I try to underline this fact too, that the Ten Secrets are a "time of grace" because it is in this time that the power of the Evil One will be conquered by the Madonna. The Madonna is here as "Queen."*

Vicka: The Madonna many times has told us that the Evil One knows where we are the weakest and he looks for empty places not dedicated to God that he can inhabit and he has found many places among the young and in families, breaking them up. The Evil One does a lot of things like this you know. But the Madonna has said that when we feel peace in our hearts and joy and tranquility, then you can see very clearly that this comes from God. If, instead, there is fear in our hearts and we feel disturbed, then we must be very careful, because this doesn't come from God. We must be able to distinguish immediately that which comes from God and that which does not, we need to keep awake and persevere with making the change in our lives so that we can keep the Evil One at bay.

Fanzaga: *This means that if we stay close to the Madonna we will feel joy in our hearts and we will not feel anxious fear about our future. In fact, the Madonna once said that he who prays has no fear about the future.*

Vicka: Certainly, he who prays has no fear about the future and he who fasts has no fear of the Evil One. We have a great grace—we are living in "a time of grace." I have never heard a word come from the Madonna that created fear—she always gives you hope. She gives joy and tranquility. You can see that the Madonna and her Son defeat all that evil that exists. We shouldn't have any fear but we must follow what They want. He who follows the Madonna and lives her messages has no motive for being afraid. He who has fear, is afraid even of himself—he must do something to start himself going in the right direction and then he can follow the messages of the Madonna.

Fanzaga: *Power is of God, evil is dangerous and Satan is strong. Anxious fear for the future certainly is not befitting of believers, but today there exists a worrying concern which is not to be undervalued. On two occasions, John Paul II affirmed that the world was in danger of destroying itself. The seer Ivan declared in a video broadcast that the Madonna had said the very same thing to him, that is, that the world was at risk of destroying itself. So, it's not wise to be too superficial. In one message, the Madonna said, "I will pray to my Son to not punish the world, but I beg you: convert yourselves. You cannot imagine what will happen and neither that which God the Father will send upon the Earth. For this, I repeat, convert yourselves. Renounce everything. Do penance (April 25, 1983)." Here one sees how hope and concern can coexist.*

Vicka: The Madonna has been with us all these many years precisely so that we might come near to God and convert ourselves. As a mother, the Madonna does not want to lose even one of her children. She comes from Heaven to the Earth to save us, but we are still too far away from her. But she never forces anyone. She never says, "You must convert, you must do this and that." No, she doesn't force anyone. She says to each one of us, "*My son, do what your heart tells you to do.*" And, she waits for us like a mother. She waits for everyone. She does all that she can do, but apparently our hearts are still very, very hard.[16]

The Secrets of Medjugorje are secret.

Needless to say, they will remain so until otherwise.

After forty years, expecting to learn something new at this time is folly. It is also unwise to place any trust in those who offer whimsical predictions as to when the Secrets will unfold. Theologians say that God is often found to move slow and with a divine precision that dictates the schedule of His plan.

The present age of the visionaries at Medjugorje, seen in this light, is not a determining factor with the coming of the Secrets, even though they have all indicated that the Secrets will unfold in their lifetimes.

Many key biblical characters were quite old when some important events found in Scripture took place in their lives. It should also be pointed out that Sister Lúcia was seventy-seven years old when Pope

John II performed the 1984 consecration; she was ninety-three years of age when the third part of the Secret of Fátima was at last revealed in 2000.

With this in mind, Father Slavko Barbarić says people should try to temper their curiosity about the arrival time of the Secrets:

> The language of Secrets is like a mother speaking to a child… the words refer to something other than what the words themselves suggest…So don't be a "literalist" about the Secrets. The rule here is "the less you know, the better."
>
> I've had discussions with some people who've written books about Medjugorje…Some of these have spoken about the "delay of the Secrets." I've said to them, "Look, who's late, in your view? God? Well, surely He knows His ways. And what precisely do you think you know, in any case, about the Secrets, or about some sort of timetable? Hypothetically?"
>
> No, it's a great mistake to focus on these things. After all, the very reason they're called Secrets is to make it clear that no one except the visionaries knows anything about them at all.[17]

One point about the Secrets of Medjugorje may be surprising to some.

God has protected the visionaries from disclosing too much about them. In fact, asserts Mirjana, the visionaries are "incapable" of divulging the Secrets.[18]

Furthermore, stresses Ivanka, although the Secrets hold some challenging moments, they are not what the Virgin Mary wants anyone to be thinking about, "The Blessed Mother told us never to focus on bad things. She told us to stay focused on God—on His love for us and on the future He has planned for us." [19]

This proper focus, emphasizes Father Barbarić, is the *true* message of Medjugorje, the real purpose behind the Secrets.

"If you knew something about the Secrets," asks Barbarić hypothetically, "would it make it easier to say fifteen decades of the Rosary each day? I think not. Would it make it easier to fast two days a week? No. Well, these things—prayer, fasting, making peace, going to confession— this is the real message, the heart of the message of Medjugorje!" [20]

The biggest secret has been revealed, adds Barbarić, "Peace is possible, it depends on you!" [21]

The visionaries agree.

If people are to focus on anything with regard to the future and the Secrets, it's the Virgin Mary's promise of a welcomed outcome in the end—that the world is going to change for the better, and peace is to come.

Mary's many conversations with the visionaries about the future of the Church is the greatest testament to this truth.[22] Ivan, in a talk given in Australia in 2003, spoke passionatly of the Church of the future:

> She wants to lift up this weary world, the weary families, the weary Church. She desires to lift us up and strengthen us. She says, "Dear children, if you be strong, the Church will be strong. If you are weak, the Church will be weak. You are the living Church. Dear children, this world, this mankind, has hope and has a future. But you have to begin to change. You have to come back to God." [23] *

"What the Madonna started in Fátima," Mirjana is often heard to say, "She will finish in Medjugorje." [24]

At the annual National Conference on Medjugorje at Notre Dame University on May 30, 2004, Mirjana participated in a question and answer forum that saw her give perhaps the best explanation of this prophetic promise.

"From what I know about Fátima," Mirjana told the large gathering there that day, "everything continues in Medjugorje. What she said in Fátima—what she started—I think through these Ten Secrets, it will be finished in Medjugorje. Her heart will win—she will win the part in this war. Everything will be finished in Medjugorje." [25]

Mirjana's reasoning is thought provoking. This is because she has—whether she meant to or not—connected the Secrets of Fátima with the Secrets of Medjugorje.

---

*   The future of the Church, according to Ivan, is part of the Ten Secrets. In his book, *Fear of Fire*, author Michael Brown writes: "At Medjugorje, one reputed seer, Ivan Dragecevic, when asked if when the Blessed Mother's Secrets unfold there will be a great trial for the Church, said, "Yes, absolutely so." (*Fear of Fire*, p. 229)

The Virgin Mary said at Medjugorje in1991 that she has come to fulfill "the Secrets she began at Fátima," now we see from Mirjana's words that this will only be accomplished "through the Secrets" of Medjugorje.

"I cannot divulge much more about the contents of the Secrets," wrote Mirjana about the coming end of an age of evil in her book, *My Heart Will Triumph*, "but I can say this—Our Lady is planning to change the world. She did not come to announce our destruction; she came to save us, and with her Son, she will triumph over evil." [26]

"I'm not personally called to interpret the Secrets of Fátima, but Our Lady affirmed in Medjugorje that both apparitions are connected to the Triumph of her Heart. [27]

Yes, Fatima and Medjugorje are " both" connected to the Triumph of Mary's Immaculate Heart. And, this truth is becoming a more visible reality.

As with so many historical events related to Fatima that mysteriously fall on the anniversary date—May 13—of the Virgin's first apparition there, the proof that Mary's Triumph is unfolding in the world through Medjugorje is often identifiable in the same manner.

This happened again in 2022.

On June 24, 2022—the anniversary date of Mary's first apparition at Medjugorje in 1981—the United States Supreme Court overturned *Roe vs. Wade*, the 1973 case which legalized abortion in the United States.

For decades, the faithful had beseeched the intercession of the Virgin to help end this holocaust, and now it could be said that she had heard their anguished cry.

But what made the announcement of this court decision even more attributable to Mary was the fact that June 24th is not just the anniversary date of Medjugorje. It holds another intimate connection to the issue at hand—one even more target specific.

June 24th is also the date of the annual feast in the Catholic Church of the birth of John the Baptist, who as an "unborn" baby "leapt in the womb" (Lk 1:41) upon hearing the Virgin Mary greet his mother, Elizabeth.[28] **

**   The June 24 date of the Supreme Court ruling in the overturning of *Roe vs Wade* holds further significance in the spiritual war at hand. It is the same date as the official founding of Freemasonry. On June 24, 1717, four lodges came together in London to form the Premier Grand Lodge of England, which became the Grand Lodge of England, the first Masonic Grand Lodge in history. Freemasonry—whose principles are still considered irreconcilable with the teachings of the Catholic Church (See *Quaesitum est*, November 26, 1983, by Joseph Cardinal Ratzinger)—is understood to have exercised considerable influence on the U.S. Supreme Court over the years. (See *Behind the Lodge Door* by Paul Fisher and *Hope of the Wicked* by Ted Flynn)

PART VI

THE TRIUMPH OF THE CHURCH

"Being a lover of freedom, when the revolution came in Germany, I looked to the universities to defend it, knowing that they had always boasted of their devotion to the case of truth; but no, the universities immediately were silenced.

Then I looked to the great editors of the newspapers, whose flaming editorials in days gone by had proclaimed their love of freedom. But they, like the universities were silenced in a few short weeks.

Only the Church stood squarely across the path of Hitler's campaign for suppressing truth. I had never any special interest in the Church before, but now I feel a great affection and admiration because the Church alone has had the courage and persistence to stand for intellectual truth and moral freedom.

I am forced thus to confess, that what I once despised, I now praise unreservedly."

—Albert Einstein,
Time Magazine,
December 23, 1940

CHAPTER SEVENTY-THREE

THE TRAGEDY OF FATIMA

"As he drew near, he saw the city and wept over it, saying, "If you only knew what makes for peace—but now it is hidden from your eyes."
—Lk 19:41-43

"I OFFER FOR THE HOLY FATHER...FOR THE HOLY FATHER...FOR THE Holy Father." [1]

United to the end with Pope John Paul II, the last words of one of the towering greats of the twentieth century helped shine the brightest of lights on an alliance that did much to help combat the evil of their times.

As Fátima's Sister Lúcia's soul slipped into eternity, she held tightly in her hands a communique received from the one she had just devoted her final sacrifice.

"I was informed of the state of your health." wrote the Holy Father to the 97-year-old Lúcia. "I come to affirm our affectionate union with a special remembrance of your personal union with God..." [2]

United to John Paul II in the most intimate of ways until the very end, God would ensure that the world would also never forget Lúcia's union with Fátima.

It had been the 13th of May that the Virgin Mary first came to her, and it would be on the 13th of October that the apparitions to her and her cousins, Jacinta and Francisco, would conclude. Now, in 2005, Lúcia would depart for paradise on the most appropriate of days, the 13th of February.

"Let me go to the house of the Father," uttered Pope John Paul II in Polish about six hours before passing away at his apartment in the Apostolic Palace on April 2, 2005, less than two months after the death of Sister Lúcia. ³

The 84-year-old Pontiff spoke his last words, as thousands prayed for him outside in St. Peter's Square.⁴

Like Sister Lúcia, God would mark Pope John Paul II's passing in an indelible way.

He died on the eve of Divine Mercy Sunday, a feast that he established on April 30, 2000.

The feast is based on the pre-World War II revelations (1934-1938) of Sister Maria Faustina Kowalska, a fellow Pole whom he canonized the same day he instituted the feast.⁵

This special feast, celebrated on the Octave of Easter—the Sunday after Easter Sunday—was requested by Christ for a reason. Sister Faustina, in her acclaimed book, *Divine Mercy in My Soul*, writes,

"Jesus looked at me and said, 'Souls perish in spite of My bitter passion. I am giving them that last hope of salvation; that is, the feast of My mercy. If they will not adore My mercy, they will perish for all eternity. Secretary of My mercy, write, tell souls about this great mercy of Mine…'" ⁶

"It is God, who is rich in mercy." ⁷

This was the truth that Pope John Paul II tried to illuminate in his encyclical letter, *Dives in Misericordia*, which brought to life the mercy of the Father, as seen in Christ:

> The truth, revealed in Christ, about God the "Father of Mercies," enables us to see Him as particularly close to man especially when man is suffering, when he is under threat at the very heart of his existence and dignity. ⁸

Through Christ, the Father bathed the twentieth century in this mercy, for truly man's very existence had come under threat.

It was a special grace that He delivered to the world through chosen souls, such as Sister Lúcia and Pope John Paul II—two saints that personally weathered this threat of the times in order to accomplish their mission.

Lúcia—hidden away in convents in Spain and Portugal—lived through World War I, the Spanish Flu pandemic, the Spanish Civil War, World War II, and the almost half-century long Cold War. Patiently, persistently, she struggled in the service of the Lord. For over eighty years, Lúcia fought to bring to light the mercy that Fátima offered humanity.

Pope John Paul II lost his family at a young age, endured the horrors of the Nazi occupation, and found himself somewhat a prisoner in his own land after Communism consumed Poland. Proving in many eyes to be the foretold *spark* that Faustina announced would prepare the world for the coming of Christ, [9] he courageously emerged from behind the Iron Curtain to become the first non-Italian to ascend to the Chair of Peter in 455 years.

Together, the Carmelite nun and the Polish pontiff strived to bring the Cold War to a close, helping a merciful God to save the world from nuclear ruin and ready it for the great changes that are to be coming in the world as promised at Fátima.

But like Moses, who was not permitted to cross the Jordan River and enter into the Land of Milk and Honey, like David who was denied his heart's desire to build a magnificent temple to the Lord, neither Lúcia nor John Paul II would live to see these changes.

"The Immaculate Heart will triumph...the Fátima week has not ended," said Lúcia, but the aging visionary added, "I may not get to see out the whole week." [10]

"Mary appeared to the three children at Fátima in Portugal and spoke to them the words that now, at the end of this century, seem to be close to their fulfillment," wrote John Paul II.[11] But, the end of the 20th century came and went without that fulfillment.

Like Lúcia, it would be a crossing the Polish Pope was not to see.

It can be said that both these giants of their day had simply aged beyond the anointed time that God reserved for the manifestation of His victory.

But this would invalidate the Virgin Mary's most perfect timing for coming to Fátima.

Mary had come at that moment in time, she would say after previewing to the visionaries the perilous future the world could face, "to prevent this"—to prevent the horrors that would befall the 20th century, and to bring her "Triumph."

Indeed, Mary came to Fátima to rescue humanity from self-destruction, to halt the Marxist, atheistic errors of Russia before they could spread, to reunite the Church, not to prognosticate the dire times at hand and then do nothing about it.

"The Virgin said that the wars—all of the wars that have occurred—could have been avoided through prayer and sacrifice," revealed Sister Lúcia. "This is the reason Our Lady asked for the Communion of Reparation and for the Consecration (of Russia)." [12]

Lúcia's words confirmed what many lament.

Fátima, despite the unprecedented amount of good it has brought upon the world, carries a most tragic part to its history. World War II, Communism, the spread of Russia's errors, and the age of nuclear annihilation ultimately were not prevented.

In their widely-circulated book, *Our Lady of Fatima: Prophecies of Tragedy or Hope?* authors Antonio Borelli and John Spann explored the history of Fátima. They concluded:

"Objectivity demands that we recognize that the goal established by Our Lady of Fátima has not been reached and that the conditions set down by her to prevent the chastisement have not been met." [13]

Brother Michael of the Holy Trinity—known more by his French name, Frère Michel de la Sainte Trinité—was born in 1948. He studied at Sorbonne, where he received a Master's degree, and then at the Institute Catholique of Paris, where he earned a Licentiate in Philosophy. [14]

In 1970, he entered the Community of the Brothers of the Sacred Heart, in France. [15] There, he authored an acclaimed four volume study on Fátima, *The Whole Truth About Fatima*, first published in French in 1983 and then in English in 1989. [16]

In this impressive work, Brother Michael meticulously outlined the history of Fátima, including the human errors that impeded its fulfillment. He called to task by name those he identified as being chiefly responsible, either by commission or omission, whether innocently or deliberately.

Brother Michael explicitly bemoaned the lack of response by the Church in the late 1920s and early 1930s, when both Jesus and Mary insisted to Lúcia that the time had come for the Church to halt what was emerging out of Russia: "It is in this tragic context of 1929, when Stalin was bringing the bloody terror and horrors of the Gulag to their height, that the great divine promise must be understood: It was at this time, Lúcia writes, that 'Our Lord had informed me that the moment had come for me to let the Holy Church know His desire for the consecration of Russia and His promise to convert it.'" [17]

But, Brother Michael emphasizes, nothing was done. [18]

The French scholar noted that, as the 1930s unfolded, more and more horrific reports were leaking out of Russia—yet, what was needed to bring the fulfillment of Fátima was still not procured. Multiple letters from Sister Lúcia in 1936 would even insist on the consecration, yet it did not transpire.[19] Finally, the Bishop of Leiria, Dom José Alves Correia da Silva, agreed to send a personal memorandum to the Holy See, presenting an urgent request. On the 8th of April, the Holy See acknowledged it, but still no response was issued.[20]

What followed were further attempts from Lúcia and others in the early 1940s and beyond, but to no avail.[21] And what resulted thereafter included World War II, the dawn of nuclear weapons, and a third of the world succumbing to Communism.

Certainly, one can argue that it was not to be expected of the Church to act on the word of a visionary. Nevertheless, the tragedy of Fátima was at hand.

It was, in fact, a tragedy Christ Himself warned Sister Lúcia of in 1931, in a most extraordinary way.

In August of 1931, Sister Lúcia, who was experiencing health problems at the time, was sent to Rianjo, a tiny maritime village near Pontevedra. There, she was ordered by her superiors to rest. [22]

In the chapel of her convent, Lúcia reported she received a vision of Christ, who spoke to her about the unfulfillment of Mary's requests for the consecration of Russia and the spread of the First Saturday Communion of Reparation devotion.

He then told her that this was leading to a tragedy in the Church and the world similar to one that took place centuries before.[23] In a letter to her Bishop, dated August 29, 1931, Lúcia revealed what the Lord said to her that day:

> My confessor orders me to inform Your Excellency of what took place a little while ago between the Good Lord and myself: As I was asking God for the conversion of Russia, Spain, and Portugal, it seems to me that His Divine Majesty said to me: "...Make it known to My ministers that given they follow the example of the King of France in delaying the execution of my request, that they will follow him into misfortune. It will never be too late to have recourse to Jesus and Mary." [24]

In a 1936 letter to her spiritual director, Father Bernardo Goncalves, Lúcia revealed more of what the Lord told her would be the severest of consequences for the delays:

> They did not wish to heed my request. Like the King of France, they will repent, but it will be too late. Russia will have already spread her errors throughout the world, provoking wars, and persecutions of the Church; the Holy Father will have much to suffer.[25]

In His words to Sister Lúcia, Christ chose to use an example from the history of the Church in France to illustrate what can occur when divine requests go unfulfilled.

In 1689, Saint Margaret Mary Alacoque—the recipient from Christ of the Sacred Heart Revelations—delivered a message from Jesus to King Louis XIV.

Jesus promised that if the King would fulfill four requests, he would have a blessed life and eternal salvation, in addition to victory over his enemies. Those requests included:

- To have engraved on all royal flags the Sacred Heart of Jesus.

- To build a chapel in Christs' honor where He would receive homage from the royal court.
- To consecrate himself to the Sacred Heart.
- To use his influence and authority with the Holy See in Rome to get a Mass in honor of the Sacred Heart of Jesus. [26]

King Louis XIV chose to do nothing.

One hundred years later, this led directly to the imprisonment of his successor (King Louis XVI), to his eventual beheading along with his wife and sister, and to the anti-religious French Revolution which France has never recovered from to this day. [27]

As Jesus had warned Lúcia in 1931, a parallel chain of tragic events unfolded throughout the twentieth century because of the failure to fulfill Mary's two requests.

Now, in our time, another desperate plea is heard from the Queen of Peace in Medjugorje.

But is the world listening?

Will there come enough change before the time of grace is over?

Or, will a renewed mankind come with another note of regret for what could have been, if only Mary's call at Medjugorje was taken *more* to heart?

"Our Lady is trying to save the world," bemoaned Vicka during an address to a crowd of pilgrims, "but we never include ourselves in that responsibility. We usually push it away from ourselves and leave it to someone else. We need to ask: who is responsible for that world we are talking of? Our Lady says the world is not about walls. The world is not about fields or woods. The world is us. We need to start working on ourselves, start to change ourselves and the people around us. This is the way that we can change the world...We start from there, otherwise nothing will change." [28]

CHAPTER SEVENTY-FOUR

THE TRAGEDY OF MEDJUGORJE?

"I in turn will choose ruthless treatment for them and bring upon them what they fear. Because, when I called, no one answered, when I spoke, no one listened."

—Is 66:4

"I LISTENED TO THE VISIONARY MARIJA WITNESSING TO HER EXPErience and I realized that some of the words she was saying from the balcony of her tiny house in front of about a hundred people were spoken directly to me. When I listened to one of Mary's messages, I realized the words spoke directly to my heart, giving me the solution to a problem I was carrying around like a heavy burden.

"Many of you are probably thinking: he is pathetic. That is what I used to think whenever I bumped into one of the many Medjugorje devotees. Reason cannot grasp this phenomenon—at least mine can't. Reason is inclined to say that Medjugorje relies on coincidence, autosuggestion, and emotionalism.

"But these explanations no longer satisfy me. If you have experienced what I experienced, you would understand why. In fact, the point of my trip to Medjugorje has been precisely this: to discover that there is a mysterious spiritual dimension that is so far beyond our understanding that it cannot be limited by our mind. So, the only words that can be useful are these: *'Come and see.'* In Medjugorje, a new world could be unveiled inside you. At least, that is what happened to me." [1]

Paola Gambi, a prominent and influential Italian journalist and broadcaster, wrote these words after visiting Medjugorje in 2010. He says he was not converted at Medjugorje. He was completely remade—heart, mind and soul.

He stepped out of the "Kingdom of Reason", he would later write, and into the "Empire of the Heart."

Gambi had been a leading opponent of Medjugorje in Italy.[2]

What happened to Gambi?

What happened to Margnelli and Sullivan?

What happened to Ellis, Klaus, and Falana?

Why have sixty thousand priests journeyed to this sanctuary of surprises?

Why have over five hundred Bishops and Cardinals answered a call within?

Why have millions of confessions been heard in the little village?

Why have hundreds of healings and tens of thousands of spiritual renaissances occurred there, and throughout the world?

The reason—for those who believe in the Madonna of Medjugorje—is easy to understand. The heavenly graces being showered there are unprecedented in the history of the Church. Many, like Paola Gambi, say this grace needs to be seized upon while it remains available.

For a small number of opponents of the visions, though, it's another story.

The apparitions are a hoax, a fraud, a deceit of the Devil.

They are mass hallucination, pseudo-mysticism, auto-suggestion.

Epilepsy affects one of the visionaries.

These were some of the charges leveled over the years.

Not against Medjugorje.

Against Fátima.[3]

Perhaps surprisingly, though the apparitions at Fátima were approved by the Church in 1930, such comments continued well into the 1940s and 1950s—even in the Vatican. During that period, a Belgian Jesuit theologian and adviser to Pope Pius XII is seen to have been particularly hard on Fátima, questioning Lucia's memory and writing that she may have engaged in "unconscious fabrication." [4]

Similar criticisms were used—either individually or collectively—to confront Medjugorje, especially in light of the fact that the apparitions have not been approved.

It was reported, however, that the third investigative body set up in 1987 by Cardinal Joseph Ratzinger—known as the *Yugoslav Bishops' Conference on Medjugorje*—did actually arrive in favor of the apparitions, but did not want to oppose the local bishop.

Antonio Gaspari, a reporter for *Inside the Vatican*, recounted the commission's positive conclusion:

> In May 1987, the Yugoslav Bishops' Conference nominated Bishop Franjo Komarica, Auxillary Bishop of Banja Luka, ex-professor of theology at Sarajevo University, and youngest bishop in the Yugoslav episcopate, as President of the *Medjugorje Inquiry Commission*. By mid- 1988, the Commission was reported to have terminated its work with a positive judgment on the apparitions. However, not wishing to directly contradict Bishop Zanic, the group continued its proceedings at a snail's pace, hoping that the pilgrimages would diminish and disappear. [5]

When the Medjugorje commission finally released a report in 1990—although its members were supportive of the visions—the document was ambiguous and continued to reflect its worries over the local bishop. Wrote Gaspari:

> Ex-Archbishop of Split Frane Franic stated in an interview with the Italian daily *Corriere della Sera*, on January 15, 1991, that only the ferocious opposition of Bishop Zanic, who refused to budge on his own verdict, had impeded a positive decision on the Medjugorje apparitions: "The bishops do not wish to humiliate Monsignor Zanic," Franic stated, "And when it was brought to his attention that his opposition was unfounded, he began to cry and shout, and the bishops finally stopped arguing." Cardinal Franjo Kuharic, Archbishop of Zagreb and President of the Yugoslav Bishops' Conference, in an interview with Croatian public television on December

23,1990, said that the Yugoslav Bishops' Conference including himself, "has a positive opinion of Medjugorje events." [6]

In 2014, the Vatican's Ruini Commission is said to have again found the events at Medjugorje to be supernatural, but limited this finding to the first seven apparitions. It is a conclusion, however, not yet officially sanctioned by the Church, as the Vatican has issued no official judgment on the visions at this time.

Acccording to theologians, the "primary reason" as to why Medjugorje remains unapproved is simple: the Church does not traditionally render definitive decisions on reported supernatural events until the event has concluded—unless it discovers pertinent reasons to rule in the negative.

Moreover, it is the Church's responsibility to permit reported supernatural events, such as Medjugorje, to continue to unfold. This allows it to discover if they *are* of God, to examine the "fruits."

Father Rene Laurentin often tried to explain the many difficulties surrounding today's Church investigations of reported supernatural events.

"The abstract principle that is always given in such situations as Medjugorje is 'wait for the judgement of the Church' before you get interested in these apparitions and go on pilgrimages," wrote Laurentin concerning misconceptions surrounding the Church's investigative process. "This is in error, because if nobody went to these places, where the heavenly manifest itself, then the Church would have no reason to investigate or pronounce a judgement. Judgements made at Guadalupe, Pontmain, Fátima, Beauraing and Banneux came about because crowds gathered and the good fruits of these events showed themselves." [7]

As at Fátima, a small but motivated smattering of individuals spearheaded opposition to Medjugorje in the early years.

"A handful of hardline opponents, who instead of proof in support of their positions, voiced their clichés," wrote Dr. Ljudevit Rupčić and Dr. Viktor Nuić in their 2002 review of the opponents of Medjugorje. [8]

Indeed, the writings of a few shaped most of the criticism. Several books—reviewed objectively by professional, secular writers, as well as theologians during their own investigations of Medjugorje—drew an almost consensus opinion as to their literary and scholarly merit.

Regardless of the predisposed prejudice against the apparitions,[9] the books were judged to lack objectivity and professionalism,[10] to follow unsound reasoning,[11] and to be poorly written.[12]

The books attempted to mislead readers with half-truths and personal conclusions,[13] often using falsification, distortion, ridicule, slander, and the deletion of relevant information in attempting to support arguments.[14] Moreover, when one closely examines the pedigree of those who attacked the events at Medjugorje vesus those who defended the visions, it is baffling how so much traction was made by the detactors.

Over the first fifteen years, a small number of critics continued to attack Medjugorje. But, by the late 1990s, much of the opposition started to wane. "All of the controversies," wrote Laurentin in his thirteenth book on Medjugorje, "seemed to have disappeared." [15]

There is an irony here that must be noted.

A few of the early—and to this day for that matter—opponents of Medjugorje were Marian devotees. Consequently, it's disheartening to imagine how much they contributed to what could someday be "the tragedy of Medjugorje."[16]

As with Fátima, all that could have been at Medjugorje may never be. The "Empire of the Heart", as Paola Gambi came to understand, has had to struggle to broaden its reign.

In the summer of 2017, Polish Archbishop Henryk Hoser—who inspected Medjugorje for the Pope—expressed optimism that this would soon lead to more.

"The Congregation for the Doctrine of the Faith has passed all documentation to the Secretariat of State," the Jesuit magazine *America* reported Hoser stated. "Everything suggests the apparitions will be accepted before the year ends." [17]

While this has yet to occcur, in May of 2018, Hoser was entrusted on a special mission by the Holy See to acquire more in-depth knowledge of the situation in Medjugorje. In May of 2019, upon his recommendations, Church sanctioned pilgrimages to Medjugorje were authorized.
[18] According to the Catholic News Agency (CNA), the pilgrimages were

permitted as "an acknowledgement of the abundant fruits of grace that come from Medjugorje and to promote those good fruits." [19]

That same year, Cardinal Angelo De Donatis—Papal Vicar General of the Diocese of Rome—presided over the opening Mass for over 50,000 youth from around the world gathered in Medjugorje for the annual youth festival there. Archbishop Salvatore Fisichella, President of the Pontifical Council for Promoting New Evangelization, and Archbishop Jose Carbello, Secretary of the Vatican's Congregation for Orders, presided over the closing Mass.

Archbishop Luigi Pezzuto, the Vatican's nuncio to Bosnia-Hercegovina, was also part of the special delegation. In addition, five hundred priests concelebrated the Mass. [20] One year later, on August 1, 2020, Archbishop Pezzuto issued a message to the same annual gathering at Medjugorje on behalf of the Holy Father.

Pezzuto stated:

> The Church needs your momentum, your intuitions, your faith. In the race for the Gospel, inspired by this festival, I entrust you to the intercession of the Blessed Virgin Mary, invoking the light and power of the Holy Spirit, so that you may be the witnesses of Christ. [21]

By 2020, an estimated 50 million are said to have traveled to Medjugorje.[22]

Millions more have heard the story of the many wonders there.

Yet, as occurred in Fátima, there is a sense that what the Virgin Mary has come to accomplish in Medjugorje is falling short.

This is apparent when the world of today is seen in the light of Mary's time of visitation in Herzegovina. While technology connects people now in an unprecedented way, it's not any more apparent that Medjugorje's appeal is truly making a dent in the conscience of humanity at large. As Mirjana Soldo notes towards the end of her book, the apparitions are in risk of being "taken for granted." [23]

With Catholics alone, the call of Medjugorje is falling on deaf ears. The message has been ignored by many—or because Medjugorje is not approved—a great number pay it no mind. Likewise, it is undeniable that the Catholic press has been even *more* aggressive in its attempts to ignore or mischaracterize the apparitions' message than the secular news outlets. [24] Like with Fátima, an influential few may someday be seen to blame for so much free and abundant grace going unclaimed.

But every day is still one more opportunity to wake the world up, one more chance to encourage people to take notice of the Virgin Mary's incomparable call at this time in history— her "call of the ages" to humanity to come back to God—while, she adds, there is still time.

CHAPTER SEVENTY-FIVE

CALL OF THE AGES

*"Fear not, for I have redeemed you; I have
called you by name: you are mine."*

—Is 43:1

"I T IS VITAL EVERYONE BECOME AWARE NOW," ASSERTS VICKA. WE
need, the oldest of the Medjugorje visionaries says, to take the
Virgin Mary's words to our friends and relatives, to anyone and everyone who will listen:

"The Blessed Mother wants these messages known by all the people
on Earth...Ask those who hear them to tell others, to share, to help the
Blessed Mother." [1]

Vicka sounds the right alarm.

But there is an important consideration that must be recognized
and taken into account.

The faithful are not required by the Church to follow such messages
as those emanating from Medjugorje—or even the message of Fátima—
regardless of their reported urgency.

Such heavenly pronouncements are not official Church teachings,
and no matter how serious they sound—no matter if they are approved
by the Church—*no one* is required to put their faith in them.

Here in lies, some Church officials claim, a difficult situation.

It is a perplexity that especially surrounds Marian apparitions of the
past century and their prophecies, which often strike a dire tone.

The Catholic Church teaches that public revelation concluded with the death of the last Apostle, St. John.

Known as Divine Revelation, the Church teaches that these revelations are given to people for all ages, and they are preserved in Sacred Scripture and Sacred Tradition. They make up the foundation of the Church, its doctrines and dogmas. [2]

However, there are also what are known as private revelations.

These are messages from God that are given to individuals to inspire them to live more faithfully, and ultimately to draw people closer to Him. But these revelations, even when sanctioned by the Church, have no binding resolution upon the faithful, as explained in the *Catechism of the Catholic Church* (N.67).

Fátima, however, brought into question the level of importance to be given private revelations. This is because the Secret of Fátima came to involve the decisions of a series of popes over time that had far-reaching effects on the Church, and in the eyes of many, the world. [3]

"It was the first time that the Church has officially recognized the historic incisiveness of a prophecy whose source was an apparition of the Virgin. A prophecy that Cardinal Sodano has defined as 'the greatest of modern times,'" writes Fátima author Renzo Allegri.[4]

Indeed, Pope John Paul II was adamant about the importance of Fátima. He resoundly held that Fátima "imposes an obligation on the Church" and is "not optional." It is one, asserted the Holy Father, that "commands the Church"; one that is "more current and even more urgent than before." [5]

Fátima also came to be viewed by many as eschatological in make-up and, therefore, of great significance to the Church's mission. Pope Paul VI was the first to truly see this new reality emerging in regards to Fátima, the Church, and the times at hand. Paul believed the falling sun at Fátima was *not only* a warning of a possible nuclear war if mankind refused to change, but more. The Miracle of the Sun, he believed, conjured up images of the end times as revealed in Scripture. [6]

"It was eschatological in the sense that it was like a repletion or an annunciation of a scene at the end of time for all humanity, assembled together," the Holy Father told the French philosopher, Jean Guitton, on May 28, 1967, which Guitton quoted in *Journal de ma Vie*, one of his fifty books. [7]

A number of Church hierarchy echoed the Pope's view in the 1970s.

Cardinal Ciappi, Papal Theologian, revealed that he shared Paul VI's conviction at the International Seminar at Fátima in 1971: "The apocalyptical imagery of the woman glowing with the sun's light may well be applied to the person of the Mother of God, seen by the beloved Apostle as crowned with twelve stars and at the same time crying as she labored in birth." [8]

The Cardinal Patriarch of Lisbon, Antonio Ribeiro, concurred at the 8th Fátima Congress at Kevelaer, Germany, on September 18, 1977: "Fátima appears like a great supernatural light. It is God who reveals Himself with the impressive majesty of Sinai." [9]

In 1979, Abbé André Richard, the French philosopher, was even more expansive on the eschatological significance of Fátima.

> Fátima is an intervention to change the march of the entire caravan of mankind...How can any of us fail to be conscious of Our Lady appearing in the sky, reminding us of the Great Sign in Chapters 11 and 12 of the *Apocalypse*? How can any of us consider Fátima to be less than the presentation of that apocalyptic message of Our Lady, dressed with the sun and announcing her triumph over the dragon? [10]

The implications of such thinking are clear.

Fátima, and consequently its contemporary peer, Medjugorje, appear to be much too important, much too critical to our present times—an age when a nuclear sword of Damocles hangs over the world—to be casually framed as *private revelation* and cast aside.

Father Louis Kondor, the noted theologian and vice-postulator of the Causes of Francisco and Jacinta, expressed his conviction concerning this conundrum. In the 1975 July-August edition of the Fátima newsletter, *Seers of Fátima*, Kondor wrote,

"In view of this similarity, which seems to be a telling fulfillment of *Apocalypse* 12, who would venture any longer to speak of a 'private revelation'? Fátima is an eschatological Sign that reveals the saving victory of the 12th chapter of the *Apocalypse*." [11]

Kondor argued that though not Divine Revelation, some private revelations hold great importance to the will of God for His people as

He guides them through history. Fátima, he pointed out, is the model for this emerging truth: [12]

> We can consider Fátima as the great eschatological Sign given by God in our times, so that we will not deserve the rebuke that Our Lord made to the Jews: "You know how to read the face of the sky, but you cannot read the sign of the times (Mt 16:4)." Fátima is the sign of the times. [13]

Father Paul Kramer echoes Kondor's argument that Fátima is not merely private revelation:

> The (Fátima) message was conveyed in a manner that is unique in Church history, and its form and content are also unique. This puts it in a class by itself; it can't be relegated to the broad category of "private revelations." Ignoring this particular message is impossible for Catholics, and may also be unwise for everyone else on this troubled planet. [14]

"Do you believe in Fátima?" Pope Pius XII asked a group of American pilgrims in Rome led by Father Leo Goode in late August 1958, just months before he died.

When they answered in the affirmative, the Holy Father asked, "Will you do what Our Lady asked at Fátima?"

On hearing their assent, Pius stated, "If we are to have peace, we must obey the request made at Fátima. The time for doubting Fátima is long past. It is now time to take action." [15]

Not only was it time to take action, wrote acclaimed Fátima author Francis Johnston, but it was time for the Church to take action on a large, national scale. Fátima needed, he believed, to be seen as a matter of "privileged priority" by the Church. [16]

"Why are we not hearing," Johnston bemoaned in his book, *Fatima, the Great Sign*, "the message of Fátima proclaimed loudly and clearly, as the world lurches deeper into the black mire of iniquity and the threat of a global holocaust?" [17]

To a great degree, this need *was* recognized and acted upon on a grand scale in Portugal in the late 1920s and early 1930s. [18]

On May 13, 1931, all of the country's bishops responded to the call of Fátima and, before 300,000 gathered at the Cova da Iria, consecrated the nation to the Immaculate Heart of Mary.[19] They would repeat the consecration in 1938 and 1940. Their bold action, Sister Lúcia noted, kept Portugal out of World War II: "In this horrible war, Portugal will be spared because of the national consecration to the Immaculate Heart of Mary made by the Bishops." [20]

But within Portugal, the consecrations did much more.

Over the next ten years, a Catholic renaissance unfolded in the country like never before seen. Seminaries throughout the nation were filled with hundreds of students, new schools opened, and religious communities abounded. By 1941, there were 3,815 professed nuns.

Moreover, a renewal of Christian life spread throughout the nation in every way. Spiritual retreats, pilgrimages, Catholic radio shows—along with a complete political and social transformation—swept through Portugal.[21]

Cardinal Manuel Gonçalves Cerejeira—who did not at first believe in Fátima and called it a "bad counterfeit of Lourdes"—told a French journalist in 1942: [22] "In the whole country (Portugal), you can hardly manage to gather a handful of enemies of religion." [23]

In Poland, the Church also took action on a national level.

According to Grzegorz Gorny and Janusz Rosikon, in their book, *Fatima Mysteries*, it was no accident that the collapse of Communism began there. The Catholic Church's position in Poland, they write, was better than in any other nation under Communist rule in Eastern Europe. Its Marian devotion was very strong. [24] And, the authors' note, because of its former primate—Cardinal August Hlond—Poland had long before taken the urgency of Fátima to heart. [25]

While in exile during World War II, Hlond had witnessed Pope Pius XII consecrate the world in 1942 to the Immaculate Heart of Mary. [26] From this, he took very seriously Pius's call for other bishops to do the same in their countries. Consequently, he made up his mind to do just that when he returned to Poland. [27]

Poland, after Portugal, became the first country to practice the First Saturdays' devotion and to be consecrated to the Immaculate Heart of Mary, which was decided by the episcopate during Advent of 1946, and then performed in three stages. [28]

The first stage of the consecration was done in all the parishes together on July 7, 1946. All of the bishops then performed the consecration in their own diocese on August 15. Finally, on September 8, the Polish episcopate gathered together in Częstochowa and performed the consecration in the presence of pilgrims from all over Poland.[29] Over one million assembled in the town that day, delivering a great shock to the Communist authorities.[30]

Over the years, the Polish Church actively disseminated literature about Fátima throughout the country, to the point that the name *Fátima* became censored by the government. [31]

All of this can be seen to be the mystical seeds of what led to the fall of Communism in 1989, and subsequently throughout Eastern Europe and beyond.

Cardinal August Hlond—on his deathbed many years later—relayed to Cardinal Wyszyński a prophetic vision of the Virgin battling the fiery dragon of *The Book of the Revelation.* "Pray!" Hlond told Wyszyński, "difficult times are coming, difficult times. Call out! Victory, when it comes, will be the victory of Our Blessed Mother!" [32]

Today, at Medjugorje, a similar reality surfaces.

Action needs to be taken.

The times at hand, as the visionary Vicka bewailed, are urgent, serious and grave.

While the apparitions at Medjugorje remain to be sanctioned by the Church, Medjugorje's call to peace, prayer, penance, and conversion— as with the call at Fátima—is in desperate need to be widely, more aggressively proclaimed to a world still submerged in the "Errors of Russia," in Marxist atheism.

Moreover, an important question arises.

When the events contained in the First Secret of Medjugorje come to pass—after having been publicly announced just days before at

Medjugorje—will the Church be prepared to voice an urgent call to the faithful? To the nations? To all mankind?

Indeed, after the First Secret unfolds—before the Great Sign appears on Mt. Podbrdo—there will be a need for the Church to act swiftly and boldly to seize the moment at hand.

It will need to lead as perhaps it has never done before in its history.

Such a moment must become the great return to God of pilgrim humanity—the penultimate fulfillment of the parable of the Prodigal Son—through the loving guidance of the Lord's One, Holy, Catholic, and Apostolic Church on Earth.

In 1917, Fátima sounded this call of universal metanoia.

Now, the Madonna of Medjugorje—the Queen of Peace—comes to see it brought to fruition with all the nations, her last call to an age of sin and atheism now in its twilight. [33]

"One day a lady from Vietnam came up to me and told me how hard it was when she was forced to leave her home during the war," said Father Jozo Zovko in a homily he delivered at St. Elijah Church in Tihaljina, a village about twenty miles from Medjugorje.

"As she was leaving, she turned and gave one last look. In her yard, she saw the statue of Mary still sitting there. It seemed to say to her, 'Don't leave me behind.' She went back for it.

"Don't leave Mary behind here in Medjugorje.

"Let her be the Mother of your family, your parish, your community, of your nation." [34]

CHAPTER SEVENTY-SIX

THE TWILIGHT OF MARXISM

"May the stars of its twilight be blackened; may it look for daylight, but have none, nor gaze on the eyes of the dawn."
—Job 3:9

WHEN ARCHAEOLOGISTS DISCOVERED A BUST OF THE EGYPTIAN Pharaoh Akhenaten in the sands of the North African desert in the nineteenth century, no one knew at first who he was.

It was eventually discovered why. Around 1350 B.C., Pharaoh Amenhotep IV, who changed his name to Akhenaten, decreed all the gods in Egypt were false, except for Aten, the god of the sun.

His monotheistic society—believed to be the first in history— was not appreciated by his successors. Just fifty years after his death, Akhenaten's name—along with the name of his wife, Nefertiti—vanished from every inch of Egypt. Even buildings that bore his memory were razed. All evidence of his reign was expunged.

To the world, Akhenaten never existed.

Akhenaten would not be the last to suffer such a fate. In the past century alone, such purges have unfolded in Germany, China, the Soviet Union, North Korea and elsewhere. Rulers run astray in the eyes of their people and are served the ultimate punishment for their perceived indiscretions; any and all remembrance of their very existence is stricken from the records.

More recently, this practice took hold again in Egypt.

In April of 2011, an Egyptian court ordered the removal of former President Hosni Mubarak's name, and that of his wife Suzanne, from all public facilities and institutions. The legacy of the ousted president's twenty-nine years in power, almost like Akhenaten some three thousand years' prior, was totally annulled.

Mubarak's name was deleted from subway stations, highways, streets, libraries, hospitals, public squares and over five hundred schools. Posters, portraits, murals, paintings, statues, coins, and even wax masks that bared his image, were destroyed.[1]

"He should disappear from everything," said Abden Nasser Hassan, a driver for an oil company. "He was the worst thing in our history." [2]

Some say the worst thing in history is God.

Similarly, efforts to purge Him—to rid His presence and memory—have been undertaken, no different than those found when former leaders become, you may say, persona non grata.

Whether by force, deceit, or the persuasive powers of reason, God has been often shown the door.

His legacy, swept under the rug.

For the most part, the ancient Greeks and Romans were tolerant of other gods, as long as one practiced venerating the principal deities. In essence, serving your own gods was permitted, one just needed to be sure those of the state were not dishonored.

It was not until the monotheism of the Jews and then the Christians—who denied all pagan gods *en masse* and refused to worship them—that the Roman Empire's tolerance for individual gods became an issue. Quite simply, the refusal to esteem Rome's gods made by association the Jewish and Christian God unacceptable in return.

From then on, it was war.

Rome realized rather quickly that the coming of Christ's Kingdom on Earth could not succeed without the seed of the Kingdom taking hold. That seed, they knew, lived in the early Christians.

The solution? Eliminate the Christians.

From the reign of Trajan (AD 98-117) until Constantine (AD 306-337), every Roman Emperor sought to eradicate Christianity. Writing of life in second century Rome, theologian and philosopher, Titus Flavius Clemens—known today as St. Clement of Alexandria—chronicled the purging: "Many martyrs are daily burned, crucified and beheaded before our eyes."

Diocletian, who ruled right before Constantine, was tireless in his effort. Recalled Eusebius, the great Christian historian of the fourth century: "Royal edicts were published everywhere commanding that the churches be leveled to the ground and the Scriptures destroyed by fire." Diocletian is said to have boasted at one point, "I have completely exterminated the Christian writings from the face of the earth."

From the time of Rome through the French Revolution, the war against Christianity and the Church saw little respite. Voltaire, the renowned French infidel who died in 1778, predicted—like Diocletian—that within one hundred years Christianity and its Bible would be summarily vanished.

Ironically, within those hundred years, the very printing press Voltaire used to publish his antichristian propaganda ended up being used to print bibles, his home itself their store house.

But nothing that came before could compare with what Marxism would bring upon the world. Atheism, the rejection of any God, is the masked face of Marxist philosophy. More than that, Marxists understood, and Communism demonstrated, that to oppose God, without rooting out religion, was futile.

True Marxists believe that only in the abolition of religion can man be free. For them, the existence of religion indicates an incomplete emancipation. A full liberation, therefore, requires the state to suppress religion and annihlate it—to erase it not just from the present and the future, but from the past.

Once all religion is gone, God will vanish with it.

To put an end to God, though, would take much more than removing His name and tearing down churches.

As the Soviets would learn, where just one person believes, God is alive.

On an unremarkable hill, almost seven and a half miles north of the city of Siauliai in northern Lithuania, sits a sacred site going back almost two centuries.

In 1831, a series of military clashes with the Russian Empire occurred in the region. Known as the "November Uprising," the battles resulted in heavy casualties for Lithuania.

In tribute to their fallen, relatives began planting crosses and crucifixes on a hill there named Jurgaicai. Soon there were hundreds of crosses. By 1850, the site was known as Kryziu Kalnas—the Hill of Crosses.[3]

Ten years later, the rather insignificant local affair was found to have emerged into something beyond the ordinary. The hill was now the destination of people from all over Lithuania who desired to plant a cross for a deceased loved one.

Around 1863, after the Tsarist authorities outlawed the leaving of crosses on roadsides and in cemeteries as part of their onslaught on religion, even more people began to journey to Kryziu Kalnas to erect a tribute. Their actions were intended to also serve as a sign of determination to resist the government.

It wasn't until the era of the Soviets, however, and their state war on God, that the hill revealed its hidden destiny.

By then, Kryziu Kalnas was off limits. More than that, it was a dangerous place to visit. But although designated as a restricted site by the Communist leadership, it was not in the minds of the faithful. Hundreds of new crosses continued to accumulate on the hill with more popping up every day.

In April of 1961, a late-night Communist operation saw the site bulldozed, the wooden crosses burned, and any salvaged metal taken away as scrap to be melted down. This left the hill bare, cleansed of all the memorials.

Soon, though, the crosses returned under the cover of darkness.

Four more times the Soviets leveled and purged Kryziu Kalnas—all to no avail. Despite KGB agents constantly patrolling the area, the crosses arose in the hundreds, then the thousands, then in the tens of thousands.[4]

Since Lithuania gained independence in 1991, a forest of metal and wooden crosses has found a home on the hill, along with icons of saints, statues, dangling rosaries, and photographs of the fallen or missing.

Today, it's estimated that more than two hundred thousand densely-packed crosses of all shapes and sizes cover an almost one-and-a-half-mile stretch of the area.

The Hill of Crosses has become a Christian pilgrimage and international tourist site. The holy mound was even visited by Pope John Paul II, who celebrated Mass there in 1993.

In Lithuania, God is alive.

Fátima and Medjugorje bring the same realization.

God is alive.

He cannot be removed from His creation—not from a hill, or a nation or the hearts of His people. Nor can His memory be stricken from the past or His presence barred from the future.

Not then and not now.

The errors of Russia—the atheistic pandemic of Marxist sophism that came and intoxicated humanity—is what, in the end, has no home, is bereft a future.

God, though silent and unseen, remains at work. "My Father is at work until now, so I am at work," Jesus asserted. Mary's words at Fátima, "In the end, my Immaculate Heart will triumph," testify again to this truth.

As in times before, God was speaking in human history.

This time, though, He was even more unequivocal than in the past. If He was not welcomed, it was because the eyes and ears of His people were not open. "They look", Christ said, "but do not see, and listen but do not hear."

But it is a fact, the onslaught of Marxism on the world was different.

Its purveyors had a plan to not only erase God, but to mute Him.

Marxism was designed for *only* the voice of man to be heard—a voice that offers nothing except the false gods and idols of this world. [5]

But we must ask our self: how did this happen?

Marxism, in the militant form of Communism, appeared as a protest in the face of perceived injustice. At first, this was said to be an objection to the prevailing norms of human order. But it soon revealed its true identity, an objection to the inexorable presence of God in the world, one more attempt to free man from the burden of sin and its consequences, one more return to "I will not serve."

As many Popes foresaw in their encyclicals, the medicine Marxism offered to humanity proved more deadly than the disease. Pope Leo XIII predicted not just the inevitable failure of this conflict theory, but the aftereffects of its rise in the first place. [6] Pope John Paul II knew the danger was not over with the collapse of Communism, warning that the atheistic chromosomes of Marxist thought were building new life in the hearts and minds of the people.

Fátima, where three peasant children—who knew nothing of the geography of the world, or the history of the nations, or of the venomous social movements of the day—on the eve of the October Revolution, hear Mary tell them, "Russia, in the end, will convert." [7]

This becomes the sign of the times. [8]

It is the sign, not of the crisis descending upon mankind, but that God will once again be true to His covenant.[9] God cannot abandon His children. He cannot withdraw His promise that their destiny is eternal life in His Kingdom.[10]

Thus, the dark forces of Masonry, of Communism, of Cultural Marxism, of all the Errors of Russia—shadows of the "father of lies"(Jn 8:44)—become destined to surrender to the hope that lives in faith. And with this the twilight of an age of sin and atheism fades into the night, as the light of Christ *passes over*, illuminating the horizon of a new time.

Humanity, as Pope John Paul II wrote, is to become sober.[11] The ears of people's hearts are to hear. The eyes of their souls are to see. The sword of justice is be unsheathed, as an era of peace settles upon the nations as Mary foretold at Fátima and brings to fulfillment at Medjugorje.[12]

God demands that His people obtain the realization to which He Himself has destined for them.[13] The promise of this shines forth through His Word—the living truth that cannot be muted, that will not be stricken from history.

And in that Word, we recall Mary, standing at the foot of the Cross, participating in the victory of Christ. It is a victory that will be made visible once again in the purification and renewal of the Church and all the world—a resurrection God's children are to know came through the Immaculate Heart of their loving Mother.

LO, I WILL SEND YOU ELIJAH

*"Lo, I will send you Elijah, the prophet, before the day of the
Lord comes, the great and terrible day, to turn the hearts of
the fathers to their children, and the hearts of the children
to their fathers, lest I come and strike the land with doom."*
—Mal 3:23-24

FIRE IS THE MOST MYSTERIOUS OF ENTITIES.
From the Stone Age to the Nuclear Age, a compelling magnetism surrounds fire. This is because its vital properties of light and heat have always been desperately needed for human survival.

Historically, fire was not just utilized by our ancestors, but treasured and protected. In fact, fire was the first priceless commodity, more so than water and food, a rarity that likely led to countless disputes and plenty of bloodshed.

Down through the centuries, its legacy remains intact.

Horribly destructive, yet infinitely beneficial, the true nature of fire is schizophrenic; it's a Jekyll and Hyde, found throughout history at the center of events of survival or demise.

The latter we more easily note, recalling how Nero sang as Rome burned, that Sherman torched Atlanta, and the first doomsday bombs set Hiroshima and Nagasaki ablaze.

Fire takes center stage in Judeo-Christian Scripture, where it is not only a manifestation of the presence of God and a symbol of divinity, but the one everlasting sign the Lord is at work, often in a powerful way.

The Bible speaks of fire over five hundred times.[1]

While it's unknown what produced light on the first day after God declared it so, by the fourth day, *The Book of Genesis* asserts the sun and the stars were up and going, massive balls of burning hydrogen and helium, capable of spewing into the sky licks of flames thousands of miles high.

But the beginning of the world tells us nowhere near as much as the foretold finale about the significance of fire in God's plans. By the time we get to *The Book of Revelation*, we find the consummation of the world is reserved for a deluge of fire:

"Then, the angel took the censer, filled it with the fire from the altar and threw it on the earth, and there were peals of thunder, loud noises, flashes of lightening, and an earthquake… and there followed hail and fire mixed with blood which fell on the earth, and a third of the earth was burned up…" [2]

Throughout the Old Testament, one confronts people, places, and events that center around fire. Quite often, this fire is supernatural in origination.

In *Genesis*, no sooner are Adam and Eve deported from the Garden than God stations a Cherub with a fiery revolving sword in hand to guard the Tree of Life.[3] Further on in the first book of the Bible, the Lord is seen to rain down sulfurous fire on Sodom and Gomorrah,[4] the smoke from which Abraham watches rise like flames from a furnace.[5] In *Genesis,* Adam, Cain, and Abraham all offer fiery holocausts to God, with the Lord even leading Abraham to offer his son, Isaac, as a burnt offering. [6]

Over time, the Jews constantly came face-to-face with the mysterious role of fire in their salvation history.

It is through a burning bush that Moses first speaks with God the Creator— who is Himself later described in *Deuteronomy* as a consuming fire.[7] Then, as Moses leads his people out of Egypt, a towering pillar of fire prevents the Egyptians from destroying the Israelites at the Red Sea.[8] Finally, once in the desert, God's presence on Sinai is signaled by a glowing fire.[9]

In *Exodus*, a fiery cloud—known as the Shekinah Glory— hovers over the Israelites' meeting tent at night, indicating God's true presence.[10] Later in the Old Testament, in *The First Book of Kings*, the prophet Elijah calls down fire upon a holocaust to crush the prophets of Baal.[11] Fire again comes down from Heaven at the consecration of Solomon's Temple,[12] where inside on the altar a fire was to be kept burning, with orders from God that it not go out.[13]

The extraordinary, supernatural manifestations of fire found in the Old Testament, however, are not forwarded in the New Testament. Rather, we find a mighty *spiritual* manifestation of fire that is emphasized in the four Gospels.

Jesus, says John the Baptist, will baptize with the Holy Spirit and with fire.[14] On Mt. Tabor, Christ's dazzling glory in the presence of His Father during the Transfiguration is found to be in keeping with Moses' radiance in the presence of the Burning Bush.[15] And, in holding to this metaphorical theme of the power of fire, Jesus tells his followers He has come to set the Earth on fire, wishing, He adds, it were already blazing.[16] Finally, after Christ ascends, the Holy Spirit descends as tongues of fire that part and rest upon the Apostles.[17]

Over the last 2,000 years, the faith, the faithful, and fire are often sewn together as the Church marches through time. From the early Christians set aflame on crosses—to Joan of Arc's heroic finale on the fiery stake—to the fire of the Holy Spirit renewing the Church at crucial moments in its history, real and mystical accounts of fire continue to accompany the unfolding of God's plan of salvation for His wayward children.

The mysterious fire on the mountain at Medjugorje on October 27, 1981, just months after the apparitions began there, was a singular event.

Witnesses say it burned brightly for fifteen minutes—was observable from a considerable distance—and looked as real as any fire. Over five hundred people, scattered about the five villages below, attested to seeing it.[18]

In a village that would become known over the years as a haven for the unexplainable, the massive blaze on the hilltop that suddenly vanished still sits close to the top of the list.

But while it *was* mysterious, its origin is no mystery.

"The fire seen by the faithful was of a supernatural character," the Virgin Mary revealed to the visionaries the following day. "It's one of the signs; a forerunner of the Great Sign." [19]

That the Virgin Mary revealed this fire was a forerunner of the Great Sign does not imply that the Great Sign at Medjugorje will necessarily consist of fire itself. But it does have significant implications.

As in the Old Testament, the manifestation of this supernatural fire on a mountain, like the glowing Sinai, clearly appears to confirm the presence of God from whom the Great Sign will directly come. And, as in the ancient days of old, one cannot help but wonder if the fire was intended to convey the certainty of God's approaching victory over His enemies.

Marian writers say the reality of this coming victory was already prophetically symbolized at Fátima during the Miracle of the Sun on October 13, 1917. On that terrifying day—as the sun left its mooring in the sky and descended upon the thousands huddled in fear in the Cova da Iria—the children were shown three visions.

First, Saint Joseph with the Child Jesus appeared in the sky, blessing the world, as Mary stood beside them clothed in a white tunic and blue mantle. Next, Christ appeared in His glorified manhood and again made the sign of the cross. This time, Mary stood beside Him as Our Lady of Sorrows. Finally, in the third and last vision, the Virgin Mary appeared as Our Lady of Mt. Carmel.

This final vision is of prophetic significance.[20]

The vision of Our Lady of Mt. Carmel, Fatima experts write, was intended to symbolically reveal the presence of a twofold message in the Miracle of the Sun that was taking place at that moment.

Seen only by the three children, the vision of Our Lady of Mt. Carmel conveyed what Mary promised the future held—God's coming victory in the world over evil: "In the end my Immaculate Heart will triumph."

Mt. Carmel—where the prophet Elijah called fire down from Heaven—was being recalled by the appearance of Mary as Our Lady of Mt. Carmel for a reason: to evoke the immortal moment recorded in *The First Book of Kings* when God intervened in the affairs of ancient Israel to bring victory over the false prophets of Baal. [21]

At that time, Israel was on the verge of annihilation from a punishment sent by God for their idolatry.

Elijah the Tishbite—one of the most illustrious figures in the Old Testament, who, along with Moses, appeared at the Transfiguration of Jesus on Mt. Tabor—told the people that if they did not destroy their idols and return to God, they would experience a severe drought: "As the Lord, the God of Israel lives, whom I serve, during these years there shall be no dew or rain except at my word." [22]

Facing the extinction of his nation after years of no rain, King Ahab met with Elijah, who asked for the meeting by request of the Lord. Confronting the prophet face-to-face, Ahab said, "Is it you? —you disturber of Israel."

Elijah replied, "It is not I who disturb Israel but you and your family, by forsaking the commands of the Lord and following the Baals. Now summon all Israel to me on Mt. Carmel, as well as the four hundred and fifty prophets of Baal and the four hundred prophets of Asherah who eat at Jezebel's table." [23]

With all of Israel and the false prophets gathered on Mt. Carmel, Elijah presented them with a challenge. The pagan priests would erect an altar, and place a young bull upon it, and pray to Baal to send down fire to consume the sacrifice. [24]

At the same time, Elijah—the only surviving prophet of God left in Israel—would build another altar, dig a trench filled with water around it, and place a sacrifice upon it, too. [25] Then, like the prophets of Baal, he was to call upon the one true God of Israel: "You shall call on your gods, and I will call on the Lord. The God who answers with fire is God," declared Elijah. All the people answered, "Agreed!" [26]

As the day unfolded, the pagan priests hopped around their altar and pleaded with Baal from morning to noon to demonstrate his power. They even self-mutilated themselves with swords and spears until blood gushed over them, all in the hope of triggering a response. [27] Elijah, all the while, taunted them on, "Call louder, for he is a god… perhaps he is asleep and must be awakened." [28]

Finally, as it was evident that their petition was in vain, Elijah called upon Heaven in a singular prayer:

"Lord, God of Abraham, Isaac, and Israel, let it be known this day that you are God in Israel and that I am your servant and have done all these things by your command. Answer me, Lord! Answer me, that this people may know that you, Lord, are God and that you have brought them back to their senses." [29]

Immediately, fire fell from the sky and consumed not only Elijah's sacrifice but the wood and stony altar, as well as the water in the trench. With this, the people of Israel fell to their knees, "The Lord is God! The Lord is God!" they cried out. [30]

Ordering the prophets of Baal to be seized, Elijah then had them all slain. God's victory over the false gods of the age was complete and the people returned to the Lord. [31]

At Fátima, theologians say God was letting the world know that the fiery sun falling from the sky not only confirmed Mary's powerful presence, but also that His enemies of today—like the prophets of Baal—were destined to suffer the same humiliating defeat as His enemies of yesterday.

"Our Lady came under her ancient title of Mt. Carmel," [32] explains Fátima author John Haffert of the symbolism behind the vision, "Elijah had performed a miracle to show God is God, and now Mary had just done the same on this mountain of Fátima." [33]

Now, at Medjugorje, the Virgin Mary will fulfill the Secrets she began at Fátima. The appearance of the forerunning sign, the supernatural fire at Medjugorje—on a mountain top like at Carmel and Fátima—appears to confirm God's approaching victory, a victory to be forever immortalized by the manifestation of the Great Sign there.

Indeed, with the Great Sign's appearance on Mt. Podbrdo, an unparalleled moment in the history of mankind will have arrived. The era of universal atheism as never seen before; the era of massive death as never experienced before; the era of sin and Satan as never known before will be brought to its prophesied demise, defeated through the blood and tears of its tragic victims—and the faith and prayers of the Virgin Mary's children.

At last, the era of peace foretold at Fátima will begin to manifest, and the presence of the Great Sign at Medjugorje will prove to the world, as did Elijah on Mt. Carmel, that "the Lord is God."

It is to be an era presented to humanity as a gift from the hands of the Father through the Immaculate Heart of the Mother. Indeed, Mary's Immaculate Heart, the ultimate symbol of the Triumph, will now secure its rightful place in the Church next to the Sacred Heart of her Son, as people throughout the world come to realize that she—*the Woman Clothed in the Sun*—secured the grace that delivered God's victory.[34]

This coming honor of the Queen of Heaven and Earth, Church tradition holds, was also previewed in Scripture that memorable day on Mt. Carmel by the prophet Elijah.

"Go up, eat and drink," Elijah told King Ahab after the false prophets of Baal were slain, "for there is the sound of a heavy rain." [35]

With these words, the time of the three-year drought in Israel was now to be over, and as Elijah called down the fire, so now he announced to Ahab the coming of the rain, which the people of the nation so desperately longed to see. [36]

Perched on the highest point of Mt. Carmel, Elijah instructed his servant to look out over the waters of the Mediterranean Sea to see if the storm was near. "There is nothing," the servant reported to the prophet after six attempts to spot the coming rain. But on the seventh attempt, the youth told Elijah, "There is a cloud as small as a man's hand arising from the sea." [37]

That cloud, tradition has long held, symbolized the coming of the Immaculate Conception—the coming of the Virgin Mary—who at a future time would shower God's healing graces from her Immaculate Heart upon a needy world, like the cloud that day showered rain upon Mt. Carmel and all of Israel. [38]

Tradition further holds that Elijah beheld a vision that day on Mt. Carmel of the coming of the Blessed Virgin Mary. [39]

If such were the case, we know today why Mary and the presence of Elijah and Mt. Carmel have been linked together at many of her apparition sites over the centuries.

It is a mystery especially noted at Lourdes, where Mary's last apparition there was on July 16, 1858, the Feast of Our Lady of Mt. Carmel.[40]

It is seen again at Fátima, where Mary's final appearance to the three children on October 13, 1917, was as Our Lady of Mt. Carmel.[41]

At Lourdes, Mary shocked the Church by declaring, "I am the Immaculate Conception." At Fátima, she stunned the world by performing the greatest foretold miracle in history.

Now, at Medjugorje, where another supernatural fire on a mountain top sets the stage, the faithful are left to wait and wonder what is to come.

Are ancient biblical prophecies about to be fulfilled in the times that near?

Is Elijah's shadowing, mystical presence being revealed once again in what may be the last apparitions of the Virgin Mary, who first appeared at Medjugorje on the feast day of John the Baptist, the prophet who the Gospels say came in "the spirit and power of Elijah?"

Is Medjugorje to take its place next to Lourdes and Fátima in a transcendent mystery involving this great prophet?

It is a mystery that deepens with the reality that the patron saint of Bosnia and Hercegovina is none other than Elijah, the only nation in the world to proclaim him as such.

And—to add to the intrigue—he was declared patron saint in 1752 by a Franciscan Bishop named Pavao "Dragićević." Yes, the same name as the one who is to reveal the Ten Secrets to the world, the Secrets that will bring the crushing defeat of evil in these times, as Elijah brought defeat to the prophets of Baal. [42]

"Lo, I will send you Elijah," Scripture reads.

Many believe these words are being fulfilled at Medjugorje.

AFTERWORD

*"I will put enmities between thee and the woman,
and thy seed and her seed; she shall crush thy
head, and thou shalt lie in wait for her heal."* *

—Gn 3:15

ONE OF GOD'S PRECIOUS LITTLE ONES, THREE-YEAR-OLD COOPER
Kirkwood, may have been given a glimpse of God's coming victory through the Immaculate Heart of Mary.

Forced to move after a fire ravaged his family's home in the summer of 2020, little Cooper told his parents that he was having nightmares about a big black snake that was chasing him around every night.

Upon hearing of the little boy's dilemma, his grandfather gave him a 6-inch statue of the Blessed Mother that Cooper dubbed his "Trophy Lady."

The following morning, after the first night with the tiny statue of the Virgin Mary at his bedside, his mother inquired if he had any bad dreams the night before.

"The big black snake was chasing me last night," Cooper told his mom, "but the Trophy Lady came and stepped on its head and killed him." [1]

---

*   *Douay-Rheims Bible*

ACKNOWLEDGEMENTS

A S I WRITE THESE ACKNOWLEDGEMENTS, THOSE WHO DESERVE MY deepest appreciation are no longer with us. Fr. René Laurentin strongly encouraged me to keep doing the work that we spent many years together discussing. Laurentin was a model of humility, always very positive, eternally kind and optimistic. Much the same can be said about John Haffert. Haffert was a legend among legends in Fátima circles, and I am extremely grateful for all his support. Haffert loved the challenge of taking Mary's message to the world and saw this as the highest of callings. More than anything, John longed to see the Triumph of the Immaculate Heart come into the world.

I am deeply appreciative of the guidance and advice I received from Ed and Jan Connell over the years. Their work and words were with me every step of the way with this undertaking.

Since I began this book some twenty years ago, there were those at the time who helped me that I wish to thank: Denis Nolan—whose letter encouraging me to write this book I read often, Bishop Pavel Hnilica, and his two assistants, Fr. Paul Sigl and Fr. Lucia Maria Alimandi, Stan and Marge Karminski, Joan Smith, Carole McElwain, Dr. Rosalie Turton of the 101 Foundation, Sister Agnes McCormick, Sister Emanuel Maillard, Georgette Faniel, Michael Fontecchio, Fr. Guy Girard, June Klins, Fr. Richard Foley, Fr. Michael O'Carroll, Fr. Robert Herrmann, Fr. Kenny Keene, Fr. Ed O'Conner, Fr. John O' Shea, Archbishop Phillip Hannon, Fr. Richard Whetstone, Fr. Jozo Zovko, and Fr. Petar Ljubicic.

More recently, Fr. David Tourville, Fr. Bill McCarthy, Fr. Peter Murphy, and Fr. Mark Ruckpol, were instrumental in one form or another, some in ways unknown to them. I am also indebted to Amanda Defazio, Dr. Raymond Badzik, Guy Murphy, John Davis, Terry Kopp and Cathy Howe for their assistance or inspiration, and to Ted Flynn, who got me back to weekly fasting on bread and water.

Dr. Frank Novasack Jr., Mary Lou Sokol, Brad Fassenbender, Noah Ostlund, Don Kirkwood, Gerard Beer, Barbara and Richard Nozewski, my daughter Dominique and my son, Joshua, all agreed to read the manuscript and were very helpful with their insights, observations and corrections.

A special thank you to long-time editor Erica Rankin, who was again very helpful in countless ways, and to the editors at Simon and Shuster, though I decided not to proceed in that direction. Likewise, a big thank you to my son Jesse, who provided and designed the pages containing the photographs.

Finally, my wife, Emily, was again totally committed with her support, covering for my lapses in countless ways. A special thank you to my six children, who I can always count on for their love and prayers: Maria Meyers and her husband, Adam, and our grandson, Theo, Sarah, Joshua, Natasha, Dominique and Jesse. Finally, eternal appreciation to my parents, Andrew and Mary, along with my uncle Michael Petrisko, who was like a brother.

NOTES

CHAPTER 1: THE FIRE THAT WASN'T

1. Svetozar Kraljevic, O.F.M., *The Apparitions of Our Lady at Medjugorje, 1981-1983: An Historical Account with Interviews* (Chicago, IL: Franciscan Herald Press, 1984), 60-61.

2. Ibid.

3. René Laurentin and Ljudevit Rupčić, *Is the Virgin Mary Appearing at Medjugorje? An Urgent Message Given to the World in a Marxist Country* (Washington, D.C.: The Word Among Us Press, 1984), 34. Father René Laurentin writes, "At the end of October in 1981, in the place of the first apparition, a large flame suddenly shot up. It lasted ten or fifteen minutes. Several hundred people saw this, including priests and religious. A policeman who was there in order to block access to the hill also saw it. He dug around the place without finding any trace of fire or ashes."

4. Joseph A. Pelletier, A.A., *The Queen of Peace Visits Medjugorje* (Worcester, MA: Assumption Publications, 1985), 80-81.

5. Mary Craig, *Spark from Heaven* (Notre Dame: Ave Maria Press, 1988), 48.

6. Ibid.; Mirjana Soldo, *My Heart Will Triumph* (Cocoa, FL: Catholic Shop Publishing, 2016), 44, 69, 80,100. There was a second fire in Medjugorje that appeared to be real but left no evidence of ever existing. It was reportedly more mysterious than the one on the hill. In the early days of July of 1981, very high flames could be seen from the valley and the neighboring villages to be surrounding St. James Church in Medjugorje. People began to shout and hasten to St. James, believing that the Communists had set fire to the church in order to bring an end to the apparitions. Father Jozo Zovko, standing right in front of the church, could see nothing and was bewildered when the alarmed people came and asked him about the fire. Five emergency and police cars arrived at the scene rather quickly. The police asked those there who set the fire. After inspecting the area and finding not a trace of anything burning, they departed dumbfounded. (See *Medjugorje Torino* (English edition), 1992, N.1, p. 11).

CHAPTER 2: JUDGEMENT DAY

1. Craig, *Spark from Heaven*, 13.
2. Ibid.
3. Jacov Marin, *Queen of Peace in Medjugorje* (Milford, OH: The Riehle Foundation, 1989), 13. Jacov Marin is the pen name for a diocesan priest stationed in the vicinity of Zagreb in the mid-1980s. He used a pen name for security purposes because of the communist regime in Yugoslavia at the time. His book was translated into English by the Sarcevic family who ran the MIR (Peace) Center in Clarks Summit, PA. The book's original title was *Kraljica Mira Medjugorje*, published in Croatia in 1988.
4. Craig, *Spark from Heaven*, 13.
5. Robert Moynihan, "Dossier: The Third Secret," *Inside the Vatican*, Year 8, No. 6, June-July 2000, p. xii.
6. Brother Michael de la Sainte Trinite, *Fatima Revealed and Discarded* (Chulmleigh, Devon: Augustine Publishing Company, 1988), 204-208. On April 4, 1957, the third part of the Secret of Fátima was placed in a small wooden safe in the papal apartments. On May 14, 1958, a French journalist, Robert Serrou, was permitted to take photographs of the various rooms in the Vatican. Asking what was in the safe, he was told by an attendant. A photograph was taken that ultimately appeared in the periodical *Paris Weekly* on October 18, 1957. This ignited more curiosity about the supposedly dreadful contents of the third part of the Secret. The Vatican never issued a statement in 1960 on its decision not to release the third part of the Secret. It was not until February 11, 1967, that any authority in the Vatican publicly addressed the issue. On this date, Cardinal Alfredo Ottaviani, at the Antonianum in Rome, reviewed the history of the document and spoke about how Pope John XXIII read it and made the decision not to release it.
7. Ibid., 206. On February 8, 1960, the Portuguese News Agency, claiming inside Vatican sources, stated that the third part of the Secret of Fátima would probably be never revealed: "In view of the pressure exerted on the Vatican, the same sources stated that—since some are demanding the disclosure of the Secret to the whole world, while others, on the assumption that the Secret contains alarming prophecies, are against its publication—the Vatican has decided that Sr. Lúcia's text will not be revealed, and will stay a closed secret." [cf., Sebastiao Martinsdos Reis, *O Milagredo sole segredo de Fatima* (Porto, Portugal: Edicoes Salesianas, 1966), 127-128]. For more, see Grzegorz Gorny and Janusz Rosikon, *Fatima Mysteries* (San Francisco and Warsaw, Poland: Rosikon and Ignatius Press, 2017), 259-261.
8. Sandra Zimdars Swartz, *Encountering Mary* (New York, NY: Avon Books-Princeton University Press, 1991), 165-189. See my book, *The*

Fatima Prophecies (Pittsburgh, PA: St. Andrew's Productions, 1998), for a comprehensive summary of the events at La Salette, chapters 37, 38, 39, pp. 239-261.

9.   Antonio Socci, *The Fourth Secret of Fatima* (Fitzwilliam, NH: *Loreto Publications*, English language translation, 2009), 77. There were a number of fictitious versions of the so called Third Secret of Fátima in circulation prior to the Vatican's release of the official Secret on June 26, 2000. Socci quotes Pope John Paul II's alleged remarks at Fulda, Germany, in November 1980, published in the German magazine, *Stimme des Glaubens*. See Chapter 56 of this book for the text of John Paul II's words at Fulda. The second most controversial, alleged version of the reported text of the third part of the Secret of Fátima was circulated widely in 1979. In a June 4th article that appeared in the Italian daily, *La Republica*, titled, "Is This the Content of the Third Secret of the Madonna of Fatima?", journalist Domenico Del Rio reported that a group of followers of Padre Pio claimed the following text was the Third Secret of Fátima: "A great plague will befall mankind in the second half of the 20th century. Nowhere in the world will there be order, and Satan will rule the highest places, determining the way of things. Satan will even succeed in asserting himself at the top of the Church. He will succeed in seducing the spirits of the great scientists who invent arms, with which it will be possible to destroy a large part of humanity in a few minutes. Satan will have in his power the powerful who command the people and who will incite them to produce enormous quantities of arms. God will punish man more thoroughly than with the Flood. There will come the time of all times and the end of all ends. The great and powerful will perish together with the small and weak. Even for the Church, it will be the time of its greatest trial. Cardinals will oppose Cardinals; Bishops will oppose Bishops. Satan will walk in their midst and in Rome there will be great changes. The Church will be darkened, and the world will be shaking in terror. A huge war will erupt in the second half of the 20th century. Fire and smoke will fall from the sky. The waters will become mist, and the foam will rise to tremendous heights and everyone will drown. Millions and millions of men will die from hour to hour. The good will perish with the bad, the great with the small, the princes of the Church with the faithful, the rulers with their people. There will be death everywhere because of the errors committed by the crazed and followers of Satan, who will then and only then, rule the world. At the last, those who survive will at every chance newly proclaim God and His glory and they will serve Him as when the world was not so perverted." (This text was also published in the *Arlington Catholic Herald* of Arlington, Virginia, July 11,1985.) Some wonder if it is the message that Pope John Paul II was reported to have been referring to in his talk at Fulda in November, 1980.

10. Sarah Delaney, "Text of 3ʳᵈ Fatima Secret Released," *The Washington Post*, June 2, 2000. *The Washington Post* went so far as to write: "The jealously guarded prophecy described the 'end of the world.'"

11. Father Andrew Apostoli, C.F.R., *Fatima for Today: The Urgent Marian Message of Hope* (San Francisco: Ignatius Press, 2010), 213-214. Upon hearing that what was released by the Vatican was being said to not be the real third part of the Secret of Fátima, Sister Lúcia responded, "Well, if they know what it [the third part of the Secret] is, then let them tell us."

12. Ratzinger, "The Message of Fatima", published in *The Fatima Prophecies*, 270-298.

13. Ibid. Cardinal Bertone maintained this position some years later: "The prophecy is no longer open to the future, but refers to something that now belongs to the past."

14. Ratzinger, "The Message of Fatima", published in *The Fatima Prophecies*, 270-298.

15. Ibid. "The third part of the Secret is a symbolic revelation," wrote Lúcia, "referring to this (the 2ⁿᵈ) part of the message, conditioned by whether we accept or not what the message ask of us... Since we did not heed this appeal of the message, we see that it has been fulfilled, Russia has invaded the world with its errors. And if we have not yet seen the complete fulfillment of the final part of this prophecy, we are going towards it little by little with great strides." The "appeal of the message" that failed to be heeded was Mary's request for the Pope and the bishops to properly consecrate Russia to her Immaculate Heart. And, because of this failure, what was fulfilled—but not "completely fulfilled" according to Lúcia—were the "errors of Russia invading the world," the Marxist cultural and political movements that have spread theoretical and practical atheism for decades.

16. Carmel of Coimbra, *A Pathway Under the Gaze of Mary: Biography of Sister Maria Lucia of Jesus and the Immaculate Heart O.C.D.* (Easton, PA: World Apostolate of Fatima, 2015), 190.

17. Thomas Landsford, *History of Communism* (New York. NY: Cavendish Square Publishing, 2007), 9-24, 36-44.

18. Leslie H. Geib, "Soviet Might: A U.S. View; News Analysis"; Bernard Gwertzman, "Pentagon Plans to Publish Study Describing Soviet Armed Strength." Both articles were published in the *New York Times*, September 27, 1981.

19. Ibid.

CHAPTER 3: LAND OF THE DEMONS

1. Peter Jennings, "The Land of the Demons," *ABC News*, 1993. The *ABC News* anchor examined the dangers and global implications of the ongoing war in the former Yugoslavia. Televised on March, 18, 1993.

2. Rebecca West, *Black Lamb, Grey Falcon: A Journey Through Yugoslavia* (New York, NY: Viking Press, 1941).

3. Robert J. Donia and John V.A. Fine, Jr., *Bosnia &Hercegovina, A Tradition Betrayed* (New York, NY: Columbia University Press, 1994), 71.

4. Ibid.

5. Ibid.

6. Fred Singleton, *A Short History of the Yugoslav Peoples* (Cambridge: Cambridge University Press, 1985), 10.

7. Ibid., 11.

8. Ibid.

9. Ibid.

10. Ibid.

11. Ibid.

12. Ibid.

13. Ibid., 16.

14. Ibid.

15. Ibid.

16. John M. Haffert, *To Prevent This* (Asbury, NJ: The 101 Foundation,1993), 10. Right up until his death, Haffert argued that the Virgin Mary's prophecy of the "annihilation of nations" remained unfulfilled. He writes, "As we have said, of all the warnings given by Our Lady at Fátima, only one has not befallen mankind: 'Several nations will be annihilated.' In the past, some thought perhaps Ukraine, Byelorussia, Lithuania, Latvia, Estonia, etc., were annihilated by being Sovietized. Obviously this is not the case. These nations exist. The word 'annihilated' means wiped out, totally destroyed. Jesus used the same word in speaking to Lúcia in March 1939, in connection with the First Saturday Communion of Reparation: "The time is coming when the vigor of My justice will punish the crimes of various nations. Some of them will be annihilated." Three reasons cause us to believe these prophecies could mean that, if there are not enough Communions of Reparation, there will be a nuclear holocaust: 1) The Miracle of the Sun; 2) Logic; 3) Prophecy of fire."

17. Writes the renowned French Mariologist Father René Laurentin: "The messages of Fátima and Medjugorje are identical. To surmount the menaces which weigh upon the world you need prayer, penance, conversion, for mankind to return to God, and the invitation to pray the Rosary. The objective is the same—peace in spite of all the things that divide us socially and continue to destroy man. And the ways are the same, a

return to God through Mary. The progression is complimentary. Fátima told us what we had to do; Medjugorje is showing how to do it." See, *Medjugorje: A Time for Truth; a Time for Action* by Denis Nolan, 88-89.

CHAPTER 4: MAKE WAY FOR MARXISM

1. Sister Mary Lúcia of the Immaculate Heart, *Fatima in Lucia's Own Words: Sister Lucia's Memoirs* (Torres Novas, Portugal: Postulation Centre, 1976), 108. Fátima is not a Christian name. It was the name of Mohammed's daughter. The village of Fátima in Portugal was named during the area's Arabic occupation in the 12th century. Because of the high regard that Muslims have for Mary as revealed in the Koran, there has long been the opinion that the apparitions at Fátima signal the eventual assimilation of the Islamic faith into the Church.

2. Ibid., 167. Mary appeared at Fátima on the 13th of May, June, July, September and October of 1917. In August, she appeared on the 19th. It is believed she first appeared on the 13th because of the role this date played with Queen Ester and her heroic rescue of the Jewish people, who were scheduled for annihilation on the 13th of the month as described in *The Book of Ester*. (In a curious side note, Mahmoud Ahmadinejad, a former President of Iran, called for annihilation of Israel on April 13, 2006. It was a remark that drew the attention of the world at the time.)

3. Ibid., 172. On September 13th, Mary did not say the war was going to end but did ask the children to "continue to pray the Rosary in order to obtain the end of the war."

4. Some estimates have the death toll from the Spanish Flu to be as high as 135 million.

5. Hugh Thomas, *A History of the World* (New York, NY: Harper and Row, Publishers, 1979), 447-455.

6. Ibid.

7. Ibid.

8. Ibid.

9. Ibid. Henry Brooks Adams was one of the towering intellects of this period. He was a member of the Adams political family of the American Revolution, a descendant of two presidents. His father, Charles Francis Adams, was Abraham Lincoln's ambassador to the United Kingdom. Educated at Harvard, Henry Adams is best known for his masterpiece nine-volume *History of the United States During the Administrations of Thomas Jefferson and James Madison*. His memoir, *The Education of Henry Adams*, published posthumously, won the Pulitzer Prize. Adams, an American historian, understood the times at hand during the American Civil War and afterwards sought to expose political corruption. As for the Civil War, he once

remarked, "I think that Lee should have been hanged. It was all the worse that he was a good man and a fine character and acted conscientiously. It's always the good men who do the most harm in the world." (Quoted in the Ken Burns documentary, *The Civil War*.)

10. Petrisko, *The Fatima Prophecies*, 11-51.
11. David Blackbourn, *Marpingen: Apparitions of the Virgin Mary in a Nineteenth Century German Village* (New York, NY: Vintage Books,1995), 5.
12. Ibid., XXVI, 20.
13. Joseph I. Dirvin, C.M., *St. Catherine Laboure of the Miraculous Medal* (Rockford, IL: TAN Inc., Books and Publishers, 1987).
14. Swartz, *Encountering Mary*, 165-189.
15. Petrisko, *The Fatima Prophecies*, 23.
16. Ibid.
17. Swartz, *Encountering Mary*, 165-189. Pope Pius IX – Giovanni Maria Mastia Ferretti of Italy—was born on May 13, 1792, the future anniversary of the first apparition at Fátima in 1917.
18. Petrisko, *The Fatima Prophecies*, 37. During this time, it was clear to Pope Pius IX that the world was not being molded into the image of God. Humanism was slowly being institutionalized, especially in government and education, and it would be only a matter of time before generations were forcibly indoctrinated into it from childhood. Pius IX's *Syllabus of Errors* in 1864 confronted the emerging crisis of worldwide liberalism but, unfortunately, his message was ignored and instead the enemies of the Church explicated the document as evidence of the Church's inflexible attitude towards Modernism. Pius, though, warned of what lay ahead: "Wicked groups think they had already become masters of the world and that they have almost reached their pre-established goal...that is power." With the rise of Communism in Russia, National Socialism in Germany, Fascism in Italy, and Ultra Nationalism and Fascism in Japan, that power would finally be at hand less than a century later.
19. Thomas A. Kselman, *Miracles & Prophecies in Nineteenth Century France* (New Brunswick, NJ: Rutgers University Press, 1983), 62.
20. Blackbourn, *Marpingen*, 112.
21. Kselman, *Miracles & Prophecies in Nineteenth Century France*, 91.
22. Catherine M. Odell, *Those Who Saw Her* (Huntington, IN: Our Sunday Visitor Publishing, 1986), 76-92.
23. Father Marie Richard, *What Happened at Pontmain?* (Washington, NJ: Ave Maria Institute, 1971), 13-78.
24. Odell, *Those Who Saw Her*, 103-112.
25. Blackbourn, *Marpingen*, 326.
26. Kselman, *Miracles and Prophecies in Nineteenth Century France*, 122.

27. Joe Tremblay, "The 100 Year Test," *CNA* (*Catholic News Agency*), February 1, 2013, catholicnewsagency.com.; Kevin J. Symonds, *Pope Leo XIII and the Prayer to St. Michael* (Booneville, NY: Preserving Christian Publications, 2015). Symonds's book is the definitive work on Pope Leo's reported vision. He attempts to trace back the roots of the vision and finds that today's most common version of the story appears to be a synthesis of older accounts. Symonds, for all his work on the subject, draws a conclusion: "This book has attempted to answer the question whether or not a vision was behind Pope Leo XIII's composing the Prayer to St. Michael. From the solid foundation herein established, one can now ask a secondary question: what does it all mean? Reliable evidence has been presented in favor of the claim that a vision was granted to Pope Leo. The vision preceded and influenced the composition of the Prayer to St. Michael that was inserted into the Leonine Prayers in 1886. The primary witness for this comes from Cardinal Nasalli who in turn named his source as Msgr. Rinaldo Angeli, Leo's private secretary. There is no reason to disbelieve the cardinal's claim and so his testimony will be taken at face value in this interpretation. In the preceding pages, we have endeavored to separate fact from fiction. Based upon this separation, it must be clearly stated that very little is known of the contents of Pope Leo's vision."

28. Mt 24: 3-51.

29. Richard, *What Happened at Pontmain?* 71.

30. Letter of Pope Benedict XV to Cardinal Pietro Gasparri, Library of the Vatican, April 27,1915. On October 31, 2019, the Feast of Our Lady of Loreto was added to the Roman calendar as an optional memorial to be celebrated on December 10th.

31. With the birth of Portugal in 1139, after the defeat of the Moors at Qurica, the new king, Alfonso Henriques, immediately chose the Virgin Mary as Portugal's Protectress and Mother. A document recording this vow, dated April 28, 1142, was found in the monastery of Alcobaca. It was written on parchment and stamped with the royal seal.

32. Lúcia, *Fatima in Lucia's Own Words*, 167. The prophetic warning at Fátima of the coming of a Second World War was not the only of its kind. A Belgian stigmatist, Berthe Petit, reported that Christ told her that Germany would rise again and that the world would feel the consequences: "The nation which is thought to be conquered, but whose strength is only diminished, remains a threat to your nation (Belgium) and to France. Trouble and danger will spread to all countries. Humanity is rushing towards a great storm, which will divide the nations more and more." See my book, *The Fatima Prophecies,* for more on this subject.

CHAPTER 5: THE MUSEUM OF THE WORLD

1. Lúcia, *Fatima in Lucia's Own Words*, 72.
2. Ibid., 73.
3. Ibid., 75.
4. Sister Mary Lúcia of the Immaculate Heart, *Fatima in Lucia's Own Words II, Sister Lucia's Memoirs, Volume II, 5th and 6th Memoirs* (Fátima, Portugal: Grafica de Coimbra, Lda., 1999), 147-148.
5. Ibid., 82.
6. Ibid., 85; Francis Johnston, *Fatima: The Great Sign* (Rockford, IL: TAN Books and Publishers, Inc., 1980), 50.
7. Lúcia, *Fatima in Lucia's Own Words II*, 70. The mere thought that the apparitions could be a deceit of the Devil was a much greater worry of Lúcia than being killed by the crowd. In Lúcia's mind, a seed of doubt had been sown by Father Ferreira, who had authority and commanded the utmost respect from Lúcia. It finally took the words of little Jacinta to turn Lúcia away from such a torment. Writes Lúcia, "I told my cousins of my doubts and Jacinta said, 'No, no, it's not the Devil. People say the Devil is very ugly and lives under the Earth in Hell, but that Lady was so beautiful and we saw her go up to Heaven.'" But even after this, Lúcia was sometimes plagued by the thought.
8. Ibid.
9. Ibid., 104.
10. Ibid. Francisco died at home. Right before he passed, he said, "Mother, look at that lovely light by the door." He was originally buried in the parish cemetery of St. Anthony in Fátima. On March 12, 1952, his remains were transferred to a side chapel in the Basilica of Our Lady of the Rosary in the Cova da Iria at Fátima.
11. Ibid. Jacinta was taken to St. Augustine's Hospital in Villa de Qurem on July 1 and eventually left there on August 31, 1919. On January 21, 1920, she was taken to Lisbon where she was admitted to an orphanage run by Madre Godinho. On February 2, she was taken to the Dona Estefania Hospital. There, Mary appeared to her three times and revealed the following: "War is a punishment for sin; many fashions in the future would offend God very much; many marriages are not of God; priests must be pure and concentrate on their service to souls and the Church; more souls go Hell because of sins of impurity than any other sin." The Virgin Mary last visited her four days before she died. Jacinta passed on February 20, 1920, at 10:30 p.m. in the hospital all alone, as Mary had foretold. She was at first buried in a cemetery in Qurem. In 1935, her remains were transferred to the parish cemetery of Saint Anthony in Fátima, where she was buried next to Francisco. On March 1, 1951,

she was transferred to the side chapel of the Basilica of Our Lady of the Rosary.

12. Ibid.

13. Lúcia, *Fatima in Lucia's Own Words*, 9.

14. Ibid., 189.

15. Ibid., 98.

16. Carmel of Coimbra, *A Pathway Under the Gaze of Mary*, 149. Lúcia became a Carmelite in 1948.

17. Apostoli, *Fatima for Today*, 148-150. Christ's words to Lúcia in 1929 are timely, as He warns Lúcia of the impending darkness approaching. The world stage was heating up. Originally a revolutionary socialist, Benito Mussolini, who formed the first cell of his Fascist Party in 1919, was on the move. By 1922, his black-shirt bully boys had so intimidated the government that he was able to seize power and become prime minister. The German Nazi Party was also formed in 1919. It began as the miniscule German Workers Party and swiftly came under the control of the rabble-rousing orator Adolf Hitler. As with the communists in Russia in 1917, the masses in Europe were ripe for the taking, and governments everywhere were bracing for confrontations in the streets by the late 1920s.

18. Ibid., 159-164.

19. Carmel of Coimbra, *A Pathway Under the Gaze of Mary*, 142.

20. Lúcia, *Fatima in Lucia's Own Words*, 100.

21. Ibid., 108.

CHAPTER 6: AN UNKNOWN LIGHT

1. Frere Michel de la Sainte Trinite, *The Whole Truth About Fatima* (Buffalo, NY: Immaculate Heart Publications, 1986), 665-708.

2. Ibid.

3. Lúcia, *Fatima in Lucia's Own Words*, 114.

4. Michel de la Sainte Trinite, *The Whole Truth About Fatima*, 677.

5. Gorny and Rosikon, *Fatima Mysteries*, 194-195; Michel de la Trinite, *The Whole Truth About Fatima*, 708. There have been auroras which were visible at equally low altitudes, or even lower: at Honolulu in1859, at Bombay in1872, at Singapore in 1909, at Samoa in 1921.

6. Michel de la Trinite, *The Whole Truth About Fatima*, 665-677.

7. J. Rand McNally, "The Nuclear Tornado Effect," 11-12. This was a report by Dr. Rand McNally that was presented to the American Physical Society on April 28-May 1, 1986. (See Chapter 23 of this book: "The Song of the Sword.")

8. Michel de la Trinite, *The Whole Truth About Fatima*, 670-677, 706-707.

9. *Le Petit Dauphinois*, January 26, 1938.

10. "The Aurora Borealis of January 25-26,1938," *Bulletin of the Astronomical Society of France and Monthly Review of Astronomy, Meteorology, and Global Physics*, 43-68, 113-125, 306-310.
11. *Le Nouvelliste de Lyon*, January 26,1938.
12. *Bulletin of the Astronomical Society of France and Monthly Review*, 54-77.
13. Ibid., 123.
14. Ibid., 61.
15. Ibid., 63.
16. Ibid., 65.
17. Barbara Ernster, "An Unknown Light in 1938 Demands Our Attention Even Today," *Soul Magazine*, January 25, 2018, https://www.bluearmy.com/an-unknown-light-in-1938-demands-our-attention-even-today/. Portions of this article were first published in *Soul Magazine*, September-October 2003, by Father Edward Atzert.
18. *Bulletin of the Astronomical Society of France and Monthly Review*, 68.
19. Ibid., 114.
20. Ibid., 309.
21. Ibid.
22. Ernster, "An Unknown Light in 1938 Demands Our Attention Even Today," January 25, 2018, https://www.bluearmy.com/an-unknown-light-in-938-demands-our-attention-even-today/.
23. Lúcia, *Fatima in Lucia's Own Words*, 114.
24. The Blue Army, "The Great Sign," *Soul Magazine*, May-June, 1984, 8-9. Fr. O'Leary's experience must precede Lúcia's memoir containing the revelation of this prophecy. However, there was a general knowledge within the religious communities that Fátima's message warned of future trials and perhaps the coming of a war. Jacinta is well known to have spoken about it with Lúcia. Did she mention it to others? It is not likely that Fr. O'Leary fabricated the story, so it remains to be understood exactly what the priests at the seminary knew of Fátima at the time, and how they learned of it.
25. Lúcia, *Fatima in Lucia's Own Words*, 114.
26. Joaquin Maria Alonso, C.M.F., *The Secret of Fatima, Fact and Legend* (Cambridge: Ravengate Press, Revised Edition, 1990), 23.
27. Michel de la Sainte Trinite, *The Whole Truth About Fatima*, 667.
28. Cf. *Deutsche Allgemeine Zeitung* of January 31, 1939, quoted by Gabriel Louis-Jarray, op.cit., 12.
29. Michel de la Trinite, *The Whole Truth About Fatima*, 684.
30. Ibid., 686.
31. Ibid.
32. Ibid., 687.

33. William Thomas Walsh, *Our Lady of Fatima* (New York, NY: Doubleday, 1947), 222-223.

34. Michel de la Sainte Trinite, *The Whole Truth About Fatima*, 683, 698.

35. Walsh, *Our Lady of Fatima*, 222-223.

36. Michel de la Sainte Trinite, *The Whole Truth About Fatima*, 698. This fulfilled Mary's words to the letter, "...if people do not stop offending God, a worse one (war) will break out during the pontificate of Pius XI."

37. Ibid., 699.

38. Ibid.

39. Ibid.

40. Lúcia, *Fatima in Lucia's Own Words*, 112-113.

41. Ibid. Father Christopher Rengers, who I had the pleasure to know, offers some insight into Jacinta's thinking: "Jacinta thought much. Often Lúcia found her in a pensive mood and asked what she might be thinking about. Often, Jacinta answered, 'Of that war which is coming, of the many people who are going to die and go to Hell. What a shame! If they would stop offending God, neither the war would come, nor would they go to Hell.' Sometimes the comment is made: 'War is Hell.' Jacinta linked war and Hell together for she knew they both came from the disorder of sin, and both could be prevented by turning to the order and love that was the complete opposite of war and Hell-the Immaculate Heart of Mary." (For an excellent book on Jacinta, see Rengers's, *The Youngest Prophet*.)

CHAPTER 7: A GRUESOME WAR

1. Elizabeth Nix, "Were They Always Called World War I and World War II?" The History Channel, March 6, 2013, https://www.history.com. https://www.history.com/news/were-they-always-called-world-war-i-and worldwarii#:~:text=The%20short%20answer%20is%20noSecond%20World%20War%E2%80%94monikers%20arose.

2. Bill O'Reilly & Martin Dugard, *Killing the Rising Sun* (New York, NY: Henry Holt and Company, 2016), 47.

3. Ibid., 47-48.

4. Ibid.

5. Ibid.

6. Ibid.

7. Timothy Snyder, *Bloodlands: Europe Between Hitler and Stalin* (New York, NY: Basic Books, 2010), 187. This book opens up a new level of reality on the horrors of World War II and what might have been if the war had followed a different path. It is highly recommended.

8. Ibid., ix.

9. Evan Presser, "My Jewish Grandfather: Handpicked by Hitler to Curate the Museum of Extinct Races," April 11, 2019, https://lithub.com/my-jewish-grandfather-handpicked-by-hitler-to-curate-the-museum-of-extinct-races/; Magda Veselska, "The Museum of an Extinct Race: Fact vs Legend," 2016, https://www.ceeol.com.

10. Snyder, *Bloodlands: Europe Between Hitler and Stalin*, ix.

11. Ibid.

12. Ibid.

13. Ibid., x.

14. Randy Roughton, "Air Superiority: Advantage Over Enemy Skies for 60 Years," *Air Force News Service*, April 19, 2013, https://www.af.mil/News/Article-Display/Article/109356/air-superiority-advantage-over-enemy-skies-for-60-years/. To understand what a dropped bomb hurling from the sky at 500 mph meant once it hit the ground, it's vitally necessary to place oneself on the ground as the object of the descending projectile's wrath. Besides the blatant destruction that occurred with the explosion, there came the high-pitched whistling overhead, which gradually grew louder and louder as the bomb descended, creating a horrifying reality on the ground for its potential victims. Over time, the wallowing, whistling sound of cascading bombs became synonymous with death to all that recognized the sound approaching out of the vast emptiness of the sky. It was the same with the sound of swooping dive-bombers that emitted terrifying noise from their engines. Once heard, those on the ground knew they were seconds away from a lacerating machine gun attack or from a bomb being dropped on their heads. The Nazis, aware of the terror factor from the sound, even equipped their planes with sirens that screamed out when they dive-bombed during a Blitzkrieg air raid. Repeatedly shown scenes from the Japanese sneak attack on Pearl Harbor, this nightmare reality became etched into tens of millions of people's minds during the 1950s and 1960s. General Eisenhower appears to not only have been an expert on human warfare but also perhaps somewhat on spiritual warfare, though unknowingly. To respond to the communist threat on the nation, he added "Under God" to the Pledge of Allegiance in 1954. Two years later, he signed a law officially declaring "In God We Trust" to be the nation's official motto (P.L.-140), mandating that the phrase be printed on all American paper currency. In 1953, Eisenhower also began the tradition of the National Prayer Breakfast. Historians say Eisenhower was known for making the case for religion in the public sphere, often invoking the words "God Almighty," "God Our Creator," and "God Our Father."

15. The number of bombers and tonnage of bombs are taken from a USAF document written in 1953 and classified secret until 1978: United States

Air Force Department Document, "Bombing of Dresden in World War II," 1953. Various authors have published comparable statistics.

16. Accounts on the ground during Dresden are from "Time Witnesses," moderated by Tom Holloway, and *The Fire-bombing of Dresden: An Eyewitness Account*, archived, September 26, 2006, at the *Wayback Machine*. Account of Lothar Metzer, rerecorded in May,1999, in Berlin.

17. New World Encyclopedia, "Bombing of Dresden in World War II," March 27, 2018, https://www.historylearningsite.co.uk/world-war-two/the-bombing-campaign-of-world-war-two/the-bombing-of-dresden/.

18. C.N. Truman, "The Bombing of Dresden," *The History Learning Site*, May 19, 2015, https://www.historylearningsite.co.uk/world-war-two/the-bombing-campaign-of-world-war-two/the-bombing-of-dresden/. The true intent of bombing missions was often not revealed or spoken. Like ancient walled cities that fell under siege, the initial aim of an aerial attack was often to sap the morale of the people. Hitler ordered London bombed specifically to break the will of the people of England. But with civilian populations now open game, the objective became complete annihilation when possible and if convenient. Ordering 329 B-29 bombers to strike Tokyo, U.S. General Curtis Lemay stated that he wanted the city burned down and wiped off the map to shorten the war.

19. Haffert, *To Prevent This*, 12.

20. Eric Lichtblau, "The Holocaust Just Got More Shocking," *The New York Times, Sunday Review,* March 1, 2013. Lichtblau's article reviews the 2013 Holocaust Memorial Museum Study. The thirteen-year study cataloged some 42,500 Nazi ghettos and camps throughout Europe from 1933-1945. The lead editors of the study, Geoffrey Megargee and Martin C. Dean, estimate 15 to 20 million died or were imprisoned at the sites. There had previously been thought to be 10,000 sites. The authors conclude from the number of sites that every German citizen *must* have known about this.

21. Anastasio Ballestrero, the Father General of the Carmelite Order at the time and the future Cardinal Archbishop of Turin, requested of Lúcia in 1955 that she explain in what sense World War II would be worse than World War I. Lúcia revised the text sometime after the year 2000 and it was published on February 13, 2006, in the book *Come Vedo il Messaggio di Fatima nel corso del tempo e degli avvenimenti*, with a foreword by Father Geremia Carlo Vechina.

22. In "The Secret of Fatima", Mary states, "The war is going to end, but if people do not cease offending God, a worse one will break out during the Pontificate of Pius XI." See my book, *The Fatima Prophecies*, p. 279.

23. Jeremy Noakes, "Hitler and 'Lebensraum' in the East," *History-World Wars*, March 30, 2011, http://www.bbc.co.uk/history/worldwars/wwtwo/

hitler_lebensraum_01.shtml. The invasion of Russia by Germany in 1941 was the first step in Hitler's attempt to acquire more land for the German people to populate.

24. Snyder, *Bloodlands*, xvii, 67, 101, 231-232.
25. This was known as Churchill's "Finest Hour" speech. His first speech to the House of Commons as Prime Minister, known as his "Blood, Toil, Tears and Sweat" speech, is also revered and has a direct Fátima connection—it was delivered on May 13, 1940, the anniversary date of the Virgin Mary's first apparition at Fátima in 1917.
26. Socci, *The Fourth Secret of Fatima*, 185.
27. Michel de la Trinite, *The Whole Truth About Fatima*, 736-742.
28. Ibid.
29. Ibid.
30. Ibid., 795-811.
31. Gorny and Rosikon, *Fatima Mysteries*, 209-210.
32. Ibid.
33. Ibid., 209.
34. Anders Stephanson, "Cold War Origins," Cold War Origins Encyclopedia of American Foreign Policy, https://www.americanforeignrelations.com/A-D/Cold-War-Origins.html. Bernard Baruch is credited with the term "Cold War." By his own account, however, Baruch took it from his friend and speech writer, Herbert Bayard Swope, who claims he came up with it while considering the so called "Phony War" of 1939-1940, the early phase of the Second World War in Europe when nothing militarily took place.
35. Ibid.
36. Apostoli, *Fatima for Today*, 210. Lúcia wrote the Secret on a single piece of lined paper and folded it as to make four pages. This is relevant with regards to the controversy surrounding the argument that there are two separate communiques from Lúcia involving the Secret. One is alleged to pertain only to the Third Secret. For more on this, see Kevin Symonds's excellent, *On the Third Part of the Secret of Fatima*.
37. Gorny and Rosikon, *Fatima Mysteries*, 210. January 3, 1947, is the date most often cited that the third part of the Secret of Fátima was written by Sister Lúcia. But the official documentarian of Fátima, Father Joaquin Alonso, writes that *this* is not certain. We *do know* for certain, he says, that it had to be written sometime between December 25, 1943, and January 9, 1944. On June 17, 1944, the Bishop of Gurza, Archbishop Ferreira, traveling with others who were unaware of his mission, arrived at the border of Portugal and Spain at a place named Valença do Minho. There he received from Lúcia, personally, the third part of the Secret. Later that day, he arrived at the Bishop of Leira's country estate in Braga,

where he handed the envelope containing the Secret to Bishop Dom José Correia da Silva. The Bishop put it in a larger envelope and wrote on it: *This envelope with its contents is to be given to His Eminence, Cardinal Dom Manuel, Patriarch of Lisbon, after my death.* Bishop da Silva then deposited the envelope in his safe in the chancery, where it remained until it was transferred to the Vatican, arriving there on April 16, 1957. Bishop da Silva could have opened it, states Alonso, but had no desire to know its contents. The sealed envelope ultimately made its way to Pope John XXIII, who broke the seal, opened it and read it on August 17, 1959. Although it was in Portuguese, he allegedly understood the text in its entirety. Then, he re-sealed it within another envelope and had it archived. According to Alonso, the Secret was kept in Pope John's quarters until his death on June 3, 1963, and then turned over to Pope Paul VI. States Alonzo, "We believe with all probability that Pope Paul VI also read the letter. We may likewise affirm that this had a decisive influence on his decision to go to Fátima for the fiftieth anniversary of the apparitions on May 13, 1967, and that the contents of the Secret are reflected in the homily delivered by him at the Pontifical Mass celebrated there." While the Church has officially documented that Lúcia wrote "1960" on the outside of the envelope, the Secretary of Pope John XXIII, Monsignor Loris Capovilla, wrote in his book, *John XXIII as Remembered by Secretary Monsignor Loris Capovilla* (p.116), that Pope John knew nothing about the 1960 date: "The fact is that no one spoke to him of it, no one hinted at that deadline." The entire matter surrounding the 1960 date for the opening of the third part of the Secret may be even more contentious. Cardinal Bertone says that he asked Lúcia why only after 1960 could the Secret be read? Lúcia told him that it was not Our Lady that fixed that date but her. "It was not Our Lady. I fixed the date because I had the intuition that before 1960 it would not be understood. But only later would it be understood. Now one can understand better." But this issue gets even more murkier. On November 25, 1985, Fátima scholar Frere Michel de la Sainte Trinite gave a talk at a Vatican symposium in Rome, there he stated, in fact, that Our Lady had asked that the Secret be published in 1944 or, at the latest, 1960 since its meaning "would become clearer at that time." (See *The Fatima Crusader*, July, 1986.)

38. Apostoli, *Fatima for Today*, 210.
39. Ibid. See 'De Nuevo el Secreto de Fatima, *Ephemerides Mariologicae*,' 1982, p.6.
40. Gorny and Rosikon, *Fatima Mysteries*, 254.
41. Ibid., 214. The reporter who took the famous photograph for *Life Magazine* was Joseph Pazen.

42. Ibid., 254. The article in *Paris Match* was on the papal apartments, written by a reporter named Robert Serrou. A nun in charge of the papal household at the time, Sister Pascalina, pointed to a box bearing the label "Secret of the Holy Office, and told Serrou, "In that box is the Third Secret of Fatima."

43. Ratzinger, "The Message of Fatima," published in *The Fatima Prophecies*, 275.

CHAPTER 8: A DIVINE COLLISION

1. Kraljevic, *The Apparitions of Our Lady at Medjugorje*, 3. Theologians studying Medjugorje have noted three pre-signs that the Virgin Mary was coming to Medjugorje: 1) The towering cross on Mt. Krizevac; 2) the oversized St. James Church built in Medjugorje; 3) the painting of Mary afloat in the sky over the village of Medjugorje that hung on the wall in the rear of St. James.

2. Randall Sullivan, *The Miracle Detective* (New York: Grove Press, 2004), 70.

3. Ibid.

4. Ibid., 71.

5. Ibid.

6. Ibid., 70-71.

7. Ibid., Andrew Thull, ed., *What They Say About Medjugorje: A Contemporary Mystery* (Cincinnati, OH: Precision Built Corporation, 1991), 839; Medjugorje *Messenger*, July-September, 1989.

8. Ibid. This account of the history of Mt. Krizevac and the construction of the cross came from a variety of sources, Sullivan's being just one of many that I pieced together. Father Grgo Vasilj celebrated the first Mass on Krizevac on March 15, 1934. On the cross is engraved, "TO JESUS CHRIST, THE REDEEMER OF THE HUMAN RACE, AS A SIGN OF OUR FAITH, LOVE AND HOPE: IN MEMORY OF THE 1900TH ANNIVERSARYOF THE PASSION OF JESUS CHRIST." Around this same time in the 1930s, a local woman named Mariciusa, who tended sheep on the hillsides there, is said to have foretold the coming of the Virgin Mary to the area in the future. She also said that a "White Army" was coming, amidst other great changes. Not only did the apparitions at Medjugorje in 1981 fulfill her words, but when UN peacekeepers arrived in the mid-90s wearing white helmets in a caravan of white painted vehicles, many of the locals became convinced that she had been a true prophet.

9. Kraljevic, *The Apparitions of Our Lady at Medjugorje*, 5.

10. Ibid.

11. Ibid.

12. Bulletin 2000, No.157, December 26,2008, www.medjugorje.hr.
13. James Mulligan, *Medjugorje, What's Happening?* (Brewster, MA: Paraclete Press), 18.
14. Kraljevic, *The Apparitions of Our Lady at Medjugorje*, 5.
15. Ibid., 3.
16. John Thavis, *The Vatican Prophecies*, (New York, NY: Viking, 2015), 58. Thavis notes that by the late 1980s' many families in the five villages had abandoned their tobacco fields and vineyards and turned to businesses related to the tourism.

CHAPTER 9: "IS IT A SNAKE?"

1. Father Janko Bubalo, *A Thousand Encounters with the Blessed Virgin Mary in Medjugorje* (Chicago, IL: Friends of Medjugorje, 1987), xi. The *Book of Haggai* in the Old Testament speaks of June 24th: "Then the Lord stirred up the spirit of the governor of Judah, Zerubbabel, son of Shealtiel, and the spirit of the high priest Joshua, son of Jehozadak, and the spirit of all the remnant of the people, so that they came and set to work on the house of the Lord of hosts, their God, on the twenty-fourth day of the sixth month." (Hg 1: 15)
2. Soldo, *My Heart Will Triumph*, 11.
3. Ibid., 67.
4. Ibid., 11.
5. Craig, *Spark from Heaven*, 15.
6. Ibid.
7. Ibid.
8. Kraljevic, *The Apparitions of Our Lady at Medjugorje*, 7. As many icons convey, the Virgin Mary often appears with the baby Jesus in her arms or the child Jesus by her side. At Tui, Spain, on December 10, 1925, the Virgin Mary appeared to Sister Lúcia with the child Jesus by her side, elevated on a cloud of light.
9. Soldo, *My Heart Will Triumph*, 15.
10. Ibid.
11. Marin, *Queen of Peace in Medjugorje*, 8. Vicka told Father Bubalo that the reason she thought it was a snake at the time was because the three of them (Ivanka, Mirjana, and Milka) were staring at something and seemed to be in "some kind of fear."

CHAPTER 10: THE MOTHER OF GOD IS VISITING EARTH

1. Janice T. Connell, *The Visions of the Children* (New York, NY: St. Martin's Griffin, revised and updated edition, 2007), 111.

2. Bubalo, *A Thousand Encounters with the Blessed Virgin Mary in Medjugorje*, xii, xiii.

3. Sullivan, *The Miracle Detective*, 126.

4. Pelletier, *The Queen of Peace Visits Medjugorje*, 42.

5. Craig, *Spark from Heaven*, 86.

6. Ibid.

7. Ibid., 19. Two months before the apparitions, a strange episode occurred involving Vicka and her family. One of Vicka's brothers, Franjo, found two sets of rosary beads mysteriously left on the family tractor at 6 a.m. in the morning. Vicka has always believed that this event was related to the coming apparitions.

8. Connell, *The Visions of the Children*, 52.

9. Ibid.

10. Kraljevic, *The Apparitions of Our Lady at Medjugorje*, 142.

11. Bubalo, *A Thousand Encounters with the Blessed Virgin Mary in Medjugorje*, 7.

12. Connell, *The Visions of the Children*, 160.

13. Craig, *Spark from Heaven*, 16.

14. Connell, *The Visions of the Children*, 141.

15. Craig, *Spark from Heaven*, 15.

16. Lucy Rooney S.N.D. and Robert Faricy, S.J., *Mary Queen of Peace: Is the Mother of God Appearing in Medjugorje* (New York, NY: Alba House, 1984), 16.

17. Ibid., 17. Milka gave the following account of the first day: "I also saw one person, as all of us were moving. She was wearing white and was standing on one big white cloud. She had something in her hand which she was covering and uncovering. She beckoned us to come closer. I think that it lasted between fifteen and twenty minutes. When Vicka and the two Ivans came, we invited them to join us. At that time, then, there were six of us and later while watching we were overcome by fear and simply went home. When we came home, we told everybody, but no one believed. We told our parents but they said we were too young. I was only thirteen. "You are only children and would be better off in bed," they said. The following day I did not go, but Marija did. They had a feeling inside which made them go to that spot. On their way, they called for me but I was not at home. I was with my mother in the field working, so Marija went with them. Nobody believed. But it was hard for anyone to believe. But on the second day, a few went there with them. On the third, there were already many people gathered. After the first day, everyone said to keep quiet because it was not possible." See *Medjugorje Herald*, Vol. 3, No. 12, December 1989, p. 9.

18. Laurentin and Rupčić, *Is the Virgin Mary Appearing at Medjugorje?* 41, 65.

19. Sullivan, *The Miracle Detective*, 74; Rooney and Faricy, *Mary Queen of Peace*, 17.

20. Rooney and Faricy, *Mary Queen of Peace*, 17.

21. Sullivan, *The Miracle Detective*, 74.

22. Craig, *Spark from Heaven*, 16.

23. Bubalo, *A Thousand Encounters with the Blessed Virgin Mary in Medjugorje,* 17; Sullivan, *The Miracle Detective*, 74.

24. Ibid., 9.

25. Sullivan, *The Miracle Detective*, 74.

26. Craig, *Spark from Heaven*, 16.

27. Ibid.

28. Laurentin and Rupčić, *Is the Virgin Mary Appearing at Medjugorje?* 49.

29. Ibid.

30. Ibid.

31. Bubalo, *A Thousand Encounters with the Blessed Virgin Mary in Medjugorje*, 9.

32. Craig, *Spark from Heaven*, 16, 218. See Craig's endnotes for BBC interview, pp. 218-223.

33. Ibid.,16. Like at Fátima, there is the presence of a cloud that Mary is seen standing upon. Both white and gray have been said to be its color.

34. Sullivan, *The Miracle Detective*, 75.

35. Ibid.

36. Craig, *Spark from Heaven*, 16.

37. The use of the word "errors" (of Russia) by the Virgin Mary at Fátima on July 13, 1917, seems to have been deliberate and for a reason. Mary can be seen to be possibly repeating Pope Pius IX's exact words in his 1846 encyclical *Qui Pluribus* (On Faith and Reason). Communism, wrote Pius in the encyclical, was dark, deceitful, cunning and depraved— "a filthy medley of errors." Hindsight reveals Pope Pius IX to be innovative and prophetic. The encyclical was released two years before the publication of the German philosophers Karl Marx and Friedrich Engels's *Manifesto of the Communist Party* in 1848, better known as *The Communist Manifesto*. It is also worthy to note that Mary never said Communism or Marxism at Fátima. She said "errors of Russia" which, although this was immediately understood after the Bolshevik Revolution in Russia to be Communism, left the door open to understand that there would be other "errors," such as we find today in Cultural Marxism by way of subcategories of post-modernist, so called progressive (socialist) movements. Atheism is the glue that binds them.

CHAPTER 11: THE ERRORS OF RUSSIA

1. L.I. Brezhnev, "Report of the Central Committee of CPSU to the XXVI Congress of the Communist Party of the Soviet Union and the Immediate Tasks of the Party in Home and Foreign Policy," https://archive. org. [Scanned by anonymous figure, uploaded by Thomas Mrett, March 26, 2015.] The 26th Congress of the Communist Party of the Soviet Union opened on February 23, 1981, with Brezhnev's five-hour opening address. A transcript of this event is also available from Bolerium Books, a used book store in San Francisco.

2. UPI Archives, "Brezhnev Warns of a Nuclear War," October 27, 1981, https://www.upi.com/Archives/1981/10/27/ Brezhnev-warns-of-nuclear-war/6773373006800/.

3. John M. Haffert, *Her Own Words to the Nuclear Age* (Asbury, NJ: The 101 Foundation, Inc.,1993), 236. At the time of the apparitions at Fátima, the revolutionary leaders of Portugal described Lisbon "as the most atheist city in the world." (See also *Fatima in the Light of History* by Costa Brochado, p. 230.)

4. Ibid.

5. Gorny and Rosikon, *Fatima Mysteries*, 56-57.

6. Ibid.

7. Ibid.

8. Apostoli, *Fatima for Today*, 13. With the October 1910 removal of the Braganca Dynasty, Portugal was thrown into an almost constant state of revolution. Writes Father John DeMarchi, "Revolution succeeded revolution. There was continual party discord, religious persecution, general discontent, cowardice, and willful blindness of the people. Since the establishment of the Republican regime (1910), the country lived in a continual state of alarm. It seemed that the various governments, one after another, were inspired by the sole purpose of furthering the powers of darkness. From 1910 until May 28, 1926—when the military coup d'état led by Marshall Gomes da Costa inaugurated an era of stability and peace—there occurred sixteen revolutions. These were authentic revolts, not mere skirmishes. The worst and most to be feared occurred in October, 1921, and became known as the revolt of the 'White Ants,' a Communist-anarchist party whose favorite weapon was the bomb."

9. Johnston, *Fatima: The Great Sign*, 23.

10. Ibid.

11. Paul Kengor, *The Devil and Karl Marx: Communism's Long March of Death, Deception, and Infiltration* (Gastonia, NC: TAN Books,2020), 29.

12. Ibid.

13. Paul Kengor, "The War on Religion," *Faith and Society*, September 25, 2010, https://www.faithandfreedom.com/special-featurethe-war-on-religion/.
14. Kengor, *The Devil and Karl Marx*, 29.
15. Ibid., xx.
16. Ibid.
17. Ibid., xxi.
18. Ibid.
19. Rev. Gianbattista Mondin S.X., "The Atheism of Karl Marx," *L'Osservatore Romano*, p.12, April 20, 1978, https://www.ewtn.com/catholicism/library/atheism-of-karl-marx-9902. Marx especially saw the traditional family as an enemy of freedom and equality. For an excellent look at this see Apostoli's *Fatima Today*.
20. Dale Yeager, "The Curious Case of Karl Marx, Satan, and the Occult," *The Dale Yeager Blog*, September 18, 2020, https://daleyeagerdotcom.wordpress.com/2020/09/13/the-curious-case-of-karl-marx-satan-and-the-occult/.
21. Ibid.
22. Ibid. For an excellent look at this subject see Kengor's, *The Devil and Karl Marx*.
23. Peter Popham, "Italy Blames KGB for Plot to Kill Pope John Paul II," March 3, 2006, https://www.fulcrum-anglican.org.uk/newswatch/italy-blames-kgb-for-plot-to-kill-pope-john-paul/.
24. Ibid.
25. Ibid. In retrospect, the fingerprints of Brezhnev and the Soviet leadership can be seen to be all over this affair by merely examining the Soviets behavior in the months leading up to the attempted assassination. Historian Paul Kengor writes that by the end of March 1981, the Soviets appeared to be "losing it." They were poised to invade Poland; they openly detested Reagan and Washington, and hated the Polish Pope in the Vatican. Moreover, their press revealed this rage. On March 26, a Ukrainian newspaper accused the Vatican of "malicious anti-Soviet and anti-communist propaganda" being forwarded "by dyed in the wool anti-Soviets and Nazi remnants." The inference was clear. Karol Wojtyła was a Nazi remnant. A worse attack came in the Soviet Journal *Polimya* that same month. The publication wrote that John Paul II was "militantly anti-communist," a "cunning and dangerous ideological enemy." The journal accused the Pope of being sympathetic to a secret Nazi-Vatican plan during the war that aimed to exterminate the Polish people, including Jews and clergy. The *Polimya* article labeled John Paul II as "malicious, lowly, perfidious, and backward," a man who was the puppet of American militarists. The Pope was, they said, "battling socialism with overseas accomplices" and "his new boss in the White House." Writes Kengor of the Soviets' view of Pope John Paul II, "The Soviets were not concerned; they were terrified."

(For a comprehensive look at all of this, see Kengor's excellent, *A Pope and a President*).

26. Author Antonio Socci calls the Secret of Fátima, "the greatest mystery of the 20ᵗʰ century." (*The Fourth Secret of Fatima*, p.4)
27. Ratzinger, "The Message of Fatima", published in *The Fatima Prophecies*, 284-286.
28. Ibid., 296.

CHAPTER 12: VISAGES OF LUCIFER

1. Gorny and Rosikon, *Fatima Mysteries*, 129.
2. Kengor, *The Devil and Karl Marx*, 114.
3. Ibid., 111,112.
4. Paul Le Blanc, "How They Saw Lenin," May 18, 2017, https://socialistworker.org/2017/05/18/how-they-saw-lenin. The information was excerpted from John Reed's *Ten Days that Shook the World* (New York, NY: Penguin Classics (1990) [1919]). The Gnostic ideas that shaped Lenin's thinking are said to be the intellectual roots of Russian Bolshevism. Lenin's great grandmother is even reported to have been burned at the stake by the Inquisition for using black magic and witchcraft.
5. Ibid. The last ten days leading up to this moment are noteworthy. On December 16, the Bolshevik Central Committee authorized Lenin's trip to Petrograd. Several days later, he secretly entered the city disguised in a gray wig and large eyeglasses, with his beard shaved off. One witness said he looked like a Lutheran minister, another thought he appeared to be an elderly music teacher. Lenin boarded at the fifth floor apartment of a woman named Margarita Fofanova, a student who worked in a publisher's office and was a Communist since the age of nineteen. On October 21, he comprised an article on what makes a successful revolution. "The success of both the Russian revolution and the world revolution," Lenin wrote that day, "depends upon two or three days of struggle." On October 22, Lenin called a meeting of the party's Central Committee for the next evening in the apartment of journalist Nikolai Sukhanov. During the five-hour meeting, Lenin relentlessly put down all doubt, indecision and question. "Revolution now! Seize power now! Wait for nothing and no one. Set a date!" "Delay is death," he repeated over and over, a maxim attributed to Czar Peter the Great. A vote was eventually taken: ten to two for revolution. Kamenev and Zinoviev voted against the motion. Lenin then wrote with a blunt lead pencil, "Recognizing, therefore, that an armed uprising is inevitable and that the time is fully ripe, the Central Committee proposes to all party organizations to be guided accordingly." (See Warren Carroll's *1917: Red Banners,*

White Mantle for an in depth look at this history from a Catholic perspective.) The revolution in Russia had long before been predicted. At the height of the French Revolution, Count Semyon Voronstov, Russia's ambassador to Great Britain, foretold a future revolution in Russia. Not in his lifetime would it occur, he told his brother in a letter, but in "the lifetime of their children."

6. Kengor, *The Devil and Karl Marx*, 10.
7. Jean Ousset, *Le Marxisme–Leninisme* (La Catholique,1960), 344. Lenin almost immediately incorporated the All-Russian Extraordinary Commission, the CHEKA. It was a secret police unit that was in charge of fighting sabotage and counterrevolution. But its primary ambition was to keep the masses in line through unrelenting terror and random violence. The CHEKA was repeatedly renamed. By the time of the Cold War it had evolved into the KGB. It slowly became a massive, twenty division operation with a half million employees serving in a wide range of intelligence gathering functions, both domestically and with foreign affairs. Just in Moscow, there were 50,000 employees assigned to espionage activities.
8. Michel Heller and Aleksandr Nekrich, *L'utopia au Pouvoir. Historie de URSS de 1917 a nos jours*, (Calmann-Levy,1982), 55-56.
9. Ibid., 114.
10. Kengor, *The Devil and Karl Marx*, 11.
11. Robert Payne, *The Life and Death of Lenin* (New York, NY: Simon and Schuster,1964), 418-419.
12. Gorny and Rosikon, *Fatima Mysteries*, 140.

CHAPTER 13: THE SPREAD OF RED

1. Arthur Ransome, "Death of Lenin-Archive, 1924," May 23, 2017, https://theguardian.com. On January 21, 1924, after suffering two previous strokes over the past few years, Lenin was pronounced dead at 6:00 p.m. Approximately eleven years later, in a Soviet prison, a woman named Elizabeth Lermola, who survived to write a book, met a Bolshevik man named Gavril Volkov. He had been the cook for Lenin at Gorki when he died. Gavril said that on January 21, 1924, he entered Lenin's room at 11:00 a.m. to take him his "second breakfast." Lenin attempted to get up and talk, but was unable to do either. Lenin then put a note in Gavril's hand, just as a doctor attempted to give Lenin an injection. The note read, "Gavrilushka, I've been poisoned...go fetch Nadyda [Krupskaya] at once...tell Trotsky...and tell everyone you can."

2. Malcolm Higgins, "Joseph Stalin-A Terrifying Titan on the Eastern Front," *War History Online,* https://www.warhistoryonline.com/war-articles/joseph-stalin-man-steel-titan.html.
3. Ibid.
4. Dariusz Stusowski, "Joseph Stalin Led a Life of Crime Before Becoming Russia's Leader," 2019, https://historycollection.com/stalin-bank-robber/. The Tiflis Bank Robbery was also known as Erivansky Square Expropriation. It netted the equivalent of 3.96 million dollars in today's (2018) monetary value.
5. Dmitry Sudakov, "Joseph Stalin's Occult Knowledge and Experiments," Pravda.ru, June 23, 2011, https://english.pravda.ru/science/118290-joseph_stalin/. [original article in Russian]
6. "Zinoviev," Encyclopedia of Marxism (Glossary of People), https://www.marxists.org/encyclopedia/.
7. Walsh, *Our Lady of Fatima*, 1, 2. (See Foreword by Rt. Rev. William C. McGrath, April, 1954.)
8. In 1917, ten-year old Lúcia thought at the time that "Russia" was the name of a very bad woman who lived in a village down the road. Lúcia's fellow visionary, Francisco, believed Mary was referring to his uncle's finicky mule, "Russa."
9. Walsh, *Our Lady of Fatima*, 221-223.
10. Harpal Brar, "Stalin and the Chinese Revolution," November / December 2009, https://www.marxists.org/encyclopedia/. Brar's quote is originally from *Stalin on the Chinese Revolution* by Chen Po Ta. This information is found on marxist/lennistwordpress.com., and originally published in *Trotskyism or Leninism* (Chapter 13), by Harpal Brar. *LALKAR is* a bi-monthly, self-described "anti-imperialist newspaper" written in Britain.
11. Ibid.
12. Rv 12:4.

CHAPTER 14: KILLING GOD

1. "Lenin: 55. To Maxim Gorky," https://www.marxists.org. The letter from Vladimir Lenin to Maxim Gorky was written on November 13 or 14 in 1913, and published in *Pravda,* No. 51, March 2, 1924. Original source: Lenin Collected Works, Progress Publishers, [1976], Moscow, Volume 35, pages 121-124. Public domain: Lenin Internet Archive. Source: Marxist Internet Archive.
2. Gorny and Rosikon, *Fatima Mysteries,*137.
3. Father Michael d' Herbigny S.J., *La Tyrannie Sovietique et le Malheur russe,* 1923, 237. Sergei Petrovich Melgunov, a Russian socialist and

historian, escaped the Soviet Union in October 1922. While there, he accumulated information and testimonies on the crimes the Communists were committing and published them in a book in 1924, titled *Red Terror*. Melgunov chronicled that each Soviet police agency had a reputation for its own way of murdering prisoners.

4.   Kengor, *The Devil and Karl Marx*, 107.
5.   Heller and Nekrich, *L'utopia au Pouvoir. Historie de URSS de 1917 a nos jours*, 183-201. On November 18, 1920, the Soviet Union became the first nation to legalize abortion, classifying it as a contraceptive. Nazi Germany became the second country to legalize abortion in the nations that it controlled. On March 9, 1943, abortions were sanctioned in Nazi-controlled territories in Poland, but only for women from what the Nazi's referred to as "lower" race nations, i.e., Slavs. Not only did the Soviets eliminate Sundays, but they established with it what was called the "Continuous Work Week." For eleven years, the USSR had no weekends.
6.   Pavi Dixon, "Religion in the Soviet Union," April 17, 2006, https://www.bolshevik.info/religion-soviet-union170406.htm.
7.   Ibid.
8.   Michel de la Sainte Trinite, *The Whole Truth About Fatima*, 451. Patriarch Tikhon was canonized a Saint by *The Russian Orthodox Church Outside of Russia*, on November 1, 1981.
9.   Dixon, "Religion in the Soviet Union," https://www.bolshevik.info/religion-soviet-union170406.htm.
10. Ibid.
11. Geoffrey York," Why Father of Glasnost is Despised in Russia," March 9, 2001, https://www.theglobeandmail.com/news/world/why-father-of-glasnost-is-despised-in-russia/article22399254/. See Alexander Yakovlev's, *The Maelstrom of Memory, From Stolypin to Putin* (2001), for a more in- depth understanding of how Communism ravaged the U.S.S.R.
12. Dimitri Pospielovsky, *A History of Soviet Atheism in Theory and Practice and the Believer* (New York, NY: Palgrave Macmillan, 1988).
13. John Das, "The Persecution of the Church in the Soviet Union: A Story that Needs to Be Told," *The American Society for the Defense of Tradition, Family and Property*, November 5, 2016, https://www.tfp.org/persecution-church-soviet-union-story-needs-told/.
14. Ibid. While Christianity was being virtually wiped off the map in the Soviet Union and under great persecution in Europe from 1920-1940, a virtual deluge of the miraculous was being reported across Europe and throughout the world. These events have been widely documented. Father Johann G. Roten, Director of the International Research Institute

at the University of Dayton, estimated that close to a thousand major, minor, and related apparitions occurred between 1830 and 1981.

15. Michel de la Sainte Trinite, *The Whole Truth About Fatima*, 449. Stalin's assault on religion, especially Catholicism, was not just external but also internal. According to Alice von Hildebrand, the wife of the German Catholic philosopher and theologian Dietrich von Hildebrand, Stalin ordered the subversion of Catholic seminaries with communist plants. Reportedly, some 1,200 men were infiltrated into the system by a communist agent named Bella Dodd with the intent to morally wreck the seminaries and to advocate and spread Liberation Theology, a synthesis of Christian theology and Marxism.

16. Gorny and Rosikon, *Fatima Mysteries*, 147.

17. Ibid., 277.

18. Josyp Terelya with Michael H. Brown, *Josyp Terelya: Witness to the Apparitions and Persecution in the U.S.S.R.* (Milford, OH: Faith Publishing, 1991), 42-43. I became very close friends with Josyp Terelya and spent many days with him. In December 1993, Josyp Terelya, Roman Churski, his English translator, Ted Flynn, a Marian author, and I traveled to the Ukraine for the purpose of bringing Catholic literature, financial assistance, and other materials to the recently liberated communist nation. While the country was no longer under Moscow's authority, many communists still maintained positions of power and exercised it to attempt to monitor and impede our efforts. We learned months later that we were considered by the authorities to be CIA operatives. We were followed across the lengthy country from Kiev to L'viv and pulled over by police and other government officials more than a dozen times. Everywhere we traveled throughout Ukraine, Terelya was welcomed as a national hero.

19. Ibid.

20. Ibid.

21. Ibid.

22. Ibid.

23. Ibid., 42-43, 60.

24. Gorny and Rosikon, *Fatima Mysteries*, 239.

25. Ibid., 222.

26. "Marxist Theology, Chou En Lai, at the Bandung and Indonesian Conference in April 1955," https://www.allaboutworldview.org/marxist-theology.htm.Quoted from James D. Bale, *Communism: Its Faith and Fallacies* (Grand Rapids, MI: Baker Book House, 1962), 37. Not much has changed for the Communist Party in China since Mao and Chou En Lai. Atheism is still the status quo, according to a July 2017 official announcement. In the Communist Party CPC Central

Committee flagship magazine, *The Qiuishi Journal,* Wang Zuoan, director of state administration for religious affairs, said that religion undermined the party. The leader warned China's estimated 85 million party members that they are forbidden to have religious beliefs. They must be, he said, "firm Marxist atheists, obey party rules and stick to the party's faith." Officials who had religious faith had to give it up, and those who resisted, the magazine said, would be punished by the organization.

27. "Religion and Communism in China," http://factsanddetails.com/china/cat3/sub8/entry-5545.html [Last updated, September 2016].
28. Alexander Yakovlev, *A Century of Violence in the Soviet Union* (New Haven, CT: Yale University Press, 2004).
29. Mt 10:28.
30. For one of the best general accounts of the Yugoslav system of Communism, see *Yugoslavia and the New Communism* by G.W. Hoffman and F.W. Neal.

CHAPTER 15: ENEMY OF THE STATE

1. Kraljevic, *The Apparitions of Our Lady at Medjugorje,* 11; Craig, *Spark from Heaven,* 16-17.
2. Sullivan, *The Miracle Detective,* 75; Craig, *Spark from Heaven,* 16.
3. Sullivan, *The Miracle Detective,* 75.
4. Bubalo, *A Thousand Encounters with the Blessed Virgin Mary in Medjugorje,* 10.
5. Craig, *Spark from Heaven,* 17, Pelletier, *The Queen of Peace Visits Medjugorje,* 14.
6. Soldo, *My Heart Will Triumph,* 27-28.
7. Ibid.
8. Connell, *The Visions of the Children,* 142.
9. Wayne Weible, *Medjugorje: The Message,* (Orleans, MA: Paraclete Press, 1989), 11.
10. Sullivan, *The Miracle Detective,* 75.
11. Soldo, *My Heart Will Triumph,* 28.
12. Craig, *Spark from Heaven,* 85.
13. Ibid.
14. Kraljevic, *The Apparitions of Our Lady at Medjugorje,* 71.
15. Ibid. In 1998, Cardinal Aloysius Viktor Stepinac (May 8, 1898-February 10,1960), former Archbishop of Zagreb, was beatified as a martyr for his defiance of Tito's regime by Pope John Paul II.
16. Pelletier, *The Queen of Peace Visits Medjugorje,* 44.
17. Kraljevic, *The Apparitions of Our Lady at Medjugorje,* 11.

18. Craig, *Spark from Heaven*, 17. Nothing says more about Marija Pavlović than her donation of one of her kidneys to her brother Andrija in 1988 at a hospital in Birmingham, Alabama. Andrija died on February 4, 2004. During the transplant surgery in 1988, Marija reportedly experienced an apparition.

19. Ibid., 86.

20. Connell, *The Visions of the Children*, 99. Jacov's father, Ante, died in Sarajevo on April 25, 1986.

21. Craig, *Spark from Heaven*, 87.

22. Connell, *The Visions of the Children*, 99.

23. Ibid., 53. Jacov, being just a little 10-year-old boy at the time, was known for some amusing anecdotal incidents. It is said he asked the Virgin Mary in the fall of 1981 if his favorite soccer team, Dinamo, would win the national title. Mary just smiled. (See *Medjugorje: An Affirmation and Defense* by Father Albert Hebert, p. 27, and *Queen of Peace in Medjugorje* by Jacov Marin. p.41)

24. Ibid., 43-82.

25. Pelletier, *The Queen of Peace Visits Medjugorje*, 88-93.

26. Michael O'Carroll CSSp, *Medjugorje: Facts, Documents Theology* (Dublin: Veritas Publications, 1986), 44. Father O'Carroll documented Father Petar Ljubicic's official statement concerning his selection to be the one who will announce the Ten Secrets, dated September 4, 1985: "Sometime previously Mirjana had told me that I would be the priest to whom she would entrust the Secrets; her confidant that is. After hearing the inner voice on 1 June, she told me definitely that she would confide the Secrets to me. She told me that ten days before the occurrence of the Secret she would give me a paper similar to a parchment. Three days before the event I am to make the Secret in question known to the public. When the event takes place, I will give the paper back to Mirjana and wait for the next Secret."

27. Soldo, *My Heart Will Triumph*, 37-39.

28. Craig, *Spark from Heaven*, 31-32.

29. Donia and Fine Jr., *Bosnia and Hercegovina*, 144-149.

30. Ibid., 144.

31. Ibid.

32. Ibid., 145.

33. Ibid.

34. Stephen Clissold, ed., *A Short History of Yugoslavia* (Cambridge: Cambridge University Press,1966).

35. Donia and Fine Jr., *Bosnia and Hercegovina*, 143.

36. Ibid., 144.

37. Ibid., 155.

38. Ibid., 156.
39. Craig, *Spark from Heaven*, 33. Craig's figure of "as many as 16,000 in one day" is from Nora Beloff's *Tito's Flawed Legacy, Yugoslavia and the West 1939-84*, published by Victor Gollancz, London, 1985.
40. Singleton, *A Short History of the Yugoslav Peoples*, 220.
41. Verna Peric, "Thirty Years After His Death, Tito's Legacy Lives On in the Balkans," May 3, 2010, https://www.independent.co.uk/news/world/europe/30-years-after-his-death-tito-s-legacy-lives-balkans-1960884.html.
42. Singleton, *A Short History of the Yugoslav Peoples*, 220. Tito may have known Stalin long before his becoming president of Yugoslavia. In January 1913, Tito and Stalin were both staying in Vienna. In a curious oddity, it is on record that Tito, Stalin. Hitler, Trotsky, and Freud were all living in Vienna that same month and year. They all are known to have frequented the same café, Café Central.
43. Ibid., 209.
44. Ibid., 210.
45. Ibid., 212.
46. Ibid., 211.
47. Ibid.
48. Ibid., 238.
49. Ibid., 239.
50. Ibid., 215.
51. Ibid.
52. Daniel Ebner, "Being Catholic in Croatia is more Nationality than Religion," July 17, 2014, http://www.catholicmessenger.net/2014/07/being-catholic-in-croatia-is-more-nationality-than-religion/.
53. Singleton, *A Short History of the Yugoslav Peoples*, 216.
54. Ibid., 241.
55. Ibid., 280.
56. Ibid., 254.
57. Ibid., 278.
58. Joze Pirjevec, *Tito and His Comrades* (Madison, WI: University of Wisconsin Press, 2018). Stalin may have had a stroke in 1945 and in 1947. He was a chronic smoker and drinker who had progressive arteriosclerosis.
59. Soldo, *My Heart Will Triumph*, 18.
60. Ibid., 19.
61. Ibid.
62. Ibid.
63. Ibid. In a bizarre historical footnote to the whole cult of adulation surrounding the Soviet Communists and their leadership's penchant for being worshipped, there is in Moscow a park known as Fallen

Monument Park, or Muzeon Park or Park of the Fallen Heroes. It is the largest open air museum in Russia. Founded in 1992, the park is filled with statues and relics of former Soviet leaders that were rounded up and brought there after the collapse of the Soviet Union. Throughout the park, often mutilated busts of Lenin, Stalin, Brezhnev, Dzerzhinsky and others, along with massive Soviet emblems and other figurines, compete with each other for attention—or at least it seems. The park displays over 700 sculptures with another 200 in storage.

64. Ibid.
65. Ibid.
66. Ibid., 102.
67. Ibid., 36.
68. Ibid.
69. Ibid., 35-36.
70. Ibid., 113.
71. Ibid., 3, 99.
72. Ibid., 33.
73. Ibid., 39.

CHAPTER 16: "THEY'LL SAY WE'RE MAD"

1. "Dayan Says Israelis Have the Capacity to Produce A-Bombs," *New York Times*, (Page A-1, Column 4), June 25, 1981, https://www.nytimes.com.
2. "A Pakistan Pledge on Nuclear Arms was Reported by Under Secretary James L. Buckley at a Senate Hearing," *New York Times*, (Page A-6, Columns 3-6), June 25, 1981, https://www.nytimes.com/1981/06/25/world/us-cites-pakistani-pledge-not-to-make-atom-arms.html. (The Times reported that same day that Microsoft incorporated as a legal entity.)
3. Bubalo, *A Thousand Encounters with the Blessed Virgin Mary in Medjugorje,* 10.
4. Kraljevic, *The Apparitions of Our Lady at Medjugorje*, 11.
5. Craig, *Spark from Heaven*, 16.
6. Ibid.
7. Ibid.
8. Sullivan, *The Miracle Detective*, 75. Vicka told Bubalo "15 or more" were there on the second day. Mirjana wrote that "half" of the village was there.
9. Pelletier, *The Queen of Peace Visits Medjugorje*, 17.
10. Ibid. The flashes of celestial light are described almost exactly in the way the children of Fátima said they experienced the impending arrival of the Virgin. Fr. John De Marchi writes of the first apparition at Fátima, May 13, 1917: "After grace, they pulled their rosaries out of their pockets

as usual, and began to pray. We can imagine that Our Lady must have heard their innocent prayer with special pleasure on that day... At that moment, there was a flash of light, which the children for wont of a better word called lightning. They dropped their stones in alarm, knowing well that lightning was the herald of a thunderstorm. They looked up and around to see where it was coming from. But neither from the east nor the west was there the least sign of a storm, nor any cloud staining the deep blue of the sky."

11. Ibid. Father Pelletier reports that Father Rupčić's Croatian books on Medjugorje detail this fact. Laurentin and Kraljevic emphasize it also, as it is seen as a connection to Fátima.

12. Craig, *Spark from Heaven*, 17. Every account of the second day reports Ivanka as once again being the first to see the apparition.

13. Bubalo, *A Thousand Encounters with the Blessed Virgin Mary in Medjugorje*, 10.

14. Ibid.

15. Sullivan, *The Miracle Detective*, 76.

16. Connell, *The Visions of the Children*, 55.

17. Pelletier, *The Queen of Peace Visits Medjugorje*, 15.

18. Soldo, *My Heart Will Triumph*, 28. Every early account notes this mystery, citing different witnesses to corroborate it.

19. Laurentin and Rupčić, *Is the Virgin Mary Appearing at Medjugorje?* 25.

20. Soldo, *My Heart Will Triumph*, 28.

21. BBC transcript of the film, *The Madonna of Medjugorje*.

22. Craig, *Spark from Heaven*, 17; Pelletier, *The Queen of Peace Visits Medjugorje*, 15. Similarly, at Fátima, Francisco could not at first see the Virgin.

23. Craig, *Spark from Heaven*, 17.

24. Bubalo, *A Thousand Encounters with the Blessed Virgin Mary in Medjugorje*, 11; Pelletier, *The Queen of Peace Visits Medjugorje*, 15.

25. Ibid.

26. Ibid.

27. Bubalo, *A Thousand Encounters with the Blessed Virgin Mary in Medjugorje*, 12.

28. Ibid.

29. Jan Connell, *Queen of the Cosmos: Interviews with the Visionaries at Medjugorje* (Brewster, MA: Paraclete Press, 1990, Revised Edition, 2004), 14.

30. Soldo, *My Heart Will Triumph*, 28-29.

31. Ibid. Mirjana would come to reveal that Mary wears a gold dress on Christmas and Easter.

32. Ibid.

33. Ibid.

34. Marin, *Queen of Peace in Medjugorje*, 9.

35. Soldo, *My Heart Will Triumph*, 29. All accounts confirm Ivanka is the first to speak to Mary.

36. Kraljevic, *The Apparitions of Our Lady at Medjugorje*, 13.

37. Soldo, *My Heart Will Triumph*, 29. As with Ivanka, Jacov has also been told by the Virgin that his mother, Jaka, is in Heaven with her. (*Visions of the Children*, p. 99). Ivanka, as reported by Jan Connell in the same book (p. 85), has seen her deceased mother four times during her apparitions.

38. Kraljevic, The *Apparitions of Our Lady at Medjugorje*, 13.

39. Bubalo, *A Thousand Encounters with the Blessed Virgin Mary at Medjugorje,*12.

40. Kraljevic, The *Apparitions of Our Lady at Medjugorje*, 13.

41. Ibid.; Sullivan, *The Miracle Detective*, 77.

42. Craig, *Spark from Heaven*, 18.

43. Pelletier, *The Queen of Peace Visits Medjugorje*, 17-18.

44. Petrisko, ed., *Our Lady Queen of Peace* newspaper, Vol. 1, August, 1990, Pittsburgh Center for Peace, Pittsburgh, PA.

45. Pelletier, *The Queen of Peace Visits Medjugorje*, 17.

46. Sullivan, *The Miracle Detective*, 77.

47. Ibid.,78.

48. Ibid.

49. Ibid.

50. Ibid.

51. Ibid.

52. Thull, ed., *What They Say About Medjugorje*, 23. Quoted from *A Message for Peace for You*, by Franz Hummer, Center for Peace, Concord, MA, 1987.

53. Pelletier, *The Queen of Peace Visits Medjugorje*, 17-18, Kraljevic, *The Apparitions of Our Lady at Medjugorje*, 15.

54. Ibid.

55. Ibid.

56. Pelletier, *The Queen of Peace Visits Medjugorje*, 16.

57. Ibid.

58. Ibid.

59. Soldo, *Mt Heart Will Triumph*, 30.

60. Bubalo, *A Thousand Encounters with the Blessed Virgin Mary at Medjugorje*, 18.

61. Ibid., 17.

62. Kraljevic, *The Apparitions of Our Lady at Medjugorje*, 14.

63. Ibid.

64. Ibid.

CHAPTER 17: "GOD EXISTS"

1.   Kraljevic, *The Apparitions of Our Lady at Medjugorje*, 15.
2.   Ibid.
3.   Craig, *Spark from Heaven*, 19.
4.   Kraljevic, *The Apparitions of Our Lady at Medjugorje*,15; Pelletier, *The Queen of Peace Visits Medjugorje*, 19.
5.   Kraljevic, *The Apparitions of Our Lady at Medjugorje*, 15; Craig, *Spark from Heaven*, 19.
6.   Craig, *Spark from Heaven*, 19; Sullivan, *The Miracle Detective*, 79.
7.   Craig, *Spark from Heaven*, 19; Pelletier, *The Queen of Peace Visits Medjugorje*, 19; Kraljevic, *The Apparitions of Our Lady at Medjugorje*, 16; Bubalo, *A Thousand Encounters with the Blessed Virgin Mary at Medjugorje*, 17-18.
8.   Bubalo, *A Thousand Encounters with the Blessed Virgin Mary at Medjugorje*, 18.
9.   Ibid.
10. Ibid., 17.
11. Ibid.; Kraljevic, *The Apparitions of Our Lady at Medjugorje*, 16.
12. Sullivan, *The Miracle Detective*, 78.
13. Bubalo, *A Thousand Encounters with the Blessed Virgin Mary at Medjugorje*, 17.
14. Kraljevic, *The Apparitions of Our Lady at Medjugorje*, 16.
15. Bubalo, *A Thousand Encounters with the Blessed Virgin Mary at Medjugorje*, 18.
16. Kraljevic, *The Apparitions of Our Lady at Medjugorje*, 19.
17. Ibid.
18. Craig, *Spark from Heaven*, 44.
19. Sullivan, *The Miracle Detective*, 102-103.
20. Ibid., 394.
21. Ibid.
22. Ibid.
23. Thavis, *The Vatican Prophecies*, 73.
24. Craig, *Spark from Heaven*, 19-20. Craig's source is an October 6, 1985, article on Medjugorje from the *Sunday Times* (London) titled "A Village Sees the Light," by Gitta Sereny.
25. Denis Nolan, *Medjugorje: A Time for Truth, a Time for Action* (Santa Barbara, CA: Queenship Publishing,1993) 1; René Laurentin, *Latest News of Medjugorje: June 1987*(Milford, Ohio: The Riehle Foundation, 1987), ix; Sullivan, *The Miracle Detective*, 80. Sullivan writes that "all six children reported hearing Mary say, 'I have come to tell you God exists." This fact is documented in other accounts, but for some reason these words of the Virgin Mary are not

recorded on this date in Laurentin's and Lejeune's book on Mary's messages at Medjugorje, *The Messages and Teachings of Mary at Medjugorje: Chronological Corpus of the Message*. Consequently, all other books and websites that have based their accounts of the early messages from this book fail to include these significant words that were spoken by her on this day.

26. Kraljevic, *The Apparitions of Our Lady at Medjugorje*, 17. According to Vicka, Mary said on this date that her message was calling the world to peace, conversion, prayer, and penance.
27. Marin, *Queen of Peace in Medjugorje*, 10.
28. Ibid.
29. Ibid. Kraljevic, *The Apparitions of Our Lady at Medjugorje*, 18.
30. Ibid. Theologians say the peace Mary speaks of is in the traditional understanding of the Jewish word "Shalom." At Fátima, a commission of six experts appointed by the Bishop to interpret Mary's message rendered the opinion that the "era of peace" implied a true "reign of Christ" on Earth. This was because there "could be no other meaning of the word peace on the lips of the Mother of Christ" and "no other meaning to her words my Immaculate Heart will triumph."
31. Sullivan, *The Miracle Detective*, 81
32. Craig, *Spark from Heaven*, 20.
33. Soldo, *Mt Heart Will Triumph*, 153.
34. Gitta Sereny, "A Village Sees the Light," *Sunday Times* (London), October 6, 1985.
35. Kraljevic, *The Apparitions of Our Lady at Medjugorje*, 19.
36. Pelletier, *The Queen of Peace Visits Medjugorje*, 20-21.
37. Craig, *Spark from Heaven*, 20.
38. Ibid.
39. Ibid.

CHAPTER 18: A CRUEL BOMB

1. Fletcher Knebel and Charles W. Bailey II, "The Ultimate Weapon", *Reader's Digest Illustrated Story of World War II* (Pleasantville, NY: Readers Digest Association, Inc., 1969), 500-514.
2. Ibid.
3. Ibid.
4. Ibid.
5. Ibid.
6. Ibid.
7. Ibid.
8. Ibid.
9. Ibid.

10. Ibid. A 1945 Gallup Poll found 85% of Americans approved the bombings of Hiroshima and Nagasaki. The atom bomb dropped on Hiroshima was made of uranium. At Nagasaki, the bomb was made of plutonium.

11. Johnston, *Fatima: The Great Sign*, 139.

12. Ibid. Father Hubert Shiffner was German. He and all seven of his colleagues that day lived for decades after surviving the August 6, 1945, atomic bombing of Hiroshima. This puzzled the scientists, too, since not only did they survive an almost ground zero hit, but they did not succumb to the radiation over time as would so many other victims. Schiffner was not quiet about this miracle, appearing and speaking on television shows and with other media outlets, constantly pointing to Fátima and the power of the Rosary. Another survivor story is worthy of mention. Tsutomu Yamaguchi was in Hiroshima on the day the Atom Bomb was dropped. He fled wounded to Nagasaki and arrived the day before the 2nd atomic bomb was dropped. His employer in Nagasaki said he was "crazy" saying "one bomb" had destroyed Hiroshima. He survived both bombings and lived to 93. He is one of 70 known people to have been in both cities at the time of the bombings, but the only person officially recognized by the government of Japan in 2009.

13. Ibid.

14. Tsuyoshi Hasegawa, *Racing the Enemy: Stalin, Truman, and the Surrender of Japan* (Cambridge, MA: Belknap Press, 2006).

15. "Imperial Rescript on the Termination of the War, https://en.wikipedia.org/wiki/File:Imperial_Rescript_on_the_Termination_of_the_War.ogg. Known as the "Jewel Voice Broadcast," this was the full text in which Emperor Hirohito read out the Imperial Rescript on the "Termination of the Greater East Asia War." Hirohito announced to the people that the Japanese government had accepted the Potsdam Declaration demanding the unconditional surrender of the Japanese military at the end of World War II. The speech was broadcast at noon Japan Standard Time on August 15, 1945. A digitally remastered version of the broadcast was released on June 30, 2015.

16. Ibid.

17. Ibid.

18. "General Douglas MacArthur: Radio Broadcast to the Nation Following the USS Missouri Surrender Ceremony," delivered September 2, 1945, USS Missouri, Tokyo Bay, Japan, https://www.americanrhetoric.com/speeches/douglasmacarthurradiojapanesesurrenderceremony.htm. Certified text version of General MacArthur's radio address to the nation following the surrender ceremony aboard the USS Missouri, transcribed from compiled radio audio.

19. Ibid.
20. Joann Lamm, "The Island Is Missing," October 29, 2010, U.S. Army Heritage and Educational Center, https://www.army.mil/article/47341.
21. Ibid.
22. Ibid. Teller, the father of the H-bomb, was perhaps the most polarizing player in the Cold War, even more than Oppenheimer. Besides the H-bomb, he opposed arms control, worked for a second federal weapons lab, advocated nuclear power in every form, and was involved in missile defense. Nobel laureate, physicist Isidor Rabi, said about him, "I really do feel it would have been a better world without Teller. I think he is an enemy of humanity." The "Left in America," wrote John J. Miller in a 2003 article for *National Review*, saw Teller as "the very incarnation of Dr. Strangelove, a one-man axis of lunacy."
23. Ibid.
24. Ibid.
25. Ibid. Eisenhower had to carefully make his way through the mine field that was post World War II and the dawn of the age of nuclear weapons. He desired, after the Soviets had developed their own nuclear weapons, to establish a new era of détente with them, but needed to be careful not to incite Catholic conservatives like Bill Buckley and Cardinal Francis Spellman of New York.
26. "Tsar Bomba," Cold War History, *The Atomic Heritage Foundation*, August 8, 2014, [Alex Wargowski is given an article assistance credit], https://www.atomicheritage.org/history/tsar-bomba.
27. Ibid.
28. Ibid.
29. Paul Kengor, *A Pope and a President: John Paul II, Ronald Reagan, and the Extraordinary Untold Story of the 20th Century* (Wilmington, DE: ISI Books, 2017), 428-429.
30. Ibid.
31. Ibid.

CHAPTER 19: SO ALL MAY BELIEVE

1. Lúcia, *Fatima in Lucia's Own Words*, 173. Most published estimates of the size of the crowd at Fátima on October 13, 1917, have it at approximately 75,000. However, author John De Marchi, in his book, *Fatima: From the Beginning* (p. 132), originally published in 1950 in Portugal, uses the 100,000 figure based upon the precise calculations of Professor Almeida Garrett, a well-known scholar from Coimbra University.
2. Ibid., 173. Lúcia, according to Professor William Thomas Walsh in his *Our Lady of Fatima* (p.145), said she had no recollection of her remark

concerning the sun because she was in ecstasy. Walsh adds that "many" say they heard her.

3. Ibid., 165. No Fátima writer devoted more effort in his writing and over-all work on behalf of the apparitions to the importance and significance of the Miracle of the Sun than John Haffert. Haffert tried desperately to get his listeners and readers to grasp not only the uniqueness of the miracle in all of history but also its great symbolic message to the world. In his book, *Meet the Witnesses*, Haffert recounts how he traveled to Portugal and spent months searching for and interviewing the surviving witnesses of the miracle. He wanted to grasp their personal experiences of that day. The book is a historical treasure and is quoted by scholars and novices alike. It truly captures the enormity of not just the miracle but of that day itself. In another of his books, *Her Words to the Nuclear Age*, Haffert tried again to emphasize the magnitude of the supernatural event. He writes: "On the same day, after the children had been released from the jail in Qurem, Our Lady reassured them that the miracle she had promised to perform on October 13th would indeed take place. But she added that because of what those evil men had done to them, the miracle would not be as great as Heaven had intended. One must wonder what the miracle would have been, when indeed it turned out to be the greatest miracle in two thousand years! Over 100,000 people gathered on the mountain of Fátima were terrified by what seemed to be the sun falling upon the Earth. Many thought it was the end of the world. It was seen up to 32 miles away. After I wrote a book about that miracle in 1960, based on interviews with over 200 witnesses, I came to the conclusion that it is impossible for anyone really to understand its impact without having actually witnessed it. It was the first miracle in the history of the world at a predicted time and place "so everyone might believe." Never before, never had God permitted any prophet or seer to announce to the world that witnesses should be at a certain place, at a certain time, to see something beyond the laws of nature, attributable only to God Himself, and performed for the sole purpose of confirming belief in a message from Heaven."

4. Johnston, *Fatima: The Great Sign*, 17.

5. Walsh, *Our Lady of Fatima*, 138.

6. John M. Haffert, *Meet the Witnesses* (Washington, NJ: AMI International Press, 1961), 21-32.

7. Ibid.

8. Ibid., 72-78.

9. Ibid., 89-91.

10. Walsh, *Our Lady of Fatima*, 139-140.

11. Haffert, *Meet the Witnesses*, 85-89.

12. Ibid.

13. Lúcia, *Fatima in Lucia's Own Words*, 165.

14. Ibid., 103-104. Lúcia would later mistakenly write in her *Fourth Memoir* that this apparition occurred on August 15th. She writes, "…the apparition, which, in my opinion, took place on the 15th." Lúcia then noted that "it could be that I am mistaken." (See footnote No.18 of the *Fourth Memoir* in which the editor of the memoir notes her mistake and confirms that the apparition took place on the 19th.)

15. Ibid., 169.

16. Ibid., 172.

17. Johnston, *Fatima: The Great Sign*, 50.

18. Reverend V. Montes De Oca, CSSp., *More About Fatima* (USA: L. Owen Traynor, 1945, Reprint 1979), 43. Originally titled *Le Prodige Inoui de Fatima*, the book sold 250,000 copies in Europe. Translated into English by Reverend J. Dacruz, CSSp.

19. Ibid., 50.

20. Ibid., 54.

21. John De Marchi, *Fatima from the Beginning* (Torres Novas, Portugal: Missoes Consolata, 1950), 127. Originally titled, *Fatima: The Facts.* Father De Marchi lived near Fátima and knew well the environment, the customs and the characteristics of the people, which is reflected in his account. Some consider his book to be the most profound, informative, and accurate look into the apparitions at Fátima.

22. De Oca, *More About Fatima*, 40.

23. Johnston, *Fatima: The Great Sign*. 54-61.

24. Walsh, *Our Lady of Fatima*, 3. The names Cova da Iria, Qurem, Santarem, Leiria all come from the martyred Portuguese Saint Irene or Iria. (See John De Marchi's, *Fatima: From the Beginning*, p. 25.)

25. Johnston, *Fatima: The Great Sign*, 51.

26. Ibid.

27. Haffert, *Her Own Words to the Nuclear Age*, 9.

28. Lúcia, *Fatima in Lucia's Own Words,* 172.

29. Ibid.

30. Johnston, *Fatima: The Great Sign*, 51. While Mary appeared to all three of the children at Fátima, only Lúcia and Jacinta could hear her, and the Virgin conversed with only Lúcia. Francisco, at first, could not see the Virgin. After the apparitions, Lúcia and Jacinta would tell Francisco everything Mary had said, leaving him, Lúcia noted in her Memoirs, "overjoyed." Jacinta would eventually converse with Mary herself after being afflicted with the illness that killed her, especially in the hospital in Lisbon where she died.

31. A great controversy erupted surrounding Lúcia's disclosure of the coming end to World War I. She mistakenly believed, Lúcia said that evening of October 13th, that the Virgin had said "the war will end today." This

controversy dragged on for years and was seen to have the potential to seriously harm the approval by the Church of the apparitions. See Chapter 68, "The Lost Prophecy of Fátima", which explores this matter in detail.

32. Lúcia, *Fatima in Lucia's Own Words*, 173. Throughout her life, Lúcia chose to continually emphasize these last words of Mary at the end of the apparition that day. In her book, *Calls: From the Message of Fatima*, she devotes an entire chapter (No. 17) to them, titled: "The Call to Stop Offending God."

CHAPTER 20: THE DANCE OF THE SUN

1. Haffert, *Meet the Witnesses*, 76.
2. Ibid., 27.
3. Ibid., 91-92.
4. De Oca, *More About Fatima*, 43.
5. Johnston, *Fatima: The Great Sign*, 52.
6. Haffert, *Meet the Witnesses*, 91-92.
7. Ibid., 89-90.
8. Ibid., 107.
9. Johnston, *Fatima: The Great Sign*, 62.
10. De Oca, *More About Fatima*, 44.
11. Haffert, *Meet the Witnesses*, 84.
12. Ibid., 111.
13. Ibid., 32. As discussed in note Number 3, Chapter 19, as great as the miracle was on October 13, 1917, it had been intended to be even more extraordinary. But, because the children had been detained by the authorities and were unable to come to the Cova da Iria on August 13th, it was lessened. At Valinhos, on August 19th, the Virgin appeared to the children and said the following, "In October, I will perform a miracle so that everyone can believe in the apparitions. If they had not taken you to the town (Qurem), the miracle would have been greater. St. Joseph will come with the Holy Child to bring peace to the world. Our Lord will also come to bless the people. Our Lady of the Rosary and Our Lady of Dolours will come too."

CHAPTER 21: MORE THAN A SIGN?

1. Johnston, *Fatima: The Great Sign*, 55. *Diario de Noticias* means *The Daily News*.
2. Ibid., 57-58. *O'Seculo* means *The Century*.
3. Ibid., 63.
4. Haffert, *Meet the Witnesses*, 95.

5.   Ibid., 91-92.
6.   Ibid., 133.
7.   Ibid., 98-99.
8.   Ibid., 76-78.
9.   Johnston, *Fatima: The Great Sign*, 65.
10. Ibid.
11. Haffert, *Meet the Witnesses*, 66.
12. Ibid., 64-65.
13. Ibid., 66.
14. Gorny and Rosikon, *Fatima Mysteries*, 108.
15. De Oca, *More About Fatima*, 49-50.
16. Johnston, *Fatima: The Great Sign*, 60.
17. Ibid., 66.
18. Haffert, *Meet the Witnesses*, 140-141.
19. Socci, *The Fourth Secret of Fatima*, 13.

CHAPTER 22: A TURNING POINT IN HISTORY

1.   *Soul Magazine*, March-April, 1950, 3-4.
2.   De Marchi, *Fatima: From the Beginning*, 132.
3.   De Oca, *More About Fatima*, 43.
4.   De Marchi, *Fatima: From the Beginning*, 136.
5.   Johnston, *Fatima: The Great Sign*, 67.
6.   President Harry S. Truman, "Statement of the President of the United States, August 6, 1945," https://www.trumanlibrary.gov/education/lesson-plans/atomic-bomb-august-6-1945.
7.   Fulton Sheen, *World's First Love* (New York, NY: McGraw Hill, 1952), 88.
8.   Johnston, *Fatima: The Great Sign*, 68.
9.   Ibid., 67- 69.
10. Ibid.
11. Ibid., 69.
12. Walsh, *Our Lady of Fatima*, Foreword.
13. Johnston, *Fatima: The Great Sign*, 68.
14. Ibid., 131.
15. Alonso, *The Secret of Fatima*, 75. There is an abundance of circumstantial evidence that clearly appears to indicate that while there is no official interpretation of the symbolism contained in the terrifying unfolding of the Miracle of the Sun at Fátima—nor could there ever be—Fátima's key players were not opposed to the view that it was a divine warning of the coming dangers of the nuclear age. Perhaps, it appears, they were in complete agreement with this conclusion. Both Sister Lúcia and Father Joachim Alonso were very close with John Haffert, the co-founder of the

Blue Army and a leading proponent of the theory. Haffert was one of the first, if not the first, non-religious to meet privately with Sister Lúcia in 1946. Over the years, he would continue to meet with her. Likewise, Father Joachim Alonso, the official documentarian of Fátima, who was chosen by the Bishop of Leiria to prepare the critical and definitive study of Fátima and its message, was extremely close with Haffert. Alonso came to Haffert and "offered him his complete collection of notes on the memoirs and the right to publish them." Haffert's almost 400-page book on Lúcia's memoirs was titled "*Her Own Words to the Nuclear Age,*" a clear reflection of his thinking as to the urgency of Fátima's message. It was an urgency that he saw as being undeniably revealed in the nuclear symbolism found in the Miracle of the Sun in 1917 and in the Great Sign of 1938. One of my great regrets is that in my many conversations with Haffert, I failed to ask him if he discussed this matter with Lúcia.

16. John M. Haffert, *Deadline: The Third Secret of Fatima* (Asbury, NJ: 101 Foundation, 2001), 229.

17. Tony Jesse, "The Smoke of Satan Has Entered the Church," August 22, 2018, https://www.catholic365.com/article/9237/the-smoke-of-satan-has-entered-the-church.html.

18. Ratzinger, "The Message of Fatima," published in *The Fatima Prophecies,* 275.

19. Haffert, *Her Own Words to the Nuclear Age,* 9-12.

CHAPTER 23: THE SONG OF THE SWORD

1. Father Edward D. O'Conner, C.S.C., *Marian Apparitions Today* (Santa Barbara, CA: Queenship Publishing Company, 1996), 15.

2. Mcnally, "The Nuclear Tornado Effect," 1-14.

3. Ibid.

4. Ibid.

5. Ibid. In a 1994 article, McNally writes, "According to *Teller's War* author, William J. Broad, Dr. J. Robert Oppenheimer called a secret meeting in Berkely to discuss the A-Bomb project in the summer of 1942. After treating the primary purpose of the meeting, Edward Teller disclosed his ideas on the 'Super' H-Bomb possibilities. Then, he startled the audience with the thought that the 'Super' might ignite the atmosphere. Oppenheimer went to Michigan to discuss this matter with Nobel Prize winning American physicist Arthur H. Compton, who said, 'This would be the ultimate catastrophe.' Subsequently, nuclear scientist Emil Konopinski and Teller wrote a one-page paper: 'Ignition of the Atmosphere' (LAA-01, December 2, 1943), which concluded that the safety factor (bremsstrahlung radiation loss rate/nuclear power production rate) was about 60. Later, after

two A-bombs were dropped on Japan, Konopinski, Marvin, and Teller, in a much longer paper, concluded the safety factor might be as low as 2.67 (LA-602, August 14,1946). In 1954, Dr. McNally visited Fátima. There, he became intensely interested in what occurred with the Miracle of the Sun and with the Great Sign. His curiosity piqued when he discovered what Lúcia had written concerning the Great Sign in her 1941, *Third Memoir*: "I don't know for certain, but I think if they investigated the matter, they would discover that, in the form in which it appeared, it could not have been an aurora borealis." Upon reading Lúcia's words, McNally set out to investigate the solar phenomenon of 1938 to ascertain if it was not an aurora borealis. Finally, in 1982, he came upon a major discovery. The 1938 aurora borealis had revealed in its center what he termed to be "two giant red spots," one rising more than 300 miles tall as measured by triangulation methods. These concentrated red areas in the solar phenomenon were confirmed by gross magnetic perturbations and later by eye witnesses that McNally interviewed. And, these "red spots" in the aurora were similar, he then realized, to what had been observed in an August 1958 TEAK fission/fusion bomb test over Johnston Island. That test had produced a magnetic dynamo in the upper atmosphere and disturbed the Earth's local magnetic field for ten to twenty minutes. It also, six minutes after the megaton explosion, started a nuclear fireball that lifted and expanded to two hundred miles in diameter, with an accompanying red shock six hundred miles in diameter. "Shades of the Great Sign in 1938," thought McNally as he pieced all of this together. The icing on the cake, however, was yet to come. McNally discovered that "giant red spots," as were seen in the Johnston Island test, are not a phenomenon of an aurora borealis, a fact which both an astrophysicist and a geophysicist informed him of. This, then, could only mean one thing: the 1938 aurora borealis was *not* a natural aurora since it contained two giant red spots. According to McNally, the presence of the red spots proved that the Great Sign was truly sent by God, just as Mary's words to Lúcia in 1917 specifically state: "When you see a night illumined by an unknown light, know that this is the Great Sign given to you by God…" McNally also believed that The Great Sign seemed to be symbolically proving that his theory of a greater, hidden danger with the detonation of a large nuclear bomb was accurate.

6. Ibid. I obtained Dr. Rand McNally's paper, titled "The Nuclear Tornado Threat." His report reveals that in 1952, with the development of the hydrogen bomb, so-called "H-Bomb expert" Professor Gregory Breit of Yale University, who was also a consultant at Los Alamos, was asked to reconsider the earlier "secret" calculations on the ignition of the atmosphere that was carried out in the early 40's. Breit gave a "private" lecture in 1952 at the Oak Ridge National Laboratory that led to *cyclotron experiments* at ORNL. These experiments

convinced researchers that there was no danger of igniting the atmosphere in a gigantic nuclear conflagration. However, with the declassification of more top secret documents on the potential ignition of the atmosphere in 1973, which contradicted previous assumptions by scientists who worked on the Manhattan Project, McNally "repostulated fusion chain reactions and the question of the ignition" of the atmosphere. His findings again alluded to the nuclear tornado hazard. McNally's paper on this possibility was rejected by *Science Magazine*, but he sent a copy to a Russian scientist known for his opposition to the massive Soviet tests of 1961. In October 1975, Soviet leader Leonid Brezhnev expressed great concern about the "possibility of a new weapon" which, according to an article published in the *Knoxville News Sentinel* on November 19, 1975, could "wipe out entire cities in seconds and set whole countries ablaze endangering the rest of the world." McNally writes that it is thought that Brezhnev may have received information concerning this danger at hand.

7. Ibid. McNally writes; "The Soviet Union prepared in 1960 a series of massive nuclear test explosions which were conducted in 1961 and were capped by a 58 megaton detonation at 12,000 feet altitude. Prior to this largest test, Chairman Nikita Khrushchev claimed the Soviets possessed a 100 megaton device. Also prior to and after this 58 megaton explosion, the author (McNally) sent letters to a Soviet scientist suggesting quite high efficiency for this explosion and warned of the danger of igniting the atmosphere in a thermonuclear tornado which could annihilate entire nations if not the world." Much later, Edward Teller, in his book *"Energy from Heaven and Earth,"* posed the same question with reference to the world's first nuclear test, code named TRINITY: "There were some who said, 'Perhaps the explosion will run away. Perhaps we will blow up the world.'" McNally writes that according to the known laws of physics, this could not happen. But, he also asks if there could be "other laws of which we were ignorant? Could anyone dream up such laws, laws that could magnify beyond all expectations the effect of what we were going to do? Could one imagine natural laws that had therefore remained hidden?"

8. Ibid.

9. Ibid.

10. Ibid.

11. Ibid.

12. Haffert, *Her Own Words to the Nuclear Age*, 11.

13. McNally, "The Nuclear Tornado Effect," 1-14. I obtained copies of McNally's two letters to the Soviet scientist. Written on official Oak Ridge National Laboratory stationary, the letters are addressed to Professor A. N. Zaidel at the Physical Technical Institute in Leningrad, dated September 26, 1961, and November 13, 1961. The September letter, states: "Your study on nitrogen and oxygen ions at high temperatures brings to mind that each cube

of ordinary air, 20 meters on a side, contains over 100 megatons of fusion energy which might be released in a very high temperature reaction." In November, McNally writes to the Soviet scientist again, this time warning more specifically of what he suspects could happen if he is correct about the dangers of the atmospheric testing of an extremely large nuclear bomb: "Should there be a stable thermonuclear configuration, which might be generated, and I believe there is, such a system might persist or even grow indefinitely so long as fuel is available unless an appropriate control element or rod can be discovered and applied in time. Consider, for example, tornados and hurricanes which, once initiated, do just that so long as water vapor fuel is available. A thermonuclear tornado would probably generate power at a rate one million times that of an ordinary tornado. Ignition of the atmosphere by such a mechanism could destroy whole nations if not the entire world."

14. Haffert, *Her Own Words to the Nuclear Age*, 10.
15. Ibid., 3.
16. *Soul Magazine*, "The Great Sign" (Washington, NJ: The Blue Army, May-June, 1984), 8-9.
17. John M. Haffert, *The Meaning of Akita* (Asbury, NJ: The 101 Foundation, Inc., 1989), 35-36.
18. Ibid. The approval by Bishop John Ito of the supernatural events at Akita, unlike at La Salette, included the gravely apocalyptic message from the Virgin Mary to Sister Agnes Sasagawa that warned of fire falling from the sky and wiping out a great part of humanity. This approval occurred on April 22, 1984, just one month after Pope John Paul II's "Entrustment of the World" to the Immaculate Heart of Mary, in which his words spoke of the danger of "incalculable self-destruction."
19. Ibid. Sister Agnes was miraculously cured of her deafness a year later on October 13, 1974.
20. Ibid. If the message of Akita is the message of Fátima, as Akita's Bishop Ito replied, then the danger of "the annihilation of nations" prophecy, as stated at both miraculous sites, is still very much an unfulfilled prophecy. This is something John Haffert and others always maintained. Moreover, the fulfillment of such a prophecy, as they repeatedly noted, would come through the hands of man. It must be also noted that Dr. McNally's theory of a nuclear tornado is still viable to this day. Throughout the 1990's, both Dr. McNally and John Haffert continued to warn of its reality. Haffert wrote a half a dozen books that addressed the issue and McNally published a paper in *Fusion Technology* (January, 1991), titled "The Nuclear Dynamo – Can a Nuclear Tornado Annihilate Nations?" On August 17, 1995, McNally wrote a guest column for a Tennessee newspaper, *The Oak Ridger*, in which he presented a history of his efforts to warn of the dangers of a nuclear tornado. The perceived threat of

nuclear annihilation greatly diminished after the SALT Treaties were signed and even more after the Cold War ended. In his 1995 article, McNally noted two items of relevant and significant importance. He cited the discovery of another declassified report by Konopinski, Marvin, and Teller titled, "Ignition of the Atmosphere with Nuclear Bombs" and he very carefully noted that *The Partial Nuclear Test Ban Treaty*—which was signed by many nations in 1963, except for France and the People's Republic of China—banned nuclear test explosions in the atmosphere, outer space and underwater, but *did not ban* underground testing. This fact remains quite significant to the world of today. McNally's theory—that the detonation of a nuclear bomb of 50 megatons or more could trigger a nuclear tornado—was perhaps in play in 2017-18 when North Korea announced it successfully tested a hydrogen bomb underground. The Communist government also stated at the time that it might test another bomb in the Pacific Ocean. The underground blast in North Korea, *The New York Times* reported on September 3, 2017, caused tremors to be felt in South Korea and China. Moreover, *Time Magazine* (February 22, 2017) reported the blast yield of the detonation could potentially have been as great as 100,000 kilotons, well above the minimal threshold of 50,000 kilotons that McNally postulated was needed to trigger a nuclear tornado. North Korean Foreign Minister Ri Yong Ho told reporters at the United Nations about North Korea's future plans on September 22, 2017: "I think that it could be a H-Bomb test at an unprecedented level, perhaps over the Pacific Ocean. It's up to our leader." As of October 2018, North Korea was listed as a "non-signatory state" with regard to the United Nations' *Partial Nuclear Test Ban Treaty*. One also must suspect that North Korea has never heard of Dr. McNally's theory of the inherent danger of testing high megaton fusion explosives and their potential to ignite an atmospheric nuclear tornado.

CHAPTER 24: THE LANGUAGE OF TEARS

1. Jeff Thomas, "We Will Bury You," November 26, 1956, https://internationalman.com.
2. Eugene Emmery Jr., "The Curious Case of the Khrushchev Shoe," January 18, 2015, https://www.politifact.com/factchecks/2015/jan/18/arthur-cyr/curious-case-khrushchev-shoe/. Photographs of Khrushchev's shoe pounding incident at the U.N. landed on the front page of newspapers throughout the world the next day—October 13, 1960, the anniversary date of Fátima's Miracle of the Sun and its nuclear symbolism. Khrushchev's instigated Cuban Missile Crisis, it must be noted, was also marked by another Fátima connection of sorts in the fact that it lasted "13 days."

3. Moynihan, "Dossier: The Third Secret," *Inside the Vatican*, Year 8, No. 6, June-July 2000, p. xiii. The German magazine *Neues Europa* reported on October 3, 1963, that Pope Paul VI may have caused an extract of the Third Secret to be received by Kennedy and Khrushchev and that it had played a role in the signing of an accord between the superpowers to stop the proliferation of nuclear weapons. The Vatican never issued a denial of the story but Fátima historian Father Alonso dismembered the report point by point as having no relevancy to the Secret of Fátima. For the record, President John F. Kennedy was a member of the Blue Army.

4. Ibid., xi.

5. Joan Ashton, *Mother of All Nations*, (San Francisco, CA: Harper & Row, 1989), 117-120.

6. The Blue Army, *There Is Nothing More* (Washington, NJ: AMI Press, circa 1975), 324.

7. Ibid., 324.

8. Ibid.

9. Johnston, *Fatima: The Great Sign*, 67.

10. The Blue Army, *There Is Nothing More*, 322.

11. Johnston, *Fatima: The Great Sign*, 125.

12. Gorny and Rosikon, *Fatima Mysteries*, 227.

13. Johnston, *Fatima: The Great Sign*, 11.

14. The Blue Army, *There Is Nothing more*, 328.

15. Ibid., 330.

16. Ibid., 333.

17. Ibid., 334.

18. Gorny and Rosikon, *Fatima Mysteries*, 15.

19. Michael H. Brown, *The Final Hour* (Milford, OH: Faith Publishing Company, 1992), 102.

20. Ibid.

21. The Blue Army: *There Is Nothing More*, 331.

22. Ibid.

23. Ibid.

24. Alonso, *The Secret of Fatima*, 108-110.

25. Ibid.

26. Ibid. As vice postulator of the causes for the beatification of Jacinta and Francisco, Father Fuentes Anguiano held quite a lofty position in the overall scheme of things surrounding Fátima. After interviewing Lúcia on December 26, 1957, he returned to Mexico and held a conference on May 22, 1958, in which he gave an account of his interview. After a text of the conference was published, drastic changes were made to it that led to a great uproar and upset Father Fuentes' superiors in Portugal. Upon investigating, Father Alonso was able to vindicate Father Fuentes. Wrote

Alonso, "The genuine text, the only one that can be justly attributed to Fr. Fuentes, does not in my opinion, contain anything that could give rise to the condemnatory notice issued from Coimbra."

27.   Ibid. Lúcia's disclosure that "the Virgin is very sad because no one heeds her message, neither the good nor the bad. The good continue in their life of virtue, but without paying attention to the message of Fátima. Sinners keep following the road of evil," is virtually echoed by Mirjana words nearly thirty years later when she tells Father Slavko Barbarić, "The Virgin is very sad with all the unfaithful people." "Which unfaithful people?" asks Slavko, "Those who go to Church...or those who do not know God?" "They are both the same," Mirjana says, "... the sin of the world consists that they are not interested in God." (See Laurentin's, *The Apparitions at Medjugorje Prolonged.*)

28.   Walsh, *Our Lady of Fatima*, 220.

29.   The Blue Army, *There Is Nothing More*, 331.

30.   Petrisko, *The Fatima Prophecies*, 7-9. Lúcia's letters indicate she firmly believed 1960 was a line of demarcation of sorts. It's not entirely clear why. One biographer attributes it to her personal conviction that she would be dead by this time, which is what she reportedly said. Besides the year's relationship with the Third Secret's opening, Lúcia also appears to have known about the spread of the errors of Russia in a more intricate and complex way. In a letter to Pope Pius XII on June 6, 1958, she writes, "Your Holiness knows of the so-called Secret of Fátima, enclosed in a sealed envelope that can be opened in 1960. Although I cannot speak of the text and because the time is approaching, I must say that in 1960, Communism will reach its maximum height, which can be decreased in intensity and duration, and to which it must comply with the Triumph of the Immaculate Heart and the reign of Christ. To achieve this purpose, God wants to intensify all apostolic works, beyond which He wants to be heard in the world."

31.   Gorney and Rosikon, *Fatima Mysteries*, 382-383.

32.   Father Richard Heilman, "Did Archbishop Fulton Sheen Prophesy About the Condition of our World Today," September 28, 2018, https://www.romancatholicman.com/archbishop-fulton-sheen-prophesy-condition-church-today-2/.

33.   Gorny and Rosikon, *Fatima Mysteries*, 112.

34.   Lúcia, *Fatima in Lucia's Own Words*, 173.

CHAPTER 25: THE DAWN OF SOMETHING GOOD

1.   Marin, *Queen of Peace in Medjugorje*, 13.

2.   Ibid. Father Jozo Zovko (Jozo means Joseph in Croatian) was born on the Feast Day of St. Joseph, March 19, 1941, in the village of Uzarici,

near Siroki Brijeg. Jozo was one of ten children born to Mate and Milka Zovko. He earned a theology degree from the University of Ljbuljana in Slovenia and was ordained in Sarajevo in 1967.

3. Ibid. It has been reported that Jozo had perhaps too much success at Posusje, especially with the youth, and was forced to leave by the local Communist authorities.

4. Craig, *Spark from Heaven*, 39.

5. Ibid.

6. Marin, *Queen of Peace in Medjugorje*, 12.

7. Ibid., 13.

8. Ibid.

9. Ibid.

10. Craig, *Spark from Heaven*, 37.

11. Marin, *Queen of Peace in Medjugorje*, 13.

12. Craig, *Spark from Heaven*, 39.

13. Ibid.

14. Marin, *Queen of Peace in Medjugorje*, 13.

15. Craig, *Spark from Heaven*, 39.

16. Ibid.

17. Ibid.

18. Andrew Thull, ed., *What They Say About Medjugorje*, 121. Transcript of interview with Dragica Ivanković from *Spirit of Medjugorje* video, filmed October 6, 1988.

19. Ibid.

20. Ibid.

21. Riehle Foundation, the eds., *A Man Named Father Jozo* (Milford, OH: The Riehle Foundation, 1989), 4.

22. Kraljevic, *The Apparitions of Our Lady at Medjugorje*, 69.

23. Marin, *Queen of Peace in Medjugorje*, 14.

24. Craig, *Spark from Heaven*, 40.

25. Ibid.

26. Sullivan, *The Miracle Detective*, 83.

27. Craig, *Spark from Heaven*, 40.

28. Ibid., 38.

29. Ibid.

30. Ibid.

31. Sullivan, *The Miracle Detective*, 78.

32. Ibid.

33. Ibid.

34. Ibid.

35. Thull, ed., *What They Say About Medjugorje*, 68.

36. Ibid.

37. Ibid
38. Ibid.
39. Craig, *Spark from Heaven*, 39.
40. Thull, ed., *What They Say About Medjugorje*, 68.
41. Ibid., 68-69.
42. Ibid., 68. One of those in the crowd late that evening was a beekeeper named Ivan Dugandzic. A skeptic when he arrived, the heat, the crowd, and his inability to get close enough to see anything left him leaving Marinko's house after 11:00 p.m. that night more convinced than ever that it was all a lark. That was until he happened to walk right into the path of Vicka who was also headed home. The second he gazed upon her face, everything inside him changed instantly: "I knew it was true. From that moment, I have never doubted, the intensity was so enormous."
43. Sullivan, *The Miracle Detective*, 82.
44. Thull, ed., *What They Say About Medjugorje*, 69.

CHAPTER 26: NO BETTER THAN AN ATHEIST

1. Craig, *Spark from Heaven*, 38. Recalls Zrinko, "Dragica came to see me early on Saturday morning and really let fly… She tore into me, shrieking that everyone was going to the hill…I shook her by the shoulders and said, "Dragica, calm down."
2. Ibid.
3. Sullivan, *The Miracle Detective*, 83.
4. Craig, *Spark from Heaven*, 38. Father Zrinko Cuvalo O.F.M. would eventually be transferred to the parish of Posuski Gradac. He became a great believer in the apparitions and credited them with his own spiritual growth. He died of cancer on June 1, 1991, and is buried in Humac at the monastery cemetery.
5. Sullivan, *The Miracle Detective*, 83.
6. Ibid.
7. Ibid.
8. Ibid.
9. Thull, ed., *What They Say About Medjugorje*, 68-69.
10. Ibid.
11. Ibid.; Craig, *Spark from Heaven*, 39.
12. Craig, *Spark from Heaven*, 39.
13. Ibid., 40.
14. Ibid.
15. Ibid.
16. Ibid.

17. Ibid.
18. Sullivan, *The Miracle Detective*, 83-84.
19. Ibid.
20. Craig, *Spark from Heaven*, 40.
21. Ibid.
22. Ibid., 41.
23. Ibid.
24. Ibid.
25. Ibid.
26. Some accounts have this initial police interrogation of the children occurring on Sunday, June 28, 1981, the fifth day. Marin, Pelletier, and Craig report it to have occurred on Saturday, right after their interview with the priests. Kraljevic also reports it occurred on Saturday, although he does not mention the interrogation of the children that morning by the priests. Bubalo sees it the same as Kraljevic in his interview with Vicka. In her book, Mirjana writes that the police interrogation takes place on the fifth day. However, much of Mirjana's account of the early days is summarily presented, with many specific details not addressed. She does not, for example, mention the presence of Milka Pavlović during the apparition on the first day. Her book is not an attempt to give a precise historical record.
27. Kraljevic, *The Apparitions of Our Lady at Medjugorje*, 21. If there is one element of the apparitions that Fátima and Medjugorje share in a most profound way, it is the extraordinary effort government authorities made to intimidate the children. At Fátima, like at Medjugorje, it was on the day of the fourth apparition that the children were physically seized and taken away against their will to be interrogated. On August 13, the expected day of the fourth apparition at Fátima, the three children were taken to the town of Vila Nova de Qurem, known simply as Qurem. There they were kept overnight and then put in jail the following day with hardened criminals. When asked by the "Administrator," Arturo de Oliveira Santos, a fallen away Catholic and a leading Freemason, to reveal their "Secret," the children refused under the penalty of death. To intimidate them, Santos questioned each child separately and when they failed to cooperate, he had them taken away to be cast into a cauldron of boiling oil—or so he allowed them to think as they were escorted out the door one by one. At Medjugorje, to maximize intimidation (somewhat in the spirit of Arturo de Santos), the children were left in a morgue and an insane asylum, both on the same day. That they could die, or be put into a mental hospital, remained a steady part of the Communist's ongoing efforts to intimidate them.
28. Bubalo, *A Thousand Encounters with the Blessed Virgin Mary in Medjugorje*, 20.

29. Craig, *Spark from Heaven*, 41.
30. Ibid.; Kraljevic, *The Apparitions of Our Lady at Medjugorje*, 21. Zrinko himself had been attempting to arrange for the children to be examined.
31. Soldo, *My Heart Will Triumph*, 3.

CHAPTER 27: EYES TO THE SKY

1. Soldo, *My Heart Will Triumph*, 45.
2. Kraljevic, *The Apparitions of Our Lady at Medjugorje*, 21. Ivan was the first examined that day, for more than an hour. The finding that the children were healthy was not only a diagnosis that the authorities were unhappy with, but also Zrinko. He was said to be "disgusted to learn" so few blood and urine tests were done. "We'll have to call in experts," he recommended, wishing to pursue more exams with the hope of finally finding evidence of drug use.
3. Soldo, *My Heart Will Triumph*, 45.
4. Ibid.
5. Ibid.
6. Ibid.
7. Sullivan, *The Miracle Detective*, 84.
8. Kraljevic, *The Apparitions of Our Lady at Medjugorje*, 21.
9. Ibid., 22.; Sullivan, *The Miracle Detective*, 84.
10. Marin, *Queen of Peace in Medjugorje*, 15.
11. Craig, *Spark from Heaven*, 41.
12. Sullivan, *The Miracle Detective*, 85.
13. Pelletier, *The Queen of Peace Visits Medjugorje*, 23.
14. Marin, *Queen of Peace in Medjugorje*, 15.
15. Bubalo, *A Thousand Encounters with the Blessed Virgin Mary in Medjugorje*, 85.
16. Sullivan, *The Miracle Detective*, 84.
17. Ibid., 84-85.
18. Thull, ed., *What They say About Medjugorje*, 255.
19. Kraljevic, *The Apparitions of Our Lady at Medjugorje*, 22.
20. Bubalo, *A Thousand Encounters with the Blessed Virgin Mary in Medjugorje*, 22.
21. Ibid., 21.
22. Pelletier, *The Queen of Peace Visits Mejugorje*, 24.
23. Ibid.
24. Ibid.
25. Ibid.
26. Ibid., 25.
27. Kraljevic, *The Apparitions of Our Lady at Medjugorje*, 23.

28. Ibid.
29. Ibid. Vicka would later tell Fr. Bubalo in her interview for his book that it was actually Jacov and Mirjana who asked for the sign that day.
30. Ibid.
31. De Marchi, *Fatima from the Beginning*, 88.
32. Kraljevic, *The Apparitions of Our Lady of Medjugorje*, 23.
33. Sullivan, *The Miracle Detective*, 86.
34. Ibid.
35. Pelletier, *The Queen of Peace Visits Medjugorje*, 25.
36. Weible, *Medjugorje: The Message*, 15. The self-proclaimed atheist, Dr. Darinka Glamuzina, who worked with the ambulance squad in Čitluk, did indeed touch the Virgin Mary's left shoulder, according to Vicka. She stopped by Vicka's home later that same evening to report she had "felt some sort of tingling in her hand" at that moment. Some accounts report that Dr. Glamuzina later converted from that experience alone. Laurentin and Lejeune report in their corpus, *Messages and Teachings of Mary at Medjugorje*, that Mary said, "There have always been doubting Thomases, but she can approach" not the words, "Let her come forward, there will always be Judases who do not believe." This conflict caused critics of Laurentin to accuse him of deliberately altering the text. No mention of Lejeune is cited in these criticisms. From his meticulous work on Lourdes and other efforts, those who know Laurentin attention's to fact and truth are most aware he would be never consider such a deception involving Mary. This reflects poorly on not just those who would make such an allegation but on their overall agenda. It is a fact that there is seen with Medjugorje, as with Fátima, different versions of the same message. This is especially true with Medjugorje in its earliest days. For a significant example of this at Fátima, see Chapter 68 of this book, "The Lost Prophecy of Fatima."
37. Sullivan, *The Miracle Detective*, 87.
38. Ibid.
39. Marin, *Queen of Peace in Medjugorje*, 15.
40. Sullivan, *The Miracle Detective*, 86-87.
41. Ibid.
42. Ibid.
43. Ibid.
44. Ibid.
45. Ibid.
46. Ibid.
47. Ibid.
48. Ibid.
49. Ibid.
50. Ibid.
51. Kraljevic, *The Apparitions of Our Lady at Medjugorje*, 24.

52. Ibid.
53. Pelletier, *The Queen of Peace Visits Medjugorje*, 25.

CHAPTER 28: HEROES AND VILLAINS

1. Craig, *Spark from Heaven*, 43.
2. Ibid.
3. Ibid.
4. Ibid.
5. Ibid.
6. Kraljevic, *The Apparitions of Our Lady at Medjugorje*, 25.
7. Craig, *Spark from Heaven*, 43.
8. Ibid.
9. Ibid.
10. Ibid.
11. Ibid.
12. Bubalo, *A Thousand Encounters with the Blessed Virgin Mary in Medjugorje*, 27.
13. Sullivan, *The Miracle Detective*, 88.
14. Craig, *Spark from Heaven*, 44.
15. Sullivan, *The Miracle Detective*, 88-90. The fact that the visionaries are able to communicate with Grgo Kozina while in ecstasy with the Virgin Mary on this day is in sharp contrast with later apparitions at Medjugorje, in which the children appear to be immune to any sensory intrusion, including communication with others. This is well-documented during the apparitions, and some experiences were later video recorded at St. James, especially during medical exams that they voluntarily submit to for researchers. Different states of ecstasy have been seen before. At Lourdes during the apparition of Thursday, February 18, 1858, Bernadette communicated with friends while in ecstasy, as they reminded her to ask the Lady to write her name with the paper and pen that they brought to the grotto. Upon hearing this, Bernadette held the paper and pen out at arm's length in the direction of the Virgin Mary, who moved slightly towards them and then said, "It is not necessary." Yet, during the previous apparition on Sunday, February 14th, the two girls that were with Bernadette found her in a trance that was impenetrable. Bernadette apparently heard nothing, and her face was pale. Even a deliberate attempt to create a small rock slide on the nearby hillside to distract her from the vision could not get Bernadette to budge. When the girls got a man named Nicolau, the operator of a nearby mill, to help, he was also unable to communicate with her. As he carried the still ecstatic girl back to his mill, he noticed that she was extremely heavy. Along the way, Nicolau recalled, "I put my hands over her eyes and tried to get her to bend her head,

but she would raise her head again and reopen her eyes with a smile." At the apparition after Easter on April 7th, a physician, Dr. Dozous, appeared at Bernadette's side during the ecstasy. He noticed, as did the crowd surrounding Bernadette, that the flames of a candle she was holding were licking up and into her hands and fingers. Yet, she remained smiling, and no effort to remove her hands from the blaze was made. Afterwards, Dr. Dozous found no burns on her. It is not known for certain if the visionaries at Fátima also experienced different types of ecstasies. After the fifth apparition at Fátima, a priest from Lisbon named Dr. Manuel Formigão came to Fátima to study and question the children. Having been present at the September 13th apparition, he returned to Fátima on September 27th and then once again prior to the October 13th apparition. On his second interrogation, he asked Lúcia a battery of questions in the presence of four witnesses. "Do you hear the voices and the cries of the people while you are talking to the Lady?" he asked. Lúcia responded, "No." Father John De Marchi reports that during the October 13th apparition, once Lúcia "entered into communication with the vision," she "did not hear her mother's warning voice behind her." There is, however, evidence that something was different during the October 13th apparition. While still in ecstasy, Lúcia suddenly told the crowd to "look at the sun." She then saw a series of visions in the sky herself after, it must be assumed, returning to some state of ecstasy. That evening, Dr. Formigão returned to question the children a third time. While it has been generally established in accounts that the children did not see the Miracle of the Sun at all, Lúcia claimed, "I saw it going round." Lúcia's answer appears to indicate that the state she was in still permitted her to interact with her environment, unlike previous states of ecstasy in which she herself stated she could not hear anyone once the apparition began.

16. Ibid. I used several sources to attempt to accurately assemble this dialogue, especially Vicka's interview with Bubalo.
17. Kraljevic, *The Apparitions of Our Lady at Medjugorje*, 26-27.
18. Ibid.
19. Ibid.
20. Ibid.
21. Sullivan, *The Miracle Detective*, 87.
22. Ibid., 88.
23. Ibid.
24. Ibid.
25. Ibid.
26. Ibid.
27. Ibid.
28. Ibid.
29. Ibid., 90.

30. Ibid., 91.
31. Ibid.
32. Ibid.
33. Ibid.
34. Ibid.
35. Ibid.
36. Ibid.
37. Craig, *Spark from Heaven*, 45.
38. Ibid.
39. Sullivan, *The Miracle Detective*, 91.
40. Ibid.
41. Ibid.
42. Kraljevic, *The Apparitions of Our Lady at Medjugorje*, 31.
43. Ibid.
44. Ibid.
45. Bubalo, *A Thousand Encounters with the Blessed Virgin Mary in Medjugorje*, 32.
46. Craig, *Spark from Heaven*, 46.
47. Ibid.
48. Ibid.
49. Bubalo, *A Thousand Encounters with the Blessed Virgin Mary in Medjugorje*, 32. Bubalo's book on Vicka was awarded the 1985 *Sapienza Award* in Italy given by the "Lettera ai Credenti". Its jury was headed by Cardinal Angelo Rossi. The award recognized it as the most widely read religious book in Italy for 1985. Fr. Janko Bubalo played an enormous role in promoting Medjugorje in the early years of the apparitions. He didn't care much about them at first: "I heard about the Medjugorje events on the 3rd or 4th day of the apparitions, but I didn't take any notice. I simply wasn't thinking about it." His book remains one of the best sources on the subject. He died on February 21, 1997.
50. Ibid. The authorities threatened to lock Vicka up in the basement with mice. To which Vicka told them immediately, "I'm not afraid of mice!" (See *Medjugorje: An Affirmation and a Defense* by Fr. Albert Hebert.)
51. Sullivan, *The Miracle Detective*, 93.
52. Bubalo, *A Thousand Encounters with the Blessed Virgin Mary in Medjugorje*, 33.
53. Kraljevic, *The Apparitions of Our Lady at Medjugorje*, 33.
54. Ibid.
55. Laurentin and Rupčić, *Is the Virgin Mary Appearing in Medjugorje?*, 155.
56. Sullivan, *The Miracle Detective*, 102.
57. Ibid.
58. Ibid.

59. Ibid.
60. Bubalo, *A Thousand Encounters with the Blessed Virgin Mary in Medjugorje*, 35.
61. Ibid.
62. Sullivan, *The Miracle Detective*, 101.
63. Craig, *Spark from Heaven*, 47.
64. Sullivan, *The Miracle Detective*, 102.
65. Craig, *Spark from Heaven*, 47.
66. Sullivan, *The Miracle Detective*, 102.
67. Ibid.
68. Craig, *Spark from Heaven*, 47.
69. Ibid.
70. Ibid.
71. Ibid.
72. Ibid. The government on this day began taking action in other ways. When Ivan returned home that night, he discovered armed guards from the state security police had been assigned to the home of each visionary, including himself. They were ordered to follow the visionaries' every move and to make sure none of them went near the hill. The agents barred doors, looked into windows, and climbed up on top of rooftops if needed. "Stay out of sight," one officer told the visionaries, "The people are taking off work. Nobody wants to do anything. Everybody thinks only of seeing you."

CHAPTER 29: "PROTECT THE CHILDREN"

1. Craig, *Spark from Heaven*, 49. Father Pervan would become Pastor of St. James in 1982.
2. Ibid.
3. Ibid.
4. Sullivan, *The Miracle Detective*, 97. Jozo's insistence that it could be the Devil is striking similar to Father Ferreira, the pastor in Fátima, with his treatment of Lúcia and the apparitions. "This is the Devil's work, "said Ferreira once to Maria Rosa, Lúcia's mother. See DeMarchi's *Fatima: From the Beginning* for a detailed look at this matter.
5. Ibid.
6. Ibid.
7. Ibid.
8. Ibid.
9. Ibid.
10. Ibid.
11. Ibid.

12. Ibid.
13. Ibid.
14. Craig, *Spark from Heaven*, 50.
15. Sullivan, *The Miracle Detective*, 98.
16. Ibid.
17. Craig, *Spark from Heaven*, 51.
18. Sullivan, *The Miracle Detective*, 98.
19. Ibid.
20. Ibid., 98-99.
21. Ibid., 99.
22. Ibid.
23. Ibid.
24. Craig, *Spark from Heaven*, 52.
25. Ibid.
26. Sullivan, *The Miracle Detective*, 99. Father Jozo was unaware of the apparition that day taking place at Cerno and believed, because of all the people on the hill, it had occurred at the regular time on Podbrdo.
27. Ibid.
28. Kraljevic, *The Apparitions of Our Lady at Medjugorje*, 40.
29. Sullivan, *The Miracle Detective*, 103.
30. Ibid.
31. Ibid.
32. Craig, *Spark from Heaven*, 55.
33. Ibid., 53.
34. Ibid.
35. Ibid.
36. Ibid.
37. Ibid.
38. Ibid.
39. Bubalo, *A Thousand Encounters with the Blessed Virgin Mary in Medjugorje*, 47.
40. Ibid., 48.
41. Sullivan, *The Miracle Detective*, 104.
42. Ibid.
43. Ibid., 103.
44. Ibid.
45. Ibid.
46. Ibid.
47. Kraljevic, *The Apparitions of Our Lady at Medjugorje*, 42.
48. Ibid.
49. Ibid.
50. Ibid.

51. Ibid.
52. Ibid. Some accounts have this event with Father Jozo hearing a voice and then protecting the children in the Church as occurring on the next evening. For all intents and purposes, it is a similar story, with the SUP pursuing the children except without the van, which they write occurred the day before. Vicka relays it to Bubalo as occurring on the next day. Mirjana writes of the event also, but it's not clear exactly what day she is saying this event occurred on. Sullivan's version, which I chose to agree with, appears the best researched of the conflicting accounts. It is very detailed, and draws upon unpublished sources.
53. Craig, *Spark from Heaven*, 56.
54. Sullivan, *The Miracle Detective*, 104.

CHAPTER 30: THE TWO MADONNAS

1. Getty Images, https://www.gettyimages.com. A photograph of Lech Walesa wearing the lapel pin that held the image of the Black Madonna of Czestochowa is available to be viewed at Getty Images.
2. Jeffery Donovan, "Poland: Solidarity- The Trade Union That Change the World," Radio Free Europe/Radio Liberty, August 24, 2005, https://www.rferl.org/a/1060898.html. Solidarity was founded on August 14, 1980.
3. "Chronology of Events Leading to Polish Crisis," *The New York Times*, December 14, 1981, https://www.nytimes.com/1981/12/14/world/chronology-of-events-leading-to-polish-crisis.html.
4. Cynthia Sularz, "The Women of Solidarity: How History Ignored Fifty Percent of Poland's Solidarity Movement", March 31, 2016, https://www.girlsglobe.org/2016/03/31/the-women-of-solidarity-how-history-ignored-fifty-percent-of-polands-solidarity-movement/.
5. "1980: The Birth of Solidarity." BBC on This Day, August 30, 1980, https://www.google.com/search?q=1980+The+birth+of+solidarity+bbc+onthis+day+august+30+1980&rlz=1C1PRFI_enUS780US781&oq=1980+The+birth +of+solidarity+bbc+onthis+day+august+30+1980&aqs=chrome.69i57.53827j0j15&sourceid=chrome&ie=UTF-8.
6. "Wojciech Witold Jaruzeliski: Polish General." https://www.google.com/search?q=wojciech+witold+jaruzelski+%3A+polish+general+obituary+encyclopedi+britanic&rlz=1C1PRFI_enUS780US781&oq=W&aqs=chrome. 0.69i59l2j35i39j69i57j0i131i433j46i199i291i433l2j0i433.4745j0j15&source id=chrome&ie=UTF-8.
7. Gorny and Rosikon, *Fatima Mysteries*, 279.
8. Ibid.
9. Craig, *Spark from Heaven*, 60.
10. Ibid.

11. Ibid.
12. Ibid.
13. Ibid.
14. Ibid.
15. Ibid.
16. Ibid.
17. Ibid.
18. Father Richard Foley, SJ, *The Drama of Medjugorje* (Dublin: Veritas Publications, 1992), 55.
19. Riehle Foundation, *A Man Named Father Jozo*, 53-54.
20. Laurentin and Rupčić, *Is the Virgin Mary Appearing in Medjugorje?* 152.
21. Ibid.
22. Kraljevic, *The Apparitions of Our Lady at Medjugorje*, 167-172.
23. Ibid.
24. Ibid., 173-179.
25. Craig, *Spark from Heaven*, 115-116. By 1995, journalist Randall Sullivan, in reviewing the official parish records, found a list of more than 500 reported miraculous healings. Sullivan notes that Dr. Luigi Frigero had been the first to review the growing list in 1986 and "admitted amazement at the level of documentation the Franciscans had maintained." One of the most extraordinary healings was a woman from Pittsburgh who was healed of multiple sclerosis in 1986. It was remarkable for three reasons. The healing was instantaneous; it was total; and Rita had not been healed in Medjugorje, but in Pittsburgh by praying to the Virgin of Medjugorje. Rita Klaus first heard of Medjugorje in 1986 and began praying to the Madonna. On the evening of June 26th, Rita heard a voice she believed was that of the Virgin Mary. She began to pray and suddenly felt an electric jolt travel through her entire body. The next morning, for the first time in years, she could feel her legs. All day long, this sensitivity grew. By the afternoon, she unbuckled her leg brace and discovered her deformed leg had been straightened. Seconds later, she stood up. That evening, she walked up the stairs to her bedroom. The next morning, she ran up and down the steps repeatedly. That same day, she walked over a mile to the home of the person who told her about Medjugorje. It was indeed a miracle, and the doctors would concur. Rita Klaus became a close personal friend of mine and I greatly admired her for how hard she worked to tell the world about Medjugorje. (See *Rita's Story* by Rita Klaus in the bibliography.) Another extraordinary story of a healing through Medjugorje is the case of Colleen Willard of Chicago, who I have met, along with her husband, on several occasions. Colleen suffered from an inoperable brain tumor that affected her pituitary gland and all of her fine and gross motor skills. She had rickets, her thyroid

had dried up, was afflicted with multiple sclerosis, lupus, fibromyalgia and nine other diagnosed diseases. The Mayo Clinic considered it a miracle that she was just alive. In the last stages of cancer, though deeply in debt, Collen and her husband John received a sign that they should go to Medjugorje. Colleen simply wanted to go for the peace and grace, and was not seeking a healing. In Medjugorje, during a group audience with Vicka, and as Vicka hugged and prayed over her, Colleen suddenly felt a rush of physical changes in her body. "My head is like coals. My head is burning," she exclaimed. "It's like a spiral going through my body." Then, Colleen was taken to Mass at St. James. There, as the priest was consecrating the Host, she heard a voice say, "My daughter, will you surrender to God the Father? Will you surrender to my Spouse, the Holy Spirit? Will you surrender to my Son, Jesus?" Colleen replied, "Yes, I will surrender now, all for the glory of Heaven, all for the glory of God." At that moment, she felt a tingling sensation sweep through her body. By the time the Mass was over, she knew she was healed and got up and out of her wheelchair immediately. When she visited the Mayo Clinic, the doctor pushed his chair back from his desk, smiled and said, "So, you have been to Medjugorje! You are our third major unexplainable healing coming from there."

26. Ibid., 63.
27. Ibid., 62-63.
28. Ibid.
29. Ibid., 63-64.
30. Ibid.
31. Ibid.
32. Kraljevic, *The Apparitions of Our Lady at Medjugorje*, 61. The UK periodical *Good News* reported in its December 83-February 84 issue that the word MIR was seen in "letters of fire" in the sky over Medjugorje. On the night of December 5, 1984, at 7:30 p.m., the letters MIR were clearly seen spelled out in the sky over Ayrshire, Scotland. A man named John Watters painted the scene as exactly he saw it and a week later learned about Medjugorje. The style of the letter "M" as Watters saw in the sky and painted it would later be found to match perfectly with the letter "M" written on the altar cloth at St. James Church in Medjugorje.
33. Craig, *Spark from Heaven*, 64-65.
34. Ibid., 65. From 1981 through 1984, there was an attempt to document in the parish chronicle many different phenomena that was seen at Medjugorje. Here is what was compiled and written: SIGNS IN THE SUN – There have been thirty-two cases as of June 24, 1984. Many of these are compared to the Miracle of the Sun at Fátima. The sun spins, pulsates, and throws off colors. In a certain number

of the cases, the center of the sun, whose brilliance can harm the eyes, becomes white or grey, and this acts as a barrier to eye damage for some reason. Many of these solar phenomena were captured on photographs and video cassettes. PHENOMENA AROUND THE CROSS ON MT. KRIZEVAC – While noted to have occurred before this date, on October 21, 1981, and on six more occasions that month from the 22nd to 27th and then repeatedly from the 17th through the 22nd of March, 1982, the entire cross, disappeared. In its place appeared a luminous column, or a rather brilliant silhouette— often mounted on a globe, which recalled the Virgin seen on the Miraculous Medal. STELLAR PHENOMENA – Pilgrims reported seeing at night phenomena with the stars and the moon. Some have reported seeing faces on the moon and even two moons. MYSTERIOUS FIRE –As described in the text, the phenomenon of the large fire that appeared for 15 minutes and then vanished on Mt. Crnica occurred on October 28, 1981. DIVERSE LIGHTS – On the hill of apparitions, celestial-looking lights have been seen before and after apparitions and at other times. INSCRIPTIONS – The word MIR was seen written in the sky on August 6 and 24, and in June, July and October (dates unrecorded),1981. The words "MIR LJUDIMA" (Peace to the People) was written in light on a wall during the apparition of December 29, 1981. Thirty-five phenomena of this kind were noted in the parish chronicle from October 14, 1981 to October 3, 1983. The accounts in the parish chronicle are accompanied by approximately 50 written testimonies, photos and videos.

35. Kraljevic, *The Apparitions of Our Lady at Medjugorje*, 163-165.
36. Craig, *Spark from Heaven*, 65-66. Over the last three decades, reports of supernatural phenomena being seen and experienced in Medjugorje, both on the ground and in the air, have continued on a regular basis. One of the more recent mysteries concerns a statue of the Risen Savior that stands in a rotunda near the rear of St. James Church. It was created by a Slovenian sculptor named Andrei Ajdia, who first presented it at Pope John Paul II's Mass in Ljubljana in 1999. The pope liked it so much he was given a miniature silver replica of it. The statue was set up in Medjugorje in 2002. Not long after it was put in place in Medjugorje, a steady stream of water began to ooze and flow out of the right knee of the figure of Christ. This mystery has continued with no natural cause yet to be determined. Geophysicists, engineers, geologists, meteorologists, and other experts have studied the phenomenon and confess to being stumped.
37. Ibid., 66.
38. Ibid.
39. Ibid., 70.

40. **CHAPTER 31: THE JUST WILL PREVAIL**
41. Craig, *Spark from Heaven*, 72.
42. Ibid.
43. Ibid.
44. Ibid., 73.
45. Ibid.
46. Ibid.
47. Ibid.
48. Sullivan, *The Miracle Detective*, 116.
49. Soldo, *My Heart Will Triumph*, 80. Sullivan reports that Podbrdo was sealed off for two years, that ringing the church bells was prohibited, and that the rectory was searched numerous times by government officers looking for propaganda literature hostile to the state. Church services were also often drowned out by low-flying helicopters, and the collection box was confiscated almost a dozen times.
50. Craig, *Spark from Heaven*, 71.
51. Ibid.
52. Ibid., 72. The visionaries report that they were given by Mary a vision of Ivan Ivanković in his prison cell. During it, only his head and shoulders could be observed. They inquired of Mary why they could only see him like that. "Because Ivan is being witness to the truth," Mary answered.
53. Sullivan, *The Miracle Detective*, 122.
54. Craig, *Spark from Heaven*, 67.
55. Sullivan, *The Miracle Detective*, 122.
56. Craig, *Spark from Heaven*, 72.
57. Ibid, 74; This account was taken from the St. James Parish ledger, August 17, 1981.
58. Ibid.
59. Ibid.; Čitluk Commune Press Release, August 17, 1981.
60. René Laurentin, *Medjugorje: 12 Years Later, War, Love Your Enemies* (Santa Barbara, CA: Queenship Publishing Company, 1993), 127-128.
61. Craig, *Spark from Heaven*, 75-76.
62. Sullivan, *The Miracle Detective*, 119. Jozo was shipped off to the infamous Foca Prison outside of Sarajevo and worked in a sawmill. Abused at first by prison authorities and fellow inmates, he gradually earned their respect and friendship.
63. Craig, *Spark from Heaven*, 76.
64. Sullivan, *The Miracle Detective*, 115.
65. Soldo, *My Heart Will Triumph*, 82.
66. Ibid.
67. Ibid.
68. Ibid.

69. René Laurentin and René Lejeune, *Messages and Teachings of Mary at Medjugorje: Chronological Corpus of the Messages* (Milford, OH: The Riehle Foundation, 1988), 157.

70. Ibid.

71. Ibid., 161.

72. Ibid., 166.

73. Ibid., 158. Per October 19, 1981, Laurentin and Lejeune write: "Mary tells the visionaries, 'Pray for Fr. Jozo and fast tomorrow on bread and water. Then you will fast for a whole week on bread and water. Pray my angels. Now, I will show you Fr. Jozo.' The seers have a vision of Fr. Jozo in prison. He tells them not to be afraid for him, that everything was well."

74. Ibid., 171. See *Spark from Heaven* for a full account of the questions of Fr. Ivica Vego to Marija Pavlović, p. 84.

CHAPTER 32: SOLIDARITY

1. Filip Mazurczak, "The Cannonization of Karol Wojtyla: Son Oj Jagiellonian Poland," April 26, 2014, https://visegradinsight.eu/the-the-cannonization-of-john-paul-ii/.

2. Kengor, *A Pope and a President*, 203.

3. Mikotaj Glinski, "The Day Poland Stood Still: Memories from the Introduction of Martial Law," December 13, 20016, https://culture.pl/en/article/the-day-poland-stood-still-memories-from-the-introduction-of-martial-law.

4. Ibid.

5. Jefferey Donovan, Poland: Solidarity-The Trade Union that Changed the World," August 24, 2005, https://www.rferl.org/a/1060898.html.

6. Kengor, *A Pope and a President*, 270.

7. Ibid.

8. Ibid.

9. Ibid.

10. Ibid., 271.

11. The transcript of Jaruzelski's statement was published in all the newspapers throughout the world on December 14 and 15, 1981.

12. David Cross, "Shooting Reported in Poland as Troops Break Wave of Strikes," *The Times* (London), December 16, 1981.

13. Peter Schweizer, *Victory: The Reagan Administration's Secret Strategy that Hastened the Collapse of the Soviet Union* (New York, NY: Atlantic Monthly Press,1996), 29, 31.

14. Kengor, *A Pope and a President*, 275.

15. Ibid., 272.

16. Ibid., 279.

17. Sullivan, *The Miracle Detective*, 120.

18. Ibid.

19. Ibid.

20. Ibid., 121. Fr. Vlašić's arrival in Medjugorje fulfilled for him two personal prophecies he received in Rome at a charismatic conference that he attended at the beginning of June, 1981. There, Sister Briege McKenna, a Poor Clare nun based in the United States, told Vlašić that she experienced a vision of a church with two large steeples high in the mountains where she saw him sitting on a celebrant's chair. A spring of water gushed from behind him and flowed through the church. Thousands were arriving to drink of this water. A priest at the same conference, Father Emiliano Tardif, prayed over Vlašić and gave him a message, "Have no fear, I am sending you my Mother."

21. Ibid. Some of the visionaries, in interviews published after 2010, deny that Father Vlašić was ever officially considered the spiritual director of the group or of certain members. A review of the documentation during this period concurs with that position. While he certainly, as did all the friars, advised them at times on all types of matters, he was never officially named or designated their spiritual director by anyone in authority. This misconception arises from authors who merely assumed such and used that terminology in reference to his perceived role at the time. Upon examination, Vlašić is found to have been more involved with the two reported locutionists in the village than with the primary group of six.

22. Laurentin and Rupčić, *Is the Virgin Mary Appearing at Medjugorje?* 146.

23. Ibid.

24. Ibid.

25. Sullivan, *The Miracle Detective*, 119.

26. Laurentin and Rupčić, *Is the Virgin Mary Appearing at Medjugorje?* 146-147.

27. Ibid., 147.

28. Craig, *Spark from Heaven*, 87.

29. Ibid., 89.

30. Ibid.

31. Ibid.

32. Ibid., 90.

33. Ibid.

34. Ibid.

35. Ibid. Fr. Tomislav Pervan, who was soon to become the Pastor at St. James, recalled in a 2008 interview those stormy days in Medjugorje, "In a very real sense, those days were biblical for me, something like the dawn after

a long night of Communist darkness, especially when I saw how many came to the church and the countless numbers who experienced new life through the Sacrament of Reconciliation. For me, this was a powerful sign and proof that the Blessed Mother was, and is, here; that she is conquering the kingdom of Satan. These were truly biblical times, a re-lecture or re-reading of the *Acts of the Apostles*."

36. Sullivan, *The Miracle Detective*, 119.
37. Craig, *Spark from Heaven*, 91.
38. Ibid.
39. Ibid.
40. Laurentin and Lejeune, *Messages and Teachings of Mary at Medjugorje*, 171.
41. Ratzinger, "The Message of Fatima," published in *The Fatima Prophecies*, 280.

CHAPTER 33: THE WORLD IS IN GRAVE DANGER

1. Gorny and Rosikon, *Fatima Mysteries*, 299.
2. Ibid., 291-293.
3. Rory Carroll, "KGB Plotted to Kill Pope and Bug Vatican," November 3, 1999, *The Guardian*, https://www.theguardian.com/world/1999/nov/04/ rorycarroll#:~:text=The%20KGB%20plotted%20to%20 kill,documents% 20published%20in%20Italy%20yesterday.
4. Ibid.
5. Ibid.
6. David Remnick, *Lenin's Tomb: The Last Days of the Soviet Empire* (New York, NY: Random House, 1993), 191.
7. Ibid.
8. Ibid.
9. Kengor, *A Pope and a President*, 313.
10. Ibid.
11. Gorny and Rosikon, *Fatima Mysteries*, 299.
12. Ibid.
13. Ibid.
14. Ibid.
15. Michael Getler, "Pershing II Missile: Why it Alarms Soviets," March 17, 1982, *The Washington Post*, https://www.washingtonpost.com/archive/politics/1982/03/17/pershing-ii-missile-why-it-alarms-soviets/20e-ca6f0-3a64-4bdf-9957-ae54261b6ca6/.
16. Laurentin and Lejeune, *Messages and Teachings of Mary at Medjugorje*, 188.

17. Ratzinger, "The Message of Fatima," published in *The Fatima Prophecies*, 279.

18. Laurentin and Lejeune, *Messages and Teachings of Mary at Medjugorje*, 173. On the date of the one-year anniversary of the apparitions in Medjugorje, an estimated 50,000 people filled St. James and surrounded the area around the church. On June 26th, a day after, an extraordinary phenomenon was reported. After the morning Mass, the people reported seeing a shining white cloud descend on Mt. Krizevac; the huge cross then totally vanished. In the cloud, a silhouette of a person dressed in a long white garment appeared. This person could be seen radiating through the cloud. Then, a completely round white circle, like a large white host with a small cross above it, appeared. Many people from a distance reported seeing the phenomenon and photographs captured it. The vision lasted thirty minutes, from 6:30 to 7:00 a.m.

19. Laurentin and Rupčić, *Is the Virgin Mary Appearing at Medjugorje?* 71. Mrs. E. McFadden of Dublin analyzed the messages at Medjugorje from 1984 to January 2000. She then graphed and charted the primary words used by Mary in her messages. She found the word prayer was used over 400 times. She pie-grafted the following specific words and got these results: prayer (31%), love (14%), heart (10%), peace (8%), messages (7%), joy 7%), sacrifice [fasting, cross] (6%), Satan (5%), conversion (4%), grace (3%) holy (3%), and surrender (2%).

20. Ibid.

21. Ibid.

22. Ibid.

23. Laurentin and Lejeune, *Messages and Teachings of Mary at Medjugorje*, 173.

24. Ibid., 181.

25. Ibid., 186.

26. Father Tomislav Vlašić and Fr. Slavko Barbarić, *I Beseech You, Listen to My Messages and Live Them* (Milan, Italy: The Association of Friends of Medjugorje,1987), 117.

27. Ibid.

28. Laurentin and Lejeune, *Messages and Teachings of Mary at Medjugorje*, 67.

29. Ibid., 69.

30. Ibid., 181.

31. Ibid., 185.

32. Ibid.

33. Ibid., 191.

34. Ibid. The apparitions during this time were taking place at several different secret locations, including the homes of the visionaries. On

August 12, five days before the arrest of Jozo, militia from the Civil Defense Bureau showed up at Podbrdo at 3:00 a.m. in the morning and sealed of all access to the hill, as well as to Mts. Crnica and Krizevac. The three hills were designated as "restricted areas" by the authorities.

35. Ibid., 189.
36. Ibid., 207.
37. Ibid., 171.
38. Ibid.
39. Ibid., 189.
40. Soldo, *My Heart Will Triumph*, 368, 369.

CHAPTER 34: GOD HAS A PLAN

1. Vlašić and Barbarić, *I Beseech You, Listen to My Messages and Live Them*, 13.
2. Ibid., 51.
3. Ibid., 70.
4. Ibid., 102.
5. Gabriel Meyer, *A Portrait of Medjugorje* (Studio City, CA: Twin Circle Publishing Company, 1990), 54.
6. Ibid., 53.
7. Ibid.
8. Ibid.
9. Ibid.
10. Ibid., 54.
11. Ibid.
12. Laurentin and Lejeune, *Messages and Teachings of Mary at Medjugorje*, 243.
13. Ibid. 255.
14. Meyer, *A Portrait of Medjugorje*, 33.
15. Laurentin and Lejeune, *Messages and Teachings of Mary at Medjugorje*, 243.
16. Meyer, *A Portrait of Medjugorje*, 54.
17. Ibid.
18. Albert J. Herbert, S.M., *Medjugorje: An Affirmation and Defense* (Paulina, LA: Albert Herbert, S.M., 1990), 45. The Virgin Mary's "thank you for responding to my call" is found at the conclusion of her messages to Marija Pavlović. However, there is an important distinction to be made concerning the messages that each visionary receives and how the visionaries interact as a whole concerning this matter. Sister Emmanuel Maillard, who has lived in Medjugorje for many years, explains, "The visionaries are very strict when it comes to their testimony. They will only speak about

messages they personally receive. Marija is the one to whom the Gospa has spoken of this special monthly blessing, and it is useless to ask the other visionaries about it; they will only answer, 'The Gospa didn't tell me anything about that.' Similarly, on the subject of sickness, it is Vicka who has received the messages, and the others will not talk about them. When one of the visionaries says, 'The Gospa hasn't said anything about this,' he or she is speaking only for himself. This attitude is the guarantee of the truthfulness of their testimony." (For more on this, see Sr. Emmanuel's *Medjugorje: The 90's*, p. 50.)

19. Ibid.
20. Laurentin and Lejeune, *Messages and Teachings of Mary at Medjugorje*, 263.
21. Herbert, *Medjugorje: An Affirmation and Defense*, 45.
22. Connell, *The Visions of the Children*, 53.
23. Ibid., 45.
24. Ibid.
25. Ibid.
26. Ibid.
27. Ibid.
28. Ibid., 53.
29. Ibid., 54.
30. Ibid.
31. Ibid.
32. Ibid., 55.
33. Ibid., 73.
34. Ibid., 43-82; Connell, *Queen of the Cosmos*, 9-34.
35. Connell, *The Visions of the Children*, 87.
36. Ibid., 88.
37. Ibid.
38. Ibid.
39. Ibid., 93.
40. Ibid.
41. Ibid., 84-97; Connell, *Queen of the Cosmos*, 37-49.
42. Connell, *The Visions of the Children*, 111.
43. Ibid., 117.
44. Ibid.
45. Ibid.
46. Ibid., 119.
47. Ibid.
48. Ibid., 120.
49. Ibid.
50. Ibid., 111-135; Connell, *Queen of the Cosmos*, 51-85.

51. Connell, *The Visions of the Children*, 161. At first considered to be exceptionally introverted, Ivan matured greatly in his role as spokesperson for the call of the Madonna. Although he didn't succeed in the seminary, he became a very good and sought-after speaker with a powerful and sincere message that he took to the world. Ivan was the first of the visionaries to come to the United States on November 12, 1988. His hosts, the Malik family, reported that he prayed 2 to 3 hours a day. During that visit, Ivan traveled to Birmingham, Alabama, where he visited with Mother Angelica of EWTN and gave her a special message from Mary.

52. Ibid., 167.

53. Ibid., 158.

54. Ibid., 165.

55. Ibid.

56. Ibid., 167-167.

57. Ibid., 166.

58. Ibid., 167.

59. Ibid., 156-172; Connell, *Queen of the Cosmos*, 89-95.

60. Connell, *The Visions of the Children*, 141. Marija is the only visionary reporting an "official message" at Medjugorje from Jesus. The Virgin Mary appeared to Marija with the Christ Child on Christmas, December 25, 2012. He said, "*I am your peace. Live My Commandments.*"

61. Ibid., 145-146.

62. Ibid., 143.

63. Ibid., 147.

64. Ibid.

65. Ibid., 149.

66. Ibid., 150.

67. Ibid., 150-151.

68. Ibid., 151.

69. Ibid., 137-154; Connell, *Queen of the Cosmos*, 111-131.

70. Connell, *The Visions of the Children*, 99.

71. Ibid., 101.

72. Ibid., 102.

73. Ibid., 103.

74. Ibid.

75. Ibid., 104.

76. Ibid.

77. Ibid., 99-109; Connell, *Queen of the Cosmos*, 97-108.

CHAPTER 35: "I HAVE SHOWN YOU HELL"

1. Eduardo Siguenza, *John Paul II: The Pope Who Understood Fatima* (Goleta, CA: Queenship Publishing, 2007), 107.

2. Lúcia, *Fatima in Lucia's Own Words*, 167. Witnesses at the Cova da Iria on July 13, 1917, the day the children saw Hell—although not realizing what the children had seen—said that after the apparition their faces showed signs of shock, fear, and terror.

3. Ibid., 29-30. Some, such as William Thomas Walsh, have this conversation between Lúcia and Jacinta on the subject of Hell taking place a few days after the July 13th apparition, which seems unlikely since Mary had shown them a vision of Hell on the 13th and told them: "You have seen Hell."

4. Ibid.

5. Ibid.

6. Ibid. Jacinta sacrificed for sinners to save them from Hell until the very end of her life. After she was stricken with the Spanish Flu, the Virgin appeared to her and said she would be taking Francisco to Heaven soon. She then asked the visionary if she wanted to stay longer on Earth to save more sinners from Hell. Jacinta told Mary she wanted to stay.

7. Ibid., 108.

8. Ibid., 109.

9. Ibid.

10. Ibid.

11. Ibid.

12. Ibid.

13. Ibid., 110.

14. Ibid., 113. At times, Jacinta would cover her face with her hands on hearing people swearing. "O my God, don't these people realize this kind of talk might send them to Hell? Forgive them, Jesus and convert them. They certainly don't know how they are offending God," she remarked.

15. Michel de la Sainte Trinite, *The Whole Truth About Fatima*, 41.

16. Alonso, *The Secret of Fatima*, 106.

17. Ibid., 42.

18. Ibid.

19. Lúcia, *Fatima in Lucia's Own Words*, 109.

20. Michel de la Sainte Trinite, *The Whole Truth About Fatima*, 44.

21. Ibid.

22. Walsh, *Our Lady of Fatima*, 219.

23. Ibid.

24. Lúcia, *Fatima in Lucia's Own Words*, 159-160.

25. Alonso, *The Secret of Fatima*, 22

26. Alonso, *La Verite sur le Secret de Fatima*, 92.
27. Quoted by the review, *Les Voyants de Fatima*, bulletin for the beatification causes for Francisco and Jacinta, September-December,1978, p.7.

CHAPTER 36: THE CENTURY OF SATAN

1. Laurentin and Lejeune, *Messages and Teachings of Mary at Medjugorje*, 172.
2. Connell, *Queen of the Cosmos*, 67.
3. Connell, *The Visions of the Children*, 126.
4. Connell, *Queen of the Cosmos*, 67.
5. Ibid.
6. Ibid.
7. Ibid.
8. Connell, *The Visions of the Children*, 127.
9. Connell, *Queen of the Cosmos*, 67.
10. Connell, *The Visions of the Children*, 127.
11. Connell, *Queen of the Cosmos*, 67.
12. Ibid.
13. Ibid., 68.
14. Ibid., 69. In an unpublished interview conducted by Chuck Peurs on October 20,1988, and translated by Father Tony Petrusic of Omaha, Nebraska, Vicka said of Hell, "It was horrible. The skin of those there was blackened. Most troublesome was seeing a beautiful girl pass through, her skin becoming blackened and then seeing her indescribably beastly and grotesque."
15. Ibid., 101.
16. Ibid., 130.
17. Ibid.
18. Ibid.
19. Ibid., 94.
20. Ibid., 40. In January of 1983, Father Tomislav Vlašić inquired of Mirjana if many souls went to Hell. Mirjana told him, "I recently asked the Gospa just that question. She says that nowadays the majority of people go to Purgatory, the second category go to Hell, and only a small number of people go directly to Heaven. She told me that those who are in Hell have ceased to think about God positively; they blaspheme more and more and are already a part of Hell."
21. Soldo, *My Heart Will Triumph*, 149, Connell, *The Visions of the Children*, 77. Between the times of Fátima (1917) and Medjugorje (1981), there occurred another very significant revelation of Hell that deserves mentioning. In 1936, St. Faustina Kowalska had a powerful experience

of Hell that she recorded in her acclaimed book, *Diary of Sister Maria Faustina Kowalska: Divine Mercy in my Soul*: "Today, in the company of an angel, I visited Hell. It is a place of great agony and it covers a large area! Of all the torments I have seen, the greatest is the loss of God...I would have died as I watched the tortures, if the power of the Almighty had not supported me. Let sinners know that the nature of their sufferings shall be that of their sins, for all eternity. I am writing this on an order from God so that no one will seek an excuse, saying that 'nobody ever went there' and that 'nobody really knows what happens there'! I, Sister Faustina, by an order of God, went into the depths of Hell to testify that Hell does exist... I noticed one thing: that most of the souls there are those who disbelieved that there is a Hell." (October 20, 1936, No. 741.)

22. Connell, *Queen of the Cosmos*, 24-25. Mirjana's encounter with Satan took place on April 14, 1982. This is 8-9 months before the January 10, 1983, interview, not the "approximately 6 months" that she states in the interview. She obviously, like all of us, lost track of the time that had gone bye. See *Open Your Hearts to Mary Queen of Peace* by Vlašić and Barbarić, p.14.

23. Kraljevic, *The Apparitions of Our Lady at Medjugorje*, 125. In the book, *Open Your Hearts to Mary Queen of Peace* (p.14), Mirjana said the following about Satan, "He was ugly, horribly ugly. You cannot even imagine how ugly, he almost killed me with his gaze. I almost fainted."

24. Lúcia, *Fatima in Lucia's Own Words*, 70.

25. Ibid. Father Ferreira was no friend of the apparitions, and entirely against any supernatural explanation of the visions. Ti Marto, the father of Jacinta and Francisco and the person considered to be the *first* believer in the apparitions, once said the priest was the last person in all of Portugal to believe in Fátima. Father Ferreira told Lucia's mom and another man, Jose Alves of Moita, on one occasion, "This is the Devil's work."

26. Ibid., 71.

27. Rev 12:1-3

28. Alonso, *The Secret of Fatima*, 110.

29. Kraljevic, *The Apparitions of Our Lady at Medjugorje*, 124.

30. Laurentin and Lejeune, *Messages and Teachings of Mary at Medjugorje*, 162.

31. Ibid., 181.

32. Ibid.

33. Ibid., 206.

34. Ibid., 207.

35. Ibid., 241.

36. Ibid., 244.

37. Ibid.
38. Ibid., 253.
39. Connell, *The Visions of the Children*, 166-167.
40. Ibid.
41. Ibid.
42. Ibid., 171.
43. Dr. Mars Domej, "Conversation with Jacov Colo on April 2, 1990, in Medjugorje," *Mary's People* (*The National Catholic Register*), September, 1990, p. 9. Excerpted from *Medjugorje Gebetsaktion*. Translated by Teresa M. Reimers.
44. Connell, *Queen of the Cosmos*, 80-82.
45. Ibid.
46. Connell, *The Visions of the Children*, 75.
47. Connell, *Queen of the Cosmos*, 42.
48. Ibid., 120.
49. Connell, *The Visions of the Children*, 143.
50. Ibid.
51. *The Pilgrim*, March, 1994.
52. Connell, *Queen of the Cosmos*, 23.
53. Ibid., 24-25.
54. Ibid., 25.
55. Ibid.
56. Ibid.
57. Ibid., 25-27.
58. Ibid., 27.
59. Ibid., 34. At Medjugorje, the Virgin has given messages that warn of Satan's desire to destroy the planet. The January 21, 1991, message, delivered during the Gulf War, is a good example: "Dear children, today, like never before, I invite you to prayer. Let your prayer be a prayer for peace. Satan is strong and desires to destroy not only human life, but also nature and the planet on which you live. Therefore, dear children, pray that through prayer you can protect yourselves with God's blessing of peace. God has sent me among you so that I may help you. If you so wish, grasp for the rosary. Even the Rosary alone can work miracles in the world and in your lives. I bless you and I remain with you for as long as it is God's will. Thank you for not betraying my presence here, and I thank you because your response is serving the good and the peace."

CHAPTER 37: 1983: ON THE BRINK

1. Diane Montagna, "What John Paul II Intended to Say the Day He Was Shot," May 7, 2016, https://www.

riz=1C1PRFI_enUS780US781&sxsrf=ALeKk 01HxfjoCW_63C-
gxawCFLnu5ydI_Q:1613416838960&q=Diane+Montgna +What+
John+Paul+Intended+to+say+the+day+he+was+shot+may+7+
2016&spell=&sa+X&ved=2ahUKEwjs!L2MzuzuAhXFjFkKHdq
KDIsQBS gAegQICRAw&biw+1600&bih=757.

2. Ibid.

3. "Fatima Visionary Predicted 'Final Battle' Would be over Marriage, Family," December 31, 2016, https://www.catholicnewsagency.com/news/fatima-visionary-predicted-final-battle-would-be-over-marriage-family-17760.

4. Ibid.

5. Gorny and Rosikon, *Fatima Mysteries*, 17. Some mistakenly report Ağca's gun was a 9-millimeter Walther. Besides the 13 cartridges in Ağca's gun that once again point to Fátima's May 13th anniversary date, some say the actual time of the shooting that day was 5:13, instead of 5:19, the same numbers as the *date* of the day. George Weigel, in his biography of John Paul II, *Witness to Hope*, has the time at 5:13 (p. 412). John O' Sullivan, author of *The President, the Pope, and the Prime Minister: Three Who Changed the World*, also has the time of the shooting at 5:13 (p. 66), as does Paul Kengor in his *A Pope and a President* (p. 4). Kengor noted other oddities surrounding the number 13 and Pope John Paul II. The Pope was shot on the thirteenth; he beatified Jacinta and Francisco on the thirteenth; the numbers in the date of his death, 4-2-2005, add up to thirteen; even the numbers of his official time of death in 2005, 21:37 (9:37 p.m.), add up to thirteen. The number 13, Cardinal Bertone noted in *The Last Secret of Fatima* (p. 12), seems to have been "fated" to play a role in John Paul's life.

6. Ibid. More than two shots were fired in St. Peter's Square that day. The exact total is not known. Three bullets were found. As many as five shots were reported heard. Two other Turkish assassins were identified. Ağca's gun jammed after the third shot. Italy's finest police investigators, the *Carabinieri*, could not find the cause after a lengthy investigation.

7. Ibid., 22.

8. Ibid.

9. Ibid., 31.

10. Ibid., 309.

11. Transcript of Ronald Reagan's remarks at the Conservative Political Action Conference Dinner, Washington, DC, February 18, 1983.

12. Gorny and Rosikon, *Fatima Mysteries*, 30.

13. Timothy Tindal-Robertson, *Fatima, Russia, & Pope John Paul II* (Still River, MA: The Ravengate Press, 1992), 2.

14. Ratzinger, "The Message of Fatima," published in *The Fatima Prophecies*, 273.

15. Apostoli, *Fatima for Today*, 189.

16. Ibid., 190.

17. Wlodzimierz Redzioch, "Assassination Attempt: I Reminded Him of Fatima," *Inside the Vatican*, October, 2001, pp.40-43; Gorny and Rosikon, *Fatima Mysteries*, 309. Redzioch's article gives a very revealing look at the Pope's recovery from the assassination attempt. Professor Gabriel Turowski was a member of a six-man team of doctors that consulted on Pope John Paul II's case. Turowski was Polish and had been Karol Wojtyła's physician when he was Archbishop of Krakow. He was the head of the Transplantation and Immunology Unit in the surgery department at the Copernicus Medical School in Krakow.

18. Ratzinger, "The Message of Fatima," published in *The Fatima Prophecies*, 273; Bertone, *The Last Secret of Fatima*, 47.

19. Nolan, *Medjugorje, A Time for Truth a Time for Action*, xx.

20. Apostoli, *Fatima for Today*, 191.

21. Ibid.

22. Father Gruner and other Fátima Experts, *World Enslavement or Peace... It's Up to The Pope* (Ontario, Canada: Fatima Crusader, circa 1988), 194.

23. Rev. Robert Fox, *Rediscovering Fatima* (Huntington, IN: Our Sunday Visitor, Inc., 1982), 127.

24. Walsh, *Our Lady of Fatima*, 221.

25. Ratzinger, "The Message of Fatima," published in *The Fatima Prophecies*, 277.

26. Ibid.

27. Kengor, *A Pope and a President*, 312.

28. Ibid.

29. Ibid., 317.

30. Ibid., 319.

31. Ibid., 327.

32. Ibid., 328.

33. Ibid.

34. Ibid., 320.

35. Ibid.

36. Ibid.

37. Ibid.

38. On February 3, 1983, at the annual National Prayer Breakfast, President Ronald Reagan designated 1983 as the "National Year of the Bible." Public Law 97-280 passed Congress and was approved on October 4, 1982.

39. Ibid.

40. Kengor, *A Pope and President*, 132.

41. Ibid., 325.

42. Ibid.

43. Presidential Speeches | Ronald Reagan Presidency / March 8,1983: Transcript of "Evil Empire Speech," UVA Miller Center, https://millercenter.org/the-presidency/presidential-speeches/march-8-1983-evil-empire-speech.

44. Kengor, *A Pope and a President*, 325.

45. Ibid., 326.

46. Ibid.

47. Presidential Speeches | Ronald Reagan Presidency / March 8,1983: Transcript of "Evil Empire Speech," UVA Miller Center, https://millercenter.org/the-presidency/presidential-speeches/march-8-1983-evil-empire-speech.

48. Kengor, *A Pope and a Presidency*, 327-328.

49. Ronald Reagan, "Remarks at the Annual Convention of the National Religious Broadcasters," January 31, 1983.

50. Paul Shillito, "Did Reagan's Real Star Wars Bankrupt the Soviet Union?" June 20, 2017, https://curious-droid.com/258/reagans-real-star-wars-bankrupt-soviet-union/.

51. Charles Moyer, "Star Wars in Strategy in Russian Response," December 17, 1985, https://www.nytimes.com.

52. Gorny and Rosikon, *Fatima Mysteries*, 318.

53. Yuri Andropov was a ruthless spy master, seemingly destined for his role. In a curious bit of fate, he was born only a few hundred yards away from the Lubyanka, the Soviet police headquarters in Moscow and the national headquarters of the KGB. This was an ominous oddity historians note since he would rise to become the head of the KGB. The building's outside façade is still marked by a number of Soviet 'Hammer and Cycle' emblems.

54. "Yuri Andropov," https://www.newworldencyclopedia.org/entry/Yuri_Andropov.

55. Ibid.

56. Ibid.

57. Kengor, *A Pope and a President*, 308.

58. Ibid.

59. *Il Giornale Nuovo*, January 6, 1983. (Cited in Claire Sterling, *The Time of the Assassins*, 184-185.)

60. Kengor, *A Pope and a President*, 312.

61. Korean Airlines Flight 007, October 16,1992, Conservapedia, https://www.conservapedia.com/Korean_Airlines_Flight_007.

62. Nuclear Close Calls: Able Archer 83 | Atomic Heritage Foundation, June 15, 2018, https://www.atomicheritage.org/history/nuclear-close-calls-able-archer 83#:~:text=The%20election%20of%20President%20Ronald,exercise%20almost%20 prompted%20nuclear%20war.

63. Kengor, *A Pope and a President*, 339-341.

CHAPTER 38: A REHEARSAL OF ARMAGEDDON

1. "Stanislav Petrov-Man Who Saved the World Dies at 77," September 8, 2017, https://www.npr.org.
2. Ibid.
3. Dylan Matthew, "Thirty-five Years Ago Today, One Man Saved Us from World Ending Nuclear War," September 26, 2018, https://www.vox.com/2018/9/26/17905796/nuclear-war-1983-stanislav-petrov-soviet-union.
4. Ibid.
5. Ibid.
6. Ibid.
7. Transcript of Ronald Reagan's remarks at the annual Pulaski Day Banquet in New York City on September 25, 1983.
8. Kengor, *A Pope and a President*, 341.
9. Ibid.
10. Strobe Talbott, *The Russians and Reagan*, (New York, NY: Vintage, 1984), 122.
11. Colin Brown, "US Troops Invade Granada," October 26, 2016, https://www.theguardian.com/world/2016/oct/26/us-troops-invade-grenada-archive.
12. Ibid. Dr. Crucitti removed 22 inches of Pope John Paul II's intestines.
13. Serge Schemann, "Reaction to Invasion a Gain for Moscow," November 2, 1983, www.nytimes.com.
14. Ibid.
15. Ibid.
16. Ibid.
17. Ibid.
18. Ibid.
19. Ibid.
20. Ibid.
21. Todd Avery Raffensperger, "How a NATO Military Exercise Freaked Out Russia (And Nearly Started a Nuclear War)," *The National Interest*, May 20, 2018, https://nationalinterest.org/blog/the-buzz/how-nato-military-exercise-freaked-out-russia-nearly-started-25864?page=0%2C1.
22. Douglas Birch, "The U.S.S.R. and U.S. Come Closer to Nuclear War Than We Thought," May 28, 2013, https://www.theatlantic.com/ international/archive/2013 /05/ the-ussr-and- us-came-closer-to-nuclear-war-than-we-thought/276290/.
23. Ibid.

24. Ibid.
25. Ibid.
26. Nate Jones and J. Peter Scoblic, "The Week the World Almost Ended," April 23, 2017, https://slate.com/news-and-politics/2017/06/able-archer-almost-started-a-nuclear-war-with-russia-in-1983.html.
27. Ibid.
28. Raffensperger, "How a NATO Military Exercise Freaked Out Russia (And Nearly Started a Nuclear War)," https://nationalinterest.org/blog/the-buzz/how-nato-military-exercise-freaked-out-russia-nearly-started-25864?page=0%2C1.
29. "Nuclear Close Calls-Able Archer 83, Cold War History," *Atomic Heritage*, June 15, 2018, https://www.atomicheritage.org/history/nuclear-close-calls-able-archer83#:~:text=The%20election%20of%20President%20Ronald,exercise%20almost%20prompted%20nuclear%20war.
30. Ibid.
31. Ibid.
32. Ibid.
33. Ibid.
34. Ibid.
35. Ibid.
36. Ibid.
37. Ibid.
38. Birch, "The U.S.S.R. and U.S. Come Closer to Nuclear War than We Thought," https://www.theatlantic.com/international/archive/2013/05/the-ussr-and-us-came-closer-to-nuclear-war-than-we-thought/276290/.
39. "Nuclear Close Calls-Able Archer 83, Cold War History," June 15, 2018, https://www.atomicheritage.org/history/nuclear-close-calls-able-archer83#:~:text=The%20election%20of%20President%20Ronald,exercise%20almost%20prompted%20nuclear%20war.
40. Ibid.
41. Birch, "The U.S.S.R. and U.S. Come Closer to Nuclear War than We Thought," https://www.theatlantic.com/international/archive/2013/05/the-ussr-and-us-came-closer-to-nuclear-war-than-we-thought/276290/.
42. Nate Jones, "War Scare." May 21, 2013, https://foreignpolicy.com/2013/05/21/war-scare/.
43. Tom Nichols, "Five Ways Nuclear Armageddon Was Almost Unleashed," May 9, 2014, https://nationalinterest.org/feature/five-ways-nuclear-armageddon-was-almost-unleashed-11044; Sam Roberts, "NATO War Games Unwittingly Put Soviet and US in Hair Trigger in 83, Analysis Suggests." November 11, 2009, https://www.nytimes.com/2015/11/10/world/europe/nato-war-games-unwittingly-put-soviets-and-us-on-hair-trigger-in-83-analysis-suggests.html.

44. "Nuclear Close Calls-Able Archer 83, Cold War History," June 15, 2018, https://www.atomicheritage.org/history/nuclear-close-calls-able- archer83#:~: text=The%20election%20of%20 President 20Ronald,exercise%20almost%20prompted%20nuclear%20 war.

45. Birch, "The U.S.R.R. and U.S. Come Closer to Nuclear War than We Thought," https://www.theatlantic.com/international/archive/2013/05/the-ussr-and-us-came-closer-to-nuclear-war-than-we-thought/276290/.

46. Scott Shane, "Cold War's Riskiest Moments", August 31, 2003, https://www.baltimoresun.com/news/bs-xpm-2003-08-31-0308310294-story.html.

47. "Yuri Andropov", https://www.newworldencyclopedia.org/entry/Yuri_Andropov.

48. Remnick, *Lenin's Tomb: The Last Days of the Soviet Empire*, 191.

49. Brandon Weichert, "What Yuri Andropov Can Tell Us About Vladimir Putin's Mind Set," October 16, 2016, https://theweichertreport.wordpress.com/2016/10/16/what-yuri-andropov-can-tell-us-about-vladimir-putins-mindset/.

50. Kiron Skinner, Martin Anderson, and Annelise Anderson, *Reagan in his Own Hand* (New York, NY: Free Press, 2001), 10-12.

51. Kengor, *A Pope and a President*, 327.

52. Benjamin Fischer, "A Cold War Conundrum: The 1983 Soviet War Scare," https://www.cia.gov/readingroom/docs/19970901.pdf.

53. Ibid.

54. G. Barrass, "Able Archer 83: What Were the Soviets Thinking? Survival: Volume, No 6," Nov. 21, 2016, https://www.google.com/search?q=G.+Barass+Able+archer+83+What+were+the+Soviets+thinkingtand+fontline&rlz=1C1PRFI_enUS780US781&oq=G.+Barass+Able+archer+83+What+were+the+Soviets+thinkingtand+fontline&aqs=chrome.69i57.56294j0j15&sourceid=chrome&ie=UTF-8.

55. Ibid.

56. 'What Effect Did Yuri Andropov Have on the Cold War," June 3, 2018, https://www.quora.com/What-changed-in-the-USSR-when-Yuri-Andropov-became-a-leader.

57. Ibid.

58. Ibid.

59. Ibid.

60. Hank Stuever, "Yes, 'The Day After' Really Was the Profound TV Moment the Americans Make It Out to Be," May 11, 2016, www.washingtonpost.com. https://www.washingtonpost.com/news/arts-and-entertainment/

wp/2016/05/11/yes-the-day-after-really-was-the-profound-tv-moment-the-americans-makes-it-out-to-be/. The film and its subject matter were heavily promoted in the news media before and after it was broadcasted. *Newsweek, Time, TV Guide* and *U.S. News and World Report* all ran cover stories. Critics saw the film as sensationalizing nuclear war. Others said it was too soft. The film received 12 Emmy nominations and won 2 Emmy awards. It was eventually released in the Communist nations of the Eastern Bloc as well as China, North Korea and Cuba.

61. William Drozdiak, "Soviets Discontinue Talks on Medium Range Missiles," November 24,1983, https://www.washingtonpost.com/archive/politics/1983/11/24/soviets-discontinue-talks-on-medium-range-missiles/95bc40d7-4776-45a4-b149-010286fb3586/.

62. William Drozdiak, "Soviets Halt Strategic Arms Talks." December 9,1983, https://www.washingtonpost.com/archive/politics/1983/12/09/soviets-halt-strategic-arms-talks/5ec90e4c-8b95-4be0-9265-1e622f706176/.

63. Laurentin and Lejeune, *Messages and Teachings of Mary at Medjugorje*, 216.

64. Laurentin and Rupčić, *Is the Virgin Mary Appearing at Medjugorje?* 142-144.

65. Apostoli, *Fatima for Today*, 188.

66. Charles Ridley, "Pope Meets His Would Be Assassin," December 27, 1983, https://www.upi.com/Archives/1983/12/27/Pope-meets-his-would-be-assassin/4402441349200/.

67. Text of Pope John Paul II remarks of December 27,1983, after his meeting in Rebibbia Prison with Mehmet Ali Ağca.

68. Pope John Paul II, *Memory and Identity: Conversations at the Dawn of the Millennium* (New York, NY: Rizzoli, 2005), 163.

69. Cardinal Stanislaw Dziwisz, *Life with Karol* (New York, NY: Doubleday, 2008), 142.

70. Bertone, *The Last Secret of Fatima*, 76. The nun named Lúcia who blocked and tackled Ağca was just one of many Fátima connections in Ağca's life. Referring to the shadow of Fátima hanging over Ağca's life, Bertone writes that Ağca said he felt like the "plaything" of some obscure mystery.

71. Alex Q. Arbuckle, "1981-1983: Violence and Forgiveness," https://mashable.com/2015/09/30/pope-john-paul-ii-assassin/.

72. "Pope Gunman Mehmet Ali Ağca Visits John Paul II's Tomb in the Vatican," Sunday, December 28, 2014, https://www.abc.net.au/news/2014-12-28/pope-john-paul-would-be-assassin-visits-his-vatican-tomb/5990056.

73. "Ağca Leaves Flowers on John Paul's Tomb in Vatican," *Associated Press*, December 27, 2014, https://www.toledoblade.com/news/Religion/2014/12/27/Agca-leaves-flowers-on-John-Paul-s-tomb-in-Vatican/stories/.

CHAPTER 39: BIG BROTHER

1. Laurentin and Rupčić, *Is the Virgin Mary Appearing at Medjugorje?* 18.
2. Sullivan, *The Miracle Detective*, 201.
3. René Laurentin, *Medjugorje Testament: Hostility Abounds, Grace Super-abounds* (Toronto, Ontario: Ave Maria Press, 1998), 233.
4. Ibid.
5. Ibid.
6. Ibid.
7. Ibid.
8. Ibid.
9. Meyer, *A Portrait of Medjugorje*, 27.
10. Laurentin and Rupčić, *Is the Virgin Mary Appearing in Medjugorje?* 1-21.
11. Ibid., 7.
12. O'Carroll, *Medjugorje: Facts, Documents, and Theology*, 56. O'Carroll was no light weight theologian, having authored a couple dozen books of his own, including an encyclopedia on the faith. I had the pleasure of staying with him in Ireland for a week at Blackrock College. Like Laurentin, his humility was extraordinary, constantly heaping praise and admiration on everyone that crossed his path. He could never say enough about Laurentin, believing him to be a God sent grace for not only Medjugorje, but the times at hand.
13. Meyer, *A Portrait of Medjugorje*, 27.
14. O'Carroll, *Medjugorje: Facts, Documents, and Theology*, 13. In his book, O'Carroll masterfully outlines the pedigree of Laurentin and shows how his presence in Medjugorje is of incomprehensible significance to the importance and progression of the visions in every way (see pages 48-57). I had the great honor of working with Father Laurentin over the years. In the 1990s, he would spend almost a week at my home in the summer before going to the University of Dayton to lecture at the renowned Marian library there. His work certainly speaks for itself. But what is probably less understood about him was his gentlemanly character and how he lived the message of the Gospel in a most impressive way. He truly loved his enemies and never surrendered to his emotions in the heat of controversy. He was, quite simply, a living saint. It is difficult to read those who take up a pen against his work knowing it is like a first year art student critiquing Michelangelo. I believe this small excerpt from one of his books on Medjugorje illustrates somewhat my

poor attempt to capture his outstanding character and consummate professionalism. Laurentin writes, "The controversy which judges these events with an opposite view gathers a mixture of pieces of gossip and free interpretations. To refute these wild imaginings; one would need two or three times more space. In doing this, the essential would be forgotten or neglected. It is better, then, to stop here, not disgusted at all for those who have a solid and lucid heart, but tired of having lost so much time on it when the rest is so much more interesting and fruitful. The Proverb says: 'The dogs bark while the caravan passes.' Let it be said without wanting to offend those who rant, that such is indeed the situation in Medjugorje. But when a man rants from anger or ideology, it is appropriate to invite him to stop ranting, for this disfigures him. The need is to find again a look, a voice, a human intelligence and a spiritual discernment which weighs realities." (From Laurentin's *Eight Years: Reconciliation, Analysis, the Future.*)

15. Ibid., 56. Laurentin wrote approximately twenty books on Medjugorje and related subject matter. The full historical value of his work on Medjugorje is not understood or appreciated yet. In terms of comparison with the record on Fátima, it appears he singlehandedly did the work of dozens of individuals who together helped construct the full story of Fátima. Future historians will begin and end with Laurentin in assembling the most factual picture of the first twenty years of Medjugorje.

16. Laurentin and Rupčić, *Is the Virgin Mary Appearing in Medjugorje?* 6.

17. Ibid.

18. Ibid.

19. Ibid., 74.

20. Ibid., 1.

21. Ibid., 134-136.

22. O'Carroll, *Medjugorje: Facts, Documents, and Theology*, 58.

23. Ibid., 59.

24. Ibid.

25. Ibid.

26. Ibid.

27. Ibid., 60.

28. Ibid., 64-69.

29. Laurentin and Rupčić, *Is the Virgin Mary Appearing in Medjugorje?* 121.

30. Craig, *Spark from Heaven*, 159.

31. Sullivan, *The Miracle Detective*, 201. In England, as in France, Medjugorje was becoming a household name around this time. In the fall of 1983, *The Catholic Herald* published a series of front-page stories and editorials about the apparitions of the Virgin Mary in Medjugorje.

32. Laurentin, *Eight Years: Reconciliation, Analysis, the Future* (Milford, OH: The Riehle Foundation, 1989), 29.

33. Laurentin and Lejeune, *Messages and Teachings of Mary at Medjugorje*, 221-228. Mary's call to prayer is found to be answered. Father Petar reported he was told there were 2,000 prayer groups in Australia. In Italy, it was said there were 2,500 known. In the United States, there were "several thousand," along with over 200 "Peace Centers."

34. Ibid., 223.

35. Ibid.

36. Ibid., 226.

37. Laurentin and Lejeune, *Is the Virgin Mary Appearing at Medjugorje?* 161. The appearance of the written word "Mir" in the sky at Medjugorje is documented to have occurred on no less than six different occasions in 1981: once in late June, again in late July, another on "the afternoon of August 24th," and once in both September and October. Laurentin retrieved the August 6th date from the church logue. Father Joseph Pelletier confirmed the multiple "MIR" sightings in his book: "A most important sign was the word *Mir* (Peace) that was written one evening in large bright letters in the sky above the cross on Mount Krizevac. This occurred in the early days of the apparitions and was seen by the pastor and many people from the village. It has been witnessed a number of times."

38. Transcript of Reagan's speech on Soviet-American relations, January 17, 1984, https://www.nytimes.com/1984/01/17/world/transcript-of-reagan-s-speech-on-soviet-american-relations.html.

39. Nicolas Bonnal, "George Orwell and the American Complex Terror," April 25, 2013, https://english.pravda.ru/history/124418-orwell_american_terror/.

40. John Burns, "Andropov is Dead. Reagan asks Productive Contacts and Names Bush to Attend Funeral," February 2, 1984, https://www.nytimes.com/1984/02/11/world/andropov-dead-moscow-69-reagan-asks-productive-contacts-names-bush-attend.html.

41. Douglas Birch, "The U.S.S.R. and the U.S.A. Come Closer to Nuclear War than We Thought." May 28, 1983, https://www.theatlantic.com/international/archive/2013/05/the-ussr-and-us-came-closer-to-nuclear-war-than-we-thought/276290/.

42. Bonnal, "George Orwell and the American Complex Terror," April 25, 2013, https://english.pravda.ru/history/124418-orwell_american_terror/. Orwell's work was fiction but another book, more than a decade before, dreamed of a real life totalitarian state being established in America. William Z. Foster, a radical Marxist and an American labor organizer, was General Secretary of the Communist Party USA from 1945 to 1957. His book *Toward Soviet America*, published in 1932, documented the Communist revolution in the Soviet Union and what such

a society in America would look like. The book remains popular today among Marxists-Leninists and Stalinists.

CHAPTER 40: DELIVER US

1. Apostoli, *Fatima for Today*, 163.
2. Carlos Evaristo, *"Two Hours with Sister Lucia"* (Fátima, Portugal: Evaristo, 1996), 37. Fátima writers point out that if the main reason the consecration attempts by the different popes over the decades were not accepted was the failure to have all the Bishops join in with the Holy Father, that problem could have been easily addressed if Pope John XXIII or Pope Paul VI would have done the consecration during Vatican II. In attendance were 108 cardinals, 543 archbishops, and 2,171 bishops representing 141 nations from around the world.
3. Ratzinger, "The Message of Fatima," published in *The Fatima Prophecies*, 271.
4. Korean Airlines Flight 007, https://www.conservapedia.com/Korean_Airlines_Flight_007.
5. Ibid.
6. Kyle Mizokami, "Revealed: How the Warsaw Pact Planned to Win World War III in Europe," July 2, 2016, https://nationalinterest.org/feature/revealed-how-the-warsaw-pact-planned-win-world-war-three-16822.
7. Socci, *The Fourth Secret of Fatima*, 207.
8. Gorny and Rosikon, *Fatima Mysteries*, 343.
9. Gruner, *World Enslavement or Peace*, 183-185.
10. Gorney and Rosikon, *Fatima Mysteries*, 326.
11. Apostoli, *Fatima for Today*, 193.
12. Gruner, *World Enslavement or Peace*, 188.
13. Transcript of Pope John Paul II's Act of Entrustment of the World to the Immaculate Heart of Mary of March 25, 1984.
14. Ratzinger, "The Message of Fatima," published in *The Fatima Prophecies*, 271.
15. Ibid., 274.
16. Gorney and Rosikon, *Fatima Mysteries*, 328-330.
17. Transcript of Pope John Paul II's Act of Entrustment of the World to the Immaculate heart of Mary of March 25,1984.
18. *L' Osservatore Romano*, March 27, 1984.
19. Gruner, *World Enslavement or Peace*, 188, 190-191.
20. Apostoli, *Fatima for Today*, 252. The consecration was performed during the time of Konstantin Chernenko's leadership of the Soviet Union.

He became head of the nation just one month before on February 13, 1984. This would be the same date that Sister Lúcia died in 2005.

21. Gorney and Rosikon, *Fatima Mysteries*, 223.
22. Ibid., 225.
23. Ibid., 226.
24. Ibid.
25. Ibid.
26. Kengor, *A Pope and a President*, 347.
27. Ibid.
28. Apostoli, *Fatima Today*, 197.
29. Ratzinger, "The Message of Fatima," published in *The Fatima Prophecies*, 271.
30. Kengor, *A Pope and a President*, 351.
31. Letter of Sister Lúcia to Sister Mary of Bethlehem, dated August 29, 1989.
32. Apostoli, *Fatima for Today*, 251. A close look at the exact historical record of the consecration, specifically Lúcia's words as found mostly in her letters over the years, does somewhat corroborate the validity of the objections. Over time, however, it appears Lúcia came to understand a degree of flexibly was needed to get the consecration done and perhaps was even led to realize this by the Virgin Mary. By the 1980s, the late date and the urgency of the times at hand almost demand a compromised solution. I cover this issue in depth in chapters 46-50 of this book. Father Apostoli's *Fatima for Today* also addresses this ongoing matter rather well in a Question/Answer format at the end of his book, see pp. 249-268.
33. Laurentin and Lejeune, *Messages and Teachings of Mary at Medjugorje*, 230.
34. Ibid.
35. Soldo, *My Heart Will Triumph*, 154.
36. "Soviet Naval Blast Called Crippling," July 11,1984, https://www.nytimes.com/1984/07/11/world/soviet-naval-blast-called-crippling.html.
37. Ibid.
38. "Backgrounder on Chernobyl Nuclear Power Plant Accident," August 15, 2018, https://www.nrc.gov/reading-rm/doc-collections/fact-sheets/chernobyl-bg.html.
39. Irvin Baxter, "Chernobyl: Third Trumpet of Revelation?" May 5, 2011, *End Time Ministries*, https://www.endtime.com/articles-endtime-magazine/chernobyl-third-trumpet-revelation/.
40. Robert Pear, "Blast Reported at Soviet Nuclear Plant that Makes Vital Nuclear Parts," May 18,1988, https://www.nytimes.com/1988/05/18/world/blast-reported-at-soviet-plant-that-makes-vital-missile-part.html.

41. Kari Hawkins, "Tragedy Probed to Prevent Repeat," May 19, 2010, https://www.army.mil/article/39380/tragedy_probed_to_prevent_repeat.

42. Orka Manna, "Pepcon Worker Remembers Massive 1988 Explosion," May 4, 1988,
https://www.8newsnow.com/news/pepcon-worker-remembers-massive-
1988-explosion/.

43. "What to know about 4:22 Pepcon Explosions 30 Years Later," May 3, 2018,
https://www.ktnv.com/news/
what-to-know-about-pepcon-explosions-30-years-later.

44. Apostoli, *Fatima Today*, 257.

45. Bertone, *The Last Secret of Fatima*, 87. Bertone writes that the Communist system seemed invincible, and it looked as if it were going to endure for centuries. But then, he says, the whole thing collapsed like a house of cards. He writes, "The synodal assembly of the Bishops (1991) got it right: 'even many nonbelievers have seen these events as a sort of miracle.'"

CHAPTER 41: THE END OF THE EVIL EMPIRE

1. Odell, Catherine M., *Those Who Saw Her* (Huntington, IN: Our Sunday Visitor Publishing Division, 1986), 95.

2. Ibid. It is believed that several small children being held in their mother's arms were able to see Mary at Pontmain that evening. This opinion was based upon their eye movements and the fact that they clapped their hands and reached out towards the location of the vision, as if begging to be picked up by Mary. On June 25, 1988, a similar incident occurred in Medjugorje during Ivanka's annual apparition at her home. Her daughter, Christina—who was being held in the arms of Ivanka's husband, Rajko, as he knelt next to her—appears in a photograph to be visually locked in on the exact location that her mother is seeing the apparition. The picture can be found on page 489 of this book. One of the visionaries at Pontmain, Jean Marie Lebosse, retracted her claim to the vision in 1920, at the age of 58.

3. Abbe Marie Richard, *What Happened at Pontmain?* 42.

4. Odell, *Those Who Saw Her*, 113.

5. Richard, *What Happened at Pontmain?* 58. Bernadette Soubirous, the visionary of Lourdes, France, gave an interview to a man named Gougenot des Mousseaux in 1872 around the time Mary appeared at Pontmain. He asked her if the invading Prussian army was foretold by the Virgin Mary. She told him "no". He then asked her if there was nothing to fear. Bernadette replied that she feared only one thing: "bad

Catholics." See *LaSalette, Lourdes, Pontmain: Journey of a Believer* by Edmond Lafond, p. 238.

6. Thomas W. Petrisko, *The Last Crusade* (Pittsburgh, PA: St. Andrews Productions, 1996), 7.

7. Apostoli, *Fatima for Today*, 174-175.

8. Ibid., 163-164. Only the bishops of Portugal gathered in the Cathedral of Lisbon to join in with the Holy Father. Six weeks later, on December 8th, Pope Pius XII repeated the consecration in St. Peter's Basilica in Rome in the presence of 40,000 people. A few bishops were present.

9. Frere Francois de Marie des Agnes, *Fatima: The Only Way to World Peace* (Buffalo, NY: Immaculate Heart Publications,1993),144.

10. Michele de la Sainte Trinite, *The Whole Truth About Fatima*, 806.

11. Socci, *The Fourth Secret of Fatima*, 187-188. Socci quotes *Fatima, the Prophecy Revealed* by Mantero and Valentina, p. 52.

12. Ibid.

13. Francois de Marie des Agnes, *Fatima: The Only Way to World Peace*, 156.

14. Alonso, *The Secret of Fatima*, 73.

15. Socci, *The Fourth Secret of Fatima*, 191.

16. Ibid.

17. Apostoli, *Fatima for Today*, 176.

18. Fellows, *Fatima in Twilight*, 117.

19. Ibid. *In Sacro Vergente Anno*, Pope Pius XII consecrated Russia without mentioning the request of Mary, without the bishops, and with no references to Fátima. Some have written that he "deliberately" did not want the act associated with private revelation. While Pope Pius XII is known as the Pope of Fátima, it is believed he came under the heavy influence in his later years of a Father Edouard Dhanis, a Belgian Jesuit who was a fierce opponent of the Fátima apparitions. Dhanis is cited in Cardinal Ratzinger's *The Message of Fatima: Theological Commentary* of June 26, 2000, a serious concern of many Fatima apologists. Kevin Symonds, in his *On the Third Part of the Secret of Fatima*, takes a look at the "Dhanis effect" on Fátima.

20. Michel de la Sainte Trinite, *Fatima Revealed...and Discarded*, 187-188.

21. Gorney and Rosikon, *Fatima Mysteries*, 233.

22. Socci, *The Fourth Secret of Fatima*, 192.

23. Ibid., 196. According to Cardinal Ottaviani, Pope John XXIII received the envelope containing the third part of the Secret still sealed. This was also attested to by Mgr. Loris Capovilla, the private secretary and confidant of John XXIII. This fact confirmed that Pope Pius XII did not read the Secret. In 1990, Cardinal Silvio Oddi revealed to an Italian journalist at *30 Giorni* that he had an intimate conversation with Pope John XXIII about the third part of the Secret. It reveals that the

Pope held some curious thoughts concerning Fátima. The following is an excerpt: "Like the priests and all the faithful, I was interested in the Third Secret of Fátima. Since it was known that it was to be revealed in 1960 unless Sister Lúcia had died earlier, we were all waiting for that year to arrive. But 1960 came and went, and nothing was announced. As secretary to John XXIII, when he was in Paris, I took advantage of the trust he placed in me to tell him frankly, "Most Holy Father, there is one thing for which I cannot forgive you for." "What?" he asked. "Having kept the world in suspense for so many years and then watching 1960 come, several months have gone by and nothing about the Secret has been made known." "Let's not talk about that," Pope Roncalli answered. "If you don't want me to I will say no more, but I can't keep people from doing so, I replied. The interest is spontaneous; I must have delivered a hundred sermons and speeches announcing the revelation." "I told you not to mention it." Continues Oddi, "I, who knew Pope John very well, am sure that the Secret contained nothing good. Roncalli didn't like to hear about scandals or punishments. From that I conclude that it contained something about prohibition, punishment, or disaster." [This disclosure of Oddi is seen by some as further evidence that there is a text to the third part of the Secret that was not released in 2000. Cardinal Oddi was sensitive to the times at hand and a follower of private revelation. I called Oddi at his personal residence in the late 1990s after he became ill, on the advice, and with the assistance of a close associate. I had the hope that he could assist me in moving forward with the powers that be in Rome to help bring about a feast in the Church in honor of God the Father. He was said to be very devoted to the Father. I was unable to speak directly with him.]

24. Ibid., 197. Cardinal Angelo Roncalli made a private pilgrimage to Fátima on May 13,1956, and delivered a homily on the Rosary. In *Miris Modis*, his document of December 13, 1962, he proclaimed the Virgin of Fátima principal patroness of the Leiria Diocese.

25. Ibid., 112,113, 194. At first, the Holy See authorized that only persons that had met previously with Lúcia, could meet with her again, without permission of the Holy See. The second decree forbade all meetings with Lúcia, except for family. Even her former spiritual director, Father Jose Aparicio, who returned from Brazil in 1960, could not see Lúcia. After the Third Secret was released in 2000, Lúcia remained under an order of silence. (See Socci's, *The Fourth Secret of Fátima* for a look at this issue, pp. 112,113.)

26. Ibid., 194-195.

27. Ibid., 195.

28. Robert Moynihan, "Dossier: The Third Secret", *Inside the Vatican*," Year 8, No. 6, June-July, 2000, p. xii.

29. Apostoli, *Fatima for Today*, 178.

30. Alonso, *The Secret of Fatima*, 122.

31. Bertone, *The Last Secret of Fatima*, 61. Bertone firmly clarifies that Sister Lúcia, in her meeting with Cardinal Luciani, did not foretell to Luciano his elevation to the Chair of Peter or his short reign. This ended, once and for all, both rumors. *Inside the Vatican* (December, 1993, p.56) ran an interesting article on this subject called "Foul Play?" The journal wrote, "When the future Pope Luciani, then Patriarch of Venice, was leading a pilgrimage to Fátima in 1977, Sister Lúcia asked to see him. During their conversation, she addressed him repeatedly as 'Holy Father.' According to some who saw him as he came away from that encounter, he was shaken because Lúcia had told him he would become Pope and would have a very brief pontificate. "One year later," the *ILL Sabatao* article concludes, 'another visionary, a few hours after the tragic night of September 28, claims to have relived the last moments of the pontiff's life. What she saw in those moments was a murder, minutely described in a book prepared by Hans Urs von Balthasar, theologian, nominated to become a cardinal by Papa Wojtyla. Luciano wrote of his visit to Fátima in an article which appeared in the January 1978 issue of the Italian journal, *IL Cuore de la Madre*. It was reprinted in *L' appel de Notre Dame*, April-June, 1995. In it, Luciano talks of his belief in the Miracle of the Sun at Fátima on October 13, 1917. Wrote Luciani, "There is also an article of faith contained in the Gospels: namely, that signs will accompany those who believe. It is the fashion today to scrutinize the signs of the times, and there is quite a proliferation of signs. So I believe it is allowable to put human faith in the sign of October 13th, recognized even by anticleric and unbelievers, and I think it is opportune to pay attention to the things emphasized by this sign." A longtime Colombo mafia mobster named Anthony Raimondi stated in his 2019 book, *When the Bullet Hits the Bone*, that he went to Rome in 1978 with a team of hit men and killed Pope John Paul I by cyanide poisoning.

32. Apostoli, *Fatima for Today*, 190. According to Antonio Socci, Msgr. Pavel Hnilica testified: "When he left the hospital, He {the Pope} told me verbatim: "I understand that the only solution to save the world from war, to save it from atheism, is the conversion of Russia according to the message of Fatima. (*30 Giorni*, March 1990. See Socci's, *The Fourth Secret of Fatima* (p.19). Mirjana points out in her book (p. 154) that Mary comes to Medjugorje just weeks after the June 7, 1981, Act of Entrustment by Pope John Paul II.

33. Fox, *Rediscovering Fatima*, x, 127.Concerning the 1982 consecration, Fox writes, "The hope of millions was fulfilled." American Cardinal John Joseph Carberry writes, "In this way, he (Pope John Paul II) fulfilled a request that the Blessed Mother had made to Sister Lúcia on June 13, 1929." Both men were incorrect concerning the validity of the 1982 consecration.

34. Apostoli, *Fatima for Today*, 191.The Apostolic Nuncio to Portugal, Archbishop Santé Portalupi, would die on March 31, 1984, one week after the 1984 consecration.

35. Fox, *Rediscovering Fatima*, 127.

36. Evaristo, *"Two Hours with Sister Lucia,"* 9.

37. Ibid., 39. Lucia explains to Evaristo how a nuclear war was prevented in 1985, a truly inconceivable reality.

38. "Crafting a US Response to an Eastern Europe in Turmoil," *The Heritage Foundation Report*, August 31, 1988, https://www.heritage.org/europe/report/crafting-us-response-eastern-europe-turmoil.

39. Ibid.

40. Ibid.

41. Donia and Fine, Jr., *Bosnia & Hercegovina*, 194-219.

42. "Revolutions of 1989", https://www.newworldencyclopedia.org/entry/Revolutions_of_1989.

43. "Freedom! The Berlin Wall," by George J. Church, *Time Magazine*, November 20, 1989, http://content.time.com/time/subscriber/article/0,33009,959058-5,00.html. Khrushchev and the East German government deliberately decided to start to build the Berlin Wall on a weekend to minimize any observance of the activity surrounding its construction. On Sunday, August 13, 1961, hundreds of police began unrolling barbed wire. Two days after, concrete barriers were put up. The Berlin Wall cut through 192 streets, 8 city train lines, 32 railroad lines, 4 subway lines and the Autobahn at four locations. A no man's land of 328 feet existed between the two parallel walls.

44. Carl E. Olson, "The Untold Story of John Paul II and Ronald Reagan: Mary is Central," May 7, 2017, https://www.catholicworldreport.com/2017/05/07/the-untold-story-of-john-paul-ii-and-ronald-reagan-mary-is-central/

45. Besides the end of the Cold War, one Catholic news source estimated that eighty-seven dictatorships have fallen since the 1984 consecration.

CHAPTER 42: DEMOCIDE

1. Rudy J. Rummel, "Mass Murder Under Communism: A Few Statistics", *Inside the Vatican*, Year 10, No.1, January, 2002, p. 6-7.

CHAPTER 43: THE DIVINE PLAN

1. Bertone, *The Last Secret of Fatima*, 87.
2. Kengor, *A Pope and a President*, 46.
3. Michael Reagan, "Stories of Faith: Ronald Reagan, Mikhail Gorbachev," https://www.beliefnet.com/faiths/storiesoffaith/reagan-andgorbachev.aspx.
4. Ibid.
5. Kengor, *A Pope and a President*, 48.
6. Ibid., 47.
7. Ibid., 47-48.
8. Ibid., 260.
9. Ibid., 261.
10. Words of George Gipp (played by Ronald Reagan) in 1940 Warner Bothers movie, *Knute Rockne, All American*.
11. Kengor, *A Pope and a President*, 263. Although Reagan's assassination attempt was a dark moment, his humor is recalled throughout it all. To the surgeons as he entered the operating room, he said, "Please tell me you are all Republicans." To his wife Nancy, he said, "Honey, I forgot to duck." Upon waking from surgery, he asked about the shooter, "Anyone know what this guy's beef was?" To his daughter Maureen, he said the shooting "ruined one of my best suits."
12. Ibid., 263-264.
13. Ibid., 264.
14. Laurence I. Barrett, *Gambling with History: Reagan in the White House* (New York, NY: Doubleday,1983), 124.
15. Kengor, *A Pope and a President*, 263-264.
16. Barret, *Gambling with History: Reagan in the White House*, 124.
17. Ibid., 263.
18. Ibid.
19. Ibid., 432.
20. Carl Olson, "The Untold Story of John Paul II and Ronald Reagan: Mary is Central," May 7, 2017, https://www.catholicworldreport.com/2017/05/07/the-untold-story-of-john-paul-ii-and-ronald-reagan-mary-is-central/.
21. Ibid.
22. Kengor, *A Pope and a President*, 385.
23. Ibid., 595.
24. Ibid.
25. Olson, "The Untold Story of John Paul II and Ronald Reagan: Mary is Central," https://www.catholicworldreport.com/2017/05/07/the-untold-story-of-john-paul-ii-and-ronald-reagan-mary-is-central/.
26. Kengor, *A Pope and a President*, 385.

27. Ibid.
28. Ibid., 387.
29. Ibid.
30. "Reagan in Lisbon, Says Communism is on the Decline," by Edward Schumacher, *New York Times*, May10, 1985. p.1.
31. Ibid., 385.
32. Ibid., 422.
33. Ibid.
34. Ibid.
35. Ibid., 385.
36. Ibid., 444-445.
37. Ibid., 445.
38. Nolan, *Medjugorje and the Church*, 33.
39. Robert Moynihan, "Dossier: The Third Secret-The Key to the 20th Century?", *Inside the Vatican*, Year 8, No.6, June-July, 2000, p. xiv. The article makes this claim about Reagan in a Fátima timeline on the release of the third part of the Secret. It does not explain or cite a source.
40. Kengor, *A Pope and President*, 434.
41. Ibid.
42. Ibid.
43. Ibid.
44. Ibid.
45. Ibid.
46. Ibid., 435.
47. Ibid.
48. Ibid.
49. Ibid.
50. Ibid., 436.
51. Ibid.
52. Thull, ed., *What They Say About Medjugorje*, 929.
53. Ibid.
54. Ibid., 920.
55. Ibid.
56. Kengor, *A Pope and a President*, 436.
57. Ibid., 436,437. Wayne Weible is on record as saying that President Ronald Reagan did attempt to personally call Marija Pavlović in Medjugorje. Weible says that he was in the village in December of 1987 and that during his stay at Marija's home, the visionary said to him, "Your President, he called me— here at my house!" Kathleen Parisod, Marija's translator, said Reagan "tried to reach Marija by telephone" but "was cut off twice" because of the deficient Yugoslavian telephone system. Later, on December 8th, Reagan's secretary called and thanked her for the letter.

58. Ibid., 436.

59. Olson, "The Untold Story of John Paul II and Ronald Reagan: Mary is Central," https://www.catholicworldreport.com/2017/05/07/the-untold-story-of-john-paul-ii-and-ronald-reagan-mary-is-central/.

60. Ibid.

61. Kengor, *A Pope and a President*, 9.

62. David Neff, "Gorbachev and God," Oct.1, 2000, https://www.christianitytoday.com/ct/2000/octoberweb-only/57.0b.html.

63. Ibid.

64. Kengor, *A Pope and a President*, 424.

65. Neff, "Gorbachev and God," https://www.christianitytoday.com/ct/2000/octoberweb-only/57.0b.html

66. "What was Pope John Paul II's Role in the Fall of the U.S.S.R?", https://catholicstraightanswers.com/pope-john-paul-iis-role-fall-soviet-union/.

67. Kengor, *A Pope and a President*, 423.

68. Ibid.

69. Ibid. While Gorbachev began to reveal his spiritual roots to Reagan at the first summit in 1985, he also revealed his uncertainties involving the cosmic landscape, telling Reagan that in the event of an alien invasion, the Soviets would ally with the United States. (See *Someone is Out to Get Us* by Brian Brown.)

70. Ibid., 429.

71. Michael Reagan, "Stories of Faith. Ronald Reagan and Mikhail Gorbachev," https://www.beliefnet.com/faiths/storiesoffaith/reagan-andgorbachev.aspx.

72. Kengor, *A Pope and a President*, 429. In his book, *Memoirs* (p.457), Gorbachev writes that he said, "I am convinced it is God's will that we should cooperate, I added."

73. Edward Morris, *Dutch: A Memoir of Ronald Reagan* (New York: Modern Library, 2000), 519.

74. Michael Deaver, *A Different Drummer: My Thirty Years with Ronald Reagan* (New York, NY: Harper Paperbacks), 118.

75. Talk given by Alfred Kingon at the May 1992 National Conference on Medjugorje at the University of Notre Dame.

76. Paul Kengor, "Red Herring: Mikhail Gorbachev's Not Quite Conversion," April 4, 2008, https://www.christianitytoday.com/ct/2008/aprilweb-only/114-52.0.html.

77. Vladimir Shiapentokh, "Gorbachev Gets Religion," March 4, 1990. https://www.washingtonpost.com/archive/opinions/1990/03/04/gorbachev-gets-religion/f5a90d02-fa2b-4784-9e6c-5a94961a1976/.

78. Clyde Haberman, "The Kremlin and the Vatican: Gorbachev Visits the Pope at the Vatican, Ties Forged," December 2, 1989, https://www.nytimes.com/1989/12/02/world/

the-kremlin-and-the-vatican-gorbachev-visits-pope-at-vatican-ties-are-forged.html.

79. "Gorbachev Saved the World from Nuclear Holocaust," March 3, 1998, https://www.independent.ie/world-news/gorbachev-saved-world-from-nuclear-holocaust-26192064.html.

80. George Weigel, *The End and the Beginning* (New York, NY: Image, 2011), 177. Gorbachev's meeting with Pope John Paul II was the first meeting ever between a Soviet leader and a pope. Writes historian Paul Kengor about this event: "Stalin and Lenin would have shaken hands with a pope only when Hell freezes over." Kengor writes that George Weigel said to him in an email, "Many good things have happened to individuals at Medjugorje but the Church has never pronounced on the veracity of the visions or the visionaries." (See *A Pope and a President*, 603.)

81. Neff, "Gorbachev and God," https://www.christianitytoday.com/ct/2000/octoberweb-only/57.0b.html.

82. "Mikhail Gorbachev Discovered at the Tomb of St. Francis of Assisi," March 21, 2008, http://forums.orthodoxchristianity.net/threads/mikhail-gorbachev-discovered-praying-at-the-tomb-of-francis-of-assisi.15142/.

83. Ibid.

84. Ibid.

85. Kengor, "Red Herring: Mikhail Gorbachev's Not Quite Conversion," https://www.christianitytoday.com/ct/2008/aprilweb-only/114-52.0.html.

86. Malcolm Moore, "Mikhail Gorbachev Now Claims He's a Christian," https://www.mostholyfamilymonastery.com/news/mikhail-gorbachev-now-claims-he-is-a-christian/#.YCxuAWhKiM8.

87. "St. Francis and Gorbachev," March 24, 2008, https://www.commonweal-magazine.org/st-francis-and-gorbachev.

88. "Gorbachev Saved the World from Nuclear Holocaust," March 3, 1998, The *Times* (London), https://www.independent.ie/world-news/gorbachev-saved-world-from-nuclear-holocaust-26192064.html; Evaristo, "*Two Hours with Sister Lucia*," 10-11, 38-39.

89. Kengor, *A Pope and a President*, 438-440.

90. Ibid.

91. Frontline, "The Millennial Pope," September, 28, 1999, https://www.pbs.org/wgbh/pages/frontline/shows/pope/.

92. "What was the Nature of Pope John Paul II's Devotion to Our Lady?", https://catholicstraightanswers.com/st-john-paul-iis-devotion-to-our-lady/.

93. Ibid.

94. Ibid.

95. Ibid.

96. Ibid.

97. Ibid.

98. Apostoli, *Fatima for Today*, 183.
99. "Karol Wojtyla-Biography," June 26, 2014, https://culture.pl/en/artist/karol-wojtyla. Karol Wojtyła almost did not become a priest, coming close to becoming one of the victims of Black Sunday in August of 1944. This was the day the Germans seized some 8,000 Polish men in order to try to prevent another Warsaw uprising. The Gestapo that day raided Karol Wojtyła's building, but did not search the basement, where he knelt in prayer in his apartment.
100. Ibid.
101. "What was the Nature of Pope John Paul II's Devotion to Our Lady? https://catholicstraightanswers.com/st-john-paul-iis-devotion-to-our-lady/.
102. Ibid.
103. Ibid. A sister who preceded Karol Wojtyła died in infancy.
104. Ibid.
105. Ibid.
106. "Mosaic of Virgin Mary in St. Peter's Square Turns 30 Years Old," https://catholicismpure.wordpress.com/2011/12/09/mosaic-of-virgin-mary-in-st-peters-square-turns-30-years-old/.
107. "Why John Paul II Placed an Icon of Mary over St. Peter's Square," May 2,2014, https://aleteia.org/2017/05/02/why-pope-john-paul-ii-placed-an-image-of-the-virgin-mary-over-st-peters-square/.
108. David Kerr, "Inside Story of Marian Mosaic Told on Blessed John Paul II's Birthday," https://www.catholicnewsagency.com/news/inside-story-of-marian-mosaic-told-on-bl.-john-paul-iis-birthday.
109. Tindal-Robertson, *Fatima, Russia & Pope John Paul II*, 153-154.
110. Kengor, *A Pope and a President*, 346.
111. Gorny and Rosikon, *Fatima Mysteries*, 34.
112. Nolan, *Medjugorje and the Church*, 81.
113. David Michael Lindsey, *The Woman and the Dragon* (Gretna, LA: Pelican Publishing Company, 2000), 317, 378.
114. Sullivan, *The Miracle Detective*, 211.
115. Pelletier, *The Queen of Peace Visits Medjugorje*, 215.
116. Johnston, *Fatima: The Great Sign*, 138.
117. Ibid.
118. René Laurentin, *Ten Years of Apparitions: New Growth and Recognition of Pilgrimages* (Milford, OH: Faith Publishing Company, 1991), 86-87. Monsignor Kim was the Bishop of Su-Wen. This quote originally appeared in the *Catholic Weekly of Korea*, reprinted in *l' Homme Nouveau*, February 3, 1991.
119. Talk given by Alfred Kingon at the May 1992 National Conference on Medjugorje at the University of Notre Dame. Historian Paul Kengor notes that some saw the three Christian leaders linked by a special

grace that held a deeper message: Reagan the Protestant; Gorbachev the Orthodox, and Wojtyła the Catholic. Were they guided by some grace to come together, some speculate, like the Three Magi in the Gospels?

120. Brown, *The Day Will Come*, 86.
121. Connell, *The Visions of the Children*, 169.
122. Ibid. On October 30, 1990, Ivan Dragićević spoke at Our Lady Help of Christians Church in Doylestown, Pa. near Philadelphia. He was interviewed at the home of Marge and Stan Karminski in Wayne, Pa. Question: "There have been many changes in Europe in the past year. Do you believe this has something to do with the message of Mary?" Ivan: "I absolutely believe this is so. This is the manifestation that Our Lady's messages are coming true... This is the fulfillment through people." Question: "Has Our Lady, in any of her manifestations, ever made any references to previous appearances, for instance Fátima?" Ivan: "She has never talked about them to me."

CHAPTER 44: "LET THE PEOPLE GO TO MEDJUGORJE"

1. Evaristo, "*Two Hours with Sister Lucia.*" 39.
2. Ibid., 30.
3. Ibid., 40. Lúcia spoke of "diabolical disorientation" at work in the present times. See *The Fatima Crusader* (Autumn, 2005, Issue 81, p.2)
4. Antonio Gaspari, "Medjugorje: Deception or Miracle? *Inside the Vatican*, Year 4, No.9, November, 1996, p. 25.
5. Laurentin, *Ten Years of Apparitions*, 124. The statistic on the number of confessions and Communions comes from a November 30, 1990, interview with Father Ludevit Rupcic, O.F.M.
6. Craig, *Spark from Heaven*, 122. The more Laurentin observed the fruits of Medjugorje, especially the changes in people, the more he marveled at what was taking place there. One person told him, "At Medjugorje, I did not see the face of the Virgin, but I saw her reflection in the face of the people there. I do not know if Our Lady appeared to the young people, but I see that she has appeared to the world. And if Our Lady has not appeared there, the receptive atmosphere will make her appear."
7. Kraljevic, *The Apparitions of Our Lady at Medjugorje*, 83.
8. Laurentin and Rupčić, *Is the Virgin Mary Appearing at Medjugorje?* 2. At Medjugorje, this explosion was measurable in many ways. Medjugorje was not only making its way out to the world, but the world was making its way to Medjugorje. By 1985-86, over 3 million had visited Medjugorje. The largest number came by bus. Sometimes up to a hundred busses a day could be seen weaving through the narrow streets. The Italians would make the entire trip by bus, with a brief ferry across the Adriatic. The

Portuguese came by bus too, flying initially to Lisbon, then to Milan or Trieste. Other foreigners would fly to Split or Dubrovnik and then get a bus; or they would arrive by train into Čitluk, Čapljina, or Mostar and find a taxi to Medjugorje. By this time, there were pilgrims who had come from Israel, Egypt, Japan, Korea, Vietnam, the Philippines, the Ivory Coast, Zaire, Haiti, Brazil, the Caribbean Islands, Nicaragua, Argentina, Uruguay, Peru, the Dominican Republic, and Mexico. Eastern Europeans, concerned about the Communists, would apply to visit Yugoslavia to go shopping and then covertly slip into Medjugorje. Many reported that they came to Medjugorje by foot. At least 3,000 reportedly walked over 50 miles, often fasting on bread and water all the way. Some said it took them ten days to come from Zagreb, or two weeks from Austria, and four weeks from West Germany. A man from Belgium said it took him forty-nine days to cover the distance to Medjugorje.

9. Weible, *Medjugorje: The Message*, 8, 23.
10. Ibid.
11. Weible, *Medjugorje: The Mission*, 2.
12. Ibid. Weible's talks took him everywhere, even into Russia. Everything was made a lot easier once the Yugoslavian government reversed its opposition to the visions. This decision officially came about through a simple press release by the government in early 1987. It stated: "The pilgrimage to Medjugorje is a purely religious phenomenon, not political, thus legal."
13. Thull, ed., *What They Say About Medjugorje*, 527.
14. Ibid. As I stated in the *Author's Foreword*, the Karminskis' are one of the primary reasons I decided to write this book. They appeared to be God's chosen vehicle to help launch Medjugorje in America, probably because, as I see it, their humility was deserving of such a grace. For a great look into their lives and their story, see "The Medjugorje 'First Family' in the United States," by Larry and Sue Eck, printed in *Medjugorje Magazine*, Summer, 2006.
15. Connell, *The Visions of the Children*, back cover.
16. *Medjugorje Magazine*, Westmont, IL.
17. Connell, *The Visions of the Children*, 359-378. See Antonio Gaspari, "Medjugorje: Deception or Miracle?", *Inside the Vatican*, November 1996, for an objective look at the magnitude of Medjugorje by the mid-90s.
18. Brown, *The Day Will Come*, 111.
19. Meyer, *A Portrait of Medjugorje*, 29, 80.
20. Denis Nolan, *Medjugorje: A Time for Truth a Time for Action*, 47.
21. Ibid., ix.
22. Ibid., 60.

23. Denis Nolan, *Medjugorje and the Church* (Goleta, CA: Queenship Publishing Company, 1995), 46.

24. Ibid., 50.

25. Ibid., 112.

26. Ibid.

27. Ibid.

28. Ibid., 51, 151-174; Nolan, *Medjugorje: A Time for Truth, a Time for Action*, 29-33. There is a preponderance of favorable statements attributed to Pope John Paul II concerning Medjugorje that are too numerous to list here. Nolan's two books, however, are the best sources for cumulative references on this matter.

29. Nolan, *Medjugorje: A Time for Truth, a Time for Action*, 29.

30. Antonio Gaspari, "Medjugorje: Deception or Miracle?" *Inside the Vatican*, Year 4, No. 9, November 1996, p. 27.

31. Thavis, *The Vatican Prophecies*, 74.

32. Sullivan, *The Miracle Detective*, 45.

33. Nolan, *Medjugorje: A Time for Truth. A Time for Action*, 31.

34. Nolan, *Medjugorje and the Church*, 24.

35. Nolan, *Medjugorje: A Time for Truth, A Time for Action*, 31.

36. Nolan, *Medjugorje and the Church*, 107.

37. Nolan, *Medjugorje: A Time for Truth, A Time for Action*, 31.

38. Nolan, *Medjugorje and the Church*, 26; *The Medjugorje Network*, May 1, 1995.

39. Nolan, *Medjugorje and the Church*, 27.

40. Nolan, *Medjugorje: A Time for Truth, A Time for Action*, 30. Pope John Paul II never made it to Medjugorje. But, as Mirjana Soldo revealed in her 2016 book, a pair of his shoes at least did. She reveals that approximately a year after the Pope's death, a close friend of John Paul II left a pair of his shoes one day at the apparition site in the Cenacolo Community, where Mirjana was to have an apparition that same day. Although she noticed the shoes under a statue of the Virgin Mary, she forgot about them by the time the apparition was over. Afterwards, a man approached her and told her that he was a good friend of the Pope and that he promised John Paul II, since he knew the Holy Father always wanted to go to Medjugorje, that he would go there for him and take his shoes in his place. It would be as if you were able to "set foot on that holy ground," Mirjana said the man told her that he had said to the Pope. Mirjana keeps the elegant pair of leather shoes that the man gifted to her in a glass case in her home. She also received from the shoemaker in Rome who made the shoes, after hearing Mirjana possessed them, a matching pair in her size. Bishop Pavel Hnilica had weekly meetings with Pope John Paul II as reported in the April, 1986, issue of *Madre di*

Deo and *Medjugorje Gebetsaktion*, 1986, No.4 and *Medjugorje Gebetsaktion*, 1988, No.3.

41. Nolan, *Medjugorje and the Church*, 30.
42. Ibid., 155.
43. Ibid., 171.
44. Ibid., 157.
45. Bertone, *The Last Secret of Fatima*, 2.
46. Nolan, *Medjugorje and the Church*, 23. The Swarnicki's tell of a dinner they attended with the Pope in which he was given a book by Fr. Jozo, one of many that day. At the end of the evening, the Pope retrieved the book by Jozo from the pile that his aide, Msgr. Stanislaw Dziwisz, was carrying, remarking to him, "No. This one I will take with me to my room."
47. Ibid.
48. Ibid.
49. Ibid.
50. Ibid.
51. Ibid.
52. Ibid., 24.
53. Antonio Gaspari, "Medjugorje: Deception or Miracle?", *Inside the Vatican*, Year 4, No. 9, November, 1996, p. 27.
54. Laurentin, *Medjugorje Testament*, 200.
55. Connell, *The Visions of the Children*, 244.
56. Ibid.
57. Nolan, *Medjugorje: A Time for Truth, A Time for Action*, 11.
58. Ibid.
59. Laurentin and Lejeune, *Messages and Teachings of Mary at Medjugorje*, 292-293.
60. Nolan, *Medjugorje: A Time for Truth, A Time for Action*, 11.
61. Ibid.
62. Ibid.
63. Laurentin and Lejeune, *Messages and Teachings of Mary at Medjugorje*, 189.
64. Nolan, *Medjugorje: A Time for Truth, A Time for Action*, 12.
65. Laurentin and Lejeune, *Messages and Teachings of Mary at Medjugorje*, 29.
66. Nolan, *Medjugorje and the Church*, 29.
67. Nolan, *Medjugorje: A Time for Truth, A Time for Action*, 12.
68. Nolan, *Medjugorje and the Church*, 29.
69. Laurentin and Lejeune, *Messages and Teachings of Mary at Medjugorje*, 297.
70. Ibid., 296-297.

71. Medjugorje.Org, *The Medjugorje Messages:1981-2013* (DeKalb, IL: *The Medjugorje Web*, 2013), 143.
72. Laurentin and Lejeune, *Messages and Teachings of Mary at Medjugorje*, 260.
73. Ibid., 150.
74. Ibid., 189-190.
75. Ibid., 220.
76. Ibid., 298.
77. Ibid., 279.
78. Ibid., 273.
79. Nolan, *Medjugorje, A Time for Truth, Time for Action*, 16.
80. Laurentin and Lejeune, *Messages and Teachings of Mary at Medjugorje*, 244.
81. Ibid., 188-189.
82. Ibid., 244.
83. Ibid., 297. During the early days of the apparitions, the children told of a time when they were all praying together with the Virgin Mary and one of them started to giggle. Soon, the entire group was laughing in the middle of the prayer session. Mortified that they had offended the Virgin in some terrible way, they were all relieved to see that she was smiling and in no way perturbed with them.
84. Ibid., 291-292.
85. Ibid., 292.
86. Ibid., 292-293.
87. Ibid., 233.
88. Ibid., 253.
89. Medjugorje.Org, *The Medjugorje Messages:1981-2013*, 122.
90. Ibid., 146.
91. Laurentin and Lejeune, *Messages and Teachings of Mary at Medjugorje*, 249.
92. Ibid., 257.
93. Medjugorje.Org, *The Medjugorje Messages: 1981-2013*, 116.
94. Ibid., 243.
95. Ibid., 139.
96. Message from the Virgin Mary to Mirjana Soldo at Medjugorje, November 2, 2019.
97. Medjugorje.Org, *The Medjugorje Messages :1981-2013*, 242.
98. Ibid.
99. Ibid., 249.
100. Medjugorje. Org, *The Medjugorje Messages: 1981-2013*, 243.
101. Medjugorje. Org, *The Medjugorje Messages: 1981-2013*, 250. Both Fátima and Medjugorje point to God the Father in a special way with

regards to the prophesied coming of the "Triumph of the Immaculate Heart" and the foretold "era of peace." On June 13, 1929, at Tui, Spain, Sister Lúcia experienced a vision of the Most Holy Trinity in the chapel of the novitiate house, where she was staying at the time. Known as "The Last Vision," she reported seeing the Eternal Father, with a dove of light upon His breast, towering over a cross with Christ crucified on it. Standing beneath the outstretched right arm on the cross was Our Lady of Fátima. Various interpretations of the vision all stress the significance of the presence of God the Father to the message of Fátima. Over the last twenty years at Medjugorje, a significant number of Mary's messages have spoken of the Father and His great love for all of His children. These revelations are especially found in Mirjana Soldo's second-of-the-month messages over the last ten years. Many prophecies concerning the coming era of peace have associated it synonymously with a coming "Era of the Father," foretelling that the Church will finally proclaim a feast day in honor of God Our Father during this epoch. Some see this as the crowning moment of the Triumph. (For more on this see my books, *The Mystery of the Divine Paternal Heart of God Our Father* and *Living in the Heart of the Father*, also see Father Jean Galot's *Abba Father, We Long to See Your Face*.)

CHAPTER 45: THE PROMISED LAND

1. Petrisko, *Inside Heaven and Hell*, 19, 29, 87-89, 121.
2. Pelletier, *The Queen of Peace Visits Medjugorje*; 148, Bubalo, *A Thousand Encounters with the Blessed Virgin Mary in Medjugorje*, 213.
3. Ibid., 215-217.
4. Ibid., 217.
5. Sullivan, *The Miracle Detective*, 156.
6. Bubalo, *A Thousand Encounters with the Blessed Virgin Mary in Medjugorje*, 214.
7. Sullivan, *The Miracle Detective*, 155. Jacov's resistance to going to Heaven with the Madonna, Mirjana would explain in her book many years later, was because, she writes, Jacov first thought that Mary "meant forever."
8. Bubalo, *A Thousand Encounters with the Blessed Virgin Mary in Medjugorje*, 214.
9. Kraljevic, *The Apparitions of Our Lady at Medjugorje*, 58-59.
10. Sullivan, *The Miracle Detective*, 155.
11. Connell, *The Visions of the Children*, 102.
12. Connell, *Queen of the Cosmos*, 100.
13. Kraljevic, *The Apparitions of Our Lady at Medjugorje*, 58.

14. Bubalo, *A Thousand Encounters with Blessed Virgin Mary in Medjugorje*, 214-215.
15. Ibid.
16. Ibid.
17. Ibid.
18. Connell, *Queen of the Cosmos*, 65.
19. Bubalo, *A Thousand Encounters with the Blessed Virgin Mary in Medjugorje*, 214-215.
20. Ibid.
21. Ibid.
22. Ibid.
23. Connell, *Queen of the Cosmos*, 65.
24. Sister EmanuelMaillard, *Medjugorje: The 90s* (Pittsburgh, PA: St Andrew's Productions, 1997), 34-35.
25. Ibid.
26. Ibid
27. Ibid.
28. Bubalo, *A Thousand Encounters with the Blessed Virgin Mary in Medjugorje*, 217.
29. Connell, *Queen of the Cosmos*, 94.
30. Ibid.
31. Ibid., 40-41.
32. Connell, *The Visions of the Children*, 85.
33. Connell, *Queen of the Cosmos*, 28.
34. Connell, *The Visions of the Children*, 78.
35. Connell, *Queen of the Cosmos*, 28.
36. Ibid.
37. Connell, *The Visions of the Children*, 78; Connell, *Queen of the Cosmos*, 28.
38. Connell, *Queen of the Cosmos*, 28.
39. Ibid.
40. Connell, *The Visions of the Children*, 78-79.
41. Ibid., 78. While Heaven exceeded their imaginations, the children's experiences with Purgatory left them somewhat stunned. It awakened them, they indicate, to the seriousness of the soul's plight. As with Heaven, Jacov and Vicka experienced Purgatory in a special way, as they "passed by it" during their visit to Heaven and Hell. The two recall Purgatory being a great darkness, in which the faces of the people there seemed dim and vague. It was, their words allude, not a place of happiness like Heaven. Jacov, keeping his thoughts again to a minimum, has only said that he was shown Purgatory in order to be a witness to its reality—as with Heaven. And, yes, he added that people need to pray for the souls

in Purgatory. Vicka, on the other hand, was again eager to share her experience with the mysterious world of purification. Like Heaven, Purgatory is a very big space—a "dark chasm" between Heaven and Hell. To her, it looked awful. Vicka remembers that they couldn't see people in Purgatory, only a misty, ashy gray fog. She did, however, sense how the souls present were going through a trial. They were weeping, trembling, and moaning, in what seemed to be terrible suffering. The Virgin told them that the people there needed prayers, especially the ones that had no-one to pray for them. This was in order for their souls to be purified. Prayers, Vicka explains to people, were the only way for them to be released from Purgatory into Heaven. Mary also told them that souls in Purgatory can see who is praying for them on Earth and that family members needed to help their deceased relatives. After their trip to Purgatory, a disturbed Vicka pleaded with Mary to allow her to take on a special suffering to help the souls there. The Virgin immediately warned her of the seriousness of her request and that she needed to pray about it. After praying and fasting for three days to discern this desire, Vicka received an illness that stayed with her for months. It then vanished on the exact date the Virgin promised it would. Vicka feels she now knows the poor souls in Purgatory well and can *feel* them. Many there, she tells her listeners, are abandoned by their loved ones on Earth. The other four visionaries at Medjugorje have seen Purgatory, too. Ivan tells pilgrims that the souls in Purgatory are extremely lonely. They were, he says, often people who prayed and believed only occasionally. Some did not know how to pray while on Earth, or if they did, they chose not to. Some were filled with doubt, uncertain of God's existence. Souls truly suffer in Purgatory, he explains, and if no one prays for them, they suffer more. Marija recalled Purgatory as being foggy, with people in deep clouds. She says the souls seemed to be moving in a daze, hitting into each other. Those in Purgatory, Marija learned, failed to recognize God in their lifetime. Now, their greatest suffering is their longing to come close to Him. They also now understand how much they hurt God, how many chances on Earth they had to change their ways, and how they often chose to disregard Him. Purgatory, remembers Ivanka, was only darkness. She says she saw Purgatory only as a "picture." The people were there, Ivanka was told, as a result of their choices. Mirjana mostly recalls the misery she witnessed in Purgatory. Many people, she remembers, were in some way physically suffering. She recalls seeing people shivering, thrashing, and withering in pain. Although Mirjana says she did not hear them, she understood that God's justice was cleansing them. Mirjana was told there are different levels of Purgatory, and the more one prayed on Earth, the higher their level. As many of the Saints have described, the lowest level is closest to Hell, and the highest is closest to Heaven, where the suffering is the least. The level you are on depends on the state of a soul's purity at death. Like the others also noted, Mirjana says the people in Purgatory are helpless to pray for themselves. They are dependent, Mary told her, on the people on Earth to help them get out. Christmas Day, Mary revealed to Mirjana, is when the most souls are released from Purgatory. [Author Jan Connell reports Vicka was told to discuss her "desire to suffer for the souls in Purgatory" with her confessor. She was then instructed by him to pray and fast for three days to help her discern. After this, she received permission from her spiritual director to undertake this sacrifice. The medical community as well as the Franciscans were made aware of this entire situation. "I know the value of suffering," explains Vicka," All suffering is for someone."]

CHAPTER 46: UNFULFILLED?

1. Nesho Djuric, "Slovenia, Croatia Declare Independence," June 25, 1991, https://www.upi.com/Archives/1991/06/25/Slovenia-Croatia-declare-independence-from-Yugoslavia/6636677822400/. The war became known as the "Croatian Homeland War 1991-1995." Croatia's declaration of independence on the official anniversary day of Medjugorje was no accident, June 25, 1991. It was chosen by Franjo Tudjman, Croatia's first president, who served in office from 1991 until his death on December 10, 1999. Tudjman's speech on that day was designed to have the people see that Mary's arrival in Medjugorje was a "call to the Croatian people."
2. John R. Lampe, "Bosnian War: Facts, Summary, War Crimes," March 27, 2019, https://www.britannica.com/event/Bosnian-War.
3. Wikipedia, List of Wars, 1990-2002, https://en.wikipedia.org/wiki/Category: Lists_of_wars.
4. Soldo, *My Heart Will Triumph*, 272.
5. Petrisko, *The Fatima Prophecies*, 141.
6. Ibid.
7. "Violence Erupts in Rwanda, Foreshadowing Genocide of 800,000," 1994, https://www.history.com/this-day-in-history/civil-war-erupts-in-rwanda.
8. Ibid.
9. Ibid.
10. *Newsweek Magazine,* August 1, 1994.
11. *Time Magazine,* May 16, 1994.
12. Ibid.
13. Petrisko, *The Fatima Prophecies*, 141.
14. Ibid., 143.

15. Ibid.

16. Ibid., 142.

17. "Jubilee year for the 25th Anniversary of the Apparitions in Kibeho, presided by Cardinal Ivan Dias and a Report on Rwanda Ecclesial Situation," http://www.fides.org/en/news/10928-AFRICA_RWANDA_Jubilee_Year_for_the_25th_anniversary_of_the_apparitions_in_Kibeho_presided_by_Cardinal_Ivan_Dias_and_a_report_on_Rwanda_s_ecclesial_situation.

18. Ibid.

19. Ibid.

20. Evaristo, *"Two Hours with Sister Lucia"*, 37.

21. Ibid. Lúcia, in many ways, repeatedly hinted that the world would remain a very hostile and dangerous place after the consecration. This was primarily because she understood that the consecration, originally intended to "contain the errors of Russia," was long past due and the "errors" were now "uncontainable."

22. Ibid., 30.

23. Ibid., 74-88. There can be no surprise to the reaction to Lúcia's words. It was no secret that many longed to hear prophetic words of doom. Said Cardinal Bertone about the release of the third part of the Secret, seven years after Lúcia's controversial interview: "There are legions of people itching for apocalypse, and we didn't want to give them ammunition, or provide an outlet for their totally absurd theories."

24. Apostoli, *Fatima for Today*, 249-252.

25. Evaristo, *"Two Hours with Sister Lucia,"* 81. See *Fatima Crusader*, Spring 1993, Issue 44, "A False Lúcia Substituted for the True?" by Brother Francois De Marie des Agnes, CRC. (article written October, 1992.)

26. Ibid., 79. Carlos Evaristo was an official Portuguese government translator. Evaristo's role in this affair appears to be quite remarkable. In short, he is accused of actions in events he had no desire to be a part of in the first place. To review the complete matter in this forum is not possible. In summary, however, his interviews with Sister Lúcia on October 11, 1992, in the presence of his Eminence Antony Cardinal Padiyara, and his subsequent interview with her on the same date a year later, in the presence of his Eminence Ricardo Cardinal Vidal, though challenged and discredited, are indisputable. The photographic history in itself of the events is more than credible as is the fact that, except for one, the numerous witnesses at both interviews have never disputed Evaristo's account. While his small book, *"Two Hours with Sister Lucia"*, has been criticized for its lack of professional quality, it is this fact in itself that lends even more credibility to the validity of its contents. For many, his interviews with Sister Lúcia seem to have resolved significant questions surrounding Fátima. Evaristo, in one of

his videos, posed an interesting hypothesis. He postulates that the prophecy in the second part of the Secret of Fátima, in which the Virgin speaks of "the annihilation of nations", is referring to a "spiritual annihilation of nations," not a physical one. Sister Lúcia is not on any "known record," however, of ever discussing this theory. Excerpts of his interviews with Lúcia and Cardinal Padiyara (1992) and Cardinal Vidal (1993) were published throughout the world in mainstream Catholic publications, including *The National Catholic Register* on September 26,1993, thus further diffusing any questions concerning their validity. A letter written by a priest in attendance disputes some of the Cardinal Padiyara interview of Sister Lúcia, which critics have tried to use to discredit all of his work. But the second interview with Vidal more than dismisses any attack on his credibility, and validates the truth of the first interview.

27. Ibid. (See inside of the front cover of Evaristo's book.)
28. Ibid., 38-39.
29. Sister Maria Lúcia of Jesus and of the Immaculate Heart, *How I See the Message* (Coimbra, Portugal: Carmel of Coimbra and the Secretary Office of the Shepherds, 2nd Edition, 2007), 65.
30. Fox, *Rediscovering Fatima*, 116; Tossati, *The Secret Revealed*, op.cit. p.138.
31. Alonso, *The Secret of Fatima*, 83-84.
32. Evaristo, *"Two Hours with Sister Lucia,"* 5,10. Cardinal Bertone, who spent long hours discussing the Secret with Lúcia, confirms this was Lúcia's understanding, "I want to make it clear Lúcia didn't conceive of the consecration of Russia as a strategy for capturing this great Christian country (Russia) for Catholicism."
33. Apostoli, *Fatima for Today*, 249-260.
34. Carmel of Coimbra, *A Pathway Under the Gaze of Mary*, 190.
35. Michel de la Sainte Trinite, *The Whole Truth About Fatima*, Vol. II, 729. Writes Michel, "Until this time, to obey the very clear and firm requests of July, 13, 1917, and June 13, 1929, Sister Lucy never asked anything except the consecration of Russia alone to the Immaculate Heart of Mary. In the collection of letters already published, she mentions the consecrating of the world for the first time on September 1, 1940, writing to Father Aparicio. Nor is it something Our Lady herself had requested to her. She writes: 'Recently, several important people have spoken to me about the consecration of the world and Russia to the Immaculate Heart of Mary.'"
36. Ibid.
37. Ibid.
38. *30 Giorni*, March, 1990.
39. Socci, *The Fourth Secret of Fatima*, 22.

40. Walsh, *Our Lady of Fatima*, 221. Walsh writes, "It was plain that she (Lúcia) felt that Our Lady's wishes had not been carried out," in reference to the errors of Russia spreading over time throughout the world.

41. Apostoli, *Fatima for Today*, 79.

42. Carmel of Coimbra, *A Pathway Under the Gaze of Mary*, 190.

43. Ibid.

44. Ibid.

45. Evaristo, "*Two Hours with Sister Lucia*," 37.

46. Walsh, *Our Lady of Fatima*, 221.

47. Pope John Paul II, *Centesimus annus* (London, United Kingdom: Catholic Truth Society, 1991).

48. "Fatima Writings," https://www.lasvegasmariancenter.com/page43.html. Pope John Paul II seems to have understood long before the collapse of the Soviet Union that a great spiritual battle was underway that would unfold over time. In August of 1976, while in the United States, the then Cardinal Karol Wojtyla of Poland stated, "We are now standing in the face of the greatest historical confrontation humanity has gone through. I do not think that wide circles of the American society or wide circles of the Christian community realize this fully. We are now facing the final confrontation between the Church and the anti-Church, of the Gospel versus the anti-Gospel. This confrontation lies within the plans of Divine Providence; it is a trial which the whole Church, and the Polish Church in particular, must take up. It is a trial of not only our nation and the Church, but, in a sense, a test of 2,000 years of culture and Christian civilization with all of its consequences for human dignity, individual rights, human rights, and the rights of nations." (See the *National Catholic Register*, October 5, 2018.)

CHAPTER 47: A PANDEMIC OF ATHEISM

1. Friedrich Nietzsche: "God is Dead," http://www.philosophy-index.com/nietzsche/god-is-dead/.

2. *Time Magazine*, "Is God Dead?", April 8, 1986.

3. Friedrich Nietzsche: "God is Dead", http://www.philosophy-index.com/nietzsche/god-is-dead/.

4. Lily Rothman, "Is God Dead at 50?", https://time.com/isgoddead/.

5. Ibid.

6. Deirdre Manifold, *Fatima and the Great Conspiracy* (Galway, Ireland: The Militia of Our Immaculate Mother,1991), 69.

7. Ibid., 83.

8. Henri Delassus, *La Conjuration Antichretienne* (Paris, France: Desclee De Brouwer, 1910), 816.

9. Ibid., 70.

10. Ibid.

11. Ibid., 71.

12. Ibid., 81.

13. Ibid., 72.

14. Tindal-Robertson, *Fatima, Russia, and John Paul II*, 144.

15. Most Reverend Joao Venancio, ed., *A Heart for All: The Immaculate Heart of Mary in the Apparitions of Fatima* (Washington, NJ: AMI Press, 1972), 114-115. Theologian Father Andre Richard sees the prayer as designed by Heaven to prempt the coming Marxist onslaught against Christianity. This book, perhaps as much Michel de la Sainte Trinite's, *The Whole Truth About Fatima*, chronicles with historical documentation the tragic aspect of Fátima. Moreover, since it is edited by the Reverend Jao Venancio, the Bishop of Leiria-Fátima, it makes the failures of the age even more clear and indisputable. It is highly recommended and rather short, approximately 200 pages.

16. Gorney and Rosikon, *Fatima Mysteries*, 382-383. If Mary first came to Fátima to defeat atheism in the form of systematic, militant Marxism (Communism), she appears to have come to Medjugorje to defeat atheism in the form of cultural, practical Marxism. Her early words at Medjugorje seem to lend support to this argument: "God exists!" Indeed, by 1981, cultural Marxism could be seen to be erasing God from the picture in a more effective way than militant Communism. At Fátima, Mary asks the institutional Church to take on institutional atheism (Communism) by enacting the consecration and spreading the First Saturday's devotion. At Medjugorje, she goes directly to the people to help them defeat the cancer that's now in them, the Marxist thought (practical atheism) that has set up home in their minds and hearts. Prayer, fasting, conversion, she says over and over, is now needed. God is needed. This is why the visionaries at Medjugorje cannot be directly compared to the Fátima visionaries. Their mission, though linked, is different, much the same as Mary's mission is not exactly the same at Medjugorje. Their message, therefore, is different, too. The words of Ivan on February 1, 1997, are relevant to this understanding: "The Mother of God asks for our prayers. She asks for unity, love, harmony and solidarity. We must give up the world through prayer. We must make it more secure and better, because it is a fact that *the world cannot exist without God.* I say: Nothing works without God. When we have decided for God, everything will flourish again. Goodness and peace will reign. This certainty gives a perspective for a better world. God did not give us power in order to lead ourselves into anarchy. The purpose of power is a better world. I would like to conclude by saying: let us follow the call of the Mother of God. By practicing her teachings,

we will learn and we will see many things!" (See Laurentin, *Medjugorje Testament, No. 17.*)

17. Ibid. Divorce, abortion, homosexuality, birth control, etc., all thrive from a lack of belief in God, in His revelation. Cultural atheism seeks to legitimize through law and other formal institutional processes these actions and practices. Through the words of Lúcia, we see all of this is related to Mary's warning at Fátima of the "errors of Russia." Grzegorz Gorny and Janusz Rosikon, in their 2016 book, *Fatima Mysteries*, concisely capture this reality: "Practical atheism prevails...furthermore Russia's errors are still being spread throughout the world. Cultural Marxism did not disappear with the Soviet Union. It is not merely a subject for academic considerations, as it is systematically becoming an element in education programs, the media, and the legal system. The sexual revolution too is enjoying great success in more and more countries and the legalization of abortion continues to extend to more regions throughout the world. The family is the object of merciless attacks, its form and essence ceaselessly undermined. It was no accident that in her letter to Father Carlo Caffarra, Sr. Lúcia wrote—mindful that she had a vision of the Holy Family during the October apparition in 1917—that the future of the Church and the world would be determined in marriages and families."

18. Robert Moynihan, "Prodigal Sons," *Inside the Vatican*, Year 17, No.8, October, 2009, p.4.

19. Ibid.

20. John L. Allen Jr., "Benedict Battles the Dictatorship of Relativism," September 16, 2010, https://www.ncronline.org/blogs/ncr-today/benedict-battles-dictatorship-relativism.

21. Pope Benedict XVI and Peter Seewald, "Dictatorship of Relativism," (Excerpted from Chapter 5 of *Light of the World: The Pope, The Church and the Signs of the Times*, 2010), https://www.catholiceducation.org/en/culture/catholic-contributions/dictatorship-of-relativism.html.

22. Bertone, *The Last Secret of Fatima*, 56.

23. *L' Osservatore Romano*, March 27, 1984; Gruner, *World Enslavement or Peace*, 188, 190-191; Apostoli, *Fatima for Today*, 252.

24. Robert Moynihan, "Woman Behold Your Son," *Inside the Vatican*, Year 8, No. 10, November, 2000, p.10.

25. Ibid.

26. Ibid.

27. Ibid.

28. *30 Giorni*, March, 1990.

29. Maike Hickson, "Cardinal Cordes on John Paul II and the Consecration of Russia," May 15, 2017, https://onepeterfive.com/

cardinal-cordes-pope-john-paul-ii-consecration-russia/. (See www. kath.net. /news/. 59585, May 15, 2017.)

30. "Interview with Lúcia," September, 1985, *Sol de Fátima* (Spanish Blue Army); Kramer, *The Devil's Final Battle*, 115.

31. Kramer, *The Devil's Final Battle*, 116.

32. Francois, *Fatima: Tragedy and Triumph*, 172.

33. *La Repubblica*, February 17, 2005.

34. Bertone, *The Last Secret of Fatima*, 56.

35. Evaristo, *"Two Hours with Sister Lucia,"* 10, 35-40.

36. Bertone, *The Last Secret of Fatima*, 87.

37. Petrisko, *The Fatima Prophecies* (revised edition), 280.

38. Apostoli, *Fatima for Today*, 163-164.

39. Michel de la Trinite, *The Whole Truth About Fatima*, 524-529.

40. Ibid. 631.; Carmel of Coimbra, *A Pathway Under the Gaze of Mary*, 187.

41. Michel de la Trinite, *The Whole Truth About Fatima*, 736-742. Lucia's letter of October 24, 1940, to Pius XII was never sent.

42. Ibid.

43. Lucia, *Fatima in Lucia's Own Words*, 114. (See *Third Memoir.*)

44. Father John De Marchi, *The Crusade of Fatima*, (New York, NY: P.J. Kennedy and Sons, 1948), 168-171.

45. Walsh, *Our Lady of Fatima*, 221.

46. Francois, *Fatima: Tragedy and Triumph*, 21, 37. Francois quotes *Il Pellegrinaggio Della Meraviglie*, Rome,1960, p.440. Canon Barthas mentions this apparition in his communication to the Mariological Congress of Lisbon-Fátima in 1926.

47. Alonso, *The Secret of Fatima*, 109.

48. Francois, *Fatima: Tragedy and Triumph*, 129, 130, 223.

49. Kramer, *The Devil's Final Battle*, 113,114.

50. Ibid.

51. Ibid., 114,115.

52. Ibid., 115, 306.

53. Carmel of Coimbra, *A Pathway Under the Gaze of Mary*, 188, 189.

CHAPTER 48: THE LIGHT COMES FROM THE EAST

1. Apostoli, *Fatima Today*, 190, 251.

2. Evaristo, *"Two Hours with Sister Lucia"*, 39.

3. Socci, *The Fourth Secret of Fatima*, 20.

4. Apostoli, *Fatima for Today*, 250.

5. Ibid., 193.

6. Moynihan, "Dossier: The Third Secret," *Inside the Vatican*, Year 8, No. 6, June-July 2000, p. xiv.

7. Kramer, *The Devil's Final Battle*, 115.

8. Ibid., 250. While Lúcia's apparent concurrence with the consecration of the world instead of Russia is contentious, it can be explained by simply accepting that perhaps the Virgin was influential on this matter due to the circumstances in the world by 1984. Much more mysterious, however, is her explanation in 2000 that it was she who decided that "1960", the date written on the outside of the envelope containing the third part of the Secret of Fátima, was her idea versus her previous statements over the decades that declared it was the desire of the Virgin Mary. Most cited is the text published in 1952 by Canon Barthas, who on the 17th and 18th of October, 1946, interviewed Lúcia on this subject. Asked by Barthas why it was necessary to wait until 1960 to reveal the Secret, Lúcia answered: 'Because the Virgin Mary wishes it so." On April 27, 2000, the following Vatican account stated: "Since Sister Lúcia, before consigning the sealed envelope containing the third part of the "Secret" to the then Bishop of Leiria-Fátima, had written on the external envelope that it could be opened only after 1960 by the Patriarch of Lisbon or by the Bishop of Leiria, His excellency Monsignor Bertone asked her, "Why only after 1960? Was it Our Lady who fixed that Date?" Sister Lúcia replied, "It was not Our Lady. I fixed the date because I had the intuition that before 1960 it would not be understood, but that only later would it be understood. Now, one can understand better." See Socci's, *The Fourth Secret of Fatima* for a thorough look at this issue, pp. 23-31.

9. Carmel of Coimbra, *A Pathway Under the Gaze*, 184-185.

10. Ibid.,185.

11. Ibid.

12. Ibid.

13. Ibid.

14. Socci, *The Fourth Secret of Fatima*, 20.

15. Evaristo, *"Two Hours with Sister Lucia"*, 10.

16. Robert Moynihan, "Dossier: The Third Secret: Questions Concerning the Consecration of Russia," *Inside the Vatican*, Year 8, No. 6, June-July, 2000, p. xiii.

17. Ibid. Many Fátima—as well as Medjugorje—followers point to the revelations of the Virgin Mary to Father Stefano Gobbi with regard to the consecration of Russia. On March 25,1984, the same day as Pope John Paul II's Entrustment of the World, Father Gobbi reported the Virgin Mary said to him (in the form of interior locution): "...Before all I ask it (the consecration) of Pope John Paul II, the first of my beloved sons, who on the occasion of this feast(Annunciation), performed the consecration in a solomn manner, after writing to the bishops of the world and inviting them to do so in union with him. Unfortunately, the invitation was not

welcomed by all the bishops; particular circumstances have not yet permitted the explicit concecration of Russia which I have requested many times. As I have already told you, this consecration will be made to me when the bloody events are well on the way to actuality. I bless the courageous act of my Pope in his wish to entrust the world and all the nations to my Immaculate Heart; I receive it with love and gratitude, and because of it I promise to intervene to shorten greatly the hours of the purification and to lessen the gravity of the trial.But I ask this consecration also from all the bishops, from all the priests, from all religious, and from all the faithful.This is the hour in which the whole Church must assemble in the secure refuge of my Immaculate Heart." On May 13, 1990, Father Gobbi reported that he received a second message from Mary in regards to the consecration: "…Russia has not been consecrated to me by the Pope together with all the Bishops, and thus she has not received the grace of conversion and has spread her errors throughout all parts of the world…" [From the book, *To the Priests Our Lady's Beloved Sons,* Message # 287, "I Ask for the Cosecration of All," and Message # 425, "I am Coming Down from Heaven."] Up until his death, Father Gobbi maintained he received interior locutions from the Virgin Mary. At this time, the Church has not approved his messages as supernatural and a letter from a CDF official refers to them as a product of his own personal meditations.

18. Paul L. Miller, "The Great Schism that Divided the East and the West," https://www.ewtn.com/catholicism/library/great-schism-that-divided-east-and-west-10794. [This article originally appeared in the August 4, 1994, issue of the *Arlington Catholic Herald.*]
19. Ibid.
20. George T. Dennis, "1054: The East West Schism," https://www.christianitytoday.com/history/issues/issue-28/1054-east-west-schism.html.
21. Miller, "The Great Schism that Divided the East and the West," https://www.ewtn.com/catholicism/library/great-schism-that-divided-east-and-west-10794.
22. Ibid.
23. Ibid.
24. Ibid.
25. Ibid.
26. Aiden Nichols O.P., *Rome and the Eastern Churches: A Study in Schism* (Collegeville, MN: The Liturgical Press, 1992), 1.
27. Ibid.
28. Ibid.
29. Ibid., 2.
30. Lumen Gentium, 1.
31. Nichols, *Rome and the Eastern Churches,* 2.

32. Ibid.
33. Ibid., 3.
34. Ibid.
35. Ibid.
36. Jn 12: 20-22.
37. Nichols, *Rome and the Eastern Churches*, 3.
38. Eph 2:19.
39. Nichols, *Rome and the Eastern Churches*, 5.
40. 1 Cor 1:10.
41. Nichols, *Rome and the Eastern Churches*, 6.
42. Ibid.,21.
43. Ibid.
44. Hugh Owen, *The Light Comes from the East*, (Mt. Jackson, VA: Hugh Owen, 2015), 3.
45. Ibid.
46. Ibid.
47. Ibid., 39.
48. Ibid., 42.
49. Ibid., 43.
50. Ibid., 37.
51. Ibid., 37, 38.
52. Ibid.
53. Ibid.

CHAPTER 49: A DIVINE FORMULA?

1. Rose Marie Borngaesser and Gernot Facius, "We Need People Who Live the Faith," *Inside the Vatican*, June-July, 2002, 55.
2. Haffert, *Her Own Words to the Nuclear Age*, 305.
3. Owen, *The Light Comes from the East*, 48-55.
4. Ibid., 86.
5. Augustin Joseph Schulte, "Consecration", *The Catholic Encyclopedia*, Vol. 4 (New York, NY: Robert Appleton Company, 1908), 9-20.
6. Venancio, ed., *A Heart for All*, 137.
7. Ibid., 95, 106,107,110.
8. Ibid.,129-130.
9. Ibid.,131.
10. Ibid., 115.
11. Ibid., 115-116.
12. Ibid.,118.
13. Ibid.,138.
14. Ibid., 204. (see footnote N.3.)

15. Laurentin and Lejeune, *Messages and Teachings of Mary at Medjugorje*, 171.
16. Owen, *The Light Comes from the East*, 105.
17. Ibid.,108.
18. Evaristo, *"Two Hours with Sister Lucia,"* 37.
19. Petrisko, *The Fatima Prophecies*, 279.
20. Michel de la Trinite, *The Whole Truth About Fatima*, 798-799.
21. Ibid., 405-437.
22. Michel de la Trinite, *The Whole Truth About Fatima*, 405.
23. See Chapter 69 of my book, *The Call of the Ages*, for more on the extraordinary changes in Portugal. See Fre Michel's *The Whole Truth About Fátima*, (Chapter IV: A Triple Miracle; Portugal, A Showcase of Our Lady) for an even greater review of this matter.

CHAPTER 50: "I WANT MY WHOLE CHURCH TO KNOW"

1. Martins, *Documents on Fatima and the Memoirs of Sister Lucia*, 286.
2. Ibid.
3. Blue Army, *There is Nothing More*, 325.
4. Fox, *Rediscovering Fatima*, 116; Tossati, *The Secret Revealed*, 138.
5. Alonso, *The Secret of Fátima*, 83, 84.
6. Owen, *The Light Comes from the East*, 98, 99.
7. Fellows, *Fatima in Twilight*, 74.
8. Ibid.
9. Ibid.
10. Michel de la Trinite, *The Whole Truth About Fatima*, 495.
11. Ibid.
12. Fellows, *Fátima in Twilight*, 107.
13. Venancio, ed., *A Heart for All*, 127.

CHAPTER 51: THE CONSECRATION OF RUSSIA

1. Laurentin and Lejeune, *Messages and Teachings of Mary at Medjugorje*, 204.
2. Craig, *Spark from Heaven*, 84. Fr. Ivica Vego got caught in some of the aftermath of the entire "Herzegovinian Affair," which led to the "Mostar Case." In January 29, 1982, he was dismissed from the Order by the Franciscan General. The dismissal was overturned by the Apostolic Signatory on March 27, 1993, but by then he had left the priesthood and married. For an indepth look at this issue, see *Once Again, the Truth About Medjugorje* by Rupčić and Nuić.
3. Ibid.

4. Laurentin and Rupčić, *Is the Virgin Mary Appearing at Medjugorje?* 80. (Also see a different version of this message in Laurentin and Lejeune, *Messages and Teachings of Mary at Medjugorje*, 171.)
5. Kraljevic, *The Apparitions of Our Lady at Medjugorje*, 96.
6. Ibid.
7. Ibid.
8. Venancio, ed., *A Heart for All*, 137.
9. Ratzinger, "The Message of Fatima," published in *The Fatima Prophecies*, 270-298.
10. Venancio, *A Heart for All*, 107.
11. Glenn Ellis and Viktoryia Kolchyna, "Putin and the 'Triumph of Christianity' in Russia, October 19, 2017, https://www.aljazeera.com/features/2017/10/19/putin-and-triumph-of-christianity-in-russia.
12. Steve Rosenberg, "Russia's Putin Wants Traditional Marriage and God in Constitution," March 3, 2020, https://www.bbc.com/news/world-europe-51719764.
13. Gene Zubovich, "Russia's Journey from Orthodoxy to Atheism, and Back Again," October 16, 2018, https://religionandpolitics.org/2018/10/16/russias-journey-from-orthodoxy-to-atheism-and-back-again/.
14. Ibid.
15. Ellis and Kolchyna, "Putin and the 'Triumph of Christianity' in Russia, https://www.aljazeera.com/features/2017/10/19/putin-and-truimph-of-christianity-in-russia.
16. "The Russian Orthodox Church and the Impact of Bolshevism," Nov. 3, 2017, https://www.themoscowtimes.com; Lena Surzhko Harned, "Holy Wars: How a Cathedral of Guns and Glory Symbolizes Putin's Russia," March 2, 2022, https://www.yahoo.com; Giles Fraser, "Putin's Spiritual Destiny," Feb. 24, 2022, https:// unherd.com.
17. Bradley Eli, "Consecrate Russia Now," May 21, 2020, https://www.churchmilitant.com/news/article/consecrate-russia-now.
18. Maike Hickson, "Archbishop Vigano: Third Secret of Fatima Has Not Been Fully Published," April 22, 2020, https://www.lifesitenews.com/blogs/archbishop-vigano-third-secret-of-fatima-has-not-yet-been-fully-published.
19. Pete Balinski, "Catholic Historian: We Need Consecration of Russia to Save Church," April 12, 2017, https://www.lifesitenews.com/news/catholic-historian-we-need-consecration-of-russia-to-save-the-church.
20. Ibid.
21. John Henry Weston, "Bishop Schneider: Consecration Will Bring Russia to the Fullest of Conversion," May 30, 2017, https://www.lifesitenews.com/news/bishop-schneider-consecration-will-bring-russia-to-the-fullness-of-conversi.

22. Eli, "Consecrate Russia Now," May 21, 2020, https://www.churchmilitant.com/news/article/consecrate-russia-now.

23. Dorothy Cummings McLean, "Catholic Leaders Sign Petition to Consecrate Russia Now," August 8, 2017, https://www.lifesitenews.com/news/catholic-leaders-sign-petition-to-consecrate-russia.

24. Apostoli, *Fatima for Today*, 254-259.

25. Ibid., 260.

26. Pope John Paul II wasn't the only one warning about the mounting danger of practical atheism. Writes Fr. Rene Laurentin in 1984: "The official atheism of the East has tried to eliminate God, and the practical materialism of the West has sometimes done this more thoroughly." (See *Is the Virgin Mary Appearing at Medjugorje?* p. 88.) It is also worth noting that Fr. Stefano Gobbi, the Italian priest who founded the worldwide organization known as the *The Marian Movement of Priests*, wrote that the Virgin Mary told him in a locution that Practical Atheism was in fact the greatest evil of the 20th Century. Officially, the Church presently has not rendered an opinion on the supernatural character of Gobbi's writings. In Message No. 577, titled "The Evil of Your Century" and dated September 2, 1996, Gobbi writes that Mary said to him: "But now you are being menaced with an even more serious and insidious danger. It is practical atheism, the evil of your century.... With the triumph of my Immaculate Heart in the world, you will be completely liberated from every form of practical atheism, which has been the greatest evil of your century." (*To the Priests, Our Lady's Beloved Sons*, English edition, 1998, p. 917-918).

27. Martins, *Documents on Fatima and the Memoirs of Sister Lucia*, 286.

28. Michele de la Trinite, *The Whole Truth About Fatima*, 685.

29. Michele de la Trinite, *The Whole Truth About Fatima*, 686.

30. Martins, *Documents on Fatima and the Memoirs of Sister Lucia*, 329.

31. While the consecration of Russia was originally intended to bring conversion to the nation of Russia and therefore "prevent" militant Marxism (Communism) from spreading throughout the world (which was finally stymied through the 1984 consecration), it would not be surprising that someday it will be seen that the March 25, 2022, consecration sparked the beginning of the defeat of cultural Marxism, which has become (due to its attack on life and the family) as toxic and lethal to humanity as Communism. This consecration, while it appeared to be aimed at resolving a mounting danger in the East, may likely be seen to have been the cure for the West.

32. **CHAPTER 52: "THE SECRETS I BEGAN AT FATIMA"**
33. Evaristo, *"Two Hours with Sister Lucia."* 37.
34. Pelletier, *The Queen of Peace Visits Medjugorje*, 215.
35. Mark Miravalle S.T.D., *Heart of the Message of Medjugorje* (Steubenville, OH: Franciscan University Press, 1988), 72-78.
36. Ibid.
37. Ibid.
38. Rev. Edward Carter, S.J., *The Spirituality of Fatima and Medjugorje* (Milford, OH: Faith Publishing Company,1994), 43.
39. Craig, *Spark from Heaven*, 203.
40. Ibid.
41. Carter, *The Spirituality of Fatima and Medjugorje*, 43.
42. Nolan, *Medjugorje and the Church*, 24. Although there is no way to confirm whether or not Sister Lúcia felt Medjugorje was the fulfillment of Fátima, in an article published in a 1987 issue of the *Mir Recorder* [News Sheet of Medjugorje Information Service] of Sussex, England, editor Peter Batty reports that on June 25, 1986, "an important representative from Fátima was in Medjugorje with a Fr. Gioacchino." The Fátima representative gave the following surprise information: "On the 14th of last December, Bishop Hnilica had a meeting with Sister Lúcia of Fátima at Coimbra, lasting nearly two hours, at which I was present. When she was asked whether Medjugorje completes Fátima, Sister Lúcia agreed it did." (*Mir Recorder*, Annunciation, 1987, p. 5). Blatty appears to have gotten the story from the July 11, 1986, issue of *Echo of Medjugorje*. Sister Emmanuel Maillard of Medjugorje, in her book *Medjugorje the 90s*, also reported that Sister Lúcia commented on and was favorable to Medjugorje. Emmanuel writes: "And how could I fail to mention here the happiness of Sr. Lucy herself, whose visions of Our Lady have continued since 1917, and to whom Mary now speaks of her work in Medjugorje." Sr. Emmanuel footnoted the source of her information: "This was reported by Sr. Lucy's nephew, Father Salinho, a Salesian priest who lives in Portugal. Needless to say, these apparitions pertain to Sr. Lucy's private mystical life and, therefore, will not be the object of an official statement during her lifetime. Happily, John Paul II maintains a close relationship with Sr. Lucy." (See *Medjugorje: the 90s*, pp. 68-69.) There have been published denials of Lucia having ever said anything about Medjugorje, publicly or privately.
43. Medjugorje.Org, *The Medjugorje Messages: 1981-2013*, 151.
44. René Laurentin, *Medjugorje-13 Years Later*, (Milford, OH: The Riehle Foundation, 1994), 46.
45. The Medjugorje Web, *The Medjugorje Messages: 1981-2013*, 152. In a message given to Mirjana on June 2, 2019, Mary states, "My children,

follow me. My way is the way of peace and love, the way of my Son. It is the way that leads to the *triumph of My heart*."

46. Ibid.

47. Soldo, *My Heart Will Triumph*, 208.

48. Ibid., 210.

49. Laurentin, *Medjugorje – 13 Years Later*, 25.

50. Official statement released by Mirjana at Medjugorje, dated March 19, 1989, titled, "The Regular Apparition of Our Lady to Mirjana for her Birthday, March 18, 1989."

51. Laurentin, *Medjugorje: Testament*, 27.

52. Soldo, *My Heart Will Triumph*, 208.

53. Ibid., 210.

54. Said Mirjana: "I carry out my mission of praying for unbelievers. The terrible things that happen in the world are the consequences of this unbelief." See *Spirit of Medjugorje*, Vol.15, No. 3, April, 2002, p.7.

55. Soldo, *My Heart Will Triumph*, 209.

56. Vlašić and Barbarić, *Open Your Hearts to Mary Queen of Peace*, 134-135.

57. Vlašić and Barbarić, *Abandon Yourselves Totally to Me*, 109.

58. Laurentin, *Ten Years of Apparions*, 120. Ivan's words come from an interview with him by the *National Catholic Register* in November, 1990, at an event held in Herndon, Virginia.

59. Laurentin and Lejeune, *Messages and Teachings of Mary at Medjugorje*, 186. It appears, in some way, that Mary came to Fátima (in the West) to convert the East (from Marxism in the form of militant atheism). And she came to Medjugorje (in the East) to convert the West (from Marxism in the form of practical atheism).

CHAPTER 53: ONE SOUL AT A TIME

1. Sullivan, *The Miracle Detective*, 207.

2. Ibid., 206.

3. Ibid.

4. O'Carroll, *Medjugorje: Facts, Documentation, and Theology*, 72.

5. Ibid., 61.

6. Ibid., 63.

7. Ibid., 62

8. Ibid.

9. Ibid.

10. Ibid.

11. Antonio Gaspari, "Medjugorje: Deception or Miracle?", *Inside the Vatican*, Year 4, No. 9, November, 1996, p.24.; Sullivan, *The Miracle Detective*, 207. Sullivan describes Margnelli as an atheist.

12. Ibid.
13. Ibid.
14. O'Carroll, *Medjugorje: Facts, Documents, and Theology*, 70.
15. Sullivan, *The Miracle Detective*, 208.
16. Ibid., 207.
17. O'Carroll, *Medjugorje: Facts, Documents, and Theology*, 70.
18. Sullivan, *The Miracle Detective*, 208.
19. Ibid., 207.
20. Ibid., 208.
21. O'Carroll, *Medjugorje, Facts, Documents and Theology*, 71.
22. Ibid.
23. Ibid.
24. Ibid.
25. Sullivan, *The Miracle Detective*, 208.
26. Ibid., 20.
27. Ibid., 19.
28. All six visionaries at Medjugorje are married. Ivanka married Rajko Elez on December 18, 1986, at St. James Church in Medjugorje. They have three children, Kristina, Josip, and Ivan, and live in Medjugorje. Mirjana was married to Marko Soldo on September 16, 1989, at St. James. They have two children, Veronica and Marija, and live in Medjugorje. Jacov was married to Annalisa Barozzi on Easter Sunday, April 11, 1993, at St. James. They have three children, Arijianna, David Emmanuel, and Myriam, and live in Medjugorje. Marija was married to Paolo Lunetti on September 8, 1993, in Milan. They have four children, Michaele, Francesca, Marco, and Giovanni, and live in Medjugorje and Monza, Italy. Ivan was married to Laureen Murphey on October 23, 1994, at St. Leonard's Church in Boston. They have three children, Kristina Marija, Mikela, and Daniel, and live in Medjugorje and Boston. Vicka was married to Mario Mijatovic on January 26, 2002, in Gruda, a small village near Medjugorje. They have two children, Marija-Sofia and Ante, and live in Krehin Gradac. On February 1, 2002, Sr. Emmanuel Maillard published a story about a Croatian marriage tradition that merits inclusion here. Wrote Sister Emmanuel: "In the town of Siroki-Brijeg, not one single divorce has been recorded among its 13,000 inhabitants. Not one single family has broken up in living memory. Does Hercegovina enjoy a special favor from Heaven? Is there a magic formula that keeps the demon of division at bay? The answer is very simple! For centuries because of the pressure from the Turks and then the Communists, the people suffered cruelly as their Christian faith was always threatened. They knew through experience that salvation comes through the Cross of Christ. It does not come from disarmament plans, from humanitarian aid or peace treaties, even if these things may bring limited benefits. The source of salvation is the Cross of Christ! These

people possess a wisdom that does not allow them to be duped over questions of life and death. That is why they have indissolubly linked marriage with the Cross of Christ. They have found marriage, which brings forth human life, on the Cross, which brings forth divine life. The Croatian marriage tradition is so beautiful that it is beginning to take hold in Europe and America. When a young couple is preparing for marriage, they are not told that they have found the ideal partner. No! What does the priest say? "You have found your Cross. And it is a Cross to be loved, to be carried, a Cross not to be thrown away, but to be cherished." In Hercegovina, the Cross represents the greatest love and the Crucifix is the treasure of the home. When the bride and groom set off for the church, they bring a Crucifix with them. The priest blesses the Crucifix, which takes on a central role during the exchange of vows. The bride places her right hand on the Crucifix and the groom places his hand over hers. Thus the two hands are bound together on the Cross. The priest covers their hands with his stole as they proclaim their vows to be faithful, according to the rules of the Church. Fr. Jozo Zovko explains that the bride and groom do not kiss each other, they rather kiss the Cross. They know that they are kissing the source of love. Anyone close enough to see their hands joined over the Cross understands clearly that if the husband abandons his wife or if the wife abandons her husband, they let go of the Cross. And if they abandon the Cross, they have nothing left. They have lost everything, for they have abandoned Jesus. They have lost Jesus. After the ceremony, the newlyweds bring the Crucifix back and give it a place of honor in their home. It becomes the focal point of family prayer, for the young couple believes deeply that the family is born of the Cross. When a trouble arises, or if a conflict breaks out, it is before the Cross that they will seek help. They will not go to their lawyer, they will not consult a fortune teller, or an astrologer, they will not rely on a psychologist to solve the problem. No, they will go straight before the Cross. They will get on their knees and in front of Jesus, they will weep their tears and pour out their hearts, and above all exchange their forgiveness. They will not go to sleep with a heavy heart because they will have turned to their Jesus, the only one who has the power to save. They will teach their children to kiss the Cross every day and not go to sleep like pagans without having thanked Jesus first. As for the children, as far back as they can remember, Jesus has always been a friend of the family, respected and embraced. They say nighty-night to Jesus and kiss the Cross. As Father Jozo says, they go to sleep with Jesus, not with a teddy bear. They know that Jesus is holding them in His arms and that there is nothing to be afraid of, and their fears melt away in their kiss to Jesus. **Dearest Gospa, please extend the blessing of this beautiful marriage to the whole family of your children on Earth."**

29. Biography of Randall Sullivan, *Wikipedia*. A story on Sullivan's conversion appeared on *Fox News* on February 20, 2005. The program was

titled "Heartland." Silloo Maria Therese Madan wrote a story on this program that was published in *The Spirit of Medjugorje*, April, 2005.

30. Ibid.
31. Ibid.
32. Interview with author Randall Sullivan by Michael Jones, http://www.medjugorjeusa.org/sullivan.htm.
33. Ibid.
34. Ibid.
35. Sullivan, *The Miracle Detective*, 280.
36. Ibid., 41-43.
37. Ibid., 45. One of those said to also be favorable to Medjugorje at the time, though not publicly, was Cardinal Ratzinger. He reportedly told Bishop Martin of Brazil that there were "good fruits" with Medjugorje. (*Mir Information Centre*, press bulletin, December 3, 1997.)
38. Ibid., 62.
39. Ibid., 153.
40. Ibid., 129.
41. Ibid.
42. Ibid.
43. Ibid.
44. Ibid., 130.
45. Ibid., 131-132.
46. Ibid., 131.
47. Ibid.
48. Ibid., 80.
49. Thull, ed., *What They Say About Medjugorje*, 469.
50. Ibid., 512.
51. Ibid., 468. Mother Angelica was a strong believer in the apparitions of Our Lady at Medjugorje. In a discussion I had with her at the Basilica of the National Shrine of the Immaculate Conception during the International Prayer and Fasting Conference in Washington, DC, on October 9, 2000, it became apparent to me that she had read many books on Mary's apparitions and lived in great expectation of the foretold Triumph of the Immaculate Heart. She seemed to know Mary in an intimate, personal way, one that displayed great confidence and revealed to me why EWTN became a reality and survived so many challenges to its existence.
52. Ibid., 477.
53. "The Miracles of Medjugorje: The Meaning and Purpose of Life," November 3, 2009, wwwstlechemindcroix.blogspot.com. I became good friends with Lola Falana, who lived in Philadelphia, my wife's hometown. We did radio shows together—*The Dom Latteiere Show*—where we discussed Medjugorje and the Virgin Mary's powerful presence there. Lola was not only

physically healed but experienced a radical conversion. We often spoke about her past days as a star entertainer and the tragedy of where that kind of life can take one if not grounded in God. Lola, as I recall, possessed a great love of Christ that was passionate and profound. She centered her life around adoration of Christ in the Blessed Sacrament.

54. "Jim Caviezel: If It Weren't for Medjugorje, He Would Have Never Played Christ in the Passion," August 6, 2010, https://www.medjugorjemiracles. com/2010/08/actor-james-caviezel-says-if-it-wasnt-for-medjugorje-he-would-have-never-played-christ-in-the-passion/. I spent three days with Jim Caviezel and his wife at the annual Conference on Medjugorje at Notre Dame. We spoke at length about his upcoming role in the *Passion*, which he was to begin filming in the upcoming months. I remember thinking at the time that this movie would be unsuccessful. For some reason, I could not imagine an entire movie based just on Christ's Passion. Jim was a class act, very soft spoken, humble and unpretentious.

55. Thull, ed., *What They Say About Medjugorje*, 211.

56. Ibid., 199. Archbishop Phillip Hannon was a good friend of mine who asked me to edit and format two of his books. Hannon gave the homily at President John F. Kennedy's funeral and also presided at the funerals of Robert F. Kennedy and Jackie Onassis. I was privileged to read dozens of his private letters in the preparation of one of his books. I also got an inside look at the role he played in Washington during the Sixties and Seventies with many prominent government leaders (Richard Nixon, Spiro Agnew, Lyndon Johnson, etc.) who he knew intimately in addition to the Kennedy family. He gave to me, at the time, many of his private papers and correspondences that detailed his intimate memories of them. My publishing company, *St. Andrew's Productions*, published his book, *Rome: Living Under the Axis*.

57. "Oregon Running Champ Salazaar Puts Faith Over the Finishing Line," April 7, 2012, www.oregonlive.com.

58. Hebert, *Medjugorje: An Affirmation and a Defense*, 99.

59. James Mulligan, *Medjugorje: What's Happening?* (Toronto, Ontario: Ave Maria Center for Peace, 2009), 220. This is a fine book to get updated on Medjugorje over the last ten years or so.

60. Bernard Ellis, "A Jewish Man is Brought to His Knees Three Times by the Blessed Mother," Gloria TV, Evelin de Jacarei, 2017. Of all the extraordinary people I had the pleasure to get to know over the last thirty years, perhaps Bernard Ellis is one of the most memorable. I stayed with him and his wife Sue at their home outside of London on occasion, where he arranged for me to speak to different Medjugorje groups in the region over a period of several days. I remember Bernard asked me to meet with a prominent member of the House of Lords who asked to speak

to me about his desire to produce a first-rate, highly professional Marian video. He was, however, extremely concerned the British tabloids might revisit some of his youthful indiscretions. This English gentleman of nobility did tell me that Princess Diana desired to go to Medjugorje, but was forbidden to do so by the Queen. As I recall, he explained to me that Diana often skied in the Alps nearby and was going to use this connection as her opportunity to slip quietly into Medjugorje. On the first night that I stayed at the Ellis home, Bernard told me that Father Slavko Barbarić had slept in the same bed the night before. Slavko, he said, didn't sleep much when he was there, preferring to walk up and down the street outside every night for long hours in the cold, dark and rain as he prayed his Rosary.

CHAPTER 54: "PROTECT MEDJUGORJE"

1. Soldo, *My Heart Will Triumph*, 236. Sullivan writes about this, too. Reportedly in 1982, one of the visionaries was asked after an apparition if Croatia would ever be free. "Yes," was the response, "after a small war." In various interviews over the years, Father Petar Ljubicic has also spoken about the visionaries knowing to some degree what was coming in the Balkans. Father Petar stayed at my home in February 2000 and we spoke at length on many subjects, including the Secrets. When I finally began to work again on this book, I reread the transcript of the interview I did with him then and came to the conclusion that I should finally publish it. (See Chapter 70, "A Conversation with Father Petar Ljubicic.") The Franciscans at Medjugorje during the early and mid-1980s, in my opinion, were privileged to much more of the confidences of the visionaries concerning their experiences—especially surrounding the Secrets—than has ever been realized, yet alone revealed. Their loyalty and trustworthiness with these matters adds greatly to their already impressive legacy.
2. Laurentin, *Medjugorje: 12 Years Later*, 143.
3. Ibid., 1.
4. Ibid., 2.
5. Emanuel, *Medjugorje: The 90s*, 126.
6. Michael Brown, *The Day Will Come* (Ann Harbor, MI: Servant Publications, 1996), 118.
7. Nolan, *Medjugorje and the Church*, 34.
8. Laurentin, *Medjugorje: 12 Years Later*, 2.
9. Ibid.

10. Father Ljudevit Rupčić, "The Silenced Situation of the Catholic Church in Bosnia and Hercegovina." (Vienna, Austria: *Medjugorje Gebetsaktion*, No.30, August, 1993), 22.

11. Laurentin, *Medjugorje: 12 Years Later*, 27. Some accounts report the Mostar cathedral library held as many as 50,000 books.

12. Soldo, *My Heart Will Triumph*, 259.

13. Emanuel, *Medjugorje: The War Day by Day*, 102-103. Pope John Paul II's favorable disposition, if not all out support, of Medjugorje is well documented. But what also appears to emerge is Cardinal Ratzinger's support. Randall Sullivan, during his trip to Rome to meet with Vatican officials, became convinced this was the case. He writes, "The Cardinal encouraged the praying of the Rosary and was lavish in his praise for the Lourdes and Fátima movements. Ratzinger did not mention Medjugorje, but it was common knowledge in the Vatican that the prefect—at the behest of John Paul, perhaps, and certainly with the pope's support—had blocked those most intent upon seeing that the devotions there were condemned." Other sources reveal that Ratzinger, while viewed to be at the service of John Paul II's wishes concerning Medjugorje, was actually quite favorable himself. Ratzinger is said to have visited Medjugorje incognito.

14. Mulligan, *Medjugorje: What's Happening*? 172.

15. Wayne Weible, *The Final Harvest* (Brewster MA: Paraclete Press, 1999), 195-196.

16. Ibid.

17. Ibid.

18. Ibid. U.S. Presidents Reagan and Clinton are not the only Presidents that have crossed paths with Medjugorje. During his October 24 through December 13,1990, visit to the United States, Ivan is believed to have met with President George H. Bush. While preferring to keep the meeting confidential, he is said to have spoken about it on May 26, 1991, during a talk in Medjugorje. Like Marija did with President Reagan and Premier Gorbachev, Ivan wrote President Bush a letter, telling him of the Virgin's efforts to bring peace to the world through Medjugorje. (The letter in its entirety can be found in the book, *The Best of the Spirit of Medjugorje*, Vol. I, p. 61-62.) Over a decade later, Ivan was rumored again to have met with President George W. Bush. This time he reportedly attended a dinner at the White House on April 29, 2008.

19. Soldo, *My Heart Will Triumph*, 259.

20. Mulligan, *Medjugorje: What's Happening*? 110.

21. Soldo, *My Heart Will Triumph*, 263.

22. Ibid.

23. The Dayton University Marian Library is known as a center of scholarship of the Blessed Virgin Mary. By 1993, it had grown to include

85,000 books and other publications on Mary, the world's largest collection of literature on the Blessed Virgin. Some of the items date back to the 15th century. It is also where Father René Laurentin would lecture for a week or more during the summer months throughout the 1990s. Fr. Johann Roten, a Marianist priest, directed the International Marian Research Institute at the University of Dayton during the 1990s and developed a lesson plan that incorporated modern Marian apparitions into the Catholic high school curriculum. Said Roten about Medjugorje and its effect on the Church and the world, "Medjugorje brought apparitions into the mainstream of the Catholic Church. The increase in the reports of apparitions may suggest that there is a spiritual hunger today that goes beyond institutional churches. There's a need for mystery to be put back into people's lives. Apparitions may be one of God's answers to these needs." The 1990s Balkans war is considered to have officially begun on April 6, 1992, and to have ended on December 14, 1995.

24. Bishop Girolamo Grillo, *Our Lady Weeps: Report on Civitavecchia* (Toronto, Ontario: Ave Maria Press, 1997), 22. See *Inside the Vatican*, "Did the Statue Really Weep?", May, 1998.
25. Ibid., 22.
26. Sullivan, *Miracle Detective*, 46.
27. Ibid., 48.
28. Ibid.
29. Laurentin and Lejeune, *Messages and Teachings of Mary at Medjugorje*, 173.

CHAPTER 55: OPENING SECRETS

1. Soldo, *My Heart Will Triumph*, 137.
2. Ibid. In his book, *Medjugorje, What's Happening?* Father James Mulligan reports the parchment like material containing the Ten Secrets is approximately 8" x 11" in size.
3. Ibid., 138.
4. Ibid.
5. Ibid., Laurentin, *The Apparitions in Medjugorje Prolonged*, 27.
6. Soldo, *My Heart Will Triumph*, 138.
7. Ibid.
8. Craig, *Spark from Heaven*, 165. René Laurentin, unreserved in his positive opinion on Medjugorje, did express being baffled over the existence of the parchment with the Ten Secrets written on it. He writes, "Mirjana makes no secret of having this document. But other than her cousin, the Swiss engineer, only another cousin (a girl) and her mother have seen it. This singular

point perplexed me, because such means of revelation more resembles magic than the habitual manner of God, according to the tradition of the Church. It is necessary to be a little more reserved on this point. The seers are not exactly infallible. Other than the three persons mentioned, Mirjana has shown the paper to no one, not even to the priest of her parish." (See Laurentin, *The Apparitions at Medjugorje Prolonged*).

9. Soldo, *My Heart Will Triumph*, 263-266.
10. Ibid.
11. Ibid.
12. Craig, *Spark from Heaven*, 165.
13. Soldo, *My Heart Will Triumph*, 136.; Klins, *The Spirit of Medjugorje*, 65.
14. Ante and Grgo Kozina, "The Spirit of Medjugorje: Local Interviews-Mirjana Recalls," *Medjugorje Herald*, Volume 3, No.7, August, 1989, 12.
15. Soldo, *My Heart Will Triumph*, 187.
16. Laurentin, *The Apparitions at Medjugorje Prolonged*, 34.
17. Craig, *Spark from Heaven*, 166.
18. Ibid.
19. Joan Ashton, *The People's Madonna: An Account of the Visions of Mary at Medjugorje* (London, UK: Harper Collins Publishers, 1991), 13-14.
20. Ibid., 14.
21. Sister Emmanuel, *Medjugorje News*, February 15, 1997. From 1995 through the turn of the millennium, there was a constant flow of rumors concerning the unfolding of the Ten Secrets. This type of commotion surrounding the Ten Secrets of Medjugorje had been seen before in the months that preceded the Gulf War (1991) in the summer of 1990. "We are all concerned about the crisis in the Middle East and many wonder what this mean in terms of the apparitions in Medjugorje. Is this one of the Secrets? What is going to happen?" wrote Bill and Fran Reck in their article, "Is It One of the Secrets? Is it a Sign?", published in *Mary's People* (*The National Catholic Register*), September 30, 1990, p.7.
22. Inside the Vatican Staff, "The Third Secret: Is the End Near?", *Inside the Vatican*, Year 4, No. 9, November, 1996, p.15. While in Fátima in October of 1996, Ratzinger was a guest on the Portuguese Catholic radio show *Radio Renascenca*. He spoke about the third part of the Secret and any apocalyptic speculation, including talk of the end of the world. While Ratzinger emphasized Mary does not engage in sensationalism, his words were viewed as being very selective. Vatican expert Orazio Petrosillo noted in *Il Massaggero* on October 14th that "this is not the same thing as saying there is 'nothing' catastrophic in the Third Secret."
23. "Text of Third Fatima Secret Released," *The Washington Post*, May 13, 2000, https://www.washingtonpost.com/archive/politics/2000/06/27/text-of-3rd-fatima-secret-   released/bdf90e36-590f-4bc0-b333-7d0e92201f13/.

In several interviews after the announcement, Cardinal Sodano said the Pope had been planning to reveal the Secret "for some time." The cardinal told reporters it was "a decision tied to the closing of the millennium, to the century just passed, a century full of suffering and tribulation."

24. Ratzinger, "The Message of Fátima" published in *The Fatima Prophecies*, 284-286.

25. Ibid., 281. Sister Lúcia was very ill when she wrote down the third part of the Secret. In June of 1943, she was found to have a fever and in September was diagnosed with pleurisy. Continuing to experience the fevers, she suffered several serious setbacks. After meeting with the Bishop of Leiria, Bishop da Silva, who came to see her and departed feeling that she could die, he ordered her to write the third part of the Secret down. Lúcia struggled with this order and repeatedly failed in her early attempts to fulfill the Bishop's request.

26. Thavis, *The Vatican Prophecies*, 7, 86.

27. Ratzinger, "The Message of Fatima," published in *The Fatima Prophecies*, 293-298.

28. Socci, *The Fourth Secret of Fatima*, 46.

29. Ibid.

30. Father Paul Kramer, "The Impending Great Chastisement Revealed in the Third Secret of Fatima," *The Fatima Crusader*, Spring 2003, pp. 11-12.; Ratzinger, "The Message of Fatima," published in *The Fatima Prophecies*, 297.

31. Bertone, *The Last Secret of Fatima*, 67.

32. Ratzinger, "The Message of Fatima," published in *The Fatima Prophecies*, 285; Bertone, *The Last Secret of Fatima*, 52.

33. Ibid., 295.

34. Jonah 3:1-10.

35. Ratzinger, "The Message of Fatima," published in *The Fatima Prophecies*, 295.

36. Moynihan, "Dossier: The Third Secret," *Inside the Vatican*, Year 8, No. 6, June-July 2000, p. xiv.

37. Socci, *The Fourth Secret of Fatima*, 53. Some have written, but not supported with documentation, that Sister Lúcia said the third part of the Secret of Fátima could be found in the *Book of Revelation*, Chapters 8-13.

38. Ibid., 54. Socci writes that "doubts, suspicions, rumors and critical observations circulated" after the release of the third part of the Secret in 2000, turning it into a "detective story."

39. Ibid., 89-96. Thull, ed., *What They Say About Medjugorje*, 162-164. (See section 2-C on 'Cardinal Joseph Ratzinger', which contains excerpts from *The Ratzinger Report* that concern Fátima and Medjugorje).

40. Moynihan, "Dossier: The Third Secret," *Inside the Vatican*, Year 8, No. 6, June-July, 2000, p. xii.

41. Ibid.

42. Father Gerald Mura, "The Third Secret of Fatima: Has it been Completely Revealed?", *Catholic*, March, 2002. Mura quotes a 1995 personal communication from Cardinal Ciappi to a Professor Baumgartner in Salzburg, Austria.

43. *Il Giornale*, June 26, 2000. Laurentin is not the only prominent "doubting Thomas" to publicly say he believed a part of the third part of the Secret was not released. On May 16, 2001, Mother Angelica of EWTN, with a guest priest seated next to her, told her viewers that she too believed there was more. "As for the Secret," said the trailblazing nun, "Well, I happen to be one of those individuals who thinks we didn't get the whole thing. I told ya! I mean, you have the right to your own opinion, don't you, Father? There, you know, that's my opinion. Because I think *it's scary*. And I don't think the Holy See is going to say something that does not happen, that might happen. Then what does it do if it doesn't happen? I mean the Holy See cannot afford to make prophecies." (See *The Fatima Crusader*, August, 2001, p. 12.) Critics of the Vatican's interpretation of the Secret especially focused on the role of Cardinal Sodano, who they viewed as long pursuing an agenda not supportive to the principles of the Triumph as predicted by Mary at Fátima. Sodano, they say, deliberately sought "to spin" the third part of the Secret in order to put to an end to any more talk of Fátima that could interfere with the new age of growing global solidarity that was emerging. To Sodano's credit, no evidence of any serious wrong doing has been demonstrated. (See Fátima Network's *Fatima News: The Third Secret Handwritten Text Essential: An Interview with Fr. Paul Kramer*, June 5, 2000.)

CHAPTER 56: A FOURTH SECRET OF FATIMA?

1. *La Republica*, June 27, 2000. *La Republica* was not the only newspaper to express bewilderment. The headline of the *Los Angeles Times* on June 27, 2000, read, "Catholic Church Unveils Third Secret: The Vatican's Top Theologian Gently Debunks a Nun's Account of Her 1917 Vision that Fueled Decades of Speculation."

2. "Pope John Paull II in Fulda, Germany (1980)", *The Fátima Center*, https://fatima.org/about/the-third-secret/pope-john-paul-ii-in-fulda-germany-1980/. For more on Fulda, see Socci, *The Fourth Secret of Fatima*, p. 77, and *Inside the Vatican*, "The Third Secret: Is the End Near?", November, 1996. (Some have written that Pope John Paul II's true inspiration behind his comments at Fulda was an article about the

apocalyptic nature of the Third Secret of Fatima that appeared in Stimme des Glaubens in 1980. (See *Fear of Fire*, by Michael Brown, pp.44-45.)

3.   Ibid., Thull, ed., *What They say About Medjugorje*, 153. Thull includes a remaining, often unpublished portion of John Paul II's reported talk at Fulda. The talk is controversial since no other sources confirm it took place or published his reportedly sensational words. An excerpt from Lúcia's diary adds a curious twist to the entire matter surrounding the third part of the Secret. In 1943, Lúcia struggled greatly with writing the Secret down as she had been ordered to do by her bishop. She writes about this and how she sought divine assistance with her travails: "While I was waiting for an answer, on January 3, 1944, I knelt beside the bed which sometimes served as a writing table, and again I experienced the same without success. What most impressed me was that at that same moment I could write anything else without difficulty. I then asked Our Lady to let me know if it was the Will of God. I went to the chapel at 4p.m. in the afternoon, the hour that I always made a visit to the Blessed Sacrament because I was ordinarily alone. I do not know why, but I liked being alone with Jesus in the Tabernacle. Then I knelt in the middle, next to the rung of the Communion rail and asked Jesus to make known to me what was His Will. Accustomed as I was to believe that the order of the superiors was the expression of the Will of God, I couldn't believe that this wasn't. Feeling puzzled and half absorbed under the weight of a dark cloud that seemed to hang over me, with my face between my hands, I hoped without knowing how for a response. I then felt a friendly, affectionate hand touch me on the shoulder and I looked up and saw the beloved Mother from Heaven. 'Do not be afraid, God wanted to prove your obedience, faith and humility. Be at peace and write what they order you, but not what has been given you to understand its meaning. After writing it, place it in an envelope, close it and seal it and write on the outside that this can be opened in 1960 by the Cardinal Patriarch of Lisbon or by the Bishop of Leiria.' I felt my spirit flooded by a mystery of light that is God and in Him saw and heard: - 'The tip of the spear as a flame unlatches and touches the axis of the Earth. It shudders. Mountains, cities, towns, and villages with their inhabitants are buried. The sea, the rivers, and the clouds emerge from their limits, overflowing and bringing with them in a whirlwind, houses and peoples in numbers that are not possible to count. It is the purification of the world because of sin as it plunges. Hatred and ambition cause the destructive war!' Then I felt the rapid beating of my heart and in my mind the echo of a gentle voice saying: In time, one faith, one baptism, one Church, Holy, Catholic, and Apostolic. In eternity, Heaven! The word Heaven filled my soul with peace and happiness, so that almost without realizing it, I was repeating for a long time: -Heaven! Heaven! As soon as the full force of the

supernatural passed, I went to write, without difficulty on January 3, 1944, on my knees, resting on the bed that served as a table." (See Lúcia's, *My Pathway*, p.155). In Cardinal Bertone 's interview with *La Repubblica* of February 17, 2005, he again states, "Its (the third part of the Secret) interpretation is not definitive."

4. "Pope John Paul II in Fulda, Germany (1980)", *The Fatima Center,* https://fatima.org/about/the-third-secret/pope-john-paul-ii-in-fulda-germany-1980/.

5. Socci, *The Fourth Secret of Fatima*, 129-167. This controversy found more wind again in April of 2020. In an interview with *Dies Irae,* a Portuguese website, Archbishop Carlo Maria Vigano, the former papal nuncio in Washington D.C., publicly stated that he did not believe that the Vatican to this day had published the full third part of the Secret of Fátima. Vigano also insisted that the consecration of Russia has not taken place as requested and is responsible for the state of affairs in the Church and the world today. He did not comment on Lúcia's words to the contrary on these issues or any other historical facts that make up both sides of the dialogue surrounding these controversial mysteries. (See *Life Site News,* April 22, 2020.)

6. Bertone, *The Last Secret of Fatima*, 66.

7. Ibid., 65.

8. Bertone, *The Last Secret of Fatima*, 48.

9. Moynihan, "Dossier: The Third Secret," *Inside the Vatican*, Year 8, No.6, June-July 2000, p.xii.

10. Apostoli, *Fatima for Today*, 264.

11. Ibid., 214.

12. Socci, *The Fourth Secret of Fatima*, 106. The Pope was in attendance at Fátima on May 13, 2000. He received 300 rosaries as a gift from Lúcia that she made herself. But it was decided for several reasons that he should not personally make the announcement concerning the third part of the Secret. The primary reason was that he was the Pope believed to be shot in the foretelling vision.

13. Ibid.

14. Ibid.

15. Wlodzimierz Redzioch, "Sister Lucia Speaks," *Inside the Vatican*, Year 10, No.1, January, 2002, p.13.

16. Socci, *The Fourth Secret of Fatima*, 107.

17. Wlodzimierz Redzioch, "Sister Lucia Speaks," *Inside the Vatican*, p.13.

18. Socci, *The Fourth Secret of Fatima*,105.

19. Ibid.

20. "Special Report, Bertone's Cover-up of Third Secret Continues to Unravel," *The Fatima Crusader*, Autumn, 2007, pp. 16-21. Also see "Declaration

of Solideo Paolini" and "The Third Secret Cover-up" by Christopher A. Ferrara in this same issue.

21. Philip Pullella, "The Man Who Tried to Kill Pope John Paul," January 18, 2010, https://www.reuters.com/article/us-turkey-agca-factbox/factbox-the-man-who-tried-to-kill-pope-john-paul-idUSTRE60H1PH20100118.

22. Moynihan, "Dossier: The Third Secret," *Inside the Vatican*, Year 8, No.6, June-July 2000, xv.

23. The most significant controversy surrounding the third part of the Secret from 2015-2020 has revolved around the claims of Fr. Ingo Dollinger, a very elderly, retired German priest. He remarked that not long after the release of the third part of the Secret in June 2000, Cardinal Joseph Ratzinger (Pope Benedict XVI) told him in an in-person conversation that there is still a part that has not been published. The Vatican responded with a direct denial attributed to Pope Emeritus Benedict XVI himself. (See: "Cardinal Ratzinger: 'We Have Not Published the Whole Third Secret of Fatima,'" by Maike Hickson, May 15, 2016, and May 17, 2020, www.spiritdaily.com and www.onepeterfive.com.) See also "Fatima: The Prophecy, the Envelope, the Missing Words, and the Denial of Ratzinger," by Andrea Torniella, May 23, 2016, *Vatican Insider* (*La Stampa*).

24. Maike Hickson, "Robert Moynihan Keeps Fatima Questions Alive," August 8, 2016, https://onepeterfive.com/robert-moynihan-keeps-fatima-questions-alive/.

25. Ibid. The mystery surrounding Cardinal Loris Capovilla is unending. Paul Kengor reports in *A Pope and a President* (p. 611) that Capovilla also said in 2007, "There are not two truths from Fátima and nor is there any Fourth Secret. The text which I read in 1959 is the same that was distributed by the Vatican." Kengor reports Capovilla added, apparently with some annoyance: "I have had enough of theses conspiracy theories. It just isn't true. I read it, I presented it to the Pope and we resealed the envelope." (See "Last Surviving Witness Says Third Fátima Secret is Fully Revealed," *Catholic News Agency*, September 12, 2007.)

26. Kevin Symonds, *On the Third Part of the Secret of Fatima* (St. Louis, MO: En Route Books and Media, 2017), 51.

27. Ibid. The Carmelite Sisters of the Convent of St. Teresa in Coimbra, Portugal, published in 2013 a biography of Sister Lúcia titled, *Um Caminho sob o Olhar da Maria*. It was translated into English and published on April 13, 2015, by the World Apostolate of Fatima, USA, Inc. under the title *A Pathway Under the Gaze of Mary*. Symonds's *On the Third Part of the Secret of Fatima* and *A Pathway Under the Gaze of Mary* are the two

best works in English released on the subject of Fátima in the last two decades. They are highly recommended and invaluable to anyone who wishes to study the subject.

28. Ibid.,53. Symonds reports that the entire letter of Pope Benedict XVI was published by Chiron in *Aletheia* (# 247) on the website TradiNews, dated June 5, 2016.

29. Matthew Culligan Hoffman, "The Third Secret of Fátima and the Hermeneutic of Conspiracy," November 27, 2017, https://www.catholicworldreport.com/2017/11/27/the-third-secret-of-fatima-and-the-hermeneutic-of-conspiracy/.

30. "World War III and Worse? -The Fatima Crusader Interviews Father Paul Kramer," *The Fatima Crusader,* Issue 82, Spring, 2006, 60-61.

31. Soldo, *My Heart Will Triumph*, 155.

32. Ibid., 155-156.

CHAPTER 57: ABORTION: THE GREATEST "ERROR OF RUSSIA"

1. John Thavis, *The Vatican Prophecies* (New York, NY: Viking, 2015), 86. Thavis's account on relics is an excellent read.

2. Symonds, *On the Third Part of the Secret of Fatima*, 378-379.; Bertone, *The Last Secret of Fatima*, 68. Symonds's book contains the complete transcript of the June 26, 2000, Vatican press conference on the third part of the Secret of Fátima. (See Appendix C of his book.) This entire work is a must read for anyone who is serious about understanding this complex issue. The book, as time goes by, will become appreciated for not just its content but its clear and poignant examination of the subject.

3. Homily of His Holiness, Benedict XVI, Thursday, May 13, 2010, given at the Shrine of Our Lady of Fátima, http://www.vatican.va/content/benedict-xvi/en/homilies/2010/documents/hf_ben-xvi_hom_20100513_fatima.html.

4. Peter Seewald, *Benedict XVI-Light of the World: The Pope, The Church and the Signs of the Times* (San Francisco, CA: Ignatius Press, 2010), 165-166. Seewald's interview with the Pope reveals that Benedict's overall interpretation of Fátima's message appears considerably distant from Pope John Paul's understanding of it. This causes one to better grasp two apparent realities. Benedict was not hostile to the visions as perceived, just not in step with the same understanding of what they meant to the Church and the world as many Fátima followers. It also makes him innocent of much of the criticism of his *Theological Commentary*

on the Secret, since his perception of private revelation does not hold, as seen in the full interview with Seewald, any expectance of what he calls "a huge turnaround in the course of history" through Fátima, or perhaps any prophetic revelation.

5. Symonds, *On the Third Part of the Secret of Fatima*, 292.

6. Ratzinger, "The Message of Fátima" published in *The Fatima Prophecies*, 277.

7. Evaristo, "*Two Hours with Sister Lucia*," 36, 37.

8. Robert Moynihan: "Editorial: The Fatima Prophesy," *Inside the Vatican*, Year 8, No. 1, January, 2000, p. 5. On November 18, 1920, the Soviet Union became the first country to legalize abortion. Nazi Germany became the second. On March 9, 1943, Hans Frank legalized abortion in Nazi-occupied territories in Poland. It was for the "lower" races, the Nazi's said.

9. See Abort 73.com for abortion statistics and charts.

10. These statistics come from the *American Life League*. They can be contacted at all.org.

11. Socci, *The Fourth Secret of Fatima*, 217.

12. Ibid.

13. Ibid.

14. Ted Flynn, "Medjugorje and the Great Spiritual Reset," *Signs and Wonders for Our Times*, Vol. 31, Spring/Summer, 2021, 46-54.

15. Laurentin and Rupčić, *Is the Virgin Mary Appearing in Medjugorje*, 73.

16. Ibid.

17. Ibid., 28.

18. Soldo, *My Heart Will Triumph*, 136. Through Father Petar Ljubicic, Mirjana will reveal the Ten Secrets, one by one. The question arose many years ago as to whether the visionaries could reveal the Secrets to anyone beforehand, such as Church authorities, as occurred at La Salette and Fátima. Jacov Marin, a Croatian priest, in his 1989 book, *Queen of Peace Visits Medjugorje*, writes: "None of the Secrets can be revealed by the seers to anyone, not even to the Holy Father. At the suggestion of the local pastor, the visionaries asked Our Lady whether they could at least reveal the Secrets to the Church superiors. Our Lady answered that she herself will tell them when, to whom, and how they should reveal the Secrets." (p. 35). In her 2016 book (p. 187), Mirjana writes that if the Pope asked for the Secrets, she could not say "no".

19. Foley, *The Drama of Medjugorje*, 16.

20. Lucy Rooney SND and Robert Faricy SJ, *Medjugorje Up Close: Mary Speaks to the World* (Chicago, IL: Franciscan Herald Books, 1985), 87.

21. Pelletier, *The Queen of Peace Visits Medjugorje*, 192.

22. Hebert, *Medjugorje: An Affirmation and Defense*, 48,76.

23. René Laurentin, *The Latest News of Medjugorje* (Milford, OH: The Riehle Foundation,1987), 36-37. As Father Bianchi notes, Fátima and Medjugorje share much in common. The children were kidnapped by the authorities; persecuted by atheist governments; shown Hell; given Secrets; and told by the Virgin of her coming Triumph. Medjugorje is to bring to an end Fátima's Secret. But Medjugorje does not exactly share in that end. Its end involves a beginning; the beginning of the future of the world as revealed in parts to all the visionaries. As Father Bubalo notes in his book, "Vicka then told me that the Virgin said: 'So, today you are coming to the end of your first notebook wherein you are recording my narration of the future of the world.'"

24. Soldo, *My Heart Will Triumph*, 84.

25. Kraljevic, *The Apparitions of Our Lady at Medjugorje*, 128.

26. Transcript of Interview with Ivan Dragićević by Fr. Zoran Ostojich in Chicago on November 19, 1989.

27. Medjugorje.Org., *The Medjugorje Messages: 1981-2013*, 261.

28. Medjugorje.Org., *The Medjugorje Messages: 1981-2013*, 270.

29. O'Leary, *Vicka: Her Story*, 48.

30. O'Carroll, *Medjugorje: Facts, Documents and Theology*, 189.

31. Nolan, *Medjugorje: A Time for Truth, A Time for Action*, 10.

32. Pelletier, *The Queen of Peace Visits Medjugorje*, 145.

33. Laurentin and Lejeune, *Messages and Teachings of Mary at Medjugorje*, 204.

CHAPTER 58: THE WINTER OF TOMORROW

1. Rooney and Faricy, *Mary Queen of Peace*, 42.

2. Ibid.

3. Peter Heintz, *A Guide to Apparitions* (Sacramento, CA: Gabriel Press, 1993), 59-67. Ivan spoke at Beauraing on August 24, 1994.

4. Petrisko, *The Fatima Prophecies*, 249.

5. Lúcia, *Fatima in Her Own Words*, 46. Lúcia was very protective of the Secret. This was due to an order from the Virgin herself not to not talk about the Secret given on July 13, 1917. It was a command that was of the greatest concern to her. Then, after Jacinta was exhumed on September 12, 1935, and a picture of her corpse was sent to her from the Bishop, the beginning of the revelation of the Secret begins to unfold. Lúcia responds with a letter to the Bishop, who is inspired to order Lúcia to write down her memories of Jacinta. This leads to Lúcia 's four memoirs. The first, on December 25, 1935, concerns Jacinta. The *Second Memoir* was written between November 7th and the 21st of 1937. The third on August 31, 1941, and the last on December 8th of the same year. Several decades later

she would pen a 5th and a 6th memoir. The revelation of the Secret begins now to see some light, but Lúcia is still reluctant to speak of it, claiming at different times that she was not asked by her superiors or did not have permission from Heaven. But beginning with the *First Memoir* and throughout the next three, the greatest mystery of the 20th century begins to have a public face. One Fátima author, Kevin Symonds, described the early glimpses of the Secret seen in the *First Memoir*, "In said Memoir, Lúcia halts her narrative on Jacinta at one point in order to tell the Bishop that some details touch upon the Secret and she will proceed cautiously. After this note, the narrative on Jacinta largely concerns her processing the vision of Hell and her heroic sacrifices for sinners up to her death in 1920. Still, however Lúcia provides scanty information about the "Secret" of July,1917. In fact, very close to the end of the *First Memoir*, Lúcia relays one of the last words from Jacinta: never to reveal the Secret." Symonds writes that by the *Third Memoir* in 1941, Lúcia begins to tell more, but is still very guarded in exactly what she reveals. In this memoir, though, she states that she believes Heaven gave her permission to reveal the Secret, and so begins to explain there is three parts to it, of which she will reveal the first two. After the 4th memoir, the Bishop was well aware of Lúcia's wish to not disclose the third part of the Secret and he was inclined not to force her. But Lúcia became seriously ill in 1943, and out of concern she might die, he ordered her to write the third part of the Secret, which she did on January 3, 1944. It was then kept by the Bishop in the diocese until 1957, when it was transferred to Rome. For her part, Lúcia remained vigilant in her silence concerning this part of the Secret and its contents. (See Symonds's *On the Third Part of the Secret of Fatima*.)

6. Eph 3:1-6.
7. Joseph Dirvin I.C.M., *St. Catherine Laboure of the Miraculous Medal* (Rockford, IL: TAN Books & Publishers, 1987).
8. Zimdals-Swartz, *Encountering Mary*, 165-189.
9. Ibid.
10. Ibid.
11. Ibid.
12. Ibid.
13. Ibid.
14. Ibid.
15. Ibid.
16. Ibid.
17. Ibid.
18. Ibid.
19. Ibid.
20. Ibid.

21. Ibid.
22. Ibid.
23. Ibid.
24. Ibid. While the apparitions of the Virgin Mary at La Salette received full approval of the Church, the Secret of La Salette did not. The contents of the Secret, however, continued to be circulated, with eventually Mélanie herself releasing a version. This version of Mélanie Calvat's secret message is actually what is known today as the "Secret of La Salette." This is because Mélanie's long secret message contained the apocalyptic language only, not Maxim's. As time went by, the Church moved to silence all versions of the Secret by issuing official Church decrees ordering the faithful to "refrain from treating and discussing the matter in any form." The last decree came in 1923, more than seventy-five years after the apparition at La Salette. To this day, however, the Secret of La Salette still circulates among the faithful and beyond.
25. Brown, *The Day Will Come*, 49.
26. Abbey Francois Trochu, *Saint Bernadette Soubirous 1844-1879* (Rockford. IL: TAN Books and Publishers, 1957), 89-100.
27. Pelletier, *The Queen of Peace Visits Medjugorje*, 143. The magical effects of Mary's secrets that Father Pelletier speaks of is undeniable. Investigative journalist Randall Sullivan, in questioning Mirjana about the Secrets, says she told him that what makes Secrets necessary is "part of the Secrets." The ultimate Catch-22, Sullivan says he thought to himself.
28. Laurentin and Lejeune, *Messages and Teachings of Mary at Medjugorje*, 55.
29. Ibid, 240. Laurentin writes that the messages of Medjugorje have an "apocalyptic propensity." (See Laurentin's *The Apparitions of Medjugorje Prolonged.*)
30. Rooney and Faricy, *Medjugorje Up Close*, 87.
31. Ibid.
32. Ibid.
33. Ibid.
34. Ibid.
35. Ibid.
36. Ibid.
37. Ibid.
38. Ibid.
39. Ibid, 90-91.
40. Laurentin and Lejeune, *Messages and Teachings of Mary at Medjugorje*, 194.
41. Craig, *Spark from Heaven*, 104.

42. *Queen of Peace Newsletter*, Vol. 1, No. 3 (Coraopolis, PA, Pittsburgh Center for Peace, 1988), p.5.

43. Medjugorje.Org, *The Medjugorje Messages: 1981-2013*, 88. In essence, at Medjugorje, the revelations reveal a countdown has begun to transition the world from one era to another—from an era of unprecedented evil to an era of relative harmony. The transitory stage is referred to as a "period of grace" in the revelations. The many special graces emanating from Medjugorje throughout the world are meant to illuminate God's call "to change willingly." This call, which comes from God's love, also harbors his approaching justice, the consequence of refusing "to change willingly."

44. Laurentin and Lejeune, *Messages and Teachings of Mary at Medjugorje*,269.

45. Medjugorje.Org, *The Medjugorje Messages:1981-2013*, 195.

46. John Paul II, Apostolic Letter, *Tertio Millenio Adveniente*, 1994.

47. Medjugorje.org., *The Medjugorje Messages: 1981-2013*, 82.

CHAPTER 59: THERE WILL BE THREE WARNINGS

1.   Lk 1:15.

2.   Soldo, *My Heart Will Triumph*, 327.

3.   Sabrina Smetko, "The Time in Which We Live is a Time of Decision," *Medjugorje Magazine*, Vol. 17, No.1, Spring, 2007, p. 26. Originally printed in *Glas Mira*. Translated by Marianne Sajn. Also see Mirjana's book, *My Heart Will Triumph*, p. 337.

4.   Soldo, *My Heart Will Triumph*, 148. Many false visionaries, even religious and those who claim ties to Medjugorje, have called for physical places of refuge and to accumulate goods. Mary has made clear through her authentic voices that the safest refuge is her Immaculate Heart, nothing else.

5.   1 Thes 5:2.

6.   Soldo, *My Heart Will Triumph*, 191.

7.   Lefevbre-Filleau, J.P., *L'Affaire Bernadette Soubirous*, Cerf, 1972, p.152, Ivonides, L., *Fatima, da ili ne? (Fatima, Yes or No)*, Zagreb,1997, p.17. Both footnotes are cited according to D. Klanac, *Medjugorje: Responses aux Objections*, op.cit., p. 66., as documented in *Once Again the Truth About Medjugorje* by Dr. Ljudevit Rupčić and Dr. Viktor Nuić, p. 97.

8.   De Marchi, *Fatima: From the Beginning*, 169.

9.   Ibid.

10. Transcript of interview with Father Svetozar Kraljevic at the Franciscan Monastery in Ljubuski, Yugoslavia, circa 1985, 1-2.

11. Soldo, *My Heart Will Triumph*, 101. Father Rupčić was imprisoned by the Communists in 1945, 1947, and again from 1952 through 1956.

12. Ibid.
13. *Center for Peace Newsletter*, Concord, MA: February, 1986.
14. Laurentin and Rupčić, *Is the Virgin Mary Appearing at Medjugorje?* 17.
15. Laurentin, *Ten Years of Apparitions*, 124.
16. Laurentin and Rupčić, *Is the Virgin Mary Appearing at Medjugorje?* 20.
17. Laurentin and Lejeune, *Messages and Teachings of Mary at Medjugorje*, 7.
18. Ibid., 146-147, 354-355; Rupčić and Nuić, *Once Again, The Truth About Medjugorje*, 63.
19. Laurentin and Lejeune, *Messages and Teachings of Mary at Medjugorje*, 145.
20. Rupčić and Nuić, *Once Again, The Truth About Medjugorje*, 169.
21. Alonso, *The Secret of Fatima*, 108-110.
22. Heintz, *A Guide to Apparitions*, 61.
23. Vlašić and Barbarić, *Open Your Hearts to Mary Queen of Peace*, 12. Establishing an accurate timeline on the revelation of the Secrets is challenging. Jacov Marin in his *Queen of Peace Visits Medjugorje*, writes, "Our Lady promised the visionaries that she will reveal ten secrets to each of them. The first three Secrets she told them when they were *all* together. By the beginning of September, 1982, Ivanka received eight Secrets all together, and of the remaining visionaries, some had received seven and some had received six Secrets. On the Feast of the Assumption, 1982, the other seers received the Secret which was the eighth one for Ivanka." If Jacov Marin's timeline is accurate, this would mean the Secrets were being revealed very early in the apparitions, before Mirjana returned to Sarajevo at the end of August. (Mirjana reports in her book [p. 98] that she was ordered to Čitluk, locked in a holding cell, and then driven three hours to her parents' home in Sarajevo by the authorities near the end of August, 1981.)
24. Connell, *Queen of the Cosmos*, 15.
25. Laurentin and Lejeune, *Messages and Teachings of Mary at Medjugorje*, 216.
26. Ibid., 50.
27. Laurentin and Rupčić, *Is the Virgin Mary Appearing at Medjugorje?* 142-144. Rupčić and Nuić report there were other written letters to the pope besides the December 2, 1983 letter. See *Once Again, The Truth About Medjugorje*, p. 46.

CHAPTER 60: WHILE THERE IS TIME

1. Alonso, *The Secret of Fatima*, 68-71. Lúcia wrote an initial draft of the first two parts of the Secret in 1927.
2. Francois, *Fatima: Tragedy and Triumph*, 24.

3.   Unpublished original transcript of Fr. Rupčić interview of the six visionaries in December, 1982. It was titled: "*Questions Asked of the Six Visionaries in Medjugorje, Yugoslavia*." See Laurentin's, *Is the Virgin Mary Appearing at Medjugorje?* (pp.42-62), for the edited version of the same interview.

4.   Kraljevic, *The Apparitions of Our Lady at Medjugorje*, 121-140. This interview with Mirjana was published in its entirety in the June, July, August, and September issues of the *Medjugorje Herald* in 1988. Father Vlašić found himself at the eye of the storm not long after his interview with Mirjana—not because of the interview, but due to everything that was going on in Medjugorje at that time. Criticized by the bishop for what was unfolding in the village, he would be transferred out of Medjugorje to a parish in Vitina nine miles down the road in July of 1984. But the overwhelming mystery of the Secrets was upon Vlašić. He understood that the world and the Church were at a crossroad in history: "Look, the experience at Medjugorje is different to that of Fátima and Lourdes," Vlašić told Fr. Kraljevic in an interview with him, "As you know, Our Lady is appearing here every day and has been doing so for nearly thirty-nine months. It is a pilgrimage. At Fátima, the apparitions were only once a month for a number of months and only several times at Lourdes. Here it is a pilgrimage, a path, as I feel quite sure that the time has come in which Our Lady will help the Church to come out of exile." Vlašić's ears were the first to pick up the apparent magnitude of the implications of Medjugorje and the Secrets, and it appears from everything that unfolded with him, the extremely amiable priest was never the same after his time there. Fr. Vlašić was laicized in 2009 and, primarily because he reportedly continued to carry out priestly activities, was excommunicated in 2020. The critics of Medjugorje in the media seized upon this news and immediately attempted to use it to discredit the apparitions even though Vlašić had not been involved there since 1984, some 36 years prior.

5.   Sister Emmanuel, "Sister Emmanuel's Medjugorje Network," *Medjugorje Gebetsaktion*, No. 30, Vienna, Austria, October 1993, p. 31.

6.   Kraljevic, *The Apparitions of Our Lady in Medjugorje*,141-150.

7.   Marin, *Queen of Peace in Medjugorje*, 109.

8.   Unpublished interviews with the Franciscan priests at Medjugorje by a French journalist in 1984 who chose not to put his name on the interviews.

9.   Meyer, *Portrait of Mary*, 63.

10. Bubalo, *A Thousand Encounters with the Blessed Virgin Mary in Medjugorje*, xiii. All of the visionaries, it was written early on, have been told by Mary of some of the events that occurred in her own earthly life. It is unclear at this point which of them, like Vicka, are going to release what they have learned in a book, or some other type of report. Vicka says she

was given "something like a complete biography of Mary." Some of it was shown to her, as Mirjana often says, "like a movie, in pictures, as in a film."

11. Ibid, 152-155.
12. Laurentin, *Medjugorje: 12 Years Later*, 120-121.
13. Medjugorje. Org., *The Medjugorje Messages: 1981-2013*, 151. Message of June 25,1991. This message was given by Mary just two months before her singular message announcing that she would fulfill at Medjugorje "the secrets I began at Fátima." Perhaps, there is more than what meets the eye here. The Medjugorje messages from May through December of 1991 are of particular significance in understanding Medjugorje in terms of its mission to fulfill Fátima.
14. Brown, *The Final Hour*, 251.
15. Connell, *The Visions of the Children*, xvii-xviii.
16. Ibid., 23.
17. Hebert, *Medjugorje: An Affirmation and a Defense*, 43.
18. Johnston, *Fatima: The Great Sign*, 8.
19. Ibid., 70.; Socci., *The Fourth Secret of Fatima*, 8. See also Chapter 55 of my book, *Call of the Ages*, for a more in-depth look at this question.
20. Alonso, *The Secret of Fatima*, 170.
21. "Fatima Visionary Predicted 'Final Battle' Would Be Over Marriage, Family," December 31, 2016, https://www.catholicnewsagency.com/news/fatima-visionary-predicted-final-battle-would-be-over-marriage-family-17760.
22. Diane Monagna, "(Exclusive) Cardinal Caffarra: 'What Sr. Lucia Wrote to Me Is Being Fulfilled Today,'"May 19, 2017, https://aleteia.org/2017/05/19/exclusive-cardinalcaffarra-what-sr-lucia-wrote-to-me-is-being-fulfilled-today/.
23. Ibid.
24. Jonathan Liedl, "Back to the Sixties? Pontifical Academy for Life Pushes for Departure From Doctrine on Contraceptive Sex", July 13, 2022, National Catholic Register, https://www.ncregister.com/news/analysis-pontificalacademy-for-life-pushes-to-changechurchs-opposition-to-contraception.

CHAPTER 61: THE POWER OF SATAN WILL BE BROKEN

1. Thull, ed., *What They Say About Medjugorje*, 121-122. Draga Ivanković is a cousin to three of the visionaries. She lived in Bijakovići at the time of the first apparition.
2. The visionaries speak often about the joys of the afterlife. They speak of the virtues of the next world over this one. Spoken by them in all sincerity, their remarks, however, inadvertently sometime add to the apocalyptic

suspicions of readers or listeners. Some have said they get the feeling that the visionaries know the harsh future, and so this is why they stress the positive view of the next life.

3. Connell, *Queen of the Cosmos*, 30.

4. Sullivan, *Miracle Detective*, 189.

5. Kraljevic, *The Apparitions of Our Lady at Medjugorje*, 126. There is no specific message directly attributable to the Virgin Mary at Medjugorje concerning the "First Secret" breaking the power of Satan. In the December 16, 1983, letter to Pope John Paul II, the report states that Mirjana said that the Virgin Mary told her, "This century is under the power of the Devil, but when the Secrets confided to you come to pass, his power will be destroyed." The original source of the understanding that the "First Secret" will end Satan's power is from Mirjana's interview of January 10, 1983, that was initially published in Fr. Kraljević's book (p. 126). In this interview, Mirjana states that the Devil "will rule until the first Secret is unfolded." In an interview with Archbishop Frane Franic of Split in Medjugorje on January 24, 1985, it is again repeated that the Devil's power will end with the unfolding of the First Secret: "His power will end when the Secret comes true." Confirmation of this disclosure by Mirjana is found again eight years later in an interview that Janice T. Connell did with Mirjana for her book, *Queen of the Cosmos* (p. 23). Mirjana tells Connell that Satan will rule "until the First Secret is unfolded." Several years after this, in another interview with Connell for her second book on Medjugorje, *Visions of the Children* (p. 67), Mirjana again tells Connell that "the First Secret will break the power of Satan." Connell is seen to be clear with this exact understanding, as she repeats it in a question to Marija in the same book (p. 145): "Marija, Mirjana told me that one of the reasons Satan is so aggressive right now is that he has little time left since his power will be broken when the "First Secret" happens. Will life be more pleasant after the "First Secret" occurs?" For the record, no one knows when the "century of Satan" began or when it will end. But it is, according to Mirjana's words, not an officially designated calendar century, such as the 20th century. This is found to be clearly understood by Mirjana's answer to a question posed during her January 20, 1983, interview. Question: "You mean the century until the year 2000, or generally speaking?" Mirjana: "Generally, *part* of which is in the twentieth century, until the First Secret is unfolded. The Devil will rule till then." With this answer— "part of which is in the twentieth century"—Mirjana was inadvertently revealing in1983, although not understood by anyone at the time, that the Ten Secrets would not begin to be revealed until at least after the year 2000. (See *The Apparitions of Our Lady at Medjugorje*, by Fr. Svetozar Kraljevic, p. 138.)

6. Ibid., 124.

7. Symonds, *Pope Leo XIII and the Prayer to St. Michael*, 1-264. There is no known definitive Vatican documentation on Pope Leo XIII's reported vision involving the Devil. But it is often repeated in Catholic publications, especially Marian publications. (See *Soul Magazine*, May 1, 1984.) However, the *Prayer to St. Michael*, which is often said to have originated from Leo's vision, *is* directly attributable to him and was authorized to be said after every Mass. The *Prayer to St. Michael* continued to be recited after Mass through the remainder of the 19th century and into the 20th century until September 26, 1964, when the Congregation of the Sacred Liturgy decreed: *"The Last Gospel is omitted; the Leonine prayers after Mass are no longer to be said."* (See Chapter Four, note N. 27, in Kevin Symonds's book, *Pope Leo XIII and the Prayer to St. Michael*, for a summary on the question of Pope Leo's vision. This book is the only known work on the subject. It is well researched, and highly recommended.)

8. Laurentin and Rupčić, *Is the Virgin Mary Appearing in Medjugorje?* 142-144.

9. Kraljevic, *The Apparitions of Our Lady at Medjugorje*, 126.

10. Laurentin and Lejeune, *Messages and Teachings of Mary at Medjugorje*, 194; Soldo, *My Heart Will Triumph*, 136.

11. Soldo, *My Heart Will Triumph*, 137. As noted, Mirjana has stated that her annual apparition on her birthday, March 18th, has nothing to do with her birthday. The real reason for that date, she says, will eventually become known with unfolding of the Secrets. (See Chapter 66 of this book for a more indepth look at this whole issue.)

12. Laurentin, *The Apparitions at Medjugorje Prolonged*, 25.

13. Soldo, *My Heart Will Triumph*, 191. With the addition of the 2nd of the month apparitions in 1987, Mirjana would now be receiving a total of 13 apparitions a year. Perhaps, some would say, a fitting number in lieu of the Medjugorje connection to Fátima.

14. Rooney and Faricy, *Mary Queen of Peace*, 93.

15. Ibid.

16. Laurentin, *The Apparition at Medjugorje Prolonged*, 25.

17. Ibid.

18. Craig, *Spark from Heaven*, 165.

19. Laurentin, *The Apparitions at Medjugorje Prolonged*, 25.

20. Ibid., 26-27. The twelve dates Mirjana experienced locutions or apparitions in 1985 were: end of February; March 18; March 19; June 1; June 15; July 19; July 27; August 11; August 17; September 13; October 25; and December 25. In her book (p.191), Mirjana states that her locutions continued throughout 1985. This could mean there were perhaps more than what was documented by the Franciscans.

21. Thull, ed., *What They Say About Medjugorje?* 34.

22. Laurentin and Lejeune, *Messages and Teachings of Mary at Medjugorje*, 271-272.
23. Laurentin, *The Apparitions at Medjugorje Prolonged*, 29-30; "Maria Konigin des Friedens," *Medjugorje Gebetsaktion*, 1986, No.2, 25.
24. Rooney and Faricy, *Medjugorje Journal*, 9.
25. Ibid., 34.
26. Laurentin, *The Apparitions at Medjugorje Prolonged*, 30.
27. Rooney and Faricy, *Medjugorje Journal*, 39.
28. Vlašić and Barbarić, *I Beseech You, Listen to My Messages and Live Them* (Milan, Italy: The Association of the Friends of Medjugorje, 1987), 23.
29. Rooney and Faricy, *Medjugorje Journal*, 136.
30. Thull, ed., *What They Say About Medjugorje*, 841.
31. Soldo, *My Heart Will Triumph*, 121.
32. Sullivan, *The Miracle Detective*, 189.
33. Brown, *The Tower of Light*, 208- 303; Brown, *The Final Hour*, 246; "Seer at Famous Apparition Gave Enthralling Hints of What May Be Her First 'Secrets,'" *Spirit Daily*, June 24, 2011, www.spiritdaily.org/mirjanainterview.htm.
34. Brown, *The Day Will Come*, 223; Brown, *The Tower of Light*, 303-305; "Seer at Famous Apparition Gave Enthralling Hints of What May Be Her First Secrets,"; *Spirit Daily*, June 24, 2011, www.spiritdaily.org/mirjanainterview.htm. The Virgin Mary gave Mirjana the last indications of the realization of the First Secret on June 4, 1986, according to the June, 1986, *Queen of Peace Newsletter* of St. Laurent, Quebec, Canada.
35. Fr. Petar Ljubicic, "The Secrets," *Medjugorje Herald*, Volume 3, N.2, February 1989, p.16.
36. Connell, *The Visions of the Children*, 145.

CHAPTER 62: AN APOCALYPTIC MOOD

1. Ivan Kordic, *The Apparitions of Medjugorje* (Zagreb, Croatia: K. Kresimir, 1994), 56. Kordic's quote of Pervan is out of K. Knotzinger's, *Antwort auf Medjugorje*, p. 191.
2. Wintz, "The Secret of Medjugorje," *St. Anthony's Messenger*, August, 1988, 33.
3. Sullivan, *The Miracle Detective 191; Queen of Peace Newsletter*, Vol. 1, No 3, p 5. Over the centuries, many visionaries have received startling revelations and have been asked to convey them to the world. Each does so in their own way, according to how they interpret what they have received. Though it is important to take seriously what true visionaries reveal, it must be remembered that their personal subjectivity is always involved, as every visionary sees, comprehends, and communicates their visions and revelations differently. "Whatever is received," wrote the Dominican friar St. Thomas Aquinas

in the thirteenth century, "is received according to the measure of the receiver." (Cf. *Summa Theologiae*, 1a, q.75, a.5; 3a, q.5). This understanding is especially significant when dealing with prophecy, because prophecy is not etched in stone. Father René Laurentin explains, "Predictions, even those inspired by God, are not infallible because they are subjected to human confusion on the part of the seers. The first Christians waited for the return of Christ in their lifetime, and He has not yet returned." Medjugorje, adds Laurentin, is especially challenging because of the Ten Secrets, a fact that he believes must be kept in perspective. "The Secrets are not the essence of the message." writes Laurentin. "They are prophecies, words given in the name of God for the reality of the world and its future. Prophecies and forecasts have always played an important role, in order to guide the lives of the people of God—in the Bible and in our days—with discontinuance. But one needs to be careful. Predictions are not made in order to satisfy one's curiosity. They are always given in clear obscurity, or light and shade, that has the function of forecasting, a guide to the future. In itself, it is of the future, but a provision which cannot be history before history exists. Further, it is incomprehensible before existing, according to its cultural context."

4. Vlašić and Barbarić, *Pray with Your Heart* (Milan, Italy: The Association of the Friends of Medjugorje, 1986), 185-186.
5. Ibid., 212.
6. Connell, *Queen of the Cosmos*, 144.
7. Wintz, "The Secret of Medjugorje," *St. Anthony's Messenger*, p.36.
8. Vlašić and Barbarić, *Pray with Your Heart*, 162-163.
9. Ibid., 168-169.
10. Ibid., 173-175.
11. I have seen at least four versions of the account of the October 25, 1985, apparition/vision. Fr. Laurentin's account, which I used, was obtained from the official parish logue kept by the Franciscans.
12. Connell, *The Visions of the Children*, 67-68.
13. Ibid. A man named Brother David Lopez from Texas visited Medjugorje in August of 1987 and reported that while there on August 15th, he received a locution from the Virgin Mary that spoke of the "Three Days of Darkness." At the time, and for years after, this purported revelation continued to experience wide spread circulation. Brother David died in February, 1988. (For more information see *The Michael Journal*, Rougemont, Canada, January-February, 1990.)
14. Michael H. Brown, *Fear of Fire* (Palm Coast, FL: *Spirit Daily Publishing*, 2013), 103.
15. Connell, *Visions of the Children*, 143.
16. June Klins, "Ivan's Talk," *Spirit of Medjugorje*, Vol. 17, No. 9, September, 2004, p.3. From Ivan's talk given in Mentor, Ohio, April 20, 2004.

17. June Klins, "Ivan Speaks of Family Prayer", *Spirit of Medjugorje*, May, 2009, p. 3. Klins article is from a talk given by Ivan in Chagrin Falls, Ohio, on April 26, 2008.

18. Klins, *The Best of the Spirit of Medjugorje, Vol. I*, 28. This quote is from a talk given by Ivan in Windsor, Ohio, on September 8, 1996.

19. Linda Rogers recorded and transcribed this talk given by Ivan in Seattle, Washington, on October 29, 1997. It was published in the *Children of Mary Center for Peace* newsletter in November, 1997, and reprinted in the *Spirit of Medjugorje* newsletter of February, 2006.

20. The first stage of the Russian Revolution took place from February 24 to 28, 1917. At this time, the Romanov monarchy of Czar Nicholas II was overthrown and replaced by a provisional government formed by the Duma, an elected semi-representative body in Russia. The October Revolution, the second stage of the Russian Revolution, is officially known in Soviet history as the Great October Socialist Revolution. It is also called the October Uprising, the October Coup, the Bolshevik Revolution, the Bolshevik Coup, and Red October. It successfully overthrew the provisional government of the Duma. The October 25th date of the Bolshevik Revolution in Russia is according to the Julian calendar which was still in effect in the country at the time. According to the Gregorian calendar used in the West, the date of the revolution was November 7, 1917. Curiously, 'thirteen days' separate the dates of the different calendars, which again reminds of Fátima. On February 14, 1918, the Communists changed Russia from the Julian calendar to the Gregorian calendar pursuant to a decree signed by Lenin on January 24, 1918. The Orthodox Church, however, stubbornly retained the Julian calendar. In 1923, the government dropped both calendars and a new calendar was introduced in which the weeks were changed and religious feasts and holy days were replaced by five national public holidays associated with the October Revolution. The October 25th date appears at other memorable times in Catholic Church history. One of the most significant is that it is the date that St. Bernadette Soubirous made her religious vows, October 25, 1866. (October 25th is also the date of my own birthday, which may attribute to my fascination with the date and this matter in general.)

21. Sullivan, *The Miracle Detective*, 189.

22. Wayne Weible, *The Last Apparition: How it Will Change the World* (Hiawassee, GA: New Hope Press, 2013), 208-212.

23. Thomas W. Petrisko, *The Miracle of the Illumination of All Consciences* (Pittsburgh, PA: St. Andrews Productions, 2000).

24. June Klins, ed., "Fr. Petar Speaks About the Secrets," *Spirit of Medjugorje*, Vol. 20, No.7, July, 2007. Transcript of a panel discussion at the Notre Dame Conference on Medjugorje held on May 27, 2007.

CHAPTER 63: THIS WILL CHANGE EVERYTHING

1. Laurentin and Lejeune, *Messages and Teachings of Mary at Medjugorje*, 53. At Fátima, the third part of the Secret was mostly hidden and the rest of the Secret revealed. At Medjugorje, the Third Secret (The Great Sign) is relatively revealed, and the rest of the Secrets hidden.

2. Ibid., 169.

3. Ibid., 54.

4. Rooney and Faricy, *Mary Queen of Peace*, 97.

5. The prediction concerning the Adriatic Sea circulated far and wide during the 1990s. Some even claimed one of the visionaries said it. There is no evidence of such a statement on record. A man named Mate Sago who lived in Bijakovići and died in 1979, two years before the apparitions, predicted that the Gospa was coming and someday the town would be a holy place where hotels would be constructed for the many visitors. He foretold there would be a large lake in Medjugorje, so big it would have boats moored in it. Mate also envisioned that hundreds of steps would run up Podbrdo, like a staircase in the hillside, which has virtually taken shape today from all the pilgrim traffic up the hill over the years. While it did not directly concern the Great Sign, Mary Craig, in her book, *Spark from Heaven*, writes that Padre Pio reportedly told a group of pilgrims from Mostar that the Blessed Mother will "soon be visiting your land." Craig conjectures that possibly this prophecy inspired the painting (see p. 564) that hung above the main door in St James at the time of the commencing of the apparitions. Painted in 1974 by a parishioner, seven years before the apparitions, it depicts the Blessed Virgin Mary in a white robe, blue girdle, white veil, and blue cloak floating in the sky above the church and the village of Medjugorje. In the background, on the Madonna's left side, can be seen Mt. Krizevac with the massive cross at its peak.

6. Bruce Cyr, *After the Warning* (Alberta, Canada: Bruce A. Cyr, 2013), 142.

7. Rooney and Faricy, *Mary Queen of Peace*, 97.

8. Mulligan, *Medjugorje: What's Happening?* 212.

9. Ibid.

10. Connell, *The Visions of the Children*, 146.

11. Bubalo, *A Thousand Encounters with the Blessed Virgin Mary in Medjugorje*, 158.

12. Ibid.

13. Laurentin and Rupčić, Is *the Virgin Mary Appearing at Medjugorje?* 142-143.

14. Bubalo, *A Thousand Encounters with the Blessed Virgin Mary in Medjugorje*, 158.

15. Ibid., 158-159.

16. Connell, *Queen of the Cosmos*, 30.

17. Bubalo, *A Thousand Encounters with the Blessed Virgin Mary in Medjugorje*, 158.
18. Ibid.
19. Connell, *Queen of the Cosmos*, 30.
20. Brown, *The Day Will Come*, 229.
21. Connell, *Queen of the Cosmos*, 78; Kraljevic, *The Apparitions of Our Lady at Medjugorje*, 59. There is reportedly a promise from Mary to the visionaries that when the Great Sign appears a man from the parish will have his leg miraculously healed. He had it severely injured in a farm accident.
22. Bubalo, *A Thousand Encounters with the Blessed Virgin Mary in Medjugorje?*, 158.
23. Ibid., 159. In Vlašić's and Barbarić's book, *Open Your Hearts to Mary Queen of Peace*, it is reported on April 22, 1984, that five of the six children know the date on which the Sign will occur. By this time, all six were certainly aware of the coming of the Great Sign on Podbrdo. It is not known which of the visionaries reported to not know the date, or if known, perhaps simply chose not to disclose such an awareness.
24. Ibid.
25. Laurentin and Rupčić, *Is the Virgin Mary Appearing at Medjugorje?* 143.
26. Ibid.
27. Connell, *The Visions of the Children*, 108.
28. Ibid.
29. Ibid., 146.
30. Ibid., 145.
31. Ibid., 146; Connell, *Queen of the Cosmos*, 21.
32. Connell, *The Visions of the Children*, 108.
33. Soldo, *My Heart Will Triumph*, 120.
34. Ibid.
35. Ibid.
36. Ibid.
37. Ibid.
38. Michael Brown, *The Tower of Light: The 1990 Prophecy* (Palm Coast, FL: Spirit Daily Publishing, 2007), 298-305.
39. June Klins, ed., "The Period of Conversion and the Ten Secrets," *The Spirit of Medjugorje*, Vol. 22, No. 8, August, 2009, p. 6-7. (Transcript of radio broadcast by *Radio Maria Italia* from Medjugorje, January 2, 2008.)
40. Bubalo, *A Thousand Encounters with the Blessed Virgin Mary in Medjugorje*, 156-159.
41. Brown, *The Day Will Come*, 225. Brown writes: "She (Vicka) believes she'll see the Virgin less than an hour before the Sign appears..."
42. June Klins, ed., "The Period of Conversion and the Ten Secrets," *Spirit of Medjugorje*, Vol. 22, No. 8, August, 2009, p. 6-7. (Transcript of radio broadcast by *Radio Maria Italia* from Medjugorje, January 2, 2008.)
43. Laurentin, *Medjugorje-Thirteen Years Later*, 27, 117.

44. *Medjugorje Network*, August 1, 1995.

45. Emmanuel, *Medjugorje, The 90s*, 93.

46. Ibid.

47. Michael Brown, *The Tower of Light: The 1990 Prophecy*, 298-305. According to two of the visionaries, Vicka and Maria, the Great Sign will occur at a time when belief and interest in Medjugorje will have extremely waned. Marija reportedly told Father Lube Kurtosis, O.F.M., an assistant pastor at Medjugorje who arrived after Father Slavko died, that even the most loyal will become skeptical: "The Sign on Apparition Hill will appear when even the most convinced believers doubt in the authenticity of the messages." (See Father James Mulligan's *Medjugorje: What's Happening?*)

48. Helen Sarcevic, (translator), "A Talk by Petar Ljubicic: April 22, 1989", *Queen of Peace Journal: Medjugorje Center of Poughkeepsie, New York*, No. XI, December, 1989, 8-9.

49. Laurentin, *The Apparitions at Medjugorje Prolonged*, 32.

50. Unpublished parts of the original transcript of the interview of Mirjana on January 10, 1983, which was originally published in books by Father Kraljevic and Father Laurentin, contained footnotes of observations concerning Mirjana's testimony that day. The final, published form of the interview in the two books is an edited version that can be seen to be missing these notes, some of which are insightful and valuable in better understanding Mirjana's words and experiences. A second interview, dated June 16, 1984, is also part of this original transcript. It is titled: "How Mirjana Prays Now that Our Lady Has Stopped Appearing to Her." It discusses her daily prayer life and her advice to people who write to her, such as a man from Sarajevo who could not walk and was partially healed through "Mirjana's prayers to Our Lady for help."

51. Fr. Tomislav Vlašić, *Our Lady Queen of Peace, Queen of Apostles is Teaching us the Way to the Truth and Life at Medjugorje, Yugoslavia* (East Sussex, England: Peter Batty / Pika Print Limited, 1984), 10.

52. Laurentin, *Eight Years*, 102.

53. Ibid. Father Rupčić's second interview with the visionaries—a repetition of the same 60 questions as previous—conducted in 1987, was published in its entirety in Father René Laurentin's 1989 book, *Eight Years: Reconciliation, Analysis, the Future* (pp. 102-130). Rupčić was indeed one of Medjugorje's greatest advocates and defenders. Father Ljudevit Rupčić died on June 25, 2003, the 22nd anniversary of the Medjugorje apparitions.

54. Ibid., 118.

55. Ibid.

56. Thavis, *The Vatican Prophecies*, 57.

57. Kraljevic, *The Apparitions of Our Lady at Medjugorje*, 148; *Medjugorje Torino*, July,1995.

58. Ibid. Laurentin says Mirjana once told him, "After the Sign will be shown, one will be obliged to believe." It was an indication to Laurentin of the confidence the visionaries have in the overwhelming impact the Sign will have on those with faith. (See Laurentin, *The Apparitions at Medjugorje Prolonged*.)
59. Connell, *The Visions of the Children*, 107.
60. Rupčić, "The Silenced Situation of the Catholic Church in Bosnia and Hercegovina," 22.
61. Thull, ed., *What They Say About Medjugorje*, 171-172.
62. Ibid.
63. Ibid. The December 16-17, 1984, interview with Archbishop Frane Franic was also published and distributed by the Center for Peace in Boston as a special 13-page report in 1985.
64. Connell, *Queen of the Cosmos*, 20-21.
65. John Brockman, ed., *This Will Change Everything* (New York, NY: Harper Perennial, 2009).

CHAPTER 64: "I KNOW THE FUTURE OF THE WORLD"

1. Laurentin and Lejeune, *Messages and Teachings of Mary at Medjugorje*, 291.
2. Thull, ed., *What They Say About Medjugorje*, 277. Thull quotes British Theologian Fr. Richard Foley, "The ten secrets being confided to the visionaries out-number anything given in other apparitions." There is a possible exception, although somewhat circumspect. In Gala, Croatia, apparitions were reported beginning on August 27, 1983. One visionary reported receiving 12 secrets, others 10. (See Brown, *The Day Will Come*, 267.)
3. Sullivan, *The Miracle Detective*, 189. The Virgin, as noted, has continued over the years to speak with Mirjana about the Secrets and to give her public messages. However, on the 2nd of the month in June, 2006, Mirjana stated, "Our Lady did not give a message." Mirjana said Mary explained some things that are supposed to happened and that her face reflected concern.
4. Connell, *Queen of the Cosmos*, 53.
5. Connell, *Queen of the Cosmos*, 44.
6. Vlašić and Barbarić, *Open Your Hearts to Mary Queen of Peace*, 12.
7. Laurentin, *Eight Years*, 95.
8. Ibid., 93.
9. Ibid., 94.
10. Connell, *Queen of the Cosmos*, 45.
11. Ibid.

12. Ibid., 46. Ivanka's statement, "I know the future of the world—not just my own history —but the future of the world," is revealing. Janice Connell has written that Ivanka is God's choice for a "great project" involving the future. Likewise, many of Ivanka's comments also appear to hint of something ahead for her that is of significance with regards to the future and the Secrets. Ivanka was the first to see Mary on day one, and on day two. She was also the first to speak to her. This was of significance. It must be remembered that although Mirjana is the visionary who will announce the Ten Secrets, all six are receiving them. This is for a reason. It is not far-fetched to believe that each of them have some role to play in the unfolding of the Secrets that has not yet been revealed. Some of Vicka's later interviews appear to allude of this possibility. Perhaps Mirjana, due to unforeseen circumstances, may not be the one who reveals the Secrets. In her book, she speculates on different scenarios arising that can change our present expectations and assumptions. Mirjana went so far as to write, "Of course, there is no guarantee I will be alive when the Secrets are revealed." (See *My Heart Will Triumph*, p. 327)

13. Ibid., 48.

14. Ibid.

15. René Laurentin, *Seven Years of Apparitions: Latest News from Medjugorje* (Milford, OH: The Riehle Foundation, 1988), 5.

16. Medjugorje.Org., *The Medjugorje Messages: 1981-2013*, 264.

17. Laurentin, *Seven Years of Apparitions*, 5.

18. Laurentin, *Eight Years*, 2.

19. Ibid.

20. Ibid., 95.

21. Medjugorje.Org, *The Medjugorje Messages: 1981-2013*, 261.

22. Ibid., 264.

23. Ibid.

24. Ibid., 261.

25. Ibid., 263.

26. Connell, *Queen of the Cosmos*, 47.

27. Laurentin, *Eight Years*, 95.

28. Laurentin and Rupčić, *Is the Virgin Mary Appearing at Medjugorje?* 54.

29. Ibid.

30. Ibid.

31. Ibid.

32. Bubalo, *A Thousand Encounters with the Blessed Virgin Mary in Medjugorje*, xiii.

33. Laurentin and Rupčić, *Is the Virgin Mary Appearing in Medjugorje*, 54.

34. Brown, *The Final Hour*, 249. Author Michael Brown quotes Ivan, from an August 14, 2012, *Radio Maria* interview with Father Livio Fanzaga, as saying, "When the prophetic Secrets of the Blessed Mother are revealed in

Medjugorje, the Catholic Church will find itself in a great ordeal, as much for the world as the faithful, and a little of this suffering has already started." (See Brown's *Fear of Fire*, p. 93).

35. Weible, *Medjugorje: The Last Apparition*, 213.

36. Laurentin, *The Apparitions at Medjugorje Prolonged*, 97. Maria Pavlović told Father Rupčić that "all her Secrets concern the world." This is the same as what Mirjana has stated about her Secrets. However, some early statements by the visionaries, particularly Vicka, are on record as saying that they have received secrets that are personal, or not just for themselves, but for the Franciscans and others.

37. Laurentin and Rupčić, *Is the Virgin Mary Appearing at Medjugorje?* 55.

38. Transcript of interview with Archbishop Frane Franic on January 24, 1985. This document was released by Father Serra to the Center for Peace in Concord, Massachusetts.

39. Soldo, *My Heart Will Triumph*, 325.

40. Linda Rogers, "Question and Answer Session with Ivan," *Children of Mary Center for Peace Newsletter*," November, 1997. (Ivan's talk and Q & A session was on October 29, 1997, in Seattle, Washington.) Reprinted in *Spirit of Medjugorje* newsletter, February, 2006, p.7.

41. Connell, *Queen of the Cosmos*, 19.

42. Ibid., 21.

43. Ibid., 30.

44. René Laurentin and Henri Joyeux, *Scientific & Medical Studies on the Apparitions at Medjugorje* (Dublin, Ireland: Veritas Publications, 1987), 112.

45. Ibid., 114.

46. Ibid.

47. Soldo, *My Heart Will Triumph*, 120.

48. Kraljevic, *The Apparitions of Our Lady at Medjugorje*, 148.

CHAPTER 65: THE DESTINY OF HUMANITY

1. Connell, *The Visions of the Children*, 91.

2. Ibid., 108.

3. June Klins, ed., *Spirit of Medjugorje*, Vol. 24, No. 9., Erie, PA, September 5, 2011, 6-7. Concerning the Seventh Secret, Sister Emmanuel Maillard writes, "This reminds me of something Marthe Robin [a French mystic/ stigmatist from Chateauneuf-de-Galaure,1902-1981] said to a priest of my community: 'The prophecy in the *Apocalypse*, concerning the death of two-thirds of the human race, does not refer to an atomic war or any other catastrophe, but to a spiritual death.' Prayer and fasting can alleviate and even prevent chastisements. This is the case for the Seventh Secret in Medjugorje." (See Sister Emmanuel's *Medjugorje the 90s*, p. 92-93.)

4. Marin, *Queen of Peace in Medjugorje*, 77.

5. Ibid.

6. Marin, *Queen of Peace in Medjugorje*, 121; Sullivan, *Miracle Detective*, 191. Marin has this event occurring on August 22, 1986, while Sullivan has it on April 22. Marin relied on Bubalo's first book, *Testimonies: Medjugorje Blessed Land*, and is more likely to be accurate.

7. Bubalo, *A Thousand Encounters with the Virgin Mary in Medjugorje*, 153.

8. All of the annual apparitions in which the Virgin Mary and Ivanka reviewed the Secrets can be found in Medjugorje.Org., *The Medjugorje Messages :1981-2013*, 253-271.

9. Connell, *The Visions of the Children*, 47.

10. Soldo, *My Heart Will Triumph*, 192.

11. Ibid., 209, 336.

12. Kraljevic, *The Apparitions of Our Lady at Medjugorje*, 128,129.

13. Laurentin and Lejeune, *Messages and Teachings of Mary at Medjugorje*, 51.

14. O'Carroll, *Medjugorje: Facts, Documents and Theology*, 189.

15. Laurentin and Lejeune, *Messages and Teachings of Mary at Medjugorje*, 269. Mirjana received this message by interior locution as reported in the *MIR Recorder*, January 5, 1986, p.3.

16. Connell, *Queen of the Cosmos*, 53.

17. Ibid., 75.

18. Connell, *The Visions of the Children*, 129.

19. Klins, ed., *The Best of the Spirit of Medjugorje*, Vol. I, 75. Ivanka's statement is from an interview on June 6, 1996, at St. George's Church in Erie, Pa. Writes Laurentin, "On the evening of May 6, 1985, Ivanka was in the rectory with Marija, Ivan and Jacov, for the apparition. At the end of two minutes, the apparition terminated for the three others. They got back up. Ivanka still sees the apparition. The others were stupefied, for they had never seen another of their group in this kind of ecstasy. For Ivanka, the apparition lasted for six minutes after which she explained: 'The Virgin has ended her messages to me on the coming chastisement of the world. She confided to me the Tenth Secret. Our Lady said to me, 'The apparitions are finished for you, but I will see you again every year on the anniversary of the first apparition (June 25th) starting the next year (1986).' She will come to say her good-byes tomorrow at my house at the same time.' 'Can we come?' asks Fr. Slavko. 'The Gospa asked to see me alone,' she answered." Ivanka's use of the word chastisement here should not be viewed as contradicting her statement that Mary had never said anything about chastisements. But it does reveal perhaps a level of innocence and naivety for her age at the time about the meaning of the word in the first place. (See Laurentin's, *The Apparitions at Medjugorje Prolonged*.)

20. Bubalo, *A Thousand Encounters with the Blessed Virgin Mary in Medju-gorje*, 194.
21. Haffert, *To Prevent This*, 11,12.
22. Lucia, *"Calls" From the Message of Fatima*, 53.
23. Vlašić and Barbarić, *Pray with Your Heart*, 185
24. Gal 4: 4-7.
25. Nolan, *Medjugorje: A Time for Truth, A Time for Action*, xxx.
26. Laurentin, *Latest News of Medjugorje*, 37.
27. Laurentin and Lejeune, *Messages and Teachings of Mary at Medju-gorje*, 130.
28. Bubalo, *A Thousand Encounters with the Blessed Virgin Mary in Medju-gorje*, 270.
29. *Catechism of the Catholic Church* (New Hope, Kentucky: Et Orbi Com-munications,1994), N. 1040.
30. Laurentin, *Medjugorje: 12 Years Later*, 121.
31. Laurentin, *Ten Years of Apparitions*, 121. Ivan was interviewed by *The National Catholic Register* (published in the newspaper's *Mary's People* supplement of January 27, 1991) at a gathering in Herndon, Virginia, in November, 1990.
32. Connell, *Queen of the Cosmos*, 19.
33. Ibid., 163.
34. Vlašić and Barbarić, *Pray with Your Heart*,185-186.
35. Ibid., 204-205.
36. Ibid., 167-168.
37. Laurentin, *Latest News of Medjugorje*, 18.
38. Thull, ed., *What They Say About Medjugorje*, 797.
39. Ibid,105. Thull quotes the article, "Fr. Vlašić Answers Questions About the Second Coming of Christ," as reported in *The Echo from Medju-gorje*, June 7, 1987. This story also appeared in the August 1987 issue of *Mir Recorder*, p.12. There has been foretold a coming manifestation of Christ in the heavens that is to accompany the times at hand. Writes Michael Brown in his excellent book, *The Day Will Come*, "We await a manifestation or unveiling in which the presence of Jesus, preceded or accompanied by tribulations, will break the power of evil (see 2 Thes-salonians 2:8). Then the century of Satan, the modernistic heresy, will be over and Satan will be bound by the "angel come down from heaven" (Rv 20:1-20). Brown concludes, "If the period of evil ends with a man-ifestation of Christ, as opposed to the formal Second Coming, then obviously we are in a stage leading up to the End Times but not at its conclusion. The End Times might still have a way to go. It might go through the Third Millennium. For all we know, it may go beyond. Or, it may conclude next month." See *The Day Will Come*, 341-342.
40. Ibid.

CHAPTER 66: THE WOMAN CLOTHED IN THE SUN

1. Soldo, *My Heart Will Triumph*,137.
2. Ibid.,157.
3. Ibid.,136.
4. Ibid.,137.
5. CLR James, "Karl Marx and the Paris Commune," January 3, 2006, https://libcom.orglarticle/karl-marx-and-paris-commune-clr-james.
6. Katherine Connolly, "Karl Marx and the Paris Commune," March 17, 2021,https://www.counterfire.org/articles/history/22167-karl-marx-and-the-paris-commune.
7. Ibid.
8. Ibid.
9. Vladimir Lenin, "The Experience of the Paris Commune of 1871: Marx's Analysis" (Chapter 3, *The State and Revolution* by Vladimir Lenin), Summer, 1917, https://www.wsws.org/en/special/library/lenin-state-and-revolution/experience-paris-commune-html.
10. John Westmoreland, "The Paris Commune: When Workers Ran a City," March 10, 2021, https://www.counterfire.org/articles/history/21095-the-paris-commune-150-when-workers-ran-a-city; Marx, Karl. *The Civil War in France: The Paris Commune.* (New York, NY: International Publishers Co., 1968).

CHAPTER 67: TIME IS SHORT

1. Craig, *Spark from Heaven*, 152-153. The controversy surrounding Ivan while in the seminary was in regards to his response to the Bishop's request for the visionaries to write down on a piece of paper everything they knew about the Great Sign. Separated from the other visionaries, who all refused to answer the question, Ivan said at first that he wrote nothing on the paper. He later admitted to writing something. What he did write did not reveal the Great Sign or anything about it, but still led to a lot of trouble for him, and indirectly, the apparition itself. (For a full account of this matter, see Nolan's *Medjugorje: A Time for Truth, A Time for Action*.)
2. Ivan's remarks were made on March 25,1988, and are quoted in *St. Anthony Messenger*, Cincinnati, OH, August, 1988, p. 32.
3. "Excerpts from an Interview with Ivan Dragićević", Pittsburgh Center for Peace, *Queen of Peace* newsletter, Vol. I, N. 4., 1990. (Interview of Ivan Dragićević conducted by Jan Connell on August 5, 1989 in Medjugorje.); Connell, *Queen of the Cosmos*, 90.
4. "I Am Striving to Be Better: Conversation with Ivan at the Franciscan Monastery of Vienna," *Medjugorje Gebetsaktion*, No. 28, January, 1993, 12-16.

5. Klins, ed., *Spirit of Medjugorje*, Vol. 24, No. 9., 6-7. Ivan's remark about "physical changes in the world," followed almost immediately by his mentioning of the Secrets, is a perfect example of how the visionaries often subtly allude to the contents of the Secrets. This remark is especially revealing, as it seems to clearly indicate that something in the Secrets is going to contain an event that will result in a physical alteration of the planet as we presently know it. It hints of a sizeable occurrence that will have universal recognition.

6. Carolanne Kilichowski, "Message to Ivan's Prayer Group: September 10, 2004," *Spirit of Medjugorje*, Vol. 17, No. 10, October, 2004, p. 3.

7. June Klins, "Ivan Speaks About Family Prayer," *Spirit of Medjugorje*, Vol. 22, No. 5., May, 2009, p. 3. Talk given by Ivan on April 26, 2008, in Chagrin Falls, Ohio. Because of Ivan marrying an American and thereby living in the Unites States half of every year, he has perhaps given the most talks outside of Medjugorje. There are a good number of recordings and transcripts of his talks throughout the United States over the last 25 years. In many ways, he has become somewhat of an American, even in support of some of the sports teams such as the Chicago Bulls and the Pittsburgh Steelers, whose t-shirt he has been photographed wearing. When in St. Mary's, Pa. (of all places), he was taken to meet the Steelers players and received a jacket and a miniature replica of Heinz Field, the stadium the team plays in at Pittsburgh. (Source: *Spirit of Medjugorje*, February, 2010.)

8. Connell, *Queen of the Cosmos*, 49.

9. Medjugorje.Org, *The Medjugorje Messages: 1981-2013*, 263.

10. Ibid., 264.

11. Ibid.

12. Ibid., 262.

13. June Klins, ed., "Question and Answer Session with Ivanka," *Spirit of Medjugorje*, Vol. 19, No. 7., p. 3, July, 2006. Interview with Ivanka conducted in Medjugorje on August 6, 2001. Videotaped by Mark Dicarlo of Michigan.

14. Laurentin, *Medjugorje-13 Years Later*, 13-14.

15. Ibid., 14.

16. Ibid.

17. Ibid.

18. Fr. Edward O'Conner, C.S.C., "The Lady Behind the Iron Curtain," *Queen*, Nov-Dec 1986, 23.

19. Connell, *The Visions of the Children*, 143.

20. Ibid., 145.

21. Ibid., 146.

22. "We Should Grow from Day to Day: Interview with Marija Pavlović on January 2, 1994, in Medjugorje," *Medjugorje Gebetsaktion*, No.33, October, 1994, 10-13.

23. "Interview of Marija Pavlović," Pittsburgh Center for Peace, *Queen of Peace Newsletter*, Vol.1, N.2., p. 9, July, 1988. (Interview conducted by Jan Connell on January 25, 1988, in Medjugorje.)
24. "Special Message," *Medjugorje Herald*, October, 1987, 4.
25. Renzo Allegri, "Marija Tells Her Story," *Mejugorje Torino* (English Edition), Vol. 10, No.35, July, 2001, 8-12.
26. Connell, *Queen of the Cosmos*, 53,54.
27. Laurentin, *Medjugorje: 12 Years Later*, 16.
28. Connell, *Queen of the Cosmos*,75.
29. Ibid.,120-121.

CHAPTER 68: THE LOST PROPHECY OF FATIMA

1. Martins, *Documents on Fatima & the Memoirs of Sister Lucia*, 145
2. De Marchi, *Fatima: From the Beginning*, 4.
3. Ibid., back inside cover.
4. Ibid., 5.
5. Ibid.
6. Ibid.
7. Ibid.,7.
8. Martins, *Documents on Fatima & the Memoirs of Sister Lucia*, 143.
9. De Marchi, *Fatima: From the Beginning*, 115.
10. Ibid., 116.
11. Ibid., 120.
12. Ibid., 121.
13. Ibid.
14. Ibid., 142.
15. Ibid.
16. Ibid.
17. Martins, *Documents on Fatima & the Memoirs of Sister Lucia*, 154.
18. De Marchi, *Fatima: From the Beginning*, 149.
19. Ibid., 150.
20. Martins, *Documents on Fatima & the Memoirs of Sister Lucia*, 163.
21. De Marchi, *Fatima: From the Beginning*, 154
22. Ibid.,149.
23. Ibid.,154.
24. Ibid.
25. Ibid.,155.
26. Ibid., 56.
27. Martins, *Documents on Fatima & the Memoirs of Sister Lucia*, 163.
28. Johnston, *The Great Sign*, 67-80.
29. Antonio Socci, *The Secret of Benedict XVI: Is He Still Pope?* (Brooklyn, NY: Angelico Press, 2019), 149-150.

30. Ibid., 150.
31. Ibid.
32. Ibid.
33. Ibid.

CHAPTER 69: "IT'S THE END OF THE WORLD"

1. Socci, *The Secret of Benedict XVI*, 149.
2. Ibid., 150.
3. Ibid.,151-152. Socci cites one official source of Formigão, *Documentacao Critica de Fátima* I, p.142. His research assistant also documents Formigão's interview in Volume III. Jacinta's remark concerning "the end of the world" is her answer to Formigão's eighth question. Father Antonio Martin's book, *Documents on Fatima & the Memoirs of Sister Lucia*, contains all of Formigão's' interviews as well Fr. Lacerda's interview with the visionaries. Jacinta's complete answers to these questions, however, are missing. There is no mention in any of the interviews of what Jacinta said about the "end of the world." The original responses, one must presume, were edited out. De Marchi is found to have this information and perhaps more from what is seen in the details he provides in his book, especially the quotes from the investigation proceedings.
4. Ibid.,152.
5. Ibid. This letter is also documented in the official record. See DCF, Vol I, 2nd ed., Doc 47, p.316.
6. Ibid.
7. Ibid.
8. Lúcia, *Fatima: In Lucia's Own Words*, 81-82.
9. Ibid., 172-173.
10. De Marchi, *Fatima: From the Beginning*, 155.
11. Ibid.78.
12. Ibid.,154.
13. Ibid.
14. Walsh, *Our Lady of Fatima*, 220; Alonso, *The Secret of Fatima*, 110.
15. Haffert, *Her Own Words to the Nuclear Generation*, 9-10.
16. Haffert, *Meet the Witnesses*, 27.
17. Ibid., 67.
18. Ibid., 91,92.
19. Ibid., 98, 99.
20. Ibid., 99,100.
21. Ibid.,129.
22. Johnston, *Fatima: The Great Sign*, 67-68.
23. Ibid., 68-69.

24. Jean Guitton, *Paola VI Segreto* (Cinisello Balsamo: Edizioni San Paulo,1985), 152-153. On January 25, 1995, the Italian journal *L'Italia Settimanale*, published a long interview with Guitton, who was 93 at the time. Guitton had recently been in the news because of his role in the conversion of former French President Francois Mitterrand, who was dying of cancer. Guitton spoke of Fátima and what he saw ahead: a worldwide experience similar to the Miracle of the Sun: "My intuition tells me that something catastrophic will happen, followed by an event which will be absolutely extraordinary and unique in the history of humanity: a theophany, a manifestation of the divine in a way such as has never occurred since the coming of Christ...I like to recall something which took place at Fátima, something that clearly must be seen as an anticipation of that great manifestation of the divine that lies ahead: the Miracle of the Sun." (For an excerpt of this interview in English, see *Inside the Vatican*, February, 1995, p. 48-51.)

25. Socci, *The Secret of Benedict XVI*, 154-155.

26. Ratzinger, "*The Message of Fatima*," published in *The Fatima Prophecies*, 271-298.

27. Laurentin, *Medjugorje: Twelve Years Later*, 120.

28. Socci, *The Secret of Benedict XVI*, 155.

29. Vlašić and Barbarić, *I Beseech You, Listen to My Messages and Live Them*, 69.

30. Medjugorje.Org, *The Medjugorje Messages 1981-2013*, 169. Message of January 25, 1997.

31. Ibid., 201. Message of October 25, 2008.

32. Ibid., 211. Message of July 25, 2012.

33. Medjugorje Message of September 25, 2020. [Available through various Medjugorje web sources.]

34. Connell, *The Visions of the Children*, 66.

35. Author's interview of Father Petar Ljubicic, February 2, 2000.

CHAPTER 70: A CONVERSATION WITH FATHER PETER LJUBICIC

1. The interview with Father Petar Ljubicic was conducted by the author on February 2, 2000, at Franciscan University in Steubenville, Ohio. It has not been previously published. Father Petar's talk that day at the college was recorded and is available through St. Andrew's Productions.

2. Father Petar Ljubicic and Mirjana, according to Mirjana, will fast for seven days. It seems Father Petar was perhaps indicating that he might fast the additional three days before a Secret comes to realization.

3. Father Petar's comment about the Communists being "back in power" was understood to be mostly in jest at the time.

4. Three visionaries are directly tied to the letter sent to the pope. After the apparition of November 30, Marija Pavlović revealed that the Virgin wanted a letter sent to the Pope. According to Laurentin, much of the information in the letter was incorporated from a November 5,1983, meeting with Mirjana Dragićević. Vlašić writes in the letter that Ivan Dragićević reported to him that the visionaries had approved its contents. No response from the pope has ever been publicly cited. At the time of my interview with Father Ljubicic, I was curious if he was aware if there ever was such a response from the Holy Father that had not been disclosed.

CHAPTER 71: "PRAY, PRAY, PRAY"

1. Connell, *Queen of the Cosmos*, 104. The Virgin Mary's assertion at Medjugorje to the visionaries that she has "come for everybody" is in keeping with Christ's words in Scripture that not one of the Father's children be lost: "Now the will of him who sent me is that I should lose nothing of all that he has given to me, but I should raise it up on the last day. It is my Father's will that whoever sees the Son and believes in him should have eternal life, and that I should raise that person up on the last day" (Jn 6: 39-40).

2. Connell, *The Visions of the Children*, 108. Jacov's certainty here carries implications that are important to consider. It has been pointed out that the fulfillment of all of Mary's Secrets at Fátima were visible happenings in time—i.e., the end of World War I, World War II, Communism, religious persecutions, the attempted assassination of Pope John Paul II, etc. They were, as author Antonio Socci writes, historical/political prophecies directly linked to Fátima that unfolded through undeniable realities, not hidden/rumored events. Consequently, it is expected with Medjugorje that this will continue, that the events that are to fulfill the Secrets will be visibly connectible to what was foretold. Jacov's words reflect a confidence that appears to imply that all will be able to see that what he is saying will come true. This means they will again be historical related prophecies in time, and that their fulfillment will be undeniable and directly related to the words of the Madonna of Medjugorje. The Triumph, in essence— through the fulfilled prophecies of Fátima and Medjugorje— is to be visible. Mirjana and Ivan, like Jacov, have also implied as much in their public comments.

3. Connell, *Queen of the Cosmos*, 101.

4. Father Milan Mikulich, "The Apparitions of Our Lady in Medjugorje, Croatia, Yugoslavia." From a talk given by Mikulich at St. Patrick's Church, Portland, Oregon, on April 4, 1984.

5. Unpublished interview with Jacov Čolo conducted by Robert Petrisko in Medjugorje for the Pittsburgh Center for Peace, April, 1992. The questions were written by the author.

6. Larry and Mary Sue Eck, "Jacov Čolo, the Youngest Visionary," *Medjugorje Magazine*, Winter 2001-2002, 10.

7. Sean Bloomfield, "Jacov's Last Daily Apparition and the Tenth Secret," *Spirit of Medjugorje*, Vol. 23, No.1, January, 2010, p. 3.

8. Ibid.

9. Ibid.

10. Medugorje.Org., *The Medjugorje Messages: 1981-2013*, 206.

11. Connell, *The Visions of the Children*, xviii. Jan Connell was present that day in Florida and witnessed all that took place during and after Jacov's final daily apparition. In a June 21, 2006, interview, Jacov recalled that day: "You have to remember, I was having apparitions on a daily basis for seventeen years and I grew up with Our Lady. As you see, I knew only about this life. And, of course, it is normal when I was given the Tenth Secret and when Our Lady told me that she would not appear to me on a daily basis any more, I cannot describe the pain I felt in my heart. And I tell you that was the most difficult moment in my life." (*Spirit of Medjugorje*, May, 2007, p. 7.)

12. Laurentin, *Medjugorje Testament*, 216. Laurentin, at the time, was pondering the longevity of the apparitions and the fact that each of the visionaries was often experiencing the visions privately. This to him posed a concern for different reasons, mostly being the lack of objective witnesses at the apparitions. Critics, at the time, were also casting doubts. The announcement of Jacov's final apparition served, he would write, as a conviction to him that the apparitions were truly still occurring: "The end of the apparitions for him (Jacov) not only destroys this hypothesis but also tends to confirm that Our Lady's apparitions were authentic." (See Laurentin's *Medjugorje Testament*, pp. 215-218).

13. Bloomfield, "Jacov's Last Daily Apparition and the Tenth Secret," *Spirit of Medjugorje*, Vol. 23, No. 1, January, 2010, p. 3.

14. Medjugorje.org, *The Medjugorje Messages:1981-2013*, 270.

CHAPTER 72: "EVERYTHING WILL BE FINISHED IN MEDJUGORJE"

1. Thavis, *The Vatican Prophecies*, 65.

2. Ibid.

3. Weible, *Medjugorje, The Last Apparition*, 214-217.

4. Connell, *The Visions of the Children*, 129.

5. Connell, *Queen of the Cosmos*, 48. Mirjana is quoted by Connell with stating the exact same thing as Ivanka. See *The Visions of the Children* (2007, revised edition), p.81. In explaining to Connell how each person on earth will have a role to play, Mirjana also revealed that those who follow the Virgin Mary's messages are going to be persecuted at some point. Question (Connell): Is this apparition just for the faithful ones? Answer (Mirjana): No. This apparition is for all people on earth. Each person on earth will have a role to play as the Secrets unfold. Many already know their role in this apparition, as I do. There will be suffering. Those who follow the Blessed Mother's messages will know persecution, but in the end all will be well. The rewards are great. They are worth every bit of persecution and suffering." See *The Visions of the Children* (2007, revised edition), p. 81.

6. Soldo, *My Heart Will Triumph*, 121.

7. Ibid.

8. Vlašić and Barbarić, *Open Your Hearts to Mary Queen of Peace*, 116. Mary's exact words were: "Do not ask for all the Secrets to be removed because God has His plan. You must be converted and live your faith."

9. Ps(s) 85, 11.

10. Laurentin and Lejeune, *Messages and Teachings of Mary at Medjugorje*, 186,188. Mary said this twice in early 1982, first on May 2nd and then on June 23rd.

11. June Klins, ed., "The Period of Conversion and the Ten Secrets," *Spirit of Medjugorje*, Vol. 22, No. 8, August, 2009, p.6.

12. Laurentin, *Eight Years*, 135.

13. "Interview with Marija Lunetti," *Words of the Harvesters: Caritas of Birmingham*, Vol. 103, March 2004, p. 4.

14. Ibid.

15. Connell, *The Visions of the Children*, 56.

16. June Klins, ed., "An Interview with Vicka," *Spirit of Medjugorje*, Vol. 22, No. 2., Erie, PA, February, 2009, 6-7. Father Albert Hebert reports that Vicka has said the apparitions will not only continue after the Secrets *begin* but will be still taking place after the Great Sign (the Third Secret) appears on Mt. Podbrdo. (See Hebert's *Medjugorje: An Affirmation and Defense*, p. 22.) One must suspect the crowds that will come for the apparitions at this time, especially after the Third Secret is fulfilled and the Great Sign manifests, will be tens, if not hundreds of thousands of people.

17. "An Interview with Father Slavko Barbarić," *Mary's People* (*The National Catholic Register*), October 25, 1992, p.16.

18. Brown, *The Day Will Come*, 233.

19. Ibid., 235.

20. Nolan, *Medjugorje: A Time for Truth, A Time for Action*, 10. (Nolan quoted *Mary's People*, October 25,1992.)

21. Thull, ed., *What They Say About Medjugorje*, 805. Father Slavko Barbarić's mark on the events at Medjugorje is immeasurable. Slavko died on Friday, November 24, 2000, immediately after completing the Way of the Cross near the top of Mt. Krizevac. In the monthly message of Mary at Medjugorje given the following day to Marija, Mary revealed that Slavko was "born into Heaven."

22. Throughout the many accounts of the visionaries reporting their conversations with Mary concerning the Secrets, talk of the future of the Church is found, especially with those visionaries that have received all ten Secrets and only experience annual apparitions. For example, there is the report of Ivanka Ivankovic Elez's annual apparition that took place on June 25, 2001: "The visionary Ivanka Elez had her annual apparition on June 25, 2001, in presence of her family. The Gospa was joyful and spoke to Ivanka about the future of the Church. Our Lady gave the following message: Dear angels, thank you for your prayers, because through them my plan is being realized. This is why, angels, pray, pray, pray, so that my plan may be realized. Receive my motherly blessing." Interviews with the visionaries reveal other conversations with Mary that appear to concern the Church *after* the Ten Secrets are underway or have been fully realized.

23. June Klins, ed., "Interview with Ivan," *Spirit of Medjugorje*, Vol.16, No. 9, September, 2003, p. 4. Interview with Ivan by Damir Govorcin of the *Catholic Weekly* in Australia, February, 2003.

24. Mary Kemper, "Mirjana's Talk at the Medjugorje Conference in Irvine, California," *Spirit of Medjugorje*, Vol. 22, No. 3, March, 2009, p.3. Mirjana has often repeated this statement about what Mary said to her concerning Fátima. On October 24, 2008, at the Medjugorje Conference in Irvine, California, Mirjana said, "The true faith is the faith that comes out of love. Our Lady said, 'What I started at Fátima, I will finish, accomplish, in Medjugorje; My heart will triumph.'"

25. June Klins, ed., "Mirjana's Question and Answer Session," *Spirit of Medjugorje*, Vol. 18, No. 4, April, 2005, p.7. The question and answer forum took place on May 30, 2004.

26. Soldo, *My Heart Will Triumph*, 142.

27. Ibid., 155.

28. June 24, 2022, was also the feast of the Sacred Heart of Jesus in 2022. The following day, June 25, 2022, was the feast of the Immaculate Heart of Mary and the annual feast of Our Lady of Medjugorje. All of these feasts together on June 24/25 send one message to the world: God's hand was on the overturning of Roe v Wade. Thus, any attempt, in any fashion, to circumvent this court decision will not only fail, but be, as Gamaliel observed (Acts 5: 33-41), a fight with God Himself.

CHAPTER 73: THE TRAGEDY OF FATIMA

1.   Barb Earnster, "Sister Lucia Offered Her Death for the Holy Father," January 31, 2019, www.bluearmy.com.

2.   "Pope John Paul II Sent Letter of Encouragement to Sister Lúcia Day Before her Death," February 16, 2005, https://www.catholicnewsagency.com/news/pope_john_paul_ii_sent_letter_of_encouragement_to_sister_lucia_day_before_her_deat; Carmel of Coimbra, *A Pathway Under the Graze of Mary*, 421. If we think of visionaries in the same light as the prophets of the Old Testament, one must look at the life of Lúcia and recognize that the fulfillment of her duties was beyond extraordinary. She boldly announced to the world, over a lengthy period of time, all that she was asked of by God to do. Moreover, in the spirit of the Old Testament prophets, she was obedient, courageous and indefatigable in her effort, yet humble as Christ would want in this age. Besides taking her message to the highest levels of the Church, she wrote hundreds of letters and several books, all with a singular purpose: to bring the triumph of the Immaculate Heart into the world. Her life, when examined closely, is every bit as inspiring and forceful, in the name of God and His work, as Moses, David, and others who are thought of as the superheroes of the Old Testament.

3.   Brian Wingfield, "Vatican Details Final Days of Pope John Paul II," *The New York Times*, September 18, 2005, https://www.nytimes.com/2005/09/18/international/europe/vatican-details-final-days-of-pope-john-paul-ii.html.

4.   Ibid.

5.   ThoughtCo., "The History and Meaning of Divine Mercy Sunday," https://www.learnreligions.com/divine-mercy-sunday-542469 [Updated June 25, 2019].

6.   Sister M. Faustina Kowalska, *Divine Mercy in My Soul: Diary* (Stockbridge, MA: Marian Helpers, 1990), N. 965.

7.   John Paul II, *Dives in Misercordia*, November 30, 1980.

8.   Ibid.

9.   Kowalska, *Divine Mercy in My Soul*, N. 1732.

10. Evaristo, "*Two Hours with Sister Lucia*," 36-37.

11. His Holiness John Paul II, *Crossing the Threshold of Hope* (New York, NY: Alfred A. Knopf, 1994), 221.

12. Evaristo, *Two Hours with Sister Lucia*, 37. One of Fatima's foremost experts in the world agreed that this was the sad, but true case with Fátima; it must be viewed as a tragedy of sorts. Writes Father Andrew Apostoli, "In World War II about 50 million people were killed, and there were many more atrocities visited upon civilians. Sister Lúcia wrote that the mass murder of the Jews was a main reason World War II was worse than World War I. In addition to the Nazi concentration

camps, there were fire bombings of cities and two atomic explosions in Japan. To think such suffering could have been avoided if people had heeded the Blessed Mother's message…"

13. Anthony A. Borelli and John R. Spann, *Our Lady at Fatima: Prophecies of Tragedy or Hope?* (York, PA: The American Society for the Defense of Tradition, Family and Property, 1975), 95-96. This book was revised in1994.

14. Thull, ed., *What They Say About Medjugorje*, 893.

15. Ibid.

16. Ibid. While Brother Michael is known for his acclaimed work on Fátima, he is found to have voiced opposition to Medjugorje. Brother Michael wrote a series of articles (1984-1988) that were published in the French newsletter, *The Catholic Counter-Reformation in the XXth Century*. A dossier consisting of reprints of all these articles, totaling 164 pages, was later distributed in French and English. Brother Michael was the literary spearhead of a group, led by Abbe Georges de Nantes, who also opposed Pope John Paul II at the time. Laurentin describes Brother Michael as "the most finicky and the most tenacious adversary of Medjugorje." Nevertheless, when Brother Michael left *The Catholic Counter-Reformation* and Abbe Georges de Nantes to seek admission into the *Grand Chartreuse*, Laurentin traveled to his hermitage to pray with him "so that his high vocation would be confirmed." While Laurentin defended Medjugorje from Brother Michael's polemics, he reveals that Brother Michael was aware that there was a weakness to his argument against Medjugorje. His organization, *The Catholic Counter–Reformation*, did not allow him "to go see" personally what he was judging, and he was aware this affected his perspective. Their standard rule for discernment was there was to be "no personal" interaction with the subject matter. Thus, argues Laurentin, since the "Father" of the community did "not permit him to go" to Medjugorje, Brother Michael "stayed in a closed circle of objections." Laurentin believed that if Brother Michael would have been permitted to see and visit Medjugorje, he would have had a different opinion. Writes Laurentin, "He (Brother Michael) tried to destroy Medjugorje without knowing either the places, the milieu, the local culture, which is greatly misunderstood in his book (the dossier of articles). From that we have enormous misrepresentations from him who has not seen or known anything: either the Franciscans, the visionaries, the sick who have been cured, the innumerable conversions. If Michel de la Trinite had been able to pray, converse, to hear confessions in Medjugorje, his polemic would have been affected by it. He would have risked to change his opinion like Fr. Radogost Grafenauer S.J., the expert on discernment who was summoned by Msgr. Zanic, and who was converted in Medjugorje." Writes Laurentin in regards to Brother Michael's dossier of articles that was published as a book after he left the community, "Briefly, this book is a brilliant exercise of dialectics, powerfully oriented, where the

analysis of these apparently negative elements, drawn from a vast written documentation, is treated with a spirit which hides everything positive and blows the negative aspects out of proportion. I hope that these clarifications do not incite indignation against the Counter Reformation. They are Christians and they are sincere, although passionate and taken in the trap of their ideology. May we pray for them as for brothers. I am the first to hasten to go to meet them as brothers, even beyond discussions, as I did with Michel de la Trinite, since he laid down his arms. The love of neighbor does not require one to masochism, or to take risks under fire."

17. Michel de la Sainte Trinite, *The Whole Truth About Fatima*, 493-494.
18. Ibid., 495.
19. Venancio, ed., *A Heart for All*, 55-56.
20. Ibid., 56.
21. Michel de la Sainte Trinite, *The Whole Truth About Fatima*, 724-757.
22. Ibid., 543.
23. Ibid.
24. Alonso, *Fatima Ante a Esfinge*, 97.
25. Michel de la Sainte Trinite, *The Whole Truth About Fatima*, 544.
26. Apostoli, *Fatima for Today*, 169.
27. Ibid.
28. O'Leary, *Vicka: Her Story*, 58-59.

CHAPTER 74: THE TRAGEDY OF MEDJUGORJE?

1. Mulligan, Medjugorje: *What's Happening?* 293-294.
2. Ibid.
3. De Marchi, *Fatima from the Beginning*, 5, 9, 72, 88, 121.
4. Michel de La Sainte Trinite, *Fatima Revealed...and Discarded*, 134-159; Symonds, *On theThird Part of the Secret of Fatima*, 31- 33.
5. Antonio Gaspari, "Medjugorje: Deception or Miracle?", *Inside the Vatican*, Year 4, No. 9, November, 1996, 26.
6. Ibid., 27.
7. René Laurentin, *The Apparitions of the Blessed Virgin Mary Today* (Paris, France: Veritas Publications,1991), 17-38. Based on Church tradition and what has been foretold to come at Medjugorje, it's highly likely that the apparitions will *not* be approved before the Ten Secrets are revealed. This is because the Virgin Mary has stated that the apparitions will still be occurring when the Secrets begin to be announced (See January 2, 2008, interview with Vicka by Father Livio Fanzaga in Chapter 72, *"Everything Will be Finished in Medjugorje."*) Essentially, this means the Church will not have been able to render a decision on Medjugorje since the apparitions had not officially concluded, unless the Church chooses to break precedence with the

approval process as historically undertaken. On May 18, 2017, *The Catholic News Agency* (CNA) reported, based upon an article that appeared in *The Vatican Insider*, that the latest commission set up to investigate Medjugorje had reached a conclusion on the first seven apparitions that occurred there in 1981. The commission, known as the Ruini Commission because it was chaired by Cardinal Camillo Ruini, was formed by Pope Benedict XVI in 2010. It ran from March 17, 2010, to January 17, 2014, and besides Cardinal Ruini, consisted of multiple cardinals, psychologists, anthropologists, theologians, a canonist, and others. Their assignment was to "collect and examine all the material" about Medjugorje and to "present a detailed report" followed by a vote on the "supernatural nature or not" of the apparitions as well as the most appropriate "pastoral solutions" needed in the village. The committee met seventeen times and screened all documents on file in the Vatican, the parish of Medjugorje, and the archives of the secret services of the former Yugoslavian government. The commission interviewed all the visionaries and select witnesses that have been or still are involved in the events at Medjugorje. In April 2012, members of the Ruini Commission visited the village and carried out an inspection. Upon reviewing the long history of Medjugorje, the commission determined it wanted to differentiate between the beginning of the apparitions and what later followed. Consequently, it chose to divide the events into two phases. The first phase consisted of what was reported as the first seven apparitions at Medjugorje, dated between June 24 and July 3, 1981. The second phase consisted of all that occurred after that designated period. After almost four years of investigation, the members and experts of the Ruini Commission voted, thirteen in favor and one in opposition, in recognizing the supernatural nature of the first seven apparitions. One other vote was characterized as a "suspensive" vote. The commission found the six visionaries were psychologically normal and that nothing they had experienced was influenced by the Franciscan priests in Medjugorje at the time or by any other parties. They acknowledged the visionaries remained steadfast in their faith, despite police arrests and death threats. The Ruini Commission also rejected the hypothesis of a demonic origin of the apparitions. The report found mixed opinion on everything from the Secrets to the personal behavior of the visionaries, voting eight to four that an opinion could not be expressed. Noting the spiritual fruits of Medjugorje and that the visionaries have not been a group for a long time, the Commission endorsed an end of the ban on official Church pilgrimages to Medjugorje. Thirteen of the fourteen members voted in favor of the constitution of "an authority dependent on the Holy See" in Medjugorje as well as the transformation of the parish into a pontifical sanctuary. This was a decision based on pastoral reasons, primarily the care of millions of pilgrims and clarity on economic issues. After examining the Ruini Report and the opinion of the members of the

Congregation of the Doctrine of the Faith, no official decision on the first seven apparitions was rendered by the Catholic Church. Rather, in May 2018, Polish Archbishop Henryk Hoser was entrusted on a "special mission of the Holy See" to "acquire more in-depth knowledge of the pastoral situation in Medjugorje and "above all, the needs of the faithful who come to pilgrimage" there. This was in order to "suggest any pastoral initiatives for the future." In May 2019, upon recommendations from Archbishop Hoser after his investigation was completed, the ban on official Church-sanctioned pilgrimages was lifted. Two years later, on August 1 to 6, 2019, several high-level Vatican officials participated in the annual international youth festival, "Miadifest," in Medjugorje for the first time, attended by over 50,000 youth from around the world. Cardinal Angelo De Donatis, Papal Vicar General of the Diocese of Rome, presided over the opening Mass while Archbishop Salvatore Fisichella, President of the Pontifical Council for Promoting New Evangelization, and Archbishop Jose Carballo, Secretary of the Vatican's Congregation for Orders, presided over the closing Mass. Archbishop Luigi Pezzuto, the Vatican's Nuncio to Bosnia- Herzegovina, was also part of the official delegation. The Masses were reportedly concelebrated by over 500 attending priests. In a July 2019 interview with the Italian publication *Avvenire*, Polish Archbishop Henryk Hoser said Medjugorje had experienced "an intense year, lived fully under the sign of God's Mother," and was generating "conversions, priestly and religious vocations and continuous confessions without any traces of heresy." In a separate interview with Poland's Catholic information agency, *KAI*, Hoser said Medjugorje was now an "object of special Vatican care," and should be seen as a "living, dynamic reality, which is growing and needing accompaniment." He added that with over 700 vocations so far recorded and at least twenty-two communities now functioning permanently at Medjugorje, the shrine's formal recognition was just a matter of time. This was not meant to imply, however, the formal approval of the apparitions. Said Hoser, "Medjugorje is an international place of pilgrimage, which attracts 3 million people annually and where huge pastoral labours are undertaken— but since its Church status isn't regulated, these people are often like sheep without a shepherd." Added Hoser, "People come here from countries where confessional practices have vanished, and where the Church has flattened out and reduced its activities to the superficial. Once here, they encounter a deep faith and a totally different perspective of being." As for the apparitions, Archbishop Hoser said that he believed the Ruini Commissions' findings on the first seven apparitions would be formally approved by the Church. The journal *America: The Jesuit Review*, reported in its August 22, 2017, issue that Archbishop Hoser stated, "The Congregation for the Doctrine of the Faith has passed all documentation to the Secretariat of State—everything suggests the apparitions will be accepted before the year ends. It's difficult to believe the six visionaries have been lying for 36 years. What they say is coherent, and none is mentally disturbed, while the apparitions' faithfulness to Church doctrine is also a powerful argument for their authenticity." Archbishop Hoser died in August 2021. The former Apostolic Nuncio to the Netherlands, Bishop Aldo Cavalli, replaced Hoser in November of the same year as papal envoy to Medjugorje.

8. Rupčić and Nuić, *Once Again, the Truth About Medjugorje*, 179; Nolan, *Medjugorje and the Church*, 178. Opponents of Medjugorje, noted Laurentin, came from the right and the left. Writes Laurentin: "The opposition to Medjugorje comes from two opposite directions: the right and the left – reactionary traditionalism on one hand, liberal progressivism on the other." In an article titled, *"Report by R. Laurentin, The National Conference on Medjugorje"* (May 12-13,1990), Laurentin goes into great detail in presenting both sides orientations and motivations, as well the leading voices. This article was published by the Riehle Foundation of Milford, Ohio, in the summer of 1990.

9. Meyer, *A Portrait of Medjugorje*, 33. Prejudice was especially noted in a book, *The Hidden Side of Medjugorje*, written by a priest who was originally from Medjugorje. Writes Pulitzer Prize nominated investigative reporter Randall Sullivan after he read the book, "This volume was an astonishingly shoddy compendium of rumor, gossip, and outright falsehoods that concluded the apparitions had been produced by a combination of imagination and fabrication, and clearly were a copy of Lourdes. The opinion was based mainly upon the fact that Mirjana had been given a book about the visions of Bernadette a few days after the apparitions in Medjugorje began." Sullivan further dismissed the book in his bibliography of *The Miracle Detective*, "I found *The Hidden Side of Medjugorje* to be without merit."

10. Nolan, *Medjugorje: A Time for Truth, A Time for Action*, 281-366. Nolan cites *Fatima Family Messenger*, July/September, 1992. In it, Fátima expert Father Robert Fox is quoted describing the unprincipled tactics of certain opponents of Medjugorje. Nolan reviews this entire matter in great detail, providing excellent documentation.

11. Meyer, *A Portrait of Medjugorje*, 33.

12. O'Carroll, *Medjugorje: Facts, Documents, and Theology*, 55. Another priest from the UK, Father James Mulligan, especially noted this fact concerning the writings of Medjugorje's most vitriolic foes. (See Mulligan's *Medjugorje, What's Happening?* p. 115). Randall Sullivan noted similar concerns. (See *The Miracle Detective* p. 377, 445).

13. Nolan, *Medjugorje: A Time for Truth, A Time for Action*, 308. Nolan quotes Laurentin here concerning the deliberate withholding of all the facts by critics: "What is lacking is first-hand knowledge of the facts: the visionaries, the ecstasy, parish life, the admirable movement toward

conversion, the innumerable attestations (oral and written) of these conversions, which are the principle elements in this debate according to the Gospel saying, 'A tree is judged by its fruit'. It is illusory to attempt a second hand examination of Medjugorje, purely at the level of dialectical argument and without any critical examination of the sources… The dialectical method used to discover the devil at Medjugorje consists of stringing together a number of most unusual studies, all guided by initial hypothesis, thus tying in minute details to suit the pre-established position. The method is attractive, but artificial."

14.   Ibid. See Nolan, *A Time for Truth, A Time for Action*, 181-268. The thread that ties all of the opponents of Medjugorje together, even to this day, was the aggressive opposition to the apparitions that emerged from the local Bishop, Pavao Zanic. Zanic was said by Archbishop Franic and many others to be immune to all reason and launched a world wide effort to stymie Medjugorje on many levels. This effort centered on a position paper he wrote and aggressively circulated. Writes Mary Craig, who herself was not convinced of the visions, in *Spark from Heaven*: "Zanic's position paper almost came near to torpedoing Medjugorje, as the international press danced to his tune. Tomislav Vlašić was pilloried and reviled, his reputation irremediably tarnished. In Italy, in America, the document was given maximum publicity; but nowhere was the onslaught deadlier or longer-lasting than in France." Craig concludes, "Zanic wrote to all the French bishops himself, said a Franciscan in Medjugorje angrily, it was a real campaign of disinformation. His efforts bore immediate fruit. In France, public opinion veered sharply against Medjugorje; books on the subject disappeared overnight from bookshop windows and shelves. Pilgrimage places were cancelled; charter flights stood empty. Many who had been pilgrims to Medjugorje felt let down and disillusioned… In an adroit move, Bishop Zanic had all but swept his opponents from the board, dealing Medjugorje a far more effective blow than the Marxists had ever managed." Even after Zanic's authority in the matter had been withdrawn by the Vatican, the bishop continued his campaign. Writes Father René Laurentin in *Seven Years of Apparitions* (p. 14-15), "In effect, given the good reception to his provoking indictment (the bishop's position paper), Monsignor Zanic had translations made of it, notably in Italian and English, and had them widely published. These publications began in Italy, where he personally went during the month of August, 1987, to contact the journal with the widest circulation in the peninsula (2 million readers), *Famiglia Christiana* (Christian Families-September 2, 1987) and other Catholic weeklies. The article and second hand dispatches often simplified the question by stating that 'the bishop of the place, responsible for the matter, condemned the apparitions,' (while forgetting to reveal that Rome had removed him from this judgement in May, 1986)." These actions by Bishop Zanic maintained a state of confusion surrounding

the question of whether or not it was permissible for Catholics to travel to Medjugorje. It was a confusion that affected thousands of bishops and priests throughout the world. Laurentin furthers explains this conundrum: "For the third time, news circulated in the world that the bishop responsible had given a negative judgement, forbidden the pilgrimages, and taken sanctions against whomever exceeded this order. And, many of the faithful, who owed their deep conversion to Medjugorje, received orders or instructions from their priests not to go there anymore, in the name of obedience to the Church. It presented trouble for their consciences, because some asked themselves: 'Should we not believe anymore? If what faith has given us is false, according to the Church herself, what then is her faith worth? We find here again, the same old story, spreading false news. We, and others have covered it before in previous books. The causes are all the same: the adversaries of Medjugorje (the press and religious), endorse by magnifying the opposition of Monsignor Zanic to the apparitions. Of course, he is still the Bishop of Mostar. In this regard, he deserves the respect and obedience which the parish of Medjugorje is first to manifest to him. But, since Rome removed him from the judgment, it is no longer correct that he declares himself as "the responsible bishop." In order to be clear, Bishop Zanic did have the right to speak, but only in a personal capacity. Archbishop Frane Franic of Split, a great defender of Medjugorje, explains, "He [Zanic] can express his opinion, just like I do when I say that I am favorable to it. I am convinced that the Madonna appears in Medjugorje, but it is my personal opinion, and one must wait for the definitive judgement of the Church. My personal opinion is worth as much as is the opinion of the Bishop of Mostar." (See Laurentin's *Seven Years of Apparitions*, p. 116). The same problem exists to this day (See statements made by the local bishop in 2018 concerning Medjugorje). The irony of all of this is how open Zanic was to the visions at first. Zanic visited Medjugorje five times in the first weeks of the apparitions and was convinced of the visionaries' sincerity. He was especially impressed with Marija, whose manner he felt was reminiscent of Bernadette Soubirous of Lourdes. The bishop told Father Jozo Zovko on Tuesday, July 1,1981, after an extensive meeting with the visionaries, "I am one hundred percent sure that it is Our Lady who is appearing to these children. I am even more certain of it than of Fátima and Lourdes. I am going to preach on this subject." On the Feast of St. James, the parish patron, Zanic returned to Medjugorje and administered Confirmation. He was the chief celebrant and delivered the homily: "The public expects us to say something about the events in the parish of Medjugorje where six children claim Our Lady appears to them. Six simple children like these would have told all in half an hour if anybody had been manipulating them. I assure you that none of the priests has done any such thing. The accusation is insulting and must be firmly rejected. Furthermore, I am convinced the children are not lying. They are saying only what they must profoundly believe. Yet the most difficult question remains: is this a supernatural experience of the children or not?" Zanic, in his own defense, maintained that he never said he believed for certain the apparitions were real. But it seems apparent that he went from being open to the question to fiercely opposing the visons almost overnight. This extremely evident behavior is suspected to be at the core of why Rome moved in and instituted a change in the Church's approach to the discernment of the visions. Many have stated that Zanic's radical opposition was triggered by threats from the Communist authorities at the time, and not really any of the problems that have been cited concerning some of the actions of the visionaries and the Franciscans that occurred in the early years. Author Sabrina Covic, in her 2003 book, *Encounters with Father Jozo*, reports a conversation that Father Jozo stated he had with Bishop Zanic in August 1981: "Our relationship was good... The bishop was very harshly accused. One day he asked me to come. Since I hadn't slept for several days and was exhausted, I was afraid of taking the driver's seat in the car, so I asked Father Ivan Cilic to take me to Mostar. The bishop wanted to see me alone. He took me to the window of the drawing room and, with tears in his eyes, he said: 'Father Jozo, I've been summoned to Sarajevo... They told me that if I protected Medjugorje, if I stood by Medjugorje, they would lock me up. I cannot go to prison for Medjugorje. I'm a Bishop!' I remained speechless, dumbfounded. Later, a dozen priests, among whom two were Franciscans, came to put pressure on him and threatened to take action to have the diocese withdrawn from him. He then said to me: 'Father Jozo, I cannot become curate of a country parish. In your opinion, can I, a Bishop, become a country curate?'" An in-depth look at this whole period of assault on the apparitions at Medjugorje during the 1980s reveals one thing: the combined efforts of Father René Laurentin, Archbishop Frane Franic. Pope John Paul II, and Cardinal Ratzinger [to a degree] is what prevented Medjugorje from being shut down from Zanic's coordinated and relentless effort and the so called "Hercegovina issue," which involved a long running dispute between the Franciscans and diocesan authority.

15. Laurentin, *Medjugorje-Thirteen Years Later*, 46. At the time, in Laurentin's eyes, the opponents of Medjugorje were becoming less in number. With the birth of the age of the Internet, however, there certainly appears to have come a resurgence. These critics almost all sound the same mantra; Medjugorje is a hoax. They also like to accuse the visionaries of financial gain with no evidence to support their claims. While such opposition is very similar to Fátima and to be expected, it is seen to lack any historical understanding of the visions, presents no new factual evidence, and often relies on Bishop Zanic's original arguments, which have been summarily dismissed for quite some time as being irrelevant to the present Church investigation. The one criticism that needs to be better addressed is the accusation of the visionaries

profiting from the apparitions. Since the 1980s, some of them have worked menial jobs indirectly related to the events (parish store, restaurants, etc.). Early on, Mirjana worked at the *Atlas* travel agency in town. They also have rented rooms to pilgrims, which has drawn criticism. These activities have led, however, to outrageous claims by some that the visionaries have become rich. It must be recognized that the visionaries have families and that they and their spouses have trade skills or degrees that permit them to earn a living. This, in the eyes of the Church, is perfectly permissible since none of them are religious. Laurentin, who is familiar with such controversy from other apparitions that he studied, first wrote of this matter when Ivanka and her husband began to work in Medjugorje in the late 1980s: "Rajko Branko (Ivanka's husband) had begun his veterinarian studies at Sarajevo, but had to stop them. The economy there is difficult. His brother had built a small restaurant at Medjugorje and he is working with him—and Ivanka is also. Certain people have regretted that the seer has become a worker in this way. But these two young homemakers must have to earn their living for themselves and their family in a country where there is an employment and economic crisis. The possibilities of local commerce are for them, as formerly for the Soubirous at Lourdes, an obvious solution… This local work eliminates the immigration of a husband, a current resource and often a necessary one in Yugoslavia, but which tears families apart."

16. Meyer, *A Portrait of Medjugorje*, 33. *Fatima International*, a monthly publication, advised its readers in its February 1987 issue to stay away from Medjugorje. Editor Robert Bergin writes, "Much is made of the sound doctrine coming from Medjugorje. …We strongly recommend to our readers that they do not support or promote so-called revelations that are not approved by the Church."

17. Jonathon Luxmoore, "Polish Archbishop Thinks Vatican Will Recognize Apparitions," August 22, 2017, https://www.archbalt.org/polish-archbishop-thinks-vatican-will-recognize-medjugorje-apparitions/.

18. Andrea Tornielli, "Medjugorje: The Findings of the Ruini Report," *CNA* (*Catholic News Agency*), May 17, 2017. While official pilgrimages to Medjugorje are permitted, they are not to be based on a supernatural origin to Medjugorje at this time.

19. "Medjugorje Visionary Says Monthly Apparitions Have Come to an End," *CNA* (*Catholic News Agency*), March 18, 2020.

20. Andrea Tornielli, "Medjugorje: The Findings of the Ruini Report," *CNA* (*Catholic News Agency*), May 17, 2017.

21. "Pope Francis Tells Youth at Medjugorje: Be Inspired by the Virgin Mary," *CNA* (*Catholic News Agency*), August 2, 2020.

22. *ABC News* reported in 2011 that 40 million had traveled to Medjugorje, with an average of over 2.2 million a year.

23. Soldo, *My Heart Will Triumph*, 366.

24. Nolan, *Medjugorje: A Time for Truth, A Time for Action*, 186. The Catholic press was brutal on Fátima, too. Writes Father John De Marchi, "The newspapers of the period, especially the *Seculo*, the *Diario de Noticias*, the *Mundo*, all at the time were anti-clerical in tone. They referred largely to the events which took place on the Serra de Aire and show clearly the religious strife which was the background of the apparitions as well as the conflicting opinions on the events themselves. It is an interesting fact that the Catholic Press did not lag behind its secular contemporaries in skepticism." (See, *Fatima: From the Beginning*, p. 5.)

CHAPTER 75: CALL OF THE AGES

1. Connell, *Queen of the Cosmos*, 61-62.

2. *The New American Bible*, (Wichita, KS: Catholic Bible Publishers, 1994-95 Edition), xiii. See Dogmatic Constitution of Divine Revelation.

3. Siguenza, *John Paul II: The Pope Who Understood Fatima*, 51. Fr. Paul Kramer, who was critical of the Church's response to the importance of the message of Fátima to the world, writes, "To both insiders and outsiders, the Vatican's treatment of this matter seems strangely inconsistent with its own standards and traditions. It also seems to show a reckless disregard for the safety not only of the Catholic Church, but the rest of humanity as well. If the Fátima threat is genuine, the price of the Vatican's reluctance could be very high indeed—and it would be paid by all mankind." (See *The Devil's Final Battle*, p.ix).

4. Renzo Allegri, *The Pope of Fatima* (Milan, Italy: Mondadori, 2006), 21.

5. Socci, *The Fourth Secret of Fatima*, 8.

6. Johnston, *Fatima: The Great Sign*, 69.

7. Ibid., Socci. *The Fourth Secret of Fátima*, 8. Jean Guitton was very sensitive to the historical uniqueness of the times in relation to the theological implications of nuclear weapons. As he put it, "At the hinge of history, before and after Hiroshima, dividing history forever." (See *Portrait de Marthe Robin*, 1986, p. 248.) Guitton also told Paul VI, "Holy Father, Fátima is more interesting than Lourdes. It is both cosmic and historical…thus it is linked to the history of salvation, to universal history."

8. Johnson, *Fatima: The Great Sign*, 70.

9. Ibid.

10. Ibid., 70-71. Fátima became so significant that some Muslim factions claim it was not a Christian miracle but a Muslim miracle. *Inside the Vatican*, quoting the Lefebvrist bulletin *Si Si No No* (July, 1996), stated, "The news was first reported on October 25,1995, by the Italian newspaper *Il Giornale* (p.15), which wrote, "According to a documentary

aired on Iranian television, what occurred in Fátima, Portugal, was not a Christian miracle but a Muslim miracle. In fact, Iranian TV affirms, it was not the Virgin Mary who appeared to three shepherd children, but Fatima herself, daughter of the prophet of Islam, Mohammed." (*Inside the Vatican*, November 1996, reports the full story.)

11. Ibid., 71.
12. Ibid.
13. Ibid.
14. Father Paul Kramer, *The Devil's Final Battle*, (Buffalo, NY: Good Counsel Publications,2002), vii. Fátima lay advocate John Vennari wrote that Fátima should not be considered just a private revelation, that it was in a different category. Wrote Vennari: "It is the notion that Fátima is supposedly only a private revelation. And because it is a private revelation, then it is no part of the Deposit of Faith, so you may take it or leave it. But, Fátima is actually in a different category from that of a mere private revelation. It is in the category of a Public Prophetic Revelation that imposes an obligation upon the Church. I will quote what theologian Joseph de Sainte-Marie and Bishop Rudolph Graber had to say about it." (For Vennari's complete article see, "Prophecy and Miracle", *The Fatima Crusader*, Autumn, 2004, pp. 24-28.)
15. Johnson, *Fatima: The Great Sign*, 73.
16. Ibid.
17. Ibid.
18. Michel de la Saint Trinite, *The Whole Truth About Fatima*, 380-388.
19. Ibid., 390. In a letter to Pope Pius XII from Sister Lúcia, dated December 2, 1940, Lúcia notes that the action of Portugal's bishops has kept Portugal out of World War II, and "that this grace was available to other nations" if they would follow the bishops of Portugal's lead. She writes: "Most Holy Father, If I am not mistaken, it is in the union of my soul with God that Our Lord promised to be attentive to the consecration made by the bishops of our nation to the Immaculate Heart of Mary, that a special protection would be granted to our country in this war and this protection will be proof of graces that would be granted to other nations if they are consecrated to her."
20. Ibid., 429-434; Kramer, *The Devil's Final Battle*, 25. There is no greater lesson to be learned from the history surrounding the consecration to the Immaculate Heart than the fact that the grace attached to the act is available on a nation to nation basis. Moreover, it is granted on a diocese to diocese basis. The reason why Mary asked for all the Bishops to join in unison with Pope was so that each nation, each diocese could be individually protected from the "errors of Russia." Like Portugal, each country, every diocese in each country, was being invited to experience what Portugal experienced in the 1930-40's.

21. Ibid., 405-410.

22. Ibid., 405-406.

23. Ibid., 410. Lucia 's revelation of how the consecration by the Bishops of Portugal helped to keep the country out of World War II, and aided the nation as a whole in many positive ways, is thought provoking. When this truth is applied to the world as a whole in reverse, one must wonder if individual bishops, who refused to participate in the 1984 consecration of the world, have left their dioceses and nations in some degree of peril because of their decision.

24. Gorny and Rosikon, *Fatima Mysteries*, 233. In 1960, the Bishop of Leiria (Fátima), Joao Venancio, sent two small statues of Our Lady of Fátima to Cardinal Stefan Wyszynski in Poland. In order to prevent them from being seized by the Communist authorities, the little statues (designated as dolls on the shipping papers) were initially sent to Holland and then transferred by ship to Gdynia, a port city on the Baltic coast of Poland. Wyszynski gave one of the Fátima statues to the Warsaw Theological Seminary. He sent the other one to the Pallottine Order in Zakopane, where it was received by the young Bishop of Krakow in 1961- Karol Wojtyła. The Pallotines made their chapel, where they kept the statue, the first Polish center of devotion to Our Lady of Fátima. They spread devotion to Our Lady of Fátima by secretly moving the statue from parish to parish in a suitcase. They called their effort the *Family Rosary Retreat*, carefully avoiding the use of the name of "Fátima."

25. Ibid., 233.

26. Ibid., 234.

27. Ibid.

28. Ibid.

29. Ibid.

30. Ibid.

31. Ibid., 237.

32. Ibid., 235.

33. Based on Mary's own words at Medjugorje, Fátima cannot be fulfilled without Medjugorje. The Virgin Mary said at Medjugorje on August 25, 1991, that she had "come to fulfill" the "Secrets I began at Fátima." She would not have said this if it were not true. She, therefore, needs Medjugorje to fulfill Fátima. At the time when Fátima could have been fulfilled, her wishes were opposed or not followed to the letter, as Saul failed to fully listen to Samuel. With Fátima, the consecration was unfortunately not done in a timely manner. The faithful also did not learn about the Five First Saturdays from the Church as requested, and then failed to respond in the numbers needed that the lay organizations tried to make up for after the fact. Although great good was done, it was not enough. Consequently, Mary has come to Medjugorje to finish the Triumph

begun at Fátima. At Medjugorje, she can be seen to be going straight to the people. In essence, the focus shifts from the dangers of the "errors of Russia" to all nations, to the dangers of the "errors of Russia" to all people.

34. Thull, ed., *What They Say About Medjugorje*, 113.

CHAPTER 76: THE TWILIGHT OF MARXISM

1. Jeffery Fleishman, "Egypt Tries to Erase Hosni Mubarak's Name," *The Los Angeles Times,* May 10, 2011.
2. Ibid.
3. Christine Blau, "Thousands of Crosses Cover This Eerie Hill in Europe," *National Geographic*, February 26, 2018, https://www.nationalgeographic.com/travel/article/things-to-do-hill-of-crosses-religious-tourism.
4. Ibid.
5. John Paul II, *Crossing the Threshold of Hope*, 130-131.
6. Ibid., 131.
7. Ibid.
8. Ibid., 132.
9. Ibid., 133.
10. Ibid.
11. Ibid.
12. Ibid.
13. Ibid., 222-223.

EPILOGUE: LO, I WILL SEND YOU ELIJAH

1. The number of times the Bible speaks of fire varies according to version.
2. Rv 8.
3. Gn 3:24.
4. Gn 19:24.
5. Gn 15:17.
6. Gn 22:7-8.
7. Dt 4:24.
8. Ex 13:17-22.
9. Ex 19:18.
10. Ex 40:38.
11. 1 Kgs 18:38
12. 2 Chr 7:1.
13. Lv 6:12-13.
14. Lk 3:16.
15. Mt 17:1-8; Mk 9:2-8; Lk 9:28-36; 2Pt 1:16-18.
16. Lk 12:49.

17. Acts 2:3-4.
18. Craig, *Spark from Heaven*, 87; Laurentin and Lejeune, *Is the Virgin Mary Appearing at Medjugorje?* 34; Thul, ed., *What They Say About Medjugorje*, 499.
19. Laurentin and Lejeune, *Is the Virgin Mary Appearing at Medjugorje?* 169.
20. Haffert, *Her Own Words to the Nuclear Age*, 265. The final three visions at Fátima to the three children on October 13,1917, are also seen as a warning of the coming spiritual attack on the family, the so called "final battle" according to the words of Lúcia. She spoke of this on occasion. It is noted especially in her letter to Cardinal Carlo Caffarra, the founding President of the John Paul II Institute for Studies on Marriage and the Family: "The final battle between the Lord and Satan will be about marriage and the family...because this is the decisive issue." The John Paul II Institute for Studies on Marriage and the Family was founded on December 13, 1981, at the Pontifical Lateran University in Rome, seven months after the attempted assassination of Pope John Paul II. Our Lady of Fátima is its patroness. It had been scheduled to be formally announced by Pope John Paul II on May 13, 1981, the day of his shooting in Vatican Square. The appearance of the Holy Family at Fátima in October of 1917 had been foretold at the September apparition. Today, the attack on the family is recognized as seen in many forms: divorce, infidelity, cohabitation, birth control, abortion, homosexual acts, same sex marriage, gender reassignment and more. The key to defeating this attack also lies in the model of the Holy Family.
21. 1 Kgs 18: 20-40.
22. Ibid.
23. Ibid.
24. Ibid.
25. Ibid.
26. Ibid.
27. Ibid.
28. Ibid.
29. Ibid.
30. Ibid.
31. Ibid.
32. Haffert, *Her Own Words to the Nuclear Age*, 265.
33. John M. Haffert, *Her Glorious Title: Our Lady of Mount Carmel, Star of the Sea* (Washington, New Jersey: 101 Foundation, 1993), 6.
34. Apostoli, *Fatima for Today*, 170.
35. 1 Kgs 18: 20-40.
36. Ibid.
37. Ibid. Haffert, in his book *Her Glorious Title*, writes that the cloud was "foot shaped" not "hand shaped." Haffert then further connects this to

Genesis 3:15, where the woman is to crush the head of the serpent. The woman is Mary, traditionally seen as Our Lady of All Grace, which corresponds with the account on Mt Carmel. All contemporary Catholic bibles that I reviewed described the cloud as a hand, not a foot.

38. Ibid.

39. Haffert, *Sign of Her Heart* (Washington, New Jersey: 101 Foundation, 1998),136. Haffert's two books, *Sign of Her Heart* and *Her Glorious Title*, are both exceptional sources for the mystery of the prophet Elijah and his role in the coming of the Virgin Mary, and his role in the coming Triumph of the Immaculate Heart.

40. Haffert, *Her Glorious Title*, 12, 17. This understanding of Mt. Carmel and the Immaculate Conception was seen to be confirmed with the apparitions at Lourdes. In 1883, at the Silver Jubilee celebration at Lourdes, the Bishop of Nines(France), Francois-Nicolas Bessson, said in his address, "Lourdes is the new Carmel where Mary has deigned to appear. Mary Immaculate appeared to the prophet (Elijah) upon the height of Carmel, raising herself from the midst of the waves under the image of a light cloud. But at Lourdes the cloud assumes color, it is transfigured. Mary is arranged in light and splendor. She speaks and reveals her name. She designates herself, she declares, 'I am the Immaculate Conception.' O! Sacred Mountain of the Orient! Great though thy glory, thou hast beheld but the shadow of what here today we possess in reality!" At Lourdes, it has been noted that Bernadette wore the brown scapular of Our Lady of Mt. Carmel before the apparitions, as was common amongst the youth in France during the time.

41. Ibid., 60, 62. At Fátima, there were other signs that connected the Miracle of the Sun with the Miracle of Fire on Mt. Carmel. During both events, after the miracles occurred, all of the water on the ground was found to have been consumed by the force of the miracle—the water filled trench around the altar on Mt. Carmel, and the water from the days of rainfall that left the Cova da Iria at Fátima a virtual swamp on October 13, 1917. Likewise, at both Mt. Carmel and Fátima, the people immediately voiced aloud that what they experienced was truly of God. Finally, it is seven times that Elijah's young servant on Mt. Carmel went to look out over the Mediterranean to see if the clouds had appeared yet, and it was seven times that the Virgin Mary appeared at Fátima. At the first apparition on May 13th, Mary told the children she would appear "seven" times. The seventh apparition occurred on June 16, 1921, at the Cova da Iria to Lúcia only. It is also noted that Mary told the children on September 13th that she *would* appear in October as Our Lady of All Sorrows and as Our Lady of Mt. Carmel.

42. Elijah has been venerated as the patron saint of Bosnia and Hercegovina since August 26, 1752. He replaced Saint George of Lydia at the request

of Bishop Pavao Dragićević. Pope Benedict XIV approved the request. It has been speculated in documents that Elijah was chosen because of his importance and significance to all three main religious groups in Bosnia and Hercegovina—Muslims, Orthodox Christians and Catholics. Pope Benedict XIV is said to have granted Bishop Dragićević's request with the remark that "a wild nation deserved a wild patron." (For more information see: https://www.deviantart.com/stanoklee/art/Elijah-the-Prophet-830112981and https://en.wikipedia.org/wiki/Pavao_Dragi%C4%8Devi%C4%87.)

AFTERWORD

1. The true story of Cooper Kirkwood as described to the author by his grandfather.

BACK COVER QUOTATIONS

1. Pope Benedict XVI: *Fatima Mysteries* by Grzegorz Górny and Janusz Rosikon (back cover)
2. Fr. Rene Laurentin, *Latest News of Medjugorje, June 1987* (p.37), *Messages and Teachings of Mary at Medjugorje* (p. 130-131)
3. Fr. Robert Faricy, *Medjugorje Up Close* (p. 87)
4. Antonio Socci, *The Fourth Secret of Fatima* (p.217)

SCRIPTURAL QUOTATIONS

All Scriptural quotations, unless otherwise indicated, are from *The New American Bible*, (revised New Testament), Catholic Bible Publishers, Wichita, Kansas, 1994-1995 EDITION.

COVER IMAGE: Shutterstock (Enhanced License Subscriber/Member). Image by Dream Perfection.

The decree of the Congregation for the Propagation of the Faith, A.A.S.58, 1186, (approved by Pope Paul VI on October 14, 1966), states that the Nihil Obstat and Imprimatur are no longer required on publications that deal with private revelations, provided they contain nothing contrary to faith and morals. The author submits to the final and official judgment of the magisterium of the Church regarding the events discussed in this book that are presently under investigation.

SELECTED BIBLIOGRAPHY

There is an extensive amount of literature on Fatima and Medjugorje. The following are some of the primary sources drawn upon in researching this book.

ARTICLES AND DOCUMENTS (CHRONOLOGICAL ORDER)

J. Rand McNally, "Letter to Professor A.N. Zaidelon on Atmospheric Testing of High Megaton Nuclear Bombs," (unpublished), September 26, 1961.

Christopher Civic, "A Fatima in a Communist Land," *Religion in Communist Lands*, Vol.10, No.1, Spring, 1982.

Fr. Ljudevit Rupčić, "Transcript of the 64 questions (with replies) asked of the six visionaries in Medjugorje, Yugoslavia," (unpublished), December, 1982.

John Christopher Mathews, "Report [to the United Nations] on Gross Violations of Fundamental Human Rights in the Village of Medjugorje, Croatia, Yugoslavia since June 24, 1981," (unpublished), International Helsinki Federation for Human Rights, January 27, 1983.

Fr. Milan Mikulich, O.F.M., S.T.D., "Apparitions of Our Lady in Medjugorje, Croatia, Yugoslavia; Still are on Full Course," *Orthodoxy of the Catholic Doctrine*, June, 1983.

Fr. Tomislav Vlašić, "The Message of Medjugorje," (unpublished draft), August 15, 1983.

Theresa Karminski, "Apparition Report: Both Plausible and Convincing," *The Catholic Standard and Times: The Official Newspaper of the Archdiocese of Philadelphia*, August 25, 1983.

Tomislav Vlašić, "Are the Apparitions in Yugoslavia for Real?", (unpublished), August 25, 1983.

John Haffert, "Confidential Interview with General Paul Tibbits on the Bombing of Hiroshima," [unreleased cassette recording – no transcript], Washington, NJ, circa 1983.

"The Messages for the Parish of Medjugorje, 1984," (unpublished), circa 1984.

Unnamed French Journalist, "Interviews with the Franciscans: Frs. Bubalo, Vlasic, Pervan, Barbaric and Kraljevic." (unpublished), circa 1984.

Ann Hermans (translator), "At Medjugorje, the Inhabitants Believe, Pray and Fast," *Le Libre Belgique,* January 9, 1984.

Theresa M. Karminski, "Reported Apparitions of Mary to Six Young Yugoslavians Being Scrutinized," *Lake Shore Visitor-Catholic Diocese of Erie,* February 17, 1984.

Bonny Rodden, "Priest a Believer After Pilgrimage to Madonna Site," *Philadelphia Dailey News,* March 13, 1984.

Robert and Annabelle Baldwin, "A Miracle in Medjugorje," *Our Sunday Visitor,* March, 1984.

John M. Haffert, "The Great Sign," *Soul Magazine,* May-June, 1984.

Dudley Plunkett, "Visions that can Contribute to the Peace of the World," *The Guardian,* July 9, 1984.

Peter Batty, "The Vision of Pope Leo XIII," *Peter Batty Newsletter,* July 26, 1984.

Fred Lilly, "What "Mr. Pentecost" Thinks About Medjugorje," *New Covenant,* October, 1984.

Rev. Michael C. Crowdy (translator), "The Present (Unofficial) Position of the Episcopal Curia of Mostar Regarding the Events at Medjugorje," *Approaches,* No. 88, Mostar, 30 October, 1984.

Jim Tibbets, "Interview of the Bishop of Mostar", (unpublished), November 8, 1984.

Fr. Milan Mikulich, O.F.M., S.T.D., "The Statement of the Commission on the Medjugorje Apparitions-March 23-24,1984," *Orthodoxy of the Catholic Doctrine,* October -December, 1984.

V. Mess, "Have You Seen the Miracles in Medjugorje?" *Danitza* (Croatian publication), December 14, 1984. (This article was published in the review *Jesus* and was written by an Italian journalist after visiting Medjugorje in June, 1984. The author's name is believed to be a pseudonym he used for the article.)

James Tibbets, "An Interview with Father Svetozar Kraljevic OFM at the Franciscan Monastery in Ljubuski, Yugoslavia," (unpublished), 1984.

Hans Urs von Balthasar (Translated by Fr. Milan Mikulich O.F.M., S.T.D.), "The Letter of Hans Urs von Balthasar, A Prominent Theologian from Switzerland, Sent to Pavao Zanic, Bishop of Mostar," *Orthodoxy of the Catholic Doctrine,* January-June, 1985.

Fr. Milan Mikulich, O.F.M., S.T.D., "Chronological Analysis of the Case of the Medjugorje Apparitions," *Orthodoxy of the Catholic Doctrine,* January-June, 1985.

Michael O'Carroll, CSSp. "Our Lady of Medjugorje–Hallucination or Apparition?", *The Sunday Press* (Dublin), January 20, 1985.

Fr. Serra, "Highlights of an Interview with One of the Visionaries by Archbishop Franic of Split and a Group of Italians," (unpublished interview conducted on January 24, 1985), Boston: MA: Center for Peace, February, 1985.

Fred Lilly, "David Du Plessis: "This is a Working of the Holy Spirit," *The Catholic Digest,* February, 1985.

Fr. Kvirin Vasily, O.F.M., "The Bishop of Mostar and the Facts," (unpublished), Beaver Falls, PA, Franciscan Fathers, March, 1985.

Rev. Milan Mikulich, O.F.M., S.T.D., "Commentary: What Happened at Medjugorje?", *Fidelity,* March, 1985.

Giorgio Sanguineti, "Critical Testimony About the Visionaries from Medjugorje", (unpublished), May 4, 1985.

Theresa Marie Karminski, "Scientists Investigate Medjugorje Apparitions," *National Catholic News Service,* May 10, 1985.

Giles Dimock, O.P., "Medjugorje: Fruits of the Spirit," *National Catholic Register,* June 16, 1985.

Mary Kenny, "Whatever is Here it Works," *The Sunday Press* (Ireland), July 28, 1985.

John Dart, "Explaining Visions of Mary: Professor Points to Psychological Origins," *The Philadelphia Inquirer,* August 4, 1985.

Orazio Petrosillo, "The Results of Scientific Tests of Two Medical Teams Agree that the Seers of Medjugorje are Neither Sick nor Deceivers," *Il Tempo* (p.21), October 9, 1985.

Fr. Slavko Barbarić, PhD, "Phenomenological Comparative Account of the 'Inner Locutions' of Jelena Vasilj and Marijana Vasilj," ['not for publication study'], October, 1985.

Henry Kamm, "Yugoslavs are Abashed: Money from a 'Miracle,'" *The New York Times,* November 18, 1985.

John Primeau, "Medjugorje; Peace or Judgement?", *The Spirit and the Word,* November, 1985.

Paul A. Fisher, "Our Lady's Secrets at Medjugorje," *The Wanderer,* December 26, 1985.

Gitta Sereny, "A Village Sees the Light," *Reader's Digest,* February, 1986.

J. Rand McNally, "The Nuclear Tornado Effect." Unpublished research paper presented at *The American Physical Society,* Washington D.C., Spring Meeting: April 28-May 1, 1986.

Agostino Bono, "Vatican Will Pursue Apparition Claims," *The Catholic Standard and Times,* June 26, 1986.

Edward O'Connor, C.S.C., "The Lady Behind the Iron Curtain," *Queen,* Sept-Oct (Part I), Nov-Dec (Part II), 1986.

Angela Dire, "McNally's Discovery of Nuclear Prophesy Led to 'Emergency'", *Gazette Telegraph,* November 16, 1986.

Bishop Paulo Hnilica, "By Their Fruits You Will Know Them (Mt 7:16)," *Medjugorje Gebetsaktion,* No. 4, December, 1986.

John M. Haffert, "A Terrible Warning", *Soul Magazine*, January-February, 1987.

Richard Szczepanowski, "Medjugorje: Despite No Official Church Statement, Reported Marian Apparitions Draw Many," *Catholic Standard: Weekly Newspaper of the Archdiocese of Washington*, March 26, 1987.

Mark Miravalle, "Medjugorje and the Media," *National Catholic Register*, June 14, 1987.

Jackson Diehl, "Crowds Visit Vision Site: Rite Occurs Daily in Rural Yugoslavia," *Washington Post Foreign Service*, July 17, 1987.

Bishop Pavao Zanic, "Homily of Bishop of Mostar for Confirmation Day," (unpublished transcript), St. James Church, Medjugorje, July 25, 1987.

Julie Asher, "Medjugorje Fever: Alleged Apparitions have Supporters and Detractors," *The Catholic Standard and Times*, July 30, 1987.

Jeanine Jacob, "Medjugorje Experiences," *The Florida Catholic* (Diocese of St. Petersburg), July 31, 1987.

Sura Rubenstein, "Is it Really a Miracle at Medjugorje? Believers Say Virgin Mary Appears Daily in Yugoslavian Village," *The Sunday Oregonian*, December 6, 1987.

Deborah Daisy, "Medical Mystery: Teacher's Recovery is Investigated as Miracle," *The Pittsburgh Press*, January 24, 1988.

Dorothy Glojek (translator), "The President of America was Inspired with the Message of Medjugorje," *Sveta Bastina* (*Holy Inheritance* newspaper, Duvno, Hercegovina), February, 1988.

John Thavis, "Alleged Apparitions Can Be Headache for Vatican Office," *Catholic Standard*, March 10, 1988.

Fr. Tomislav Vlašić, "A Calling in the Marian Year," *Mariji K Isusu Association*, March 25, 1988.

John Thavis, "Medjugorje: Pilgrims Become 'Missionaries'," *Catholic Herald*, April 7, 1988.

Vittorio Messori, "A Modern Apologist for Mary: An Interview with Father René Laurentin," *Homiletic and Pastoral Review*, May, 1988.

Richard McSorley, S.J., "Medjugorje Journal I, II, III," *Georgetown University Center for Peace Studies*, September, 1986-May, 1988.

Henry Rene Ayoub, "Medical and Scientific Studies of the Apparition at Medjugorje," *Editions of O.E.L.L.*, Paris, May, 1988.

Peter Toscani, "Medjugorje Overview," *Homiletic &Pastoral Review*, May, 1988.

Tomislav Vlašić O.F.M., "Documents: Interview with Mirjana Dragicevic," *Medjugorje Herald*, June, July, August, September, 1988.

Rev. Louis Garbacik, "Medjugorje; Is It Another Fatima?", *Hazelton Standard-Speaker*, June 23, 1988.

Alberic Stacpoole O.S.B., "My Medjugorje Experience," *Priests and People,* July-August, 1988.

Bishop Michael D. Pfeifer, O.M.I., "The Gospel, Mary and Medjugorje," *Catholic Diocese of San Angelo, Press Release,* Texas, August 5, 1988.

Jack Wintz, "The Secret of Medjugorje," *St. Anthony Messenger,* August, 1988.

Ann Marie Hancock, "Medjugorje: Signs and Wonders of Her Love," *Venture Inward-The Magazine for the Association for Research and Enlightenment,* September-October, 1988.

Rev. John Szantyr, "Medjugorje and the Miracle of the Sun," (unpublished), November, 1988.

Jack Wintz, O.F.M., "What I Saw at Medjugorje," *Catholic Digest,* November, 1988.

Fr. Tony Petrusic. "Interview with Visionary Vicka Ivankovic," (unpublished), December 12, 1988.

Fr. Slavko Barbarić, "The Immaculate Heart of Mary Will Triumph: An Interview with Cardinal Frantisek Tomasek," *Medjugorje Gebetsaktion,* No.1, 1988.

Zoran Krzelj, "Miracle of the Red Madonna," *Yugoslav Airlines Magazine,* 1988.

Fr. Tomislav Vlašić, "A Calling in the Marian Year," *Po Mariji K Isusu Association,* 1988.

Fr. Ljudevit Rupčić, "The Great Falsification: The Hidden Face of Medjugorje," (unpublished), circa 1989.

Father Robert F. Griffin, C.S.C., "Medjugorje, Miracles and a Bit of Smugness," *Our Sunday Visitor,* January 29, 1989.

Fr. Petar Ljubicic, "The Secrets", *Medjugorje Herald,* February, 1989.

NC, "Bishop Quinn Sees 'Indisputable' Spiritual Energy in Medjugorje," *The Catholic Standard and Times,* February 16, 1989.

Loretta Seyer, "Catholic Controversy: Is Mary Appearing at Medjugorje?" *The Catholic Twin Circle National Weekly Magazine,* March 19, 1989.

Thomas C. Fox, "Medjugorje: Miracle or Hoax?", *National Catholic Reporter* (Forum), Vol 25, No.22., March 24, 1989.

Michael Davies, "Letter from London: More on Medjugorje," *The Remnant,* March 31, 1989.

Helen Sarcevic, "Apparitions in Split," *Mir Peace Group,* April 23, 1989.

Helen Sarcevic, "Interviews with Vicka, Mirjana, Ivan, Jelena, and Bishop Hnilica," (unpublished), April 18-25, 1989.

Zrinko Cuvalo, O.F.M., "The Spirit of Medjugorje...The Early Dawn Days," *Medjugorje Herald,* May, 1989.

Richard Foley, "Mother Angelica Talks About Medjugorje-An Interview by Father Richard Foley, S.J.", *The Medjugorje Messenger –Canadian Edition,* May, 1989.

Greg Burke, "Medjugorje: The View from Rome," *National Catholic Register*, December 10, 1989.

Peter Hyun and Barbara J. Tyner, "The Miracle of Medjugorje," *Morning Calm-Korean Air*, December, 1989.

Rev. Leonard Orec O.F.M., "A Sanctuary in the Making," *Medjugorje Gebetsaktion*, No. 16, December,1989.

Gianni Cardinale, "Medjugorje Decision by Spring," *30 Days*, February, 1990.

CNS, "Bishop Zanic Rejects Medjugorje Claims," *The Remnant*, April 30, 1990.

Riehle Foundation, ed., "The National Conference on Medjugorje: Report by R. Laurentin," *Riehle Foundation-Pres Release*, May 12-13, 1990.

Lou Baldwin, "Medjugorje Defended: Yugoslavian Archbishop Confident Apparitions Are Genuine," *The Catholic Standard and Times of the Archdiocese of Philadelphia*, May 17, 1990.

René Laurentin, "Response by Fr. René Laurentin to the Most Recent Objections of His Excellency Bishop Zanic against Medjugorje," *The Riehle Foundation: Press Release*, May, 1990.

Msgr. Pavao Zanic, "The Truth About Medjugorje," *Fidelity Magazine*, May, 1990.

Steven Crabill, "A Little Piece of Heaven on Earth: Seeking a Miracle in Yugoslavia," *Passaic Record*, July 22, 1990.

Tihomir Karacic, "The Public Confession of a Perjured Witness" (Witness in the trial of Fr. Jozo Zovko), *Nasa Ognijista* (English translation: Fr. Chris Coric and Marie Leman), March, 1991.

Inga Saffron, "Madonna in the Balkans," *The Philadelphia Inquirer Daily Magazine*, June 21, 1991.

Anne McGlone, "The Third Secret of Fatima," *Mary's People (The National Catholic Register)*, October 25, 1992.

M.D., "I am Striving to be Better- A Conversation with Ivan," *Medjugorje Gebetsaktion*, No. 28, January 18, 1993.

Father Ljudevit Rupčić, "The Silenced Situation of the Catholic Church in Bosnia and Hercegovina," *Medjugorje Gebetsaktion*, No. 30, August, 1993.

Uta Herrmann, "David Parkes Tells How He Was Healed on Yugoslav Trip," *Naples Dailey News*, January 16, 1994.

I.D., "My Task is to be at the Disposal of the Pilgrims: Interview with Fr. Petar Ljubicic," *Medjugorje Gebetsaktion*, No. 33, January 19, 1994.

J. Rand McNally, "This Would Be the Ultimate Catastrophe," *Voice of the Sacred Hearts*, January-February, 1994.

N.M., "Prayer is the Spiritual Nourishment for Every Person: Interview with Marija Pavlovic-Lunetti," *Medjugorje Gebetsaktion*, No. 37, September 9, 1994.

Robert Moynihan, "Why is Mary Weeping," *Inside the Vatican*, Year 3, No.5, March, 1995.

VIS., "Vatican Issues Declaration on Pilgrimages to Medjugorje," *The Wanderer*, July 11, 1996.

Daniele Palmieri, "Our Lady of Akita," *Inside the Vatican*, Year 4, No.8, October, 1996.

Antonio Gaspari," Medjugorje: Deception or Miracle?", *Inside the Vatican*, Year, 4, No.9, November, 1996.

Inside the Vatican Staff, "The Third Secret: Is the End Near?", *Inside the Vatican*, Year 4, No. 9, November, 1996.

Renzo Allegri, "An Interview with René Laurentin," *Medjugorje -Torino*, December, 1996.

Antonio Gaspari, "Fatima: Faith, Marvels and Messages," *Inside the Vatican*, August-September, 1997.

Antonio Gaspari, "Did the Statue Really Weep," *Inside the Vatican*, Year 6, No. 5, May, 1998.

Frank Brown, "Vatican's Representative to Russia Attends Burial of Romanovs," *The Byzantine Catholic World*, August 2, 1998.

Robert Moynihan, "Editorial: The Fatima Prophecy", *Inside the Vatican*, Year 8, No.1, January, 2000.

Christa Kramer von Reisswitz, "Will John Paul II Reveal the Third Fatima Secret," *Inside the Vatican*, Year 8, No. 3, March, 2000.

Wlodziermierz Redzioch, "Seen from Fatima," *Inside the Vatican*, Year 8, No. 3, March, 2000.

Raymond De Souza, "The Third Secret is Out," *The National Catholic Register*, May 21-27, 2000.

"Pope Reveals Third Secret", www.cwnews.com., May, 23, 2000.

Brian McGuire, "The Third Secret: Doom or Triumph?", *National Catholic Register*, June 3, 2000.

Lucio Brunelli, "The Third Secret Involves Apostasy in the Church," www. fatima.org., June 5, 2000.

Michael Brown, "Fatima Mystery: How did a German Publication Guess at the Third Secret?" *Spirit Dailey*, March 20, 2001.

Wlodzimierz Redzioch, "Assassination Attempt: 'I Reminded Him of Fatima," *Inside the Vatican*, Year 9, No.8, October, 2001.

Joseph Pronechen, "Marian Apparitions, Why Fatima is the Key to Understand Them: She Still Warns Us," *Marian Helper*, Winter, 2001-2002.

Rudy J. Rummel, "Mass Murder Under Communism: A Few Statistics," *Inside the Vatican*, Year 10, No.1, January, 2002.

Wlodzimierz Redzioch, "Sister Lúcia Speaks," *Inside the Vatican*, Year 10, No.1, January, 2002.

Father Gerard Mura, "The Third Secret of Fatima: Has it Been Completely Revealed?", *Transalpine Redemptorists* [Orkney Isles, Scotland (Great Britain)], March, 2002.

Sandra Miesel, "A Quiet Death in Rome: Was John Paul I Murdered," *Crisis*, July-August, 2003.

Larry and Mary Sue Eck, "The Medjugorje 'First Family' in the United States," *Medjugorje Magazine*, Summer, 2006.

"Last Surviving Witness Says Third Fatima Secret is Fully Revealed," *CNA* (*Catholic News Agency*), September 12, 2007.

Inside the Vatican Staff, "Mary's Role in the Last Battle," *Inside the Vatican*, Year 16, No. 1, January, 2008.

Andrea Torniella, "Medjugorje: Communists Against Apparitions," www.lastampa.com., July, 9, 2011.

Daniel Klimek, "Fatima Visionary Saw and Confirmed the Apparitions of Our Lady of Medjugorje," www.medjugorjemiracles.com., July, 21, 2011.

Joe Tremblay, "The 100 Year Test," *CNA* (*Catholic News Agency*), February 1, 2013.

Kevin Symonds, *In Defense of the World Apostolate of Fatima*, www.catholic-stand.com.July 5, 2015.

Orth, Maureen, "Mary: The World's Most Powerful Woman," *National Geographic*, 30-59, December 2015.

"Alice Von Hildebrand Sheds New Light on Fatima," www.onepeterfive.com., May 12, 2016.

Dr. Maike Hickson, "Cardinal Ratzinger: We Have Not Published the Whole Secret of Fatima," www.onepeterfive.com., May 15, 2016.

Simcha Fisher, "The Lady of Medjugorje Is Not Your Mother," www.catholicweekly.com.,March 17, 2017.

Kevin Symonds, "Fatima and Fr. Dollinger: A Response," www.kevinsymonds.com., May 17,2016.

Steve Skojec, "On Fatima Story: Pope Emeritus Benedict XVI Breaks Silence," www.onepeterfive.com., May 21, 2016.

George Weigel, "The Ostpolitik Failed. Get Over It," *First Things*, July 20, 2016.

Maike Hickson, "A Further Confirmation of Father Dollinger's Claim About Cardinal Ratzinger and Fatima, www.onepeterfive.com., March 10, 2017.

Jonathon Luxmoore, "Polish Archbishop thinks Vatican Will Recognize Medjugorje Apparitions," www.americamagazine.org.,August 22, 2017.

Melissa Chan, "What is the Difference Between a Hydrogen and an Atomic Bomb," *Time*, September 22, 2017.

Jonathan and Clara Fleischmann, "Lúcia of Fatima, Part I: Marian Genius," www.onepeterfive.com., October 11, 2017.

Jonathan and Clara Fleischmann, "Lúcia of Fatima, Part II: The Vow of Perfection," www.onepeterfive.com.,October 12, 2017.

Jonathon and Clara Fleischmann, "Lúcia of Fatima, Part III: The Infamous Third Secret," www.onepeterfive.com.,October 13, 2017.

Jonathan and Clara Fleischmann, "Lúcia of Fatima, Part IV: Calls from Our Lady," www.onepeterfive.com., October 14, 2017.

Steve Skojec, "As 2017 Comes to a Close, Fatima Warnings Still Resonate," www.onepeterfive.com., November 21, 2017.

Michael K. Jones, "Is Medjugorje the Sequel to Fatima and the Woman Clothed with the Sun," http://www.medjugorjefatimasequel.htm., November 25, 2017.

Matthew Culligan Hoffman, "The Third Secret of Fatima and the "Hermeneutic of Conspiracy," www.catholicworldreport.com., November 27, 2017.

Antonio Socci, "Do the Hierarchies in the Church Still Have the Faith," www.roratecaeli.com., March 10, 2018.

Maike Hickson, "The Church and the World in Vertigo-We Are Still in Need of the Full Fatima Message," www.onepeterfive.com., April 3, 2018.

Fr. Richard Heilman, "Father Joseph Ratzinger's 1969 Prediction: What the Church Will Look Like in 2000," www.romanatholicman.com., April 10, 2018.

Christopher Ferrara, "The Prophecy of Bella Dodd," *Cristian Order Magazine*, November, 2,000. Reprinted by Brian Kelly, "Bella Dodd's Prophecy of Communist Tactics in Infiltrating the Church," *Fatima Perspectives*, www.archive.fatima.org., June 11, 2018.

Jonathan Luxmoore, "Pope's Delegate Outlines Plans for Expansion at Medjugorje Shrine," *Crux*, September 20, 2018.

Fr. Richard Hellman, "Things Accelerate Toward the End: Prophecy of Archbishop Fulton Sheen," www.romancatholicman.com.,October 27, 2018.

Andrea Tornielli, "Fatima: The Prophecy, the Envelope, the Missing Words, and the Denial of Ratzinger," www.lastampa.com., October 27, 2018.

Sarah MacDonald, "Vatican Official: Church Must Be Prudent Judging Medjugorje Apparitions", www.Americamagazine.org., August 16,2019.

Richard Chonak, "A Leak from the Medjugorje Study Commission," *Catholic Light*, www.catholiclight.stblogs.org/Inc., February 12, 2020.

Pope Francis Tells Youth at Medjugorje: Be inspired by the Virgin Mary," *CNA (Catholic News Agency)*, www.catholicnewsagency.com., August 2, 2020.

BOOKS

Allegri, Renzo. *The Pope of Fatima*. Milan, Italy: Arnoldo Mondadori Editore, 2006.

Alonso, Joaquin Maria, C.M.F. *The Secret of Fatima*. Cambridge: The Ravengate Press, 1976.

Alonso, Joaquin Maria and Ribeiro, Abilio Pina. *Fatima: Message and Consecration*. Fatima, Portugal: Consolata Missions' Publications, 1984.

Anderson, Annelise, Anderson, Martin, and Skinner, Kiron. *Reagan, In His Own Hand*. New York: Free Press, 2001.

Apostoli, Fr. Andrew, C.F.R. *Fatima for Today: The Urgent Marian Message of Hope*. San Francisco: Ignatius Press, 2010.

Ashton, Joan. *Mother of All Nations*. New York: Harper and Row, 1989.

——. *The People's Madonna: An Account of the Visions of Mary at Medjugorje*. London, UK: Harper Collins Publishers, 1991.

Baker, Peter and Glasser, Susan. *Kremlin Rising: Vladimir Putin's Russia and the End of Revolution*. Washington D.C.: Potomac Books, Inc., 2005, revised edition, 2007.

Barbarić, Fr. Slavko. *In the School of Love*. Milford, OH: Faith Publishing Company, 1993.

——. *Pearls of the Wounded Heart*. Medjugorje: Mir Information Center, 1998.

——. *Pray with the Heart*. Steubenville, OH: Franciscan University Press, 1988.

Barrett, Lawrence I. *Gambling with History: Reagan in the White House*. New York: Doubleday, 1983.

Bartholomew, Professor Courtney, M.D. *The Last Help Before the End of Time: The Ultimate message of Fatima*. Goleta, CA: Queenship Publishing Company, 2005.

Bartulica, Nicholas, M.D. *Are the Seers Telling the Truth?* Chicago, IL: Croatian Franciscan Press, 1991.

Bedard, Fr. Bob. *Medjugorje Reflections*. Toronto, Ontario: Koinonia Enterprises, 1989.

——. *Medjugorje: Prophecy for Our Time*. Ottawa, Canada: Catholic Renewal Centre, 1982.

——. *Medjugorje: A Second Look*. Ottawa, Canada: Catholic Renewal Centre, 1984.

Bertone, Cardinal Tarcisio. *The Last Secret of Fatima*. New York: Image, Doubleday, 2008.

Beyer, Rev. Richard. *Medjugorje: Day by Day*. Notre Dame, IN: Ave Maria Press, 1993.

Bianchi, Fr. Luigi. *Fatima and Medjugorje* (4th Edition). Gera Lario, Italy: Bianchi, 1985.

Blackbourn, David. *Marpingen: Apparitions of the Virgin Mary in a Nineteenth Century German Village*. New York: Vintage Books, 1993.

Blue Army. *There is Nothing More*. Washington, NJ: AMI Press, circa 1975.

Borelli, Anthony A. and Spann, John R. *Our Lady at Fatima: Prophecies of Tragedy or Hope?* York, PA: The American Society for the Defense of Tradition, Family and Property, 1975.

Brochado, Costa, Boehrer, George C.A., ed. and trans. *Fatima in the Light of History*. Milwaukee, WI: Bruce Publishing Company, 1955.

Brockman, John, ed. *This Will Change Everything: Ideas That Will Shape the Future*. New York: Harper Perennial, 2009.

Brown, Hilary. *The Great War: History's Most Tragic Conflict,1914-1918*. London, UK: Go Entertainment Group, 2014.

Brown, Michael. *The Final Hour*. Milford, OH: Faith Publishing Company, 1992.

——. *Fear of Fire*. Palm Coast, FL: Spirit Daily Publishing, 2013.

——. *Sent to Earth*. Goleta, CA: Queenship Publishing, 2000.

——. *The Day Will Come*. Ann Arbor, MI: Servant Publications, 1996.

——. *The Last Secret*. Ann Harbor, MI: Servant Publications, 1998.

——. *Tower of Light*. Palm Coast, FL: Spirit Daily Publishing, 2007.

Brown, Wilmott G. *The Significance of Lourdes, Fatima, and Medjugorje as Explained in Scripture*. Winter Park, FL: Wilmot G. Brown, 1995.

Bubalo, Fr. Janko, O.F.M. *A Thousand Encounters with the Blessed Virgin Mary in Medjugorje*. Chicago, IL: Friends of Medjugorje, 1987.

——. *Testimonies: Medjugorje, Blessed Land*. Croatia: Jesla, 1986.

Cacella, Rev. Joseph. *Fatima and the Rosary: A Brief History of the Wonders of Fatima, Portugal*. New York: St. Anthony's Welfare Center, circa 1948.

Cappa, Alphonse M. S.S.P. *Fatima: Cove of Wonders*. Boston, MA: St. Paul Editions, circa 1980.

Carberry, Thomas F. *Medjugorje and Guadalupe: Parallels and Speculation. Will Medjugorje Lead to the Conversion of Russia?* Burlington, MA: T.F. Carberry, 1988.

Carmel of Coimbra. *A Pathway Under the Gaze of Mary: Biography of Sister Maria Lucia of Jesus and the Immaculate Heart*. Coimbra, Portugal: World Apostolate of Fatima, 2015.

Carroll, Rev. Msgr. Richard L. *Oasis of Peace: Our Refuge in the Tribulations*. Diamondhead, MI: Signs and Wonders, 2002.

Carroll, Warren H. *1917: Red Banners, White Mantle*. Front Royal, VA: Christendom Publications, 1981.

Carter, Rev. S.J. *The Spirituality of Fatima and Medjugorje*. Milford, OH: Faith Publishing Company, 1994.

Casaletto, Thomas. *A State of Emergency*. New York: Richardson & Steinman, 1987.

Catechism of the Catholic Church-Liberia Editrice Vaticana. New Hope, KY: Urbi et Orbi Communications, 1994.

Cheston, Sharon E. *Mary the Mother of All: Protestant Perspectives and Experiences of Medjugorje*. Chicago, IL: Loyola University Press, 1992.

Christian, William A. Jr. *Visionaries*. Berkeley, CA: University of California Press, 1996.

Cirrincione, Msgr. Joseph A. with Nelson, Thomas A. *St. Joseph, Fatima and Fatherhood: Reflections on the Miracle of the Sun*. Rockford, IL: TAN Books and Publishers, 1989.

——. *The Forgotten Secret of Fatima and the Silent Apostolate*. Rockford, IL: TAN Books and Publishers, 1988.

——. *The Rosary and the Crisis of Faith: Fatima and World Peace*. Rockford, IL: TAN Books and Publishers, 1986.

Cirrincione, Msgr. Joseph A. *Venerable Jacinta Marto of Fatima*. Rockford, IL: TAN Books and Publishers, 1992.

——. *Fatima's Message for Our Times*. Rockford, IL: TAN Books and Publishers, 1990.

Citrano, Louis J. *Jesus, Mary, Medjugorje, and Me*. Metairie, LA: New Writers' Inc., 2005.

Clissold, Stephen, ed. *A Short History of Yugoslavia*. Cambridge: Cambridge University Press, 1966.

Connell, Jan. *Queen of the Cosmos*. Orleans, MA: Paraclete Press, 1990.

Connell, Janice T. *The Secrets of Mary: Gifts from the Blessed Mother*. New York: St. Martin's Press, 2009.

——. *The Triumph of the Immaculate Heart*. Santa Barbara, CA: Queenship Publishing Company, 1993.

——. *The Visions of the Children*. New York: St. Martin's Griffin, 1992, Revised Edition, 2007.

Covic-Radojicic, Sabrina. *Mirjana Dragićević Soldo: Visionary of Our Lady in Medjugorje: Guardian of the Secrets*. Paris, France: Les Editions Sakramento, 2018.

Covic, Sabrina. *Encounters with Father Jozo*. Paris, France: Les Editions Sakramento, 2003.

Craig, Mary. *Spark from Heaven: The Mystery of the Madonna of Medjugorje*. Notre Dame, IN: Ave Maria Press, 1988.

Cyr, Bruce. *After the Warning 2016*. Alberta, Canada: Bruce A. Cyr, 2013.

Danish, Peter. *Medjugorje-The Final Prophecy*. Bulverde, TX: True North Publishing, 2015.

Davies, Michael. *Medjugorje, A Warning*. St. Paul, MN: The Remnant Press, 1988.

——. *Medjugorje: After Fifteen Years* (2nd Edition). St. Paul, MN: The Remnant Press, 1998.

——. *Medjugorje: After Twenty Twenty-One Years (1981-2002)*. [Full text], Archive. Org. 2005.

Delaney, John J., ed. *A Woman Clothed with the Sun*. New York: Doubleday, 1961.

De Marchi, John. *Fatima: From the Beginning*. Torres Novas, Portugal: Missoes Consolata, 1950.

De Marchi, John I.M.C. *Mother of Christ Crusade*. Billings, MT: Mother of Christ Crusade, Inc., 1947.

DeMers, John. *Invited to Light: A Search for the Good News in Medjugorje*. Chicago, IL: Trinakria Press, 1990.

De Oca, Rev. V. Montes CSSp. *More About Fatima*. USA: L. Owen Traynor, K.M., 1945.

Dinolfo, John. *A Place of Healing: The Virgin Mary in Medjugorje*. Toronto, Canada: Ave Maria Centre of Peace, 2001.

Dirvin, Joseph I.C.M. *St. Catherine Laboure of the Miraculous Medal*. Rockford, IL: TAN Books and Publishers, 1987.

Donia & Fine, Jr. *Bosnia &Hercegovina*. New York: Columbia University Press, 1994.

Dziwisz, Cardinal Stanislaw. *A Life with Karol: My Forty Year Friendship with the Man Who Became Pope*. New York: Image, Doubleday, 2008.

Eck, Larry & Mary Sue. *The Embrace of the Gospa: Miraculous Stories from Medjugorje Magazine*. Westmont, IL: Epiphany Formations, Inc., 1995.

——. *Will You Be My Priest? Stories of Men Who Said "Yes" to God's Call through Medjugorje*. Westmont, IL: Medjugorje Magazine, 2009.

Ellis, Sue. *Dear Children: Words from the Mother of God at Medjugorje*. Surrey, UK: Marian Spring Centre, 1993.

Emanuele; Lane, Edmund C., S.S.P., translator. *Medjugorje: A Portfolio of Images*. New York: Alba House, 1987.

Evaristo, Carlos. *Saint Michael and the Fatima Connection*. Fatima, Portugal: Evaristo, 1992.

——. *"Two Hours with Sister Lucia."* Fatima, Portugal: Evaristo, 1996.

Fellows, Mark. *Fatima in Twilight*. Niagara Falls, Canada-USA: Marmion Publications, 2003.

Ferrara, Christopher A. *The Secret Still Hidden*. Pound Ridge, New York: Good Counsel Publications, 2008.

Ficocelli, Elizabeth. *Bleeding Hands, Weeping Stone*. Charlotte, NC: Saint Benedict Press, 2009.

——. *The Fruits of Medjugorje: Stories of True and Lasting Conversion*. New York/Mahwah, N.J: Paulist Press, 2006.

Flynn, Ted and Maureen. *The Thunder of Justice*. Herndon, Virginia: MaxKol Communications, 1993, revised edition, 2010.

Flynn, Ted. *The Great Transformation*. Herndon, Virginia: MaxKol Communications, Inc., 2015.

Foley, Donel Anthony. *Medjugorje Revisited: 30 Years of Visions or Religious Fraud?* Nottingham, England: Theotokas Books, 2011.

Foley, Fr. Richard, SJ. *The Drama of Medjugorje*. Dublin: Veritas Publications, 1992.

Fonseca, Luigi Gonzaga. *The Marvels of Fatima*. San Paulo, Italy: Cinisello Balsamo, 1997.

Fox, Rev.Robert J. *Rediscovering Fatima*. Huntington, IN: Our Sunday Visitor, Inc., 1982.

Fox, Father Robert J. *The Intimate Life of Sister Lucia*, Hanceville, AL: Fatima Family Apostolate, 2001.

Fox, Fr. Robert J. and Martins, Fr. Antonio Maria, S.J. *Documents on Fatima & the Memoirs of Sister Lucia: Pictorial Documentary & Historical Update* (English Edition). Waite Park, MN: Family Fatima Apostolate, Park Press, Inc., 1992.

Francois, Frere de Marie des Agnes. *Fatima: The Only Way to World Peace*. Buffalo, NY: Immaculate Heart Publications, 1993.

——. *Fatima: Tragedy and Triumph*. Buffalo, NY: Immaculate Heart Publications, 1994.

Galot, Jean, S.J. *ABBA, Father, We Long to See Your Face: Theological Insights into the First Person of the Trinity*. New York: Alba House, 1992.

Girard, Fr. Guy, S.SS.A.; Girard, Fr. Armand., S.SS.A. and Bubalo, Fr. Janko., O.F.M. *Mary Queen of Peace Stay with Us*. Montreal, Canada: Editiones-Paulines, 1988.

Golob, D.R. *"Live the Messages": The Messages of Mary, Mother of Jesus Christ Lord God, Mary, Queen of Peace Medjugorje*. Harahan, LA: D.R. Golob, 1987.

Gorny, Grzegorz, and Rosikon, Janusz. *Fatima Mysteries*. San Francisco and Warsaw, Poland: Rosikon Press and Ignatius Press, 2017.

Gress, Carrie, Ph. D. *The Marian Option: God's Solution to a Civilization in Crisis*. Charlotte, NC: TAN Books, 2017.

Grillo, Bishop Girolamo. *Our Lady Weeps: Report on Civitavecchia*. Toronto, Ontario: Ave Maria Press, 1997.

Gruner, Father Nicholas, and other Fatima Experts. *World Enslavement or Peace...It's Up to the Pope*. Ontario, Canada: The Fatima Crusader, circa 1988.

Guerrera, Fr. Vittorio. *Medjugorje: A Closer Look*. Meriden, CT: Maryheart Crusaders, 1995.

Haffert, John M. *Deadline: The Third Secret of Fatima*. Asbury, NJ: The 101 Foundation, Inc., 2001.

——. *Dear Bishop: The History of the Blue Army*. Washington, NJ: AMI International Press, 1982.

——. *Explosion of the Super-Natural*. Washington, NJ: Pillar, AMI Press, 1975.

——. *Finally, Russia!* Asbury, NJ: The 101 Foundation, Inc., 1993.

——. *From a Morning Prayer: Autobiography*. Washington, NJ: Ave Maria Institute, Inc., 1947.

——. *God's Final Effort*. Asbury NJ: The 101 Foundation, Inc., 1999.

——. *Her Own Words to the Nuclear Age*. Asbury, NJ: The 101 Foundation, Inc., 1993.

——. *Meet the Witnesses*. Washington, NJ: AMI Press, 1961.

——. *Night of Love*. Asbury, NJ: The 101 Foundation, Inc., 1996, revised edition, 1997.

——. *Now, The Woman Shall Conquer*. Asbury, NJ: The 101 Foundation, Inc., 1997.

——. *Sign of Her Heart*. Washington, NJ: Ave Maria Institute, 1971.

——. *The Brother and I*. Washington, NJ: Ave Maria Institute, 1971.

——. *The Day I Didn't Die*. Asbury NJ: Lay Apostolate Foundation, 1998.

——. *The Great Event*. Asbury, NJ: The 101 Foundation, Inc., 2000.

——. *The Hand of Fatima*. Washington, NJ: AMI Press, 1984.

——. *The World's Greatest Secret*. Washington, NJ: AMI Press, 1967.

——. *Too Late?* Asbury, NJ: Queen of the World Center, 1999.

——. *To Prevent This*. Asbury, NJ: The 101 Foundation, Inc., 1993.

——. *To Shake the World: Life of John Haffert*. Asbury, NJ: The 101 Foundation, Inc., 2001.

——. *You, Too, Go into the Vineyard*. Asbury, NJ: The 101 Foundation, Inc., 1989.

Hardiman, James. *The Incredible Story of the Song of Three Shepherds: A non-Catholic Meets the Miracles of Fatima*. New Hope, KY: Family Fatima Apostolate, 1993.

Herbert, S.M., Albert J. *Medjugorje: An Affirmation and Defense*. Paulina, LA: Albert J. Herbert, S.M., 1990.

Heintz, Peter. *A Guide to Apparitions*. Sacramento, CA: Gabriel Press, 1993.

Howe, Cathy. *A Heavenly Promise: In Search of My Mother's Garden, I Found My Own*. Tarentum, PA: World Association Publishers, 2018.

Hummer, Franz. *Medjugorje*. West Concord, MA: Center for Peace, 1987.

Hummer, Franz, and Jungwirth, Christian. *Medjugorje, Reports, Pictures, Documents*. Duvno, Bosnia-Hercegovina: Sveta Rastina, 1986.

John Paul II, His Holiness. *Crossing the Threshold of Hope*. New York: Alfred A. Knopf, 1994.

John Paul, II. *Centesimus Anus*. London, UK: Catholic Truth Society, 1991.

——. *Memory and Identity: Conversations at the Dawn of the Millennium*. New York: Rizzoli, 2005.

Johnston, Francis. *Fatima: The Great Sign*. Rockford, IL: TAN Books and Publishers, 1980.

Jones, E. Michael, Ph.D. *Medjugorje: The Untold Story*. South Bend, IN: Fidelity Press, 1988.

Jones, E. Michael. *The Medjugorje Deception*. South Bend, IN: Fidelity Press, 2010.

Jones, Michael Kenneth. *Medjugorje Investigated*. Medjugorje, Bosnia & Hercegovina: Devotions, Catholic Books, Music, and Souvenir Shops, 2006.

Kaczmarek, Louis. *The Wonders She Performs*. Manassas, VA: Trinity Communications, 1986.

Kelly, Cynthia J., ed. *The Manhattan Project*. New York: Black Dog and Leventhal Publishers, 2007.

Kengor, Paul. *A Pope and a President*. Wilmington, DE: ISI Books, 2017.

——. *The Devil and Karl Marx: Communism's Long March of Death, Deception, and Infiltration*. Gastonia, NC: TAN Books, 2020.

Klanac, D. *Medjugorje, Responses aux Objections*. Canada: Le Serment, 2001.

Klaus, Rita. *Rita's Story*. Orleans, MA: Paraclete Press, 1993.

Klimek, Daniel Maria. *Mejugorje and the Supernatural: Science, Mysticism, and the Extraordinary Religious Experience*. Oxford, United Kingdom: Oxford University Press, 2018.

Klins, June. *The Best of "The Spirit of Medjugorje: Volume I, 1988-1997."* Bloomington, IN: Authorhouse, 2005.

Knotzinger, Kurt. *Antwort Auf Medjugorje (Answer to Medjugorje)*. Germany: Styria Graf, 1985.

Kordic, Ivan, Ph.D. *The Apparitions of Medjugorje: A Critical Conclusion*. Zagreb, Croatia: K. Kresimir, 1994.

Kotkin, Stephen. *Armageddon Averted: The Soviet Collapse 1970-2000*. New York: Oxford University Press, 2001.

Kowalska, M. Faustina. *Diary of Sister Maria Faustina Kowalska: Divine Mercy in My Soul*. Stockbridge, MA: Marian Press, 1987.

Kraljevic, Svetozar, O.F.M. *In the Company of Mary*. Nashville, TN: St. Francis Press, 1988.

——. *Pilgrimage: Reflections of a Medjugorje Priest*. Orleans, MA: Paraclete Press, 1991.

——. *The Apparitions of Mary at Medjugorje*. Chicago, IL: Franciscan Herald Press, 1984.

Kramer, Father Paul. *The Devil's Final Battle*. Terryville, CT: Good Counsel Publications, 2002.

Krepinevich, Andrew F. *7 Deadly Scenarios: A Military Futurist Explores War in the Twenty-First Century*. New York: Bantam Books, 2010.

Kselman, Thomas A. *Miracles and Prophecies in Nineteenth Century France*. New Brunswick, NJ: Rutgers University Press, 1983.

Laurentin, Fr. René, and Joyeux, Henri. *Scientific and Medical Studies on the Apparitions at Medjugorje*. Dublin, Ireland: Veritas Publishers, 1987.

Laurentin, Fr. René, and Lejeune, Fr. René. *Messages and Teachings of Mary at Medjugorje*. Milford, OH: Riehle Foundation, 1988.

Laurentin, Fr. René. *Eight Years: Reconciliation, Analysis, the Future*. Milford, OH: Riehle Foundation, 1989.

——. *Is the Virgin Mary Appearing in Medjugorje?* Washington, D.C.: The Word Among Us Press, 1984.

——. *Latest News of Medjugorje: June 1987*. Milford, OH: Riehle Foundation, 1987.

——. *Learning from Medjugorje*. Gaithersburg, MD: The Word Among Us Press, 1988.

——. *Medjugorje Testament: Hostility Abounds, Grace Superabounds*. Toronto, Ontario: Ave Maria Press, 1998.

——. *Medjugorje -13 Years Later*. Milford, OH: The Riehle Foundation, 1994.

——. *Medjugorje: 12 Years Later, War, Love Your Enemies*. Santa Barbara: CA: Queenship Publishing, 1993.

——. *Nine Years of Apparitions*. Milford, OH: Riehle Foundation, 1991.

——. *Report on Apparitions*. Milford, OH, Riehle Foundation, 1989.

——. *Seven Years of Apparitions: Time for the Harvest?* Milford, OH: Riehle Foundation, 1988.

——. *Sixteen Years of Apparitions: Peace and Deepening in the Expectation of the Ten Secrets*. Paris, France: F.X. de Guibert, 1997.

——. *Ten Years of Apparitions: New Growth and Recognition of Pilgrimages*. Milford, OH: Faith Publishing Company, 1991.

——. *The Apparitions of Medjugorje Prolonged*. Milford, OH: Riehle Foundation, 1987.

——. *The Apparitions of the Blessed Virgin Mary Today*. Dublin, Ireland: Veritas Publishers, 1990.

——. *The Cause of Liberation in the USSR*. Santa Barbara, CA: Queenship Publishing Company, 1993.

——. *The Church and Apparitions - Their Status and Function: Criteria and Reception*. Milford, OH: Riehle Foundation, 1989.

Lindsey, David Michael. *The Woman and the Dragon*. Gretna, LA: Pelican Publishing Company, 2000.

Ljubicic, Petar. *The Call of the Queen of Peace*. Zagreb, Croatia: Glas Mira Medjugorje, 1996.

Lord, Bob and Penny. *The Many Faces of Mary: A Love Story*. Slidell, LA: Journeys of Faith, 1987.

Lynch, Dan. *The Ten Secrets of the Blessed Virgin Mary: How to Prepare for their Warnings*. St. Albans, VT: John Paul Press, 2011.

Maillard, Sister Emanuel. *Medjugorje: The 1990's*. Pittsburgh, PA: St. Andrew's Productions, 1997.

——. *Medjugorje: The War Day by Day*. Miami, FL: Florida Center for Peace, 1993.

Maillard, Sister Emanuel and Nolan, Denis. *Medjugorje: What Does the Church Say?* Santa Barbara, CA: Queenship Publishing Company, 1995, revised edition, 1998.

Manifold, Deirdre. *Fatima and the Great Conspiracy*. Galway, Ireland: The Militia of Our Immaculate Mother, 1982.

Manuel, David. *Medjugorje Under Siege*. Orleans, MA.: Paraclete Press, 1992.

Maria Lucia of Jesus and of the Immaculate Heart, Sr. *How I See the Message*. Coimbra, Portugal: Carmel of Coimbra and the Secretary office of the Shepherds, revised edition, 2007.

Marin, Jacov. *Queen of Peace in Medjugorje*. Milford, OH: Riehle Foundation, 1989.

Martins, Antonio S.J. *Fatima: Way of Peace*. Devon, Chulmleigh: Augustine Publishing Company, 1989.

Martins, Fr. Antonio Maria, S.J. and Fox, Father Robert J. *Documents on Fatima and the Memoirs of Sister Lucia; Pictorial Documentary & Historical Update*. Hanceville, AL: Fatima Family Apostolate, 2001.

McFadden, Eleanor. *Words of Our Lady: Medjugorje Messages (Map Form)*. Dublin, Ireland: Eleanor McFadden, 2000.

McGlynn, Fr. Thomas. *Vision of Fatima*. Manchester, NH: Sophia Institute Press, 2017.

McKenna, Thomas J. *The Fatima Century*. San Diego, CA: Catholic Action for Faith and Family, 2017.

McNamara, Joseph E., ed. *Medjugorje-The Sunset and the Need for Prayer Groups*. Milford, OH: Riehle Foundation, 1990.

Medjugorje, A Friend of. *Look What Happened While You Were Sleeping*. Sterret, AL: Caritas of Birmingham, 2007.

Medjugorje,.Org. *The Medjugorje Messages: 1981-2013*. DeKalb, IL: The Medjugorje Web, 2013.

Meyer, Gabriel. *A Portrait of Medjugorje*. Studio City, CA: Twin Circle Publishing Company, 1990.

Michel, Frere de la Sainte Trinite. *Fatima Revealed...and Discarded*. Chulmleigh, Devon: Augustine Publishing Company, 1988.

——. *The Whole Truth About Fatima, Volume I, Science and the Facts*. Buffalo, NY: Immaculate Heart Publications, 1983.

——. *The Whole Truth About Fatima, Volume II, The Secret and the Church*. Buffalo, NY: Immaculate Heart Publications, 1989.

——. *The Whole Truth About Fatima, Volume III, The Third Secret*. Buffalo, NY: Immaculate Heart Publications, 1990.

Mikulich, Fr. Milan O.F.M. *The Apparitions of Our Lady in Medjugorje*. Portland, OR: Orthodoxy of the Catholic Doctrine, 1984.

Miller, Rev. Frederick L., ed. *Exploring Fatima*. Washington, NJ: AMI Press, 1989.

Minutoli, Armando. *Medjugorje: A Pilgrim's Journey*. Medford, NY: The Morning Star Press, 1991.

Miravalle, Mark, S.T.D. *Heart of the Message of Medjugorje*. Steubenville, OH: Franciscan University Press, 1988.

——. *Introduction to Medjugorje*. Goleta, CA: Queenship Publishing, 2004.

——. *The Message of Medjugorje*. Lanham, MD: University Press of America, 1986.

Morin Jerry. *To the World: A Conversion Story*.Des Moines, IA: Respond Ministry, Inc. Publications, 1998.

Mulligan, James. *Medjugorje: What's Happening?* Brewster, MA.: Paraclete Press, 2008.

Murphey, Guy, O.P. *The Weapon of Medjugorje*. Hillside, IL: Totally Yours, 2006.

Nichols, Aiden, O.P. *Rome and the Eastern Churches: A Study in Schism*. Collegeville, MN: The Liturgical Press, 1992.

Nolan, Denis. *Medjugorje: A Time for Truth, A Time for Action*. Santa Barbara, CA: Queenship Publishing, 1993.

——. *Medjugorje and the Church*. Goleta, CA: Queenship Publishing Company, 1995.

O'Carroll, Michael, CSSp. *Is Medjugorje Approved?* Dublin, Ireland: Veritas Publishers, 1991.

——. *Medjugorje: Facts, Documents, Theology*. Dublin, Ireland: Veritas Publishers, 1986.

O'Conner, Edward D., C.S.C. *I Am Sending You Prophets; The Role of Apparitions in the History of the Church*. Goleta, CA: Queenship Publishing, 2007.

——. *Marian Apparitions Today*. Santa Barbara, CA: Queenship Publishing Company, 1996.

O'Connor, Fr. John O.S.A. *Medjugorje: The Story and the Message*. Galway, Ireland: Marian Promotions, 1989.

——. *Medjugorje: Where the Cock Crows and the Birds Sings*. Galway, Ireland: Marian Promotions, 1986.

Odell, Catherine M. *Those Who Saw Her*. Huntington, IN: Our Sunday Visitor Publishing Division, 1986.

O'Leary, Finbar. *Meeting with our Lady of Medjugorje: With Prayer Group Messages from Ivan, Marijana, Marija, and Jelena*. Dublin, Ireland: Columba Books, 2014.

——. *Vicka: Her Story*. Dublin, Ireland: The Columba Press, 2015.

O'Neil, Michael. *Exploring the Miraculous*. Huntington, IN: Our Sunday Visitor, 2015.

O'Reilly, Bill and Dugard, Martin. *Killing the Rising Sun*. New York, NY: Henry Holt and Company, 2016. w

O'Sullivan, Desmond and O'Carroll, Fr. Michael., CSSp. *The Alliance of the Hearts of Jesus and Mary: Testimonies*. Dublin, Ireland, 1997.

Owen, Hugh. *The Light Comes from the East*. Mount Jackson, Virginia: Hugh Owen, 2015.

Parsons, Heather. *A Light Between the Hills*. Dublin, Ireland: Robert Andrew Press, 1994.

Paolini, Solideo. *Fatima: Do Not Despise Prophecies*. Tavagnacco, Italy: Edizioni Segno, 2005.

Pelletier, Joseph, A.A. *The Queen of Peace Visits Medjugorje*. Worcester, MA.: Assumption Publications, 1985.

———. *The Sun Danced at Fatima*. Garden City, NY: Image Books, Doubleday, 1951.

Pervan, Tomislav, O.F.M. *Queen of Peace: Echo of the Eternal Word*. Steubenville, OH: Franciscan University Press, 1986.

Petrisko, Thomas W. *Call of the Ages*. Santa Barbara, CA: Queenship Publishing, 1996.

———. *Fatima's Third Secret Explained*. Pittsburgh, PA: St. Andrew's Productions, 2001.

———. *Inside Heaven and Hell*. Pittsburgh, PA: St. Andrew 's Productions, 2000.

———. *Inside Purgatory*. Pittsburgh, PA: St. Andrews Productions, 2000.

———. *Living in the Heart of the Father*. Pittsburgh, PA: St. Andrew's Productions, 2013.

———. *The Fatima Prophecies: At the Doorstep of the World*. Pittsburgh, PA: St. Andrew 's Productions, 1998.

———. *The Last Crusade*. McKees Rocks, PA: St. Andrew's Productions, 1996.

———. *The Miracle of the Illumination of All Consciences*. Pittsburgh, PA: St. Andrew's Productions, 2000.

———. *The Mystery of Divine Paternal Heart of God Our Father*. Pittsburgh, PA: St. Andrew's Productions, 2015.

———. *The Sorrow, the Sacrifice, and the Triumph*. New York: Simon and Schuster, Inc., 1995.

Pilgrim Virgin Committee. *Our Lady of Fatima: Our Mother Comes to Us*. Asbury, NJ: Pilgrim Virgin Committee, 1998.

Pirjevec, Joze. *Tito and His Comrades*. Madison WI: University of Wisconsin Press, 2018.

Plunkett, Dudley. *Queen of Prophets: The Gospel Message of Medjugorje*. New York: Doubleday, 1992.

Proctor, Jim d'Urfe. *Sailing Beyond the Sea*. Santa Barbara, CA: Queenship Publishing Company, 1996.

Pronechen, Joseph. *The Fruits of Fatima: A Century of Signs and Wonders*. Manchester, NH: Sophia Institute Press, 2019.

Rangers, Christopher, OFM Cap. *The Youngest Prophet: The Life of Jacinta Marto, Fatima Visionary*. New York: Alba House, 1986.

Reader's Digest, the eds. *Reader's Digest Illustrated Story of World War II*. Pleasantville, NY: The Reader's Digest Association, Inc., 1969.

Remnick, David. *Lenin's Tomb: The Last Days of the Soviet Empire*. New York: Random House, 1993.

Riehle Foundation, the eds. *A Man Named Father Jozo*. Milford, OH: The Riehle Foundation, 1989.

Richard, Abbe M. *What Happened at Pontmain?* Washington, NJ: Ave Maria Institute, 1971.

Riehle Foundation, the eds. *Medjugorje and Meditations, Witnesses, and Teachings*. Milford, OH: The Riehle Foundation, 1988.

Rooney, Lucy, S.N.D. and Faricy, Robert, S.J. *A Medjugorje Retreat*. New York: Alba House, 1989.

——. *Mary, Queen of Peace*. New York: Alba House, 1984.

——. *Medjugorje Journal*. Essex, England: McCremmon Publishing Co., Ltd., 1987.

——. *Medjugorje Unfolds*. Steubenville, Ohio: Franciscan University Press, 1985.

——. *Medjugorje Up Close*. Chicago, IL: Franciscan Herald Books, 1985.

Rosage, Msgr.David E. *Mary, Star of the New Millennium: Guiding Us to Renewal*. Ann Harbor, MI: Servant Publications, 1997.

Rosenbaum, Ron. *How the End Begins: The Road to a Nuclear World War III*. New York, NY: Simon and Shuster, 2011.

Ruane, Rev. Gerald P., and Williams, Ruthann, op. *Thank You for Hearing My Call: Living the Messages of Medjugorje*. Caldwell, NJ: Sacred Heart Press, 1990.

Rupčić, Fr. Ljudevit. *Medjugorje in the History of Salvation*. Zagreb, Yugoslavia: Duvno, 1988.

Rupčić, Dr. Ljudevit and Nuic, Dr. Viktor. *Once Again, The Truth About Medjugorje*. Zagreb, Croatia: K. Kresimir, 2002.

Rupčić, Ljudevit. *The Truth About Medjugorje*. Yugoslavia: Lubiski-Hume, 1990.

Rutkoski, Thomas. *Apostles of the Last Days: The Fruits of Medjugorje*. Evans City, PA: Gospa Missions, 1992.

Santos, Lucia dos. *Fatima in Lucia's Own Words: Sister Lucia's Memoirs*. [Edited by Fr. Louis Kondor, SVD]. Translated by Dominican Nuns of the Perpetual Rosary. Fatima, Portugal: Postulation Centre, 1976.

——. *Fatima in Lucia's Own Words II: Sister Lucia's Memoirs, Volume II*. Edited by Fr. Louis Kondor SVD. Translated by the Dominican Nuns of the Perpetual Rosary (Fatima) and the Dominican Nuns of Monteiro de Santa Maria (Lisbon). Fatima, Portugal: Secretariado dos Pastorinhos, 1999.

Schweizer, Peter. *Victory: The Reagan Administration's Secret Strategy that Hastened the Collapse of the Soviet Union*. New York: Atlantic Monthly Press, 1996.

Seewald, Peter. *Benedict XVI-Light of the World: The Pope, the Church and the Signs of the Times*. San Francisco, CA: Ignatius Press, 2010.

Sharkey, Don. *The Woman Shall Conquer*. Libertyville, IL: Franciscan Marytown Press, 1954.

Schiffer, Hubert F. SJ. *The Rosary of Hiroshima.*Washingtom, NJ: The Blue Army, 1953.

Shamom, Rev. Albert J.M. *The Power of the Rosary.* Milford, OH: The Riehle Foundation, 1990.

Siguenza, Eduardo. *John Paul II: The Pope Who Understood Fatima.* Goleta, CA: Queenship Publishing Company, 2007.

Singleton, Fred. *A Short History of the Yugoslav Peoples.* Cambridge: Cambridge University Press, 1985.

Sister Lucia of Jesus and of the Immaculate Heart. *'Calls': From the Message of Fatima.* Still River, MA: The Ravengate Press, 2001.

Sivric, Fr. L.O.F.M. *The Hidden Side of Medjugorje.* Quebec, Canada: Psilog, Inc., 1989.

Snyder, Timothy. *Bloodlands: Europe Between Hitler and Stalin.* New York: Basic Books, 2010.

Socci, Antonio. *Mistero Medjugorje.* Milan, Italy: Piemme Edizioni, 2013.

——. *The Fourth Secret of Fatima.* Fitzwilliam, NH: Loreto Publications, 2006.

——. *The Secret of Benedict XVI.* Brooklyn, NY: Angelico Press, Ltd., 2019.

Soldo, Mirjana. *My Heart Will Triumph.* Cocoa, FL: CatholicShop Publishing, 2016.

Srouji, Jacqueline. *Mystic Medjugorje.* Nashville, TN: St. Francis Press, 1988.

Stromberg, Johannes Maria. *Our Blessed Mother Leads Her Children Out of Sarajevo.* Santa Barbara, CA: Queenship Publishing Company, 1993.

Sullivan, Randall. *The Miracle Detective.* New York: Grove Press, 2004.

Symonds, Kevin. *On the Third Part of the Secret of Fatima.* St. Louis, MO: En Route Books and Media, 2017.

——. *Pope Leo XIII and the Prayer to St. Michael.* Boonville, NY: Preserving Christian Publications, 2018.

Talbott, Strobe. *The Russians and Reagan.* New York: Vintage, 1984.

Tardo, Russell K. *Apparitions at Medjugorje: Divine of Demonic?* Kenner, LA: Faith Word Publications, 1989.

Thavis, John. *The Vatican Prophecies: Investigating Supernatural Signs Apparitions, and Miracles in the Modern Age.* New York, NY: Viking Press, 2015.

Terelya, Joseph, with Brown, Michael. *Josyp Terelya: Witness to the Apparitions and Persecution in the U.S.S.R.* Milford, OH: Faith Publishers, 1991.

The New American Bible. Wichita, KS: Catholic Bible Publishers, revised edition, 1994-95.

Thull, Andrew, ed. *What They Say About Medjugorje 1981-1991: A Contemporary Mystery.* Cincinnati, OH: Precision Built Corporation, 1991.

Tindal-Robertson, Timothy. *Fatima, Russia & Pope John Paul II.* Still River, MA: The Ravengate Press, 1992.

Toye, Charles. *Miracle of the Sun at Medjugorje.* Reading, MA: Send Your Spirit Prayer Ministry, 1988.

——. *Prayer of the Heart from Our Lady of Medjugorje*. Reading, MA: Send Your Spirit Prayer Ministry, 1987.

Trinchard, Fr. Paul. *The Awesome Fatima Consecrations*. Metairie, LA: META, 1992.

Tutto, Fr. George. *Medjugorje: Our Lady's Parish*. East Sussex, England: Medjugorje Information Service, 1985.

Two Friends of Medjugorje. *Words from Heaven*. Birmingham, AL.: St. James Publishing, 1990.

Ulicny, Joan. *A Greater Vision: Back from Abortion*. Santa Barbara, CA: Queenship Publishing Company, 1995.

Varghese, Roy Abraham. *Great Thinkers on Great Questions*, Oxford, England: Oneworld Publications, 1998.

Venancio, Most Rev. Joao, D.D., Bishop of Leiria-Fatima, ed. *A Heart for All: The Immaculate Heart of Mary in the Apparitions at Fatima*. Washington, NJ: AMI Press, 1972.

——. *Lucia Speaks on the Message of Fatima*. Washington, NJ: AMI Press, 1968.

Vlašić, Fr. Tomislav, O.F.M. *Our Lady Queen of Peace, Queen of Apostles is Teaching Us the Way to the Truth and Life at Medjugorje, Yugoslavia*. East Sussex, England: Peter Batty / Pika Print Limited, 1984.

Vlašić, Tomislav, O.F.M., and Barbarić, Slavko, O.F.M. *Abandon Yourselves Totally to Me*. Milan, Italy: The Association of the Friends of Medjugorje, 1985.

——. *I Beseech You, Listen to My Messages and Live Them*. Milan, Italy: The Association of the Friends of Medjugorje, 1987.

——. *Open Your Hearts to Mary*. Milan, Italy: The Association of the Friends of Medjugorje, 1986.

——. *Pray with Your Heart*. Milan, Italy: The Association of the Friends of Medjugorje, 1986.

Wallace, Mary Joan. *Medjugorje: Its Background and Messages*. Huntington Beach, CA: Follow Me Communications, 1989.

Walsh, William Thomas. *Our Lady of Fatima*. New York: Image Books, Doubleday, 1947.

Watkins, Christine. *Full of Grace. Miraculous Stories of Healing and Conversion Through Mary's Intercession*. Notre Dame, IN: Ave Maria Press, 2010.

Weible, Wayne. *A Child Shall Lead Them*. Brewster, MA: Paraclete Press, 2005.

——. *Letters from Medjugorje*. Orleans, MA: Paraclete Press, 1991.

——. *Medjugorje: The Last Apparition. How It Will Change the World*. Hiawassee, GA: New Hope Press, 2013.

——. *Medjugorje: The Message*. Orleans, MA: Paraclete Press, 1989.

——. *Medjugorje: The Mission*. Orleans, MA: Paraclete Press, 1994.

——. *The Final Harvest: Medjugorje at the End of the Century*. Brewster, MA: Paraclete Press, 1999.

Weigel, George. *The End and the Beginning*. New York: Image Books, Doubleday, 2011.

——. *Witness to Hope: The Biography of Pope John Paul II*. New York: Harper Perennial, 2004.

West, Rebecca. *Black Lamb, Gray Falcon: A Journey Through Yugoslavia*. New York, Viking Press, 1941.

White, Lottie. *I Will Save the World: Mary's Promise*. Pittsburgh, PA: FEB Company, 1979.

Williams, Alfred W. and Elizabeth, the "Blue Army Betty." *Gems of Wit and Wisdom: Supplement of Two Hearts of Wit and Wisdom*. Cape Coral, FL: Alfred and Elizabeth Williams, circa 1990.

——. *Two Hearts of Wit & Wisdom*. Cape Coral, FL: Alfred and Elizabeth Williams, 1990.

Yakovlev, Alexander. *A Century of Violence in the Soviet Union*. New Haven, CT: Yale University Press, 2004.

Yeung, Andrew Jerome. *Our Lady Speaks from Medjugorje*. Toronto, Ontario: The Ave Maria Centre for Peace, 2005.

——. *The Way to Medjugorje, Yugoslavia*. Toronto, Ontario: The Ave Maria Centre for Peace, 1984.

Zimdals-Swartz, Sandra L. *Encountering Mary: From La Salette to Medjugorje*. Princeton, N.J.: Princeton University Press, 1991.

NEWSPAPERS, PERIODICALS AND WEBSITES, 1981–2021

1. *Fatima International,* London, England.
2. *Medjugorje Gebetsaktion,* Vienna, Austria.
3. *Medjugorje Sentinel,* New South Wales, Australia.
4. *The Medjugorje Star,* New Orleans, LA.
5. *Via Ad Pacem,* Auburn, NY.
6. *Children of Medjugorje Newsletter,* Notre Dame, IN.
7. *The Spirit of Medjugorje,* Erie, PA.
8. *The Pilgrim,* Voorhees, NJ.
9. *Queen of Peace Center Update,* Dallas, TX.
10. *Medjugorje Torino,* Torino, Italy.
11. *Theotokas News,* Toledo, OH.
12. *Hawaii Catholic Herald,* Honolulu, HI
13. *Mary's People,* Studio City, CA.
14. *Mary's Mantle,* Yonkers, NY.
15. *The Medjugorje Messenger,* London, England.
16. *Orthodoxy of the Catholic Doctrine,* Portland, OR.
17. *The Mir Response,* New Orleans, LA.
18. *Medjugorje: Queen of Peace Newsletter,* Notre Dame, IN.
19. *Queen of Peace Journal,* Poughkeepsie, NY.
20. *30Days,* Rome, Italy.
21. *Our Sunday Visitor,* Huntington, IN.
22. *Catholic Counter-Reformation in the 20th Century,* Paris, France.
23. *The Wanderer,* Saint Paul, MN.
24. *Evangelist,* Albany, NY.
25. *Glas Koncila,* Catholic Newspaper, Yugoslavia.
26. *Guardian,* London, England.
27. *Catholic Worker,* New York, NY.
28. *Furrow,* County Kildore, IE.
29. *Catholic Twin Circle,* Los Angeles, CA.
30. *Month,* London, England.
31. *Mary's Newsroom,* Pittsburgh, PA.
32. *Libre Belgique,* Belgium.
33. *Queen of All Hearts,* Bay Shore, NY.
34. *Fidelity,* South Bend, IN.
35. *Catholic Standard and Times,* Philadelphia, PA.
36. *London Times,* London, England.
37. *Philadelphia Inquirer,* Philadelphia, PA.
38. *US News and World Report,* Washington, D.C.
39. *Time Magazine,* New York, NY.
40. *Tablet,* London, England.
41. *Criterion,* Indianapolis, IN.
42. *Our Lady Queen of Peace Newsletter,* Chicago, IL.
43. *Echo of Mary Queen of Peace,* Treviso, Italy.
44. *Caritas of Birmingham,* Sterret, AL.
45. *ABC News* (20/20), TV News Network, New York, NY.
46. *Queen of Peace Newsletter,* Coraopolis, PA.
47. *Center for Peace-West Newsletter,* Portland, OR.
48. *Medjugorje Queen of Peace Newsletter,* Las Vegas, NV.
49. *Weible Columns: Medjugorje*

Newsletter, Myrtle Beach, SC.

50. *Words of Our Lady*, Dublin, Ireland.
51. *New York Times*, New York, NY.
52. *Michigan Catholic*, Detroit, MI.
53. *Miami Herald*, Miami, FL.
54. *Cincinnati Enquirer*, Cincinnati, OH.
55. *Newsweek Magazine*, New York, NY.
56. *Medjugorje Magazine*, Riverside, IL.
57. *Our Lady Queen of Peace Newspaper*, McKees Rocks, PA.
58. *Voice of the Sacred Hearts*, Dover, DE.
59. *Crusade Magazine*, Hanover, PA.
60. *Pro Ecclesia Magazine*, New York, NY.
61. *HLI Reports*, Front Royal, VA.
62. *Echo from Medjugorje*, Italy.
63. *St. Louis Review*. St. Louis, MO.
64. *Reader's Digest*, Pleasantville, NY.
65. *L'Osservatore Romano*, Vatican City, Rome, Italy.
66. *Queen of Peace Newsletter*, St. Laurent, Quebec, CA.
67. *Columbia*, New Haven, CT.
68. *Providence Journal*, Providence, RI.
69. *Marian Helper Bulletin*, Stockbridge, MA.
70. *Texas Catholic*, Dallas, TX.
71. *Catholic Herald*, London, England.
72. *New Covenant*, Ann Harbor, MI.
73. *Signs and Wonders for Our Times*, Herndon, VA.
74. *Our Lady's Courier*,

Fairview, PA.
75. *Catholic Family News*, Niagara Falls, NY.
76. *Priests and People*, London, England.
77. *The Marian Library Newsletter*, Dayton, OH.
78. *Catholic Telegraph*, Cincinnati, OH.
79. *National Catholic Reporter*, Kansas City, MO.
80. *Soul Magazine*, Washington, NJ.
81. *Spectator*. London, England.
82. *Liquorian*, Liquori, MO.
83. *Catholic Almanac*, Huntington, IN.
84. *America*, New York, NY.
85. *Catholic Digest*, Saint Paul, MN.
86. *Good News*, Wales, UK.
87. *Omni Magazine*, New York, NY.
88. *The Catholic Thing*, https:wwwthecatholicthing.org.
89. *Immaculata Magazine*, Libertyville, IL.
90. *Crisis: Politics, Culture & the Church*, Washington, D.C.
91. *Divine Mercy Messenger*, Erie, PA.
92. *Dallas Morning News*, Dallas, PA.
93. *Mystic Post*, https://mysticpost.com.
94. *The 101 Times*, Asbury, N.J.
95. *The Triumph*, Buffalo, NY.
96. *LifesiteNews*, https://lifesitenews.com.
97. *Spirit Dailey*, Palm Coast, FL.
98. *Catholic Times*, Columbus, OH.
99. *Saint Anthony Messenger*, Cincinnati, OH.
100. *Medjugorje: Its Time Newspaper*, Weyburn, Saskatchewan.

101. *National Catholic Register*, Los Angeles, CA.
102. *Sunday Times Magazine*, London, England.
103. *LAF News*, Washington, NJ.
104. *Washington Post*, Washington, D.C.
105. *Orlando Sentinel*, Orlando, FL.
106. *NBC News* (*Inside Edition*), [TV news], New York, NY.
107. *Listener*, London, England.
108. *Cincinnati Post*, Cincinnati, Ohio.
109. *Long Island Catholic*. Long Island, NY.
110. *Dedicated Decades*, Dickinson, Texas.
111. *Insight (Washington Times)*, Washington, D.C.
112. *International Herald Tribune*, London, England.
113. *Salem News*, Salem, PA.
114. *Homiletic and Pastoral Review*, St. Louis, Mo.
115. *La Vita Populo*, Treviso, Italy.
116. *Marian Observer*, Berkley, MI.
117. *Clarion Herald*, New Orleans LA.
118. *Dayton Daily News*, Dayton, OH.
119. *Lamplighters Bulletin*, Ottawa, CA.
120. *South Bend Tribune*, South Bend, IN.
121. *Arizona Republic*, Phoenix, AZ.
122. *The Catholic Review*, Baltimore, MD.
123. *Medjugorje Center Newsletter*, Kansas City, MO.
124. *Leaves*, Detroit MI.
125. *The Children of Mary Center for Peace Newsletter*, Mossyrock, WA.
126. *Pittsburgh Center for Peace World Report*, McKees Rocks, PA.
127. *Gospa Missions Catholic News Periodical*, Evans City, PA.
128. *Inside the Vatican*, Front Royal, VA.
129. *Church Militant*, www.church-militant.com.
130. *The Spirit and the Word*, Providence, RI.
131. *One Peter 5*, https://onepeterfive.com.
132. *The Mir Recorder*, Middlesex, England.
133. *Medjugorje USA*, https://www.medjugorjeusa.org.
134. "*Hvaljen Isus I Marija (Praised Be Jesus and Mary Newsletter)*, Wayne, PA.
135. *The Fatima Crusader*, Constable, NY.
136. *Medjugorje*, Nashville, TN.
137. *Medjugorje Monthly*, London, England.
138. *Medjugorje Herald*, Galway, Ireland.

VIDEOS AND DOCUMENTARIES

1. *Medjugorje: Our Mother's Last Call with Sister Emmanuel*. Children of Medjugorje: Notre Dame, IN.,1997.
2. *The Madonna of Medjugorje*. Franciscan University Press, Steubenville, OH.,1997.

3. *Medjugorje: Responding to the Call from the Heart.* Respond Ministry, Inc,1991.
4. *Apparitions at Fatima.* EWTN Global Catholic Network, 1994.
5. *Medjugorje, Queen of Peace: A Message of Peace by the Karminski Family.* Wayne, PA, 1984.
6. *The Message of Medjugorje.* Wayne Weible, 1992.
7. *Medjugorje: Transforming Your Heart.* Marian Communications, LTD, 1988.
8. *The Little Shepherds of Fatima.* Fatima Productions, 1981.
9. *Madonna of Medjugorje.* BBC, Everyman / Westhanger Film, London, UK, 1985.
10. *Prophecy in the New Times.* MaxKol Productions, Herndon, VA, 1996.
11. *The Triumph of the Immaculate Heart of Mary: Volume I: Medjugorje.* Gray Haven Films, Diamond Bar, CA.,1994.
12. *Medjugorje in the New Millennium.* QOP Productions, Sean Patrick Bloomfield, 2002.

RECCOMENDED READING / VIEWING FATIMA

1. *Fatima: In Lucia's Own Words Vol.I & II*...Sr. Maria Lucia of the Immaculate Heart
2. *A Pathway Under the Gaze of Mary*...Carmel of Coimbra / World Apostolate of Fatima
3. *The Whole Truth About Fatima*...Frere Michel de la Sainte Trinite
4. *Fatima: The Great Sign*...Francis Johnston
5. *Our Lady of Fatima*... William Thomas Walsh
6. *Two Hours with Sister Lucia*...Carlos Evaristo
7. *Meet the Witnesses*...John Haffert
8. *Fatima: From the Beginning*...John De Marchi
9. *The Secret of Fatima*...Joaquin Maria Alonso, C.M.F.
10. *The Fourth Secret of Fatima*...Antonio Socci
11. *Fatima for Today*...Fr. Andrew Apostoli, C.F.R.
12. *On the Third Part of the Secret of Fatima*...Kevin J. Symonds
13. *Fatima Mysteries*...Grzegorz Gorny and Janusz Rosikon
14. *The Last Secret of Fatima*...Cardinal Tarcisio Bertone
15. *1917: Red Banners, White Mantle*...Warren H. Carroll
16. *The Fatima Prophecies*...Thomas W. Petrisko
17. *A Heart for All*...Most Reverend Joao Venancio, D.D, (ed.)
18. *Rediscovering Fatima*...Reverend Robert J. Fox
19. *The Youngest Prophet*...Christopher Rengers, OFM Cap.
20. *Calls from the Message of Fatima*...Sister Lucia of Jesus and the Immaculate Heart

21. *More About Fatima*...Reverend V. Montes De Oca, C.S.Sp.
22. *Documents on Fatima &the Memoirs of Sister Lucia*...Father Antonio Maria Martins, S.J.
23. *Fatima in Twilight*...Mark Fellows
24. *The Devil's Final Battle*...Father Paul Kramer (ed.)

MEDJUGORJE

1. *My Heart Will Triumph*...Mirjana Soldo
2. *The Visions of the Children*...Janice T. Connell
3. *Queen of the Cosmos*...Jan Connell
4. *Apparition Hill* (Documentary)...Sean Bloomfield
5. *Is the Virgin Mary Appearing in Medjugorje*...René Laurentin and Ljudevit Rupčić
6. *The Miracle Detective*...Randall Sullivan
7. *A Thousand Encounters with the Blessed Virgin Mary in Medjugorje*...Fr. Janko Bubalo
8. *Medjugorje: A Time for Truth, A Time for Action*...Denis Nolan
9. *Medjugorje: Facts, Documents, Theology*...Michael O'Carroll, CSSp
10. *Spark from Heaven*...Mary Craig
11. *Medjugorje: The 90's*...Sister Emmanuel Maillard
12. *What They Say About Medjugorje*...Andrew B. Thull, (Editor)
13. *Medjugorje Testament: Hostility Abounds, Grace Superabounds*...René Laurentin
14. *The Apparitions of Our Lady at Medjugorje*...Svetozar Kraljevic, O.F.M.
15. *Medjugorje Journal*...Lucy Rooney, SND and Robert Faricy, SJ
16. *Words from Heaven*...A Friend of Medjugorje
17. *The Apparitions of Medjugorje*...Ivan Kordic, Ph.D.
18. *Medjugorje: What's Happening?*... James Mulligan
19. *The Medjugorje Messages: 1981-2013*...Medjugorje.org.
20. *The Best of the Spirit of Medjugorje: Volume I, 1988-1997*...June Klins

RELATED / MISCELLANEOUS

1. *A Pope and a President*...Paul Kengor
2. *The Embrace of the Gospa*... Larry and Mary Sue Eck,
3. *Saint Michael and the Fatima Connection*...Carlos Evaristo
4. *The Day Will Come*...Michael Brown
5. *The Light Comes from the East*...Hugh Owen
6. *Invited to Light*...John DeMers
7. *The Thunder of Justice*...Ted Flynn
8. *A Heavenly Promise*...Cathy Howe

ABOUT THE AUTHOR

Dr. Thomas Petrisko is the former editor of an international Catholic newspaper and the author of 25 books on health and spiritual topics, including the best-selling *The Sorrow, the Sacrifice* and *the Triumph* (Simon and Schuster, 1995). He has appeared on or advised numerous newspapers, magazines, radio programs and TV shows such as *Oprah Winfrey, Newsweek, The Joan Rivers Show, CBS-48 Hours, Coast to Coast AM (Art Bell Radio Show), The Today Show, Inside Edition, The Washington Times, The Pittsburgh Post-Gazette, The Los-Angeles Times, The Washington Post* and others. He lives in Ave Maria, Florida, with his wife and children.

[Thomas Petrisko writes a freelance subscriber email (digital) news-letter for **SUBSTACK** (see *substack.com*), under the title ***Consider the Fig Tree***. It deals with Catholic themed issues including prophecy, mystics, apparitions, miracles, saints, contemporary news, related Church and secular events, and excerpts from his books that are relevant to the times at hand.]

AVAILABLE TO SPEAK

Dr. Thomas Petrisko is available to come to your Church or organization to speak. He is also available to do radio, television, internet and print media interviews. If you desire to schedule him, please call St. Andrews Productions at 412-787-9735 or email your request at standrewsproductions@yahoo.com.

INDEX

CPSIA information can be obtained
at www.ICGtesting.com
Printed in the USA
BVHW030943030523
663428BV00005BA/497

9 781891 903601